Organizational Behavior

13th Edition

Don Hellriegel
Texas A & M University

John W. Slocum, Jr.
Southern Methodist University

SOUTH-WESTERN
CENGAGE Learning

Australia • Brazil • Japan • Korea • Mexico • Singapore • Spain • United Kingdom • United States

SOUTH-WESTERN
CENGAGE Learning™

Organizational Behavior,
Thirteenth Edition
Don Hellriegel & John W. Slocum, Jr.

VP Editorial, Director: Jack W. Calhoun

Editor-in-Chief: Melissa Acuña

Executive Editor: Scott Person

Developmental Editor: Erin Guendelsberger

Senior Editorial Assistant: Ruth Belanger

Marketing Manager: Clinton Kernen

Senior Marketing Communications Manager:
Jim Overly

Marketing Coordinator: Julia Tucker

Director, Content and Media Production:
Barbara Fuller-Jacobsen

Content Project Manager: Emily Nesheim

Media Editor: Rob Ellington

Senior Frontlist Buyer: Kevin Kluck

Production Service: Elm Street Publishing
Services

Copyeditor: Lorretta Palagi

Compositor: Integra Software Services Pvt. Ltd.

Senior Art Director: Tippy McIntosh

Cover and Internal Design: Kim Torbeck,
Imbue Design

Cover Image: © Getty Images, Photodisc

Senior Rights Acquisitions
Account Manager, Text: Katie Huha

Text Permissions Researcher: Karyn Morrison

Rights Acquisitions Account Manager,
Images: John Hill

Senior Image Researcher: Kelly Franz,
Pre-PressPMG

Exam*View*® is a registered trademark of eInstruction Corp. Windows is a registered trademark of the Microsoft Corporation used herein under license. Macintosh and Power Macintosh are registered trademarks of Apple Computer, Inc. used herein under license.

© 2008 Cengage Learning. All Rights Reserved.

Cengage Learning WebTutor™ is a trademark of Cengage Learning.

Library of Congress Control Number: 2009932083

ISBN-13: 978-1-4390-4225-0

ISBN-10: 1-4390-4225-X

South-Western Cengage Learning
5191 Natorp Boulevard
Mason, OH 45040
USA

Cengage Learning products are represented in Canada by Nelson Education, Ltd.

For your course and learning solutions, visit **www.cengage.com.**

Purchase any of our products at your local college store or at our preferred online store **www.ichapters.com.**

Printed in China
3 4 5 6 7 14 13 12

To Lois (DH)
To Gail (JWS)

Brief Contents

Contents

Part 3: Leadership and Team Behaviors 251

Part 4: The Organization   411

Chapter 17

Preface

As we started to write the 13th edition of this book, many of our friends asked us why we were revising it. Our answer was that we believe we have the desire and the ability to help students learn about important issues that they will face as leaders. After all, we have been writing, teaching, and consulting as a team for a combined total of more than 80 years. When we published the first edition of this book in 1976, a number of the topics, concepts, and models presented in this edition were not covered. Of course, leaders continue to face many of the same challenges they faced during the mid-1970s, such as attracting, retaining, and motivating employees; forming and leading high-performance teams; managing conflicts; and changing their organizations' processes to be more effective. However, the complexity of leading people has changed. With the development of the Internet, Twitter, Facebook, and a host of other communication vehicles, issues facing employees and leaders are instantly broadcast around the globe. At times, the decisions of leaders may impact millions of employees. Just recently, we have witnessed the failure of General Motors and Chrysler being sold to an Italian automobile company (Fiat); major changes in the U.S. banking system; the expanded "reach" of the U.S. government into the management of private firms; leaders of major institutions, such as Bernie Madoff and Allen Stanford, being convicted of ethical violations; the rise of developing nations, especially India and China, as major players in almost every industry; and the global recession. This edition presents how employees and leaders from around the globe have sought to respond to these pressing issues.

Snapshot of What's New

As employees and leaders conduct business around the world, they face many ethical challenges. New to this edition is Chapter 2, "Individual and Organizational Ethics." This chapter highlights ethical concepts and concerns that are relevant to all employees and leaders. Some of the major concerns that we believe need to be addressed by employees and leaders include workforce diversity, stakeholder responsibility, outsourcing, and ethical values. The ethical competency is so important that we present **9 NEW** ethical competency features. They appear in various chapters throughout the book. These features enable the reader to consider a variety of ethical situations and how they were addressed. In addition, ethics-based exercises and cases at the end of each chapter require the reader to make decisions and choose a course of action. In addition to this **NEW** chapter, we have completely revised major portions of each chapter, especially the leadership, decision making, and organization design chapters.

If the 13th edition is a major revision that reflects the challenges facing today's and tomorrow's leaders, what's new?

- First, all *Learning from Experience* features are new. A wide variety of organizations are represented in these chapter-opening features, including Xerox, PepsiCo, Costco, Lowe's, and Petrobras. Each chapter-opening feature introduces you to the major themes developed in the chapter and illustrates some of the challenges facing employees and leaders.

- Second, the Competency features, four per chapter, are virtually all new. These give you an opportunity to quickly read about an issue and then use the materials in the chapter to gain a new perspective on the issue.

- Third, at the end of select chapters, we have included **NEW** Experiential Exercises. We have retained some exercises that you thought were effective and developed others that are new to this edition.

- Fourth, **13 NEW** and **4** revised cases appear at the end of the chapters. These cases serve to reinforce the major concepts developed within the chapter and are based on real incidents from a variety of organizations.
- Fifth, we have added **14 NEW** and retained **3** BizFlix videos that we have found to enrich student learning. These short videos provide keen insights into real-life challenges facing employees and leaders.
- Sixth, we have updated and added new Integrating Cases for those instructors who wish to have complex cases that span a chapter's content. A total of **9** integrated cases are included for those instructors who wish to use more comprehensive cases that span the content found in several chapters.
- Seventh, we have added new PowerPoints® to reflect our new content. All PowerPoints have been redesigned based on the recommendations of our users.
- Eighth, Susan Leshnower has completely updated the Instructor's Manual to accompany the text. This valuable resource will help new and practiced professors, providing text notes, enrichment modules, and more.
- Lastly, John Hite and Scott Tarcy have developed and tested almost 4,000 true/false, multiple-choice, short answer, and essay questions for this edition.

Snapshot of What Stayed the Same

First, as in all previous editions, we have pursued the goal of presenting core concepts and foundation principles that are fundamental to individual and organizational effectiveness. These are highlighted through the use of contemporary examples, issues, and leadership practices. Second, to actively engage the readers in the learning process and assist them in developing their individual and management competencies, we have included more than **30** self-assessment instruments for them to complete. We have found that these instruments enrich the students' learning experience and expose them to competencies that they need to develop to become effective employees and successful leaders. Third, our approach has also been to develop and integrate a few major concepts well rather than to expose students to a "laundry list" of concepts without any real-world takeaway. Therefore, we continue to use real-life examples from a variety of organizations to support student learning. Finally, the *Instructor's Manual* has been a continuing source of strength for many faculty members. We have retained its author, and she has added new enrichment modules to help faculty members explain each chapter's content to students.

The Learning Process

Our road map to the learning process starts in Chapter 1. In this chapter, we discuss differences between leaders and managers, introduce you to the learning framework for the entire book, and illustrate the key attributes of the seven key competencies that are woven into the text. Based on research and our own experience, we present seven competencies that we believe all employees and leaders need to master.

Key Competencies

Ethics Competency

This includes the knowledge, skills, and abilities to incorporate values and principles that distinguish right from wrong when making decisions and choosing behaviors.

Self Competency

This includes the knowledge, skills, and abilities to assess personal strengths and weaknesses, set and pursue professional and personal goals, balance work and personal life, and engage in new learning.

Diversity Competency

This includes the knowledge, skills, and abilities to value unique individual, group, and organizational characteristics, embrace such characteristics as potential sources of strength, and appreciate the uniqueness of each.

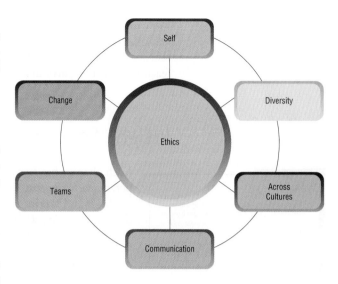

Across Cultures Competency

This includes the knowledge, skills, and abilities to recognize and embrace similarities and differences among nations and cultures.

Communication Competency

This includes the knowledge, skills, and abilities to use all modes of transmitting, understanding, and receiving ideas, thoughts, and feelings—verbal, listening, nonverbal, and written—for accurately transferring and exchanging information.

Teams Competency

This includes the knowledge, skills, and abilities to develop, support, and lead groups to achieve goals.

Change Competency

This includes the knowledge, skills, and abilities to recognize and implement needed adaptations or entirely new transformations in people, tasks, strategies, structures, or technologies.

Individual Learning

Throughout the book, students are provided with rich opportunities to become actively involved in their own learning. These opportunities include self-assessment instruments, experiential exercises, case studies, BizFlix, and discussion questions. Self-assessment instruments are found in all chapters and often provide students with benchmarks against which they can gauge their competencies in relation to other students and practicing leaders.

Learning from Experience Feature

This feature introduces the reader to the major themes developed within each chapter. To do so, we often use leaders and organizations that most students are familiar with, such as Indra Nooyi of PepsiCo, Jim Sinegal of Costco, Steve Jobs of Apple, and Anne

Mulcahy of Xerox. Fifteen of these features are **NEW** to this edition. We wrote these features to illustrate effective or ineffective use of one or more of our seven competencies. Within the chapter, there are flashbacks to how the *Learning from Experience* feature illustrates particular concepts or practices.

Insight Feature

> **Ethics Insight**
>
> Senior leaders typically emphasize the importance of performance and the bottom line. But if they don't also emphasize ethical behavioral messages, then all employees hear is that it's all about the numbers. Get the numbers at all costs, they think—and that causes some to compromise ethics.
>
> *Ronald James, President and CEO, Center for Ethical Business Cultures*

Each chapter has two *Insight* features that are related to one of our seven competencies. This feature emphasizes a leader's thinking about an issue. These are brief and are intended to highlight a particular theme in the text. Some of the *Diversity Insights* are from Ronald Parker of PepsiCo, Magda Yrizarry of Verizon Communications, and David George of United Technologies. Other leaders included in different *Insight* features include Jim Sinegal of Costco, Martin Coles of Starbucks, Stacy Guinn of Sherwin-Williams, Patricia Woertz of Archer Daniels Midland, and Olli-Pekka Kallasvuo of Nokia.

Competency Features

Following a tradition we started several editions ago, there are **4** competency features in each chapter. These features aid student learning by reinforcing each chapter's content and challenge the student to consider it in relation to a model, concept, or practice presented in that section of the chapter. These reflect real-world challenges or issues that have faced employees and leaders. We have **68** competency features that help students develop their own competencies. Eighty percent are **NEW** to this edition. Those that have been retained have been updated and revised. Let's briefly highlight some of the organizations and/or leaders that are included in this feature.

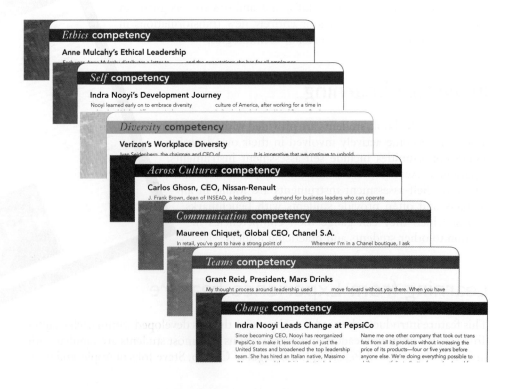

Ethics Competency

Of the 10 features, 9 are **NEW** to this edition and include organizations such as Johnson & Johnson, Mattel, The Gap, CitiMortgage, and Enron.

Self Competency

Of the 11 features, 7 are **NEW** to this edition and include leaders such as John Schnatter of Papa John's Pizza, Indra Nooyi of PepsiCo, Colin Powell, and Chesley Sullenberger (Sully) of US Airways.

Diversity Competency

Of the 8 features, 6 are **NEW** to this edition and include insights from Aetna, Deloitte & Touche, Lockheed Martin, WellPoint, and Chubb.

Across Cultures Competency

Of the 11 features, 9 are **NEW** to this edition and include examples of leaders and organizations such as Carlos Ghosn of Nissan-Renault, Tahir Ayub of PricewaterhouseCoopers, Hewlett-Packard, Alcoa, and Ricardo Semler of Brazil-based Semco.

Communication Competency

All 9 features are **NEW** to this edition. Included are leaders from Chanel, Intuit, Chroma Technology, DreamWorks, United Technologies, and Texas Nameplate.

Teams Competency

Of these 8 competency features, 4 are **NEW** to this edition. Teams from Mars, Starbucks, SEI Investments, Jeff Gordon's Rainbow Warriors, Gore & Associates, and IBM are highlighted.

Change Competency

Nine of the 11 competency features are **NEW** to this edition. Leaders and teams discussed range from PepsiCo to Boeing to Yahoo and Harley-Davidson.

Key Terms and Concepts

Key terms and concepts appear in blue and definitions immediately follow in italics. A list of all terms introduced in the chapter is given at the end of each chapter, along with the page on which it is defined.

Discussion Questions

More than **160** questions are **NEW** to this edition. In these end-of-chapter questions, the first question requires the student to use the Internet to search for an answer. This question is based on the *Learning from Experience* feature that opens each chapter. The ethical and diversity discussion questions also require the student to use the

Internet. All questions engage students to use their diagnostic skills and various key competencies.

Experiential Exercises and Cases

Each chapter has at least one experiential exercise and one case that are keyed to one of the seven competencies. These end-of-chapter features provide additional means for learners to actively participate in the development of their own competencies. All of these have been class tested and have proven to stimulate active classroom discussion. Some of the Experiential Exercises include a foundation competency inventory, ethical decision making, a creativity inventory, a communication climate inventory, coping with work-related stress, team assessment, conflict handling styles, and cultural values. A few of the organizations included in cases are Accenture, Oracle, SAS Institute, Wegmans, Virgin Airlines, Allstate, and the Ladies Professional Golf Association. At the end of each case, we pose several questions that have been found to stimulate learners' competencies.

Chapter Summary

Every chapter ends with a summary of the chapter's main points. These summaries are organized around the chapter's *Learning Goals*. Readers can use these summaries to assess their mastery of the material presented in the chapter.

Assessment Instruments

Throughout the book, we present more than **30** self, team, and organizational assessment instruments. Typically, they focus on one or more of the key competencies in the chapter. Usually these are found within the chapter and learners are invited to complete them as they read the text to enhance their understanding of the concept being presented. They are designed to help individuals (1) gain self-insights, (2) gain knowledge about teams that they have worked with, (3) gain understanding about organizations that they have worked with or used, (4) more readily understand the concepts in the text, (5) identify their own strengths and weaknesses, and (6) gain insights about how to be more effective employees and future leaders. Some examples are:

- Chapter 1: Competencies Inventory
- Chapter 2: Ethical Intensity
- Chapter 3: Big Five Personality Inventory
- Chapter 4: Impression Management Assessment
- Chapter 5: What Is Your Self-Efficacy?
- Chapter 6: Designing a Challenging Job
- Chapter 7: Goal Commitment Questionnaire
- Chapter 8: Workplace Bullying

- Chapter 9: Polychronic Attitude Index (How Do You Use Time?)
- Chapter 10: Behavioral Leadership Questionnaire
- Chapter 11: Globe Leadership Instrument
- Chapter 12: Team Assessment Inventory
- Chapter 13: Conflict Handling Styles
- Chapter 14: Personal Creativity Inventory
- Chapter 15: Analyzing Your Organization's Design
- Chapter 16: What Do You Value at Work?
- Chapter 17: Diversity Perceptions Scale

Integrating Cases

We have included **9** integrating cases in Part 5. Each case poses questions that require learners to draw from a variety of concepts and models presented in various chapters. The goal of these cases and questions is to foster the critical and analytical thinking capabilities of readers. The questions require the learner to have mastered the materials. We have posed questions linked to the seven competencies that have been illustrated throughout the book.

Learning Framework

The framework for learning about organizational behavior and how learners can develop their competencies is presented in Chapter 1, pages 5–8. As shown in Figure 1.1 on page 7, our framework starts with a focus on the individual, then moves to leadership and the team level, and concludes with a focus on the organization. We believe that it is impossible to understand why employees and leaders make certain decisions without first understanding something about their ethics, personality, motivations, leadership abilities, and the like.

Part 1 of the book presents an introduction to the seven competencies and a **NEW** chapter that focuses on individual and organizational ethics. Given the ethical challenges facing employees and leaders, we believed that a chapter dedicated to ethical issues early on in the book was needed. This chapter focuses learners' attention on ethical issues of individual differences, decision making, diversity, and stakeholder responsibility.

Part 2 of the book (Chapters 3 through 8) focuses on key aspects of the individual by discussing personality,

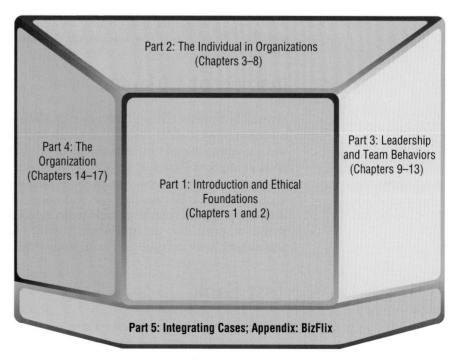

Part 2: The Individual in Organizations
(Chapters 3–8)

Part 4: The Organization
(Chapters 14–17)

Part 1: Introduction and Ethical Foundations
(Chapters 1 and 2)

Part 3: Leadership and Team Behaviors
(Chapters 9–13)

Part 5: Integrating Cases; Appendix: BizFlix

attributions, emotions, learning, motivation, goal setting, reward systems, workplace aggression, cultural values, and much more. These six chapters are full of examples of how leaders and individuals in global organizations use these concepts to lead and manage others.

Part 3 of the book (Chapters 9 through 13) moves the learner from a focus on the individual to the interpersonal processes that influence individual, team, and organizational effectiveness. We start this five-chapter sequence with a focus on interpersonal communications and how individuals, leaders, and organizations can effectively create communication channels to increase effectiveness. Communications do not occur in a vacuum but through people. Therefore, in the next two chapters, we explore how leaders' behaviors can impact the commitment, performance, and overall effectiveness of both individuals and teams. Developing and leading teams, the focus of Chapter 12, is a major part of a leader's job. Teams must be led in order for them to be successful. At times, leaders and team members may be in conflict with each other over goals to pursue and negotiating strategies to use to reach an agreement. Chapter 13 addresses these issues.

Part 4 of the book (Chapters 14 through 17) considers the factors that influence individual, team, leader, and organizational effectiveness. The part opens with a focus on factors and processes that influence how individuals and leaders make decisions. Decision making in many organizations is not orderly because the outcomes are usually not clear. For leaders to make decisions that will allow the organization to maintain or increase its effectiveness, however, the organization must be designed properly in order to pursue its goals. Chapter 15 addresses how the business strategy of an organization affects its choice of organizational design. This chapter reviews the core vertical and horizontal dimensions of an organization's structure. Chapter 16 addresses the importance of creating an organizational culture that supports decision-making processes and the leader's influence style. Corporate culture is the "soul" of an organization and, therefore, knowing how to create, sustain, and change a culture becomes a vital part of any leader's goals. Finally in Chapter 17, we conclude with a discussion of how to manage organizational change. This discussion draws on concepts presented throughout the book in an integrated fashion.

Resources for Instructors

A full range of teaching and learning supplements and resources is available for use with the 13th edition of *Organizational Behavior*.

Instructor's Manual

Written by Professor Susan Leshnower of Midland College, the Instructor's Manual contains comprehensive resource materials for lectures, including enrichment modules for enhancing and extending relevant chapter concepts. This supplement also presents suggested answers to all end-of-chapter discussion questions. It includes notes on using the end-of-chapter *Experiential Exercise and Case* features, including suggested answers to case questions and notes for the integrating cases. Finally, the Instructor's Manual contains a guide to the videos available for use with the text. This manual is available on the Instructor's Resource CD-ROM and on the product support website, www.cengage.com/management/hellriegel.

Test Bank

Written by John Hite and Scott Tarcy, the Test Bank contains almost 4,000 questions from which to choose. Each question is tagged to AACSB learning standards to allow for the assessment of student achievement as it relates to these key measures. A selection of new and revised true/false, multiple-choice, short answer, and critical thinking essay questions is provided for each chapter. For this edition, the selection of short answer questions has been expanded. Each question in the Test Bank is classified according to type, difficulty level, and learning goal. Cross-references to materials in the textbook and pages where answers can be found are included. Explanations are provided for why statements are false in the true/false sections of the test bank. The Test Bank is available on the Instructor's Resource CD-ROM and on the product support website, www.cengage.com/management/hellriegel.

ExamView®

Available on the Instructor's Resource CD-ROM, ExamView contains all of the questions in the printed Test Bank. This program is easy-to-use test creation software that is compatible with  Microsoft® Windows®. Instructors can add or edit questions, instructions, and answers and select questions (randomly or numerically) by previewing them on the screen. Instructors can also create and administer quizzes online, whether over the Internet, a local-area network (LAN), or a wide-area network (WAN).

PowerPoint® Presentation Slides

Developed by Argie Butler of Texas A&M University and prepared in conjunction with the Instructor's Manual, more than 500 PowerPoint slides are available to supplement course content, adding structure and a visual dimension to the learning experience. With a new, improved design, these PowerPoint slides present the dynamic nature of the materials while also allowing for easy customization. Available on the website (www.cengage.com/management/hellriegel) and the Instructor's Resource CD-ROM, all of the PowerPoint slides include meaningful captions that tie in directly to the concepts in the book. Material is organized by chapter and can be modified or expanded for individual classroom use. PowerPoint slides are easily printed to create customized transparency masters. We want learners to engage with their classroom experience and grow from it.

Instructor's Resource CD-ROM (ISBN: 0-538-74201-1)

Key instructor ancillaries (Instructor's Manual, Test Bank, ExamView, and PowerPoint slides) are provided on the Instructor's Resource CD-ROM. This CD-ROM provides instructors with the ultimate tool for customizing lectures and presentations.

Reel to Real Video Package DVD (ISBN: 1-439-07888-2)

A video library is available to users of the 13th edition to show how real organizations and managers deal with organizational behavior issues. This unique video package is available on DVD for classroom use.

BizFlix videos use short film scenes from popular Hollywood films, including *In Good Company*, *Friday Night Lights*, and *Hot Fuzz*, to illustrate organizational behavior concepts from the text. These film scenes help learners synthesize and reflect on key concepts. Each film clip is associated with a specific text chapter, but many could be utilized to accompany several chapters. The 17 *BizFlix* videos—14 **NEW** and 3 retained—are presented in brief form, along with key questions, in the Appendix at the end of the text.

Workplace videos are from organizations including Evo and Numi Organic Tea. They give learners a look inside the situations faced by organizations and the subsequent solution.

Cengage Learning Custom Solutions and TextChoice.com

Create your perfect text, casebook, or reader with TextChoice from Cengage Learning Custom Solutions. TextChoice provides the fastest, easiest way for instructors to create their own learning materials. A list of suggested cases from Harvard Business School Publishing can be found on the companion website (www.cengage.com/management/hellriegel), but more than 13,000 cases are available on TextChoices.com through our Case Net database. Case Net is a collection of business cases from prestigious partners such as Harvard Business School Publishing, Ivey, and Darden Business Publishing. Contact your local South-Western/Cengage Learning sales representative for more information on these additional case resources, or for more information about providing your students a customized edition of this text.

Learner and Instructor Resources

Student Premium Website (www.cengage.com/login)

New to this edition, this optional premium website features text-specific resources that enhance student learning by bringing concepts to life. Dynamic interactive learning tools include online quizzes, flash cards, PowerPoint slides, concept tutorials, learning games, competency assessments, and more. Access to the Hellriegel/Slocum Premium Student Website is pincode protected. Learn more by adding this text to your bookshelf at www.cengage.com/login. Ask your local South-Western/Cengage Learning sales representative about this optional package item.

Enriching Competency Instrument

Through the text's new student premium website, learners can access a detailed self-assessment competency instrument to use and reuse as their competencies develop. Individual ratings can be compared with those of practicing professionals and others. These comparisons give learners feedback on their developmental needs. In addition, videos, glossaries, and links to other online resources complete this collection of technology-based tools and content. The Premium Student Website is free when bundled with a new textbook.

WebTutor™ (0-538-49561-8 on WebCT® or 0-538-49553-7 on BlackBoard®)

WebTutor is an interactive, web-based learner supplement on WebCT and/or BlackBoard that harnesses the power of the Internet to deliver innovative learning aids that actively engage learners. Instructors can incorporate WebTutor as an integral part of their course, or the learners can use it on their own as a study guide. Benefits to learners include automatic feedback from quizzes and exams; interactive, multimedia-rich explanation of concepts; online exercises that reinforce what they have learned; flash cards that include audio support; and greater interaction and involvement through online discussion forums.

Complementary Website

The website at www.cengage.com/management/hellriegel complements and enriches the text, providing extras for learners and instructors. Resources include interactive chapter quizzes and flash cards.

The Business & Company Resource Center

The Business & Company Resource Center (BCRC) puts a business library at the learner's fingertips. The BCRC is a premier online business research tool that allows learners to seamlessly search thousands of periodicals, journals, references, financial information, industry reports, company histories, and much more. This all-in-one reference tool is invaluable to learners, helping them to quickly research their case analysis, presentation, or business plan. Learners can save time and money by building an online coursepack using BCRC InfoMarks. It links learners directly to the assigned reading without the inconvenience of library reserves, permissions, or printed materials.

Contact your local South-Western/Cengage Learning sales representative to learn more about this powerful tool and how the BCRC can save valuable time for both instructors and learners.

Acknowledgments

We express our sincere and grateful appreciation to the following individuals who provided thoughtful reviews and useful suggestions for improving this edition of *Organizational Behavior*. Their insights were critical in making a number of important revisions.

Maryann Albrecht, *University of Illinois at Chicago*

Barry Bales, *University of Texas*

Cecily Cooper, *University of Miami*

Edward Cox, *EDS, a HP Company*

Thomas Fairchild, *University of North Texas Health Science Center*

Sue Hammond, *Thin Book Publishing*

MaryRose L. Hart, *Rogers State University*

Howard Johnson, *Lowe's Corporation*

William Joyce, *Dartmouth College*

Any Kohlberg, *Kisco Senior Living*

Maribeth Kuenzi, *Southern Methodist University*

David Lei, *Southern Methodist University*

Fred Luthans, *University of Nebraska*

Antoinette Phillips, *Southeastern Louisiana University*

Consuelo M. Ramirez, *University of Texas, San Antonio*

William Reisel, *St. John's University*

Ralph Sorrentino, *Deloitte Consulting*

David Stoner, *ViewCast*

Charlotte Sutton, *Auburn University*

Paul D. Sweeney, *University of Dayton*

Bill Wallick, *University of Scranton*

Ben Welch, *Texas A&M University*

For their assistance with the previous edition, we would like to thank the following individuals:

Eileen Albright, *Cinemark Theaters*

Lucinda Blue, *Strayer University*

Alicia Boisnier, *State University of New York at Buffalo*

Rupert Campbell, *St. Joseph's College*

Robin Cheramie, *Kennesaw State University*

David Ford, *University of Texas at Dallas*

Lynda Fuller, *Wilmington College*

Amy Henley, *Kennesaw State University*

Peter Heslin, *Southern Methodist University*

Homer Johnson, *Loyola University, Chicago*

Morgan R. Milner, *Eastern Michigan University*

Padmakuma Nair, *University of Texas at Dallas*

Rhonda Palladi, *Georgia State University*

Alesia Stanley, *Wayland Baptist University*

Barbara Thomas, *Hewlett-Packard*

Roger Volkema, *American University*

William Walker, *University of Houston*

For their valuable professional guidance and collegial support, we sincerely thank the following individuals who served on the team responsible for this edition:

- Michele Rhoades, the senior acquisition editor, who supported us in framing the revisions for this edition

- Scott Person, the executive editor, who also offered support in this revision

- Erin Guendelsberger, the developmental editor, who demonstrated many competencies on all facets of this edition and also provided a key interface with the authors of the various supplements

- Lorretta Palagi, the copyeditor, who was outstanding in improving the flow and readability of the manuscript

- Emily Nesheim, the content project manager, who so deftly handled the myriad issues in the production process

- Clint Kernen, the marketing manager, who provided the fine leadership in presenting this edition to potential adopters

- Tina Potter, John Slocum's associate at Southern Methodist University, who superbly supported manuscript preparation

- Argie Butler, Don Hellriegel's long-time associate at Texas A&M University, who creatively designed and developed the PowerPoint slides for this edition and superbly supported manuscript preparation

- Amanda Zagnoli, the project editor at Elm Street Publishing Services, who ensured that excellent page proofs were developed and provided on schedule
- Patsy Hartmangruber, Don Hellriegel's associate at Texas A&M University, who ably assisted him with various tasks.

Don Hellriegel expresses his appreciation to colleagues at Texas A&M University who collectively create a work environment that nurtures his continued learning and professional development. In particular, the learning environment fostered by Jerry Strawser, Dean, and Murray Barrick, head of the Management Department, is gratefully acknowledged. They continue the tradition of supporting a positive and learning-based work environment.

John Slocum acknowledges his colleagues at Southern Methodist University, especially Tom (aka "The Lion") Perkowski, for their constructive input and reviews. Also, special thanks are extended to Bill Dillon, Associate Dean of the Cox School, for his intellectual support and warm friendship. To all of the executive MBA students who listened to countless stories and wrote cases for this book, John is forever grateful. John also thanks his golfing group at Stonebriar Country Club (Jack Kennedy, Cecil Ewell, Ed Cox, Wally Schortmann, and Mark Gilbert) for understanding that books do not get written on the fairways or on putting greens.

Finally, we celebrate the 13th edition, some 35 years after the publication of our first edition in 1976. We wish to thank many hundreds of reviewers, adopters, students, and our families who have supported the development of these 13 editions for more than three decades. Moreover, Don and John thank each other for being close friends since 1962. We met each other in an industrial relations class during our MBA days at Kent State University in 1962 and are still close and special friends. It's been a unique and enriching experience for both of us and well as our wives. Don and Lois have raised three girls and now have 13 grandchildren. John and Gail have raised three boys and now have seven grandchildren. Most importantly, we are happily married to our wives for more than 45 years.

Don Hellriegel, Texas A&M University
John W. Slocum, Jr., Southern Methodist University

Author Page

Don Hellriegel

Don Hellriegel is Emeritus Professor of management within the Mays Business School at Texas A&M University. He received his B.S. and M.B.A. from Kent State University and his Ph.D. from the University of Washington. Dr. Hellriegel became a member of the faculty at Texas A&M in 1975. He has served on the faculties of the Pennsylvania State University and the University of Colorado.

His research interests include organizational behavior, the effects of organizational environments, managerial cognitive styles, and organizational innovation and strategic management processes. His research has been published in a number of leading journals.

Professor Hellriegel served as Vice President and Program Chair of the Academy of Management (1986), President Elect (1987), President (1988), and Past President (1989). In September 1999, he was elected to a three-year term as Dean of the Fellows Group of the Academy of Management. He served a term as Editor of the *Academy of Management Review* and served as a member of the Board of Governors of the Academy of Management (1979–1981 and 1982–1989). Dr. Hellriegel has performed many other leadership roles, among which include President, Eastern Academy of Management; Division Chair, Organization and Management Theory Division; President, Brazos County United Way; Co-Consulting Editor, *West Series in Management*; Head (1976–1980 and 1989–1994), Department of Management (TAMU); Interim Dean, Executive Associate Dean (1995–2000), Mays School of Business (TAMU); and Interim Executive Vice Chancellor (TAMUS).

He has consulted with a variety of groups and organizations, including 3DI, Sun Ship Building, Penn Mutual Life Insurance, Texas A&M University System, Ministry of Industry and Commerce (Nation of Kuwait), Ministry of Agriculture (Nation of Dominican Republic), AACSB, and Texas Innovation Group.

John W. Slocum, Jr.

John W. Slocum, Jr., is an Emeritus Professor in the Cox School of Business at Southern Methodist University, Dallas, Texas. He has taught on the faculties of the University of Washington, Penn State, Ohio State, International University of Japan, and the Amos Tuck School, Dartmouth College. He holds a B.B.A. from Westminster College, a M.B.A. from Kent State, and a Ph.D. in organizational behavior from the University of Washington.

Professor Slocum is Past President of the Eastern Academy of Management, the 39th President of the Academy of Management (1983–1984), and Editor of the *Academy of Management Journal* (1979–1981). He is a Fellow of the Academy of Management, Decision Science Institute, and the Pan-Pacific Institute. He has been awarded the Alumni Citation for Professional Accomplishment by Westminster College, and the Nicolas Salgo, Rotunda, and Executive MBA Outstanding Teaching Awards at SMU. Currently, he is serving as Co-Editor of the *Journal of World Business* and the *Journal of Leadership and Organizational Studies* and Associate Editor of *Organizational Dynamics*.

Professor Slocum has served as a consultant to such organizations as ARAMARK, Baylor Hospital, University of North Texas Health Science Center, LBJ School at the University of Texas, Celanese Chemical Corporation, Pier 1, NASA, and Brakke Consulting. He is a regular speaker for many senior executive development programs, including the University of Oklahoma, Oklahoma State University, SMU, and Lockheed Martin. He is currently on the Board of Directors of ViewCast Corporation, Kisco Senior Living, and GoToLearn.

Introduction and Ethical Foundations

chapter 1

Learning about Organizational Behavior

Learning Goals

After studying this chapter, you should be able to:

1 State the core differences between leadership and management.

2 Outline the framework for learning about organizational behavior.

3 Describe the ethics competency and its contribution to effective performance.

4 Describe the self competency and its contribution to effective performance.

5 Describe the diversity competency and its contribution to effective performance.

6 Describe the across cultures competency and its contribution to effective performance.

7 Describe the communication competency and its contribution to effective performance.

8 Describe the teams competency and its contribution to effective performance.

9 Describe the change competency and its contribution to effective performance.

Learning Content

Learning from Experience
Indra Nooyi, Chairman and CEO, PepsiCo

Leadership versus Management

Learning Framework

Ethics Competency
Ethics Competency
Robert A. Eckert, Chairman and CEO, Mattel, Inc.

Self Competency
Self Competency
Indra Nooyi's Development Journey

Diversity Competency
Diversity Competency
Aetna's Diverse Discoveries Program

Across Cultures Competency
Across Cultures Competency
Carlos Ghosn, CEO, Nissan-Renault

Communication Competency
Communication Competency
Maureen Chiquet, Global CEO, Chanel S.A.

Teams Competency
Teams Competency
Grant Reid, President, Mars Drinks

Change Competency
Change Competency
Indra Nooyi Leads Change at PepsiCo

Experiential Exercise And Case
Experiential Exercise: Self Competency
Key Competencies Self-Assessment Inventory

Case: Diversity Competency
Accenture's Work–Life Balance Programs

Indra Nooyi, Chairman and CEO, PepsiCo

Indra Nooyi became the CEO of PepsiCo in 2006 and was elected to the additional role of chairman of the board in 2007. PepsiCo has 185,000 employees. It manufactures, markets, and sells hundreds of different snacks and beverages worldwide. This opening feature provides a few insights about Indra Nooyi in her own words.

My father was an absolutely wonderful human being. From him I learned to always assume positive intent. Whatever anybody says or does, assume positive intent. You will be amazed at how your whole approach to a person or problem becomes very different. When you assume negative intent, you're angry. If you take away that anger and assume positive intent, you will be amazed. Your emotional quotient goes up because you are no longer almost random in your response. You don't get defensive. You don't scream. You are trying to understand and listen because at your basic core you are saying, "Maybe they are saying something to me that I'm not hearing." So "assume positive intent" has been a huge piece of advice for me.

In business, sometimes in the heat of the moment, people say things. You can either misconstrue what they're saying and assume they are trying to put you down, or you can say, "Wait a minute. Let me really get behind what they are saying to understand whether they're reacting because they're hurt, upset, confused, or they don't understand what it is I've asked them to do." If you react from a negative perspective—because you didn't like the way they reacted—then it just becomes two negatives fighting each other. But when you assume positive intent, I think often what happens is the other person says, "Hey, wait a minute, maybe I'm wrong in reacting the way I do because this person is really making an effort."

Since becoming chairman and CEO, I've seen that one of the ways to inspire people is by having a vision that everyone can get behind. At PepsiCo, that vision is "Performance with Purpose." It's our company's long-term strategy for delivering strong financial results while responding to the changing demands of our consumers and the marketplace.

Performance with Purpose rests on three pillars: human sustainability, environmental sustainability, and talent sustainability. For example, we're transforming our product portfolio in order to offer consumers healthier choices—everything from nourishing beverages and snacks that are good for you, to healthier, fun-for-you treats. This is human sustainability. We're also driving initiatives to sustain the environment where we and our consumers live and work. And we're committed to attracting, training, and retaining the best talent because the ability of PepsiCo to meet our performance goals and deliver our purpose agenda rests in the hands of our 185,000 associates around the globe.[1]

NEVILLE ELDER/CORBIS

To learn more about PepsiCo, go to www.pepsico.com.

Indra Nooyi is a highly competent person and leader, as suggested in her remarks and confirmed through many forms of recognition by others. This opening feature suggests just a few of the elements in her rich portfolio of personal competencies. We will have more to say about these and the other competencies demonstrated by Nooyi as the chapter unfolds.

The Organizational Behavior Division of the Academy of Management, the leading professional association dedicated to creating and disseminating knowledge about management and organizations, identifies the major topics of organizational behavior as follows:

> individual characteristics such as beliefs, values and personality; individual processes such as perception, motivation, decision making, judgment, commitment and control; group characteristics such as size, composition and structural properties; group processes such as decision making and leadership; organizational processes and practices such as goal setting, appraisal, feedback, rewards, behavioral aspects of task design; and the influence of all of these on such individual, group, and organizational outcomes as performance, turnover, absenteeism, and stress.[2]

We address all of these topics and more in this book.

One theme of this book is to demonstrate the importance of organizational behavior to your own performance. You are or probably will be an employee of an organization—and in all likelihood of several organizations—during your career. You may eventually become a team leader, a manager, or an executive. Studying organizational behavior will help you attain the knowledge and competencies needed to perform effectively in all of these roles. The knowledge and competencies that you acquire will help you diagnose, understand, explain, and act on what is happening around you in your job.

In the first section of this chapter, we introduce the elements of leadership versus management. Our general learning framework for achieving effective performance by individuals, teams, and organizations is presented next. In the remaining sections of this chapter, we explain each of the seven key competencies that are woven into the chapters throughout the book.

Organizational behavior is the study of individuals and groups within an organizational context, and the study of internal processes and practices as they influence the effectiveness of individuals, teams, and organizations. It does this by taking a system approach. That is, organizational behavior strives to understand and improve people–organization relationships in terms of the individual, team, organization, and broader social system.

Leadership versus Management

Learning Goal

1. State the core differences between leadership and management.

Leadership *is the process of developing ideas and a vision, living by values that support those ideas and that vision, influencing others to embrace them in their own behaviors, and making hard decisions about human and other resources.* Noel Tichy, who has studied many outstanding leaders, describes contemporary leadership in these words:

> Leadership is accomplishing something through other people that wouldn't have happened if you weren't there. And in today's world, that's less and less through command and control, and more and more through changing people's mindsets and hence altering the way they behave. Today, leadership is being able to mobilize ideas and values that energize other people.[3]

A **leader** *is a person who exhibits the key attributes of leadership—ideas, vision, values, influencing others, and making tough decisions.* Indra Nooyi demonstrates all of these attributes. Throughout this book, you will develop a deep appreciation for the fact that leadership is like a prism—something new and different appears each time it is looked at from another angle. Our purpose is to identify and describe diverse leadership issues, ideas, and approaches. In doing so, we present various leadership perspectives, along with their strengths, limitations, and applications. We also wrote the book to give you personal insights into your own leadership abilities and those that need further development. Our assumption is simple: Leadership can be learned but not taught. Learning leadership means that you are actively seeking to develop the competencies and make the personal changes required to become a leader.[4]

In contrast to leadership, management focuses on looking inward, improving the present, tight controls, directing, coordinating, efficiency, and the like. Likewise, in contrast to being a leader, a **manager** *directs, controls, and plans the work of others and is responsible for results.* Effective managers bring a degree of order and consistency to the work for their employees. To be effective, managers need to exhibit the attributes of leadership and/or management in various situations. Within business and other types of organizations, all managers are not leaders. Leaders are usually identified by such titles as *manager, executive, supervisor, team leader,* and the like. We often use the generic title of *manager* to refer to such individuals. Regardless of title, effective leaders and managers in organizations usually accept three key functions in their roles:

- *Authority*: the right to make decisions,
- *Responsibility*: assignment for achieving a goal, and
- *Accountability*: acceptance of success or failure.[5]

Table 1.1 provides an overview of the differences between the essentials of contemporary leadership and management. The pairs of attributes within each category are presented as contrasts; however, most managers don't function at these extreme contrasts. However, patterns that tend toward leadership on the one hand or management on the other hand are likely to emerge as managers develop and utilize their competencies.

As you review Table 1.1, think about the relative emphasis placed on leadership or management by a person for whom you have worked. How would you assess Indra Nooyi on each of the contrasts in Table 1.1? Managers may lean more heavily toward either the leadership or management profile at various times as they face different issues and problems. However, most tend to operate primarily in terms of either the leadership or the management profile.[6]

Being a leader in an organization is not limited to a very few. Consider the remarks by Indra Nooyi: "I believe that each one of PepsiCo's 185,000 employees is a leader. There are two reasons for this. First, PepsiCo is a meritocracy. Hard work gets recognized and small wins are celebrated. Second, PepsiCo has an entrepreneurial culture, so people have the ability to constantly take risks and seek ways to both improve and grow."[7]

Learning Framework

Learning Goal

2. *Outline the framework for learning about organizational behavior.*

The long-term effectiveness of an organization is determined by its ability to anticipate, manage, and respond to changes in its environment. Shareholders, unions, employees, financial institutions, and government agencies, among others, exert numerous and ever-changing pressures, demands, and expectations on the organization. The seven competencies presented in this chapter are linked to the actions of individuals, teams, and organizations as a whole. Throughout this book, therefore, we discuss the relationships among these various competencies and organizational behavior in general.

TABLE 1.1 Leadership and Management: A Comparison

CATEGORY	LEADERSHIP	MANAGEMENT
Model the Way	• Leads by example • Aligns values with actions • Understands your personal values	Leads by remote control Tells people what to do
Inspire a Shared Vision	• Imagines exciting possibilities • Appeals to shared aspirations • Paints big picture of what we aspire to be	Focuses on day-to-day activities Does things right
Challenge the Process	• Takes risks and learns from mistakes • Searches for opportunities to change, grow, and improve • Asks "What can we learn?"	Goes by the book Tight controls
Enable Others to Act	• Fosters collaboration by building trust • Shares power and decision making • Actively listens to diverse points of view	Makes all decisions Directs and controls
Encourage from the Heart	• Recognizes contributions from others • Celebrates victories • Is passionate about helping others grow	Little recognition of others' accomplishments Rewards not aligned with results

Source: Adapted from Kouzes, J. M., and Posner, B. Z. *The Leadership Challenge,* 4th ed., San Francisco: Jossey-Bass, 2007; Taylor, T., Martin, B. N., Hutchinson, S., and Jinks, M., Examination of leadership practices of principals identified as servant leaders. *International Journal of Leadership in Education,* 2007, 10, 401–419; Ergeneli, A., Gohar, R., and Temirbekova, Z., Transfer national leadership: Its relationship to culture value dimensions. *International Journal of Intercultural Relations,* 2007, 31, 703–725.

The framework for learning about organizational behavior and improving the effectiveness of employees, teams, and organizations consists of five basic parts: (1) the key competencies, with particular emphasis on individual and organizational ethics in Chapter 2, that underlie and integrate the next four parts; (2) the individual in organizations; (3) leadership and team behaviors in organizations; (4) the organization itself; and (5) integrating cases at the end of the book, as shown in Figure 1.1. This figure suggests that these parts are not independent of each other. The relationships among them are much too dynamic—in terms of variety and change—to define them as laws or rules. As we discuss each part here and throughout this book, the dynamics and complexities of organizational behavior will become clear. Most of this chapter focuses on explaining each of the seven key competencies that are developed and illustrated throughout the book.

The Individual in Organizations

Each individual makes assumptions about those with whom she or he works or spends time in leisure activities. To some extent, these assumptions influence a person's behavior toward others. An effective employee understands what affects her or his own behavior before attempting to influence the behaviors of others. In Part 2, Chapters 3 through 8, we focus on the behavior, attitudes, personality, motivations,

FIGURE 1.1 Learning Framework for Enhanced Individual, Team, and Organizational Effectiveness

Part 2: The Individual in Organizations
(Chapters 3–8)

Part 4: The
Organization
(Chapters 14–17)

Part 1: Introduction and Ethical
Foundations
(Chapters 1 and 2)

Part 3: Leadership
and Team Behaviors
(Chapters 9–13)

Part 5: Integrating Cases; Appendix : BizFlix

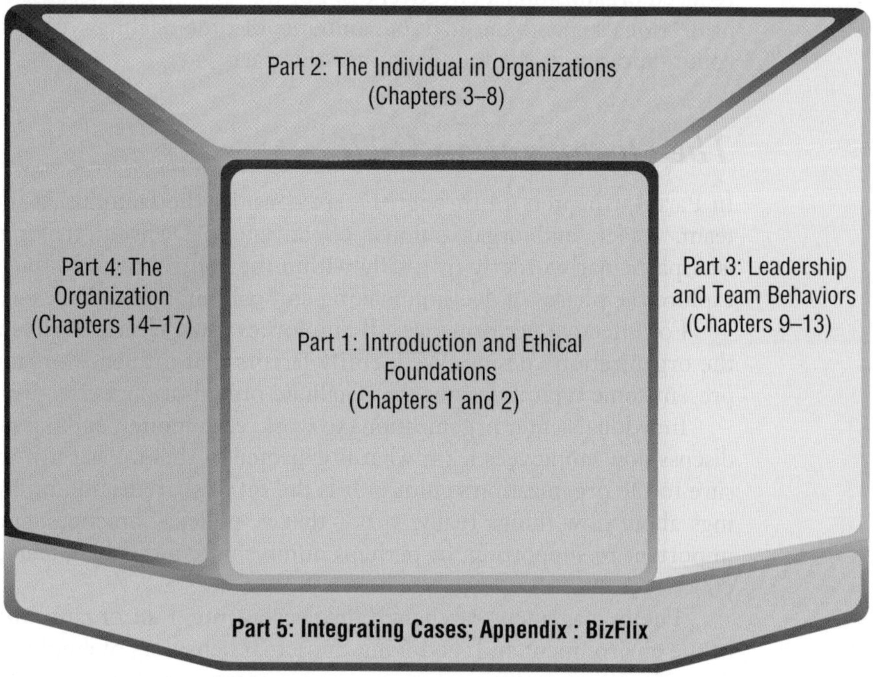

and stressors of each individual. The individual is the starting point of organizational effectiveness. Understanding the individual is crucial for enhancing individual, team, and organizational effectiveness. Each person is a physiological system composed of various subsystems—digestive, nervous, circulatory, and reproductive—and a psychological system composed of various subsystems—attitudes, perceptions, learning capabilities, personality, needs, feelings, and values. In Part 2, we concentrate on the individual's psychological system. Both internal and external factors shape a person's behavior on the job. Among others, internal factors include learning ability, motivation, perception, attitudes, personality, and values. Among the external factors that affect a person's behavior are the organization's reward system, groups and teams, managerial leadership styles, organizational culture, and the organization's design. We examine these and other factors in Parts 3 and 4.

Leaders and Teams in Organizations

Being inherently social, an individual generally doesn't choose to live or work alone. Most of the individual's time is spent interacting with others. Each person is born into a family, worships in groups, works in teams, and plays in groups. A person's identity is influenced by the ways in which other people and groups perceive and treat that person. For these reasons—and because many managers and employees spend considerable amounts of time interacting with others—a variety of competencies are usually vital to each person, team, and organization as a whole.

Effective organizations have leaders who can integrate customer, employee, and organizational goals. The ability of organizations to achieve their goals depends on the degree to which leadership abilities and styles enable managers and team leaders to plan, organize, control, influence, and act effectively. In Part 3, Chapters 9 through 13, we examine how leaders influence others and how individuals can develop their leadership competencies. Effective leadership involves developing multiple competencies.

How employees communicate with superiors, peers, subordinates, and others can help make them effective team members or lead to low morale, lack of commitment, and reduced organizational effectiveness. For that reason and because most managers and professionals spend considerable amounts of time dealing with others, interpersonal communication is the foundation for this part.

The Organization Itself

In Part 4, Chapters 14 through 17, we consider the factors that influence individual, team, leader, and organizational effectiveness. Decision making in organizations isn't particularly orderly or totally within the control of individuals. We identify and explore the phases of decision making and core models of decision making.

For effective performance, all employees must clearly understand their jobs and the organization's design. We identify factors that influence organization design and present some typical designs that facilitate organizational effectiveness.

Individuals enter organizations to work, earn money, and pursue career goals. We discuss how employees learn what is expected of them. Basically, they do so by exposure to the organization's culture. It is the set of shared assumptions and understandings about how things really work—that is, policies, practices, and norms—that are important to supporting, or perhaps diminishing, individual, team, or organizational effectiveness.

The management of change involves adapting an organization to the demands of the environment and modifying the actual behaviors of employees. We explore the dynamics of organizational change and present several basic strategies for achieving change to improve organizational effectiveness.

Competencies for Individual, Team, and Organizational Effectiveness

The first part in Figure 1.1 is competencies for individual, team, and organizational effectiveness, with special emphasis on ethical foundations. Seven competencies are the focus of this chapter. With the exception of the self competency, which is inherent to individuals, the other six competencies apply to individuals, teams, and the organization as a whole. Indra Nooyi has developed a mosaic of individual competencies over time that enables her to be a successful leader at PepsiCo. A **competency** *is an interrelated cluster of knowledge, skills, and abilities needed by an individual, team, or organization for effective performance.* A number of competencies are critical to the effectiveness and performance of most organizations.[8] The seven key competencies affect the behavior and effectiveness of each individual, team, and organization. Our emphasis is on the human side of the organization. The competencies apply to individuals and teams in all functional areas and levels of the organization as well as the organization as a whole. There are a number of other functional competencies (marketing, planning, accounting, finance, production, personnel, and so on) as well as technical competencies that are essential for individual, team, and organizational effectiveness.

The competencies emphasized are important to the effectiveness of virtually all employees, not just those in managerial and leadership roles. One of the goals of this book is to define, describe, and illustrate how the seven key competencies can be used by individuals, teams, and members of the entire organization. These ideas are woven into the discussion of organizational behavior and effectiveness throughout.

Another goal of this book is to help you to fully understand and further develop these seven competencies. Before reading further, we invite you to assess yourself in these seven key competencies. Again, with the exception of the self competency, these competencies also need to be understood, developed, and applied at the team and organizational levels. They are developed throughout the book. Go to the end of this chapter and complete the *Key Competencies Self-Assessment Inventory* on pages 27–28. Figure 1.2 suggests that these competencies are interrelated and that drawing rigid boundaries between them isn't feasible. Moreover, this figure conveys that the ethics competency plays a foundational role in implementing the other six competencies. All of the competencies are discussed in considerable depth in specific chapters.

Many leading organizations use competency frameworks, including the types of competencies we use. The competencies are used to select, develop, assess, and promote employees to foster team and organizational effectiveness. A few of these organizations include PepsiCo, Bank of America, Exxon-Mobil, John Hancock, Merck & Co., and AT&T.[9] Why do they use competency models? For years, many top-level executives believed that there were two ways to think about identifying successful individuals. From a selection perspective, the approach was to identify the common characteristics of effective individuals and try to identify them early in their career. The other perspective was to identify those employees who management thought were best able to take advantage of developmental opportunities, if provided. At the individual level, the competency-based approach identifies employees who can develop or possess key competencies and provides them with challenging opportunities to learn. Throughout this book, there are opportunities to learn how successful leaders, employees, teams, and the organization as a whole use these competencies. One successful outcome of using this book is your further development of the competencies needed to be an effective professional or leader and to understand how they apply to teams and the organization as a whole.

FIGURE 1.2 Competencies for Individual, Team, and Organizational Effectiveness

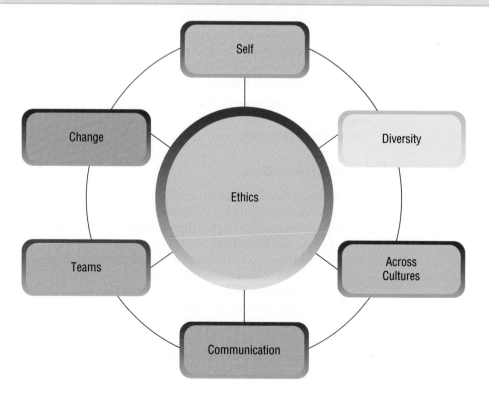

Note: These competencies focus on the human side of the organization. They apply to individuals and teams in all functional areas and levels of the organization as well as the organization as a whole. There are a number of other functional competencies (marketing, planning, accounting, finance, production, personnel, and so on) as well as technical competencies that are essential for individual, team, and organizational effectiveness.

3. *Describe the ethics competency and its contribution to effective performance.*

Ethics Competency

The **ethics competency** *includes the knowledge, skills, and abilities to incorporate values and principles that distinguish right from wrong when making decisions and choosing behaviors.* **Ethics** *are the values and principles that distinguish right from wrong.*[10]

Key Attributes

The key attributes of the ethics competency include the knowledge, skills, and abilities of individuals, teams, and the organization to be effective in doing the following:

- Identifying and describing the principles of ethical decision making and behavior.

- Assessing the importance of ethical issues in considering alternative courses of action. The decision to shop at Walmart versus Best Buy is not related to any ethical issue of consequence for most individuals. In contrast, when purchasing a new car, some individuals consider the gasoline mileage an important ethical issue that allows them to make a decision to help reduce air pollution to improve the atmosphere.

- Applying governmental laws and regulations, as well as the employer's rules of conduct, in making decisions. In general, the greater a person's level of responsibilities and authority, the more the person is likely to face increasingly complex and ambiguous ethical issues and dilemmas. For example, an associate at Best Buy does not make decisions about purchasing goods from foreign countries that often involve ethical issues. The associate has no authority and responsibility in this decision-making area at Best Buy.

- Demonstrating dignity and respect for others in working relationships, such as taking action against discriminatory practices as individually feasible and in terms of a person's position. The manager at a Walmart store is more able to stop an employee from showing disrespect to members of a minority group than is a checkout associate in the store.

- Being honest and open in communication, limited only by legal, privacy, and competitive considerations (e.g., do what you or the organization say and say what you or the organization do).

Ethics Insight

Senior leaders typically emphasize the importance of performance and the bottom line. But if they don't also emphasize ethical behavioral messages, then all employees hear is that it's all about the numbers. Get the numbers at all costs, they think—and that causes some to compromise ethics.

Ronald James, President and CEO, Center for Ethical Business Cultures

Ethical Dilemmas

The ethical issues facing organizations, leaders, and other employees have grown significantly in recent years, fueled by public concern about how business is conducted. This point is developed through Ethics Competency features throughout the book. Ethical behavior can be difficult to define, especially in a global economy with its varied beliefs and practices. Although ethical behavior in organizations clearly has a legal component, it involves more than that.

Managers, employees, and organizations alike face situations in which there are no clear right or wrong answers. An **ethical dilemma** *occurs when a decision must be made that involves multiple values.* An ethical dilemma doesn't always involve choosing right over wrong because there may be several competing values. Some ethical dilemmas arise from competitive and time pressures, among other factors.[11] Consider these two real-life examples of ethical dilemmas:

- A fellow employee told me that he plans to quit the company in two months and start a new job that has been guaranteed to him. Meanwhile, my manager told me that she wasn't going to give me a new opportunity in our company because she was going to give it to my fellow employee now. What should I do?

- The vice president told me that one of my subordinates is among several to be laid off soon and that I'm not to tell him yet or he might tell the whole organization, which would soon be in an uproar. Meanwhile, I heard from my subordinate that he plans to buy braces for his daughter and new carpet for his house. What should I do?[12]

Top-management leadership, policies and rules, and the prevailing organizational culture can do much to reduce, guide, and help individuals, teams, and organizations confront and resolve ethical dilemmas.[13]

Robert Eckert is the chairman and chief executive officer of Mattel, Inc., which is headquartered in El Segundo, California. Mattel is a worldwide firm that designs, manufactures, and markets toys and family products. The firm has 30,000 employees in 43 countries.[14] Several years ago, Mattel had recalls of 18 million toys with potentially harmful tiny magnets and 1.5 million toy railroad sets with impermissible lead paint levels. Eighty percent of the world's toys are manufactured in China by outsourcing to approximately 5,000 Chinese contractors.[15]

How this happened and what Mattel has done to strengthen its safety and testing standards since this crisis are beyond our scope here; however, the following Ethics Competency feature focuses on the transparent and assertive ways in which Eckert strived to ethically address this crisis.[16] This feature also reflects the communication competency of Eckert. It presents a few excerpts of Eckert's statements on coping with this crisis.

Ethics competency

Robert A. Eckert, Chairman and CEO, Mattel, Inc.

When the tough times hit at Mattel, consumers wanted to hear directly from me on how the company was addressing the issues. In order to maintain consumer trust in Mattel through those difficult weeks, I had to be visible. Taking responsibility was simply the right thing to do. I had to communicate widely and talk about the problems we were facing as both a company and an industry. I had to tell people how we were fixing things. That communication effort was very personal to me because it consisted of some of the most grueling days I've experienced in my professional career—from extremely tough media interviews to conversations with our business partners, and from testimony at congressional hearings to direct communications with consumers through videos on our website and other means.

Employee communications were especially important during this time. I sent numerous company-wide e-mails as we made our way through the crisis to keep employees informed about what was happening, so that they didn't first read about it in the morning newspaper. During

KARL-JOSEF HILDENBRAND/DPA/LANDOV

Robert A. Eckert, Chairman and CEO of Mattel, Inc.

Mattel's recalls, we had a crisis team that met daily in person or by phone and I made it a point to participate. People, no matter how senior or how experienced, need leadership during challenging times. As the CEO, I knew it was my responsibility to set the tone for how the company responded by making the tough calls in full view of the team.

I believe that in order to solve these challenges, unwavering integrity is one of the most important characteristics a leader can possess for effective and ethical crisis management throughout the organization.

Placing blame is not only divisive, but also wastes valuable time when people should be working together toward solutions. Leaders need to empower people and teams to make decisions and set an ethical tone through example. As an organization, I believe that Mattel has embraced a difficult test of our company and found the opportunity to become better. As an organization, we have been open about the issues we face and how we are acting to fix those issues. And we are committed to facing future challenges in the same way: with integrity—out of the shadows, and on the ethical course.

To learn more about Mattel, go to **www.mattel.com**.

Learning Goal

4. *Describe the self competency and its contribution to effective performance.*

Self Competency

The **self competency** *includes the knowledge, skills, and abilities to assess personal strengths and weaknesses, set and pursue professional and personal goals, balance work and personal life, and engage in new learning.*

Key Attributes

The key attributes of the self competency include the knowledge, skills, and abilities of individuals to be effective in doing the following:

- Understanding one's own and others' personality and attitudes.
- Perceiving, appraising, and interpreting accurately oneself and others.
- Understanding and acting on one's own and others' work-related motivations and emotions.
- Assessing and establishing one's own developmental, personal (life-related), and work-related goals.
- Taking responsibility for managing oneself and career over time and through stressful circumstances.

The self competency is the most individual-focused of the seven competencies. Its achievement creates the underlying personal attributes needed for successfully developing the other six competencies. For example, it is not possible to develop the communication competency if the individual is unable to perceive, appraise, and interpret individual differences and attitudes. We continue our discussion of Indra Nooyi's journey to understand how her self competency developed.[17]

Self competency

Indra Nooyi's Development Journey

Nooyi learned early on to embrace diversity rather than hide her differences in the corporate world. Long fascinated by the opportunities and culture of America, after working for a time in India, she headed to the United States. Coming out of Yale in 1980 with a master's in public and private management, Nooyi wore a sari to an interview at Boston Consulting Group and was offered the job. She later held corporate strategy posts at Motorola, Inc. and what is now ABB Group. She was drawn to PepsiCo by the chance to make a difference in a company that was struggling.

At PepsiCo, Nooyi has long been known for two things: a keen business sense and an irreverent personal style. The combination became obvious soon after she joined the company as its chief strategist some years ago. She pushed Chief Executive Roger Enrico to spin off Taco Bell, Pizza Hut, and KFC in 1997 because she didn't feel PepsiCo could add enough value to the fast-food business. She later was instrumental in the purchase of Tropicana, the spinoff of Pepsi's bottling business, and the $13 billion merger with Quaker Oats Co. Each of these strategic moves has paid off financially.

"She challenges you," says Tim Minges, president of the Asia Pacific region. When his team couldn't find an inexpensive alternative to palm oil for its products in Thailand, she kept pushing and pushing, saying, "I hear you, I hear you, so what's the right solution?" until they came up with one: rice bran oil. Minges continues: "Don't try to delegate up, because she will bounce it right back in your face."

Nooyi says she wishes she had reacted differently to allegations in India that traces of pesticide had been found in both Pepsi and Coke. The company denied the claims and did scientific analysis to support its position. At the time, it was not her direct responsibility. However, Nooyi reflects: "I was the face of India. I should have hopped on a plane right away and said, 'Guys, I assure you, these products are the safest.' At that point, it didn't occur to me. That's the thing I regret. Now if it happened—man, I would be there in an instant."

In a recent speech, Nooyi stated: "We're in the midst of transformation done willingly, voluntarily, and enthusiastically not in response to legislation or litigation. Our Performance with a Purpose philosophy includes fostering a culture where employees feel valued—looking for ways to advance minorities and women. The company also gives employees time and opportunities to volunteer with causes. We want people to look at this company and think it is the model for how to conduct business in the global world."

To learn more about PepsiCo, go to **www.pepsico.com.**

Career Development

A **career** *is a sequence of work-related experiences occupied by a person during a lifetime.*[18] It embraces attitudes and behaviors that are part of ongoing work-related tasks and experiences. The popular view of a career usually is restricted to the idea of moving up the ladder in an organization. At times, this opportunity is no longer available to many people because of downsizing, mergers, and the increasing tendency of managers to place the responsibility on employees to develop their own competencies. A person may remain at the same level, acquiring and developing new competencies, and have a successful career without ever being promoted. A person also can build a career by moving among various jobs in different fields, such as accounting, management information systems, and marketing, or among organizations such as Toyota, IBM, and Nike. Thus, a career encompasses not only traditional work experiences but also the opportunity for career alternatives, individual choices, and individual experiences.[19] Let's briefly consider five aspects of a career:

- The nature of a career in itself doesn't imply success or failure or fast or slow advancement. Career success or failure is best determined by the individual, rather than by others.

- No absolute standards exist for evaluating a career. Career success or failure is related to a person's self-concept, goals, and competencies. An individual should evaluate her own career goals and progress in terms of what is personally meaningful and satisfying. Unfortunately, too often the individual falls into the trap of comparing his own career progress to that of others. This can undermine the person's experience of career success.

- An individual should examine a career both subjectively and objectively. Subjective elements of a career include one's values, attitudes, personality, and motivations, which may change over time. Objective elements of a career include job choices, positions held, income earned, challenges overcome, and competencies developed.

- **Career development** *involves making decisions about an occupation and engaging in activities to attain career goals.* The central idea in the career development process is time. The shape and direction of a person's career over time are influenced by many factors (e.g., the economy, availability of jobs, skill acquisition, personal characteristics, family status, and job history).[20]

- Cultural factors play a role in careers. Cultural norms in countries such as Japan, the Philippines, and Mexico also influence the direction of a person's career. By U.S. standards, women are discriminated against as managers in these cultures. In India and South Korea, social status and educational background often influence an individual's career paths.

Ralph Waldo Emerson's classic essay "Self-Reliance" offers good advice for a person's career: "Trust thyself." To be successful, the individual needs to commit to a lifetime of learning, including the development of a career plan. A **career plan** *is the individual's choice of occupation, organization, and career path.*

Learning Goal

5. *Describe the diversity competency and its contribution to effective performance.*

Diversity Competency

The **diversity competency** *includes the knowledge, skills, and abilities to value unique individual, group, and organizational characteristics, embrace such characteristics as potential sources of strength, and appreciate the uniqueness of each.*[21] This competency includes the ability to help people work effectively together even if their interests and backgrounds are different. At PepsiCo, the importance of the diversity competency is illustrated by Indra Nooyi: "It's important to create an inclusive culture: a place where people can 'bring their whole selves to work.' A place where diverse values, beliefs, and practices are treated with respect."[22]

Diversity Insight

To truly understand the needs of our customers and consumers—and succeed in the marketplace—PepsiCo must reflect that diversity in our employees, our suppliers and in everything we do. Offering a workplace where diversity is valued helps us build the top-quality workforce so crucial to our success—by enabling us to attract and retain great people from a wide spectrum of backgrounds.

Ronald G. Parker, Chief Diversity and Inclusion Officer, PepsiCo

Key Attributes

The key attributes of the diversity competency include the knowledge, skills, and abilities of individuals, teams, and the organization to be effective in doing the following:

- Fostering an environment of inclusion with people who possess characteristics different from themselves.

- Learning from individuals, teams, or organizations with different characteristics, experiences, perspectives, and backgrounds. Diversity of thought and behavior is vital to stimulating creativity and innovation.

- Embracing and developing personal, team, or organizational tendencies—such as conscientiousness and attitudes that demonstrate respect for people of other cultures and races—that support diversity in the workplace and elsewhere.

- Communicating and personally practicing a commitment to work with individuals and team members because of their talents and contributions, regardless of their personal attributes.

- Providing leadership—*walk the talk*—in confronting obvious bias, promoting inclusion, and seeking win–win or compromise solutions to power struggles and conflicts that appear to be based on diversity issues.

- Applying governmental laws and regulations as well as organizational policies and regulations concerning diversity.

Categories of Diversity

As suggested in Figure 1.3, diversity includes many categories and characteristics. Even a single aspect of diversity, such as physical abilities or heredity, contains various characteristics that may affect individual, team, or organizational behaviors. One challenge for the individual is to determine whether those effects (1) deny opportunity and are counterproductive, (2) simply reflect a tolerance of differences, or (3) lead to embracing diversity as a value-added organizational resource. A second challenge is to assist others in valuing and embracing diversity as a source of creativity and strength.

Figure 1.3 identifies the more common categories of diversity dealt with in organizations. They are subdivided into *primary categories*—genetic characteristics that affect a person's self-image and socialization—and *secondary categories*—learned characteristics that a person acquires and modifies throughout life. As suggested by

FIGURE 1.3 Selected Categories of Diversity

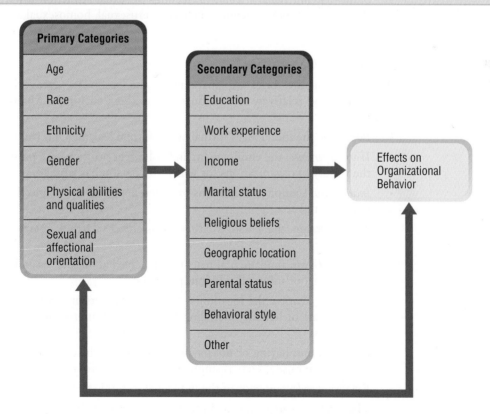

Source: Adapted from Bradford, S. Fourteen dimensions of diversity: Understanding and appreciating differences in the workplace. In J. W. Pfeiffer (ed.), 1996 *Annual: Volume 2, Consulting.* San Diego: Pfeiffer and Associates, 1996, 9–17.

the arrows, these categories aren't independent. For example, a woman (gender) with children (parental status) is likely to be directly affected by an organization with *family-friendly* or *family-unfriendly* policies and attitudes. An example of a family-unfriendly attitude would be "Your job must always come first if you are to get ahead in this organization."

Primary Categories

The following are brief explanations of the primary categories of diversity. Individuals have relatively little influence over these characteristics.

- *Age*: the number of years a person has been alive and the generation into which the individual was born in the United States [e.g., baby boomers born from 1946 through 1964; Generation X born from 1965 through 1981, or Generation Y (Millennials) born from 1982 through 2000].

- *Race*: the biological groupings within humankind, representing superficial physical differences, such as eye shape and skin color. Race accounts for less than 1 percent of the difference in a person's genetic heredity.

- *Ethnicity*: identification with a cultural group that has shared traditions and heritage, including national origin, language, religion, food, and customs. Some people identify strongly with these cultural roots, others do not.

- *Gender*: biological sex as determined by XX (female) or XY (male) chromosomes.

- *Physical abilities and qualities*: a variety of characteristics, including body type, physical size, facial features, specific abilities or disabilities, and visible and invisible physical and mental talents or limitations.

- *Sexual and affectional orientation*: feelings of sexual attraction toward members of the same or opposite gender, such as heterosexual, homosexual, or bisexual.

Secondary Categories

The following are brief explanations of the secondary categories of diversity. Individuals have relatively more influence over them during their lifetimes by making choices.

- *Education*: the individual's formal and informal learning and training.

- *Work experience*: the employment and volunteer positions the person has held and the variety of organizations for which the person has worked.

- *Income*: the economic conditions in which people grow up and their current economic status.

- *Marital status*: the person's situation as never married, married, widowed, or divorced.

- *Religious beliefs*: fundamental teachings received about deities and values acquired from formal or informal religious practices.

- *Geographic location*: the location(s) in which the person was raised or spent a significant part of her life, including types of communities and urban areas versus rural areas.

- *Parental status*: having or not having children and the circumstances in which the children are raised, such as single parenting and two-adult parenting.

- *Behavioral style*: tendency of the individual to think, feel, or act in a particular way.

The primary categories of diversity are discussed throughout the book. In the following feature, a few highlights of the diversity competency for one organization are provided. Aetna is widely recognized for its Diverse Discoveries Program.[23] A few characteristics of their program are presented in the following feature. Aetna, Inc., headquartered in Hartford, Connecticut, is a major provider of all types of insurance and pension products. It has over 35,000 employees.[24]

Diversity competency

Aetna's Diverse Discoveries Program

Ron Williams, the chairman and CEO of Aetna, introduces what it means to embrace diversity:

> We see diversity as a strategic business advantage: The simple act of knowing that what works for some might not work for all is what makes our commitment to diversity come to life every day. Our commitment becomes action when we take our understanding of differences and apply that insight to everything from how we service customers and design products to how we communicate with each other.

Each year, every Aetna employee completes web-based diversity training. It is designated to raise awareness of diversity and addresses the business case for diversity. Diversity in Action lectures assist employees in thinking about diversity in new and different ways. A Leadership Development Program focuses on identifying and developing needed competencies among underrepresented groups. A talent acquisition strategy aims to attract motivated individuals, including members of underrepresented groups, and a commitment to their development. The support of employee resource groups allows employees to share their cultures, give back to the communities, network with senior management, and attain career-building competencies. Three of these eight resource groups include African American Resource Group, Hispanic Employee Resource Group, and Women's Employee Resource Group.

How have these and other diversity values and initiatives at Aetna made a difference? A variety of external groups have recognized Aetna for its leadership and commitment to diversity, such as *Black Enterprise* magazine, the National Association for Women Executives, DiversityInc, and *CRO* magazine. Of approximately 35,000 employees, 76 percent are women and 31 percent are people of color. Women represent 64 percent of management/supervisory positions, and people of color represent 16 percent. Eleven percent of senior leaders are people of color and 30 percent are women.

To learn more about Aetna, go to **www.aetna.com**.

Across Cultures Competency

Learning Goal

6. Describe the across cultures competency and its contribution to effective performance.

The **across cultures competency** *includes the knowledge, skills, and abilities to recognize and embrace similarities and differences among nations and cultures.* **Culture** *is the dominant pattern of living, thinking, feeling, and believing that is developed and transmitted by people, consciously or unconsciously, to subsequent generations.*[25] For a *culture* to exist, it must

- be shared by the vast majority of the members of a major group or entire society;
- be passed on from generation to generation; and
- shape perceptions, judgments, and feelings as well as subsequent decisions and behavior.[26]

As discussed further in Chapter 3, a key feature of a culture is its **cultural values**—*those deeply held beliefs that lead to general preferences and behaviors and views of what is right and wrong.* Cultural values are reflected in a society's morals, customs, and established practices.

Key Attributes

The key attributes of the across cultures competency include the knowledge, skills, and abilities of individuals, teams, and the organization to be effective in doing the following:

- Understanding and appreciating the characteristics that make a particular culture unique and are likely to influence behavior.
- Understanding how work-related values, such as individualism and collectivism, influence the decisions made by individuals and groups.
- Understanding, leading, and motivating employees with different values and attitudes. These may range from the more individualistic, Western belief, to paternalistic, non-Western attitudes, to the extreme "the-state-will-take-care-of-me" collectivist mind-set.
- Communicating in the language of the host country in which the individual is working. This ability is crucial for employees who have ongoing communications with people whose native language is different from their own.
- Working with those from foreign countries. This ability applies if the assignment is abroad or the person has international responsibilities from the home office.
- Addressing leadership, organizational, and other issues through a **global mind-set**—*viewing the environment from a worldwide perspective, always looking for unexpected trends that may create threats or opportunities for a unit or an entire organization.* Some call this the ability to *think globally, act locally.*

Avoiding Stereotypes

The development of the across cultures competency is useful for diagnosing, understanding, and relating to individuals with different cultural values. Of course, there may be wide variations of behavior and values by various individuals and groups within a given society.

There is a need to be wary of stereotyping others in a particular society by glossing over the nuances and complexities of a culture.[27] Furthermore, specific issues and situations—such as work, family, friends, and recreation—can play a significant role in understanding the impact of different cultural values on behaviors. For example, when Japanese businesspeople develop contracts, they want them to be more general than detailed, as preferred by U.S. managers. They believe that those entering into an agreement are joined together and share something in common; thus, they should rely on and trust one another.

Carlos Ghosn is the cochairman, president, and CEO of Nissan Motor Co. Ltd. As a result of an alliance between Nissan and Renault in 2005, he also serves as CEO of Renault.[28] The following Across Cultures Competency feature provides several insights on Ghosn's across cultures leadership.[29]

Across Cultures competency

Carlos Ghosn, CEO, Nissan-Renault

J. Frank Brown, dean of INSEAD, a leading business school in France, comments: "Increased globalization is changing the landscape of the business climate and creating a demand for business leaders who can operate in and across different cultures. Carlos Ghosn personifies the essence of a transcultural leader by recognizing that cultural diversity is an integral component to his organization's future success."

Ghosn notes: "I think one of the basics of transcultural leadership is empathy and respect. It is essential for leaders to develop a deeper understanding of the country and the culture in which they operate and try to learn about its strengths. I would say even though the term today is not very popular, love the country and love the culture in which you are in. And try to learn about its strengths, don't focus on the weaknesses, and make sure that all the people you are transferring with you are of the same opinion. If you have to work and particularly do something significant in a country, it is much easier if somehow you connected with the country and you like the country and you respect the people and you are curious about the culture."

One of Ghosn's tasks was to help revive Nissan, but Ghosn contends the experience wasn't simply about performing a job—it was about discovering a new culture and it was very rewarding. He states: "When you have a very diverse team—people of different backgrounds, different culture, different gender, different age, you are going to get a more creative team— probably getting better solutions, and enforcing them in a very innovative way and with a very limited number of preconceived ideas."

Ghosn says that when he started at Nissan, only 1 percent of the top management at Nissan were women. Although that was twice as good as his competitors, he was determined to increase the number of women in management still further. Today, the number of women in management is 5 percent, and the goal is to raise that figure to 10 percent within a few years. Ghosn says that, although such targets are good, it's more important to set a lasting, achievable trend for women that will prove that diversity delivers.

To learn more about Nissan, go to **www.nissan-global.com.**

Communication Competency

Learning Goal

7. *Describe the communication competency and its contribution to effective performance.*

The **communication competency** *includes the knowledge, skills, and abilities to use all the modes of transmitting, understanding, and receiving ideas, thoughts, and feelings—verbal, listening, nonverbal, and written—for accurately transferring and exchanging information.*[30] This competency may be thought of as the *circulatory system* that nourishes the other competencies. Just as arteries and veins provide for the movement of blood in a person, communication allows for the exchange of information and feelings.

The communication competency is a strength of Indra Nooyi. Recall her comment in the Learning from Experience feature: "In business, sometimes in the heat of the moment, people say things. You can either misconstrue what they're saying and assume they are trying to put you down, or you can say, 'Wait a minute. Let me really get behind what they are saying to understand whether they're reacting because they're hurt, upset, confused, or they don't understand what it is I've asked them to do.'"

Key Attributes

The key attributes of the communication competency include the knowledge, skills, and abilities of individuals, teams, and the organization to be effective in doing the following:

- Conveying information, ideas, and emotions to others in such a way that they are received as intended. This ability is strongly influenced by a person's **describing skill**—*identifying concrete, specific examples of behavior and its effects.* This skill also includes recognizing that the communicator needs to avoid the tendency to jump quickly to generalizations and judgments.

- Providing constructive feedback to others.

- Engaging in **active listening**—*the process of integrating information and emotions in a search for shared meaning and understanding.* Active listening requires the use of the **questioning skill**—*the ability to ask for information and opinions in a way that gets relevant, honest, and appropriate responses.* This skill helps to bring relevant information and emotions into the dialogue and reduce misunderstandings.

- Using and interpreting **nonverbal communication**—*facial expressions, body movements, physical contact, and symbols that are often used to send messages.* The **empathizing skill** *refers to detecting and understanding another person's values, motives, and emotions.* It is especially important in nonverbal communication and active listening. The empathizing skill helps to reduce tension and increase trust and sharing.

- Engaging in **verbal communication** effectively—*presenting ideas, information and emotions to others, either one to one, between teams, or between organizations.* In a recent speech, Indra Nooyi demonstrated this personal ability when she stated: "It's vital that people are shown respect by speaking to them with truth and candor. Give people honest feedback. Let them know where they stand. Be clear about what they need to do to improve or to reach their career goals. In this same vein, managers must be approachable. Associates need to feel that they are able to talk to their leaders informally to address issues and ask questions."[31]

- Engaging in **written communication** effectively—*the ability to transfer data, information, ideas, and emotions by means of reports, letters, memos, notes, and e-mail.*

- Using a variety of computer-based (electronic) resources, such as e-mail and the Internet. Through an array of computer-based information technologies, the Internet directly links organizations and their employees to customers, suppliers, information sources, the public, and millions of individuals worldwide. We help you develop this skill throughout the book by presenting numerous Internet addresses and encouraging you to learn more about the organizations, issues, and people discussed.

In the following feature, we provide several examples of the communication competency, especially active listening, exhibited by Maureen Chiquet, the Global CEO of Chanel S.A.[32] Chanel is a private corporation headquartered in Paris, France. The firm specializes in luxury goods, handbags, perfumes, and cosmetics. It operates boutiques across the world.[33]

Communication **competency**

Maureen Chiquet, Global CEO, Chanel S.A.

In retail, you've got to have a strong point of view and present it effectively. But to lead effectively and achieve real business results as the head of any enterprise, you have to listen. You've got to constantly ask questions and seek out diverse opinions, and remain humble enough to change your mind—whether about a product or a person.

Whenever I'm in a Chanel boutique, I ask the store employees what's selling, how consumers are responding, and what we should be doing differently. Their observations help me refine my own thoughts about the business—and sometimes change my mind outright about a piece of merchandise or even a big strategy. Back in the office, I spend about 75 percent of my time listening to my direct reports' insights, and I make regular dates with our partners around the world to hear their perspectives, too. I'm always seeking information from as many varied sources as possible: I'll check YouTube, for example, just to see what people are watching. I keep my ears open and my eyes peeled for new trends in culture, the arts, film, theater, and the like.

Listening has its drawback because sometimes you realize that people are just telling you what they want you to hear. Yet, ultimately, what's good for this business—surrounding myself with talented teams and relying on their expertise—is good for me personally, too.

To learn more about Chanel S.A., go to **www.chanel.com.**

JEAN-MARC CHARLES/PHOTOLIBRARY

Chanel store in Paris, France.

Teams Competency

Learning Goal

8. *Describe the teams competency and its contribution to effective performance.*

The **teams competency** *includes the knowledge, skills, and abilities to develop, support, and lead groups to achieve goals.*[34] Howard Guttman, author of *Great Business Teams,* has studied over 300 executive teams.[35] He comments:

> Leadership is no longer about one-person rule. Today's organizations are too complex and far-flung for the "leader" to make all the decisions. That doesn't mean that organizations should be ruled by consensus—that's dysfunctional, because it's virtually impossible to get everyone to agree on every issue. Effective leaders balance the need for speed and a quality outcome with the need to involve members of their team.[36]

Key Attributes

The key attributes of the teams competency include the knowledge, skills, and abilities of individuals, teams, and the organization to be effective in doing the following:

- Determining the circumstances in which a team approach is appropriate and, if using a team is appropriate, the type of team to use.
- Engaging in and/or leading the process of setting clear performance goals for the team.
- Participating in and/or providing the leadership in defining responsibilities and tasks for the team as a whole, as well as its individual members.
- Demonstrating a sense of mutual and personal accountability for the achievement of team goals, not just an individual's own goals. That is, the individual doesn't approach problems and issues with a mind-set of "That's not my responsibility or concern."
- Applying decision-making methods and technologies that are appropriate to the goals, issues, and tasks confronting the team.

- Resolving personal and task-related conflicts among team members before they become too disruptive.
- Assessing a person's own performance and that of the team in relating to goals, including the ability to take corrective action as needed.

Teams and Individualism

People in some countries strongly believe in the importance and centrality of the individual. In the United States, the United Kingdom, and Canada, educational, governmental, and business institutions frequently state that they exist to serve individual goals. As we discuss further in Chapter 3, two cultural values that strongly affect decisions about whether to use teams and groups in organizations are *individualism* and *collectivism*.

Employees in individualistic cultures are expected to act on the basis of their personal goals and self-interest. In collectivistic countries, such as China and South Korea, the use of teams by organizations is a natural extension of their nations' cultural values. Uneasiness revolves around the relative influence of individuals in teams. We might characterize the basic difference as "fitting into the team" versus "standing out from the team." Even in societies that value individualism, teams are widely used in such firms as Mattel, PepsiCo, and Hewlett-Packard (HP).

The potential for teams and individuals to have incompatible goals clearly exists, but these goals need not always be in conflict. In fact, they often are compatible.[37] The potential strengths and weaknesses of teams is captured in the following statements: (1) teams do exist, and employees need to take them into account; (2) teams mobilize powerful forces that influence individuals; (3) teams may create both good and bad results; and (4) teams can be managed to increase the benefits from them.

Grant Reid is the president of Mars Drinks North America, headquartered in West Chester, Pennsylvania. This firm provides a wide variety of nonalcoholic beverages, coffees, teas, and the like under the Flavia brand. It is a subsidiary of Mars, Inc., a privately owned firm. In the following Teams Competency feature, Grant Reid's evolving perspective on teams is presented.[38]

Teams competency

Grant Reid, President, Mars Drinks

My thought process around leadership used to be that I would make decisions, everyone would come in, I would give them the charter for the day, and they would all run off. Now, I recognize that it's not about *me*—it's about getting the right team together, with the right expertise in that particular area, and getting the best out of that team. No one is as smart as everyone.

There are lots of meetings I no longer need to go to. If you're command-and-control, you have to be there to command and control; no major decision, no major recommendation can move forward without you there. When you have teams capable of making decisions, there are a lot of things you can let go. When I took over Mars Drinks, we were meeting globally, as a management team, every month. People were flying in from America and different parts of Europe; it was very time consuming. Now, we meet four times a year. We have scheduled telephone conversations with the whole team once a month so everybody's clear on what they're doing, and then we get on with it.

You can't keep setting up teams that do nothing, because the first thing that happens is that teams sit down and say, "OK, what are we trying to achieve here?" And if there's no real goal, each of the team members will want out. It's a self-governing process. Back in the 1980s, when I was working in Europe, you'd have teams that were more like bagel clubs—everybody would come in, have a nice chat. Everybody was pleasant to each other; nobody really called anybody out; if somebody said something that didn't make any sense, it was glossed over. The difference now is that people here ask, "What are we trying to achieve here?" And if you can't answer that question, then chances are that team doesn't have a purpose.

Teams should meet with a clear goal in mind.

To learn more about Mars, Inc., go to **www.mars.com.**

Change Competency

Learning Goal

9. *Describe the change competency and its contribution to effective performance.*

The **change competency** *includes the knowledge, skills, and abilities to recognize and implement needed adaptations or entirely new transformations in the people, tasks, strategies, structures, or technologies.*[39] The challenge of change is well stated by Grant Reid, the focus of the preceding Teams Competency feature when he adds: "In my experience, when you bring people together, everybody's uncomfortable with change to different degrees. Some say, 'OK, I get this,' and others say, 'This is never going to work in my lifetime.' Those people frequently self-select and go off and do something else. For the others, the team will hold them accountable.'"[40]

Key Attributes

The key attributes of the change competency include the knowledge, skills, and abilities of individuals, teams, and the organization to be effective in doing the following:

- Applying the six previously discussed competencies in the diagnosis, development, and implementation of needed changes.
- Providing leadership in the process of planned change. The approaches to change vary under different conditions.
- Diagnosing pressure for and resistance to change in specific situations. These pressures may be internal—such as the organizational culture—or external—such as new technologies or competitors.
- Applying processes to introduce and achieve organizational change. This includes the ability to identify key issues and diagnose them by examining the basic factors of *who, what, why, when, where,* and *how.*
- Seeking, gaining, sharing, and applying new knowledge in the pursuit of constant improvement, creativity, and entirely new approaches or goals.[41]

The following Change Competency feature provides additional insights by Indra Nooyi. It reveals several aspects of her effectiveness in leading major changes at PepsiCo.[42] Of course, Nooyi is the first to acknowledge that these changes are a result of many individuals at PepsiCo. Recall the opening Learning from Experience feature in which we highlighted Nooyi's Performance with Purpose vision, which rests on three pillars: human sustainability, environmental sustainability, and talent sustainability.

Change competency

Indra Nooyi Leads Change at PepsiCo

Since becoming CEO, Nooyi has reorganized PepsiCo to make it less focused on just the United States and broadened the top leadership team. She has hired an Italian native, Massimo d'Amore, to lead the division that includes the troublesome U.S. soft drink business. She recruited a former Mayo Clinic endocrinologist to head up the research and development division.

PepsiCo recently spent $1.3 billion on acquisitions such as Naked Juice, a California maker of soy drinks and organic juice. According to Nooyi, it essentially boils down to balancing the profit motive with making healthier snacks, striving for a net-zero impact on the environment, and taking care of the workforce. She asserts: "If all you want is to screw this company down tight and get double-digit earnings growth and nothing else, then I'm the wrong person. Companies today are bigger than many economies. We are little republics. We are engines of efficiency. If companies don't do responsible things, who is going to? Why not start making change now?"

In a speech to the food industry, Nooyi pushed the group to tackle obesity. She asked: "Do you remember campaigns like 'Keep America Beautiful'? What about 'Buckle Up'? I believe we need an approach like this to attack obesity. Let's be a good industry that does 100% of what it possibly can—not grudgingly but willingly. I am extremely proud of our track record.

Name me one other company that took out trans fats from all its products without increasing the price of its products—four or five years before anyone else. We're doing everything possible to shift our portfolio to 'better for you' or 'good for you' products."

In an interview, Nooyi notes: "I do market tours all the time. Every weekend I hop in the car and go somewhere. I listen to kids talk about what they're consuming, what they're doing, what they're not doing. I read a range of things to keep in touch with cultural and lifestyle trends—the usual business press but also *People* and *Vanity Fair* and anything close to the cutting edge of the culture. Even the AARP magazine."

Confronted by high commodity prices, a downturn in U.S. beverage sales, and other consequences of the souring economy in 2008 and 2009, Nooyi concluded some bold steps were necessary. She launched an aggressive belt-tightening program to generate more than $1.2 billion in savings by 2011. Nooyi says the tough measures—including the elimination of 3,300 jobs (much of which will be achieved through normal turnover) and the closing of some plants—were necessary to put PepsiCo ahead of the curve in a fast-changing economic environment. Most of the savings from cost cutting will be invested in fast-growing emerging markets, the U.S. beverage business, and accelerating development of new beverages and snacks.

To learn more about PepsiCo, go to **www.pepsico.com**.

Blur: Constant Change

New technologies are increasing the need for constant learning, adaptation, and innovation by individuals, teams, and entire organizations.[43] In *Blur: The Speed of Change in the Connected Economy*, S. Davis and C. Meyer proposed a formula to represent the rapidly accelerating rate of technological and other changes:

$$\text{Speed} \times \text{connectivity} \times \text{intangibles} = \text{blur.}$$

Speed	Every aspect of how organizations operate and change in real time.
Connectivity	Everything is becoming electronically connected to everything else: products, people, companies, countries—everything.

Intangibles	Every transaction has both tangible (e.g., monetary) and intangible (e.g., reputational) value. The intangible is growing faster; it is the increasing role of personal services for many organizations and the economy as a whole.
Blur	The new world in which we will come to live and work.[44]

The revolution in technologies is a driving force in creating the state of *blur* and the need to actively manage change. Throughout this book, we discuss topics from the human side of the organization that are related to the introduction and use of technology and which, in turn, are affected by it.

The rapid rise in use of the Internet throughout the world is the most obvious expression of economies and businesses that focus on technology.[45] The Internet seems to bring the entire world to a person's desktop, laptop, or personal digital assistant instantaneously and to quickly address any query or curiosity. The ever-expanding online World Wide Web is but the most recent indication of a trend during the past few decades that has brought businesses, customers, and others continually closer in real time. Technologies have shaped our expectations about acceptable time frames for communicating, performing tasks, and seeing results.

Chapter Summary

Leadership is the process of developing ideas and a vision, living by values that support those ideas and that vision, influencing others to embrace them in their own behaviors, and making hard decisions about human and other resources. Leadership includes the seven foundation competencies developed throughout this book and more. In contrast, management focuses on looking inward, improving the present, tight controls, directing, coordinating, efficiency, and the like. Both leaders and managers must accept three key functions to be effective: authority, responsibility, and accountability.

1. State the core differences between leadership and management.

Organizational behavior involves the dynamic interplay among employees, leaders, teams, and the organization itself. We introduced seven competencies in this chapter and suggested the dynamic interplay among these competencies.

2. Outline the framework for learning about organizational behavior.

The ethics competency includes the knowledge, skills, and abilities to incorporate values and principles that distinguish right from wrong when making decisions and choosing behaviors. Managers and employees often experience ethical dilemmas—situations in which a decision must be made that involves multiple values.

3. Describe the ethics competency and its contribution to effective performance.

The self competency includes the knowledge, skills, and abilities to assess a person's own strengths and weaknesses; set and pursue professional and personal goals; balance work and personal life; and engage in new learning—including new or modified skills, behaviors, and attitudes. This competency is especially inherent to the individual. Mastering it requires a lifelong process of learning and career management.

4. Describe the self competency and its contribution to effective performance.

The diversity competency includes the knowledge, skills, and abilities to value unique individual and group characteristics, embrace such characteristics as sources of organizational strength, and appreciate the uniqueness of each individual and group. These characteristics can act as potential sources of organizational strength. The core components of this competency are related to a framework of six primary categories of diversity: age, race, ethnicity, gender, physical abilities and qualities, and sexual orientation. These types of diversity are important because they often reflect differences in perspectives, lifestyles, attitudes, values, and behaviors. How leaders and employees embrace and respond to diversity influences an organization's effectiveness.

5. Describe the diversity competency and its contribution to effective performance.

6. *Describe the across cultures competency and its contribution to effective performance.*	The across cultures competency includes the knowledge, skills, and abilities to recognize and embrace similarities and differences among nations and cultures and then approach key organizational and strategic issues with an open and curious mind. Individuals' and groups' perceptions, communication, decisions, and behaviors are influenced by their culture. Too often, one's culture may influence the development of sweeping negative stereotypes about those from other cultures.
7. *Describe the communication competency and its contribution to effective performance.*	The communication competency includes the knowledge, skills, and abilities to transmit, receive, and understand data, information, thoughts, and emotions—nonverbal, verbal, written, listening, electronic, and the like—for accurately transferring and exchanging information and emotions. Core components of this competency are describing, active listening, questioning, nonverbal communication, empathizing, verbal communication, and written communication. This competency is like the body's circulatory system, nourishing and carrying information to other competencies to enhance individual, team, and organizational effectiveness.
8. *Describe the teams competency and its contribution to effective performance.*	The teams competency includes the knowledge, skills, and abilities to develop, support, and lead teams to achieve organizational goals. Recognition of the potential for individual and team differences is stressed.
9. *Describe the change competency and its contribution to effective performance.*	The change competency includes the knowledge, skills, and abilities to recognize and implement needed adaptations or entirely new transformations. New technologies are one of the primary sources of change, which creates a state of *blur*. The Internet is a primary enabler of increasing organizational effectiveness and efficiency.

Key Terms and Concepts

Across cultures competency, **17**

Active listening, **20**

Career, **13**

Career development, **14**

Career plan, **14**

Change competency, **23**

Communication competency, **19**

Competency, **8**

Cultural values, **17**

Culture, **17**

Describing skill, **19**

Diversity competency, **14**

Empathizing skill, **20**

Ethical dilemma, **10**

Ethics, **10**

Ethics competency, **10**

Global mind-set, **18**

Leader, **4**

Leadership, **4**

Manager, **5**

Nonverbal communication, **20**

Organizational behavior, **4**

Questioning skill, **20**

Self competency, **12**

Teams competency, **21**

Verbal communication, **20**

Written communication, **20**

Discussion Questions

1. In the Learning from Experience feature, Indra Nooyi states: "Performance with Purpose rests on three pillars: human sustainability, environmental sustainability, and talent sustainability." Go to the PepsiCo website at www.pepsico.com. Click on "Company" and choose "PepsiCo Values and Philosophy." Which attributes of the ethics competency are illustrated in PepsiCo's statement of "Guiding Principles"?

2. Review the Ethics Competency feature entitled "Robert A. Eckert, Chairman and CEO, Mattel, Inc." Which attributes of the ethics competency are illustrated in this feature?

3. Review the Diversity Competency feature on "Aetna's Diverse Discoveries Program." Which attributes of the diversity competency are illustrated in this feature?

4. Review the Self Competency feature on "Indra Nooyi's Development Journey." Which attributes of the self competency are illustrated in this feature?

5. Review the Across Cultures Competency feature on "Carlos Ghosn, CEO, Nissan-Renault." Which attributes of the across cultures competency are illustrated in this feature?

6. Review the Communication Competency feature on "Maureen Chiquet, Global CEO, Chanel S.A." In addition to active listening, what other attributes of the communication competency appear to be illustrated in this feature?

7. Review the Teams Competency feature on "Grant Reid, President, Mars Drinks." Which attributes of the teams competency are illustrated in this feature?

8. Review the Change Competency feature on "Indra Nooyi Leads Change at PepsiCo." Which attributes of the change competency are illustrated in this feature?

9. What aspect of your life or role that you play reflects some or all of the variables that go into creating the state of blur? Explain.

Experiential Exercise and Case

Experiential Exercise: Self Competency

Key Competencies Self-Assessment Inventory

Instructions

The statements in this inventory describe specific knowledge/skills/abilities that are needed to be an effective leader or professional. This inventory focuses on the individual rather than teams or the organization as a whole with respect to the key competencies developed in this book. For each specific knowledge/skill/ability statement, you are to assess yourself on a scale from 1 to 10, according to the descriptive statements provided on the scale shown here.

10 I am outstanding on this knowledge/skill/ability.
9   I am very good on this knowledge/skill/ability.
8   I am good on this knowledge/skill/ability.
7   I am average on this knowledge/skill/ability.
6   I am barely adequate on this knowledge/skill/ability.
5   I am lacking on this knowledge/skill/ability.
4   I am weak on this knowledge/skill/ability.
3   I am very weak on this knowledge/skill/ability.
2   I have little relevant experience on this knowledge/skill/ability, but the experiences I have had are poor.
1   I have no relevant experience. I have not yet begun to develop this knowledge/skill/ability.

Fill in the blank next to each listed specific knowledge/skill/ability with a number from the preceding scale that you think is most descriptive of yourself. It is important that you choose a number that is most descriptive of what you are *actually like* rather than what you would prefer to be like or how you would like others to see you.

Statements of Knowledge/Skills/Abilities

_____ 1. Maintains an awareness of own behavior and how it affects others.

_____ 2. Is able to set priorities and manage time.

_____ 3. Knows own limitations and asks for help when necessary.

_____ 4. Assesses and establishes own life- and work-related goals.

_____ 5. Takes responsibility for decisions and managing self.

_____ 6. Perseveres in the face of obstacles or criticism.

_____ 7. Is not self-promoting or arrogant.

_____ 8. Recovers quickly from failure, including learning from mistakes.

_____ 9. Tries to learn continuously.

_____ 10. Pursues feedback openly and nondefensively.

_____ 11. Organizes and presents ideas effectively.

_____ 12. Detects and understands others' values, motives, and emotions.

_____ 13. Presents written materials clearly and concisely.

_____ 14. Listens actively and nonjudgmentally.

_____ 15. Responds appropriately to positive and negative feedback.

_____ 16. Is aware of and sensitive to nonverbal messages.

_____ 17. Holds people's attention when communicating.

_____ 18. Shares information willingly.

_____ 19. Expresses own needs, opinions, and preferences without offending others.

_____ 20. Uses a variety of computer-based (electronic) resources to communicate.

_____ 21. Encourages the inclusion of those who are different from self.

_____ 22. Seeks to learn from those with different characteristics and perspectives.

_____ 23. Embraces and demonstrates respect for people of other cultures and races.

_____ 24. Shows sensitivity to the needs and concerns of others.

_____ 25. Seeks positive win–win or appropriate compromise solutions to conflicts based on diversity issues.

_____ 26. Embraces unique individual and group characteristics as potential sources of organizational strength.

_____ 27. Is sensitive to differences among people and seeks ways to work with them.

_____ 28. Respects the ideas, values, and traditions of others.

_____ 29. Identifies opportunities to promote diversity.

_____ 30. Invests personal effort in helping people with attributes different from self to succeed.

_____ 31. Demonstrates dignity and respect for others in working relationships.

_____ 32. Is honest and open in communication, limited only by privacy, legal, and competitive considerations.

_____ 33. Assesses the right or wrong in own decisions and behaviors.

_____ 34. Adheres to professional and organizational codes of conduct.

_____ 35. Resists pressures from others to engage in unethical conduct.

_____ 36. Understands ethical principles and rules.

_____ 37. Is seen by others as a person of integrity.

_____ 38. Sets clear expectations of ethical behavior and regularly reinforces this expectation with others.

_____ 39. Is sensitive to the rights of others.

_____ 40. Takes responsibility for own decisions and actions—doesn't place blame on others to escape responsibility.

_____ 41. Seeks to understand and appreciate the characteristics that make a particular culture unique.

_____ 42. Treats people from different cultures with respect.

_____ 43. Considers managerial and other issues from a worldwide perspective, that is, the ability to think globally, act locally.

_____ 44. Works effectively with members from different cultures.

_____ 45. Likes to experience different cultures.

_____ 46. Learns from those with different cultural backgrounds.

_____ 47. Knows which cultures have the expectation that individuals are to take care of themselves.

_____ 48. Possesses firsthand knowledge that different cultures are risk adverse and use rules to minimize trying to deal with uncertainty.

_____ 49. Knows how masculinity and femininity in different societies affect interpersonal relationships.

_____ 50. Works effectively with people from different cultures who value unequal distribution of power in society.

_____ 51. Works effectively in team situations.

_____ 52. Encourages teams to celebrate accomplishments.

_____ 53. Demonstrates mutual and personal responsibility for achieving team goals.

_____ 54. Observes dynamics when working with groups and raises relevant issues for discussion.

_____ 55. Promotes teamwork among groups, discourages "we versus they" thinking.

_____ 56. Supports and praises others for reaching goals and accomplishing tasks.

_____ 57. Encourages and supports creativity in teams.

_____ 58. Shares credit with others.

_____ 59. Motivates team members to work toward common goals.

_____ 60. Is able to use groupware and related information technologies to achieve team goals.

_____ 61. Demonstrates the leadership skills to implement planned change.

_____ 62. Understands how to diagnose pressures for and resistances to change.

_____ 63. Prepares people to manage change.

_____ 64. Learns, shares, and applies new knowledge to improve a team, department, or whole organization.

_____ 65. Knows how to diagnose a firm's culture.

_____ 66. Uses a variety of technologies to achieve successful change.

_____ 67. Understands how various organizational designs can be used to bring about successful organizational change.

_____ 68. Possesses a positive attitude toward considering changes and new ideas.

_____ 69. Is able to negotiate and resolve conflicts that are often part of any significant change.

_____ 70. Understands how organizational cultures influence organizational change.

Scoring and Interpretation

The _Key Competencies Self-Assessment Inventory_ seeks your self-perceptions on characteristics and dimensions that are representative of seven key competencies. Total your responses for each competency as instructed. The sum of your responses is your score. The maximum score is 100 points for each competency.

Self Competency:
Includes the knowledge, skills, and abilities to assess your own strengths and weaknesses; set and pursue professional and personal goals; balance work and personal life; and engage in new learning—including new or changed skills, behaviors, and attitudes.
- Add your responses for items 1 through 10 = _____, which is your self-assessment on the self competency.

Communication Competency:
Includes the knowledge, skills, and abilities to use all of the modes of transmitting, understanding, and receiving ideas, thoughts, and feelings—verbal, listening, nonverbal, written, electronic, and the like—for accurately transferring and exchanging information and emotions.
- Add your responses for items 11 through 20 = _____, which is your self-assessment on the communication competency.

Diversity Competency:
Includes the knowledge, skills, and abilities to value unique individual, group, and organizational characteristics, embrace such characteristics as potential sources of strength, and appreciate the uniqueness of each.
- Add your responses for items 21 through 30 = _____, which is your self-assessment on the diversity competency.

Ethics Competency:
Includes the knowledge, skills, and abilities to incorporate values and principles that distinguish right from wrong when making decisions and choosing behaviors.
- Add your responses for items 31 through 40 = _____, which is your self-assessment on the ethics competency.

Across Cultures Competency:
Includes the knowledge, skills, and abilities to recognize and embrace similarities and differences among nations and cultures and then approach key issues with an open and curious mind.
- Add your responses for items 41 through 50 = _____, which is your self-assessment on the across cultures competency.

Teams Competency:
Includes the knowledge, skills, and abilities to develop, support and lead groups to achieve goals.
- Add your responses for 51 through 60 = _____, which is your self-assessment on the teams competency.

Change Competency:
Includes the knowledge, skills, and abilities to recognize and implement needed adaptations or entirely new transformations in the people, tasks, strategies, structures, or technologies.
- Add your responses for items 61 through 70 = _____, which is your self-assessment on the change competency.

Your Overall Profile and Comparisons

Determine your overall profile of competencies by using the summary (total) score for each competency. Compare and contrast your scores with those of two sample populations: (1) experienced managers and professionals (shown in the table below) and (2) undergraduate students at colleges and universities (shown in the table to the right). Mean scores and standard deviations are based on a sample of more than 300 individuals. One standard deviation from the mean covers 68 percent of the sample population; that is, if your score falls within one standard deviation of the mean score of either the managerial or the student sample, your score is similar to the scores of 68 percent of the students.

Managerial Sample Population

Competency	Mean	One Standard Deviation From Mean	Numerical Range for 68% of Population (High and Low)
Self	78	9	87–69
Communication	75	9	84–66
Diversity	75	11	87–63
Ethics	84	9	93–75
Across Cultures	72	14	86–58
Teams	77	12	89–65
Change	69	14	83–52

Student Sample Population

Competency	Mean	One Standard Deviation from Mean	Numerical Range for 68% of Population (High and Low)
Self	77	8	85–69
Communication	74	9	84–65
Diversity	75	12	88–63
Ethics	83	8	91–75
Across Cultures	66	16	84–50
Teams	79	11	90–68
Change	67	16	84–52

Overall Interpretations

Scores	Meaning
20–39	You see yourself as having little relevant experience and are deficient on this competency.
40–59	You see yourself as generally lacking on this competency but may be satisfactory or better on a few of its knowledge/skill/ability components.
60–74	You see yourself as average on this competency—probably below average on some of its knowledge/skill/ability components.
75–89	You see yourself as generally above average on this competency and very good on a number of its knowledge/skill/ability components.
90–100	You see yourself as generally outstanding on this competency.

Questions
1. What does your overall profile suggest in relation to your needs for personal and professional development?
2. Based on the competency most in need of development, identify three possible actions that you might take to reduce the gap between your current and desired level for that competency.
3. Would others who work with you closely or know you well agree with your self-assessment profile? In what dimensions might their assessments of you be similar to your own? Why? In what dimensions might they differ? Why?

Case: Diversity Competency

Accenture's Work–Life Balance Programs[46]

Accenture is a global management consulting, technology services, and outsourcing company. It has over 186,000 employees with offices and operations in 200 cities within 52 countries. Accenture is headquartered in New York City.

Time and Flexibility

Internal surveys at Accenture revealed that time is highly valued among employees—regardless of age—as are daily and career flexibility. Eighty-one percent of the employees reported that their job satisfaction would increase significantly with additional time and location flexibility. Eighty-three percent said the ability to balance work and life impacts their commitment to stay with Accenture. Sixty-one percent indicated that sabbaticals (career flexibility) are one of the top five most-favored resources. Equally between genders, 32 percent have turned down a new position in the past several years or considered leaving because of work–life balance concerns. Seventy-one percent said wellness is a priority.

Work–Life Initiative at Accenture

As a result of these findings and other considerations, Accenture developed two dozen work–life initiatives to give employees more time and flexibility. They range from flexible work arrangements to programs such as *Back-Up Dependent Care* and *Lifeworks*. In-home or center-based care is available for any dependent when regular care arrangements break down. *Lifeworks* is a free and confidential resource that provides information on a broad range of topics—from online health coaching to ergonomics assessments. This initiative also provides access to experts in many areas, including legal and financial.

Future Leave is among the most successful new programs at Accenture. It provides Gen X (born 1965–1981) and Gen Y (born 1982–2000) employees and baby boomers alike the flexibility to address the personal and family issues they face at their particular stage of life while preserving promising or well-established careers. This initiative makes it possible for employees to take a self-funded sabbatical lasting from one to three months to teach English in another country, trek through Alaska, or meet family commitments. Any activity that employees believe will enrich their lives, their families, or their communities is eligible for approval. Employees may take *Future Leave* after every three years of work. It offers participants the option of planning ahead and putting aside savings in a special account at Accenture to fund a future leave. On average, 50 employees each quarter are away from their jobs on such sabbaticals. This number is expected to increase in the future.

Chris Tserng

Chris Tserng, the Human Resources Demand Lead for Accenture's insurance practice in North America, supervises a staff of four in the Cincinnati, Ohio, office. This office supports executives when they work at client sites across the country. Ten years into her career at Accenture and eight months pregnant with her first child, Tserng earned a promotion. As planned, she took eight weeks of maternity leave and four weeks of accrued vacation time.

Tserng states: "I didn't know how hard it would be to leave my baby, Nicholas. I was feeling guilty and nervous. The guilt was compounded when I learned that the sitter I'd lined up had a change in plans. I didn't know what to do or where to turn for child care. I began to think that my only option was to consider leaving the company, the job, and the colleagues I loved."

Future Leave was the answer for Tserng, making it possible for her to add one additional month to her maternity leave and paid time-off. During that extra time away, she and her husband located an appropriate day-care facility for Nicholas. Tserng adds: "It's the best thing I ever did for my family. It was only 30 days, but it gave me the time to make important decisions about Nicholas and about my own future."

At the end of her leave, Tserng said her colleagues welcomed her back with open arms. She adds, "A lot of our executives, the men especially, recognize that once women become mothers, they do feel guilty about leaving their child and some decide not to return to work."

To learn more about Accenture, go to **www.accenture .com.**

Questions
1. Which key attributes of the diversity competency are illustrated in this case? Give a specific example of each attribute identified.
2. Which key attributes of the self competency are illustrated by Chris Tserng in this case? Give a specific example of each attribute identified.
3. Which key attributes of the change competency are illustrated in this case? Give a specific example of each attribute identified.

chapter 2

Individual and Organizational Ethics

Learning Goals

After studying this chapter, you should be able to:

1
Describe the stages of moral and ethical development.

2
Explain and apply the core concepts used by individuals and organizations to make ethical decisions.

3
Describe some ethics-based initiatives for fostering diversity in organizations.

4
Explain the nature of stakeholder responsibility and its ethical basis.

Learning Content

Anne Mulcahy, Chairman and Former CEO of Xerox, Commits to Business Ethics

Anne M. Mulcahy is the chairman and former CEO of the Xerox Corporation, headquartered in Norwalk, Connecticut. Xerox is best known for its copiers, but it also makes printers, scanners, and fax machines. The company sells document software and copier supplies and also provides consulting and document outsourcing. In this feature and throughout the chapter, we present a number of aspects of Anne Mulcahy's personal commitment to ethics and Xerox's initiatives for nurturing an ethically based organization.

When Mulcahy was appointed the CEO in 2001, it was not the best time to be the company's leader. On May 11, 2000, Xerox fired CEO Richard Thoman (later charged with, but not convicted of, accounting fraud), and promoted Mulcahy to chief operating officer (COO). Acting CEO Paul Allaire (also later charged with, but not convicted of, accounting fraud) made it clear that Mulcahy was running the show. At the time, the company was $18 billion in debt and its stock price tanked. In their settlements with the U.S. Securities and Exchange Commission, Barry Romeril, the chief financial officer, was barred for life from serving as an officer or director of any corporation; Allaire was barred for five years; Thoman for three years.

Mulcahy believes in transparency and on October 3, 2000, she candidly told analysts, "Xerox's business model is unsustainable." She was thanked for her honesty by a stock sell-off. Rumors of bankruptcy

and takeovers flourished. Things got worse. In January 2001, word got out that an assistant treasurer had been fired six months earlier for reporting to his superiors that accounting irregularities were widespread. This contradicted management's earlier claims that the problems were confined to its Mexican operations. Four months later, Xerox announced it was restating three years of financials. In late July 2001, the Xerox board offered Mulcahy the top job. "I had never been on the board," Mulcahy remembered. "I didn't even know the board." She had, however, been viewed favorably by outsiders, even as her peers were being pilloried for their governance failures. "I went about preparing myself with a vengeance," Mulcahy said.

Mulcahy has since ensured that Xerox's ethics and governance practices and policies are

STEFAN ZAKLIN/GETTY IMAGES

To learn more about Xerox, go to www.xerox.com.

among the best in business today. *Business Ethics* magazine, the Ethisphere Institute, and others consider Xerox among the world's most ethical companies. Recently, Mulcahy was selected as Chief Executive of the Year by *Chief Executive* magazine. She is the first woman CEO to be chosen by her peers for this honor. It is based on multiple criteria and competencies. Mulcahy decided to resign as CEO in July 2009 and continues as chairman.[1]

Ethical concepts and issues are being increasingly recognized as vital components of decision making in leading organizations, such as Xerox and Johnson & Johnson. In the Learning from Experience feature, Anne Mulcahy provides a glimpse into her efforts to instill and shape an ethical environment. It is the obligation of every organization's top leaders to model and champion the core values and ethical principles that employees should use to guide their behaviors and decision making.

The issues, concepts, and processes related to making ethical decisions are the focus of this chapter. First, we discuss the stages of moral and ethical development. Second, we discuss core concepts and principles that are fundamental to ethical decision making and behavior. Next, we describe some ethics-based initiatives for nurturing diversity in organizations. Then, we conclude with a discussion of several ethics-based initiatives for fostering stakeholder responsibility.

Individual Differences and Ethics

Learning Goal

1. *Describe the stages of moral and ethical development.*

Because of the importance of ethics in organizations, we recognize it throughout this book in the Ethics Competency features.[2] As discussed in Chapter 1, the *ethics competency* involves the knowledge, skills, and abilities needed by individuals, teams, and organizations to incorporate values and principles that distinguish right from wrong when making decisions and choosing behaviors. We also noted in Chapter 1 that *ethics* are values and principles that help individuals distinguish right from wrong. In the broadest sense, *ethics* refers to the study of moral values, principles, and rules, including the determination of standards of conduct and obligations for individuals and organizations. Ethical issues in organizations are common and complex. In fact, ethical issues influence the decisions that employees make daily. Some ethical issues involve factors that blur individual perceptions between "right" and "wrong." As a result, some employees may differ in their opinions about what is ethical or unethical in various situations.[3]

Stages of Moral Development

Lawrence Kohlberg probably is the best known scholar in the field of the psychology of ethical decision making and behavior. Kohlberg's model of moral development is useful for exploring questions about how members of an organization regard ethical dilemmas, including how they determine what is right or wrong in a particular situation.[4] Kohlberg held that people develop morally, much as they do physically, from early childhood to adulthood. As they develop, their ethical criteria and patterns of moral reasoning go through stages, as suggested in Figure 2.1. **Stages of moral development** *are stages through which individuals evolve, ranging from the lowest stage (obedience and punishment orientation) to the highest stage (universal ethical principles).* Kohlberg didn't assume that everyone progresses through all of the stages. For example, an adult criminal could be stuck in the first stage. Moreover, Kohlberg contended that what defines a person's stage of moral development is *not* the specific ethical choice, but the person's ethical *reasoning* used to justify that choice. For example, individuals may talk and think at a higher moral level, but may not always behave accordingly. Situational forces, such as threatening peer pressure or demands from higher management, may lead to behaviors that the person would not otherwise exhibit.[5]

FIGURE 2.1 Kohlberg's Stages of Moral Development

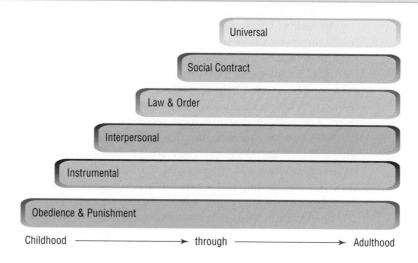

Universal

Social Contract

Law & Order

Interpersonal

Instrumental

Obedience & Punishment

Childhood ——————→ through ——————→ Adulthood

An individual at the *obedience and punishment stage* does the right thing mainly to avoid punishment or to obtain approval. In other words, only the immediate consequences of an action determine whether it's good or bad. An employee stuck at this stage might think that the only reason not to steal money from an employer is the certainty of getting caught and then fired or even arrested. Obviously, organizations don't want employees who use such simple reasoning to guide their behavior when faced with ethical issues.

An individual at the *instrumental stage* becomes aware that others also have needs and begins to defer to them to get what the individual wants. Proper behavior is what satisfies the person's self-interest. At times, self-interest can be satisfied by making deals or exchanges with other people. An employee at this stage might be willing to defer to the needs of the employer to reduce absenteeism, but only if the employer gives something in return.

An individual at the *interpersonal stage* considers appropriate behavior as that which pleases or is approved by friends or family. Proper behavior exhibits conformity to conventional expectations, often of the majority. At this stage, being seen as a "good person" with basically good motives is important. An employee at this stage might focus on the importance of being a loyal employee and colleague who is always friendly and who avoids or remains calm during conflict. For example, if a work absence creates conflicts or work overload for other employees, some individuals at this stage might be willing to reduce their absences even if that meant not using all of their allotted sick days.

An individual at the *law and order stage* recognizes that ethical behavior consists of doing a person's duty, showing respect for authority, and maintaining the social order for its own sake. Loyalty to the nation and its laws is paramount. The person sees other people as individuals and also as parts of the larger social system that gives them their roles and obligations. An employee at this stage might rigidly adhere to organizational rules and regulations and legitimate orders from superiors. The employee is likely to resist or criticize the efforts of coworkers or superiors to bend or break the rules. In some organizations, employees commonly take paid sick days even when they aren't sick. Employees may even encourage each other to take all of their sick days. They view these leave days as something the organization owes them. However, the organization's policy or union contract may state that sick days are allowed only for legitimate illnesses. In this situation, employees at the law and order stage might resist peer pressure to take a day off if they aren't ill. They would view the organization's rules or the union contract as overriding the pressures from their peers. At this stage of moral reasoning, rules are considered to be necessary for the effective functioning of the entire organization, and they should be followed even when it requires some self-sacrifices or resisting pressures from peers.

An individual at the *social contract stage* is aware that others hold a variety of conflicting personal views that go beyond the letter of the law. An individual at this stage understands that, although rules and laws may be agreed on and for the most part must be followed, they can be changed if necessary. Some absolute values, such as life and liberty, are held regardless of different individuals' values or even majority opinion. "The greatest good for the greatest number" is a key characteristic at this stage. The individual at this stage recognizes that employees are expected to follow the rules but also accepts the idea of breaking the rules when those rules conflict with accepted social values. They accept the organization permitting employees to be absent for only a specified number of days. But if the employee believes that the absentee rules unduly restrict freedom, he or she might also feel justified in breaking the rule or working to make it less restrictive.

Finally, an individual at the *universal principles stage* views appropriate conduct as determined by a person's conscience, based on universal ethical principles. Kohlberg felt that universal principles are founded in justice, the public welfare, the equality of human rights, and respect for the dignity of individual human beings. In his model, people at the most advanced stage of ethical reasoning recognize these universal principles and act in accordance with them rather than rules or laws.

Moral Intelligence

The contributions of Kohlberg and others are the foundation for the development of the concept of *moral intelligence*, which has been advanced in the field of education, medicine, and more recently business. It partially overlaps with *emotional intelligence* (EQ), which is discussed in Chapter 3.

Moral intelligence is the mental capacity to determine how universal human principles that cut across the globe should be applied to personal values, goals, and actions.[6] The moral principles in moral intelligence include:

- *Integrity:*   acting consistently with principles, values, and belief; telling the truth; standing up for what is right; and keeping promises.

- *Responsibility:*   taking responsibility for personal choices; admitting mistakes and failures; embracing responsibility for serving others.

- *Compassion:*   actively caring about others.

- *Forgiveness:*   letting go of one's own mistakes; and letting go of others' mistakes.[7]

Our concept of the *ethics competency* includes these moral principles. The following provides more insights about Anne Mulcahy, the chairman of Xerox who was discussed in the chapter-opening feature, as a person who reflects moral intelligence and champions the ethics competency.[8]

Ethics competency

Anne Mulcahy's Ethical Leadership

Each year, Anne Mulcahy distributes a letter to all Xerox employees on business ethics. It reflects her personal commitment to ethical principles and the expectations she has for all employees. The following paragraphs are excerpts from one of Mulcahy's letters.

In our highly competitive environment, where the pressure to perform is intense and relentless, we must constantly strive to do more and do better. Results are important—vital, in fact—and the pressure to improve results will always be with us. But, equally important is the means we use to achieve results. We must conduct ourselves and our business dealings with the highest degree of ethical conduct. This means not only complying with laws, regulations and company policies, but also doing so in a way that reflects our core values.

When it comes to business ethics, there is no choice and there can be no change in our position. Ethic issues are so serious that, in some instances, violations could result in serious legal penalties for Xerox Corporation and for the individual. Furthermore, violations of our ethics policy could damage the reputation of Xerox, as well as the individual. To make certain that we protect our reputation and ensure compliance with applicable laws, regulations, company policies and values, every violation of the ethics policy will be treated severely by the management of this Corporation. We must have zero tolerance in this regard.

We have a duty to assure that Xerox people understand their ethical obligations. For this reason, we have a written Xerox Code of Conduct, available to all employees in multiple languages, and we cascade a letter like this throughout the company every year. It is important to rededicate ourselves periodically to our unwavering commitment to ethical conduct.

We are committed to an absolute standard of the highest ethical behavior and unquestionable integrity in our financial reporting and business activities. For a Xerox manager, regardless of the division or the location, compliance with our policies and code of conduct is a non-negotiable requirement.

To learn more about Xerox, go to **www.xerox.com**.

Decision Making and Ethics

Learning Goal

2. Explain and apply the core concepts used by individuals and organizations to make ethical decisions.

The Ethics Resource Center, headquartered in Washington, D.C., conducts ethical surveys of employees in the United States. In their most recent survey, more than half of the American employees surveyed observed at least one type of ethical misconduct a year in their workplace despite an increase in employees' awareness of formal ethics programs. The importance of having an ethical culture in organizations cannot be underestimated. Employees in organizations with a weak ethical culture reported a much higher level of observing at least one type of misconduct (theft, lying, etc.) than employees in an organization with a strong ethical culture (52 percent compared to 4 percent, respectively). Employees in organizations with a weak ethical culture were much more likely to experience pressure to break rules than those in strong ethical culture organizations (18 percent compared to one-half of 1 percent). Culture had a stronger impact on the results reported by employees than an organization's formal ethics and compliance programs. Patricia Harned, the president of the Ethics Resource Center, comments: "Creating a strong ethical environment should be a top priority of all companies. We know formal programs are critical and work well initially, but we must now focus greater attention on building the right culture in which ethics programs operate. This data shows, for example, that leaders needs to behave by example to set an ethical culture throughout the whole organization."[9] Anne Mulcahy and the other top executives at Xerox show their commitment to a strong ethical culture by using their own behavior as an example.

In some situations, there are no simple rules for making ethical decisions. Our goal here is to help you develop your ethics competency. The five key components that comprise the basics of ethical decision making include ethical intensity, ethics-based principles, concern for affected individuals, benefits and costs, and determination of rights. As suggested in Figure 2.2, these basic components are interrelated and need to be considered as a whole in order to make ethical decisions and create an ethical culture.

FIGURE 2.2 Basic Components for Making Ethical Decisions

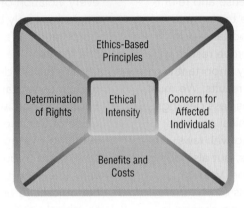

Ethical Intensity

Ethical intensity *is the degree of moral importance given to an issue.* It is determined by the combined impact of six factors, which are shown in Figure 2.3 and described as follows[10]:

- **Magnitude of consequences** *is the harm or benefits accruing to individuals affected by a decision or behavior.* An action that causes 1,000 people to suffer a particular injury has greater consequences than an action that causes 20 people to suffer the same injury. A decision that causes the death of a human being is of greater consequence than one that causes a sprained wrist.

- **Probability of effect** *is the likelihood that if a decision is implemented it will lead to the harm or benefit predicted.* The production of an automobile that would be dangerous to occupants during normal driving has greater probability of harm than the production of a NASCAR race car that endangers the driver when curves are taken at high speed. The sale of a gun to a known armed robber has a greater probability of harm than the sale of a gun to a law-abiding hunter.

- **Social consensus** *is the amount of public agreement that a proposed decision is bad or good.* Actively discriminating against minority job candidates is worse than

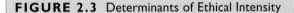

FIGURE 2.3 Determinants of Ethical Intensity

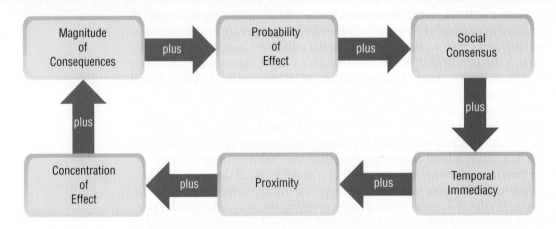

not actively seeking out minority job candidates. Bribing a customs official in the United States or Canada evokes greater public condemnation than bribing a customs official in a country (e.g., Nigeria or Chad) where such behavior is an accepted way of doing business. Managers and employees will have difficulty deciding what is and isn't ethical if they aren't guided by a reasonable amount of public agreement or if the organization's ethical culture is weak.

- **Temporal immediacy** *is the length of time that elapses between making a decision and when the consequences of that decision are known.* A shorter length of time implies greater immediacy. Assume Merck releases a drug that causes 1 percent of the people who take it to have acute nervous reactions within one week. This has greater temporal immediacy than releasing a drug that will cause 1 percent of those who take it to develop nervous disorders after 25 years of use. A reduction in the retirement benefits of current retirees at GM, Ford, and Chrysler has greater temporal immediacy than a reduction in the future retirement benefits of employees who are currently 25 years of age.

- **Proximity** *is the sense of closeness (social, cultural, psychological, or physical) that the decision maker has for victims or beneficiaries of the decision.* Recently, Citigroup cut 53,000 jobs. This reduced its labor force to 300,000 employees with more layoffs anticipated. This action had a greater impact on the remaining employees than the personal impact the news reporters feel when announcing this layoff. Citigroup CEO Vikrim Pandit reflected this more personal impact when he addressed the job cuts at an employee town hall meeting. He stated: "There is nothing easy about these decisions and the impact on our people. We do this because we must and not because we want to."[11]

- **Concentration of effect** *is the inverse function of the number of people affected by a decision.* A change in an insurance policy denying coverage to 40 people with claims of $50,000 each has a more concentrated effect than a change denying coverage to 4,000 people with claims of $500 each. Cheating an individual or small group of individuals out of $10,000 has a more concentrated affect than cheating an organization, such as the IRS, out of the same sum.

Insights for Individuals

The six factors of ethical intensity are influenced by the characteristics of the decision itself. Ethical intensity rises with increases in one or more of its factors and declines with reductions in one or more of these factors, assuming that all other conditions remain constant. However, you may rate the ethical intensity of the same decision differently than another person because you place different values on the principles and rules of ethics in decision making. Table 2.1 provides a questionnaire for you to take in rating the ethical intensity of 10 different behaviors.

Ethics-Based Principles

There are no universally accepted principles and rules for resolving all ethical issues. In addition, individuals and groups differ over what influences ethical and unethical behaviors and decisions. Numerous principles and rules have been suggested to provide an *ethical justification* for a person's decisions and behaviors.[12] They range from those that justify self-serving decisions to those that require careful consideration of others' rights and costs. In presenting all of these principles, we recognize that the individual generally cannot use a principle to justify an act or decision if it is illegal.

Self-Serving Principles

The following three ethical principles are used to justify self-serving decisions and behaviors.

TABLE 2.1 Ethical Intensity of Selected Behaviors

Instructions: Evaluate each of the 10 behaviors shown in this questionnaire in terms of its ethical intensity. The overall scale of ethical intensity varies from −5, which indicates highly unethical behavior, to +5, which indicates a highly acceptable and ethical behavior. Write down the number on each scale at or near the point that reflects your assessment. What factors were most important in arriving at your rating of the ethical intensity for each behavior?

ETHICAL INTENSITY

BEHAVIORS		UNETHICAL/ NEGATIVE −5	NEUTRAL 0	ETHICAL/ POSITIVE +5
_____	1.	Covering up mistakes by coworkers.		
_____	2.	Giving a favor to a client out of friendship.		
_____	3.	Giving a favor to a client for a bribe.		
_____	4.	Discriminating against an employee on the basis of race.		
_____	5.	Presenting misleading information to a customer.		
_____	6.	Presenting only positive features of your organization's products to a customer.		
_____	7.	Manipulating performance data and indicators to give the appearance of reaching your goals.		
_____	8.	Rewarding people differently based on differences in performance.		
_____	9.	Bending the rules to help the organization.		
_____	10.	Using an office PC for personal use.		

- **Hedonist principle:** *You do whatever is in your own self-interest.*
- **Might-equals-right principle:** *You do whatever you are powerful enough to impose on others without respect to socially acceptable behaviors.*
- **Organization interests principle:** *You act on the basis of what is good for the organization.*

Some of the statements that might reflect self-serving principles include the following: (1) "This act really won't hurt anybody"; (2) "I don't feel comfortable doing this, but if this is what it takes to get ahead (via money/work/promotion/prestige), I should probably do it"; (3) "Everybody else does it, so why shouldn't I"; (4) "Because _____ is my boss and told me to do this, I have no choice but to comply"; and (5) "Since this is such a small matter to most people and it will help our organization, who will notice."

The large bonuses paid to or requested by top executives at some U.S. financial institutions with huge losses after the near collapse of the financial system and in the face of a deep recession appear to reflect the hedonist principle and might-equals-right principle. John Thain, the CEO of Merrill Lynch, initially proposed in early December 2008 to the board of directors that he receive a bonus of $10 million for 2008, despite huge losses and the need to sell the floundering firm to Bank of America to avoid bankruptcy. His argument: Things would have been worse if he had not orchestrated the sale of the firm. There were enormous losses for Merrill's shareholders and major layoffs. Thain received a $15 million signing bonus when he joined Merrill in December 2007. The public and media hullabaloo that ensued when his bonus request hit the news presumably led him to withdraw his bonus proposal to the board on December 8, 2008. We suspect, but do not know, that Thain received a phone call from Kenneth Lewis, the CEO of Bank of America, to withdraw the bonus proposal. Lewis announced no bonuses for top executives at Bank of America in 2008. Three weeks later, Lewis fired Thain over the way he handled billions in losses at Merrill Lynch.[13]

Balancing Interests Principles

The following three ethical principles are used to justify decisions intended to balance the interests of multiple individuals or groups[14]:

- **Means–end principle:** *You act on the basis of whether some overall good justifies a moral transgression.*

- **Utilitarian principle:** *You act on the basis of whether the harm from the decision is outweighed by the good in it—that is, the greatest good for the greatest number.*

- **Professional standards principle:** *You act on the basis of whether the decision can be explained before a group of your peers.*

These principles provide the ethical foundation for some decisions in organizations. They create the basis for helping to resolve ethical dilemmas. For example, organizations—Citigroup, General Motors, and others—are able to justify employee layoffs for the good of the organization. However, they recognize certain responsibilities for providing career counseling and severance packages to the employees affected.

The Internet, new surveillance technologies, privacy issues, and governmental legislation in the United States and many other countries have created major concerns in the attempt to balance the interests of individuals, organizations, and the public at large.[15] The growing perception is that employees and consumers have lost too much of their privacy to employers, marketers, and governmental agencies. Although a variety of U.S. laws have been passed that attempt to protect the privacy of individuals in their roles as citizens, an employee's legal right to privacy in the workplace is quite limited.[16]

Privacy issues in the workplace pose ethical dilemmas in terms of (1) distribution and use of employee data from computer-based human resource information systems; (2) increasing use of paper-and-pencil honesty tests, resulting from polygraph testing being declared illegal in most situations; (3) procedures and biases for substance abuse and acquired immune deficiency syndrome (AIDS) testing; and (4) genetic testing. The ethical dilemmas in each of these areas revolve around balancing the rights of the individual, the needs and rights of the employer, and the interests of the community at large.[17]

New surveillance technologies have created concerns in the attempt to balance the interests of individuals, organizations, and the public at large.

Most employers want to ensure a reasonable degree of employee privacy even when they are not legally obligated to do so. This perspective is based on the balancing interests ethical principles. There is, however, wide consensus that employers must protect against the actions of employees who download pornography or copyrighted music, send harassing e-mail, reveal company secrets, disclose personal information, sell drugs, or spend too much time surfing the Internet for personal use. New technologies make it possible for employers to monitor many aspects of their employees' jobs, especially on telephones, computer terminals, through electronic and voice mail, and when employees are using the Internet. Monitoring of employees by employers is virtually unregulated by the U.S. government. Therefore, unless company policy specifically states otherwise (and even this is not assured), there are no legal prohibitions against an employer listening, watching, and reading almost all workplace communications by employees.[18]

Concern-for-Others Principles

The following three ethical principles focus on the need to consider decisions and behaviors from the perspective of those affected and the public as a whole:

- **Disclosure principle:** *You act on the basis of how the general public would likely respond to the disclosure of the rationale and facts related to the decision.*

- **Distributive justice principle:** *You act on the basis of treating an individual or group equitably rather than on arbitrarily defined characteristics (e.g., gender, race, age).*

- **Golden rule principle:** *You act on the basis of placing yourself in the position of someone affected by the decision and try to determine how that person would feel.*

These three ethical principles are often *imposed* on certain categories of decisions through laws, regulations, and court rulings. Governments impose ethical principles and rules that organizations are expected to follow. For example, U.S. civil rights laws forbid organizations from considering personal characteristics—such as race, gender, religion, or national origin—in decisions to recruit, hire, promote, or fire employees. These laws are based on the ethical principle of distributive justice, which requires the same (or substantially the same) treatment of individuals regardless of age, disability, race, national origin, religion, and sex. The U.S. Equal Pay Act of 1963 asserts that paying women and men different wages is illegal when their jobs in the same organization require substantially equal skills, effort, and responsibility and are performed under similar working conditions. This act applies to organizations with 15 or more employees. There are limited exceptions for pay differentials when an employer can show that

- the difference is due to a seniority or merit system or
- the difference is due to an employee's education, training, and experience.[19]

The scenario in Table 2.2 lets you choose a course of action based on the nine ethical principles just described. If you were Ray, what would you do?

Ethics Insight

Our system of capitalism is built on investor trust—trust that corporate leaders and boards of directors will be good stewards of their investments and provide investors with a fair return. There is no doubt that some leaders of corporations have violated that trust.

William George, Former Chairman and CEO, Medtronic, and Author, True North: Discover Your Authentic Leadership

---

TABLE 2.2   Ethical Assessment of a Scenario

Scenario

Ray manages a unit in a company that calls itself a "total quality" organization. Part of the organization's mission statement says that employees should strive to continually improve their performance. Lately, Ray's unit has been extremely busy trying to get its work done on several important projects. Ray asked his vice president for advice about how to meet all of the deadlines, and the VP basically told him that his unit would have to cut corners on quality in order to get everything done on time. The VP also told Ray that meeting deadlines is the best way to keep clients off their backs, and that the clients rarely complain about substandard work because its effects show up much later. However, Ray knows that doing substandard work for clients will only hurt the company's reputation in the long run.

Questions

1. What should Ray do?
2. How would you evaluate the ethics of your decision with respect to the degree to which it is based on each of the following ethical principles?

Ethical Principle

HIGH DEGREE		UNCERTAIN/ UNDECIDED		LOW DEGREE (NONE)
5	4	3	2	1

To what degree is your decision based on this ethical principle:

1. Hedonist		5	4	3	2	1
2. Might-equals-right		5	4	3	2	1
3. Organization interests		5	4	3	2	1
4. Means-end		5	4	3	2	1
5. Utilitarian		5	4	3	2	1
6. Professional standards		5	4	3	2	1
7. Disclosure		5	4	3	2	1
8. Distributive justice		5	4	3	2	1
9. Golden rule		5	4	3	2	1

Source: Scenario adapted from Loviscky, G. E., Treviño, L. K., and Jacobs, R. R. Assessing managers' ethical decision-making: An objective measure of managerial moral judgment. *Journal of Business Ethics*, 2007, 73, 263–285.

Insights for Leaders

As noted previously, no single factor influences the degree to which decisions and behaviors are likely to be ethical or unethical. However, the following actions can help integrate ethical decision making into the day-to-day culture of an organization[20]:

- Leaders must demonstrate their commitment to ethical behaviors and decisions made by other managers and employees. Recall Anne Mulcahy's commitments to ethics in the opening feature and her annual letter to all employees in the Ethics Competency feature. Elsewhere, she has stated, "We all believe we are part of an ongoing experiment to demonstrate that business success and business ethics are not mutually exclusive."[21]

- A clear code of ethics should be promulgated and followed. Xerox has a clear and well-stated code of ethics titled *Code of Conduct: A Handbook for Xerox People*. On the opening page to this document, Anne Mulcahy states, in part: "This handbook is one of the most important documents you will ever read at Xerox. It summarizes and synthesizes all of our policies relating to business ethics. It's a document I hope you will read and internalize. Even more important, I hope you will keep it and refer to it whenever the slightest question arises as to what is and isn't ethical behavior."[22]

    If truly part of the organization's ethical culture, a code of ethics can clarify for all parties, internal and external, the principles and standards that govern its conduct. This helps convey its commitment to responsible practice wherever it operates. Codes of ethics may serve a variety of other practical purposes. They can help employees from diverse backgrounds work more effectively across geographic and cultural boundaries. Recall Mulcahy's statement in her letter to all employees: "For a Xerox manager, regardless of division or the location, compliance with our policies and code of conduct is a non-negotiable requirement." A code may serve as a reference point for decision making. A code enables organizations to respond quickly and uniformly to a crisis. It may even aid in recruitment by helping to attract individuals who want to work for an organization that advocates world-class principles and standards. A code that is enforced can also help an organization manage risk by reducing the likelihood of employee misconduct.

- A whistle-blowing policy to forbid retaliation against those who report wrong-doing or other ethical procedures should be established and followed. Xerox addresses this in a variety of ways. Patricia Nazemetz, the chief ethics officer at Xerox, sets forth on the firm's website (www.xerox.com) the nine components of the Xerox Ethics and Compliance Program.

- Managers and employees alike should be involved in the identification of ethical problems and efforts to solve them. Xerox does this extensively by providing annual ethics training, an annual ethics certification process, and an Ethics Helpline.

- The performance appraisal process should include consideration of ethical issues. Xerox does this, as suggested in the chapter-opening feature.

- The organizational priorities and efforts related to ethical issues should be widely publicized. Xerox does this in a variety of ways, for example, with the annual ethics letter discussed earlier that is sent to all employees.

Concern for Affected Individuals

The highest form of ethical decision making involves a careful determination of who will receive benefits or incur costs as a consequence of a decision. For major decisions, this assessment may include a variety of stakeholders—shareholders, customers, lenders, suppliers, employees, and governmental agencies, among others.[23] The more specific an individual or group can be about who may benefit and who may incur costs from a particular decision, the more likely it is that ethical implications will be fully considered.

UN Global Compact

Launched in 2000, the UN Global Compact is the largest "corporate citizenship" initiative in the world.[24] This voluntary initiative includes more than 4,700 corporate participants from 130 countries as well as 700 civil societies, labor organizations, and academic institutions. This compact represents a partnership between the private sector and other sectors to promote responsible corporate citizenship as one means of encouraging business to be part of the solution to a more sustainable and inclusive global economy.

The UN Global Compact works to advance 10 universal principles in the areas of human rights, labor standards, the environment, and anticorruption. For example, Principle 1 states: "Businesses should support and respect the protection of internationally proclaimed human rights." The compact provides extensive information, specific guidelines, and suggestions for implementing this principle. The UN Global Compact is not a regulatory agency—it does not "police," enforce, or measure the behavior or actions of companies. Rather, it relies on public accountability, transparency, and the enlightened self-interest of companies to initiate and share the actions they take in pursuing the principles on which the UN Global Compact is based.

Employment at Will

Employment at will *is an employment relationship in which either party can terminate the employment relationship at will with no liability if there was not an express contract for a definite term governing the employment relationship.*[25] Although employment at will allows an employee to quit for no reason, it is also used when an employer wants to fire an employee at any time for any reason or no reason. At-will employment is a creation of U.S. law.

All 50 states recognize retaliatory discharge as an exception to the at-will rule. Under the retaliatory discharge exception, an employer may not fire an employee if it would violate a state or federal statute. For example, an employee who reported illegal behavior by the organization to a government agency cannot be fired. Most states also recognize an implied contract as an exception to at-will employment. Implied employment contracts are most often found when an employer's personnel policies or handbooks indicate that an employee will not be fired except for good cause. If the employer fires the employee in violation of an implied employment contract, the employer may be found liable for breach of contract.

The employment-at-will doctrine increasingly has been challenged successfully in alleged wrongful termination cases in the courts. These challenges are based on the distributive justice principle and the golden rule principle. Before 1980, companies in the United States were free to fire most nonunion employees "at will." Employees were fired for any reason without explanation and rarely went to court to challenge a termination. The vast majority who did had their suits dismissed. However, the courts have recently ruled in favor of exceptions to the employment-at-will doctrine, especially if questionable termination procedures were followed.[26]

Benefits and Costs

An assessment of the ethical implications of the benefits and costs of a decision or issue requires a determination of the interests and values of those affected by the decision(s). Those affected might be the organization as a whole, all employees or specific groups of employees, customers, suppliers, a community, society as a whole, and other affected parties. *Benefits* refer to whatever a party considers desirable. *Costs* refer to whatever a party considers undesirable. Benefits and costs can refer to monetary or nonmonetary effects. A low-cost, coal-burning power plant (monetary effect) that produces high levels of pollution (nonmonetary effect) results in a benefit to the firm and a cost to the public.

The rub comes in considering the implications of the benefits and costs of particular decisions through the interests and "eyes" of those affected. One party's benefits in a decision may create or be perceived to create costs for one or more other parties. A few of these potential tensions with ethical implications are briefly noted as follows:

- *Greater profits for shareholders versus higher wages for employees.* Within the United States, the legally mandated minimum wage for workers was raised in 2008 with subsequent required increases in 2009. The concern-for-others ethical principles were presented as the rationale for the minimum wage that should be paid by U.S. employers, with a few exceptions.

- *Increased production of electrical energy with lower per unit costs versus the need for lower levels of pollution.* Traditionally, electric utilities used the organization interests principle to suggest that if greater pollution would lower production costs and increase profits, it was justifiable. Today, an increasing number of energy companies (e.g., Duke Energy, TXU) are recognizing the need to proactively address pollution problems and not simply wait for government regulatory agencies and laws that require them to do so. This is consistent with the views expressed in the UN Global Compact.

- *Higher prices needed by suppliers to pay better wages, provide a safer work environment, and pollute less versus providing lower prices to consumers.* The self-serving principles suggest that firms (e.g., Walmart, Nike, Dell) should seek to obtain products or services from suppliers at the lowest possible cost with the highest possible quality from any source in the world.

- *Survival of the business through layoffs and reduced compensation versus the desires of employees for greater job security and increased pay.* Various combinations of ethical principles often come into play in such situations, including self-serving, balancing interests, and concern for others.

Care must be taken to guard against assuming that all stakeholders attach the same importance or ethical principles to the costs versus benefits of particular decisions. Conflicting assessments can lead to different interpretations of ethical responsibilities. For example, Greenpeace and other environmental groups emphasize the benefits of "preservation of nature" and that the costs of doing so are well worth it. Steven Biel, the Greenpeace USA Global Warming Campaign Director, released a statement prior to the U.S. car manufacturers being given financial support by the U.S. government in 2008. He stated: "Should Congress bail out the auto companies, they should require Detroit to make real, significant changes in the way they do business, not just small tweaks around the edges, like cutting executive salaries and selling corporate jets. At a minimum, Congress should institute the following changes as a condition of any bailout: (1) Increase fuel economy standards to at least 50 mpg by 2028; (2) Put one million plug-in hybrids—cars that can get up to 150 miles per gallon—on the road by 2015; and (3) Establish a national standard for tailpipe global warming emissions modeled on the California clean cars program."[27]

Insights for Leaders

The utilitarian principle is commonly used by leaders to weigh the benefits and costs of organizational decisions. Utilitarianism emphasizes the greatest good for the greatest number in judging the ethics of a decision. For example, a leader who is guided by utilitarianism considers the potential effect of alternative actions on affected employees. All else equal, the leader selects the alternative benefiting the greatest number of employees. The leader accepts the fact that this alternative may harm others. As long as potentially positive results outweigh potentially negative results, the leader considers the decision to be both good and ethical.

According to some critics, such as Greenpeace, utilitarianism has been misused by business leaders in U.S. organizations. They suggest that there is too much short-run maximizing of personal advantage and too much discounting of the long-run costs of disregarding ethics. Those costs are claimed to include rapidly widening gaps in income between rich and poor, creation of a permanent underclass with its hopelessness, and harm done to the environment. These critics believe that too many people and institutions are acquiring wealth for the purpose of personal consumption and power and that the end of acquiring wealth justifies any means of doing so. As a result, these critics suggest that trust of leaders and institutions, both public and private, has declined.[28] Perhaps individuals such as Anne Mulcahy will help to increase trust in the ethics of business leaders and institutions. Also, greater transparency in decisions that affect others will enhance a sense of trust in the leadership of corporations. Of course, a reduction in fraudulent and unethical decision making by some businesspeople such as Bruce Marlow of AIG and Richard Fuld, Jr., of Lehman Brothers would help. They and others receive widespread publicity and shape the public's general negative stereotype of top business leaders.[29]

Determination of Rights

The notion of rights also is complex and continually changing. One dimension of rights focuses on who is entitled to benefit from or participate in decisions. If rights change, then the mix of benefits and costs changes. Union–management negotiations frequently involve conflicts and dilemmas over management's rights to hire, promote, fire, and reassign union employees and to outsource work. Slavery, racism, gender, and age discrimination and invasion of privacy often have been challenged by appeals to values based on concepts of fundamental rights, especially in terms of the distributive justice and golden rule principles.[30]

Insights for Leaders

Issues of responsibilities and rights in the workplace are numerous and vary greatly over time.[31] A few examples include unfair and reverse discrimination, sexual harassment, employee rights to continued employment, employer rights to terminate employment "at will," employee and corporate free speech, due process, the right to test for substance abuse and AIDS, and the right to privacy. Some experts believe that workplace rights and the establishment of trust with employees is a crucial internal issue facing organizations today.

Procedural and Interactional Justice

Procedural justice *refers to the perceived fairness of the rules, guidelines, and processes for making decisions.*[32] As you recall, *distributive justice* focuses on treating an individual or group equitably rather than on arbitrarily defined characteristics (gender, race, age, and so on). We are mindful that culture may exert important and wide ranging effects on justice behaviors—distributive, procedural, and interactional—and often shapes individuals feelings of injustice or justice.[33] The expectation is that fair procedures, such as a formal and well-developed appeals process, will result in more just decisions (e.g., distributive justice). For example, Xerox has well-developed procedures in place for employees to report fraudulent and harassing behaviors.

It is now recognized that procedural justice needs to be accompanied by a sense of interactional justice. **Interactional justice** *refers to the quality of interpersonal treatment individuals receive during the use of organizational procedures.*[34] A few examples of procedural and interactional justice include disciplinary appeals procedures; procedures for reporting ethical misconduct, such as Boeing's Ethics Line; procedures for appealing dismissals or annual performance reviews; and sexual or racial harassment appeal procedures. Four criteria that typify the presence or absence of interactional justice include (1) respect (whether decision makers treat individuals politely), (2) propriety (whether decision makers are free of bias), (3) truthfulness (whether decision makers are engaged in deceptions), and (4) justification (whether decision makers adequately explain procedures to individuals).[35] Individuals who have high moral intelligence are likely to find it natural to implement the interactional justice criteria when striving to implement both procedural justice and distributive justice in their leadership roles.

Leaders who use procedural and interactional justice believe that employees are going to be more motivated to perform at a high level when they perceive the procedures and their implementation as fair. In organizations, these two types of justice are very important to most employees. Reactions to pay raises, for example, are greatly affected by employees' perceptions about procedural and interactional fairness issues. If in the minds of the employees the pay raises were administered fairly, the employees are usually more satisfied with their increases than if the employees judged the way the raises were made to be unfair. The perceived fairness of how pay raises were allocated is a better predictor of satisfaction than the absolute amount of pay received.

In both the pay and performance evaluation situations, the individual can't directly control the decision but can react to the procedures used to make it. Even when a particular decision has negative outcomes for the individual, procedural and interactional fairness can help ensure that individuals will feel their interests are being protected.

Procedural and interactional justice have also been found to affect the attitudes of workers who survive a layoff. When workers are laid off, survivors are often in a good position to judge the fairness of the layoff in terms of how it was handled. When a layoff is handled fairly, survivors feel more committed to the organization than when they believe that the laid-off workers were treated unfairly.

A number of best practices have been identified for implementation in performance reviews that are intended to achieve both procedural and interactional justice. In brief, five of them are as follows[36]:

- Managers should be given specific and clear instructions on procedures.
- Managers should be trained in how to administer the review.
- Results should be discussed with employees.
- Employee participation should be allowed in the review process (e.g., setting goals, providing input on performance).
- The review should be developmental (e.g., indicate how to improve).

The following Change Competency feature focuses on the leadership of James McNerney, CEO of Boeing. It reports on some of the ways that he has led the changes to restore and reinforce the firm's ethical culture. His selection as CEO followed the public revelations of a series of unethical and illegal actions by a few of Boeing's key leaders and others.[37] Prior to becoming CEO, McNerney was the chairman and CEO of 3M and had served on the board of directors of Boeing, among other organizations. Boeing is a major aerospace company, maker of commercial jets, and defense contractor. This firm is headquartered in Chicago, Illinois, and has approximately 160,000 employees with major operations in the Seattle, Washington, region.[38]

Change competency

James McNerney, CEO of Boeing

The following are excerpts of comments by James McNerney.

A few years ago, Boeing was stunned to find itself among the companies that made headlines for some very high-profile ethical lapses. Several external reviews found that Boeing's ethical breaches were not part of a systemic problem. But the reviews found that weaknesses within the corporation's culture permitted some employees to look the other way. Too many people who thought something "didn't feel right" failed to raise a red flag for a variety of reasons. They wanted to

M. SPENCER GREEN/AP PHOTO

James McNerney, CEO of Boeing.

win a contract, they feared retaliation, they just didn't want to rock the boat, or they lacked the courage to speak up in a command-and-control culture.

Companies doing business with the U.S. government are expected to adhere to the highest legal and ethical standards. I acknowledge that Boeing did not live up to those expectations in the cases addressed by the settlement we're discussing here today. We take full responsibility for the wrongful acts of the former employees who brought dishonor on a great company and caused harm to the U.S. government and its taxpayers. Boeing is accountable for what occurred. And we have cooperated with the government throughout this process.

To strengthen the ethics of our culture, we are changing in a number of ways, several of which follow:

- We are getting committed and getting aligned. For example, every employee, each year, *personally* recommits to ethical and

compliant behavior three ways: by going through a thorough training regimen; re-signing the Boeing Code of Conduct; and participating in one of our Ethics Recommitment stand-downs with his or her business or function.

- Boeing established a new organization—the Office of Internal Governance (OIG)—which reports directly to me and has regular, and routine, visibility with our board of directors. OIG's role includes: (1) Acting as a strong check and balance for key functional disciplines. An example would be monitoring and tracking such things as potential conflicts of interest throughout hiring, transfer and proposal processes. (2) Providing significantly greater visibility into—and oversight of—specific ethics and compliance concerns and cases for our top leaders. (3) Consolidating, in one organization, our various investigative, audit and oversight resources. This way, we were able to identify potential problems and take corrective actions earlier.

- We are opening up the culture. And this is critical. We are creating a work environment that encourages people to talk about the tough issues and to make the right decisions when they find themselves at the crossroads between meeting a tough business commitment and doing the right thing. There simply can be no trade-offs between Boeing's values and Boeing's performance. We want people to know that it's OK to question what happens around them, because that's what surfaces problems early. Silence that ignores the misconduct of fellow workers is not acceptable.

- We are driving ethics and compliance through our core leadership development model, not just off to the side of other things we do every day. At the end of the day, the character of an organization—its culture—comes down to the behavior of its leaders. I believe this is key: Ethics and compliance must be—*and must be seen to be*—a central part of the whole system of training and developing leaders, and of the whole process of evaluating, paying and promoting people.

To learn more about Boeing, go to **www.boeing.com.**

Diversity and Ethics

Learning Goal

3. *Describe some ethics-based initiatives for fostering diversity in organizations.*

The diversity competency must be accompanied by an ethical foundation, as suggested in Chapter 1, to be meaningful.[39] Just as importantly, the diversity competency needs to reflect *proactive* efforts by organizations and leaders to nurture positive and constructive diversity that is difficult to achieve in the absence of an ethical culture.[40]

There are varied and conflicting points of view on diversity.[41] Individual employees may view diversity initiatives as a threat, an opportunity, a blow for justice, harmless fluff, a learning opportunity, a ploy of the disenfranchised, a source of discomfort, or a cultural learning experience.[42]

In the following section, we address several domains that are important to ethics and diversity.

Diversity and Ethical Cultures

Cultural diversity in an organization is embedded in its culture.

Role of Organizational Culture

Organizational culture *reflects the shared and learned values, beliefs, and attitudes of its members.*[43] In a sense, organizational culture is the personality of the organization—difficult to fully express in words. Yet, most employees in the organization sense it and know it because it guides their day-to-day behaviors and decisions. Organizational cultures may vary from having a weak ethical culture to a strong one. Recall the leadership initiatives of James McNerney, CEO of Boeing, in the Change Competency feature to strengthen the ethics of the organization's culture.

Organizational culture appears to affect ethical behavior and diversity in several ways. For example, a culture that emphasizes ethical norms provides support for ethical behavior. Top leadership plays a key role in fostering ethical behavior by exhibiting the correct behavior. A few of the organizations identified as having strong ethical cultures include Xerox, Canon, Medtronic, and the Mayo Clinic. Top leaders in these organizations nurture a culture that rewards ethical priorities and influences how employees behave. If lower level managers observe top-level leaders sexually harassing others, falsifying expense reports, diverting shipments to preferred customers, misrepresenting the organization's financial position, and other forms of unethical behavior, they assume that these behaviors will be acceptable, ignored, or possibly rewarded. Thus, the presence or absence of ethical behavior in leaders' actions both influences and reflects the culture. The organizational culture may promote taking responsibility for the consequences of actions, thereby increasing the probability that employees will behave ethically. Alternatively, the culture may diffuse responsibility for the consequences of unethical behavior, thereby making such behavior more likely.[44]

Diversity Insight

We're focused on maintaining a culture of diversity and inclusion, one that benefits our shareholders and customers. It also allows us to tap into the creativity and vitality of our workforce and suppliers....We recognize that diversity is about everyone. So we're creating an inclusive culture where the talents of every employee are maximized and everyone feels respected and valued.

Magda N. Yrzarry, Vice President, Workplace Culture, Diversity and Compliance, Verizon Communications, Inc.

Increasing Diversity as Opportunity

Organizations have become increasingly diverse in terms of gender, race, ethnicity, and nationality. More than half of the U.S. workforce consists of women, minorities, and recent immigrants. The growing diversity of employees in many organizations may bring substantial benefits, such as more successful marketing strategies for different types of customers, improved decision making, and greater creativity and innovation. The U.S. Department of Labor forecasts that 60 percent of all new employees entering the U.S. workforce during the period through 2010 will be women or people of color.

Anne Mulcahy, the chairman of Xerox, comments on diversity as an opportunity:

> Diversity is about more than race and gender. It's about more than numbers. It's about inclusion. Diversity means creating an environment where all employees can grow to their fullest potential. I'm convinced diversity is a key to success. Experience tells us that the most diverse companies—companies ruled by a hierarchy of imagination and filled with people of all ages, races, and backgrounds—are the most successful over time. Somehow, diversity breeds creativity. Maybe it's because people with different backgrounds challenge each other's underlying assumptions, freeing everybody from convention and orthodoxy. We provide a shining proof point that diversity in all its wonderful manifestations is good for business… good for our country… and good for people.[45]

Mulcahy's remarks reflect several ethical principles: the organization interests principle, distributive justice principle, and golden rule principle. However, employee diversity does not automatically foster creativity, market share, or competitive advantage. Left unmanaged and with a weak ethical culture, increased employee diversity may well damage morale, increase turnover, and cause more communication problems and interpersonal conflict.[46]

Insights for Leaders

There are no easy answers to the challenges of fostering a culturally diverse workforce. There are some common characteristics in organizations, for example, AT&T, Motorola, and Campbell Soup Co., with an effective diversity culture. These characteristics include the following helpful insights:

- Leaders and employees need to understand that a diverse workforce will have people with different perspectives and approaches to issues and problems at work and must truly value a variety of opinions and insights.

- Leaders should recognize both the learning opportunities and the challenges that a culturally diverse workforce presents for the organization.

- The organizational culture should create an expectation of high standards of performance and ethics from everyone.

- The organizational culture should stimulate personal development and support openness to ideas.

- The organizational culture should make workers feel valued.[47]

Generation Diversity and Ethics

From a diversity perspective, a **generation** *refers to an identifiable group that shares years of birth and significant historical and social life events at critical stages of their development.* Most researchers agree that there are four broad categories of generations, as follows:

- *Mature:* born from 1925 through 1944.
- *Baby boomers:* born from 1945 through 1964.
- *Generation X:* born from 1965 through 1981.
- *Generation Y:* born from 1982 through 2000.

There are considerable differences as to the relevance of generation diversity in general and ethics in particular. In one study published by the Center for Creative Leadership, the researcher found 10 commonalities among generations that challenge generational stereotypes. Six of the commonalities are summarized as follows[48]:

1. All generations have similar values. In fact, they all value family the most. They also attach importance to integrity, achievement, love, and competence.

2. Everyone wants respect; they just define it differently.

3. Trust matters. Distrust of the organization and in upper management is prevalent among all age groups.

4. All generations want leaders who are credible and trustworthy. They also want them to listen, be farsighted and encouraging.

5. Organizational politics are a problem. Employees of all ages know that political savvy is a critical component in career advancement and upper-level management.

6. No one really likes change. Resistance to change has nothing to do with age; it is all about how much one has to gain or lose with the change.

We are not claiming there are no differences between the generations. Rather, on a number of important workplace issues, the presumed conflicts and differences are more stereotypes than real. In later chapters, we address some of the differences that appear to exist among generations. For now, we note several ethics results from the *2008 World of Work* report[49]:

- *Generation Y respondents* think that 22 percent of their Gen Y coworkers as a group are ethical, 33 percent of Gen X coworkers as a group are ethical, 38 percent of baby boomer coworkers as a group are ethical, and 44 percent of mature coworkers as a group are ethical. Clearly, the Generation Y respondents did not think highly of the ethics of their coworkers. In contrast, 58 percent of Gen Y respondents perceived themselves as ethical, which is greater but still troubling.

- *Generation X respondents* think that 36 percent of their coworkers as a group are ethical, 28 percent of Gen Y coworkers as a group are ethical, 41 percent of baby boomer coworkers as a group are ethical, and 50 percent of mature coworkers as a group are ethical. In contrast, 71 percent of Gen X respondents perceived themselves as ethical. Once again, a significant gap exists between self-perception of being ethical and the perceptions of coworkers' ethics in the four generations.

- *Baby boomer respondents* think that 56 percent of baby boomer coworkers as a group are ethical, 16 percent of Gen Y coworkers as a group are ethical, 29 percent of Gen X coworkers as a group are ethical, and 61 percent of mature coworkers as a group are ethical. In contrast, 78 percent of baby boomers describe themselves as ethical. There is a substantial gap between baby boomers perceiving most (61 percent) of their coworkers as ethical versus Gen Y coworkers (only 16 percent).

The Gen Y employees, by definition, are newest to their organizations. They have not had as much opportunity to demonstrate that they are ethical and their peers may be presumed as unethical because of generation gap stereotypes. Also, consider the concept of **small numbers bias**, which *refers to the tendency to view a few incidents, cases, or experiences with individuals as representative of a larger population.* For example, observations of unethical conduct by a few Gen Y coworkers may be seen as applying to the supermajority of them and fits the popular stereotype of this generation as not being very ethical as a whole. The contrasting interpretation is that the findings for Gen Y are accurate, which would be a sobering generality.

A recent study of ethics of U.S. high school students (Gen Y), who will be employees within several years, presents mixed messages. The data were gathered through a national sample of almost 30,000 respondents in public and private high schools.[50] The attitudes and intentions expressed are ethical. In brief, (1) 98 percent said "It's important for me to be a person with good character"; (2) 96 percent said, "It's important to me that people trust me"; (3) 93 percent agreed with the statement "In business and the workplace, trust and honesty are essential"; (4) 91 percent said, "People should play by the rules even if it means they lose"; and (5) 84 percent affirmed, "It's not worth it to lie or cheat because it hurts your character."

In contrast, a large majority of the high school respondents (Gen Y) admitted personal behaviors that did match their ethical aspirations and attitudes. Perhaps this is influenced by the 59 percent of respondents who agreed with the following survey statement: "In the real world, successful people do what they have to do to win, even if others consider it cheating."

Most of the users of this text are members of Gen Y. If the data presented are representative, the vast majority of Gen Y respondents did not characterize their coworkers as a group to be ethical. In addition, only 28 percent of Gen X respondents and 16 percent of baby boomer respondents perceived their Gen Y coworkers as a group to be ethical.

Sexual Harassment

Sexual harassment is one of the many categories of harassment that may occur in the workplace. Harassment *refers to verbal or physical conduct that denigrates or shows hostility or aversion toward an individual because of that person's race, skin color, religion, gender, national origin, age, or disability.* Harassment can also occur if conduct is directed toward a person's relatives, friends, or associates.[51] Harassment does one or more of the following:

- Has the purpose or effect of creating an intimidating, hostile, or offensive work environment.

- Has the purpose or effect of unreasonably interfering with an individual's work performance.

- Otherwise adversely affects an individual's employment opportunities.

Harassment in its more serious and aggressive forms, such as sexual harassment, reflects (1) the obedience and punishment stage of moral development; (2) the absence of moral intelligence; (3) the absence or lack of consideration of ethical intensity; (4) the use of the self-serving hedonist and might-equals-right principles; (5) violation of all balancing interests principles—means–end, utilitarian, and professional standards; and (6) violation of all concern-for-others principles—disclosure, distributive justice, and golden rule.

Sexual harassment *generally refers to unwelcome sexual advances, requests for sexual favors, and other verbal or physical conduct of a sexual nature.*[52] Sexual harassment consists of two types of prohibited conduct in the United States: (1) *quid pro quo*—in which submission to harassment is used as the basis for employment decisions, and (2) *hostile environment*—in which harassment creates an offensive working environment. Consider these basic questions from a legal perspective in the United States:

- If an employee "voluntarily" has sex with a manager, does this mean that she (or he) has not been sexually harassed? Not necessarily. If an employee by her or his conduct shows that sexual advances are unwelcome, it does not matter that she (or he) eventually "voluntarily" succumbs to the harassment. In deciding whether the sexual advances are "unwelcome," the courts will often allow evidence concerning the employee's dress, behavior, and language as indications of whether the employee "welcomed" the advances.

- Is an employer liable for *quid pro quo* harassment engaged in by its managers? In general, an employer is held to be strictly liable when a manager engages in *quid pro quo* harassment.

- What is hostile environment harassment? A hostile work environment *occurs when an employee is subjected to comments of a sexual nature, offensive sexual materials, or unwelcome physical contact as a regular part of the work environment.* In general, a single isolated incident will not be considered evidence of hostile environment harassment unless it is extremely outrageous and egregious conduct. The courts look to see whether the conduct is both serious and frequent. Courts are more likely to find a hostile work environment as being present when the workplace includes sexual propositions, pornography, extremely vulgar language, sexual touching, degrading comments, or embarrassing questions or jokes. Supervisors, managers, coworkers, and even customers can be responsible for creating a hostile environment.

- Is an employer liable for hostile environment harassment? It depends on who has created the hostile environment. The employer is liable when supervisors or managers are responsible for the hostile environment, unless the employer can prove that it exercised reasonable care to prevent and promptly correct sexually harassing behavior and that the employee unreasonably failed to take advantage of any preventive or corrective opportunities provided by the employer.

Any harassment policy, including one on sexual harassment, should contain (1) a definition of the harassment, (2) a harassment prohibition statement, (3) a description of the organization's complaint procedure, (4) a description of disciplinary measures for such harassment, and (5) a statement of protection against retaliation.[53]

All individuals need a clear understanding of harassment. California has a fairly well-developed law on the dimensions that constitute sexual harassment. The law reflects the ethical concepts and principles we noted previously. Organizations with strong ethical cultures that embrace diversity incorporate these provisions both formally and informally. The core provisions with examples of unacceptable behaviors include the following[54]:

- *Verbal harassment:* epithets, derogatory comments or slurs. *Examples:* Name-calling, belittling, sexually explicit or degrading words to describe an individual, sexually explicit jokes, comments about an employee's anatomy and/or dress, sexually oriented noises or remarks, questions about a person's sexual practices, use of patronizing terms or remarks, verbal abuse, graphic verbal commentaries about the body.

- *Physical harassment:* assault, impeding or blocking movement, or any physical interference with normal work or movement, when directed at an individual. *Examples:* Touching, pinching, patting, grabbing, brushing against or poking another employee's body, requiring an employee to wear sexually suggestive clothing.

- *Visual harassment:* derogatory posters, cartoons, or drawings. *Examples:* Displaying sexual pictures, writings, or objects, obscene letters or invitations, staring at an employee's anatomy, leering, sexually oriented gestures, mooning, unwanted love letters or notes.

- *Sexual favors:* unwanted sexual advances that condition an employment benefit on an exchange of sexual favors. *Examples:* Continued requests for dates, any threats of demotion, termination, etc., if requested sexual favors are not given, making or threatening reprisals after a negative response to sexual advances, propositioning an individual.

Sexual harassment continues to be a problem in the United States.[55] In a review of a number of studies of the incidence of sexual harassment in the United States, it was found that 58 percent of the women respondents reported having experienced potentially harassing behaviors, and 24 percent report having experienced sexual harassment at work.[56] Sexual harassment represents a serious form of workplace aggression. Leaders have a strong responsibility to do everything in their power to prevent sexual harassment from occurring. When it does occur, it needs to be dealt with quickly and firmly.[57]

Insights for Leaders

Diversity programs and initiatives often run into unanticipated problems. Diversity awareness training programs may backfire if they seem to reinforce stereotypes or highlight differences that employees have tried to minimize in order to fit into the organization's culture. Special diversity programs offered only to some groups may feed the belief that they are gaining an unfair advantage. Employees assigned to work in markets that match their individual diversity-based differences may view that as limiting rather than maximizing the contributions that they can make. Affirmative action programs implemented with a heavy hand may create a stigma for all members of groups targeted to benefit. As a result, even the best qualified people are presumed to have acquired their positions because of their demographic attributes rather than on the basis of merit. Networking or caucus groups may lead to increased segregation and fragmentation if implemented in ways that focus on their diversity differences rather than on their common goals.

Leading diversity successfully requires developing a strong organizational and ethical culture that values individual differences and ensures that the talents of all employees are used to their fullest extent. Implementing the variety of changes that may be needed to lead diversity changes effectively takes time in most organizations. During that time, many challenges will arise along the way. Among the most difficult challenges that leaders face as they attempt to implement these diversity-based changes are

- anticipating and addressing the reactions of members of the dominant culture, who may think that they are about to lose the influence they previously had;

- capturing and synthesizing opinions on diversity initiatives from employees and using them as input for reaching a shared understanding on them; and

- avoiding real and perceived tokenism and quota systems that may help the organization achieve its quantitative diversity goals, but can be destructive to developing a positive culture.[58]

Perhaps the biggest challenge to leaders, however, is understanding that diversity initiatives often have organizational consequences. On the one hand, diversity can enhance a team's ability to solve problems creatively. On the other hand, the price of such creativity may be heightened conflict within the team. Similarly, changing the mix of men and women in a team or department toward a 50–50 split may improve the attitudes of the women involved while irritating the men. Leaders shouldn't expect diversity-related initiatives to affect members of the organization in uniformly positive ways. They should consider carefully which initiatives are most important for the organization to achieve, and be prepared for some resistance from employees who do not gain personally from them.[59]

Leaders need to recognize that the foundational elements for achieving positive diversity (1) start with understanding and perhaps changing key aspects of the organization's culture, (2) proceed to understanding and perhaps changing key aspects of the ethical dimensions of the organization culture, leadership that models ethical behaviors, and formal policies and mechanisms to ensure ethical decisions; and (3) conclude with a portfolio of diversity initiatives, diversity policies, and supportive diversity practices.

Verizon Communications has been ranked as a corporate leader in diversity by a number of organizations and magazines, such as *Business Week*, *Fortune*, *DiversityInc*, *Black Enterprise*, *LATINA Style*, and *Working Mother*. Verizon, headquartered in New York, is the second largest U.S. telecommunications services provider with operations in 28 states and approximately 235,000 employees.[60]

The following Diversity Competency feature provides diversity leadership insights that are relevant to many organizations.[61] You will see that diversity is integrated with Verizon's culture (core values) and ethics.

Diversity competency

Verizon's Workplace Diversity

Ivan Seidenberg, the chairman and CEO of Verizon, set the tone and top-level leadership expectations through these words (and in many other ways):

It is imperative that we continue to uphold the Verizon commitment and core values: put customers first, act with integrity, treat people with respect, be accountable, and raise our standards of performance. This means that we also have to do more than simply follow the law: instead, we have to do the right thing—and we have to do it every day. Ethical conduct is the foundation of any lasting business success. For Verizon to succeed and win in the competitive marketplace, our brand must stand for integrity, trust and solid ethical standards. Each of us contributes to Verizon's success in unique ways, but we share a collective responsibility to "do the right thing" and behave ethically at all times.

Diversity is viewed as an integral part of Verizon's business. The extensive discussion of diversity on its website (www.verizon.com) states: "At Verizon, diversity means embracing differences and variety including age, ethnicity, education, sexual orientation, work style, race, gender and more. When diversity is a part of a company's culture, as it is at Verizon, everyone benefits—customers, suppliers and employees. Diversity isn't just a concept at Verizon. It's an integral part of the business.

Diversity drives everything from workforce development and supplier relationships to economic development, marketing and philanthropy. Verizon's *Code of Business Conduct* clearly spells out what is expected from employees when it comes to valuing and respecting the diversity of others. The commitment to diversity

begins at the top of the company, and progress is measured like any other business objective. Executives are accountable for promoting diversity within their units. They are rewarded for successes through a performance incentive linked to their short-term compensation."

Verizon has an explicit diversity strategy. It is expressed as follows: "The goal of our diversity strategy is to have an aligned and integrated workplace where diversity is transparent, and where Verizon is an inclusive organization that leverages the diversity of employees, customers and supplies for increased productivity, profitability and an enhanced reputation." The components of the strategy include:

- *The Inclusion Index*—Measures employees' sense of belonging through an index developed by our research team based on responses to our Employee Opinion survey. The survey also measures employee satisfaction.
- *Diversity Performance Incentive*—A measure that tracks the workforce composition in each line of business, as well as the number of hires and promotions of diverse candidates. Each line of business has a unique goal, depending upon their individual unit's composition.
- *Supplier Diversity*—Measure derived from the procurement opportunities and developing and advocating a diversified supplier base.

To learn more about Verizon, go to **www.verizon.com**.

Stakeholder Responsibility and Ethics

Stakeholder responsibility *holds that leaders and other employees have obligations to identifiable groups that are affected by or can affect the achievement of an organization's goals.*[62] Various ethical principles are used by different parties as a basis for justifying stakeholder responsibility. The organization interests principle suggests that leaders should consider the desires or demands of different stakeholders for the good of the organization. The utilitarian principle suggests that leaders should act on the basis of the relative harm or good from their decisions on each stakeholder group. The distributive justice and golden rule principles suggest that the leaders' decisions should strive to be equitable and take into account how each stakeholder group might experience and feel about their decisions.

Stakeholders *are individuals or groups that have interests, rights, or ownership in an organization and its activities.* Customers, suppliers, employees, and shareholders are examples of primary stakeholder groups. Each has an interest in how an organization acts. These stakeholder groups can benefit from an organization's successes and can be harmed by its mistakes. Similarly, an organization has an interest in maintaining the general well-being and effectiveness of stakeholder groups. If one or more stakeholder

4. Explain the nature of stakeholder responsibility and its ethical basis.

groups were to dissolve their relationships with the organization, the organization would suffer.[63]

For any particular organization, some stakeholder groups may be relatively more important than others. The most important groups—the primary stakeholders—are those whose concerns the organization must address to ensure its own survival. They directly impact the financial resources available to the firm. At colleges and universities, these stakeholders include students, parents, faculty members, staff, and suppliers (e.g., food services, utilities, bookstores). They are directly impacted by various decisions of the top leaders of the colleges and universities. Secondary stakeholders are also important because they can take actions that can damage or assist the organization. Secondary stakeholders often include governments (especially through regulatory agencies), unions, nongovernmental organizations, activists, political action groups, and the media. During the recent economic crisis in the United States, the federal government became a primary stakeholder to a number of financial institutions as a result of providing billions of dollars in financial support to them.[64]

Stakeholder Pressures

Each stakeholder group has somewhat different expectations of the organization. Each group cares more about some aspects of an organization's activities and less about others. Leaders have to assess the relative importance of primary and secondary stakeholders, including identification and assessment of the many pressures and issues that must be considered in their decision making. Table 2.3 provides examples of these general types of pressures. All of these stakeholders are demanding to be treated ethically with renewed expectations and pressures for truthfulness and fairness.[65] In some situations, there are trade-offs in addressing the preferences of different stakeholders, such as improved benefits being sought by employees versus higher dividend payouts being sought by shareholders. Ethical dilemmas occur for leaders who strive to implement a stakeholder responsibility approach in their decision.

TABLE 2.3 Examples of Types of Pressures from Primary Stakeholders

EMPLOYEES

- Pay and benefits
- Safety and health
- Rights at work/global labor standards
- Fair/ethical treatment in hiring, reviews, promotion, and related areas

SHAREHOLDERS

- Demands for efficiency/profitability
- Viability (sustainability)
- Growth of investment
- Ethical disclosure of financial information

CUSTOMERS

- Competitive prices
- Quality and safe products
- Respect for customers' privacy
- Concern for environment
- Truthful/ethical advertising and sales practices

SUPPLIERS

- Meet commitments
- Repeat business
- Fair trade practices/ethical treatment

Leaders in the same organization may even differ among themselves with respect to[66]

- the importance they place on various stakeholders,
- their beliefs as to the positive/negative consequences that different stakeholders will enjoy/suffer, and
- their beliefs as to the likelihood that certain consequences will occur.

Consider a sample of stakeholder issues that have ethical implications by leaders within an organization as well as between organizations.[67] Some leaders think it is ethically right to give uniform raises to all employees when raise money is extremely limited. Others think it is ethically right to continue to give performance-based raises in such circumstances. Some leaders think it is ethically right to focus only on performance evaluations when conducting layoffs. Others think it is ethically right to consider employee personal considerations. Some leaders think it is ethically right to monitor employees' nonworkplace conduct. Others think it is ethically right to limit surveillance to workplace conduct such as theft and personal use of the Internet. Some leaders think it is ethically right to outsource as much work as possible to firms in foreign countries as a means of cutting labor and other costs to maximize profits for shareholders. Others think it is ethically right to retain as much work as possible in house within the home country.

The following Ethics Competency feature reports on the importance of multiple stakeholders to Johnson & Johnson's in striving to behave ethically as expressed through its credo.[68] Johnson & Johnson (J&J) invents, develops, and produces healthcare products for the consumer, including pharmaceutical, medical devices, and diagnostic markets. J&J is headquartered in New Brunswick, New Jersey, and has more than 250 companies operating in 60 countries. The firm has approximately 119,000 employees.[69] Over a number of years, Johnson & Johnson has received numerous awards for "walking the talk" with respect to living stakeholder ethics as expressed through its credo. Three of the recent ones include (1) rated number one by Barron's on their world's most respected companies list, (2) rated top 10 in *Fortune* magazine's most admired companies, and (3) honored by Boston College's Center for Corporate Citizenship as one of the most socially responsible companies.[70]

Ethics competency

Johnson & Johnson's Stakeholder Ethics and Principles

William C. Weldon, chairman and CEO, comments "Johnson & Johnson is governed by the values set forth in our Credo, created by General Robert Wood Johnson in 1943. These principles have guided us for many years and will continue to set the tone of integrity for the entire Company ..." The J&J statement of Our Credo follows:

We believe our first responsibility is to the doctors, nurses and patients, to mothers and fathers and all others who use our products and services. In meeting their needs, everything we do must be of high quality. We must constantly strive to reduce our costs in order to maintain reasonable prices. Customers' orders must be serviced promptly and accurately. Our suppliers and distributors must have an opportunity to make a fair profit. We are responsible to our employees, the men and women who work with us throughout the world. Everyone must be considered as an individual. We must respect their dignity and recognize their merit. They must have a sense of security in their jobs. Compensation must be fair and adequate, and working conditions clean, orderly and safe. We must be mindful of ways to help our employees fulfill their family responsibilities. Employees must feel

AP PHOTO

Robert Wood Johnson, author of Johnson & Johnson credo.

To learn more about Johnson & Johnson, go to **www.jnj.com.**

free to make suggestions and complaints. There must be equal opportunity for employment, development and advancement for those qualified. We must provide competent management, and their actions must be just and ethical.

We are responsible to the communities in which we live and work and to the world community as well. We must be good citizens—support good works and charities and bear our fair share of taxes. We must encourage civic improvements and better health and education. We must maintain in good order the property we are privileged to use, protecting the environment and natural resources.

Our final responsibility is to our stockholders. Business must make a sound profit. We must experiment with new ideas. Research must be carried on, innovative programs developed and mistakes paid for. New equipment must be purchased, new facilities provided and new products launched. Reserves must be created to provide for adverse times. When we operate according to these principles, the stockholders should realize a fair return.

Sustainable Development

The protection of the natural environment is a key area of growing commitment and interest by organizations and stakeholders. Anne Mulcahy, chairman of Xerox, reflects this perspective in commenting: "Sustainable development is a proven catalyst for Xerox innovation. Repeated recognition by independent groups affirms both the economic and social value of our long-standing commitment to corporate sustainability."[71]

Sustainable development *is a pattern of resource use that strives to meet current human needs without compromising the ability of future generations to meet their own needs.*[72] The issues addressed under the umbrella of sustainable development are wide ranging. For example, the United Nations Division for Sustainable Development identifies 96 core indicators of sustainable development within a framework that contains 14 themes. A few of these themes include atmosphere, consumption and production patterns, land, freshwater, oceans, seas, and coasts, economic development, and natural hazards.[73] Sustainable development is an area of major interest and increasing commitment by organizations—both private and public. Businesses often make reference to *sustainability* rather than sustainable development, a term that dominates the public and academic sectors.[74]

The ethical rationales used for pursuing sustainability are many and often vary among business firms and their stakeholders. As one might expect, business firms are attracted to sustainability initiatives when top management comes to recognize that these are good for the organization. Sustainability initiatives often require capital investments with possible positive financial returns in the long run, but until recent years, were often perceived by top executives as costs incurred at the expense of current profits. At McDonald's, one of the driving forces for sustainability is increased energy efficiency. McDonald's spends more than $1.5 billion a year around the world to power its restaurants. About 80 percent of an average restaurant's energy use is devoted to heating and cooling systems and running cooking appliances. Lighting is another significant draw. Robert Langert, McDonald's vice president for corporate responsibility, comments: "Energy is really our No. 1 issue. When you look at the dollars we spend, and the impact we have on the environment, and the progress we can make to do better, and use our size and influence to make a difference, it's energy."[75] A few of the sustainability initiatives for addressing energy management at McDonald's include[76]:

- Pilot projects with a handful of recently built green restaurants. The one completed in Chicago in 2008 has a green roof, a permeable parking lot, a 20,000-gallon underground cistern to capture runoff water, LED lighting outside and a daylight harvesting system inside. Elsewhere green stores are planned for Brazil, France, Canada, and Germany.

- Internally, it provides employee education and operates an Energy All-Star recognition program that showcases innovations, best practices and outstanding efforts on the part of workers.

- Externally, the company requires its suppliers to join McDonald's in working to improve any aspect of their business operation that affects the environment. The company does not mandate goals, but does require suppliers to provide annual measurements to McDonald's in four environmental areas: energy use, water consumption, waste and recycling, and air pollution.

Organizations that actively address sustainability issues benefit in a variety of ways. Most obviously, it often benefits their long-term profitability and, thus, shareholder interests. They build reputations for being responsible with multiple stakeholders. But they also develop new and valuable organizational capabilities. They learn to integrate the concerns of multiple stakeholders when planning and making key decisions. These organizations further develop abilities to innovate and learn. This is not to suggest that the leaders of business firms will always perceive sustainability initiatives and their relative merits as do other stakeholders.[77] Yet, the opportunities for win–win relationships between stakeholders, especially shareholders and others, are increasingly evident in new organizational initiatives.

For example, DuPont seeks to increase its financial prosperity through strategies that simultaneously produce reductions in the organization's environmental footprint. Its strategies for sustainable development include integrated science and knowledge intensity. DuPont integrated the scientific fields of chemistry and bioengineering to produce a new line of polymers, called Sorona. This material has most of the desirable characteristics of older materials such as nylon, Dacron, and Lycra. However, unlike its predecessors, Sorona is produced using fermented corn sugar, a renewable resource, rather than the petrochemical-derived materials it replaces. Knowledge intensity is increased by initiatives including the creation of Simplyengineering, which generates revenue from selling copyrighted engineering guidelines, calculations, and models, as well as SafeReturns, a DuPont consultancy that helped Texas Instruments reduce its workplace injuries by 65 percent.

The environmental sustainability attained by DuPont's integrated science and knowledge intensity strategies is assessed with a customized metric called the "shareholder value added per pound of production" (SVB/lb). This metric helps DuPont focus on shareholder value creation through increased productivity, waste reduction, and the development of new services and other sources of revenue generation. At the same time, it assists DuPont in meeting its goals for decreasing energy consumption and toxic emissions—all essentially by producing "more value and less stuff."[78]

Assessing Responsibility to Stakeholders

With heightened interest in stakeholder responsibility, many organizations are discovering that they can't avoid having others assess how well they perform in this respect. Business sources, such as *Fortune*, *Forbes*, and the Dow Jones Sustainability Index, rate various aspects of organizational and stakeholder achievements annually. Many stakeholders are pressuring business leaders to abandon the practice of placing their sole emphasis on short-term shareholder profits and to instead contribute more actively to other stakeholders. One approach to assessing an organization's stakeholder and ethical responsibility is to consider whether it merely reacts to ethical pressures as they arise or anticipates and addresses ethical concerns proactively. Several themes found in firms with a proactive commitment to assessing its stakeholder ethics and responsibility are discussed next.[79]

Disclosure

The firm is transparent, providing comprehensive stakeholder environmental information to the public. The firm produces reports annually that review its stakeholder and environmental policies, goals, and achievements as well as financial performance. The firm often provides stakeholder and environmental information on its company website or in other published materials, as with McDonald's, Xerox, and Johnson & Johnson.

A strong corporate responsibility report might use the Global Reporting Initiative (GRI) guidelines as a framework for reporting. The GRI is a not-for-profit organization located in Amsterdam, The Netherlands. It suggests global standards that improve the consistency and comparability of reports. Some companies are now producing "In Accordance with GRI" reports. This is the highest level of disclosure recognized by the GRI. The organization also provides disclosure of goals and performance for key stakeholder and environmental metrics, such as workplace diversity data, workplace safety data, and energy consumption data.[80]

Communication and Engagement

The firm actively seeks to communicate with various groups about its environmental performance. This allows the organization to present progress made and to learn from the groups about what future expectations may be. In some cases, such as AT&T, Xerox, and Walmart, the firm will have established a "road show" through which it meets with various groups about stakeholder and environmental performance or development areas of concern. The firm uses advisory committees to solicit regular input on key issues. Communication is a precursor to action. The firm takes what it learns from the interaction with stakeholders and strives to ensure that business practices adapt to meet changing needs.

Proactive Management

The firm is committed to going beyond minimum compliance requirements and integrating stakeholder responsibility into board governance, executive compensation, and management policies. Compliance is no longer enough—if indeed it ever was. The leaders integrate stakeholder and environmental issues into both day-to-day operations and into its managerial, executive, and fiduciary governance. This can mean creating a stand-alone corporate responsibility department and a cross-functional executive committee. At the board level, the firm has a corporate stakeholder responsibility committee to regularly evaluate and oversee social and environmental issues. It has a formal chain of command to handle these issues—from the board through line employees—to ensure that progress is not driven solely by crises.

The organization recognizes that these issues will not be led properly unless they are included in management compensation incentives and reviews. There are ways to measure stakeholder and environmental progress, determining the proper metrics and setting up systems to collect relevant data, such as air and water pollution levels, workforce diversity, employee turnover, employee safety, energy consumption, and product safety.

Creating Shareholder Value

The organization views stakeholder responsibility as central to its long-term efforts to create shareholder value. It looks at how stakeholder and environmental issues can affect sales, costs, and reputation. For example, on the sales side, the firm recognizes that future sales depend on delivering products that are kinder to the environment, such as fuel-efficient cars or energy-efficient computers. The well-managed company recognizes the need for diverse workforces, managers, and boards to relate to the increasing diversity of its consumer base. From a cost perspective, it recognizes that proactive leadership of environmental and stakeholder risks can substantially lessen the uncertainties and liabilities created by changing regulatory requirements and new knowledge of emerging risks. Top leaders recognize that costs can be reduced through environmental initiatives, such as reducing energy intensity or minimizing waste. There is a recognition that its customers, suppliers, employees, and others would rather do business with a company that is mindful of its power and its ability to affect people's lives.

Xerox's Self Assessment

Xerox is a firm that mirrors these four themes. The 58-page Xerox document titled *Our Commitment to Global Citizenship: The 2008 Report* illustrates our point. A few of the comments by Anne Mulcahy, the chairman of Xerox, suggests the firm's sense of stakeholder and environmental responsibility and ethics. She comments[81]:

> Our people take great pride in the culture they have created—a culture that values Xerox both as a profit-making enterprise and as an institution that strives to be a positive force in the world around us. You will see that philosophy running throughout this report. It's organized around five themes that capture the essence of our citizenship efforts.
>
> * Conducting our business with integrity and transparency builds credibility and attracts investors.
> * Aligning our resources around customer need provides the revenue stream that enables investment in innovation and future growth.
> * Nurturing a greener world through sustainable innovation and development saves money, creates value and helps develop new markets.
> * Creating a great workplace for our people strengthens our competitiveness.
> * Leveraging our resources to make our world better improves the quality of life for our people and the economic climate for our customers.

A number of specific measures (data) and discussions are presented for each of these themes. Consider this one example. Xerox is well on the way to achieving the goal of a 25 percent reduction in greenhouse gas emissions by 2012. In the five years between 2002 and 2007, it cut energy consumption by 19 percent and greenhouse gas emissions worldwide by 21 percent. And in support of customer climate protection goals, 80 percent of new products introduced in 2007 met the U.S. Environmental Protection Agency's tougher ENERGY STAR requirements.

Chapter Summary

1. *Describe the stages of moral and ethical development.*

Stages of moral development are stages through which individuals evolve, ranging from the lowest stage (obedience and punishment orientation) to the highest stage (universal ethical principles). These personal phases of moral development focus on the ethical reasoning used to justify choices in decision situations. The higher stage of moral development is used by some as an indicator of moral intelligence—the mental capacity to determine how universal ethical principles that cut across the globe should be applied to personal values, goals, and actions.

2. *Explain and apply the core concepts used by individuals and organizations to make ethical decisions.*

Ethical misconduct in the workplace continues to be demonstrated by some individuals from the top through the lowest levels of the organization. The creation of a strong ethical culture by leaders makes a major difference in the frequency and severity of ethical misconduct. Severity of misconduct is illustrated through the six factors that comprise ethical intensity—the degree of moral importance given to an issue. Numerous principles and rules have been suggested to provide an ethical justification for a person's and organization's decisions and actions. We highlighted three self-serving principles, three balancing interests principles, and three concern-for-others principles. The complexity of applying these principles and rules is often played out in decision-making situations in which the parties assess their relative concern for the affected individuals, the benefits and costs of alternative courses of action, and determination of who has what rights. The parties' satisfaction with how these thorny ethical issues are resolved depends somewhat on the presence of procedural justice—the perceived fairness of the rules and guidelines used to make decisions—and interactional justice.

3. *Describe some ethics-based initiatives for fostering diversity in organizations.*

Diversity must be accompanied by an ethical foundation to be meaningful. The implementation of diversity initiatives is typically anchored in one or more of the balancing interests principles and concern-for-others principles. Positive diversity is very much influenced by the presence of an ethical culture. We reviewed a profile of organizational characteristics that foster an effective diversity environment. We reviewed the four broad categories of generation diversity and how each of these generations tends to view the ethical standards of those in their own generation and those in other generations. Harassment and sexual harassment, in particular, was discussed as an ongoing challenge in organizations. The legal, ethical, preventive, and corrective dimensions of sexual harassment were reviewed.

4. *Explain the nature of stakeholder responsibility and its ethical basis.*

Stakeholder responsibility holds that leaders and other employees have obligations to identifiable groups that are affected by or can affect the achievement of an organization's goals. Various stakeholder groups use various ethical principles as a basis for justifying stakeholder responsibility. Each stakeholder group typically has somewhat different expectations of the organization. Leaders of organizations are increasingly challenged by stakeholder pressures, each with its own configuration of ethical justifications, to make decisions and pursue goals consistent with its own interests. Sustainable development was presented as a domain with ethical underpinnings and one in which stakeholders may find common grounds for action. Leading for-profit organizations are increasingly embracing the need to accept and assess responsibility to multiple stakeholders—not just their shareholders. However, shareholders continue to be the dominant stakeholder group for top executives. Effective means of accepting responsibility to stakeholders include indicators of (1) disclosure, (2) communication and engagement, (3) proactive management, and (4) creating long-term shareholder value.

Key Terms and Concepts

Concentration of effect, **39**
Disclosure principle, **41**
Distributive justice principle, **41**
Employment at will, **44**
Ethical intensity, **38**
Generation, **50**
Golden rule principle, **41**
Harassment, **52**
Hedonist principle, **40**
Hostile work environment, **52**
Interactional justice, **46**
Magnitude of consequences, **38**
Means–end principle, **41**
Might-equals-right principle, **40**
Moral intelligence, **36**

Organization interests principle, **40**
Organizational culture, **49**
Probability of effect, **38**
Procedural justice, **46**
Professional standards principle, **41**
Proximity, **39**
Sexual harassment, **52**
Small numbers bias, **51**
Social consensus, **38**
Stages of moral development, **34**
Stakeholder responsibility, **55**
Stakeholders, **55**
Sustainable development, **58**
Temporal immediacy, **39**
Utilitarian principle, **41**

Discussion Questions

1. Go to www.xerox.com. In the search box, type in "corporate governance guidelines." Open the document titled "Corporate Governance Guidelines at Xerox." Identify at least two of the specific ethical principles that are reflected in this document. What is a specific provision that illustrates each of the principles identified?

2. Review the Learning from Experience feature on Anne Mulcahy, chairman of Xerox, and other discussions of her leadership in this chapter. How would you evaluate her in relation to each of the six attributes of the diversity competency presented in Chapter 1? For each attribute on which Mulcahy is evaluated, identify the specific statement(s) about her that serve as a basis of your assessment.

3. Think of an organization in which you have been employed (or are currently employed). What are your assessments of the stage of moral development and moral intelligence of the manager for whom you worked? What specific examples of this manager's behaviors and decisions serve as the basis for your assessments?

4. What are the similarities and differences between the organization interests principle and the utilitarian principle?

5. What are the similarities and differences between the professional standards principle and the distributive justice principle?

6. From your personal perspective, what is your assessment of the ethical intensity of the grading system and practices used by an instructor in a course that you have completed? Your assessment should include an assessment of each of the six components of ethical intensity.

7. What specific aspects of procedural justice are suggested in the Change Competency feature on James McNerney, CEO of Boeing?

8. How would you assess Generation Y individuals as a group with respect to their general pattern of ethical behaviors and decision making within the work environment? Explain. If a generalization is possible, what is your overall assessment? Explain.

9. How did (or does) an organization for which you have worked (or do work) compare with the policies, practices, and goals of Verizon's workplace diversity as presented in the Diversity Competency feature? Give specific comparisons of similarities and/or differences.

10. What specific ethical principles for guiding decisions and actions are illustrated in the Ethics Competency feature titled "Johnson & Johnson's Stakeholder Ethics and Principles"? You should relate specific statements in the code to specific ethical concepts.

11. Sustainable development is discussed as an application of stakeholder responsibility. Think of an organization for which you have worked (or currently work). In what ways did it implement or fail to implement sustainable development initiatives?

Experiential Exercise and Case

Experiential Exercise: Ethics Competency

What Is Your Decision?[82]

Instructions

Mark the preferred decision for each of the four incidents and reply to the two questions that follow each incident. This exercise may also be undertaken in a small group. The group members should make their choices individually and then discuss them with each other. They should attempt to reach a consensus on the preferred decision for each incident and the responses to the questions.

Ethical Incidents

1. Barbara is a sales representative for Global Fashions Inc. One of her best customers, George, places a large order for linen jackets for the coming spring season. Barbara knows that Global has had production and delivery problems with these jackets. She also knows that George's order will assure her year-end bonus. Should she:

   _____ A   Take the order. There's no guarantee that Global won't meet the deadline, and George is sophisticated enough to know that sometimes problems happen in manufacturing.

   _____ B   Warn George of the risk and put the sale at risk before taking the order, if George still wants to place it.

   _____ C   Refuse the order, since she's likely to disappoint a long-time customer by promising something that may not happen.

   Questions
   1. What ethical principle or principles reflect your decisions?
   2. How would you assess the ethical intensity in this situation?

2. Jose is a general manager of a division of Global Operations. In that capacity, he knows that his company is planning on making layoffs soon. Juan, a good friend in another division, tells Jose he is about to buy a new house that is much more expensive, but he's confident that he can make the higher payments, because his career at Global is going well. Jose doesn't know if Juan will be laid off but is concerned. Should he:

   _____ A   Warn Juan of the upcoming layoffs.

   _____ B   Encourage Juan to hold off on buying the house because "something is up" and he can't say more.

   _____ C   Let Juan's direct supervisor know what Juan is doing.

   _____ D   Stay out of the issue. Since Jose doesn't know what's going to happen to Juan, there's really nothing to do.

   Questions
   1. What ethical principle or principles reflect your decision?

2. How would you evaluate the ethical intensity in this situation?

3. Don is a sales representative for a local moving company. His friend Adam works as an auto salesman. Adam informs Don that people who move are surprisingly likely to buy new cars shortly thereafter because their commute has now changed. He tells Don, "I'll tell you what. Give me the names of people you meet with to discuss moving, I'll send them a welcome-to-the-neighborhood note. If any of them buy a car, I'll give you a piece of my commission." Don should:

   _____ A   Give Adam the names—there's no harm done.

   _____ B   Offer to take Adam's cards and give them to customers.

   _____ C   Decline the offer.

   Questions
   1. What ethical principle or principles reflect your decision?
   2. How would you assess the ethical intensity in this situation?

4. You've been a manager at your company for five years and have developed an excellent reputation. Your future looks bright, which is a good thing since you have a family to support. Yesterday a fellow employee, Kim, came to you with a problem. Kim, an African-American woman who used to report to you, had just been turned down for a promotion. You believe she was very qualified for the position and perfectly capable of doing it with excellence. The candidate chosen was a white male with good qualifications but not as much experience or, in your opinion, ability as Kim. Steve, the manager who did not select Kim, happens to be a "rising star" whom you've known for years and with whom you get along pretty well. Steve couldn't make you CEO and couldn't get you fired, but he is in a position to help or hinder your career. What do you do?

   _____ A   Encourage Kim to speak to the Human Resources department and offer to speak to them as well about your excellent opinion of Kim.

   _____ B   Talk to Steve.

   _____ C   Tell Kim that many (legitimate) factors go into a promotion decision and that such a decision can't be judged from the outside.

   _____ D   Talk to Steve's supervisor.

   Questions
   1. What ethical principle or principles reflect your decision?
   2. How would you assess the ethical intensity in this situation?

Case: Diversity Competency

Consensual Relationship Agreements[83]

If you put individuals with common interests together for 40-plus hours per week, office romance is bound to happen. Statistics seem to bear that out: According to a survey by Valut.com, an online career center, 47 percent of the 1,000 professionals surveyed had been involved in an office romance, and another 19 percent would consider it. Of those individuals who had a romance, 11 percent had dated their managers or another manager.

"This issue is not going away," says Helaine Olen, coauthor of *Office Mate: The Employee Handbook for Finding—and Managing—Romance on the Job* (Adams Media, 2007). It's crucial, she says, for managers to accept the likelihood of office romance and have policies and procedures in place to address it when it occurs. Most experts warn against forbidding office romance altogether. They see it as futile. "Our experience was if a company tried to forbid it, more people started dating for the thrill of it. It was counter-productive," Olen says. This is an issue among every employee demographic, not just single 20-somethings, although in her experience members of each group handle the situation differently. For instance, "The average 22-year-old wasn't concerned about who knew what and when. The older employees were more likely to keep it quiet. But it was still fairly common," Olen says.

Seventy-two percent of companies had no policy regarding workplace romance, according to the Society for Human Resource Management (SHRM) Workplace Romance Poll. "The vast majority of companies do not have rules around dating, and they should. Of the few that do, most of them involve a boss dating a subordinate. If they perceive a conflict of interest or see the relationship as disruptive or potentially disruptive, human resources should step in," asserts Olen.

One type of workplace policy that is being adopted is a consensual relationship agreement (CRA). A CRA is essentially a written "contract" in which the romantically involved parties acknowledge the following:

- Their relationship is voluntary and consensual.
- They agree to abide by the employer's antidiscrimination, antiharassment, and workplace conduct policies.
- They promise to report any perceived harassment to management, if it occurs.
- They agree to behave professionally and not to allow the relationship to affect their performance.
- They agree to avoid behavior that offends others in the workplace.
- They agree not to engage in favoritism. This is especially an issue if one of the employees is in a higher management position and has the authority to influence rewards available to the other employee.

Some individuals believe that the reasons for expecting employees who are in a relationship to sign a CRA include:

- *Decreasing sexual harassment litigation risk.* After a workplace romance fails, the employee sometimes claims to have been pressured into the relationship. A CRA signed after the relationship has started can effectively refute such claims because it provides compelling evidence that the employees entered the relationship voluntarily. But what if employees refuse to sign? The CRA could be a condition of employment. Some individuals advise approaching employees about signing "love" contracts by showing them how the documents protect them, too, in the event the relationship turns sour. Even though an employee wants to keep things private, there's always the risk of something going wrong. If there is a helpful, responsible way of working with the employee in place, the situation is more like to be normalized.
- *Reducing perceptions of favoritism.* Favoritism—or the appearance of it—isn't just poor employee relations. In some cases, it is a cause for sexual harassment lawsuits. In a few states, the interpretation of sexual harassment laws includes third parties. If an employee views a supervisor as favoring a subordinate due to their relationship, the employee can sue the company—and the supervisor personally—for sexual harassment.
- *Creating a forum to discuss professional workplace behavior.* A CRA provides a forum for human resource professionals to talk to dating employees about what is appropriate and inappropriate workplace behavior. They can remind employees to be sensitive to their coworkers, especially concerning displays of physical affection, verbal affection, or lovers' quarrels.
- *Reminding dating employees of lack of privacy in the workplace.* When employees bring their relationships into the workplace, they don't have a legal right to privacy. They are governed by a no-harassment policy. This doesn't mean the employer has the right to ask about intimate details, but when employees are in the workplace, the employer has the right to set reasonable rules. Dating employees should not instant message or e-mail each other about intimate issues. Even an innocuous note such as "Where do you want to go to dinner tonight?" can be misconstrued if the relationship goes sour. Employees in a relationship should only speak privately and in person about personal issues.

Questions

1. Critics of CRAs assert that they are too intrusive, ineffective, and unnecessary and that they can cause as many problems as they solve. Identify the specific reasons and examples that might justify these criticisms.
2. How would you assess the ethical intensity of CRAs from the perspective of the employer? From the perspective of the employees in a consensual relationship?
3. What specific ethical principles might be used to justify the use of CRAs? Explain.
4. What ethical principles might be used by employees in consensual relationships to oppose signing such an agreement? Explain.
5. Do you personally favor or oppose the use of CRAs in the workplace? Explain.

The Individual in Organizations

chapter 3

Understanding Individual Differences

Learning Goals

After studying this chapter, you should be able to:

1
Explain the basic sources of personality formation.

2
Identify a set of personality dimensions that affect performance.

3
Describe the attitudes that affect performance.

4
Explain how emotions impact employees' performance.

Learning Content

Steve Jobs at Apple

When Steve Jobs returned to Apple in 1997, he was remembered as the wonder boy who, with Steve Wozniak, at the age of 21 founded Apple Computer in his parents' garage back in 1976. Worth more than $300 million by the age of 30, he was thrown out of Apple in 1985 because of his "personality" clashes with others. Now more than two decades later, he has been called by Jack Welch and others the most successful CEO today.

Jobs is a controversial leader. He publicly ridicules Apple's competitors, who he casts as mediocre, evil, and lacking taste. His subordinates are geniuses or "bozos," indispensable or no longer relevant. Individuals at Apple know they can flip from one category to another at a moment's notice. Jobs doesn't live with his mistakes; he simply rationalizes them away and moves on. Subordinates have been made to cry at meetings and have been fired during his angry tantrums. Former Apple public relations executive Laurence Clavère said that before going into a meeting with Jobs, she had to develop a mind-set like a bullfighter entering the ring—kill or be killed. According to Jean-Louis Gassée, a former Apple executive who once worked with Jobs: "Democracies don't make great products. You need a competent tyrant" and Jobs fit the bill. When John Sculley led the fight to ouster Jobs in 1985 and then replaced Jobs at Apple, Sculley likened Jobs to the Russian revolutionary Leon Trotsky saying that he was a zealot with visions so pure that he couldn't accommodate the imperfections of the world.

When Jobs returned to Apple in 1997, Apple was losing money and market share. Jobs immediately dug into the details of the business. He created a sense of urgency that led the company back to profitability. No engineering spec, no design detail was too small for his scrutiny. Today, he lists himself as co-inventor on 103 separate Apple patents, everything from the user interface for the iPod to the support systems for the glass staircases used in Apple's retail stores.

He makes his own rules. He drives a Mercedes without a license plate and parks it in handicapped spaces. When doctors discovered an abdominal cancerous tumor in 2003, they told him that surgery was the best decision. Jobs sought treatment with a special diet while launching a lengthy exploration of alternative approaches instead of undergoing surgery. Several of the Apple board members said that this was probably not the best thing for his health. Jobs was stubborn and

ROBERT GALBRAITH/REUTERS/LANDOV

To learn more about Apple Computer, go to www.apple.com.

resisted surgery for almost a year. After finding no cure on his own, he had a successful operation in 2004. Jobs only told a few individuals in his inner circle about the surgery. When he had health issues in 2009, however, he announced that he was taking a leave of absence from his role as CEO and temporarily appointed Tim Cook as CEO. When Jobs ran Pixar before selling it to Disney, Jobs personally negotiated bonuses with key executives. He often went to the board meetings saying that

this is what he wanted to do for compensation—he didn't wait for input from others.

Unlike Microsoft, Apple has been labeled one of America's least philanthropic companies. Jobs ended all of Apple's long-standing corporate philanthropy programs when he returned in 1997 and has not restored any of these. He also has not shown any interest in handing over the reins to another person to create a different kind of personal legacy.[1]

As the Learning from Experience feature indicates, individuals react to how they are treated by others. You might ask yourself whether you would be willing to work for Jobs. Depending on your personality, preferences, and goals, your answer might be either *yes* or *no*. As an employee and future leader, you must recognize and appreciate individual differences in order to understand and respond appropriately to the behavior of individuals in organizations.[2]

In Part 2 of this book, we cover individual processes in organizations. In this chapter, we focus first on the individual to help you develop an understanding of organizational behavior.

Individual differences *are the physical, personality, attitudinal, and emotional attributes that vary from one person to another*. What are some individual differences about Steve Jobs that stand out for you? What are your individual differences? The individual differences that characterize you make you unique. Perhaps you have a dynamic personality and enjoy being the center of attention, whereas others you know avoid crowds and do not have the same energy level as you. Is that good or bad? The answer, of course, is that it depends on the situation. Whenever you attempt to understand individual differences, you must also analyze the situation in which the behavior occurs. A good starting point in developing this understanding is to appreciate the role of personality in organizations. In this chapter, we discuss individual differences in personality, attitudes, and emotions. We begin by addressing the concept of personality. Later in the chapter, we explore the role of attitudes and emotions in organizational behavior.

Learning Goal

1. *Explain the basic sources of personality formation.*

Bases of Personality

Behavior always involves a complex interaction between the person and the situation. Events in the surrounding environment (including the presence and behavior of others) strongly influence the way individuals behave at any particular time; yet individuals always bring something of themselves to the situation. This "something," which represents the unique qualities of the individual, is *personality*.[3] No single definition of personality is accepted universally. However, one key idea is that personality represents personal characteristics that lead to consistent patterns of behavior. Individuals quite naturally seek to understand these behavioral patterns in interactions with others.

Personality *represents the overall profile or combination of stable psychological attributes that capture the unique nature of a person*. Therefore, personality combines a set of physical and mental characteristics that reflect how a person looks, thinks, acts, and feels. This definition contains two important ideas.

First, theories of personality often describe what individuals have in common and what sets them apart. To understand the personality of an individual, then, is to understand both what that individual has in common with others and what makes that particular individual unique. Thus, each employee in an organization is unique and may or may not act like someone else will act in a similar situation. This uniqueness makes managing and working with individuals extremely challenging.

Second, our definition refers to personality as being "stable," meaning that it remains somewhat the same through time. Most individuals intuitively recognize this stability. If your entire personality could change suddenly and dramatically, your family and friends would confront a stranger. Although significant changes normally don't occur suddenly, an individual's personality may change over time. Personality development occurs to a certain extent throughout life, but the greatest changes occur in early childhood.

How is an individual's personality determined? Is personality inherited or genetically determined, or is it formed after years of experience? There are no simple answers because too many variables contribute to the development of each individual's personality. As Figure 3.1 shows, two primary sources shape personality differences: heredity and environment. An examination of these sources helps explain why individuals are different.

> ### Self Insight
>
> If individuals are products of biology, life would have no higher meaning and purpose. It is personality that gives individuals meaning and purpose. Personality is what makes individuals different.
>
> *Steve Pinker, Author,* The Blank Slate

Heredity

Deeply ingrained in many individuals' notions of personality is a belief in its genetic basis. Expressions such as "She is just like her father" or "He gets those irritating qualities from your side of the family, dear" reflect such beliefs. Genes determine height, eye color, size of hands, and other basic physical characteristics. Some individuals believe that personality is inherited; others believe that a person's experiences determine personality. Our thinking is balanced—both heredity (genes) and environment (experiences) are important. Of course, some personality characteristics may be influenced more by one factor than the other. Some personality traits

FIGURE 3.1 Sources of Personality Difference

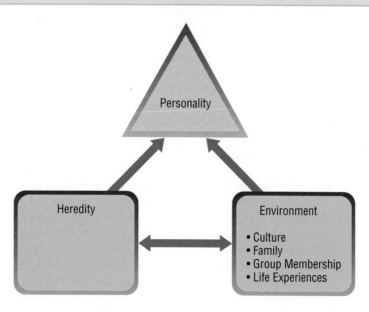

seem to have a strong genetic component, whereas other traits seem to be largely learned (based on experiences).[4]

Heredity sets limits on the range of development of characteristics, and within this range environmental forces influence personality characteristics. However, recent research on the personalities of twins who have been raised apart indicates that genetics may play a larger role than many experts had believed. Some studies of twins suggest that as much as 50 to 55 percent of personality traits may be inherited. Further, inherited personality traits seem to explain about 50 percent of the variance in occupational choice. In other words, you probably inherited some traits that will influence your career choices. Furthermore, there is not one single gene that determines a person's personality but a combination of genes.[5]

Environment

Other individuals think that the environment plays a large role in shaping personality; in fact, the environment may have a more important role than inherited characteristics. That is, beyond what genes are inherited from your parents, the environment a person experiences as a child has an important role in molding one's personality development. How a child is treated by adults and playmates and others influences the child's personality. A person growing up in a warm and nurturing household is much more likely to be a well-adjusted person than a child growing up in a cold and sterile environment. Aspects of the environment that influence personality formation include culture, family, group membership, and life experiences.

Culture

Anthropologists have clearly demonstrated the important role that culture plays in personality development.[6] A culture is not a symbolic pattern, but evolves under the stress of competing goals and other cultures. Cultures do not exist as simply static differences to be celebrated, but compete with one another as better or worse ways of getting things done. Individuals born into a particular society are exposed to family and societal values and to norms of acceptable or unacceptable behavior—the culture of that society. Culture also defines how various roles in that society are to be performed. For example, U.S. culture generally rewards individuals for being independent and competitive, whereas Japanese culture generally rewards individuals for being cooperative and group oriented.[7]

Culture helps determine broad patterns of behavioral similarity among individuals. However, differences in behavior—which at times can be extreme—usually are seen among individuals within a society. Most societies aren't homogeneous (although some are more homogeneous than others). For example, one characteristic of Western cultures is that people often follow a work ethic in which hard work is valued and an unwillingness to work is sinful. But this value doesn't influence everyone within Western cultures to the same degree. Although culture has an impact on the development of employees' personalities, not all individuals respond to cultural influences equally. Indeed, one of the most serious errors that leaders can make is to assume that their subordinates are just like themselves in terms of societal values, personality, or any other individual characteristic.

Cultural Values. A number of cultural values impact a person's behavior at work. We believe that is particularly helpful in understanding individual and societal differences. To determine your cultural value profile, please go to the first Experiential Exercise at the end of this chapter on page 97 and complete the questionnaire. These values in combination influence the behaviors and decisions of employees in many organizations.[8] Figure 3.2 shows how the five cultural dimensions covered in the Experiential Exercise vary between France, the United States, Canada, and Japan. Let's explore each of these five cultural dimensions more closely.

FIGURE 3.2 Cultural Values in Four Countries

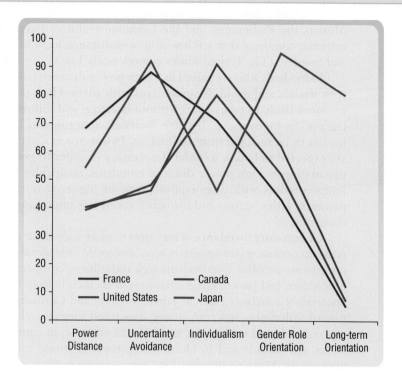

Individualism versus collectivism is a fundamental work-related value that leaders must thoroughly understand to be effective in today's global world. **Individualism** *is the tendency of individuals to look after themselves and their immediate families.* A culture high on individualism emphasizes individual initiative, decision making, and achievement. Everybody is believed to have the right to privacy and personal freedom of expression. Individuals in these countries generally do not believe that they share a common fate with others. They view themselves as independent, unique, and special. They are less likely to conform to the expectations of others. When group goals conflict with personal goals, individuals commonly pursue their own goals. In addition, seeking personal identity is highly valued in individualistic cultures. Personal achievement, pleasure, and competition are all highly valued. Countries characterized by an emphasis on individualism include the United States, Canada, New Zealand, the United Kingdom, and Australia.

At the other end of the continuum, **collectivism** *is the tendency of individuals to emphasize their belonging to groups and to look after each other in exchange for loyalty.* Groups (relatives, communities, and organizations) focus on their common welfare. Collectivism usually involves emotional dependence of the individual on groups, organizations, and institutions. The sense of belonging and "we" versus "I" in relationships is fundamental. Individuals' private lives are shaped by the groups and organizations to which they belong. Group goals are generally thought to be more important than the individual's personal goals. Individuals in China, Japan, Taiwan, and South Korea care about whether their behavior would be considered shameful by the other members of their groups. They also avoid pointing out other individuals' mistakes in public so that the others won't lose face and harmony is maintained. Face-saving is important in these cultures because it allows individuals to retain their dignity and status.

Power distance *is the extent to which individuals in a society accept status and power inequalities as a normal and functional aspect of life.* Countries that are "high in power distance" are those whose citizens generally accept status and power inequalities; those "low in power distance" are those whose citizens generally do *not*. Countries that are high in power distance include Argentina, India, Malaysia, Mexico, the Philippines, and the Commonwealth of Puerto Rico. At the opposite extreme, countries that are low in power distance include Finland, Israel, Norway, and Sweden. (The United States is moderately low.)

Individuals who are raised in a high power distance culture behave submissively with leaders and avoid disagreements with them. High power distance employees are more likely to take orders without question and follow the instructions of their leaders. In high power distance societies, subordinates consider bypassing their leaders to be an act of insubordination. In low power distance countries, employees are expected to bypass a leader if necessary in order to get their work done. When negotiating in high power distance countries, companies find it necessary to send representatives with titles equivalent to or higher than those of their bargaining partners. Titles, status, and formality are of less importance in low power distance countries.

Uncertainty avoidance *is the extent to which individuals rely on procedures and organizations (including government) to avoid ambiguity, unpredictability, and risk.* With "high" uncertainty avoidance, individuals seek orderliness, consistency, structure, formalized procedures, and laws to cover situations in their daily lives. Societies that are high on uncertainty avoidance, such as Japan, Sweden, and Germany, have a strong tendency toward orderliness and consistency, structured lifestyles, clear specification of social expectations, and many rules and laws. In contrast, in countries such as the United States and Canada and in Hong Kong, there is strong tolerance of ambiguity and uncertainty. More secure and long-term employment is common in "high" uncertainty avoidance countries. In contrast, job mobility and layoffs are more commonly accepted in "low" uncertainty avoidance countries.

Gender role orientation *is the extent to which a society reinforces, or does not reinforce, traditional notions of masculinity versus femininity.* A society is called *masculine* when gender roles are clearly distinct. Men are supposed to be assertive, tough, and focused on material success. Women are supposed to be more modest, tender, and concerned with the quality of life. In masculine-dominated cultures, gender roles are clearly distinct. Japan, Austria, Italy, Mexico, and Ireland are a few of the countries ranked as high in masculinity. Dominant values are material success and progress and money. A society is called *feminine* when gender roles overlap: Both men and women are supposed to be modest, tender, and concerned with the quality of life. In feminine-dominated societies, roles are often merged or overlap for sexes. A few of the countries ranked high on femininity are Denmark, Costa Rica, Finland, and Portugal. Dominant values include caring for others, emphasizing the importance of individuals and relationships, accepting that both men and women can be gentle, stressing the quality of work life, and resolving conflict by compromise and negotiation.

Long-term orientation *is the extent to which the society embraces the virtues oriented toward future rewards.* A long-term orientation ranking indicates that the society prescribes to the values of sustained commitments, perseverance, and thrift. This is thought to support a strong work ethic in which long-term rewards are expected as a result of today's hard work. A few of the countries with a long-term orientation are China, Japan, India, and the Netherlands. These countries include characteristics such as adaptation of traditions to the modern context, respect for tradition and obligation within limits, thrift (saving resources), perseverance toward slow results, willingness to subordinate oneself for a purpose, and concern with virtue.

A short-term orientation is seen in those societies that expect and reward quick results, view leisure time as important, have little respect for old-time traditions, and reward the risk taking and adaptability required of entrepreneurs. A few of the societies with a short-term orientation include Canada, Czech Republic, Pakistan, Spain, and the United States. From a business perspective, several of the features of a strong short-term orientation include the following:

- The main work values are freedom, individual rights, achievement, and thinking for oneself.
- The focus is on the bottom line with an emphasis on the importance of this year's profits.
- Leaders and workers view themselves as highly distinct groups.
- Personal loyalties vary with business needs (versus investment in life-long personal networks).[9]

After reading this section and examining your Experiential Exercise scores on these five dimensions, some of you are probably questioning whether you have the ability to work in a foreign setting. We hope that we have given you some information about how key cultural differences can shape one's personality. Understanding the role of culture can make you a better leader even if you never leave your home country. How do you believe that the culture of the United States impacted the development of Steve Jobs' personality?

Family

The primary vehicle for socializing an individual into a particular culture is the person's immediate family. Both parents and siblings play important roles in the personality development of most individuals. Members of an extended family—grandparents, aunts, uncles, and cousins—also can influence personality formation. In particular, parents (or a single parent) influence their children's development in three important ways:

Family is the primary vehicle for socializing an individual into a particular culture.

- Through their own behaviors, they present situations that bring out certain behaviors in children.
- They serve as role models with which children often strongly identify.
- They selectively reward and punish certain behaviors.[10]

The family's situation also is an important source of personality differences. Situational influences include the family's size, socioeconomic level, race, religion, and geographic location; birth order within the family; and parents' educational level. A firstborn usually has the undivided parental attention for some time without siblings around. And because they identify with their parents, they tend to grow up more conservative and conscientious. Laterborns, in contrast, are often more conciliatory and open to new ideas and experiences. Also, a person raised in a poor family from China simply has different experiences and opportunities than does a person raised in a wealthy family. Children do not spend their waking hours trying to become more like their parents, but are also influenced by the culture in which they were raised. Cultural norms inform children what it takes to survive in that society.

Group Membership

The first group to which most individuals belong is the family. Individuals also participate in various groups during their lives, beginning with their childhood playmates and continuing through teenaged schoolmate groupings and sports teams to adult work and social groups. The numerous roles and experiences that individuals have as members of groups represent another important source of personality differences. Although playmates and school groups early in life may have the strongest influences on personality formation, social and group experiences in later life continue to influence and shape personality. Understanding someone's personality requires understanding the groups to which that person belongs or has belonged in the past.

Life Experiences

Each person's life also is unique in terms of specific events and experiences, which can serve as important bases of personality. For example, the development of self-esteem (a personality dimension that we discuss shortly) depends on a series of experiences that include the opportunity to achieve goals and meet expectations, evidence of the ability to influence others, and a clear sense of being valued by others. A complex series of life experiences with others helps shape the adult's level of self-esteem.

As we weave an understanding of personality and other individual differences into our exploration of a variety of topics in organizational behavior, we hope that you will come to understand the crucial role that personality plays in explaining behavior. Individuals clearly pay a great deal of attention to the attributes of the personalities of the coworkers with whom they interact. The following Self Competency feature shows how JetBlue's former CEO David Neeleman's personality was shaped by various forces and how these affected his leadership at JetBlue.[11]

Self competency

David Neeleman of JetBlue

If you want to understand the culture of a company that is led by its founder, it helps to understand the personality of that founder. Neeleman spent the first five years of his life in Brazil where his father was a journalist. His family moved from Brazil, but he visited every summer. Brazil is a country that is divided between the haves and have-nots. He grew up in the rich part of the country and enjoyed a big house, a membership in country clubs, and so forth. During his junior year in Utah, he decided to return to Brazil to go on a mission for his church and ended up living in the slums or *favelas* of Brazil. The slums are where the desperately poor individuals live behind barbed wire fences in cardboard shacks.

He was struck by a few things living in the slums. First, most wealthy individuals have a sense of entitlement. They thought that they were better than the individuals in the slums. This bothered him tremendously. Second, most of the poor individuals were happier than the rich individuals and they generously shared what little they had. He experienced enormous pleasures and satisfactions from working with these individuals.

These experiences had a tremendous impact on the formation of his personality and his drive to manage JetBlue differently when he was CEO. When he traveled on a business trip, he flew coach class. There was no Lincoln Town Car waiting for him at the airport. At JetBlue, there are no reserved parking places. The coffee in the kitchen down the hall from his office was the same brand as that in the employee lounge at J. F. Kennedy airport. There is only one class on JetBlue planes. The seats at the back have slightly more legroom, so individuals who get off the plane last actually have roomier seats in-flight. The desk and other furniture in his office were the same as that used by everyone else. He told pilots: "There are individuals who make more money at this company than others, but that doesn't mean they should flaunt it."

He was seen frequently on flights from Florida to New York City. Once the plane settled into its cruising altitude, Neeleman walked to the front of the cabin, grabbed the microphone, and introduced himself. He explained that he would be coming through the cabin serving drinks and snacks along with the crew. He took out the garbage when the flight was over just like the cabin attendants. It was his chance to speak directly to JetBlue's customers. JetBlue also started a Crewmember Crisis fund when he was CEO. Everyone donated to it and it was used to help employees in crisis. If someone at JetBlue gets cancer, they have health benefits, but they might tap the fund to pay a babysitter while at chemotherapy.

Employees and customers both continue to like the "touchy-feely" aspect of JetBlue.

"When you have a leader who's so friendly, it makes everybody feel good about what they're doing," says Jim Small, a general manager for JetBlue in San Juan. JetBlue continues to be generous with travel vouchers when passengers are inconvenienced. Neeleman himself once drove an elderly couple from JFK to Connecticut, where he lives and they were headed, rather then let them spend $200 on a taxi.

To learn more about JetBlue, go to **www.jetblue.com.**

Insights for Leaders

Leaders should realize that their ability to change an individual's personality is very limited and almost impossible. The idea that both nature and nurture interact to shape an individual's personality is important. Heredity and the environment both play major roles in shaping personality. Also important is the fact that behavior is embedded in the way leaders think about subordinates.

In an increasingly global market, leaders in every country must think globally. Global competition is a reality and the number of leaders and others who are taking assignments in countries other than their own is rapidly increasing. These workers bring aspects of their own cultures into their organizations, neighborhoods, school systems, and homes.

Personality and Behavior

Learning Goal

2. Identify a set of personality dimensions that affect performance.

You don't see a person's personality, instead you see behaviors that reflect these internal characteristics.[12] For our purposes, personality describes a person's most dominant characteristics—shy, sensitive, reliable, creative, and the like. This meaning of personality is useful to employees because it contains a profile of characteristics that tell employees about the behaviors they can expect from their leaders. This profile also serves as a guide for how we might communicate with a manager or fellow employee. The main reason that we are interested in individual personality in the study of organizational behavior is because of the link between personality and individuals' competencies. Most individuals believe that there is a relationship between personality traits and behavior. Chet Cadieux, CEO of QuikTrip, a $4 billion privately held firm in Tulsa, Oklahoma, that operates more than 460 convenience stores in nine states, put all applicants through a personality assessment. He believes that extroverted salesclerks sell more than introverted ones and that extroverted clerks will like each other and stay longer in the job than introverts.[13]

The vast number and variety of specific personality traits or dimensions are bewildering. The term **personality trait** *refers to the basic components of personality.* Researchers of personality have identified literally *thousands* of traits over the years. Trait names simply represent the terms that individuals use to describe each other. However, a list containing hundreds or thousands of terms isn't very useful either in understanding the profile of personality in a scientific sense or in describing individual differences in a practical sense. To be useful, these terms need to be organized into a small set of concepts or factors. Recent research has done just that, identifying several general factors that can be used to describe a personality.[14] Before reading any further, please take time to complete the questionnaire in Table 3.1.

Big Five Personality Factors

The "Big Five" personality factors, as they often are referred to, describe an individual's emotional stability, agreeableness, extraversion, conscientiousness, and openness.[15] As shown in Figure 3.3, each includes a potentially large number and range of specific

TABLE 3.1 Assessing Your Personality Using the Big Five

The following questionnaire gives you a chance to gain insights into your Big Five personality dimensions. Please answer the following 25 statements using the following scale:

5 = Strongly agree

4 = Agree

3 = Moderate

2 = Disagree

1 = Strongly disagree

STATEMENTS

_____ 1.   I am the life of the party.
_____ 2.   I sympathize with others' feelings.
_____ 3.   I get chores done right away.
_____ 4.   I have frequent mood swings.
_____ 5.   I have a vivid imagination.
_____ 6.   I don't talk a lot. (R)
_____ 7.   I am not interested in other people's problems. (R)
_____ 8.   I often forget to put things back in their proper place. (R)
_____ 9.   I am relaxed most of the time. (R)
_____ 10. I am not interested in abstract ideas. (R)
_____ 11. I talk to a lot of different people at parties.
_____ 12. I feel others' emotions.
_____ 13. I like order.
_____ 14. I get upset easily.
_____ 15. I have difficulty understanding abstract ideas. (R)
_____ 16. I keep in the background. (R)
_____ 17. I am not really interested in others. (R)
_____ 18. I make a mess of things. (R)
_____ 19. I seldom feel blue. (R)
_____ 20. I do not have a good imagination. (R)
_____ 21. I don't mind being the center of attention.
_____ 22. I make people feel at ease.
_____ 23. I pay attention to details.
_____ 24. I am easily disturbed.
_____ 25. I am full of ideas.

SCORING

NOTE: If a statement has an "(R)" at the end of it, the scoring for that statement is reversed. That is, strongly agree is worth 1 point, agree is worth 2 points, etc.

1. Add your score for statements 1, 6, 11, 16, and 21: _____. This is your score for extraversion. The higher the score, the more likely you are to be energetic, outgoing, and gregarious.

2. Add your score for statements 2, 7, 12, 17, and 22: _____. This is your score for agreeableness. The higher the score, the more warm, tactful, and considerate you are toward others.

3. Add your score for statements 3, 8, 13, 18, and 23: _____. This is your score for conscientiousness. The higher the score, the more careful, neat, and dependable you are likely to be.

4. Add your score for statements 4, 9, 14, 19, and 24: _____. This is your score for emotional stability. The lower the score, the more stable, confident, and effective you are likely to be.

5. Add your score for statements 5, 10, 15, 20, and 25: _____. This is your score for openness. The higher the score, the more imaginative, curious, and original you are likely to be.

traits. That is, each factor is both a collection of related traits and on a continuum as shown in Figure 3.3.

Researchers have investigated extensively the relationships between the Big Five personality factors and performance. Their findings indicate that employees who

FIGURE 3.3 The Big Five Personality Factors

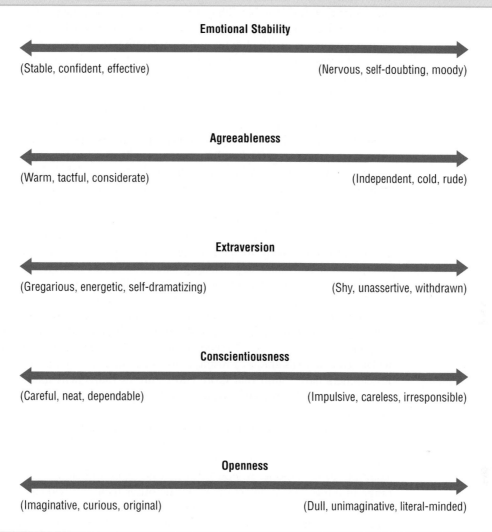

Emotional Stability

(Stable, confident, effective)   (Nervous, self-doubting, moody)

Agreeableness

(Warm, tactful, considerate)   (Independent, cold, rude)

Extraversion

(Gregarious, energetic, self-dramatizing)   (Shy, unassertive, withdrawn)

Conscientiousness

(Careful, neat, dependable)   (Impulsive, careless, irresponsible)

Openness

(Imaginative, curious, original)   (Dull, unimaginative, literal-minded)

have emotional stability, agreeableness, and conscientiousness perform better than those who lack these (the extremes of the *conscientiousness* continuum in Figure 3.3). An individual with a personality at one extreme of the *agreeableness* factor continuum might be described as warm and considerate. But with a personality at this factor's other extreme, the person would be considered cold or rude. Let's define the terms used for the Big Five personality factors and relate these to Steve Jobs.

Emotional stability *is the degree to which a person is calm, secure, and free from persistent negative feelings.* Individuals who are emotionally stable are relaxed, poised, slow to show anger, handle crises well, resilient, and secure in their interpersonal dealings with others. Individuals with less emotional stability are more excitable, insecure in their dealings with others, reactive, and subject to extreme swings of moods. Teams composed of emotionally unstable individuals usually come up with relatively fewer creative ideas than teams composed of emotionally stable individuals. Individuals with emotional stability handle the stress of managing others better than those who are less emotionally stable. How would you rate Steve Jobs' emotional stability?

Agreeableness *is a person's ability to get along with others.* Agreeable individuals value getting along with others. They are considerate, friendly, helpful, and willing to compromise their interests. Agreeable individuals also have an optimistic view of human nature. They believe individuals are basically honest, decent, and trustworthy. Individuals who demonstrate low agreeableness are often described as short tempered, uncooperative, and irritable. They are generally unconcerned with others' well-being and are unlikely to extend themselves for other individuals. Highly agreeable individuals are better at developing and maintaining close relationships with others at work, whereas less agreeable individuals are not likely to have particularly close working relationships with others, including customers and suppliers. How would you rate Steve Jobs on the agreeableness dimension?

Extraversion *is the degree to which a person seeks the company of others.* Extraverts enjoy being with individuals, are full of energy, and often experience positive emotions. Sociable individuals are extraverts. Extraverts are comfortable talking with others, speak up in a group, and are assertive, talkative, and open to establishing new interpersonal relationships. Less sociable individuals are labeled *introverts.* They tend to be low key, quiet, and deliberate. Their lack of social involvement should not be interpreted as shyness; the introvert simply needs less stimulation and more time alone to recharge his batteries. Research has shown that sociable individuals tend to be higher performing individuals than those who are less sociable. These individuals are also more likely to be attracted to managerial positions that require good interpersonal skills, such as marketing, sales, and senior management positions. How would you rate Steve Jobs on the extraversion dimension?

Conscientiousness *is concerned with self-discipline, acting responsibly, and directing our behavior.* Individuals who focus on a few key goals are more likely to be organized, reliable, careful, thorough, responsible, and self-disciplined because they concentrate on doing a few things well. Individuals who are less conscientious tend to focus on a wider array of goals and, as a result, tend to be more disorganized and less thorough. Researchers have found that more conscientious individuals tend to be higher performers than less conscientious individuals, especially in sales. How would you rate Steve Jobs on this dimension?

Openness *describes imagination and creativity.* Individuals with high levels of openness are willing to listen to new ideas, have vivid imaginations, appreciate art and beauty, prefer variety to routine, and change their own ideas, beliefs, and assumptions in response to new information. Open individuals tend to have a broad range of interests and be creative. On the other hand, individuals who demonstrate low openness tend to be less receptive to new ideas and less willing to change their minds. They prefer the plain, straightforward, and obvious over the complex, ambiguous, and subtle. Leaders who are high on openness tend to be better performers because of their ability to adapt to new situations and their willingness to listen to others who have different points of view. How would you rate Steve Jobs on openness?

Insights for Leaders

We must caution you that before a link can be established between job performance and any personality measure, it must satisfy two concerns. One is that the measure must be reliable. **Reliability** *refers to how consistently a measure gets the same results.* If you get on a scale and its reads 188 pounds, step off and then on again and the scale reads 170, it is not reliable. For a measure to be reliable, it must be consistent. Second, a scale must be valid. **Validity** *refers to how important the measure is to other things that are important*, such as job performance. Many of you took the ACT or SAT test prior to applying for college. Many admissions individuals believe that your test score is a valid measure of your past achievements and your capacity to compete academically at their institution.

Although each personality factor represents a collection of related traits, the link between personality and specific behaviors often is most valid when the focus is on a single factor rather than all five factors at once. Organizations are using the Big Five as an assessment device for screening new employees as part of their interviewing process. Nordstrom's requires sales individuals to be cheerful, energetic, and serve very demanding customers with a smile. Therefore, individuals are required to show extraversion, agreeableness, and emotional stability. Nordstrom's human resource managers have found that these are valid measures leading to high performance for its sales staff. At Outback Steakhouse, the turnover of employees varies between 40 and 60 percent a year. Using the Big Five inventory, Outback managers found that by recruiting employees who were extraverted and agreeable, they were able to cut down on turnover and increase customers' satisfaction with their dining experiences. Similarly, Outsourcing Solutions, a debt collection firm, found that those employees high in conscientiousness and introversion were able to sit for hours by themselves to make calls regarding past-due accounts and stayed with the organization longer than those employees who did not demonstrate these traits. New Horizons Computer Learning Centers also faced high turnover until it discovered that those employees who were high in conscientiousness and extraversion made the best employees for them.[16]

Some individuals question these findings noting that one's personality traits can undergo change. We recognize that one's personality can evolve over time as a person becomes exposed to new experiences and situations. Graduating from college, breaking away from one's parents, starting a career, getting married, raising children, and being managed by various "bosses" can all shape the development of an individual's personality. Also by examining our own behavior, we may learn to behave differently from situation to situation. Have you ever noticed how your behavior at a Super Bowl party is different than your behavior at work?

Self-Esteem

Self-esteem *is the extent to which an individual believes that he or she is a worthwhile and deserving individual.* In other words, individuals develop, hold, and sometimes modify opinions of their own behaviors, abilities, appearance, and worth. These general self-assessments reflect responses to individuals and situations, successes and failures, and the opinions of others. Such self-evaluations are sufficiently accurate and stable to be widely regarded as a basic personality dimension. In terms of the Big Five personality, self-esteem most likely would be part of the *emotional stability* dimension (see Figure 3.3).

Self-esteem affects behavior in organizations and other social settings in several important ways. It influences initial vocational choice. For example, individuals with high self-esteem are more likely to take risks in job selection, to seek out high-status occupations (e.g., medicine or law), and to choose unconventional or nontraditional jobs (e.g., forest ranger or jet pilot) than are individuals with low self-esteem. A study of college students looking for jobs reported that those with high self-esteem (1) received more favorable evaluations from recruiters, (2) were more satisfied with the job search, (3) received more job offers, and (4) were more likely to accept jobs before graduation than were students with low self-esteem.[17]

Self-esteem influences numerous behaviors. Employees with low self-esteem are more easily swayed by the opinions of coworkers than are employees with high self-esteem. Employees with low self-esteem set lower goals for themselves than do those with high self-esteem. Employees with high self-esteem place more value on actually attaining their goals than do those with low self-esteem. That is, high self-esteem individuals break down jobs into specific tasks and prioritize their work so they can accomplish their jobs. Employees with low self-esteem are more susceptible than employees with high self-esteem to procrastinate, suffer stress, conflict, ambiguity, poor supervision, poor working conditions, and the like. In brief, high self-esteem is positively related to achievement and a willingness to expend effort to accomplish goals. Clearly, self-esteem is an important individual difference in terms of work behavior. Both Steve Jobs and David Neeleman appear to be individuals with high self-esteem.

Locus of Control

Locus of control *is the degree to which individuals believe that they can control events affecting them.*[18] Individuals who have a high **internal locus of control** (internals) *believe that their own behavior and actions primarily, but not necessarily totally, determine many of the events in their lives.* On the other hand, individuals who have a high **external locus of control** (externals) *believe that chance, fate, or other individuals primarily determine what happens to them.* Locus of control typically is considered to be a part of the *conscientiousness* factor (see Figure 3.3). Table 3.2 contains a measure that you can use to assess your own locus of control beliefs. What is your locus of control?

Many differences between internals and externals are significant in explaining aspects of behavior in organizations and other social settings.[19] Internals control their own behavior better, are more active politically and socially, and seek information about their situations more actively than do externals. Compared to externals, internals are more likely to try to influence or persuade others and are less likely to be influenced by others. Internals often are more achievement oriented than are externals. Compared to internals, externals appear to prefer a more structured, directive style of supervision. As we pointed out in Chapter 1, the ability to perform effectively in the global environment is increasingly important. Individuals with a high internal locus of control often adjust more readily to international assignments than do those with a high external locus of control. What do you think Steve Jobs' locus of control score is?

Figure 3.4 shows some of the important relationships between locus of control and job performance.

TABLE 3.2 A Locus of Control Measure

For each of these 10 questions, indicate the extent to which you agree or disagree, using the following scale.

1 = strongly disagree	5 = slightly agree
2 = disagree	6 = agree
3 = slightly disagree	7 = strongly agree
4 = neither disagree nor agree	

_____ 1.   When I get what I want it's usually because I worked hard for it.
_____ 2.   When I make plans I am almost certain to make them work.
_____ 3.   I prefer games involving some luck over games requiring pure skill.
_____ 4.   I can learn almost anything if I set my mind to it.
_____ 5.   My major accomplishments are entirely due to my hard work and ability.
_____ 6.   I usually don't set goals, because I have a hard time following through on them.
_____ 7.   Competition discourages excellence.
_____ 8.   Often people get ahead just by being lucky.
_____ 9.   On any sort of exam or competition I like to know how well I do relative to everyone else.
_____ 10. It's pointless to keep working on something that's too difficult for me.

To determine your score, reverse the values you selected for questions 3, 6, 7, 8, and 10 (1 = 7, 2 = 6, 3 = 5, 4 = 4, 5 = 3, 6 = 2, 7 = 1). For example, if you strongly disagreed with the statement in question 3, you would have given it a value of "1." Change this value to a "7." Reverse the scores in a similar manner for questions 6, 7, 8, and 10. Now add the 10 point values together.

Your score: _____

A study of college students found a mean of 51.8 for men and 52.2 for women using this questionnaire. The higher your score, the higher your internal locus of control. Low scores are associated with external locus of control.

Source: Adapted from Burger, J. M. *Personality: Theory and Research.* Belmont, Calif.: Wadsworth, 1986, pp. 400–401.

FIGURE 3.4 The Effects of Locus of Control on Performance

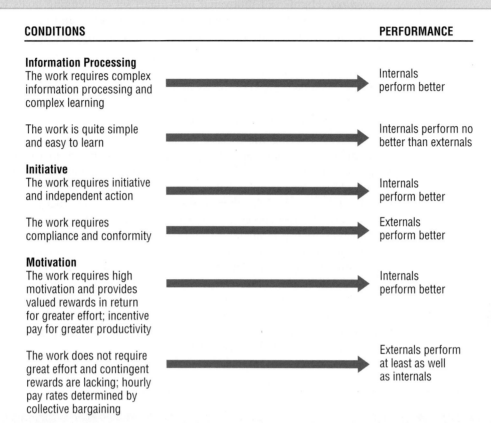

CONDITIONS	PERFORMANCE
Information Processing The work requires complex information processing and complex learning	Internals perform better
The work is quite simple and easy to learn	Internals perform no better than externals
Initiative The work requires initiative and independent action	Internals perform better
The work requires compliance and conformity	Externals perform better
Motivation The work requires high motivation and provides valued rewards in return for greater effort; incentive pay for greater productivity	Internals perform better
The work does not require great effort and contingent rewards are lacking; hourly pay rates determined by collective bargaining	Externals perform at least as well as internals

Source: From J. B. Miner, *Industrial-Organizational Psychology*. McGraw-Hill, 1992, 151.

Emotional Intelligence

Psychologist Daniel Goleman contends that emotional intelligence (EQ) is actually more crucial than general intelligence (IQ) in terms of career success.[20] **Emotional intelligence** *refers to how well an individual handles oneself and others rather than how smart or how capable the individual is in terms of technical skills.* Goleman suggests that leaders need a high EQ to be effective in their leadership positions. A high EQ enables a leader to accurately assess their subordinates' needs, analyze the situation, and then suggest the proper course of action. The leader processes this information to tailor her behaviors to fit the situation. To assess your emotional intelligence, turn to the second Experiential Exercise at the end of this chapter on page 99 and complete the questionnaire. Emotional intelligence includes the attributes of self-awareness, social empathy, self-motivation, and social skills:

- **Self-awareness** *refers to recognizing one's emotions, strengths and limitations, and capabilities and how these affect others.* Individuals with high self-awareness know their emotional state, recognize the links between their feelings and what they are thinking, are open to feedback from others on how to continuously improve, and are able to make sound decisions despite uncertainties and pressures. They are able to show a sense of humor.

- **Social empathy** *refers to sensing what others need in order for them to develop.* Individuals who are socially aware of themselves show sensitivity, understand other individuals' needs and feelings, challenge bias and intolerance, and act as trusted advisers to others. They are good at acknowledging an individual's strengths, accomplishments, and development. As a mentor, they give timely coaching advice and offer assignments that challenge a person's competencies.

- **Self-motivation** *refers to being results oriented and pursuing goals beyond what is required.* Highly self-motivated individuals set challenging goals for themselves and others, seek ways to improve their performance, and readily make personal sacrifices to meet the organization's goals. They operate from hope of success rather than a fear of failure.

- **Social skills** *refer to the ability of an individual to influence others.* Individuals with effective social skills are good at persuading others to share their vision; stepping forward as a leader, regardless of their position in the organization; leading by example; and dealing with difficult interpersonal situations in a straightforward manner.

Think of EQ as being the social equivalent of IQ. At GM, Ford, AT&T, and other organizations undergoing rapid change, emotional intelligence may determine who gets promoted and who gets passed over or who gets laid off and who stays. Studies have consistently shown, for example, that the attributes associated with emotional intelligence (e.g., the ability to persuade others, the ability to understand others, and so on) are twice as important for career success as intelligence (IQ) or technical competencies.[21] Using all the dimensions of EQ, evaluate Steve Jobs' EQ. What aspects of Jobs' personality seem to be most important in influencing his behavior(s)? Why was he so successful at Apple?

By any measure, Starbucks is among the most successful retailing companies in the world. While much has been written about Starbucks' successes and challenges during the worldwide recession, the role of the barista's personality is critical because he or she is the person who talks to the customers and serves them. In the following Teams Competency feature, we have put brackets around the personality characteristics so you can identify them as you read.[22]

Teams competency

Why Personality Is Important at Starbucks

Starbucks' baristas are important for store success.

TED S. WARREN/AP PHOTO

Enter any Starbucks and you'll see baristas (the associates who take orders and make and serve coffee and food) at work. They work like a well-oiled machine with all moves well choreographed to serve the customer. These baristas work together as a team and are important for the store's success.

How does Starbucks train them to work together as a team? All baristas receive 24 hours of in-store training in customer service (how to meet, greet, and serve customers) and basic retail skills. They also take "Coffee Knowledge" and "Brewing the Perfect Cup" classes. Baristas are taught to anticipate the customer's needs, and to make eye contact while carefully explaining the various flavors and blends. They are also trained in the care and maintenance of the machinery and how to treat each other.

One of the guiding principles at Starbucks is to provide a great working environment and to employ individuals who treat each other with high respect and dignity (emotional stability).

A company survey found the top two reasons individuals want to work for Starbucks are "the opportunity to work with an enthusiastic team" and "to work in a place where I feel I have value" (agreeableness). Therefore, Starbucks looks to hire individuals with high self-esteem who are sensitive to the feelings of others and who want participation from and success for all team members.

Highly effective baristas are also stable individuals who do not show anxiousness or hostility to others even under stressful conditions. Finally, Starbucks wants barista partners who combine their passion for great coffee and quality customer service, listen to others, are reliable, organized, and can focus on completing their tasks.

To learn more about Starbucks, go to **www.starbucks.com**.

Insights for Leaders

It should be evident by now that the various personality dimensions have important implications for understanding behavior and improving performance. However, leaders or groups should not try to change or otherwise directly control employee personality because being able to do so is generally impossible. Even if such control were possible, it would be highly unethical. Rather, the challenge for leaders and employees is to understand the crucial role played by personality in explaining some aspects of human behavior in the workplace. Knowledge of important individual differences provides leaders, employees, and students of organizational behavior with valuable insights and a framework that they can use to diagnose events and situations.

Although understanding differences in personality is important, behavior always involves an interaction of the person and the situation. Sometimes the demands of the situation may be so overwhelming that individual differences are relatively unimportant for leaders. For example, if an office building is burning, everyone in it will try to flee. However, the fact that all employees behaved the same way says nothing about the personalities of those individuals. In other situations, individual differences may explain more about behavior.

Under normal working conditions, a person's personality has a role in determining how that person behaves at work. Just reflect on how Steve Jobs' personality affects others at Apple, or the characteristics of baristas that Starbucks looks for when hiring new employees. We believe that considering both the personality of the individual and the demands of the job are needed to help leaders understand why individuals behave as they do in organizations. When an individual's personality does not fit the demands of the job, that person will be less satisfied and productive. Job applicants should assess the fit between their personal characteristics and the demands of the job and organization. However, if all individuals share common characteristics and preferences, leaders need to recognize that the organization might be more resistant to change. To remain competitive over the long term, leaders are probably well served to hire some individuals who do not fit the mold. For that reason, this perspective is consistently used throughout this book. Many of the topics covered in this book, such as leadership, interpersonal communication, conflict management, stress, and resistance to change, examine both *personal* and *situational causes* for the organizational behavior discussed. Both *interact* to determine behavior.

Work-Related Attitudes

Learning Goal

3. *Describe the attitudes that affect performance.*

It is often very difficult to separate personality and attitudes. You cannot see either one, but you can see the results of each through a person's behavior. Attitudes are another type of *individual difference* that affects an individual's behavior in organizations. **Attitudes** *are relatively lasting feelings, thoughts, and behaviors aimed at specific* *individuals, groups, ideas, issues, or objects.*[23] Attitudes are influenced by an individual's background and experiences. They are formed by a variety of forces, including their personal values, experiences, and personalities. Attitudes are important for three reasons. First, attitudes are reasonably stable over time. Unless individuals have strong reasons to change, they will persist. Individuals who have a favorable attitude toward buying domestic cars will probably like domestic cars in the future, unless important reasons occur to change their automobile preferences. Second, individuals hold attitudes that are directed toward some object—job, supervisor, company, college. If a barista likes coffee and serving individuals, they probably won't have a negative attitude toward working at Starbucks as a barista. Third, attitudes influence our behavior. That is, individuals tend to behave in ways that are consistent with their feelings. If we have a specific attitude toward an object or person, we tend to form other consistent attitudes toward related objects or individuals. Therefore, to change a person's attitude, you need to change a person's behavior.

Components of Attitudes

Individuals often think of attitudes as a simple concept. In reality, attitudes and their effects on behavior are complex. An attitude consists of:

*   an *affective* component—the feelings, sentiments, moods, and emotions about some specific person, idea, event, or object;

*   a *cognitive* component—the thoughts, opinions, knowledge, or information held by the individual about a specific person, idea, event, or object; and

*   a *behavioral* component—the predisposition to act on a favorable or unfavorable evaluation to a specific person, idea, event, or object.

These components don't exist or function separately. An attitude represents the *interplay* of a person's affective, cognitive, and behavioral tendencies with regard to something—another person or group, an event, or an issue. For example, suppose that a college student has a negative attitude about the use of tobacco. During a job interview with the representative of the Altria Group, he discovers that Philip Morris, a maker of cigarettes, is owned by the Altria Group. He might feel a sudden uneasiness during the interview (the affective component) because a close friend's parent recently died from lung cancer. He might form a negative opinion of the interviewer based on beliefs and opinions about the type of person who would work for such a company (the cognitive component). He might even be tempted to make an unkind remark to the interviewer or suddenly terminate the interview (the behavioral component). However, the person's *actual* behavior may or may not be easy to predict and will depend on several factors, including the current state of the job market, that we will discuss shortly.

Diversity Insight

Individuals working together and respecting one another so that they can achieve their common goal is all I want. We need all sorts of individuals to succeed as an organization.

Albert Black, CEO, On-Target Supplies and Logistics

Attitudes Affecting Job Performance

Individuals form attitudes about many things. Employees have attitudes about their manager, pay, working conditions, promotions, where they park, coworkers, and the like. Some of these attitudes are more important than others because they are more closely linked to performance. Especially important to job performance are attitudes of hope, job satisfaction, and organizational commitment.

Hope

Hope *involves a person's mental willpower (determination) and waypower (road map) to achieve goals.*[24] Simply wishing for something isn't enough; a person must have the means to make it happen. However, all the knowledge and skills needed to solve a problem won't help if the person doesn't have the willpower to do so. Therefore, a simple definition of hope is

$$\text{Hope} = \text{mental willpower} + \text{waypower to achieve goals.}$$

Answering the questions in Table 3.3 will help you understand this definition of *hope*. You need to have a high level of both the willpower and the waypower to have a high level of hope to accomplish your goals. This concept applies to a variety of work-related attitudes. The high-hope person enjoys the pursuit of challenging goals and pursues them with a positive attitude. High-hope individuals engage in self-talk, such as "This should be an interesting task" or "I am ready for this challenge." High-hope individuals are attentive and focused on the appropriate behaviors for the situation. They commit themselves to desired positive work outcomes (e.g., good performance) and distance themselves from negative outcomes. They possess an internal locus of control. As such, they need a high degree of autonomy in order to express themselves and be productive. They can be easily offended and discouraged if micromanaged and will likely try to search for alternative pathways to regain control. Hopeful employees tend to be creative and resourceful.

In contrast, low-hope individuals are apprehensive about what is to come. Their attention is quickly diverted from task-relevant behavior to such thoughts as "I'm not doing very well." Low-hope individuals may feel a lot of negative emotions very quickly. Low-hope individuals are especially susceptible to feeling great amounts of stress in their jobs and becoming easily derailed by issues in their pursuit of goals. With such derailments, low-hope individuals perceive that they are not going to reach their desired goals. Their natural tendency is to withdraw from friends and become "loners." For high-hope individuals, however, the stressor is

---

TABLE 3.3 Hope Scale

Read each item carefully. For each item, what number best describes you?

1 = definitely false
2 = mostly false
3 = mostly true
4 = definitely true

_____ 1. I energetically pursue my work (academic) goals.
_____ 2. I can think of many ways to get out of a jam.
_____ 3. My past experiences have prepared me well for my future.
_____ 4. There are lots of ways around any problem.
_____ 5. I've been pretty successful in life.
_____ 6. I can think of many ways to get things in life that are most important to me.
_____ 7. I meet the goals (work/academic) that I set for myself.
_____ 8. Even when others get discouraged, I know I can find a way to solve the problem.

Scoring: Total the eight numbers. If you score higher than 24, you are a hopeful person. If you score less than 24, you probably aren't hopeful. Items 1, 3, 5, and 7 relate to will power, and items 2, 4, 6, and 8 relate to waypower.

Source: Adapted from Snyder, C. R. Managing for high hope. *R&D Innovator,* 1995, 4(6), 6–7; Snyder, C. R., LaPointe, A. B., Crowson, J. J., and Early, S. Preferences of high- and low-hope people for self-referential input. *Cognition and Emotion,* 1998, 12, 807–823.

seen as a challenge that needs to be worked around. What happens when high-hope individuals are blocked from reaching their goal? They are not filled with anger, self-pity, and negative emotions, as is the case for low-hope individuals in similar circumstances. Rather, high-hope individuals will find another goal that will fulfill similar needs. This is because high-hope individuals have several goals that can bring them happiness. Leaders who are hopeful spend more time with employees, establish open lines of communication with employees and others, and help others set difficult, but achievable, goals. High-hope individuals tend to be more certain of their goals, value progress toward achieving those goals, enjoy interacting with individuals, readily adapt to new relationships, and are less anxious in stressful situations than are low-hope individuals.

Leaders can help employees increase their level of hope by using one or more of the following management practices.[25] First, they can help subordinates set clear and specific *goals* that have benchmarks so that the employees can track progress toward their goals. Vague goals may actually lessen hope because the result sought is unclear and tracking progress is therefore difficult, if not impossible. Employees who set performance goals that are slightly higher than previous levels of performance learn to expand their range of hope. They also learn a great deal about which goals are best for them. Second, leaders can help employees break overall, long-term goals into *small subgoals* or *steps*. Remember how you learned to ride a bike? Through many falls and wobbles, you learned that each consecutive subgoal (moving the pedals, balancing, going a block without falling) is a stretch. These small steps provided you with positive mental maps about how to reach your goal—riding a bike. Third, leaders can help employees figure out how to *motivate* themselves to reach their goals.

Job Satisfaction

An attitude of great interest to managers and team leaders is job satisfaction.[26] **Job satisfaction** *reflects the extent to which individuals find fulfillment in their work*. Job satisfaction has been linked to employees staying on the job and low job turnover. With the cost of replacing employees being about 30 to 40 percent of their salary, job turnover can become quite expensive. Similarly, employees who are highly satisfied with their jobs come to work regularly and are less likely to take sick days.

Do employees generally like their jobs? Despite what you may hear in the news about dissatisfied employees going on strike or even acting violently toward their coworkers and/or managers, they are generally quite satisfied with their jobs. Low job satisfaction can result in costly turnover, absenteeism, tardiness, and even poor mental health. Because job satisfaction is important to organizations, we need to look at the factors that contribute to it.

A popular measure of job satisfaction used by organizations is shown in Table 3.4. It measures five facets of job satisfaction: pay, security, social, supervisory, and growth satisfaction. Take time now to complete it. Obviously, you may be satisfied with some aspects of your job and, at the same time, dissatisfied with others.

The sources of job satisfaction and dissatisfaction vary from person to person. Some individuals may find that being an animal control officer, mortician, correctional/probation officer, or a used car salesperson might not offer sources of personal satisfaction. Yet, individuals who perform these jobs often think that they are performing important jobs and derive a great sense of job satisfaction from performing them. Important sources of satisfaction for many employees include the challenge of the job, the interest that the work holds for them, the physical activity required, working conditions, rewards available from the organization, the nature of coworkers, and the like. Table 3.5 lists work factors that often are related to various levels of job satisfaction. An important implication is that job satisfaction be should considered an outcome of an individual's work experience. Thus, high levels of dissatisfaction should indicate to leaders that problems exist, say, with working conditions, the reward system, or the employee's role in the organization.

TABLE 3.4 Measuring Job Satisfaction

Think of the job you have now, or a job you've had in the past. Indicate how satisfied you are with each aspect of your job below, using the following scale:

1 = Extremely dissatisfied
2 = Dissatisfied
3 = Slightly dissatisfied
4 = Neutral
5 = Slightly satisfied
6 = Satisfied
7 = Extremely satisfied

_____ 1. The amount of job security I have.
_____ 2. The amount of pay and fringe benefits I receive.
_____ 3. The amount of personal growth and development I get in doing my job.
_____ 4. The people I talk to and work with on my job.
_____ 5. The degree of respect and fair treatment I receive from my boss.
_____ 6. The feeling of worthwhile accomplishment I get from doing my job.
_____ 7. The chance to get to know other people while on the job.
_____ 8. The amount of support and guidance I receive from my supervisor.
_____ 9. The degree to which I am fairly paid for what I contribute to this organization.
_____ 10. The amount of independent thought and action I can exercise in my job.
_____ 11. How secure things look for me in the future in this organization.
_____ 12. The chance to help other people while at work.
_____ 13. The amount of challenge in my job.
_____ 14. The overall quality of the supervision I receive on my work.

Now, compute your scores for the facets of job satisfaction.

Pay Satisfaction:
Q2 + Q9 = _____ Divided by 2:

Security Satisfaction:
Q1 + Q11 = _____ Divided by 2:

Social Satisfaction:
Q4 + Q7 + Q12 = _____ Divided by 3:

Supervisory Satisfaction:
Q5 + Q8 + Q14 = _____ Divided by 3:

Growth Satisfaction:
Q3 + Q6 + Q10 + Q13 = _____ Divided by 4:

Scores on the facets range from 1 to 7. (Scores lower than 4 suggest there is room for change.) This questionnaire is an abbreviated version of the Job Diagnostic Survey, a widely used tool for assessing individuals' attitudes about their jobs.

Source: J. Richard Hackman & Greg R. Oldham, *Work Redesign*, © 1980. Reprinted by permission of Pearson Education, Inc., Upper Saddle River, NJ.

A commonsense notion is that job satisfaction leads directly to effective performance. (A happy worker is a good worker.) Yet, numerous studies have shown that a simple, direct link between job satisfaction and job performance often doesn't exist.[27] Research has shown that job satisfaction and job performance are influenced by one's personality. That is, a person's locus of control and Big Five personality characteristics affect the relationship between job satisfaction and job performance. The difficulty of relating attitudes to behavior is important. For example, individuals who hold a positive attitude toward their job but are low in conscientiousness may not necessarily work harder because they end up coming in late to work, fail to show up at all, are unorganized, and the like. General attitudes best predict general behaviors, and specific attitudes are related most strongly to specific behaviors. These principles explain,

TABLE 3.5 Effects of Various Work Factors on Job Satisfaction

WORK FACTORS	EFFECTS
Work itself	
Challenge	Mentally challenging work that the individual can successfully accomplish is satisfying.
Physical demands	Tiring work is dissatisfying.
Personal interest	Personally interesting work is satisfying.
Reward structure	Rewards that are equitable and that provide accurate feedback for performance are satisfying.
Working conditions	
Physical	Satisfaction depends on the match between working conditions and physical needs.
Goal attainment	Working conditions that promote goal attainment are satisfying.
Self	High self-esteem is conducive to job satisfaction.
Others in the organization	Individuals will be satisfied with supervisors, coworkers, or subordinates who help them attain rewards. Also, individuals will be more satisfied with colleagues who see things the same way they do.
Organization and management	Individuals will be satisfied with organizations that have policies and procedures designed to help them attain rewards. Individuals will be dissatisfied with conflicting roles and/or ambiguous roles imposed by the organization.
Fringe benefits	Benefits do not have a strong influence on job satisfaction for most workers.

Source: Adapted from Landy, F. J. Psychology of Work Behavior, 4th ed. Pacific Grove, Calif.: Brooks/Cole, 1989, 470.

at least in part, why the expected relationships often don't exist. Job satisfaction is a collection of numerous attitudes toward various aspects of the job and represents a general attitude. Performance of a specific task, such as preparing a particular monthly report, can't necessarily be predicted on the basis of a general attitude. However, studies have shown that the level of overall workforce job satisfaction and organizational performance are linked. That is, organizations with satisfied employees tend to be more effective than organizations with unsatisfied employees.

Mercedes-Benz leaders learned how to create a high-performing and satisfied workforce when it developed its M-Class SUV built in Vance, Alabama. Experts from around the globe met with the leadership of Mercedes-Benz to offer them advice on how to create this new factory. The following Across Cultures Competency feature describes how Mercedes-Benz designed the Alabama factory to let workers derive a sense of high job satisfaction from working in this plant.[28]

Across Cultures competency

Mercedes-Benz

Mercedes-Benz is one of the world's most widely recognized brands. It represents quality and luxury. In Germany, engineers are highly trained experts who develop their skills by working as an apprentice to a *Meister* (master in the profession). Workers accept the authority of the Meister and don't expect to be treated as equals to the Meister. Once they learn the skills they need, they expect to carry out their tasks without close supervision. This is a sign that they are respected and can be trusted to do a good job. Strong norms exist concerning the importance of producing cars and SUVs of superior quality. In many U.S. automobile plants, managers control workers through a division of labor and narrow spans of control. Henry Ford's assembly-line approach to motivating workers still dominates many production plants. Employees are driven to get their job done. Leaders are not concerned with employees deriving much job satisfaction.

When the Vance plant was built, German engineers spent two years helping to train Americans to perform their work as part of multidisciplinary teams. Each team was autonomous and managed its particular operations. The teams are accountable for meeting quality standards, controlling costs, and meeting production schedules. When Jack Duncan, a supervisor, noticed that workers had to "slant walk" zigzag style to reach parts in a bin, he called the workers together to find a better arrangement for

them. The workers made a change, and that change saved 2 seconds off the line for all SUVs. All workers are looking for small changes that will make their job more satisfying. According to George Jones, a 38-year-old who inspects raw materials at the plant, "job satisfaction is all about having a voice in what goes on."

At Mercedes-Benz, teams are accountable for meeting quality standards.

To learn more about Mercedes-Benz, go to **www.mercedesbenz.com.**

Take a look at the various work factors in Table 3.5. How many can you identify in the Mercedes-Benz example? How do these contribute to employee job satisfaction?

Organizational Commitment

Organizational commitment influences whether a person stays on the job. **Organizational commitment** *is the strength of an employee's involvement in the organization and identification with it.*[29] Employees who stay with their organization for a long period of time tend to be more committed to the organization than those who work for shorter periods of time. For long-time employees, the thought of packing up and moving on is not taken lightly. Strong organizational commitment is characterized by:

*   a support of and acceptance of the organization's goals and values,
*   a willingness to exert considerable effort on behalf of the organization, and
*   a desire to remain with the organization.[30]

Highly committed employees will probably see themselves as dedicated members of the organization, referring to the organization in personal terms, such as "We make high-quality products." They will overlook minor sources of job dissatisfaction. In contrast, less committed employees often view their relationship with the organization in less personal terms ("They don't offer quality service"), will express their dissatisfaction more openly about things, and will have a short tenure with the organization.

Organizational commitment goes beyond loyalty to include an active contribution to accomplishing organizational goals. Organizational commitment represents a broader work-related attitude than job satisfaction. It applies to the entire organization rather than just to the job. Further, commitment typically is more stable than satisfaction because day-to-day events are less likely to change commitment.

As with job satisfaction, the sources of organizational commitment may vary from person to person. Employees' initial commitment to an organization is determined largely by their individual characteristics (e.g., cultural values, personality, attitudes) and how well their early job experiences match their expectations. If you have ever visited Seattle's Pike Place Fish Market, you probably saw John Yokoyama. John encourages employees to work hard, have fun, be kind, and develop positive attitudes. Tossing the fish and joking with customers, practices that may not work at Exxon, seem to work at Yokoyama's fish market.

Organizational commitment continues to be influenced by job experiences, with many of the same factors that lead to job satisfaction also contributing to organizational commitment or lack of commitment: pay, relationships with supervisors and coworkers, working conditions, opportunities for advancement, and so on. How would you describe workers' job commitment in the Mercedes-Benz plant in Vance, Alabama? Over time, organizational commitment tends to become stronger because (1) individuals develop deeper ties to the organization and their coworkers as they spend more time with them, (2) seniority often brings advantages that tend to develop more positive work attitudes, and (3) opportunities in the job market may decrease with age, causing employees to become more strongly attached to their current organization.

A highly committed organization is one in which everyone feels equally committed to the organization's goals. Members of majority and minority groups feel respected; everyone has an equal chance to express views and influence decisions; and everyone has equal access to both formal and informal networks within the organization. Scott McQuillan describes how Deloitte & Touche earns its employee commitment in the following Diversity Competency feature.[31]

Diversity competency

Deloitte & Touche

At the accounting firm of Deloitte & Touche, employment numbers alerted partners to a disturbing trend. Only about 5 percent of the firm's partners were women, and the turnover rate for women throughout the firm was 30 percent. When Diana O'Brien left Deloitte & Touche to work for another firm, she was just one of the many women who did so. Subsequently, partners at the firm realized that they needed to change their diversity policy. The changes they made were so successful that Diana O'Brien decided to return. "Before I left, I couldn't have a life and still do consulting. Now, enough has changed that I have been able to do that," she explained.

One of the most significant changes was the company's flexible work arrangements, which includes compressed workweeks, telecommuting, job sharing, and paid child-care leave. For Jeff McLane, the changes made it possible for him to have a more balanced personal life, which included time to train for competing as an Olympic cyclist. For Scott McQuillan, the firm's diversity and inclusion program helped him win the war for talent at college campuses. Getting the message out that the firm wanted applicants to be able to balance work and family was critical for McQuillan's college recruiting program success. The firm was also committed to hiring college seniors with different backgrounds. McQuillan started to recruit earlier and attend conferences sponsored by the National Association of Black, Hispanic and Latino Accountants. Such tactics helped the firm bring in a variety of diverse individuals.

To learn about Deloitte & Touche, go to **www.deloitte.com**.

Emotions at Work

4. *Explain how emotions impact employees' performance.*

Anger, jealousy, guilt, shame, happiness, and relief are all feelings that you have probably experienced in organizations. These feelings are all part of your emotions. **Emotions** *are the complex patterns of feelings toward an object or person.* We have all seen how emotions affect workplace attitudes and behaviors. When performing your job, you experience a variety of emotions during the day. You also know that how employees and leaders handle their emotions at work has a tremendous impact on their productivity.[32] The more positive emotions we experience while at work, the more we form positive attitudes toward the organization. Positive emotions, such as joy, affection, and happiness, serve many purposes. When employees experience these positive emotions, they tend to think more creatively, seek out new information and experiences, behave more flexibly, have greater confidence in their competencies, and be more persistent.

Positive emotions also help individuals bounce back from adversity and live longer and healthier lives. Individuals who experience positive emotions, especially during stressful times, tend to tolerate pain better, cope with and recover from illness faster, and experience less depression. In contrast, negative emotions, such as anger, disgust, and sadness, tend to narrow an individual's focus and limit his or her options to seek alternatives. For example, anger tends to lead to a desire to escape, attack, or take revenge, and guilt/shame can result in a person's desire to withdraw from the situation rather than creatively problem solve. Negative emotions also tend to produce larger, more long-lasting effects than positive emotions. That is, negative emotions tend to stay with individuals longer than positive ones.

The distinction between positive and negative emotions is shown in Figure 3.5. Negative emotions are incongruent with the goal you are striving to achieve. For example, which of the six emotions are you likely to experience if you fail the final exam for this course, or if you are dismissed from a job? Failing the exam or losing a job is incongruent with the goal of graduating or being perceived as an accomplished professional. On the other hand, which of the four positive emotions, shown in Figure 3.5, will you likely experience if you graduate with honors or receive a promotion? The emotions experienced in these situations are positive because they are congruent with your goals. Therefore, emotions are goal directed.

Positive emotions have been linked to organizational effectiveness. Leaders who express positive emotions encourage employees to feel positive emotions as well. When individuals have positive emotions, they are more likely to set high goals, see and fix mistakes, feel more competent, and have greater problem-solving capabilities. In organizations that recently cut staff, such as AT&T and Hewlett-Packard, those organizations with leaders who displayed positive emotions in such trying times had significantly higher productivity, higher quality, and lower voluntary employee turnover than those leaders who displayed negative emotions. After the attacks on the Hotel Oberoi and Taj Mahal in Mumbai, India, in November 2008, employees at a local restaurant near the hotels were told by their manager that they could leave to protect their safety. Instead, employees and the store supervisors chose to stay. They literally pulled stunned individuals passing by into the store, giving them food, drink, shelter, and emotional support. As one reporter said: "Embedded in a crisis is an opportunity for employers to build loyalty and wholeheartedly provide positive emotions."

A Model of Emotions

A model of how emotions affect behavior is shown in Figure 3.6.[33] The process starts with a goal. A **goal** *refers to what an individual is trying to accomplish.* That is, a goal is your purpose or intent. An eye doctor may have a goal of serving 30 patients a week. **Anticipatory emotions** *refer to the emotions that individuals believe they will feel*

FIGURE 3.5 Positive and Negative Emotions

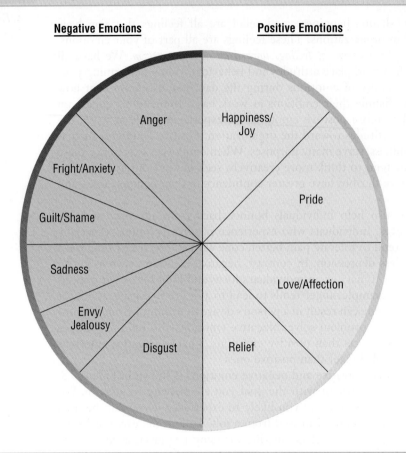

after achievement of or failure to reach their goal. For example, at Sewell Automotive in Dallas, Texas, a salesperson's goal is to sell 9 cars a month. If they sell between 9 and 19 cars, they receive special recognition from their manager (e.g., flowers, round of golf, choice of cars to drive for the next month). If they sell more than 20 cars in any month, they receive a special letter from Carl Sewell, a weekend package at a local hotel with all expenses paid, as well as flowers, golf, etc. If they sell fewer than 9 cars a month, they will receive coaching on their selling tactics. If they sell fewer than 27 cars in three months, they are dismissed.

The key motivational device is to have each salesperson imagine the emotions she will feel when she reaches her goal. The more desirable the implications are for achieving the goal, the more intense will be the anticipated emotions from achieving that goal. Jenny Craig, Weight Watchers, and other diet organizations ask individuals to write down the emotions they anticipate they will experience when they reach their weight goals. Individuals who anticipated positive emotions (e.g., I will feel excited, delighted, etc.) lost more weight than those who didn't have such positive anticipatory emotions.

If the anticipatory emotions are of sufficient intensity to motivate the individual, the individual will engage in those behaviors in order to reach his goal. That is, a person will need to develop a plan, outline the behaviors needed to reach his plan, and exert effort to exhibit those behaviors. Returning to our diet example, if individuals can imagine strong positive emotions from achieving their weight goals, they need to behave in ways that will enable them to reach that positive emotion. That is, they need to start exercising and dieting. Both of these behaviors are linked to loss of weight. As shown in Figure 3.6, goal

FIGURE 3.6 Role of Emotions in Performance

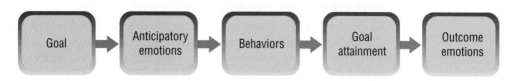

attainment is the next step. Did they reach their goals? Yes or no? If yes, then they would experience positive emotions; if no, then they would experience negative emotions. In our dietary plan, researchers found that those individuals who could anticipate positive emotions from achieving their goal were more likely to diet and exercise and reach their goal than those individuals who didn't engage in these behaviors.

Cross-Cultural Differences

There are cross-cultural differences in the display of emotions. Most Japanese managers believe that it is inappropriate to get emotional doing business, compared with 40 percent of Americans, 34 percent of French managers, and 29 percent of Italians. Italians, for example, are more likely to accept individuals who display their emotions at work, whereas this would be considered rude in Japan. In the Japanese culture, hiding one's emotions is considered a virtue because the lack of expression minimizes conflict and avoids drawing attention to the individual. Tomoko Yoshida is a customer relations training expert who works at the Sheraton Hotels in Japan. He teaches hotel employees never to show emotions while talking with a guest. In particular, even if the employee is upset, they are instructed never to point with a finger. Pointing is considered rude. Using one's whole hand shows more effort and is considered more polite and business-like. Similarly, if a customer is sitting in a restaurant and the waiter raises his or her voice, it signals to the customer that the waiter wants the guest to leave and isn't welcome any longer. Yoshida also instructs bellmen not to use their feet to close a door or move a customer's bags or toys even if the bellman is upset. Why? In Japan, individuals believe that the ground is where they walk in shoes. When they go home, they take their shoes off because they don't want to mix the outside ground with the inside ground. So not using their shoes to move bags—and possibly mixing inside and outside ground—is a sign of respect Yoshida would like the bellmen to exhibit.

Yoshikihiko Kadokawa, author of *The Power of Laughing Face*, found that even in Japan's culture, the friendliest clerks in some of Japan's biggest retail stores consistently rang up the highest sales. His research found that smiling salesclerks reported 20 percent more sales than nonsmiling salesclerks. McDonald's Corporation is using Kadokawa's techniques in Japan to screen applicants. The company screens out individuals who are too poker faced. When asked by the company to describe a pleasant experience, those applicants who don't smile and indicate that they find pleasure in what they're discussing aren't hired. McDonald's wants all of their employees to provide the friendly service at the price stated on its menu: "Smiles, 0 yen."[34]

Insights for Leaders

Let's consider six ways by which leaders can create positive emotions in their organization:

- Express positive emotions—gratitude, generosity, optimism, trust—regularly at work. Start meetings with sincere words of appreciation. Remember that positive emotions are contagious, especially when expressed by direct supervisors and organizational leaders.

- A rule of thumb is that the number of positive communications sent by the leader should outnumber the number of negative communications by a ratio of 5:1 if the employee is to have positive emotions at work.

- Give unexpected kindness and reach out to others when it is least expected. When the leader engages in positive emotions and behaviors when it goes against the norm, the element of surprise and courage becomes a powerful example to others, both strengthening individuals' trust in their leader and role-modeling behavior for others to follow.

- Help individuals find positive meaning in their day-to-day work lives. The leader should assist employees with seeing how their work contributes to a greater good and whom they are helping through their efforts.

- Provide opportunities for employees to help each other and to express appreciation for the help they receive from others.

- Celebrate small wins with employees so that they experience ongoing success and the associated positive emotions.

Chapter Summary

1. *Explain the basic sources of personality formation.*

Personality is a person's set of relatively stable characteristics and traits that account for consistent patterns of behavior in various situations. Each individual is like other individuals in some ways and in some ways is unique. An individual's personality is determined by inherited genes and the environment. Experiences occur within the framework of the individual's biological, physical, and social environment—all of which are modified by the culture, family, and other groups to which the person belongs. We reviewed five basic cultural values—individualism and collectivism, power distance, uncertainty avoidance, gender role orientation, and long-term orientation—that impact the development of a person's personality.

2. *Identify a set of personality dimensions that affect performance.*

An individual's personality may be described by a set of factors known as the Big Five personality factors. Specifically, these personality factors describe an individual's degree of emotional stability, agreeableness, extraversion, conscientiousness, and openness. We hope that you took the opportunity to assess your own Big Five personality dimensions in Table 3.1. Many specific personality dimensions, including self-esteem, locus of control, and emotional intelligence, have important relationships to work behavior and outcomes. In addition, an understanding of interactions between the person and the situation is important for comprehending organizational behavior.

3. *Describe the attitudes that affect performance.*

Attitudes are patterns of feelings, beliefs, and behavioral tendencies directed toward specific individuals, groups, ideas, issues, or objects. Attitudes have affective (feelings, emotions), cognitive (beliefs, knowledge), and behavioral (a predisposition to act in a particular way) components. The relationship between attitudes and behavior isn't always clear, although important relationships exist. We reviewed how the attitudes of hope, job satisfaction, and organizational commitment affect behavior in many organizations.

4. *Explain how emotions impact employees' performance.*

Employees show a variety of emotions during the day. Some of these are positive and can lead to more effective performance, whereas others are negative and can lead to poor performance. We introduced how emotions can influence the productivity of employees.

Key Terms and Concepts

Agreeableness, 79
Anticipatory emotions, 93
Attitudes, 85
Collectivism, 73
Conscientiousness, 80
Emotional intelligence, 83
Emotional stability, 79
Emotions, 93
External locus of control, 82
Extraversion, 80
Gender role orientation, 74
Goal, 93
Hope, 87
Individual differences, 70
Individualism, 73
Internal locus of control, 82

Job satisfaction, 88
Locus of control, 82
Long-term orientation, 74
Openness, 80
Organizational commitment, 91
Personality, 70
Personality trait, 77
Power distance, 73
Reliability, 80
Self-awareness, 83
Self-esteem, 81
Self-motivation, 84
Social empathy, 83
Social skills, 84
Uncertainty avoidance, 74
Validity, 80

Discussion Questions

1. Visit Apple's website (www.apple.com) and enter "Steve Jobs" in the search icon. Then click on the feature showing him deliver a speech. How does this speech illustrate the factors in the Big Five personality profile?

2. Atlas Sports Genetics (www.atlasgene.com.) offers to test parents to determine whether their children have inherited the genes to be a successful football player, marathon runner, etc. What are some ethical issues raised by doing this?

3. How might the values of a culture impact the development of a person's personality? What cultural dimensions seem to have the most influence on this developmental process?

4. What influences on personality development seem most important to you? Why?

5. Using the Big Five personality factors, describe the personality of (a) a close family member and (b) a person

for whom you have worked. How do these factors affect your behavior toward them?

6. Can individuals change their attitude without changing their behavior? Give an example.

7. Describe how you can develop your hope attitude to improve your performance.

8. Don Tuttle, CEO of Top Gun Ventures, thinks that satisfied workers are more productive than less satisfied workers. Do you agree or disagree with him? Explain.

9. Think of an organization that you have worked for. What factors seemed to influence your commitment to this organization?

10. In what ways does the model of emotions affect your attitude and performance?

Experiential Exercises and Case

Experiential Exercise: Self Competency

What Are Your Cultural Values?[35]

Instructions
In the following questionnaire, we ask you about your perception of your own culture's values. Please indicate the extent to which you agree or disagree with each statement. For example, if you **strongly agree** with a particular statement, you would circle the **5** next to that statement.

1 Strongly disagree
2 Disagree
3 Neither agree nor disagree
4 Agree
5 Strongly agree

Questions

_____ 1. It is important to have job requirements and instructions spelled out in detail so that employees always know what they are expected to do.   1 2 3 4 5

_____ 2. Managers expect employees to follow instructions and procedures closely.   1 2 3 4 5

_____ 3. Rules and regulations are important because they inform employees about what the organization expects of them.   1 2 3 4 5

_____ 4. Standard operating procedures are helpful to employees on the job.   1 2 3 4 5

_____ 5. Instructions for completing job tasks are important for employees on the job.   1 2 3 4 5

_____ 6. Group welfare is more important than individual rewards.   1 2 3 4 5

_____ 7. Group success is more important than individual success.   1 2 3 4 5

_____ 8. Being accepted by the members of the work group is very important.   1 2 3 4 5

_____ 9. Employees should only pursue their goals after considering the welfare of the group.   1 2 3 4 5

_____ 10. Managers should encourage group loyalty even if individual goals suffer.   1 2 3 4 5

_____ 11. Individuals should be expected to give up their goals in order to benefit group success.   1 2 3 4 5

_____ 12. Managers should make most decisions without consulting subordinates.   1 2 3 4 5

_____ 13. Managers must often use authority and power when dealing with subordinates.   1 2 3 4 5

_____ 14. Managers should seldom ask for the opinions of employees.   1 2 3 4 5

_____ 15. Managers should avoid off-the-job social contacts with employees.   1 2 3 4 5

_____ 16. Employees should not disagree with management decisions.   1 2 3 4 5

_____ 17. Managers should not delegate important tasks to employees.   1 2 3 4 5

_____ 18. Managers should help employees with their family problems.   1 2 3 4 5

_____ 19. Management should see to it that workers are adequately clothed and fed.   1 2 3 4 5

_____ 20. Managers should help employees solve their personal problems.   1 2 3 4 5

_____ 21. Managers should see that health care is provided to all employees.   1 2 3 4 5

_____ 22. Management should see that children of employees have an adequate education.   1 2 3 4 5

_____ 23. Management should provide legal assistance for employees who get in trouble with the law.   1 2 3 4 5

_____ 24. Management should take care of employees as they would treat their children.   1 2 3 4 5

_____ 25. Meetings are usually run more effectively when they are chaired by a man.   1 2 3 4 5

_____ 26. It is more important for men to have professional careers than it is for women to have professional careers.   1 2 3 4 5

_____ 27. Men usually solve problems with logical analysis; women usually solve problems with intuition.   1 2 3 4 5

_____ 28. Solving organizational problems usually requires an active, forcible approach typical of men.   1 2 3 4 5

_____ 29. It is preferable to have a man in a high-level position rather than a woman.   1 2 3 4 5

Interpretation

The questionnaire measures each of the five basic culture dimensions. Your score can range from 5 to 35. The numbers in parentheses that follow the title of the value are the question numbers. Add the scores for these questions to arrive at your total score for each cultural value. The higher your score, the more you demonstrate the cultural value.

Value 1: Uncertainty Avoidance (1, 2, 3, 4, 5). Your score _____. A high score indicates a culture in which individuals often try to make the future predictable by closely following rules and regulations. Organizations try to avoid uncertainty by creating rules and rituals that give the illusion of stability.

Value 2: Individualism–Collectivism (6, 7, 8, 9, 10, 11). Your score _____. A high score indicates collectivism, or a culture in which individuals believe that group success is more important than individual achievement. Loyalty to the group comes before all else. Employees are loyal and emotionally dependent on their organization.

Value 3: Power Distance (12, 13, 14, 15, 16, 17). Your score _____. A high score indicates a culture in which individuals believe in the unequal distribution of power among segments of the culture. Employees fear disagreeing with their bosses and are seldom asked for their opinions by their bosses.

Value 4: Long-Term Orientation (18, 19, 20, 21, 22, 23, 24). Your score _____. A high score indicates a culture in which individuals value persistence, thrift, and respect for tradition. Young employees are expected to follow orders given to them by their elders and delay gratification of their material, social, and emotional needs.

Value 5: Gender Role Orientation (25, 26, 27, 28, 29). Your score _____. A high score indicates masculinity, or a culture in which individuals value the acquisition of money and other material things. Successful managers are viewed as aggressive, tough, and competitive. Earnings, recognition, and advancement are important. Quality of life and cooperation are not as highly prized.

Questions

1. According to your perception of your culture, what values are most important in your culture?
2. How do these values influence the behaviors of individuals?

Experiential Exercise: Self Competency

What's Your Emotional IQ?[36]

An individual difference that has recently received a great deal of interest is *emotional intelligence* (EQ). You can assess your EQ by using the following scale.

Instructions

Using a scale of 1 through 4, where 1 = strongly disagree, 2 = somewhat disagree, 3 = somewhat agree, and 4 = strongly agree, respond to the 32 statements.

_____ 1. I know when to speak about my personal problems to others.

_____ 2. When I'm faced with obstacles, I remember times I faced similar obstacles and overcame them.

_____ 3. I expect that I will do well on most things.

_____ 4. Other individuals find it easy to confide in me.

_____ 5. I find it easy to understand the nonverbal messages of other individuals.

_____ 6. Some of the major events of my life have led me to reevaluate what is important and not important.

_____ 7. When my mood changes, I see new possibilities.

_____ 8. Emotions are one of the things that make life worth living.

_____ 9. I am aware of my emotions as I experience them.

_____ 10. I expect good things to happen.

_____ 11. I like to share my emotions with other individuals.

_____ 12. When I experience a positive emotion, I know how to make it last.

_____ 13. I arrange events others enjoy.

_____ 14. I seek out activities that make me happy.

_____ 15. I am aware of the nonverbal messages I send to others.

_____ 16. I present myself in a way that makes a good impression on others.

_____ 17. When I am in a positive mood, solving problems is easy for me.

_____ 18. By looking at facial expressions, I can recognize the emotions that others are feeling.

_____ 19. I know why my emotions change.

_____ 20. When I am in a positive mood, I am able to come up with new ideas.

_____ 21. I have control over my emotions.

_____ 22. I easily recognize my emotions as I experience them.

_____ 23. I motivate myself by imagining a good outcome to the tasks I do.

_____ 24. I compliment others when they have done something well.

_____ 25. I am aware of the nonverbal messages other individuals send.

_____ 26. When another person tells me about an important event in his or her life, I almost feel as though I have experienced this event myself.

_____ 27. When I feel a change in emotions, I tend to come up with new ideas.

_____ 28. When I am faced with a challenge, I usually rise to the occasion.

_____ 29. I know what other individuals are feeling just by looking at them.

_____ 30. I help other individuals feel better when they are down.

_____ 31. I use good moods to help myself keep trying in the face of obstacles.

_____ 32. I can tell how individuals are feeling by listening to the tone of their voices.

Scoring

Add your responses to questions 1, 6, 7, 8, 12, 14, 17, 19, 20, 22, 23, and 27. Put this total here_____. This is your *self-awareness* score.

Add your responses to questions 4, 15, 18, 25, 29, and 32. Put this total here_____. This is your *social empathy* score.

Add your responses to questions 2, 3, 9, 10, 16, 21, 28, and 31. Put this total here_____. This is your *self-motivation* score.

Add your responses to questions 5, 11, 13, 24, 26, and 30. Put this total here_____. This is your *social skills* score.

Discussion and Interpretation

The higher your score is in each of these four areas, the more emotionally intelligent you are. Individuals who score high (greater than 36) in *self-awareness* recognize how their feelings, beliefs, and behavior affect others. They accurately assess their strengths and limitations, and have a strong sense of their self-worth and capabilities.

Individuals who score high (greater than 18) in *social empathy* are thoughtful and consider others' feelings when making decisions and weigh those feelings along with other factors when making a decision. They are good at understanding others, taking an active interest in their concerns, empathizing with them, and recognizing the needs of others.

Individuals who score high (greater than 24) in *self-motivation* can keep their disruptive emotions and impulses under control, maintain standards of integrity and honesty, are conscientious, adapt their behaviors to changing situations, and have internal standards of excellence that guide their behaviors. That is, these individuals always want to do things better and seek feedback from others about their performance. They are passionate about their work.

Individuals who have high (greater than 18) *social skills* sense others' developmental needs, inspire and lead groups, send clear and convincing messages, build effective interpersonal relationships, and work well with others to achieve shared goals. They build effective bonds between individuals. Often, they appear to be socializing with coworkers, but they are actually working to build solid relationships at work.

Questions

1. Use EQ to describe a friend. What are this person's strengths and weaknesses?
2. Is EQ genetic or shaped by experience?

Case: Self Competency

Larry Ellison at Oracle Computer[37]

Larry Ellison, founder and CEO of Oracle Computer whose net worth is in the billions, has been the driving force at Oracle since he started the company more than two decades ago. He is now the fourth richest man in America with an annual salary of more than $72 million, a pay package that is 12 times bigger than the average pay of CEOs in the technology industry. Addressing his stockholders at Oracle's Redwood Shores, California, headquarters in 2008, he delivered a 30-minute profanity-laced speech in which he attacked his partners, competitors, the government, and most individuals in the room. PeopleSoft CEO Craig Conway called him the modern-day "Genghis Khan" because of his atrociously bad corporate behavior. In 2008 when Ellison proposed to buy PeopleSoft, Conway noted that the takeover was nothing more than a sham intended to disrupt PeopleSoft's sales. PeopleSoft employees openly criticized Ellison. Pleasanton City officials, home of PeopleSoft, questioned the integrity of a man who would insensitively target thousands of jobs just to claim a corporate victory. He is known for his corporate ruthlessness, which is outlined in a book by Mike Wilson titled *The Difference Between God and Larry Ellison*. Go to Oracle's blog (www.oracle.com) and read the blogs from irate customers and employees.

Ellison's brash disdain for failure and obsession with reaching the top started as a child when his adoptive father tried to lower his self-esteem, telling him that he would never amount to anything. His father fled Russia in the early 1900s, but was able put together enough money to make down payments on some apartment buildings in Chicago. He then leveraged those properties to buy more. When the tenants didn't pay rent during the Great Depression of the 1930s, he evicted them. His father was very hard on him also, but that made Ellison tough and competitive. He dropped out of the University of Illinois in 1964 because college was holding him back. He nearly died in a high-profile yachting race off the coast of Australia in 1998. His boat, named the *Sayonara*, ran into a hurricane and nearly sank, but Ellison was able to win the Sydney-to-Hobart race by his sheer persistence and determination to win at all costs. One of Ellison's favorite quotes is from a Zen proverb: "Your garden is never complete until there is nothing left to take out of it." To his competitors, the message is clear: Ellison will not be satisfied until there is no more business to take away from competitors.

Ellison runs Oracle without much input from others. He is famous for firing individuals because he doesn't like them. He lost Oracle's President Raymond Lane and senior executive Gary Bloom and refused to name successors, calling such a move dumb. He runs a tight ship that rewards employees who produce and squeezes out those who don't measure up to his standards. Individuals stay at Oracle because they are paid very well and fear recrimination. According to Thomas Siebel, founder of Siebel Systems, which Oracle bought a few years ago, "Larry is a control freak. He has the knack for taking the best and the brightest and trying to destroy them." Ellison defectors often end up competing against him. "Larry Ellison is a silver-backed alpha male gorilla," says his former friend and Oracle employee David Roux. "He will respond only to a direct challenge." Ellison likes to compete rather than collaborate. For example, he gave out gold coins as sales bonuses when Oracle drove Ingres Sybase out of business. In his bid for PeopleSoft, he said that if he and PeopleSoft CEO Craig Conway and Conway's dog were standing next to each other and Ellison had only one bullet, it wouldn't be for the dog.

Ellison might be a nightmare to work for, but his methods have created unimaginable wealth for the company's shareholders, managers, and employees. Since its initial stock offering in 1986, Oracle's share price has risen by more than 1,000 percent. It began with a staff of 3; today it employees more than 50,000 worldwide. Oracle's share of the database market is 49 percent.

Questions
1. Using the Big Five personality factors, describe Ellison's personality characteristics. How do these affect others?
2. What's Ellison EQ? Why do individuals work for him?

chapter 4

Perceptions and Attributions

Learning Goals

After studying this chapter, you should be able to:

1
Describe the major elements in the perceptual process.

2
Identify the main factors that influence what the individual perceives.

3
Identify the factors that determine how one person perceives another.

4
Describe the primary errors in perception that people make.

5
Explain how attributions influence behavior.

Learning Content

Learning from Experience
Jim Sinegal, Cofounder and CEO of Costco

Perceptual Process
Across Cultures Competency
McDonald's Use of Feng Shui

Perceptual Selection
Communication Competency
Hand Gestures

Person Perception
Self Competency
Doing Business in Arab Countries

Perceptual Errors

Attribution Process
Ethics Competency
The Gap

Experiential Exercise and Case
Experiential Exercise: Self Competency
The Perception Process

Case: Self Competency
Joan Murphy

Jim Sinegal, Cofounder and CEO of Costco

Jim Sinegal is the cofounder, president, and CEO of Costco Wholesale, America's fourth largest retailer, which opened its first warehouse in 1983. Costco is a leading warehouse-club operator with 546 warehouses worldwide. The firm has 142,000 employees, 53 million gold star members, and 5.6 million business members, each paying $50 per year to join. Revenues have grown by 70 percent in the last five years to exceed $72 billion. Costco has an 87 percent membership renewal rate. A typical Costco store stocks 4,000 types of items, with a limited number of each type, such as four brands of toothpaste.

Unlike the stereotypical CEO, Sinegal doesn't try to distance himself from his employees. He even wears a name tag—but not one that says "Jim, the CEO" or "Jim, Costco Founder." It just says "Jim." He easily could be mistaken for a stock clerk when he visits warehouses, sometimes up to 12 a day. On Costco's website, where executive officers are listed, his name appears in alphabetical order—not what you would expect of a corporate CEO.

His management philosophy is simple. He states: "We have said from the very beginning: 'We're going to be a company that's on a first-name basis with everyone.'" That also includes answering his own phone and doing his own faxes. He continues: "If a customer's calling and they have a gripe, don't you

think they kind of enjoy the fact that I picked up the phone and talked to them?" Because he listened to customers, Costco started its Kirkland Signature Wines brand, which has sold very well, but also had to exit the home-improvement and magazine businesses. Sinegal believes that customers shop at Costco for quality. Sinegal looks at a warehouse from the standpoint of a customer. Does the building have the right goods out? Is it well stocked, clean, and safe? He believes that when you have a sloppy building, it's a sign that there is pilfering and shoplifting.

Many executives think shareholders are best served if they do all they can to hold down costs, including the costs of labor. Costco's approach is different, in terms of how employees are treated. Sinegal says, "[Paying high wages] absolutely

ATSUSHI TSUKADA/AP PHOTO

To learn more about Costco, go to www.costco.com.

makes good business sense. Most people agree that we're the lowest-cost provider. Yet we pay the highest wages. So it must mean we get better productivity. It's axiomatic in our business—you get what you pay for." He is working on having employees work 10-hour days so they don't have to drive to work every day. This could save employees 20 percent on their gasoline purchases. Sinegal remarks: "Obviously it's not just wages that motivate people. How much they are respected, and whether they feel they can have a career at a company, are also important."

One of Sinegal's cardinal rules is that no branded item, such as a Xerox printer, can be marked up by more than 14 percent and no private-label item, such as Costco gasoline, by more than 15 percent. In contrast, supermarkets generally mark up merchandise by 25 percent and department stores by 50 percent or more. The secret to Costco's profit is simple. Its margin on each item isn't very high—but Sinegal says they make it up on volume. Some Wall Street analysts think Costco is also overly generous to its customers. One analyst states: "At Costco, it's better to be an employee or a customer than a shareholder." Another analyst asserts: "Whatever goes to employees comes out of the pockets of shareholders." Sinegal replies: "On Wall Street, they're in the business of making money between now and next Thursday. I don't say that with any bitterness, but we can't take that view. We want to build a company that will still be here 50 and 60 years from now." Interestingly, Costco stock has done very well.

For the past several years, Sinegal has received a salary of $350,000, plus stock options. That is low for a CEO of a $72 billion-per-year business. By comparison, the typical CEO of a large American company makes more than 430 times the pay of the average worker. Sinegal states, "I figured that if I was making something like 12 times more than the typical person working on the floor that was a fair salary." Of course, as a cofounder of the company, Sinegal owns a lot of Costco stock.[1]

The Learning from Experience feature illustrates the importance of how a leader's perceptions of his employees influence employees' behavior. People base their behaviors on what they *perceive*, not necessarily on what reality *is*. In this chapter, we explore the importance of *perception* and *attribution*. First, we describe the perceptual process. Then, we examine the external and internal factors that influence perception, the ways that people organize perceptions, the process of *person perception*, and various errors in the perceptual process. Finally, we explore the attributions that people make to explain their behaviors and those of others.

Perceptual Process

Learning Goal

1. *Describe the major elements in the perceptual process.*

As Jim Sinegal discovered, it is the *perception* of reality—not reality—that influences behavior. **Perception** *is the process by which the individual selects, organizes, interprets, and responds to information.* Employees are constantly exposed to a variety of information. They know when leaders are being phony. This information is processed in a person's mind and organized to form concepts pertaining to what is sensed or experienced. What happens when Tina Potter goes to Costco to buy a bouquet of flowers? Before buying it, she looks at the types of flowers in the bouquet, looks at the size of the bouquet and other bouquets that are available in her price range, and smells the flowers to see if they are fresh. After all of those activities, she decides whether or not to purchase the bouquet. Her mind processes all of this information to make a decision about whether to buy the bouquet and where it would look nice in her home. She gathers this information by using her three senses—touch, sight, and smell. This represents the psychological process whereby individuals take information from their environment and make sense of it.[2]

The key words in the definition of perception are *select* and *organize*. Different people often perceive a situation differently, both in terms of what they selectively perceive and how they organize and interpret what is perceived. Figure 4.1 summarizes the basic elements in the perceptual process from initial observation to final response.

Everyone selectively pays attention to some aspects of the environment and selectively ignores other aspects. For example, when shoppers pull into the gasoline station at Costco, what objects in their environment are they paying attention to and what do they ignore? What do they observe? A well-lit station, clean areas to pump gas, fully stocked paper towel dispensers with squeegees to wipe and clean windshields, etc., are objects people notice when they pull into a gas line at Costco. They might ignore

FIGURE 4.1 The Perceptual Process

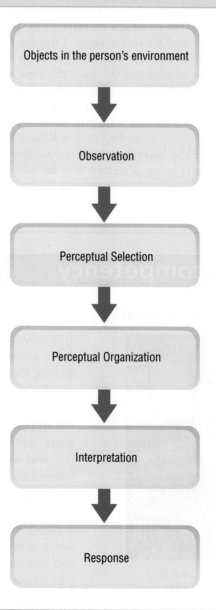

signs advertising freshly brewed coffee or the price of Coke. A person's selection process involves both external and internal factors. In other words, a complex set of factors, some internal to the person (attitudes) and some in the external environment, combine to determine what the person perceives. We discuss this important process in more detail shortly.

The individual organizes the stimuli selected into meaningful patterns. How people interpret what they perceive varies considerably. The Experiential Exercise at the end of this chapter titled *The Perception Process* permits you to test your current level of perceptual skills. For example, a wave of the hand may be interpreted as a friendly gesture or as a threat, depending on the circumstances and the state of mind of those involved. Leaders and employees need to recognize that perceptions of events and behaviors may vary among individuals and be inaccurate.

As suggested in Figure 4.1, people's interpretations of their environments affect their responses. Everyone selects and organizes things differently, which is one reason why people behave differently in the same situation. In other words, people often perceive the same things in different ways, and their behaviors depend, in part, on their perceptions.

The following Across Cultures Competency feature shows how McDonald's is using feng shui to design its restaurants. **Feng shui** *is the belief that space needs to be in harmony with the environment.*[3] Literally, *feng* means "wind" and *shui* "water." Feng shui was developed thousands of years ago in a village in China. Villagers studied the formations of land and the ways the wind and water worked together to help them survive. Over time feng shui developed and was used by emperors to ensure their successes. According to feng shui experts, when a harmonious arrangement is created between the wind and water, the individual or organization prospers and the quality of life improves. According to Tan Khoon Yong, a feng shui master, this balance can be achieved by balancing the magnetic flow in which people live. According to feng shui, what is being perceived may be subtle and greatly influences perceptions and behaviors.[4]

Across Cultures competency

McDonald's Use of Feng Shui

McDonald's restaurants in the L.A. Asian community use red accents to symbolize fire, good luck, laughter, and prosperity.

RENE MACURA/AP PHOTO

The only familiar signs at the McDonald's in the Asian community in Los Angeles are the golden arches, the drive-through, and the menu. Gone are the plastic furniture, Ronald McDonald, and the red and yellow palette that has symbolized the world's largest hamburger chain. Leather seats, earth tones, bamboo plants, a wood ceiling, and water trickling down glass panels have taken their place. Red accents are used throughout the restaurant to symbolize fire and "good luck, laughter and prosperity." The restaurant is designed using the principles of feng shui, which is meant to help diners achieve happiness and fortune. McDonald's uses the basic principles of placing the five elements—earth, water, fire, metal, and wood—around the restaurant to increase the flow of chi or energy. The number 4, considered bad luck in some Asian cultures, is absent in the street address and the phone number. The walls are curved. The ceiling and floor tiles are placed at distinctive angles, and the doors swing open and shut in opposite directions. There is also a wall displaying three pieces of brushed aluminum graphic art, one featuring a crane, because it represents fertility; another featuring a koi fish, representing prosperity; and the third an iguana, a symbol for the community.

According to Bryan Carmack, the manager, "We wanted to make the restaurant a little bit more of a destination. The goal is to bring harmony and a peaceful place to be."

To learn more about Feng Shui, go to **www.fengshuisociety.org.uk.**

Perceptual Selection

Learning Goal

2. Identify the main factors that influence what the individual perceives.

The phone is ringing, your TV is blaring, a dog is barking outside, your PC is making a strange noise, and you smell coffee brewing. Which of these events will you ignore? Which will you pay attention to? Can you predict or explain why one of these events grabs your attention at a particular time?

Selective screening *is the process by which people filter out most information so that they can deal with the most important matters.* Perceptual selection depends on several factors, some of which are in the external environment and some of which are internal to the perceiver.

External Factors

As we noted in Chapter 3, a common external force affecting behavior is culture. Different cultures train people to respond to different cues. Do the French and Chinese see the world in the same way? No. In fact, no two national groups see the world in exactly the same way. When Mexican children simultaneously see a picture of a bullfight and a baseball game, they generally remember only seeing the bullfight. American children, on the other hand, remember seeing only the baseball game. Why do the children not remember both pictures? This is the nature of perception. Perceptual patterns are not absolute. Misperceptions cause some managers to fail in their international assignments. Many U.S. firms, such as Procter & Gamble, Microsoft, and PepsiCo, are competing in global markets where English is not the first language either read or spoken. Therefore, language is becoming an increasingly important consideration when choosing product names and slogans.

Frito-Lay, a division of PepsiCo, is trying to become a dominant supplier of salty nuts and chips to China's $450 million market. Frito-Lay's senior management believes that China has tremendous growth potential. However, its managers realize that Chinese consumers have different perceptions of their product depending on where they live. People in Hong Kong like salty chips, in Beijing they like meaty ones, and in Xian, they like spicy flavors. Frito-Lay introduced "cool lemon" potato chips. These yellow, strongly lemon-scented chips are dotted with greenish lime specks of mint and are sold in a package featuring images of breezy blue skies and rolling green grass. Why "cool lemon"? Chinese people consider fried foods hot and therefore do not eat them in the summer months. Cool is better in the summer months.[5]

What are some other external factors that influence our perceptual process? What does Jim Sinegal want customers to notice when they arrive at Costco? Factors present in the warehouse can affect whether customers sense important information and these factors can influence whether this information is used in perceptions. Let's review some external factors that may affect perception. In each case we present an example to illustrate the principle.

- *Size.* The larger the object, the more likely it is to be perceived. The size of the new buildings to be built where the Twin Towers in New York City were destroyed by terrorist attacks on September 11, 2001, will get noticed more than an alleyway on 42nd street. The new 421-meter (1,368-feet) Jin Mao Tower in Shanghai's Pudong District is more likely to be seen than the eight-story Howard Johnson Hotel in Shanghai.

- *Intensity.* The more intense an external factor (bright lights, loud noises, and the like), the more likely it is to be perceived. The language in an e-mail message from a manager to an employee can reflect the intensity principle. For example, an e-mail message that reads "Please stop by my office at your convenience" wouldn't fill you with the same sense of urgency as an e-mail message that reads "Report to my office immediately!"

- *Contrast.* External factors that stand out against the background or that aren't what individuals expect are the most likely to be noticed. In addition, the contrast of objects with others or with their backgrounds may influence how they are perceived. Salespeople at JCPenney, Macy's, Saks, and other department stores are instructed to show men the most expensive suit first. After being exposed to the most expensive suit, a man sees the price of the less expensive suit as appearing smaller by comparison. Presenting a least costly suit first and following with an expensive one makes the expensive one seem even more costly. Another advantage of this tactic is that when it comes time to buy accessories, such as ties, shirts, and belts, these things don't seem that expensive next to the cost of the suit.

- *Motion.* A moving factor is more likely to be perceived than a stationary factor. PlayStation games use motion to attract people to play them.

- *Repetition.* A repeated factor is more likely to be noticed than a single factor. Marketing managers use this principle in trying to get the attention of prospective customers. An advertisement may repeat key ideas. The ad itself may be presented many times for greater effectiveness. Marketing managers at Nike developed the Nike "swoosh" symbol that is used consistently worldwide on all of its products.

- *Novelty and familiarity.* Either a familiar or a novel factor in the environment can attract attention, depending on the circumstances. A Korean businessman entered a client's office in Stockholm and was greeted by a woman sitting behind a desk. He asked to see the president. The woman responded by saying that she (the president) would be glad to see him. The Korean was confused because he assumed that most women are secretaries and not presidents of a company. The misinterpretation of the situation was caused by a novel situation for him.[6]

A combination of these or similar factors may be existing at any time and, hence, affecting perception. Along with a person's internal factors, they determine whether any particular stimulus is more or less likely to be noticed.

Nowadays the visual aspects of nonverbal communications are receiving increasing attention because of the global markets for organization. Managers may offend someone in a different culture with hand gestures without ever knowing that these are offensive. For example, thumbs up may signal "okay" in America, but in parts of the Arab world, it means "Go to hell." Look at some common hand gestures in the following Communication Competency feature. Did you know what you might be communicating across different cultures with your hand gestures?

Communication competency

Hand Gestures

HOW WE SAY IT	WHERE IT'S NOT OKAY	WHAT TO DO INSTEAD

HELLO/GOOD-BYE

Wave the full arm side to side.

*In **East Asian** countries, it's considered overly demonstrative—and can also be confused in **Japan, Europe,** and **Latin America** for no and in **India** for "Come here."*

In northern Europe, wag your hand back and forth from the wrist.

In Greece and Italy, the palm faces inward, fingers curled in. Don't mistake this for a beckoning motion.

In Japan, bow slightly. In India and other Buddhist/Hindu areas, place your hands together and say "Namaste."

STOP/EXCUSE ME

Hand and arm out in front, fingers outspread.

*In **Lebanon,** it simply means no. In **Greece,** it's an awful curse called the moutza (made worse by using both hands and pushing the palms forward), and it has similarly rude meanings in **Spain, Nigeria,** and **Chile.***

In Greece, just avoid putting your hand out with fingers outstretched, no matter what the intention. Count and beckon with the palm facing inward and downward.

➕ *The **Japanese** excuse themselves when pushing through a crowd by holding the hand up in a chopping motion; this is not considered rude.*

COME HERE

Either curl the index finger, or four fingers, toward you.

*In the **Philippines** and other parts of **East Asia,** the index finger is used only to beckon dogs. In **Latin American** countries, it's a come-on, and in **Indonesia** and **Australia,** it's for soliciting prostitutes. In **southern Europe,** the all-finger version would be mistaken for good-bye.*

In most of Asia (including India) and parts of Latin America, the palm faces downward and the fingers are curled below in tandem in a scratching motion.

In Korea, hold your arm out and move your fingers up and down, as if signaling a good-bye in Europe.

Internal Factors

The perception process is also influenced by several factors that are related to the perceiver. These are internal factors that influence what the individual sees. Effective leaders are able to develop more complete and accurate perceptions of various situations and people with whom they communicate than ineffective leaders. An effective manager knows when people are sincere, honest, and dependable. These accurate perceptions are crucial to being an effective leader. The powerful role that internal factors play in perception shows itself in many ways. Let's review how personality, learning, and motivation influence the process of perceiving other people.

Personality

Personality has an interesting influence on what and how individuals perceive things. Any of the several personality dimensions that we discussed in Chapter 3, along with numerous other traits, may influence the perceptual process.[7] Personality appears to affect strongly how an individual perceives other people. In Chapter 3, we introduced you to the Big Five personality factors. To illustrate how personality can influence perception, let's examine one of the Big Five factors, conscientiousness. A conscientious person tends to pay more attention to external environmental cues than does a less conscientious person. On the one hand, less conscientious people are impulsive, careless, and irresponsible. They see their environment as hectic and unstable, which affects the way in which they make perceptual selections. On the other hand, more conscientious people are likely to organize their perceptions into neat categories, allowing them to retrieve data quickly and in an organized manner. In brief, this person is more careful, methodical, and disciplined in making perceptual selections.

Learning

Another internal factor affecting perceptual selection is learning. Among other things, learning determines the development of perceptual sets. A **perceptual set** *is an expectation of a particular interpretation based on the person's past experience with the same or a similar object.* What do you see in Figure 4.2? If you see an attractive, elegantly dressed woman, your perception concurs with the majority of first-time viewers. However, you may agree with a sizable minority and see an ugly, old woman. The woman you first see depends, in large part, on your perceptual set.

Leaders' and employees' past experiences and learning strongly influence their perceptions. Leaders are influenced by their functional backgrounds (e.g., accounting, engineering, marketing, or production) when making decisions. Because perceptions influence how employees and managers behave toward one another, it is important to understand a leader's perceptual set. What are the factors that influence Jim Sinegal's perceptions of Costco?

Ethical Insight

Obey the law means obey the law. There is no exception. Sloppy behavior is not going to be tolerated. We want all our employees to be careful and treat customers with respect.

Jim Sinegal, CEO, Costco

Motivation

Motivation also plays an important role in determining what a person perceives. A person's most urgent needs and desires at any particular time can influence perception. For example, imagine that, while taking a shower, you faintly hear what sounds like the telephone ringing. Do you get out of the shower, dripping wet, to answer it? Or do you conclude that it is only your imagination? Your behavior in this situation may depend on factors other than the loudness of the ringing. If you are expecting an important call, you're likely to leap from the shower. If you aren't expecting a call, you're more likely to attribute the ringing sound to shower noises. Your decision is influenced by your expectations and motivations.

In general, the individual perceives things that promise to help satisfy their needs and that they have found rewarding in the past. The individual tends to ignore mildly disturbing events (a barking dog), but will react to dangerous events (the house being on fire). Summarizing an important aspect of the relationship between motivation and perception is the **Pollyanna principle,** *which states that people process pleasant events more efficiently and accurately than they do unpleasant events.* For example, an employee who receives both positive and negative feedback during a performance appraisal session may more easily and clearly remember the positive statements than the negative statements.[8]

FIGURE 4.2 Test of Perceptual Set

Person Perception

Learning Goal

3. *Identify the factors that determine how one person perceives another.*

The preceding discussion shows that perceiving others accurately can be challenging. Because perceptions influence how people behave toward one another, there is a need to understand the factors that influence both the perceiver and the situation in general.

Person perception *is the process by which the individual attributes characteristics or traits to other people.* The person perception process relies on the same general process of perception shown in Figure 4.1. That is, the process follows the same sequence of observation, selection, organization, interpretation, and response. However, the object being perceived is another person. Perceptions of situations, events, and objects are important, but individual differences in perceptions of other people are crucial at work. For example, suppose that you meet a new employee. To get acquainted and make him feel at ease, you invite him to lunch. During lunch, he begins to tell you his life history and focuses on his accomplishments. Because he talks only about himself (he asks you no questions about yourself), your first impression is that he is very self-centered.

In general, the factors influencing person perception are the same as those that influence perceptual selection: Both external and internal factors affect person perception. However, we may usefully categorize factors that influence how a person perceives another as:

- characteristics of the perceived,
- characteristics of the perceiver, and
- the situation or context within which the perception takes place.

The Perceived

When perceiving someone else, you need to be aware of various cues given by that person: facial expressions, general appearance, skin color, posture, age, gender, voice quality, personality traits, behaviors, and the like. Such cues usually provide important information about the person. Each individual seems to have implicit ideas about the relationships among physical characteristics, personality traits, and specific behaviors.[9] **Implicit personality theory** *is a person's beliefs about the relationships between another's physical characteristics and personality.* Table 4.1 illustrates the implicit personality theory in action. A person may believe that some voice-quality characteristics indicate that

TABLE 4.1 Personality Judgments on the Basis of Voice Quality

VOICE QUALITY: HIGH IN	MALE VOICE	FEMALE VOICE
Breathiness	Younger, artistic	Feminine, pretty, petite, shallow
Flatness	Similar results for both sexes:	Masculine, cold, withdrawn
Nasality	Similar results for both sexes:	Having many socially undesirable characteristics
Tenseness	Cantankerous (old, unyielding)	Young, emotional, high-strung, not highly intelligent

Source: Adapted from Hinton, P. R. *The Psychology of Interpersonal Perception*, London: Routledge, 1993, 16.

the speaker has certain personality traits. However, the relationships presented in Table 4.1 have no scientific basis. Similarly, think about your first contact with someone you met on MySpace, Facebook, or an online dating service. It is not the person's voice that you consider, but perhaps the person's physical appearance. Later, on meeting, did that person look and act as you expected?

The Perceiver

Listening to an employee describe the personality of a coworker may tell you as much about the personality of the employee doing the describing as it does about that of the person being described. That shouldn't surprise you if you recall that factors internal to the perceiver, including personality, learning, and motivation, influence perception. A person's own personality traits, values, attitudes, current mood, and past experience influence how that person perceives someone else.

Accurately perceiving an individual raised in another culture often is difficult. In China, for example, the communication style is generally indirect. Chinese may talk around the point and hedge their speech using words such as *maybe* or *perhaps* because they must protect their social face and respect social roles (e.g., manager, employee). The Chinese will lose social face if they fail to understand what is being asked or cannot do what is requested. Therefore, by being vague, Chinese businesspeople save face and can continue to build and maintain relationships. Rick Linck, CEO of Asia Pacific for Heineken Brewing Company, learned that when communicating with beer distributors in China, distributors frequently say "Let me look into this further" to avoid a direct no or to avoid admitting that they cannot do what he asked. Linck learned to communicate with distributors by saying "What do you think about this?" instead of saying "Is this acceptable?"[10]

Cross-cultural negotiations are an important part of every global manager's job, and the dynamics of negotiating reflect each culture's values and beliefs. In Mexico, personal qualities and social connections influence the selection of a negotiator, whereas in the United States, many companies select negotiators on the basis of position and competence. In U.S.–Chinese negotiations, U.S. companies often prefer to send a small team or only a single person to represent them, whereas the Chinese prefer to send a large group. The large group allows them to have representatives from different areas of the organization present at the negotiations.

The Situation in Foreign Assignments

As more and more employees are asked to take assignments in foreign countries, opportunities for living and working in different countries arise. Siemens, the German electronics firm with headquarters in Munich, Germany, estimates that almost 25 percent of its managers take expatriate assignments. **Expatriates** *are employees who live and work outside of their home country.*[11] There are now more than 500,000 U.S. expatriate managers living around the globe. Because of the high cost of sending employees and their families to foreign countries for extended periods of time (usually three years), it is important for this experience to be successful. Unfortunately, some expatriates cannot adapt to the new situation (culture) and fail in their assignments. Why do people fail? According to Global Relation Services, the top reasons for expatriate failure are as follows:

* Lowered security and safety,
* Lower quality of life,
* Job doesn't meet expectations,
* Inability to adapt to new situation,
* Family concerns, and
* Spouse/partner dissatisfaction.[12]

Running down the list, the reasons for failure are personal and not related to technical competence. China and India were the two countries that presented expatriates with the greatest challenge. Why do you think these two countries were singled out?

What are some characteristics that human resource managers are looking for in the person who takes a foreign assignment? Patience, flexibility, openness to new experiences, and tolerance for other beliefs are among the top characteristics.[13] Tips for successfully handling a foreign assignment include making sure that the family supports the foreign assignment, developing foreign language competencies, getting strong support from your manager, and making sure that your accomplishments are widely visible.

Are women more likely to succeed or fail in expatriate assignments? A number of male leaders still think that women aren't interested in overseas jobs or won't be effective in them. These male managers typically perceive dual career issues, a presumed heightened risk of sexual harassment, and gender prejudices in many countries as reasons why their female employees often aren't seriously considered for international assignments. In contrast, a recent survey of female expatriates and their managers revealed that women, on average, are just as interested as men in foreign assignments and every bit as effective once there.[14] Indeed, some of the traits considered crucial for success overseas—such as knowing when to keep your mouth shut, being a strong team player, and soliciting a variety of opinions and perspectives when solving problems—are more often associated with women's management styles than with men's.

Misinterpretation of the situation occurs when an individual gives certain meaning to observations and their relationships. Interpretation organizes our experience and guides our behavior. Read the following sentence and quickly count the number of Fs:

FINISHED FILES ARE THE RESULT OF YEARS OF SCIENTIFIC STUDY COMBINED WITH THE EXPERIENCE OF YEARS.

Most people who do not speak English see all six Fs. By contrast, many English speakers see only three Fs; they do not see the Fs in the word *of*. Why? Because English-speaking people have learned that the word *of* is not important for overall understanding of the sentence. We selectively see those words that are important according to our cultural upbringing.

A way to understand the norms and values of a culture is to pay attention to the behaviors that are rewarded in that society. The following Self Competency feature illustrates a sample of important behaviors that you should be aware of when conducting business in Arab countries.[15]

Self competency

Doing Business in Arab Countries

- *Greeting women.* When greeting a female employee, never greet her with a kiss on the cheek. If the employee extends her hand to greet you, you may shake it; otherwise greeting with words is appropriate. Do not compliment your host on the beauty of his wife, sister, or daughter. Such statements will not be taken as compliments.
- *Gift giving.* When Arab businesspeople receive a gift, it is not customary to open it in front of the giver. Never give alcohol or products made out of pigs.
- *Face concept.* Saving face involves withholding one's reactions to give the other party a way to exit the situation with minimal discomfort. It involves compromise, patience, and sometimes looking the other way to allow things time to get back to normal. Pressure sales tactics should be avoided because the Arab managers will associate you with an unpleasant experience.
- *Dress.* The majority of men wear a long-sleeved, one-piece dress called a *thoub* that covers the entire body. This garment allows air

to circulate in hot summer days. Women dress conservatively in a garment called an *abayah*. This is a long black garment that covers a woman's body from the shoulders down to her feet.

- *Social duties.* Managers perform a variety of social duties, including greeting an employee who returns from a trip, visiting an employee who is ill, bringing a gift to a newly wed couple, and visiting the husband and wife after the wife has delivered a new baby.
- *Privacy.* Privacy is important in Arabian societies. Therefore, houses and offices are built with walls that maintain privacy from others. People are not permitted to enter until the manager or host extends his right hand with his palm up saying "Tafaddal," which means "Come in."
- *Social gatherings.* Men and women may meet in separate rooms in some Arab countries. Men gather in rooms that are outside the main entrance of a home, away from the rest of the house. Women guests meet in a room inside the house and go through an entrance specifically assigned to female visitors.

To learn more about Arab countries, go to **www.montclair.edu/orgs/aso/arab6.html.**

Learning Goal

4. *Describe the primary errors in perception that people make.*

Perceptual Errors

The perceptual process may result in errors in judgment or understanding. An important part of understanding individual differences in perception is knowing the source of these errors. First, we examine the notion of accuracy of judgment in person perception. Then, we explore five of the most common types of perceptual errors: perceptual defense, stereotyping, the halo effect, projection, and impression management.

Perceptual Accuracy

How accurate are people in their perceptions of others? This question is important in organizational behavior. For example, misjudging the characteristics, abilities, or behaviors of an employee during a performance appraisal review could result in an inaccurate assessment of the employee's current and future value to the organization. Another example of the importance of accurate person perception comes from the employment interview. Considerable evidence suggests that interviewers can easily make errors in judgment and perceptions when basing employment decisions on information gathered in face-to-face interviews. In fact, managers often make a decision about hiring a person within the first 10 minutes of an interview and spend the remainder of the interview just confirming their first impressions.[16] After reading the following types of errors, what are some types of errors that you have committed in the past few days?

- *Similarity error.* Interviewers tend to be positively predisposed toward job candidates who are similar to them (in terms of background, interests, hobbies, jobs, and the like) and may be negatively biased against job candidates who are unlike them.

- *Contrast error.* Interviewers have a tendency to compare job candidates to other candidates interviewed at about the same time, rather than to some absolute standard. For example, an average candidate might be rated too highly if preceded by several mediocre candidates. However, an average candidate might be scored too low if preceded by an outstanding applicant.

- *Overweighting of negative information.* Interviewers tend to overreact to negative information as though looking for an excuse to disqualify a job candidate.

- *Race, gender, and age bias.* Interviewers may be more or less positive about a candidate on the basis of the candidate's race, gender, or age.

- *First-impression error.* The primacy effect may play a role in the job interview, because some interviewers are quick to form impressions that are resistant to change.

There are no easy answers to the general problem of ensuring perceptual accuracy. Some people accurately judge and assess others, and some people do so poorly. Some basic guidelines to make more accurate judgments include the following: (1) Avoid generalizing from an observation of a single trait (e.g., tactful) to other traits (e.g., stable, confident, energetic, dependable); (2) avoid assuming that a behavior will be repeated in all situations; and (3) avoid placing too much reliance on physical appearance. Your accuracy in person perception can be improved when you understand these potential biases.

Perceptual Defense

Perceptual defense *is the tendency for people to protect themselves against ideas, objects, or situations that are threatening.* A well-known folk song suggests that we "hear what we want to hear and disregard the rest." Once established, an individual's way of viewing the world may become highly resistant to change. Sometimes perceptual defense may have negative consequences. This perceptual error can result in a manager's inability to perceive the need to be creative in solving problems. As a result, the manager simply proceeds as in the past even in the face of evidence that "business as usual" isn't accomplishing anything.

Stereotyping

Stereotyping *is the belief that all members of a specific group share similar traits and behaviors.* The use of stereotypes can have powerful effects on the decisions that managers make. There are many exceptions to any stereotype. In a study of *Fortune* magazine's top 500 CEOs, researchers found that CEOs are mostly white males. The study also found that on the average, male CEOs were almost six feet tall, which reflects a kind of implicit stereotype of the height of CEOs. Given that the average American male is five foot nine, it means that CEOs as a group are about three inches taller. In the United States, about 14.5 percent of all men are six feet or taller and 3.9 percent of white males are six foot two or taller. In this sample, almost a third were six foot two or taller. Furthermore, it was calculated that each inch of height is worth $789 a year in salary.[17] That means an individual who is six feet tall, but otherwise identical to someone who is five foot five, will make on average $5,525 more per year. Over a career, the difference is hundreds of thousands of dollars.

In another study, it was found that attractive people earn about 5 percent more than do average-looking employees, who in turn earn 9 percent more than plain-looking employees. Thus, if an average-looking college graduate starts at $47,000, their good-looking friends start at \$49,350, while their least attractive friends start at \$42,770. Plain-looking employees may also receive fewer promotions than those awarded to their better looking colleagues.[18]

An interesting challenge for organizations is to determine in what ways female managers essentially are like their male counterparts. To the extent they are alike, gender differences should be only a marginal concern. Unfortunately, stereotyping exists in many retailing organizations. A federal judge has granted a class-action lawsuit against Costco on behalf of more than 700 female department managers. The suit claims the company has discriminated against women seeking promotion to store manager. A debate is raging in scientific and management circles around the world with regard to gender differences in thought, emotions, and information processing styles. Some research suggests that women are, on average, superior to men in many organizational roles. Such roles include communicating with customers or clients, facilitating discussions, and smoothing conflicts. With regard to the latter two roles, one study indicated that female project team leaders were more effective, on average, than males in leading cross-functional teams designed to foster high rates of innovation.[19]

Halo Effect

The **halo effect** *occurs when one positive or negative characteristic dominates the way that person is viewed by others.* As we pointed out earlier, the evidence is clear that physical attractiveness and height are often such characteristics. It is hardly any wonder that Nordstrom's, Dillard's, Kohl's, and other retail stores like to hire attractive salespeople. Their sales training programs include grooming hints to make their salespeople more attractive.

The halo effect is based on general assessments of the overall person. That is, if the manager regards the person as "good," that manager will tend to review that person's performance in a positive way. In other words, a halo blinds the perceiver to other attributes that also should be evaluated to obtain a complete, accurate impression of the other person. Managers have to guard against the halo effect when rating employee performance. A manager may single out one trait and use it as the basis for judging all other performance measures. Students have been known to evaluate the overall effectiveness of a faculty member in just the first two seconds of the first class. The rankings they gave after these two seconds were almost identical to rankings made after sitting through the instructor's course the entire semester. That's the power of the halo effect.

An important aspect of the halo effect is the self-fulfilling prophecy. The **self-fulfilling prophecy** *is the tendency for someone's expectations about another to cause that individual to behave in a manner consistent with those expectations.*[20] Expecting certain things to happen shapes the behavior of the perceiver in such a way that the expected is more likely to happen. Self-fulfilling prophecies can take both positive and negative forms. In the positive case, *holding high expectations of another tends to improve the individual's performance,* which is known as the **Pygmalion effect.** The Pygmalion effect has its roots in Greek mythology. According to mythology, Pygmalion was a sculptor who hated women yet fell in love with a statue he carved of a beautiful woman. He became so infatuated with the statue that he prayed to a goddess to bring her to life. The goddess granted him his wish. The essence of the Pygmalion effect is that people's expectations determine their behavior or performance, thus serving to make their expectations come true. In other words, we strive to validate our perceptions of reality no matter how faulty they may be. Subordinates whose managers expect them to perform well do perform well. Subordinates whose managers expect them to perform poorly do in fact perform poorly. Obviously, this effect can be quite devastating.[21] Some top executives believe that a manager who puts in long hours and works on Saturday is a better performer than those who do not put in these hours. Long hour expectations help create and foster a reward system that uses long hours as one criterion for a manager's success.

The **Golem effect** *refers to the loss in performance that results from low expectations by the manager.*[22] If a manager notices that a subordinate's sales reports are always late, this leads the manager to doubt whether the employee is committed to being a high achiever. This results in the manager watching the employee more closely, and the employee becoming afraid to make suggestions that could improve the sales report for fear of turning the report in late. The manager then interprets this as a lack of initiative.

How can managers create positive performance expectations? We believe that managers need to consider three things:

1. *Individuals behave toward others consistent with others' expectations of them.* Managers who have high expectations of their employees are supportive and generally give employees more training and challenging jobs. By contrast, managers who have low expectations of their employees aren't supportive and generally won't give employees training and challenging jobs.

2. *A person's behavior affects others.* Not only will those treated positively benefit from special opportunities, but these opportunities will also bolster their self-esteem.

3. *People behave in response to how they are treated.* People who have benefited from special treatment and who have confidence in their abilities are likely to be high performers.

> ### Diversity Insight
>
> We must treasure openness in every single thing we do, from ideas to beliefs in people. We need to be positive Pygmalions for all of our diversity programs.
>
> *George David, CEO, United Technologies*

Projection

Projection *is the tendency for individuals to see their own traits in other people.* That is, the individual projects his or her own feelings, personality characteristics, attitudes, or motives onto others. For example, during the recession of 2008 and 2009 when the automobile and financial industries were in turmoil, people in other industries, such as education and entertainment, also assessed their jobs to be in more jeopardy than they actually were. Advertisers love to inform people when a product is the "fastest growing" or "largest selling" because they don't have to convince consumers directly that the product or service is good. They need only to say that many others think so.

Falsely believing that others share one's beliefs can lead to poor performance. Projection may be especially strong for undesirable traits that perceivers possess but fail to recognize in themselves. The individual whose personality traits include stinginess, obstinacy, and disorderliness tends to rate others higher on these traits than does the individual who doesn't have these personality traits.

Impression Management

Impression management *is an attempt by an individual to manipulate or control the impressions that others form about them.* This includes everything from how people talk to how they dress, and the hand gestures they use to how they walk.[23] In Ecuador, you can hire a person or groups of people (called *lloronas*) to come to the funeral of a family member. The job of these people is to cry while the dead person is being buried, making sure that more people start to cry. Bartenders often put their own money in their tip jars at the beginning of the evening to give the impression to customers that others have tipped them. Evangelical preachers are known to seed their audience with ringers, who are rehearsed to come forward at a specified time to give witness and donations.

Employees in organizations use several impression management tactics to affect how others perceive them. They are especially likely to use these tactics when talking with managers who have power over them and on whom they are dependent for raises, promotions, and good job assignments. Impression management is used by individuals at all organizational levels as they talk with suppliers, coworkers, managers, and others—and vice versa. To determine how much you rely on impression management tactics, take a moment to complete the self-assessment questionnaire in Table 4.2.[24]

TABLE 4.2 Impression Management Assessment

To assess the impression tactics you use, please answer the following 22 questions using the following scale:

How often do you behave this way?

	Never		Occasionally		Often
	1	2	3	4	5

_____ 1. Talk proudly about your experience or education.

_____ 2. Make people aware of your talents.

_____ 3. Let others know how valuable you are to the organization.

_____ 4. Make people aware of your accomplishments.

_____ 5. Compliment your colleagues so they will see you as likable.

_____ 6. Take an interest in your colleagues' personal lives to show them that you are friendly.

_____ 7. Praise your colleagues for their accomplishments so they will consider you a nice person.

_____ 8. Do personal favors for others to show them that you are friendly.

_____ 9. Be pushy with coworkers when it will help you get your job done.

_____ 10. Let others know you can make things difficult for them if they push you too far.

_____ 11. Deal forcefully with others when they hamper your ability to get the job done.

_____ 12. Deal aggressively with others who interfere in your business.

_____ 13. Use intimidation to get others to behave appropriately.

_____ 14. Act like you know less than you do so people will help you out.

_____ 15. Try to gain sympathy from people by appearing needy in some areas.

_____ 16. Pretend not to understand something to gain someone's help.

_____ 17. Act like you need assistance so people will help you out.

_____ 18. Pretend to know less than you do so you can avoid an unpleasant assignment.

_____ 19. Stay late so people will know you are working hard.

_____ 20. Try to appear busy, even at times when things are slow.

_____ 21. Arrive early to work to look dedicated.

_____ 22. Come to the office at night or on weekends to show that you are dedicated.

Scoring:

To determine your impression management tactics, please add your answers to decide your score.

Questions:

1–4	_____	This is your *self-promotion score*. The higher your score, the more likely you are to use this tactic.
5–8	_____	This is your *ingratiation score*. The higher your score, the more likely you are to use this tactic.
9–13	_____	This is your *intimidation score*. The higher your score, the more likely you are to use this tactic.
14–18	_____	This is your *supplication score*. The higher your score, the more likely you are to use this tactic.
19–22	_____	This is your *exemplification score*. The higher your score, the more likely you are to use this tactic.

Source: Adapted from Bolino, M. C., and Turnley, W. H. Measuring impression management in organizations: A scale development based on Jones & Pittman taxonomy. *Organizational Research Methods,* 1999, 2, 187–206.

Impression management involves the systematic manipulation of the perceptual process. The CEOs of Chrysler, Ford, and General Motors went to Congress in 2008 and 2009 to ask for financial support of their companies. The first time before Congress they arrived in separate private jets and were earning millions in salary and other benefits. These behaviors did not create the impression that their companies were in dire financial straits.

Table 4.3 describes five common impression management tactics: self-promotion, ingratiation, intimidation, supplication, and exemplification. These five tactics can lead to either positive or negative perceptions depending on how the individual uses them. Individuals who are high in political skills have the ability to create better managerial impressions when they use these tactics frequently. On the other hand,

TABLE 4.3 Impression Management Tactics

TACTIC	DESCRIPTION	EXAMPLE
Self-promotion	The person tries to present himself in a positive light	Employee reminds boss about accomplishments
Ingratiation	The person flatters others so they will see the person as likable	Employee compliments manager on good customer service after the manager handled a complaint from an irate customer
Intimidation	The person lets others know that she can make life difficult for them if they push her	Employee tries to push others to get things done on schedule or else
Supplication	The person acts like he needs help so others will help him	Employee asks for help on a task that he could perform himself
Exemplification	The person stays late so others know she is working hard	Employee is the last one to leave the parking lot and the first one to arrive

Source: Harris, K. J., Zivnuska, S., Kacmar, K. M., and Shaw, J. D. The impact of political skill on impression management effectiveness. *Journal of Applied Psychology,* 2007, 92, 278–285.

individuals who use these impression management tactics but have low political skills are less likely to be viewed favorably and should instead avoid using them. Also, if superior performance evaluations are used to make key organizational decisions (e.g., pay raises, promotions, job assignments), there is a potential for employees to receive these outcomes because of their ability to use impression management tactics rather than more job-related criteria.

Attribution Process

Learning Goal

5. Explain how attributions influence behavior.

A question often asked about others is "Why?" "Why did this engineer use these data in his report?" or "Why did Jim Sinegal, CEO and founder of Costco, start Costco?" Such questions are an attempt to get at why a person behaved in a particular way. The **attribution process** *refers to the ways in which people come to understand the causes of their own and others' behaviors.*[25] In essence, the attribution process reflects the person's need to explain events through the deliberate actions of others rather than viewing them as random events. To maintain the illusion of control, the individual needs to create causal attributions for events. Attributions also play an important role in perceptions. Attributions made about the reasons for someone's behavior may affect judgments about that individual's basic characteristics (that is, what that person is really like).

The attributions that employees and managers make concerning the causes of behavior are important for understanding behavior. For example, a leader who attributes poor performance directly to his subordinates tends to behave more punitively than does a leader who attributes poor performance to circumstances beyond his subordinates' control. A manager who believes that an employee failed to perform a task correctly because he lacked proper training might be understanding and give the employee better instructions or more training. The same manager might be quite angry if she believed that the subordinate made mistakes simply because he didn't try very hard.

Responses to the same outcome can be dramatically different, depending on the attributions made about the reasons for that outcome. Table 4.4 lists some of the possible differences in managerial behavior when employees are perceived positively versus when they are perceived negatively. The relationships between attributions and behavior will become clearer as we examine the attribution process.

TABLE 4.4 Possible Results Stemming from Differences in Perceptions of Performance

BOSS'S BEHAVIOR TOWARD PERCEIVED STRONG PERFORMERS	BOSS'S BEHAVIOR TOWARD PERCEIVED WEAK PERFORMERS
Discusses project objectives. Gives subordinate the freedom to choose own approach to solving problems or reaching goals.	Gives specific directives when discussing tasks and goals.
Treats mistakes or incorrect judgments as learning opportunities.	Pays close attention to mistakes and incorrect judgments. Quick to emphasize what subordinate is doing wrong.
Is open to subordinate's suggestions. Solicits opinions from subordinate.	Pays little attention to subordinate's suggestions. Rarely asks subordinate for input.
Gives subordinate interesting and challenging assignments.	Gives subordinate routine assignments.
May frequently defer to subordinate's opinions in disagreements.	Usually imposes own views in disagreements.

Making Attributions

The individual makes attributions in an attempt to understand why others behave as they do and to make better sense of their situations. An individual doesn't consciously make attributions all the time (although he may do so unconsciously much of the time).[26] However, under certain circumstances the individual is likely to make causal attributions consciously. For example, causal attributions are common in the following situations:

- The perceiver has been asked an explicit question about another's behavior. (Why did she do that?)
- An unexpected event occurs. (I've never seen him behave that way. I wonder what's going on?)
- The perceiver depends on another person for a desired outcome. (I wonder why my manager made that comment about my expense account?)
- The perceiver experiences feelings of failure or loss of control. (I can't believe I failed my midterm exam!)

Figure 4.3 presents a model for making attributions. The individual infers "causes" to behaviors that she observes in others. These interpretations often largely determine her reactions to those behaviors. The perceived causes of behavior reflect several antecedents: (1) the amount of information the perceiver has about the people and the situation and how that information is organized by the perceiver; (2) the perceiver's beliefs (implicit personality theories, what other people might do in a similar situation, and so on); and (3) the motivation of the perceiver (e.g., the importance to the perceiver of making an accurate assessment). Recall our discussion of internal factors that influence perception—learning, personality, and motivation. These same internal factors influence the attribution process. The perceiver's information and beliefs depend on previous experience and are influenced by the perceiver's personality.

Internal versus External Causes of Behavior

In applying attribution theory, you should be especially concerned with whether a person's behavior has been internally or externally caused. Internal causes are believed to be under an individual's control—you believe that your website designer's performance is poor because she is often late to work. External causes are believed to be beyond a person's control—you believe that her performance is poor because

FIGURE 4.3 The Attribution Process

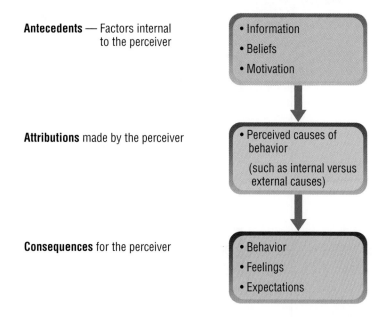

Antecedents — Factors internal to the perceiver

- Information
- Beliefs
- Motivation

Attributions made by the perceiver

- Perceived causes of behavior
  (such as internal versus external causes)

Consequences for the perceiver

- Behavior
- Feelings
- Expectations

her Windows operating system is old. According to attribution theory, three factors influence the determination of internal or external cause:

- *Consistency*—the extent to which the person perceived behaves in the same manner on other occasions when faced with the same situation. If your website designer's behavior has been poor for several months, you would tend to attribute it to an internal cause. If her performance is an isolated incident, you would tend to attribute it to an external cause.

- *Distinctiveness*—the extent to which the person perceived acts in the same manner in different situations. If your website designer's performance is poor, regardless of the computer program with which she's working, you would tend to make an internal attribution; if her poor performance is unusual, you would tend to make an external attribution.

- *Consensus*—the extent to which others, faced with the same situation, behave in a manner similar to the person perceived. If all the employees in your website designer's team perform poorly, you would tend to make an external attribution. If other members of her team are performing well, you would tend to make an internal attribution.[27]

As Figure 4.4 suggests, under conditions of low consistency, high distinctiveness, and high consensus, the perceiver will tend to attribute the behaviors of the perceived to external causes. When consensus and distinctiveness are low, but consistency is high, the perceiver will tend to attribute the behaviors of the perceived to internal causes. For example, when all employees are performing poorly (high consensus), when the poor performance occurs on only one of several tasks (high distinctiveness), and the poor performance occurs only during the last week of the month (low consistency), a manager may attribute poor performance to an external source, such as peer pressure or an overly difficult task. In contrast, performance may be attributed to an employee (internal attribution) when only the individual in question is performing poorly (low consensus), when the inferior performance is found across several tasks (low distinctiveness), and when the low performance has persisted over time (high consistency). Other combinations of high and low consistency, distinctiveness, and consensus are possible. Some combinations may not provide the perceiver with a clear choice between internal and external causes.

FIGURE 4.4 Example of Attribution Process

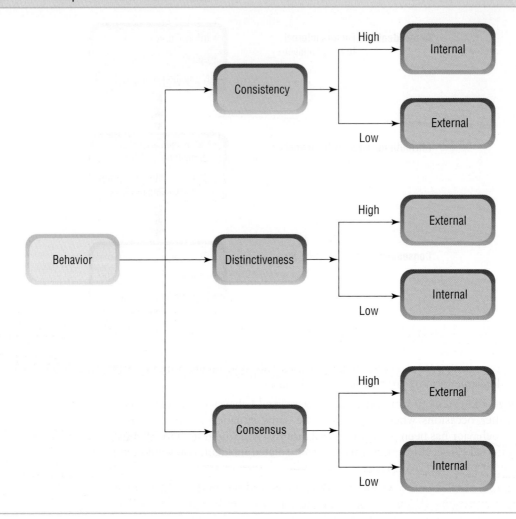

With regard to internal versus external causes of behavior, individuals often make what is known as the fundamental attribution error.[28] The **fundamental attribution error** *is the tendency to underestimate the influence of situational factors and to overestimate the influence of personal factors in evaluating someone else's behavior.* This error causes the perceiver to ignore important environmental factors that often significantly affect another person's behavior. In organizations, employees may assign blame to other departments or individuals and fail to recognize the effect of the situation. For example, a CEO might attribute a high level of political behavior on the part of her vice presidents to aspects of their personalities, not recognizing that competition for scarce resources is causing much of the political behavior.

Some cultural differences exist in the fundamental attribution error. For example, in North America, this type of error would be as just described (underestimating external causes and overestimating internal causes). In India, however, the more common attribution error is for a manager to overestimate situational or external causes for the observed behaviors. This difference in attributions may reflect the way that the individual views personal responsibility or perhaps differences in "average" locus of control beliefs in the different societies.

The fundamental attribution error isn't the only bias that can influence judgments concerning internal versus external causes of behavior. A study of supervisors showed that they were more likely to attribute effective performance to internal causes for high-status employees. The supervisors were less likely to attribute success to internal causes for low-status employees. Similarly, supervisors were more likely to attribute ineffective performance to internal causes for low-status employees and less likely to attribute failure to internal causes for high-status employees.[29]

Perceptions of people and their behaviors are subjective. How others perceive events has important implications as the following Ethics Competency feature illustrates.[30] Before reading any further, what is your perception of overseas factories, especially those in China, that manufacture clothing for JCPenney, Macy's, Levi Strauss, and the Gap? Are these factories clean and well maintained? Are workers treated well? Are their products safe? How did you form these perceptions?

The Gap, a $15.7 billion retailer, has issued a 42-page social responsibility report that spells out some of the problems found in operating garment factories in 60 countries around the world to produce clothes for the Gap, Old Navy, GapBody, GapKids, and Banana Republic. It found persistent wage, health, and safety violations in many factories. These violations ranged from failure to provide protective wear to physical abuse and coercion. The Gap pulled its business from more than 140 factories and turned down business from hundreds of others when they failed to meet the Gap's labor standards.

Ethics **competency**

The Gap

High worker turnover (more than 60 percent) is common in the apparel industry and is a significant contributor to production costs. The Gap found that good factory practices and better working conditions lead to these results: (1) Factories that treated their workers better had significantly lower turnover than those that treated their workers poorly, (2) factory managers who maintained close relationships and frequent communications with buyers tended to have better human resource management systems and experienced lower management turnover than those with limited buyer contact, and (3) a factory's production efficiency declined by 16 percent for each 1 percent increase in monthly turnover.

Armed with these data, the Gap's vice president for social responsibility, Dan Henkle, took a variety of actions, three of which are discussed here. First, the Gap built an elaborate monitoring system with about 90 members who perform more than 8,500 factory inspections each year. The inspections have focused on working conditions, such as child or forced labor (prisoners), unrealistic production cycles, requiring employees to work more than 60 hours a week, and expecting employees to work unpaid overtime.

The Gap discovered that good factory practices and working conditions lead to positive results.

As a result of the inspections, 136 factories were found in violation and dropped from the Gap's supplier list.

Second, the Gap outlined specific goals for each of its supplier factories to achieve. For example, in its Southern China plant, plant management redefined the role of sewing supervisors to focus on workers' wages and operational efficiency as well as output. The result was a decrease of 99 percent in the missing units from theft, a 9 percent decrease in worker turnover, a 35 percent reduction in overtime, and a 50 percent average increase in workers' monthly pay. In India, the Gap added benefits like on-site child care and health care, as well as free meals. These have reduced turnover and improved productivity. Third, Henkle and his staff met with several labor-advocacy groups in an effort to clarify the Gap's labor policies.

To learn more about The Gap, to go **www.gap.com**.

JEFF GROSS/GETTY IMAGES

▲

Tiger Woods' key to success relies on internal attribution processes.

After reading this competency feature, did your perceptions of the Gap's use of foreign manufacturers change?

Attributions of Success and Failure

The attributions that employees and leaders make regarding success or failure are very important. Leaders may base decisions about rewards and punishments on their perceptions of why subordinates have succeeded or failed at some task. In general, individuals often attribute their own and others' success or failure to four causal factors—ability, effort, task difficulty, and luck[31]:

- I succeeded (or failed) because I had the competencies to do the task (or because I did not have the competencies to do the task). Such statements are *ability attributions*.

- I succeeded (or failed) because I worked hard at the task (or because I did not work hard at the task). Such statements are *effort attributions*.

- I succeeded (or failed) because the task was easy (or because the task was too hard). Such statements are attributions about *task difficulty*.

- I succeeded (or failed) at the task because I was lucky (or unlucky). Such statements are attributions about *luck* or the circumstances surrounding the task.

Causal attributions of ability and effort are internal. Causal attributions of task difficulty and luck are external. These attributions about success or failure reflect differences in self-esteem and locus of control—personality dimensions discussed in Chapter 3. Accordingly, the **self-serving bias** *refers to individuals attributing their success to internal factors (ability or effort) and attributing their failure to external factors (task difficulty or luck)*. For example, an individual with high self-esteem and high internal locus of control is likely to assess his own performance positively and to attribute his good performance to internal causes.

The tendency of employees to accept responsibility for good performance but to deny responsibility for poor performance often presents a serious challenge for managers during performance appraisals.[32] A self-serving bias may also create other types of problems. For example, it prevents individuals from accurately assessing their own performance and abilities and makes it more difficult to determine why a course of action has failed. The general tendency to blame others for a person's own failures often is associated with poor performance and an inability to establish satisfying interpersonal relationships at work and in other social settings. In general, a version of the self-serving bias seems to operate when people are asked to compare themselves to others in the work setting. That is, managers and employees often view themselves to be more ethical, more effective, better performing, and so on, than the "average" other person.

One of the more traumatic events that can occur to anyone is being fired.[33] Today losing a job doesn't carry the stigma that it once did. But—it still hurts! Inevitably the person asks herself: What went wrong? What could I have done differently? And, perhaps most important: What am I going to do now?

For most people, undertaking a job search at any time is always stressful. Undertaking a job search *after* suffering the psychological blow of being fired can be a formidable challenge for anyone. Suppose that you have just been fired. You can take certain constructive actions to increase your chances of success and even end up with a more satisfying job. All of these tips assume that you have not been fired for unethical behaviors, including theft, bullying, sexual harassment, and other issues.

1. *Work through the firing psychologically.* Emotionally, you might feel like hiding or taking a sabbatical. Experts suggest, however, that beginning the search for a new job immediately is crucial. The first contact or two may be hard, but the sooner you get started and the more people you talk to, the quicker you will find another position. Of course, reestablishing your normal good spirits may be either a long or slow process, depending on your ability to bounce back. Maintaining a sense of humor helps. Hal Lancaster, of the *Wall Street Journal,* suggests that "getting fired is nature's way of telling you that you had the wrong job in the first place."

2. *Figure out what went wrong.* This step is an important part of coming to grips, psychologically, with the situation. If you don't understand what led to your being fired, you're likely to repeat the same mistakes in the future. Moreover, you need to talk to your former employer, coworkers, and friends and seek honest feedback to help you understand your strengths and weaknesses. Doing so may well be difficult. Many firms' human resource professionals prefer to say as little as possible at the time of dismissal in order to minimize lawsuits. If you can't get insights from your former employer, experts suggest utilizing a career counselor to help you make the same evaluation.

3. *Work with your former employer to develop an exit statement.* If possible, you should have something in writing from your former employer that will be an asset in your job search. Specific suggestions include having a paragraph that describes what you accomplished in your former job followed by a paragraph that explains why you are no longer with the firm. There are lots of "socially acceptable" reasons that can be given in such a document: a change in management style, a change in strategy, the desire to pursue interests that no longer fit what the employer wants, and so on. Surprisingly, the fired employee can often get a former manager or a senior manager to sign such a document. Managers often want to be helpful, and if such a request is approached in a constructive, problem-solving manner, many times the former manager is willing to help create a letter or other document that does not condemn the company or you. This approach has the advantage of creating a situation where prospective future employers hear the same "story" from both the former employer and you.

4. *Avoid negative attributions as part of your explanation.* Experts say that you should never say anything bad about your former employer. Don't make excuses, don't trash the people you used to work for, and don't blame everything on others. Focus on the positive aspects of any written understanding that you have obtained. Accept responsibility for both your failures and successes. Quickly move the discussion to the future, stressing what you've learned from previous jobs and focusing on what you can do for a new employer.

Chapter Summary

1. *Describe the major elements in the perceptual process.*

Perception is the psychological process whereby the individual selects information from the environment and organizes it to make sense of his world. Environmental stimuli are observed, selected, organized, interpreted, and responded to as a result of the perceptual process. Understanding the two major components of this process—selection and organization—is particularly important.

2. *Identify the main factors that influence what the individual perceives.*

Perceptual selection is used to filter out less important information in order to focus on more important environmental cues. Both external factors in the environment and factors internal to the perceiver influence perceptual selection. External factors (i.e., size, motion) can be thought of as characteristics of the event. These influence whether the event is likely to be noticed. Internal factors include personality, learning, and motivation.

3. *Identify the factors that determine how one person perceives another.*

How the individual perceives another is particularly important for organizational behavior. Person perception is a function of the characteristics of the person perceived, the characteristics of the perceiver, and the situation within which the perception takes place. Individuals may go to great lengths to manage the impressions that others form about them.

4. *Describe the primary errors in perception that people make.*

The perceptual process may result in errors of judgment or understanding in various ways. The more important and common perceptual errors include perceptual defense, stereotyping, the halo effect, projection, and impression management. However, through training and experience, individuals can learn to judge or perceive others more accurately.

5. *Explain how attributions influence behavior.*

Attribution deals with the perceived causes of behavior. Individuals infer causes to understand the behavior of others. Their perceptions of why certain behaviors occur influence their own subsequent behaviors and feelings. Whether behavior is internally caused by the nature of the individual or externally caused by circumstances over which the individual has little control has important implications for leaders. Individuals also make attributions concerning task success and failure that have important implications for organizational behavior.

Key Terms and Concepts

Attribution process, **119**
Expatriates, **113**
Feng shui, **106**
Fundamental attribution error, **122**
Golem effect, **116**
Halo effect, **116**
Implicit personality theory, **111**
Impression management, **117**
Perception, **104**
Perceptual defense, **115**

Perceptual set, **110**
Person perception, **111**
Pollyanna principle, **110**
Projection, **117**
Pygmalion effect, **116**
Selective screening, **107**
Self-fulfilling prophecy, **116**
Self-serving bias, **124**
Stereotyping, **115**

Discussion Questions

1. Go to www.google.com and enter "Jim Sinegal." Scroll down until you find "ABC News: Costco CEO Finds Pro-Worker Means Profitability." What is your perception of him?

2. The individual forms perceptions of how ethical principles are portrayed in organizations through the behaviors of leaders, advertisements, news stories, and the like. Go to the Gap's website (www.gap.com). What

attributions can you make about their ethical principles from visiting this website?

3. Review the Communication Competency feature showing different hand gestures on page 109. Do you use any of these gestures? How might these be interpreted by people in different countries?

4. What are your scores on the *Impression Management Assessment* questionnaire in Table 4.2? Based on these, how might the overuse of any tactic backfire on you and hurt your career advancement?

5. If you take an assignment with an organization in a foreign country, what are some of the perceptual errors that you should avoid to complete the assignment successfully?

6. Give three examples of the halo effect that you have observed personally.

7. Give an example of a situation in which you attributed someone's behavior to internal or external factors. What influenced your attribution?

8. Describe an important task at which you failed. Describe a second important task at which you succeeded. Identify the attributions that you made to explain your failure and your success.

9. Provide two real examples of the Pygmalion effect.

10. Which stereotypes do you believe are most widely held by leaders in organizations? Why?

Experiential Exercise and Case

Experiential Exercise: Self Competency

The Perception Process[34]

The *Perception Process Questionnaire* (PPQ) is designed to help you evaluate your current level of perceptual skills. If you do not have experience in a management-level position, consider a project you have worked on either in the classroom or in an organization such as a fraternity, sorority, club, church, or service group. You will find that the statements are applicable to your own experience even if you are not yet a manager.

Use the following scale to rate the frequency with which you perform the behaviors described in each statement. Place the corresponding number (1–7) in the blank space preceding the statement.

1 = Rarely
2 = Irregularly
3 = Occasionally
4 = Usually
5 = Frequently
6 = Almost Always
7 = Consistently

_____ 1. I search for verified facts and observations to support inferences or conclusions.

_____ 2. I examine available information related to my area of job responsibility.

_____ 3. I note organizational changes and policies that might affect my information.

_____ 4. I ask others for their opinions and observations to get access to more information.

_____ 5. I note inconsistencies and seek explanations for them.

_____ 6. I look at information in terms of similarities and differences.

_____ 7. I generate possible explanations for available information.

_____ 8. I check for omissions, distortions, or exaggerations in available information.

_____ 9. I verbally summarize data that are not completely quantified (e.g., trends).

_____ 10. I distinguish facts from opinions.

_____ 11. I am aware of my own style of approaching problems and how this might affect the way I process information.

_____ 12. I put quantitative information in tables, charts, and graphs.

_____ 13. I am aware of the personality characteristics of my peers, colleagues, subordinates, and superiors.

_____ 14. I am aware of my own biases and value systems that influence the way I see people.

_____ 15. I am aware of patterns of people's performance and how these patterns might indicate characteristics.

_____ 16. I recognize differences and similarities among people.

_____ 17. I actively seek to determine how pieces of information might be related.

_____ 18. I relate current information to past experiences.

_____ 19. I relate my own attitudes and feelings and those of others to job performance.

_____ 20. I relate work methods to outcomes.

PPQ Scoring Sheet

Behavioral Area	Statements	Score
Searching for information	1, 2, 3, 4	
Interpreting and compre-hending information	5, 6, 7, 8	
Determining essential factors	9, 10, 11, 12	
Recognizing characteris-tics of people	13, 14, 15, 16	
Identifying relationships	17, 18, 19, 20	
TOTAL SCORE		

Questions
1. What competencies need to be further developed to improve your perceptual skills?
2. Have your scores affected your communications with others? Explain.

Case: Self Competency

Joan Murphy[35]

Instructions

Joan Murphy is a computer engineering programmer for the aerospace division of Lockheed Martin Company. Please read the case and then identify the causes of her behavior by answering the questions following the case. Then determine whether you made an internal or external attribution. After completing the task, decide on the appropriateness of various forms of corrective action. A list of potential recommendations has been developed. The list is divided into four categories. Read each action, and evaluate its appropriateness by using the scale provided. Next, compute a total score for each of the four categories.

The Case

Joan Murphy, 42, received her baccalaureate degree in aerospace engineering from a school in the Northeast. She graduated with a 3.4 GPA and had a minor in international relations. During the summer between her junior and senior years, she took an internship with Texas Instruments in Japan. Immediately upon graduation, she took a permanent position with Lockheed Martin and was assigned to its Fort Worth, Texas, jet fighter division. Joan is currently working in the aerospace engineering department as a senior engineer. During the past year, she has missed 12 days of work. She seems unmotivated and rarely has her assignments completed on time. Joan is usually given the harder engineering designs to work on because of her technical competency.

Past records indicate Joan, on average, completes programs classified as "routine" in about 45 hours. Her coworkers, on the other hand, complete "routine" programs in an average time of 32 hours. Further, she finishes programs considered "major problems," on average, in about 115 hours. Her coworkers, however, finish these same "major problems" assignments, on average, in about 100 hours. When she has worked in engineering teams, her peer performance reviews are generally average to marginal. Her peers have noted she is not creative in attacking problems and she is difficult to work with.

The aerospace engineering department recently sent a questionnaire to all customers to evaluate the usefulness and accuracy of its designs. The results indicate many departments are not using its designs because they cannot understand the reports. It was also determined that many customers found Joan's work unorganized and they could not use her work unless someone redid it.

Causes of Performance

To what extent was each of the following a cause of Joan's performance? Use the following scale:

	Very Little			Very Much	
	1	2	3	4	5
a. High ability	1	2	3	4	5
b. Low ability	1	2	3	4	5
c. Low effort	1	2	3	4	5
d. Difficult job	1	2	3	4	5
e. Unproductive coworkers	1	2	3	4	5
f. Bad luck	1	2	3	4	5

Internal attribution (total score for causes a, b, and c)
_____

External attribution (total score for causes d, e, and f)
_____

Appropriateness of Corrective Action

Evaluate the following courses of action by using the scale below:

Very Inappropriate			Very Appropriate	
1	2	3	4	5

Coercive Actions
a. Reprimand Joan for her performance.
  1   2   3   4   5
b. Threaten to fire Joan if her performance does not improve.
  1   2   3   4   5

Change Job
c. Transfer Joan to another job.
  1   2   3   4   5
d. Demote Joan to a less demanding job.
  1   2   3   4   5

Coaching Actions
e. Work with her to help her do the job better.
  1   2   3   4   5
f. Offer her encouragement to help her improve.
  1   2   3   4   5

No Immediate Actions
g. Do nothing.
  1   2   3   4   5
h. Promise her a pay raise if she improves.
  1   2   3   4   5

Compute a score for the four categories:
  Coercive actions = a + b = _____
  Change job = c + d = _____
  Coaching actions = e + f = _____
  No immediate actions = g + h = _____

Questions
1. What is your evaluation of Joan's performance in terms of consistency, distinctiveness, and consensus?
2. Do you attribute Joan's performance to internal or external causes? What is the rationale for your decision?
3. Which of the four types of corrective actions do you think is most appropriate? Explain.

chapter 5

Learning Concepts to Improve Performance

Learning Goals

After studying this chapter, you should be able to:

1
Explain the role of classical and operant conditioning in fostering learning.

2
Describe the contingencies of reinforcement that influence behavior.

3
Explain how positive reinforcement, negative reinforcement, punishment, and extinction affect an individual's performance.

4
Describe how social learning theory can be used by individuals to improve their performance.

Learning Content

Working at United Parcel Service

With revenues of more than $49.7 billion dollars, 425,300 employees worldwide, and 1,800 locations, UPS is the world's largest package-delivery company. UPS transports 16 million packages and documents per business day throughout the United States and to more than 200 countries and territories. Its delivery operations use a fleet of about 100,000 motor vehicles and nearly 600 aircraft. How does UPS deliver?

Service providers are trained to perform their tasks over and over again without wasted effort. Veteran service providers earn $29 per hour and can earn more with overtime. They are told to keep the DIAD (Delivery Information Acquisition Device) under the right arm and the package under the left. Keys are on the pinky finger. They are told to look at the package only once to fix the address in their mind. They walk to the customer's place of business or home at three feet a second. The service provider's left foot should hit the truck's first step. They are told to put their seat belt on with their left hand, while at the same time turning on the ignition with their right hand. During an average day, a service provider will make about 100 stops to deliver 246 packages and pick up 70 others. Each service provider participates in hours and hours of classroom and on-the-road training during which they learn the Five Seeing Habits: (1) Look down the road to uncover traffic patterns, (2) maintain the proper following distance, (3) constantly keep your eyes on the road, (4) make sure that the truck has an escape route, and (5) communicate in traffic with your horn, lights, and signals. Those service providers who use these Five Seeing Habits effectively are rewarded with T-shirts, free lunches, and the like.

United Parcel Service gives its supervisors personal digital assistants (PDAs) to use in on-road driver evaluations. The PDAs are equipped with proprietary software that standardizes the evaluation process, helping to ensure that each driver review is as objective as possible. "Our supervisors do ride-alongs to see if the service provider is following procedures and adhering to our health and safety policies," says Cathy Callagee, vice president of applications development for UPS's operations portfolio. "But this was problematic because supervisors used to have to write notes on paper, and then bring their notes back to the office and type them into reports."

Paper is eliminated with the help of PDAs, which display a series of checklists for the

MARK DUNCAN/AP PHOTO

To learn more about UPS, go to www.ups.com.

supervisor to use during the evaluation. The checklists guide the supervisors through a list of duties the service provider should be performing. The supervisor simply checks off each duty as the service provider completes it. Additionally, the checklists are uniform across the UPS network, so each service provider receives the same evaluation, regardless of who is conducting the review. The PDAs identify training needs to help make service providers safer and provide better customer service. The PDAs permit the supervisor to immediately reward an employee for excellent service with a congratulatory note.

The PDAs also serve as a remote office, allowing supervisors to receive e-mail and check the status of other activities while they are on the road with drivers. "Supervisors can now electronically write how their drivers are doing and [whether] they are following procedures," Callagee says. "If [they're] not, the supervisor can bring the applied methods right up on the PDA and walk the driver through it."[1]

Companies in all industries are recognizing the importance of customer satisfaction and how the quality of frontline customer service providers can make or break a company. Turnover and competition are pushing organizations to focus on ways to keep top-quality employees satisfied and motivated. A recent survey conducted by WorldatWork found that recognition and reward programs remain a top priority for all managers.[2] As you read in the feature on UPS, managers have in place opportunities to recognize and reward good performance. UPS asks service providers, via surveys and team meetings, what they value most in terms of recognition and rewards and then designs their motivational program around these employee expectations and values. UPS also knows that unless there is a consistent way to track and recognize superior performance, such motivational programs lose their effectiveness.

UPS managerial practices are based on specific principles drawn from an area of psychology called *learning*. **Learning** *is a relatively permanent change in knowledge or observable behavior that results from practice or experience.*[3] Desirable work behaviors contribute to achievement of organizational goals; conversely, undesirable work behaviors hinder achievement of these goals. Labeling behavior as *desirable* or *undesirable* may be somewhat subjective and depends on the value systems of the organization (most often represented by an employee's leader) and the employee exhibiting the behavior. For example, a service provider at UPS who returns late from lunch exhibits undesirable behavior from the supervisor's viewpoint, desirable behavior from the viewpoint of friends with whom the worker chats during the break, and desirable behavior from the worker's viewpoint because of the satisfaction of social needs. Employees quickly learn whether their behavior is desirable or undesirable based on the leader's reaction to the behavior, and also learn how to change an undesirable to a desirable (from the leader's viewpoint) behavior.

Usually, however, the work setting and organizational norms provide objective bases for determining whether a behavior is desirable or undesirable. The more a behavior deviates from organizational expectations, the more undesirable it is. At UPS, undesirable behavior includes anything that results in lost packages and late or missed deliveries. Expectations about behavior vary considerably from one organization to another. For example, at Microsoft's research and development laboratory, engineers and scientists are encouraged to question top management's directives because innovation and professional judgment are crucial to the organization's success.

Effective leaders do not try to change employees' personalities or basic beliefs. As we pointed out in Chapters 3 and 4, an individual's personality, emotions, and perceptual processes influence his behavior and directly influencing those traits is often difficult, if not impossible. Rather, effective leaders focus on identifying observable employee behaviors and the environmental conditions that affect these behaviors. They then attempt to influence external events in order to guide employee behaviors—to help employees learn and exhibit desirable behaviors. In this chapter, we explore three major concepts of learning: classical conditioning, operant conditioning, and social learning theory. Each theory proposes a different way by which people learn, but focusing on observable behaviors is common to all three.

Learning Through Rewards and Punishments

Learning Goal

1. *Explain the role of classical and operant conditioning in fostering learning.*

Employees need to learn and practice productive work behaviors. Learning new work assignments often depends on many factors. The leader's task, then, is to provide learning experiences in an environment that will simplify the learning process and promote the employee behaviors desired by the organization. For learning to occur, some types of behavioral change are required. In the sterile processing department at Children's Hospital in Denver, Colorado, good attendance is critical. Absenteeism impacts the entire department because the work must get done regardless, so team members have to pick up the slack for their missing colleagues. To encourage perfect attendance, staff members who have not missed work in the previous three months are announced at the department's meetings. Various rewards are handed out, such as ribbons, perfect attendance pins, prizes, tote bags, alarm clocks, and the like. As an added incentive, the individual with the longest record of perfect attendance is allowed to choose first from the list of "gifts." In addition, each quarter a list of employees who have not missed any days of work is posted in the staff lounge along with the length of their perfect attendance. If the entire department has perfect attendance for a quarter, the whole department celebrates with events like an ice cream social or root beer float party to acknowledge everyone's efforts and accomplishments.[4]

Classical Conditioning

Classical conditioning *is the process by which individuals learn to link the information from a neutral stimulus to a stimulus that causes a response.* This response may not be under an individual's conscious control.[5] In the classical conditioning process, an unconditioned stimulus (environmental event) brings out a natural response. Then a neutral environmental event, called a *conditioned stimulus*, is paired with the unconditioned stimulus that brings out the behavior. Eventually, the conditioned stimulus alone brings out the behavior, which is called a *conditional response.*

The individual most frequently associated with classical conditioning is Ivan Pavlov, the Russian physiologist whose experiments with dogs led to the early formulations of classical conditioning theory. In Pavlov's famous experiment, the sound of a metronome (the conditioned stimulus) was paired with food (the unconditioned stimulus). The dogs eventually exhibited a salivation response (conditioned response) to the sound of the metronome alone. The classical conditioning process is illustrated in Figure 5.1.

The classical conditioning process helps explain a variety of behaviors that occur in everyday organizational life. At Presbyterian Hospital's emergency room in Plano, Texas, special lights in the hallway indicate that a patient who needs treatment has just arrived. Nurses and other hospital staff report that they feel nervous when the lights go on. In contrast, at a recent luncheon in the dining room at Stonebriar Country Club in Frisco, Texas, Ralph Sorrentino, a partner at Deloitte Consulting, was thanked by his friend Jack Kennedy for suggesting a new personnel performance evaluation system. When Sorrentino dines in the dining room, he remembers that recognition and feels good.

Some organizations spend millions of dollars on advertising campaigns designed to link the information value of a stimulus to customers' purchasing behaviors. In a TV ad, AFLAC has successfully created a link between its duck and supplemental

FIGURE 5.1 Classical Conditioning

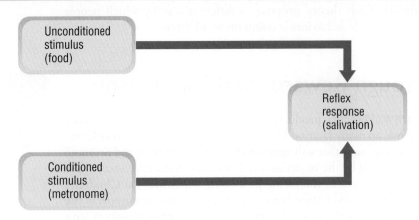

insurance. The duck is the unconditioned stimulus, and insurance is the conditioned stimulus. The positive feelings that buyers have toward the duck are associated with insurance, which AFLAC hopes will lead people to buy its products.

Classical conditioning isn't widely used in work settings. Employee behaviors usually don't include responses that can be changed with classical conditioning techniques. Instead, there is greater interest in the voluntary behaviors of employees and how they can be changed via operant conditioning.

Operant Conditioning

The individual most closely linked with operant learning is B. F. Skinner.[6] He coined the term **operant conditioning** *to refer to a process by which individuals learn voluntary behavior*. Voluntary behaviors are called *operants* because they operate, or have some influence, on the environment. Learning occurs from the consequences of behaviors, and many employee work behaviors are operant behaviors. In fact, most behaviors in everyday life (e.g., talking, walking, reading, or working) are forms of operant behavior. Leaders are interested in operant behaviors because they can influence the results of such behaviors. For example, the frequency of an employee behavior can be increased or decreased by changing the results of that behavior. The crucial aspect of operant conditioning is what happens as a consequence of the behavior. The strength and frequency of operantly conditioned behaviors are determined mainly by consequences. Thus, leaders and team members must understand the effects of different types of consequences on the task behaviors of employees. For example, at Virgin Life Care in Boston, Massachusetts, the company's rewards program motivated 40 percent of its more than 940 employees to establish a habit of walking up stairs instead of taking the elevator. Thanks to the program, employees reduced their body fat by 68 percent, saving the company money in terms of decreased medical claims and reduced absenteeism.[7]

In operant conditioning, a response is learned because it leads to a particular consequence (reinforcement), and it is strengthened each time it is reinforced. The success of Denver's Children's Hospital motivational program to encourage perfect attendance relies on rewarding behavior (perfect attendance) or not rewarding behavior when individual calls in sick. At school, you've probably learned that if you study hard, you are likely to receive good grades. If you keep up with your reading throughout the semester, you can more easily cope with the stress of finals week. Thus, you've learned to operate on your environment to achieve your desired goals.

Contingencies of Reinforcement

Learning Goal

2. *Describe the contingencies of reinforcement that influence behavior.*

A **contingency of reinforcement** *is the relationship between a behavior and the preceding and following environmental events that influence that behavior.* A contingency of reinforcement consists of an antecedent, a behavior, and a consequence.

An **antecedent** *precedes and is a stimulus to a behavior.* Antecedents are instructions, rules, goals, and advice from others that help individuals to know which behaviors are acceptable and which are not and to let them know the consequences of such behaviors. At UPS, service providers are trained on how to deliver a package. Antecedents play an essential educational role by letting service providers know in advance the consequences (rewards) of different behaviors.

A **consequence** *is the result of a behavior, which can be either positive or negative in terms of goal or task accomplishment.* A leader's response to an employee is contingent on the consequence of the behavior (and sometimes on the behavior itself, regardless of consequence). The consequence for service providers at UPS is delivering all their packages on time and going home on time. The consequence for staff members of the sterile processing department at Children's Hospital who have perfect attendance for the quarter is that they receive tote bags, their name is posted in the break room, etc.

Figure 5.2 shows an example of contingent reinforcement. First, the employee and leader jointly set a goal (e.g., selling $100,000 worth of equipment next month). Next, the employee performs tasks to achieve this goal (e.g., calling on four new customers a week, having regular lunches with current buyers, and attending a two-day training program on new methods of selling). If the employee reaches the sales goal, the leader praises the employee—an action contingent on achievement of the goal. If the employee fails to reach the goal, the leader doesn't say anything or reprimands the employee.

The contingency of reinforcement concept involves three main types of contingencies. First, an event can be presented (applied) or withdrawn (removed), contingent on employee behavior. The event also may be positive or aversive. **Positive events** *are desirable, or pleasing, to the employee.* **Aversive events** *are undesirable, or displeasing, to the employee.* Figure 5.3 shows how these events can be combined to produce four types of contingencies of reinforcement. It shows whether a particular type of contingency

---

FIGURE 5.2 Examples of Contingent Reinforcement

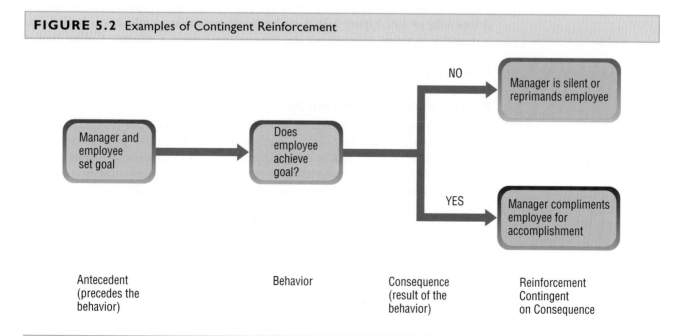

FIGURE 5.3 Types of Contingencies of Reinforcement

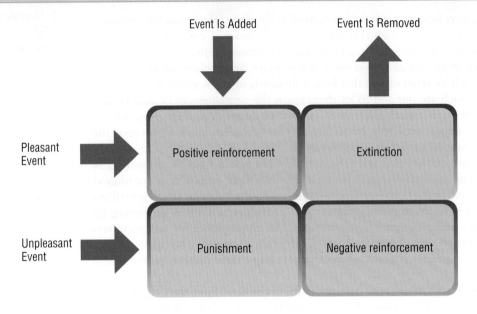

is likely to increase or decrease the frequency of the behavior. This figure also is the basis for the following discussion of contingencies of reinforcement. **Reinforcement** *is a behavioral contingency that increases the frequency of a particular behavior that it follows.* Whether positive or negative, reinforcement always increases the frequency of the employee behavior. If you want a behavior to continue, you must make sure that it is being reinforced. In contrast, extinction and punishment always decrease the frequency of the employee behavior.

Positive Reinforcement

Positive reinforcement *entails presenting a pleasant consequence after the occurrence of a desired behavior* (see Figure 5.3). A leader might reward an employee's behavior that is desirable in terms of achieving the organization's goals. Catherine Collins took a cup of coffee to Bobbie Watson and then discussed the improved quality of her work. Bobbie's work continued to improve (positive reinforcement).

Reward versus Reinforcement

The terms *reinforcement* and *reward* are often confused in everyday usage. A **reward** *is an event that an individual finds desirable or pleasing.* An individual's culture influences whether a reward acts as a reinforcer.[8] For example, praise and appreciation of employees in family-dominated cultures such as Greece, Italy, and South Korea may mean just as much to the recipient as money. Certain material rewards can also carry unexpected consequences. In China, for example, cashiers and clerks at Walmart and Sam's typically earn between 1500 and 2500 RMB per month (roughly $200 to $300). This is a competitive wage in China. In addition, Walmart distributes food to employees as holiday gifts and gives them a housing allowance. Employees in higher positions get more and better food and housing than lower level workers.[9]

To qualify as a reinforcer, a reward must increase the frequency of the behavior it follows. Money can be regarded as a positive reinforcer for a particular individual only if the frequency of the desired behavior (in this case, high performance) increases.

A reward doesn't act as a reinforcer if the frequency of the behavior decreases or remains unchanged.

Primary and Secondary Reinforcers

A **primary reinforcer** *is an event for which the individual already knows the value.* Food, shelter, and water are primary reinforcers. However, primary reinforcers don't always act as reinforcers, given a particular situation. For example, food may not be a reinforcer to someone who has just completed a five-course meal.

In organizations, secondary reinforcers influence most behaviors. A **secondary reinforcer** *is an event that once had neutral value but has taken on some value (positive or negative) for an individual because of past experience.* Money is an obvious example of a secondary reinforcer. Although it can't directly satisfy a basic human need, money has value because an individual can use it to purchase both necessities and discretionary items. Calvert, a Bethesda, Maryland, financial firm, groups its secondary reinforcers into three categories:

* *core benefits,* such as life insurance, sick leave, holiday pay, and a retirement savings plan;

* *optional benefits,* such as dental and eye care coverage, and spending accounts for health and dependent care; and

* *other benefits,* such as tuition reimbursement, car pooling, and career planning.

At Costco, employees are offered challenging jobs and participate in the management of their own jobs. Management teaches employees quality control techniques so that they can monitor their own behavior, learn to control costs, and assume responsibility for tasks traditionally viewed as managerial prerogatives. Costco also provides employees with health and education benefits, flexible working arrangements, maternity/paternity leave, and child and elder care. It also sponsors social events for employees. Does it work? Costco employees, on average, earn $31,000 per year and receive an additional $7,065 in benefits, whereas the average Sam's Club employee earns $24,680 per year with $4,247 in benefits. Yet the labor costs at Costco are actually lower because Costco's employees generated roughly twice the revenue ($72 versus $39.7 billion) as did Sam's Club's employees—and Costco did it with thousands of fewer employees. When the costs of turnover, employee theft, and productivity are considered, it is more efficient for Costco to pay its employees more. For more information on Costco and its leaders, see Chapter 4.[10]

David Stoner, president of ViewCast Corporation, has discovered that when people are given a choice of things to do, whatever they consistently choose can be used as a secondary reinforcer. In fact, you are invited to make a list of all the tasks that you need to do in the next two days. Rank these from things you most want to do or enjoy doing to the tasks you least like to do. Then start working at the bottom of the list. You will quickly notice that when you start at the bottom, every time you finish a task, the next one on the list is more desirable. If you start at the top of your list, the consequence of completing that task is that the next one is more undesirable, difficult, or boring. Using this approach, you quit. Starting from the bottom and working to the top, you don't want to quit until all tasks are done.

The nation's 300 largest employers estimate that unscheduled absenteeism costs their business more than $760,000 per day in direct payroll costs and even more when lower productivity, lost revenue, and the effects of poor morale are considered. The following Self Competency feature illustrates how JCPenney designed a positive reinforcement system to tackle this problem.[11]

> ### Communication Insight
>
> Encouraging positive behavior takes much less effort on a leader's part than having to address poor performance issues. I try to give out five positive comments for every one negative one to reinforce good performance.
>
> *Jack Gustin, President, Lakewood Hospital*

Self competency

Coming to Work Today?

On any given day, about 1,500 JCPenney Company employees do not show up for work at one of the company's more than 11,000 stores—with a costly result. And in recessionary times when profits are slim, that's a cost that most leaders do not want to incur. In an effort to cut down on unscheduled absenteeism, JCPenney implemented a program that is staffed by a team of employees to work on this problem. If an employee is sick and cannot come to work for more than three days, the employees must call Penney's PowerLine team. The team determines the type of benefit, if any, the employee can receive. The team notifies the leader of the department where the employee works and sends the employee the necessary forms to complete. The PowerLine team follows up with absent employees until they return to work.

Jim Cuva, Penney's benefit leader, learned that when individuals check on the person to see how they are doing, it shows the individual that someone cares and is thinking about them.

The PowerLine team also discovered that only a third of all absences were related to an illness. The rest of the times absences were related to having to be somewhere else or the individual just didn't feel like going to work. They also found that authoritarian leaders who make employees feel it's "their way or the highway" created more absences than leaders who make employees feel important. They recommended leadership development programs for these leaders in an effort to educate them on the consequences of their autocratic leadership style. Finally, the PowerLine team, working with a consultant, designed a survey to find out whether a job applicant might have a problem with absences. Some of the questions that they ask job applicants to either agree or disagree with include:

- I have asked a friend to punch my time card when I knew I was going to be late for work.
- It's okay to say you're sick and go home if you don't feel like working.
- It's okay to get around rules, as long as you don't actually break them.

The PowerLine team uses these and other questions to understand the applicant's character. The team has learned that if the individual is not going to be satisfied at work, they're more likely to be absent.

JCPenney has created a PowerLine team to follow up with absent employees.

SUSAN GOLDMAN/BLOOMBERG NEWS/LANDOV

To learn more about JCPenney's PowerLine, go to **www.jcpenney.com.**

Concepts of Positive Reinforcement

Several general principles influence the effectiveness of positive reinforcement. The following general principles help to explain optimum reinforcement conditions[12]:

- The **principle of contingent reinforcement** *states that the reinforcer must be administered only if the desired behavior is performed.* A reinforcer administered when the desired behavior has not been performed is ineffective.

- The **principle of immediate reinforcement** *states that the reinforcer will be most effective if administered immediately after the desired behavior has occurred.* This is what supervisors at UPS do. The more time that elapses after the behavior occurs, the less effective the reinforcer.

- The **principle of reinforcement size** *states that the larger the amount of reinforcer delivered after the desired behavior, the more effect the reinforcer will have on the frequency of the desired behavior.* The amount, or size, of the reinforcer is relative. A reinforcer that may be significant to one person may be insignificant to another person. Thus, the size of the reinforcer must be determined in relation both to the behavior and the individual. ARAMARK, a supplier of food services to college campuses, gives T-shirts to workers with perfect attendance for a month and a $50 gift certificate to those with perfect attendance for a semester.

- The **principle of reinforcement deprivation** *states that the more an individual is deprived of the reinforcer, the greater effect it will have on the future occurrence of the desired behavior.* However, if an individual recently has had enough of a reinforcer and is satisfied, the reinforcer will have less effect.

Organizational Rewards

Material rewards—salary, bonuses, fringe benefits, and the like—are obvious. Most leaders also offer a wide range of other rewards to reinforce the behaviors they want. For example, the Dallas Independent School System recently spent more than $12 million on substitute teachers. The average teacher was absent 10 days during the school year. The district launched its Staff and Teacher Attendance Reward program as a financial incentive for teachers to show up for class. According to Marita Hawkins, the district's benefits director, if a teacher had only one absence during the school year, the district matched 100 percent of the teacher's contribution to a retirement account, up to $1,000 a year. Teachers out two days got a 75 percent match, up to $700. Those with three to five absences earned 50 percent match, up to $500 a year. Hawkins hopes to save the district more than $2 million with this reward system.[13]

At Toyota's Camry assembly plant in Georgetown, Kentucky, management rewards employees for *kaizens*. A **kaizen** *is a suggestion that results in safety, cost, or quality improvements.*[14] The awards are distributed equally among all members of a team. The awards aren't cash payments; rather, they are gift certificates redeemable at local retail stores. Toyota learned that an award that could be shared by the employees' families was valued more than extra money in the paycheck. These awards instill pride and encourage other teams to scramble for new ideas in the hope that they, too, will receive them. In addition, self-administered rewards are important. For example, self-satisfaction for accomplishing a particularly difficult assignment can be an important personal reinforcer. Table 5.1 contains an extensive list of organizational rewards. Remember, however, that such rewards will act as reinforcers only if the individuals receiving them find them desirable or pleasing.

Negative Reinforcement

Negative reinforcement (see Figure 5.3) *occurs when an unpleasant event that precedes the employee behavior is removed when the desired behavior occurs.* Negative reinforcement increases the likelihood that the desired behavior will occur. Negative reinforcement is sometimes confused with punishment because both use unpleasant events that influence behavior. Negative reinforcement is used to increase the frequency of a desired behavior. In contrast, punishment is used to decrease the frequency of an undesired behavior. On NBC's TV show *The Biggest Loser*, the station agreed to pay $250,000 to the individual who lost the biggest percentage of his or her body weight. In the primetime reality show, unless a contestant lost 15 pounds in two months, the show would air unflattering photos of them on TV. Cynthia Nacson-Schechter explained that she knew all about the dangers of being overweight and yet these dangers and the money weren't enough to scare her into losing weight. What she feared most was

TABLE 5.1 Rewards Used by Organizations

MATERIAL REWARDS	SUPPLEMENTAL BENEFITS	STATUS SYMBOLS
Pay	Company automobiles	Corner offices
Pay raises	Health insurance plans	Offices with windows
Stock options	Pension contributions	Carpeting
Profit sharing	Vacation and sick leave	Drapes
Deferred compensation	Recreation facilities	Paintings
Bonuses/bonus plans	Child-care support	Watches
Incentive plans	Club privileges	Rings
Expense accounts	Parental leave	Private restrooms

SOCIAL/INTERPERSONAL REWARDS	REWARDS FROM THE TASK	SELF-ADMINISTERED REWARDS
Praise	Sense of achievement	Self-congratulation
Developmental feedback	Jobs with more responsibility	Self-recognition
Smiles, pats on the back, and other nonverbal signals	Job autonomy/self-direction	Self-praise
Requests for suggestions	Performing important tasks	Self-development through expanded knowledge/skills
Invitations to coffee or lunch		Greater sense of self-worth
Wall plaques		

the possibility that her ex-boyfriend would see her in a bikini on national TV. She lost weight and then some. It was the fear of being on national TV in a bikini that acted as a negative reinforcer for her to lose weight.

Leaders and team members frequently use negative reinforcement when an employee hasn't done something that is necessary or desired. For example, air-traffic controllers want the ability to activate a blinking light and a loud buzzer in the cockpits of planes that come too close to each other. Air-traffic controllers wouldn't shut these devices off until the planes moved farther apart. This type of procedure is called *escape learning* because the pilots quickly learn to move their planes away from each other to escape the light and buzzer. **Escape learning** *refers to an unpleasant event that occurs until an employee performs a behavior or terminates it*. In most instances, use of negative reinforcements generates enough behavior to escape or avoid punishment. Doing "just enough to get by" is typical.

Extinction

Extinction *is the removal of all reinforcing events*. Whereas reinforcement increases the frequency of a desirable behavior, extinction decreases the frequency of an undesirable behavior (see Figure 5.3). Leaders use extinction to reduce undesirable employee behaviors that prevent achievement of organizational goals. The extinction procedure consists of three steps:

1. identifying the behavior to be reduced or eliminated,

2. identifying the reinforcer that maintains the behavior, and

3. stopping the reinforcer.

Extinction is a useful technique for reducing and eventually eliminating behaviors that disrupt normal workflow. For example, a team reinforces the disruptive behavior of a member by laughing at it. When the team stops laughing (the reinforcer), the disruptive behavior will diminish and ultimately stop.

Extinction can be regarded as a failure to reinforce a behavior positively. In this sense, the extinction of behaviors may be accidental. If leaders fail to reinforce desirable behaviors, they may be using extinction without recognizing it. As a result, the frequency of desirable behaviors may inadvertently decrease.

Some leaders think that doing nothing has no effect on performance. When leaders do nothing following a behavior, they change the contingencies of reinforcement. If employees are taking the initiative to go beyond what is required, those behaviors will stop if they are not reinforced. If employees are taking shortcuts in areas of safety and quality and nothing is said, then extinction will cause the undesirable behaviors to continue.

Punishment

Punishment (see Figure 5.3) *refers to an unpleasant event occurring following a behavior and decreasing that behavior's frequency.* Remember when you tried to use a PC for the first time? You may have inadvertently deleted a document you had been working on for hours (punishment). If that happened, now you probably hit the "Save" option regularly. As in positive reinforcement, a punishment may include a specific antecedent that cues the employee that a consequence (punisher) will follow a specific behavior. A positive contingency of reinforcement encourages the frequency of a desired behavior. In contrast, punishment decreases the frequency of an undesired behavior. To qualify as a punisher, an event must decrease the undesirable behavior. Just because an event is thought of as unpleasant, it isn't necessarily a punisher. The event must actually reduce or stop the undesired behavior before it can be defined as a punisher.

Organizations typically use several types of unpleasant events to punish employees. Material consequences for failure to perform adequately include a cut in pay, a disciplinary suspension without pay, a demotion, or a transfer to a dead-end job. The final punishment is the firing of an employee for failure to perform. In general, organizations reserve the use of unpleasant material events, such as demotions, reassignments, dismissals, and the like, for cases of serious behavior problems.

Interpersonal punishers are used extensively. They include a leader's oral reprimand of an employee for unacceptable behavior and nonverbal punishers such as frowns, grunts, and aggressive body language. Certain tasks themselves can be unpleasant. The fatigue that follows hard physical labor can be considered a punisher, as can harsh or dirty working conditions. However, care must be exercised in labeling a punisher. In some fields and to some employees, harsh or dirty working conditions may be considered as just something that goes with the job.

Three of the principles of positive reinforcement discussed earlier have equivalents in punishment. For maximum effectiveness:

- a punisher should be directly linked to the undesirable behavior (principle of contingent punishment);

- the punishment should be administered immediately (principle of immediate punishment); and,

- in general, the greater the size of the punisher, the stronger the effect on the undesirable behavior (principle of punishment size).

Negative Effects of Punishment

A criticism for using punishment is the chance that it will have negative effects, especially over long or sustained periods of time.[15] Punishment stops an undesirable employee behavior. However, the potential negative consequences may be greater than the original undesirable behavior. Figure 5.4 illustrates some potential negative effects of punishment, as discussed next.

FIGURE 5.4 Potential Negative Effects of Punishment

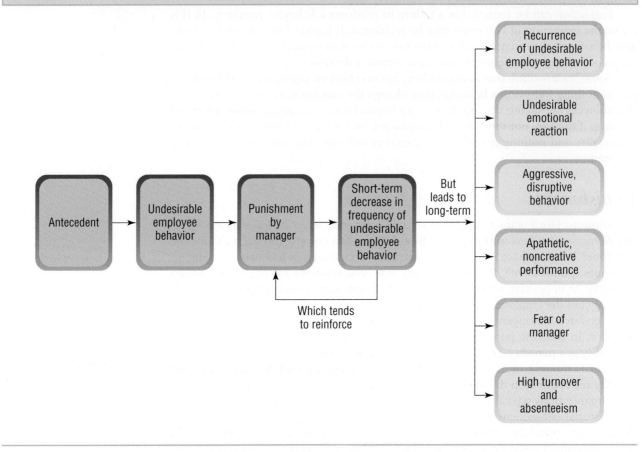

Punishment may cause undesirable emotional reactions. An employee who has been reprimanded for staying on break too long may react with anger toward the leader and the organization. Such reactions may lead to behavior detrimental to the organization. Sabotage, for example, may be a result of a punishment-oriented management system. Chapter 8 discusses aggressive behavior in the workforce more completely.

Punishment frequently leads only to short-term suppression of the undesirable behavior, rather than to its elimination. The suppression of an undesirable behavior over a long period of time usually requires continued and, perhaps, increasingly severe punishment. Another problem is that control of the undesirable behavior becomes contingent on the leader's presence. When the leader isn't around, the undesirable employee behavior is likely to recur.

In addition, the punished individual may try to avoid or escape the situation. From an organizational viewpoint, this reaction may be unacceptable if an employee avoids a particular, essential task. High absenteeism is a form of avoidance that may occur when punishment is used frequently. Quitting may be the employee's final form of escape. Organizations that depend on punishment are likely to have high rates of employee turnover. Some turnover is desirable, but excessive turnover is damaging to an organization. Todd Diener, president of Chili's at Brinker International based in Dallas, Texas, says that recruitment and training costs average more than $600 per employee at Chili's restaurants.

Punishment suppresses employee initiative and flexibility. Reacting to punishment, many an employee has said: "I'm going to do just what I'm told and nothing more."

Such an attitude is undesirable because organizations depend on the personal initiative and creativity that employees bring to their jobs. Overusing punishment produces apathetic employees who are not an asset to an organization. Sustained punishment can also lead to lower self-esteem. Lower self-esteem, in turn, undermines the employee's self-confidence, which is necessary for performing most jobs (see Chapter 3).

Punishment produces a conditioned fear of management. That is, employees develop a general fear of punishment-oriented leaders. Such leaders become an environmental cue, indicating to employees the probability that an aversive event will occur. So if operations require frequent, normal, and positive interaction between employees and a leader, such a situation can quickly become intolerable. Responses to fear, such as "hiding" or reluctance to communicate with a leader, may well hinder employee performance.

A leader may rely on punishment because it can produce fast results in the short run. In essence, the leader is reinforced for using punishment because the approach produces an immediate change in an employee's behavior. Thus, the leader may ignore punishment's long-term detrimental effects, which can be cumulative. A few incidents of punishment may not produce negative effects. The long-term, sustained use of punishment most often results in negative outcomes for the organization.

Individuals have also learned how to "game" the situation to avoid the punisher as the following Ethics Competency feature illustrates.[16]

Ethics competency

Time Off for Bad Behavior

Samuel Waksal, former CEO of the biotech firm ImClone, was serving time in a federal prison for insider trading. He was released nine months early. Why? He was rewarded for participating in a prison rehab program for substance abusers. The rehab program is a 500-hour program focusing on behavioral and cognitive treatments, during which time participants are housed in a dorm-like unit set apart from the general prison population. The problem was that he was not a substance abuser. Waksal told the probation officer and judge that he was a "social drinker" and that he had never been treated for alcohol addiction. In prison, he learned from his fellow inmates that in 1994, Congress passed a law offering up to 12 months off a sentence for nonviolent offenders if they complete a counseling program for alcohol addiction. In 1994, only 3,755 inmates were in the program, but in 2008, there were more than 18,000 prisoners in the program, with a waiting list of more than 7,000.

The rehab program is so attractive to prisoners that it is now a big business. For a fee of up to $5,000, lawyers advise their clients how to get into the program and how to maximize their chances of getting a reduction in their sentence. For example, one lawyer advised his clients to show up drunk on the day of their sentencing so they get interviewed right away about their substance abuse problem. They also arrange for doctors to testify, for a consulting fee, that they purportedly treated the individual for alcohol abuse. Drug-dealer-turned celebrity chef Jeff Henderson wrote in his book, *Cooked*, that even though he never used drugs and hadn't been around them since he stopped selling them, he was admitted to the program. While the Bureau of Prisons has rigid eligibility requirements designed to keep out fakers, there are no rigid standards on what constitutes substance abuse.

Despite its problems, the program has had some societal benefits. Male inmates who have participated in the program are 16 percent less likely to commit another crime and 15 percent less likely to relapse into future drug abuse.

Effective Use of Punishment

Positive reinforcement is more effective than punishment over the long run, but effectively used punishment does have an appropriate place in management. The most common form of punishment in organizations is the oral reprimand. It is intended to diminish or stop an undesirable employee behavior. An old rule of thumb is "Praise in public; punish in private." Private punishment establishes a different type of contingency of reinforcement than public punishment. A private reprimand can be constructive and informative. A public reprimand is likely to have negative effects because the employee has been embarrassed in front of her peers.

Vague and general oral reprimands should not be given about behavior and especially not about a so-called "bad attitude." An effective reprimand pinpoints and specifically describes the undesirable behavior to be avoided in the future. It focuses on the target behavior and avoids threatening the employee's self-image. The effective reprimand punishes specific undesirable behavior, not the employee. Behavior is easier to change than the employee.

Punishment (by definition) trains an employee in what not to do, not in what to do. Therefore, a leader must specify an alternative behavior to the employee. When the employee performs the desired alternative behavior, the leader must then reinforce that behavior positively. Finally, a leader should strike an appropriate balance between the use of pleasant and unpleasant events. The absolute number of unpleasant events isn't important, but the ratio of pleasant to unpleasant events is. A good rule of thumb is that this ratio should be 5 to 1: five positive reinforcements to one punishment. When a leader primarily uses positive reinforcement, an occasional deserved punishment can be quite effective. However, if a leader never uses positive reinforcement and relies mostly on punishment, the long-run negative effects are likely to counteract any short-term benefits. Positive management procedures should dominate in any well-run organization.

Insights for Leaders

For a positive reinforcer to cause an employee to repeat a desired behavior, it must have value to that employee. If the employee is consistently on time, the leader or team leader positively reinforces this behavior by complimenting the employee. What happens if the employee has been reprimanded in the past for coming to work late and then reports to work on time? The leader or team leader uses negative reinforcement and refrains from saying anything. Why? The employee is expected to come to work on time.

What happens if the employee continues to come to work late? The leader or team leader can use either extinction or punishment to try to stop this undesirable behavior. The team leader who chooses extinction doesn't praise the tardy employee but simply ignores the employee. The use of punishment may include reprimanding, fining, or suspending—and ultimately firing—the employee if the behavior persists.

The following guidelines are recommended for using contingencies of reinforcement in the work setting:

- Do not reward all employees in the same way.
- Carefully examine the consequences of nonactions as well as actions.
- Let employees know which behaviors will be reinforced.
- Let employees know what they are doing wrong.
- Don't punish employees in front of others.
- Make the response equal to the behavior by not cheating workers out of their just rewards.[17]

Can global leaders use these guidelines to motivate employees? BMW's factory located in Oxford, England, produces one of the company's new products, its 7 series.[18] The factory has seen big changes from a few years ago, when Rover owned the factory. Then the buildings were crumbling and the plant was often half-empty. After acquiring the Rover factory, the first challenge for BMW was modernizing the facilities.

They installed the newest production technology, expanded the parking lot, created more appealing landscapes, and in other ways created a more pleasant work environment. As employee Bernard Moss explained, "We had an open day for old employees and they just couldn't believe the transformation of the plant."

The improvements were badly needed, but they were costly, too. For the plant to become profitable, productivity had to improve. BMW relies on the factory workers themselves to find ways to cut costs and boost output. To motivate their employees and align their efforts with the needs of BMW, leaders and union leaders designed a new pay system. It offers all employees an annual bonus of £260 (approximately $400) for their ideas. To receive the full bonus, each employee must come up with an average of three ideas, and the ideas must save an average of £800 (about $1,200).

Other changes were also made in the way employees were paid. Under the old system, when production stopped and employees didn't come to work, they were paid anyway. When the plant was extra busy, they earned overtime pay. Now, when the plant is closed, employees are paid, but there is a new twist. Employees make up the time by putting in extra hours when needed. When things are busy, employees are expected to put in longer hours. Instead of overtime pay, they build up an account of extra time off. Each week quality reports are posted in a plaza that employees pass on their way to lunch. Employees are made aware of any quality problems.

The employees resented the new pay arrangements at first, but now they like it. According to Moss, "they [employees] are starting to see the advantages of longer holidays." Today the plant is even more productive than BMW leaders had hoped for. Employees offered more than 10,000 ideas for improvements, saving the company £6 million ($7.79 million). "If people are highly satisfied, they are more likely to be productive. If they are not satisfied, they are not going to bother [making] suggestions," says Moss.

Schedules of Reinforcement

Learning Goal

3. *Explain how positive reinforcement, negative reinforcement, punishment, and extinction affect an individual's performance.*

Leaders using reinforcement to encourage the learning and performance of desired behaviors must choose a schedule for applying reinforcers. The schedule of reinforcement often depends on practical considerations (e.g., the nature of the person's job and the type of reinforcer being used, deliberately or not). However, reinforcement is always delivered according to some schedule.

Continuous and Intermittent Reinforcement

Continuous reinforcement *means that the behavior is reinforced each time it occurs and is the simplest schedule of reinforcement.* An example of continuous reinforcement is dropping coins in a soft-drink vending machine. The behavior of inserting coins is reinforced (on a continuous schedule) by the machine delivering a can of soda (most of the time!). Verbal recognition and material rewards generally are not delivered on a continuous schedule in organizations. In organizations such as Mary Kay Cosmetics, Tupperware, and Amway, salespeople are paid a commission for each sale, usually earning commissions of 25 to 50 percent of sales. Although the reinforcer (money) isn't paid immediately, the salespeople track their sales immediately and quickly convert sales into amounts owed them by the organization. Most leaders, however, supervise employees other than salespeople, and they seldom have the opportunity to deliver a reinforcer every time their employees demonstrate a desired behavior. Therefore, behavior typically is reinforced intermittently.

Intermittent reinforcement *refers to a reinforcer being delivered after some, but not every, occurrence of the desired behavior.* Intermittent reinforcement can be subdivided into (1) interval and ratio schedules and (2) fixed and variable schedules. In an **interval schedule,** *reinforcers are delivered after a certain amount of time has passed.* In a **ratio schedule,** *reinforcers are delivered after a certain number of behaviors have been performed.* These two schedules can be further subdivided into fixed (not changing) or variable (constantly changing) schedules. Figure 5.5 shows these four primary types of intermittent schedules: fixed interval, variable interval, fixed ratio, and variable ratio.

FIGURE 5.5   Four Types of Intermittent Reinforcement Schedules

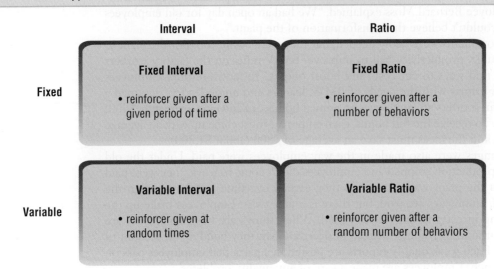

Fixed Interval Schedule

In a **fixed interval schedule**, *a constant amount of time must pass before a reinforcer is provided*. The first desired behavior to occur after the interval has elapsed is reinforced. For example, in a fixed interval, one-hour schedule, the first desired behavior that occurs after an hour has elapsed is reinforced. Administering rewards according to this type of schedule tends to produce an uneven pattern of behavior. Prior to the reinforcement, the behavior is frequent and energetic. Immediately following the reinforcement, the behavior becomes less frequent and energetic. Why? Because the individual rather quickly figures out that another reward won't immediately follow the last one—a certain amount of time must pass before it is given again. A common example of administering rewards on a fixed interval schedule is the payment of employees weekly, biweekly, or monthly. That is, monetary reinforcement comes regularly at the end of a specific period of time. Such time intervals, unfortunately, are generally too long to be an effective form of reinforcement for newly acquired work-related behavior.

Males typically send flowers to their significant other on Valentine's Day as an expression of their love, devotion, and appreciation. However, as the following Across Cultures competency feature illustrates, sending the right flowers is not as easy as it seems. What color flowers are sent can be seen as either a reward or punisher. Do you remember what the color was of the flowers you sent on Valentine's Day last year?[19]

Across Cultures competency

Flowers: A Symbol of Love?

According to FTD and Interflora Inc., which send flowers by wire to some 140 countries, the color red is used to cast spells in Mexico, and a white bouquet is necessary to lift the spell. In Spain, red roses are associated more with lust than with love. In France, a dozen yellow roses are inappropriate—yellow suggests infidelity—and cut flowers by the dozen or any even number are unlucky.

A bouquet of yellow flowers is also inappropriate in Latin America where yellow is associated with death rather than infidelity. In Africa, yellow is associated with disease. In India, sending green flowers is associated with bad luck. In Italy, roses serve as tokens of affection when they are sent in odd numbers to women. In Japan, on the other hand, men receive flowers from women.

White is an appropriate color for a wedding gown in the United States, yet white is used alternatively with black for mourning in India, Hong Kong, and Japan. Americans see red when they are angry, but red is a lucky color for the Chinese. It is customary for the Chinese to put money in red envelopes as gifts for employees and children on special occasions, especially on the Chinese New Year's Day. White flowers are used in China as a symbol of mourning.

To learn more about flowers, go to **www.teleflora.com.**

Although red flowers mean love in U.S. culture, they have other meanings across the globe.

Variable Interval Schedule

A **variable interval schedule** *represents changes in the amount of time between reinforcers.* Sherry Burnside, head of housekeeping at Presbyterian Hospital in Dallas, Texas, uses a variable interval schedule to observe and reinforce the behaviors of housekeeping personnel. An individual receives $100 for perfect attendance and a score above 92 percent on 23 performance indicators (e.g., floor swept, trash baskets emptied, room dusted, etc.). To observe their behavior, Burnside announced to all housekeeping employees that, during the month, she would make seven inspections at random times. During the first week, she observed and recorded the performance of employees on Tuesday between 3:00 and 4:00 P.M. and Wednesday from 6:00 to 7:30 A.M. The following week, she made no observations. During the third week, she observed employees on Monday between 10:00 and 11:00 A.M. and Friday from 12:00 to 1:45 P.M. During the fourth week, she observed employees on Monday between 8:00 and 9:00 P.M. and from 11:00 P.M. to 12:00 A.M. and on Thursday from 2:00 to 3:30 P.M. If she didn't change her schedule, the employees would anticipate her tours and adjust their behaviors to get a reward.

Fixed Ratio Schedule

In a **fixed ratio schedule**, *the desired behavior must occur a specified number of times before it is reinforced.* Administering rewards under a fixed ratio schedule tends to produce a high response rate when the time for reinforcement is close, followed by periods of steady behavior. The employee soon determines that reinforcement is based on the number of responses and performs the responses as quickly as possible in order to receive the reward. The individual piece-rate system used in many manufacturing plants is an example of such a schedule. In the Northern Shipping Company in China, production workers are paid on the basis of pieces. The firm allocates a number of hours per job and assigns a unit price to each piece. The number of hours allocated to each job is reviewed from time to time according to whether production targets are being met. The workers are paid 9.6 RMB (or US $1.24) per piece. Workers can complete several pieces per hour. If the job is completed on time to the required quality standard, workers will receive the full amount for the job. The norm for production workers is to work 176 hours per month, but many work up to 250 hours per month. An average production employee can earn 2,500 to 3,000 RMB per month.[20]

Variable Ratio Schedule

In a **variable ratio schedule,** *a certain number of desired behaviors must occur before the reinforcer is delivered, but the number of behaviors varies around some average.* Leaders frequently use a variable ratio schedule with praise and recognition. For example, team leaders at Alcatel vary the frequency of reinforcement when they give employees verbal approval for desired behaviors. Gambling casinos, such as Bally's and Harrah's, and state lotteries use this schedule of reinforcement to lure patrons to shoot craps, play poker, feed slot machines, and buy lottery tickets. Patrons win, but not on any regular basis. A variable ratio schedule is effective because it creates uncertainty about when the consequence will occur. The use of this schedule makes sense for giving praise or auditing the behavior of employees. Employees know that a consequence will be delivered, but not when. To avoid consequences of either punishment or extinction, the employee keeps demonstrating the desired behaviors.

Pioneer Telephone Cooperative of Kingfisher, Oklahoma, was facing severe competition from other telephone and cable companies, such as AT&T, Cingular, and Time Warner.[21] The firm's leaders had developed the idea of a triple play—high-speed Internet, phone service, and TV service—all from one company. Pioneer needed its sales representatives to sell this new service to its customers. The triple play provided customers with advanced video services, including pay-per-view, high-definition programming, and gaming.

With only 600 employees and a little more than $100 million in sales, Pioneer is a small fish in a big pond dominated by major companies. So how does Pioneer get new subscribers? All employees at Pioneer are salespeople. Employees refer qualified leads to the company via Pioneer's intranet. A lead is qualified when employees, on their own time, recommend the triple play to customers and ask them to contact them at work. Employees are rewarded for each successful lead; bonuses are deposited in their company accounts and paid each quarter. Pioneer periodically offers double points for leads. To ensure that all employees are aware of the triple play, each month they receive a computer-based learning module. Each topic is designed to be an interactive experience. Employees read the information and answer 10 questions. Those who correctly answer at least 90 percent of the questions received $5. Pioneer also introduced an e-billing service. It offered a free T-shirt to the first 100 employees who enrolled in the program to learn about its e-billing service.

Pioneer used the same type of reinforcement program to get customers involved in the triple play. Called Take 5–Win $25, this program required customers to read the information in the company's newsletter, answer five questions, and send it back to Pioneer with a chance to win $25. Each month, one winner is drawn from each of Pioneer's 13 districts. Several thousand customers participated in a chance to win $25.

Loyd Benson believes that rewarding employees to promote Pioneer achieves four things: It (1) educates employees about Pioneer's products and services, (2) increases sales through solid leads, (3) reduces sales expenses, and (4) makes employees ambassadors for the company.

Table 5.2 summarizes the four types of intermittent reinforcement schedules. The ratio schedules—fixed or variable—usually lead to better performance than do interval schedules. The reason is that ratio schedules are more closely related to the occurrence of desired behaviors than are interval schedules, which are based on the passage of time. The particular schedule of reinforcement is not as critical as the fact that reinforcement is based on the performance of desired behaviors.

TABLE 5.2 Comparison of Reinforcement Schedules

SCHEDULE	INFLUENCE ON PERFORMANCE	EXAMPLE
Fixed interval	Leads to average performance	Monthly paycheck
Fixed ratio	Leads quickly to high and stable performance	Piece-rate pay
Variable interval	Leads to moderately high and stable performance	Occasional praise by team members
Variable ratio	Leads to very high performance	Random quality checks with praise for zero defects

Social Learning Theory

Operant conditioning accurately describes some of the major factors that may influence learning. Certain aspects of learning, however, are not addressed by operant conditioning. For example, an individual's feelings and thoughts aren't considered. Albert Bandura and others have demonstrated that people can learn new behavior by watching others in a social situation and then imitating their behavior.[22] **Social learning theory** *refers to knowledge acquisition through the mental processing of information by observing and imitating others.* The social part acknowledges that individuals learn by being part of a society, and the learning part recognizes that individuals use thought processes to make decisions. People actively process information to learn. By watching others perform a task, people develop mental pictures of how to perform the task. Observers often learn faster than those who do not observe the behaviors of others because they don't need to unlearn behaviors and can avoid needless and costly mistakes that often accompany trial-and-error learning.

Social learning theory includes five dimensions—symbolizing, forethought, vicarious learning, self-control, and self-efficacy—as shown in Figure 5.6. These five dimensions can help explain why different employees may behave differently when facing the same situation.

4. Describe how social learning theory can be used by individuals to improve their performance.

Change Insight

As CEO of ViewCast, a major part of my job is to teach employees how to ask interesting questions and pose new solutions to how we do business.

David Stoner, CEO, ViewCast Corporation

Symbolizing

Symbolizing *is the process of creating a mental image to guide an individual's behavior.* People imitate parents, friends, teachers, heroes, and others because they can identify with them. If a golfer observes the swings of Tiger Woods or Anika Sorenstam on their web pages, this observation creates an image (symbol) in that individual's mind of what a good golf swing looks like. Such images or symbols help the person swing a golf club the next time he plays golf. In a social situation, when those at the head of the table at a formal dinner begin to eat, their actions let the other diners know that starting to eat now is appropriate.

Forethought

Forethought *refers to the individual planning his or her actions based on the level of performance he or she desires.* For example, when a golfer who has watched an instructional video of Woods or Sorenstam getting out of a sand trap approaches the same type of shot, she recalls what she learned in the video. As a result, she adjusts her hands, feet, and body posture to the correct playing position to hit the shot. She anticipates where the ball will land and mentally plans her next shot.

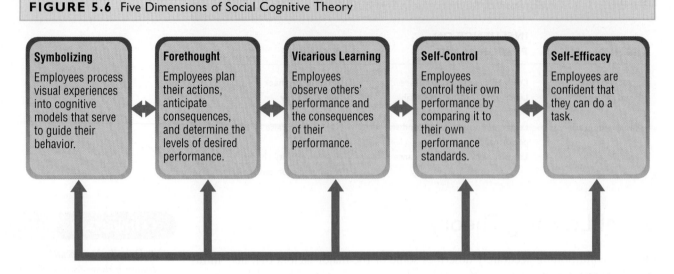

FIGURE 5.6 Five Dimensions of Social Cognitive Theory

Source: Adapted from Stajkovic, A. D., and Luthans, F. Social cognitive theory and self-efficacy. *Organizational Dynamics,* Spring 1998, 65. Reprinted with permission.

Vicarious Learning

Vicarious learning *refers to the individual observing the behavior of others and the consequences of that behavior.* Individuals learn what works and what doesn't work by watching others and studying what happens to them. Employees' capacity to learn by observation enables them to obtain accurate information without having to perform these behaviors through trial and error. All self-help videos rely on vicarious learning. For vicarious learning to occur, several conditions must be met:

- The learner must observe the other person—the model—when the behavior is being performed.
- The learner must accurately perceive the model's behavior.
- The learner must remember the behavior.
- The learner must have the competencies necessary to perform the behavior.
- The learner must observe that the model receives rewards for the behavior.[23]

Self-Control

Not everyone is cut out to work as a flight attendant, salesperson, construction worker, or leader. Many people never apply for particular jobs because what they see isn't consistent with their own ideas of the type of job they want. **Self-control** *refers to the individual selecting his or her own goals and ways of reaching them to learn new behaviors.* Tina Potter, an administrative assistant at Southern Methodist University, had a new software package for graphics on her desk for a month. She knew that she had to learn how to use it even though her leader hadn't put any pressure on her to do so. She worked Saturdays on her own to learn this new technique. Potter's goal was to learn to use the graphics software to produce figures for this book—which she achieved. Her approach exhibited self-control.

Most people engage in self-control to learn behaviors both on and off the job. Mundane tasks (e.g., learning how to use e-mail) and more complex tasks (e.g., preparing a subordinate's performance appraisal) can be learned. When an employee learns through self-control, leaders don't need to be controlling because the employee takes responsibility for learning and performing the desired behaviors. In fact, if a leader exercises control, it may well be redundant and counterproductive.

In recent years, the use of teams, especially self-directed teams, has taken the business world by storm. In many cases, management continues to exert too much direct control over teams. As a result, members then have few opportunities to apply self-control to their tasks. For most teams to be effective, leaders must empower their members to make decisions. **Empowerment** *means giving employees the authority, skills, and self-control to perform their tasks.*[24] The following Teams Competency feature highlights how Steelcase Incorporated, a Minnesota manufacturer of business furniture, empowers teams to improve productivity.[25]

Teams **competency**

Steelcase Inc.

For 18 years, Jerry Hammond had been a spot welder, making parts of business furniture without even knowing the employees in nearby departments by name. Now, he knows his coworkers because they are a team responsible for deciding how to manufacture a part and for running as many as six different pieces of equipment. Team members are cross-trained, as time permits, during their regular shifts. Often team members stay after their shifts to watch how other employees perform certain operations.

When Steelcase's leaders decided to create teams and empower its employees, it realized that barriers between workers and leaders would have to be removed. As a result, only customers now have reserved parking spaces. A common cafeteria is used by all employees and only a few walls remain in the plant.

Whenever new equipment is needed, a team of employees who are responsible for running the equipment make the decision about what to buy and how it should be installed on the shop floor. A group of employees visits the manufacturer of the equipment to learn firsthand how to use it. They are encouraged to watch videotapes provided by the manufacturer for quality and service guidelines. Forty-one self-directed production teams and four support teams tackle day-to-day problems, such as

Steelcase's implementation of teams has made workers 45 percent more productive than their competitors' workers.

waste, scrap, paint quality, shipping, and discipline. As a result, Steelcase has only one supervisor for every 33 workers, compared to a ratio of one to 12 for a competitor. Steelcase's workers are 45 percent more productive than its competitors, turning a customer's order into a finished product in three days instead of three weeks, thus reducing costs. Teams of employees working with suppliers have cut raw material inventory by half.

To learn more about Steelcase, go to **www.steelcase.com.**

Self-Efficacy

Self-efficacy *is the individual's estimate of his or her own ability to perform a specific task in a particular situation.*[26] The greater the employee's perceived ability to perform the task, the higher the employee's self-efficacy. Employees with high self-efficacy believe that (1) they have the ability needed, (2) they are capable of the effort required, and (3) no outside events will keep them from performing at a high level. If employees have low self-efficacy, they believe that no matter how hard they try, something will happen to prevent them from reaching the desired level of performance. Self-efficacy influences people's choices of tasks and how long they will spend trying to reach their goals.[27] For example, a novice golfer who has taken only a few lessons might shoot a good round. Under such circumstances, the golfer might attribute the score to "beginner's luck" and not to ability. But, after many lessons and hours of practice, an individual with low self-efficacy who still can't break 100 may decide that the demands of the game are too great to justify spending any more time on it. However, a high self-efficacy individual will try even harder to improve her game. This effort might include taking more lessons, watching videotapes of the individual's own swing, and practicing even harder and longer.

Self-efficacy has an impact on learning in three ways:

- *It influences the activities and goals that individuals choose for themselves.* In a sales contest at Pioneer Telephone Cooperative in Kingfisher, Oklahoma, employees with low self-efficacy didn't set challenging, or "stretch," goals. These people weren't lazy; they simply thought that they would fail to achieve a lofty goal. The high self-efficacy employees thought that they were capable of achieving high-performance goals—and did so.

- *It influences the effort that individuals exert on the job.* Individuals with high self-efficacy work hard to learn new tasks and are confident that their efforts will be rewarded. Low self-efficacy individuals lack confidence in their ability to succeed and see their extra effort as futile because they are likely to fail anyway.

- *It affects the persistence with which an individual stays with a complex task.* Because high self-efficacy people are confident that they will perform well, they are likely to persist in spite of obstacles or in the face of temporary setbacks. At IBM, low-performing employees were more likely than high-performing employees to dwell on obstacles hindering their ability to do assigned tasks. When people believe that they aren't capable of doing the required work, their motivation to do a task will be low.

To determine your self-efficacy, turn to the *Experiential Exercise* on page 154 at the end of this chapter.

Insights for Leaders

Leaders (and fellow team members) can use social learning theory to help employees learn to believe in themselves. Past experience is the most powerful influence on behavior. At work, the challenge is to create situations in which the employee may respond successfully to the task(s) required. A leader's expectations for a subordinate's performance—as well as the expectations of peers—also can affect a person's self-efficacy. If a leader holds high expectations for an employee and provides proper training and suggestions, the individual's self-efficacy is likely to increase. Small successes boost self-efficacy and lead to more substantial accomplishments later. If a leader holds low expectations for an employee and gives little constructive advice, the employee is likely to form an impression that he can't achieve the goal and, as a result, perform poorly.

Guidelines for using social learning theory to influence employee behavior in organizations include the following[28]:

- Identify the behaviors that will lead to improved performance.

- Select the appropriate model for employees to observe.

- Be sure that employees are capable of meeting the technical skills required by the new behaviors.

- Create a positive learning situation to increase the likelihood that employees will learn the new behaviors and act accordingly.

- Provide positive consequences (praise, raises, or bonuses) to employees who perform as desired.
- Develop organizational practices that maintain the newly learned behaviors.

The effective use of self-control in learning requires that several conditions be met. First, the individual must engage in behaviors that she wouldn't normally want to perform. This distinguishes performing activities that the individual enjoys from those involving self-control. Second, the individual must be able to use self-reinforcers, which are rewards that individuals give themselves. Some self-reinforcers include buying oneself a present, going out to a nice restaurant, playing a round of golf at a resort course, and the like. Self-reinforcers come simply from a feeling of accomplishment or achievement. Third, the individual must set goals that determine when self-reinforcers are to be applied. An individual high in self-control doesn't randomly reward himself, but sets goals that determine when to self-reinforce. In doing so, the individual relies on his own past performance, the performance of others on similar kinds of tasks, or some standard set by others. For example, one of the authors of this book is an accomplished golfer with a single-digit handicap. After playing a round in the 70s, he frequently buys himself a golf shirt as a self-reinforcer for a good round. Finally, the individual must administer the self-reinforcer only when the goal is achieved: The author buys himself a golf shirt only when he shoots a round in the 70s.

Chapter Summary

Classical conditioning began with Pavlov's work. He started a metronome (conditioned stimulus) at the same time food was placed in a dog's mouth (unconditioned stimulus). Quickly the sound of the metronome alone caused the dog to salivate. Operant conditioning focuses on the effects of reinforcement on desirable and undesirable behaviors. Changes in behavior result from the consequences of previous behavior. People tend to repeat a behavior that leads to a pleasant result and not to repeat a behavior that leads to an unpleasant result. In short, when a behavior is reinforced, it is repeated; when it is punished or not reinforced, it is not repeated.

1. Explain the role of classical and operant conditioning in fostering learning.

The two types of reinforcement are (1) positive reinforcement, which increases a desirable behavior because the individual is provided with a pleasurable outcome after the behavior has occurred; and (2) negative reinforcement, which also maintains the desirable behavior by presenting an unpleasant event before the behavior occurs and stopping the event when the behavior occurs. Both positive and negative reinforcement increase the frequency of a desirable behavior. Conversely, extinction and punishment reduce the frequency of an undesirable behavior. Extinction involves stopping everything that reinforces the behavior. A punisher is an unpleasant event that follows the behavior and reduces the probability that the behavior will be repeated.

2. Describe the contingencies of reinforcement that influence behavior.

There are four schedules of reinforcement. In the fixed interval schedule, the reward is given on a fixed time basis (e.g., a weekly or monthly paycheck). It is effective for maintaining a level of behavior. In the variable interval schedule, the reward is given around some average time during a specific period of time (e.g., the plant leader walking through the plant an average of five times every week). This schedule of reinforcement can maintain a high level of performance because employees don't know when the reinforcer will be delivered. The fixed ratio schedule ties rewards to certain outputs (e.g., a piece-rate system). This schedule maintains a steady level of behavior once the individual has earned the reinforcer. In the variable ratio schedule, the reward is given around some mean, but the number of behaviors varies (e.g., a payoff from a slot machine). This schedule is the most powerful because both the number of desired behaviors and their frequency change.

3. Explain how positive reinforcement, negative reinforcement, punishment, and extinction affect an individual's performance.

4. *Describe how social learning theory can be used by individuals to improve their performance.*

Social learning theory focuses on people learning new behaviors by observing others and then modeling their own behaviors on those observed. The five factors emphasized in social learning theory are symbolizing, forethought, vicarious learning, self-control, and self-efficacy.

Key Terms and Concepts

Antecedent, **135**
Aversive events, **135**
Classical conditioning, **133**
Consequence, **135**
Contingency of reinforcement, **135**
Continuous reinforcement, **145**
Empowerment, **151**
Escape learning, **140**
Extinction, **140**
Fixed interval schedule, **146**
Fixed ratio schedule, **147**
Forethought, **149**
Intermittent reinforcement, **145**
Interval schedule, **145**
Kaizen, **139**
Learning, **132**
Negative reinforcement, **139**
Operant conditioning, **134**
Positive events, **135**

Positive reinforcement, **136**
Primary reinforcer, **137**
Principle of contingent reinforcement, **138**
Principle of immediate reinforcement, **138**
Principle of reinforcement deprivation, **139**
Principle of reinforcement size, **139**
Punishment, **141**
Ratio schedule, **145**
Reinforcement, **136**
Reward, **136**
Secondary reinforcer, **137**
Self-control, **150**
Self-efficacy, **151**
Social learning theory, **149**
Symbolizing, **149**
Variable interval schedule, **147**
Variable ratio schedule, **148**
Vicarious learning, **150**

Discussion Questions

1. To understand what behaviors are rewarded at UPS, visit www.ups.com and in the search bar (upper right hand corner) enter "careers." Search under careers. What kinds of rewards are given to attract and retain people? What criteria are used by UPS to administer these awards?

2. In the Ethics Competency feature "Time Off for Bad Behavior," what are some ethical dilemmas created by giving prisoners time off if they legitimately enroll in a substance abuse program while in prison? What behavior(s) are being rewarded? What is the schedule of reinforcement?

3. Visit either a local health club or diet center and schedule an interview with the leader. What types of rewards does it give its members who achieve targeted goals? Does it use punishment?

4. What are some issues surrounding the use of punishment?

5. What are some positive and negative reinforcements that you have experienced either at school or work? How did these affect your behavior?

6. What schedule(s) of reinforcement did your parent(s) use with you to reinforce good behavior at school?

7. How do producers of self-help videos use social learning theory to change an individual's behavior?

8. How can a leader raise an employee's level of self-efficacy?

9. If you skipped a class or cut out of work to simply take the day off, what were the consequences of this behavior? How might your teacher or supervisor change your behavior to encourage attendance?

10. Gambling casino owners in Las Vegas, Reno, and Atlantic City use a variable ratio reinforcement schedule. Why do people find this schedule so addictive?

Experiential Exercise and Case

Experiential Exercise: Self Competency

What Is Your Self-Efficacy?[29]

The following questionnaire gives you a chance to gain insight into your self-efficacy in terms of achieving academic excellence. Using the following five-point scale, answer the following seven questions by circling the number that most closely agrees with your thinking. An interpretation of your score follows the questions.

5 = Strongly agree
4 = Agree
3 = Moderate
2 = Disagree
1 = Strongly disagree

1. I am a good student.   5 4 3 2 1
2. It is difficult to maintain a study schedule.   5 4 3 2 1
3. I know the right things to do to improve my academic performance.   5 4 3 2 1
4. I find it difficult to convince my friends who have different viewpoints on studying than mine.   5 4 3 2 1
5. My temperament is not well suited to studying.
                                                                             5 4 3 2 1
6. I am good at finding out what teachers want.
                                                                             5 4 3 2 1
7. It is easy for me to get others to see my point of view.
                                                                             5 4 3 2 1

Add your scores to questions 1, 3, 6, and 7. Enter that score here _____. For questions, 2, 4, and 5, reverse the scoring key. That is, if you answered question 2 as strongly agree, give yourself 1 point, agree is worth 2 points, and so on. Enter your score here for questions 2, 4, and 5 _____. Enter your combined score here _____. This is your *self-efficacy* score for academic achievement. If you scored between 28 and 35, you believe that you can achieve academic excellence. Scores lower than 18 indicate that you believe, no matter how hard you try to achieve academic excellence, something may prevent you from reaching your desired level of performance. Scores between 19 and 27 indicate a moderate degree of self-efficacy. Your self-efficacy may vary with the course you are taking. In courses in your major, you may have greater self-efficacy than in those outside of your major.

Questions
1. Why does self-efficacy influence an individual's behavior?
2. What actions can you take to increase your self-efficacy at either work or school?

Case: Self Competency

Joe Salatino, President of Great Northern American[30]

As president of Great Northern American, Joe Salatino gauges the success of this 35-year-old company by the amount of money he pays employees. The firm's salespeople will sell more than $20 million in office, promotional, arts-and-crafts, and computer supplies to more than 60,000 businesses around the country this year. Great Northern American sells more than 7 million yards of packaging tape, 8 million paper clips, and 11 million BIC and Papermate pens and pencils bearing customer logos, along with about 12,000 other products, each year. The head of this Dallas-based telemarketing company believes that spending money on commissions and bonuses is necessary to keep his 30-person sales force motivated, especially in the face of stiff competition from Internet users.

The company's salesroom features all kinds of motivational devices. On a recent Friday morning, rotating blue lights signal that a special deal on pens is on. For the next hour, customers can get two for one on Stars and Stripes promotional pens. When the blue-light special is off, they're back up to 39 cents apiece. When the light goes off, a leader draws a large snowball on one of the large dry-erase boards to indicate another sale has ended. The noise and pace is fast and furious.

Many of Salatino's salespeople earn more than $60,000 a year, and top producers earn more than $100,000. Gary Gieb, aka John Johnson, because it's easier to spell and sounds more all-American over the phone, earned more than $100,000 last year. During a typical day, he makes 20 to 25 calls per hour. If a customer places an order, the entire sale takes just under 5 minutes. He earns commission of between 5 and 12 percent on the list price, depending on the merchandise. A salesperson usually needs a year to build up a good account base. Many employees who can't handle the self-starting selling intensity and bedlam usually leave within the first month. To establish loyal customers, many top-selling salespeople subscribe to their customer's hometown newspaper so that they can chat with the customer about local issues, such as who had a baby and who won the local football game. Peggy Gordon topped $70,000 last year selling educational supplies that police and sheriff's departments take on visits to schools.

Salatino believes that employees who have established solid relationships with their customers earn significantly more money than those who have not been able to foster good relationships with customers. Therefore, when hiring telemarketing individuals, he looks for individuals with who have excellent communications skills (especially listening), are respectful of customers' points of view, have an "upbeat" attitude, and are highly self-motivated. Salatino also knows that customers rarely show gratitude and his telemarketers must take personal credit for the positive results as well as blame when things go bad. Finally, Salatino looks for people who recognize their own strengths and limitations and who thrive on taking the initiative without being told what to do all the time.

Questions
1. What kind of reinforcers does Salatino use to motivate his salespeople?
2. What kind of reinforcement schedule is used by Great Northern American to pay salespeople?
3. If you were Salatino, how might the concept of self-efficacy help you hire successful salespeople?

chapter 6

Motivating Employees

Learning Goals

After studying this chapter, you should be able to:

1
Explain basic motivational processes.

2
Describe two basic human needs approaches to motivation.

3
Explain how to design motivating jobs.

4
Describe how expectations can lead to high performance.

5
Explain how treating individuals fairly influences their motivation to work.

Learning Content

Working at Starbucks

Starbucks is everywhere. It is the world's largest specialty coffee retailer with more than 16,000 shops in more than 35 countries—and that doesn't include more than 7,000 shops operated by franchisees in airports and shopping centers. The company also owns Seattle's Best Coffee and Torrefazione Italia coffee brands. It has about 160,000 employees on its payroll serving more than 30 million customers a week. Annual sales exceed $10 billion. Because of recent layoffs and store closings, Howard Schultz, Starbucks' founder and CEO, sent a message to all partners emphasizing the need to reduce costs while paying attention to Starbucks' culture.

Starbucks has been named one of *Fortune* magazine's "100 Best Companies to Work for in America" for the past several years. Sheri Southern, vice president of partner resources for Starbucks, believes that Starbucks' success is strongly influenced by its individuals, called *partners*. Starbucks doesn't just sell coffee, it sells an experience and that experience is totally dependent on the attitudes and skills of the partners who serve customers. According to Alicia Caceres, a recruiter for Starbucks, Starbucks really understands Gen Y partners. Gen Y individuals (born from 1982 through 2000) want a good work/life balance and ready opportunities for advancement. They tend to bring value systems that put relationships first and quality of life very high on their lists. Southern knows what kinds of individuals will make good partners: those who are adaptable, dependable, and passionate team players. Keeping Gen

Y individuals means finding ways to motivate these individuals. All partners who work a minimum 20 hours a week receive medical and dental coverage, vacation days, and stock options as part of Starbucks Bean Stock Program. Eligible partners can choose health coverage from two managed care plans. Offering comprehensive benefits is a core value of the company and it takes priority over other benefits even when Starbucks is facing difficult economic times.

Because Starbucks partners are young and healthy, Starbucks has relatively low health-benefit costs. The company also provides disability and life insurance, a discounted stock purchase plan, and a retirement savings plan with company matching contributions. According to Southern, these benefits provide a meaningful incentive for partners, particularly those working part time, to stay with the company. This reduces Starbucks' recruiting and training costs.

LYNNE SLADKY/AP PHOTO

To learn more about Starbucks, go to www.starbucks.com.

Caceres observes that Gen Y individuals are on the go and that their attention span is a little shorter than other individuals'. Therefore, Starbucks' training focuses on being clear and concise, lasting no more than 30 to 35 minutes at a time. She has also learned that partners want rapid gratification. In-store sales competitions now last no more than a weekend, compared to the past when they lasted a week. Starbucks recognizes that its partners tend to be educated, passionate, philanthropic, and entrepreneurial. Starbucks provides grants to nonprofit organizations based on the number of hours partners volunteer on qualified projects. The purpose of the program is to offer a way to recognize and support each partner's personal volunteer efforts. This means that relationships—professional and personal—are keyed for partners.

Starbucks' mentoring program is designed to give partners the opportunity to learn new skills and provide them with a clear career path. Through its internal social networking site, MyPartnerCareer.Com, partners are encouraged to create a profile page, network with other partners, and learn about career opportunities at Starbucks. Caceres has found that partners respond with higher commitment and productivity when they know that they are truly listened to by others.[1]

Alicia Caceres and other leaders at Starbucks say that their greatest challenge is to attract, develop, and manage a worldwide workforce. Many Gen Y types don't like working for big companies because of their impersonality and size. Caceres and CEO Howard Schultz believe that Starbucks' motivational programs enable it to remain an attractive place to work. Therefore, Starbucks' motivational programs include the following features: (1) a list of duties to be performed, (2) the number of hours an employee is required to work, (3) the pay schedule and timetable for the distribution of work schedules, (4) current employee benefits, and (5) operational rules, such as limits on switching shifts or cell phone use at work. Even in tough economic times, attracting and retaining individuals is a major concern of all managers.[2]

The question of exactly what it takes to motivate individuals to work has received a great deal of attention. We begin by exploring the basic elements of the motivational process. Then, we present four different approaches for motivating employees: (1) meeting basic human needs, (2) designing jobs that motivate individuals, (3) enhancing the belief that desired rewards can be achieved, and (4) treating individuals equitably.

Motivational Processes

Learning Goal

1. *Explain basic motivational processes.*

Motivation represents the forces acting on or within a person that cause the person to behave in a specific, goal-directed manner.[3] Because the motives of employees affect their productivity, one of management's jobs is to channel employee motivation effectively toward achieving organizational goals. However, motivation isn't the same as performance. Even the most highly motivated employees may not be successful in their jobs, especially if they don't have the competencies needed to perform the jobs or they work under unfavorable job conditions. Although job performance involves more than motivation, motivation is an important factor in achieving high performance.[4]

Experts also do not agree about everything that motivates employees—and the effects of working conditions on their careers—but they do agree that an organization needs to:

- attract individuals to the organization and encourage them to remain with it,
- allow individuals to perform the tasks for which they were hired, and

- stimulate individuals to go beyond routine performance and become creative and innovative in their work.

For an organization to be effective, it must tackle the motivational challenges involved in arousing individuals' desires to be productive members of the organization.

Core Phases

A key motivational principle states that performance is a function of a person's level of ability and motivation. This principle is often expressed by the following formula:

$$\text{Performance} = f(\text{ability} \times \text{motivation}).$$

According to this principle, no task can be performed successfully unless the person who is to carry it out has the ability to do so. **Ability** *is the person's natural talent, as well as learned competencies, for performing goal-related tasks*. Regardless of a person's competence, however, ability alone isn't enough to ensure performance at a high level. The person must also *want* to achieve a high level of performance. The multiplicative formula suggests that ability and motivation are important. If an employee is 100 percent motivated and 75 percent able to perform a task, he will probably be better than average at performing the task. However, if the same individual has only 10 percent ability, no amount of motivation will enable him to perform satisfactorily. Therefore, motivation represents an employee's desire and commitment to perform and is evidenced by his performance.

The motivational process begins with identifying a person's needs, shown as phase 1 in Figure 6.1. **Needs** *are deficiencies that a person experiences at a particular time* (phase 1). These deficiencies may be psychological (e.g., the need for recognition), physiological (e.g., the need for water, air, or food), or social (e.g., the need for friendship). Needs often

FIGURE 6.1 Core Phases of the Motivational Process

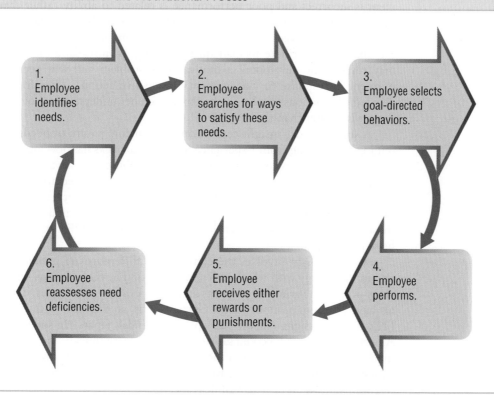

1. Employee identifies needs.

2. Employee searches for ways to satisfy these needs.

3. Employee selects goal-directed behaviors.

4. Employee performs.

5. Employee receives either rewards or punishments.

6. Employee reassesses need deficiencies.

act as energizers for behavior. That is, needs create tensions within the individual, who finds them uncomfortable and therefore is likely to make an effort (phase 2) to reduce or eliminate them.

Motivation is goal directed (phase 3). A **goal** *is a specific result that an individual wants to achieve.* An employee's goals often are driving forces, and accomplishing those goals can significantly reduce needs. J. C. Hernandez, a relationship manager at Wells Fargo Bank, has a strong drive for advancement. He expects that working long hours on highly visible projects will lead to promotions, raises, greater influence, and job security. His work on major problems facing Wells Fargo is designed to gain visibility and influence with senior leaders (phase 4). Promotions and raises are two of the ways in which organizations attempt to maintain desirable behaviors. They are signals (feedback) to employees that their needs for advancement and recognition and their behaviors are appropriate or inappropriate (phase 5). Once the employees have received either rewards or punishments, they reassess their needs (phase 6).

Insights for Leaders

The basic motivational process just described appears simple and straightforward. In the real world, of course, the process isn't as clear-cut. The first insight is that motives can only be inferred; they cannot be seen. Elaine Beecroft, head of project and systems management at Lockheed Martin, observed two employees in her department who were debugging software programs that estimate service requirements for the company. She knows that both employees are responsible for the same type of work, have received similar training, have similar competencies, and have been with the organization for about five years. One employee is able to spot problems more easily and quickly than the other. Are these observable differences a result of differences in ability or motivation? Research has shown that leaders tend to apply more pressure to a person if they feel the person is deliberately not performing up to their expectations and not due to external, uncontrollable events. Unfortunately, if the leader's assessment is incorrect and poor performance is related to ability rather than motivation, the response of increased pressure will worsen the problem. What happens if poorly performing employees feel that management is insensitive to their problems, which the employees attribute to inadequate training or unrealistic time schedules? They may respond by developing a motivational problem and will decrease their commitment in response to management's insensitive actions. Therefore, before Elaine decided what actions to take, she had to deepen her understanding of why one person's output is greater than the others.

A second leader insight centers on the dynamic nature of needs.[5] As we pointed out in the Learning from Experience feature, Starbucks has developed numerous programs in its attempts to meet partners' needs. Doing so is always difficult because, at any one time, everyone has various needs, desires, and expectations. Moreover, these factors change over time and may also conflict with each other. Employees who put in many extra hours at work to fulfill their needs for accomplishment may find that these extra work hours conflict directly with needs for affiliation and their desires to be with their families.

A third insight involves the considerable differences in individuals' motivations and in the energy with which individuals respond to them. Just as different organizations produce a variety of products and offer a variety of services, different individuals have a variety of motivations. Curtis Harris, an engineer with Texas Instruments (TI), took an assignment with TI's plant in Sendai, Japan. He soon joined a group of American leaders so he could satisfy his need to learn quickly about Japanese management practices. He discovered that Japanese do not bypass formal lines of communication. Seniority and titles are to be respected and honored and bypassing the chain of command would be a sign of disrespect.

All of these insights are things that leaders can do something about. Leaders can determine what motivates employees and use this knowledge to channel employees' energies toward the achievement of the organization's goals. With this opportunity in mind, we devote the rest of the chapter to various approaches to motivation that leaders can apply.[6]

Satisfying Human Needs

Learning Goal

2. *Describe two basic human needs approaches to motivation.*

Needs Hierarchy Model

The most widely recognized model of motivation is the **needs hierarchy model**. In this model, Abraham H. Maslow suggested *that individuals have a complex set of exceptionally strong needs, that can be arranged in a hierarchy.*[7] Underlying this hierarchy are the following basic assumptions:

- Once a need has been satisfied, its motivational role declines in importance. However, as one need is satisfied, another need gradually emerges to take its place, so individuals are always striving to satisfy some need.

- The needs network for most individuals is very complex, with several needs affecting behavior at any one time. Clearly, when someone faces an emergency, such as desperate thirst, that need dominates until it is gratified.

- Lower level needs must be satisfied, in general, before higher level needs are activated sufficiently to drive behavior.

- There are more ways of satisfying higher level than lower level needs.

This model states that a person has five types of needs: physiological, security, affiliation, esteem, and self-actualization. Figure 6.2 shows these five needs categories, arranged in Maslow's hierarchy.

FIGURE 6.2 Maslow's Needs Hierarchy

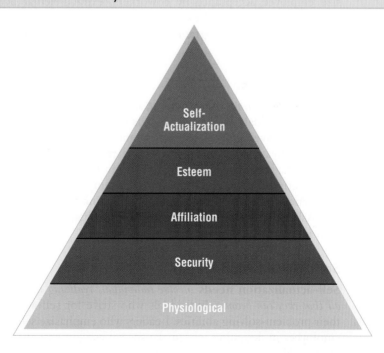

Physiological Needs

Physiological needs *are the desire for food, water, air, and shelter.* They are the lowest level in Maslow's hierarchy. Individuals concentrate on satisfying these needs before turning to higher order needs. Leaders should understand that, to the extent employees are motivated by physiological needs, their concerns do not center on the work they are doing. They will accept any job that meets those needs. Leaders who focus on physiological needs in trying to motivate subordinates assume that individuals work primarily for money. Hershey Foods, for example, offers insurance rebates to employees who live healthy lifestyles (e.g., physically fit nonsmokers) and raises premiums for those at greater risk. In this way, they offer incentives to encourage wellness activities.

Security Needs

Security needs *are the desire for safety, stability, and the absence of pain, threat, or illness.* Like physiological needs, unsatisfied security needs cause individuals to be preoccupied with satisfying them. Individuals who are motivated primarily by security needs value their jobs mainly as defenses against the loss of basic needs satisfaction. During the recent worldwide economic recession, many individuals felt that their security needs were threatened because of plant closings, permanent reductions in their company's workforce, and the outsourcing of many U.S. manufacturing jobs to foreign lands. Psychological safety is also important. By offering health, life, and disability insurance, organizations like Starbucks promote their partners' sense of security and well-being.

Affiliation Needs

Affiliation needs *are the desire for friendship, love, and a feeling of belonging.* When physiological and security needs have been satisfied, affiliation needs emerge. Leaders should realize that when affiliation needs are the primary source of motivation, individuals value their work as an opportunity for finding and establishing warm and friendly interpersonal relationships. Team leaders who believe that employees are striving primarily to satisfy these needs are likely to act supportively. They emphasize employee acceptance by coworkers, extracurricular activities (e.g., organized sports programs, cultural events, and company celebrations), and team-based norms. Starbucks' volunteer programs are examples of an organization satisfying its employees' affiliation needs.

Esteem Needs

The desires for feelings of achievement, self-worth, and recognition or respect are all **esteem needs.** Individuals with esteem needs want others to accept them for what they are and to perceive them as competent and able. Leaders who focus on esteem needs try to motivate employees with public rewards and recognition for achievements. Such leaders may use lapel pins, articles in the company paper, achievement lists on the bulletin board, and the like to foster employees' pride in their work. Mary Kay Cosmetics rewards top performers with a pink Cadillac. According to the late Mary Kay Ash, the founder of her company, individuals want recognition and praise more than money.

Self-Actualization Needs

Self-actualization needs *involve individuals realizing their full potential and becoming all that they can become.* Individuals who strive for self-actualization seek to increase their problem-solving abilities. Leaders who emphasize self-actualization may involve employees in designing jobs, make special assignments that capitalize on employees' unique skills, or give employee teams leeway in planning and implementing their work. The self-employed often have strong self-actualization needs. When Mary Kay Ash founded her firm in 1963, she acted on her belief that, when a woman puts her priorities in order, she can indeed have it all.

Insights for Leaders

Maslow's needs hierarchy model also suggests the types of behaviors that will help fulfill various needs. *The three lowest categories of needs—physiological, security, and affiliation (social)—are also known as* **deficiency needs**. According to Maslow, unless these needs are satisfied, an individual will fail to develop into a healthy person, both physically and psychologically. In contrast, *esteem and self-actualization needs are known as* **growth needs**. Satisfaction of these needs helps a person grow and develop as a human being. What needs is Starbucks satisfying for its employees?

The needs hierarchy is based on U.S. cultural values.[8] In cultures that value uncertainty avoidance, such as Japan and Greece, job security and lifelong employment are stronger motivators than self-actualization. Moreover, in Denmark, Sweden, and Norway, the value and rewards of a high quality of life are more important than productivity. Thus, social needs are stronger than self-actualization and self-esteem needs in these countries. In countries such as China, Japan, and Korea that value collectivist and community practices over individual achievements, belonging and security are considerably more important than meeting growth needs. In developing East African nations that exhibit high uncertainty avoidance, low individualism, and high power distance, the community dominates. For example, their dances and worship ceremonies are focused on the community. Clearly the motivation of employees from more collective cultures differs from that of more individualistic countries. Therefore, although the needs that Maslow identified may be universal, their importance and the ways in which they are expressed vary across cultures, as does the rank ordering of their importance.[9]

Maslow's work has received much attention from leaders, as well as psychologists.[10] Research has found that individuals are better able to satisfy their esteem and self-actualization needs than are lower level leaders; part of the reason is that top leaders have more challenging jobs and opportunities for self-actualization. Employees who work on a team have been able to satisfy their higher level needs by making decisions that affect their team and organization. At the Container Store, groups of employees are trained to perform multiple tasks, including hiring and training team members—and even firing those who fail to perform adequately. As team members learn new tasks, they start satisfying their higher level needs. The fulfillment of needs differs according to the job a person performs, a person's age and background, and the size of the company. "Not everyone is motivated in the same way. You shouldn't assume that it's a one-size-fits-all solution. You have to understand individuals' needs," says Andy Kohlberg, president of Kisco Senior Living of Carlsbad, California.

Learned Needs Model

David McClelland proposed a learned needs model of motivation that he believed to be rooted in culture.[11] He argued that everyone has three particularly important needs: for achievement, power, and affiliation. The **need for achievement** has been defined as *behavior toward competition with a standard of excellence*. In other words, individuals with a high need for achievement want to do things better and more efficiently than others have done before. The **need for power** can be defined as *the desire to influence individuals and events*. According to McClelland, there are two types of power: one that is directed toward the organization (institutional power) and one that is directed toward the self (personal power). Individuals who possess a *strong power motive* take action that affects the behaviors of others and has a strong emotional appeal. These individuals are concerned with providing status rewards to their followers. The **need for affiliation** has been defined as *the desire to be liked and to stay on good terms with others*. Individuals who have a *strong affiliation motive* tend to establish, maintain, and restore close personal relationships with others. A recent Gallup survey found that employees who have a best friend at work are more engaged and productive than those who do not report having a good friend at work.[12]

McClelland has studied achievement motivation extensively, especially with regard to entrepreneurship. His **achievement motivation model** *states that individuals are motivated according to the strength of their desire either to perform in terms of a standard of excellence or to succeed in competitive situations*. According to McClelland, almost all individuals believe that they have an "achievement motive," but probably only about 10 percent of the U.S. population is strongly motivated to achieve. The amount of achievement motivation that individuals have depends on their childhood, their personal and occupational experiences, and the type of organization for which they work. Table 6.1 shows an application of McClelland's model to managing others.

According to McClelland's model, motives are "stored" in the preconscious mind just below the level of full awareness. They lie between the conscious and

TABLE 6.1   Learned Needs Model

FOCUS ON	ACHIEVEMENT	AFFILIATION	POWER	
			PERSONALIZED POWER	SOCIALIZED POWER
Motives	Improve their personal performance and meet or exceed standards of excellence	Maintain close, friendly relationships	Be strong and influence others, making them feel weak	Help people feel stronger and more capable
Potential positive effects	Meet or surpass a self-imposed standard	Establish, restore, or maintain warm relationships	Perform powerful actions	Perform powerful actions
	Accomplish something new	Be liked and accepted	Control, influence, or persuade people	Persuade people
	Plan the long-term advancement of your career	Participate in group activities, primarily for social reasons	Impress people inside or outside the company	Impress people inside or outside the company
Potential negative effects	Try to do things or set the pace themselves	Worry more about people than performance	Be coercive and ruthless	Coach and teach
	Express impatience with poor performers	Look for ways to create harmony	Control and manipulate others	Be democratic and involve others
	Give little positive feedback	Avoid giving negative feedback	Look out for their own interests and reputations	Be highly supportive
	Give few directions or instructions			Focus on the team rather than themselves

Source: Adapted from Spreier, S. W., Fontaine, M. H., and Malloy, R. L. Leadership run amok. *Harvard Business Review*, 2006, 84(6), 75.

the unconscious, in the area of daydreams, where individuals talk to themselves without quite being aware of it. A basic premise of the model is that the pattern of these daydreams can be tested and that individuals can be taught to change their motivation by changing these daydreams.

Measuring Achievement Motivation

McClelland measured the strength of a person's achievement motivation with the **Thematic Apperception Test (TAT)**. *The TAT uses unstructured pictures that may arouse many kinds of reactions in the person being tested.* Examples include an inkblot that a person can perceive as many different objects or a picture that can generate a variety of stories. There is no right or wrong answer, and the person isn't given a limited set of alternatives from which to choose. A major goal of the TAT is to obtain the individual's own perception of the world. The TAT is called a *projective method* because it emphasizes individual perceptions of stimuli, the meaning each individual gives to them, and how each individual organizes them (recall the discussion of perception in Chapter 4).

One projective test involves looking at the picture shown in Figure 6.3 for 10 to 15 seconds and then writing a short story about it that answers the following questions:

- What are individuals doing in this picture?
- What is being felt? What is being thought? By whom?
- How will it come out? What will happen?

FIGURE 6.3 Sample Picture Used in a Projective Test

MANCHAN/DIGITAL VISION/GETTY IMAGES

Write your own story about the picture in 75 to 100 words. Then compare it with the following story written by Susan Reed, general manager, at Innovative Hospice Care[13]:

> The four individuals are working as a team to accomplish the task of getting a woman over a wall. She probably couldn't make it without the help of her teammates. They all have duties—pushing, pulling, grabbing—to perform in getting her over the wall. The woman is excited about accomplishing this task and is counting on her teammates to help her. After they achieve their goal, they can relax knowing that they reached their goal of helping a teammate.

What motivational profile did you identify? Does it match this person's?

Characteristics of High Achievers

Self-motivated high achievers have three main characteristics. First, they like to set their own *goals*. Seldom content to drift aimlessly and let life happen to them, they nearly always are trying to accomplish something. High achievers seek the challenge of making tough decisions. They are selective about the goals to which they commit themselves. Hence, they are unlikely to automatically accept goals that other individuals, including their superiors, attempt to select for them. They exercise self-control over their behaviors, especially the ways in which they pursue the goals they select. They tend to seek advice or help only from experts who can provide needed knowledge or skills. High achievers prefer to be fully responsible for attaining their goals. If they win, they want the credit; if they lose, they accept the blame. For example, assume that you are given a choice between rolling dice with one chance in three of winning, or working on a problem with one chance in three of solving the problem in the time allotted. Which would you choose? A high achiever would choose to work on the problem, even though rolling the dice is obviously less work and the odds of winning are the same. High achievers prefer to work at a problem rather than leave the outcome to chance or to other individuals.

Second, high achievers avoid selecting extremely difficult goals. They prefer *moderate goals* that are neither so easy that attaining them provides no satisfaction nor so difficult that attaining them is more a matter of luck than ability. They gauge what is possible and then select as difficult a goal as they think they can attain. The game of ring toss illustrates this point. Most carnivals have ring toss games that require participants to throw rings over a peg from some minimum distance but specify no maximum distance. Imagine the same game but with individuals allowed to stand at any distance they want from the peg. Some will throw more or less randomly, standing close and then far away. Those with high-achievement motivation will seem to calculate carefully where they should stand to have the greatest chance of winning a prize and still feel challenged. These individuals seem to stand at a distance that isn't so close as to make the task ridiculously easy and isn't so far away as to make it impossible. They set a distance moderately far away from which they can potentially ring a peg. Thus, they set personal challenges and enjoy tasks that will stretch their abilities.

Third, high achievers prefer tasks that provide *immediate feedback*. Because of the goal's importance to them, they like to know how well they're doing. That's one reason why the high achiever often chooses a professional career, a sales career, or entrepreneurial activities. Golf appeals to most high achievers: Golfers can compare their scores to par for the course, to their own previous performance on the course, and to their opponents' scores; performance is related to both feedback (score) and goal (par). It also provides immediate feedback because a person earns an individual score and receives feedback following each shot. There are no teammates to coordinate with or cover a mistake. The ultimate responsibility for your shot is yours.

Financial Incentives

Money has a complex effect on high achievers. They usually value their services highly and place a high price tag on them. High achievers are usually self-confident. They are aware of their abilities and limitations and thus are confident when they choose to do a particular job. They are unlikely to remain very long in an organization that doesn't pay them well. Whether an incentive plan actually increases their performance is an open question because they normally work at peak efficiency. They value money as a strong symbol of their achievement and adequacy. A financial incentive may create dissatisfaction if they feel that it inadequately reflects their contributions.

When achievement motivation is operating, outstanding performance on a challenging task is likely. However, achievement motivation doesn't operate when high achievers are performing routine or boring tasks or when there is no competition against goals. An example of a high achiever is John Schnatter, founder of Papa John's Pizza. Schnatter's drive is to become number one in the $28 billion dollar pizza industry.[14]

Self competency

John Schnatter of Papa John's Pizza

As a high school student working at a local pizza shop in Jeffersonville, Indiana, Schnatter in the early 1980s realized that there were no national takeout pizza chains. So in 1984, he knocked out a broom closet located in the back of his father's tavern, sold his prized Z28 Camaro, purchased $1,600 worth of used restaurant equipment, and began selling pizzas to the tavern's customers. The business grew so fast that he decided to move next door. He eventually opened his first Papa John's restaurant in 1985.

Today, Papa John's operates the third largest pizza chain behind Pizza Hut and Domino's in the delivery and takeout pizza market with more than 3,000 pizzerias worldwide and sales of more than $1.1 billion dollars annually. With 27 percent of the market share, Schnatter's goal is to take market share away from Pizza Hut (which has about 38 percent) and Domino's (which has about 30 percent) by having better ingredients, making a better pizza, and expanding internationally especially in the United Kingdom, Asia, and China. He has achieved remarkable results by being singularly obsessive about high quality and performance. He preaches to his employees about pizza in very passionate terms. He requires all employees to memorize the company's Six Core Values,

John Schnatter, founder and president of Papa John's Pizza.

TARO YAMASAKI/TIME LIFE PICTURES/GETTY IMAGES

including stay focused, customer satisfaction must be superior, and individuals are priority No. 1 *always*—and calls on employees during meetings to stand up and shout them out. He created a Ten Point Perfect Pizza Scale that measures the quality of pizzas. For example, pieces of the toppings should not touch, there should be no "peaks or valleys" along the pizza's border, all mushrooms should be sliced to a quarter inch, and no splotchy coloring should appear on the crust. The employee newsletter carries articles such as "The Papa John's Black Olive Story" or "The Papa John's Tomato Story." Such articles inform employees about how special ingredients are used to make Papa John's pizza.

At headquarters in Louisville, Kentucky, most employees (including Schnatter) wear Papa John's teal-blue polo shirts, with Pizza Wars embroidered across them. Employees even have their own clothing embroidered with Papa John's logo.

Recognizing that international consumers have different tastes (e.g., baby lobster pizza in China) and get their pizza delivered by scooters or bicycles, rather than automobile as in the United States, Schnatter believes that Papa John's can grow by 32 percent a year in these markets. By 2010, Schnatter wants Papa John's to be the number one pizza brand in the world in terms of name recognition and by 2014, the leader in sales.

To learn more about Papa John's, go to **www.papajohns.com.**

Insights for Leaders

McClelland and his associates at McBer and Company have conducted most of the research supporting the learned needs motivation model.[15] They have found that high needs for institutional power and achievement are critical for high-performing leaders. Individuals with these high needs are particularly good at increasing morale, creating clear expectations for performance, and getting others to work for the good of the organization. Interestingly the need for institutional power is more important for managerial success than the need for achievement. Individuals high in need for achievement tend to be reluctant to delegate work to others and to be patient when working toward long-term objectives, both of which are behaviors that are often necessary for effective leaders. Individuals with a high need for achievement are often attracted to organizations that have a pay-for-performance reward system because they know that if they perform, they will be financially rewarded. Finally, their research has found that successful CEOs are high in institutional power and achievement but low in affiliation needs. Why? Senior leaders often make difficult decisions and cannot worry too much about whether their decisions are liked by others.

> ### Across Cultures Insight
>
> We must be willing to reexamine our international partners' needs and offer them more chances to satisfy these at work and enhance their lives. Partners in China must be able to deliver unparalleled experiences for our customers for us to be successful.
>
> *Martin Coles, President, Starbucks Coffee International*

The following insights for leaders are recommended to foster achievement motivation in employees:

- Arrange tasks so that employees receive periodic feedback on their performance. Feedback enables employees to modify their behaviors as necessary.

- Provide good role models of achievement. Employees should be encouraged to have heroes to emulate.

- Help employees modify their self-images. High-achievement individuals accept themselves and seek job challenges and responsibilities.

- Guide employee aspirations. Employees should think about setting realistic goals and the ways in which they can attain them.

- Make it known that leaders who have been successful are those who are higher in power motivation than in affiliation motivation.

One of the main problems with the learned needs motivation model is also its greatest strengths. The TAT method is valuable because it allows the researcher to tap the preconscious motives of individuals. This method has some advantages over questionnaires, but the interpretation of a story is more of an art than a science. As a result, the method's reliability is open to question. The permanency of the model's three needs has also been questioned. Further research is needed to explore the model's validity.[16]

Designing Jobs

Motivator–Hygiene Model

Learning Goal

3. Explain how to design motivating jobs.

In a recent survey, 41 percent of employees were very satisfied with their jobs.[17] What are the reasons for high job satisfaction? Frederick Herzberg and his associates have found the answer to this question. They asked individuals to tell them when they felt exceptionally good about their jobs and when they felt exceptionally bad about their jobs. As shown in Table 6.2, individuals identified somewhat different things when they felt good or bad about their jobs. From this study they developed the *two-factor theory,* better known as the **motivator–hygiene model**, *which proposes that two sets of factors— motivators and hygienes—are the primary causes of job satisfaction and job dissatisfaction.*[18]

Motivator Factors

Motivator factors *include the work itself, recognition, advancement, and responsibility.* These factors are related to an individual's positive feelings about the job and to the content of the job itself. These positive feelings, in turn, are associated with the individual's experiences of achievement, recognition, and responsibility. They reflect lasting rather than temporary achievement in the work setting. In other words, motivators are **intrinsic factors**, *which are directly related to the job and are largely internal to the individual.* The organization's policies may have only an indirect impact on them. But, by defining exceptional performance, for example, an organization may enable individuals to feel that they have performed their tasks exceptionally well. Look back at the chapter-opening Learning from Experience feature and identify some of the motivators that Starbucks uses.

Hygiene Factors

Hygiene factors *include company policy and administration, technical supervision, salary, fringe benefits, working conditions, job security, and interpersonal relations.* These factors are associated with an individual's negative feelings about the job and are related to the environment in which the job is performed. Hygiene factors are **extrinsic factors**,

TABLE 6.2 Sources of Job Satisfaction and Job Dissatisfaction

MOTIVATOR FACTORS THAT AFFECT JOB SATISFACTION	HYGIENE FACTORS THAT AFFECT JOB DISSATISFACTION
• Achievement	• Organizational rules and policies
• Advancement	• Relationships with coworkers
• Autonomy	• Relationships with supervisors
• Challenge	• Salary
• Feedback	• Security
• Responsibility	• Working conditions

or factors external to the job. They serve as rewards for high performance only if the organization recognizes high performance. Save Mart Supermarkets rewarded three employees with a Dodge Challenger car for their excellence in customer service. It believes that giving employees rewards, such as cars, cruises, and consumer electronics, motivates them to drive for service excellence. Do you agree with these types of rewards for motivating employees? Can you identify the hygiene factors used by Starbucks to attract new employees?

It is important to note that those factors that lead to job satisfaction are not the same as those factors that lead to job dissatisfaction. Job security, benefits, and feeling safe cannot increase employee job satisfaction, but if these are *not* present, they can lead to job dissatisfaction.

Job Characteristics Model

The job characteristics model is one of the best known approaches to job design.[19] The job characteristics model uses Herzberg's recommendations of adding motivators to a person's job and minimizing the use of hygiene factors. Before reading further, complete the *Designing a Challenging Job* questionnaire found in Table 6.3.

Framework

The **job characteristics model** *involves increasing the amounts of skill variety, task identity, task significance, autonomy, and feedback in a job.* The model proposes that the levels of these job characteristics affect three critical psychological states: (1) experienced meaningfulness of the tasks performed, (2) experienced personal responsibility for task outcomes, and (3) knowledge of the results of task performance. If all three

---

TABLE 6.3 Designing a Challenging Job

Directions

The following list contains statements that could be used to describe a job. Please indicate the extent to which you agree or disagree with each statement as a description of a job you currently hold or have held, by writing the appropriate number next to the statement. Try to be as objective as you can in answering.

1	2	3	4	5
Strongly Disagree	**Disagree**	**Uncertain**	**Agree**	**Strongly Agree**

This job . . .

_____ 1. provides much variety.

_____ 2. permits me to be left on my own to do my work.

_____ 3. is arranged so that I often have the opportunity to see jobs or projects through to completion.

_____ 4. provides feedback on how well I am doing as I am working.

_____ 5. is relatively significant in my organization.

_____ 6. gives me considerable opportunity for independence and freedom in how I do the work.

_____ 7. provides different responsibilities.

_____ 8. enables me to find out how well I am doing.

_____ 9. is important in the broader scheme of things.

_____ 10. provides an opportunity for independent thought and action.

_____ 11. provides me with a considerable variety of work.

_____ 12. is arranged so that I have the opportunity to complete the work I start.

_____ 13. provides me with the feeling that I know whether I am performing well or poorly.

_____ 14. is arranged so that I have the chance to do a job from the beginning to the end (i.e., a chance to do the whole job).

_____ 15. is one where a lot of other people can be affected by how well the work gets done.

Scoring

For each of the five scales, compute a score by summing the answers to the designated questions.

Score

Skill variety: Sum the points for items 1, 7, and 11. ___

Task identity: Sum the points for items 3, 12, and 14. ___

Task significance: Sum the points for items 5, 9, and 15. ___

Autonomy: Sum the points for items 2, 6, and 10. ___

Job feedback: Sum the points for items 4, 8, and 13. ___

Total Score: ___

Summary Interpretation

A total score of 60-75 suggests that the core job characteristics contribute to an overall positive psychological state for you and, in turn, lead to desirable personal and work outcomes. A total score of 15-30 suggests the opposite. You can develop your own job profile by using the totals on the scales in the questionnaire, each of which has a score range of 3-15. You can calculate an overall measure of job enrichment, called the motivating potential score (MPS), as follows.

$$MPS = \frac{skill\ variety + task\ identity + task\ significance}{3} \times autonomy \times feedback$$

The MPS formula sums the scores for skill variety, task identity, and task significance and divides the total by 3. Thus, the combination of these three job characteristics has the same weight as autonomy and job feedback. This is because the job characteristics enrichment model requires that both *experienced responsibility* and *knowledge of results* be present for high internal job motivation. This outcome can be achieved only if reasonable degrees of autonomy and job feedback are present. The minimum MPS score is 1, and the maximum possible MPS score is 3,375. A clearly positive MPS score starts at 1,728, and a purely neutral MPS score is 729 (based on an average score of 9 per scale).

Questions

1. Visit any fast-food restaurant. Evaluate the motivating potential score of the order taker. As a manager, how might you redesign this job to increase its motivating potential score?

2. Why is a high motivating potential score more likely to lead to higher job performance than a low motivating potential score?

psychological states are positive, a reinforcing cycle of strong work motivation based on self-generated rewards is activated. A job without meaningfulness, responsibility, and feedback is incomplete and doesn't strongly motivate an employee. Figure 6.4 illustrates the elements of the job characteristic model and their relationships.

Job Characteristics

Five job characteristics hold the key to this model. They are defined as follows:

1. **Skill variety**—*the extent to which a job requires a variety of employee competencies to carry out the work*

2. **Task identity**—*the extent to which a job requires an employee to complete a whole and identifiable piece of work, that is, doing a task from beginning to end with a visible outcome*

3. **Task significance**—*the extent to which an employee perceives the job as having a substantial impact on the lives of other individuals, whether those individuals are within or outside the organization*

4. **Autonomy**—*the extent to which the job provides empowerment and discretion to an employee in scheduling tasks and in determining procedures to be used in carrying out those tasks*

5. **Job feedback**—*the extent to which carrying out job-related tasks provides direct and clear information about the effectiveness of an employee's performance.*

FIGURE 6.4 Job Characteristics Enrichment Model

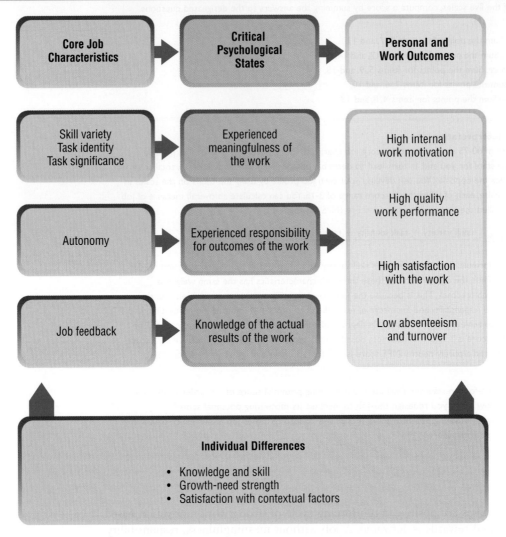

Source: J. Richard Hackman & Greg R. Oldham, *Work Redesign* (Prentice Hall Organizational Development Series), 1st © 1980. Reproduced by permission of Pearson Education, Inc. Upper Saddle River, New Jersey.

Individual Differences

The individual differences (see Figure 6.4) identified in this model influence how employees respond to enriched jobs. They include knowledge and skills, strength of growth needs, and satisfaction with contextual factors. These individual differences have an impact on the relationship between job characteristics and personal or work outcomes in several important ways. Leaders, therefore, should consider them when designing or redesigning jobs.

Employees with the *knowledge* and *skills* needed to perform an enriched job effectively are likely to have positive feelings about the tasks they perform. Employees unable to perform an enriched job may experience frustration, stress, and job dissatisfaction. These feelings and attitudes may be especially intense for employees who desire to do a good job but realize that they are performing poorly because they lack the necessary skills and knowledge. Accordingly, assessing carefully the competencies of employees whose jobs are to be enriched is essential. A training and development program may be needed along with an enrichment program to help such employees attain the needed competencies.

The extent to which an individual desires the opportunity for self-direction, learning, and personal accomplishment at work is called **growth-need strength**. This concept is essentially the same as Maslow's esteem and self-actualization needs concepts. Individuals with high growth needs tend to respond favorably to job enrichment programs. They experience greater satisfaction from work and are more highly motivated than individuals who have low growth needs. High growth-need individuals are generally absent less and produce better quality work when their jobs are enriched.

Contextual factors *include cultural values, organizational policies and administration, technical supervision, salary and benefit programs, interpersonal relations, travel requirements, and work conditions (lighting, heat, safety hazards, and the like).* The extent to which employees are satisfied with contextual factors at work often influences their willingness or ability to respond positively to enriched jobs. Contextual factors are similar to hygiene factors. Employees who are extremely dissatisfied with their superiors, salary levels, and safety measures are less likely to respond favorably to enriched jobs than are employees who are satisfied with these conditions. Other contextual factors (e.g., organizational culture, power and the political process, travel requirements, and team norms) also can affect employee responses to their jobs.

Insights for Leaders

The two most widely used approaches recommended to leaders for designing enriched jobs are vertical loading and the formation of natural work teams.

Vertical loading *is the delegation to employees of responsibilities and tasks that were formerly reserved for management or staff specialists.* Vertical loading includes the empowerment of employees to:

- set schedules, determine work methods, and decide when and how to check on the quality of the work produced;

- make their own decisions about when to start and stop work, when to take breaks, and how to assign priorities; and

- seek solutions to problems on their own, consulting with others only as necessary, rather than calling immediately for the manager when problems arise.

The formation of *natural teams* combines individual jobs into a formally recognized unit (e.g., a section, team, or department). The criteria for the groupings are logical and meaningful to the employee and include the following:

- *Geographic:* Sales individuals or information technology consultants might be given a particular region of the state or country as their territory.

- *Types of business:* Insurance claims adjusters might be assigned to teams that serve specific types of businesses, such as utilities, manufacturers, or retailers.

- *Organizational:* Word-processing operators might be given work that originates in a particular department.

- *Alphabetic or numeric:* File clerks could be made responsible for materials in specified alphabetical groups (A to D, E to H, and so on); library-shelf readers might check books in a certain range of the library's cataloging system.

- *Customer groups:* Employees of a public utility or consulting firm might be assigned to particular industrial or commercial accounts.

Many companies have used job enrichment recommendations to help them reduce turnover and absenteeism. Scott Kerslake, CEO of Athleta Corporation, a sports apparel company, tells his 60 employees to put themselves and their personal needs before jobs. Athleta's turnover rate is less than 1 percent in an industry that averages 38 percent, and employees are getting their work done because each employee is cross-trained and can fill in for one another as needed.[20]

To show the benefits of enriched jobs, the following Teams Competency feature illustrates how SEI Investments uses job enrichment concepts to maintain and increase productivity at its Oaks, Pennsylvania, headquarters.[21] After reading this feature, you should be able to identify the five job characteristics and methods used by SEI to enrich employees' jobs.

Teams competency

SEI Investments

The first sign that there's something unusual about SEI investments, a $1.3 billion financial company, is the design of its headquarters building. On the outside, it looks like a Playskool version of a farm. On the inside, it looks like a beehive. All the furniture is on wheels so that employees can create their own work area. Colorful cables spiral down from the ceiling, carrying electricity, Internet access, and telephone cords. SEI has created a software map to locate all employees. There are no secretaries, walls, or organizational charts. Tasks are distributed among its 98 employees. Some employees work in self-managed teams, while others do their job alone. Employees come together to solve a problem and disband when the task is completed. Different employees work on different financial models until the task is completed.

All employees know the goals that matter most: earnings per share and assets under management. SEI leaders establish corporate-level goals and these then translate into goals for teams. Alfred West, SEI's president, explained, "Our goals are passed out to the teams and they

figure out what they have to do to hit them. Once the team understands its goal(s), everyone on that team drives toward that goal." West and other leaders do not care how many vacation days employees take so long as they hit their goals.

To motivate employees to work in teams, West and other leaders follow this basic principle: Self-management teams need leaders. Employees must demonstrate certain competencies to be chosen by their coworkers to be team leaders. Team leaders need communication, ethical, diversity, and other competencies that enable them to use a "soft" hand to guide the team. It's up to the team leaders to describe the project in a passionate manner so that others will want to join the team.

Teamwork is a major part of an individual's pay. SEI uses incentive team-based compensation whereby employees can earn anywhere from 10 to 100 percent of their base pay. "Each team gets a pot of money," says West, and then decides how to distribute it. Some teams have members vote on each other's bonuses, while other teams defer to the team leader.

To learn more about SEI, go to **www.seic.com.**

Cultural Influences

One of the important themes of this book is recognizing and addressing cultural diversity in the workforce. As U.S. organizations continue to expand overseas and foreign organizations establish manufacturing operations in Canada, Mexico, and the United States, leaders must be aware of cultural differences and how these differences can affect the motivation of employees. Cultural values are a part of the *contextual factors* with which leaders must deal. In Chapter 3, we noted the five cultural factors—individualism/collectivism, power distance, uncertainty avoidance, gender role orientation, and long-term orientation—that impact individuals' attitudes. With the passage of the North American Free Trade Agreement (NAFTA), leaders and employees in North America began working more closely with others who don't necessarily share similar cultural values about the motivation to work. It didn't take U.S. leaders very long to realize that employees in Mexico have different attitudes toward work.[22] In the United States, workers generally favor taking the initiative, having individual responsibility, and taking failure personally. They are competitive, have high goals, and live for the future. Workers are comfortable operating in a group, with the group sharing both successes and failures. They tend to be cooperative, flexible, and enjoy life as it is now.

In Mexico, employees usually are not willing to speak up and take the initiative. Employees also prefer a management style that is more authoritarian and do not like to work in teams because of the emphasis on family rather than work teams. However, if the work team is seen as part of an individual's extended family, the team can be a powerful motivator. Employees' priorities are family, religion, and work—in that order. During the year, plant managers host family dinners to celebrate anniversaries of employees who have worked there 5, 10, 15, and 20 years. Employees may use the company clubhouse for weddings, baptisms, anniversary parties, and other family celebrations. Organizations also host a family day during which employees' families can tour the plant, enjoy entertainment and food, and participate in soccer, bowling, and other events. It is very important for families to be invited and involved.

The length of the typical workday in Mexico is similar to the U.S. workday: 8 A.M. to 5:30 P.M., but there are many differences: Employees are picked up by a company bus at various locations throughout the city. Employees like to eat their main meal in the middle of the day, the cost of which is heavily subsidized (as much as 70 percent) by the company. Interestingly, the leaders serve the employees this meal. They are mirroring a family setting, in which parents serve their children. This is not only good for morale, but it also reinforces cultural values.

Influencing Performance Expectations

Learning Goal

4. *Describe how expectations can lead to high performance.*

Besides creating jobs that individuals find challenging and rewarding, individuals are also motivated by the belief that they can expect to achieve certain rewards by working hard to attain them. Believing that you can get an "A" in this class by expending enough effort can be a very effective motivator. If you can clearly see a link between your study behaviors (effort) and your grade (goal), you will be motivated to study. If you see no link, why study at all? To better understand this approach to motivation, let's focus on you as we take a look at the expectancy model and explain how this model motivates you to choose certain behaviors and not others.

Expectancy Model

The **expectancy model** *states that individuals are motivated to work when they believe that they can achieve things they want from their jobs.* These things might include satisfaction of safety needs, the excitement of doing a challenging task, or the ability to set and achieve difficult goals. A basic premise of the expectancy model is that you are a rational person. Think about what you have to do to be rewarded and how much the rewards mean to you before you perform your job. Four assumptions about the causes of behavior in organizations provide the basis for this model.

First, a combination of forces in you and the environment determines behavior. Neither you nor the environment alone determines behavior. You go to work or attend school with expectations that are based on your needs, motivations, and past experiences. These factors influence how you will respond to an organization, but they can and do change over time.

Second, you decide your own behavior in organizations, even though many constraints are placed on your individual behavior (e.g., through rules, technology, and work-group norms). You probably make two kinds of conscious decisions: (1) decisions about coming to work, staying with the same organization, and joining other organizations (membership decisions); and (2) decisions about how much to produce, how hard to work, and the quality of workmanship (job-performance decisions).

Third, you and others have different needs and goals. You want particular rewards from your work, depending on your gender, race, age, and other characteristics. Of the many rewards that Starbucks offers to its employees, which do you find attractive? Why? In five years, are these same rewards likely to be attractive to you?

Fourth, you decide among alternatives based on your perceptions of whether a specific behavior will lead to a desired outcome. You do what you perceive will lead to desired outcomes and avoid doing what you perceive will lead to undesirable outcomes.[23]

In general, the expectancy model holds that you have your own needs and ideas about what you desire from your work (rewards). You act on these needs and ideas when making decisions about what organization to join and how hard to work. This model also holds that you are not inherently motivated or unmotivated but rather that motivation depends on the situations that you face and how your responses to these situations fit your needs.

To help you understand the expectancy model, we must define its most important variables and explain how they operate. The variables are first-level and second-level outcomes, expectancy, instrumentality, and valence.

First-Level and Second-Level Outcomes

The results of behaviors associated with doing the job itself are called **first-level outcomes**. They include level of performance, amount of absenteeism, and quality of work. **Second-level outcomes** *are the rewards (either positive or negative) that first-level outcomes are likely to produce.* They include a pay increase, promotion, and acceptance by coworkers, job security, reprimands, and dismissal.

Expectancy

Expectancy *is the belief that a particular level of effort will be followed by a particular level of performance.* An individual's degree of expectancy can vary from the belief that there is absolutely no relationship between your effort and performance to the certainty that a given level of effort will result in a corresponding level of performance. Expectancy has a value ranging from 0, indicating you see no chance that a first-level outcome will occur after the behavior, to +1, indicating certainty that a particular first-level outcome will follow from your behavior. For example, if you believe that you have no chance of getting a good grade on the next exam by studying this chapter, your expectancy value would be 0. Having this expectancy, you shouldn't study this chapter. Good teachers will do things that help their students believe that hard work will help them to achieve better grades.

Instrumentality

Instrumentality *is the relationship between first-level outcomes and second-level outcomes.* It can have values ranging from −1 to +1. A −1 indicates that your attainment of a second-level outcome is inversely related to the achievement of a first-level outcome. For example, assume that you are an IBM engineer and want to be accepted as a member of your work group, but it has a norm for an acceptable level of performance. If you violate this norm, your work group won't accept you. Therefore, you limit your performance so as not to violate the group's norm. A +1 indicates that the first-level outcome is positively related to the second-level outcome. For example, if you received an A on all your exams, the probability that you would achieve your desired second-level outcome (passing this course) approaches +1. If there were no relationship between your performance on a test and either passing or failing this course, your instrumentality would be 0.

Valence

Valence *is an individual's preference for a particular second-level outcome.* Outcomes having a positive valence include being respected by friends and coworkers, performing meaningful work, having job security, and earning enough money to support a family. Valence is just not the amount of the reward you receive, but what it means to you upon receiving it. Outcomes having a negative valence are things that you want to avoid, such as being laid off, being passed over for a promotion, or being discharged for sexual harassment. An outcome is positive when it is preferred and negative when it is not preferred or is to be avoided. An outcome has a valence of 0 when you are indifferent about receiving it.

Putting It All Together

In brief, the expectancy model holds that work motivation is determined by your beliefs regarding effort–performance relationships and the desirability of various work outcomes associated with different performance levels. Simply put, you can remember the model's important features by the saying:

> I exert work effort to achieve performance that leads to valued work-related outcomes.

The Expectancy Model in Action

The five key variables just defined and discussed lead to a general expectancy model of motivation, as shown in Figure 6.5. Motivation is the force that causes you to expend effort, but effort alone isn't enough. Unless you believe that effort will lead to some desired performance level (first-level outcome), you won't make much of an effort. The effort–performance relationship is based on a perception of the difficulty of achieving a particular behavior (say, working for an A in this course) and the probability of achieving that behavior. On the one hand, you may have a high expectancy that, if you attend class, study the book, take good notes, and prepare for exams, you can achieve an A in this class. That expectancy is likely to translate into making the effort required on those activities to get an A. On the other hand, you may believe that, even if you attend class, study the book, take good notes, and prepare for exams, your chances of getting an A are only 20 percent. That expectancy is likely to keep you from expending the effort required on these activities to achieve an A.

Performance level is important in obtaining desired second-level outcomes. Figure 6.5 shows six desirable second-level outcomes: self-confidence, self-esteem, personal happiness, overall GPA this semester, approval of other individuals, and respect of other individuals. In general, if you believe that a particular level of performance (A, B, C, D, or F) will lead to these desired outcomes, you are more likely to try to perform at that level. If you really desire these six second-level outcomes and you can achieve them only if you get an A in this course, the instrumentality between receiving an A and these six outcomes will be positive. But, if you believe that getting an A in this course means that you won't gain personal happiness and the approval and respect of other individuals, the instrumentality between an A and these outcomes will be negative. That is, if the higher the grade, the less likely you are to experience personal happiness, you might choose not to get an A in this course. Once you have made this choice, you will lessen your effort and start cutting class, not studying for exams, and so on.

Researchers are still working on ways to assess how leaders can use this model to affectively motivate others to achieve high performance. This has presented some

FIGURE 6.5 Expectancy Model in Action

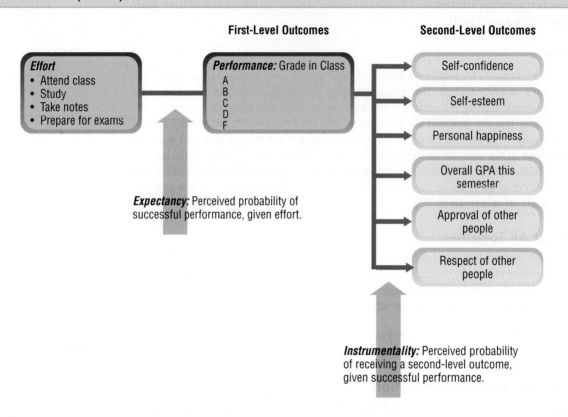

Source: VandeWalle, D., Cron, W. L., and Slocum, J. W. The role of goal orientation following performance feedback. *Journal of Applied Psychology,* 2001, 86, 629–640.

problems.[24] First, the model tries to predict choice or the amount of effort an individual will expend on one or more tasks. However, there is little agreement about what constitutes choice or effort for different individuals. Therefore, this important variable is difficult to measure accurately. Second, the model doesn't specify which second-level outcomes are important to a particular individual in a given situation. Although researchers are addressing this issue, comparison of the limited results to date is often difficult because each study is unique. Take another look at the second-level outcomes in Figure 6.5. Would you choose them? What others might you choose? Third, the model contains an implicit assumption that motivation is a conscious choice process. That is, the individual consciously calculates the pain or pleasure that he expects to attain or avoid when making a choice. The expectancy model says nothing about unconscious motivation or personality characteristics. In fact, individuals often do not make conscious choices about which outcomes to seek. Can you recall going through this process concerning your grade while taking this course? Lastly, the model works best in cultures that emphasize internal attribution. The expectancy model works best when individuals in a culture believe that they can control their work environment and their own behavior, such as in the United States, Canada, and the United Kingdom.[25]

In cultures where individuals believe the work environment and their own behavior aren't completely under their control, such as in Brazil, Saudi Arabia, Iran, Japan, and China, the assumptions of the model might not be valid. For example, a Canadian manager in Japan decided to promote one of her young female Japanese sales representatives to manager (a status and monetary reward). To her surprise, the promotion diminished the new Japanese manager's performance. Why? Japanese have a high need for harmony—to fit in with their colleagues. The promotion, an individualistic reward, separated the new manager from her colleagues, embarrassed her, and therefore diminished her work motivation.

Insights for Leaders

The expectancy model has some important implications for motivating employees. These implications can be grouped into a number of suggestions for action.[26] We present five of these here for your consideration:

1. Leaders should try to determine the outcomes that each employee values. Two ways of doing so are observing employee reactions to different rewards and asking employees about the types of rewards they want from their jobs. However, leaders must recognize that employees can and do change their minds about desired outcomes over time.

2. Leaders should define good, adequate, and poor performance in terms that are observable and measurable. Employees need to understand what is expected of them and how these expectations affect performance. When Johnson & Johnson announced the production of a new examination table for doctors, its salespeople wanted to know what behaviors, such as cold-calling on new accounts or trying to sell the new tables to their existing accounts, would lead to more sales. To the extent that the company was able to train its salespeople in selling its new product, it was able to link salespeople's efforts with performance.[27]

> ### Self Insight
>
> High performance is not a matter of chance, it is a matter of choice; it is not a thing to be waited for, it is a thing to be achieved.
>
> *Kevin Elliott, Senior Vice President, Merchandising, 7-11*

3. Leaders should be sure that the desired levels of performance set for employees can be attained. If employees feel that the level of performance necessary to get a reward is higher than they can reasonably achieve, their motivation to perform will be low. For example, Nordstrom tells its employees: "Respond to Unreasonable Customer Requests." Employees are urged to keep scrapbooks that record "heroic" acts, such as hand-delivering items purchased by phone to the airport for a customer leaving on a last-minute business trip, changing a customer's flat tire, or paying a customer's parking ticket when in-store gift wrapping has taken longer than expected. It is hardly surprising that Nordstrom pays its employees much more than they could earn at a rival store. For those who love to sell and can meet its demanding standards, Nordstrom is nirvana.

4. Leaders should directly link the specific performance they desire to the outcomes desired by employees. Recall the discussion in Chapter 5 of how operant conditioning principles can be applied to improve performance. If an employee has achieved the desired level of performance for a promotion, the employee should be promoted as soon as possible. If a high level of motivation is to be created and maintained, it is extremely important for employees to see clearly and quickly the reward process at work. Concrete acts must accompany statements of intent in linking performance to rewards.

5. Leaders should never forget that perceptions, not reality, determine motivation. Too often, leaders misunderstand the behavior of employees because they tend to rely on their own perceptions of the situation and forget that employees' perceptions may be different.

Intuit uses many of these suggested actions to motivate its employees. As described in the following Communication Competency feature, managers at Intuit understand that there are many ways besides a simple "thank-you" to communicate how much they appreciate the efforts of their employees.[28]

Communication **competency**

Intuit

Headquartered in Mountain View, California, Intuit is a $3.1 billion maker of well-known software programs, such as Quicken and Turbo-Tax. With more than 8,000 employees, the company has offices throughout the United States, United Kingdom, and Canada.

One of the internal programs that makes Intuit a great place to work is their Thanks Program. At each company location, giving out a small award is a part of every leader's job. The company's philosophy is that awards should only be given to people who perform well above what is expected. Getting an award is special—it is Intuit's way to recognize excellence and communicate appreciation. Leaders decide the criteria that will be used for giving awards and they decide what awards to give. Examples of awards given include gift certificates to restaurants, movie tickets, handwritten thank-you notes, and a Night-on-the-Town. Why do employees get these awards? Some employees get awards for going beyond the call of duty to help out their

colleagues. Some get awards for making suggestions that save Intuit money. Some get awards for technical programming achievement or outstanding service to the community. Intuit gives team leaders the authority to make decisions about awards.

To make sure that team leaders use sound judgment when giving awards, Intuit developed a website designed to help team leaders. It explains the importance of linking the awards they give to achieving business objectives. It also helps leaders ensure that awards given out are valued by individuals. To monitor how employees feel about the Thanks Program, Intuit includes a question in the annual employee satisfaction survey that reads "I am rewarded and recognized when I do a great job." As long as employees continue to agree with this statement, Intuit senior leaders believe that the Thanks Program is working and helping Intuit to be named as one of *Fortune's* "100 Best Companies to Work for in America."

To learn more about Intuit, go to **www.intuit.com.**

Ensuring Equity

Learning Goal

5. *Explain how treating individuals fairly influences their motivation to work.*

Feelings of unfairness were among the most frequent sources of job dissatisfaction reported to Herzberg and his associates. Some researchers have made this desire for fairness, justice, or equity a central focus of their models. Assume that you just received a 5 percent raise. Will this raise lead to higher performance, lower performance, or no change in performance? Are you satisfied with this increase? Would your satisfaction with this pay increase vary with the consumer price index, with what you expected to get, or with what others in the organization performing the same job and at the same performance level received?

Equity Model: Balancing Inputs and Outcomes

The **equity model** *focuses on an individual's feelings of how fairly she is treated in comparison with others.*[29] It is based on the belief that individuals are motivated to maintain a fair, or equitable, relationship between themselves and others and to avoid relationships that are unfair or inequitable. It contains two major assumptions. The first is that individuals evaluate their interpersonal relationships just as they would evaluate the buying or selling of a home, shares of stock, or a car. The model views relationships as exchange processes in which individuals make contributions and expect certain results. The second assumption is that individuals don't operate in a vacuum. They compare their situations to those of the others in the organization to determine fairness. In other words, what happens to individuals is important when they compare themselves to similar others (e.g., coworkers, relatives, and neighbors).

General Equity Model

The equity model is based on the comparison of two variables: inputs and outcomes. **Inputs** *represent what an individual contributes to an exchange;* **outcomes** *are what an individual receives from the exchange.* Some typical inputs and outcomes are shown in Table 6.4. A word of caution: The items in the two lists aren't paired and don't represent specific exchanges.

According to the equity model, individuals assign weights to various inputs and outcomes according to their perceptions of the situation. Because most situations involve multiple inputs and outcomes, the weighting process isn't precise. However, individuals generally can distinguish between important and less important inputs and outcomes. After they arrive at a ratio of inputs and outcomes for themselves, they compare it with their perceived ratios of inputs and outcomes of others who are in the same or a similar situation. These relevant others become the objects of comparison for individuals in determining whether they feel equitably treated.[30]

Equity exists whenever the perceived ratio of a person's outcomes to inputs equals that for relevant others. For example, an individual may feel properly paid in terms of what he puts into a job compared to what other workers are getting for their inputs. Inequity exists when the perceived ratios of outcomes to inputs are unequal. Jay Loar, a director of program engineering at Lockheed Martin, works harder than his coworkers, completes all his tasks on time even though others don't, and puts in longer hours than others, but receives the same pay raise as the others. What happens? Loar believes that his inputs are greater than those of his coworkers and therefore should merit a greater pay raise. Inequity can also occur when individuals are overpaid. In this case, the overpaid employees might be motivated by guilt or social pressure to work harder to reduce the imbalance between their inputs and outcomes and those of their coworkers.

Consequences of Inequity

Inequity *causes tension within and among individuals.* Tension isn't pleasurable, so individuals are motivated to reduce it to a tolerable level, as illustrated in Figure 6.6. To

---

TABLE 6.4 Examples of Inputs and Outputs in Organizations

INPUTS	OUTCOMES
Age	Challenging job assignments
Attendance	Fringe benefits
Interpersonal skills, communication skills	Job perquisites (parking space or office location)
Job effort (long hours)	Job security
Level of education	Monotony
Past experience	Promotion
Performance	Recognition
Personal appearance	Responsibility
Seniority	Salary
Social status	Seniority benefits
Technical skills	Status symbols
Training	Working conditions

FIGURE 6.6 Inequity as a Motivational Process

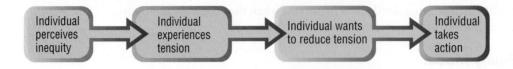

reduce a perceived inequity and the corresponding level of tension, individuals may choose to act in one or more of the following ways:

- Individuals may either increase or decrease their inputs to what they feel to be an equitable level. For example, individuals who think they are underpaid may reduce the quantity of their production, work shorter hours, and be absent more frequently.

- Individuals may change their outcomes to restore equity. Many union organizers try to attract nonmembers by pledging to improve working conditions, hours, and pay without an increase in employee effort (input).

- Individuals may distort their own inputs and outcomes. As opposed to actually changing inputs or outcomes, individuals may mentally distort them to achieve a more favorable balance. For example, individuals who feel inequitably treated may distort how hard they work ("This job is a piece of cake") or attempt to increase the importance of the job to the organization ("This really is an important job!").

- Individuals may leave the organization or request a transfer to another department. In doing so, they hope to find an equitable balance.

- Individuals may shift to a new reference group to reduce the source of the inequity. The star high school athlete who doesn't get a scholarship to a major university might decide that a smaller school has more advantages, thereby justifying a need to look at smaller schools when making a selection.

- Individuals may distort the inputs or outcomes of others. They may come to believe that others in a comparison group actually work harder than they do and therefore deserve greater rewards.

How susceptible are you to the temptation to cheat a little in order to achieve what you believe is equitable?[31] To find out, take a few minutes to consider the situations posed in the following Ethics Competency feature. When individuals feel it is okay to cheat in order to meet their goals and obtain the rewards offered by their employer, whose responsibility is it? Are the employees at fault? Is their management responsible? Or is it just "the system" that is to blame?[32]

Ethics competency

How Tempted Are You?

Read each situation. Then indicate how tempted you feel to act in ways that might be viewed as questionable. Try to be candid. Your answers will help you recognize tempting situations when they present themselves.

How Tempted Are You?

Not at All; Would Not Cheat					Very Tempted; Probably Would Cheat
1	2	3	4	5	6	7

_____ 1. You work in a retail store selling clothes. Your goal for the week is to sell $4,000 worth of merchandise. Achieving your goal earns you a red recognition ribbon for your name badge. You have sold $3,950 with one hour of time left. A colleague is in a similar situation and proposes that you each spend $50 to purchase items from each other to achieve your goals. Do you go along with your friend's suggestion?

_____ 2. The situation is almost the same as #1 above, but the reward is different. Besides the recognition ribbon, you will receive a $100 bonus if you meet your goal. Do you agree to work with your friend to reach the sales goal?

_____ 3. You work in a call center for a catalog company. The company monitors calls to measure service quality and also gives extra points to employees who process calls quickly. Your service quality is excellent but your speed is too slow. Your sister offers to help by posing as a caller. She'll keep calling until she gets you, and then ask a simple question so you can have a few fast calls. She says she learned this trick where she works, where people do it all the time. Do you tell her to call you?

_____ 4. You clean windows in homes during the summer to help pay for your college costs. You are paid by the size and number of windows you clean. You are responsible for counting the number of windows and estimating the sizes. Most of the homes you work on have a lot of windows. You are pretty sure the home owners don't really know how many windows they have. You suspect that you could easily charge for two extra windows without being caught. Do you do it?

_____ 5. You deliver frozen food products to grocery stores. To maximize profits, your employer sets goals for a variety of performance metrics. One measure used is fuel efficiency. You find it difficult to meet the fuel goals, but have figured out that one solution is to carry more products on each trip. The only space available is the passenger seat, but if you use that space you cannot keep products at the lower temperature required by state food safety regulations. You learn that other truck drivers bring their own coolers and use them to carry products in the passenger seat. They say it is the only way anyone can meet the fuel goals. Do you bring a cooler to store food on the passenger seat?

After answering all of the questions, review your ratings. Most people admit that they would be tempted to cheat in some of these situations. In which types of situations were you most tempted: When the reward was large? When the degree of cheating seemed minor? When you believed you wouldn't get caught?

Procedural Justice: Making Decisions Fairly

Equity theory focuses on the outcomes individuals receive after they have expended effort, time, or other inputs. It doesn't deal with how decisions leading to outcomes were made in the first place. Procedural justice examines the impact of the *process* used to make a decision. As we defined in Chapter 2 on page 46, *procedural justice* refers to the perceived fairness of the rules, guidelines, and processes for making decisions.[33] Procedural justice holds that employees will be more motivated to perform at a high level when they perceive as fair the procedures used to make decisions about the distribution of outcomes. Procedural justice is important to most employees. They are often motivated to attain fairness in how decisions are made, as well as in the decisions themselves.

Reactions to pay raises, for example, are greatly affected by employees' perceptions about the fairness of how the raises were determined. If in the minds of the employees the pay raises were administered fairly, the employees are usually more

DUNCAN SMITH/PHOTODISC/GETTY IMAGES

Organizational citizenship behavior may include one employee helping another with a computer problem.

satisfied with their increases than if the employees judged the procedures used to make these increases to be unfair. The perceived fairness of the procedures used to allocate pay raises is a better predictor of satisfaction than the absolute amount of pay received. ViewCast Corporation is a digital encoding company that makes equipment that digitizes live programming for transmission over the Internet. David Stoner, ViewCast's president, announced that because of the financial conditions facing the company, all salaries would be frozen. While employees were not pleased with this announcement, they understood how the recent recessions had impacted ViewCast and its industry. Many were grateful just to have a job and were willing to forgo pay raises in the short term.

In both the pay and evaluation situations, the individual can't directly control the decision but can react to the procedures used to make it. Even when a particular decision has negative outcomes for the individual, fair procedures help ensure that the individual feels that her interests are being protected.[34]

Employees' assessments of procedural justice have also been related to their trust in management, intention to leave the organization, evaluation of their supervisor, employee theft, and job satisfaction. Consider some of the relatively trivial day-to-day issues in an organization that are affected by procedural justice: decisions about who will cover the phones during lunch while others are away from their desks, the choice of the site of the company picnic, or who gets the latest software for a personal computer.

Procedural justice has also been found to affect the attitudes of workers who survive a layoff. During the recent recession when Caterpillar, Bank of America, Microsoft, and hundreds of other companies laid off thousands of employees, the survivors (those who remain on the job) are often in a good position to judge the fairness of the layoff in terms of how it was handled. When a layoff is handled fairly, survivors feel more committed to the organization than when they believe that the laid-off workers were treated unfairly. In Chapter 8, we discuss how survivors of layoffs also experience stress and some actions that they can take to relieve it.

Going Beyond the Call of Duty

In many organizations, employees perform tasks that are not formally required.[35] **Organizational citizenship behavior** *exceeds formal job duties and is often necessary for the organization's survival, including its image and acceptance.* Examples of organizational citizenship behavior include helping coworkers solve problems, making constructive suggestions, and volunteering to perform community service work (e.g., blood drives, United Way campaigns, and charity work). Although not formally required by employers, these behaviors are important in all organizations. Helping coworkers is an especially important form of organizational citizenship behavior when it comes to computers. Every organization has its computer gurus, but often it's the secretary who doesn't go to lunch who can easily fix a problem and do it without insulting the struggling user. Leaders often underestimate the amount of this informal helping that takes place in organizations.

Employees have considerable discretion over whether to engage in organizational citizenship behaviors. Employees who have been treated fairly and are satisfied are more likely to do so than employees who feel unfairly treated. Fairly treated employees engage in citizenship behaviors because they want to give something back to the organization. Most individuals desire to have fair exchanges with coworkers and others in their organization.

Barbara Thomas, manufacturing applications sales manager for Hewlett-Packard: EDS, developed a simple yet innovative method for acknowledging organizational citizenship behaviors at her office. At the beginning of the year, Thomas gives each of her 10 employees a jar containing 12 marbles. Throughout the year, employees may give marbles to others who have helped them in some way or who have provided an extraordinary service. Employees are recognized throughout the year and are proud of the number of marbles they accumulate, even though they receive no monetary reward from Thomas.

Insights for Leaders

Leaders often use the equity model in making a variety of decisions, such as taking disciplinary actions, giving pay raises, allocating office and parking space, and dispensing other perquisites (perks). The equity model leads to two primary insights for leaders. First, employees should be treated fairly. When employees believe that they are not being treated fairly, they will try to correct the situation and reduce tension by means of one or more of the types of actions identified previously in this section. A sizable inequity increases the probability that individuals will choose more than one type of action to reduce it. For example, employees may partially withdraw from the organization by being absent more often, arriving at work late, not completing assignments on time, or stealing. Leaders may try to reduce the inputs of such employees by assigning them to monotonous jobs, taking away some perks, and giving them only small pay increases.

Second, employees make decisions concerning equity only after they compare their inputs and outcomes with those of comparable employees.[36] These relevant others may be employees of the same organization or of other organizations. The latter presents major problems for leaders, who cannot control what other organizations pay their employees. For example, Ralph Sorrentino, a partner at Deloitte Consulting, hired a recent business school undergraduate for $54,500, the maximum the company could pay for the job. The new employee thought that this salary was very good until she compared it to the $65,250 that fellow graduates were getting at Boston Consulting, McKinsey, or Bain. She felt that she was being underpaid in comparison with her former classmates, causing an inequity problem for her (and the company).

The idea that fairness in organizations is determined by more than just money has received a great deal of attention from leaders. Organizational fairness is influenced by how rules and procedures are used and how much employees are consulted in decisions that affect them.

Chapter Summary

A six-stage motivational model indicates that individuals behave in certain ways to satisfy their needs. Leaders have three motivational challenges: Motives can only be inferred, needs are dynamic, and there are considerable differences in individuals' motivations.

1. Explain basic motivational processes.

Two human needs models of motivation are widely recognized. Maslow proposed that individuals have five types of needs: physiological, security, affiliation, esteem, and self-actualization, and that when a need is satisfied it no longer motivates a person. McClelland believed that individuals have three learned needs (achievement, power, and affiliation) that are rooted in the culture of a society. We focused on the role of the achievement need and indicated the characteristics associated with high achievers, including that they like to set their own moderate goals and perform tasks that give them immediate feedback.

2. Describe two basic human needs approaches to motivation.

3. *Explain how to design motivating jobs.*

Herzberg claimed that two types of factors affect a person's motivation: motivator and hygiene factors. Motivators, such as job challenge, lead to job satisfaction but not to job dissatisfaction. Hygiene factors, such as working conditions, prevent job dissatisfaction but can't lead to job satisfaction. Leaders need to structure jobs that focus on motivators because they lead to high job satisfaction and performance. The job characteristics model focuses on adding five motivators to the job (skill variety, task identity, task significance, autonomy, and feedback). Whether an employee responds favorably to an enriched job is dependent on her knowledge and skill, growth-need strength, and contextual factors.

4. *Describe how expectations can lead to high performance.*

The expectancy model holds that individuals know what they desire from work. They choose activities only after they decide that the activities will satisfy their needs. The primary components of this model are first- and second-level outcomes, expectancy, instrumentality, and valence. An individual must believe that effort expended will lead (expectancy) to some desired level of performance (first-level outcome) and that this level of performance will lead (instrumentality) to desired rewards (second-level outcomes and valences). Otherwise, the individual won't be motivated to expend the effort necessary to perform at the desired level.

5. *Explain how treating individuals fairly influences their motivation to work.*

The equity model focuses on the individual's perception of how fairly he is treated in comparison to others in similar situations. To make this judgment, an individual compares his inputs (experience, age) and outcomes (salary) to those of relevant others. If equity exists, the person isn't motivated to act. If inequity exists, the person may engage in any one of six behaviors to reduce this inequity. Both procedural justice and organizational citizenship behavior are based on the equity model and have significant implications for employees' perceptions of equity. Procedural justice examines the impact of the process (rules and procedures) used to make a decision. Organizational citizenship behaviors are employee behaviors that go above and beyond their job requirements.

Key Terms and Concepts

Ability, **159**
Achievement motivation model, **164**
Affiliation needs, **162**
Autonomy, **171**
Contextual factors, **173**
Deficiency needs, **163**
Equity model, **180**
Esteem needs, **162**
Expectancy, **176**
Expectancy model, **175**
Extrinsic factors, **169**
First-level outcomes, **176**
Goal, **160**
Growth-need strength, **173**
Growth needs, **163**
Hygiene factors, **169**
Inequity, **181**
Inputs, **181**
Instrumentality, **176**
Intrinsic factors, **169**
Job characteristics model, **170**
Job feedback, **171**

Motivating potential score (MPS), **171**
Motivation, **158**
Motivator factors, **169**
Motivator–hygiene model, **169**
Need for achievement, **163**
Need for affiliation, **164**
Need for power, **163**
Needs, **159**
Needs hierarchy model, **161**
Organizational citizenship behavior, **184**
Outcomes, **181**
Physiological needs, **162**
Second-level outcomes, **176**
Security needs, **162**
Self-actualization needs, **162**
Skill variety, **171**
Task identity, **171**
Task significance, **171**
Thematic Apperception Test (TAT), **165**
Valence, **177**
Vertical loading, **173**

Discussion Questions

1. To explore how Starbucks motivates its partners, go to www.starbucks.com. On that page, look for "career center." Click on that. What employee needs is Starbucks attempting to satisfy for its retail partners?
2. Go to www.starbucks.com, click on "about us," then click on "business ethics & compliance." Click on the link that shows all versions of Starbucks Standard of Business Conduct on the right-hand side of the screen. Scroll down to resources under which you will find Ethical Decision-Making Framework. What motivational concepts do you find Starbucks drawing on in this section?
3. Phil Jackson, after winning his tenth NBA title as a coach, said: "I don't motivate my players. You cannot motivate someone. All you can do is provide a motivating environment and the players will motivate themselves." Do you agree or disagree? What's the reasoning behind your answer?
4. Focus on some aspects of your own work in which you feel your performance is below your own expectations.

Using your answers from Table 6.3, explore some of the reasons for your level of performance.
5. How has John Schnatter, CEO of Papa John's, applied the learned needs model to motivate his employees?
6. What are your own assumptions about motivation? How do they reflect the culture in which you were raised?
7. Why is job satisfaction not strongly related to job performance?
8. Why are some individuals motivated to cheat?
9. Imagine that you have been selected for an office visit at SEI Investments for a financial analyst position. What are leaders looking for in that interview to decide whether or not to hire you?
10. Imagine that you have just been selected to become a new sales manager for Dell Computers in Mexico. What would you do to motivate employees to become high producers?

Experiential Exercise and Case

Experiential Exercise: Self Competency[37]

What Do You Want from Your Job?

We have listed the 16 most often mentioned characteristics that individuals want from their jobs in random order. Please rank them in order of both their importance to you and then in terms of satisfaction for you. Rank these characteristics 1 (most important), 2 (next most important), and so on, through 16 (least important). Use the same procedure to rank satisfaction. Then compare your answers with those of hundreds of managers working in a variety of jobs and industries provided at the end of this exercise.

Job Characteristics	Importance Rank	Satisfaction Rank
1. Working independently	____	____
2. Chance for promotion	____	____
3. Contact with people	____	____
4. Flexible time	____	____
5. Health insurance & other benefits	____	____
6. Interesting work	____	____
7. Work important to society	____	____
8. Job security (no layoffs)	____	____
9. Opportunity to learn	____	____
10. High income	____	____
11. Recognition from team members	____	____
12. Vacation time	____	____
13. Regular hours	____	____
14. Working close to home	____	____
15. Little job stress	____	____
16. A job in which I can help others	____	____

Questions
1. What things influenced your ranking? What motivational concepts did you rely on for making your decisions?
2. What aspects gave you the most job satisfaction? Why?

Answers given by managers
For job importance, the rank order of characteristics is 1–6; 2–14; 3–15; 4–16; 5–1; 6–2; 7–13; 8–3; 9–4; 10–11; 11–7; 12–5; 13–8; 14–12; 15–10; 16–9.
For job satisfaction, the rank order of characteristics is 1–3; 2–14; 3–2; 4–16; 5–13; 6–4; 7–9; 8–7; 9–11; 10–12; 11–15; 12–8; 13–5; 14–1; 15–6; 16–10.

Case: Communication Competency

SAS Institute[38]

Jim Goodnight founded the SAS Institute in Cary, North Carolina, in 1976. It is probably the least-well-known, major privately owned software company in the world. In simplest terms, SAS writes software that makes it possible to gather and understand data, to sift through mountains of information in order to find patterns and meaning.

SAS—which stands for "statistical analysis software"—started out as a tool for statisticians. Goodnight originally developed it to analyze agricultural-research data in North Carolina. These days Marriott Hotels uses the software to manage a frequent-visitor program; Merck & Co. and Pfizer Inc. use it to develop new drugs; the U.S. government uses SAS to calculate the Consumer Price Index. The software is not cheap. A charge of $50,000 a year for 50 users is typical. All but 2 of the 100 largest U.S. public companies use it. It sales exceed $2.2 billion annually. The company employs more than 11,000 people worldwide. It has been consistently listed among *Fortune* magazine's "100 Best Companies to Work for in America." Goodnight believes "If you treat employees as if they make a difference to the company, they will make a difference to the company."

What is unique about SAS is not the software it creates but the unusual way in which it does business. The freedom and exuberance associated with the new economy has a dark side: Work is so demanding, so all-consuming, that is can become unsatisfying. In that context, SAS may be the world's sanest company. Why?

First, there's the mood of the place. SAS operates in a competitive arena full of buzzwords—"data mining," "knowledge management"—and builds cutting-edge products that set the industry standard. Yet the one word that employees universally use to describe the company's work environment is "relaxed."

Second, there's also the stability of the company. It is an article of faith in the software business that the only way to attract and keep talented employees is to offer them stock options, along with extraordinary salaries. SAS, a private company, offers no stock, and its salaries are no better than its competition. But SAS treats its employees so well in other areas—there is no limit on how many sick days they can take; they can even stay home to care of sick family members—that employees remain committed to the company. Its employee turnover rate is low and it has never had a layoff.

Third, there's the sense of balance between work and family life found at SAS. At a time when companies are trying to mix work and family, SAS has the largest on-site day-care operation in North Carolina. To encourage families to eat lunch together, the SAS cafeteria supplies baby seats and high chairs. To encourage families to eat dinner together, the company has adopted a seven-hour workday. Indeed, most people at SAS keep work hours that are far from typical of the new economy. They leave the office by 5 P.M.

The history of the company's benefits is revealing. The story begins when SAS was still a startup in 1976—a startup with a number of women working for it. "Our women employees were two or three years into their careers—at the top of their talent curve—and they started deciding to stay home and have kids," says Jennifer Mann, vice president of human resources. "We knew and they knew that they'd have to start from scratch if they stepped out. Jim said, 'We can't lose those people. We're too small a company.' So we started providing day care in the basement. We began with 4 or 5 kids; now we have 528 (including some who attend a nearby private facility)." SAS was by no means obligated to offer day care. It couldn't, however, afford to lose its female employees. Today 51 percent of SAS managers are women. A group at the company meets monthly to discuss proposed new benefits, evaluating them in the context of a three-part test: Would the benefit accord with SAS's culture? Would it serve a significant number of employees? And would it be cost accountable—that is, would its perceived value be at least as high as it cost? Every benefit has to pass all three tests. Moreover, Goodnight points out that it is not just the benefits that keep employees at SAS, but "it's the challenge of work."

The benefits build a foundation of loyalty that supports the bottom line. The payoff starts with turnover. A typical software company of SAS's size loses 1,000 employees per year. At SAS, the number lost is about 130—which translates into almost 900 employees per year whom SAS doesn't have to replace. The result is a huge reduction in expenses for recruiting candidates, for flying them in for interviews, and for moving new hires across the country, as well as a reduction in the amount of work time lost while jobs remain unfilled. Two consulting companies—Top Gun and Hewitt—have estimated that the cost of replacing a worker runs between 1 and 2.5 times the salary of the open job. The more sophisticated the job, the higher the cost. Given a factor of 1.5 and an average SAS salary of $50,000, the company arguably saves millions a year, compared with what its competitors spend to attract new employees.

The informal environment at SAS can be misleading. This is a company built on accountability. SAS is a decentralized company, but tracks key performance data closely. From his computer, Goodnight can look up detailed sales and performance information; he can track data on technical support calls, which are sorted by product and by time-to-resolution; he can monitor bug reports in new software, noting how quickly testers and developers are eliminating flaws in products headed for release. The sense of accountability also extends to documentation. Every SAS product manual includes the names of the developers and testers who created or updated the software. The sense of accountability is so ingrained and the lines of reporting are so simple that the company needs no formal organization chart. As it grows, SAS tends to get wider—spawning new divisions—rather than adding more layers of management. Indeed, the company is so brutally flat that on the Cary campus, many of the several thousand frontline employees who work there—from housekeepers to coders with Ph.D.s—are just two or three levels in the corporate hierarchy from Jim Goodnight.

Larnell Lennon says that what surprised him most when he arrived at SAS—besides getting his own office—was how his manager spent his time. "My manager is doing what I'm doing," says Lennon. "She is in the trenches, writing code. Dr. Goodnight was once in the same group that I'm in. At my last job, my manager was just making sure that everything got done. Here, we all do that." Xan Gregg works in John Sall's group. Sall has plenty to say "about the details of how code is written," says Gregg. "That's unusual for an executive vice president. Usually managers are not very technical." Sall, an almost impossibly shy and unassuming billionaire, says that he sees himself primarily as "a statistician and a software developer—not a businessperson or a manager." Managers who understand the work that they oversee can make sure

that details don't slide. At SAS, groups agree on deadlines, and managers understand what their group does. Unrealistically optimistic promises about timetables and completion dates are relatively rare.

Questions
1. Go to *Fortune* magazine, February 2, 2009, and turn to pages 64–65 or go to **www.sas.com** and search under the heading "SAS Family." Using the criteria on these pages, evaluate the SAS Institute. Do these criteria reveal why SAS consistently makes the list of "Best Companies to Work for in America"?
2. What is motivating Jim Goodnight?
3. Would you like to work for SAS? Why or why not?

Motivation: Goal Setting and Reward Programs

Learning Goals

After studying this chapter, you should be able to:

1
Explain how goal setting affects performance.

2
State the effects of goal setting on an individual's behavior.

3
Describe reward programs for improving performance.

Learning Content

Enterprise Rent-A-Car

Enterprise Rent-A-Car was founded by Jack Crawford in 1957 and is now run by Pamela Nicholson, the company's first female president. She is ranked by *Fortune* magazine as the 44th most powerful woman in the United States. The company started out as a small auto-leasing business and moved into car rentals in the 1960s with a very different business strategy from that of Hertz, Avis, and Budget. It didn't rent cars at airports, but instead focused on customers whose cars were being repaired or who needed a rental for vacations or other special occasions. So, even though Enterprise recently acquired Vanguard Car Rental, a company that manages the Alamo Rent A Car and National Car Rental brands, which rent cars mostly at airports, more than 90 percent of Enterprise's car rental business still comes from customers in their home cities, as opposed to travelers. Enterprise has a fleet of more than 714,000 vehicles located at more than 7,000 rental shops and revenues exceeding $13 billion.

The company opens, on average, one new office every business day somewhere in the world. Enterprise has contracts with 70 percent of the body shops and insurance companies in North America. It provides body shops with a website tracking device that enables these shops to post estimates about when a customer's car will be ready. This saves the body shop mechanics time because they no longer have to phone customers and give them estimates about when their cars will be ready.

Enterprise's success can be traced to how it manages its employees. All employees start as trainees just like

Nicholson did in 1981 after graduating from the University of Missouri. For nine months, she washed cars, listened to customers, wrote rental agreements, and settled customer complaints. She was taught that if a customer forgets his driver's license, drive the customer home to pick it up. If the license has expired, drive the customer to a state motor vehicle registration department to obtain a new one. Based on her performance, she was promoted to assistant branch manager and during the next 12 years was promoted through the ranks to regional vice president. She assumed additional responsibilities as her performance exceeded expectations, including establishing the first national preferred provider rental agreements between Enterprise and auto manufacturers.

All Enterprise employees start with a low base salary and earn a sliding percentage of profits generated by their office. Thus, they are highly motivated to push extra services, such as GPS systems, children's car seats, collision-damage insurance, and the like. They are also rewarded

JAMES A. FINLEY/AP PHOTO

To learn more about Enterprise Rent-A-Car, go to www.enterprise.com.

for steering customers to other Enterprise outlets that sell preowned cars.

Employee turnover is a problem in the car-rental industry. Major car rental companies, such as Avis, Budget, National, and Hertz, average more than 30 percent turnover a year, because of the long hours and stress of handling customer complaints. Enterprise, however, has turnover of less than 25 percent. One reason for the lower turnover is that employees work in teams of less than 10 people. In these teams, employees can develop personal relationships with their teammates.

Nicholson has set some metrics for how to measure the company's performance. Enterprise has developed a performance management system that is simple to use and easy for employees to understand. The Enterprise Service Quality Index asks more than 175,000 customers each month these questions: (1) How would you rate your overall experience? and (2) Would you consider renting from Enterprise again? The goal is to achieve a 90 percent positive response. Employees get a chance to see how they're performing and to respond accordingly. "These scores drive everything at Enterprise," Nicholson explains. "It determines how much money you make and how you progress in the company. If the office's Index is below the mark, no one in that branch moves. If it's above, everyone gets ahead. It's equitable and it has had a big impact on teamwork."[1]

To survive in today's competitive global market, setting challenging goals that take into account the crucial factors of time and quality and providing feedback to employees are no longer options. They must happen!

The motivational practices that produced the achievements at Enterprise are based on setting goals, developing feedback systems, and providing reward systems that get individuals to strive to reach those goals. Goals play an important part in motivating individuals to strive for high performance. The basic concepts in goal setting remain an important source for motivating employees. Regardless of the nature of their specific achievements, successful people tend to set goals. Their lives are goal oriented. This is true for politicians, students, and leaders in all sorts of organizations.[2]

In this chapter, we begin by presenting a model of goal setting and performance based on the individual. In the next section, we discuss the effects of goal setting on employees' behaviors. Finally, we conclude the chapter with a discussion of four commonly used reward programs that reinforce desired behaviors of employees.

Model of Goal Setting and Performance

Learning Goal

1. *Explain how goal setting affects performance.*

Goals *are future outcomes (results) that individuals and groups desire and strive to achieve.*[3] An example of an individual goal is "I intend to graduate with a 3.2 grade point average by the end of the spring semester, 2012." **Goal setting** *is the process of specifying desired outcomes toward which individuals, teams, departments, and organizations will strive and is intended to increase organizational efficiency and effectiveness.*

Importance of Goal Setting

The goal-setting process is no easy task, but the effort is not only worthwhile, it is also becoming essential for success in today's highly competitive global business environment. Just as organizations strive to achieve certain goals, individuals also are motivated to strive for and attain goals. In fact, the goal-setting process is one of the most important motivational tools for affecting the performance of employees in organizations. In this section we consider one of the most widely accepted models of goal setting and indicate how goal-setting techniques can be applied to motivate individuals and teams.

Figure 7.1 presents a model of individual goal setting and performance.[4] According to this goal-setting model, goal setting has four motivational aspects:

- *Goals direct attention.* That is, they focus an employee's attention on what is relevant and important. What two goals does Enterprise track?

- *Goals regulate effort.* Not only do goals direct our attention, they motivate us to act. What motivates employees at Enterprise?

- *Goals increase persistence.* Persistence represents the effort expended on a task over an extended period of time. Persistent people find ways to overcome obstacles and avoid making excuses if they fail.

- *Goals foster strategies and action programs.* Goals encourage people to develop strategies and action programs that enable them to achieve their goals. Give an example of this at Enterprise.

FIGURE 7.1 Motivational Aspects of Goal Setting

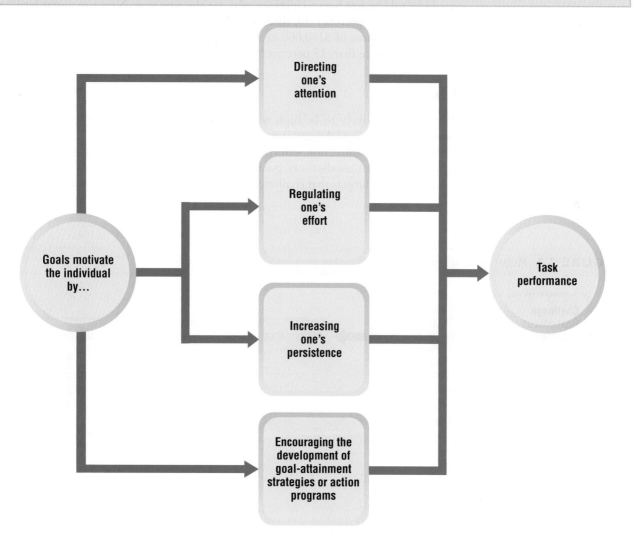

Source: E. A. Locke and G. P. Latham, *A Theory of Goal Setting and Task Performance.* Englewood Cliffs, NJ: Prentice Hall, 1990. © 1990. Adapted and reprinted by permission of the author.

Figure 7.2 presents a version of this model. It shows the key variables and the general relationships that can lead to high individual performance, some of which we have discussed in previous chapters. The basic idea behind the model in Figure 7.2 is that a goal serves as a motivator because it allows people to compare their present performance with that required to achieve the goal. To the extent that people believe they will fall short of a goal, they will feel dissatisfied and work harder to attain it as long as they believe that it can be achieved.

Having a goal also may improve performance because the goal makes clear the type and level of performance expected. At PPG, a Pittsburgh-based paint and glass manufacturer, employee objectives are called SMART goals, an acronym for "Specific, Measurable, Agreed-upon by the employee and manager, Realistic, and Timebound." Being *specific* means goals should be stated in precise rather than vague terms. *Measurable* refers to assessing the extent to which a goal is accomplished. Goals should be *attainable, challenging*, and *realistic*. Impossible goals reduce motivation because people do not like to fail. *Results-oriented* goals are needed to support the organization's mission. At Enterprise if they get a positive response to their survey questions, which are results oriented, then the organization's goal will be achieved. Finally, *timebound* means that goals need to specify target dates for completion.

Before the SMART goal system was implemented at PPG, a sales manager would be told by her boss to increase sales for the next year. Now she might be asked to develop, by September 30, three new customers in three Southeast regions with annual sales volume of $250,000 each. Using SMART, sales performance at PPG has increased by more than 25 percent.[5]

Challenge

Performance is likely to be high when (1) challenging goals have been set, (2) the moderators (ability, goal commitment, feedback, and task complexity) are present, and (3) the mediators (direction, effort, persistence, and task strategy) are operating (see Figure 7.2). Stated another way, goal setting is the process of developing, negotiating, and establishing targets that challenge the individual. Employees with unclear goals or

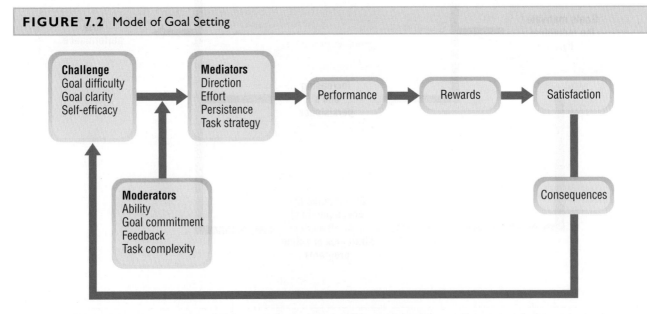

FIGURE 7.2 Model of Goal Setting

Source: Adapted from Locke, E. A., and Lantham, G. P. *A theory of Goal Setting and Task Performance.* Englewood Cliffs, NJ: Prentice Hall, 1990, 253.

no goals are more prone to work slowly, perform poorly, exhibit a lack of interest, and accomplish less than employees whose goals are clear and challenging. In addition, employees with clearly defined goals appear to be more energetic and productive. They get things done on time and then move on to other activities (and goals).

Goals may be implicit or explicit, vague or clearly defined, and self-imposed or externally imposed. Whatever their form, goals serve to guide the individual's time and effort. Two key attributes of challenging goals are particularly important:

- **Goal difficulty**: *A goal should be challenging but not impossible to achieve.* If it is too easy, the individual may delay or approach the goal lackadaisically. If it is too difficult, the individual may not really accept the goal and thus not try to meet it.

- **Goal clarity**: *A goal must be clear and specific if it is to be useful in directing effort.* The individual thus will know what is expected and not have to guess. For instance, Enterprise rental agents are expected to answer customers' calls by the third ring of the phone.

Clear and challenging goals lead to higher performance than do vague or general goals. **Management by objectives (MBO)** *is a management system that uses goal difficulty and goal clarity as its foundation for motivating employees.* In essence, this management system involves managers and employees in jointly setting goals for performance and personal development, periodically evaluating employees' progress toward achieving these goals, and then rewarding employees. One company that has made extensive use of management by objectives is Cardinal Health, an integrated health-care solutions provider located in Dublin, Ohio. At the beginning of each year, all 55,000 employees are asked to identify at least one performance objective that supports one of the four corporate goals of growth, operational excellence, leadership development, and customer focus. In addition, at the end of the year, managers are asked to rate employees on a set of core leadership competencies, such as self-management, teamwork, sound judgment, and relationship building. By combining the ratings from the manager with those from the employees, Cardinal has been able to show how MBO leads to both employee satisfaction and profits. Cardinal managers have found that goals that are difficult but not impossible lead to higher performance than do easy goals. However, unrealistically high goals may not be accepted or may lead to high performance only in the short run.[6] Individuals eventually get discouraged and stop trying, as predicted by the expectancy model (see Chapter 6).

Along with goal difficulty and clarity, a third key factor that influences the establishment of challenging goals is self-efficacy. In Chapter 5, we defined *self-efficacy* as the individual's estimate of his or her own ability to perform a specific task in a particular situation. As might be expected, individuals who set high goals perform at a high level when they also have high self-efficacy. A person's self-efficacy is dependent on the task. For example, a golfer with a low handicap has high self-efficacy on the golf course. But the same person might have low self-efficacy when meeting sales goals for a new piece of equipment that the company has just introduced.[7]

With clear and challenging goals, employee behaviors are more likely to be focused on job-related tasks, high levels of performance, and goal achievement. Table 7.1 provides a summary of the key links between goal setting and individual performance.

The following Teams Competency feature illustrates how people in teams use the basic concepts of goal challenge, goal clarity, and self-efficacy to instill teamwork. In NASCAR racing, it costs $20 million to $25 million a year to keep a driver and crew in all 36 NASCAR races. Winning is often determined by how well the pit crew performs tire changes, refueling, and other tasks. Most times, the difference between

> ### Communication Insight
>
> The list of things that we tell new employees includes an opportunity to be a part of something big, respect others, straight talk, open dialogue, good stewardship and a commitment to learn from each other.
>
> *Pamela Nicholson, President, Enterprise Rent-A-Car*

TABLE 7.1 Impact of Goals on Performance

WHEN GOALS ARE	PERFORMANCE WILL TEND TO BE
Specific and clear	Higher
Vague	Lower
Difficult and challenging	Higher
Easy and boring	Lower
Set participatively	Higher
Set by management (top down)	Lower
Accepted by employees	Higher
Rejected by employees	Lower
Accompanied by rewards	Higher
Unrelated to rewards	Lower

winning a NASCAR race and placing second is a matter of seconds and these can either be gained or lost when the driver comes in for a pit stop. Fourteen seconds or less is a goal for pit crews to make all the needed changes for the driver. For example, if the crew drops a lug nut when changing a tire, the driver will spend about half a second longer in the pit, which is equivalent to about 180 feet of track.[8]

Teams competency

Jeff Gordon's Rainbow Warriors

The Rainbow Warriors, Jeff Gordon's pit crew, work as a team with Gordon to win races.

During his career, Jeff Gordon has driven in 545 NASCAR races and won 67 races, four titles, and nearly $98 million in prize money. He's won more Chase Sprint Cup races than any other NASCAR driver. Gordon and his Rainbow Warriors, so named because of their rainbow-striped jump-suits, decided to go their separate ways after the 2007 racing season and Gordon did not win a Chase Sprint Cup race in 2008 for the first time in his career. In 2009, Steve Letarte, considered by many NASCAR people to be a premier crew chief, and the Rainbow Warriors rejoined Gordon's team. Together, Gordon and Letarte credit much of their success to the pit crew.

When the Rainbow Warriors crew was assembled, its members decided to do things differently. In the past, mechanics who had worked on a race car all week also suited up on Sunday to work as the pit crew. The car was the number one priority. The crew relied on horsepower and the driver to win the race. Pit crews didn't practice and set goals. But Letarte and Gordon knew that all drivers have essentially the same equipment, so they thought the ingredient that would separate winning from losing drivers was their ability to create a team. They decided to have two crews: The first crew was responsible for the mechanics of the car (e.g., engine and suspension components); the second—the pit crew—was responsible for the car during the race.

Under Letarte and Gordon's leadership, the team hired a coach to develop the teamwork competency of the pit crew. Training included rope climbing, scaling walls, wind sprints, guys carrying each other on their backs, and the like. All members of the pit crew were trained to perform all necessary tasks so that they could rotate tasks among themselves, depending on race conditions. By analyzing other NASCAR drivers, Letarte determined that if Gordon's car could leave the pit 1 second faster than the competition's cars, Gordon would gain 300 feet on the competition (a car going 200 mph travels nearly 300 feet a second). The pit crew set a goal of having the car exit the pit in 13 seconds or less because races are often decided by less than 1 second between the first and second place car.

During a race, all crew members listen to each other on their scanners. They use special code words to signal whether they are changing two or four tires when Gordon pulls into the pit. The crew also determines whether to gas the car fully or just to put in enough gas to finish the race. Letarte and his crew also determine when Gordon should come in for a pit stop. Before the race, all the Rainbow Warriors sit in a circle to discuss race strategy. The circle symbolizes that the team is stronger than any individual. When Gordon wins a race, signs a personal services contact, or is paid to sign autographs, all members of both crews receive a percentage of that money.

To learn more about Jeff Gordon, go to **www.jeffgordon.com.**

Moderators

Moderators act like a volume control on a TV set. By increasing or decreasing moderators, the strength between challenge and the mediators changes. Figure 7.2 shows the four moderators that buffer the relationship between goals and performance: ability, goal commitment, feedback, and task complexity. We begin with ability because it limits an individual's capacity to respond to a challenge.

Ability

The relation of goal difficulty to performance is curvilinear, not linear. That is, performance levels off as the limits of a person's ability are approached. In Chapter 6, we learned that motivation is an important part of a person's ability to perform. Some individuals believe that they have the ability to acquire new competencies and master new situations. They seek challenging new assignments that open their eyes to new ways of doing tasks. Others believe that their ability to complete a task is relatively stable and avoid placing themselves in a situation in which they might receive a negative evaluation.[9]

Goal Commitment

The second factor, **goal commitment**, *refers to an individual's determination to reach a goal, regardless of whether the goal was set by that person or someone else.*[10] What is your goal commitment in this class? Take a minute and complete the questionnaire in Table 7.2. Your commitment to achieve a goal is likely to be stronger if you make it publicly, if you have a strong need for achievement, and if you believe that you can control the activities that will help you reach that goal.

The effect of participation on goal commitment is complex. Positive goal commitment is more likely if employees participate in setting their goals, which often leads to a sense of ownership. In a study by the Corporate Leadership Council of 50,000 employees, the council found that increased commitment can lead to a 57 percent improvement in discretionary effort—employees' willingness to exceed the normal job duties. That effort produces, on the average, a 20 percent individual performance improvement and an 87 percent reduction in a desire to leave the organization. Not expecting or wanting to be involved in goal setting reduces the importance of employee participation in terms of goal commitment. Even when a leader has to assign goals without employee participation, doing so leads to more focused efforts and better performance than if no goals are set or if a person is told simply to "do their best."[11]

TABLE 7.2 Goal Commitment Questionnaire					

	RESPONSE CATEGORY				
ITEM	**STRONGLY AGREE**	**AGREE**	**UNDECIDED**	**DISAGREE**	**STRONGLY DISAGREE**
1. I am strongly committed to achieving a grade of _____.	_____	_____	_____	_____	_____
2. I am willing to expend the effort needed to achieve this goal.	_____	_____	_____	_____	_____
3. I really care about achieving this grade.	_____	_____	_____	_____	_____
4. Much personal satisfaction can be gained if I achieve this grade.	_____	_____	_____	_____	_____
5. Revising my goal, depending on how other classes go, isn't likely.	_____	_____	_____	_____	_____
6. A lot would have to happen to abandon my grade goal.	_____	_____	_____	_____	_____
7. Expecting to reach my grade goal in this class is realistic for me.	_____	_____	_____	_____	_____

Scoring:

Give yourself 5 points for each Strongly Agree response; 4 points for each Agree response; 3 points for each Undecided response; 2 points for each Disagree response; and 1 point for each Strongly Disagree response. The higher your total score, the greater is your commitment to achieve your grade goal in this class.

Source: Adapted from Cron, Wm. L., Slocum, J. W., Jr., VandeWalle, D. and Fu, F. The role of goal orientation on negative emotions and goal setting when initial performance falls short of one's performance goal. *Human Performance*, 2005, 18(1), 55–80; Hollenbeck, J. R. Williams, C. R., and Klein, H. J. An empirical examination of the antecedents of commitment to goals. *Journal of Applied Psychology*, 1989, 74, 18–23.

The expected rewards for achieving goals play an important role in the degree of goal commitment. The greater the extent to which employees believe that positive rewards (merit pay raises, bonuses, promotions, opportunities to perform interesting tasks, and the like) are contingent on achieving goals, the greater is their commitment to the goals. At Enterprise, it didn't take long for employees to realize how the goal of 90 percent positive response to the Enterprise Service Quality Index impacted their pay. Similarly, if employees expect to be punished for not achieving goals, the probability of goal commitment also is higher. Of course, punishment and the fear of punishment as the primary means of guiding behavior may create long-term problems (see Chapter 5).

Employees compare expected rewards against rewards actually received. If received rewards are consistent with expected rewards, the reward system is likely to continue to support goal commitment. If employees think that the rewards they receive are much less than the rewards they expected, they may perceive inequity. If perceived or actual inequity exists, employees eventually reduce their goal commitment.

Teamwork and peer pressure are other factors that affect a person's commitment to a goal. The Baylor HealthTexas Provider Network has successfully matched organizational goals with those of its employees. Carl Couch and his management team set five goals, including patient care and managing costs. Why five? Because they wanted to keep managers focused on a handful of high-priority items that were measurable. At the beginning of the year, department heads sit down with their employees and communicate these five goals. They discuss how the employee plans to contribute to reaching each goal. If the manager of the emergency department needs to reduce his operating costs by 5 percent, he can log into the hospital intranet to see how costs are tracking for his department during the year. A person's pay increase is based on individual and team performance. If a manager is not reaching her goal, then human resource managers give her input on how to achieve the goal. According to Ziad Haydar, director of quality control, "The monitoring system holds managers accountable to motivate their staffs to their highest performance."[12]

Feedback

Feedback makes goal setting and individual responses to goal achievement (performance) a dynamic process. **Feedback** *provides information to the employee about how well he or she is doing*. It enables the individual to relate received rewards to those expected in terms of actual performance. This comparison, in turn, can influence changes in the degree of goal commitment.[13] However, some organizations are giving employees positive feedback for just showing up. Land's End, Diamond Fiber Products, and the Scooter Store teach managers how to give positive feedback to employees using e-mails, prize packages, and public displays of appreciation. The 1,000-employee Scooter Store, for instance, has a manager who uses a power wheelchair to wheel around in while throwing confetti at employees. The manager also passes out 100 to 500 celebratory helium balloons once a week as a way of showing the company's appreciation for employees showing up. Such positive feedback, however, rarely improves performance because it is not targeted at specific goals.

Task Complexity

Task complexity *refers to the cognitive processing that is needed by a person to solve a task*. For simple tasks (e.g., answering telephones at Marriott's reservation center), the effort encouraged by challenging goals leads directly to high task performance. For more complex tasks (e.g., studying to achieve a high grade), effort doesn't lead directly to effective performance. The individual must also decide where and how to allocate effort.

Mediators

Let's assume that an individual has challenging goals and that the moderating factors support achievement of these goals. Mediators are links that join challenge and performance. How do the four links shown in Figure 7.2—direction, effort, persistence, and task strategy—affect performance? *Direction of attention* focuses behaviors on activities expected to result in goal achievement and steers the individual away from activities irrelevant to achieving the goals. At Enterprise, employees direct their attention to the two factors on the Enterprise Service Quality Index. The *effort* a person exerts usually depends on the difficulty of the goal. That is, the greater the challenge, the greater will be the effort expended, assuming that the person is committed to reaching the goal. *Persistence* involves a person's willingness to work at the task over an extended period of time until the results are achieved. Most sports require participants to practice long and hard to hone their competencies and maintain them at a high level. Finally, *task strategy* is the way in which an individual—often through experience and instruction—decides to tackle a task. That is, what to do first.

Performance

As suggested in Figure 7.2, one of the reasons why leaders and employees set goals is to achieve a level of performance that helps the entire organization achieve its goal(s). In Albuquerque, New Mexico, the Bernalillo County Parks and Recreation Department has started a program designed to create a healthy workforce. The *One Step at a Time* program was created to encourage employees to seek preventive medical care. This program awards points to employees who take care of themselves. The goal was to get 50 percent of its 400 employees to walk 10,000 steps a day by the end of its 12-week program. To track their performance, the department gave all employees pedometers to measure how many steps they actually took during the day. After reaching the desired performance level, employees were given water bottles, T-shirts, etc.[14]

Three basic types of quantitative indicators can be used to assess performance: units of production or quality (amount produced or number of errors), dollars (profits, costs, income, or sales), and time (attendance and promptness in meeting deadlines). When such measures are unavailable or inappropriate, qualitative goals (customer satisfaction, teamwork) and indicators may be used. In addition, many organizations have developed a code of ethics to support employees in setting ethical goals and making ethical decisions. Creating ethics guidelines has several advantages that the Gap, GE, and Johnson & Johnson, among others, consider important. Some of the advantages for setting ethical goals are:

- to help employees identify what their organization recognizes as acceptable behaviors,
- to legitimize the consideration of ethics as part of decision making,
- to avoid uncertainties among employees about what is right and wrong, and
- to avoid inconsistencies in decision making caused by an organizational reward system that appears to reward unethical behavior.[15]

Bonnie Nixon-Gardiner works at Hewlett-Packard (HP) and her goal is to improve the working conditions of employees in HP's overseas supply factories. As described in the following Across Cultures Competency feature, she has sought to create industry-wide changes by setting the standards for her employees and influencing what other companies should do. She understands that change cannot happen in a day, week, or even a year. If she can stimulate small changes in the way HP does its business, she feels that she has made a contribution.[16]

Across Cultures competency

Hewlett-Packard

As a program manager for HP's Supply Chain Social and Environmental Responsibility department, Bonnie Nixon-Gardiner cares about how HP treats its employees. She showed up unannounced in Long Hua, China, to inspect the working conditions at the manufacturing plant of one of HP's largest suppliers. When the company managers tried to steer her into a conference room, she refused and asked to see the manufacturing operation that employed more than 200,000 workers. She wanted to see the waste treatment center, the dorm rooms where the workers live, and the assembly line where products are assembled.

When industries such as technology suppliers and athletic gear and toy manufacturers began outsourcing manufacturing to low-wage countries, she became aware of and concerned about the sweatshop conditions that had been exposed in the media. To address those concerns, she began benchmarking how other companies monitored their suppliers. Then she set high standards for HP's suppliers. HP now has a system of 70 auditors who inspect more than 200 factories owned by 150 of their suppliers. Nixon-Gardiner also started a training program to teach Chinese suppliers how to prevent labor and environmental abuses. This was her goal: "For consumers to know that when they touch an HP product, they are guaranteed that it was made in a socially and environmentally responsible way." She also got Dell, IBM, Intel, and other companies to formulate the Electronic Industry Code of Conduct. This code bans abuses such as child labor, forced labor (use of prisoners), and excessive overtime. It also requires manufacturers to adhere to basic standards for environmental protection and participate in an inspection for monitoring working conditions in the plants. The inspection and enforcement of these standards are the responsibility of each manufacturer.

She has been tracking performance data for several years now and can see that her efforts are paying off. After six visits to one plant, the supplier had finally addressed her concerns

Hewlett-Packard factory.

one by one, which meant that the supplier had to spend lots of money to reduce employees' exposure to dangerous equipment and harmful noise. For example, during one inspection, she found that the supplier had bought an employee some flimsy orange earplugs. Not good enough for her. The plant manager described dealing with her in this way: "Dealing with Nixon-Gardiner is like being kissed and slapped at the same time. It can make you psychotic—but it needed to be done."

To learn more about HP, go to **www.hp.com**. To learn more about industry-wide standards, go to **www.eicc.info**.

Rewards

When an employee attains a high level of performance, rewards are important inducements for individuals to continue performing at that level. Rewards can be external (bonuses, paid vacations, and the like) or internal (a sense of achievement, pride in accomplishment, and feelings of success). Enterprise, PPG, and Jeff Gordon's NASCAR organization all reward people for high performance. However, what is viewed as a reward in one culture may not be viewed as a reward in another. For example, doing business in Vietnam requires the exchange of gifts during the first day of a business meeting. Although they may be small and relatively inexpensive, gifts with a company logo are highly valued. The gifts should be wrapped, but white or black paper should not be used because these colors are associated with death. In contrast, exchanging gifts at a business meeting in the United States generally is not expected. Praising an individual in public for achievement in Vietnam will embarrass the individual. Rewards are not to be given in public. Conversely, public acclaim for achievement in the United States is valued.[17]

Satisfaction

Many factors—including challenging work, interesting coworkers, salary, the opportunity to learn, and good working conditions—influence a person's satisfaction with the job (see Chapter 3). However, in the goal-setting model, the primary focus is on the employee's degree of satisfaction with performance. Employees who set extremely high, difficult goals may experience less job satisfaction than employees who set lower, more easily achievable goals. Difficult goals are less frequently achieved, and satisfaction with performance is associated with success. Thus, some compromise on goal difficulty may be necessary in order to maximize both satisfaction and performance. However, some level of satisfaction is associated with simply striving for difficult goals, such as responding to a challenge, making some progress toward reaching the goals, and the belief that benefits may still be derived from the experience regardless of the outcome.

Consequences

The consequences of a person reaching his or her goal include both a willingness to accept future challenges and to increase his or her commitment to the organization. If a person reaches a goal, it gives the leader a way to have the person become emotionally attached to achieving even more challenging assignments. For example, one of the consequences of Martin Luther King's "I Have a Dream" speech was that it captured the hearts of millions of people pushing for civil rights justice. For leaders, a consequence is that employees know what the goal is because their behaviors reflect the acceptance of the goals. If the outcomes of goal attainment are positive, goal commitment is likely.

Effects of Goal Setting

Learning Goal

2. State the effects of goal setting on an individual's behavior.

In recent years, leaders have recognized the importance of focusing their employees' efforts to achieve high organizational performance. Because leaders are not in the position to change individuals' personalities, they must try to motivate employees. As we have pointed out in previous chapters, a major problem for leaders is that motivation ultimately comes from within individuals and, therefore, cannot be directly observed. The best that leaders can do is create the conditions that will lead to high levels of performance. As you read about with Enterprise Rent-A-Car and Hewlett-Packard, goals lay the foundation for organizational effectiveness. Therefore, what conditions increase or decrease the benefits of goal setting?

Conditions for Effective Goal Setting

Five conditions must generally come together for managers to gain the benefits of a goal-setting program[18]:

1. The employee must have the knowledge and ability to attain the goal. If the goal is to increase sales by 15 percent within the next 12 months and the employee lacks the sales competencies needed to attain it, urging them to set "stretch goals" usually isn't effective. It can make employees so anxious to reach the goal that they scramble to discover ways (ethical and unethical) to reach the goal, but do not learn the behaviors that are needed to be effective.

2. The employee must be committed to the goal, especially if the goal is difficult. Achieving a difficult goal requires a great deal of effort.

3. People need feedback on their progress toward the goal. Feedback enables employees to adjust their effort and behavior necessary for goal attainment. When employees discover that they are not reaching their goals, they typically increase their efforts because of the pride they have in their performance.

4. Tasks that are complex need to be broken down so that the employee can set subgoals that can be attained. These subgoals yield information for employees as to whether their progress is consistent with what is required for them to attain their goal.

5. Situational constraints can make goal attainment difficult. One of the primary roles of a manager is to ensure that employees have the resources necessary to attain their goals and to remove obstacles in the way of accomplishing those goals.

Impact on Performance

One of the consequences of goal setting is that it motivates individuals to achieve high performance. There are several reasons for this. First, difficult but achievable goals prompt employees to concentrate on achievement of the goals. At Enterprise Rent-A-Car, agents focus on customer satisfaction goals because they know that results are measured monthly and ranked and that these rankings affect their chances for advancement. Second, difficult goals motivate employees to spend lots of time and effort on developing methods for achieving them. At Enterprise, agents communicate with customers, sometimes at length, so that the agents understand customers' needs and can provide the most suitable vehicle to them, whether it is a sedan, convertible, pickup, or SUV. Customer satisfaction and loyalty are vital to the success of the business. Third, difficult goals increase employees' persistence in trying to achieve them. If employees perceive that goals can be reached by luck or with little effort, they tend to dismiss the goals as irrelevant and not follow through with the actions needed to reach them.

To sum up, specific, difficult goals affect motivation and performance by:

- encouraging individuals to develop action programs to reach these goals,
- focusing individual's attention on these goal-relevant actions,
- causing individuals to exert the effort necessary to achieve the goals, and
- spurring individuals to persist in the face of obstacles.

One of the many firms that have put these principles into action is Lockheed Martin. Lockheed Martin is facing a major challenge because many of its 70,000 engineers are expected to retire within the near future. President and CEO Robert Stevens has emphasized that the company must create a workforce that is more diverse and inclusive, not only of racial and gender differences but also differences in beliefs, backgrounds, and experiences. The following Diversity Competency feature highlights how the Lockheed Martin MS2 team developed a program to achieve that goal.[19]

Diversity competency

Lockheed Martin MS2 Team

The Lockheed Martin MS2 employee communication and design team focused on an innovative "Embrace Diversity" print campaign. All 13,000 employees in the MS2 program would receive a series of postcards over four months that would encourage a discussion of various topics. The goals were (1) to engage employees' understanding and acceptance of inclusive behavior and (2) to set the stage for greater employee involvement in both diversity communication and the company's efforts to create a diverse, inclusive work environment. The team established two key goals: (1) to reach at least 75 percent of employees and (2) to establish a baseline of employee understanding of what constitutes a diverse environment.

The team designed 12 different postcards that explored themes such as generational differences, cultural and religious traditions, and military experience. The intent was to explore the beliefs and backgrounds that contribute to an inclusive work environment by presenting realistic scenarios. The design used "conversation bubbles" similar to those used in comic strips. The team decided on the postcard campaign because employees normally receive very little print material from the company. The postcard would stand out from the normal e-mail that people received. Second, with multiple postcards, the team could explore a wide variety of issues each month. Third, employees seated in nearby office or cubicles received different versions of the same theme, encouraging conversation about the theme.

The team also focused on measurement and evaluation. By conducting polls of employees through the intranet and discussions with employees across various locations, the team estimated that 70 percent of employees received the first set of postcards and 90 percent received the final set. They also learned that 65 percent of employees recalled that they received the postcards; 43 percent felt the diversity messages were new, different, and made them think; and 50 percent believed that the messages would cause them to change their behavior. Furthermore, more than 85 percent of employees strongly agreed that MS2 was serious about its commitment to have a diverse, inclusive work environment, and 84 percent believed that the benefits of having an inclusive work environment had been clearly communicated to them.

To learn more about the program, go to **www.lockheedmartin.com.**

Limitations to Goal Setting

Goal setting has often been shown to increase performance in a variety of settings. However, there are three potential limitations.[20] First, when employees lack the skills and abilities needed to perform at a high level, goal setting doesn't work. Giving an employee a goal of writing a computer program will not lead to high performance if the worker doesn't know how to write such a program. To overcome this limitation, new hires at the Ritz-Carlton, for example, are required to attend training sessions at which they are taught how to process requests and complaints, build customer loyalty, and establish relationships with restaurants, taxi services, golf courses, and others services frequently requested by guests.

Second, successful goal setting takes longer when employees are given complicated tasks that require a considerable amount of learning. Good performance on complicated tasks also requires that employees be able to direct all of their attention to the tasks and not be interrupted by side issues. Steve Letarte's Rainbow Warriors pit crew is able to perform complicated tasks quickly because they are the only tasks that the crew is focusing on while the car is in the pit.

Third, goal setting can lead to major problems when it rewards the wrong behaviors. Rod Rodin is the CEO of Marshall Industries, a billion-dollar electronics distributor in Los Angeles that serves more than 30,000 customers who order more than 700,000 parts a month. He quickly recognized that the company's reward program was encouraging behaviors that led to poor service, dissatisfied customers, and, ultimately, lower profits. Rodin found that more than 20 percent of each month's sales were shipped to clients during the last three days of the month. Managers were hiding customer returns or opening bad credit accounts just to make their monthly sales goals. Divisions were hiding products from each other or saying that products had been shipped when they really had none on hand. Salespeople fought over how to split commissions on revenue from a customer who did design work in Chicago but made

Change Insight

Why should I pay you to get in the batter's box? When you hit the ball, I'll increase your pay. Results are paid for; showing up doesn't count for much.

Carlos Sepulveda, CEO, Interstate Battery

purchases in Cleveland. Employee and team performance were reviewed and ranked on the basis of numerical criteria, such as receivables outstanding and gross sales dollars. Rodin's solution was to scrap the incentive compensation program. He declared that there would be no more contests, prizes, or bonuses for individual achievements. Everyone at Marshall was put on a salary and shared in a company-wide bonus pool if the organization as a whole met its goals. It worked.[21]

Insights for Leaders

As you might expect, individuals who are both satisfied with and committed to an organization are more likely to stay with and accept the challenges the organization presents. Turnover and absenteeism rates for satisfied individuals are lower. This link brings us full circle to the beginning of the goal-setting model. What might happen if things go badly and an individual who had been satisfied becomes dissatisfied? Individual responses fall into at least six categories: (1) job avoidance (quitting), (2) work avoidance (absenteeism, arriving late, and leaving early), (3) psychological defenses (alcohol and/or drug abuse), (4) constructive protest (complaining), (5) defiance (refusing to do what is asked), and (6) aggression (theft or assault). Quitting is the most common outcome of severe dissatisfaction.[22]

The goal-setting model has important implications for employees, leaders, and teams alike. First, it provides an excellent framework to assist the leader or team in diagnosing the potential problems with low- or average-performing employees. Diagnostic questions might include these: (1) How were the goals set? (2) Are the goals challenging? (3) What is affecting goal commitment? and (4) Does the employee know when he has done a good job? Second, it provides concrete advice to the leader on how to create a high-performance work environment. Third, it portrays the relationships and interplay among key factors, such as goal difficulty, goal commitment, feedback, and rewards, to achieve high performance.

Reward Programs for Improving Performance

Learning Goal

3. *Describe reward programs for improving performance.*

In Chapters 5 and 6, we discussed types of rewards that organizations make available to employees. From the concepts discussed in those chapters, along with the concepts presented so far in this chapter, you should by now recognize that one of the basic goals of leaders should be to motivate employees to perform at their highest levels. Managers agree that tying rewards to job performance is essential. However, the actual implementation of programs designed to bring about such a relationship is often quite difficult. Questions that arise include "Should rewards be tied to the performance of an individual or team?" Recall that Rod Rodin, CEO of Marshall Industries, found that rewarding individual performance only created unhealthy competition among employees and destroyed morale. Deciding to reward all employees in the organization raises another question: Should the rewards be based on cost savings or profits and be distributed annually or when employees retire or otherwise leave the organization?

Considerable research has been done on how rewards affect individual and team performance. According to the Ascent Consulting organization, the ability of rewards to motivate individuals or teams to high performance was found to depend on six factors[23]:

1. *Availability*. For rewards to reinforce desired performance, they must be available. Too little of a desired reward is no reward at all. For example, pay increases are often highly desired but unavailable. Moreover, pay increases that are below minimally accepted standards may actually produce negative consequences, including theft, falsifying records, and the like. Organizations spend an average of $850

per employee on reward and recognition programs, but there are wide variations. Fifty percent of organizations spend less than $100 per year per employee, 65 percent spend less than $500, and 10 percent spend more than $2,500 per employee annually.

2. *Timeliness.* Like performance feedback, rewards should be given in a timely manner. A reward's motivating potential is reduced to the extent that it is separated in time from the performance it is intended to reinforce. Most companies use a combination of on-the-spot awards and team/departmental performance. On-the-spot rewards are usually in the form of gift cards, dress casual days, time-off, and the like.

3. *Performance contingency.* Rewards should be closely linked with particular performances. If a goal is met, the reward is given. The clearer the link between goal achievement and rewards, the better able rewards are to motivate desired behavior. Forty percent of employees nationwide believe that there is no link between their performance and rewards, such as bonuses and pay.

4. *Durability.* Some rewards last longer than others. Intrinsic rewards, such as increased autonomy, challenge, and accountability, tend to last longer than extrinsic rewards, such as a gift card to a restaurant.

5. *Equity.* Employees' motivation to perform is improved when they believe that the reward policies of their organization are fair and equitable.

6. *Visibility.* To promote a reward program, leaders must ensure that rewards are visible throughout an organization. Visible rewards, such as assignments to important committees or promotion to a new job, send signals to employees that rewards are available, timely, and based on performance.

Many weight-loss programs, such as Jenny Craig and Diet Center, use these factors when helping clients lose weight. In *One Small Step Can Change Your Life*, author Robert Maurer challenges participants to "march in place for one minute while watching television." One minute of low-intensity exercise then becomes stretched to two, three, four, etc. As the participant sees his or her weight drop, other stretch goals can be set. As the participant's weight drops, tote bags, T-shirts, and other rewards are given to celebrate pounds and inches lost.[24]

To the extent that reward programs are used to motivate employees to achieve higher performance, we discuss four popular ones: informal, profit-sharing, skill-based pay, and flexible benefit programs. The strengths and limitations of each are summarized in Table 7.3.

TABLE 7.3 Reward Programs for Improving Performance

REWARD PROGRAMS	STRENGTHS	LIMITATIONS
Informal reward programs	Cost effective; flexible; timely; easy to use.	Often ignored by leaders as trivial; not given for specific performance.
Profit-sharing programs	Reward organizational performance.	Individuals and teams are not likely to have an impact on overall performance.
Skill-based pay programs	Reward employees with higher pay for learning new skills.	Labor costs increase as employees' skills increase; employees can "top out" at the highest skill level.
Flexible benefit programs	Tailored to fit individual employee needs.	Not directly linked to performance; difficult to use with teams.

Informal Programs

Leaders have long underestimated the importance of informal rewards for improving individuals' performance.[25] At a time when raises and promotions are scarce, the use of informal rewards by leaders is gaining in popularity. In a recent survey, 81 percent of employees say that they do not receive any reward for increased productivity, and 60 percent indicate that their compensation will not increase if their performance improves. **Informal rewards** *refer to those that result from interactions between people.* Informal rewards are designed to encourage continuous improvement. For years, one of your authors has written a personal note to all students who received an A in his class and mailed these to the students' homes. The personal note thanks the students for their hard work and dedication to the course and adds some personal statements. Many students show these notes to their fellow students and parents and keep them for years. Sherry Burnside showed up in the office after graduating 15 years earlier and said that she still remembers getting the note—in fact, she still has it—and the impact that it had on her. Now a successful leader of research programs at Presbyterian Hospital, she uses the same practice with her employees—thanking them for a job well done. Note that informal rewards are personal and flexible, easy to use, and cost effective.

Characteristics of Informal Rewards

What makes informal rewards effective? Informal rewards are most effective when they:

*   directly reinforce the desired behavior,
*   are given immediately,
*   are delivered personally, and
*   are valued by the individual.

At Blanchard Training and Development in San Diego, California, leaders have established the Eagle Award to recognize legendary service to customers—one of the organization's goal. The program was announced and explained at a company-wide meeting. The program is open to any employee who could submit the name of another employee who had gone out of his or her way to satisfy a customer request. The name is submitted with a brief description of the activity, such as staying late to ship materials, helping a customer find a lost order, resolving a billing problem, etc. The recognized employee is surprised by a visit from the Eagle Committee. The employee's picture is taken holding the award and the photo displayed on the bulletin board in the company's lobby with a brief description of the activity that is being recognized. The recipient keeps the eagle statue on his or her desk until it is needed for the next recipient. At the end of the year, by a vote of prior Eagle Award winners, one person is awarded an engraved clock at the company's celebration program.[26]

Profit-Sharing Programs

Profit-sharing programs *provide employees with a portion of the company's earnings.* As the name suggests, profit-sharing programs distribute profits to employees. Average profit-sharing figures are difficult to calculate. According to some experts, they typically range between 4 and 6 percent of a person's salary. Steve Watson, managing director at Stanton Chase, an executive-recruiting firm, contends that profit sharing may have a limited impact because employees may feel that they can do little to influence the organization's overall profitability. That is, company profits are influenced by many factors (e.g., competitor's products, state of the economy, and inflation rate) that are well beyond the employees' control. However, profit-sharing programs are very popular in Japan. For example, at Seiko Instruments many managers and workers receive bonuses twice a year that equal four or five months' salary. These bonuses are based on the company's overall performance.[27]

What are the characteristics of successful profit-sharing programs? According to John Semyan, partner at TNS Associates, an executive-recruiting firm, more than one-third of the companies that use profit sharing do not track the results of such programs. In addition, 28 percent indicate that their profit-sharing programs do not meet their goals. To reduce failure, the following recommendations are offered:

- Involve line managers and employees in the program's creation to ensure their support.
- Set clear goals for the program.
- Ensure that the employees understand the metrics that the program is measuring.
- Tie the program to the company's strategies.
- Give the program time to succeed. It takes two or three years for a program to change overall company performance.
- Provide up-to-date information that allows employees to see how well they are performing against their goals.[28]

The following Change Competency feature illustrates how Nucor uses its profit-sharing plan to reward employees. When Nucor entered the steel-making business in 1986 as a mini-mill, it was an upstart company in a business dominated by large producers, such as Bethlehem Steel, U.S. Steel, and National Steel. Faced with a successful challenge from China and other steel-producing nations, many of the steel mills in the United States have been closed. Nucor, however, survived. Today, Nucor is among the largest steel companies in the world, employing more than 18,000 and with sales exceeding $16 billion annually. Until the latest recession, Nucor's sales had been growing at more than 12 percent a year. With such growth, Nucor has not laid off any employees since it started production in 1986. One of the reasons for its success is found in its profit-sharing plan.[29]

Change competency

Nucor's Profit-Sharing Program

Nucor has developed a profit-sharing plan that works and is easy to understand. The average Nucor steelworker earns more than $70,000 per year, but only one-third of that amount is guaranteed. Jim Coblin, human resources vice president, believes that paying a low base salary, but paying high bonuses on a weekly basis, will keep employees focused on Nucor's goals of quality and customer satisfaction. The bonuses are paid based on the quality and tons produced and shipped by a team. The average base pay is between $9 and $10 an hour, but with the bonuses employees can make an additional $15 to $20 an hour. Nucor's profit-sharing plan also has some penalties. If employees catch a bad load of steel before it is shipped, they lose their bonus for that shipment. If that bad batch is shipped to a customer, the team loses three times its usual bonus.

Nucor's profit-sharing plan is also based on employees' ability to keep the mills running and discover new ways to improve the quality and amount of steel produced. For example, when the electrical grid that feeds its Hickman, Arkansas, plant failed, it could have shut down that plant for one week. When three electricians from other plants heard the news, they drove to Hickman and within three days got the business operating. Dan DiMicco, Nucor's CEO, praised them for their efforts and thanked them for giving up their weekend, but these three electricians earned no extra pay for their actions. These three electricians did what they had to do to make Nucor successful.

To learn more about Nucor, go to **www.nucor.com**.

Skill-Based Pay Programs

Paying employees according to their value in the labor market makes a great deal of sense. After all, employees with highly developed skills and those who develop multiple skills are particularly valuable assets to the organization. As we emphasized earlier, the communication, team, and change competencies are often based on mastering a number of specific skills. **Skill-based pay programs** *are based on the number and level of job-related skills that an employee has learned.*[30] Skill-based pay compensates employees for the skills they can use in the organization, rather than for the specific jobs they are performing. Pay changes do not necessarily go along with job changes. There is also little emphasis on seniority. The underlying assumption is that by focusing on the individual rather than the job, skill-based reward programs recognize learning and growth. Employees are paid according to the number of different skills they can perform.

More than 16 percent of the *Fortune* 1000 companies use skill-based pay programs to motivate employees. In the United Kingdom, the Norwich and Peterborough Building Society, a mortgage and banking business, had a 12-level reward program. It proved to be ineffective in curbing turnover, covered only some of the employees, and basically confused employees. The new program centers on a 5-level job skills reward program, such as customer service and relationship management, that are linked to pay rate changes in the market. Sixty-seven percent of employees now know that their pay progression is linked to the attainment of these 5-level job skills. As a result, employee turnover dropped to 17 percent from 25 percent, productivity increased, and customer satisfaction improved. Employees report that the new pay system is simple, transparent, and they understand what skills they need to learn to increase their pay. And managers do not have to answer the question "Why is that person earning more than I am?"[31]

Of course, skill-based pay programs have some limitations.[32] One major drawback of skill-based pay is the tendency to "top out." Topping-out occurs when employees learn all the skills there are to master and, hence, reach the top end of the pay scale, with no higher levels to attain. Some organizations, such as GE and United Technologies, have resolved the topping-out effect by installing a gain-sharing program after most employees have learned all of the required skills. Other organizations have resolved this limitation by making skills obsolete, eliminating them, and adding new ones, thus raising the standards of employee competence. Other limitations include inadequate management commitment to the program, conflicts between the employees included in and those excluded from the skill-based pay program, inadequate training of managers, and poor program designs that increase labor costs without providing offsetting organizational benefits. Skill-based pay programs also require a heavy investment in training, as well as measurement systems capable of assessing when employees have learned the new skills.

Flexible Benefit Programs

Flexible benefit programs *allow employees to choose the benefits they want, rather than having management choose for them. Flexible benefit programs often are called* **cafeteria-style benefit programs.** According to Leslie Ritter, a principal in Sagen Consulting, a human resource consulting firm located in Addison, Texas, a typical corporation's benefits program costs between 25 and 30 percent of its total employee compensation package.[33] This represents a huge cost, considering that only 3 percent or less is set aside annually for merit pay increases in most organizations. Under flexible benefit programs, employees decide—beyond a base program—which additional benefits they want, tailoring the benefits package to their needs. The idea is that employees can make important and intelligent decisions about their benefits. Some employees take all of their discretionary benefits in cash; others choose additional life insurance, child or elder care, dental

CULTURA/ALAMY

In flexible benefit programs, employees choose the benefits they want.

insurance, or retirement programs. Extensive benefit options may be highly attractive to an employee with a family. However, many benefits might be only minimally attractive to a young, single employee. Older employees value retirement programs more than younger employees and are willing to put more money into them. Employees with elderly parents may desire financial assistance in providing care for them. At Travelers Insurance Company, employees can choose benefits of up to $5,000 a year for the care of dependent elderly parents.

Thousands of organizations now offer flexible benefit programs. They are very popular because they offer three distinct advantages. First, they allow employees to make important decisions about their finances and to match their needs with their benefit programs. Second, such programs help organizations control their costs, especially for health care. Employers can set the maximum amount of benefit dollars they will spend on employees' benefits and avoid automatically absorbing cost increases. Third, such programs highlight the economic value of many benefits to employees. Most employees have little idea of the cost of benefits because the organization is willing to pay for them even though employees might not want some of them or might prefer alternatives.

Some limitations are associated with flexible benefit programs. First, because different employees choose different benefit packages, record keeping becomes more complicated. Sophisticated computer systems are essential for tracking the details of employees' records. Second, it is difficult to accurately predict the number of employees that might choose each benefit. Such uncertainty may affect the firm's group rates for life and medical insurance, because the costs of such programs are based on the number of employees covered.

Insights for Leaders

Improving performance-based reward systems has come under attack, especially during the recent recession. CEOs at JPMorgan Chase, AT&T, and Citigroup, among others, have been in the news for granting huge bonuses to key employees when their firms are experiencing major financial losses. Comcast has designed a reward system that will pay its CEO, Brian Roberts, a $47.5 million bonus if he dies on the job. Disney has even promised to keep paying CEO Robert Iger's salary to his heirs for three years after he dies! Such arrangements have stockholders and others shaking their heads and demanding to know how the company dare pay people who are dead and not performing.[34] While the compensation committees of these companies defend these deals as a kind of life insurance to maintain talent, President Obama and members of Congress have called for "anti-greed" proposals to stop such practices. Although these instances are small in number, the magnitude of these rewards is what people are disturbed about. Let's look at some of the more important practices to improve effectiveness, as shown in Figure 7.3.

First, leaders need to link rewards to performance and set a measurement system in place that measures the behaviors that lead to effectiveness. In Chapter 5, we discussed how principles of reinforcement theory can be used to channel and reward employees' behaviors. In Chapter 6, we discussed how expectancy theory concepts can be used to reward proper behavior. The foundation for the recommendations using either concept is that good performers should be rewarded more than poor performers. Leaders can improve the performance–reward linkage by using objective measures of performance along with subjective ones, such as leadership, teamwork, and communications. Objectives measures, such as volume, customer complaints, and machine downtime, need to be established and agreed

FIGURE 7.3 Deciding among Alternative Reward Programs

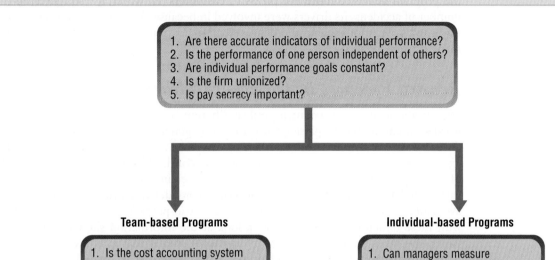

Source: Adapted from Wagner, J. A., and Hollenbeck, J. K. *Organizational Behavior*, 3rd ed. Englewood Cliffs, NJ: Simon & Schuster, 1998, 100.

on by individuals. Both subjective and objective measures need to be related to the organization's goals. Organizations also need to reward individuals soon after the performance occurs and with a sufficient size reward so that individuals experience positive emotions when receiving the rewards. This is one of the reasons why Nucor's profit-sharing program has been so successful—workers receive bonuses on a weekly basis.

Second, leaders need to make sure that rewards are relevant and valued by employees. Employees need to see a connection between their daily actions and a reward to be motivated to improve their performance. At Whole Foods Market, each department within the store is run by a team with a monthly payroll budget. If payroll money is unspent at the end of a month, the surplus is divided among the members of that Whole Foods team.

Leaders should ask employees what they value. According to Dave Stoner, CEO of ViewCast, employees don't always go for material things. They want rewards that have value for them. For example, for years, on the Monday before Thanksgiving, leaders at ViewCast gave turkeys or hams to employees who worked in the shipping department. But when asked, most of the employees said that they valued only working a half day on Wednesday, instead of receiving a turkey or ham, so they could travel to be with their families. They promised that all of their work would be done prior to noon on Wednesday even if they had to show up early to achieve the result.

Lastly, leaders need to watch out for unintended consequences. Performance-based reward systems sometimes have undesirable effects on behavior. For example when Domino's pizza started it advertising campaign "Fifteen minutes or it's free," the program delivered more hot pizzas to customers. However, it also increased the number of accidents its drivers were involved in because the program unintentionally rewarded drivers for making the delivery within 15 minutes. To make this deadline, many drivers had to speed.

Reward Practices in Different Cultures

Organizations in various countries utilize different reward programs. Cultural values learned in childhood are passed down from one generation to the next and serve to differentiate one country from another. In Chapter 3, we presented a framework for examining various feelings, ideas, values, and ways of thinking that differentiate people of one culture from another.[35] We discussed the five dimensions on which cultures can vary: power distance, individualism–collectivism, gender role orientation, uncertainty avoidance, and long-term orientation. Please reread pages 72–75 to refresh yourself with these dimensions and then take a look at the information shown in Table 7.4, which was taken from several large international studies that examined reward program differences in more than 50 cultures. Using what you've learned about the cultural dimensions and Table 7.4, let's explore how four of these five dimensions impact differences in reward programs.[36]

In high *power distance* cultures, rewards are based on one's level within the managerial hierarchy. There are wide salary ranges between the top and lower level employees. Perquisites and status symbols are popular and expected. Profit sharing and other forms of variable compensation systems are relied on to motivate employees. Subordinates are motivated by the threat of sanctions.

In *individualistic cultures*, organizations expect individuals to look out for their own personal interests. The employee–employer compensation relationship is a business deal based on what the "labor market" will pay. Incentives are given to individuals. Therefore, skill-based programs and MBO programs are popular because they reward an individual's achievements. In collective cultures, team-based pay is used to reinforce the team or group's achievements. At NSK, a ball-bearing manufacturer, and Toto, a toilet producer, when business slows down, these Japanese companies permit all workers to work shorter shifts and receive smaller paychecks.

TABLE 7.4 Cultures and Reward Systems

CULTURE	REWARD SYSTEM
Power distance	Pay based on individual performance
	Status symbols are important
	Pay tied to level in the organization's hierarchy
	Stock options to MBO
Individualism-collectivism	Pay based on team performance
	Profit sharing
	Little emphasis on extrinsic rewards
Gender role orientation	Extensive use of fringe benefits
	Gain sharing
	Goals set by participation linked to team achievements
	Pay equality
Uncertainty avoidance	Pay focuses on long-term orientation
	Seniority is important

Source: Adapted from Tosi, J. L., and Greckhamer, T. Culture & CEO compensation. *Organization Science*, 2004, 15, 657–670; and Hofstede, G. *Cultures Consequences*, 2nd ed. Thousand Oaks, CA: Sage, 2001.

In cultures that do not have a strong *gender role orientation*, equality among members is stressed. There are fewer differences in pay based on gender differences. Flexible benefit programs that allow the individual a wide choice of non–work-related benefits (e.g., child care, sabbatical leaves) are used to motivate employees to perform. For example, in Sweden, women in management take having families for granted and expect managers to find creative ways to help them work through this childbearing time.

In high *uncertainty avoidance* cultures, reward programs emphasize seniority. There is strong loyalty to the company that leads to long-term employment. Rewards based on seniority are easy to administer and understand. These programs expose the employee to little risk because they are based on the performance of the company and not on individual and/or team efforts. There is high fear of failure. In Japan and other Asian cultures, employees receive their annual pay raise on their anniversary date (the day they joined the company). Instead of dismissing an employee for poor performance, managers move people from one department to another or into a "window seat," a job with little authority and responsibility. These practices allow the employee to save face.

Chapter Summary

Goal setting is a process intended to increase efficiency and effectiveness by specifying the desired outcomes toward which employees, departments, teams, and organizations should work. The goal-setting model emphasizes the challenges provided for the individual: goal difficulty, goal clarity, and self-efficacy. Setting difficult but clear and achievable goals for individuals who believe that they have the ability to complete their tasks leads to high performance. Four moderators—ability, goal commitment, feedback, and task complexity—influence the strength of the relationship between challenging goals and performance. If the individual has the ability, is committed to the goal, and is given feedback on progress toward achievement of the goal—and if the task is complex—high performance will result. All four moderators must be present to motivate an employee to achieve goals. Four mediators—direction, effort, persistence, and task strategy—facilitate goal attainment. These four characteristics channel or focus the employee's motivational efforts. Performance, rewards, satisfaction, and consequences complete the model.

1. Explain how goal setting affects performance.

Goal setting is a key mechanism for increasing job satisfaction and performance because it permits employees to be self-motivated. Five requirements must be in place for goal setting to have positive benefits for the employee and organization: the employee's knowledge and ability, the employee's commitment to a goal, feedback on the task, establishment of subgoals on complex tasks, and a leader who removes obstacles that prevent employees from reaching their goals.

2. State the effects of goal setting on an individual's behavior.

Reward programs represent a powerful means for motivating high levels of individual and team performance. Reward programs, in particular, are designed to enhance performance: informal rewards, profit sharing, skilled-based pay, and flexible benefits. Informal rewards come about through interactions with others—coworkers, superiors, and customers. Profit sharing gives employees a portion of the department's or organization's profits. Skilled-based pay programs compensate an employee according to the number and level of job-related skills they have mastered. The value of these skills is determined by the organization. Flexible benefit programs allow employees to choose the benefits that are important to them.

3. Describe reward programs for improving performance.

Key Terms and Concepts

Cafeteria-style benefit programs, **209**
Feedback, **199**
Flexible benefit programs, **209**
Goal clarity, **195**
Goal commitment, **197**
Goal difficulty, **195**
Goal setting, **192**

Goals, **192**
Informal rewards, **207**
Management by objectives (MBO), **195**
Profit-sharing programs, **207**
Skill-based pay programs, **209**
Task complexity, **199**

Discussion Questions

1. Visit Enterprise at www.enterprise.com. Click on "Careers," on "Our Culture," then on "Our Values." How does Enterprise use goal-setting?

2. What are some ethical problems associated with performance-based reward programs? What abuses have you seen? How can leaders correct such abuses?

3. What factors influenced your level of goal commitment to this course? Did your level of commitment change after receiving feedback on an assignment or test? Explain.

4. Use the goal-setting model found on page 194 to analyze Steve Letarte's NASCAR team, the Rainbow Warriors. Why is the team effective?

5. Sandra Swann, director of human resources at ViewCast, said that many times, leaders commit the error of measuring the wrong behaviors with excruciating accuracy. What implications does this pose for leaders using management by objectives?

6. Jay Beck, general manager at Benefit Partners, a company that specializes in human resource management, said: "If you cannot define it and measure it, you are not going to get it." What implications does this statement have for setting goals? For measuring them?

7. What are some of the negative issues associated with goal-setting programs?

8. Why does the diversity program at Lockheed Martin work?

9. What are some problems that employees might face in an organization that has adopted a skill-based pay program?

10. Bella Goren, vice president for Customer Services Planning in Asia for American Airlines, is transferring a manager from American Airlines based in Dallas to Japan. What cultural issues might he encounter when rewarding employees in Japan?

Experiential Exercise and Case

Experiential Exercise: Self Competency[37]

Goal Setting

Instructions

The following statements refer to a job you currently hold or have held. Read each statement and then select a response from the following scale that best describes your view. You may want to use a separate sheet of paper to record your responses and compare them with the responses of others.

Scale

Almost Never			Almost Always	
1	2	3	4	5

_____ 1. I understand exactly what I am supposed to do on my job.

_____ 2. I have specific, clear goals to aim for on my job.

_____ 3. The goals I have on this job are challenging.

_____ 4. I understand how my performance is measured on this job.

_____ 5. I have deadlines for accomplishing my goals on this job.

_____ 6. If I have more than one goal to accomplish, I know which are most important and which are least important.

_____ 7. My goals require my full effort.

_____ 8. My manager tells me the reasons for giving me the goals I have.

_____ 9. My manager is supportive with respect to encouraging me to reach my goals.

_____ 10. My manager lets me participate in the setting of my goals.

_____ 11. My manager lets me have some say in deciding how I will go about implementing my goals.

_____ 12. If I reach my goals, I know that my manager will be pleased.

_____ 13. I get credit and recognition when I attain my goals.

_____ 14. Trying for goals makes my job more fun than it would be without goals.

_____ 15. I feel proud when I get feedback indicating that I have reached my goals.

_____ 16. The other people I work with encourage me to attain my goals.

_____ 17. I sometimes compete with my coworkers to see who can do the best job in reaching our goals.

_____ 18. If I reach my goals, my job security will be improved.

_____ 19. If I reach my goals, my chances for a pay raise are increased.

_____ 20. If I reach my goals, my chances for a promotion are increased.

_____ 21. I usually feel that I have a suitable action program(s) for reaching my goals.

_____ 22. I get regular feedback indicating how I am performing in relation to my goals.

_____ 23. I feel that my training was good enough so that I am capable of reaching my goals.

_____ 24. Organization policies help rather than hurt goal attainment.

_____ 25. Teams work together in this company to attain goals.

_____ 26. This organization provides sufficient resources (e.g., time, money, and equipment) to make goal setting effective.

_____ 27. In performance appraisal sessions, my supervisor stresses problem solving rather than criticism.

_____ 28. Goals in this organization are used more to help you do your job well rather than punish you.

_____ 29. The pressure to achieve goals here fosters honesty as opposed to cheating and dishonesty.

_____ 30. If my manager makes a mistake that affects my ability to attain my goals, he or she admits it.

Scoring and Interpretation

Add the points shown for items 1 through 30. Scores of 120 to 150 may indicate a high-performing, highly satisfying work situation. Your goals are challenging and you are committed to reaching them. When you achieve your goals, you are rewarded for your accomplishments. Scores of 80 to 119 may suggest a highly varied work situation with some motivating and satisfying features and some frustrating and dissatisfying features. Scores of 30 to 79 may suggest a low-performing, dissatisfying work situation.

Questions

1. Using the concepts found in the goal-setting model, how might you increase your performance?

2. Why don't employees use goal-setting concepts in their everyday life to control their weight and personal habits?

Case: Diversity Competency

Allstate Insurance Company[38]

In today's competitive environment, companies continue to look for ways to improve their performance and achieve corporate goals. The task is not easy, but the team of human resource (HR) executives at Allstate Corporation has found that its diversity strategy has become one of the company's most important competitive weapons. It has long been Allstate's position that diversity is about neither political mandates nor legal obligation. Rather, the company's vision is stated this way: "Diversity is Allstate's strategy for leveraging differences in order to create a competitive advantage." This strategy has two major points: one internally focused and the other externally focused. According to James DeVries, senior vice president of human resources, the internal diversity focus is about "unlocking the potential for excellence in all workers by providing them the tools, resources, and opportunities to succeed." The external focus of diversity is about making certain that the workforce matches the experiences, backgrounds, and sensitivities of the markets it serves. In this context, Allstate managers view diversity not as a goal but as a process that is integrated into the daily life of the company.

Allstate launched its first affirmative action program back in 1969. In the early days, its commitment to diversity didn't always link recruitment, development, and retention strategies to business performance. The company focused more on affirmative action and diversity awareness through education and training. Although these initiatives were considered innovative in their day, they were not linked to Allstate's business strategy. The director of diversity management notes that the key question has become "How do you take this workforce of differences and bring them together in a more powerful way so that it can impact business results?" Allstate has taken four specific steps:

Step One: Succession Programming. A diverse slate of candidates is identified and developed for each key position. Allstate's management information system enables it to track and measure key drivers of career development and career opportunities for all of its more than 36,000 employees, ensuring that the company's future workforce will be diverse at all levels. Allstate's succession programming has made a difference that is easy to measure. Employment of women and minorities has grown at a rate far surpassing national averages. Today, 50 percent of Allstate's more than 5,300 executives and managers are women, and of that percentage, 25 percent are Hispanics or people of color. Languages other than English, a total of 62, are spoken in more than 3,200 Allstate agencies. The company has a minority recruitment program that focuses on colleges and universities with the most diverse enrollments.

Step Two: Development. Through the company's employee development process, all employees receive an assessment of their current job skills and a road map for developing the critical skills necessary for advancement. Options include education, coaching and mentoring, and classroom training. Leaders are provided employee feedback on which they can base future development programs. In addition, all of Allstate's nonagent employees with service of more than one year have completed mandatory diversity training courses.

Step Three: Measurement. Twice a year the company takes a snapshot of all 36,000 employees through a survey called the Diversity Index. As a part of a larger online employee survey and feedback process called the Quarterly Leadership Measurement System (QLMS), the Diversity Index asks the following questions:

1. To what extent does our company deliver quality service to customers regardless of their ethnic background, gender, age, and so on?
2. To what extent are you treated with respect and dignity at work? To what extent does your immediate manager/team leader seek out and utilize the different backgrounds and perspectives of all employees in your work group?
3. How often do you observe insensitive behavior at work, for example, inappropriate comments or jokes about ethnic background, gender, age, and so on?
4. To what extent do you work in an environment of trust where employees/agents are free to offer different opinions?

Management communicates the results of this survey via its intranet and actively solicits feedback from employees on creating action programs to solve problems and improve work processes.

Step Four: Accountability and Reward. To link compensation to the company's diversity goals, 25 percent of each manager's merit pay is based on the Diversity Index and the QLMS. DeVries believes that this sharpens the focus on the initiative. "What you measure is what people focus on. This really sends a clear signal that management of people and doing that well are really important."

To help employees maintain a balance between work and personal life, Allstate has a number of programs in place. For example, it has an on-site child-care center at its headquarters in Northbrook, Illinois, and three near-site child-care centers, all of which offer parents discount programs. It also has on-site dry cleaning, oil change, and postal and catering services and allows for flexible work arrangements for its employees. The Allstate Center for Assistive Technology (ACAT) helps employees with disabilities that include carpal tunnel syndrome, mobility impairments, and multiple sclerosis. For example, when one information technology employee began experiencing hearing problems, the ACAT team was deployed to fit him with a special home phone for use when he was on night call.

Questions
1. Using the model found on page 194, evaluate Allstate's goal-setting process. How does it work?
2. On pages 202–203, we list some of the dimensions of an effective goal-setting program. Does Allstate meet these criteria?
3. What type of high-performance reward system should Allstate choose to motivate its employees to reach its diversity goals?

chapter 8

Workplace Stress and Aggression

Learning Goals

After studying this chapter, you should be able to:

1
Explain the concept of and influences on creating stress.

2
Identify the primary sources of work-related stressors.

3
State the potential impacts of severe stress on health, performance, and job burnout.

4
Describe how individual differences influence reactions to stressful situations.

5
Apply individual and leader insights to the management of workplace stress.

6
Explain four major types of workplace aggression.

Learning Content

Learning from Experience
Stress and Coping with a Layoff

Concept of Stress

Primary Stressors
Communication Competency
Workplace Incivility: How Not to Communicate

Severe Stress

Individual Differences and Stress
Self Competency
Chesley B. Sullenberger III, Captain of US Airways Flight 1549

Stress Management
Change Competency
Ortho-Clinical Diagnostics' Wellness Program

Workplace Aggression
Diversity Competency
Darwin Realty

Experiential Exercise and Case
Experiential Exercise: Self Competency
Work-Related Stress Inventory
Case: Ethics Competency
Coleen Colombo and Colleagues Resist Mortgage Fraud

Stress and Coping with a Layoff

Job layoffs in the recent recession showed no mercy. They struck all levels of organizations: from data entry clerks to department managers, from new hires to senior employees. This opening feature provides brief examples of the stresses and coping efforts of five employees and their families as a result of layoffs.

Charlene Jeter was laid off as vice president of marketing at SunTrust MidAtlantic, a financial institution, during a restructuring. Her 28 years there entitled her to a good severance package. She's still looking for a job after a full year. She states: "Employers can be very picky right now. There are too many people like me out there." She thought her diverse marketing skills would transfer easily, but she has found that employers want specialists. She has applied for 58 jobs and had 10 in-person interviews, but nothing has clicked yet. Adding to the stress, her husband, Duane, was laid off from his job in the construction industry. She states: "He has the kind of skills that he can hire himself out hourly, if not full time, almost more easily than I can. In his world, it seems people need him to do things but can't hire him full time." With neither of them working full time, they've cut back in little ways. For Christmas, they didn't buy big presents. They don't eat out often. They pay more attention to prices. She feels fortunate they only have themselves to worry about. Charlene adds: "I know people that this happened to and they're sweating kids or college. That kind of burden we don't have."

Life changed for Thomas and Jennifer Dodson of Sacramento, California, when he was laid off by the architecture firm where he worked. He immediately started his own consulting firm. Although the work is rewarding and fulfilling, it continues to be an "immense struggle financially," he says. He praises his wife for being "more than great" throughout this experience. He states: "She has been a rock. Despite the stress and turmoil this has brought into our life, this has made us closer than ever. I don't know how people do it without the support of their spouse. Having that other person there whispering in your ear and telling you you can do it is so powerful."

Joyce Ellis was phased out of an accounting position at a construction company. She's searching for another job but doesn't expect quick results. "I've been on the other side, so I understand what it's like to hire someone," she said. As

DAVID MUSCROFT/PHOTOLIBRARY

To learn more about stress, go to www.stress.org.

one of 10 children, she learned to be frugal and that knowledge has come in handy now and when she was laid off from another job about seven years ago. She has always planned her expenses so she will be okay financially as she searches for another job. For instance, when she purchased her house, she bought the house she could afford, rather than a bigger or fancier house. Joyce said, "That's all preplanning, not getting in over your head when the mortgage company says you can afford much more." To save on heating in her home, she keeps the thermostat low and wears layers of clothing. She hangs double-layer curtains to block cold air. Her two children are grown, so she only has herself to take care of.

Stacy Shiplett of Akron, Ohio, knows all too well the ill effects of financial stress. The mother of two has been looking for a job for months since she lost hers. She was diagnosed with a lung condition but said she can't afford her needed breathing treatments without health insurance. "I can't sleep, and now it's getting to me," she said through tears. "I'm not focused because of the stress level I'm at. Health-wise, your stomach hurts all the time. It's mental and physical." But she said she's hopeful things will improve soon. Shiplett has participated in an intensive, three-week job search and placement course at The Job Center in Akron. Stacy states: "It's a big help. It takes that stress level down."

For some individuals, the stresses of dealing with a layoff and the difficulty of finding a new job are even bad for their health. Take the cases of Raymond and Melissa Gibbons. Since Raymond unexpectedly lost his job as a truck driver when his employer closed, his blood pressure skyrocketed to 170/107, well above the normal range of 120/80. These days, Melissa often suffers from headaches. And neither can sleep more than a couple of hours most nights. They're too worried about how to pay their bills and provide for their four children, ranging in age from 11 weeks to 9 years. Raymond states: "We have young kids, so they expect Santa Claus to be there. The trucking industry was not hiring during the deep recession."[1]

The experiences of Charlene and Duane Jeter, Thomas and Jennifer Dodson, Joyce Ellis, Stacy Shiplett, and Raymond and Melissa Gibbons are snapshots of the various stress levels and coping mechanisms employed by the millions of individuals laid off in the recent recession. Even for those not laid off, 50 percent of the respondents in one recent survey indicated they are experiencing stress from financial concerns.[2] Layoffs are typically stressful experiences, but the stress is magnified when alternative and equivalent job opportunities are scarce to none. This opening feature also illustrates that individuals cope with stressful situations differently. For example, Thomas Dodson even came to perceive several positive outcomes from his layoff.

Our focus in this chapter is not simply about the stresses and coping mechanisms associated with layoffs. Rather, its scope is much broader. We discuss (1) the nature of stress, (2) the key causes of stress, (3) the effects of stress, (4) the role of personality differences in handling stress, (5) insights to help manage stress, and (6) core dimensions of workplace aggression.

Beyond the personal stress of a job layoff, on-the-job stress is a common and costly problem in the workplace, leaving few workers untouched. For example, surveys of workplace stress and aggression report the following:

- Sixty-five percent of respondents said that workplace stress had caused physical and psychological difficulties, and more than 10 percent described these as having major effects.

- Forty percent of respondents view their jobs as very or extremely stressful.

- Forty-eight percent said that excessive stress makes it hard for them to perform well on the job.

- Fourteen percent of respondents had felt like striking a coworker in the past year, but didn't.

- Twenty-five percent had felt like screaming or shouting because of job stress; 10 percent are concerned about an individual at work they fear could become violent.[3]

Leaders who ignore employee stress, or assign it a low priority, are likely to see declines in productivity and morale and increased legal costs. The negative consequences of stress are so dramatic that leaders need to (1) take action to reduce excessive employee stress in the workplace and (2) assist employees in developing stress-coping skills.

Concept of Stress

Learning Goal

1. *Explain the concept of and influences on creating stress.*

Stress *is the excitement, feeling of anxiety, and/or physical tension that occurs when the demands or stressors placed on an individual are thought to exceed the person's ability to cope.*[4] This is the most common view of stress and is often called *distress* or negative stress. Stressors can take various forms, but they all have one thing in common: Stressors create stress or the potential for stress when an individual perceives them as representing a demand that exceeds that person's ability to respond.

Fight-or-Flight Response

Numerous changes occur in a person's body during a stress reaction. Breathing and heart rates increase so that the body can operate with maximum capacity for physical action. Brain wave activity goes up to allow the brain to function maximally. Hearing and sight become momentarily more acute, and muscles ready themselves for action. An animal attacked by a predator in the wild basically has two choices: to fight or to flee. The animal's bodily responses to the stressor (the predator) increase its chances of survival. The **fight-or-flight response** *refers to the biochemical and bodily changes that represent a natural reaction to an environmental stressor.*[5] Similarly, cave-dwelling ancestors benefited from this biological response mechanism. People gathering food away from their caves would have experienced a great deal of stress upon meeting a saber-toothed tiger. In dealing with the tiger, they could have run away or stayed and fought. The biochemical changes in their bodies prepared them for either alternative and contributed to their ability to survive.

The human nervous system still responds the same way to stressors. This response continues to have survival value in a true emergency. However, for most people most of the time, the "tigers" are imaginary rather than real. In work situations, for example, a fight-or-flight response usually isn't appropriate. If an employee receives an unpleasant work assignment from a leader, physically assaulting the leader or storming angrily out of the office obviously is professionally inappropriate. Instead, the employee is expected to accept the assignment calmly and do the best job possible. Remaining calm and performing effectively may be especially difficult when the employee perceives an assignment as threatening and the body is prepared to act accordingly.

Medical researcher Hans Selye first used the word *stress* to describe the body's biological response mechanisms. Selye considered *stress* to be the nonspecific response of the human body to any demand made on it.[6] However, the body has only a limited capacity to respond to stressors. The workplace makes a variety of demands on people, and too much stress over too long a period of time will exhaust their ability to cope with those stressors.

Influences on the Stress Experience

A variety of factors influence how an individual experiences stress, especially severe stress. Figure 8.1 identifies four of the primary factors: (1) the person's perception of the situation, (2) the person's past experiences, (3) the presence or absence of social support, and (4) individual differences in reacting to stress.

Perception

In Chapter 4, we defined *perception* as the process by which people select, organize, interpret, and respond to information from the world around them. Employee perceptions of a situation can influence how (or whether) they experience stress. For example, two employees, Tina and John, have their job responsibilities substantially changed—a situation likely to be stressful for many people. Tina views the new responsibilities as an opportunity to learn new competencies. She perceives the change to be a vote of confidence from management in her ability to be flexible and take on new challenges. In contrast, John perceives the same situation to be extremely threatening. He concludes that management is unhappy with his performance and is using this as a tactic to make him fail so that he can be fired. Recall from the opening feature that when Charlene Jeter was laid off as a vice president from SunTrust MidAtlantic after 28 years, she could not find another job. This experience is highly stressful for her.

Past Experiences

John may perceive a situation as more or less stressful based on how familiar he is with the situation and his prior experiences with the particular stressors involved. Past practice or training may allow Tina to deal calmly and competently with stressors that would greatly intimidate less experienced or inadequately trained employees. The relationship between experiences and stress is based on reinforcement (see Chapter 5). Positive reinforcement or previous success in a similar situation can reduce the level of stress that a person experiences under certain circumstances. In contrast, punishment or past failure under similar conditions can increase stress under the same circumstances.

Also, recall Joyce Ellis's past experiences in the opening feature that have helped her cope with the stresses of being phased out of an accounting position at a construction company. As one of 10 children, Ellis reported that she learned to be frugal and indicated it came in handy when she was laid off from another job seven years prior to the current job. Ellis planned her expenses so she would be okay if unemployed. Remember her quote: "That's all preplanning, not getting in over your head when the mortgage company says you can afford much more." Words of wisdom, indeed!

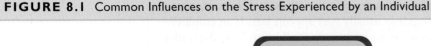

FIGURE 8.1 Common Influences on the Stress Experienced by an Individual

Social Support

The presence or absence of other people influences how individuals in the workplace experience stress and respond to stressors.[7] The presence of coworkers may increase John's confidence, allowing him to cope more effectively with stress. For example, working alongside someone who performs confidently and competently in a stressful situation may help John behave similarly. Conversely, the presence of fellow workers may irritate Tina or make her anxious, reducing her ability to cope with stress. Recall the importance of the social support Jennifer Dodson gave her spouse Thomas when he was laid off.

Individual Differences

Each person's motivation, attitudes, personality, and abilities influence the degree and nature of work stress experienced and how the individual responds.[8] What one person considers a major source of stress, another may hardly notice. Personality characteristics, in particular, may explain some of the differences in the ways in which an employee experiences and responds to stress. For example, the Big Five personality factor that we labeled *emotional stability* in Chapter 3 seems to be important in individual responses to various stressors in the work setting. Individuals who are emotionally stable (described as stable, relaxed, resilient, and confident) are more likely to cope well with a wide variety of work stressors. In contrast, individuals who are lacking in emotional stability (described as reactive, nervous, and self-doubting) typically have greater difficulty coping with the same stressors. We further discuss relationships between personality and stress in this chapter.

> ### Ethics Insight
>
> At some plants, we have six-week unpaid layoffs on a rolling basis. A big concern for a lot of employees is "Am I going to have a job?" This way, it's a comfort to them—like having six weeks off, and still having a job to come back to. We've been doing this for two years now. Employees feel like they have some sort of control, and they almost always come back.
>
> *Stacy Guinn, HR Coordinator, Sherwin-Williams*

Primary Stressors

Employees often experience stress in both their personal and work lives. Understanding these two sources of stress and their possible interaction is important. To consider either source in isolation may give an incomplete picture of the stress that an employee is experiencing. However, our primary focus is on work-related stressors.

Work-Related Stressors

Work-related sources of stress take a variety of forms. Figure 8.2 presents a framework for thinking about and diagnosing organizational sources of work-related stress. It identifies seven principal work-related stressors. This framework shows that internal individual factors influence the ways in which each employee experiences these stressors.

Workload

For some employees, having too much work to do and not enough time or resources to do it is a major stressor. **Role overload** *exists when the demands of the job exceed the capacity of the individual to meet all of the demands adequately.* Some employees may be in a continuous condition of role overload. Surveys commonly identify work overload or "having to work too hard" as a major source of stress.[9]

> **Learning Goal**
>
> **2.** *Identify the primary sources of work-related stressors.*
>
> *Having too much work to do can cause stress for some employees.*
> ▼

LWA/GETTY IMAGES

FIGURE 8.2 Work-Related Stressors and Experienced Stress

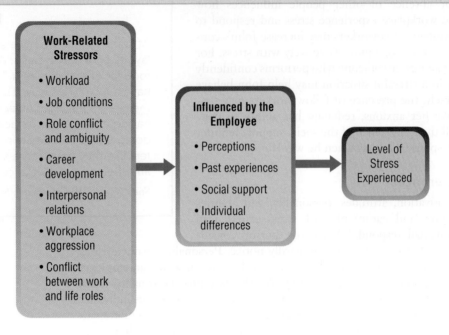

Having too little work to do also may create stress. Have you ever had a job with so little to do that the workday seemed to never end? If so, you can understand why employees may find too little work to be stressful. Leaders sometimes are guilty of trying to do their subordinates' work, or *micromanage*, when their jobs aren't challenging enough. Micromanaging might reduce the manager's stress caused by boredom, however, it is likely to increase subordinates' stress because the superior constantly watches them or second-guesses their decisions.

Job Conditions

Poor working conditions represent another important set of job stressors. Temperature extremes, loud noise, too much or too little lighting, radiation, and air pollution are but a few examples of working conditions that can cause stress in employees. Heavy travel demands or long-distance commuting are other aspects of jobs that employees may find stressful. Poor working conditions, excessive travel, and long hours all add up to increased stress and decreased performance.

Cutting-edge technology, while clearly of great benefit to society in general and many individuals in particular, nevertheless has created job conditions that may be quite stressful. Many employees are receiving massive volumes of e-mail, text messages, phone calls, and voice mail messages. It is often easy to perform work anytime, anyplace.[10] For some employees, this makes it difficult to draw mental boundaries between work and home.

Role Conflict and Ambiguity

Role conflict *refers to differing expectations of or demands on a person at work that become excessive.* (We discuss role conflict further in Chapter 13.) **Role ambiguity** *occurs when an employee is uncertain about assigned job duties and responsibilities.* Role conflict and role ambiguity may be particularly significant sources of job-related stress. Many employees suffer from role conflict and ambiguity because of conflicting expectations from leaders (e.g., cut prices, yet achieve higher profits). Having responsibility for the behavior of others and a lack of opportunity to participate in important decisions affecting their jobs are other aspects of employees' roles that may be stressful.[11]

Career Development

Major stressors related to career planning and development involve job security, promotions, transfers, and developmental opportunities. An employee can feel stress from underpromotion (failure to advance as rapidly as desired) or overpromotion (promotion to a job that exceeds the individual's competencies). The current wave of reorganizations and downsizings seriously threatens careers and causes stress. For example, the *Boston Globe* newspaper recently announced that it is eliminating 50 full-time jobs—12 percent of its news and editorial staff. The workforce reduction represents an effort to save money, be more efficient, and return to profitability. This is the fifth staff reduction since 2001. In the year prior to this announcement, there was a reduction of 42 *Boston Globe* managers and team leaders in the advertising, circulation, and marketing departments.[12] When jobs, teams, departments, or entire organizations are restructured, employees often have numerous career-related concerns: Can I perform competently in the new situation? Can I advance? Is my new job secure? Typically, the remaining employees find these concerns very stressful. At the *Boston Globe*, the employees not laid off face the stress of thinking more reductions are likely in the future since there have been so many in recent years and what that might mean for their careers. In a recent survey of downsizing survivors, two-thirds of the respondents used the following words to reflect their feelings: *guilt*, *anxiety*, and *anger*. Contrary to what might be expected, 74 percent of the survivors say their personal output has declined and 77 percent see more errors and mistakes being made.[13]

Interpersonal Relations

Teams and groups have a great impact on the behavior of employees. (We explore these dynamics in Chapter 12.) Good working relationships and interactions with peers, subordinates, and superiors are crucial aspects of organizational life, helping employees achieve personal and organizational goals. When relationships are poor, they can become sources of stress. A high level of political behavior, or "office politics," may create stress for leaders and employees. The nature of relationships with others often influences how employees react to other stressors. In other words, interpersonal relationships can be either a source of stress or the social support that helps employees cope with stressors.

In a recent survey, 53 percent of employees lost work time worrying about an incident of incivility. **Workplace incivility** *refers to rudeness, lack of regard for one another, and the violation of workplace norms for mutual respect.*[14] Forty-six percent contemplated changing jobs over incivility. In most instances, the manager is reported to be the instigator of the incivility. In addition, widespread workplace incivility has been found to negatively impact individual and organizational performance.[15] The following Communication Competency feature reports on communication incidents of several individuals who were subjected to workplace incivility.[16] It presents the violations of various attributes of the communications competency by instigators of the workplace incivility. All names have been disguised, but the incidents are real.

Communication competency

Workplace Incivility: How Not to Communicate

Lucy quit her job in university administration after finding herself routinely ignored and undermined by a manager. On one occasion, the manager returned from leave and sent everyone in the department except Lucy an e-mail thanking them for their work during her absence. On another, she told some of Lucy's peers that Lucy could not be trusted. Lucy says things rapidly went downhill. "I found it exceptionally rude. It made me extremely negative towards her. It shut me down. I felt she was someone I didn't really want to get to know or work with. Communication became very poor, which made the job difficult."

Bill comments: "One so-called member of the local management team regularly makes snide comments by e-mail and presses the 'Send' button as he puts on his coat and heads for home, knowing he won't see the people he's targeting for several days because of their work hours."

Ben reports: "I was pulling off a payoff preparation cycle for a month during December, and I entered '12' (the calendar month) when I should have entered '6' (the fiscal month). The payroll cycle was garbage therefore. The accountant called me insulting names with my new boss sitting right next to me. It was humiliating and unfair. It was my first payroll preparation cycle with the company, I was new—it was an honest mistake."

Argie recalls: "I was making a presentation to all of the company's international country managers and vice presidents. The division president stood up and shouted, 'No one is interested in this stuff.' His comment made me so nervous and upset that I could barely go on. I had been with this company for many years; you'd think he could have offered me a little respect for that alone."

Richard, a manager, says: "My two bosses, the company co-founders of an architectural interior-design firm, rarely converse with their workers. They treat employees like we're not even here. The company often receives gift baskets from vendors and the bosses hoard it in their offices. They invited only half of their employees to the holiday office party."

Susan, a public relations manager, reports: "My boss called my cell phone while I was sitting in an airplane on the runway. As the flight attendants announced that all phones had to be shut off, my boss said, 'This isn't a good fit anymore, so come by after 5:30 tomorrow to pick up your things.' "

Workplace Aggression

A disturbing source of stressors is workplace aggression. We discuss four types of workplace aggression in the last major part of this chapter: bullying, sexual harassment (which was also discussed in Chapter 2), workplace violence, and aggression toward the organization itself.

Conflict between Work and Life Roles

A person has many roles in life (employee, family member, Little League coach, church volunteer, to name just a few). Only one of these roles is associated with work (although some individuals may hold more than one job at a time). Work typically meets only some of a person's goals and needs. In addition, life goals and needs may conflict with career goals, presenting a source of stress. For example, employees' personal desires to spend time with their families or have more leisure time may conflict with the extra hours they must work to advance their careers. The large number of dual-career couples with children has brought work and family role conflicts into sharp focus. For example, when the children are sick, who takes primary responsibility for taking them to the doctor or staying home with them?

Life Stressors

The distinction between work and nonwork stressors isn't always clear, although a primary source of stress for many employees clearly is pressures between work and family demands.[17] As Figure 8.3 illustrates, both work and family pressures may contribute to work–family stress because pressures in one area can reduce a person's ability to cope with pressures in the other. These incompatible pressures trigger stress, which,

FIGURE 8.3 Path of Work–Family Pressures, Stress, and Conflict

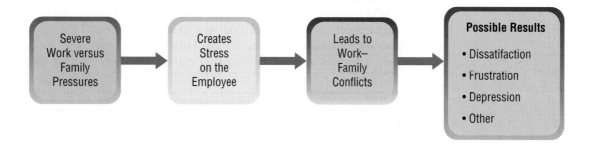

in turn, leads to work–family conflicts. These conflicts trigger possible outcomes such as dissatisfaction, frustration, and depression.

Life stressors *are tensions, anxieties, and conflicts that stem from pressures and demands in people's personal lives.* People must cope with a variety of life stressors; they deal with these stressors differently because of personality, age, gender, experience, and other characteristics. However, life stressors that affect almost everyone are those caused by significant life changes: divorce, marriage, death of a family member, and the like. People have a limited capacity to respond to stressors. Too much change too quickly can exhaust the body's ability to respond and result in negative consequences for a person's physical and mental health.

Table 8.1 presents a variety of stressful events that college students may face. Based on a current social readjustment rating scale, each event is rated on a 100-point scale,[18] with 1 indicating an event that is not stressful and 100 an extremely stressful event. An event labeled "high level of stress" might be assigned 71 to 100 points, depending on the specific stress experienced by the student. "Moderate level of stress" for an event might be scored from 31 to 70 points, and a "low level of stress" for an event may be assigned scores from 1 to 30 points by the student. During the course of a year, if a student experiences several events in the high level of stress range, there is a

TABLE 8.1 Stressful Events for College Students

EVENTS HAVING HIGH LEVELS OF STRESS	EVENTS HAVING RELATIVELY LOW LEVELS OF STRESS
• Death of parent	• Change in eating habits
• Death of spouse	• Change in sleeping habits
• Divorce	• Change in social activities
• Flunking out	• Conflict with instructor
• Unwed pregnancy	• Lower grades than expected

EVENTS HAVING MODERATE LEVELS OF STRESS

• Academic probation	• Major injury or illness
• Change of major	• Parents' divorce
• Death of close friend	• Serious arguments with romantic partner
• Failing important course	• Outstanding achievement
• Finding a new love interest	
• Loss of financial aid	

Source: Adapted from Baron, R. A., and Byrne, D. *Social Psychology: Understanding Human Interaction,* 6th ed. Boston: Allyn & Bacon, 1991, 573.

50–50 chance the student will get sick and his or her grades will suffer as a result of the excessive stress. How many of the events in Table 8.1 did you experience last year?

Recall that stress is the body's general response to any demand made on it. The list of stressful events in Table 8.1 contains both unpleasant events, such as failing a course, and pleasant events, such as finding a new love interest. This dual nature of life stressors demonstrates that they involve both negative and positive experiences. For example, vacations and holidays actually may be quite stressful for some people but very relaxing and refreshing for others. In addition, viewing unpleasant life events as having only negative effects is incorrect. People often can both cope with and grow from experiencing unpleasant events. Recall Thomas Dodson from the opening feature. He experienced severe stress as a result of being laid off by the architecture firm where he worked. He immediately started his own consulting firm. He has found the work to be rewarding and challenging, but an "immense struggle financially." Of course, people typically enjoy the positive effects and stimulation of pleasurable events, such as significant accomplishments, vacations, or gaining a new family member.

Learning Goal

3. *State the potential impacts of severe stress on health, performance, and job burnout.*

Severe Stress

High levels of stress can have both positive and negative effects. Our concern with severe and continuous work stress over time focuses on the negative effects because of their potential impacts on individual and organizational effectiveness as well as one's health. The potential impacts of severe stress levels occur in three main areas: physiological, emotional, and behavioral.[19] Examples of the effects of severe distress in these areas are as follows:

- Physiological effects of severe stress may include increased blood pressure, increased heart rate, sweating, hot and cold spells, breathing difficulties, muscular tension, gastrointestinal disorders, and panic attacks.

- Emotional effects of severe stress may include anger, anxiety, depression, low self-esteem, poor intellectual functioning (including an inability to concentrate and make decisions), nervousness, irritability, resentment of supervision, and job dissatisfaction.

- Behavioral effects of severe stress may include poor performance, absenteeism, high accident rates, high turnover rates, alcohol and substance abuse, impulsive behavior, and difficulties in communication.

The effects of severe work stress have important implications for organizational behavior and organizational effectiveness. We examine some of these effects in terms of health, performance, and job burnout.

Impacts on Health

Health problems commonly associated with severe stress include back pain, headaches, stomach and intestinal problems, upper respiratory infections, and various mental problems. Although determining the precise role that such stress plays in individual cases is difficult, some illnesses appear to be stress related.[20] Recall the layoff of Raymond and Melissa Gibbons in the opening feature. His blood pressure skyrocketed and he couldn't sleep. Melissa experienced headaches and also couldn't sleep.

Stress-related illnesses place a considerable burden on people and organizations. The costs to individuals seem more obvious than the costs to organizations. Let's review some of the organizational costs associated with stress-related disease. First, costs to employers include increased premiums for health insurance, as well as lost workdays from a serious illness (e.g., ulcers) and less serious illnesses (e.g., headaches). Estimates are that each employee who suffers from a stress-related illness loses an average of 16 days of work a year. In addition, it is estimated that health-care costs are 50 percent higher for employees who report higher levels of stress.[21] Second, more than three-fourths of all industrial accidents are caused by a worker's inability to cope with stress-related emotional problems. Third, legal problems for employers grow when they fail to address the intense stress they may be causing. The number of stress-related worker compensation claims is increasing. The link between the levels of stress in the workplace and worker compensation claims is clear. When employees experience severe stress over time, more worker compensation claims are filed. Studies have shown similar patterns in many different industries.[22]

Post-traumatic stress disorder *is a psychological disorder brought on, for example, by horrible experiences in combat during wartime, acts of violence and terrorism, and the like.*[23] Courts are now recognizing post-traumatic stress disorder as a condition that may justify a damage claim against an employer. Employees have successfully claimed suffering from this disorder as a result of sexual harassment, violence, and other traumatic circumstances in the workplace. Awards of damages in the millions of dollars have resulted from court cases involving workplace post-traumatic stress disorder claims.

Impacts on Performance

The positive and negative effects of stress are most apparent in the relationship between stress and performance. Figure 8.4 depicts the general stress–performance relationship in the shape of an arch. At low levels of stress, employees may not be sufficiently alert, challenged, or involved to perform at their best. As the curve indicates,

FIGURE 8.4 Typical Relationship between Performance and Stress Arousal

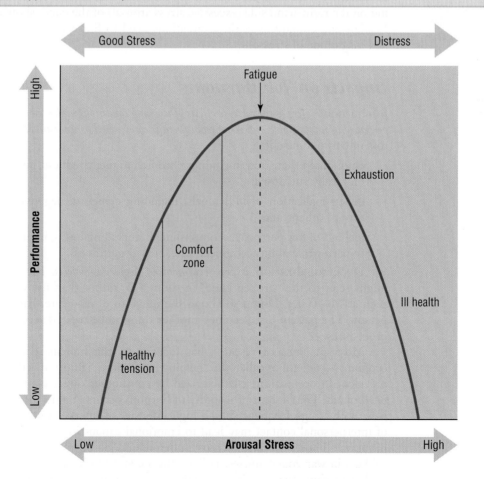

Adapted from Nixon, P. Stress: The human function curve. American Institute of Stress. www.stress.org (March 2007).

KEITH BROFSKY/PHOTODISC/GETTY IMAGES

▲

Common indicators of job burnout include emotional exhaustion, chronic fatigue, tiredness, and a sense of being physically run down.

increasing the arousal of stress may improve performance—but only up to a point. An optimal level of stress probably exists for most tasks. Beyond that point, performance begins to deteriorate.[24] At excessive levels of stress, employees are too agitated, aroused, or threatened to perform well.

Leaders need to consider the optimum stress points for both themselves and their subordinates. The causes for these points, however, are difficult to pin down. For example, an employee may be absent from work frequently because of boredom (too little stress) or because of overwork (excessive stress). The curve shown in Figure 8.4 changes with the situation; that is, it varies for different people and different tasks. Too little stress for one employee may be just right for another on a particular task. Similarly, the optimal amount of stress for a specific individual for one task may be too much or too little for that person's effective performance of other tasks.

As a practical matter, leaders should be more concerned about excessive stress than with how to add to stress. Motivating individuals to perform better is always important, but attempting to do so by increasing the level of severe stress is typically shortsighted. Studies of the stress–performance relationships in organizations often show a strong negative association between severe stress in a team or department and its overall performance. That is, high levels of employee stress over an extended period of time often lead to lower productivity. This negative relationship indicates that these work settings are operating on the right-hand side (excessive stress arousal) of the curve shown in Figure 8.4. Leaders and employees in these situations need to find ways to reduce the number and magnitude of stressors.

Impacts on Job Burnout

Job burnout *refers to the adverse effects of working conditions under which strong stressors are perceived as unavoidable and relief from them is interpreted as unavailable.* Common indicators of burnout include:

- emotional exhaustion, including chronic fatigue, tiredness, and a sense of being physically run down;
- depersonalization of individuals, including cynicism, negativity, and irritability toward others; and
- feelings of low personal accomplishment, including losing interest and motivation to perform, inability to concentrate, and forgetfulness.[25]

Depersonalization *is the treatment of people as objects.* For example, a nurse might refer to the "broken knee" in room 405, rather than use the patient's name, such as Ms. Wiley. Doing so allows the nurse to disassociate from the patient as a person. The patient just becomes another thing to be treated according to rules and procedures.

Most job burnout research has focused on the human services sector of the economy—sometimes called the "helping professions." Burnout is thought to be most prevalent in occupations characterized by continuous direct contact with people in need of aid. The highest probability of burnout occurs among those individuals who have both a high frequency and a high intensity of interpersonal contact. This level of interpersonal contact may lead to emotional exhaustion, a key component of job burnout.[26] Those who may be most vulnerable to job burnout include social workers, soldiers in war zones, nurses, police officers, and teachers. Burnout also may affect leaders or shop owners who are under increasing pressure to reduce costs, increase profits, and better serve customers. Individuals who experience job burnout seem to have some common characteristics. Three characteristics are associated with a high probability of burnout:

- experiencing a great deal of negative stress as a result of job-related stressors,
- tending to be idealistic and self-motivating achievers, and
- seeking unattainable goals.[27]

The burnout syndrome represents a combination of certain individual attributes and the job situation. Individuals who suffer from burnout often have unrealistic expectations concerning their work and their ability to accomplish desired goals, given the nature of the situation in which they find themselves. Job burnout is not something that happens overnight. The entire process typically takes a great deal of time. The path to job burnout is illustrated by Figure 8.5. One or more of the working conditions listed, coupled with the unrealistic expectations or ambitions of the individual, can lead eventually to a state of complete physical, mental, and emotional exhaustion. Under conditions of burnout, the individual can no longer cope with the demands of the job and willingness to try drops dramatically.

Individual Differences and Stress

Learning Goal

4. *Describe how individual differences influence reactions to stressful situations.*

Several individual differences are related to stress, including self-esteem and locus of control (personality attributes discussed in Chapter 3). Individual differences may affect how a person will perceive and react to a situation or an event as a stressor.[28] For example, an individual with low self-esteem is more likely to experience stress in highly demanding work situations than is a person with high self-esteem. Individuals high in self-esteem typically have more confidence in their ability to meet intense job demands than do those with low self-esteem. Employees with high internal locus of control may take more effective action, more quickly, in coping with a sudden and critical emergency (a stressor) than might employees with a high external locus of control. Individuals high in internal locus of control are likely to believe that they can moderate the highly stressful situation. Before reading further, please respond to the statements in Table 8.2. This self-assessment exercise is related to the discussion that follows.

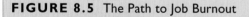

FIGURE 8.5 The Path to Job Burnout

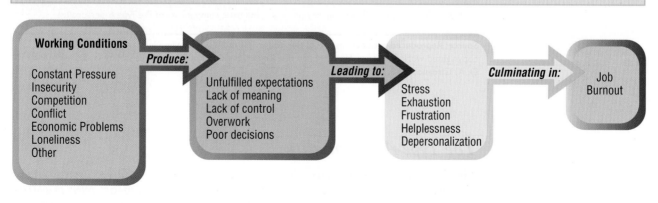

TABLE 8.2 A Self-Assessment of Type A Personality

Choose from the following responses to answer the questions below:

A. Almost always true   C. Seldom true

B. Usually true   D. Never true

_____ 1. I do not like to wait for other people to complete their work before I can proceed with my own.
_____ 2. I hate to wait in most lines.
_____ 3. People tell me that I tend to get irritated too easily.
_____ 4. Whenever possible, I try to make activities competitive.
_____ 5. I have a tendency to rush into work that needs to be done before knowing the procedure I will use to complete the job.
_____ 6. Even when I go on vacation, I usually take some work along.
_____ 7. Even when I make a mistake, it is usually due to the fact that I have rushed into the job before completely planning it through.
_____ 8. I feel guilty for taking time off from work.
_____ 9. People tell me I have a bad temper when it comes to competitive situations.
_____ 10. I tend to lose my temper when I am under a lot of pressure at work.
_____ 11. Whenever possible, I will attempt to complete two or more tasks at once.
_____ 12. I tend to race against the clock.
_____ 13. I have no patience for lateness.
_____ 14. I catch myself rushing when there is no need.

Score your responses according to the following key:

- *An intense sense of time urgency* is a tendency to race against the clock, even when there is little reason to. The person feels a need to hurry for hurry's sake alone, and this tendency has appropriately been called "hurry sickness." Time urgency is measured by items 1, 2, 8, 12, 13, and 14. Every A or B answer to these six questions scores one point.

    Your score = _____

- *Inappropriate aggression and hostility* reveal themselves in a person who is excessively competitive and who cannot do anything for fun. This inappropriately aggressive behavior easily evolves into frequent displays of hostility, usually at the slightest provocation or frustration. Competitiveness and hostility are measured by items 3, 4, 9, and 10. Every A or B answer scores one point.

    Your score = _____

- *Polyphasic behavior* refers to the tendency to undertake two or more tasks simultaneously at inappropriate times. It usually results in wasted time due to an inability to complete the tasks. This behavior is measured by items 6 and 11. Every A or B answer scores one point.

    Your score = _____

- *Goal directedness without proper planning* refers to the tendency of an individual to rush into work without really knowing how to accomplish the desired result. This usually results in incomplete work or work with many errors, which in turn leads to wasted time, energy, and money. Lack of planning is measured by items 5 and 7. Every A or B response scores one point.

    Your score = _____

    TOTAL SCORE = _____

If your score is 5 or greater, you may possess some basic components of the Type A personality.

Source: Reproduced with permission of the Robert J. Brady Co., Bowie, Maryland, 20715, from its copyrighted work *The Stress Mess Solution: The Causes and Cures of Stress on the Job*, by G. S. Everly and D. A. Girdano, 1980, 55.

The Type A Personality

The **Type A personality** *refers to a person involved in a never-ending struggle to achieve more and more in less and less time.* In contrast, the **Type B personality** *refers to a person who tends to be easygoing and relaxed, patient, a good listener, and takes a long-range view of things.* Characteristics of the Type A personality include:

- a chronic sense of urgency about time;
- an extremely competitive, almost hostile orientation;
- thinking about other things or text messaging while talking to someone;
- an impatience with barriers to task accomplishment; and
- a sense of guilt when relaxing or taking a vacation.[29]

Two medical researchers first identified the Type A personality when they noticed a recurrent personality pattern in their patients who suffered from premature heart disease.[30] In addition to the characteristics just listed, *extreme* Type A individuals often speak rapidly, are preoccupied with themselves, and are dissatisfied with life. They tend to give quick replies to questions with no pause to deliberate before answering the questions. Type A personalities may give sarcastic, rude, and hostile responses. They may try to appear to be humorous, but with the underlying intent to be hurtful.

The questionnaire in Table 8.2 measures four sets of behaviors and tendencies associated with the Type A personality: (1) time urgency, (2) competitiveness and hostility, (3) polyphasic behavior (trying to do several things at once), and (4) a lack of planning. Medical researchers have discovered that these behaviors and tendencies often relate to life and work stress. They tend to cause stress or make stressful situations worse than they otherwise might be.

Current research suggests that the Type A personality description is too broad to predict adverse health impacts accurately. Rather, research now indicates that only certain aspects of the Type A personality—particularly anger, hostility, and aggression—may be related to severe stress and health reactions.[31] Type A individuals with these specific attributes appear to be two to three times more likely to develop health problems than are Type B individuals.

The Hardy Personality

What aspects of personality might protect individuals from the negative health impacts of stress? Individual traits that seem to counter the effects of severe stress are known collectively as the **hardy personality**—*the personality of a person with a cluster of characteristics that includes feeling a sense of commitment, responding to each difficulty as representing a challenge and an opportunity, and perceiving that one has control over one's own life*.[32] The hardy personality is characterized by:

- a sense of personal control over events in one's life;
- a tendency to attribute one's own behavior to internal as opposed to external causes (recall the discussion of attribution in Chapter 4);
- a strong commitment to work and personal relationships; not detaching oneself when the going gets tough; and
- an ability to view unexpected change or potential threats as challenges and opportunities for growth.[33]

A high degree of **hardiness** *reduces the negative effects of stressful events*. Hardiness seems to reduce stress by altering the way in which people perceive stressors. An individual having a low level of hardiness perceives some events or situations as stressful; an individual having a high level of hardiness perceives fewer events or situations as stressful. A person with a high level of hardiness isn't overwhelmed by challenging or difficult situations. Rather, faced with a severe stressor, the hardy personality copes or responds constructively by trying to find a solution—to control or influence events and situations. This behavioral response typically reduces stress reactions, moderates blood pressure increases, and reduces the probability of adverse health impacts.

Through development of the *self competency*, a person may come to reflect the attributes of the hardy personality. Recall from Chapter 1 that the *self competency* involves the ability to assess your own strengths and weaknesses, set and pursue professional and personal goals, balance work and personal life, and engage in new learning—including new or changed skills, behaviors, and attitudes. Table 8.3 provides

TABLE 8.3 Assessing Your Sense of Hardiness

Instructions:
Please respond to each of the statements below as truthfully as you can. Use the following scale:

Not like me	Seldom	Sometimes	When I think about it	Usually	Always
0	1	2	3	4	5

_____ 1. I have a set of things that I would like to accomplish in my life.

_____ 2. I spend quiet time thinking about my life and my world.

_____ 3. When I think about it, I wake up in the morning full of optimism and I look forward to starting my day.

_____ 4. I have a clear picture of what the next phase of my life will look like.

_____ 5. I try to learn new things.

_____ 6. I sleep well and am able to relax when I have free time.

_____ 7. I believe that I have control over most things in my life.

_____ 8. I look forward to the changes that happen in my life and view them as challenges.

_____ 9. I have goals in life and I am clear on what they are.

_____ 10. I am usually an optimistic person when it comes to how I view my future.

_____ 11. I am adventuresome, continually pushing to try new things.

_____ 12. I would consider myself to be very goal oriented.

Score:
Add points for items 1 through 12 = _____.

Possible Interpretations of Your Hardiness Score:
- **0–24** You likely don't feel that you can control your world and you don't spend a lot of time making plans. Your ability to handle stress is not as high as you would like.
- **25–36** You do some planning, but probably wish you did more. You tend to be "other directed" and not always in control of your life.
- **37–48** You are more self-directed and normally handle stress well. You tend to be goal oriented, though you could be more focused on setting goals.
- **49–60** You are very goal oriented and know the difference between being stressed and handling stress.

Source: Adapted from Retirement Lifestyle Centers. *How hardy is your personality?* www.retirementlifestyle .com (April 2007).

a brief questionnaire for you to reflect on your own sense of hardiness. If you perceive your sense of hardiness is lacking, the good news is that you can do something about it. We provide suggestions in this chapter and others for developing your hardiness.

Captain Chesley B. Sullenberger III, the pilot of US Airways Flight 1549, which he safely landed in the Hudson River, appears to reflect the attributes of the hardy personality. The following Self Competency feature reports on his handling of the jetliner when both engines were disabled by a large flock of birds shortly after departing La Guardia Airport on January 15, 2009.[34]

Self competency

Chesley B. Sullenberger III, Captain of US Airways Flight 1549

Some individuals suggest that Sullenberger spent practically his whole life preparing for the five-minute nightmare that was US Airways Flight 1549. He obtained his pilot's license at 14, was named best aviator in his class at the Air Force Academy, flew fighter jets, investigated air disasters, mastered glider flying, and studied the psychology of how cockpit crews behave in a crisis.

When the ultimate test came on a descent over the Hudson River, he spoke into the intercom only once and gave perhaps the most terrifying instruction a pilot can give—"Brace for impact"—with remarkable calm. And as the 150 passengers of Flight 1549 marveled at their hero pilot's skills and cool head, they learned what friends and relatives of Sullenberger say they had known all along. "This is someone who has not just spent his life flying airplanes but has actually dug very deeply into what makes these things work, and I think he proved it," said Robert Bea, a civil engineer who knows Sullenberger (affectionately known as "Sully"). Bea adds: "He is, how should I call it, a humble man. But he is damned smart."

His wife, Lorraine, called her husband a "pilot's pilot" who "loves the art of the airplane." She described him, as almost everyone else had, as controlled and professional. She states: "This is the Sully I know. I always knew how he would react. So to me this is not something unusual. It's the man I know." His sister, Mary Margaret Wilson, said Sully built model airplanes, taking care to paint even the most minuscule details on the faces of the pilots. Wilson, recalling her brother's childhood crop duster flights at the age of 15, said she was usually nervous flying in small planes—but never with him. She said he was always professional and never cut corners. Wilson notes: "I think Sully is a very duty-oriented person. He is always looking to get better. He would be the one person who could land a plane in the water without any engines."

Robert Bea, cofounder of UC Berkeley's Center for Catastrophic Risk Management, said he could think of few pilots as well situated to bring the plane down safely as Sullenberger. Bea notes that Sully has been studying the psychology of helping airline crews function even in the face of a crisis. Bea adds: "When a plane is getting ready to crash with a lot of people who trust you, it is a test. Sully proved the end of the road for that test. He had studied it, he had rehearsed it, he had taken it to his heart." David Love, recently retired, has known Sully since the 1980s when he was a pilot at US Airways. Love describes his friend as a well-spoken, well-educated, dedicated pilot who takes his job and profession very seriously and is an expert on airline safety. He said Sully would brush off the notion that he was a hero. "If he were here, Sully would say that his team functioned flawlessly," Love said.

New York Mayor Michael Bloomberg commented: "The pilot did a masterful job of landing the plane in the river and then making sure that everybody got out. He walked the plane twice after everybody else was off, and tried to verify that there was nobody else on board, and he assures us there was not." As the cabin took on water, Sully climbed out of the jet only after the four other crew members and 150 passengers made their orderly exit. When he reached a raft, someone on a ferry tossed him a knife, and he cut away the tether to the jet.

Sullenberger is also a cofounder of the Safety Reliability Methods company. This firm provides consulting services in such areas as risk evaluation, improved safety, and creating high-reliability organizations.

To learn more about Safety Reliability Methods, go to **http://safetyreliability.com.**

Stress Management

Individual and leader insights to help employees cope with stress are increasingly important as stress has become a more widely recognized organizational problem. A number of insights are available to individuals and leaders for effective stress management and reducing the potential harmful impacts of stress. **Stress management** *refers to the actions and initiatives that reduce stress by helping the individual understand the stress response, recognize stressors, and use coping techniques to minimize the negative impacts of severe experienced stress.*[35]

Learning Goal

5. Apply individual and leader insights to the management of workplace stress.

Insights for Individuals

Individuals can use stress management practices that are designed to (1) eliminate or control the sources of severe stress and (2) make the individual more resistant to or better able to cope with severe stress. The first step in stress management involves recognizing the stressors that are affecting the person's life. Next, the individual needs to decide what to do about them. Personal goals and values, coupled with practical stress management skills, can help an individual cope with stressors and reduce negative stress reactions.

Some of the insights for managing severe and ongoing stress by an individual include the following:

> **Change Insight**
>
> The to-do list is infinite. For every big priority you put on the to-do list, you need a corresponding item on the stop-doing list. It's like an accounting balance.
>
> *Jim Collins, Author,* Good to Great

- Plan ahead and practice good time management. Frame your aspiration (e.g., getting a job) as something you'd really like to achieve, rather than in absolute terms (e.g., I *absolutely must* get a job now).
- Get plenty of exercise, eat a balanced diet, get adequate rest, and generally take care of yourself.
- View the difficulties you encounter as opportunities to learn and challenges to be tackled, rather than as problems to be solved or difficulties to overcome.
- Recognize and minimize the tendency to be a perfectionist.
- Concentrate on balancing your work and personal life. Always take time to have fun.
- Learn relaxation techniques and maintain a sense of humor.
- Communicate with those who can provide social support and take action to help reduce the severe and ongoing stressors.[36]

An individual can use relaxation techniques during the workday to cope with intense job demands. For example, a common "relaxation response" to stress is to (1) choose a comfortable position, (2) close your eyes, (3) relax your muscles, (4) become aware of your breathing, (5) maintain a passive attitude when thoughts surface, and (6) continue for a set period of time (e.g., 20 minutes).[37]

At work, the application of the knowledge, skills, and abilities of the communication competency is vital in coping with intense stress. Consider the insights of Steve Widom, one of the founders and chief technology officer at Chordial Solutions, a firm that provides enterprise software and services to businesses. It is located in The Colony, Texas (near Dallas). In information technology (IT) jobs, Widom contends that severe stress is more manageable when you learn to expect the occasional 2:00 A.M. call about a system that's down. He chuckles: "If systems were perfect, we would be bored. When we signed up for IT, we knew what we were getting into." Because IT is project based, Widom emphasizes that severe stress comes in waves and smart stress management involves riding those waves skillfully. When those times come, he works as hard as those employees who report to him. Widom states: "When they work all night, I'm there with them. My rule of thumb is, for every all-nighter you pull, you need two days of comp time."[38]

Insights for Leaders

Leaders often have the authority to approve organizational stress management programs that are designed to reduce the harmful effects of severe stress (distress) in one or more of the following ways: (1) Identify and reduce or eliminate intense work stressors, (2) assist employees in changing their perceptions of the stressors and experienced stress, and (3) assist employees to cope more effectively with the outcomes from severe stress.

Reducing Work Stressors

Leader insights aimed at eliminating or modifying work stressors include:

- improvements in the physical work environment;
- job redesign (see Chapter 6);
- changes in workloads and deadlines;
- changes in work schedules, more flexible hours, and sabbaticals; and
- greater levels of employee participation, particularly in planning changes that affect them.

Improvements in job responsibilities and accountabilities can be particularly useful in removing or reducing major role ambiguities and role conflicts—two main sources of severe stress. When diagnosing stressors in the workplace, leaders should be particularly aware that an employee's lack of control over the tasks they perform heightens stress. The greatest stress occurs when jobs are high in stressors and low in controllability (e.g., police, military in war zones, and disaster recovery work). Thus, work stress may be reduced through (1) involvement of employees in organizational changes that will affect them, (2) work redesign that reduces major uncertainties and increases reasonable control over the pace of work, and (3) improved clarity and understanding of roles. An important way to provide employees with more control and less stress is to give individuals more control over their time.

Larry Sanders is chairman and chief executive of Columbus Regional Healthcare System, headquartered in Columbus, Georgia. He is the recipient of a number of awards for his leadership in health-care and civic organizations. Sanders recognizes the importance of giving employees appropriate control over their work and the need for effective communication to effectively manage stress—both his own and subordinates. Sanders comments:

> *My style of management is inclusive, open, and honest. I delegate and then expect those I left in charge to use their resources and capabilities to fulfill the responsibility. I was never micromanaged, and I don't micromanage. I was allowed to use the full range of my abilities to accomplish tasks, and I expect those who work with me and around me to do the same thing. Micromanagement kills the morale of an organization faster than anything else does.*[39]

Modifying Behaviors

Improvements targeted at behaviors and experiences of severe stress include:

- team building,
- career counseling and other employee assistance programs,
- workshops on time management,
- workshops on job burnout to help employees understand its nature and symptoms, and
- training in relaxation techniques.

Dividing stress management programs into these categories doesn't mean that they are not related. In addition, such programs might overlap in terms of their impact on the three target areas mentioned previously. For example, a workshop dealing with role problems might clarify job descriptions and duties, reducing the magnitude of these potential stressors. At the same time, through greater knowledge and insight into roles and role problems, employees might be able to cope more effectively with this source of stress. Similarly, career counseling might reduce career concerns as a source of stress while improving the ability of employees to cope with career problems.

Many organizational wellness programs focus on preventing the leading causes of illness among employees, including sedentary lifestyles and poor nutrition habits.

SW PRODUCTIONS/DIGITAL VISIONS/GETTY IMAGES

Wellness Programs

One comprehensive remedy that may be approved by leaders for improving the ability of employees to cope with severe stress is a **wellness program**—*a health management initiative that incorporates the components of disease prevention, medical care, self-care, and health promotion.*[40] The Wellness Councils of America (WELCOA) is a nonprofit membership organization based in Omaha, Nebraska. It is dedicated to promoting healthy lifestyles. Its primary focus is on building *Well Workplaces*—organizations dedicated to the health of their employees. The council provides a blueprint to help organizations create programs that help employees make better lifestyle choices and that can have a positive impact on the organization's profits. To date, more than 700 organizations, such as UPS, SAS, Deloitte Institute, Microsoft, and Berkshire Hathaway, have met the rigid criteria for the *Well Workplace* award and designation. WELCOA and other wellness programs are driven by, among other factors, the continuous increases in health-care costs paid by employers and employees. The leading causes of illness are often preventable. Targets of wellness programs often include tobacco use, alcohol and substance abuse, sedentary lifestyles, poor nutritional habits, excessive and unnecessary stressors in the workplace, and inadequate employee abilities to cope with stress.[41] The scope and features of wellness programs among organizations vary widely. With skyrocketing health insurance premiums for employers and rising copayments for employees, there has been a surge in the adoption of wellness programs.[42]

The following Change Competency feature provides an overview of Ortho-Clinical Diagnostics' wellness program, which is one of the Johnson & Johnson family of companies.[43] It is headquartered in Raritan, New Jersey, with manufacturing operations in Rochester, New York, and elsewhere. This feature focuses on the Rochester operation. Ortho-Clinical Diagnostics provides solutions for screening, diagnosing, monitoring, and confirming diseases early.[44]

Change competency

Ortho-Clinical Diagnostics' Wellness Program

Ortho-Clinical Diagnostics employs multiple strategies for enhancing employee wellness and vitality. The cornerstone of the company's program is a health risk assessment and intervention program. All of Ortho-Clinical's 950 Rochester, New York, employees have completed a health profile detailing their HDL cholesterol, LDL cholesterol, triglycerides, blood sugar, blood pressure, and height, weight, hip, and waist measurements. After completing the profile, employees receive a confidential and personalized health assessment with recommendations and tips for improving their health.

By participating in this program, each employee nets a $500 annual health benefit savings. A recent Johnson & Johnson survey indicated that participants have lower medical expenses than those employees who choose not to participate. In addition, they have been able to reduce their cholesterol levels, incidents of hypertension, and cigarette smoking. "The vision of our company is to have the healthiest employees in the world," says Lorraine Cleary, occupational health nurse and a member of the company's five-person health and wellness team. "We want to create a culture of complete health, ranging from our nutritious food offerings in the company cafeteria to our outdoor walking trails," adds Melissa Kraemer, program manager of health and wellness.

Employees have many on-site opportunities to improve their personal health. There is a fitness center that offers 12 weekly group exercise classes. Other activities include a work-site Weight Watchers group, smoking cessation classes, health awareness programs and screenings, and connections with community-based health runs and walks. A stroll through the cafeteria further underscores a commitment to employee health. "Roughly 80 percent of our cafeteria food choices are nutritionally healthy, with minimal processing," Kraemer explains. "Items include a complete salad bar, whole-wheat pizza made with low-fat cheese, and veggie burgers on whole-wheat buns topped with lots of vegetables." As part of the company's Eat Complete campaign, one vending machine is dedicated to providing healthy choices, such as yogurt, trail mix, almonds, pita chips, and 100 percent fruit juice.

In addition, Ortho-Clinical uses plenty of marketing tools to spread the word about healthy lifestyles. Initiatives include web-based health resources and programs, the *Healthy People* newsletter, daily e-mail tips on healthy living, and cafeteria table tents with information on topics ranging from injury and illness prevention to work–life programs. Outside the building, employees are treated to a relaxing setting, which includes an extensive walking trail, gazebos, and two serene ponds. Cleary adds: "We fully embrace Johnson & Johnson's credo. Part of it focuses on our responsibility to employees and their families."

To learn more about Ortho-Clinical Diagnostics, Inc., go to **www.orthoclinical.com**.

Workplace Aggression

Learning Goal

6. *Explain four major types of workplace aggression.*

Workplace aggression *includes behaviors that are intended to have the effect of harming a person within or directly related to (e.g., customer, service representative, employee) the organization or the organization itself.*[45] Aggressive workplace behavior can be grouped into three broad categories: (1) hostility—abusive verbal or symbolic behavior such as "the silent treatment"; (2) obstructionism—behavior that is designed to hamper the individual's performance, such as refusing to provide needed resources; and (3) overt aggression—many types of assault, violence, and destruction of property.[46] Recent studies of the overall percentage and estimated number of U.S. employees who experience psychological and physical aggression show that it is excessive. In one study, 47 million U.S. employees reported having experienced one or more forms of psychological aggression during the previous 12 months. In addition, 7 million U.S. employees experienced one or more forms of workplace violence during the previous 12 months. In another study, nearly 45 percent of the respondents reported that they had worked for an abusive manager.[47]

Self-Serving Biases

A variety of self-serving biases have been identified for why some employees engage in workplace aggression. Some of these biases include[48]:

- **Hostile attribution bias**—*the assumption that people tend to be motivated by the desire to harm others.* This bias is used at times to explain why others behave as they do. Individuals with a strong motive to aggress may even see friendly acts by others as being driven by hidden/hostile agendas that are designed to harm them. This type of attribution enables aggressive persons to rationalize their own hostile behaviors as acts of self-defense intended to head off physical or verbal attack by others.

- **Potency bias**—*the assumption that interactions with others are contests to establish dominance versus submissiveness.* This bias rationalizes the use of aggression to dominate others as demonstrating strength, bravery, control, and fearlessness.

The failure to act aggressively is seen as weakness, fear, and cowardice. Thus, aggressive individuals see their behaviors as a means of gaining respect from others and feel that to show weakness is to encourage powerful others to take advantage of them.

- **Retribution bias**—*individuals think that taking revenge (retribution) is more important than preserving relationships.* There is a tendency to see retaliation as a more rational behavior than reconciliation. For example, aggression is seen as justifiable if it is thought to restore respect or exact retributions for a perceived wrong. Retaliation is seen by aggressive individuals as more reasonable than forgiveness, vindication is seen as more reasonable than reconciliation, and obtaining revenge is seen as more reasonable than maintaining a relationship. This bias often underlies justification for aggressions stimulated by wounded pride, reduced self-esteem, and perceived disrespect.

- **Derogation of target bias**—*individuals see those they wish to make (or have made) targets of aggressions as evil, immoral, or untrustworthy.* This type of influence enables them to see the targets of aggression as deserving of it.

- **Social discounting bias**—*individuals believe that social customs reflect free will and the opportunity to satisfy their own needs.* They have a disdain for traditional ideals and conventional beliefs and are often cynical and critical of social customs. They show a lack of sensitivity, empathy, and concern for social customs. Socially deviant behaviors intended to harm others are justified by claiming that they allow the aggressive individuals to obtain freedom of expression, relief from the cycles of social customs, and liberation from social relationships. These and other underlying mechanisms for rationalizing aggression may be seen in incidents of bullying, sexual harassment, and workplace violence.

In the remainder of this section, we present the core features of four major types of workplace aggression: bullying, sexual harassment, violence, and aggression toward the organization. There are potential overlaps and relationships among these types of workplace aggression. For example, an employee may encounter a variety of bullying behaviors, some of which may escalate into the category of workplace violence and destruction or theft of organizational property.

Workplace Bullying

Workplace bullying *is repeated and persistent negative actions directed toward one or more individuals that involve a power imbalance and create a hostile work environment.*[49] Unreasonable behavior refers to acts that a reasonable person, when considering all of the circumstances, would see as victimizing, humiliating, undermining, or threatening an employee or group of employees. Bullying often involves a misuse or abuse of power. For the employees subject to it, they can experience difficulties in defending themselves. Bullying cuts across race, religion, and gender. It involves offensive behaviors that a reasonable person would see as creating an intimidating, hostile, or abusive work environment. Normally, bullying must involve repeated incidents and a pattern of behavior.

Bullies engage in a variety of behaviors ranging from condescension to rage. Table 8.4 is a questionnaire that presents 24 negative acts that have been identified as components of workplace bullying. This questionnaire enables you to assess whether you have experienced any of these bullying behaviors over the past six months and, if so, how frequently and with what intensity (i.e., the cumulative number of negative acts experienced, which can range from 1 act to a maximum of all 24 acts). In brief, the greater the frequency of a negative act over a six-month period and the greater the number of negative acts, the more severe the degree of bullying.[50]

Women as well as men may bully others at work. Women bullies target other women an overwhelming 84 percent of the time. Men bullies target women in 69 percent of the cases. Women are most often the targets of bullying.[51]

TABLE 8.4 Negative Acts Associated with Workplace Bullying

Instructions:

Indicate how often you may have experienced each of the negative acts associated with workplace bullying during the past six months.

Use the following scale and record your response next to each statement below:

Never	Occasionally (less than monthly)	Monthly	Weekly	Daily
0	1	2	3	4

_____ 1. Had information withheld that affected your performance.

_____ 2. Been exposed to an unmanageable workload.

_____ 3. Ordered to do work below your level of competence.

_____ 4. Given tasks with unreasonable/impossible targets/deadlines.

_____ 5. Had your opinions and views ignored.

_____ 6. Had your work excessively monitored.

_____ 7. Reminded repeatedly of your errors or mistakes.

_____ 8. Humiliated or ridiculed in connection with your work.

_____ 9. Had gossip and rumors spread about you.

_____ 10. Had insulting/offensive remarks made about you.

_____ 11. Been ignored, excluded, or isolated from others.

_____ 12. Received hints or signals from others that you should quit your job.

_____ 13. Been intimidated with threatening behavior.

_____ 14. Experienced persistent criticism of your work and effort.

_____ 15. Been ignored or faced hostile reactions when you approached the person.

_____ 16. Had key tasks removed, replaced with trivial unpleasant tasks.

_____ 17. Had false allegations made against you.

_____ 18. Subjected to excessive teasing and sarcasm.

_____ 19. Been shouted at or targeted with spontaneous anger (or rage).

_____ 20. Pressured into not claiming something to which you were entitled.

_____ 21. Been subjected to demeaning practical jokes.

_____ 22. Received unwanted sexual attention.

_____ 23. Received offensive remarks or behavior related to your race or ethnicity.

_____ 24. Experienced threats of violence or abused/attacked.

Scoring:

Total the number of points assigned. In general, the greater the *frequency* (never to daily) and the greater the intensity (none to 24 acts), the greater the degree of bullying experienced. Based on your responses to this instrument, how do you perceive and interpret the degree of bullying (if any) experienced by you?

Source: Adapted from Einarsen, S., Hoel, H., Zapf, D., and Cooper, C. L. The concept of bullying at work. In Einarsen, S., Hoel, H., Zapf, D., and Cooper, C. L. (Eds.). *Bullying and Emotional Abuse in the Workplace: International Perspectives in Research and Practice.* London: Taylor & Francis, 2003, 3–30; Lutgen-Sandvik, P., Tracy, S. J., and Alberts, J. K. Burned by bullying in the American workplace. *Journal of Management Studies,* 2007, 44, 837–862.

Bullying harms the health of the individual subjected to it. Health concerns from bullying need to be distinguished from routine office politics, teasing, incivilities, and somewhat off-color stories/jokes. All of the effects of stress identified previously may be experienced as a result of bullying. In addition, individuals who report severe forms of bullying identify experiencing the following major symptoms:

- *General anxiety disorder*—evidenced by anxiety, excessive worry, disruptive sleep, stress headaches, and racing heart rate.

- *Clinical depression*—evidenced by loss of concentration, disruptive sleep, obsession over details at work, exhaustion (leading to an inability to function), and diagnosed depression.

- *Post-traumatic stress disorder*—evidenced by feeling edgy or irritable and constantly on guard, having recurrent nightmares and flashbacks, and needing to avoid the feelings or thoughts that remind the bullied person of the trauma.[52]

In addition to the potential terrible effects of bullying on the individual, the organization has much at stake in preventing or dealing with bullying in a direct way. A variety of organizational effects have been associated with bullying. These include (1) high absenteeism resulting from time taken off by the bullied employees, (2) reduced productivity among bullied workers, (3) stress-related illnesses that increase health-care costs to the organization, (4) reduced customer service due to bullied employees feeling less loyalty to the organization because it is not protecting them from bullying, and (5) increased employee turnover—82 percent of people targeted by a bully quit.[53]

Insights for Leaders

Many insights have been suggested to address bullying in the workplace. As a start, leaders should have an anti-bullying workplace aggression policy that defines expectations for interpersonal relationships. Employees should understand what is and is not acceptable behavior in the workplace. This will serve as one step toward creating a culture in which people treat each other with courtesy and respect. Leaders need to create a culture of respect by taking corrective action against those engaged in bullying behaviors. Increasingly, employers are no longer dismissing bullying as simply a socially acceptable side effect of office politics. In addition to strong sexual harassment policies, a number of firms are developing policies that address bullying. A few examples include American Express, Burger King, and JCPenney. The failure of leaders to address bullying has resulted in successful legal action against those firms.[54]

In addition to the insights reviewed, leaders can do the following: (1) Speak directly to the bully. Tell the individual that you find his or her behavior unacceptable and that it needs to stop. Often this is all that is needed. (2) In some cases, the bullying behaviors are not seen by others. Thus, tell a friend or work colleague. You may soon learn that you are not the only one who has been subject to the person's bullying. (3) Keep a diary of the specific behaviors and incidents of bullying and when each occurred. Many of the incidents in isolation may seem minor, but when put together, they can establish a serious pattern over time. (4) Discuss the experience of bullying with the bully. If your manager is the person who is doing the bullying, you may need to discuss the matter with a person in the human resources department. (5) If these initial steps are not effective, it may be necessary to file a formal complaint, consistent with the organization's policies.[55] There is no assurance that these steps will be effective. Unfortunately, too often employees have found it necessary to resign from their positions or seek a transfer to a different department to remove themselves from the bullying activity.

A special type of bullying in the workforce is **mobbing**—*the ganging up by coworkers, subordinates, or superiors to force someone out of the workplace through rumor, intimidation, humiliation, discrediting, and/or isolation.* As with the traditional form of bullying, mobbing may result in high turnover, low morale, decreased productivity, increased absenteeism, and a loss of key individuals. It may eventually lead to diminished teamwork, trust, and a toxic workplace culture. It is estimated that about 5 percent of employees are targets of mobbing sometime during their working lives.[56]

The prime targets of mobbers are often high achievers, enthusiastic employees, those of high integrity and ethical standards, those who don't belong to the "in-group," women with family responsibilities, and even those with different religious or cultural orientations.[57] Mobbing is much more difficult for an employee to deal with than bullying. Why? The employee is not simply dealing with the actions of another, but rather that of many of his or her coworkers and/or superiors. While training a work team, one anonymous employee reported about witnessing mobbing: "I noticed a young man, relatively new to the company, who sat alone. Whenever he spoke, someone hurled a wisecrack his way. If he entered or left the room, jibes from his 'teammates' followed. At a break, I asked if this harassment was typical. 'Oh,' he answered, 'it's been like that since I got here. It's not everybody, just four or five guys. I guess I have to put up with it because I'm new.' I offered to address the obnoxious behavior or get help from his manager, but he refused. 'Don't,' he pleaded. 'That'll only make it worse. I just try to put up with it.' "[58]

The employee subject to mobbing may find that colleagues no longer meet with her or him. Management may not provide the possibility to communicate, the employee may be isolated in a work area, perhaps the employee is given meaningless work assignments, or the employee may be repeatedly left out of the information loop critical to his or her work. Taken together and repeated over time, these kinds of actions may be devastating for the employee. In too many cases, the only recourse for the employee is to seek a transfer within the organization or resign the position.[59]

Sexual Harassment

Sexual harassment is one of the many categories of harassment that may occur in the workplace. As discussed in Chapter 2, *harassment* refers to verbal or physical conduct that denigrates or shows hostility toward an individual because of that person's race, skin color, religion, gender, national origin, age, or disability. Harassment can also occur if conduct is directed toward a person's relatives, friends, or associates.[60] Please recall from Chapter 2 that harassment does one or more of the following: (1) has the purpose or effect of creating an intimidating, hostile, or offensive work environment; (2) Has the purpose or effect of unreasonably interfering with an individual's work performance; or (3) otherwise adversely affects an individual's employment opportunities.

In Chapter 2, we stated that *sexual harassment* generally refers to unwelcome sexual advances, requests for sexual favors, and other verbal or physical conduct of a sexual nature.[61] Sexual harassment consists of two types of prohibited conduct in the United States: (1) *quid pro quo*—in which submission to harassment is used as the basis for employment decisions, and (2) *hostile environment*—in which harassment creates an offensive working environment. Please see Chapter 2 for a discussion of behaviors that constitute sexual harassment.

In Chapter 2, we also stated that any harassment policy, including one on sexual harassment, should contain (1) a definition of the harassment, (2) a harassment prohibition statement, (3) a description of the organization's complaint procedure, (4) a description of disciplinary measures for such harassment, and (5) a statement of protection against retaliation.[62]

Stopping Sexual Harassment

A few highlights of the insights for stopping sexual harassment, include[63]:

- Tell the person that his or her behavior is offensive. Firmly refuse all invitations. If the harassment doesn't end promptly, write a letter instructing the harasser to stop and keep a copy.

- As soon as the employee experiences the sexual harassment, she or he should start writing it down, including dates, places, times, and possible witnesses to what happened. If possible, coworkers should be asked to write down what they saw or heard, especially if the same thing is happening to them. Remember that others may (and probably will) read this written record at some point. It is a good idea for the employee to keep a duplicate record at home or in some other safe place. The employee should not keep the only record at work.

- The employee should tell the manager, human resources representative, or some other department or person within the organization who has the power to stop the harassment. If possible, tell them in writing. Keep a copy of any written complaint made to the employer. It is very important that the employee report the harassment because the employer must know or have reason to know about the harassment in order to be legally responsible for a coworker's, client's, or customer's actions. Even if the harasser was the manager, the employee may need to show that the harassment was reported to the employer or be able to give a good reason why it wasn't.

- When the employee reports the sexual harassment to the employer, it needs to be done in writing. Describe the problem and how the employee wants it fixed. This creates a written record of when the employee complained and what happened in response to it. Keep copies of everything sent and received from the employer.

- Most employers have policies for dealing with sexual harassment complaints. The employee must attempt to resolve the problem through this process. It is important to follow the employer's procedures.

- An employee in the United States has the right to file a complaint with the Equal Employment Opportunity Commission and/or a state agency. As a last resort, a lawsuit in federal or state court may be filed.

Sexual harassment continues to be a serious form of workplace aggression because it may lead to one or more of the discussed reactions outlined for bullying. As with bullying, leaders have a responsibility to do everything in their power to prevent sexual harassment from occurring. When it does occur, it needs to be dealt with quickly and firmly.

Workplace Violence

Workplace violence *is any act in which a person is abused, threatened, intimidated, or assaulted and that represents an explicit or implicit challenge to the person's safety, well-being, or health at work.*[64] A number of behaviors are considered to be forms of workplace violence. These include murder, rape, robbery, wounding, battering, kicking, throwing objects, biting, hitting, pushing, kicking, spitting, scratching, squeezing or pinching, stalking, intimidation, threats, leaving offensive messages, rude gestures, swearing, harassment (including sexual, racial, and other), intense bullying or mobbing, sabotage, theft, property damage, and arson.[65] It is generally recognized that numerous incidents of workplace violence are never officially reported or, if so, never formally recorded.[66]

Harm Model

As noted previously, there are potential overlaps in the types of aggressive workplace behaviors that are considered to constitute bullying, sexual harassment, and workplace violence. These relationships and overlaps are suggested in the **harm model of aggression**—*a continuum that ranges from harassment to aggression to rage to mayhem.*[67] The types of conduct related to each level of aggressive or threatening behavior occur on an ascending scale, as follows:

- *Harassment.* The first level of behavior on the continuum is harassment. This behavior may or may not cause harm or discomfort to the employee. But, harassment is generally considered unacceptable in the workplace. Examples of harassment include acting in a condescending way to a customer, slamming an office door, glaring at a colleague, or playing frequent practical and cruel jokes.

- *Aggression.* Aggressive behaviors are those that cause harm to or discomfort for another employee or for the organization. Such behaviors include shouting at a customer, spreading damaging rumors about a coworker, or damaging someone's personal belongings. Clearly, all of these behaviors are inappropriate for the workplace.

- *Rage*. The third level on the continuum is rage. Rage is seen through intense behaviors that often cause fear in other employees and which may result in physical or emotional harm to people or damage to property. Rage typically makes the inappropriate behaviors physical and visible. Examples of rage can range from pushing a customer to sabotaging a coworker's presentation or leaving hate statements on someone's desk.

- *Mayhem*. The final stage is mayhem. This stage represents physical violence against employees or customers or the violent destruction of property. Activity in this category can range from punching a customer or ransacking an office to physically punching a coworker or superior to destroying a facility to shooting a coworker or superior to death.

Warning Signs

Employees who engage in workplace violence at the rage and mayhem levels frequently exhibit clear observable warning signs. These warning signs include the following: (1) *violent and threatening behavior*—including hostility and approval of the use of violence; (2) *"strange" behavior*—becoming reclusive, deteriorating personal appearance/hygiene, and erratic behavior; (3) *performance problems*—including problems with attendance or tardiness; (4) *interpersonal problems*—including numerous conflicts, hypersensitivity to comments, and expressions of resentment; and (5) *"at the end of his (or her) rope"*—indicators of impending suicide, the expression of an unspecified plan to "solve all problems" and the like, and statements of access to and familiarity with weapons.[68]

Triggering Events

There are identifiable sets of triggering events. The triggering event is seen to the violence-prone individual as the last straw that creates a mind-set of no way out or no more options. The most common sets of triggering events that lead to rage or mayhem are (1) being fired, laid off, or suspended or passed over for promotion; (2) disciplinary action, poor performance review, severe criticism from one's superior or coworkers; (3) bank or court action such as foreclosure, restraining orders, or custody hearings; (4) a benchmark date—the anniversary of the employee at the organization, chronological age, a date of some horrendous event (such as September 11, 2001, or the aftermath of Hurricanes Katrina, Rita, and Ike); or (5) failed or spurned romance or a personal crisis such as separation, divorce, or death in the family.[69] These types of triggering events are indicators that allow employers to anticipate an employee who exhibits these warning signs for engaging in rage or mayhem.

Insights for Leaders

There are a number of insights for leaders to help prevent workplace violence. During the hiring process, careful interviewing and background checks are essential. For the existing workforce, leaders' application of the foundation competencies developed throughout this book will minimize the conditions that trigger incidents of workplace violence. Employee training related to workplace violence is increasingly seen as essential. When the early warning signs of the potential for an employee to engage in workplace violence occur, the appropriate use of counseling, employee assistance program referrals, sound security measures, and preventive disciplinary actions will be helpful.

A zero-tolerance violence policy that is fairly enforced and consistently communicated is a foundation guideline for minimizing and taking corrective action with respect to workplace violence.[70] First, a formal policy sends a strong signal to employees that workplace violence will not be tolerated. Second, the severity of the penalty for violent behavior should further reinforce the message. Third, a policy lets employees know exactly what conduct is prohibited.

Coping with violence among employees within the workplace is one challenge; another is coping with intimate partner violence that enters the workplace directly (the partner works in the same organization) or indirectly (the partner is not a member of the organization). **Intimate partner violence** *refers to the rage committed by a spouse, ex-spouse, or current or former boyfriend/girlfriend.*[71] Typically, it is committed by a male. This violence is not only traumatic for the victim, but difficult for leaders and the victim's peers in knowing how to respond—or if they should even attempt to respond. Although few in number, an increasing number of organizations are putting in place programs and policies to assist employees who are victims of intimate partner violence. A few of these organizations include American Express, Liz Claiborne (an early leader), CIGNA, and Kaiser Permanente. The *Corporate Alliance to End Partner Violence* provides information on intimate partner violence as related to the workplace.[72] In a recent study, only 13 percent of executives say organizations should provide formal policies and practices to address domestic violence. In contrast, 9 out of 10 employees in the study think their employers should assist in addressing the problem.

As suggested in the following Diversity Competency, the best efforts of leaders and peers are not always sufficient in helping the employee who is a victim of intimate partner violence.[73] The setting is the Darwin Realty & Development Corporation, headquartered in suburban Chicago. It is a privately held real estate brokerage, property management, investment, and development firm.[74] The president and peers of Cindy Bischof did all that was possible.

Diversity **competency**

Darwin Realty

Cindy Bischof was not the kind of woman who would normally let a boyfriend get in the way of her career. Motivated and productive, Bischof was an admired partner at Darwin Realty. She was a role model to the firm's young women, a mentor to junior brokers, a 43-year-old high achiever. Her peers voted her Industrial Broker of the Year. Bischof was neither submissive nor easily intimidated—which is why what happened to her on March 7, 2008, is all the more shocking.

For nearly a year, Bischof had been trying to untangle herself from a soured five-year relationship with an out-of-work salesman named Michael Giroux. After their breakup in May 2007, the handsome and charming Giroux turned strange and dangerous. The day of the breakup, Bischof changed the locks on her house. That night she went to stay with her parents. Giroux smashed the back windows of her house, broke in, and threw paint all over her furniture, rugs, and appliances. Giroux began calling Bischof incessantly on her cell phone. He stalked her at her house, at her parent's house, even on the golf course.

Bischof's torment became Darwin Realty's nightmare as the firm's leaders and peers rallied around her. They helped clean up the damage to her house, which cost her $70,000, according to police reports. The head of Bischof's department installed a camouflaged infrared deer hunting camera in the bushes of her backyard to take pictures of her deck at night.

In August 2007, the camera caught Giroux there with a rope, making a noose. Darwin's president, George Cibula, arranged for Bischof to move into a rental property 30 miles away in Plainfield so that Giroux couldn't find her. Cibula hired security guards for the company Christmas party. Sometimes Bischof's partners walked her out to her car at night, just in case.

But Bischof was alone that Friday afternoon in March 2008 as she left her office and headed to her car. She was looking forward to joining her parents at her condo in Estero, Florida. Minutes later, Brian Liston, a Darwin partner working in a corner office, heard four gunshots behind him. He turned and there, outside his office window, lay Bischof, face down on the parking-lot pavement. Giroux, wearing a baseball cap and a fake mustache, had been lying in wait at the tire store next door. He shot and fatally wounded her before shooting himself in the head.

While police spent hours investigating the obvious, employees huddled in the hallways and conference rooms as shock turned to horror and then to unbearable grief. "It's still not over," Cibula said months later, choking up. "All you can do is endure the shock of it." As the top executive, Cibula doesn't know what he could have done differently. He couldn't shield his staff from the trauma. No amount of security would

have stopped so determined a killer, he believes. "Cindy did not want to bring her personal problems to work. But we butted our way in anyway because she was our friend and colleague." Cathy Radek, one of Bischof's colleagues, recalls: "She was petrified, and we were petrified for her. Bischof was doing everything she could to switch up her routines. I made sure she called me multiple times a day. Check-ins were required." Radek and Darwin president Cibula attended every court hearing—to give moral support to Bischof and send Giroux a message to leave her alone. "It was an emotional roller coaster for everybody," Radek states.

To learn more about Darwin Realty, go to **www.darwinrealty.com.**

Employee attitudes, demographics, and the efforts of an increasing number of leaders are converging to bring this issue out in the open. With so many women in the workforce, and with e-mail, text messaging, and cell phones connecting them to the office around the clock, intimate partner violence comes to work whether executives like it or not. Employees are well aware of this.

Aggression toward the Organization

Our discussion has focused on three of the types of workplace aggression as they impact the employee or groups of employees. An employee who feels unjustly treated, whether for a good cause or self-serving rationalization, may also engage in aggressive behaviors against the organization. At times, the aggression toward the organization is seen as a way of retaliating against the employee's manager or higher levels of leadership. Direct aggression toward management may be seen as resulting in reprisals, such as disciplinary actions or dismissal. The employee might ignore customers and their requests or be rude to them, but not to the point that the customers are likely to complain to higher management. Or, the employee might say negative things as a way of blaming the customers' problems on higher management.[75] As suggested previously, other forms of aggression against the organization may include (1) theft of equipment, supplies, or money; (2) damaging or destroying equipment and facilities; and (3) slacking off whenever possible and withholding ideas for improvements.

Chapter Summary

Stress is the excitement, feeling of anxiety, and/or physical tension that occurs when the demands placed on individuals exceed their ability to cope. The stories of stress are often about negative stress. An individual's general biological responses to severe stressors prepare them to fight or flee—behaviors generally inappropriate in the workplace. Many factors determine how employees experience severe work stress, including their perception of the situation, past experiences, the presence or absence of social support, and a variety of individual differences.

1. *Explain the concept of and influences on creating stress.*

2. *Identify the primary sources of work-related stressors.*

Organizational sources of severe stress at work often include (1) workload, (2) job conditions, (3) role conflict and ambiguity, (4) career development, (5) interpersonal relations, (6) conflict between work and life roles, and (7) workplace aggression, especially bullying, sexual harassment, and violence. In addition, significant changes or other events in an individual's personal life may also be sources of severe stress.

3. *State the potential impacts of severe stress on health, performance, and job burnout.*

Severe stress may affect an individual physiologically, emotionally, and behaviorally. Severe stress is linked to various health problems. An arch-shaped relationship exists between stress and performance. In other words, an optimal level of stress probably exists for any particular task. Less or more stress than that level may lead to reduced performance. Job burnout is a major result of unrelieved and intense job-related stress.

4. *Describe how individual differences influence reactions to stressful situations.*

Several personality characteristics are related to differences in how individuals cope with severe stress. Individuals with a Type A personality are more prone to stress and have an increased chance of experiencing physical ailments due to it. Some dimensions of the Type A personality, such as hostility, are particularly important in terms of stress-related illness. In contrast, the collection of personality traits known as hardiness seems to reduce the effects of severe stress.

5. *Apply individual and leader insights to the management of workplace stress.*

Stress is a real issue for both individuals and organizations. Fortunately, various insights can help leaders and employees manage stress in the workplace. These insights often focus on identifying and removing workplace stressors as well as helping employees cope with stress.

6. *Explain four major types of workplace aggression.*

Workplace aggression includes a variety of behaviors: psychological acts such as shouting or intimidating remarks, physical assault, and destruction or theft of property. Four of the more common types of workplace aggression include bullying, sexual harassment, violence, and aggression toward the organization itself. There may be overlaps in the behaviors associated with each type, as suggested by the *harm model*. This model represents a continuum of levels of violence from harassment to aggression to rage to mayhem. Mayhem may include murder or the destruction of organizational property. A variety of guidelines for minimizing and taking corrective action with respect to bullying, sexual harassment, and workplace violence were reviewed.

Key Terms and Concepts

Depersonalization, **230**
Derogation of target bias, **240**
Fight-or-flight response, **221**
Hardiness, **233**
Hardy personality, **233**
Harm model of aggression, **244**
Hostile attribution bias, **239**
Intimate partner violence, **246**
Job burnout, **230**
Life stressors, **227**
Mobbing, **242**
Post-traumatic stress disorder, **229**
Potency bias, **239**
Retribution bias, **240**

Role ambiguity, **224**
Role conflict, **224**
Role overload, **223**
Social discounting bias, **240**
Stress, **221**
Stress management, **235**
Type A personality, **232**
Type B personality, **232**
Wellness program, **238**
Workplace aggression, **239**
Workplace bullying, **240**
Workplace incivility, **225**
Workplace violence, **244**

Discussion Questions

1. Go to www.howtolayoffemployees.com. What suggestions are presented that help to reduce the stresses of being laid off?
2. What are the ethical implications for leaders who ignore the impacts of severe workplace stress on their employees?
3. Assume a leader is lacking in the diversity competency. How does this deficiency link to the severe workplace stress experienced by some or all employees?
4. Give an example of your use of the fight-or-flight response. In that situation, all things considered, was your response effective or ineffective?
5. Have you experienced or observed workplace incivility? If yes, what impacts, if any, did it have on you or others? Explain.
6. Review the Self-Competency feature entitled "Chesley Sullenberger III, Captain of US Airways Flight 1549." Based on the descriptions of Sullenberger, what characteristics of the hardy personality are illustrated?

Tie the specific comments about him to each of the characteristics identified.

7. Review the Change Competency feature entitled "Ortho-Clinical Diagnostics' Wellness Program." How does this program help reduce work stressors and modify behaviors?
8. Identify and list some of the stressors in a job that you have had. Which were the most difficult to deal with? Why?
9. How would others who know you assess you in comparison to (a) the Type A personality, (b) the Type B personality, and (c) the hardy personality? Explain.
10. Have you experienced or witnessed workplace bullying? If yes, did the organization's leaders deal with it effectively? Explain.
11. Have you experienced or witnessed workplace violence? If yes, did the organization's leaders deal with it effectively? Explain.

Experiential Exercise and Case

Experiential Exercise: Self Competency

Work-Related Stress Inventory[76]

Instructions

The following statements ask about the availability of various individuals to provide support when you experience stressful problems at work or school. Please respond to each item by recording a number from the rating scale below next to each statement. Rate the support from your leader, your coworkers, and your partner/family/friends in helping you with stressful issues and events.

How much can you rely on others . . .

Not at all	A little	Somewhat	Much	Totally
1	2	3	4	5

Emotional Support

_____ 1. . . . to help you feel better when you experience work-related problems?

_____ 2. . . . to listen to you when you need to talk about work-related problems?

_____ 3. . . . to be sympathetic and understanding about your work-related problems?

Informational Support

_____ 4. . . . to suggest ways to find out more about a work situation that is causing you problems?

_____ 5. . . . to share their experiences of a work problem similar to yours?

_____ 6. . . . to provide information that helps to clarify your work-related problems?

Instrumental Support

_____ 7. . . . to give you practical assistance when you experience work-related problems?

_____ 8. . . . to spend time helping you resolve your work-related problems?

_____ 9. . . . to help when things get tough at work?

Appraisal Support

_____ 10. . . . to reassure you about your ability to deal with your work-related problems?

_____ 11. . . . to acknowledge your efforts to resolve your work-related problems?

_____ 12. . . . to help you evaluate your attitudes and feelings about your work-related problems?

Scoring

- Emotional support from others: Sum the points for items 1–3 = _____.
- Informational support from others: Sum the points for items 4–6 = _____.
- Instrumental support from others: Sum the points for items 7–9 = _____.
- Appraisal support from others: Sum the totals for items 10–12 = _____.

Interpretation

- 12 to15 points suggest you have much support for that dimension.
- 7 to 11 points suggest you have some support for that dimension.
- 3 to 6 points suggest you are on your own for that dimension.
- **Overall:** Sum the points for all 12 items. Total scores of 48 to 60 points suggest a pattern of strong support. Total scores of 12 to 24 points suggest a pattern of feeling isolated and alone in dealing with problems that create work-related stress. Total scores of 25–47 suggest a pattern of some or mixed support.

Questions

1. Do your scores suggest that you need to take action to lower your stress level? If "yes," what actions do you think would be most effective?
2. Of the seven competencies discussed in this book (communication, self, diversity, etc.), which three are likely to be most effective and important to you in managing your stress level? Explain.

Case: Ethics Competency

Coleen Colombo and Colleagues Resist Mortgage Fraud[77]

Coleen Colombo joined the Concord (California) branch of BNC in 2003. The small office, next to a Mercedes–Benz dealership and a run-down Kmart, was part of a regional group that funded some $1.2 billion worth of loans each month. Colombo initially thrived in her job as a senior underwriter. In a performance review, she received a top rating of "exceeds expectations," according to a wrongful termination and harassment suit filed in California Superior Court on behalf of Colombo and five other female employees.

The environment turned hostile in 2005 and thereafter, the suit says. At that time, one fellow employee, a male wholesaler, began bringing Colombo questionable loans with incorrect salaries, occupations, and home values, she says. In one instance, she claims in the suit, the wholesaler "tried to bribe (Colombo) to allow a loan with fraudulent information to go through."

The bribes, known as *spiffs*, were common at the BNC branch, says Sylvia Vega-Sutfin, a former wholesaler who left the firm in 2005. The mother of four, who says she made $16,000 a month during the boom, says that some underwriters demanded spiffs of $1,000 for the first 10 loans and $2,500 for the next 20 loans, whether they approved the mortgages or not. When she refused to pay them, Vega-Sutfin says, her loan files started to go missing and the size of her commission checks plummeted. Her bosses "said they would make an example of me to others: 'If you complain, this is what will happen,'" she says.

Colombo says in her lawsuit that she e-mailed the regional vice president for operations to report the wholesaler who tried to bribe her. She claims the vice president brushed off her complaints in a meeting. Colombo "left the office in tears," the suit says. After she returned from a short leave of absence, the branch manager told her a coworker "wanted her terminated for making the complaints," Colombo claims.

Meanwhile, the wholesaler who tried to bribe Colombo started sexually harassing her, according to the suit. The male colleague made her feel "uncomfortable and fearful" by "intentionally rubbing his body against hers." Colombo resigned from BNC in 2005. "You would have thought he was the pimp and we were his prostitutes," says Linda Weekes, another underwriter who is part of the suit. "It felt like a dirty place to work." The case has been on hold since BNC's owner, Lehman Brothers, filed for bankruptcy on September 15, 2008. "We dispute the allegations made by these former employees and will be contesting them on the merits in the pending litigation," says a Lehman spokesman.

The world came crashing down for wholesalers when subprime loans started going bad. Wall Street quickly reined in its mortgage factories, tightening lending standards, pulling credit lines, and forcing lenders to buy back the same risky loans it once consumed. For the thousands of wholesalers swept up in the excitement and excess of a manic market, it was time to find a new job.

Questions

1. Is the "fight-or-flight" response evident in this case? Explain.
2. What influences on the stress experience appear to be present?
3. What were the primary work-related stressors for Coleen Colombo and Sylvia Vega-Sutfin? Explain.
4. Do you think the lawsuit was warranted? Explain.
5. What defense mechanisms used by individuals to justify aggressive behaviors are evident? Explain.

Leadership and Team Behaviors

chapter 9

Interpersonal Communication in Organizations

Learning Goals

After studying this chapter, you should be able to:

1
Describe the core elements of interpersonal communication.

2
Explain the factors that foster ethical communications.

3
Diagnose nonverbal communication behaviors.

4
Understand the importance of cultural and nonverbal barriers to communication.

5
Discuss the role of communication networks.

Learning Content

Learning from Experience
Julia Stewart, Chairman and CEO of DineEquity

Elements of Interpersonal Communication

Ethical Interpersonal Communications
Change Competency
Susan Powers, Chief Information Officer, Travelport GDS

Nonverbal Communication
Communication Competency
Poor Nonverbal Signals Prior to Layoffs

Intercultural Communication
Across Cultures Competency
Tahir Ayub, Partner, PwC

Interpersonal Communication Networks
Change Competency
Michael Ward's Reflections on CSX's One Plan Redesign

Experiential Exercise and Case
Experiential Exercise: Communication Competency
Communication Inventory

Case: Communication Competency
Xographics

Julia Stewart, Chairman and CEO of DineEquity

Julia Stewart serves as chairman and chief executive officer of DineEquity, Inc. DineEquity franchises and operates a small number of restaurants under the Applebee's Neighborhood Grill & Bar and IHOP brands. A franchise is a system that enables a franchisor (DineEquity) to arrange for a franchisee to handle specific products and services under mutually agreed-on conditions. In 2007, Stewart led DineEquity's acquisition of Applebee's, which brought together two restaurant brands and created the largest full-service restaurant company in the world with more than 3,300 locations, 99 percent of which are franchised. DineEquity has approximately 200 franchise groups, each of which operates multiple restaurants. DineEquity is headquartered in Glendale, California. Stewart is a recipient of major industry awards and serves on various association and charity boards.

She says "I can tell a lot about people by the way they act toward the food server. So I typically never hire anyone without going out to eat with them. It's a great way to learn about a person. If you have a conversation with me and never acknowledge the food server, you are being disrespectful and will never work for me."

Stewart uses e-mail, but voice mail works best for her. She comments: "I feel strongly about returning people's phone calls and treating them with dignity. Everybody deserves a return phone call. Employees have to return franchisee phone calls within 24 hours. That's standard procedure." She finds e-mail sort of stale and impersonal. Stewart doesn't allow BlackBerrys to be used in meetings. "We want people's undivided attention to each other, and I can't find anything more disruptive than those," she says.

She often finds herself saying, "I thought of something in the shower. The other day my general counsel said, 'You must have the biggest water bill of anybody here.' I have a pad I keep in my bathroom, and when I get an idea, I just start writing. I bring these little pieces of paper into the office. Some of the strategies involved with the Applebee's [deal] came from shower notes."

As one of her vice presidents comments, "She's big on us all reading books. Recently, everybody in the company read *The Oz Principle*. *The Oz Principle* is that every human being goes below the line and says something catty or inappropriate about someone. It's human nature. And it's okay, but you can't just stay there. You've got to get back up above the line."

Stewart nurtures relationships with franchisees very carefully. The most important part of a relationship is communication. "I constantly talk with franchisees making certain that they

FRANK POLICH/REUTERS/LANDOV

To learn more about DineEquity, go to www.dineequity.com.

understand our vision, they understand where leaders want to take the brand, they're supportive; there's collaboration, there's buy-in. This is an ongoing process." She doesn't think you ever stop that. "At the core of continuing that re-energizing with Applebee's franchisees is the communication and ongoing conversations with them, because they have to buy in. They're doing a lot of the heavy lifting. We're certainly doing the strategic part, but they're doing the execution day in and day out. So it's making sure they feel comfortable."

Michael Smith, a restaurant analyst, comments: "I've been impressed with how she came up with a plan to execute franchisees' desires, and she's done a good job of executing. You'd have to give her an A for that. At one time, I saw IHOP as being in a box that was going to be hard to get out of, and she got them out of it." Stewart is engaged in leading the same transformation at Applebee's.[1]

In the Learning from Experience feature, Julia Stewart demonstrates the importance of effective interpersonal communications for achieving organizational effectiveness. Her commitment to ethical interpersonal communications is evident through her practice of using four factors that foster ethical dialogues: communication openness, constructive feedback, appropriate self-disclosure, and active listening. (These factors are discussed in detail later in the chapter.) Recall from Chapter 1 that the *communication competency* involves the knowledge, skills, and abilities to use all the modes of transmitting, understanding, and receiving ideas, thoughts, and feelings—verbal, listening, nonverbal, and written—for accurately transferring and exchanging information.

This chapter focuses primarily on providing a path for individuals to enhance their communication competency with an emphasis on interpersonal communication. **Interpersonal communication** *refers to a limited number of people who (1) are usually in proximity to each other, (2) use many sensory channels, and (3) are able to provide immediate feedback.*[2] First, we discuss the process, types, and patterns of verbal, nonverbal, and other forms of communication used by employees on the job. Second, we discuss ethical communications in organizations. Third, we examine the nature and importance of nonverbal communication in interpersonal communication. Fourth, we discuss the importance of cultural context and differences in communications. Fifth, we review the role of communication networks in organizations, including the impacts of e-mail and instant messaging technologies.

Learning Goal

1. *Describe the core elements of interpersonal communication.*

Elements of Interpersonal Communication

For accurate interpersonal communication to take place, the sender's message must be the same as that interpreted by the receiver. Recall Julia Stewart's views: "I constantly talk with franchisees making certain that they understand our vision, they understand where leaders want to take the brand, they're supportive; there's collaboration, there's buy-in. This is an ongoing process."

Figure 9.1 presents the elements of interpersonal communication involving only two people. This process is not easy, and by considering its components, you can readily see that it becomes increasingly complex as more people participate.

Sender and Receiver

Exchanges between people are an element of interpersonal communication. Labeling one person as the sender and the other as the receiver is arbitrary. These roles shift back and forth, depending on where the individuals are in the process. When the

FIGURE 9.1 Elements of Interpersonal Communication

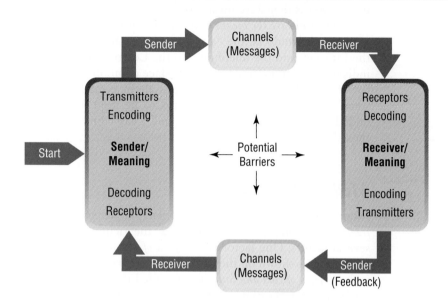

receiver responds to the sender, the original receiver becomes the sender and the initiating sender becomes the receiver.

Transmitters and Receptors

Transmitters (*used by the sender*) and **receptors** (*used by the receiver*) *are the means available for sending and receiving messages.* They usually involve one or more of the senses: seeing, hearing, touching, smelling, and tasting. Transmission can take place both verbally and nonverbally. Once transmission begins, the communication process moves beyond the direct control of the sender. A message that has been transmitted cannot be brought back. How many times have you thought to yourself "I wish I hadn't said that" or "Why did I hit send?"

Messages and Channels

Messages *include the sent data and the coded symbols that give particular meaning to the data.* By using both verbal and nonverbal symbols, the sender tries to ensure that messages are interpreted by the receiver as the sender intended. To understand the difference between an original meaning and a received message, think about an occasion when you tried to convey inner thoughts and feelings of happiness, rage, or fear to another person. Did you find it difficult or impossible to transmit your true "inner meaning"?

The greater the difference between the interpreted meaning and the original message, the poorer will be the communication. Words and nonverbal symbols have no meaning by themselves. Their meaning is created by the sender, the receiver, and the situation or context. Recall the importance of context and nonverbal communications to Stewart when interviewing potential employees. She states, "I can tell a lot about people by the way they act toward the food server. So I typically never hire anyone without going out to eat with them. It's a great way to learn about a person. If you have a complete conversation with me and never acknowledge the food server, you are being disrespectful and will never work for me." In our discussion later in this chapter of potential interpersonal barriers, we examine why messages aren't always interpreted as they were meant to be.[3]

Channels *are the means by which messages travel from sender to receiver.* Examples of channels would be the "air" during person-to-person conversations, e-mail via the Internet, and the telephone. In the Learning from Experience feature, Stewart indicated the importance of face-to-face communication with both employees and franchisees. Recall Stewart's feelings about e-mail: She finds it stale and impersonal and doesn't allow BlackBerrys to be used in meetings. "We want people's undivided attention to each other, and I can't find anything more disruptive than those," she says.

Media Richness

Media richness *is the capacity of a communication approach to transmit cues and provide feedback.*[4] As suggested in Figure 9.2, the richness of each medium is a blend of several factors. One factor is the *speed of personalized feedback* provided through the medium. It is shown on the vertical axis as varying from slow to fast. A second factor is the *variety of cues and language* provided through the medium. It is shown on the horizontal axis as varying from single to multiple. A **cue** *is a stimulus, either consciously or unconsciously perceived, that results in a response by the receiver.* Figure 9.2 relates 12 different media to these two factors. A medium may vary somewhat in richness, depending on its use by sender and receiver. For example, e-mail may be associated with slower or quicker feedback than indicated in Figure 9.2. The speed depends on accessibility to e-mail messages and the receiver's tendency to reply immediately or later. Messages that require a long time to digest are low in richness. Julia Stewart, for example, makes a special effort to employ rich media through one-on-one and

FIGURE 9.2 Examples of Media Richness

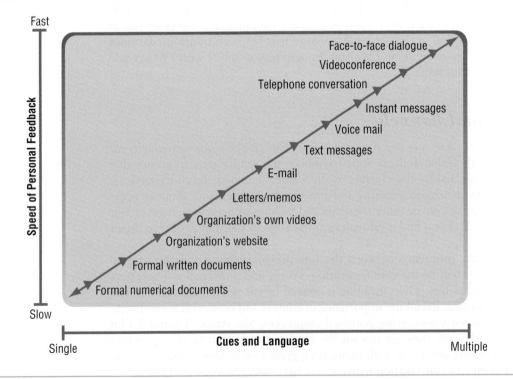

small group meetings and personal phone calls. She comments: "I feel strongly about returning people's phone calls and treating them with dignity. Everybody deserves a return phone call. Employees have to return franchisee phone calls within 24 hours. That's standard procedure."

Data are the output of the communication. Face-to-face dialogue is shown as the highest in richness in Figure 9.2 and formal numerical documents as the lowest. The data become information when they reinforce or change the receivers' understanding.

All of the media identified in Figure 9.2 clearly have their place and use. Moreover, a complex decision, such as DineEquity's decision to acquire Applebee's, requires the use of multiple media—ranging from formal documents prepared for shareholders and governmental agencies to face-to-face dialogue with executives and franchisees. The effective processing of a complex decision may start with face-to-face dialogue to gain an understanding and agreement on the issues and problems to be addressed. Then, some of the individuals may be assigned the task of developing formal documents related to the decision. These documents are likely to be the basis for further face-to-face dialogue. Recall Julia Stewart's comment that she often comes up with ideas while taking a shower. She states: "I have a pad I keep in my bathroom, and when I get an idea, I just start writing. I bring these little pieces of paper into the office."

Meaning and Feedback

The sender's message is transmitted through channels to the receiver's five senses in interpersonal communications. As Figure 9.1 suggests, received messages are changed from their symbolic form (e.g., spoken words) to a form that has meaning. **Meaning** *represents a person's thoughts, feelings, beliefs, and attitudes.*

Encoding *gives personal meaning to messages that are to be sent.* Vocabulary and knowledge play an important role in the sender's ability to encode. Unfortunately, some professionals have difficulty communicating with people in general. They use vocabulary that only other professionals in the same field can understand. Lawyers often encode (write) contracts that directly affect consumers but use language that only other lawyers can decode. Consumer groups have pressed to have such contracts written in a language that almost everyone can understand. As a result, many banks, credit card firms, and other organizations have simplified the language in their contracts.

Decoding *gives personal, interpreted meaning to messages that are received.* People decode messages so that the meanings received are reasonably close to the meanings transmitted. The accurate decoding of messages is often a major challenge in communicating. Communication accuracy should be evaluated in relation to an ideal state. This occurs when the sender's intended meaning and the receiver's interpretation of it are the same.[5] The transmission of factual data of a nonthreatening nature approximates the ideal state. For example, the sharing of the time, place, and procedures for a high school or college commencement ceremony generally results in easy and accurate interpersonal communication.

The interpersonal communication process during a meeting to terminate a long-term employee due to downsizing is a complex matter. Consider the reflections of a leader who has had to meet with and terminate employees who were performing well:

> *If you have done it as long as I have, the challenge is that you focus on the job so much that is to be done that you ignore the individual and it can become cold. You can just race through the process. If this is the first time you have done it, you can be so caught up in the sympathetic role that one must play that you are not able to convey the message. So it is striking the appropriate balance between the two extremes.[6]*

Feedback *is the receiver's response to the message.* It lets the sender know whether the message was received as intended. Interpersonal communication becomes a dynamic, two-way process through feedback, rather than just a one-way event.

Interpersonal Barriers

Barriers to interpersonal communication are numerous.[7] Let's review briefly the more important barriers that stem from individual differences and perceptions. Later in the chapter, we address cultural barriers in interpersonal communications.

Individual personality traits that serve as barriers to communication include low adjustment (nervous, self-doubting, and moody), low sociability (shy, unassertive, and withdrawn), low conscientiousness (impulsive, careless, and irresponsible), low agreeableness (independent, cold, and rude), and low intellectual openness (dull, unimaginative, and literal minded). Introverts are likely to be more quiet and emotionally inexpressive (see Chapter 3) than extroverts.

Individual perceptual errors include perceptual defense (protecting oneself against ideas, objects, or situations that are threatening), stereotyping (assigning attributions to someone solely on the basis of a category in which the person has been placed), halo effect (evaluating another person based solely on one impression, either favorable or unfavorable), projection (tendency for people to see their own traits in others), and high expectancy effect (prior expectations serve to bias how events, objects, and people are actually perceived). Individuals who make the fundamental attribution error of underestimating the impact of situational or external causes of behavior are not likely to communicate effectively. This error too readily results in communicating blame or credit to other individuals for outcomes rather than to oneself. A related attribution error is the self-serving bias (communicating personal responsibility for good performance but denying responsibility for poor performance). (See Chapter 4.) Executives at GM and Chrysler blamed unions, the recession, banks, and the government for their financial problems. They didn't place any blame on their own decisions to produce cars that many consumers didn't want to buy.

In addition to these underlying personal communication barriers, there are direct barriers, as discussed next. Five of the direct barriers include noise, semantics, language routines, lying, and distortion.

Noise

Noise *represents any interference with the intended message in the channel.* A radio playing loud music while someone is trying to talk to someone else is an example of noise. Noise sometimes can be overcome by repeating the message or increasing the intensity (e.g., the volume) of the message.

Semantics

Semantics *is the special meaning assigned to words.* Thus, the same words may mean different things to different people.[8] Consider the semantics for five words in American (U.S.) English versus British English vocabularies:

Pavement:	American—a hard road surface; British—footpath, sidewalk.
Table (verb):	American—to remove from discussion; British—to bring to discussion.
Tick off (verb):	American—to anger; British—to rebuke.
Canceled check:	American—a check paid by the bank; British—a check that is stopped or voided.
Ship:	American—to convey by boat, train, plane, truck, or other means; British—to convey only by boat.[9]

Language Routines

A person's verbal and nonverbal communication patterns that have become habits are known as **language routines**. They can be observed by watching how people greet one another. In many instances, language routines are quite useful because they reduce the amount of time needed to communicate. They also provide predictability in terms of being able to anticipate what is going to be said and how it is going to be said. The image and strategy of Intel is reinforced through language routines, including its slogan: "Intel Inside." This slogan is supported by Intel's saying "Innovations that move the world forward." Intel's slogan reinforces its brand image, namely, "Intel pushes the boundaries of innovation so our work can make people's lives more exciting, fulfilling, and manageable. And our work never stops."[10]

Language routines can cause discomfort, offend, and alienate when they put down or discriminate against others. Many demeaning stereotypes of individuals and groups are perpetuated through language routines.[11]

Lying and Distortion

Lying *means the sender states something that is believed to be false in order to seriously mislead one or more receivers.*[12] During the recent recession and collapse of the stock market, it was revealed that Bernard Madoff masterminded a Ponzi scheme that resulted in the largest fraud in history—$50 billion in losses to investors. This and events related to other distortions shook the public's trust in financial institutions and government agencies in the United States.[13] Everyday social flattery in conversations may not be completely honest, but it is normally considered acceptable and rarely regarded as dishonest (lying). **Distortion** *represents a wide range of messages that a sender may use between the extremes of lying and complete honesty.*[14] Of course, the use of vague, ambiguous, or indirect language doesn't necessarily indicate a sender's intent to mislead. This form of language may be viewed as acceptable political behavior. Silence may also be a form of distortion, if not dishonesty. Not wanting to look incompetent or make his or her manager look bad in a departmental meeting, a subordinate may remain quiet instead of expressing an opinion or asking a question.

As discussed in Chapter 4, personal distortion in interpersonal communications may occur through **impression management**, *which represents the attempt by individuals to manipulate or control the impressions that others form about them.* In Table 4.3 (page 119), we reviewed five impression management tactics: self-promotion, ingratiation, intimidation, supplication, and exemplification. An additional tactic is face-saving. Face-saving often involves (1) apologizing in a way to convince others that the bad outcome isn't a fair indication of what the sender is really like as a person; (2) making excuses to others by admitting that the sender's behavior in some way caused a negative outcome, but strongly suggesting that the person isn't really as much to blame as it seems (because the outcome wasn't intentional or there were extenuating circumstances); or (3) presenting justifications to others by appearing to accept responsibility for an outcome, but denying that the outcome actually led to problems. When the opportunity is present, shifting blame for problems or a failure to meet a goal is a common means of face-saving.[15] When Blake Jorgensen was fired as chief financial officer from Yahoo!, Carol Bartz, Yahoo's CEO, said the dismissal was necessary to speed up the decision making and have senior leaders support her strategy for turning the company around. Yahoo's two previous CFOs were removed for similar stated reasons. Do you suspect that the dismissal of the three CFOs was a form of scapegoating to minimize the acknowledgment of other problems?

Impression management strategies can range from relatively harmless minor forms of distortion (being courteous to another person even if you don't like the individual), to messages that use extreme ingratiation and self-promotion to obtain a better raise or promotion than others, to intimidation. In brief, the greater the frequency of distortion tactics and the more they approach the lying end of the distortion continuum, the more they will serve as a hurdle to interpersonal communication.[16]

Ethical Interpersonal Communications

In Chapter 2, we discussed the ethical principles and practices that provide the underlying foundation for ethical interpersonal communications. In this section of the chapter, we discuss factors that foster ethical interpersonal communications. The individual is more likely to incorporate values and principles that distinguish right from wrong in communications through effective dialogue. The barriers to effective communication—such as noise, confusing semantics, inappropriate language routines, and lying—will be reduced when effective dialogue takes place.

Dialogue *is a process whereby people suspend their defensiveness to enable a free flow of exploration into their own and others' assumptions and beliefs.* Dialogue includes (1) asking questions and listening to learn, (2) seeking shared meanings, (3) integrating multiple perspectives, and (4) uncovering and examining assumptions. As a result, dialogue can build mutual trust, common ground, and the increased likelihood of ethical interpersonal communication.[17] A necessary condition for dialogue is assertive communication. **Assertive communication** *means confidently expressing what you think, feel, and believe while respecting the right of others to hold different views.* Ethical dialogue requires that interacting individuals demonstrate multiple abilities and behaviors. Figure 9.3 illustrates the idea that ethical dialogue is characterized by a specific group of interrelated abilities and behaviors. These include communication openness, constructive feedback, appropriate self-disclosure, and active listening.

Through the factors of ethical dialogue and assertive communication, workplace honesty will be more prevalent. Julia Stewart has built a reputation for ethical dialogue and assertive communication over her career. Among many, consider these two testimonials.[18] Bill Floyd, vice president of operations at Taco Bell and Stewart's manager when she was there, comments: "We used to say that an important determinant of success was whether the crew adopted [managers] and saw them as someone who connected with them and empathized. Julia fit that to a T." Karen Eadon, senior

FIGURE 9.3 Factors that Foster Ethical Dialogue

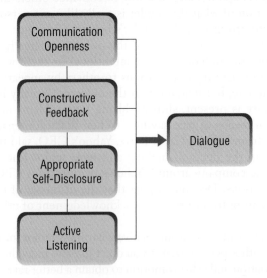

vice president of marketing at Applebee's during Stewart's tenure there as president, remembers Stewart as a "strong leader" who often invited opinions before making strategic decisions. "Julia was very open to divergent points of view and to vigorous discussion that would allow her to see all sides."

In reflecting on the importance of dialogue, Stewart states: "People don't understand, first, that franchising is highly regulated by the U.S. government and, second, that it's much harder than running a regular company. I don't demand or dictate anything: I influence, I collaborate, I persuade. Franchisors need to be mindful of the partnership. At the core of being a franchisor, you'd better desire to be a partner. If you don't want to be a partner, it will never work."

Communication Openness

Communication openness may be viewed as a continuum ranging from closed, guarded, and defensive to open, candid, and supportive.[19] Figure 9.4 shows that, at the extreme left-hand side of the continuum, messages are interpreted through low trust, hidden agendas, and concealed goals.

Communication occurs on two levels: direct and meta-communication. **Meta-communication** *brings out the (hidden) assumptions, inferences, and interpretations of the parties that form the basis of open messages.* In closed communication, senders and receivers consciously and purposely hide their real agendas and "messages." Game playing is rampant. Meta-communication focuses on inferences such as (1) what I think you think about what I said; (2) what I think you really mean; (3) what I really mean, but hope you don't realize what I mean; (4) what you're saying, but what I think you really mean; and (5) what I think you're trying to tell me but aren't directly telling me because . . . (you're afraid of hurting my feelings, you think being totally open could hurt your chances of promotion, and so on).

At the extreme right-hand side of the continuum in Figure 9.4, communication is open, candid, and supportive. Messages are interpreted through high trust, shared agendas, and revealed goals.[20] The words and nonverbal cues sent convey an authentic message that the sender chose without having a hidden agenda.

Breakdowns in communication at the right end of the continuum are due primarily to honest errors (e.g., the different meanings that people assign to words such as *soon*

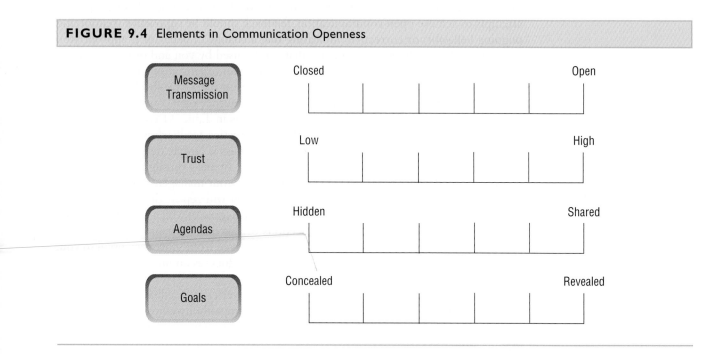

FIGURE 9.4 Elements in Communication Openness

or *immediately*). Communication openness usually is a matter of degree rather than an absolute. The nature of language, linguistics, and different situations (coworker to coworker, subordinate to superior, friend to friend, or spouse to spouse) creates situations that allow for degrees of shading, coloring emphasis, and deflection in the use of words and nonverbal cues as symbols of meaning.

Insights for Individuals

The degree of openness must be considered in relation to the setting. There are three important factors in a setting. First, the history of the relationship is perhaps the most significant factor affecting openness. Consider the case of Don and Argie's relationship. Has Don violated Argie's or others' trust in the past? Has Don been dishonest and unethical with Argie or others? Has Don provided cues (verbal and/or nonverbal) soliciting or reinforcing Argie's attempts to be open and candid? Or has Don provided cues to the contrary? Has the history of the relationship created a level of such comfort that both Argie and Don can focus on direct communication, rather than meta-communication?

Second, if the communication is likely to be partly adversarial or Don is committed to damaging or weakening Argie's position or gaining at Argie's expense through unethical acts, guarded communication is likely. Conversely, if the communication is likely to be friendly and Don is trying to be supportive of Argie, strengthen her position, or enhance her esteem, guarded communication may be viewed as irrational.

Third, when Argie communicates with someone of higher status and power, she is communicating with someone who has some control over her future. That person may be responsible for appraising her performance, judging her promotability, and determining the amount of her merit pay increase. The tendency in such a case is to project a favorable image and to state negative messages with qualifiers.

Constructive Feedback

In giving feedback, people share their thoughts and feelings about others. Feedback may involve personal feelings or reactions to others' ideas or proposals. The emotional impact of feedback varies according to how personally it is focused. When a person attempts to achieve open communication, feedback should be supportive (reinforcing ongoing behavior) or corrective (indicating that a change in behavior is appropriate).

Table 9.1 provides a questionnaire that can be used by you and other employees to diagnose interpersonal feedback practices within an organization. The greater the frequency of "agree" and "strongly agree" responses to the 15 feedback practices, the greater the degree of open, and most likely ethical, interpersonal communications you perceive within the organization. The first four items in Table 9.1 concern corrective feedback from your superiors and coworkers. Corrective feedback is not necessarily bad for the person who is receiving it. Its effectiveness is largely determined by how the feedback is given. The second section in Table 9.1 (items 5 through 8) concerns the degree to which positive feedback is given to you by your manager. Positive feedback reinforces and rewards certain behaviors so that you will repeat them in the future. The third section (items 9 through 12) concerns the degree to which positive feedback is given by your peers. The first three sections of this questionnaire all concern the degree to which positive or negative feedback is received from sources external to you. By contrast, the fourth section (items 13 through 15) focuses on internal feedback, for example, your self-talk.

This diagnostic questionnaire clearly shows the variety of feedback forms that are available to employees in organizations. A lack of compatibility among these forms of feedback for you may indicate serious interpersonal communication problems in your organization.

TABLE 9.1   Diagnosis of Feedback Practices

Read each of the following statements and record your perceptions about the feedback practices you experienced in a previous job. Respond on the continuum that ranges from strongly disagree to strongly agree, as follows:

1	2	3	4	5
Strongly Disagree	Disagree	Neutral	Agree	Strongly Agree

CORRECTIVE FEEDBACK

1.	Your manager lets you know when you make a mistake.	1 2 3 4 5
2.	You receive a formal report of poor performance.	1 2 3 4 5
3.	Coworkers tell you that you have done something wrong.	1 2 3 4 5
4.	You are told when you should be doing something else.	1 2 3 4 5

POSITIVE FEEDBACK FROM YOUR MANAGER

5.	You receive thanks after completed jobs.	1 2 3 4 5
6.	Your manager tells you when you are doing a good job.	1 2 3 4 5
7.	You have a regular performance review with your manager.	1 2 3 4 5
8.	The manager treats you as a mature adult.	1 2 3 4 5

POSITIVE FEEDBACK FROM PEERS

9.	Peers congratulate you for how much you accomplish.	1 2 3 4 5
10.	Peers compliment you for the quality of your work.	1 2 3 4 5
11.	You know more people are using the company's product or service because of your efforts.	1 2 3 4 5
12.	Peers like you very much.	1 2 3 4 5

INTERNAL FEEDBACK

13.	You know when you have met your goals.	1 2 3 4 5
14.	You can see the results of finding better ways of doing the job.	1 2 3 4 5
15.	You know how much you can do without making a mistake.	1 2 3 4 5

Insights for Individuals

The following are insights for constructive and ethical feedback that can foster open communication[21]:

- It is based on a foundation of trust between sender and receiver. When an organization is characterized by competitiveness, the emphasis is on the use of power to punish and control, rigid superior–subordinate relationships, and a lack of trust for constructive and ethical feedback.

- It is specific rather than general. Saying "You are a dominating person" isn't as useful as saying "Just now when we were deciding the issue, you did not listen to what others said. I felt I had to accept your argument or face attack from you."

- It is given at a time when the receiver appears to be ready to accept it. When a person at Dell has just been downsized, that person will probably be angry, upset, or defensive. This isn't the time for you to bring up new issues.

- It is checked with the receiver to determine whether it seems valid. The sender can ask the receiver to rephrase and restate the feedback to test whether it matches the intended message.

- It covers behaviors that the receiver may be capable of doing something about.

- It doesn't include more than the receiver can handle at any particular time. When employees are about to be laid off, they are not ready to hear about everything they do that annoys you.

Individuals, teams, and organizations all depend on feedback to improve the way they develop and perform. One approach to obtaining such feedback is through the collection of perceptions from multiple individuals about the behaviors and performance of a single individual. For example, **360-degree feedback** *is a questionnaire-based process that gathers structured feedback from a number of people about the competencies and behaviors of an individual or team*. Increasingly, this is referred to as *multisource feedback*. For a manager, questionnaires on behaviors (e.g., teamwork, leadership, goal setting) might be completed by oneself, subordinates, peers, superior, and customers. The results are compiled in a feedback report, with data from each source presented separately. These data and results are provided to the individual, who then develops a plan for building strengths and improving personal performance. Normally, this discussion would take place with the person's superior or a consultant.

The use and application of 360-degree feedback is controversial. Clearly, there needs to be an ethical environment of trust and communication openness before the implementation of a formal 360-degree feedback process. It doesn't work in a highly political or bureaucratic organization. It may not work well when the feedback is used as part of a performance review process unless specific knowledge, skills, and abilities can be linked to specific performance goals. In general, 360-degree feedback appears to work best if it is used for coaching and professional development purposes.[22]

Appropriate Self-Disclosure

Self-disclosure *is any information that individuals communicate (verbally or nonverbally) about themselves to others*. People often unconsciously disclose much about themselves by what they say and how they present themselves to others. The ability to express yourself to others usually is basic to your career and professional development.[23] Nondisclosing individuals may repress their real feelings because to reveal them is threatening. Conversely, total-disclosure individuals, who expose a great deal about themselves to anyone they meet, actually may be unable to communicate with others because they are too self-centered. The presence of appropriate self-disclosure, say, between superior and subordinate or team members and customers, can facilitate dialogue and sharing of work-related problems.

Insights for Individuals

A person's level in an organization often complicates self-disclosure. A person is more likely to reduce self-disclosure to those having greater formal power because of their ability to punish. Even when the employee is able and willing to engage in "appropriate" forms of self-disclosure at work, the perception of the manager's trustworthiness in not using the revealed information to punish, intimidate, or ridicule is likely to influence the amount and form of the employee's self-disclosure.

As discussed in the case at the end of Chapter 2, one of the more sensitive areas of appropriate self-disclosure relates to dating and romance with coworkers. Of major concern in most organizations is a romantic or dating relationship between a manager and subordinate. A concern is that the manager will treat the romantic subordinate differently than other subordinates performing at the same level through better pay raises, promotion opportunities, and assignments. As for keeping an office romance a secret, it's not possible. As one business relationship specialist comments: "If you think no one knows, everyone knows." Increasingly, organizations require employees who are romantically involved and work in the same reporting group to disclose their relationship. Such disclosure represents one way to minimize—and, it is hoped, avoid—conflicts of many types.

Active Listening

Active listening is necessary to encourage appropriate levels of ethical feedback and openness. **Active listening** *involves paying attention, withholding judgment, reflecting, clarifying, summarizing, and sharing*. Listening is effective when the receiver understands the sender's message as intended.

As much as 40 percent of an eight-hour workday for many employees is devoted to listening. Tests of listening comprehension suggest that people often listen at only 25 percent efficiency. Listening influences the quality of peer, leader–subordinate, and employee–customer relationships. Employees who dislike a manager may find it extremely difficult to listen attentively to the manager's comments during performance review sessions. Moreover, active listening is a necessary condition for learning. The Greek philosopher Epictetus wisely wrote: "It is impossible for a man to learn what he thinks he already knows."

Active listening abilities are interrelated. That is, the individual can't practice one without improving the others. Active listening is much easier to read about than to develop and practice. The more a person practices active listening skills, the more he is able to enter into effective dialogue. Moreover, the listening insights make clear that active listening is not feasible without constructive feedback.[24]

Insights for Individuals

Adapted from the book *Active Listening: Improve Your Ability to Listen and Lead*, we offer the following insights to increase active listening skills[25]:

- A primary goal of active listening is to set a comfortable tone and allow time and opportunity for the other person to think and speak. The individual should pay attention to one's frame of mind, body language, and the other person. The individual should be present, focus on the moment, and operate from a place of respect.

- Active listening requires an open mind. As a listener, the individual needs to be open to new ideas, new perspectives, and new possibilities. Even when good listeners have strong views, they suspend judgment, hold their criticism, and avoid arguing or selling their point right away. The individual should think: "I'm here to understand how the other person sees the world. It is not time to judge or give my view."

- Active listening is first about understanding the other person, then about being understood. As the individual gains a clearer understanding of the other person's perspective, she can then introduce her ideas, feelings, and suggestions and address any concerns. The individual might talk about a similar experience she had or share an idea that was triggered by a comment made previously in the conversation.

- Active listening involves the use of questions to double-check any issue that is ambiguous or unclear, which is a component of constructive feedback. Open-ended, clarifying, and probing questions are important tools. Open-ended questions draw people out and encourage them to expand their ideas (i.e., "What are their thoughts on . . . ?" or "What led them to draw this conclusion?") Clarifying questions ensure understanding and clear up confusion. Any *who, what, where, when, how,* or *why* questions can be clarifying questions, but those are not the only possibilities. An employee might say, "I must have missed something. Could you repeat that?" or "I am not sure that I got what you were saying. Can you explain it again another way?" By asking questions, he invites reflection and a thoughtful response instead of telling others what to do. He might ask, for example, "More specifically, what are some of the things you've tried?" or "What is it in your own style that might be contributing to the trouble with others?"

- Restating key themes as the conversation proceeds confirms and solidifies the listener's grasp of the other person's point of view. It also helps both the listener and other person(s) to be clear on mutual responsibilities and follow-up. The listener should briefly summarize what she understood as she listened (i.e., "It sounds as if your main concern is . . ." or "These seem to be the key points you have expressed . . ."). She could also ask the other person to summarize.

The following Change Competency feature reports on the use of active listening by Sue Powers, the chief information officer of Travelport GDS.[26] In her role, Powers oversees the global product and development initiatives of the Worldspan, Apollo, Galileo GDS, and Airlines Services units. These are lines of businesses within Travelport. Travelport GDS is a major provider of multi-host technology platforms for airlines worldwide. Each day Travelport GDS processes more than 1 billion transactions. It is a major provider of web-based travel e-commerce and services in the global travel industry.[27] In this feature, Sue Powers focuses on the communication processes used to achieve an organizational change.

Change competency

Susan Powers, Chief Information Officer, Travelport GDS

Susan Powers relies on a communication process that she calls *socializing an idea* to nudge and encourage her colleagues to consider a new information technology system or business process. The approach is an active one. It requires more than simply running an idea up the flagpole. Socializing means practicing active listening and communication outside formal meetings, where people are less guarded. Powers finds that during casual conversations (in the hallway, in their offices, over lunch), people are more at ease and more willing to discuss change. They also are more likely to discuss their objections to an idea, making it possible to come up with solutions. In a formal setting, people can feel pushed into an idea. In informal settings, they feel they can be more honest.

For example, a few years ago Powers wondered why they couldn't get the same Internet access deal she had at home: an inexpensive DSL connection. At the time, the business, which operated travel reservation systems, used a fairly low-band connection linking the company to its travel agent customers. Powers and David Lauderdale, the chief technology officer, began talking with the 650-member technology group about how much more flexible and efficient a standard Internet protocol network could be. The technology group was sold, but they had to convince the rest of the company. Objections to the new technology came fast and furious. Some business managers speculated that travel agents wouldn't want to buy their own PCs and Internet service, preferring to have them provide their connectivity. Others worried about the technology

transition. Salespeople said they could not get out of their contracts, which required them to provide dedicated service and equipment.

Powers and her team spent several weeks bringing the idea up again and again with employees and customers during lunch, after company meetings, at after-hours get-togethers, at company functions, and during any casual conversation. Powers didn't emphasize cost savings at first (although the new system would ultimately save tens of millions of dollars). Instead, she asked for reactions to the potential benefits of the change (the new system would be more reliable, easier to maintain, and simpler to use). Powers says, "The early feedback caused us to think more about what was in this for everybody, and we were able to better think through the benefits for customers and salespeople. We ended up with a better plan."

Powers used the feedback from these informal discussions to write a business case for the new system, and her plan was immediately approved. When it came time to rewrite customer contracts, the travel agents were sold on the added benefits they would get. The company soon completed its rollout of the DSL network. Power notes "getting people involved early by just talking with them [through active listening] allowed us to address objections and actually have a better plan. By the time we did the business plan, we had everybody pretty much on board."

Powers thinks "The next big thing in our business will be 'green' initiatives. This will range from providing carbon-tracker information to corporations and travelers to ensuring that our company, our employees, and the data center operate in a 'green' fashion."

She concludes: "The best advice I can give to future leaders is it's all about the people, and communication is key. Make sure your front-line managers understand the strategy, objectives, metrics, and business drivers. If you have a committed, well-informed, well-prepared, and motivated staff, you will be successful."

To learn more about Travelport, go to **www.travelport.com.**

Nonverbal Communication

Learning Goal

3. *Diagnose nonverbal communication behaviors.*

Nonverbal communication *includes the process of sending "wordless" messages by means such as facial expressions, gestures, postures, emotional tones of voice, grooming, clothing, colors, and use or type of space.*[28] Nonverbal cues may contain many direct or hidden messages and can influence the process and outcome of "words" in communication. Even when individuals are silent, they are sending messages, which may or may not be the intended messages (including boredom, fear, anger, or depression). Nonverbal signals are a rich source of information for a leader. A person's own nonverbal behavior can be useful in responding to others, making stronger connections with others, and conveying certain impressions about oneself. The proportion of *emotional* reactions that are expressed through nonverbal signals may exceed 90 percent.[29]

Types of Nonverbal Cues

A framework for considering types of *personal* nonverbal cues is *PERCEIVE*, an acronym that stands for the following terms: (1) **P**roximity, (2) **E**xpressions, (3) **R**elative orientation, (4) **C**ontact, (5) **E**yes, (6) **I**ndividual gestures, (7) **V**oice, and (8) **E**xistence of adapters. A brief review of each follows[30]:

*   *Proximity* is the physical distance between individuals. Generally, individuals sit, stand, and want to be near those they like. Increased proximity is usually an indication of feelings of liking and interest.

*   *Expressions* are observed on the face and can last as little as 1/15th of a second. These very brief expressions occur when people are trying to hide a feeling. Interestingly, when people begin to experience an emotion, their facial muscles are triggered. If they suppress the expression, it's shown for only 1/15th of a second. If they do not suppress it, the expression will appear prominently. The six universal expressions that most cultures recognize are happiness, sadness, anger, fear, surprise, and disgust. Smiling can be real or false, interpreted by differences in the strength and length of the smile, the openness of the eyes, and the symmetry of expression.

*   *Relative orientation* is the degree to which individuals face one another. Individuals sitting side by side is usually an indication that they are interested in and focused on the other person. As individuals become less interested in another person, they tend to angle their bodies away. A good way to understand relative orientation is to observe where a person's feet are placed. Often individuals will point their feet in the direction they truly want to go.

*   *Contact* refers to physical contact. Generally, the amount and frequency of physical contact demonstrate closeness, familiarity, and degree of liking. A lot of touching usually indicates strong liking for another person.

- *Eyes* primarily show whom or what people are most interested in or like. One can gauge liking and interest by the frequency and duration of time spent looking. Few gestures carry more weight than looking someone in the eyes or face. Eye and face contact displays your willingness to listen and your acknowledgment of the other person's worth. Although eye contact does not indicate truthfulness or honesty (as some people believe), it does usually show interest in the other person's idea or point of view. However, prolonged and intense eye contact does not usually occur unless feelings of hostility, defensiveness, or romantic interest are present. Lack of interest may be indicated through contractions of the pupils or wandering eyes.

- *Individual gestures* can convey an image in a person's mind that is sometimes not spoken. Some typical gestures are ones that describe an emotion or experience (e.g., sobbing gesture or frenetic moving of the hands) or gestures that identify where objects are in relation to one another. Gestures also reveal how people are feeling. People tend to gesture more when they are enthusiastic, excited, and energized. People tend to gesture less when they are demoralized, nervous, or concerned about the impression they are making. For more about nonverbal communication, see the Communication Competency feature in Chapter 4 entitled "Hand Gestures." The feature addressed the different meanings of three hand gestures used in the United States and how they would be interpreted in certain other cultures.

- *Voice* or speech often provides information about the demographics of a speaker (e.g., gender, age, area of origin, social class). Voice can also reveal emotions, which are transmitted through the tone of the voice, accentuation of words, rapidity of speech, and number of speech errors. Typically, speech errors indicate discomfort and anxiety. A person who begins to produce a lot of speech errors may be anxious and ill at ease.

- *Existence of adapters* is the last element of *PERCEIVE*. Adapters are small behaviors that tend to occur when people are stressed or bored with a situation. Examples are playing with rings, twirling a pen, or touching one's hair. As meetings become too long, an increasing number of adapter behaviors tend to emerge among the people in the room.

Physical Environment

Some organizations are attempting to influence interpersonal communications through the physical environment with use of feng shui, which we introduced in Chapter 4. *Feng shui* is the belief that space needs to be in harmony with the environment. We noted that the Chinese phrase *feng shui* means "wind and water" to represent the flow of energy and harmony. Recall the Across Cultures Competency feature in Chapter 4 entitled "McDonald's Use of Feng Shui." A few of the common recommendations for office arrangements related to nonverbal communication based on feng shui include the following: (1) You should have a full view of the room's entrance door by merely looking up from your desk. (2) You should be able to see outside while sitting at your desk. If the office doesn't have a window, brighten up the lighting and use a picture of the outdoors. (3) Your desk should not be placed at the side of the door. You can place a screen in the space between your desk and the doorway if necessary. (4) You should have a wall at your back while seated. Presumably, it gives you a "commanding" position.[31]

Although the ability of feng shui to impact "harmony and energy" has been questioned, its principles for designing buildings and offices, including the placement of furniture and objects, are increasingly being used to varying degrees in Western societies.[32] For people in North America who are interested in feng shui, the American Feng Shui Institute is a good place to start for more details about its concepts and principles.[33]

Importance to Verbal Messages

Nonverbal communication is an important complement to verbal communication; neither is adequate by itself for effective dialogue. A few of the ways in which verbal and nonverbal cues can be related are as follows:

- Repeating, such as when verbal directions to some location are accompanied by pointing.

- Contradicting, such as when you say "What, me nervous?" while fidgeting and perspiring anxiously before taking a test. This is a good example of how the nonverbal message might be more believable when verbal and nonverbal signals conflict.

- Substituting nonverbal for verbal cues, such as when you return from the manager's office with a stressful expression that says "I've just had a horrible meeting with my manager"—without a word being spoken.

- Complementing the verbal cue through nonverbal "underlining," such as when you pound on a table, place a hand on the shoulder of a coworker, use a tone of voice indicating the great importance attached to the message, or give a gift as a way of reinforcing an expression of gratitude or respect.

Since the recent downturn and resulting distress in the U.S. and other economies, more and more companies have been downsizing their workforces. Layoffs at Yahoo!, *The New York Times*, JPMorgan Chase, and others make daily newscasts. Therefore, leaders need to learn how to handle laying off employees. The following Communication Competency feature presents the poor use of nonverbal communications by leaders related to layoffs.[34]

Communication competency

Poor Nonverbal Signals Prior to Layoffs

Marcia Finberg's relationship with her CEO had been cordial during the three years she worked as vice president of marketing and business developments for a Phoenix hospital. The CEO always made small talk and followed up with her on projects. When this rapport suddenly stopped, she knew something was up. Three months later her job was eliminated. Finberg's CEO went from being friendly with her to avoiding her and being curt. She knew the hospital was losing patients to a new medical center in the area and that her employer's financial situation had become precarious. Finberg says her CEO's cold response leading up to her being let go could have been a defense mechanism. "You don't want to admit that under your stewardship the finances were such that you had to let someone from your executive team go," she says.

Ron Shewchuk, now a communications consultant, comments that he worked for an organization that went on a 15-year acquisition binge. This meant the company was constantly integrating acquired companies, which always meant consolidation and the job losses that come with it. The workplace became so cynical that some people kept "300-day clocks." They morbidly would count down the days before the next layoff. Inevitably, the pink slips would come before the clocks ran out. The clocks became stark and daily nonverbal reminders of impending layoffs. Shewchuk notes that the CEO hadn't directly communicated with employees for at least a decade.

When John Boyd was chief intellectual property counsel of a midsize technology company, he says, the CEO and other executives made him feel like he wasn't in the "inner circle." He says he was continually left off of e-mail announcements congratulating teams on projects, even when he was on those teams. He didn't wait to see what his fate might be; instead, Boyd left the company.

Simma Lieberman, who owns a consulting firm in Albany, California, reflects on one technology company that hired her to deal with the aftermath of a layoff. The company laid off more than 200 people, many of whom were preparing for retirement. They received no benefits except outplacement services for one day. Security guards immediately escorted them out of the building. Senior management didn't provide any explanations or communicate with existing staff about what had occurred. This turned otherwise loyal employees against the company. Lieberman states: "It was horrific what the company had done. The remaining employees were so demoralized. I couldn't fix it." The silence by higher management in this whole incident became a powerful and negative nonverbal signal to both the remaining and laid-off employees.

Status Differences

Nonverbal cues often strongly reveal status differences. The following are only three of the many relationships between nonverbal cues and organizational status:

- Employees of higher status typically have better offices than do employees of lower status. For example, executive offices are typically more spacious, located on the top floors of the building, and have finer carpets and furniture than those of first-line managers. Most senior offices are at the corners, so they have windows on two sides.

- The offices of higher status employees are better "protected" than those of lower status employees. *Protected* refers to how much more difficult it would be for you to, say, arrange to visit the governor of your state than for the governor to arrange to visit you. Top executive areas are typically least accessible and are often sealed off from others by several doors and assistants. Of course, having an office with a door and a secretary who answers the telephone protects even lower level managers and many staff personnel.

- The higher the employee's status, the easier that employee finds it to invade the territory of lower status employees. A superior typically feels free to walk right in on subordinates, whereas subordinates are more careful to ask permission or make an appointment before visiting a superior.[35]

Insights for Leaders

Carried to excess, these and other nonverbal status cues are likely to create barriers to dialogue, especially from the perspective of the employees with lower formal status. However, effective leaders often use supportive nonverbal cues when meeting with subordinates, such as (1) lightly touching subordinates on the arm when they arrive and shaking hands, (2) smiling appropriately, (3) nodding to affirm what was said, (4) slightly pulling their chairs closer to subordinates and maintaining an open posture, and (5) engaging in eye contact to further demonstrate listening and interest.[36]

Learning Goal

4. *Understand the importance of cultural and nonverbal barriers to communication.*

Intercultural Communication

Cultural Barriers

Intercultural communication *occurs whenever a message sent by a member of one culture is received and understood by a member of another culture.*[37] The effects of cultural differences on interpersonal communication can be wide ranging. They depend on the degrees of difference (or similarity) between people in terms of language, religious beliefs, economic status, social values, physical characteristics, use of nonverbal cues, and the like. The greater the differences, the more likely it is that there will be barriers to achieving effective communication.

In Iran, there is a concept called **taarof**, *which is a set of social manners that seem polite or deceitful depending on one's point of view.* Taarof is a form of etiquette intended to harmonize social meetings and communications. It often involves displays of flattery and deference.[38] In interpersonal communications among Iranians, people are expected to tell you what you want to hear to avoid conflict, or to offer hope when there is none. Iranians understand such practices and are not offended by them. Nasair Hadian, a political science professor at the University of Iran, comments: "You have to guess if people are sincere, you are never sure. Symbolism and vagueness are inherent in our language." Kian Tajbakhsh, a social scientist who lived for many years in England and the United States before returning to Iran in 1996, continues: "Speech has a different function than it does in the West. In the West, 80 percent of language is explicit and as stated. In Iran 80 percent is implied." Translation: In the West, *yes* generally means "yes." In Iran, *yes* can mean "yes," but it often means "maybe" or "no." In Iran, "Listeners are expected to understand that words don't necessarily mean exactly what they mean."[39]

Cultural Context

The conditions that surround and influence the life of an individual, group, or organization are its **cultural context**. Differences in cultural context may represent a barrier to communication.[40] Nations' cultures vary on a continuum from low context to high context. Figure 9.5 shows the approximate placement of various countries along this continuum.

A **high-context culture** *in interpersonal communication is characterized by (1) the establishment of social trust before engaging in work-related discussions, (2) the high value placed on personal relationships and goodwill, and (3) the importance of the surrounding circumstances during an interaction.* In a high-context culture such as China, Korea, and Japan, people rely on paraphrasing, tone of voice, gesture, posture, social status, history, and social setting to interpret spoken words, all of which require time to cultivate. Factors such as trust, relationships among friends and family members, personal needs and difficulties, weather, and holidays must be taken into consideration. For example, Japanese executives—when meeting foreign executives for the first time—do not immediately "get down to business." They engage in a period of building trust and getting to know each other that foreign executives often are impatient with but must conform to.

In contrast, a **low-context culture** *in interpersonal communication is characterized by (1) directly and immediately addressing the tasks, issues, or problems at hand; (2) the high value placed on personal expertise and performance; and (3) the importance of clear, precise, and speedy interactions.* Within low-context cultures such as Germany, Switzerland, and the United States, the purpose of communication is to often reveal actual intent, not conceal it. The individuals often express what they mean and mean what they convey. Leaders motivate employees with statements focusing on positive or corrective feedback and goal setting. In a heterogeneous country, such as the United States, multiple subcultures have their own unique characteristics. In contrast, the cultural context of a homogeneous country, such as South Korea or Japan, reflects the more uniform characteristics of its people.

IMAGE SOURCE

▲
Differences in cultural context may represent a hurdle to communication because low-context countries, such as the United States, and high-context countries, such as Japan, have different communication norms.

Across Cultures Insight

So much of our office jargon in the U.S. is colloquial, and we don't even realize it. Comments like "cover all the bases" or "three strikes and you're out" don't have any context value here in India at all. People just don't know what we are talking about with such phrases.

Nina E. Woodward, Director, Business Development, Strategic Human Resource Management India

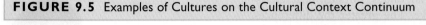

FIGURE 9.5 Examples of Cultures on the Cultural Context Continuum

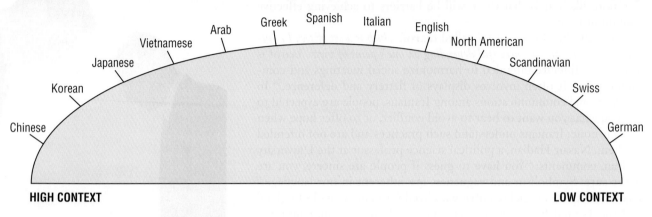

HIGH CONTEXT   LOW CONTEXT

Source: Based on Hall, E. *Understanding Cultural Differences*. Yarmouth, ME: Intercultural Press, 1989; Munter, M., *Guide to Managerial Communication: Effective Business Writing and Speaking*, 5th ed. Englewood Cliffs, NJ: Prentice Hall, 1999.

Ethnocentrism

Ethnocentrism *occurs when individuals believe that only their culture makes sense, has the "right" values, and represents the "right" and logical way to behave.*[41] This may be the greatest barrier to communication because it involves judging others from our own cultural point of view. It also involves making false assumptions about the ways others behave based on our own limited experiences. Individuals are not even aware that they are being ethnocentric because "we don't understand that we don't understand." When two highly ethnocentric people from different cultures interact, there is little chance that they will achieve a common understanding. Ethnocentric reactions to differing views may be anger, shock, or even amusement. Ethnocentric people view all others as inferior and may recognize cultural diversity, but only as a source of problems. Their strategy is to minimize the sources and impacts of cultural diversity. Ethnocentric individuals ignore or deny that cultural diversity can lead to advantages.

Ethnocentrism is best viewed along a continuum—everyone is, to some extent, ethnocentric.[42] At one end of the continuum, ethnocentrism may be functional when one's group or even nation is under attack or threat of attack. It forms the basis for patriotism and the motivation to sacrifice for one's group. At the other end, it results in the tendency for people to see their own way as the only right way. This can be dangerous and may lead to poor communication that results in prejudice and discrimination.

All intercultural exchanges are, to a lesser or greater degree, influenced by ethnocentrism. It acts as a perceptual filter (see our discussion of perception and attributions in Chapter 4) that affects verbal and nonverbal messages and how individuals see their source. We tend to initiate and continue communication with those to whom we are attracted. When we interact with someone from another culture, our perception of the other's attractiveness is influenced by our degree of ethnocentrism. By definition, high ethnocentric individuals perceive themselves as very different and superior from other groups—within the same or other countries. Because of their sense of superiority, high ethnocentric individuals tend to judge other group members as less competent and less trustworthy, which adversely influences intercultural communications.

The following Across Cultures Competency feature reports on Tahir Ayub's experiences as a participant in PricewaterhouseCoopers' (PwC's) Ulysses Program.[43] Tahir Ayub is an Audit and Assurance Group partner and the Alberta Private Company Services leader of PricewaterhouseCoopers LLP in Canada. As a business adviser, he provides advice and acts as a sounding board to the owners and management of private companies in the various Canadian industries. The Ulysses Program is a global leadership development program at PwC. It was started in 2001 and has sent 80 partners from 32 territories on 26 projects. Among other purposes, this program enhances the participants' intercultural communication abilities and appreciation for cultural context. PwC has 155,000 employees who work in 150 countries. They provide a variety of services in the fields of assurance, tax, human resources, performance improvement, and the like.[44]

Across Cultures competency

Tahir Ayub, Partner, PwC

Tahir Ayub's role in the Ulysses Program at PricewaterhouseCoopers was to help village leaders in Africa's Namibian outback grapple with their community's growing AIDS crisis. Faced with language barriers, cultural differences, and limited access to electricity, Ayub and two colleagues learned that they needed to garner community support for programs to combat the disease. Ayub learned an important lesson as well: Technology isn't always the answer. "You better put your beliefs and biases to one side and figure out new ways to look at things," he said.

PwC arranged for the trip and Ayub's stay there as part of their Ulysses Program to develop global leaders. The partners "go local"—they are stripped of all the comforts they have grown to take for granted and given a specific task to complete. They must rely on their own resourcefulness to succeed. PwC believes such hands-on experience is essential to developing global leaders.

On arrival, Ayub paired up with two other PwC partners whom he had never met before— one from the Netherlands and the other from Mexico. Having grown up in the United Kingdom and having gone to college in Vancouver, British Columbia, it was a life-changing experience: "When you work in a (culturally diverse) place like Vancouver, you work with people from different backgrounds and you think you are culturally aware," he recalls. But working as part of the Namibia team, he was less sure of his openmindedness. He also learned that "perhaps the way you see things isn't necessarily the best way"—a humbling experience for someone as successful as a PwC partner.

After returning from Namibia, Ayub says he can still see the faces of the orphans he met, whose parents had died from AIDS. PwC says it can see that Ayub benefited from the experience. Today, he recognizes the importance of listening to different perspectives before making decisions. "Before, when I came across an issue that I thought I knew how to deal with, I would say that I didn't have a lot of time to listen to everyone involved to make sure it was the right way to go. Now I am much more open to listening and to other people's points of view," he says. In reflecting on the Ulysses Program and other experiences, Tahir comments: "As a leader, you have to communicate clearly and most of all walk the talk; actions really do speak louder than words."

To learn more about PwC, go to **www.pwc.com.**

Nonverbal Differences

Because of the many differences in nonverbal expression, people from different cultures often misunderstand each other. This is a significant barrier to cross-cultural communication.[45] We now review three forms of nonverbal cross-cultural communication: chromatics, chronemics, and body language.

Chromatics

Chromatics *is communication through the use of color.* Colors of clothing, products, packaging, or gifts send intended or unintended messages when people communicate cross-culturally. For example, in Hong Kong red signifies happiness or good luck. The traditional bridal dress is red, and at the Chinese New Year luck money is distributed in *hong bao*, red envelopes. Men in Hong Kong avoid green because of the Cantonese expression "He's wearing a green hat," which means "His wife is cheating on him." In Chile, a gift of yellow roses conveys the message "I don't like you," and in the Czech Republic giving red roses indicates a romantic interest.

In the United States, it is common to wear black when one is mourning, whereas in some locations in India, people wear white when they are mourning. In Asia, people like colored shampoos because they like the shampoo to be the color of their hair because they believe different or lighter colors change the color of their hair. In the United States, shampoos tend to be light colored because people see this as a sign of cleanliness and hygiene.

Chronemics

Chronemics *reflects the use of time in a culture.*[46] Before reading any further, please complete the instrument in Table 9.2 to determine how you use your personal time. **A monochronic time schedule** *means that things are done linearly, or one activity at a time.* Time is seen as something that can be controlled or wasted by people. Time schedules are followed by employees in individualistic cultures, such as those in Northern Europe, Germany, and the United States. Being a few minutes late for a business appointment is an insult, so punctuality is extremely important. Keith Hughes is the former CEO

TABLE 9.2 The Polychronic Attitude Index

Please consider how you feel about the following statements. Circle your choice on the scale provided: strongly agree, agree, neutral, disagree, or strongly disagree.

	STRONGLY DISAGREE	DISAGREE	NEUTRAL	AGREE	STRONGLY AGREE
1. I do not like to juggle several activities at the same time.	5	4	3	2	1
2. People should not try to do many things at once.	5	4	3	2	1
3. When I sit down at my desk, I work on one project at a time.	5	4	3	2	1
4. I am comfortable doing several things at the same time.	5	4	3	2	1

Add up your points, and divide the total by 4. Then plot your score on the scale.

1.0	1.5	2.0	2.5	3.0	3.5	4.0	4.5	5.0
Monochronic								Polychronic

The lower the score (below 3.0), the more monochronic your organization or department is; the higher the score (above 3.0), the more polychronic it is.

Source: Adapted from Bluedorn, A. C., Kaufman, C. F., and Lane, P. M. How many things do you like to do at once? An introduction to monochronic and polychronic time. *Academy of Management Executive*, 1992, 6(4), 17–26. Used with permission.

of Associates First Capital Corporation, a consumer finance company that has been acquired by Citigroup. He used to lock the doors when a meeting was supposed to start and didn't unlock them until the meeting was over.

A **polychronic time schedule** *means that people tend to do several things at the same time.*[47] A more fluid approach is taken to scheduling time. Many people may like to drive and conduct business at the same time (cars and cellular phones) or watch the news and a ball game at the same time (picture-in-picture TV). Schedules are less important than personal involvement and the completion of business. In Latin America and the Middle East (e.g., Saudi Arabia and Egypt), time schedules are less important than personal involvement. In Ecuador, businesspeople come to a meeting 15 or 20 minutes late and still consider themselves to be on time.

Polychronic cultures are deeply steeped in tradition rather than in tasks—a clear difference from their monochronic counterparts. They are more focused on relationships, rather than watching the clock. They have no problem being "late" for an event if they are with family or friends, because the relationship is what really matters. As a result, polychronic cultures have a much less formal perception of time. These cultures are much less focused on the preciseness of accounting for each and every moment. They are not as ruled by precise calendars and schedules as are monochronic cultures. Rather, they may even schedule multiple appointments simultaneously such that keeping on schedule is an impossibility. Many polychronic cultures have a past orientation toward time. The Chinese, for example, place great significance on the past.

Body Language

Posture, gestures, eye contact, facial expression, touching, voice pitch and volume, and speaking rate differ from one culture to another.[48] As a simple, but potentially disastrous example, nodding the head up and down in Bulgaria means "no," not "yes." You must avoid using any gestures considered rude or insulting. For instance, in Buddhist cultures, the head is considered sacred, so you must never touch anyone's head. In Muslim cultures, the left hand is considered unclean, so never touch, pass, or receive with the left hand. Pointing with the index finger is rude in cultures ranging from the Sudan to Venezuela to Sri Lanka. The American circular "A-OK" gesture carries a vulgar meaning in Brazil, Paraguay, Singapore, and Russia. Crossing your ankle over your knee is rude in Indonesia, Thailand, and Syria. Pointing your index finger toward yourself insults the other person in Germany, the Netherlands, and Switzerland. Avoid placing an open hand over a closed fist in France, saying "tsk tsk" in Kenya, and whistling in India.

Body language, including gestures, eye contact, facial expressions, and touching, varies from one culture to another.

Prepare yourself to recognize gestures that have meaning only in the other culture. Chinese stick out their tongues to show surprise and scratch their ears and cheeks to show happiness. Japanese suck in air, hissing through their teeth to indicate embarrassment or "no." Greeks puff air after they receive a compliment. Hondurans touch a finger to the face below the eye to indicate caution or disbelief.

Finally, resist applying your own culture's nonverbal meanings to other cultures. Vietnamese may look at the ground with their heads down to show respect, not to be "shifty." Russians may exhibit less facial expression and Scandinavians fewer gestures than Americans are accustomed to, but that doesn't mean that they aren't enthusiastic. The British may prefer more distant personal and social space and might consider it rude if you move too close. Closely related is the concept of touch. Anglos usually avoid touching each other very much. In studies of touching behaviors, researchers observed people seated in outdoor cafes in each of four countries and counted the number of touches during an hour of conversation. The results were San Juan, Puerto Rico, 180 touches per hour; Paris, 110 per hour; Gainesville, Florida, 1 per hour; and London, 0 per hour.[49]

THE STUDIO DOG/PHOTODISC/GETTY IMAGES

Interpersonal Communication Networks

5. *Discuss the role of communication networks.*

An **interpersonal communication network** *is the pattern of communication flows, relationships, and understandings developed over time among people, rather than focusing on the individual and whether a specific message is received as intended by the sender.* Networks involve the ongoing flow of verbal, written, and nonverbal messages between two people or between one person and others. Communication networks can influence the likelihood of a match between messages as sent and as actually received and interpreted. The more accurately the message moves through the channel, the more clearly the receiver will understand it.

Individual Network

The elements of interpersonal communication shown earlier in Figure 9.1 are based on a network of only two people. Obviously, communication often takes place among many individuals and larger groups. Claudia Gonzales, a telecommunications manager for Abaco Grupo Financiero in Mexico, normally has ongoing links with many people both inside and outside her organization. Her communication network extends laterally, vertically, and externally. *Vertical networks* typically include her immediate superior and subordinates and the superior's superiors and the subordinates' subordinates. *Lateral networks* include people in the same department at the same level (peers) and people in different departments at the same level. *External networks* include customers, suppliers, regulatory agencies, pressure groups, professional peers, and friends. Thus, a person's communication network can be quite involved.

Size limits the possible communication networks within a team or informal group. In principle, as the size of a team increases arithmetically, the number of possible communication interrelationships increases exponentially. Accordingly, communication networks are much more varied and complex in a 12-person team than in a 5-person team. Although each team member (theoretically) may be able to communicate with all the others, the direction and number of communication channels often are somewhat limited. In committee meetings, for example, varying levels of formality influence who may speak, what may be discussed, and in what order. The relative status or ranking of team members also may differ. Members having higher status probably will dominate communications more than those with lower status. Even when an open network is encouraged, a team member may actually use a limited network arrangement.

A common prescription, especially for college graduates when they join an organization, is to work on developing an individual communication network. At present or in the future, how might you know if you have developed a strong inside individual network? If you are able to answer "yes" to most of the following questions, you are probably on the right track[50]:

1. Do I know people at more than one level of the organization? Do they know my name and what I do?

2. Do I know a number of the people whose work relates to mine in any way beyond my own department?

3. Am I involved in any interdepartmental activities (temporary assignments, committees, task forces, special projects, volunteer activities)?

4. Am I plugged into the grapevine? Do I find out quickly what's up?

5. Do I take every opportunity to meet face to face to define and discuss complex problems, shifting priorities, areas of responsibility?

6. Do I know and talk with others about trends that will impact my job in the future and methods to get the job done today?

7. When I become aware of a problem that involves people from various areas, do I take the initiative to indicate my willingness to work on it?

8. Do I drop by to see people—even when I don't need anything—as time permits?

Effective individual networking focuses on serving customers, streamlining internal processes, solving problems, and achieving organizational and unit goals. Networking that focuses on immediate and apparent self-serving interests and goals is often counterproductive and even more so when it serves to hurt or take advantage of others.[51] For individual network effectiveness, the individual needs **political skill**—*the ability to effectively understand others at work, and to use such knowledge to influence others to act in ways that enhance one's long-term personal and/or organizational goals.*[52] Consider four of the dimensions of political skill[53]:

* *Networking ability*—the degree to which individuals are adept at developing and using diverse networks of people. People in these networks tend to have capabilities seen as valuable and necessary for successful personal and organizational functioning.

* *Apparent sincerity*—the degree to which individuals appear to others as possessing high levels of integrity, authenticity, sincerity, and genuineness. They are, or appear to be, honest, open, and forthright.

* *Social astuteness*—the degree to which individuals are savvy observers of others and are keenly attuned to diverse social situations. They understand social interactions and accurately interpret their behavior, as well as that of others, in social settings. They have strong powers of discernment and high self-awareness.

* *Interpersonal influence*—the degree to which individuals use a subtle and convincing personal style that exerts a powerful influence on those around them. Individuals high on interpersonal influence nonetheless are capable of appropriately adapting and calibrating their behavior to each situation in order to elicit particular responses from others. Because their actions are not interpreted as manipulative or coercive, individuals high in apparent sincerity inspire trust and confidence in and from those around them.

A major study identified the primary causes of managerial failure in changing organizations. More than 1,000 successful U.S. managers participated in this study.[54] Table 9.3 shows the top 10 major themes that were cited as causes of managerial failures. Although a failed manager is likely to be characterized by several themes, it is apparent that "ineffective communication skills/practices" is cited by the vast majority (81 percent) of managers. The failed managers typically did not effectively share critical information with individual employees and/or work teams. Also, they failed to listen to the concerns of those around them, with potentially devastating outcomes. In essence, these failed managers were poor networkers and lacked political skill.

TABLE 9.3 Themes in Causes of Managerial Failure: Perceptions of More Than 1,000 Successful Managers

THEMES	FREQUENCY OF MENTIONS
1. Ineffective communication skills/practices	81%
2. Poor work relationships/interpersonal skills	78%
3. Person job mismatch	69%
4. Fail to clarify direction/performance expectations	64%
5. Failing to adapt and break old habits quickly	57%
6. Delegation and empowerment breakdown	56%
7. Lack of personal integrity and trustworthiness	52%
8. Unable to develop cooperation/teamwork	50%
9. Unable to lead/motivate others	47%
10. Poor planning practices/reactionary behavior	45%

Source: Adapted from Longenecker, C. O., Neubert, M. J., and Fink, L. S. Causes and consequences of managerial failure in rapidly changing organizations. *Business Horizons*, 2007, 50, 148.

Informal Group Network

An informal group network involves the communication pattern of multiple individual networks. By *informal* we mean those communication channels and messages that do not strictly follow the formal organization paths, such as when the president meets with or sends all employees an e-mail, or when a manager holds a weekly meeting with employees.

The most common form of informal group network is the **grapevine**—*the unofficial, and at times confidential, person-to-person or person-to-group chain of verbal, or at times e-mail, communication.*[55] The most common messages of the grapevine are rumors—unverified information, which may be of uncertain origin, that is usually spread by word of mouth or perhaps e-mail. Rumors are often a result of stress circumstances, like the perceived threats from major organizational changes. Of course, rumors themselves, especially when false, can be a source of stress and dissatisfaction. In general, the frequency of negative rumors is much greater than positive rumors in organizations.[56] Four of the major ways that messages move through grapevines in organizations are as follows[57]:

- *Single-strand chain* refers to one person telling a rumor to the next, who then tells the next person, who tells the next, and so on. As such, the rumor is told to one person at a time and passed on to others. Accuracy is lower in this type of chain than in the others because of the many alterations the story is subject to with each retelling.

- *Gossip chain* refers to only one person spreading the message, telling the story to most everyone with which the person comes in contact. This chain is likely to be the most slow moving.

- *Probability chain* refers to one person randomly contacting several others and telling them the message. Those individuals, in turn, randomly contact several others and continue to spread it. This chain is not a definite channel because the message is spread to different people, bypassing others altogether.

- *Cluster chain* refers to one person telling several close contacts who then pass it on to several people with whom they have close contacts. Regardless, people receive and transmit the message in terms of their personal biases, which results in the general theme being maintained but the details potentially being changed. It is often used to spread rumors and other news in organizations.

Informal group networks, like grapevines, cannot be eliminated by leaders. In fact, leaders often participate in them. The best approach is to understand grapevines and develop strategies to use in preventing and combating false or inaccurate rumors and gossip both internally and externally to the organization.[58] In an organization with low levels of communication openness, it is to be expected that informal group networks are likely to conflict with the formal employee network established by senior management. As you will recall from Figure 9.4, low communication openness is characterized by (1) closed, guarded, and defensive message transmission; (2) low trust; (3) hidden agendas; and (4) concealed goals. In this situation, it is likely that different informal group networks are likely to conflict with each other and be engaged in continuous power struggles. In contrast, with high levels of communication openness and other attributes of ethical interpersonal communication, individual networks, informal group networks, and formal employee networks will more often be mutually supportive and reasonably consistent with one another, thereby reducing barriers, inconsistencies, and confusion in communications within the organization.[59]

Formal Employee Network

A **formal employee network** *is the intended pattern and flows of employee-related communication vertically—between levels—and laterally—between individuals, teams, departments, and divisions.* In this chapter, we discussed several of the practices undertaken by Julia Stewart at DineEquity to shape, develop, and use informal and formal employee networks. Our discussion of Tahir Ayub at PwC emphasized the importance of cultural context in a formal employee network such as the Ulysses Program at PwC. In our Change Competency feature on Susan Powers at Travelport GDS, she and her team used individual, informal, and formal employee networks to introduce ideas, receive feedback, and foster organizational change.

In most chapters throughout this book, we present competency features on how leaders can foster or hinder the development of effective formal employee networks. Our discussion of six types of formal teams in Chapter 12—such as self-managed, virtual, and global—are examples of top leaders' initiatives to form and influence various lateral and vertical formal employee networks. Also, we discuss the *network design* as one of the contemporary organizational designs in Chapter 15, *Organization Design*.

Insights for Leaders

All types of networks are important for day-to-day communication in organizations.[60] No single network is likely to prove effective for a team or organization faced with a variety of tasks, problems, and goals. The apparently efficient, low-cost, and simple method of a superior instructing subordinates is likely to be ineffective if used exclusively. Dissatisfaction may become so great that members will leave the team or lose their motivation to contribute. Individuals and teams that face complex problems requiring a lot of discussion and coordination may deal with them ineffectively because of this top-down pattern. Leaders must consider trade-offs or opportunity costs. The overuse of formal meetings results in members becoming bored and dissatisfied with them. They often simply come to feel that their time is being wasted. Employees may spend too much time on a problem and its solution with excessive use of formal meetings. Hence, leaders should use the level of networking that is most appropriate to the specific goals and tasks.

Major organizational changes typically require the use of all types of networks—electronic, informal, and formal employee networks. One of the key leadership challenges is in creating vision so that these networks are reasonably consistent with and reinforce each other. The following Change Competency feature emphasizes the importance of leadership in creating employee networks and introducing information technologies to bring about a major turnaround at CSX.[61] CSX has a 21,000-route-mile rail network that serves 23 states and two Canadian provinces. It operates an average of 1,200 trains per day with a fleet of 3,800 locomotives and 110,000 freight cars. CSX is headquartered in Jacksonville, Florida, and has 30,000 employees.[62] The change and communication competencies of Michael J. Ward, the chairman and CEO of CSX, were key ingredients in the turnaround at CSX. He was recognized for his leadership by *Railway Age* as the 2009 Railroader of the Year.

Change competency

Michael Ward's Reflections on CSX's One Plan Redesign

Upon becoming CEO, we outlined some real core values that we had to believe in as a company. They're very basic to our business and very appropriate for our company. People make a difference. It starts with the customer. Safety is a way of life. Be fact-based. Get the right results the right way. One of the things I'm actually the proudest of is our One Plan Redesign, which looked at our entire scheduled merchandise, automotive and intermodal networks. We needed to put consistency into the plan and operate in a disciplined manner so that we could give our customers the kind of service they require. When we first rolled One Plan out, it really worked well for a couple of quarters. All of our key measures started improving. The customers were satisfied

CSX train.

DMAC/ALAMY

and we thought, wow, this is really a good program. Then, all of a sudden, we stopped paying attention. All those great improvements went by the wayside.

I'm really proud of what we did then. Traditionally, we would have come out with a new program. But we said, no, we're going to do the One Plan and we are going to do it right. So we went back and we examined what some of the issues were. One of them was that the locomotive plan was not adequately matched up and networked with the train operating plan. We made those improvements. We rolled out the One Plan again, and ever since then, it's been working well and we continue to improve it.

To learn more about CSX, go to **www.csx.com.**

On the operating plan itself, we're actually doing a redesign, if you will, a rerunning of our One Plan. It's a several-month process because it's a very complicated computer model that looks at all the traffic demands and how to best "build" the trains. It isn't just a computerized, headquarters-originated process. We take the preliminary results and go out to the field personnel. We say, this is what we think you should or could be able to do; do you agree with this? Many times the local personnel will have some refinements. Sometimes they'll change what that recommendation is and will improve it and make it more executable. We want to make sure it's not just an exercise in computer modeling. It needs to be something that people feel like they can execute on a day-in, day-out basis. It takes a couple of iterations to get it refined properly, and we're in the process of doing that as well.

We recently implemented a new dispatch system. Before, everything was centrally decided in Jacksonville, Florida. The new dispatch system is much more portable and flexible. There's real value in having dispatching close to the actual operations. It's my view that having the dispatcher closer to the operations is actually very beneficial. They get to know the people, they get to know the territory better. This makes it less of a video game, realizing that there are physical locations, there are sidings, and understanding the ebbs and flows. Having dispatchers closer to the field operating people is much more effective.

Impacts of E-Mail

E-mail impacts individuals, informal groups, and formal employee networks as well as interpersonal communications throughout the organization. Just as face-to-face meetings can be overused and misused in organizations, so too can e-mail. The average manager receives over 250 e-mails a week. The potential perils of e-mail are greater than many assume. Research suggests that less than 50 percent of users grasp the tone or intent of an e-mail. Moreover, most people vastly overestimate their ability to relay and comprehend e-mail messages accurately. Misinterpretation is highest when the e-mail comes from the person's manager.[63]

E-mail is different from a live conversation in two important ways: First, the individual cannot modify the content of a message based on the nonverbal reactions of the other party. Second, e-mails are permanent documents. Once sent, an e-mail can't be taken back and the sender loses all control over who views the message. Unfortunately, the permanent nature of e-mail often is forgotten in the hubbub of everyday communications and can come back to haunt the sender in unanticipated ways.

Three major challenges have been identified with the use of e-mail: First and foremost, e-mails lacks cues like facial expression and tone of voice. That makes it difficult for recipients to decode meaning. Second, the prospect of instantaneous communication creates an urgency that pressures e-mailers to think and write quickly, which can lead to carelessness in grammar, spelling, and tone. Third, the inability to develop personal rapport over an e-mail makes relationships fragile in the face of conflict.[64] In effect, e-mail cannot adequately convey emotion. When it does, unintended emotions are often received. The sender may soon wish the message sent could be retrieved or revised. Recall how Julia Stewart in the opening Learning from Experience feature felt about e-mail: She uses it, but says voice mail works best for her because she finds e-mail to be stale and impersonal.

The emotional dimension conveyed thru e-mail has been termed *e-body language* by one author.[65] E-body language is primarily conveyed in three main areas: tone, timing, and tension.

Tone

How the person structures and phrases e-mails can play a large part in how they are interpreted. For example, the overuse of personal pronouns—*I, me, my*—makes the writer sound parochial or egotistical. Too much use of the words *we* and *they* signals a competitive atmosphere. Overuse of exclamation points, sentences in all caps and bold font, and messages marked "high importance" when that is not really so are pitfalls associated with using e-mail. These practices can easily create unintended tones and related reactions.

Timing

Because people open e-mail messages at different times, a person might reply to a message that has been superseded by another, leading to confusion. Sometimes e-mail messages arrive with an expected quick reply when the recipient is in an overload situation. In a recent survey, one-quarter of the 7,800 responding managers reported being overwhelmed by their daily communications, especially through e-mail.[66]

Tension

Interpersonal conflict may leave a bloody and ugly trail in e-mail communications. Outbursts of anger via e-mails usually make both parties look foolish, especially when individuals escalate the conflict into heated exchanges. The way to stop an online battle is to refrain from taking the bait. Don't respond to the attack in kind. Acknowledge a difference of opinion, but don't escalate the situation. Switching to a different form of communication will help avoid a trail of embarrassing messages.[67] Chapter 13 explores approaches for managing conflict and negotiating effectively.

Impacts of Text and Instant Messaging

Text messaging *allows short text messages, generally no more than a couple of hundred characters in length, to be sent and received on a mobile phone.*[68] Most phones and carriers also allow messages to be sent directly to an e-mail address. Outside of the United States, text messaging is more commonly known as SMS—short messaging service. *Instant messaging*, sometimes called mobile messaging, includes a variety of capabilities—such as chat, video, web links, streaming content, and file sharing—beyond texting.[69]

The use of text messaging in the United States began to explode in 2002, but was well under way in a number of other countries at that time. Text messaging, as many readers of this book know, started as a communication tool of the younger generation, but that is changing rapidly.[70]

A review of the new instant messaging innovations is beyond the scope of this discussion,[71] however, the e-body language issues of e-mail also apply, for the most part, to text messaging. The increasing adoption of instant messaging as a business communication medium has been driven by employees, rather than through formal initiatives by the organization. This is changing. To date, the primary functions of instant messaging in the workplace include (1) quick (brief) questions and clarifications; (2) coordinating and scheduling day-to-day tasks; (3) coordinating impromptu social meetings, such as lunch or after-work "happy hours"; and (4) letting friends and family know of work-related schedule changes, such as being home early or late from work.[72] As expected, instant and text messaging have the advantage of being more "real time" than e-mail.

Gartner, headquartered in Stamford, Connecticut, is a leading provider of market research covering the information technology industry. David Smith, a senior research analyst at Gartner, comments: "Although consumer IM [instant messaging] use has been predominant, we expect penetration levels for enterprise grade IM to rise from around 25 percent currently to nearly 100 percent by 2011 or earlier. The business benefits that IM can bring are considerable. The ability to connect people in disparate locations by text, voice and video in one application is useful and is equally well suited to an informal 'water cooler' atmosphere as well as more formal group communications."[73] IM is increasingly being used as a vehicle for rapidly disseminating critical information to the entire enterprise, to groups of users, or to individuals in cases such as natural disasters, health issues, network outages, or schedule changes. In some cases, the IM network remains operational when phone or e-mail systems are down.[74]

Chapter Summary

1. Describe the core elements of interpersonal communication.

The basic elements in the communication process—senders, receivers, transmitters, receptors, messages, channels, meaning, encoding, decoding, and feedback—are interrelated.

Face-to-face interpersonal communication has the highest degree of information richness. An information-rich medium is especially important for performing complex tasks and resolving social and emotional issues that involve considerable uncertainty and ambiguity. Important issues usually contain significant amounts of uncertainty, ambiguity, and people-related (especially social and emotional) problems.

There are many potential challenges to effective interpersonal communication. Direct barriers include aggressive communication approaches, noise, semantics, demeaning language, and lying and distortion.

2. Explain the factors that foster ethical communications.

Through mastering the factors that constitute dialogue, the likelihood of engaging in ethical interpersonal communications is magnified. Dialogue includes communication openness, constructive feedback, appropriate self-disclosure, and active listening. Dialogue requires senders and receivers to play a dynamic role in the communication process. In open communication, senders and receivers are able to discuss, disagree, and search for understanding without resorting to personal attacks or hidden agendas. Feedback received from others provides motivation for individuals to learn and change their behaviors. How much individuals are willing to share with others depends on their ability to disclose information. By being an active listener, the receiver hears the whole message without interpretation or judgment.

3. Diagnose nonverbal communication behaviors.

Nonverbal cues play a powerful role in supporting or hindering communications. There are many types of personal nonverbal cues. They were presented through the acronym PERCEIVE, which stands for the following terms: proximity, expressions, relative orientation, contact, eyes, individual gestures, voice, and existence of adapters. Formal organizational position is often tied to status. Status symbols—office size, the floor on which the office is located, number of windows, location of a secretary, and access to senior-level employees—all influence communication patterns. We noted some cautionary comments on the need to avoid simplistic stereotypes as to the meaning of nonverbal cues employed by an individual.

To provide a sense of how much the interpersonal communication process can vary between cultures, we reviewed the concept of taarof in Iran. The barriers stemming from cultural differences are always present. They are more likely to be high when the interaction takes place between individuals from high-context and low-context cultures. We noted how certain nonverbal messages—the use of color, time, and gestures—can affect intercultural communications.

4. Understand the importance of cultural and nonverbal barriers to communication.

An individual's communication network extends laterally, vertically, and externally. The development of a strong inside individual network can be determined by being able to respond "yes" to most of the eight questions presented in the chapter text, such as "Do I know a number of the people whose work relates to mine in any way beyond my own department?" For individual networking effectiveness, the individual needs political skill. The informal group network involves the pattern of multiple individual networks. The most common form of informal group network is the grapevine, which may take the pattern of a single-strand chain, gossip chain, probability chain, or cluster chain. The formal employee network focuses on the intended pattern of employee-related communication vertically and laterally. Leaders need to be proactive in creating an open and ethically based pattern to ensure that individual and employee group networks are not in conflict with the formal employee network, but are instead, for the most part, supportive of it. This network may be influenced and supported by a variety of information technologies.

5. Discuss the role of communication networks.

The potential impacts of e-mail as well as text and instant messaging technologies on interpersonal communication were reviewed. We focused on the overuse and misuse of e-mail. Of course, despite the limitations, e-mail, text messaging, and instant messaging are vital in today's organizations and society.

Key Terms and Concepts

Active listening, **264**
Assertive communication, **260**
Channels, **256**
Chromatics, **274**
Chronemics, **274**
Cue, **256**
Cultural context, **271**
Decoding, **257**
Dialogue, **260**
Distortion, **259**
Encoding, **257**
Ethnocentrism, **272**
Feedback, **258**
Formal employee network, **278**
Grapevine, **278**
High-context culture, **271**
Impression management, **259**
Intercultural communication, **270**
Interpersonal communication, **254**
Interpersonal communication network, **276**

Language routines, **259**
Low-context culture, **271**
Lying, **259**
Meaning, **257**
Media richness, **256**
Messages, **255**
Meta-communication, **261**
Monochronic time schedule, **274**
Noise, **258**
Nonverbal communication, **267**
Political skill, **277**
Polychronic time schedule, **275**
Receptors, **255**
Self-disclosure, **264**
Semantics, **258**
Taarof, **271**
Text messaging, **281**
360-degree feedback, **264**
Transmitters, **255**

Discussion Questions

1. Visit DineEquity's home page at www.dineequity.com. Click on "Corporate Governance," then "DineEquity Policies on Business Conduct." Read Julia Stewart's statement and the section on "Conflicts of Interest." Do you think these are effective statements on ethical business conduct? Explain.
2. In what ways do the barriers to interpersonal communication interfere with your development of the diversity competency?
3. Review the Change Competency on Susan Powers. What key attributes of the communication competency were used by Susan Powers and her team to achieve the changes at Travelport GDS?
4. How would you assess the level of ethical interpersonal communication in an organization at which you are or have been employed? Give concrete examples that serve as the basis of your assessment.
5. Based on your diagnosis of feedback practices you experienced in a current or previous job through the completion of the instrument in Table 9.1, which practices are least effective? How might they be improved?
6. Why is media richness important in interpersonal communication? Do changes need to be made in the pattern and frequency of use of the various media employed by the leadership in the organization for which you currently work or have worked? Explain.
7. Describe the common nonverbal cues used by someone you have worked for. Are they usually consistent or inconsistent with that person's verbal expressions? Explain.
8. Describe your individual communication network at work or at school. Is it effective? Would you like to make any changes in it? Why or why not?
9. In what ways can you both agree and disagree with the following statement: "The Internet, e-mail, text messaging, and instant messaging are making it easier to communicate with people from different cultures." Explain.
10. Review the Change Competency feature entitled "Michael Ward's Reflections on CSX's One Plan Redesign." What factors that foster effective communications are illustrated in this feature? Explain.

Experiential Exercise and Case

Experiential Exercise: Communication Competency

Communication Inventory[75]

The following statements relate to how your current or former manager and you communicate on the job. There are no right or wrong responses. Respond honestly to each statement using the following scale:

Strongly Agree	Agree	Uncertain	Disagree	Strongly Disagree
1	2	3	4	5

_____ 1. My manager criticizes my work without allowing me to explain.

_____ 2. My manager allows me as much creativity as possible in my job.

_____ 3. My manager always judges the actions of his or her subordinates.

_____ 4. My manager allows flexibility on the job.

_____ 5. My manager criticizes my work in the presence of others.

_____ 6. My manager is willing to try new ideas and to accept other points of view.

_____ 7. My manager believes that he or she must control how I do my work.

_____ 8. My manager understands the problems that I encounter in my job.

_____ 9. My manager is always trying to change other people's attitudes and behaviors to suit his or her own.

_____ 10. My manager respects my feelings and values.

_____ 11. My manager always needs to be in charge of the situation.

_____ 12. My manager listens to my problems with interest.

_____ 13. My manager tries to manipulate subordinates to get what he or she wants or to make himself or herself look good.

_____ 14. My manager does not try to make me feel inferior.

_____ 15. I have to be careful when talking to my manager so that I will not be misinterpreted.

_____ 16. My manager participates in meetings with employees without projecting his or her higher status or power.

_____ 17. I seldom say what really is on my mind because it might be twisted and distorted by my manager.

_____ 18. My manager treats me with respect.

_____ 19. My manager seldom becomes involved in employee conflicts.

_____ 20. My manager does not have hidden motives in dealing with me.

_____ 21. My manager is not interested in employee problems.

_____ 22. I feel that I can be honest and straightforward with my manager.

_____ 23. My manager rarely offers moral support during a personal crisis.

_____ 24. I feel that I can express my opinions and ideas honestly to my manager.

_____ 25. My manager tries to make me feel inadequate.

_____ 26. My manager defines problems so that they can be understood but does not insist that his or her subordinates agree.

_____ 27. My manager makes it clear that he or she is in charge.

_____ 28. I feel free to talk to my manager.

_____ 29. My manager believes that if a job is to be done right, he or she must oversee it or do it.

_____ 30. My manager defines problems and makes his or her subordinates aware of them.

_____ 31. My manager cannot admit that he or she makes mistakes.

_____ 32. My manager tries to describe situations fairly without labeling them as good or bad.

_____ 33. My manager is dogmatic; it is useless for me to voice an opposing point of view.

_____ 34. My manager presents his or her feelings and perceptions without implying that a similar response is expected from me.

_____ 35. My manager thinks that he or she is always right.

_____ 36. My manager attempts to explain situations clearly and without personal bias.

Scoring and Interpretation

Place the numbers that you assigned to each statement in the appropriate blanks. Now add them to determine a subtotal for each communication category. Place the subtotals in the proper blanks and add your scores.

Part I: Defensive Scores

A. Evaluation: Add point values for statements (1) ___ + (3) ___ + (5) ___ = _____

B. Control: Add point values for statements (7) ___ + (9) ___ + (11) ___ = _____

C. Strategy: Add point values for statements (13) ___ + (15) ___ + (17) ___ = _____

D. Neutrality: Add point values for statements (19) ___ + (21) ___ + (23) ___ = _____

E. Superiority: Add point values for statements (25) ___ + (27) ___ + (29) ___ = _____

F. Certainty: Add point values for statements (31) ___ + (33) ___ + (35) ___ = _____

Subtotals for Defensive Scores

A. Evaluation _____   D. Neutrality _____
B. Control _____   E. Superiority _____
C. Strategy _____   F. Certainty _____

Add subtotals for A thru F = _____

Place an X on the scale below to indicate what your perception is of your manager's communication skills.

18 25 30 35 40 45 50 55 60 65 70 75 80 85 90
Defensive   Neutral   Supportive

Part II: Supportive Scores

A. Provisionalism: Add point values for statements (2) ___ + (4) ___ + (6) ___ = _____

B. Empathy: Add point values for statements (8) ___ + (10) ___ + (12) ___ = _____

C. Equality: Add point values for statements (14) ___ + (16) ___ + (18) ___ = _____

D. Spontaneity: Add point values for statements (20) ___ + (22) ___ + (24) ___ = _____

E. Problem Orientation: Add point values for statements (26) ___ + (28) ___ + (30) ___ = _____

F. Description: Add point values for statements (32) ___ + (34) ___ + (36) ___ = _____

Subtotals for Supportive Scores

A. Provisionalism _____   D. Spontaneity _____
B. Empathy _____   E. Problem Orientation _____
C. Equality _____   F. Description _____

Add subtotals for A thru F = _____

Place an X on the scale below to indicate what your perception is of your manager's communication skills.

18 25 30 35 40 45 50 55 60 65 70 75 80 85 90
Supportive   Neutral   Defensive

Interpretation

You will note that low _defensive scores_ in Part I indicate a high degree of defensiveness, whereas low supportive scores in Part II indicate a high degree of supportiveness.

Questions

1. Based on the assessment of your manager on the defensive scores (Part I), what suggestions and comments would you have for him or her if you were serving as a communication consultant to this individual?

2. Based on the assessment of your manager on the supportive scores (Part II), what suggestions and comments would you have for her or him if you were serving as a communication consultant to this individual?

3. Using the factors that foster ethical dialogue from Figure 9.3, what changes would you propose in your own communications with your manager?

Case: Communication Competency

Xographics[76]

Part A

Xographics is a division of a large telecommunications company. Ellen Bohn, the vice president of production, had recently moved to Xographics from a firm where she had been the manager of a large office staff. The three managers reporting to Bohn at her new job all had 20 or more years of experience with Xographics. They had seen it go from an effective production division to one that was badly troubled with problem workers and poor performance.

Shortly after her arrival, while talking with one of the managers, Bohn learned that many of them were upset because of the previous vice president's insistence that employees report any machine breakdown to him or one of his assistants within 15 minutes of the breakdown. They felt that this didn't give the employees the opportunity to repair the machine themselves. The manager told Bohn that the word was that once an employee had five breakdown reports, he or she was taken off the machine and given a lower paying job.

Questions
1. What should Bohn do?
2. What other problems (unidentified by Bohn) might be present?
3. What additional steps might the managers take?

Part B

One of the major problems that Bohn faced was that only about 40 percent of the jobs listed for scheduled maintenance shutdowns were ever performed. During an informal conversation with Ken Viet, Xographics' human resources manager, Bohn learned that the maintenance department was operating at about 60 percent efficiency. Viet said that the maintenance employees had recently staged a slowdown in order to force the company to increase their wages. Viet also told Bohn that maintenance employees usually quit about an hour early in order to wash up.

The head of the maintenance department had worked his way up through the ranks. He started with Xographics immediately after graduation from high school and had been with the company for 25 years. His reason for the "inefficiency" was the lack of qualified maintenance people in the area, with the personnel department sending him individuals not qualified to maintain the mill's machines. He didn't have the time to train each newly hired employee, assigning this responsibility to other employees who had been around for a while.

Questions (continued)
4. How might Bohn approach the head of maintenance?
5. Who else should Bohn talk to?

Part C

Two months after Bohn joined Xographics, the company held its annual picnic at a Six Flags park. Most of the employees and their families were there. Bohn saw Viet at the picnic and handed him a soft drink. The following conversation then took place.

Viet: Hey, Ellen [Bohn], got a minute?
Bohn: Sure, what's up?
Viet: Well, I was talking with one of your managers that I know pretty well. You know, an off-the-record chat about the company.
Bohn: Yeah?
Viet: He told me that the company's management style is the mushroom style: Keep them in the dark and feed 'em a lot of manure. He said that nobody knew you were hired until you showed up at the plant. We heard that the guard didn't even know who you were.
Bohn: Yeah, I guess that's so.
Viet: This manager said that he has been doing his job for ten years and has never received any performance appraisal. His raises are just added into his check. No one has pointed out his strong and weak points.
Bohn: Yeah, I guess that's so. But, I'm not totally sure. You know that I've been here only a few months myself.
Viet: Yeah, I know that, but listen to this. Tom Kerr, the new manager of industrial engineering, hasn't talked to or even been introduced to anybody in the paper-machine area, and Tom has been on the job for three months.
Bohn: Ken [Viet], how widespread do you think this feeling is about the mushroom style of management?
Viet: I don't know, Ellen, but I think you ought to find out if you want this place to produce.

Questions (continued)
6. What steps can Bohn take?
7. What barriers to communication may exist?
8. What role has the company's informal communication network played in this situation?

chapter 10

Leadership Effectiveness: Foundations

Learning Goals

After studying this chapter, you should be able to:

1
Describe the role of power and political behavior in the leadership process.

2
Describe three legacy models of leadership: traits, Theory X/ Theory Y, and behavioral.

3
Explain and apply the Situational Leadership® Model.

4
Explain and apply the Vroom– Jago leadership model.

Learning Content

Learning from Experience
Douglas Conant's Leadership at Campbell Soup Co.

Power and Political Behavior

Change Competency
Carol Bartz's Use of Power to Change Yahoo!

Legacy Leadership Models

Self Competency
Colin Powell's "Lessons in Leadership"

Situational Leadership® Model

Communication Competency
Paul Millman, CEO, Chroma Technology

Vroom–Jago Leadership Model

Ethics Competency
The Bank CEO

Experiential Exercise and Case

Experiential Exercise: Self Competency
Personal Power Inventory

Case: Diversity Competency
Women on Corporate Boards

Douglas Conant's Leadership at Campbell Soup Co.

Douglas R. Conant was appointed president and chief executive officer of Campbell's Soup Company in 2001. Campbell's, headquartered in Camden, New Jersey, is a global manufacturer and marketer in 120 countries of simple foods such as soup, baked foods, frozen foods, and vegetable-based beverages. The company has approximately $8 billion in annual sales and a variety of brands, such as Campbell's, Pepperidge Farm, Prego, Swanson, and V8. Its 190,000 employees are in various locations and its principal markets are in North America, Australia, France, Germany, and Belgium.

Under Conant's leadership, Campbell's has reversed a decline in shareholder value and employee commitment. The company has made significant investments to improve product quality and packaging, strengthen the effectiveness of its marketing programs, and develop a strong innovation pipeline. Campbell's also has improved its financial profile, enhanced its relationships with its customers, and consistently improved its employee satisfaction and commitment through investments in its organization. Conant did not shake up the firm through in-your-face control and domination. He readily gives others credit and deflects praise.

Conant led the development of a 10-year plan, called the "Campbell's Journey," that is based on the concept of focused, mission-driven innovation. Broken down into three phases beginning in 2001, the first was the Transformation Plan from 2001 to

2004, the second was the Quality Growth Plan, and the last is the Building for Extraordinary Growth Plan from 2008 to 2010. A process is under way to develop a revised "Campbell's Journey." The mission is to build "the world's most extraordinary food company," which Conant equates to "a sustainably good company."

When Conant first assessed employee commitment, Campbell's workforce ranked at the bottom when compared to other firms in a Gallup Organization sample. Conant set about reinvigorating the employees and firm through a variety of actions:

- *Using a personal touch.* Conant has sent out more than 20,000 handwritten thank-you notes to employees, from the chief investment officer to the receptionist at headquarters. These notes are often found hanging

MEL EVANS/AP PHOTO

To learn more about the Campbell Soup Company, go to www.campbellsoupcompany.com.

in people's offices or above their desks. "In business, we're trained to find things that are wrong, but I try to celebrate what's right," says Conant.

- *Setting expectations.* All leaders must meet with direct reports each quarter to update their progress on clearly articulated goals. However, given the poor state of leadership at Campbell's when he arrived, Conant led the process over a six-year period of replacing 300 of the company's 350 managers. Half of the replacements were from within.
- *Featuring communications.* Every six weeks, Conant has lunch with a group of a dozen or so employees to listen to problems and get

feedback. Conant knows he doesn't have all the answers, admitting mistakes with a simple but meaningful "I can do better."

- *Developing professional opportunities and learning.* Conant encourages movement among employees and led the creation of programs to develop a pipeline of talent. Conant is a serious student of leadership-related books. He even started a book club for top executives.
- *Stimulating innovation.* Conant knows that Campbell must keep developing new products and ideas to maintain its momentum. So he has focused on innovation, the lifeblood of any consumer packaged-goods company.[1]

The Learning from Experience feature provides a few insights into Douglas Conant's effectiveness as a leader and what it means to be a leader. This and the following chapter further develop and expand on those insights. Leadership embraces the seven foundation competencies developed throughout this book, but it also goes beyond them. A team's or organization's success is greatly influenced by its leadership. Conant clearly reflects leadership qualities.

In this chapter, we explore foundation concepts and models of leadership. First, we review the role of power and political behavior for managers and leaders. Second, we highlight three legacy leadership models. The third and fourth sections of this chapter present two recognized contingency models of leadership.

Before reading further, it would be useful to review the section titled "Leadership versus Management" in Chapter 1. We stated that *leadership is the process of developing ideas and a vision, living by values that support those ideas and that vision, influencing others to embrace them in their own behaviors, and making hard decisions about human and other resources.* Management, on the other hand, emphasizes planning, control, rules and procedures, authority relations, and the like. We emphasized that not all managers are necessarily leaders.

Power and Political Behavior

Learning Goal

1. *Describe the role of power and political behavior in the leadership process.*

All leaders use power and engage in political behaviors to influence others.[2] True leaders do so effectively and ethically. Others in managerial roles, but who do not qualify as effective leaders, use power and political behavior in ways that are ineffective and counterproductive. We illustrate this in a variety of chapters, especially Chapter 2.

Leaders' Use of Power

There are five important interpersonal sources of power—legitimate power, reward power, coercive power, referent power, and expert power—that leaders and others use in various situations.[3] Leaders use these sources of power to influence followers by appealing to one or more of their needs. Effective leadership depends as much on the acceptance of influence by the follower as on the leader's providing it. Let's review those sources of power in relation to the roles of leader and you as a follower.

Legitimate Power

Legitimate power is an individual's ability to influence others' behaviors because of the person's formal position in the organization. You may respond to such influence because you acknowledge the leader's legitimate right to tell you what to do. Nonmanagerial employees also may possess legitimate power. For example, when John Ogden was a safety inspector at Lockheed Martin Vought's plant in Camden, Arkansas, he had the legitimate power to shut down production if there was a safety violation, even if the plant manager objected and tried to stop him.

Legitimate power is an important concept. Typically, a manager is given the right to make decisions within a specific area of responsibility, such as customer service, quality control, marketing, or accounting. This area of responsibility defines the activities for which the manager (and sometimes other employees) can expect to exercise legitimate power to influence behavior. The further removed managers are from their specific areas of responsibility, the weaker their legitimate power becomes. You have a zone of indifference with respect to the exercise of power by your manager.[4] The **zone of indifference** *is an area within which employees will accept certain directives without questioning the leader's power.* The leader may have considerable legitimate power to influence your behavior. Outside that zone, however, legitimate power disappears rapidly. For example, an administrative assistant (male or female) may keystroke letters, answer the phone, open the mail, and do similar tasks for a manager (female or male) without question. However, if the manager asks the administrative assistant to go out for a drink after work, the assistant may refuse. The manager's request clearly falls outside the assistant's zone of indifference. The manager has no legitimate right to expect the assistant to comply.

In the Learning from Experience feature, we reported on Douglas Conant's use of legitimate power. As you will recall, over a six-year period, he replaced 300 of Campbell's 350 managers. He led and approved resources for the creation of programs aimed at developing a pipeline of talent at Campbell's.

Reward Power

Reward power *is an individual's ability to influence others' behaviors by providing them with valued things.* To the extent that the employee values the rewards that the manager can give—praise, promotions, money, time off, and so on—the employee may comply with requests and directives. A manager who controls the allocation of merit pay raises in a department has reward power over employees in that department. Accordingly, the employees may comply with some attempts by the manager to influence their behavior because they expect to be rewarded for this compliance. Conant has sent out more than 20,000 handwritten thank-you notes to employees. They are often found hanging in people's offices or above their desks. Conant stated: "In business, we're trained to find things that are wrong, but I try to celebrate what's right." As the CEO, Conant has considerable reward power; including pay raises or bonuses, many of which he is permitted to award without approval by the board of directors.

Reward power is an individual's ability to influence others' behavior by providing valued talent. Rewards might include awards, praise, promotions, money, or time off.

▼

STOCKBYTE/GETTY IMAGES

Coercive Power

Coercive power *is an individual's ability to influence others' behaviors by punishing them.* For example, employees may comply with a manager's directive because they expect to be punished if they fail to do so. Punishment may take the form of reprimands, undesirable work assignments, closer supervision, tighter enforcement of work rules, suspension without pay, and the like.

Recall, however, that punishment can have undesirable side effects (see Chapter 5). For example, employees who receive an official reprimand for shoddy work may find ways to avoid punishment, such as by refusing to perform tasks, falsifying performance reports, or being absent frequently. Coercive power doesn't necessarily encourage desired behavior, but it may stop or reduce undesirable behaviors.

At times, leaders do need to exercise coercive power, which is based on their legitimate power. Demoting or dismissing subordinates for poor performance, unacceptable behaviors (e.g., sexual harassment, bullying, workplace violence), and the lack of integrity (e.g., lying, deceitful conduct, and the like) may require the use of coercive power. The 300 managers removed by Conant over a six-year period may have experienced his action as a form of punishment, but these actions were within his legitimate power to do so. He made replacements after careful assessment.

Referent Power

Referent power *is an individual's ability to influence others because they respect, admire, or like the person.* For example, subordinates' identification with a leader often forms the basis for referent power. This identification may include the desire by subordinates to be like the leader. A young manager might copy the style of an older, admired, and more experienced leader. The senior leader, thus, has some referent power to influence the younger manager's behavior.

Referent power usually is associated with individuals who possess admired personality characteristics, charisma, or a good reputation. It often is associated with political leaders, movie stars, sports figures, or other well-known individuals (hence, their use in advertising to influence consumer behavior). However, leaders and employees in business firms also may have considerable referent power because of the strength of their character and competencies. Conant has considerable referent power. Recall that he did not transform Campbell's through in-your-face control and domination. He readily gives others credit and deflects praise. Recall that he has lunch with a group of a dozen or so employees to listen to problems and get feedback.

Expert Power

Expert power *is an individual's ability to influence others' behaviors because of recognized competencies, talents, or specialized knowledge.* To the extent that leaders can demonstrate their competencies, they will acquire expert power. However, expert power often is relatively narrow in scope. For example, an employee at Overhead Door Company might carefully follow the advice of the manager about how to program a garage door opener, yet ignore advice from the manager regarding which of three company health plans to select. In this instance, the employee recognizes expertise in one area while resisting influence in another.

A lack of expert power often causes problems for new managers and employees. A junior accountant might possess a great deal of knowledge about accounting theory and procedures. This expertise must be correctly demonstrated and applied over time to be recognized and accepted.

When Conant became the CEO of Campbell's in 2001, he arrived with 25 years of food industry experience from three of the world's leading food companies: General Mills, Kraft Foods, and Nabisco. Prior to joining Campbell's, he was president of Nabisco Foods Co., where he led that firm to five consecutive years of double-digit earnings growth. Upon arrival, he was recognized and accepted throughout Campbell's as a person with considerable expertise for the CEO role.[5]

An effective manager who is also a leader—whether a first-line manager or top-level executive—uses a variety of sources of power. For successful leaders and organizations, the emphasis is on reward, referent, and expert power, with less reliance on coercive and legitimate power.

Political Behavior in Organizations

Political behavior *involves attempts by individuals to influence the behaviors of others as a means to protect their self-interests, meet their own needs, and advance their own goals.*[6] Defined in this way, almost all behavior may be regarded as political. Labeling behavior as political, however, usually implies that certain people are gaining something at the expense of others or the organization as a whole. However, a balanced understanding of political behavior and its consequences is needed. People often are self-centered and biased when labeling actions as political behavior. Employees may justify their own political behavior as defending legitimate rights or interests. Some may say it's "playing politics."

Organizational Politics

Organizational politics *involves actions by individuals, teams, or leaders to acquire, develop, and use power and other resources in order to obtain preferred outcomes.*[7] When people share power but differ about what must be done (e.g., invest in expanding in North America versus China), many decisions and actions quite naturally will be the result of a political process.

Employees are often concerned about organizational politics.[8] Many believe that an ideal work setting would be free from political behavior. Negative attitudes about political behavior and organizational politics can hinder organizational effectiveness. Examples of behaviors often seen as political are shown in Table 10.1. Employees tend to assume that political behavior doesn't yield the best organizational decisions or outcomes—that somehow, by pushing for their own positions, they cause inferior actions or decisions to be made. Although this result can occur, political behavior isn't always detrimental to an organization. For example, a study involving managers in 30 organizations indicated that they were able to identify beneficial, as well as harmful, effects of political behavior.[9]

> ### Self Insight
>
> Success is to be measured not so much by the position that one has reached in life as by the obstacles which the individual has overcome while trying to succeed.
>
> *Booker T. Washington, Author, Up from Slavery, and Civil Rights Leader*

Beneficial effects included career advancement, recognition and status for individuals looking after their legitimate interests, and achievement of organizational goals—getting the job done—as a result of the normal political process in the organization. Harmful effects included demotions and loss of jobs for "losers" in the political process, a misuse of resources, and creation of an ineffective organizational culture. Organizational politics may arouse anxieties that cause employees to withdraw emotionally from the organization. Their withdrawal makes creating an organization characterized by high performance and high commitment very difficult.

Political behavior, then, can meet appropriate and legitimate individual and organizational needs, or it can result in negative outcomes. In any event, leaders and employees must understand political behavior because it definitely does occur. Eliminating political behavior isn't possible—it can only be influenced.

Conant provides strong leadership to minimize the negative aspects of political behavior. To help bring employees together, he led the creation of a new mission for Campbell's that states: "Together we will build the world's most extraordinary food company by nourishing people's lives everywhere, every day." From this, a

TABLE 10.1	Common Political Tactics
Taking counsel	The individual exercises great caution in seeking or giving advice.
Maneuverability	The individual maintains flexibility and never completely commits to any one position or program.
Communication	The individual never communicates everything. Instead information is withheld and/or at times it's released carefully.
Compromising	The individual accepts compromise only as a short-term tactic, while continuing to press ahead with one's own agenda.
Confidence	Once individuals make a decision, they must always give the impression of knowing what they are doing, even when they do not.
Always the boss	An atmosphere of social friendship limits the power of the leader; thus the leader always maintains a sense of distance and separation from subordinates.

Source: Adapted from Buchanan, D., and Badham, R. *Power, Politics, and Organizational Change*. London: Sage 1999.

"Success Model" was developed that states: "Our Success Model recognizes that to maximize shareowner value we need to 'win in the workplace' in order to 'win in the marketplace,' and we must do both with integrity." The mission and Success Model are based on three core values that include statements on *character*, *competence*, and *teamwork*.[10]

Drivers of Political Behavior

The probability of political behavior occurring typically increases in proportion to disagreements over goals, different ideas about the organization's problems, different information about the situation, the need to allocate scarce resources, and so on.[11] If these forces didn't exist, perhaps political behavior would be minimal or wouldn't exist. Results are never certain, resources are never infinite, and people must make difficult choices between competing goals and methods to attain them. Thus, political behavior will naturally occur as individuals, teams, and departments attempt to obtain their preferred outcomes. Leaders shouldn't try to prevent the inevitable. Rather, they should try to ensure that these activities do not have negative consequences for the organization and its employees.

Employees are more likely to act politically when (1) decision-making procedures and performance measures are uncertain and complex, and (2) competition for scarce resources is strong. Conversely, in less complex situations where decision-making processes are clear and competitive behavior is not rewarded, excessive political behavior is unlikely.

Even though individual differences (e.g., attitudes, personality, needs, etc.) may contribute to political behavior, such behavior is typically more strongly influenced by aspects of the situation. Managers make political behavior more likely to occur when they provide a weak vision, mission, and values that reflect their own behaviors, for example, when they fail to "walk the talk." Conant's leadership is seen by the vast majority of employees and other stakeholders as reflecting a person who "walks the talk" and expects it of others as well. Ambiguous circumstances allow individuals to define situations in ways that satisfy their own needs and desires. Further, when employees focus on wanting more resources (e.g., equipment, promotions, pay raises, or office space) than are available, political behavior may be more likely to occur.

Political behavior is greater when managers reward it. A reward system may focus solely on individual accomplishment and minimize team contributions. When that's the case, individuals may be tempted to behave politically to ensure that they receive much more of the rewards than other team members. If their actions result in more rewards, employees are even more likely to engage in such political actions in the future. Similarly, individuals who had avoided political behavior may start behaving politically when they observe such behavior being rewarded by managers. In sum, the organizational reward system can be a significant factor in the occurrence of political behavior.

Insights for Leaders

The performance appraisal process provides a good example of a situation in which managers may encourage political behavior among employees. Performance for employees in many departments—accounting, human resources, quality control, legal, information systems, and so on—isn't easily measured. Thus, the process used by managers results in the allocation of scarce resources (pay, bonuses, benefits, etc.) based on complex subjective criteria as opposed to objective criteria (e.g., sales).[12]

Some managers ignore the existence of politics in the appraisal process or may assume that the use of a quantitative performance appraisal method (e.g., number of units sold, downtime, wastes) will minimize it. But political behavior is a fact of life in the appraisal process. In particular, because of the ambiguous nature of managerial work, appraisals of managers by higher level leaders are susceptible to political manipulation. What is the risk, ethical or otherwise, of using performance appraisal as a political tool? Among other things, political performance appraisals by managers can

- undermine organizational goals and performance,
- compromise the link between performance and rewards,
- increase political behavior in other organizational processes and decisions, and
- expose the organization to litigation if employees are terminated.[13]

Leaders tend to adopt the following behaviors to help reduce the problem of politically based performance appraisals:

- Develop goals and standards that are as clear and specific as possible.
- Link specific actions and performance results to rewards.
- Conduct structured, professional reviews, including specific examples of observed performance and explanations for ratings given.
- Offer performance feedback on an ongoing basis, rather than just once a year.
- Acknowledge that the potential for politics in performance appraisals exists and make this topic a focus of ongoing discussions throughout the organization.[14]

The following Change Competency reports on the change efforts of Carol Bartz to lead Yahoo! out of the internal power struggles and political turmoil that had become prominent by the time of her appointment as CEO in early 2009.[15] This feature provides examples of how Bartz effectively used her power to achieve the desired results. Bartz serves on several corporate boards and had been a successful chairman, CEO, and president of Autodesk, Inc., a major provider of design and engineering software. The success of her use of power and change initiatives at Yahoo! is not likely to be known for several years.

Yahoo!, which is an acronym for *Yet Another Hierarchical Officious Oracle*, is an online portal that draws more than 400 million to its network of websites and other services. Yahoo! publishes online content in 20 languages and has approximately 13,000 employees. It is headquartered in Sunnyvale, California.[16]

Change competency

Carol Bartz's Use of Power to Change Yahoo!

In February 2009, Carol Bartz announced a reorganization of Yahoo! Excerpts from her blog post follow.

A month and a half in the saddle and today I have the perfect excuse to get blogging. I've been on a whirlwind tour for the last six weeks, talking with everybody from executive leaders to the guys who configured my laptop. I've been in student mode, slowly getting smarter about what makes this place tick. And most recently, I've been gathering information on what it's going to take to get Yahoo! to a great place as an organization—and one that brings you killer products.

People here have impressed the hell out of me. They're smart, dedicated, passionate, driven, and really nice. There's so much great energy and frankly lots of optimism. But there's also plenty that has bogged this company down. For starters, you'd be amazed at how complicated some things are here. So today, I'm rolling out a new management structure that I believe will make Yahoo! a lot faster on its feet. For us working at Yahoo!, it means everything gets simpler. We'll be able to make speedier decisions, the notorious silos are gone, and we have a renewed focus on the customer. For you using Yahoo! every day, it will better enable us to deliver products that make you say, "Wow."

I've noticed that a lot of us on the inside don't spend enough time looking to the outside. That's why I'm creating a new Customer Advocacy Group. After getting a lot of angry calls at my office from frustrated customers, I realized we could do a better job of listening to and supporting you. Our Customer Care team does an incredible job with the amazing number of people who come to them, but they need better resources. So we're investing in that. After all, you deserve the very best. We're also leaning on this team to make sure we're all hearing the voice of our customers (consumers and advertisers). I'm singularly focused on providing you with awesome products. Period. The kind that gets you so excited, you have to tell someone about them. Whether on your desktop, your mobile device, or even your TV.

The new management organization has all major executives reporting directly to Bartz, who lamented in her blog post that there's "plenty that has bogged this company down." "It looks like she isn't afraid to go in with a chain saw," said Kevin Lee, CEO of search marketing firm Didit. Bartz has reorganized the company into two regions— North American and international—compared to four in the past. People in mobile and product development now report directly to Bartz to emphasize their increased level of accountability.

A number of people noted that the new organization is a vast improvement over the previous "matrix management" system that handed multiple executives oversight over many products and new projects. That led to slow decision making and little accountability, Yahoo! insiders say. By most accounts, the swing to strong line authority is the right move for Yahoo! after so many years of decentralized product groups around the world, each with their own engineering and other functions. Yahoo! has an "inability to stop doing good things that don't fit with their strategy," says Robert Sutton, a professor of management science and engineering at Stanford University. That will change under Bartz's leadership.

To learn more about Yahoo!, go to **www.yahoo.com.**

Legacy Leadership Models

The traits, Theory X/Theory Y, and behavioral models are probably the most basic, oldest, and well known of the leadership models. The more recent and complex leadership models often draw on parts of these three models. Thus, these three models provide an important legacy to the contingency leadership models and the contemporary leadership literature in general.

Traits Model of Leadership

The **traits model of leadership** *is based on characteristics of many leaders—both successful and unsuccessful—and is used to predict leadership effectiveness.* The resulting lists of traits are then compared to those of potential managers to assess their likelihood of success or failure as leaders. There is some support for the notion that successful leaders have interests and abilities and, perhaps, even personality traits that are different from those of less effective leaders.

Key Traits

Some evidence suggests that four traits are shared by most (but not all) successful leaders:

- *Intelligence.* Successful leaders tend to have somewhat higher intelligence than their subordinates.
- *Maturity and breadth.* Successful leaders tend to be emotionally mature and have a broad range of interests.
- *Achievement drive.* Successful leaders are results oriented; when they achieve one goal, they seek another. They do not depend primarily on employees for their motivation to achieve goals.
- *Integrity.* Successful leaders, over the long term, usually have integrity. When individuals in leadership positions state one set of values but practice another set, followers quickly see them as untrustworthy. Many surveys show that honesty is the key attribute when employees are asked to rank and comment on the various traits of successful and unsuccessful leaders. Trust is crucial and translates into the degree of willingness by employees to follow leaders. Confusion over the leader's thinking and values creates negative stress, indecision, and personal politics.[17]

Insights for Leaders

The traits model of leadership is inadequate for successfully predicting leadership effectiveness for at least three reasons.[18] First, in terms of personality traits, there are no consistent patterns between specific traits or sets of traits and leadership effectiveness. More than 100 different traits of successful leaders in various managerial positions have been identified. For example, the traits pattern of successful leaders of salespeople includes optimism, enthusiasm, and dominance. The traits pattern of successful leaders of production workers usually includes being progressive, introverted, and cooperative. These descriptions are simply generalities. Many successful leaders of salespeople and production workers do not have all, or even some, of these characteristics. There also is often disagreement over which traits are the most important to be an effective leader.

The second limitation of the traits model is that it often attempts to relate physical traits—such as height, weight, appearance, physique, energy, and health—to effective leadership. Most of these factors, however, are related to situational factors that can have a significant impact on a leader's effectiveness. For example, people in the military or law enforcement must be a particular minimum height and weight in order to perform certain tasks well. Although these traits may help an individual rise to a leadership position in such organizations, neither height nor weight correlates highly with effective leadership. In business and other organizations, height and weight generally play no role in performance and, thus, are not requirements for a leadership position.

The third limitation of the traits model is that leadership itself is complex. A relationship between specific traits and a person's interest in particular types of jobs could well exist, which a study relating personality and effectiveness might not identify. The traits approach paints a somewhat fatalistic picture, suggesting that some people, merely because of their traits, are destined not to be effective leaders.

Theory X and Theory Y Model

The behavior of managers is often influenced by their assumptions and beliefs about followers and what motivates their followers. Thus, differences in the behaviors of managers can be understood by looking at the different assumptions they make. One of the most widely cited and recognized models for describing differences in these assumptions was developed by Douglas McGregor in 1957. He coined the labels "Theory X" and "Theory Y" as a way to contrast two sets of assumptions and beliefs held by managers. Theory X and Theory Y managers both understand that they are responsible for the resources in their units—money, materials, equipment, and people—in the interest of achieving organizational goals. What sets them apart are their propositions about what motivates their subordinates and what are the best ways to carry out leadership responsibilities.[19] Before proceeding, take a few minutes to respond to the propositions in Table 10.2.

TABLE 10.2 Theory X/Theory Y Propositions Instrument

Indicate your degree of agreement or disagreement with each of the eight propositions by recording the point value next to each numbered proposition. Determine the appropriate score by noting the points for the response you made to each proposition. For example, if your response to proposition 1 was strongly agree you would give yourself five points; disagree is worth two points; and so on. Add the eight scores together. Use the following scale:

STRONGLY DISAGREE (5)	AGREE (4)	UNDECIDED (3)	DISAGREE (2)	STRONGLY DISAGREE (1)

_____ 1. The average human being prefers to be directed, wishes to avoid responsibility, and has relatively little ambition.

_____ 2. Most people can acquire leadership skills regardless of their particular inborn traits and abilities.

_____ 3. The use of rewards (for example, pay and promotion) and punishment (for example, failure to promote) is the best way to get subordinates to do their work.

_____ 4. In a work situation, if the subordinates can influence you, you lose some influence over them.

_____ 5. A good leader gives detailed and complete instructions to subordinates rather than giving them merely general directions and depending on their initiative to work out the details.

_____ 6. Individual goal setting offers advantages that cannot be obtained by group goal setting, because groups do not set high goals.

_____ 7. A superior should give subordinates only the information necessary for them to do their immediate tasks.

_____ 8. The superior's influence over subordinates in an organization is primarily economic.

_____ Total Score

Scoring Key:
A score of more than 32 points may indicate a tendency to manage others according to the propositions in Theory X. A score of 16 or less may indicate a tendency to manage others according to the propositions in Theory Y. A score somewhere between 16 and 32 may indicate flexibility in the management of others.

Theory X

When McGregor developed his model, he knew many managers with the Theory X point of view. **Theory X** *is based on a set of beliefs that managers should take a command-and-control approach to management.*[20] Theory X beliefs embrace the following negative views of human nature:

- People are inherently lazy and must therefore be motivated by incentives.

- People's natural goals run counter to those of the organization; hence, individuals must be controlled by formal rules and management to ensure that they're working toward organizational goals.

- Because of irrational feelings, people are basically incapable of self-discipline and self-control.

- The average person prefers to be directed, wishes to avoid responsibility, and wants security above all.

Theory X managers view leadership as a process that involves directing, controlling, and modifying their subordinates' behaviors to fit the needs of the organization. This perspective assumes that, without the strong intervention of managers, most employees would be passive—even resistant—to organizational needs. Therefore, employees must be persuaded, rewarded, punished, and their activities tightly controlled. Doing so is management's primary task. McGregor found that Theory X managers were everywhere in U.S. organizations and perhaps more common today than recognized. According to him, Theory X management was largely ineffective because it ignored the social, self-esteem, and self-actualization needs of most employees.

Theory Y

McGregor concluded that a different view of leading employees was needed—one based on more adequate assumptions about human nature and human motivation. **Theory Y** *is based on a set of beliefs that managers should take an empowering approach to management.* Theory Y beliefs embrace the following positive views of human nature:

- The average human does not inherently dislike work. Depending on controllable conditions, work may be a source of satisfaction.

- Rules, top-down managerial control, and the threat of punishment are not the only means for achieving organizational goals. Employees will exercise self-direction and control in the service of goals to which they are committed.

- The average person learns, under proper conditions, not only to accept but to seek responsibility.

- The capacity to exercise a relatively high degree of imagination, ingenuity, and creativity in the solution to organizational problems is widely, not narrowly, distributed in the population.

According to the Theory Y view, employees are not *by nature* passive or resistant to organizational goals. They have become so as a result of their experiences in organizations. The motivation, the potential for development, the capacity for assuming responsibility, and the readiness to direct behavior toward organizational goals are all present in these employees. Management does not put them there. Leaders recognize that their responsibility is to make it possible for employees to recognize and develop these human characteristics for themselves. Whereas Theory X managers attempt to gain control over their

According to Theory Y, most employees have the capacity to exercise a relatively high degree of imagination, ingenuity, and creativity in finding solutions to organizational problems.

DIGITAL VISION/GETTY IMAGES

Ethics Insight

Courage and humility are more complementary than contradictory. This means you know, as CEO, that your role is really to serve the company. This perspective makes you appreciate how much you depend on others to do the right things.

Olli-Pekka Kallasvuo, President and CEO, Nokia

subordinates, Theory Y leaders rely more on the self-control and self-direction of their subordinates.

Insights for Leaders

McGregor's Theory X and Theory Y model spawned many new leadership models, concepts, and approaches. Compared to about 50 years ago, the assumptions of Theory Y and its concern for employees are much more widely accepted in the United States nowadays among leaders. Nevertheless, there are managers who find it difficult to give up some or all of the assumptions that make up the Theory X perspective and its emphasis on management's top-down approach to accomplishing goals.

McGregor's model of more than 50 years ago has been very influential in contemporary leadership thinking. An increasing number of leaders realize that skilled and knowledgeable employees, who have been identified as the key contributors to future wealth, thrive primarily under Theory Y.[21]

Behavioral Model of Leadership

The **behavioral model of leadership** *focuses on what leaders actually do and how they do it.* There are several versions of this model. The model we present suggests that effective leaders help individuals and teams achieve their goals in two ways. First, they build task-centered relations with employees that focus on the quality and quantity of work accomplished. Second, they are considerate and supportive of employees' attempts to achieve personal goals (e.g., work satisfaction, promotions, and recognition). Also, they work hard at settling disputes, keeping employees satisfied, providing encouragement, and giving positive reinforcement.

The greatest number of studies of leader behavior has come from the Ohio State University leadership studies program, which began in the late 1940s. This research was aimed at identifying leader behaviors that are important for attaining team and organizational goals. These efforts resulted in the identification of two main dimensions of leader behavior: consideration and initiating structure.[22] Our review of the behavioral model is based on that leadership studies program. Table 10.3 provides the opportunity for you to diagnose your own leadership style according to the behavioral style of leadership.

Consideration

Consideration *is the extent to which the leader has relationships with subordinates that are characterized by mutual trust, two-way communication, respect for employees' ideas, and empathy for their feelings.* This style emphasizes the satisfaction of employee needs. The leader typically finds time to listen, is willing to make changes, looks out for the personal welfare of employees, and is friendly and approachable. A high degree of consideration indicates psychological closeness between the leader and subordinates; a low degree shows greater psychological distance and an impersonal manager.

When is consideration effective? The most positive effects of leader consideration on effectiveness and job satisfaction occur when (1) the task is routine and denies employees little, if any, satisfaction from the work itself; (2) followers are predisposed toward participative leadership; (3) team members must learn something new; (4) employees feel that their involvement in the decision-making process is legitimate and affects their job performance; and (5) employees feel that strong status differences should not exist between them and their leader.

TABLE 10.3 Behavioral Leadership Style Questionnaire

The following statements can help you diagnose your leadership style according to the behavioral model of leadership. Read each item carefully. Think about how you usually behave when you are the leader (or if you were in a leader role). Then, using the following, record the letter that most closely describes your style next to the item.

A = Always
O = Often
? = Sometimes
S = Seldom
N = Never

_____ 1. I take time to explain how a job should be carried out.
_____ 2. I explain the part that others are to play in the team.
_____ 3. I make clear the rules and procedures for others to follow in detail.
_____ 4. I organize my own work activities.
_____ 5. I let people know how well they are doing.
_____ 6. I let people know what is expected of them.
_____ 7. I encourage the use of uniform procedures for others to follow in detail.
_____ 8. I make my attitude clear to others.
_____ 9. I assign others to particular tasks.
_____ 10. I make sure that others understand their part in the team.
_____ 11. I schedule the work that I want others to do.
_____ 12. I ask that others follow standard rules and regulations.
_____ 13. I make working on the job more pleasant.
_____ 14. I go out of my way to be helpful.
_____ 15. I respect others' feelings and opinions.
_____ 16. I am thoughtful and considerate of others.
_____ 17. I maintain a friendly atmosphere in the team.
_____ 18. I do little things to make it more pleasant for others to be a member of my team.
_____ 19. I treat others as equals.
_____ 20. I give others advance notice of change and explain how it will affect them.
_____ 21. I look out for others' personal welfare.
_____ 22. I am approachable and friendly toward others.

Scoring:
The point values for Always (A), Often (O), Sometimes (?), Seldom (S), and Never (N) are as follows: A=5; O=4; ?=3; S=2; and N=1. Sum the point values for items 1 through 12. Then, sum the point values for items 13 through 22.

Point values for initiating structure:

_____ 1, _____ 2, _____ 3, _____ 4, _____ 5, _____ 6, _____ 7, _____ 8, _____ 9, _____ 10, _____ 11, _____ 12 = Total _____

Point values for consideration:

_____ 13, _____ 14, _____ 15, _____ 16, _____ 17, _____ 18, _____ 19, _____ 20, _____ 21, _____ 22 = Total _____

Interpretation:
Items 1 through 12 reflect an initiating structure or task leadership style. A score greater than 47 indicates that you describe your leadership style as high on initiating or task structure. You see yourself as planning, directing, organizing, and controlling the work of others. Items 13 through 22 reflect a considerate or relationship style. A score greater than 40 indicates that you see yourself as a considerate leader. A considerate leader is one who is concerned with the comfort, well-being, and personal welfare of her subordinates. In general, individuals rated high on initiating structure and at least moderate on consideration tend to be in charge of more productive teams than those whose leadership styles are low on initiating structure and high on consideration.

Source: Schriesheim, C. *Leadership Instrument*. Used by permission, Miami, Florida: University of Miami, 2005.

Initiating Structure

Initiating structure is the extent to which a leader defines and prescribes the roles of subordinates in order to set and accomplish goals in their areas of responsibility. This style emphasizes the direction of team or individual employee activities through planning, communicating, scheduling, assigning tasks, emphasizing deadlines, and giving orders. The leader sets definite standards of performance and expects subordinates to achieve them. In short, a leader with a high degree of initiating structure is concerned with accomplishing tasks by setting performance goals, giving directions, and expecting them to be followed.

When is initiating structure effective? The most positive effects of leader initiating structure on effectiveness and job satisfaction occur when (1) a high degree of pressure for output is imposed by someone other than the leader; (2) the task satisfies employees; (3) employees depend on the leader for information and direction on how to complete the task; and (4) employees are psychologically predisposed toward being instructed in what to do, how to do it, and when it should be achieved.

The dimensions of consideration and initiating structure are not necessarily mutually exclusive and, in fact, may be related in various ways. An individual may be high, low, or moderate on both consideration and initiating structure, as suggested in Figure 10.1. Conant, the CEO of Campbell's, appears to be a leader who is high on consideration and high on initiating structure, depending on the leadership issue.

Insights for Leaders

Some studies suggest that a leader who emphasizes initiating structure generally improves productivity, at least in the short run. However, managers who rank high on initiating structure and low on consideration generally have large numbers of grievances, absenteeism, and high employee turnover rates. Our view is that effective leaders can have high consideration and initiating structure at the same time. Showing consideration is beneficial insofar as it leads to high levels of team morale and low levels of turnover and absenteeism. At the same time, high levels of initiating structures are useful in promoting high levels of efficiency and performance.

Perhaps the main limitation of the behavioral model is the lack of attention it gives to the effects of the situation. It focuses on relationships between leaders and subordinates but gives little consideration to the situation in which the relationships occur. A better understanding of behavior usually results when both the person and the situation is examined.

FIGURE 10.1 Behavioral Leadership Grid

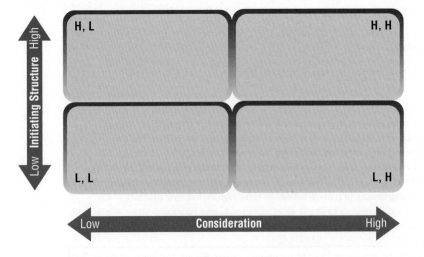

The following Self Competency feature presents Colin Luther Powell's "lessons in leadership."[23] They are based on his 50 years of professional experiences in the U.S. Army and his roles as a four-star general, chairman of the Joints Chief of Staff, national security adviser, and secretary of state. He is currently a partner at the venture capital firm Kleiner Perkins Caufield & Byers. He has received numerous military and civilian awards, including awards from two dozen countries. Powell is a widely sought keynote speaker on leadership, project management, and social responsibilities.[24] As you read about Powell's lessons in leadership, reflect on the leadership behaviors that are high on both consideration and initiating structure. Based on a review of multiple sources, Powell appears to possess the four leadership traits of intelligence, maturity and breadth, achievement drive, and integrity.

Self competency

Colin Powell's "Lessons in Leadership"

A dream doesn't become reality through magic, it takes sweat, determination, and hard work. If you are going to achieve excellence in big things, you develop the habit in little matters. Excellence is not an exception, it is a prevailing attitude. Perpetual optimism is a force multiplier.

Leaders are primarily responsible for setting strategic goals. Too often leaders give nice speeches and make PowerPoint presentations, but it's the followers who either accomplish the mission or not. So, in times of crisis, challenge, or great opportunity, I've always tried to make sure the followers understood the opportunities, risks and dangers, and why it was important to move forward.

It is essential that people have a plan to follow and know they will receive the resources required to get the job done. Too often, leaders talk a good game but they don't follow through with the resources or executable plan needed to achieve the goal. I've always tried to create a team environment where everyone trusts each other, we all understand what we're trying to accomplish and everybody knows that they have a role to play.

The best leaders are those who face reality and avoid trying to spin the problem away. They confront issues, share their anxiety and uncertainty with the followers, and let them become part of the solution. Leadership is all about problem-solving. In the military, there is a lot of discussion about where a leader should

Colin Powell.

be on the battlefield. Should the leader be up front where it's possible to become a quick casualty or should the person be at the rear? The correct answer is that you should be at the point of decision. You should be where you can make the most difference. The trick of leadership is being at the right place at the right time.

Obviously, everyone can't prevail in decision situations where there is uncertainty and different points of view. The way I've always gone about it is to let people have their say. I want them to argue with me for their position. I want people to jab at me when they think my position is wrong and point out why. At every organization, I've allowed—actually encouraged—the most junior people to argue with me. I want a lot of debate and dialogue because it draws out the best of them and it draws out the best of me. But at some point you can't keep debating and arguing and looking at options, you've got to do something. That's when the leader says, "Fine, I've got all the information I need and I thank you for all your input. This is what we are going to do." At that point, I expect people to behave as if they've thought of it themselves and to attack the problem or project with the passion I have. I won't tolerate anybody saying, "Well, that's what he decided, but it's a bad idea."

Ultimately, you have to create an environment where people are freed from demonstrating their ego because it contaminates the decision-making process. How many times have you seen a leader close down debate or discussion? They say, I know what we're going to do. Then everybody thinks, "Let's just sit around and wait for the leader to tell us what to do. We don't have to use our brains." Well, that's not the maximum use of all the brains available. In high-performance organizations, you get the right people, you manage risk, do your contingency planning, tap into expertise. Above all else, you maintain open lines of communication.

I believe the techniques and principles that work are timeless. It's all about collaborating with people, building trust and confidence, and making sure you take care of the followers. You also need to give them what they need to do their work well, solve problems, face reality, create opportunities and monitor risks. This is all fairly universal and it applies to any time or era.

To learn more about Colin Powell, go to **http://en.wikipedia.org/wiki/Colin_Powell.**

Developers of the legacy leadership models—traits, Theory X/Theory Y, and behavioral—sought to find characteristics and personal attributes that apply to most leadership situations. In contrast, situational (contingency) leadership models identify variables that permit certain leadership characteristics and behaviors to be effective in given situations. In the next two sections, we present two contingency models of leadership: the Situational Leadership® Model, and the Vroom–Jago leadership model.

Learning Goal

3. *Explain and apply the Situational Leadership® Model.*

Situational Leadership® Model

The **Situational Leadership® Model** *states that the style of leadership should be matched to the level of readiness of the followers.*[25] Like other contingency models of leadership, this one contains three basic components: a set of several possible leadership styles, a description of several alternative situations that leaders might encounter, and recommendations for which leadership styles are most effective in each situation.

Leadership Styles

According to the model, leaders can choose from among four styles. These four leadership styles involve various combinations of task behavior and relationship behavior. Task behavior is similar to initiating structure and relationship behavior is similar to consideration as described in the behavioral model. More specifically, **task behavior** *includes using one-way communication, spelling out duties, and telling followers what to do and where, when, and how to do it.* An effective leader might use a high degree of task behavior in some situations and only a moderate amount in other situations. **Relationship behavior** *includes using two-way communication, listening, encouraging, involving followers in decision making, and giving emotional support.* It is similar to consideration in the behavior model. Again, an effective leader may sometimes use a high degree of relationship behavior, and at other times less. By combining different amounts of task behavior with different amounts of relationship behavior, an effective leader may use four different leadership styles. The four leadership styles are called *telling*, *selling*, *participating*, and *delegating*. These styles are shown in Figure 10.2.[26]

Situational Contingency

According to this model, a leader should consider the situation before deciding which leadership style to use. The situational contingency in this model is the degree of follower readiness. **Readiness** *is a follower's ability to set high but attainable task-related goals and a willingness to accept responsibility for reaching them.* Readiness is not a fixed characteristic of followers—it depends on the task. The same group of followers may have a

FIGURE 10.2 The Situational Leadership® Model

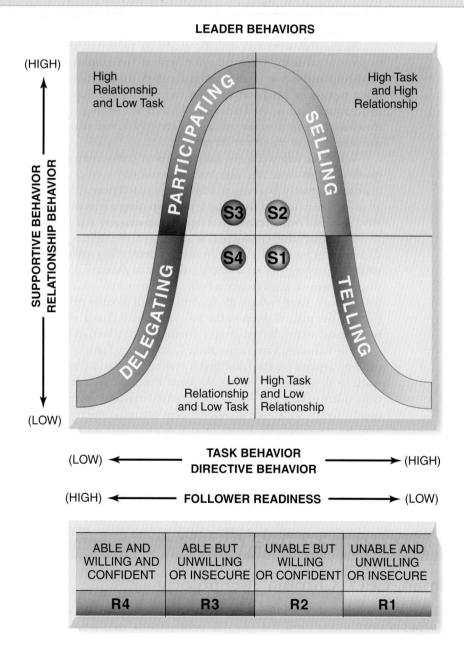

high degree of readiness for some tasks, but a low degree of readiness for others. The readiness level of followers depends on how much training they have received, how committed they are to the organization, their technical expertise, experience with the specific task, and so on.

Choosing a Leadership Style

As Figure 10.2 shows, the appropriate leadership style depends on the level of follower readiness. The curve running through the graph indicates the leadership style that best fits each readiness level of the individual or team. Note that at the bottom of the figure high readiness levels appear on the left and low readiness levels appear on the right.

For a follower who is at the stage of low readiness for a task, a telling style is effective. In using a **telling style**, *the leader provides clear instructions, gives specific directions, and supervises the work closely.* The telling style helps ensure that new employees perform well, which provides a solid foundation for their future success and satisfaction.

As the follower's task-specific readiness increases, the leader needs to continue to provide some guidance behavior because the employee isn't yet ready to assume total responsibility for performing the task. In addition, the leader needs to begin using supportive behaviors in order to build the employee's confidence and maintain enthusiasm. That is, the leader should shift to a selling style. In using a **selling style**, *the leader provides direction, encourages two-way communication, and helps build confidence and motivation on the part of the follower.*

When the follower feels confident about performing the task, the leader no longer needs to be so directive. The leader should maintain open communication but now does so by actively listening and assisting the follower as he or she makes efforts to use what has been learned. In using a **participating style**, *the leader encourages followers to share ideas and facilitates the work by being encouraging and helpful to subordinates.*

Finally, when an employee is at a high level of readiness for the task, effective leadership involves more delegation. In using a **delegating style**, *the leader turns over responsibility for making and implementing decisions to followers.* Delegating is effective in this situation because the follower is both competent and motivated to take full responsibility for his work. Even though the leader may still identify problems, the responsibility for carrying out plans is given to the follower. The follower who is fully ready for a project is permitted to handle the project deciding how, when, and where tasks are to be done.

The following Communication Competency feature, with aspects of the self competency, reports on Paul Millman's realization that a single leadership style does not work in all situations.[27] He is the chief executive officer and one of the six member cofounders of Chroma Technology, located in Rockingham, Vermont. This firm makes optical filters, which are components in scientific microscopes. Chroma Technology, with 88 employees, is a very unique firm in that it's entirely employee owned and run.[28] This has created leadership challenges for the organization and especially Paul Millman who recognizes the need for more contingency-based styles of leadership.

Communication competency

Paul Millman, CEO, Chroma Technology

Early on, employees at Chroma Technology, which was founded in 1991, made decisions on their own or by consensus. Most major decisions—whether to raise salaries, for example—were made with a one-person, one-vote system, so a worker with two months' tenure had as much say as a cofounder. No one was officially in charge of strategy or long-term planning. "I never expected the company to grow to the size we are now," says Wendy Cross, a cofounder and Millman's partner of almost 20 years. "My best hope was that we would keep ourselves employed and have some of our friends work here. We never really planned for the future."

Now that has become a problem. In the past few years, the industry has changed, and Chroma has struggled to keep up. Optical filters selectively transmit light, so a researcher can dye a portion of a cell—say, the nucleus—and then look at it exclusively, without viewing the rest of the cell. In 2002, a new competitor emerged: Semrock, a small company in Rochester, New York. By some standards, Semrock's filters worked better than Chroma's, but it took two years before Chroma started developing its own version of Semrock's technology. "There was nobody who thought that he or she had the authority to push the issue," Millman says. Meanwhile, one of Chroma's biggest customers started shifting its orders to Semrock. Chroma began selling its new, improved filters in 2005, but by then, growth had slowed to less than 3 percent.

Millman realized that a lack of clarity about his role was hindering the company's progress. Because Chroma supposedly had no bosses, workers complained when Millman acted like a boss. And because he was frustrated by his lack of authority, he frequently lashed out when other employees questioned his decisions. "He can be punishing," says cofounder Wim Auer. "If he thinks the company is doing something wrong, he can punish people in a public way." Tension reached a high point in early 2007, when the steering committee sent a memo giving members of the sales team guidelines on the hotels they could choose when they traveled. Millman was furious at the interference and sarcastically proposed eliminating the entire committee, which in turn infuriated committee members, who felt Millman was undermining their authority. The tension lasted for months. "Sales had always been my domain," Millman says, "and everybody else knew to stay out of it."

Millman wants to establish clear lines of authority, to get in writing that certain people are in charge of certain things—though he refuses to admit that this will turn anyone into a boss. He knows it will be a tough sell. Millman used to think a company could be structured as an inverted pyramid, with the leader largely subservient to the employees. Now, he believes there needs to be someone on top, a person with a long-term outlook. He wishes it were different, but he is not looking back. Says Millman, "I just wish more people had a broader view of the world."

To learn more about Chroma Technology, go to **www.chroma.com.**

Insights for Leaders

The Situational Leadership® Model helps leaders recognize that the same leadership style may be effective in some situations but not others. Furthermore, it highlights the importance of considering the followers' situation when choosing a leadership style. This model has generated interest among practitioners and researchers. The idea that leaders should be flexible with respect to the leadership style they use is appealing.[29] An inexperienced employee may perform as well as an experienced employee if properly directed and closely supervised. An appropriate leadership style should also help followers gain more experience and become more competent. Thus, as a leader helps followers develop to higher levels of readiness, the leader's style also needs to evolve. Therefore, this model requires the leader to be constantly monitoring the readiness level of followers in order to determine the combination of task and relationship behaviors that is most appropriate.

Like other contingency models, this one assumes that leaders can accurately assess each situation and change their leadership styles to match different situations. Some leaders can read situations and adapt their leadership style more effectively than others. For those who can't, what are the costs of training them to be able to do so?

Do these costs exceed the potential benefits? Before an organization adopts a development program to train leaders to use this model of leadership, they need to answer questions such as these.

Vroom–Jago Leadership Model

Victor Vroom and Arthur Jago developed a model that focuses on the leadership role in decision-making situations.[30] They developed this model to (1) assess variations that may exist in situational factors, (2) present five leadership styles, and (3) emphasize the choice of leadership style in relation to decision-making situations. The **Vroom–Jago leadership model** *prescribes a leader's choice(s) among five leadership styles based on seven situational factors, recognizing the time requirements and costs associated with each style.*[31]

Leadership Styles

There are five core leadership styles that vary in terms of the levels of empowerment and participation available to the leader's subordinates. These styles are summarized here in increasing levels of empowerment and participation:

- **Decide style**—*the leader makes the decision alone and either announces or sells it to the team.* The leader uses personal expertise and collects information from the team or others who can help solve the problem. The role of employees is clearly one of providing specific information that is requested, rather than generating or evaluating solutions.

- **Consult individually style**—*the leader presents the problem to team members individually, getting their ideas and suggestions and then makes the decision without bringing them together as a group.* This decision may or may not reflect their influence.

- **Consult team style**—*the leader presents the problem to team members in a meeting, gets their suggestions, and then makes the decision.* It may or may not reflect their influence.

- **Facilitate style**—*the leader presents the problem to the team in a meeting, acts as a facilitator, defines the problem to be solved, and sets the boundaries within which the decision must be made.* The goal is to get agreement on a decision. Above all, the leader takes care to ensure that her or his ideas are not given any greater weight than those of others simply because of her position. The leader's role is much like that of chairperson, coordinating the discussion, keeping it focused on the problem, and being sure that the essential issues are discussed. The leader doesn't try to influence the team to adopt her or his solution. The leader is willing to accept and implement any solution that has the support of the entire team.

- **Delegate style**—*the leader permits the team to make the decision within prescribed limits.* The team undertakes the identification and diagnosis of the problem, developing alternative procedures for solving it and deciding on one or more alternative solutions. The leader doesn't enter into the team's deliberations unless explicitly asked, but plays an important role by providing needed resources and encouragement. This style represents the highest level of subordinate empowerment.

Situational Variables

The Vroom–Jago leadership model focuses on seven situational factors (contingency variables) that should be assessed by the leader to determine which of the five leadership styles to use. An implicit assumption is that a leader has the ability to use any one of the styles, as the situation demands. Victor Vroom developed a Windows-based computer program called Expert System that enables the leader to record judgments on a five-point scale as to the extent to which a factor is present in a particular situation. Specifically, 5 = high presence, 3 = moderate presence, and 1 = low presence. Following our presentation of the seven situational factors, we demonstrate their use with a simplified "high" or a "low" presence evaluation.

- *Decision significance*—the degree to which the problem is highly important and a quality decision is imperative. In brief, how important is the technical quality of the decision?

- *Importance of commitment*—the degree to which subordinates' personal willingness to support the decision has an impact on the effectiveness of implementation. In brief, how important is subordinate commitment to the decision? Employees are more likely to implement enthusiastically a decision that is consistent with their goals, values, and understanding of the problem.

- *Leader expertise*—the degree to which the leader has relevant information and competencies to understand the problem fully and select the best solution to it. In brief, does the leader believe that he or she has the ability and information to make a high-quality decision?

- *Likelihood of commitment*—the degree to which subordinates will support the leader's decision if it is made. Followers who have faith and trust in the judgments of their leaders are more likely to commit to a decision, even if the subordinates were not heavily involved in making it. In brief, if the leader were to make the decision, would subordinate(s) likely be committed to it?

- *Team support*—the degree to which subordinates relate to the interests of the organization as a whole or a specific unit in solving the problem. In brief, do subordinates share the goals to be achieved by solving this problem?

- *Team expertise*—the degree to which the subordinates have the relevant information and competencies to understand fully the problem and select the best solution to it. In brief, does the leader think that subordinates have the abilities and information to make a high-quality decision?

- *Team competence*—the degree to which team members have the abilities needed to resolve conflicts over preferred solutions and work together in reaching a high-quality decision. In brief, are team members capable of handling their own decision-making process?

Solution Matrix

The solution matrix shown in Table 10.4 represents the basic features of the Vroom–Jago leadership model. This matrix begins on the left where you evaluate the significance of the situation—high (H) or low (L). The column headings denote the situational factors that may or may not be present. The leader progresses across the matrix by selecting high (H) or low (L) for each relevant situational factor. After the leader determines the significance of the decision, then there is an evaluation of the degree (high or low) to which employee commitment is important to implementation of the decision. As one proceeds across the matrix, a value (H or L) is recorded for only those situational factors that call for a judgment, until the recommended leadership style is reached.

The more participative styles (especially the delegate and consult team versions) require more time and energy. As suggested in our Communication Competency on Paul Millman at Chroma Technology, they can require too much time and energy. Of course, as we emphasize throughout this book, participative leader behaviors help develop the technical skills and competencies of employees, build teamwork, and foster loyalty and commitment to organizational goals. The Vroom–Jago model considers the trade-offs among the criteria by which a leader's decision-making style can

TABLE 10.4 Vroom–Jago Leadership Model

Note: A dashed line (–) in a cell means the leader does not consider the situational variable a factor.

SITUATIONAL VARIABLES/QUESTIONS							Suggested Leadership Styles
1 → Decision Significance	2 → Importance Of Commitment	3 → Leader Expertise	4 → Likelihood Of Commitment	5 → Team Support	6 → Team Expertise	7 → Team Competence	
H	H	H	H	—	—	—	Decide
			L	H	H	H	Delegate
					H	L	Consult Team
					L	—	
				L	—	—	
		L	H	H	H	H	Facilitate
					H	L	Consult Individually
					L	—	
				L	—	—	
			L	H	H	H	Facilitate
					H	L	Consult Team
					L	—	
				L	—	—	
	L	H	—	—	—	—	Decide
		L	—	H	H	H	Facilitate
					H	L	Consult Individually
					L	—	
				L	—	—	
L	H	—	H	—	—	—	Decide
			L	—	—	H	Delegate
						L	Facilitate
	L	—	—	—	—	—	Decide

Source: Vroom, V. H. Leadership and decision-making. *Organizational Dynamics*, Spring 2000, 82–94.

be evaluated: decision quality, employee commitment to implementation, costs, and employee development. The consult and delegate styles are viewed as most supportive of employee development.

The following Ethics Competency feature places you in the role of chief executive officer of a relatively small regional bank.[32] You are to use the matrix in Table 10.4 to select the leadership style for this situation.

Ethics competency

The Bank CEO

The bank examiners have just left, insisting that many of your commercial real estate loans be written off, thereby depleting already low capital. Along with many other banks in your region, your bank is in serious danger of being closed by the regulators. As the financial problems surfaced, many of the top managers left to pursue other interests. Fortunately, you were able to replace them with three highly competent younger managers. While they had no prior knowledge of one another, each is a product of a fine development program with one of the money center banks in which they rotated through positions in each of the banking functions.

Your extensive experience in the industry leads you to the inevitable conclusion that the only hope is a two-pronged approach involving reduction of all but the most critical expenses and the sale of assets to other banks. The task must be accomplished quickly and ethically. Further deterioration in the quality of the loan portfolio could result in a negative capital position, forcing regulators to close the bank. Funds from the U.S. government are no longer available to help you survive.

The strategy is clear to you, but you have many details that will need to be worked out. You believe that you know what information will be needed in order to get the bank on a course for future prosperity. You are fortunate in having three junior executives to help you out. Although they have had little or no experience in working together, you know that each is dedicated to the survival of the bank. Like you, they know what needs to be done and how to do it.

Instructions

As you make each assessment (high or low) based on the situational variables in Table 10.4, what leadership style should you choose when making a decision about how to lead? Start with *decision significance* on the left-hand side of the matrix. This first column requires that you make a decision about the importance of the issue. After you make that decision, go to the next column,

importance of commitment. Again, you must make a decision about the importance of having staff members committed. After you make this decision, you face another decision and then another. As you make each decision, follow the columns across the matrix. Eventually, at the far right-hand side of the matrix, you will arrive at the suggested best style of leadership to use in this situation, which is based on your previous seven decisions in relation to each situational variable that you assessed; for example, high, low, or not a factor.

We used this method and obtained the results shown below. Based on this analysis, we selected the style of leadership that we recommend for this situation. Do you agree?

SITUATIONAL VARIABLES

• Descision significance	H
• Importance of commitment	H
• Leader expertise	H
• Likelihood of commitment	L
• Team support	H
• Team expertise	H
• Team competence	L

We suggest the use of the consult team style with the junior managers. A different assessment to one or more of these situational factors would probably result in a different suggested leadership style.

Insights for Leaders

The Vroom–Jago leadership model is consistent with work on group and team behaviors, as we will discuss in Chapter 12. If leaders diagnose situations correctly, choosing the best leadership style for those situations becomes easier. These choices, in turn, enable them to make high-quality, timely decisions. If the situation requires delegation, the leader must learn how to establish the desired goals and limitations and let employees determine how best to achieve the goals within those limitations. If the situation calls for the leader alone to make the decision, the leader should be aware of potential positive and negative consequences of not asking others for their input.

The model does have some limitations. First, subordinates in various countries (e.g., United States, Canada, United Kingdom) may have a strong desire to participate in decisions affecting their jobs, regardless of the model's recommendation of a style for the leader to use. If subordinates aren't involved in the decision, they may become frustrated and not be committed to the decision. In societies high in power distance and uncertainty avoidance such as China, Mexico, and Malaysia, there is often a much greater employee acceptance of taking orders without participation in decision making. Second, certain competencies of the leader play a key role in determining the relative effectiveness of the model. For example, in situations involving conflict, only leaders skilled in communication and conflict resolution may be able to use the kind of participative decision-making strategy suggested by the model. A leader who hasn't developed such competencies may obtain better results with a more directive style, even though this leadership style is different from the style that the model proposes. Third, the model is based on the assumption that decisions involve a single cycle. Often, decisions go through several cycles and are part of a solution to a bigger problem than the one being addressed at the time.

Choosing the most appropriate leadership style can be difficult. A theme of employee empowerment has begun to prevail in many leading business organizations. Evidence shows that this leadership style can result in productive, healthy organizations. Participative management is not appropriate for all situations, as the model in Table 10.4 suggests.

Chapter Summary

1. *Describe the role of power and political behavior in the leadership process.*

Leaders draw on five sources of power to influence the actions of followers: legitimate, reward, coercive, referent, and expert. All leaders engage in political behavior to influence others—sometimes ineffectively. Political behavior and organizational politics focus on efforts to protect or enhance self-interests, goals, and preferred outcomes. The drivers of political behavior were noted with special emphasis on how leaders can foster or minimize political behaviors of subordinates in relation to the performance appraisal process.

2. *Describe three legacy models of leadership: traits, Theory X/Theory Y, and behavioral.*

Three of the legacy leadership models are the traits, Theory X/Theory Y, and behavioral models. The traits model emphasizes the personal qualities of leaders and attributes success to certain abilities, skills, and personality characteristics. This model fails to explain why certain managers succeed and others fail as leaders. The primary reason is that it ignores how traits interact with situational variables. The Theory X/Theory Y model is based on the premise that the behavior of managers is often influenced by their assumptions and beliefs about followers and what motivates their followers. Theory X is a composite of propositions and underlying beliefs that take a command-and-control approach to leadership that is based on a negative view of human nature. In contrast, Theory Y is a composite of propositions and beliefs that take an empowering approach to leadership that is based on a positive view of human nature. The behavioral model emphasizes leaders' actions instead of their personal traits. We focused on two leader behaviors—consideration and initiating structure—and how they affect employee performance and job satisfaction. The behavioral model tends to ignore the situation in which the leader is operating. This omission is the focal point of the two contingency models of leadership that we reviewed. The contingency approach emphasizes the importance of various situational factors for leaders and their leadership styles.

3. *Explain and apply the Situational Leadership® Model.*

The Situational Leadership® Model states that leaders should choose a style that matches the readiness of their subordinates. If subordinates are not ready to perform a task, a directive leadership style will probably be more effective than a relationship style. As the readiness level of the subordinates increases, the leader's style should become more participative and less directive.

4. *Explain and apply the Vroom–Jago leadership model.*

The Vroom–Jago model presents a leader with choices among five leadership styles based on seven situational (contingency) factors. Time requirements and other costs associated with each style are recognized in the model. The leadership styles lie on a continuum from decide (leader makes the decision) to delegate (subordinate or team makes the decision). A solution matrix is used to diagnose the situation and arrive at the recommended leadership style.

Key Terms and Concepts

Behavioral model of leadership, **300**
Coercive power, **292**
Consideration, **300**
Consult individually style, **308**
Consult team style, **308**
Decide style, **308**
Delegate style, **308**
Delegating style, **306**
Expert power, **292**
Facilitate style, **308**
Initiating structure, **302**
Legitimate power, **291**
Organizational politics, **293**
Participating style, **306**

Political behavior, **293**
Readiness, **305**
Referent power, **292**
Relationship behavior, **304**
Reward power, **291**
Selling style, **306**
Situational Leadership® Model, **304**
Task behavior, **304**
Telling style, **306**
Theory X, **299**
Theory Y, **299**
Traits model of leadership, **297**
Vroom–Jago leadership model, **308**
Zone of indifference, **291**

Discussion Questions

1. Visit Campbell's Soup home page at www.campbell soupcompany.com. Click on "Governance" and then "Code of Ethics for the CEO and Senior Financial Officer." What leadership concepts presented in this chapter are illustrated in this code? Is this code consistent with the presentation of Douglas Conant in the Learning from Experience feature? Explain.

2. Based on the five sources of power presented in the chapter text, which ones are relevant to fostering the diversity competency by leaders?

3. Review the Change Competency feature related to Carol Bartz. What sources of power and political behavior are suggested in this feature?

4. Think of a manager for whom you have worked. Did this manager reflect any of the propositions related to Theory X and/or Theory Y? Explain with specific examples.

5. Review the Self Competency feature on Colin Powell's lessons in leadership. What statements in the feature reflect "high consideration" and what statements reflect "high initiating structure"?

6. Review the Communication Competency feature on Paul Millman, CEO, Chroma Technology. Which behaviors and decisions *do* and which *do not* reflect elements of the Situational Leadership® Model? Assume you are a consultant to Millman. Based on this model, what advice would you give him?

7. Based on a problem situation in which you were a team member or leader, was the appropriate leadership style used according to an assessment of the situational variables in the Vroom–Jago leadership model? Use Table 10.4 to guide your assessment.

8. Assume that you have been selected as a team leader for four other classmates. The team's assignment is to develop a 15-page paper on leadership and then present the paper to the class. This project represents 30 percent of the course grade. How might the Vroom–Jago leadership model be helpful to you as the team leader? What limitations does this model impose on you as team leader?

9. Are people born to be leaders?

Experiential Exercise and Case

Experiential Exercise: Self Competency

Personal Power Inventory[33]

Instructions
Think of a group of which you are a member. For example, it could be a team at work, a committee, or a group working on a project at your school. Use the following scale to respond to the numbered statements:

1 = Strongly disagree
2 = Disagree

3 = Slightly disagree
4 = Neither agree nor disagree
5 = Slightly agree
6 = Agree
7 = Strongly agree

_____ 1. I am one of the more vocal members of the group.
_____ 2. People in the group listen to what I have to say.

_____ 3. I often volunteer to lead the group.

_____ 4. I am able to influence group decisions.

_____ 5. I often find myself on "center stage" in group activities or discussions.

_____ 6. Members of the group seek me out for advice.

_____ 7. I take the initiative in the group for my ideas and contributions.

_____ 8. I receive recognition in the group for my ideas and contributions.

_____ 9. I would rather lead the group than be a participant.

_____ 10. My opinion is held in high regard by group members.

_____ 11. I volunteer my thoughts and ideas without hesitation.

_____ 12. My ideas often are implemented.

_____ 13. I ask questions in meetings just to have something to say.

_____ 14. Group members often ask for my opinions and input.

_____ 15. I often play the role of scribe, secretary, or note taker during meetings.

_____ 16. Group members usually consult me about important matters before they make a decision.

_____ 17. I clown around with other group members.

_____ 18. I have noticed that group members often look at me, even when not talking directly to me.

_____ 19. I jump right into whatever conflict the group members are dealing with.

_____ 20. I am very influential in the group.

Scoring and Interpretation

Visibility		Influence	
Item	Your Score	Item	Your Score
1.	_____	2.	_____
3.	_____	4.	_____
5.	_____	6.	_____
7.	_____	8.	_____
9.	_____	10.	_____
11.	_____	12.	_____
13.	_____	14.	_____
15.	_____	16.	_____
17.	_____	18.	_____
19.	_____	20.	_____
Total	_____	Total	_____

Use the scores calculated and mark your position on the power matrix shown in Figure 10.3. The combinations of visibility and influence shown are described as follows:

1. *High power.* Individuals in quadrant I exhibit behaviors that bring high visibility, and they are able to influence others. In organizations, these individuals may be considered to be on the "fast track."

2. *Low power.* Individuals in quadrant II are highly visible but have little real influence. This condition could reflect their personal characteristics but also could indicate that formal power resides elsewhere in the organization. Often these people may hold staff, rather than line, positions that give them visibility but that lack "clout" to get things done.

FIGURE 10.3 Power Matrix

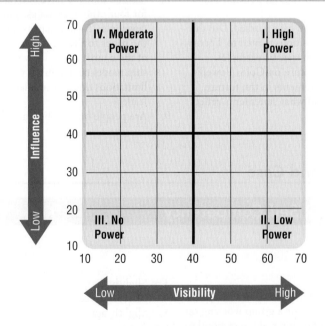

Source: Adapted from Reddy, W. B., and Williams, G. The visibility credibility inventory: Measuring power and influence. In J. W. Pfeiffer (ed.), *The 1988 Annual: Developing Human Resources.* San Diego: University Associates, 1988,124.

3. *No power.* Individuals in quadrant III, for whatever reason, are neither seen nor heard. Individuals in this category may have difficulty advancing in the organization.
4. *Moderate power.* Individuals in quadrant IV are "behind-the-scenes" influencers. These individuals often are opinion leaders and "sages" who wield influence but are content to stay out of the limelight.

Questions
1. Based on your scores, what changes, if any, do you propose for yourself in the use of power? Explain.
2. Would other individuals who know you well agree with your self assessment on the power matrix? Explain.
3. What competencies are most important to you in your use of power? Explain.

Case: Diversity Competency

Women on Corporate Boards[34]

In recent years, the absolute number of accomplished and successful women leaders invited to serve on the board of directors of major corporations, such as the *Fortune 1000* list, has increased. However, the absolute number of female leaders on any one board, relative to the total members on a board, remains relatively small. To have just one woman member on a board is quite common. This case presents some of the diversity-related experiences and issues of board composition in terms of male and female membership. The stories presented in this case are from those female leaders and a few male CEOs who are highly successful in their own right. For obvious reasons, most of these stories are based on experiences of female leaders who need to remain anonymous.

One Woman on the Board

Woman director: I was the only woman in a room of guys. I'm not shy, but trying to get your voice heard around the table is not easy. You can make a point that is valid. Two minutes later "Joe" says exactly the same thing, and all the guys congratulate him. It is hard, even at our level, to get your voice heard. You have to find a way to wedge in, and they come to realize you are not going away.

Woman director: It is kind of like "Who is this person? She's a lot different than we are." Not collegial. Not a lot of conversation, not a lot of interaction. On this board, where I'm the only woman and the only African American, it's very different than the other two boards on which I serve where there are two women—the interaction with board members, openness, and acceptance of new members like me.

Woman director: Initially it felt like I was playing catch-up. Other directors seemed to understand, and I didn't. A lot of what happened seemed to have been worked out in committees I didn't sit on or on golf courses. It was an old-boy network until I asked, "How did that get decided?" Then they began to ask what I thought.

Woman director: They look at you skeptically as to how you got there. First you'd better show men why you're there—women don't get the benefit of the doubt. Board meetings are pretty brutal.

Male CEO on a board: Shareholders had been asking, "When are you going to have a woman?" So they put a woman on just to say they had a woman. She had to break down brick walls to be heard. She had to work hard to get into the conversation, almost like not being there. Management was not interested in her competency. It was an old boys' club, and no one on the board wanted a female.

Two or More Women on the Board

Woman director: On this board, from day one it was so special. Amazing! Actually that board has the most women. It is very much a team. Professionalism—everyone did their homework and everyone is supportive of each other but very challenging—a lot of dialogue and constructive criticism.

Woman director: Three women board members is kind of a charm. When the third woman came, it was easier. The dynamic among the women became slightly more interactive. It isn't based on the fact that the first woman is not a friend. In fact, she is someone I didn't know at all. She's become a friend, but before all that happened, it changed the dynamic between us as women. If the three of us got into a conversation, there was no awkward feeling.

Woman director: On my board with four women, the invisibility issue never happened. I became effective quickly. I happen to be the lead director of that board. If you look at that board, the head of the governance committee is a woman, the head of the compensation committee is a woman, the CEO is a woman, and the head of the audit committee is a guy. There is no problem with women in leadership on that board.

Woman director: For the time being, women and people of color are outsiders in the boardroom. The dynamics of being someone who hasn't had the same experiences are that one asks different questions. One of the most valuable things in the boardroom is the questions asked. Why are we doing that? I see this increasingly on the dynamic on compensation. There was difficulty in setting limits by those who have benefited from the non-limits in the past—former CEOs. I don't want them to question mine; I won't question yours. Most women and minorities have not been CEOs and bring different perspectives to corporate compensation.

Male CEO and chairman of the board: As there were more women, the first woman became more active. They were all more active as the number of women increased. It's a group dynamic. When you bring on one of any demographic group, they're trying to figure out how they fit. With more, that's not an issue. They were more vocal, more willing to push their issues when more women were added to the board. More relaxed.

Woman corporate secretary to the board: The women board members are incredibly humanizing. They treat staffers better. They are less hierarchical. They are affirming of staff. They compliment them on reports—in meetings and outside. They are also critical but are much more likely to find time to be positive and personal. Thanking people publicly. That makes the board less remote and intimidating to staff. People talk differently now that there are more women. I did not notice this when there were two women. It is happening more now. At audit committee meetings, there are now several top executives who are women. So with the women on the audit committee, there are a lot of women in the room. It is much more conversational and less hierarchical and, as a result, all the directors get better information.

Questions
1. What aspects of power and political behaviors are suggested in these stories?
2. What personality traits are suggested in the stories of the women leaders who serve on these various boards?
3. Based on these stories, did the male members of these boards tend to reflect Theory X or Theory Y propositions?
4. Based on these stories, how would you tend to characterize the female board members in relation to the behavioral model of leadership?

chapter 11

Leadership Effectiveness: New Perspectives

Learning Goals

After studying this chapter, you should be able to:

1
Explain the characteristics of transactional leadership.

2
Describe the core elements of leader–member exchange.

3
Discuss the attributes of authentic leadership.

4
Explain the essentials of transformational leadership.

5
Explain the core features of Global Leadership and Organizational Behavior Effectiveness.

Learning Content

Learning from Experience

John W. Thompson, Chairman of Symantec

Symantec, headquartered in Cupertino, California, is a major software company with approximately 17,000 employees in 40 countries. The firm provides security, storage, and systems management solutions to numerous types of businesses and consumers. Its most well-known antivirus, antispyware, and Internet security software and services are marketed under the Norton brand.

John W. Thompson serves as chairman of the board of Symantec and until recently had served as the chief executive officer for 10 years. Thompson led the company through a tremendous growth phase—from a $600 million consumer antivirus company in 1999 to an enterprise security, virus, and storage provider with more than $6 billion in sales. His most criticized strategic initiative by some analysts was the acquisition of Veritas storage management software, which was one of 25 acquisitions by Symantec during Thompson's tenure as CEO. Before becoming CEO of Symantec, Thompson had a distinguished 28-year career at IBM.

Upon announcing his retirement as CEO, Thompson noted that this transition had been in place for two years. He commented: "I've always believed that 10 years was long enough for a CEO to run a company." One columnist in information technology observed that under Thompson's watch, Symantec was dramatically transformed and has emerged as a powerhouse security and storage provider.

For Thompson, the Symantec job offered a chance to be a true leader. "It's one thing to be a part of a great team, recognized as doing well in the industry. It's another to be a leader of the team trying to create an image for the company and its product," he explained. By all accounts, he is a true leader. During challenging times, Thompson's confidence and resolve served him well. For example, one executive observed: "He did not back off [for] one moment on everything he said about Veritas and the need and the value of that acquisition, despite the pressure that he was under. He did not cave. The leadership he demonstrated under difficult circumstances was admirable."

With a reputation for taking calculated and thoughtful risks that paid off, Thompson became an excellent choice to lead the company forward. Besides having excellent business competencies, he also was known to be ambitious, likable, and very persuasive. Thompson's style is friendly

JUSTIN SULLIVAN/GETTY IMAGES

To learn more about Symantec, go to www.symantec.com.

and easygoing. He's a good storyteller, and the kind of person people describe as a leader of change. Based on decades of business experience, Thompson thinks he understands what it takes to be a good leader. Besides being able to work with numbers, he says, leaders need personal integrity and a relentless focus on people. Leaders also need to take time to rest and reflect. "You cannot run 24/7, 365 days a year. You need to take time to enjoy the fruits of your labors." Thompson has always strived to keep a healthy balance between working hard and having fun.

When asked how others can achieve what he has achieved, Thompson points to the important role of mentors. Reflecting on his own experience, he observed: "I had the belief that if I could produce good results, the rest would take care of itself. But along the way, I also was fortunate enough to have support from some really well-placed people who took an interest in my career. . . . Success is a combination of hard work and a good support structure that helps to get you going, but it's determination along the way that keeps you moving along. I had enough of all of those to get me where I am today." Thompson is spending more of his time encouraging young African Americans to pursue engineering careers. He takes this responsibility personally, inviting young talent to his home and treating them to a barbecue. Periodically, he also coaches students at Florida A&M University, his alma mater.[1]

Leadership is like a prism—there is something new and different each time you look at it from a new angle. In this chapter, we present additional lenses for understanding and addressing the range of leadership issues and the pressures that leaders face. Our focus is on new perspectives and models of leadership: transactional, leader–member exchange, authentic, transformational, and GLOBE (an acronym for Global Leadership and Organizational Behavior Effectiveness).

Leadership is future oriented. It involves influencing people to move from where they are (here) to some new place (there).[2] Clearly, John Thompson's leadership had a significant influence in continuously transforming Symantec. In the Learning from Experience feature, this future orientation is illustrated by the way in which Thompson guided the dramatic transformation of Symantec into a powerhouse security and storage provider. Of course, various leaders define or perceive *here* and *there* differently. For some, the journey between here and there is relatively routine, like driving a car on a familiar road. Others see the need to chart a new course through unexplored territory. Such leaders perceive fundamental differences between the way things are and the way things can or should be. They recognize the shortcomings of the present situation and offer a sense of passion and excitement to overcome them. Recall Thompson's comments: "It's one thing to be part of a great team, recognized as doing well in the industry. It's another to be a leader of the team trying to create an image for the company and its product."

Transactional Leadership

Learning Goal

1. Explain the characteristics of transactional leadership.

Transactional leadership *involves motivating and directing followers primarily through appealing to their own self-interest.* Transactional leadership focuses on a carrot (and sometimes a stick) approach, setting performance expectations and goals and providing feedback to followers. The primary power of transactional leaders comes from their formal authority in the organization. They focus on the basic management processes of controlling, organizing, and short-term planning.

Core Components

Three primary components of transactional leadership are as follows[3]:

- *Provides contingent rewards.* Transactional leaders identify paths that link the achievement of goals to rewards, clarify expectations, exchange promises and resources for support, arrange mutually satisfactory agreements, negotiate for resources, exchange assistance for effort, and provide commendations for successful performance. These leaders set and clarify detailed goals to obtain short-term and measurable results. They give their subordinates extrinsic things they want (like bonuses and stock options) in direct exchange for measurable things that these leaders want.

- *Exhibits active management by exception.* Transactional leaders actively monitor the work performed by subordinates, take corrective actions if deviations from expected standards occur, and enforce rules to prevent mistakes.

- *Emphasizes passive management by exception.* Transactional leaders intervene after unacceptable performance or deviations from accepted standards occur. They may wait to take action until mistakes are brought to their attention. Corrective actions and possibly punishment are used as a response to unacceptable performance.

Insights for Leaders

Transactions clearly in place form the basis for leader–follower interactions.[4] Effective transactional leaders are likely to engage in the following five practices:

- They ask: "What needs to be done?"
- They ask: "What is right for the organization?"
- They develop action plans.
- They take responsibility for decisions.
- They take responsibility for communicating.[5]

Transactional leaders may tend to overemphasize detailed and short-term goals, standard operating procedures, rules, and policies. This emphasis may tend to stifle creativity and the generation of new ideas at lower organizational levels. The pure form of transactional leadership may work only where organizational problems and goals are clear and well defined. There may be a tendency for transactional leaders to not reward or ignore ideas that do not fit with their plans and goals. In other cases, transactional leaders have been known to spur innovation by clarifying exactly what performance standards and innovations are desired by others and stating the extrinsic rewards that will be forthcoming if they are reached. This is more likely when the transactional leaders focus on making innovations that refine and improve existing products and services.

Transactional leaders attempt to influence others by exchanging good performance for extrinsic rewards, such as wages, financial incentives, benefits, and status symbols—a large private and corner office, first-class hotels when traveling, use of private jets or first-class air travel, membership in country clubs, top-of-the line company-provided cars, generous expense accounts, and the like. The failure to perform is often followed by punishment. Transactional leaders may be quite effective in guiding efficiency initiatives designed to cut costs and improve productivity in the short term.[6] They tend to be highly directive and action oriented, if not dominating. The relationships between transactional leaders and followers tend to be transitory and not based on emotional bonds.

The following Change Competency feature presents a sampling of behaviors by Mark Hurd, the CEO of Hewlett-Packard, that suggests his orientation tends toward that of a transactional leader.[7] Hewlett-Packard (HP) is headquartered in Palo Alto, California. The firm has annual sales of approximately $118 billion, 170,000 employees, and operations in 170 countries. HP provides a comprehensive portfolio of IT products, software, and services.[8]

Change **competency**

Mark Hurd, CEO, Hewlett-Packard

Mark Hurd became the chief executive officer of HP in 2005 after serving in a variety of leadership positions at NCR over a 25-year period. Since his arrival, HP's stock price more than doubled until the recent recession. Sales grew and costs shrunk. To make these changes possible, shortly after arrival at HP, Hurd imposed a hardheadedness. He laid off 15,000 employees after four months on the job. To increase accountability, he gave executives more control over their budgets but also tougher standards for managing them. They were required to cut costs from slower businesses such as black-and-white laser printers and invest the savings in fast-growing areas. Top execs were interrogated by Hurd on minute details of their performance. He questioned their projections and then set them loose to solve problems. He reduced the number of people who weighed in on major decisions, providing more autonomy and responsibility to executives and managers. That move sped up the decision-making process and also saved almost $2 billion. HP acquired EDS, an information technology firm, in 2008 and within months downsized HP by 24,000 employees, mostly from EDS.

One of the big initial changes was to demand improvements in consumer marketing. He split up the sales and marketing group, dividing them among the major business units. This decision again granted executives and managers more power to direct their sales spending, simplifying what used to be a complicated process. Hurd stated: "My principles: Do it simple, and have accountability and responsibility." Rob Enderle, president and principal analyst of Enderle Group, contends that pushing his managers has been one of Hurd's tools for success. He has granted them more responsibility, but, in return, he expects more from them and has recognized their efforts when they perform. Hurd knows who's playing him and who's not, and he pushes his people to make commitments a little ahead of what they think they can do and then drives them to meet them. The results have been noticeable, especially for the once-maligned PC business, which struggled to turn a profit. It has been suggested that Hurd "lives by the numbers and the numbers don't lie," which is easier said in manufacturing than in services, such as those provided by EDS.

In a 2009 letter to HP employees, in relation to mandated pay cuts, Hurd comments, in part:

> We have decided to further variabilize our cost structure by reducing base pay and some benefits across HP. My base pay will be reduced by 20 percent. The base pay of other executives will be reduced by 10 percent. The base pay of all other exempt employees will be reduced by 5 percent. For non-exempt employees, base pay will be reduced by two-and-a-half percent. Additional efficiencies, including changes to the US 401(K) plan and the share ownership plan, will also be implemented. Follow-up communications will detail the timing and the plans in your location.

HP hasn't increased its overall R&D expenditures of around $3.5 billion for four years. As a result, R&D spending as a percentage of sales has fallen as HP's sales have climbed. Michael Tushman is a Harvard Business School professor whose research has quantified the shortcomings of stressing operations and efficiency at the expense of innovation. He comments: "The religion of efficiency has a dark, dark side. For too many general managers, the certainty of today trumps the uncertainty of the future." Time will tell if Hurd's change competency will serve HP well over the long term.

To learn more about HP, go to **www.hp.com.**

Leader–Member Exchange

Learning Goal

2. *Describe the core elements of leader–member exchange.*

Leader–member exchange (LMX) *suggests that leaders develop different relationships with each of their subordinates through a series of work-related transactions.* Each manager–subordinate relationship is proposed as falling along a continuum that ranges from *low quality*, where the relationship is based strictly on the transactional part of employment requirements, to *high quality*, where the relationship is based on mutual liking, trust, respect, and a sense of loyalty or obligation to each other.[9]

Core Components

Before reading further, please complete the leader–member exchange (LMX) instrument in Table 11.1. It asks your perceptions as a subordinate in relation to your views of a current or former manager (supervisor) for whom you have worked.

The *low* or *high* quality of the LMX between a manager (supervisor) and each subordinate has been proposed more recently as unfolding over three phases, as follows:

- *Stranger phase.* The LMX relationship begins with the stranger phase. The leader and a new (recently hired) employee occupy formal organizational roles (superior and subordinate). They begin their relationship by interacting on a formal basis that focuses on an exchange relationship that is absent a sense of caring and commitment. Presumably, if the subordinate does not meet minimal performance standards within the leader's expected time horizon, the subordinate is likely to be fired.

- *Acquaintance phase.* In this phase, the leader and subordinate begin to share greater information on both a work and personal level. This is a critical stage. If this stage is not successful, the dyad (leader–subordinate) is likely to revert to the stranger phase, even if the subordinate is meeting performance expectations (exchange relationship).

- *Mature partnership phase.* In this phase, the exchanges are not just task (performance) based. They include emotional bonds. The leader and subordinate begin to count on each other for mutual affection, mutual loyalty and support, work-related contributions and obligations to each other, mutual professional respect, and mutual trust. The leader counts on the subordinate to provide her or him with assistance whenever needed (e.g., I need you to work this weekend to finish our project on time) and vice versa by the follower (e.g., I would appreciate Thursday and Friday off from work because I have relatives unexpectedly coming to town). In brief, the follower relies on the leader for support, encouragement, and a willingness to invest in the subordinate's career. This might include mentoring, assignment to projects that have high visibility and impact, special professional development and training opportunities, and the like.

Assessing LMX

Table 11.1 asked about LMX from your point of view. The other side would be to ask the leader (manager) about her or his LMX quality with each of his or her subordinates. The same dimensions and types of statements in Table 11.1 might be assessed through the leader's perceptions. The same five-point scale (strongly disagree, 1 point—to strongly agree, 5 points) might be presented to the leader about each subordinate. For example, a *mutual affection* item might state: "I like this subordinate very much as a person." A *loyalty* item might state: "This subordinate will come to my defense if attacked by others." A *contribution to work activities* item might state: "I provide support and resources to this subordinate that goes beyond what is required in my job description." A *professional respect* item might state: "I admire this subordinate's knowledge of and competence on the job." Based on your completion of the instrument in Table 11.1, how do you think the leader (manager) selected would reply to these items about you? Does (did) this manager see you in a *low-* or *high-quality* LMX relationship with her or him?

TABLE 11.1 Leader–Member Exchange (LMX) from a Subordinate's Perspective

Instructions

Think of a manager (supervisor) you have reported to or currently report to. Respond to the following 12 statements based on the scale shown below. There are no right or wrong responses. Record the numerical value of your response/perception next to each statement. Use the scoring key in the Results and Interpretation section to compute your assessment of each LMX dimension and overall assessment.

1	2	3	4	5
Strongly Disagree	Disagree	Neither Agree nor Disagree	Agree	Strongly Agree

Record your numerical value next to each statement.

_____ 1. I like my manager (supervisor) very much as a person.

_____ 2. I think my manager defends my work to a superior, even without complete knowledge of the issue in question.

_____ 3. I carry out work tasks for my manager that go beyond what is specified in my job description.

_____ 4. I am impressed with my manager's knowledge of his or her job.

_____ 5. I think my manager is the kind of person I would like to have as a friend.

_____ 6. I think my manager would defend me if I were "attacked" by others.

_____ 7. I am willing to apply extra effort, beyond that normally required, to further the interest of the work group.

_____ 8. I respect my manager's knowledge of and competency on the job.

_____ 9. I think my manager is a lot of fun to work with.

_____ 10. I think my manager would defend me to others in the organization if I made an honest mistake.

_____ 11. I do not mind working my hardest for my manager.

_____ 12. I admire my manager's professional skills.

Results and Interpretation

Sum the point values for items 1, 5, and 9 = _____. This is you level of *mutual affection*. Is it low (3–6) or high (12–15)?

Sum points for items 2, 6, and 10 = _____. This is your level of *loyalty*. Is it low (3–6) or high (12–15)?

Sum points for items 3, 7, and 11 = _____. This is your level of *contribution to work activities*. Is it low (3–6) or high (12–15)?

Sum points for items 4, 8, and 12 = _____. This is your level of *professional respect*. Is it low (3–6) or high (12–15)?

For your overall score, sum items 1 through 12 = _____. Is your overall LMX low (12–24) or high (48–60)? Scores in between these numbers (25–47) may reflect leaning one way or the other, or perhaps a neutral perception about your manager.

Source: Adapted from Liden, R. C., and Maslyn, J. M. Multidimensionality of leader-member exchange: An empirical assessment through scale development. *Journal of Management*, 1998, 24, 43–72. Also see Greguras, G. J., and Ford, J. M. An examination of the multidimensionality of supervisor and subordinate perceptions of leader-member exchange. *Journal of Occupational and Organizational Psychology*, 2006, 79, 433–465.

LMX assumes that the leader establishes high LMX relationships with a limited number of subordinates, referred to as the *in group*. The in-group subordinates presumably are more likely to receive inside and advance information from the leader, learn of forthcoming developments before others, and receive more rewards than other subordinates. In contrast, *out-group* subordinates are less likely to receive these. They are also more likely to be assigned less desirable tasks and have leader–subordinate relationships based on formal authority interactions.

LMX also assumes that the leader essentially categorizes each subordinate as an *in* or *out* member early in their relationship and it usually remains that way over time.

Figure 11.1 captures the results in an LMX process for a leader with nine subordinates. Unlike a number of other leadership models, LMX suggests that the leader does not have one major style of leadership or varies the style based on situation factors. Rather, high- or low-quality LMX is based on the specific relationships with the subordinates. This is coupled with the assumption that the leader does not likely have the time or inclination to have high-quality LMX relationships with all of his or her subordinates.

Insights for Leaders

The level of LMX has a significant relationship to subordinates' satisfaction with their manager. Thus, subordinates with a low-quality level of LMX are more likely to become dissatisfied, less motivated, and more prone to quit.[10] The employees who perceive a low-quality level of LMX and see themselves as members of the *out group*, but are competent performers, are not being effectively led. Managers who want to be good leaders must guard against this possibility. In Chapter 9, "Interpersonal Communication in Organizations," we emphasized that true leaders strive to achieve effective dialogue, assertive communication, appropriate communication openness, and constructive feedback with all of their subordinates, not just an *in group* of subordinates within the unit. Further, it is difficult and perhaps impossible to develop a *team-oriented* environment if a leader fosters relationships with subordinates based on behaviors that emphasize an *in group* and *out group*.[11]

Several studies suggest that leader–member relationships develop quickly. Leaders and subordinates need to take this possibility into account when they interact early on as these initial relationships may too strongly affect the development of low- or high-quality LMX.[12] In our view, a leader who has the most power relative to subordinates also has the most responsibility to avoid processes such as stereotyping and the like in relation to each subordinate (see Chapter 4). These perceptual errors often occur prior to or during early interactions with others.

The diversity competency requires that these and other biases be minimized and, to the extent possible, eliminated. There is some evidence that certain leaders tend to select in-group members, in part, because they have similar personal attributes—race, ethnicity, gender, and so on (see our discussion of "Diversity and Ethics" in Chapter 2).[13] Also, leaders need to guard against selecting in-group members based substantially on the political skills of one or more of these subordinates (see our discussion of "Power and Political Behavior" in Chapter 10).[14]

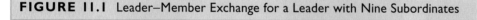

FIGURE 11.1 Leader–Member Exchange for a Leader with Nine Subordinates

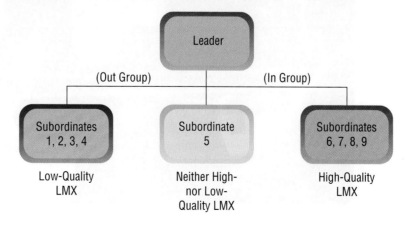

Authentic Leadership

Authentic leadership *refers to individuals who (1) know and understand themselves, (2) know what they believe and value, and (3) act on their values and beliefs through open and honest communications with subordinates and others.*[15] As a result of these attributes, subordinates are more willing to trust and follow the authentic leader. These leaders can be directive or participative. The person's leadership style is not what distinguishes inauthentic leaders from authentic leaders. Authentic leaders build credibility and win the respect of followers by encouraging and respecting diverse viewpoints. They seek to foster collaborative and trusting relationships with followers, customers, shareholders, and other stakeholders.

These leaders convey a genuine desire to serve rather than primarily control others through their leadership. These leaders strive to find ways to empower employees in the pursuit of making a difference. Authentic leaders recognize and value individual differences in goals and competencies. They also have the ability and desire to identify the underlying talents of subordinates and to help build them into workable strengths and competencies.

Core Components

Authentic leadership includes the interrelated components discussed next and shown in Figure 11.2.[16]

Stimulates Follower Identification

Authentic leaders influence followers' attitudes and behaviors, which, in turn, positively affects their self-esteem. These leaders are able to determine their followers' strengths and develop them. Authentic leaders help followers link their strengths to a common purpose or mission. This is accomplished through leading by example and setting high moral standards of honesty and integrity. They are open, positive, and highly ethical. There is an orientation toward doing "what is right and fair" for the leader and followers. Authentic leaders identify with their followers by being up front, openly discussing their own and followers' limitations while constantly nurturing the growth of followers. They have a clear sense of how their roles require them to act responsibly, ethically, and in the best interests of others. Through their high moral values, honesty, and integrity, followers' social identification with the work

An authentic leader wins the respect of followers by encouraging and respecting diverse viewpoints and in general by fostering collaborative relationships.

FIGURE 11.2 Interrelated Core Components of Authentic Leadership

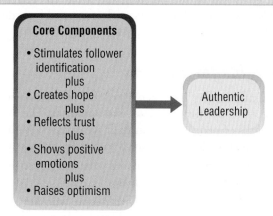

team, department, or organization is increased. Followers are able to connect and identify with the leader over time. The followers' self-concept and related self-control become identified with or tied to the purpose or mission of the organization.

Creates Hope

Authentic leaders create positive motivations for followers by fostering goal setting and helping them identify how to achieve their goals. The role of hope was discussed in Chapter 3. We noted that *hope* involves a person's willpower (determination) and waypower (road map) to achieve goals. Followers accept and become committed to the goals that can be achieved. Also, they believe that successful plans can be developed to achieve these goals. Authentic leaders are able to enhance followers' sense of hopefulness by (1) showing high levels of commitment, sharing, and openness; (2) communicating important information needed for them to reach their goals; and (3) encouraging questioning and open discussions.

Reflects Trust

Authentic leaders are more likely to be trusted by followers and others. They build trust by encouraging open two-way communications; sharing critical information, both good and bad; and revealing—in a constructive way—their perceptions and feelings, both good and bad, about the people with whom they work. Followers come to know what the leader values and stands for. In turn, the leader comes to know what the followers value and stand for.

Shows Positive Emotions

The positive emotions of authentic leaders broaden followers' thoughts on how to achieve goals and solve problems, discover novel ways for doing things, and foster creative thinking. They are more likely to stimulate positive feelings among followers and a sense of identification with the purposes being championed.

Raises Optimism

Authentic leaders tend to be optimists and stimulate a sense of optimism among followers. Optimists persevere in the face of obstacles or difficulties, assess personal failures and setbacks as temporary, and exhibit high levels of work motivation, performance, and job satisfaction. Optimism includes the assumption that individuals can do something to change situations for the better. Pessimism includes the assumption that probably nothing individuals do will

Self Insight

For me, being an authentic leader begins with knowing yourself, your values, and what motivates you and understanding what you enjoy doing. At a higher level, being an authentic leader means understanding the gifts you've been given.

Paula R. Autry, President and Chief Operating Officer, Mount Carmel East Hospital (Columbus, Ohio)

make much of a difference. Optimists want to take action, which increases the likelihood that goals will be set, pursued, and achieved. That's how optimism may create a self-fulfilling outcome. Optimists are less stressed by ordinary ups and downs. They tend to see bad situations as temporary and specific—as something they can address.

Insights for Leaders

Authentic leaders influence followers' attitudes and behaviors through identification, hope, trust, positive emotions, and optimism. The focus is on the positive attributes and strengths of people—not on their weaknesses. Authentic leadership focuses on understanding enough about yourself to be able to make confident statements such as these:

- I know what I'm good at and what I'm not so good at. I will build on my strengths and shore up my weaknesses.

- I will surround myself with people who are good, really good, at what I neither have the time for or the ability to do myself. I will build a truly diversified team who can get the job done, who can achieve the focus.

- When I mess up, I will fess up. I will forgive myself and move on. I will do the same with other committed team players. I recognize that when I trip up and fall, it's because I am moving, and that without movement there can be no progress.

- I will be myself at all times. I will not wear a mask.

The leader is, in part, a "servant" to followers. The leader is called on to engage employees' hearts and minds in a purpose greater than any of them.[17] Authentic does not mean being "soft." Tough assignments, accountability, and high standards of performance are part of being an authentic leader.

Authentic leadership advocates assert that it will, over the long run, result in superior organizational performance. Although this may prove to be the case, data supporting this claim are limited. Moreover, many factors and forces are likely to influence the leadership process. Some of these include organizational power and politics, organizational structure, and organizational culture. Top executives may be able to shape and influence many of these factors. However, that may not be as feasible for first- and middle-level managers who must work at developing their own authentic leadership style if their top-level executives do not exhibit or model this kind of leadership.

The following Self Competency feature is primarily an adaption of the perspectives of Bill George on lessons for leading in a crisis.[18] Bill George is professor of management practices at the Harvard Business School and former chairman and CEO of Medtronics. He serves as a director of several corporate boards and is a trustee and board member of several major charitable and civic organizations. He has been named one of the "Top 25 Business Leaders of the Past 25 Years" by the Public Broadcasting Company, named "Executive of the Year" by the Academy of Management, and has been the recipient of other major recognitions. George is the author or coauthor of a number of articles and books on authentic leadership, such as *True North: Discovering Your Authentic Leadership*.[19] Finally, he is a principal in the Authentic Leader Institute (http://authleadership.com) at the Harvard Business School.[20]

Self competency

Lessons for Leading in a Crisis

Bill George comments that virtually every American institution is facing major crises these days, from declining business to evaporating financial portfolios. To get out of these crises, authentic leaders must step forward and lead their organizations through them. According to

George, it's obvious that many of the people who have been in charge for the past 10 years haven't really led. Inauthentic leaders (Thain, Fuld, Madoff, auto execs, etc.) have gotten us into this mess. He feels it's going to take authentic leaders to get us out. Here are several lessons from George and others for leaders charged with leading their organizations through a crisis:

Lesson 1: "Leaders must face reality." Reality starts with the person in charge. Leaders need to look at themselves in the mirror and recognize their role in creating the problems. Then they should gather their teams together and gain agreement about the root causes. Widespread recognition of reality is a crucial step that must be taken before problems can be solved. Attempting to find short-term fixes that address the symptoms of the crisis only ensures that the organization will wind up back in the same predicament. To understand the real reasons for the crisis, everyone on the leadership team must be willing to tell the whole truth.

Lesson 2: "No matter how bad things are, they will get worse." Faced with bad news, many leaders cannot believe that things could really be so grim. Consequently, they try to convince the bearers of bad news that things aren't so bad and that swift action can make problems go away. This causes leaders to undershoot the mark in terms of corrective actions. As a consequence, they wind up taking a series of steps, none of which is powerful enough to correct the downward spiral. It is far better for leaders to anticipate the worst and get out in front of it. If they restructure their cost base for the worst case, they can get their organization healthy for the turnaround when it comes and take advantage of opportunities that present themselves.

Lesson 3: "Get the world off your shoulders." In a crisis, many leaders act like Atlas, carrying the weight of the world on their shoulders. They go into isolation, and think they can solve the problems themselves. In reality, leaders must have the help of all their people to devise solutions and to implement them. This means bringing people into their confidence, asking them for help and ideas, and gaining their commitment to painful corrective actions.

Lesson 4: "Before asking others to sacrifice, first volunteer yourself." If there are sacrifices to be made—and there will be—then the leaders should step up and make the greatest sacrifices themselves. Crises are the real tests of leaders. Everyone is watching to see what the leaders do. Will they stay true to their values? Will they bow to external pressures, or confront the crisis in a straightforward manner? Will they be seduced by short-term rewards, or will they make near-term sacrifices in order to fix the long-term situation?

Lesson 5: "Fear doesn't create leadership." At best, fear is the other side of the coin from arrogance. None of us fully know how things will turn out in the next few years. However, doing what everyone else is doing won't be your finest moment. As Warren Buffett said about his experience of the herd mentality, "When everyone is greedy, I am fearful. When everyone is fearful, I get greedy."

To learn more about authentic leadership, go to **http://authleadership.com**.

Transformational Leadership

Transformational leadership *involves anticipating future trends, inspiring followers to understand and embrace a new vision of possibilities, developing others to be leaders or better leaders, and building the organization or group into a community of challenged and rewarded learners.*[21] Transformational leadership may be found at all levels of the organization: teams, departments, divisions, and the organization as a whole. *Visionary, inspiring, daring,* and *ethical* are words that describe transformational leaders. They are assertive risk takers who seize or create new opportunities. They are also thoughtful thinkers who understand the interactions of technology, culture, stakeholders, and external environmental forces.

As suggested in Figure 11.3, transformational leadership is challenging to implement. As you will see, there are some similarities between transformational and authentic leadership.

4. Explain the essentials of transformational leadership.

FIGURE 11.3 Interrelated Core Components of Transformational Leadership

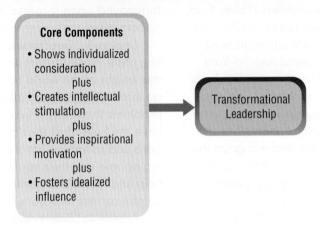

Core Components

The interrelated core components of transformational leadership include individualized consideration, intellectual stimulation, inspirational motivation, and idealized influence.[22]

Shows Individualized Consideration

Individualized consideration *is the degree to which the leader attends to followers' needs, acts as a mentor or coach, and listens to followers' concerns.* In particular, transformational leaders provide special attention to each follower's needs for achievement and growth. Followers and colleagues are encouraged to develop to successively higher levels of their potential. Individual differences are embraced and rewarded to enhance creativity and innovation. An open dialogue with followers is encouraged and "leadership by continuous engagement" is standard practice. Listening skills are sharp and reflect this observation: It's not what you tell them, it's what they hear.

Transformational leaders empower followers to make decisions. At the same time, they monitor followers to determine whether they need additional support or direction and to assess progress. With trust in leaders' intentions, followers think, "This person is trying to help me by noting mistakes, as opposed to pointing a finger at me in some accusatory way." Moreover, trust is important when leading change because change itself requires risk taking. As we have noted in a number of places, a foundation for trust is built on consistency between a person's words and actions. Individuals are often willing to take considerable risks for their leader if she practices what she preaches.

A few of the possible performance criteria that higher level leaders and others might use to assess a manager's leadership effectiveness in relation to the *shows individualized consideration* component appear below. A 10-point rating scale is used (1 = poor to 10 = outstanding).[23]

_____ 1. Communicates in open, candid, clear, complete, and consistent manner—invites response/dissent.

_____ 2. Listens effectively and probes for new ideas.

_____ 3. Delegates whole task; empowers team to maximize effectiveness. Is personally a team player.

_____ 4. Fully utilizes diversity of team members (cultural, race, gender, other) to achieve organizational success.

Creates Intellectual Stimulation

Intellectual stimulation *is the degree to which the leader challenges assumptions, takes risks, and solicits followers' ideas.* Transformational leaders encourage followers to "think out of the box" by being innovative and creative. They urge followers to question assumptions, explore new ideas and methods, and approach old situations with new perspectives. In addition, such leaders actively seek new ideas and creative solutions from followers. Followers' ideas aren't criticized just because they may differ from those of the leader. Leaders have a relatively high tolerance for mistakes made by followers, who aren't publicly criticized for those errors. Transformational leaders focus on the "what" in problems rather than "who" to blame for them. Followers feel free to encourage leaders to reevaluate their own perspectives and assumptions.

Transformational leaders are willing to abandon practices that are no longer useful even if they developed them in the first place. Nothing is too good, fixed, political, or bureaucratic that it can't be changed or discontinued. As demonstrated by John Thompson in the opening feature, they have the ability to live in the moment, and appreciate the past but not be burdened by it, which is extremely important. The prevailing view of transformational leaders is that it is better to question ourselves than to leave all of the questioning about us to our competitors. They view risk taking as necessary and desirable for the long-term development and success of the organization. In brief, they promote creativity, rationality, and thoughtful problem solving from multiple points of view.

A few of the possible performance criteria that might be used to assess a manager's leadership effectiveness in relation to the *creates intellectual stimulation* component appear below. A 10-point rating scale is used (1 = poor to 10 = outstanding).

_____ 1. Possesses and readily shares functional/technical knowledge and expertise. Constant interest in learning.

_____ 2. Trusts others; encourages responsible and thoughtful risk-taking behavior.

_____ 3. Encourages everyone to be heard. Open to ideas from anywhere.

_____ 4. Creates real and positive change. Sees change as an opportunity.

Provides Inspirational Motivation

Inspirational motivation *is the degree to which the leader articulates a vision that appeals to followers.* Of course, the transformational leader requires more than a vision to foster change. A **vision** *expresses fundamental aspirations and purpose, usually by appealing to peoples' emotions and minds.* The leader needs the competencies to translate abstract and intangible concepts of a broad vision into understandable and concrete goals with which followers can associate and identify required actions.

Transformational leaders guide followers by providing them with a sense of meaning and challenge. Leaders, such as Anne Mulcahy at Xerox and John Thompson at Symantec, get followers involved in and eventually committed to a vision of a future that may be significantly different from the present. They inspire others by what they say and do. These leaders appeal to followers' sense of pride, self-esteem, and other intrinsic motivators. The framing and inspirational promotion of a consistent vision and set of values is the foundation of transformational leadership.

A few of the possible performance criteria that might be used to assess a manager's leadership effectiveness in relation to the *provides inspirational motivation* component appear below. A 10-point rating scale is used (1 = poor to 10 = outstanding).

_____ 1. Has developed and communicated a clear, simple, customer-focused vision/direction for the unit.

_____ 2. Is forward thinking. Stretches horizons. Challenges imaginations.

_____ 3. Inspires and energizes others to commit to vision. Captures minds. Leads by example.

_____ 4. Inspires and demonstrates a passion for excellence in every aspect of work.

Fosters Idealized Influence

Idealized influence is the degree to which the leader behaves in charismatic ways that cause followers to identify with him or her. **Charisma** *involves motivating and directing followers by developing in them a strong emotional commitment to a vision and set of shared values.* Transformational leaders, such as Indra Nooyi at PepsiCo and Jim Sinegal at Costco, demonstrate the behaviors that followers strive to mirror. Followers typically admire, respect, and trust such leaders. They identify with these leaders as people, as well as with the vision and values that they are advocating. Positive idealized influence allows followers to feel free to question what is being advocated. The goals of followers are often personally meaningful and consistent with their self-concepts. They willingly give extra effort because of the intrinsic rewards obtained from performing well, not just because of the potential for receiving greater monetary and other extrinsic rewards. Immediate short-term goals are viewed as part of the commitment to reaching a greater vision.

To further earn such idealized influence, transformational leaders often consider the needs and interests of followers over their own needs. They may willingly sacrifice personal gain for the sake of others. Transformational leaders can be trusted and demonstrate high standards of ethical and moral conduct. Followers come to see such leaders as operating according to a pattern of open communication. Thus, they can be very direct and challenging to some followers (e.g., poor performers) and highly empathetic and supportive of others (e.g., those with a seriously ill family member).

Although transformational leaders minimize the use of power for personal gain, they will use all of the sources of power—expert, legitimate, reward, referent, and coercive—at their disposal to move individuals and teams toward a vision and its related goals.

A few of the possible performance criteria that might be used to assess a manager's leadership effectiveness in relation to the *provides idealized influence* component appear below. A 10-point rating scale is used (1 = poor to 10 = outstanding).

_____ 1. Maintains unequivocal commitment to honesty/truth in every facet of behavior.

_____ 2. Follows through on commitments; assumes responsibility for own mistakes.

_____ 3. Fair and compassionate, yet willing to make difficult decisions.

_____ 4. Values and promotes full utilization of global and workforce diversity.

Across Cultures Insight

If you fail to honor your people, they will fail to honor you. It is said of a good leader that when the work is done, the aim fulfilled, the people will say, "We did this ourselves."

Lao Tzu, 604–531 B.C., Founder of Taoism, Tao Te Ching

Insights for Leaders

Our presentation on transformational leadership included a variety of insights for leaders. Thus, we will not repeat them here, but will instead note that, faced with increasing turbulence in their environments, organizations need transformational leadership more than ever—and at all levels, not just at the top. The need for managers of vision, confidence, and determination, whether they are leading a small team or an entire organization, is increasing rapidly. Such leaders are needed to motivate others to assert themselves, to join enthusiastically in team efforts, and to have positive feelings about what they're doing. Top leaders must come to understand, appreciate, and support as never before employees who are willing to make unpopular decisions, who know when to reject traditional ways of doing something, and who can accept reasonable risks. A "right to fail" must be nurtured and be an integral part of an organization's culture. This leadership is vital to the most difficult, complex, and vague organizational threats, opportunities, and weaknesses.

Transformational leadership fosters synergy. **Synergy** *occurs when people together create new alternatives and solutions that are better than their individual efforts.* The greatest chance for achieving synergy is when people don't see things the same way; that is, differences present opportunities. Relationships don't break down because of differences but because people fail to grasp the value of their differences and how to take advantage of them. Synergy is created by people who have learned to think win–win, and who listen in order to understand the other person.

When higher management forms teams with members who are diverse, it is especially important to try to select qualified team leaders who exhibit transformational leadership behaviors. If the selected team leader is somewhat lacking in transformational leadership capabilities, a good investment is to develop such capabilities.[24] This might occur through mentoring and having the person attend leadership development programs offered within the organization or by other organizations such as the Center for Creative Leadership and a number of universities.[25] In our opinion, these programs need to be at least two weeks in length, but not necessarily at one time. A variety of other influences of transformational leadership on individual, group, and organizational outcomes and effectiveness have been found in research studies. They provide additional insights for leaders.[26]

The following Ethics Competency feature highlights Ruben Vardanian, the CEO of Russia's Troika Dialog and a transformational leader.[27] He led an *ethical turnaround* of the firm when he became the CEO and has solidified his role as a key figure in Russia's capital markets. Among many awards and recognitions, he was named "Businessperson of the Year" by the American Chamber of Commerce in Russia, which included recognition for his "commitment to highest standards of business ethics." Also, he was recently awarded "Best Reputation on the Financial Market" by *Finance* magazine.[28] Troika Dialog is one of Russia's largest brokerages and asset management firms with about $5.5 billion in assets. In describing itself, Troika Dialog states: "We pioneered independent research and reporting into corporate governance standards in Russia. We play a leading part in all the key elements of the securities market and regulatory infrastructure. Our philosophy is that by helping guide the markets to global standards, we build the credibility of the market, and ultimately benefit many times over relative to pursuing shorter-term objectives. We also take pride in helping to build Russia as an economic and financial leadership globally." Outside parties concur with this description.[29]

Ethics competency

Ruben Vardanian, CEO of Russia's Troika Dialog

This discussion of Ruben Vardanian is *keyed to* the four core components of transformational leadership.

Individualized consideration. Vardanian is a strong believer in professional development, starting with his own, taking the role of leadership seriously and reading extensively on the

topic. He believes that part of his leadership role is to instill consistent values throughout the organization. He has created a strong culture by communicating directly and frequently with employees at all levels, sharing information, and leading by example. Vardanian is accessible in his office and is described by colleagues as a

JAMIE RECTOR/BLOOMBERG NEWS/LANDOV

Ruben Vardanian, CEO of Russia's Troika Dialog.

loving father, caring older brother, and spiritual leader. While valuing employee development, he realizes that the organization cannot tolerate resistance to change.

Intellectual stimulation. Demonstrating his understanding of the Russian environment and its restrictive effects on employees and potential employees, Vardanian states: "Every day you need to prove what you say. I think worthless slogans—like some in the old Communist system—are a big problem. As soon as you start doing things differently from what you claim to believe, you destroy everything. So each day I try to show people we're in the same boat, that I'm not a big boss who has a separate life."

He recognizes the need to provide a safe and supportive environment for employees if he expects them to be creative and courageous. Vardanian emphasizes that when you try to be fair, you need to be sustainable and provide long-term confidence that people can operate in the environment and achieve results. He doesn't

want people to be scared, and doesn't want them to lose everything because they didn't realize that the rules of the game had changed overnight.

Inspirational motivation. Vardanian feels Russian business needs to be more ethical. He states: "As for ethics, people joke about it and compare Russia with America a hundred years ago. Many oligarchs (wealthy and powerful people) used this as an excuse for their questionable behavior."

In the longer term, he looks beyond business to other forms of social responsibilities, focusing on charity: "We have to develop a charity industry as we have developed a financial industry here in Russia. That's what I really want to do." And even in discussing his personal circumstances, Vardanian's vision of improving Russian society is not forgotten: "Having good kids is the most important thing for me—but contributing to the development of a strong and stable Russian economy is an almost equal passion."

Idealized influence. One of the key elements in fostering idealized influence is creating a sense of trust by others in the transformational leader. Consider Vardanian's comments and behaviors about creating such trust: Vardanian comments: "In our business, traders can work only by telephone, which means there is no legal contract and no guarantee. With securities, the trader simply says: I sold for you and I bought for you, and the deal is done. My word is my bond. This was one of the first rules I learned when I went to learn about successful investment banking services."

Further emphasizing the crucial importance of trust as well as the potential for Russians to exhibit trustful behavior, he explains: "I wanted to show that we could make money without being crooks." He adopted practices to support this sense of trust. For example, Troika Dialog uses international auditors because of Vardanian's insistence on transparency and high standards of corporate governance. He explains that these ethical standards are not only important for Troika Dialog, but for Russia as a whole.

To learn more about Troika Dialog, go to **www.troikadialog.com**.

Global Leadership and Organizational Behavior Effectiveness

Learning Goal

5. *Explain the core features of Global Leadership and Organizational Behavior Effectiveness.*

Global Leadership and Organizational Behavior Effectiveness (GLOBE) *examines the interrelationships between societal culture, organizational culture, and organizational leadership.* Approximately 170 social scientists and management scholars from 62 cultures/countries representing all major regions throughout the world are engaged in a long-term study of cross-cultural leadership.[30] The 62 "societal cultures" are grouped into 10 societal clusters. Four of these clusters and some of the countries in each cluster are as follows: Anglo (Australia, Canada, United States), Arabic (Egypt, Morocco, Kuwait), Germanic (Austria, Germany, Switzerland), and Southern Asian (India, Indonesia, Malaysia).

GLOBE draws on data from more than 17,000 managers in almost 1,000 organizations in 62 societies. It addresses leadership qualities within those cultural clusters, and makes recommendations on how managers should conduct business in cultural clusters other than their own. Given the massive research efforts to develop GLOBE, it is only possible to provide illustrative highlights of this project here. For comprehensive discussions of the many facets, findings, and recommendations with respect to GLOBE, the interested reader should see the references cited.[31]

Let's begin with a few definitions in GLOBE:

- **Organizational leadership**—*the ability of an individual to influence, motivate, and enable others to contribute toward the effectiveness and success of the organizations of which they are members.*

- **Societal culture**—*shared motives, values, beliefs, identities, and interpretations or meanings of significant events that result from common experiences of members of collectives and are transmitted across generations.*

The GLOBE model addresses leadership qualities within cultural clusters and makes recommendations on how managers should conduct business in cultural clusters other than their own.

Core Components

According to GLOBE, individuals have implicit beliefs, convictions, and assumptions about the attributes and behaviors that distinguish certain leaders from others—for example, effective leaders from ineffective ones, and moral leaders from evil ones. Implicit leadership models influence the importance that individuals place on selected leader behaviors and attributes.

Dimensions of Culture

In our discussion of culture in Chapter 3, we used a framework of culture based on five value orientations: individualism/collectivism, power distance, uncertainty avoidance, gender role orientation, and long-term orientation. Also, recall our discussion of McClelland's learned needs motivation model in Chapter 6. It too is based on culture, including the need for power, need for affiliation, and need for achievement. GLOBE's cultural dimensions have been adapted and expanded from these two models. As presented in Table 11.2, GLOBE includes nine cultural dimensions. The meaning of each dimension is presented in this table.

A significant aspect of GLOBE's nine cultural dimensions is that each one is defined in two ways: *practices* (or "as is") and *values* (or "should be"). *Practices* reflect the respondents' day-to-day realities. *Values* reflect their aspirations and ideals. The

---

TABLE 11.2 Cultural Dimensions of the GLOBE Model

CULTURAL DIMENSION DEFINITION

1. Assertiveness	• The degree to which individuals are bold, forceful, dominant, confrontational, or demanding in relationships with others.
2. Collectivism–group	• The degree to which individuals express and show pride, loyalty, and cohesiveness to their organizations or families.
3. Collectivism–societal	• The degree to which organizational and societal institutional (such as government) practices encourage and reward collective (joint) distribution of resources (such as under socialism) and collective action.
4. Future orientation	• The degree to which a society encourages and rewards behaviors such as planning, investing in the future, and delaying gratification.
5. Gender egalitarianism	• The degree to which a society minimizes differential treatment between men and women, such as through equal opportunity based on ability and performance.
6. Humane orientation	• The degree to which a society or organization encourages and rewards individuals for being fair, altruistic, generous, caring, and kind to others.
7. Performance orientation	• The degree to which a society encourages and rewards group members for performance improvement, excellence, high standards, and innovation.
8. Power distance	• The degree to which members of a society accept and endorse the equal (lower power distance) or unequal (higher power distance) distribution of authority, control, and status privileges (such as a class structure).
9. Uncertainty avoidance	• The degree to which a society, organization, or group relies on social norms, formal rules, and formal procedures to alleviate the unpredictability of future events.

Source: Based on House, R. J., Hanges, P. J., Javidan, M., Dorfman, P., and Gupta, V. (Eds.). *Culture, Leadership, and Organizations: The GLOBE Study of 62 Societies.* Thousand Oaks, CA: Sage, 2004.

17,370 managers were asked about both practices and values. Their answers led to some intriguing findings. The values score ("should be") in most cases was noticeably different from the practices score ("as is"). The values score was often higher than the practices score. For example, managers worldwide valued gender egalitarianism more than they said they were experiencing it in practice.

Another surprising finding emerged. A high value score was often associated with a low practice score on a cultural dimension. This is contrary to conventional wisdom that people behave in a certain way because they hold certain values in high esteem. However, if employees "in practice" experience a low degree of something perceived as good, its absence may lead them to value ("should be") it all the more. But if employees in practice have a high degree of something perceived as good, the value they put on it doesn't need to be high.[32]

When it came to examining the societal culture dimensions in relation to the leadership dimensions, the GLOBE researchers thoughtfully concluded:

> *When individuals think about effective leader behaviors, they are more influenced by the value ("should be") they place on the desired future than their perception of current realities ("as is"). Our results, therefore, suggest that leaders are seen as the society's instruments for change. They are seen as the embodiment of the ideal state of affairs.*
>
> *In general, cultural dimension values, not practices, are related to the cultural leadership dimensions. Both values and leadership dimensions represent desired end states; values reflect culture; the other leadership attributes.*[33]

Impacts of Culture on Leadership

GLOBE, more than the others we have reviewed, emphasizes the central role of societal culture through its values and beliefs in understanding what leadership styles and practices will be seen by subordinates as effective and desirable. A few of the GLOBE findings on the relationships between culture and leadership follow: (1) Societal cultural values and practices affect what leaders do. (2) Societal cultural values and practices affect organizational culture and practices. (3) Organizational culture and practices also affect what leaders do. (4) A leader's acceptance by followers is influenced by the interaction of cultural and organizational factors in relation to the leader's attributes and behaviors. (5) A leader's effectiveness is influenced by the interaction of the leader's attributes and behaviors in relation to organizational and cultural factors.

GLOBE Leadership Dimensions

GLOBE has six dimensions of leadership. To obtain a personal sense of your leadership style, complete the GLOBE questionnaire that appears in the Experiential Exercise and Case section at the end of this chapter (page 342).

The six global leadership dimensions and their basic definitions are as follows:

- *Charismatic/value based*—visionary, inspirational, decisive, has integrity.
- *Team oriented*—collaborative, diplomatic, considerate.
- *Self-protective*—self-centered, status conscious, face-saver.
- *Participative*—democratic, delegator, values group needs.
- *Human oriented*—modest, helps others, displays empathy to others.
- *Autonomous*—individualistic, independent, unique.

Leadership across Cultures

There is no question that one of the most important facets of a global leader's job is to effectively influence people from other parts of the world. Effective leadership requires the ability to listen, to frame the message in a way that is understandable to the receiver, and to accept and use feedback. Effective global leadership involves finding solutions in a way that allow decisions to be implemented by members of diverse cultures. Although this may sound simple, it can be quite complicated.

The U.S. respondents in the GLOBE study reported very high performance-oriented values. To a typical American manager, effective leadership means direct and explicit directions. Facts and figures are important. Effective leaders focus their attention and thinking on rational means of solving problems. To these leaders, leadership means delivering the results. People from cultures with lower performance-oriented values, such as Russia or Greece, are not comfortable with strong results-oriented leaders. In these cultures, facts and figures are often hard to come by and are not taken seriously when they are available. Therefore, to a Greek employee, effective leaders do not necessarily rely on facts and figures. Their approach to discussions and explorations of issues tend to be without any clear commitment to explicit results.

Employees from countries with lower assertive values, such as Sweden and the Netherlands, say they prefer leaders to use two-way communication. They want to participate in decisions that will impact them. Employees want leaders who not only deliver results, but improve the interpersonal relations between them.

In cultures with higher gender-differentiated values, such as South Korea and Japan, employees expect effective leaders to use different language for males and females. For females, the leadership style is more paternalistic and one way and most of the time it is initiated by the leader. In Denmark, Sweden, and other countries with gender-egalitarian values, women are offended if they are patronized or in any way treated differently from men.

Effective leadership was also found to differ by power distance values in a culture. In countries like Russia or Thailand with high power distance values, effective leadership is mostly one way, top to bottom (Theory X or transactional). The effective leader is expected to know more than his employees. Input or feedback from subordinates is seldom asked for and, in fact, may be seen as impolite and disloyal.

A culture's uncertainty avoidance values also influence leaders' behaviors. In countries with high levels of uncertainty avoidance values, such as Switzerland and Austria, the leader's message needs to be clear and explicit and based on facts. The leader needs to be very clear on what needs to be done and the rules to follow to get things done. Meetings are planned in advance with a clear agenda, highly structured, and formal. Leaders are not likely to use a participative style of leadership. In countries with lower uncertainty avoidance values, like Russia or Greece, people are not used to highly structured procedures. Effective leaders, therefore, are not expected to announce agendas in advance, and meetings can last for hours without any clear decision being made.

In cultures with strong collectivist values, the leader is expected to stress group harmony and cohesion. An effective leader's influence is soft and indirect. Conflict is to be avoided. Both charismatic/valued-based leaders and team-oriented leaders are usually found in such societies. Therefore, the effective leader tends to use indirect language to influence employees and wants employees to enter into discussions about issues facing them.

Finally, in countries like the Philippines and Malaysia, which are high on the humane-oriented values, the effective leader is seen as being caring and paternalistic. The leader's influence is focused on being supportive rather than leading others based on facts. The process is more important than the result because it helps build group cohesiveness. On the other hand, in countries like France or Spain, which are lower on the humane-oriented values, people do not expect their leaders to be highly supportive or caring. Generosity is not important. Employees want their leader to give them clear, simple directions.

Insights for Leaders

Our insights represent just a snapshot of the many findings with respect to leadership behaviors across cultures from GLOBE. One implication of GLOBE is that leadership is in the eye of the beholder. That is, *leader* is a term applied by observers (think of them as followers, at least potentially) to someone whose behaviors and characteristics match the observers' implicit leadership preferences.[34]

The GLOBE researchers set out to demonstrate that possessing an implicit leadership model is true of groups as well as individuals. The researchers' main contention was that each societal culture is associated with a specific set of beliefs by followers about leadership. Put another way, the researchers wanted to show that societal and organizational culture influence the kind of leadership found to be outstanding by people within that culture—and that is what they found.

But this isn't the only finding about leadership that the research team hoped to demonstrate. They expected that any individual's implicit leadership model would include beliefs about unacceptable and ineffective leadership as well as beliefs about acceptable and effective leadership. So another question was "Are both the positive and the negative attributes of leadership shared by the members of a cultural cluster?" They confirmed that it was. The GLOBE team identified which leadership attributes are positive, negative, and different across cultural clusters. A few of the findings with insights for leaders for 4 of the 10 societal clusters are as follows:

- *Anglo cluster* (Australia, Canada, England, Ireland, New Zealand, South Africa [white sample], and United States): The outstanding leader demonstrates charismatic influence and inspiration while encouraging participation. Outstanding leaders are viewed as being diplomatic, delegating authority, and allowing everyone to have their say.

- *Arabic cluster* (Egypt, Morocco, Turkey, Kuwait, and Qatar): Outstanding leaders need to balance a paradoxical set of expectations. On one hand, they are expected to be charismatic and powerful, but on the other, they are expected not to differentiate themselves from others and to have modest styles. Leaders are also expected to have a great deal of power and control and to direct most decisions and actions.

- *Germanic cluster* (Austria, Germany, the Netherlands, and Switzerland): The outstanding leader is one who is charismatic, highly team oriented, and participative.

- *Southern Asian cluster* (India, Indonesia, Iran, Malaysia, the Philippines, and Thailand): The outstanding leader is humane, participative, and charismatic. Leaders are expected to be benevolent while maintaining a strong position of authority.

The following Across Cultures Competency feature provides insights and emerging themes related to culture and leadership in Mexico that are primarily based on GLOBE.[35]

Across Cultures competency

Culture and Leadership in Mexico

A corollary of the high assertiveness (tough and dominating) and high power distance of traditional Mexican culture is that individuals with little formal power have had very little influence and involvement in determining organizational policies and practices. This was shown in the GLOBE data where *participative leadership* approaches in Mexico were ranked 59th out of 62 GLOBE countries in importance. Historically, participative leadership has generally had little impact on followers' attitudes and performance in Mexico.

The traditional view of participation, however, may be changing. In several industrial centers, including the urban border areas shared with the United States, there is an increased interest in participative management approaches. This corresponds with the increasing number of joint ventures and *maquiladora* operations in Mexico, where popular international management styles are being tried with some apparent success. The participative approach in Mexico differs from approaches that are popular in the United States and Europe. With the participative approach in Mexico, leaders make decisions and develop strategies and then discuss these with followers who will eventually carry them out. In Mexico, there may be an active give and take between leaders and followers regarding how decisions and strategies made by the leaders are implemented. These discussions may jump from one issue to another, but the skillful leader can apparently manage multiple discussions at one time. The key point of these discussions is that all individuals who are involved have an opportunity to provide input related to the implementation of strategies and decisions made by leaders.

Leaders in Mexico who obtain follower input on how to implement decisions represent a significant change from the autocratic leadership practices that have been traditionally followed in Mexico. The increasing popularity of a participative approach is suggested by the GLOBE culture data, which show that Mexicans believe there should be much less emphasis on power distance in their society. The changing portrait of Mexican society and organizations is likely to include more participative leadership of some type in the future. However, these changes are evolving and were hardly universal among the 13 top-level leaders from Monterey, Mexico, who participated in a recent study through in-depth interviews. The research found that the leaders studied (from industry, health care, education, and government) were more like managers who rely on transactional leadership approaches and directive decision-making styles. Part of the need for the transactional approach is based on the paternalistic ideal that exists in Mexican business culture and is very much aligned with the cultural expectations between leaders and followers. That being said, the leaders in Mexico also have very traditional beliefs about women in leadership roles. They want the rationalization of cultural norms to advance their ideals as evidenced by comments made about the nature of women's roles. They emphasized the notion that motherhood was preeminent and that maternity was similar to a disability.

The increasing importance of collective/team efforts inside Mexican organizations is indicated by the high score for *team-oriented leadership* in the GLOBE data. Team-oriented leadership is rated the highest of the leadership factors that contribute to outstanding leadership in Mexico. This leadership includes being diplomatic, collaborative, integrative, and administratively competent.

GLOBE respondents from Mexico also expressed a strong desire for more *performance orientation* and *future orientation* in their institutions and organizations. This probably reflects the many changes occurring in Mexican society as Mexico becomes an increasingly important member of the international business community. Mexicans increasingly recognize the importance of planning and performance in order to compete successfully in international markets.

To learn more about Mexico's culture, go to **http://en.wikipedia.org/wiki/culture_of_Mexico.**

Chapter Summary

1. *Explain the characteristics of transactional leadership.*

Transactional leadership calls for managers to influence followers primarily through contingent reward-based exchanges. They attempt to identify clear goals for followers, the specific paths for achieving the goals, and the rewards that will be forthcoming for achieving them. A follower's performance is monitored and corrective actions are taken if there are deviations from the expected path. The emphasis is on exchanging units of work for units of rewards (salary, bonuses, size of office, etc.).

Leader–member exchange (LMX) suggests that leaders develop different relationships with each of their subordinates through a series of work-related exchanges. Over time, one group of subordinates is said to have a low-quality LMX with their leader and another group a high-quality LMX. The time dimension is said to be represented over three phases: stranger, acquaintance, and mature partnership. The latter phase develops for those who establish high-quality LMX. The degree of LMX quality may be assessed in terms of dimensions such as mutual affection, loyalty, contribution to work activities, and professional respect.

2. Describe the core elements of leader–member exchange.

Authentic leadership involves influencing followers' attitudes and behaviors through the core interrelated processes of stimulating follower identification, creating hope, reflecting trust, showing positive emotions, and raising optimism. Individuals who are authentic leaders know and understand themselves, know what they believe and value, and act on their values and beliefs through open and honest communications with subordinates and others. They are highly ethical.

3. Discuss the attributes of authentic leadership.

Transformational leadership involves influencing followers through a complex and interrelated set of behaviors and abilities. Individuals who are transformational leaders anticipate the future, inspire relevant stakeholders (especially followers) to embrace a new vision or set of ideas, develop followers to be leaders or better leaders, and guide the organization or group into a community of challenged and rewarded learners. It extends and incorporates features of authentic leadership. The core interrelated components of transformational leadership that primarily relate to followers include showing individualized consideration, creating intellectual stimulation, providing inspirational motivation, and fostering idealized influence. Transformational leaders are both challenging and empathetic—and they are people of integrity.

4. Explain the essentials of transformational leadership.

GLOBE examines the interrelationships between societal culture, organizational culture, and organizational leadership. We provided a snapshot of the concepts and findings with respect to the interrelationships between the nine cultural dimensions and six global leadership dimensions in GLOBE. It provides many insights on why and how individual leaders need to cope with and adjust to cross-cultural issues when leading organizations.

5. Explain the core features of Global Leadership and Organizational Behavior Effectiveness.

Key Terms and Concepts

Authentic leadership, **326**
Charisma, **332**
Global Leadership and Organizational Behavior
    Effectiveness (GLOBE), **335**
Idealized influence, **332**
Individualized consideration, **330**
Inspirational motivation, **331**
Intellectual stimulation, **331**

Leader–member exchange (LMX), **323**
Organizational leadership, **335**
Societal culture, **335**
Synergy, **333**
Transactional leadership, **320**
Transformational leadership, **329**
Vision, **331**

Discussion Questions

1. In the Learning from Experience feature, John Thompson is reported as emphasizing that leaders need personal integrity and a relentless focus on people. Also, he says leaders need to take time to rest and reflect. Go to Symantec's website at www.symantec.com. Click the "About Symantec" tab, go to the "Careers" drop-down menu, and find "Working at Symantec." Does the presentation in this section reflect or fail to reflect Thompson's perspectives? Explain.

2. Review the Change Competency feature titled "Mark Hurd, CEO, Hewlett-Packard." Do the perspectives in this feature support or work against achieving the diversity competency or are they irrelevant to it? Explain.

3. In what three ways did a manager you have worked for use transactional leadership?
4. Based on the manager identified in Question 3, in what ways did that person exhibit or fail to exhibit each of the components of leader–member exchange (LMX)? Did you have a *high* or *low* LMX with that manager? Explain. If you have not done so, it will be helpful to complete the instrument in Table 11.1.
5. Review the Self Competency titled "Lessons for Leading in a Crisis." For each lesson presented, does the lesson reflect one or more of the core components of authentic leadership? Explain.
6. Assume that you have just taken a job with a professional services firm. What insights provided in this chapter can help you be an effective "follower" in this situation?
7. Think of a person that you know who comes closest to exhibiting transformational leadership. Describe at least one behavior of this person that is consistent with each of the components of transformational leadership.
8. Review the nine cultural dimensions of GLOBE (see Table 11.2). How would you describe your societal culture as you understand it with respect to each of these dimensions? In what ways do you think your experiences with leaders reflect this cultural profile?

Experiential Exercise and Case

Experiential Exercise: Self Competency

GLOBE Leader Behaviors Instrument[36]

Introduction

The GLOBE leader behaviors instrument presented here represents an adapted and much shortened version of the leadership instruments used in the GLOBE project. This adapted instrument is for instructional purposes only. It is designed to give you a more personal understanding of each of the six global leadership dimensions and a profile of what you think represents an outstanding leader.

Instructions

You are probably aware of people who are exceptionally skilled at motivating, influencing, or enabling you, others, or groups to contribute to the success of an organization or task. We might call such people "outstanding leaders." This instrument presents behaviors and characteristics that can be used to describe these leaders. Each behavior or characteristic is accompanied by a short definition to clarify its meaning. Using the description of outstanding leaders as a guide, rate the behaviors and characteristics on this instrument. On the line next to each behavior or characteristic, write the number from the scale below that best describes how important that behavior or characteristic is to you for a leader to be considered as outstanding.

Scale

1 = This behavior or characteristic *greatly inhibits* a person from being an outstanding leader.
2 = This behavior or characteristic *somewhat inhibits* a person from being an outstanding leader.
3 = This behavior or characteristic *slightly inhibits* a person from being an outstanding leader.
4 = This behavior or characteristic *has no impact* on whether a person is an outstanding leader.
5 = This behavior or characteristic *contributes slightly* to a person being an outstanding leader.

6 = This behavior or characteristic *contributes somewhat* to a person being an outstanding leader.
7 = This behavior or characteristic *contributes greatly* to a person being an outstanding leader.

	Behavior or Characteristic	Definition
_____ 1.	Diplomatic	Skilled at interpersonal relations, tactful
_____ 2.	Evasive	Refrains from making negative comments to maintain good relationships and save face
_____ 3.	Listener	Seeks inputs from subordinates in an authentic way
_____ 4.	Intragroup competitor	Tries to exceed the performance of others in his or her group
_____ 5.	Autonomous	Acts independently, does not rely on others
_____ 6.	Independent	Does not rely on others; self-governing
_____ 7.	Improvement oriented	Seeks continuous performance improvement
_____ 8.	Inspirational	Inspires emotions, beliefs, values, and behaviors of others, inspires others to be motivated to work hard
_____ 9.	Anticipatory	Anticipates, attempts to forecast events, considers what will happen in the future
_____ 10.	Trustworthy	Deserves trust, can be believed and relied on to keep his or her word

_____ 11. Worldly — Interested in temporal events; has a world outlook

_____ 12. Just — Acts according to what is right or fair

_____ 13. Win–win problem-solver — Able to identify solutions that satisfy individuals with diverse and conflicting interests

_____ 14. Self-interested — Pursues own best interests

_____ 15. Integrator — Integrates people or things into cohesive, working whole

_____ 16. Calm — Not easily distressed

_____ 17. Loyal — Stays with and supports friends even when they have substantial problems or difficulties

_____ 18. Unique — An unusual person; has characteristics of behaviors that are different from most others

_____ 19. Collaborative — Works jointly with others

_____ 20. Encouraging — Gives courage, confidence, or hope through reassuring and advising

_____ 21. Democratic — Makes decisions in a joint way

_____ 22. Secretive — Tends to conceal information from others

_____ 23. Asocial — Avoids people or groups; prefers own company

_____ 24. Generous — Willing to give time, money, resources, and help to others

_____ 25. Formal — Acts in accordance with rules, convention, and ceremonies

_____ 26. Modest — Does not boast; presents self in a humble manner

_____ 27. Consultative — Consults with others before making plans or taking action

_____ 28. Loner — Works and acts separately from others

_____ 29. Compassionate — Has empathy for others; inclined to be helpful or show mercy

_____ 30. Intellectually stimulating — Encourages others to think and use their minds; challenges beliefs, stereotypes, and attitudes of others

_____ 31. Balanced orientation — Places appropriate value on both individual and group needs

_____ 32. Egalitarian — Believes that individuals should have equal rights and privileges

_____ 33. General manager — An agile manager, one who does not insist on making all decisions

_____ 34. Delegator — Willing and able to relinquish close control of projects or tasks

_____ 35. Self-effacing — Presents self in a modest way

_____ 36. Patient — Has and shows patience

_____ 37. Individualistic — Behaves in a different manner than peers

Scoring

Sum the scores for each item shown within each global leadership dimension and divide by the number of items to obtain an average score on that dimension. These average scores reflect your model of what it means to be an outstanding leader.

- Charismatic/value based

____7; ____8; ____9; ____10; ____12; ____20; ____30 = Total _____ ÷ 7 = _____ = Average score on charismatic/value based

- Team oriented

____1; ____11; ____13; ____15; ____17; ____19; ____27 = Total _____ ÷ 7 = _____ = Average score on team oriented

- Self-protective

____2; ____4; ____14; ____22; ____23; ____25; ____28 = Total _____ ÷ 7 = _____ = Average score on self-protective

- Participative

____3; ____21; ____31; ____32; ____33; ____34 = Total _____ ÷ 6 = _____ = Average score on participative

- Humane oriented

____16; ____24; ____26; ____29; ____35; ____36 = Total _____ ÷ 6 = _____ = Average score on humane oriented

- Autonomous

____5; ____6; ____18; ____37 = Total _____ ÷ 4 = _____ = Average score on autonomous

Interpretation

The six average scores represent your model of what it means to be an outstanding leader. An average score that ranges from 1 to 3.5 suggests that you think the global leadership dimension inhibits, to varying degrees, the person from being an outstanding leader. An average score that ranges from 3.6 to 4.9 suggests that you think the leadership dimension has little to no impact on whether a person is an outstanding leader. An average score that ranges from 5 to 7 suggests that you think the leadership dimension slightly to greatly contributes to a person being an outstanding leader. In the GLOBE research, the charismatic/value-based leadership dimension emerged as the most strongly endorsed contributor, worldwide, to acceptable and effective leadership. Is your score on this leadership dimension consistent with this finding? The team-oriented leadership dimension is also endorsed worldwide as a strong contributor to outstanding leadership. Is your score on this leadership dimension consistent with this finding?

Case: Change Competency

Sir Richard Branson, Chairman, Virgin Group, Ltd.[37]

Sir Richard Branson, founder and chairman of the London-based Virgin Group Ltd., has turned a lifelong disdain for conventional business wisdom into a multibillion-dollar global conglomerate and one of the world's most recognizable brands. The Virgin Group has ventured into many lines of business such as retail stores, air travel, financial services, books and music, and telecommunication. The Virgin Group consists of approximately 200 companies that operate in numerous countries. Virgin has approximately 50,000 employees and more than $20 billion in annual sales.

Some have suggested that Branson and the Virgin brand attract almost a cult following, and it works both ways—many people admire Branson, but some detest him. Many find it refreshing that Branson is willing to candidly reveal setbacks in his business career. Branson reflects: "Virgin has gotten it right when we've taken on a Goliath and offered a much-better-quality product at good value. We've gotten it wrong when we've taken on a giant with a product or service where we can't differentiate." Three of the significant setbacks, among others, that he discusses openly are:

- Virgin tried launching a portable MP3 player (the Virgin Pulse). It was a total disaster—they were crushed by the Apple iPod. It was a $20 million write-off.
- Branson ignored his top management's advice and insisted on holding onto the Virgin MegaStore retail outlets for too long. When he finally agreed to sell them, they lost the Virgin Group a "lot of money."
- Branson tried to take on the Coca-Cola company with Virgin Cola. Coca-Cola sent a SWAT team to the United Kingdom to systematically destroy Virgin Cola. Coca-Cola succeeded. Again, big losses for Virgin. Virgin Cola is "still the number one cola drink in Bangladesh!"

One aspect of Branson's philosophy is centered on finding the best people to run the diverse businesses in the Virgin Group. He is not as much concerned about industry-specific expertise as he is with recruiting employees with strong communication and teamwork competencies that mesh with the Virgin culture. Branson states, "What makes somebody good is how good they are at dealing with people. If you can find people who are good at motivating others and getting the best out of people, they are the ones you want. There are plenty of so-called experts, but not as many great motivators of people." Virgin tends to promote from within. The desired profile, not surprisingly, is someone like Branson—someone who gets charged up when told that something cannot be done; someone who is unafraid of industry barriers and will not take no for an answer.

Many executives devote their attention primarily to serving customers and shareholders. Branson thinks that the correct pecking order is employees first, customers next, and then shareholders last. His logic is this: If your employees are happy, they will do a better job. If they do a better job, the customers will be happy, and thus business will be good and the shareholders will be rewarded.

Branson is frequently on the road to visit Virgin businesses, talking with employees and customers. He is known for his ever-present notebook and pen, which he pulls out whenever he chats with employees and customers. Branson insists that this is a crucial element in his role as chairman. By writing things down, he creates a regular list of items for immediate action. He reads e-mail from employees every morning before he does anything else. This habit, which he started in Virgin's early days, influences company–employee dynamics. Employees do not hesitate to air their grievances directly to him. Branson has proved with his actions that he actively listens. Although Virgin has about 50,000 employees around the world, he gets only about 50 e-mails or letters each day from nonmanagerial employees. They vary from small ideas to frustrations with middle management to significant proposals. He addresses every one by answering personally or by initiating some action. Branson states, "Instead of needing a union when they have a problem, they come to me. I will give the employee the benefit of the doubt on most occasions."

For Branson, retaining the standards he has instilled as the company grows is his major task. He states, "You've got to treat people as human beings—even more so as the company gets bigger. The moment I start to think 'I've made lots of money, I'm comfortable. I don't need to bother with these things anymore,' that's when Virgin will be at risk."

David Rooke, a managing consultant at Harthill Consultants, states: "Branson is the consummate people's man. He is not a smooth operator that people may feel inclined to distrust, but a genuine strategist, who thinks outside the box, who achieves, and given some of his crazier pastimes, someone who manifestly enjoys life." In an article entitled *Integrity to What Matters Most*, three leadership experts make this comment, among others, about Branson: "Steadfast integrity to his unique sense of personal meaning has always been one of Branson's values."

In a recent visionary commitment, Branson pledged as much as $3 billion during the next 10 years (through 2017) to tackle global warming. The money is an estimate of his anticipated personal profits from his airlines and rail company, so the amount is not precise. But anything close would be a dramatic investment in a cleaner environment through developing new and cleaner sources of energy. Branson states: "We must not be the generation responsible for irreversibly damaging the environment."

Branson has other ideas on leadership:

Ultimately, the entrepreneur will only succeed if he or she has good people around them and they listen to their advice. My colleagues know me as Dr. Yes because I always find it hard to say "No" to new ideas and proposals. I rely on them to guide me but ultimately, I'm also prepared to trust my intuition, as long as I feel it is well informed. It is impossible to run a business without taking risks. Virgin would not be the company it is today if risks had not been taken.

I think one of the reasons for our success is the core values which Virgin aspires to. This includes those that the general public thinks we should aspire to, like providing quality service. However, we also promise value for money, and we try to do things in an innovative way, in areas where consumers are often ripped-off, or not getting the most for their money. I believe we should do what we do with a sense of fun and without taking ourselves too seriously, too! If Virgin stands for anything, it should be for not being afraid to try out new ideas in new areas.

Whenever I experience any kind of setbacks, I always pick myself up and try again. I prepare myself to have another stab at things with the knowledge I've gained from the previous failure. My mother always taught me never to look back in regret, but to move on to the next thing. The amount of time that people waste on failures, rather than putting that energy into another project, always amazes me. I have fun running the Virgin businesses, so a setback is never a bad experience, just a learning curve. Loyalty means a lot to me. Working with people I know and trust makes me feel secure. I guess that's why I prefer to promote from within. People who join Virgin know that there are plenty of opportunities to progress in their careers.

Questions

1. What specific statements in this case appear to reflect individualized consideration, a core component of transformational leadership, by Branson?

2. What specific statements in this case appear to reflect intellectual stimulation by Branson?

3. What specific statements in this case appear to reflect inspirational motivation by Branson?

4. What specific statements in this case appear to reflect idealized influence by Branson?

5. Would you like to work for one of the Virgin Group companies? Explain.

chapter 12

Developing and Leading Teams

Learning Goals

After studying the chapter, you should be able to:

1
State the basic features of groups and teams.

2
Explain the stages of team development.

3
Describe the attributes of common types of work-related teams.

4
Describe the core influences on team effectiveness.

5
Explain five of the potential dysfunctions of teams.

Learning Content

Learning from Experience
Boeing's Development of Teams and Their Leaders

Introduction to Groups and Teams

Teams Competency
Empowered Teams at W. L. Gore & Associates

Stages of Team Development

Types of Work-Related Teams

Across Cultures Competency
Alcoa's Global Virtual Teams

Core Influences on Team Effectiveness

Ethics Competency
Sanjiv Das's Leadership at CitiMortgage

Diversity Competency
Angela Braly, CEO and President, WellPoint, Inc.

Potential Team Dysfunctions

Experiential Exercise and Case

Experiential Exercise: Teams Competency
Team Assessment Inventory

Case: Teams Competency
Absence of Teamwork

Boeing's Development of Teams and Their Leaders

Boeing is a major aerospace company and manufacturer of commercial jetliners and military aircraft. Headquartered in Chicago, Boeing employs more than 160,000 people in the United States and 70 other countries. In Chapter 2, we featured James McNerney, the CEO of Boeing, in a Change Competency feature.

Consider this brief scenario. Minutes before his plane went down over the glaciers of southeast Alaska, the captain was poking fun at his new first officer. He was streaking toward Ketchikan, eager to land before his favorite snack bar closed. The first officer warned that the plane was flying too high and too fast, but the captain brushed him off. "What's the difference between a duck and a first officer?" the engineer chimed in. "The duck can fly." That wisecrack silenced the first officer. The silence was deadly. The plane crashed, killing 1 passenger and injuring 34.

"That's an example of how creating an environment of fear and distrust can prevent you from assessing information," explains Phil Polizatto, an instructional media designer for Boeing. Polizatto's job is not to train pilots to fly Boeing's planes. It's to train team leaders to build planes more effectively. His course is the most dramatic in a series of offerings designed for team leaders at Boeing. In Polizatto's developmental course, he uses disastrous cockpit conversations, among other techniques, to teach team leaders how to communicate. "Just as a flight crew is dependent on the captain's behavior, the work of a team is dependent on its leader's behavior," says Polizatto. His course at Boeing is always full.

Boeing also has an intranet site devoted to teamwork. It offers a wealth of instructional materials and diagnostic tools for team leaders and others. The site provides learning that is "just in time, just for me," says Chuck Welter, an organization development specialist at the company. The intranet site focuses on the most sensitive realities of life in teams. If a person is disrupting a meeting, for example, the site offers a menu of options. It also offers hands-on advice about learning from mistakes. It encourages leaders to call a meeting to discuss the following questions: What did we expect to happen? What actually happened? How did we respond?

Boeing also conducts a two-day workshop aimed at the whole team, not just the leader. "The original intent was to train people to lead in new ways," says Mary Jo Svendsen of Boeing's Center for Leadership and Learning. "But we

LARRY W. SMITH/GETTY IMAGES

To learn more about Boeing, go to www.boeing.com.

found that people learn best when they're in the environment they work in every day. So, we required leaders to bring their teams."

The workshop uses a series of leading questions to explore a team's vision and division of responsibilities. If you were an investor in your team's vision, would there be enough hope, energy, and intent to get your attention? If your team left Boeing and formed your own business, how would you determine roles and make decisions? What analogies would you use to describe how your team operates?[1]

The Learning from Experience feature illustrates three important points about teams: (1) Boeing's top leadership recognizes that individual performance by committed and competent individuals is crucial, (2) Boeing's employees need to work together as a team on complex projects to achieve goals, and (3) team leaders make a difference in the functioning of teams.

In this chapter, we primarily focus on one of the seven core competencies introduced in Chapter 1. Recall that the *teams competency* includes the knowledge, skills, and abilities to develop, support, and lead groups to achieve goals. Throughout the chapter, we discuss ways to understand and increase the effectiveness of groups and teams. We focus on (1) the basic features of groups and teams, (2) the ways in which team members develop and learn, (3) the types of teams commonly used in organizations, (4) the principal factors that influence team effectiveness, and (5) the potential dysfunctions of teams if not effectively developed, used, and led.

Introduction to Groups and Teams

Learning Goal

1. State the basic features of groups and teams.

For our purposes, a **group** *is any number of people who share goals, often communicate with one another over a period of time, and are few enough so that each individual may communicate with all the others, person to person.*[2]

Classifications of Groups

Most individuals belong to various types of groups, which can be classified in many ways. For example, a person concerned with obtaining membership in a group or gaining acceptance as a group member might classify groups as open or closed to new members. A person evaluating groups in an organization according to their primary goals might classify them as friendship groups or task groups. A **friendship group** *evolves informally to meet its members' personal security, esteem, and belonging needs.* A friendship group may form over time among some or many coworkers. In addition, friendship groups are now being fostered electronically. MySpace, Facebook, Twitter, Blogger, YouTube, and instant messaging are all electronic ways that are used to form and foster friendship groups. A **task group** *is created by management to accomplish certain organizational goals.* Of course, a single group in the workplace may serve both friendship and task purposes.

The primary focus of this chapter is on types of task groups, commonly known today as teams, such as the Stuffed Tailcone Team that works on Boeing's C-17 plane. The tailcone of the C-17 is located at the aft (rear) of the airplane and houses (is "stuffed" with) numerous components.

Informal Group

An **informal group** *is one that develops out of the day-to-day activities, interactions, and sentiments that the members have for each other.* Informal groups typically satisfy their members' security and social needs. Informal groups can provide their members with desirable benefits (e.g., security and protection). An informal group can also provide positive feedback to other members.

At work, informal groups may oppose senior management and organizational goals, reinforce and support such goals, or simply be unrelated to the organizational goals. The organization often has considerable influence on the development of informal groups through the physical layout of work, the leadership practices of managers, and the types of technology used.[3] For example, when the Smeal College of Business at Pennsylvania State University opened its new building, over time the design of the building affected the development of informal groups. The open atrium and food services in the new building fostered the development of more and different informal groups among faculty, staff, and students.

The physical distance between members may make face-to-face communication difficult and cause groups to disband or re-form themselves. In contrast, a new manager taking over a department and telling its employees to "shape up or ship out" may cause an informal group to form, with its members uniting against the manager.

Some managers believe that close-knit informal groups have undesirable effects on an organization. They view groups as a potential source of antiestablishment power, as a way of holding back information when the group doesn't identify with organizational goals, or as a means of pressuring individuals to slow production. For instance, an informal group might set production limits for their members, fearing that management might use an outstanding worker as a standard for output and that increased production might lead to some workers being laid off. The all-too-common belief that higher productivity will work against the interests of workers is kept alive and enforced by some informal groups within organizations.[4]

Informal groups can also exercise undesirable power over individual members. Such power usually falls into two categories. First, a group may be able to use rewards and punishments to pressure members to conform to its standards. Second, a group may restrict the ways by which social needs can be satisfied on the job. Informal groups have been known to ridicule certain members or give them the silent treatment for not conforming to group standards of "acceptable" behavior. This treatment may threaten the individual's safety, social, and esteem needs.

Informal groups in organizations can't be classified simply as positive or negative. They may exhibit both characteristics from time to time, depending on the circumstances or issues facing the organization.[5] Therefore, leaders should try to minimize the undesirable effects of informal groups rather than try to eliminate them.[6]

Team

A **team** *is a small number of employees with complementary competencies who are committed to common performance goals and working relationships for which they hold themselves mutually accountable.*[7] The heart of any team is a shared commitment by its members for their joint performance. Team goals could be as basic as responding to all customers' calls within 24 hours or as involved as reducing defects by 20 percent during the next year. The key point is that such goals can't be achieved without coordination, cooperation, and communication among team members.

When a team is formed, its members must have (or quickly develop) the right mix of competencies to achieve the team's goals. Also, its members need to be able to influence how they will work together to accomplish those goals. Boeing's C-17 Stuffed Tailcone Team recently set forth a set of goals, three of which included (1) employee satisfaction with having a safe work environment as measured by a yearly employee survey and other metrics, (2) a 10 percent increase in quality, and (3) a two-day reduction in the time required to complete tailcone tasks.[8]

Effective Teams

Leaders must know how to recognize effective and ineffective teams. An effective team or group has the following core characteristics. Its members

- know why it exists and have the shared goals of getting things done (task-oriented behaviors) and building constructive interpersonal ties and processes (relations-oriented behaviors),

- support agreed-on guidelines or procedures for making decisions,

- communicate openly and have achieved trust among themselves,

- receive help from one another and give help to one another,

- deal with conflict openly and constructively,

- diagnose its own processes and improve their own functioning, and

- experience a sense of freedom to be themselves while feeling a sense of belonging with others.[9]

The degree to which a team lacks one or more of these characteristics determines whether—and to what extent—it is ineffective. These basic characteristics apply to all teams. Recall the commitment by Boeing in the Learning from Experience feature to develop teams and their leaders. With the complex tasks, technologies, and diverse competencies that need to be brought together to meet stringent requirements for safety and reliability with each of an airplane's components, effective teams are a must at Boeing.

Team Empowerment

All types of teams and groups need the degree of empowerment that will help them achieve their goals. Accordingly, **team empowerment** *refers to the degree to which its members perceive the group as (1) being competent and able to accomplish work-related tasks (potency), (2) performing important and valuable tasks (meaningfulness), (3) having choice (autonomy) in how they carry out their tasks, and (4) experiencing a sense of importance and significance (impact) in the work performed and goals achieved.*[10] You may relate the key dimensions of empowerment—*potency, meaningfulness, autonomy,* and *impact*—to your own experience by responding to the brief questionnaire in Table 12.1. To obtain your team empowerment score, follow the directions in the table.

Our discussion of Boeing's development of teams and their leaders, such as the C-17 Stuffed Tailcone Team, recognizes that teams need the appropriate level of empowerment to function effectively and achieve their goals. The following Teams Competency feature reports on the use of highly empowered teams at W. L. Gore & Associates.[11] Perhaps best known for its consumer products like GORE-TEX fabric and Elixir guitar strings, Gore is a leading manufacturer of thousands of advanced technology products for the electronics, industrial, fabrics, and medical markets. The company is headquartered in Newark, Delaware, and employs approximately 8,000 associates at 45 facilities throughout the world in the Asia Pacific, Australia, Europe, North America, and South America. It is a privately held company with annual sales of approximately $2 billion. Gore has received many awards for its innovativeness. It is one of the few companies to appear on all of the U.S. "100 Best Companies to Work For" lists and to do so over a number of years.[12] We do not suggest that the Gore approach can be made to fit the context of all organizations. However, it does provide a dramatic example of a firm that is organized and led through the use of highly empowered teams.

TABLE 12.1   Team Empowerment Questionnaire

Instructions: Think of a team that you are (or have been) a member of in a work setting. Respond to each statement below by indicating the degree to which you agree or disagree with it in terms of the team identified. The scale is as follows:

1	2	3	4	5
Strongly Disagree	Disagree	Undecided/ Neutral	Agree	Strongly Agree

Place the appropriate number value next to each item.

Potency Items

_____ 1.   The team has confidence in itself.
_____ 2.   The team believes that it can be very good at producing high-quality work.
_____ 3.   The team expects to be seen by others as high performing.
_____ 4.   The team is confident that it can solve its own problems.
_____ 5.   The team views no job as too tough.

Meaningfulness Items

_____ 6.   The team cares about what it does.
_____ 7.   The team thinks that its work is valuable.
_____ 8.   The team views its group goals as important.
_____ 9.   The team believes that its projects are significant.
_____ 10.   The team considers its group tasks to be worthwhile.

Autonomy Items

_____ 11.   The team can select different ways to do its work.
_____ 12.   The team determines how things are done.
_____ 13.   The team has a lot of choice in what it does without being told by management.
_____ 14.   The team has significant influence in setting its goals.
_____ 15.   The team can rotate tasks and assignments among team members.

Impact Items

_____ 16.   The team assesses the extent to which it makes progress on projects.
_____ 17.   The team has a positive impact on other employees.
_____ 18.   The team has a positive impact on customers.
_____ 19.   The team accomplishes its goals.
_____ 20.   The team makes a difference in the organization.

Total: Add points for items 1 through 20: _____. This total is your perceived team empowerment score. Scores may range from 20 to 100. Scores of 20 through 45 suggest low team empowerment. Scores of 46 through 74 indicate moderate levels of team empowerment. Scores of 75 through 100 reveal a state of significant to very high team empowerment.

Source: Adapted from Kirkman, B. L., and Rosen, B. Beyond self-management: Antecedents and consequences of team empowerment. *Academy of Management Journal,* 1999, 42, 58–74; Kirkman, B. L., and Rosen, B. Powering up teams. *Organizational Dynamics,* Winter 2000, 48–65.

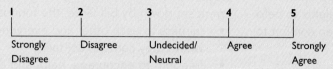

Teams competency

Empowered Teams at W. L. Gore & Associates

When new associates start at Gore, they receive a first-day induction much as they would at any company. This introduction is followed up with a three-day workshop known as "Building on the Best," which takes them through 15 modules about the team culture at Gore. Associates are each assigned a "sponsor" when they join the company to help them identify "quick wins" and create their own network. The new associates are chosen to work in general areas, not specific jobs. Their sponsors (not bosses) help them identify opportunities to use their talents to help meet team goals, and associates then commit to projects that match their skills.

Teams "adopt" associates and associates can seek out new sponsors if they wish, but the general sense is one of feeling part of a huge corporate family. This is helped by the fact that facilities are not generally allowed to grow to more than 200 people.

Gore is based on a "lattice structure," which revolves around personal relationships and trust. Each person interacts with other people directly, and associates volunteer themselves for jobs. Teams have heavy input into recruiting new associates and deciding other associates' contribution to the organization. Some associates earn the title of leader. They are selected by other members of their team rather than someone senior to them. All associates are responsible to their teams, rather than a boss.

Gore's team-based culture provides associates with considerable freedom and in return expects them to work cooperatively. To be successful and remain with Gore, associates are required to embrace four guiding principles that were set down by Bill Gore, the founder:

- fairness to each other and everyone with whom they come in contact;
- freedom to encourage, help, and allow other associates to grow in knowledge, skill, and scope of responsibility;
- the ability to make one's own commitments and keep them; and
- consultation with other associates before undertaking actions that could impact the reputation of the company.

Anne Gillies, a human resource leader at Gore, notes that this organization does not suit everyone. She comments: "We know pretty quickly if it's not working. And the individual knows it too. We tend to either lose people in the first 18 months or keep them for a long time. Bringing on new associates who have held senior positions in other businesses can be especially difficult at times."

To learn more about W. L. Gore & Associates, go to **www.gore.com.**

When to Use Teams

Different types of goals, problems, and tasks confronting an organization require varying degrees of coordination and cooperation among individuals and teams.[13] Some require both individual and team problem solving. Organizations can incur excessive costs if either individual or team decision making is used improperly. The unnecessary use of teams is wasteful because the employees' time could have been used more effectively on other tasks; it creates boredom, resulting in a feeling that time is being wasted, and reduces motivation. Conversely, the improper use of individual problem solving can result in poor coordination, little creativity, and numerous errors. In brief, the use of teams is likely to be superior to individual problem solving when

- the greater diversity of information, experience, and approaches to be found in a team is accessed to perform the important tasks and achieve the goals at hand;
- acceptance of the decisions arrived at is crucial for effective implementation by team members;
- participation is important for reinforcing the values of representation versus authoritarianism and demonstrating respect for individual members through team processes; and
- team members rely on each other in performing their jobs.

Stages of Team Development

Learning Goal

2. Explain the stages of team development.

Social scientists have developed many different models to explain how teams develop.[14] Because many of these models overlap, we present only one of them, as outlined in Figure 12.1. The vertical axis indicates that work teams develop on a *continuum of maturity*, which ranges from low, or immature (e.g., inefficient and ineffective) to high, or mature (e.g., efficient and effective). The horizontal axis represents a *continuum of time together*, which ranges from start (e.g., the first team encounter) to end (e.g., the point at which the team adjourns).

No particular period of time is needed for a team to progress from one stage to the next. For example, a team whose members have effective interpersonal skills and high initial commitment to the team's goals could move rapidly to the performing stage. In contrast, an informal group may never make much progress and quickly disband voluntarily if its members aren't satisfied with it. A work team may be discontinued in a variety of ways. It may simply stop cooperating and communicating and continue to exist only on paper. It may communicate rarely and only engage in routine tasks. Its membership may change (e.g., adding, losing, or changing members), weakening its purpose or commitment. It may be terminated officially by the leader who created it. In general, however, the speed of team development seems to reflect the team's deadlines. Work teams develop slowly at first. As deadlines approach, team members feel more pressure to perform and often respond by resolving or setting aside personal differences in order to complete the task.

FIGURE 12.1 Stages of Team Development

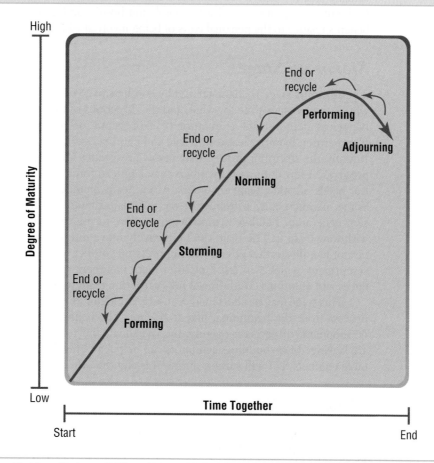

Source: Adapted and modified from Tuckman, B. W., and Jensen, M. A. C. Stages of small-group development revisited. *Group and Organization Studies*, 2, 1977, 419–422; and Tuckman, B. W. Developmental sequence in small groups. *Psychological Bulletin*, 63, 1965, 384–389.

Figure 12.1 also shows the possibility of a team ending at each stage or recycling to a previous stage. For example, a mature work team could lose the majority of its members in a short period of time to promotions, retirements, and/or rotation of membership. With so many new members, the team may recycle to an earlier stage of development. The stages identified represent general tendencies, and teams may develop by going through repeated cycles rather than linearly, as shown. Each stage simply reveals the *primary* issues facing team members. Behaviors from other stages may occur at times within each stage.

Pinpointing the developmental stage of a team at any specific time is difficult. Nevertheless, leaders and team members need to understand these developmental stages because each can influence a team's effectiveness. In the following discussion, we describe behaviors that might occur at each stage. As suggested, a team or group does not necessarily develop in the straightforward manner depicted in this model. Team members with high levels of the seven core competencies presented throughout this book are likely to speed up and alter the stages of development presented here. As you read about each stage, does it reflect your experiences in becoming a member of a new group or team?

Forming Stage

In the forming stage, team members often focus on defining goals and developing procedures for performing their jobs. Team development in this stage involves getting acquainted and understanding leadership and other member roles. In terms of interpersonal behaviors, it should also deal with members' feelings and the tendency of most members to depend too much on one or two of the team's members. Otherwise, individual members might (1) keep feelings to themselves until they know the situation; (2) act more secure than they actually feel; (3) experience confusion and uncertainty about what is expected of them; (4) be nice and polite, or at least certainly not hostile; and (5) try to size up the personal benefits relative to the personal costs of being involved with the team or group.

Storming Stage

The storming stage is characterized by conflicts over work, relative priorities of goals, who is to be responsible for what, and the directions of the team leader. Interpersonal behaviors demonstrate a mixture of expressions of hostility and strong feelings. Competition over the leadership role and conflict over goals may dominate this stage. Initially, the storming process may involve resistance and impatience with the lack of progress. A few dominant members may begin to force an agenda without regard for the needs of other team members. A few team members may challenge the leader. Some members may withdraw or try to isolate themselves from the emotional tension generated. The key is to manage conflict during this stage, not to suppress it or withdraw from it. The team can't effectively move into the third stage if its members do not handle conflict effectively. Suppressing conflict will likely create bitterness and resentment, which will last long after team members attempt to express their differences and emotions. Withdrawal may cause the team to fail.

This stage may be shortened or mostly avoided if the members use a team-building process from the beginning, like at Boeing. The team-building process involves the development of decision-making, interpersonal, and technical capabilities when they are lacking. Team-building facilitators can help team members work through the inevitable conflicts that will surface during this and the other stages.

Norming Stage

In the norming stage, member behaviors evolve into a sharing of information, accepting of different options, and attempting to make decisions that may require compromise. During this stage, team members set informal rules by which the team will operate. For teams that become effective, interpersonal behaviors often focus on empathy, concern, and positive expressions of feelings that lead to a sense of cohesion. Cooperation and a sense of shared responsibility develop among members of effective teams. Thus, team members become increasingly positive about the team as a whole, the other members, and what the team is doing. At the beginning of the norming stage, the dominant view might be "We are in this together, like it or not. Let's make the most of it."

Rules of behavior develop that are widely shared and enforced by the members of the team. If the team gets to the end of this stage, most members may like their involvement a great deal. Sometimes, however, the team focuses too much on "*we-ness*," harmony, and conformity. When that happens, team members may avoid task-related conflicts that need to be resolved to achieve optimal performance. That failure to deal with conflict may, in turn, cause the quality and/or quantity of performance to slip.

Performing Stage

Some work teams never reach their full potential, regardless of how long they exist. Nevertheless, by the performing stage, members usually have come to trust and accept each other. To accomplish tasks, diversity of viewpoints (rather than we-ness) is supported and encouraged. Members are willing to risk presenting "wild" ideas without fear of being put down by the team. Listening carefully and giving accurate feedback to others can help focus team members on the team's tasks and reinforce a sense of clear and shared goals. Leadership within the team is flexible and may shift among members in terms of who is most capable of solving a particular problem. In terms of relations-oriented behaviors (discussed later in the chapter), the team accepts the reality of differences and disagreements and works on them cooperatively. The team tries to reach consensus on important issues and to avoid internal politics.[15]

Teams that diagnose and improve their own functioning are especially valued because they can adapt to changing circumstances. Important adaptive behaviors include handling unpredictable work situations, emergencies, and crises; managing interactions across team boundaries; handling work stress; solving problems creatively; and learning new technologies and procedures. Teams that make good use of the diversity on the team tend to be more able to adapt, and teams that are more adaptive tend to be more successful. In summary, high-performing teams reflect the core characteristics of effective teams presented previously.

Adjourning Stage

The termination of task-related behaviors and disengagement from interpersonal behaviors occur during the adjourning stage. A team created to investigate and report on a specific issue within six months has a well-defined point of adjournment. This stage isn't always planned and may be rather abrupt. However, a planned team conclusion often involves recognition for participation and achievement as well as an opportunity for members to say personal good-byes. Many work teams (e.g., the executive committee of an organization's board of directors) are ongoing. As members turn over, some recycling through earlier stages rather than adjournment may occur. Staggered terms of appointment can minimize the amount of recycling required.

Types of Work-Related Teams

There are many types of work-related teams. We consider six of the most common: functional teams, problem-solving teams, cross-functional teams, self-managed teams, virtual teams, and global teams. As shown in Figure 12.2, all of these types of teams may be found in a single organization. It is quite possible that you may work in all of these types of teams during your career.

Learning Goal

3. *Describe the attributes of common types of work-related teams.*

FIGURE 12.2 Common Types of Work-Related Teams

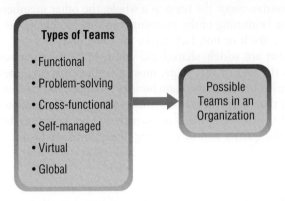

Functional Team

A **functional team** *usually includes employees who work together daily on similar tasks and must coordinate their efforts.* These teams often exist within functional departments: marketing, purchasing, production, engineering, finance, auditing, human resources, and the like. Within a human resource department, one or more functional teams could perform recruiting, compensation, benefits, safety, training and development, affirmative action, industrial relations, and similar functions.

Stoner, Inc., is headquartered in Quarryville, Pennsylvania, and has fewer than 100 employees. The firm manufactures more than 300 cleaning, lubrication, and coating products for other businesses. The firm has a leadership team and six functional teams. The functional teams include (1) inside sales; (2) manufacturing, warehousing, and purchasing; (3) technology; (4) outside sales; (5) marketing; and (6) accounting, logistics, and information technology. Stoner's functional teams are connected to the leadership team through representatives, but each has the authority to make a variety of decisions related to its functions. Stoner team members are both empowered and rewarded to fulfill the needs of customers and meet performance goals.[16]

Problem-Solving Team

A **problem-solving team** *is a team that has members who focus on a specific issue, develop a potential solution, and can often take action within defined limits.* These teams often address quality or cost problems. Members may be employees from a specific department who meet at least once or twice a week for an hour or two or members from several units. Such a team might even include representatives from outside the organization, such as suppliers and customers. Teams may be empowered to implement their own solutions if those solutions don't require major changes that might adversely affect other operations or require substantial new resources. Problem-solving teams do not fundamentally reorganize work or change the role of managers. In effect, managers delegate certain problems and decision-making responsibilities to a team.

Cross-Functional Team

A **cross-functional team** *is a team that has members drawn from various work areas whose goal is to identify and solve mutual problems.* Cross-functional teams draw members from several areas to deal with problems that cut across departmental and functional lines. Cross-functional teams may operate on an extended basis, or they may be disbanded after the problems addressed have been solved and their goals achieved.

Cross-functional teams are frequently used to foster innovation, speed, and a focus on responding to customer needs. They may design and introduce quality improvement programs and new technology, meet with customers and suppliers to improve inputs or outputs, and link separate functions (e.g., marketing, finance, manufacturing, and human resource) to increase product or service innovations.[17] Increasingly, such teams include members from outside the organization such as customer representatives, consultants, and suppliers.

The recent escalation of piracy in the Gulf of Aden and elsewhere has resulted in a number of shipping firms forming special crisis cross-functional teams. Their purposes are typically to (1) assess and develop new ways to prevent and cope with piracy that goes beyond paying ransom fees and (2) develop proposals for consideration by the maritime industry and governments as a whole.[18] Many of these teams include members from outside the shipping firm, such as a maritime lawyer from a law firm like Holman Fenwick that has piracy expertise, a member from a specialized insurance company like Hiscox Insurance Company, and a representative from Xe (formerly Blackwater Worldwide) that has security (military-like) expertise.[19]

Self-Managed Team

A **self-managed team** *refers to a team with highly interdependent members who work together effectively on a daily basis to manufacture an entire product (or major identifiable component) or provide an entire service to a set of customers.*[20]

Self-managed teams, sometimes called self-directed work teams, are often empowered to perform a variety of traditional managerial tasks, such as (1) scheduling work and vacations by members, (2) rotating tasks and assignments among members, (3) ordering materials, (4) deciding on team leadership (which can rotate among team members), (5) setting key team goals within overall organizational goals, (6) budgeting, (7) hiring replacements for departing team members, and (8) sometimes even evaluating one another's performance. Each member may even learn all tasks that have to be performed by the team.[21]

The impact of teams in general and self-managed teams, in particular, on efficiency and effectiveness may be considerable. In some cases, they have raised productivity and quality substantially.[22] The development of a team-based organization may fundamentally change how work is organized and leadership is practiced.[23] The introduction of self-managed teams may eliminate one or more managerial levels such as at Gore & Associates, thereby creating a flatter organization. Even if a managerial level is not eliminated, the role of management and supervision changes. Consider this typical pattern when self-managed teams are adopted in manufacturing settings: Traditional supervision is eliminated. The once-supervisor (if he or she still exists) serves in the same role as functional specialists such as process specialists or quality specialists. Supervisors (usually called something else such as team development coordinator) are often viewed as training coordinators. They manage a process to ensure that each team member is constantly learning new information and skills about the manufacturing process. Functional experts also serve as trainers providing hands-on training to team members. The team development coordinators often provide mentoring and coaching of individual team embers.[24]

Insights for Leaders

Self-managed teams aren't necessarily right for every situation or organization. Both costs and benefits accompany such a system. A number of questions need to be addressed in considering the introduction of self-managed teams, including the following:

1. Is the organization fully committed to aligning all management systems with empowered work teams, including selection of leaders, team-based rewards, and open access to information?

2. Are organizational goals and the expected results from the teams clearly specified?

3. Will the teams have access to the resources they need for high performance?

4. Will team members carry out tasks that require a high degree of coordination and communication?

5. Do employees have the necessary competencies to effectively carry out peer evaluations, selection and discipline decisions, conflict management, and other administrative tasks?[25]

Virtual Team

All teams may operate as virtual teams. A **virtual team** *refers to a team with members who collaborate through various information technologies on one or more tasks while geographically dispersed at two or more locations and who have minimal face-to-face interaction.*[26] Unlike teams that operate primarily in person-to-person settings with members of the same organization, virtual teams work primarily across distance (any place), across time (any time), and increasingly across organizational boundaries (members from two or more organizations). Accordingly, some of the potential benefits of virtual teams include these:

• Members can work anywhere and at anytime.

• Members can be recruited for their competencies, not just the physical location where they primarily work and live.

• Members with physical handicaps that limit travel can participate.

• Expenses associated with travel, lodging, and leasing or owning physical space may be reduced.

The core features of a virtual team are goals, technology links, and people. Goals are important to any team, but especially so to a virtual team. Clear, precise, and mutually agreed-on goals are the glue that holds a virtual team together. The need for a superior to do hiring and firing and reliance on rules and regulations are minimized in effective virtual teams.

Desktop videoconferencing systems re-create aspects of face-to-face interactions for virtual teams.

LEFT LANE PRODUCTIONS/CORBIS

As in all teams, people are at the core of effective virtual teams, but with some unique twists. Everyone in a virtual team needs to be self-reliant while simultaneously working collaboratively with others. This duality requires a certain type of person and a foundation of trust among team members. The most apparent feature of a virtual team is the array of technology-based links used to connect members and enable them to carry out the team's tasks. Virtual teams are often used by movie studios, book publishers, and consulting firms because of rapid advances in computer and telecommunications technologies.[27]

Technology Links

Three broad categories of technologies are often used in the operation of virtual teams: desktop videoconferencing systems, collaborative software systems, and Internet/intranet systems.[28] Virtual teams can function with only simple e-mail and telephone systems, including voice mail. However, *desktop videoconferencing systems* (DVCSs) re-create some of the aspects of face-to-face interactions of conventional teams. This technology makes possible more complex communication among team members. The DVCS is a relatively simple system for users to operate. A small camera mounted atop a computer monitor provides the video feed to the system; voice transmissions operate through an earpiece–microphone combination or speakerphone. Connection to other team members is managed through software on the user's computer.

With improvements in bandwidth-related technologies and reduced costs, videoconferencing systems—increasingly referred to as *telepresence systems*—are starting to provide another tool for creating more face-to-face–like meetings for all types of teams where the members are physically dispersed. The costs of these systems vary greatly. For example, Cisco has a low-cost system at $90,000 and a top-of-the-line system at $300,000. In addition, there is the cost of purchasing bandwidth.[29] Recently, the National Basketball Association (NBA) and ESPN used Cisco's TelePresence system during the NBA All-Star Game. One application allowed fans to interact "face to face" with NBA stars who were on the show floor while the fans were in a convention "green room" and backstage at the arena.[30]

Collaborative software systems (group support systems) comprise the second category of technologies that enable the use of virtual teams. Collaborative software is designed for both independent and interactive use. It helps people perform tasks and achieve individual and team goals.[31] For example, IBM Lotus Quickr, a major collaborative software product, is designed specifically for communication and data sharing in virtual teams. It combines numerous features, a few of which include scheduling (calendaring), e-mail (electronic messaging), discussion forums, blogs, and document and data sharing (including editing and queries).[32] IBM Lotus Quickr and other such systems are increasingly used to support teamwork in a traditional work environment. Of course, they are vital to the operation of empowered virtual teams. Instant Messaging (IM) is a virtual Post-it note. It is informal and interactive. IM, as well as text messaging, helps team members keep tabs on each other's availability.

> ## Change Insight
>
> In my mind, the 3-D virtual world is the future of the Internet. In the future, you don't need to be in the same room to look each other in the eye and understand the issues and collaborate on projects. Our researchers around the world are now having some meetings in *Second Life*—a full online virtual world.
>
> *Sophie Vandebroek, Innovation Chief, Xerox Corporation*

Internet and intranet technologies represent the third main enabler of virtual and often other types of teams. Intranets give organizations the advantage of using Internet technology to disseminate information and enhance interemployee communication while maintaining system security. They allow virtual teams to archive text, visual, audio, and numerical data in a user-friendly format. The Internet and intranets also allow virtual teams to keep other organizational members and important external stakeholders, such as suppliers and customers, up to date on a team's progress and even to participate in a team's deliberations.[33]

Insights for Leaders

A variety of insights for leaders have been offered for enhancing the *people* dimension of virtual teams.[34] We share seven of them here:

- Keep the team as small as possible, preferably no more than 12 people.

- Develop clear and specific goals in collaboration with the team members. Clear goals are absolutely critical for virtual teams whose members do not see or meet each other frequently. These goals serve as a unifying force.

- If the members will be working together for any length of time, it is important to bring the members together for an initial face-to-face session. This session could last one to three days depending on the scope and complexity of the team's responsibilities and goals. Members need to be given adequate time to get to know and understand one another. This initial session may include team-building activities. Work-related goals, team member roles, and team responsibilities should be thoroughly discussed and agreed on in this session. With advances in communication technologies, there are some who hold the view that an initial face-to-face session may not be essential and could be too costly for team members located around the world. This view may be more applicable to teams that have a narrow set of tasks and a short-time goal.

- For long-term or permanent teams, establish a schedule of periodic face-to-face meetings—quarterly, semiannual, or at least annual. These meetings refresh connections, enable the meaningful discussion of possible communication and emotional barriers that may have developed, and minimize the development of "out-of-site, out-of-mind" attitudes. Remember, virtual team members often serve on other teams at their own work site and have other individual tasks, responsibilities, and goals.

- Agree on what, when, and how information, issues, and problems will be shared as well as on how the team leader and team members will respond to them.

- Establish clear norms and procedures for reducing, surfacing, and resolving conflicts. As suggested above, serious emotional and interpersonal conflicts may require a face-to-face team meeting and/or a face-to-face meeting by the team leader with each of the team members who are in conflict.

- Encourage team members to interact one on one, without feeling obligated to copy every e-mail message or share phone conversations with the entire team. This approach can help prevent misunderstandings from needlessly escalating into crises.

Global Team

A **global team** *has members from a variety of countries who are separated significantly by time, distance, culture, and language.*[35] Global teams may operate like any of the other types of teams we have discussed—functional, problem solving, cross-functional, self-managed, and virtual. Global teams typically conduct a substantial portion of their tasks as virtual teams.

Four of the principal reasons for the use of global teams are as follows[36]:

1. The desire to develop goods and services in a variety of countries with a minimum level of customization. In this circumstance, global teams help to define common features of goods and services that will appeal to customers in different countries. Coca-Cola and IBM use global teams to market their products.

2. In contrast to reason 1 just given, there is a desire to develop goods or services that are tailored to the unique needs and requirements of local markets, such as Campbell's development of soups for Russian markets. The global team members from different countries can provide insight into and input about these unique market needs and requirements for specific attributes of goods and services.

3. Global teams enable organizations to leverage and capitalize on expertise that exists in different countries, such as at Google and Microsoft. This eliminates the need to bring the required expertise to a single country by relocating team members and incurring the costs of doing so.

4. For organizations such as Alcoa and Elsevier Publishing, the location of manufacturing facilities, distribution centers, and marketing units in various countries requires the use of global teams. The teams serve as a mechanism for coordinating worldwide resources. Global teams allow companies to take advantage of lower manufacturing costs in one country, the central location of a distribution center in another, and "on-site" marketing units by bringing together individuals virtually. These global teams usually need to meet face to face only on occasion.

Insights for Leaders

Global virtual teams face a variety of special leadership challenges relative to most virtual or face-to-face teams because of differences in the members' cultures and native languages as well as significant time zone differences in their normal working hours. For example, virtual teams with members from China, Germany, Japan, France, and the United States are more culturally, socially, and linguistically diverse (even if the work-related communications are undertaken in English) than virtual teams with members from California, Colorado, Florida, Massachusetts, and New York.[37] In a number of chapters, we discuss the special challenges associated with differences across cultures and the suggested leadership insights related to them.

With respect to time, the normal working hours for global virtual team members may vary by 12 or more hours due to differences in the time zones. Moreover, the cultural meaning of *time* may vary among team members in different societies, which we discussed in more detail in Chapter 9. Cultural orientations about time may affect team members' perceptions of schedules and deadlines. In some cultures, for instance, the Germanic and Scandinavian countries, schedules and deadlines are seen as absolutes. In other countries, such as Mexico and Italy, they are often seen as guidelines. In recognition of the potential for different views of time among global virtual team members, leaders should (1) create an awareness of the different views members may have with respect to time after the formation of the team, (2) facilitate the development of agreed-on norms and expectations with respect to time, and (3) encourage the use of precise language with respect to time and avoid the use of time-related language such as "Wait a minute," "I'll be in touch shortly," and "Let's keep in contact as time permits." Of course, all of the leader insights for virtual teams apply to global virtual teams as well.[38]

The following Across Cultures Competency feature presents the insights by four leaders of four different global virtual teams at Alcoa.[39] This feature is based on Alcoa's initiatives to create a web of global virtual teams that operate outside and across the traditional operational and divisional lines of authority. In recent years, Alcoa has established 80 of these teams. The overall goals of these teams are the identification, codification, and dissemination of new or revised operational practices across units that are in various locations. The team members have formally assigned positions at their locations which require the bulk of their time and energy. The teams do not have the authority to implement their proposed new or revised "best practices" at each location.[40]

Alcoa is a major producer of primary aluminum, fabricated aluminum, and alumina combined. It also produces and markets various aluminum products such as wheels, fastening systems, and building systems. The company has 87,000 employees in 35 countries. Alcoa has been recognized as one of the world's most ethical companies by Ethisphere and named one of the most sustainable corporations of the world at the World Economic Forum in Davos, Switzerland. It has been a member of the Dow Jones Sustainability Index for eight consecutive years.[41]

Across Cultures competency

Alcoa's Global Virtual Teams

This feature presents insights and perspectives from four global virtual team leaders at Alcoa. The specific identity of each team is not revealed, but their comments are real.

Getting Supported: One of the growing challenges for the teams is their ability to meet face to face. I do not know where the funding is going to come from for this to occur. We do not have formal funding for the lead-team. We try to meet when the majority of us are at one place. The rest of us manage to find a way to get there

somehow. We do not have a budget for the lead-team to meet twice a year, or the support groups to meet at least once a year. So the lack of resources is a challenge, which again boils down to whether or not there is true recognition for the value of work we are doing.

Enriching Communication: To make best use of the group teleconferences, we make sure that we have all the information in hand. In the team meetings, I may ask a particular site to help another site. I generally send an e-mail in this regard and they know they will be asked about this in the meeting. This is to make efficient use of the meeting time. Sometimes, there is spontaneity in the discussions, but I try to keep the meetings mostly structured. For a typical team meeting, I will send the agenda beforehand. In the meeting, I ask each representative to give a two-minute synopsis on how they deal with the work mentioned in the agenda (at their site). Also, I ask them to highlight any issue and try to make sure that I am not emphasizing one refinery over the others. I also ask about matrices and calculations, how each refinery has come to a certain figure. I also make sure that all the spreadsheets and data are in front of me, so that I can correlate what people are talking about.

Building and Sustaining Relationships: In terms of improving of trust and familiarity among members over time and the practices which led to this trust, certainly over time people have started feeling more comfortable. They come to know the rewards of sharing knowledge over time and certainly are much more open in discussions. In the early days . . . there was a lot of initial reticence. This is because of cross-cultural gaps. Some people were quite blunt in their comments . . . which could be interpreted as insensitive to [another] person. This may be one

reason for reticence. Also political correctness in some countries like Australia is much more advanced than in other countries like those in the Caribbean or, say, Brazil. So, I will say that the reticence was because of these cultural sensitivities, and as time has passed, team members have gotten along better.

Getting People to Talk and Listen: In virtual teams, sometimes getting people to talk and listen becomes a problem when you are not able to observe the body language. The language problem adds to this dilemma. You can grasp the engineering stuff, but it is difficult to grasp people's emotions and sentiments. In a virtual environment, sometimes it becomes difficult trying to be assertive without being pushy. This becomes even more difficult when English is not their first language. Even if English is somebody's first language, the culture is quite different. People from Brazil will say "yes" even if they have not understood. They do not feel comfortable asking you to repeat what they have not understood. Jamaicans will commit to do almost anything (quite willingly) in the meeting, but it doesn't get done. I know this, and I will say that I know you guys are not going to do this . . . but still they will say they will do it . . . "It's cool, man. . . ."

To learn more about Alcoa, go to **www.alcoa.com**.

Learning Goal

4. *Describe the core influences on team effectiveness.*

Core Influences on Team Effectiveness

The core influences on team and group effectiveness are interrelated. Figure 12.3 identifies eight of the core influences. Each influence needs to be analyzed separately and in relation to each other. This approach fosters a fuller understanding of team dynamics and effectiveness—and helps to develop the competencies needed to be an effective team member and leader.

Context

The **context** *refers to the external conditions within which a team works.* Moreover, the context can directly affect each of the seven other factors that affect a team. Examples of a team's context include technology, organization design, physical working conditions, management practices, and organizational rewards and punishments.[42] Our earlier discussion of virtual teams illustrated the contextual influence of technology.

If the members of a team are more focused on themselves than their peers, perhaps the organization's reward system (a contextual factor) should be tailored so that

FIGURE 12.3 Core Influences on Team Effectiveness

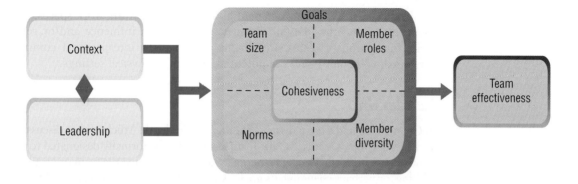

individuals see how their own interests are being served by being strong team contributors. This notion is based on three perspectives:

1. Motivation primarily comes from the individual, not the team.

2. The development of competencies, such as those emphasized in this book, are individual undertakings.

3. Fairness in dealing with teams does not necessarily mean equal pay for all members of the team.

The team system at the Mayo Clinic considers these perspectives in its recruitment and selection process (a contextual factor) by not hiring physicians and others who want to maximize their own personal income. A physician at the Mayo Clinic states:

> *The Mayo culture attracts individuals who see the practice of medicine best delivered when there is an integration of medical specialties functioning as a team. It is what we do best, and most of us love to do it. What is most inspiring is when a case is successful because*

RYAN MCVAY/PHOTODISC/GETTY IMAGES

In an office, the placement and types of furniture and work spaces can influence the social interaction of teams.

of the teamwork of a bunch of docs from different specialties; it has the same feeling as a home run in baseball.[43]

In office settings, the placement and types of furniture, work spaces, conference rooms, halls, and the like (all contextual factors) can influence and/or regulate the social interaction of teams. Recall our discussion of interpersonal communication networks in Chapter 9 and the potential impacts of physical settings.

Leadership

In Chapters 10 and 11, we discussed leadership in depth. Much of that discussion applies to the leadership of teams as well. Team leaders may be formally designated to their roles. In other cases, informal leaders emerge to develop and guide the team or group in accomplishing, or perhaps changing, its goals. An **informal leader** *is an individual whose influence in a team grows over time and usually reflects a unique ability to help the team reach its goals.*

Multiple Leaders

Team leadership is often thought of in terms of one person. Because a team often has both relations-oriented and task-oriented tasks and goals, it may have two or more leaders. These two categories of tasks and goals may require different skills and leadership styles, creating a total set of demands that one person may have difficulty satisfying. Informal task-related leaders of teams aren't likely to emerge unless the formal leader ignores task-related responsibilities or lacks the necessary skills to carry them out. In contrast, relations-oriented leaders of teams may well emerge informally. (Task-oriented and relations-oriented behaviors are discussed later in the Member Roles section.)

Insights for Leaders

As suggested in Figure 12.3, team leaders may influence virtually all aspects of a team (e.g., goals, size, member roles, diversity, norms, cohesiveness, and even context).[44] A leader often assumes a key role in the relations between the team and external groups, such as customers or suppliers, and often influences the selection of new members. Even when the team heavily participates in the selection process, the team leader may screen potential members, thereby limiting the number and range of candidates, which is how it is done at the Mayo Clinic.

The following Ethics Competency feature reports on the ethical and change-based leadership of Sanjiv Das regarding his decisions to set the context for decision making by the many teams and individual employees at CitiMortgage.[45] Das became the CEO and president of CitiMortgage in 2009. CitiMortgage is a subsidiary of Citigroup and primarily provides and services home mortgages. It is headquartered in St. Louis, Missouri, and has 10,000 employees.[46]

Ethics **competency**

Sanjiv Das's Leadership at CitiMortgage

Upon becoming the CEO and president of CitiMortgage, Sanjiv Das found himself charged with motivating 10,000 employees and revitalizing a firm caught in the throes of one of the biggest housing crises to hit the United States.

It's the riskiest thing Das says he has ever done. He comments: "The single biggest issue I face is to be able to deal with this onslaught of unemployment and negative sentiment (toward banks) out there that none of us control. We all feel, in our own small way, if we can ebb the tide, it will go toward turning around the economy of this great country, and belief in the housing market and trust in the banking system." Das indicates that one of his goals is to bolster employee morale during a time of intense business demand and shrinking public respect toward financial institutions. Another goal is to do what they can to avert as many of the foreclosures as possible that have been crippling the housing market.

Das's leadership has already made a difference. He helped pioneer a first-of-a-kind program at CitiMortgage that was designed to help homeowners who have lost their jobs. Under the program, CitiMortgage allows eligible borrowers who have been newly laid off to have their monthly mortgage payments lowered by up to $500 for a defined period.

The performance of CitiMortgage's loan modifications also has beaten national averages. The firm reported that 23 percent of delinquent home loans it modified during the past year fell into default again, far below the figures showing that about 55 percent of modified loans done by national banks were in default after six months. Das states: "Our people and teams are driven by the ability to find innovative solutions, as opposed to doing the same thing we do in good times. Our mantra is very clear: It's about keeping people in their homes."

Trevor Harris, professor at Columbia Business School, worked with Das at Morgan Stanley. Harris comments: "He tries to understand the issue and problem and takes a lot of different input. He identifies what he believes the right solution is (for a problem) and works hard to execute it. Das tries to make everybody feel comfortable with the outcome."

With thousands of employees at CitiMortgage, Das says he tries to do as he was taught when growing up by, for instance, nurturing morale. He states: "You do that by integrity, and servant leadership is at the heart of my values. The No. 1 thing I talk about are the customers. Each day, my business is to keep them in their homes, no matter what. That goes back to the values I was brought up with."

He starts every morning with a team meeting of other CitiMortgage executives to review the previous day's key performance measures. Other meetings often follow—with the CitiHoldings management team or with other teams to discuss new programs and ways to keep people current on their mortgages. He holds conference calls with teams implementing the new White House program to avert foreclosures, monitors Citi's progress, and resolves impediments.

To learn more about CitiMortgage, go to **www.citimortgage.com.**

Goals

Team goals *are the outcomes desired for the team as a whole.* Many aspects of goals were discussed in Chapter 7. Throughout the book, we focus on how goals influence individual, team, and organizational effectiveness. Obviously, individual and organizational goals are likely to influence team goals and behaviors in pursuit of these goals. Both compatible and conflicting goals may exist within a team.[47] Moreover, teams typically have both relations-oriented and task-oriented goals (discussed later in the Member Roles section). Effective work-related teams spend two-thirds or more of their time on task-oriented issues and roughly one-third or less of their time on relations-oriented issues. The pursuit of only one or the other type of goal over the long run can hurt performance, increase conflicts, and cause a team to disband. The influence of goals on group dynamics and outcomes becomes even more complex when the possible compatibilities and conflicts among member goals, broader team goals, and even broader organizational goals are considered.

One mechanism for dealing with these issues is the use of **superordinate goals,** *which two or more individuals, teams, or groups might pursue but can't be achieved without their cooperation.* These goals do not replace or eliminate individual or team goals and may be either qualitative or quantitative. An example of a qualitative goal is "We need to pull together for the good of the team." An example of a quantitative goal is "We need to work together if we are to reach our goal of launching a new line within nine months." Superordinate goals may have a more powerful effect on the willingness of individuals or teams to cooperate if they are accompanied by team rewards established by higher management. Team rewards are given to team members and are determined by the results of their joint efforts. Team rewards may also be in the form of a sense of mutual satisfaction and accomplishment for having performed well by serving customers, achieving high quality, and making a difference.

At times, the way the organization's principles and values are expressed and implemented may serve as superordinate goals. For example, the core principles set forth by Dr. William J. Mayo late in his life continue to serve as superordinate goals at the Mayo Clinic. They include, among others,

- continuing pursuit of the ideal of service and not profit,

- continuing primary and sincere concern for the care and welfare of each individual patient, and

- continuing interest by every member of the staff in the professional progress of every other member.[48]

In Chapter 5, we discussed self-efficacy—the individual's estimate of his or her own ability to perform a specific task in a particular situation. In a similar sense, **collective efficacy** *is a team's or group's shared perception of its capability to successfully perform specific tasks.* Collective efficacy helps teams to achieve their goals. If a team lacks in collective efficacy, the impact of setting team goals is often diminished.[49] Just look at winning teams in the NFL, NBA, and NHL. Typically, they display collective efficacy.

Team Size

The effective size of a team can range from 3 members to a normal upper limit of about 16 members.[50] Collaborative software systems, the Internet, and other technologies are enabling larger teams to work effectively on some tasks. Twelve members probably is the largest size that allows each member to interact easily with every other member face to face, especially when the team members are not highly interdependent in performing their tasks on a day-to-day basis. Table 12.2 shows six dimensions of teams that change as team size increases. The likely effects of team size on each dimension are highlighted. Note that members of teams of 7 or fewer interact differently than do members of teams or groups of 13 to 16. A 16-member board of directors will operate differently from a 7-member board. Large boards of directors often form committees of 5 to 7 members to consider specific matters in greater depth than can the entire board.

TABLE 12.2 Typical Effects of Size on Teams

	TEAM SIZE		
DIMENSION	2–7 MEMBERS	8–12 MEMBERS	13–16 MEMBERS
1. Demands on leader	Low	Moderate	High
2. Direction by leader	Low	Moderate	Moderate to high
3. Member tolerance of direction by leader	Low to moderate	Moderate	High
4. Member inhibition	Low	Moderate	High
5. Use of rules and procedures	Low	Moderate	Moderate to high
6. Time taken to reach a decision	Low	Moderate	High

Source: I. D. Team size and technology fit: Participation, awareness, and rapport in distributed teams. Professional Communication, 2005, 48, 68–77.

As with all influences on teams, the effects identified in Table 12.2 need to be qualified. For example, adequate time and sufficient member commitment to a team's goals and tasks might lead to better results from a team of seven to nine than from a hurried and less committed team of five members. If a team's primary task is to tap the knowledge of the members and arrive at decisions based primarily on expertise rather than judgment, a larger team won't necessarily reflect the effects identified in Table 12.2. Of course, many teams that are formed with professionals (experts and leaders) are intended to integrate expertise and judgments.

Member Roles

A universally agreed-on framework of team roles does not exist.[51] For our purposes, member roles in teams can be classified as to whether they are task-oriented, relations-oriented, or self-oriented roles. Each member has the potential for performing each of these roles over time.[52] This classification underlies most other models of team member roles.[53]

Task-Oriented Role

The **task-oriented role** *of a team member involves facilitating and coordinating work-related behaviors and decision making*. This role may include

- *initiating* new ideas or different ways of considering team problems or goals and suggesting solutions to difficulties, including modification of team procedures;
- *seeking information* to clarify suggestions and obtain key facts;
- *giving information* that is relevant to the team's problem, issue, or task;
- *coordinating* and clarifying relationships among ideas and suggestions, pulling ideas and suggestions together, and coordinating members' activities; and
- *evaluating* the team's effectiveness, including questioning the logic, facts, or practicality of other members' suggestions.

Relations-Oriented Role

The **relations-oriented role** *of a team member involves fostering team-centered attitudes, behaviors, emotions, and social interactions*. This role may include

- *encouraging* members through praise and acceptance of their ideas, as well as indicating warmth and solidarity;
- *harmonizing* and mediating intrateam conflicts and tensions;
- *encouraging* participation of others by saying, "Let's hear from Susan" or "Why not limit the length of contributions so all can react to the problem?" or "Juan, do you agree?";
- *expressing* standards for the team to achieve or apply in evaluating the quality of team processes, raising questions about team goals, and assessing team progress in light of these goals; and
- *following* by going along passively or constructively and serving as a friendly member.

Self-Oriented Role

The **self-oriented role** of a team member *involves the person's self-centered attitudes, behaviors, and decisions that are at the expense of the team or group*. This role may include

- *blocking progress* by being negative, stubborn, and unreasoningly resistant—for example, the person may repeatedly try to bring back an issue that the team had considered carefully and rejected;

- *seeking recognition* by calling attention to oneself, including boasting, reporting on personal achievements, and in various ways avoiding being placed in a presumed inferior position;
- *dominating* by asserting authority, manipulating the team or certain individuals, using flattery or proclaiming superiority to gain attention, and interrupting the contributions of others; and
- *avoiding* involvement by maintaining distance from others and remaining insulated from interactions.

Effective teams often are composed of members who play both task-oriented and relations-oriented roles over time. A particularly adept individual who reveals behaviors valued by the team probably has relatively high *status*—the relative rank of an individual in a team. A team dominated by individuals who exhibit mainly self-oriented behaviors is likely to be ineffective because the individuals don't adequately address team goals or engage in needed collaboration.

Table 12.3 provides a questionnaire for evaluating some of your task-oriented, relations-oriented, and self-oriented behaviors as a team member. The questionnaire asks you to assess your tendency to engage in each role, on a scale of 1 to 5 (or almost never to almost always). Member composition and roles greatly influence

---

TABLE 12.3   Assessing Your Role-Oriented Behavior as a Team Member

Instructions: Assess your behavior on each item for the team that you selected by using the following scale.

1	2	3	4	5
Almost Never	Rarely	Sometimes	Often	Almost Always

Place the appropriate number value next to each item.

Task-oriented behaviors: In this team, I . . .

_____ 1. initiate ideas or actions.
_____ 2. facilitate the introduction of facts and information.
_____ 3. summarize and pull together various ideas.
_____ 4. keep the team working on the task.
_____ 5. ask whether the team is near a decision (determine consensus).

Relation-oriented behaviors: In this team, I . . .

_____ 6. support and encourage others.
_____ 7. harmonize (keep the peace).
_____ 8. try to find common ground.
_____ 9. encourage participation.
_____ 10. actively listen.

Self-oriented behaviors: In this team, I . . .

_____ 11. express hostility.
_____ 12. avoid involvement.
_____ 13. dominate the team.
_____ 14. free ride on others.
_____ 15. take personal credit for team results.

Total: Add points for items 1 through 15.

Interpretation: Scores of 20–25 on task-oriented behaviors, 20–25 on relations-oriented behaviors, and 5–10 on self-oriented behaviors probably indicate that you are an effective team member. This conclusion assumes that other team members perceive you as you see yourself.

team or group behaviors. Either too much or too little of certain member behaviors can adversely affect team performance and member satisfaction.

Member Diversity

The growing diversity of the workforce adds complexity—beyond individuals' personalities and team roles—to understanding team behavior and processes. We have discussed how the composition of the workforce is undergoing continued change in terms of primary and secondary categories of diversity, which are increasingly reflected in the membership of teams. As you may recall from Chapters 1 and 2, primary categories, over which individuals have little influence, include age, race, ethnicity, gender, physical abilities and qualities, and sexual orientation. In contrast, the secondary categories include education, work experiences, job position, income, marital status, religious beliefs, geographical location, parental status, ways of thinking, personal style, seniority, and the like. It is common to think of the primary categories as sources of difficulties in team functioning. The general assumption is that people like to work on teams with people who are similar to themselves. In the initial time period of members working together, this is often the case. However, as team members work together over time, these primary categories in the U.S. work environment appear to become less important to understanding team difficulties. In contrast, the secondary categories often become more important to understanding difficulties in team functioning, such as the formation of subgroups in a team based on age, seniority, job position, specialty, and the like.[54]

The existence of subgroups in teams results from **fault lines**—*the process by which teams divide themselves into subgroups based on one or more attributes.*[55] In general, the development of strong fault lines works *against* a good decision-making team. Teams without strong fault lines become aware of more issues, perceive issues in different and deeper ways, propose more novel and creative courses of action, and engage in constructive task-related conflict.[56] Our years of experience with numerous student teams who have had to analyze complex cases or complete challenging projects suggests that diverse teams that do not form strong fault lines typically develop more effective cases or projects than teams that do so. Is this consistent with your experiences?

Insights for Leaders

As we have suggested in many chapters, team effectiveness will be hampered if members hold false stereotypes about each other. Although attitudes are changing, diversity all too often still is viewed more negatively than positively. This negative reaction may be due, in large part, to four underlying attitudes involving stereotypical false assumptions, as follows:

- Diversity poses a threat to the organization's effective functioning.
- Expressed discomfort with the dominant group's values is perceived as oversensitivity by minority groups.
- Members of all groups want to become and should be more like the dominant group.
- Equal treatment means the same treatment.

The goal of achieving diversity creates unique challenges in making it work for rather than against the long-term interests of individuals, teams, and organizations.[57] Once an "us versus them" distinction is perceived through strong fault lines in a team, subgroups tend to discriminate against other team members who are different. Moreover, they tend to perceive these other team members as inferior, adversarial, and competitive.

The following Diversity Competency feature reports on Angela Braly, who became president and CEO of WellPoint in 2007. It focuses on her leadership ability in drawing together teams of employees and customer groups to achieve superordinate and common goals, including the need to embrace diversity. Braly sees diversity management as a fundamental part of how WellPoint does business.[58]

WellPoint provides health coverage, primarily under the Blue Cross and Blue Shield brand, to about 35 million members. It has approximately 43,000 employees and $61 billion in revenues annually. WellPoint has received many awards and forms of recognition for its diversity initiatives and achievements. It is recognized as one of the leading companies for diversity. WellPoint is headquartered in Indianapolis, Indiana.[59]

Diversity competency

Angela Braly, CEO and President, WellPoint, Inc.

BRENDAN MCDERMID/LANDOV

Angela Braly, CEO and president of WellPoint, Inc.

In this feature, we share a few snapshots of Angela Braly as a leader, including how she sees diversity management as a fundamental part of how WellPoint operates and does business. Let's start with Braly's viewpoint on the importance of communication:

Nothing could be more important than being passionate about your organization's mission and values. When thinking about an organization's vision and goals, it's important to start with the questions, Why are we here? What is our role? Answering these questions creates the road map that then leads an organization to defining its strategy and initiatives. When rolling out a mission, vision or goals, it's also important that the communication is effective. Otherwise, there's no point in communicating. Effective communication

takes the complex and makes it simple. I believe in being straightforward, honest and transparent at every level. Good leaders have a very strong set of values. They know who they are and what they believe. They have a strong sense of what ethics mean. Every day a leader is faced with important choices— some small and some large—and the best leaders always fall back on their core set of beliefs and values in guiding them to decisions that are best.

At WellPoint, diversity management is seen as more than just a strategy. It's a fundamental part of how it does business. Focusing on diversity helps WellPoint to better understand and meet the health care needs of the unique communities it serves. Strategic diversity management also drives associate engagement and trust, which increases productivity and operational effectiveness. Diversity is seen as a shared responsibility among all associates in the organization. There is a core team of associates who serve as subject matter experts and catalysts for transformation and engagement, led by the chief diversity officer. There are more than 200 ambassadors who volunteer to infuse the corporate diversity strategy in their unique work locations throughout the company. They implement events and activities in their areas that resonate with their peers and colleagues.

There are six associate resource groups that engage in two-way communication, not only for their personal and professional development, but also in support of the company's overall business strategies. A Customer InSights Team is used to develop a link with the firm's multicultural customers. Additionally, there is a team dedicated to understanding and addressing health-care disparities from a multicultural and multigenerational perspective. WellPoint remains active in various diversity organizations in order to stay abreast of changes and best practices.

WellPoint also has a dedicated Diversity Leadership Team managed by WellPoint's chief diversity officer. The team includes a diversity program manager, an EEO compliance consultant, an affirmative action plan consultant, and three workplace culture consultants. Braly concludes: "Our programs and culture intend to ensure that all WellPoint leaders and employees understand the company's commitment to diversity and utilize the tools designed to assist them in managing and supporting this commitment in their daily practices."

To learn more about WellPoint, go to **www.wellpoint.com.**

Norms

Norms *are the rules and patterns of behavior that are accepted and expected by members of a team or whole organization.* They help define the behaviors that members believe to be necessary to help them reach their goals. Over time, every team establishes norms and enforces them on its members.[60] Norms often are more rigidly defined and enforced in informal groups—by peer pressure—than in formally organized teams. Such norms may further or inhibit achievement of organizational goals.

Norms versus Organizational Rules

Norms differ from organizational rules. Leaders and staff groups, like human resource management and quality control, typically develop and distribute formal organizational rules to employees in the form of manuals and memoranda. These are often required by governmental laws and rules developed by regulatory agencies. At times, employees refuse to accept such rules or simply ignore them. In contrast, norms are informal, unwritten expectations that are enforced by team members. If a member consistently violates these norms, the other members sanction the individual in some way. Sanctions may range from physical abuse to threats to social ostracism to positive inducements (rewards) for compliance. Those who consistently adhere to the team's norms typically receive praise, recognition, and acceptance from the other members.

Team members may be only vaguely aware of some of the norms that are operating, but they should be made aware of these norms for at least two reasons. First, awareness increases the potential for individual and team freedom and effectiveness. Second, norms can positively or negatively influence the effectiveness of individuals, teams, and organizations. For example, team norms of improving quality are likely to reinforce an organization's formal quality standards. Or, team norms toward absenteeism may affect the level of absence behavior by members.[61]

Relation to Goals

Teams often adopt norms to help them attain their goals. Moreover, some organizational development efforts are aimed at helping members evaluate whether their team's norms are consistent with organizational goals. For example, a team may claim that one of its goals is to become more efficient. However, the team members' behaviors might be inconsistent with this stated goal; that is, members take long lunch breaks, let products that are not quite up to quality standards pass to customers, ignore some quality control steps in the production process, and the like.

Even if team members are aware of such norms, they may think of them as being necessary in order to achieve their own goals. Members may claim that producing more than the norm will "burn them out" or reduce product or service quality, resulting in lower long-term effectiveness. If a team's goals include minimizing managerial influence and increasing the opportunity for social interaction, its members could perceive norms restricting employee output as desirable.

Enforcing Norms

Teams don't establish norms for every situation. They generally form and enforce norms with respect to behaviors that they believe to be particularly important. Norms express the central values and goals of the team and clarify what is distinctive about its identity. Members are most likely to enforce norms under one or more of the following conditions[62]:

- Norms aid in team survival and provide benefits. For instance, a marketing team might develop a norm not to discuss individual salaries with other members in the organization to avoid calling attention to pay inequities.
- Norms simplify or make predictable the behaviors expected of members. When coworkers go out for lunch together, there can be some awkwardness about how to split the bill at the end of the meal. A group may develop a norm that results in some highly predictable way of behaving: split the bill evenly, take turns picking up the tab, or individually pay for what each ordered.
- Norms help avoid embarrassing interpersonal situations. Norms might develop about not discussing romantic involvements in or out of the office (so that differences in moral values don't become too obvious) or about not getting together socially in members' homes (so that differences in taste or income don't become too obvious).

Conforming to Norms

Conformity may result from the pressure to adhere to norms. The two basic types of conformity are compliance and personal acceptance. **Compliance conformity** *occurs when a person's behavior reflects the team's desired behavior because of real or imagined pressure*. In fact, some individuals may conform for a variety of reasons, even though they don't personally agree with the norms. They may think that the appearance of a united front is necessary for success in accomplishing team goals. On a more personal level, someone may comply in order to be liked and accepted by others. Meeting this need may apply especially to members of lower status in relation to those of higher status, such as a subordinate and a superior. Finally, someone may comply because the costs of conformity are much less than the costs of nonconformity, which could threaten the personal relationships in the team.

The second type of conformity is based on positive personal support of the norms. In **personal acceptance conformity**, *the individual's behavior and attitudes are consistent with the team's norms and goals*. This type of conformity is much stronger than compliance conformity because the person truly believes in the goals and norms.[63]

Insights for Leaders

All of the preceding helps explain why some members of highly conforming teams may easily change their behavior (compliance type of conformity), whereas others may oppose changes and find them highly stressful (personal acceptance type of conformity). Without norms and reasonable conformity to them, teams would be chaotic and few tasks could be accomplished. Conversely, excessive and blind conformity may threaten expressions of individualism and a team's ability to change and learn.

Cohesiveness

Cohesiveness *is the strength of the members' desire to remain in a team and their commitment to it*. Cohesiveness is influenced by a variety of factors, especially the degree of compatibility between team goals and individual members' goals—in terms of both task-related goals and relations-oriented goals. Members who have a strong desire to remain in a team and personally accept its goals often form a highly cohesive team.[64]

This relationship between cohesiveness and conformity isn't a simple one. Low cohesiveness usually is associated with low conformity. However, high cohesiveness doesn't exist only in the presence of high conformity. High-performing teams may have high member commitment and cohesiveness, while simultaneously respecting and encouraging individual differences. This situation is more likely to develop when cohesiveness arises from trusting relationships and a common commitment to performance goals.

Insights for Leaders

Team performance and productivity can be affected by cohesiveness. Cohesiveness and productivity are often related, particularly for teams having high performance goals. If the team is successful in reaching those goals, the positive feedback of its successes may heighten member commitment and satisfaction. For example, a winning basketball team is more likely to be cohesive than one with a losing record, everything else being equal. Also, a cohesive basketball team may be more likely to win games. Conversely, low cohesiveness may interfere with a team's ability to win games. The reason is that members aren't as likely to communicate and cooperate with each other to the extent necessary to reach the team's goals.

High team cohesiveness actually may be associated with low efficiency if team goals conflict with organizational goals. Team members might think that the manager holds them accountable rather than that they hold themselves accountable to achieve results. Therefore, the relationships among cohesiveness, productivity, and performance can't be anticipated or understood unless the team's goals and norms are also known.

Potential Team Dysfunctions

Learning Goal

5. *Explain five of the potential dysfunctions of teams.*

If a team's members and its leader are not savvy to the concepts, models, and issues discussed in this and other chapters, a variety of team dysfunctions may come into play, especially in the performing stage of team development.[65] To enrich your understanding of the potential sources of team ineffectiveness noted in this and previous chapters, we focus here on five potential team dysfunctions: groupthink, free riding, the bad apples effect, absence of trust, and avoidance of accountability for results. As suggested in Figure 12.4, a poorly performing team is likely to suffer from more than one dysfunction.

FIGURE 12.4 Potential Team Dysfunctions

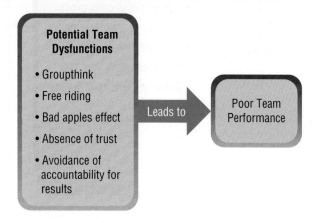

Teams Insight

We are generally more aware of the downside of individualism in organizations, and we forget that teams can be just as destructive by being so strong and controlling that individual voices and contributions and learning are lost.

J. Richard Hackman, Author, Leading Teams, *and Coauthor,* Senior Leadership Teams

Groupthink

Groupthink *is an agreement-at-any-cost mentality that results in ineffective group or team decision making and poor decisions.* Irving L. Janis, who coined the term *groupthink*, focused his research on high-level governmental policy groups faced with difficult problems in a complex and dynamic environment. Of course, team or group decision making is quite common in all types of organizations. When a team is faced with a highly stressful and anxiety-provoking situation, the possibility of groupthink exists in private sector organizations as well as those in the public sector. Figure 12.5 outlines the initial conditions that are likely to lead to groupthink, its characteristics, and the types of defective decision making that result from it. The characteristics of groupthink include the following[66]:

- An *illusion of invulnerability* is shared by most or all team members, which creates excessive optimism and encourages extreme risk taking. Statements such as "No one can stop us now" or "The other group has a bunch of jerks" may be made by members suffering from an illusion of invulnerability.

- *Collective rationalization* discounts warnings that might lead the members to reconsider their assumptions before committing themselves to major policy decisions. Statements such as "We are confident that only a small segment of auto buyers are willing to buy fuel-efficient autos" were made by U.S. auto executives until recent years.

- An *unquestioned belief* in the team's inherent morality leads members to ignore the ethical or moral consequences of their decisions.

FIGURE 12.5 The Groupthink Process

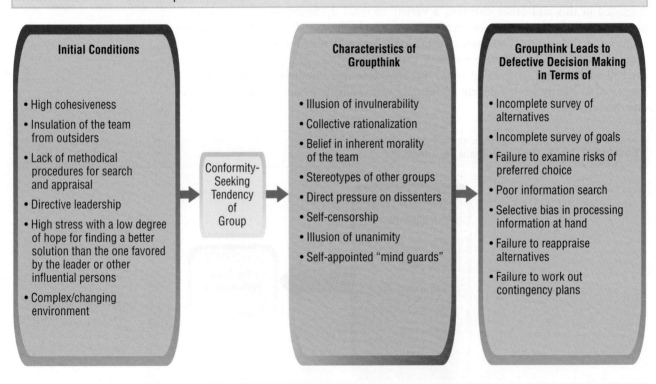

Initial Conditions	Characteristics of Groupthink	Groupthink Leads to Defective Decision Making in Terms of
• High cohesiveness • Insulation of the team from outsiders • Lack of methodical procedures for search and appraisal • Directive leadership • High stress with a low degree of hope for finding a better solution than the one favored by the leader or other influential persons • Complex/changing environment	Conformity-Seeking Tendency of Group → • Illusion of invulnerability • Collective rationalization • Belief in inherent morality of the team • Stereotypes of other groups • Direct pressure on dissenters • Self-censorship • Illusion of unanimity • Self-appointed "mind guards"	• Incomplete survey of alternatives • Incomplete survey of goals • Failure to examine risks of preferred choice • Poor information search • Selective bias in processing information at hand • Failure to reappraise alternatives • Failure to work out contingency plans

- *Stereotypical views* of rivals and enemies (other groups) picture them as too evil to warrant genuine attempts to negotiate or too weak or stupid to counter whatever attempts are made to defeat their purpose.

- *Direct pressure* is exerted on any member who expresses strong arguments against any of the team's illusions, stereotypes, or commitments, making clear that such dissent is contrary to what is expected of all loyal members. The leader might say, "What's the matter? Aren't you a team member anymore?"

- *Self-censorship* of deviations from any apparent team consensus reflects the inclination of members to minimize the importance of their doubts and not present counterarguments. A member might think, "If everyone feels that way, my feelings must be wrong."

- A *shared illusion of unanimity* results, in part, from self-censorship and is reinforced by the false assumption that silence implies consent.

- The emergence of *self-appointed "mind-guard"* members serves to protect the team from adverse information that might shatter the shared complacency about the effectiveness and morality of their decision. Example: "Those studies don't apply to our issue."

Insights for Leaders

Some research suggests that the strongest triggers leading to groupthink are (1) a strong and directive leader who expresses early endorsement for a particular solution to the problem at hand and (2) the lack of methods and established processes for making decisions. The directive leader often discourages diverse perspectives and promotes a favored solution early in the team deliberations. The stress and anxiety being experienced by the team members in considering a problem is reduced through premature concurrence seeking. Much research suggests that high levels of anxiety are a possible cause of premature concurrence seeking, which is associated with a desire to conform. A leading researcher and expert on teams contends[67]:

> *This is where what I call a* deviant *comes in. Every team needs a deviant, someone who can help the team by challenging the tendency to want too much homogeneity, which can stifle creativity and learning. Deviants are the ones who stand back and say, "Well, wait a minute, why are we even doing this at all? What if we looked at the thing backwards or turned it inside out?"*

Free Riding

The potential for conflicting team and individual interests is suggested by the free-rider concept. A **free rider** *is an individual who obtains benefits from membership but does not contribute much to achieving the team's goals.*[68] *Free riding* is referred to by some as *shirking* or *social loafing*. Students sometimes experience the free-rider problem when an instructor assigns a group project for which all of the members receive the same (group) grade. Let's assume that there are five students on the team and that one member makes little or no contribution. This free rider obtains the benefit of the team grade but does not bear a proportional share of the demands in earning it.

When team members fear that one or more other members may free ride, a phenomenon may occur known as the **sucker effect**, *which refers to one or more individuals in the team deciding to withhold effort in the belief that others (the free riders) are planning to withhold effort.* The sucker role is repulsive to many team members for three reasons. First, the free riding of others violates an equity standard: Members don't want others receiving the same levels of rewards for less input or effort. Second, it violates a standard of social responsibility: Everyone should do their fair share. Third, the free riding of others may violate a standard of reciprocity or exchange.[69] A team is doomed to ineffectiveness with both free riders and other members acting on the basis of the sucker effect.

Bad Apples Effect

The **bad apples effect** *refers to negative team or group members who withhold effort, express negative feelings and attitudes, and violate important team norms and behaviors.*[70] We already addressed one aspect of the "bad apple" in the form of withholding effort in our discussion of free riding. The common saying "a bad apple spoils the barrel" captures the basic idea of one or more negative individuals on a team having a disproportionate and adverse effect on other members of the team and, as a result, reducing its effectiveness. Bad apples may even be "destroyers" of team processes and effectiveness through their persistent negative behaviors and communications. These individuals have even been characterized as being like a cancer that spreads throughout the team or even the larger workforce.[71]

The types of negative feelings and attitudes expressed by a bad apple are reflected in our discussion of the self-oriented role. You will recall that this role includes such things as expressing hostility, avoiding involvement at one extreme or dominating the team at the other extreme, blocking progress by being stubborn and unreasonably resistant, taking personal credit for team results, and so on. The violation of important team norms and behaviors is seen at the extreme through forms of workplace aggression, as discussed in Chapter 8. Recall our discussion of workplace bullying, which includes a variety of behaviors that typically violate the norms and behaviors endorsed by most team members. These negative behaviors and communications range from condescension to threats of violence or actual attacks. (See Table 8.4 for a list of 24 negative acts associated with workplace bullying.)

Absence of Trust

The absence of trust among team members can severely hamper its effectiveness.[72] Members of teams with an absence of trust tend to act in these ways:

- Conceal their weaknesses and mistakes from one another.
- Hesitate to ask for help or provide constructive feedback.
- Hesitate to offer help outside their own areas of responsibility.
- Jump to conclusions about the intentions and aptitudes of others without attempting to clarify them.
- Fail to recognize and tap into one another's skills and experiences.[73]

The important role of trust and how to increase it in teams and organizations was addressed in Chapters 9 through 11.

Avoidance of Accountability for Results

When teams don't commit to a clear set of goals and plan of action, even the most committed individuals may hesitate to confront their peers on counterproductive actions and behaviors. Team members may put their own needs (ego, career, recognition) ahead of the goals of the team when individuals aren't held accountable. If members lose sight of the need to achieve results, the team's effectiveness suffers. For example, Gary Boomer, a CPA and president of Boomer Consulting in Manhattan, Kansas, contends:

> *Often accountants (CPA firms) are focused on effort rather than results. This often comes from the emphasis on chargeable hours. Don't misunderstand; accounting is a business*

that requires a significant investment of one's time. However, improved standards, processes and procedures can help firms reduce time requirements while improving client satisfaction.[74]

In the following chapter, "Managing Conflict and Negotiating Effectively," we discuss approaches for reducing avoidance of conflict, especially approaches that might be triggered by efforts to hold individuals or teams as a whole accountable.

As we commented at the start of this section, the potential team dysfunctions discussed here are just that—*potential*. They are not inevitable. Even if one or more of them begins to develop, this chapter and others have suggested ways for diagnosing and resolving them.

Chapter Summary

We focused on developing the *teams competency*—the knowledge, skills, and abilities to develop, support, and lead groups to achieve goals. Groups and teams are classified in numerous ways. In organizations, a basic classification is by the group's primary purpose, including informal groups and task groups (now commonly called teams). Informal groups develop out of the day-to-day activities, interactions, and sentiments of the members for the purpose of meeting their security or social needs. Informal groups may support, oppose, or be indifferent to formal organizational goals. Effective groups, formal or informal, have similar basic characteristics. We reviewed the core characteristics of effective teams. The degree to which a team lacks in one or more of these characteristics determines whether—and to what extent—it is ineffective. For a team to operate, it must have some degree of empowerment, which is reflected in terms of the teams' degree of potency, meaningfulness, autonomy, and impact. In our discussion of when to use teams, we noted that teams are not always appropriate. Four factors were identified for understanding when teams are likely to be superior to individuals in performing tasks and solving problems.

1. *State the basic features of groups and teams.*

The five-stage developmental model for teams focuses on forming, storming, norming, performing, and adjourning. The issues and challenges a team faces change with each stage. Teams do not necessarily develop in the straightforward manner presented in this model, especially when the members possess strong team management and related competencies. Several other models are available to aid in understanding the developmental sequence of teams.

2. *Explain the stages of team development.*

Functional teams include members from the same functional department, such as marketing, production, or finance. Problem-solving teams include individuals from a particular area of responsibility who address specific problems such as cost overruns or a decline in quality. Cross-functional teams include individuals from a number of specialties and departments who deal with problems that cut across areas. Self-managed teams include employees who must work together daily to manufacture an entire product (or major identifiable component) or provide an entire service to a set of customers. For maximum effectiveness, self-managed teams need to be empowered; that is, have a strong sense of potency, meaningfulness, autonomy, and impact. A variety of organizational, team, and individual factors must be satisfied for introduction of self-managed teams. Any type of task group could function somewhat or primarily as a virtual team, which collaborates through various information technologies. Global teams have members from a variety of countries and are, therefore, often separated significantly by time, distance, culture, and native language.

3. *Describe the attributes of common types of work-related teams.*

4. *Describe the core influences on team effectiveness.*

Team dynamics and effectiveness are influenced by the interplay of context, leadership, goals, size, member roles, member diversity, norms, and cohesiveness. One type of changing contextual influence on how teams work and network with other teams is that of information technology, especially the rapid developments in collaborative software systems. Other contextual influences are the nature of the organization's reward system and how it fits the basic value orientations of team members, especially in terms of individualism and collectivism. Team leaders may be appointed or emerge informally. They are often in a position to affect a number of the other influences on team effectiveness. Team members need to clearly understand and accept team goals as outcomes desired by each member of the team as a whole. Team size can substantially affect the dynamics among the members and the ability to create a sense of mutual accountability. Teams of about 16 or more members typically break into smaller task groups. Members may assume task-oriented, relationship-oriented, or self-oriented roles. Member diversity often enhances the effectiveness of teams by bringing more divergent insights into the causes of problems and their potential solutions. Of course, if not handled thoughtfully, member diversity may also be a source of conflict and poor communication among team members through the development of fault lines. Norms differ from rules in important ways and can have a positive or negative impact on performance. The pressures to adhere to norms may result in either compliance conformity or personal acceptance conformity. Another factor having an impact on the effectiveness of teams is cohesiveness. Of course, high cohesiveness is usually helpful to work-related teams if it improves their ability to perform tasks and achieve goals.

5. *Explain five of the potential dysfunctions of teams.*

The potential team dysfunctions are just that—*potential*. They are not inevitable as we indicate in this and previous chapters. Team members and leaders need to be mindful of the potential or actual development of team dysfunctions, which include groupthink, free riding, the bad apples effect, absence of trust, and the avoidance of accountability for results.

Key Terms and Concepts

Bad apples effect, **376**
Cohesiveness, **372**
Collective efficacy, **366**
Compliance conformity, **372**
Context, **362**
Cross-functional team, **356**
Fault lines, **369**
Free rider, **375**
Friendship group, **348**
Functional team, **356**
Global team, **360**
Group, **348**
Groupthink, **374**
Informal group, **348**
Informal leader, **364**

Norms, **371**
Personal acceptance conformity, **372**
Problem-solving team, **356**
Relations-oriented role, **367**
Self-managed team, **357**
Self-oriented role, **367**
Sucker effect, **375**
Superordinate goals, **365**
Task group, **348**
Task-oriented role, **367**
Team, **349**
Team empowerment, **350**
Team goals, **365**
Virtual team, **358**

Discussion Questions

1. Review the Learning from Experience feature titled "Boeing's Development of Teams and their Leaders." Go to the Boeing website at www.boeing.com. In the search box, enter "ethics" and read the statement on "The purpose of the Ethics and Business Conduct program is to. . . ." Does Boeing's approach to the development of teams and their leaders reflect this stated purpose? Explain.

2. Review the Diversity Competency feature titled "Angela Braly, CEO and President, WellPoint, Inc." What attributes of the diversity competency are suggested by Braly for herself, teams, and individual employees at WellPoint?

3. Think of one work-related team of which you are or have been a member during the past two years. In terms of the types of teams presented in this chapter, how would you classify it? Did it appear to be of more than one type? Explain.

4. Based on your responses to the statements in the *Team Empowerment Questionnaire* (Table 12.1), what actions, if any, are needed to modify the degree of empowerment for this team? Explain and justify your assessment.

5. Review the Teams Competency feature titled "Empowered Teams at W. L. Gore & Associates." What special challenges might exist if a firm's top-level management wanted to literally adopt Gore's team-based culture, but the firm was publicly owned and traded on the New York Stock Exchange?

6. Review the Ethics Competency feature titled "Sanjiv Das's Leadership at CitiMortgage." What ethical behaviors are being championed by Sanjiv Das for the teams and individual employees at CitiMortgage?

7. Review the Across Cultures Competency feature on Alcoa's global virtual teams. Assume you are a manager of a global organization and have been asked to lead a global virtual team. Based on the comments by the managers in this feature, what insights did you gain in how to lead this type of team?

8. Think of a new team or group in which you participated during the past two years. Describe and explain the degree to which the development of this team or group matched the five-stage model of team development discussed in this chapter.

9. What were the formal and informal goals of the team or group you identified in Question 8? Were the informal goals consistent and supportive of the formal goals? Explain.

10. We identified five potential team dysfunctions. What are some likely special challenges that could arise for a leader of a virtual team or global virtual team when dealing with these potential team dysfunctions?

Experiential Exercise and Case

Experiental Exercise: Teams Competency

Team Assessment Inventory[75]

Instructions

Think of a student or work-related team in which you are or have been a member and that was formed to achieve one or more goals. This team could be associated with a job, a specific course, or student organization.

1. Evaluate the *success* of your team on each *item* in this instrument. Use the following scale and assign a value from 1 to 5 to each item. Record the number next to each numbered item. How successful do you think your team was on each of the items?

   1 = Not at all successful (well below expectations)
   2 = Somewhat successful (though below expectations)
   3 = Moderately successful (meets expectations)
   4 = Fairly high level of success (exceeds expectations)
   5 = Very high level of success (far exceeds expectations)

2. Based on the item assessments and any other related dimensions for each factor, evaluate the *overall success* of your team on each of the seven summary *factors*. Sum the item scores for each factor. Divide the sum (total) by the number of items in that factor.

I. Goals Factor

_____ 1. Team members understood the goals and scope of the team.

_____ 2. Team members were committed to the team goals, and took ownership of them.

Overall Goals Factor:
Add the scores for items 1 through 2 and divide by 2 = _____.

II. Team Performance Management Factor

_____ 3. Individual roles, responsibilities, goals, and performance expectations were specific, challenging, and accepted by team members.

_____ 4. Team goals and performance expectations were specific, challenging, and accepted by team members.

_____ 5. The workload of the team was shared more or less equally among team members.

_____ 6. Everyone on my team did his or her fair share of the work.

_____ 7. No one on my team depended on other team members to do his or her work.

_____ 8. Nearly all the members on my team contributed equally to the work.

Overall Team Performance Management Factor:
Add the scores for items 3 through 8 and divide by 6 = _____.

III. Team Basics Factor

_____ 9. My team had enough members to handle the tasks assigned (i.e., small enough to meet and communicate frequently and easily, and yet not too small for the work required of the team).

_____ 10. The team as a whole possessed the competency levels required to achieve its goals.

_____ 11. The team members possessed the complementary competencies required to achieve the team's goals.

Overall Team Basics Factor:

Add the scores for items 9 through 11 and divide by 3 = _____.

IV. Team Processes Factor

_____ 12. My team was able to solve problems and make decisions.

_____ 13. My team was able to encourage desirable conflict and discourage undesirable team conflict.

_____ 14. My team members were able to communicate, listen, and give constructive feedback.

_____ 15. Team meetings were conducted effectively.

_____ 16. Members of my team were very willing to share information with other team members about our work.

_____ 17. Members of my team cooperated to get the work done.

_____ 18. Being on my team gave me the opportunity to work on a team and to provide support for other team members.

_____ 19. My team increased my opportunities for positive social interaction.

_____ 20. Members of my team helped each other when necessary.

Overall Team Processes Factor:

Add the scores for items 12 through 20 and divide by 9 = _____.

V. Team Spirit Factor

_____ 21. Members of my team had great confidence that the team could perform effectively.

_____ 22. My team took on the tasks assigned and completed them.

_____ 23. My team had a lot of team enthusiasm.

_____ 24. My team had high morale.

_____ 25. The team developed norms (i.e., expectations concerning team member behavior) that contributed to effective team functioning and performance.

_____ 26. Team members invested energy intensely on behalf of the team.

Overall Team Spirit Factor:

Add the scores for items 21 through 26 and divide by 6 = _____.

VI. Team Outcomes Factor

_____ 27. The team attained measurable results (if objective or quantifiable measures were available).

_____ 28. The product or service delivered by the team met or exceeded the expectations of those receiving it.

_____ 29. My team carried out its work in such a way as to maintain or enhance its ability to work together on future team tasks.

_____ 30. Generally, the team experience served to satisfy, rather than frustrate, the personal needs of team members.

Overall Team Outcomes Factor:

Add the scores for items 27 through 30 and divide by 4 = _____.

VII. Team Learning Factor

_____ 31. We took time to figure out ways to improve team processes.

_____ 32. Team members often spoke up to test assumptions about issues under discussion.

_____ 33. Team members got all the information they needed from others.

_____ 34. Someone always made sure that we stopped to reflect on the team's processes.

_____ 35 The team as a whole asked for feedback from others as it progressed.

_____ 36. The team actively reviewed its own progress and performance.

Overall Team Learning Factor:

Add the scores for items 31 through 36 and divide by 6 = _____.

Interpretation

An average score of 4 or 5 on a factor suggests considerable success (exceeding expectations and success). An average score of 3 on a factor suggests a satisfactory level of success and a feeling of just "okay." An average score of 1 or 2 on a factor suggests that the team processes needed considerable improvement. You might consider all seven factors as a whole to arrive at a final summary assessment. Insights for the action steps needed are likely to be learned through each factor and the specific items that are in it.

Questions

1. Based on this inventory, what specific changes do you propose to improve the effectiveness of this team?

2. Are any team dysfunctions suggested by your scores on one or more of the seven team factors? Explain. If none are identified, why do you think that was the case for this team?

Case: Teams Competency

Absence of Teamwork[76]

At 3 A.M., John was wondering what he was going to do to finish the team project that was due by 9 A.M. the same morning. Just five minutes ago, Shaun stormed out of John's apartment yelling. Perhaps the pressure was too much for Shaun. John knew somehow he would get the work done by the deadline, but he was getting sick and tired of doing the work by himself and was wondering how he got himself into the mess. Nine hours ago, John, Shaun, and the rest of his teammates got together to complete the project. The major project for the finance class had been divided up among six team members several weeks ago. It had been agreed that they would get together the night before the due date to complete the assignment.

John completed his section a day before the meeting and spent the day checking over his work. He was quite proud of his work. When John called Shaun, his best friend, Shaun told him that his work was also completed and of high quality. When John got to the meeting, he found Shaun, Brigitte, Anton, and Aliyah at the meeting, but Craig was nowhere in sight. When he asked about Craig, Shaun just shrugged his shoulders and said that he had no idea.

As it turned out, Craig's absence was the least of John's problems. Neither Brigitte nor Aliyah had completed their parts of the assignments. Brigitte had completed only 50 percent of her part, and John could see that even the completed part needed a major revision. Aliyah completed 80 percent of her assignment, but she wasn't sure whether she got it right. Anton completed 75 percent of his assignment, and his part only needed a minor revision. At this point, John felt like pulling his hair out but remained calm. He said, "OK. I think we can get the work done if we all pitch in together. . . ." Before he had a chance to finish his sentence, Brigitte said that she couldn't stay because she had to go to work. She told the group that her shift would start at 9 P.M., and she would get off at 6 A.M. the next day. Anton jumped in and said he had to leave at 7:30 P.M. to attend the NFL Monday night football game. He had two tickets to the game, and he had promised to take his fiancée to the game. John looked at Shaun and Aliyah to see what excuses they had. To his relief, John found Shaun didn't have any commitments. However, Aliyah had to leave at 9 P.M. to attend her husband's surprise birthday party.

John realized that in order to get the project done, he and Shaun would have to stay up all night doing other people's work and combining the parts. Things proceeded smoothly until John noticed that a major piece of work that was Craig's part was left out. John knew Craig could be a liability. When the team divided up the work, John insisted that Craig's critical parts also be worked on by others in the team. Despite John's careful planning, one critical piece was never assigned to anyone besides Craig. It had to be completed before other parts of the project could be consolidated. This was when Shaun became more belligerent. John understood why Shaun was frustrated. John thought if anyone should be angry, it should be him. John felt he had somehow assumed the leadership role in the team even though he didn't want to. Now, he felt responsible for the whole project.

Shaun said, "This isn't fair. Why do we always get stuck with doing all the work?" John said, "Because we want to get an A for the course. Both Brigitte and Aliyah just want to get B's. They are marketing majors, and they couldn't care less about finance. Anton is a JD/MBA student, and he just wants to practice law. Oh, Craig has already found a lucrative job in the computer industry. So, he just wants to graduate and go on with his life. So, you see it's up to us to get the project done."

Shaun became agitated and said, "John, I couldn't care less at this point. I'm exhausted and burned out. I've got to go home and get some sleep or I won't make it to my accounting exam this afternoon." (Yelling and screaming.) "Those [expletive] teammates can go [expletive] themselves! I'm going home." Shaun stormed out of John's apartment. John was left alone to work on the project. He assessed the project and realized that it would take him at least another six hours to finish it. John kept asking himself how he got himself into this mess and started to get angry at himself.

John finally finished the project around 8:30 A.M., and he was about to print out the cover page for the project. When he came to putting the names of the team members on the cover page, he hesitated. He really wanted to put only his and Shaun's names on the cover page and leave other names off. John eventually printed out two cover pages, one with all the names and the other with only John and Shaun's names. He rushed out of the apartment and walked over to Professor Michael's office to submit the project. Professor Michael was working in his office that morning. When he saw John standing outside his office, he called John in: "Hey, John. Do you want to talk to me? Come on in." Somewhat surprised at Professor Michael's prompt, John told him that he was there to hand in his team project. Pretending everything was fine, he quickly selected one of the cover pages and attached it to the main project. He handed in the project and walked out of the office.

Questions

1. How would you evaluate this team based on each of the seven characteristics of effective groups?
2. What type of work-related team is presented in this case? Explain.
3. What are the dysfunctions of this team? Explain and illustrate each.
4. Was John a good team member? Was he a responsible team member? Explain.
5. What could the team have done to avoid the situation described?
6. What should John have done at the end of the case; that is, which cover page should he have picked? What might be the consequences of either action? Did one or the other choice make him more ethical? Explain.
7. What cover page do you think John selected? Why?

chapter 13

Managing Conflict and Negotiating Effectively

Learning Goals

After studying this chapter, you should be able to:

1

Describe the primary conflict levels in organizations.

2

Explain the common interpersonal conflict-handling styles.

3

Discuss the core stages, strategies, and influences in negotiations.

4

State the unique aspects of across culture negotiations.

Learning Content

Learning from Experience
    Cathy McBroom versus Federal Judge Samuel Kent

Conflict Levels
Teams Competency
    IBM's Cross-Team Workouts

Interpersonal Conflict-Handling Styles
Self Competency
    Reflections on Conflict-Avoiding Managers

Negotiation in Conflict Management
Change Competency
    GM and UAW Negotiate for Mutual Survival

Across Culture Negotiations
Across Cultures Competency
    Business Negotiations in Germany and Italy

Experiential Exercise and Case
Experiential Exercise: Self Competency
    Conflict-Handling Styles
Case: Communication Competency
    Conflict Style Case Incidents

Cathy McBroom versus Federal Judge Samuel Kent

Cathy McBroom, a federal court case manager, faced off against a federal judge who ruled over the U.S. court in Galveston, Texas. U.S. District Judge Samuel Kent seemed untouchable. He had been appointed by a U.S. president and approved by Congress to serve for a lifetime. His sentencing to 33 months in jail brought both vindication and sorrow to Cathy McBroom. Kent admitted to sexually molesting both McBroom and his former secretary Donna Wilkerson. He pleaded guilty to obstruction of justice for lying to judges who investigated his misconduct. Wilkerson came forward after the judge's first indictment.

McBroom stated: "I'm very satisfied. Kent was treated like any other defendant." Being allowed to deliver her victim statement publicly at a federal court hearing made McBroom feel like a big weight had been lifted. She stated: "I did the right thing and didn't have to lose my job. Maybe it will give other women the opportunity to come forward . . . [but] I was not out for vengeance. For someone like the judge who had a brilliant mind, it's a horrible thing."

Through it all, McBroom continued working at the Houston federal courthouse, where she had transferred, and attended college at night. She suffered emotional conflicts, sleeplessness, and other forms of stress. Kent's criminal defense attorney repeatedly labeled her as "enthusiastically consensual" and a disgruntled employee.

"Eventually, I went into this and decided to make a complaint feeling I would have a very small voice.

But I knew I could never be happy with myself if I didn't do it," McBroom said. She said the incident that prompted her to action—though it was not the first time Kent attempted to assault her—came in 2007 when McBroom was summoned to Kent's Galveston chambers. She says the judge, a foot taller and 150 pounds heavier, attempted to force . . . [excised]. She fled in tears. McBroom reported the incident to a female supervisor who told her to brush it off—if she wanted to keep her job.

On the day of the March 2007 incident, Kent called McBroom into his office and started to sexually assault her. She got away after someone knocked on the door. That weekend, McBroom sat down to a computer and poured details into a request for immediate transfer, saying she could never return to "a hostile and dangerous workplace. I felt like I was not going to be protected by the clerk's office and if Kent wanted to go on and

F. CARTER SMITH/BLOOMBERG NEWS/LANDOV

do something worse to me, he probably felt like he had the power. . . . He had pushed things to the point where I no longer cared if I lost my job."

It was a crime, she thought. Yet contacting the police seemed unthinkable to her. "I felt like as a federal judge, he had everyone in his back pocket. Who could I report this to?" McBroom requested an immediate transfer to Houston and eventually filed a formal judicial misconduct complaint in 2007. Worried about facing a judicial disciplinary hearing alone, McBroom asked Houston attorney Rusty Hardin to help. Together in 2007, they prepared to be summoned to New Orleans to address a ruling body of federal judges. The summons never came. Instead, the Fifth Circuit judicial council voted secretly to approve the never-disclosed specific agreement between the

three investigating judges and Kent's attorney, paid by taxpayers to defend him. Kent accepted a paid four-month leave and a transfer from Galveston to Houston, where McBroom had been reassigned as well.

After open legal proceedings, Kent pleaded guilty to one count of obstruction of justice for lying to a judicial panel investigating a sexual harassment complaint. Kent also admitted he had nonconsensual sexual contact with the two employees between 2003 and 2007. The five charges relating to the sexual misconduct were dismissed in the plea agreement. Prosecutor Peter Ainsworth stressed that Kent lied not only to the judges investigating the complaint against him, but to the FBI and to prosecutors and that Kent even pressured Wilkerson that she lie, too.[1]

Conflict and the need to manage it occur every day in organizations. **Conflict** *is a process in which one party (person or group) perceives that its interests are being opposed or negatively affected by another party.*[2] This definition implies incompatible concerns among the people involved and includes a variety of conflict issues and events. **Conflict management** *refers to the diagnostic processes, interpersonal styles, and negotiation strategies that are designed to avoid unnecessary conflict and reduce or resolve excessive conflict.* The ability to understand and correctly diagnose conflict is essential to managing it.

In this chapter, we examine conflict and negotiation from several perspectives. First, we discuss the core dimensions of conflict and note different attitudes about it. Second, we present the primary levels of conflict found in organizations. Third, we share five interpersonal styles of conflict management and the guidelines under which each style may be appropriate. Fourth, we discuss negotiation and basic negotiation strategies, and highlight the role of third-party mediation in the negotiation process. Fifth, we review some of the complications and recommendations for negotiations across cultures.

Our attitude is that conflict may sometimes be desirable and at other times destructive. In Chapter 8, we reviewed a variety of situations that were related to high levels of stress, emotional conflicts, and workplace aggression, such as bullying and office politics. The Learning from Experience feature on "Cathy McBroom versus Federal Judge Samuel Kent" provides a profound example of these relationships. Although some types of conflict can be avoided and reduced, other types of conflict have to be properly managed by a competent leader. The balanced approach is sensitive to the consequences of conflict, ranging from negative outcomes (loss of skilled employees, sabotage, low quality of work, stress, and even violence) to positive outcomes (creative alternatives, increased motivation and commitment, high quality of work, and personal satisfaction).

The balanced approach recognizes that conflict occurs in organizations whenever interests collide. Sometimes, employees will think differently, want to act differently, and seek to pursue different goals. When these differences divide individuals, they must be managed constructively.[3] How easily or effectively conflict can be managed depends on various factors, such as how important the issue is to the people involved and whether strong leadership is available to address it. Table 13.1 identifies some of

TABLE 13.1 Effects of Various Dimensions of Conflict

DIMENSION	DIFFICULT TO RESOLVE	EASY TO RESOLVE
• The issue itself	A matter of principle or values	Simply clarifying misperceptions
• Size of the stakes	Large	Small
• Continuity of interaction	Single transaction	Long-term relationship
• Attitudes	Negative toward each other	Neutral to positive toward each other
• Communication competency	Weak, poor listening	Strong, active listening
• Characteristics of participants' "groups"	Disorganized, with weak leadership	Cohesive, with strong leadership
• Involvement of third parties	No neutral third party available	Trusted, prestigious, neutral third party available

Source: Adapted from Lewicki, R. J., Saunders, D. M., and Barry, B. *Negotiation*, 6th ed. New York: McGraw-Hill, 2010.

the dimensions that distinguish conflict situations that are difficult to resolve from conflict situations that are easier to resolve.

Conflict Levels

Learning Goal

1. *Describe the primary conflict levels in organizations.*

Four primary levels of conflict may be present in organizations: intrapersonal (within an individual), interpersonal (between individuals), intragroup (within a group), and intergroup (between groups). Figure 13.1 suggests that these levels are often cumulative and interrelated. For example, over a multiyear period, it appears that Cathy McBroom experienced multiple levels of conflict. Can you identify them for her?

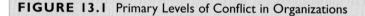

FIGURE 13.1 Primary Levels of Conflict in Organizations

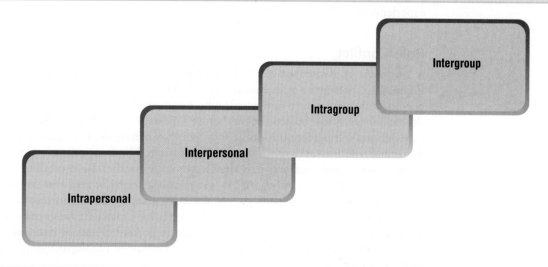

Intrapersonal Conflict

Intrapersonal conflict *occurs within an individual and usually involves some form of goal, cognitive, or affective conflict.* It is triggered when a person's behavior results in outcomes that are mutually exclusive. Inner tensions and frustrations commonly result. McBroom experienced this during her struggles of whether to stay in her job, whether to complain about Samuel Kent, and eventually whether to seek a legal remedy.

A graduating senior may have to decide between jobs that offer different challenges, pay, security, and locations. Trying to make such a decision may create one or more of three basic types of intrapersonal goal conflict:

1. *Approach–approach conflict* means that an individual must choose between two or more alternatives, each of which is expected to have a positive outcome (e.g., a choice between two jobs that appear to be equally attractive).

2. *Avoidance–avoidance conflict* means that an individual must choose between two or more alternatives, each of which is expected to have a negative outcome (e.g., relatively low pay or extensive out-of-town traveling).

3. *Approach–avoidance conflict* means that an individual must decide whether to do something that is expected to have both positive and negative outcomes (e.g., accepting an offer of a good job in a bad location).

Many decisions involve the resolution of intrapersonal goal conflict.[4] The intensity of intrapersonal conflict generally increases under one or more of the following conditions: (1) Several realistic alternative courses of action are available to the individual for handling the conflict, (2) the individual sees the positive and negative consequences of the alternative courses of action as roughly equal, or (3) the source of conflict is important to the individual.

Severe unresolved intrapersonal conflict within employees, customers, or others may trigger intense interpersonal conflict. As discussed in Chapter 8, much violence and aggression in the workplace has its source in severe intrapersonal conflict.

Interpersonal Conflict

Interpersonal conflict *occurs when two or more individuals perceive that their attitudes, behaviors, or preferred goals are in opposition.* As with intrapersonal conflict, much interpersonal conflict is based on some type of role conflict or role ambiguity. Clearly, Cathy McBroom experienced interpersonal conflict with Judge Samuel Kent over a number of years. Recall the sleeplessness and crying spells she experienced as a result of both intrapersonal and interpersonal conflicts due to the multiple harassments she experienced.

Role Conflict

A **role** *is the set of interconnected tasks and behaviors that others expect a person to perform.* Figure 13.2 presents a role episode model, which involves role senders and a focal person. Role senders are individuals who have expectations of how the focal person should behave. A role episode begins before a message is sent because role senders have expectations and perceptions of the focal person's behaviors. These, in turn, influence the actual role messages that the senders transmit. The focal person's perceptions of these messages and pressures may then lead to role conflict. **Role conflict** *occurs when a focal person is pressured by role senders to respond and behave in ways that are incompatible with the focal person's preferences.* A **role set** *is the group of role senders that directly affect the focal person.* A role set might include the employee's manager, other team members, close friends, immediate family members, and important clients or customers.

Four types of role conflict may occur as a result of incompatible messages and pressures from the role set:

FIGURE 13.2 Role Episode Model

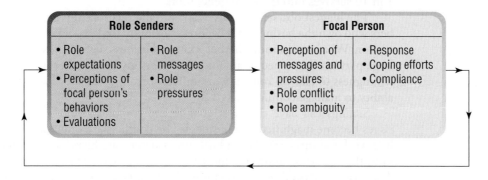

Source: Based on Kahn, R. L., et al. *Organizational Stress: Studies in Role Conflict and Ambiguity.* New York: John Wiley and Sons, 1964, 26.

- *Intrasender role conflict* may occur when different messages and pressures from a single member of the role set are incompatible, for example, when a manager wants a routine goal achieved more quickly, at a lower cost, and with higher quality.

- *Intersender role conflict* may occur when the messages and pressures from one role sender oppose messages and pressures from one or more other senders. For example, the top leaders of GM, prior to filing for bankruptcy, experienced intersender role conflict from a variety of individuals who represented the United Auto Workers, the U.S. federal government, bondholders, major shareholders, creditors, and others.

- *Interrole conflict* may occur when role pressures associated with membership in one group are incompatible with pressures stemming from membership in other groups. College friends may want you to go out to have fun on a Thursday night and you want to do so, but the members of your study group for a certain course want you to join them to help prepare for a major exam on Friday and you want to do so.

- *Person–role conflict* may occur when role requirements are incompatible with the focal person's own attitudes, values, or views of acceptable behavior. Intrapersonal conflict typically accompanies this type of role conflict.[5] For example, the demands imposed on McBroom were incompatible with her values and attitudes.

Role Ambiguity

Role ambiguity *is the uncertainty and lack of clarity surrounding expectations about a single role.* Like role conflict, severe role ambiguity causes stress and triggers subsequent coping behaviors. These coping behaviors often include taking aggressive action (e.g., verbal abuse, theft, and violence), hostile communication, withdrawing, or attempting joint problem solving. Research findings suggest that high levels of role conflict and role ambiguity have numerous dramatic effects, including stress reactions, aggression, hostility, and withdrawal behaviors (turnover and absenteeism).[6] Stress is a common reaction to severe role conflict and role ambiguity (see Chapter 8). However, effective leaders and professionals possess the ability to cope with the many ambiguities inherent in their roles.

Intragroup Conflict

Intragroup conflict *refers to disputes among some or all of a group's members, which often affect a group's dynamics and effectiveness.* For example, family-run businesses can be especially prone to intragroup and other types of conflict. Such conflicts typically become more intense when an owner–founder approaches retirement, actually retires, or dies. Only 3 in 10 family-run businesses make it to the second generation, and only 1 in 10 survives into the third generation.

The biggest obstacles to succession are the relationships among the family members who own the business and bear responsibility for keeping it alive for another generation. What determines whether a family business soars or nosedives? It depends, in large part, on the respect that family members give each other in the workplace, their willingness to take on roles at work different from those they have at home, and their ability to manage conflict effectively.[7]

Siblings can have the most volatile and complex family relationships—and the issues become magnified in a business. The conflicts are often practical. Can one sibling work for another? Should birth order determine hierarchy? Should siblings give in to the one who whines the most to preserve peace, then work around him or her? The answers depend on the situation. Ongoing factors often underlie these problems. Although they share parents and many memories, siblings often must come to grips with having different attitudes and preferences because they grew up at different times in a changing family environment. The fact that parents try to interest their children in the family business but give them little assistance in understanding how to work with each other puts the siblings in a double bind: an obligation with no road map.[8]

Intergroup Conflict

Intergroup conflict *refers to opposition, disagreements, and disputes between groups or teams.* At times, intergroup conflict is intense, drawn out, and costly to those involved. Under high levels of competition and conflict, the groups develop attitudes toward each other that are characterized by distrust, rigidity, a focus only on self-interest, failure to listen, and the like.

Intergroup conflict within organizations can occur across teams, departments, or divisions, and between different levels of the organization, such as between top management and first-level employees. At Ford, American Airlines, and other companies, this type of vertical conflict is clearly seen in union–management disputes through collective bargaining. Conflicts often occur between manufacturing and sales or internal auditors and the other business functions.

Let's consider four of the various sources of intergroup conflict[9]:

- *Perceived goal incompatibility.* Goal incompatibility is probably the greatest source of intergroup conflict. The potential conflicts between marketing and manufacturing are significant in many organizations because some of the goals for these two functions may be at odds. For example, at Josten's—a provider of class rings, yearbooks, and the like—one of the top marketing goals that will help maximize sales (for which bonuses and commissions are received) is to satisfy the unique requests of customers. Manufacturing has the priority goal of long lead times to maximize efficiency. Accordingly, marketing may state: "Our customers demand variety." Manufacturing may counter: "All of the orders for pictures and rings don't arrive until late April or early May. We cannot meet the demand for these orders by late May. We need longer lead times to maximize efficiency."

- *Perceived differentiation.* The greater the number of ways in which groups see themselves as different from each other (e.g., the Gen Y generation versus Gen X), the greater the potential for conflicts between them. These differences may actually be sources of strength, such as the specialized expertise and insights that those from different functions and backgrounds contribute to achieve the organization's goals. Unfortunately, these differences too often serve as the base for stimulating distrust and conflicts between the groups or teams.

- *Task interdependency.* **Task interdependency** *refers to the interrelationships required between two or more groups in achieving their goals.* For example, sales needs manufacturing to produce the required products on a timely and cost-effective basis. Manufacturing needs sales to generate sales of those products that it is able to produce. In general, as task interdependency increases, the potential for conflict between the groups increases. Of course, task interdependency also occurs among organizations, such as between General Motors, the United Auto Workers, and the U.S. federal government.

- *Perceived limited resources.* Limited resources create the condition for groups competing and engaging in conflict over the available resources. This circumstance was clearly seen in the situations of GM and Chrysler. In their fight for survival, multiple relationship conflicts occurred among the firms, suppliers, bond holders, divisions within those firms, banks, the U.S. federal government, and so on. Organizations have limited money, physical facilities, and human resources to allocate among different groups. The groups may think they need more of the resources than are available to meet the goals for which they will be held accountable.

The following Teams Competency feature reports on IBM's cross-team workouts, which are designed to manage conflicts between teams and groups.[10] The International Business Machines Corporation (IBM), with headquarters in Armonk, New York, is one of the world's major providers of computer products and services. IBM's service arm accounts for more than half of its sales. IBM has approximately 390,000 employees worldwide.[11]

Teams competency

IBM's Cross-Team Workouts

Several years ago, IBM's sales and delivery organization became increasingly complex as the company brought together previously independent divisions and reorganized itself to provide customers with integrated solutions of bundled products and services. Senior executives soon recognized that managers in different units were not dealing with conflicts effectively. The relationships among them were strained because they failed to consult and coordinate around cross-unit issues. This led to the creation of a forum called the Market Growth Workshop. This forum was designed to send a message throughout the company that resolving cross-unit conflict was critical to meeting customer needs and, in turn, growing market share. Monthly conference calls brought together leaders, salespeople, and frontline product specialists from across the company. They discussed and resolved cross-unit conflicts that were hindering important sales—for example, the difficulty salespeople faced in getting needed technical resources from over-stretched product groups.

IBM's Cross-Team Workouts are weekly meetings that take place in person or via conference call.

The Market Growth Workshop evolved into a more structured approach to managing escalated conflict known as Cross-Team Workouts. Designed to make conflict resolution more transparent, the workouts are weekly meetings in person and via conference calls of people across the organization who work together on sales and delivery issues for specific accounts. The sessions provide a public forum for resolving conflicts over account strategies, solution configurations, pricing, and delivery. Those issues that cannot be resolved at the local level are escalated to regional workout sessions attended by managers from product groups, services, sales, and finance. Attendees then communicate and explain the resolutions to their reports.

Issues that cannot be resolved at the regional level are escalated to an even higher level workout session attended by cross-unit executives from a larger geographic region, such as the Americas or Asia Pacific. The session is chaired by the general manager of the region present-ing the issue. The most complex and strategic issues reach this global forum. Attendance at

these sessions overlaps—the leaders who chair one level of cross-team workout sessions attend the sessions at the next higher level. This overlap allows them to observe the decision-making pro-cess at the higher level, which further enhances the transparency of the process among different levels of the company.

IBM has formalized the process for the direct resolution of conflicts between services and product sales on large accounts. A managing director in sales and a global relationship part-ner in IBM global services are designated as the ultimate point of resolution. By explicitly making the resolution of complex conflicts part of the job descriptions for both managing directors and global relationship partners—and by making that clear to others in the organization—IBM has reduced ambiguity, increased transparency, and increased the efficiency with which conflicts are resolved.

To learn more about IBM, go to **www.ibm.com.**

Learning Goal

2. Explain the common interpersonal conflict-handling styles.

Interpersonal Conflict-Handling Styles

Individuals handle interpersonal conflict in various ways.[12] Figure 13.3 presents a model for understanding and comparing five interpersonal conflict-handling styles. The styles are identified by their locations on two dimensions: *concern for self* and *con-cern for others*. The desire to satisfy your own concerns depends on the extent to which

FIGURE 13.3 Interpersonal Conflict-Handling Styles

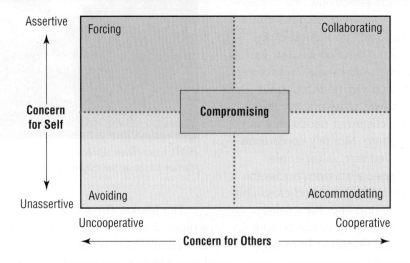

you are *assertive* or *unassertive* in pursuing personal goals. Your desire to satisfy the concerns of others depends on the extent to which you are *cooperative* or *uncooperative*. The five interpersonal conflict-handling styles thus represent different combinations of assertiveness and cooperativeness. Although you may have a natural tendency toward one or two of the styles, you may use all of them as the situation and people involved change. For example, the style you use in working through a conflict with a good friend may be quite different from the style you use with a stranger after a minor auto accident. The Experiential Exercise at the end of this chapter contains a questionnaire on page 407 that you can use to assess your own styles for handling conflict. We suggest that you complete this questionnaire now.

> ### Communication Insight
>
> You have to be willing to temporarily upset a lot of people in order to save a company. You have to withstand a lot of conflict, histrionics, screaming at meetings, and toughness on all sides.
>
> *Debra Cafaro, Chairman, President and CEO, Ventas, Inc.*

Collaborating Style

The **collaborating style** *refers to high levels of cooperative and assertive behaviors.* It is the win–win approach to interpersonal conflict handling. The person using collaboration desires to maximize joint results. An individual who uses this style tends to (1) see conflict as natural, helpful, and leading to a more creative solution if handled properly; (2) exhibit trust in and candor with others; and (3) recognize that when conflict is resolved to the satisfaction of all, commitment to the solution is likely. An individual who uses the collaborating style is often seen as dynamic and evaluated favorably by others. The following statements illustrate the collaborating style:

- I first try to overcome any distrust that might exist between us. Then I try to get at the feelings that we mutually have about the topics. I stress that nothing we decide is cast in stone and suggest that we find a position for which we can do a trial run.

- I tell the others my ideas, actively seek out their ideas, and search for a mutually beneficial solution.

- I like to suggest new solutions and build on a variety of viewpoints that may have been expressed.

- I try to dig into an issue to find a solution that works for all of us.

Insights for Individuals

With this style, conflict is open and evaluated by all concerned. Sharing, examining, and assessing the reasons for the conflict should lead to development of an alternative that effectively resolves the conflict and is acceptable to everyone involved. Collaboration is most practical in certain circumstances. A high level of cooperation is needed to justify expending the extra time and energy needed to make working through the conflict worthwhile. Ideally, a reasonable degree of parity in influence exists among the individuals so that they feel free to interact candidly, regardless of their formal status. The potential exists for mutual benefits, especially over the long run, for resolving the dispute through a win–win process. There is sufficient organizational support for investing the necessary time and energy in resolving disputes in this manner. The norms, rewards, and punishments of the organization—especially those set by top leadership—provide the framework for encouraging or discouraging collaboration.[13]

> ### Communication Insight
>
> The best conflict management executives lead by example. They are candid and encourage candor in their interactions with others, stepping up and calling out dysfunctional behavior when they see it. They really listen to what others have to say, don't resort to passive-aggressive or bullying tactics to get their way, and give and receive feedback in a healthy, depersonalized way.
>
> *Howard Guttman, Principal, Guttman Development Strategies, and Author, When Goliaths Clash: Managing Executive Conflict to Build a More Dynamic Organization*

Compromising Style

The **compromising style** *refers to behaviors at an intermediate level of cooperation and assertiveness*. The individual using this style engages in give-and-take concessions. Compromising is commonly used and widely accepted as a means of resolving conflict. The following statements illustrate the compromising style:

*   I want to know how and what others feel. When the timing is right, I explain how I feel and try to show them where they are wrong. Of course, it's often necessary to settle on some middle ground.
*   After failing to get my way, I usually find it necessary to seek a fair combination of gains and losses for all of us.
*   I give in to others if they are willing to meet me halfway.
*   As the old saying goes, half a loaf is better than nothing. Let's split the difference.

An individual who compromises with others tends to be evaluated favorably. Various explanations are suggested for the favorable evaluation of the compromising style. For many, it is seen primarily as a cooperative "holding back." It may reflect a pragmatic way of dealing with conflict. Compromise is seen as helping maintain good relations for the future.

Insights for Individuals

The compromising style shouldn't be used early in the conflict resolution process for several reasons. First, the people involved are likely to compromise on the stated issues rather than on the real issues. The first issues raised in a conflict often aren't the real ones, and premature compromise will prevent full diagnosis or exploration of the real issues. For example, students telling professors that their courses are tough and challenging may simply be trying to negotiate an easier grade. Second, accepting an initial position is easier than searching for alternatives that are more acceptable to everyone involved. Third, compromise is inappropriate to all or part of the situation when it isn't the best decision available. That is, further discussion may reveal a better way of resolving the conflict.

Compared to the collaborating style, the compromising style doesn't maximize mutual satisfaction. Compromise achieves moderate, but only partial, satisfaction for each person. This style is likely to be appropriate under various circumstances. A compromise agreement enables each person to be better off, or at least not worse off than if no agreement were reached. It may not be possible to achieve a total win–win agreement. Conflicting goals or opposing interests can block agreement on one person's proposal.

Those who use the forcing style try to achieve their own goals without concern for others, sometimes threatening demotion, dismissal, or other punishments.

Forcing Style

The **forcing style** *refers to assertive and uncooperative behaviors and represents a win–lose approach to interpersonal conflict*. Those who use the forcing approach try to achieve their own goals without concern for others. This was very evident in the behaviors exhibited by Judge Samuel Kent in his relationships with Cathy McBroom and Donna Wilkerson. This style relies on coercive power, which we explained in Chapter 10. It may help a person achieve individual goals, but, like avoidance, forcing tends to result in unfavorable evaluations by others. The following statements illustrate the forcing style:

*   I like to put it plainly: Like it or not, what I say goes.
*   I convince the other person of the logic and benefits of my position.

TRIANGLE IMAGES/PHOTODISC/GETTY IMAGES

- I insist that my position be accepted during a disagreement.
- I usually hold onto my solution to a problem after the controversy starts.

Individuals who are prone to using the forcing style assume that conflict resolution means that one person must win and the other must lose. When dealing with conflict, forcing-style managers may threaten or actually use demotion, dismissal, negative performance evaluations, or other punishments to gain compliance. When conflict occurs between peers, employees using the forcing style might try to get their way by appealing to their manager. This approach represents an attempt to use the manager to force the decision on the opposing individual.

Insights for Individuals

Overreliance on forcing by a manager lessens employees' work motivation because their interests haven't been considered. Relevant information and other possible alternatives usually are ignored. In some situations, the forcing style may be necessary. Emergencies may require quick action. An unpopular course of action might be necessary for long-term organizational effectiveness and survival (e.g., cost cutting and dismissal of employees for unsatisfactory performance). The individual needs to take action for self-protection and to stop others from taking advantage of him or her.

At times, personal decisions can escalate to the point at which both or one of the parties—employer versus employee—uses the forcing style. When the conflict is escalated and unresolved, one of the parties may even appeal to the legal system to obtain the preferred solution on the other party through court-mandated orders. Ultimately, this was the path taken by Cathy McBroom, and understandably so, after other efforts failed in coping with former federal Judge Samuel Kent.

Accommodating Style

The **accommodating style** *refers to cooperative and unassertive behaviors.* Accommodation may represent an unselfish act, a long-term strategy to encourage cooperation by others, or just complying with the wishes of others. Individuals using the accommodating style are typically evaluated favorably by others, but they may also be perceived as weak and submissive. The following statements illustrate the accommodating style:

- Conflict is best managed through the suspension of my personal goals in order to maintain good relationships with others.
- If it makes other people happy, I'm all for it.
- I like to smooth over disagreements by making them appear less important.
- I ease conflict by suggesting that our differences are trivial and then show goodwill by blending my ideas into those of the other person.

Insights for Individuals

When using the accommodating style, an individual may act as though the conflict will go away in time and appeal for cooperation. The person will try to reduce tensions and stress by providing support. This style shows concern about the emotional aspects of conflict but little interest in working on its substantive issues. The accommodating style simply results in the individual covering up or glossing over personal feelings. It is generally ineffective if used consistently. The accommodating style may be effective in the short run in some situations. The individual is in a potentially explosive emotional conflict situation, and accommodating is used to defuse it. The maintenance of harmony and avoidance of disruption are especially important in the short run. The conflicts are based primarily on the personalities of the individuals and cannot be easily resolved.

Avoiding Style

The **avoiding style** *refers to unassertive and uncooperative behaviors.* A person uses this style to stay away from conflict, ignore disagreements, or remain neutral. The avoidance approach reflects an aversion to tension and frustration and may involve a decision to let a conflict work itself out. Because ignoring important issues often frustrates others, the consistent use of the avoidance style usually results in unfavorable evaluations by others. The following statements illustrate the avoiding style:

* If there are rules that apply, I cite them. If there aren't, I leave the other person free to make her own decision.
* I usually don't take positions that will create controversy.
* I shy away from topics that are sources of disputes with my friends.
* That's okay. It wasn't important anyway. Let's leave well enough alone.

Insights for Individuals

When unresolved conflict gets in the way of accomplishing goals, the avoiding style will lead to negative results for the organization. This style may be desirable under some situations. The issue may be minor or only of passing importance and thus not worth the individual's time or energy to confront the conflict. The individual doesn't have enough information to deal effectively with the conflict at that time. The individual's power is so low relative to the other person's that there's little chance of causing change (e.g., disagreement with a new strategy approved by top management). Another individual can resolve the conflict more effectively.

Insights for Leaders

Studies conducted on the use of different interpersonal conflict-handling styles indicate that leaders who use a collaborating style tend to be (1) more successful rather than less successful managers and (2) are found more in high-performing rather than medium- and low-performing organizations. The leader's use of collaboration seems to result in positive feelings by others, as well as favorable evaluations of performance and abilities. In contrast to collaboration, the forcing and avoiding styles often have negative effects. These styles tend to be associated with a less constructive use of conflict, more negative feelings, and unfavorable evaluations of performance and abilities. The effects of the accommodating and compromising styles appear to be mixed. The use of accommodation sometimes results in positive feelings from others. But these managers do not form favorable evaluations of the performance and abilities of those using the accommodating style. The use of the compromising style generally results in positive feelings from others.[14]

As suggested in the following Self Competency feature, the avoidance style, if used as a general tendency, may be especially problematic for the manager and subordinates.[15] This feature presents a sample of comments related to avoidance-prone managers.

Self competency

Reflections on Conflict-Avoiding Managers

Lowrie Beacham admits he didn't like confronting people or making decisions that favored one staffer over another, including the time two of his people were vying to be in charge of the new fitness center. He recalls: "Instead of having one bad day and getting over it, it went on for literally years. You just kick the can a little farther down the road—'Let's have a meeting on this next month'—anything you can try to keep from having that confrontation."

Any time his employees bristled at his gentle criticisms, he'd change the subject: "You're getting to work on time; that's wonderful!" he'd say. "Never mind that your clients say you're difficult to work with." What resulted was a dysfunctional department, he admits, "with no discipline, no confidence in where they stood, lots of scheming and kvetching, backstabbing." He gave up his management role. "I'm extremely happy not managing," he says.

James Hardcastle reflects that every time he asked for feedback on a report his manager would never say anything constructive, negative or positive. Hardcastle comments: "My manager would visibly dance around the aspects of my reports that needed improvement. I never really knew exactly where I stood."

Lawrence Levine reports on witnessing a colleague spend much of his day on eBay and other such sites. There's no doubt the manager saw it, too. It mystified the staff. Levine states: "We all pondered in the absence of any action why the heck this person drawing a decent salary was allowed to do this stuff. The anger was that all the rest of us produced."

John Traylor concedes he used to be a conflict-avoiding manager. He reflects on dealing with a lazy employee. He hated giving an employee news that he thought would "crush his spirit." Traylor even once quietly arranged to have an employee transferred at the request of others. Traylor states: "The employee could leave with the dignity of having been asked by higher levels to move to a more important project—and I didn't have to confront the real issue." Traylor concedes that his handling didn't help the employee improve. He also says that the management training he received from the company didn't teach him how to deal with such conflict. "It would have been helpful," he says.

Negotiation in Conflict Management

Learning Goal

3. Discuss the core stages, strategies, and influences in negotiations.

Negotiation *is a process in which two or more interdependent individuals or groups who perceive that they have both common and conflicting goals state and discuss proposals and preferences for specific terms of a possible agreement.* Negotiation often includes a combination of compromise, collaboration, and possibly some forcing conflict-handling styles. A negotiation situation is one in which

- two or more individuals or groups must make decisions about their combined goals and interests,
- the individuals are committed to peaceful means for resolving their disputes, and
- there is no clear or established method or procedure for making the decisions.[16]

Stages of Negotiation

Negotiations can be viewed as a process with a series of distinct stages. Table 13.2 provides a list of a few of the questions that might be presented in each of the four stages of negotiations, as discussed next:

- The first stage involves *assessing the situation* to ensure that it is appropriate for negotiation, preparing to enter into negotiations, and determining that the other party has some reason to negotiate with you. A critical issue to address in this stage is for each party to establish its BATNA. **BATNA** *refers to the Best Alternative To a Negotiated Agreement and refers to the negotiator's absolute bottom line.* If an agreement isn't better than the BATNA, it actually makes the negotiator worse off. To protect negotiators from escalating to irrational commitments during negotiations, they need to identify and assess the alternatives if an agreement is not reached.

TABLE 13.2 Sample Questions in Each Stage of Negotiations

Stage 1: Assessing the Situation
- Are you clear on your interests and priority issues?
- Have you defined the criteria by which you will determine whether or not you will enter into an agreement?
- Have you defined your BATNA (Best Alternative To a Negotiated Agreement)? That is, do you know what you will do if there is no agreement?
- Have you considered the interests and constraints of the other party?

Stage 2: Establishing the Process
- Have you agreed on the scope of the issues?
- Do you understand how agreements will be approved or ratified?
- Are you in agreement on time frames and deadlines?
- Have you discussed what information may be required and how it will be acquired and managed (e.g., confidentiality)?

Stage 3: Negotiating the Agreement
- Are you entering negotiations committed to meet your interests—not your positions?
- Are you identifying and addressing the interests of the other party?
- Are you jointly identifying mutual interests and expanding the "pie"?
- Are you building a relationship that will support the agreement?

Stage 4: Implementing the Agreement
- Are all of the agreements clearly understood and perhaps spelled out in writing?
- Does the agreement spell out the responsibilities of the parties in the implementation of the agreement?
- Is there a provision for assessing the implementation of the agreement and improving it as necessary?
- Are there procedures for jointly resolving disputes under the agreement in a timely manner?

Source: Adapted from Cormick, G. W. *Negotiation Skills for Board Professionals.* Mill Creek, WA: CSE Group, 2005; Dietmeyer, B. *Strategic Negotiation: A Breakthrough Four-Step Process for Effective Business Negotiation.* Chicago: Dearborn Trade, 2004.

- The second stage is *establishing and agreeing on the process* by which the negotiations will proceed. Matters that require discussion and prior agreement between the parties include the scope of the issues, who will participate, deadlines, and understandings regarding how the negotiators will approach the problem and each other.

- The third stage is *negotiating the substantive agreement*. In this stage, the negotiators will make a number of strategic decisions regarding tactics and acceptable outcomes.

- The fourth stage is *implementing the agreement*. It is important that the agreement reached will be and can be implemented. Experienced negotiators will consider what understandings need to be reached to ensure timely and effective implementation.[17]

Distributive Negotiations Strategy

Distributive negotiations *involve traditional win–lose situations in which one party's gain is the other party's loss.* This strategy often occurs over economic issues, such as the negotiating by Ford (and other U.S. automakers) with the United Auto Workers over the costs and support of health benefits and retirement plans. Communications are guarded, and expressions of trust are limited. Threats, distorted statements, and demands are common. In short, the parties are engaged in intense, emotion-laden conflict. The forcing and compromise conflict-handling styles characterize distributive negotiations.[18]

Some individuals and groups believe in distributive (win–lose) negotiations. Negotiators have to be prepared to counter them. Awareness and understanding probably are the most important means for dealing with win–lose negotiation ploys by the other party. Four of the most common win–lose strategies that you might face as a negotiator are as follows[19]:

- *I want it all*. By making an extreme offer and then granting concessions grudgingly, if at all, the other party hopes to wear down your resolve. You will know that you have met such a negotiator when you encounter one or more forcing-like tactics. The other party's first offer is extreme. Minor concessions are made grudgingly. You are pressured to make significant concessions. The other party refuses to reciprocate.

- *Time*. Time can be used as a powerful weapon by the win–lose negotiator. When any of the following techniques are used, you should refuse to be forced into an unfavorable position: The offer is valid only for a limited time. You are pressured to accept arbitrary deadlines. The other party stalls or delays the progress of the negotiation. The other party increases pressure on you to settle quickly.

- *Good cop, bad cop*. Negotiators using this strategy hope to sway you to their side by alternating sympathetic with threatening behavior. You should be on your guard when you are confronted with various tactics such as these: The other party becomes irrational or abusive. The other party walks out of a negotiation. Irrational behavior is followed by reasonable, sympathetic behavior.

- *Ultimatums*. This strategy is designed to try to force you to submit to the will of the other party. You should be wary when the other party tries any of several tactics: You are presented with a take-it-or-leave-it offer. The other party overtly tries to force you to accept its demands. The other party is unwilling to make concessions. You are expected to make all of the concessions.

Distributive negotiations between management and labor are most visible when labor unions go on strike or when there is a stalemate in negotiations that seem to go on endlessly.

Integrative Negotiations Strategy

Integrative negotiations *involve joint problem solving to achieve results that benefit both parties.* With this strategy, the parties identify mutual problems, identify and assess alternatives, openly express preferences, and jointly reach a mutually acceptable solution. Rarely perceived as equally acceptable, the solution is simply advantageous to both sides.[20]

Principled Negotiations

A variety of principles and actions are recommended for successful integrative (win–win) negotiations. **Principled negotiations** *refer to the prescribed ways in which the parties should negotiate to resolve disputes.* It suggests that *how* the negotiation is accomplished may be as important as *what* they are negotiating about to achieve mutually satisfactory outcomes. Many individuals, especially when employing distributive negotiations, focus their attention on the *what*, thereby neglecting the *how* of negotiations. The framework and prescriptions of principled negotiations evolved out of work being done since 1979 by associates of the Harvard Negotiation Project.[21]

Principled negotiations advocate the following four principles to increase the likelihood of successful integrative negotiations[22]:

- *Separate the people from the problem*. The first principle in reaching a mutually agreeable solution is to disentangle the substantive issues of the negotiation from the interpersonal relationship issues between the parties and deal with each set of issues separately. Negotiators should see themselves as working side by side, dealing with the substantive issues or problems, instead of attacking each other.

ROB CARR/AP PHOTO

▲

Ron Shapiro, author and CEO of Shapiro Negotiation International, has negotiated many agreements.

- *Focus on interests, not positions.* People's egos tend to become identified with their negotiating positions. Furthermore, focusing only on stated positions often obscures what the participants really need or want. Rather than focusing only on the positions taken by each negotiator, a much more effective strategy is to focus on the underlying human needs and interests that caused them to adopt those positions in the first place.

- *Invent options for mutual gains.* Designing optimal solutions under pressure in the presence of an adversary tends to narrow people's thinking. Searching for the one right solution inhibits creativity, particularly when the stakes are high. These blinders can be removed by establishing a forum in which various possibilities are generated before decisions are made about which action to take.

- *Insist on using objective criteria.* The parties should discuss the conditions of the negotiation in terms of one or more standards, such as market value, expert opinion, custom, or law. This principle steers the focus away from what the parties are willing or unwilling to do. By using objective criteria, neither party has to give in to the other, and both parties may defer to a fair solution.

Ron Shapiro is coauthor of *The Power of Nice: How to Negotiate So Everyone Wins—Especially You* and CEO of the Shapiro Negotiation Institute. He has negotiated numerous agreements, ranging from real estate acquisitions to corporate mergers, from major financial packages to home loans, from settling symphony orchestra and umpire strikes to completing contracts for professional athletes. Consistent with integrative and principled negotiations, he suggests:

> *Don't negotiate as if you'll never again do business with the person across the table. . . . Forget about conquerors and victims. Negotiation is not war. It isn't about getting the other side to wave a flag and surrender. Don't think hurt. Think help. Don't demand. Listen. The best way to get most of what you want is to help the other side get some of what it wants. . . . On the surface, negotiation may seem to be about winning and losing. After all, to the victor belong the spoils. Can it be true that only the hardest, toughest and meanest negotiators will be the most successful? . . . These types of negotiators will undoubtedly achieve success in deals, but most will fall short in the long run. I believe that you can be "nice" and still get what you are after. In fact, you often get better results, achieve more of your goals, and build long-term relationships with even greater returns. Win–win simply means the best way to get what you want is to help them get what they want.*[23]

Table 13.3 provides a concise summary of the differences between integrative negotiations and distributive negotiations in terms of five core characteristics.

Common Influences on Negotiation Strategies

In this section, we highlight four common influences on the distributive and integrative negotiation strategies: attitudinal structuring, intraorganizational negotiations, the negotiator's dilemma, and mediation. Each of these influences places demands on the negotiators.

Attitudinal Structuring

Attitudinal structuring *is the process by which the parties seek to establish feelings and relationships.* Throughout any negotiations, the parties reveal certain attitudes (e.g., hostility or friendliness and competitiveness or cooperativeness) that influence their

TABLE 13.3 Integrative versus Distributive Negotiations		
CHARACTERISTIC	**INTEGRATIVE NEGOTIATIONS**	**DISTRIBUTIVE NEGOTIATIONS**
• Outcome sought	Win–win	Win–lose
• Motivation	Joint gain	Individual gain
• Interests	Congruent	Opposed
• Time horizon emphasis	Long term	Short term
• Issues	Multiple issues	Single or few issues

Source: Adapted from La Piana Associates. The difference between integrative and distributive negotiation. www.lapiana.org (July 2007).

communications. Recall our previous quote from Ron Shapiro related to the attitudes that he thinks the parties should hold to establish effective negotiations. Reflect on his statement: "I believe that you can be 'nice' and still get what you are after."

William Ury is a well-known scholar on negotiations and heads the Global Negotiation Initiative at Harvard. We share a few of his remarks related to attitudinal structuring in negotiations:

> *Deal with the people and their emotions first. Be soft on the people so that you can be hard on the problem. . . . It's important not to react without thinking, but instead to "go to the balcony," a mental place of calm and perspective where you can step back and remember what your interests are. The truth is that we can't have a whisper of a chance of influencing the other side until we are able to influence ourselves. . . . It's important to put yourself in the other side's shoes, understand their interests and how they feel. Negotiation is an exercise in influence. You're trying to influence another person. You can't influence their mind unless you know where their mind is right now. Try to be inventive. Open up to other options besides your position.*[24]

Intraorganizational Negotiations

Intraorganizational negotiations *involve negotiators building consensus for agreement and resolving intragroup conflict before dealing with the other group's negotiators.*[25] Groups often negotiate through representatives. For example, representatives of OPEC nations set oil prices for the cartel. These representatives first have to obtain agreement from the leaders of their respective nations before they can work out an agreement with each other.

Negotiator's Dilemma

Negotiators increasingly realize the importance of cooperatively creating value by means of integrative negotiations. They must also acknowledge the fact that both sides may eventually seek gain through the distributive process. The **negotiator's dilemma** *is a situation in which the tactics of self-gain tend to restrain moves to create greater mutual gain.* An optimal solution results when both parties openly discuss the problem, respect each other's substantive and relationship needs, and creatively seek to satisfy each other's interests. Such behavior doesn't always occur because of the exclusive focus on self-serving outcomes and the extensive use of questionable political and communication tactics.[26]

Win–win negotiators are vulnerable to the tactics of win–lose negotiators. As a result, negotiators often develop an uneasiness about the use of integrative strategies because they expect the other party to use distributive strategies. This mutual suspicion often causes negotiators to leave joint gains on the table. Moreover, after win–win

FIGURE 13.4 Negotiating Strategies and Outcomes

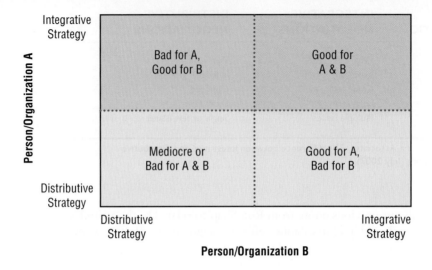

Source: Adapted from Anderson, T. Step into my parlor: A survey of strategies and techniques for effective negotiations. *Business Horizons,* May–June 1992, 75.

negotiators have been stung in several encounters with experienced win–lose strategists, they soon "learn" to become win–lose strategists. Finally, if both negotiators use distributive strategies, the probability of achieving great mutual benefits is virtually eliminated. The negotiations will likely result in both parties receiving only minimal benefits.

Graphically, the integrative and distributive negotiation strategies can be placed on vertical and horizontal axes, representing the two negotiating parties. Then, a matrix of possible outcomes emerging from the negotiating process can be developed to illustrate the negotiator's dilemma, as shown in Figure 13.4 for person A and person B.

The following Change Competency provides selected highlights on the recent complex negotiations between General Motors and the United Auto Workers.[27] Both organizations were facing dire consequences, such as the failure of General Motors and few jobs for the members of the United Auto Workers, if their negotiations failed. These negotiations involved a unique blend of distributive negotiations, integrative negotiations, and intense pressure from the U.S. federal government. The government's power was increased in these negotiations by virtue of providing monies to General Motors and providing certain types of support to members of the union.

Change competency

GM and UAW Negotiate for Mutual Survival

Under pressure from the Treasury Department of the U.S. Government, General Motors (GM) and the United Auto Workers (UAW) negotiated an agreement to cut GM's labor costs by more than $1 billion a year. Also, there had been an agreement in place to provide the UAW with $20 billion to fund a health-care program run by the union. The renegotiated agreement involves cutting in half GM's remaining cash outlays to the UAW health-care fund to about $10 billion. In exchange, the health-care fund will receive a 17.5 percent equity stake (shares) in the reorganized GM as well as $6.5 billion in preferred shares and a $2.5 billion note payable in cash. Initially, the health-care trust had been expected to end up with a 39 percent equity stake. The UAW membership employed at GM is about 60,000, whereas in 1999 nearly 200,000 union members were employed.

In 2007, the UAW moved to protect one of its key benefits: health care for retirees. At that time, GM agreed to fund a new $35 billion health-care trust—known as a Voluntary Employee's Beneficiary Association (VEBA)—that was set up to assume responsibility for retiree health-care costs starting in 2010. The trust was to end GM's exposure to health-care inflation by capping what it would pay in long-term health-care costs. The cap meant the UAW would eventually need to cut coverage for hundreds of thousands of retirees and their family members.

GM had already provided about $15 billion to the VEBA, but still owed $20 billion under an agreement that would have let it fund the trust over time. The original plan was viewed as the largest UAW concession in history. The idea was to help clear long-term obligations off GM's balance sheet, and eliminate billions of dollars a year in cash outlays.

The collapse of the U.S. auto market in 2008 and 2009 as well as continued erosion of GM's market share dramatically changed the company's financial situation and forced the parties back to the bargaining table. People involved in the negotiations say the two sides were able to approach an accord this time without the lengthy battles that hampered previous negotiations. The UAW was able to negotiate to have a union leader on GM's board of directors. A concession by the UAW was to agree to a no-strike clause that would be in effect until 2015.

Many worries remain for union officials, say people involved in the discussions. They say that the stock GM contributed to the VEBA is hard to value. This presents a major risk for UAW members. The union had initially asked for more from Treasury officials in the negotiations, but was rebuffed. GM did tentatively agree with the UAW to "substantially" cut U.S. planned imports from China and elsewhere.

To learn more about GM and the UAW, go to **www.gm.com** and **www.uaw.org**.

Mediation

At times, the parties engaged in negotiations get stuck and are not able to resolve one or more issues. As you would expect, this situation occurs more frequently with the distributive negotiations strategy than with the integrative negotiations strategy. In this situation, the parties may elect to use some form of alternative dispute resolution.[28] For example, **mediation** *is a process by which a third party helps two (or more) other parties resolve one or more conflicts*. Most of the actual negotiations occur directly between the involved individuals. But, when the parties appear likely to become locked in win–lose conflict, a mediator, acting as a neutral party, may be able to help them resolve their differences.

Mediators need special competencies. They must be able to diagnose the conflict, be skilled at breaking deadlocks and facilitating discussions at the right time, show mutual acceptance, and have the ability to provide emotional support and reassurance. In brief, an effective mediator must instill confidence in and acceptance by the parties in conflict.

Key tasks in the mediator's role include the following:

- *Ensure mutual motivation.* Each party should have incentives for resolving the conflict.

- *Achieve a balance of power.* If the power of the individuals isn't equal, establishing trust and maintaining open lines of communication may be difficult.

- *Coordinate confrontation efforts.* One party's positive moves must be coordinated with the other party's readiness to do likewise. A failure to coordinate positive initiatives and readiness to respond can undermine future efforts to work out differences.

- *Promote openness in dialogue.* The mediator can help establish norms of openness, provide reassurance and support, and decrease the risks associated with openness.
- *Maintain an optimum level of tension.* If the threat and tension are too low, the incentive for change or finding a solution is minimal. However, if the threat and tension are too high, the individuals involved may be unable to process information and envision creative alternatives. They may become polarized and take rigid positions.[29]

Learning Goal

4. *State the unique aspects of across culture negotiations.*

Across Culture Negotiations

The most obvious aspect of international business negotiations is the effect of different cultural values and practices on the process. There are two common perspectives about cross-cultural negotiations. First, negotiations in one country are totally different from negotiations in any other country. Global negotiations are likely to be completely different from domestic transactions. Second, negotiating globally is essentially the same as negotiating domestically. They're all business transactions. Both perspectives are inadequate, if not wrong. Cultural differences are critical. The core concepts of conflict management and negotiations addressed in previous sections of this chapter are useful across cultures as well. In this section, we focus on those aspects of negotiations that are unique in cross-cultural negotiations.

Differences in Negotiators

The issues and complexities relevant to all negotiations are increased—sometimes dramatically—when negotiators are from different cultures.[30] Table 13.4 provides a framework for understanding a person's negotiating style and approach based on seven dimensions. These dimensions, among others, have been used to explain how the orientations of negotiators vary across cultures.[31] Of course, we want to emphasize that there can be substantial differences among negotiators within a culture—based on their own negotiating style.[32]

TABLE 13.4 Selected Dimensions of Across Culture Negotiating Styles

Dimension		(1 2 3 4 5)	
1. Goal	Contract		Relationship
2. Attitudes	Win–Lose		Win–Win
3. Personal style	Informal		Formal
4. Communications	Direct		Indirect
5. Time sensitivity	High		Low
6. Emotionalism	High		Low
7. Agreement form	Specific		General

Source: Based on Salacuse, J. W. Negotiating: The top ten ways that culture can affect your negotiation. *Ivey Business Journal*, March/June 2005, 1–6; Graham, J. L., and Requejo, W. H. Managing face-to-face international negotiations. *Organizational Dynamics*, 2009, 38, 167–177; and *Global Negotiation Resources* (for information on negotiating in teach of 50 countries). www.globalnegotiationresources.com/resources/countries (June 2009).

For example, in one study, 39 percent of the respondent negotiators in India expressed a strong contract (e.g., legal) goal orientation versus 34 percent who expressed a strong relationship orientation. Forty-one percent expressed a desire for a one-leader team organization versus 39 percent who emphasized a consensus orientation. The bottom line is that when negotiating across cultures, you need to come prepared not only to learn about the cultures and assumptions of the negotiators, but also to appreciate their cultural values and practices.

Let's consider a few examples of negotiator orientations based on cultural influences from other studies. In one study,[33] 100 percent of the respondents from Japan emphasized win–win in their approach to negotiations. In contrast, only 37 percent of the Spanish negotiators utilized a win–win approach. A negotiator from Germany with a very formal style might insist on addressing individuals by their titles, avoid the use of personal stories and anecdotes, and avoid any mention of private or family life. In contrast, a negotiator from the United States with an informal style might use first names as a form of address, strive to develop a personal relationship with other parties, and dress more casually on purpose. The contrast between direct and indirect communications has to do primarily with how straightforward and to the point communication typically is during the negotiations. Indirect communication consists of heavy use of nonverbal communication (see Chapter 9) and many vague statements. German and U.S. negotiators are typically viewed as relatively direct in their negotiations. French and Japanese negotiators are viewed as relatively more indirect, relying a great deal on nonverbal cues to help understand the negotiations.

The traditional assumptions and generalizations about cross-cultural negotiations may not apply when long-term relationships have been established. This situation applies particularly to negotiations by the Japanese with each other. Almost by definition, Japanese businesspeople consider Westerners to be outsiders. Thus, Westerners often incorrectly assume that the Japanese never use direct or confrontational approaches to conflict resolution and negotiation. In fact, they often are very direct in resolving differences of opinion with other Japanese. They explicitly express the differences among group members and state demands, rejections, and counteroffers directly with each other.[34]

Cross-Cultural Emotional Intelligence

Negotiators and others are likely to be more effective if they possess emotional intelligence. We discussed emotional intelligence (EQ) in Chapter 3. Let's extend that discussion by noting the relationship of the components of EQ with the specific skills and abilities that increase cross-cultural effectiveness for negotiators. The components and relationships include the following:

- *Self-awareness:* Acknowledging differences between home and host cultures; realizing the impact of cultural values on performance, recognizing initial difficulties in adjusting to new cultural norms and seeking assistance; being open to new perspectives; managing uncertainties by seeking cultural coaching; resisting the urge to impose one's own values on the host culture; understanding the link between the host culture and cross-cultural conflicts; and being flexible and patient when uncomfortable situations arise during negotiations.

- *Self-motivation:* Maintaining optimism in the face of new challenges; effectively handling stress; seeking new ways of achieving goals during negotiation impasses; and consciously balancing the advantages of global negotiations against challenges and stressors in such negotiations.

- *Social empathy:* Developing good listening skills; being sensitive to differences; asking questions and seeking to understand before reacting; being willing to change so as to show respect for other negotiators; openly sharing information that provides others with more understanding; and respecting opposing viewpoints.

- *Social skill:* Being outgoing and friendly; building relationships; seeking common ground despite cross-cultural differences; being open minded and engaging in discussion rather than immediately passing judgment; and communicating informally to build rapport and future cooperation in negotiations.[35]

A mastery of these components of EQ provides the foundation for becoming an effective negotiator in cross-cultural work situations. Moreover, EQ enables the negotiator to avoid applying simplistic stereotypes and erroneous attributions to specific negotiators from other cultures.[36]

Consistent with the characteristics of EQ and the competencies emphasized throughout this book, a good approach is to focus on the individual differences of specific negotiators to gain a deeper appreciation and understanding of their values and practices.

Insights for Leaders

Many features of the negotiation process, such as the key questions in each stage of negotiations, are similar across cultures. We note here a few of the features that are unique or require tailoring to across culture negotiations[37]:

- *Dealing with people.* It is essential to take adequate time to get to know the other negotiators as professionals and people. More time is needed than in domestic business negotiations, because cultural, as well as personal, knowledge has to be acquired. Almost every negotiation involves a face-saving situation. The successful international negotiator avoids making people uncomfortable. To save face, the negotiator needs to avoid arrogance, be careful in the choice of words so as not to offend the other party, and treat the other negotiators with respect. This will help generate trust. When people trust one another, they communicate more openly and are more receptive to each other's proposals and point of view.

- *Time.* Allow plenty of time. In particular, give time to think—do not respond too quickly to new proposals. The timing of verbal exchanges is crucial in negotiations. Some Westerners find gaps or pauses in conversations to be disturbing, whereas people from other cultures (e.g., Japan, China) prefer to leave a moment of silence between statements. Patience is an asset in global negotiations, but can be destroyed by time pressures.

- *Managing issues.* Be flexible with the negotiation agenda if the other party does not stick to it. It may be somewhat frustrating when a negotiation agenda has been agreed on and then slowly eroded bit by bit. Such a situation may mean that the other party prefers a global rather than a step-by-step negotiation; the other party may not see negotiation as a linear process in which issues are addressed one after the other and settled before proceeding to the next issue.

- *Communication process.* The basic guideline for effective communication in international negotiations is to be ready for different communication styles. Be cautious when interpreting silence, emotions, threats, and any kind of manipulative communication. Start by assessing as accurately as possible the intercultural obstacles, such as language and problems of communication. Businesspeople often underestimate or even completely overlook this point, because they often share a technical or business culture with their negotiators. Beware that what is explicitly said is not necessarily what is implicitly meant. Check, verify. Spend time on checking communication accuracy, especially when the stakes are high.

- *Developing relationships.* The agreement should foster the development of the relationship and be flexible enough to deal with changes. A major concern is to balance the *relationship* and *deal orientations.* The ultimate goal of negotiation is to establish a mutually trustworthy relationship. This is, of course, true in all negotiations, but especially so in cross-cultural negotiations where so many things can and do go wrong. With trust, the parties are more able to work through the inevitable problems.

The following Across Cultures Competency feature presents a few generalizations regarding the contrasts in business negotiations in Germany and Italy.[38] As we have suggested, there is a need to be ever mindful of individual and organizational differences in approaches and styles of business negotiations *within* each of these countries.

Across Cultures competency

Business Negotiations in Germany and Italy

German businesspeople tend to be competitive negotiators. German executives in particular are technically oriented, disciplined, and orderly. Presentations can be direct and factual without giving offense. Similarly, Germans do not emphasize the personal side of business relationships. Commerce and social aspects are usually separated. Like many Europeans, they are suspicious of overbearing profit orientations.

In the preliminary stages of negotiations, German negotiators are often tough and cold. They grill their prospective partners on all of the technical aspects of their businesses. It's bad luck for them if they don't have the answers to the questions. "A mistake at this stage means that you're lost," suggests one expert. Once the German negotiators are satisfied about technical matters, they begin to think they can trust the other negotiators. The difficulty at this point is to make German negotiators change their position. At times, they can stick to one point and refuse to budge. German negotiators are, in general, quite practical at this stage. Finalizing a negotiation is not difficult with German negotiators, but it is important to know if the person you are dealing with has the authority to close the deal. Germans believe in "consensus management." Patience may be required to get the final word.

Italians are capable of dramatic flair. They tend to be conscious of their external image and the impressions they create. They use emotional arguments well. They can be hard to pin down on specific points. Italian negotiating styles can vary from being very obliging to abrasive. Presentations made to Italians should be organized, clear, and exact. Style and appearances are important. Autocratic decision making is often the norm.

Italian negotiators need to believe that they can get along as well with their foreign partners as they would with managers from Italian companies. Initial negotiations with Italians can include a lot of idle talk and subtle messages as to desired outcomes. These preliminaries will last until they feel secure and comfortable. When they do, the negotiation process actually starts. Italian negotiators may take ages to get to the point. But, it is important not to interrupt their meandering comments. As far as Italians are concerned, they are simply giving you the benefit of a complete understanding of their position. Concluding a negotiation with Italian negotiators can go quite quickly. However, a surprise may be in store for the foreign negotiator because of the fluid nature of the Italian corporate hierarchy. Titles mean relatively little in Italian companies. Very often the person who would normally have decision-making authority turns out to need approval. "Watch for someone sitting on the sidelines who's said nothing so far." That person may leap into the fray at the end, make some changes, and then conclude the negotiations.

To learn more about the cultures of Germany and Italy, go to **http://en.wikipedia.org**, or search on the Web under "culture of Germany" and "culture of Italy."

Chapter Summary

1. *Describe the primary conflict levels in organizations.*	Conflict occurs at four different levels within organizations: intrapersonal, interpersonal, intragroup, and intergroup. Intrapersonal conflict occurs within the individual. Interpersonal conflict occurs when someone's wishes or desires are perceived to be in opposition to another's. Intragroup conflict occurs between or among group members. Intergroup conflict occurs between groups or teams.
2. *Explain the common interpersonal conflict-handling styles.*	The five styles for handling interpersonal conflict are collaborating, compromising, forcing, accommodating, and avoiding. An individual may have a natural preference for one or two of these styles. Most individuals are likely to use all of them over time when dealing with various interpersonal conflict situations. As a reminder, an instrument for measuring your own conflict-handling style is presented in the Experiential Exercise at the end of this chapter.
3. *Discuss the core stages, strategies, and influences in negotiations.*	Negotiation is a component in conflict management. It is a process by which two or more interdependent individuals or groups who perceive that they have both common and conflicting goals state and discuss proposals and preferences for specific terms of a possible agreement. The four core stages of negotiation include (1) assessing the situation, (2) establishing the process, (3) negotiating the agreement, and (4) implementing the agreement. Table 13.2 provides examples of questions that need to be addressed in each stage. The two major negotiating strategies are distributive (focus is on win–lose outcomes) and integrative (focus is on win–win outcomes). Principled negotiations focus on the *how* or process of negotiations to increase the likelihood of positive outcomes for all parties. Four of the influences that affect the selection or implementation of each of these strategies are attitudinal structuring, intraorganizational negotiations, the negotiator's dilemma, and mediation when stalemates occur over particular issues.
4. *State the unique aspects of across culture negotiations.*	Negotiators across cultures may differ with respect to a variety of dimensions of negotiating style, such as those highlighted in Table 13.4. Global negotiators are likely to be more effective if they possess emotional intelligence. It increases their cross-cultural adaptation ability in the components of self-awareness, self-motivation, social empathy, and social skill. Aspects of the negotiation process that may be unique when negotiating across cultures include dealing with people, allowing enough time, managing issues, handling the communication process, and developing relationships over time.

Key Terms and Concepts

Discussion Questions

1. Reread the Learning from Experience feature entitled "Cathy McBroom versus Federal Judge Samuel Kent." Enter "Samuel B. Kent" in your Internet search feature and open the entry from Wikipedia (http://en.wikipedia.org). What additional forms of unethical misconduct that led to conflicts for Cathy McBroom can you identify?

2. What levels of conflict may be present when individuals embrace the attributes of the diversity competency but those attributes are not shared by coworkers? Explain.

3. What conflict-handling styles appear to have been used by Cathy McBroom in the Learning from Experience feature? Explain.

4. Reread the Teams Competency feature on IBM's cross-team workouts. What levels of conflict were addressed through this conflict management approach? Explain. What interpersonal conflict-handling styles are illustrated? Explain.

5. Reread the Self Competency feature entitled "Reflections on Conflict Avoiding Managers." Think

of a manager you have worked for (or currently work for). What patterns of conflict-handling styles were (are) used by this manager? Were (are) they effective?

6. Reread the Across Cultures Competency feature entitled "Business Negotiations in Germany and Italy." How would you assess the negotiating styles of the German and Italian negotiators by using the criteria listed in Table 13.4?

7. Give personal examples of (a) approach–approach conflict, (b) avoidance–avoidance conflict, and (c) approach–avoidance conflict.

8. Provide examples of (a) intrasender role conflict, (b) intersender role conflict, (c) interrole conflict, and (d) person–role conflict that you have experienced.

9. Have you been involved in negotiations in which the other party used the distributive negotiations strategy? Describe the situation. What did you do in response to the tactics used with this strategy? How did you feel? What was the outcome?

Experiential Exercise and Case

Experiential Exercise: Self Competency

Conflict-Handling Styles[39]

Instructions

Each numbered item contains two statements that describe how people deal with conflict. Distribute 5 points between each pair of statements. The statement that more accurately reflects your likely response should receive the highest number of points. For example, if response (a) strongly describes your behavior, then record

<u>5</u> a.
<u>0</u> b.

However, if responses (a) and (b) are both characteristic, but (b) is slightly more characteristic of your behavior than (a), then record

<u>2</u> a.
<u>3</u> b.

1. _____ a. I am most comfortable letting others take responsibility for solving a problem.
   _____ b. Rather than negotiate differences, I stress those points for which agreement is obvious.
2. _____ a. I pride myself on finding compromise solutions.
   _____ b. I examine all the issues involved in any disagreement.
3. _____ a. I usually persist in pursuing my side of an issue.
   _____ b. I prefer to soothe others' feelings and preserve relationships.

4. _____ a. I pride myself in finding compromise solutions.
   _____ b. I usually sacrifice my wishes for the wishes of a peer.
5. _____ a. I consistently seek a peer's help in finding solutions.
   _____ b. I do whatever is necessary to avoid tension.
6. _____ a. As a rule, I avoid dealing with conflict.
   _____ b. I defend my position and push my view.
7. _____ a. I postpone dealing with conflict until I have had some time to think it over.
   _____ b. I am willing to give up some points if others give up some too.
8. _____ a. I use my influence to have my views accepted.
   _____ b. I attempt to get all concerns and issues immediately out in the open.
9. _____ a. I feel that most differences are not worth worrying about.
   _____ b. I make a strong effort to get my way on issues I care about.
10. _____ a. Occasionally I use my authority or technical knowledge to get my way.
    _____ b. I prefer compromise solutions to problems.
11. _____ a. I believe that a team can reach a better solution than any one person can working independently.
    _____ b. I often defer to the wishes of others.

12. _____ a. I usually avoid taking positions that would create controversy.
_____ b. I'm willing to give a little if a peer will give a little, too.

13. _____ a. I generally propose the middle ground as a solution.
_____ b. I consistently press to "sell" my viewpoint.

14. _____ a. I prefer to hear everyone's side of an issue before making judgments.
_____ b. I demonstrate the logic and benefits of my position.

15. _____ a. I would rather give in than argue about trivialities.
_____ b. I avoid being "put on the spot."

16. _____ a. I refuse to hurt a peer's feelings.
_____ b. I will defend my rights as a team member.

17. _____ a. I am usually firm in pursuing my point of view.
_____ b. I'll walk away from disagreements before someone gets hurt.

18. _____ a. If it makes peers happy, I will agree with them.
_____ b. I believe that give-and-take is the best way to resolve any disagreements.

19. _____ a. I prefer to have everyone involved in a conflict generate alternatives together.
_____ b. When the team is discussing a serious problem, I usually keep quiet.

20. _____ a. I would rather openly resolve conflict than conceal differences.
_____ b. I seek ways to balance gains and losses for equitable solutions.

21. _____ a. In problem solving, I am usually considerate of peers' viewpoints.
_____ b. I prefer a direct and objective discussion of my disagreement.

22. _____ a. I seek solutions that meet some of everyone's needs.
_____ b. I will argue as long as necessary to get my position heard.

23. _____ a. I like to assess the problem and identify a mutually agreeable solution.
_____ b. When people challenge my position, I simply ignore them.

24. _____ a. If peers feel strongly about a position, I defer to it even if I don't agree.
_____ b. I am willing to settle for a compromise solution.

25. _____ a. I am very persuasive when I have to be to win in a conflict situation.
_____ b. I believe in the saying, "Kill your enemies with kindness."

26. _____ a. I will bargain with peers in an effort to manage disagreement.
_____ b. I listen attentively before expressing my views.

27. _____ a. I avoid taking controversial positions.
_____ b. I'm willing to give up my position for the benefit of the group.

28. _____ a. I enjoy competitive situations and "play" hard to win.
_____ b. Whenever possible, I seek out knowledgeable peers to help resolve disagreements.

29. _____ a. I will surrender some of my demands, but I have to get something in return.
_____ b. I don't like to air differences and usually keep my concerns to myself.

30. _____ a. I generally avoid hurting a peer's feelings.
_____ b. When a peer and I disagree, I prefer to bring the issue out into the open so we can discuss it.

Scoring

Record your responses (number of points) in the space next to each statement number and then sum the points in each column.

Column 1	Column 2	Column 3	Column 4	Column 5
3 (a) ____	2 (a) ____	1 (a) ____	1 (b) ____	2 (b) ____
6 (b) ____	4 (a) ____	5 (b) ____	3 (b) ____	5 (a) ____
8 (a) ____	7 (b) ____	6 (a) ____	4 (b) ____	8 (b) ____
9 (b) ____	10 (b) ____	7 (a) ____	11 (b) ____	11 (a) ____
10 (a) ____	12 (b) ____	9 (a) ____	15 (a) ____	14 (a) ____
13 (b) ____	13 (a) ____	12 (a) ____	16 (a) ____	19 (a) ____
14 (b) ____	18 (b) ____	15 (b) ____	18 (a) ____	20 (a) ____
16 (b) ____	20 (b) ____	17 (b) ____	21 (a) ____	21 (b) ____
17 (a) ____	22 (a) ____	19 (b) ____	24 (a) ____	23 (a) ____
22 (b) ____	24 (b) ____	23 (b) ____	25 (b) ____	26 (b) ____
25 (a) ____	26 (a) ____	27 (a) ____	27 (b) ____	28 (b) ____
28 (a) ____	29 (a) ____	29 (b) ____	30 (a) ____	30 (b) ____
Total ____	Total ____	Total ____	Total ____	Total ____

Next carry over the totals from the column totals and then plot your total scores on the following chart to show the profile of your conflict-handling styles. A total score of 36 to 45 for a style may indicate a strong preference and use of that style. A total score of 0 to 18 for a style may indicate little preference and use of that style. A total score of 19 to 35 for a style may indicate a moderate preference and use of that style.

	Total	0	10	20	30	40	50	60
Column 1 (Forcing)	____	—	—	—	—	—	—	—
Column 2 (Compromising)	____	—	—	—	—	—	—	—
Column 3 (Avoiding)	____	—	—	—	—	—	—	—
Column 4 (Accommodating)	____	—	—	—	—	—	—	—
Column 5 (Collaborating)	____	—	—	—	—	—	—	—
		0	10	20	30	40	50	60

Questions
1. Are you satisfied with this profile? Why or why not?
2. What actions, if any, do you propose for improving your conflict-handling styles?

Case: Communication Competency

Conflict Style Case Incidents[40]

Instructions: Your task is to rank the five alternatives as to your statements and/or actions in each of the following four case incidents. Rank the alternatives from the most desirable or appropriate way of dealing with the conflict to the least desirable. Rank the most desirable as 1, the next most desirable as 2, and so on, with the least desirable as 5. Enter your rank in the space next to each item. Next, identify the conflict-handling style being used with each of the possible statements and/or actions (collaborating, compromising, forcing, accommodating, or avoidance). Place your response at the end of each statement.

Case Incident 1

Peter is team leader of a production molding machine. Recently, he has noticed that one of the employees from another machine has been coming over to his machine and talking to one of his team members (not on break time). The efficiency of Peter's operator seems to be falling off, and his inattention has resulted in some rejects. Peter thinks he detects some resentment among the rest of the team. If you were Peter, you would:

_____ a. Talk to the team member and tell him to limit his conversations during on-the-job time. _____ *style.*

_____ b. Ask the manager to tell the team leader of the other machine to keep his operators in line. _____ *style.*

_____ c. Confront both men the next time you see them together (as well as the other team leader, if necessary), find out what they are up to, and tell them what you expect of your operators. _____ *style.*

_____ d. Say nothing now; it would be silly to make something big out of something so insignificant. _____ *style.*

_____ e. Try to put the rest of the team at ease; it is important that they all work well together. _____ *style.*

Case Incident 2

Johara is the senior quality control (QC) inspector and has been appointed team leader of the QC people on her crew. On separate occasions, two of her people have come to her with different suggestions for reporting test results to the machine operators. Paul wants to send the test results to the manager and then to the machine operators, since the manager is the person ultimately responsible for production output. Jim thinks the results should go directly to the lead operator on the machine in question, since he is the one who must take corrective action as soon as possible. Both ideas seem good and Johara can find no ironclad procedures in the department on how to route the reports. If you were Johara, you would:

_____ a. Decide who is right and ask the other person to go along with the decision (perhaps establish it as a written procedure). _____ *style.*

_____ b. Wait and see; the best solution will become apparent. _____ *style.*

_____ c. Tell both Paul and Jim not to get uptight about their disagreement; it isn't that important. _____ *style.*

_____ d. Get Paul and Jim together and question both of them closely. _____ *style.*

_____ e. Send the report to the manager, with a copy to the lead operator (even though it might mean a little more copy work for QC). _____ *style.*

Case Incident 3

Juan is a module team leader; his module consists of four very complex and expensive machines and five team members. The work is exacting, and inattention or improper procedures could cause a costly mistake or serious injury. Juan suspects that one of his men is taking drugs on the job, or at least showing up for work under the influence of drugs. Juan feels that he has some strong indications but knows that he doesn't have a "case." If you were Juan, you would:

_____ a. Confront the man outright; tell him what you suspect and why and that you are concerned for him and for the safety of the rest of the crew. _____ *style.*

_____ b. Ask that the suspected offender keep his habit off the job; what he does on the job is your business. _____ *style.*

_____ c. Not confront the individual right now; it might either "turn him off" or drive him underground. _____ *style.*

_____ d. Give the man the "facts of life"; tell him it is illegal and unsafe and that if he gets caught, you will do everything you can to see that he is fired. _____ *style.*

_____ e. Keep a close eye on the man to see that he is not endangering others. _____ *style.*

Case Incident 4

Argie is a supervisor of a production crew. From time to time in the past, the product development section has tapped the production crews for operators to augment their own operator personnel to run test products on special machines. This has put very little strain on the production crews, since the demands have been small, temporary, and infrequent. Lately, however, there seems to have been an almost constant demand for four production operators. The rest of the production crew must fill in for them, usually by working harder and taking shorter breaks. If you were Argie, you would:

_____ a. Let it go for now; the "crisis" will probably be over soon. _____ *style.*

_____ b. Try to smooth things over with your own crew and with the development foreman; we all have jobs to do and cannot afford conflict. _____ *style.*

_____ c. Let development have two of the four operators they requested. _____ *style.*

_____ d. Go to the development supervisor—or the supervisor's manager—and talk about how these demands for additional operators could be met without placing production in a bind. _____ *style*.

_____ e. Go to the manager of production (Argie's boss) and get her to "call off" the development people. _____ *style*.

Key

Case Incident 1: (a) compromise, (b) forcing, (c) collaboration, (d) avoidance, and (e) accommodating.

Case Incident 2: (a) forcing, (b) avoidance, (c) accommodating, (d) collaboration, and (e) compromise.

Case Incident 3: (a) collaboration, (b) compromise, (c) avoidance, (d) forcing, and (e) accommodating.

Case Incident 4: (a) avoidance, (b) accommodating, (c) compromise, (d) collaboration, and (e) forcing.

Questions

1. Did you change your ranking of the preferred five alternatives from one case incident to another? Explain.

2. Did you rank the forcing style as the first or second preferred option for any of the case incidents? Explain.

part 4

The Organization

chapter 14

Managerial Decision Making

Learning Goals

After studying this chapter, you should be able to:

1
Explain certainty, risk, and uncertainty and how these influence decision making.

2
Explain the core concepts of bounded rationality and how knowledge management helps leaders to reduce it.

3
Discuss and apply the elements of evidence-based management.

4
Describe the attributes of political decision making.

5
Explain the blocks, stages, and several methods of creative decision making.

Learning Content

David Hoover, CEO of Ball Corporation

The Ball Corporation, headquartered in Broomfield, Colorado, is a provider of metal and plastic packaging, primarily for beverages, foods, aerospace, and other services to commercial and governmental customers. The company employs approximately 14,000 people in 90 locations worldwide—10,000 in the United States and 4,000 in other countries. The firm has five major business segments: (1) Americas and Asia metal beverage packaging, (2) European metal beverage packaging, (3) Americas metal food and household products packaging, (4) Americas plastics packaging, and (5) aerospace and technologies.

R. David Hoover is the chairman, president, and chief executive officer of the Ball Corporation. The following are excerpts from an in-depth interview with Hoover in which he comments on the decision process, problems, and challenges faced by him and the members of the Ball Leadership Team (BLT).

The BLT consists of 15 people who get together monthly to discuss where we are, what we're doing, and where we are going. There is, of course, a continuing list of issues we monitor. We identify critical issues, identify owners of those issues, and report their progress, usually quarterly. They can be anything from improving the image of the can to making acquisitions to improving the overall cost benefit of the employee benefits programs. For an issue to become critical, it's got to be something we really

need to tackle. We have a dozen of those right now that we're working on.

Sensing a need for renewal, the BLT met to explore the questions, "Why is there a Ball? Why are we here?" I was a little worried some of the operations people might leave because that delved into the philosophical side of life. However, none of that happened and everyone was very participative. As a result, we came up with a new core purpose statement. We then shifted to the core values we believe drive our company. We generated a list of a half-dozen or so. Integrity was at the top of the list, particularly these days. We want it to be clear that integrity is important to us and to reinforce that throughout the company's practices. Recently, we met off-site and talked about potential areas of diversification. We looked not at specific opportunities, but [at broader issues]. Some were pretty far afield and some were pretty

COURTESY OF BALL CORPORATION

To learn more about the Ball Corporation, go to www.ball.com.

close. We decided to stay close and focus on our core products. We also pledged to stay disciplined.

In another 25 years, I think we'll be involved in some businesses we currently are not, although I don't think you'll see us in the car-making business or selling cosmetics. I suspect we'll still be in packaging but have broader offerings. We'll probably still be making beverage and food cans and PET bottles, and we'll still be in the aerospace business.

We've got lots of challenges ahead of us. I spend about 75% of my time solving problems of one sort or another. The other 25% is really wonderful, though. Watching people grow, develop, achieve, and do good things and seeing the company succeed is very rewarding and lots of fun.[1]

Decision making is an everyday fact of life for each of us. Of course, most of the time we are making decisions that do not have major life or profit consequences—like deciding on a class schedule for the following semester or where to eat. Senior leaders, however, engage daily in addressing issues that require major decisions in the near term that are likely to have major consequences—positive or negative—on one or more stakeholder groups. As implied in David Hoover's remarks, thoughtful decision making typically involves the same foundation elements: defining the problem, gathering information, identifying and assessing alternatives, and deciding what to do. Hoover's comments also suggest that a process is needed for addressing these foundation elements. One process in place at the Ball Corporation is the use of a leadership team. Recall that Hoover calls the 15 members of the Ball Leadership Team together monthly to "discuss where we are, what we're doing, and where we are going." The team monitors critical issues (problems) and is currently working on a dozen of these types of issues.

Decision making *includes defining problems, gathering information, generating alternatives, and choosing a course of action.*[2] In this chapter, we first discuss the conditions under which decisions are made. Second, we review the bounded rationality process that may characterize how decisions are made and how knowledge management can be used to improve that process. Third, this perspective for improving managerial decision making is continued as we review the elements and recommended practices of evidence-based management. Fourth, we shift to a discussion of political decision making, in which the conflicting interests and goals of the parties prevail. Fifth, we change the focus to addressing several blocks, stages, and methods of creative decision making.

Effective leaders rely on several competencies to make and implement decisions. The self competency provides a foundation for most competencies as discussed in Chapter 1. Hoover used his self competency when dealing with the difficult process of developing new strategies and goals. He used his teamwork competency to lead the BLT to address critical issues. Hoover's discussion of how the BLT explored the core questions of "Why is there a Ball?" and "Why are we here?" illustrates his communication competencies. He noted that everyone participated in the discussions. Currently, Ball's core purpose is expressed as follows:

> *Ball Corporation is in business to add value to all of its stakeholders, whether it is providing quality products and services to customers, an attractive return on investment to shareholders, a meaningful work life for employees or a contribution of time, effort and resources to our communities as we strive to make Ball a more successful and sustainable enterprise. In all of our interactions, we ask how we can get better—how we can make it better, be better and do better, for our own good and the good of those who have a stake in our success.*[3]

The senior leaders and other employees at the Ball Corporation have taken this core purpose to heart. It serves as an anchor for implementing their change and other competencies. For example, Ball's purpose statement explicitly recognizes that any decisions about alternatives being considered should take into account the alternatives' impact on multiple stakeholders, such as employees, customers, and shareholders.

Decision-Making Conditions

Learning Goal

1. *Explain certainty, risk, and uncertainty and how these influence decision making.*

Numerous developments and events—often outside of the control of leaders—influence their decision-making process and their ultimate decisions. In previous chapters, we identified a variety of domestic and global competitive, political, and cultural forces that must be considered when leaders make decisions. A number of these forces are beyond their direct control. In Chapter 2, we noted the impact that key stakeholders can have on decisions involving ethical and social responsibility issues.

Decisions are affected by many factors. In addition to identifying and measuring the strength of these factors, leaders must estimate their potential impact. The Ball Corporation has, for the most part, been successful with its acquisition strategy. However, as Hoover indicates, there may be strong forces that create unanticipated adverse impacts: ". . . we acquired a business in China and the market unexpectedly turned down. In large part, successful acquisitions depend on execution, but they also depend on good fortune and timing. You've got to have a little luck along the way to make them work."[4]

The conditions under which decisions are made can be classified as certainty, risk, and uncertainty.[5] These conditions are shown as a continuum in Figure 14.1 When individuals can identify developments and events and their potential impact with total predictability, they can make decisions under the condition of certainty. As information dwindles and becomes ambiguous, the condition of risk enters into the decision-making process. Individuals begin to base their decisions on either objective (clear) or subjective (intuition and judgment) probabilities. The decision by the top leaders of the Ball Corporation to acquire a business in China was based on the expected subjective probability that the Chinese market would continue to grow. In fact, it turned down. In the condition of uncertainty, the decision maker has little or no information about developments and forces on which to base a decision. Because of that uncertainty, decision makers may be able to make only a reasonable guess as to possible outcomes from the decision.

Certainty

Certainty *is the condition under which individuals are fully informed about a problem, alternative solutions are known, and the results of each solution are known.* This condition means that both the problem and alternative solutions are totally known and well

FIGURE 14.1 Conditions under Which Decisions Are Made

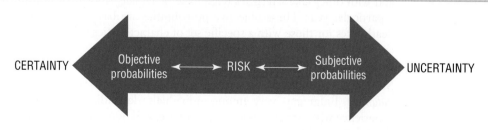

CERTAINTY — Objective probabilities ⟷ RISK ⟷ Subjective probabilities — UNCERTAINTY

defined. Once an individual has identified alternative solutions and their expected results, making the decision is relatively easy. The decision maker simply chooses the solution with the best result.

Decision making under the condition of certainty is the exception for most leaders. First-line managers often make some day-to-day decisions under conditions of certainty or near certainty. Avis Rent A Car System, Inc., headquartered in Parsippany, New Jersey, is a wholly owned subsidiary of Avis Budget Group, Inc., which also owns Budget Rent A Car. Avis has attempted to make the entire rental process as certain as possible. The process has been broken down into more than 100 incremental and prescribed steps. These steps are designed to take out the risk and uncertainty in decision making for both employees and customers at its 2,200 locations in the United States, Canada, and the Asia/Pacific Region. Employees know exactly what to do and how to deal with problems that have already been anticipated—and customers know what to expect.[6]

Risk

Risk *refers to the condition under which individuals can define a problem, specify the probability of certain events, identify alternative solutions, and state the probability of each solution leading to a result.* Risk generally means that the problem and alternative solutions fall somewhere between the extremes of being certain and being unusual and ambiguous. In its day-to-day meaning, *risk* is usually thought of as the potential harm that may arise from some decision or decision process (e.g., a safety procedure for handling chemicals) or future event (e.g., a fire). In general, *harm* may be physical (e.g., destruction of a building, loss of investment) and/or psychological/emotional to a person (work stress). The specific meaning, measurement, and assessment of risk varies widely across different professions, disciplines, and industries, as you may have already seen in your academic courses within different fields.[7]

Probability *is the percentage of times that a specific result would occur if an individual were to make the same decision a large number of times.* The most commonly used example of probability is that of tossing a coin: With enough tosses of the coin, heads will show up 50 percent of the time and tails the other 50 percent. Insurance companies make use of probabilities in setting all kinds of premium rates. The probability of a specific event is a measure between 0 (impossible) and 1 (certainty) of whether the event is likely to happen.[8]

The quality of information available to an individual about the relevant decision-making condition can vary widely—as can the individual's estimates of risk. The type, amount, and reliability of information influence the level of risk and whether the decision maker can use objective or subjective probability when estimating the result (see Figure 14.1).

Objective Probability

Objective probability *is the likelihood that a specific result will occur, based on hard facts and numbers.* Sometimes an individual can determine the likely result of a decision by examining past records. For example, although State Farm, Prudential, and other life insurance companies cannot determine the year in which each policyholder will die, they can calculate objective probabilities that specific numbers of policyholders, at various ages and with other characteristics (e.g., male or female, smoker or nonsmoker), will die in a particular year. These objective probabilities are based on the expectation that past death rates for those with a specific set of characteristics will be repeated in the future.

Subjective Probability

Subjective probability *is the likelihood that a specific result will occur, based on personal judgment.* Judgments vary among individuals, depending on their intuition, previous experience with similar situations, expertise, and personality traits (e.g., preference for risk taking or risk avoidance).

The leaders of the Ball Corporation recognize many risks—and uncertainties—in their business. In the filing of its recent annual 10-K form with the Securities and Exchange Commission, Ball Corporation management annually identifies "risk factors" for review by all interested parties. Five of the 20 general risk factors—which include uncertainties—that the Ball Corporation leadership set forth recently were as follows[9]:

- The loss of a customer or a reduction in its requirements could have a significant negative impact on our sales. Brief excerpt of explanation: "While we have diversified our customer base, we do sell a majority of our packaging products to relatively few major beverage and packaged food and household products companies."

- We face competitive risks from many sources (e.g., foreign competitors) that may negatively impact our profitability.

- We are subject to competition from alternative products (e.g., paper packaging) which could result in lower profits and reduced cash flows.

- We are vulnerable to fluctuations in the supply and price of raw materials.

- The current global credit, financial and economic crisis could have a negative impact on our results of operations, financial position or cash flows.

Uncertainty

Uncertainty *is the condition under which an individual does not have the necessary information to assign probabilities to the outcomes of alternative solutions.* In fact, the individual may not even be able to define the problem, much less identify alternative solutions and possible outcomes.[10] As suggested in the risks and uncertainties identified by the Ball Corporation, the problems and alternative solutions are often both ambiguous and highly unusual. Dealing with uncertainty is an important part of the jobs for many leaders and various professionals, such as R&D engineers, market researchers, and strategic planners. Leaders, teams, and other professionals often need to resolve uncertainty by using their intuition, creativity, and all available information to make a judgment regarding the course of action (decision) to take.

Table 14.1 provides examples of possible crises that may be sources of uncertainty and high risk for organizations. These crises involve uncertainty in terms of

---

TABLE 14.1 Possible Crises That May Be Sources of Uncertainty and High Risk

Economic Crises	Information Crises
Recessions	Theft of proprietary information
Stock market crashes	Tampering with company records
Hostile takeovers	Cyberattacks
Physical Crises	**Reputation Crises**
Industrial accidents	Rumormongering or slander
Supply breakdowns	Logo tampering
Product failures	Sick jokes
Human Resource Crises	**Natural Disasters**
Strikes	Fires
Exodus of key employees	Floods/hurricanes
Workplace violence	Earthquakes
Criminal Crises	
Theft of money or goods	
Product tampering	
Kidnapping or hostage taking	

Sources: Adapted from Mitroff, I. I., and Alpaslan, M. C. Preparing for evil. *Harvard Business Review,* April 2003, pp. 109–115; Mitroff, I. I. *Crisis Leadership: Planning for the Unthinkable.* New York: John Wiley & Sons, 2003.

their likelihood of occurrence, potential impact, and means for dealing with them should they occur. Business leaders often prepare to handle only the types of crises they've already suffered, and not even all of those.[11] The potential crises facing an organization, such as those listed in Table 14.1, cannot be totally eliminated. Through crisis anticipation and preparation, their likelihood of occurrence or severity of consequences can be reduced.

The following Change Competency reports on how Matthew K. Smith, the president of Shoes For Crews, which is headquartered in West Palm Beach, Florida, developed a unique warranty as a way to reduce customers' sense of risk and uncertainty regarding the company's shoes.[12] Most individual customers have no idea about how to assign a probability of being injured due to slipping on the job. For those customers, slipping and injuring themselves represents a condition of uncertainty. Smith considers his unique warranty to be a critical factor in the company's success. The firm has over 200 employees and annual revenue of more than $100 million. The firm provides slip-resistant footwear products at more than 100,000 workplaces in the United States and globally.

Change **competency**

Shoes For Crews Reduces Risk and Uncertainty

COURTESY OF SHOES FOR CREWS

Matthew K. Smith, President of Shoes For Crews.

On the surface, the offering of a $5,000 warranty on a $50 product sounds questionable. Matthew K. Smith, whose shoe company has honored that warranty for more than a decade, thinks that this promise was the smartest move he ever made. Shoes For Crews makes slip-resistant footwear. It had sales of only about $10 million per year before offering the unique slip and fall accident warranty. It reimburses companies up to $5,000 for each worker's compensation claim paid if an employee slips and encounters an injury while wearing a pair of the company's shoes. The limited warranty is only effective for slips and falls that occur on a level floor within the company's

workplace. This serves to reduce the risk and uncertainty for Shoes For Crews of excessive claims.

Smith thought slip injuries involving his shoes were unlikely. He started the uncertainty reduction warranty with a $500 cap and moved up to $5,000 eventually. In a recent year, Shoes For Crews honored several hundred claims—ranging from a few hundred dollars for an ambulance ride to $5,000 for an accident involving broken bones. Smith considers it a cost of doing business. He comments: "Paying $15,000 a year in claims on a $2 million account is nothing."

Kurt Leisure, a vice president of risk services at the Cheesecake Factory, a nationwide chain of restaurants based in Calabasas, California, encourages all 31,000 employees to buy their shoes at Shoes For Crews and nearly all of them do. He comments: "We have significantly increased our participation in the Shoes For Crews program and currently have 90% of our staff wearing them. Since the inception of the program, our slip/fall related claims frequency has been reduced by 72% and associated expenses have been reduced by 81%. We have tested many other brands but have not found the slip-resistance durability that we have found in Shoes For Crews. This is one of the few safety programs available that continues to deliver significant measurable results while also being fully funded and appreciated by our staff."

Smith's guarantee helped get Shoes For Crews out of a serious marketing quandary. For years, the shoes, which cost between $20 and $75, were sold mainly through payroll deduction plans, in which employers would deduct the cost of the shoes directly from workers' paychecks. Smith needed to convince factory and restaurant managers to market his shoes to their employees. It was difficult getting managers to care about where their employees shopped for work shoes. However, managers did care immensely about preventing injuries and workers' compensation claims because injuries increase costs. So Smith began promising managers that if a worker slipped while wearing his shoes, Shoes For Crews

would help pay the claim. Since launching the program more than ten years ago, 9 of the 10 largest restaurant chains in the country either buy the Shoes For Crews brand for their employees or urge them to do so.

Smith made another recent decision to reduce the risk, cost, and potential uncertainty for customers. He comments: "We introduced 'Free Exchanges and E-Z Returns.' In the past, our customers had to pay to send back their footwear purchase from us if they were not happy. Now, we have a prepaid UPS Return Label placed in every shoe box we send out. We've had an amazing response from our end-user customers and large corporate accounts. I think that we eliminated the most vexing problem and uncertainty for our customers, and improved the overall customer experience."

To learn more about Shoes For Crews, go to **www.shoesforcrews.com.**

Bounded Rationality

Learning Goal

2. *Explain the core concepts of bounded rationality and how knowledge management helps leaders to reduce it.*

Bounded rationality *describes the limitations of rationality and emphasizes the decision-making processes often used by individuals or teams.* Herbert Simon, a management scholar, introduced the bounded rationality process in the mid-1950s. It contributed significantly to the Swedish Academy of Sciences' decision to award him the 1978 Nobel Prize in economics for his "pioneering research into the decision-making process within economic organizations." This process helps to explain why different individuals or teams may make different decisions when they have exactly the same information. Bounded rationality also recognizes the reality that complete information—concerning available alternatives or the outcome of some course of action—may be impossible for an individual or team to obtain, regardless of the amount of time and resources applied to the task.[13] As portrayed in Figure 14.2, bounded rationality reflects the individual's or team's tendencies to

1. select less than the best goal or alternative solution (that is, to *satisfice*),
2. undertake a limited search for alternative solutions, and
3. cope with inadequate information and control of external and internal environmental forces influencing the outcomes of decisions.[14]

Satisficing

Satisficing *is the tendency to select an acceptable, rather than an optimal, goal or decision. Acceptable* might mean easier to identify and achieve, less controversial, or otherwise safer than the best alternative. For example, profit goals are often stated as a percentage, such as a 15 percent rate of return on investment or a 5 percent increase in profits over the previous year. These goals may not be the optimal ones. They may, in fact, reflect little more than top management's view of reasonable goals that

FIGURE 14.2 Bounded Rationality

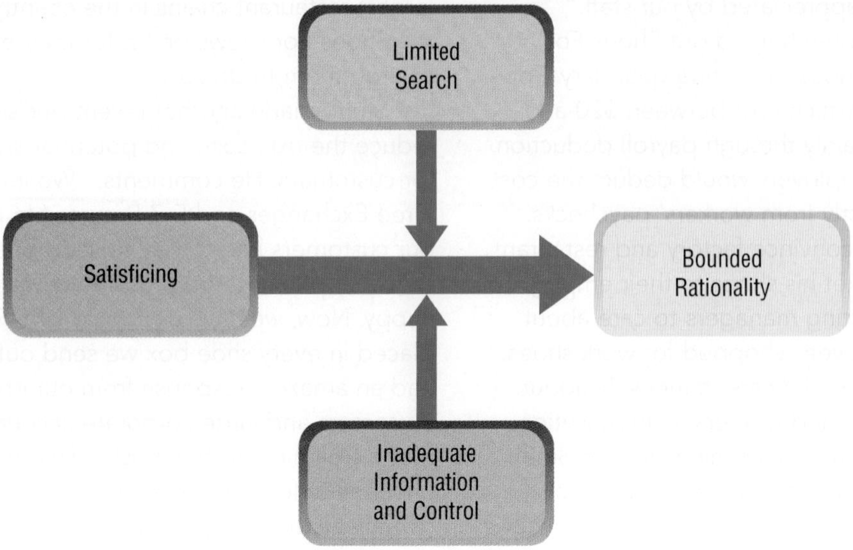

are challenging but not impossible to achieve. Herbert Simon, who introduced the bounded rationality model, comments:

> *Satisficing doesn't necessarily mean that managers have to be satisfied with what alternative pops up first in their minds or in their computers and let it go at that. The level of satisficing can be raised—by personal determination, setting higher individual or organizational standards, and by the use of an increasing range of sophisticated management science and computer-based decision-making and problem-solving techniques.*
>
> *As time goes on, you obtain more information about what's feasible and what you can aim at. Not only do you get more information, but in many, if not most, companies there are procedures for setting targets, including procedures for trying to raise individuals' aspiration levels [goals]. This is a major responsibility of top management.*[15]

Limited Search

Individuals and teams often make a limited search for possible goals or solutions to a problem, considering alternatives only until they find one that seems adequate. For example, in choosing the "best" job, you won't be able to evaluate every available job in your particular field. You might hit retirement age before obtaining all of the information needed for a decision! In the bounded rationality model, an individual or team stops searching for alternatives as soon as an acceptable ("good enough") goal or solution is discovered.[16]

One form of limited search is escalating commitment—*a process of continuing or increasing the allocation of resources to a course of action even though a substantial amount of feedback indicates that the choice made is wrong.* This process is often called "throwing good money after bad." One of the explanations for escalating commitment is that individuals feel responsible for negative consequences. This motivates them to justify their previous choices. Individuals may become committed to a choice simply because they believe that consistency in action is a desirable form of behavior.[17] This process may be more likely if groupthink exists, a concept we discussed in Chapter 12.

A number of years ago, there was an escalating commitment to a single, integrated baggage-handling system for all airlines at the Denver International Airport. Although numerous problems with the integrated system continued after repeated and expensive failed efforts to resolve them, the managers continued for more than a year to increase their commitment to making it work. They refused to recognize that the problem was the system itself. Finally, as a result of increased pressures from various stakeholders to open the new airport, the integrated baggage-handling system was scrapped.[18]

Inadequate Information and Control

Decision makers often have inadequate information about problems and face environmental forces that they cannot control. This means they have to make decisions under conditions of risk or uncertainty. These conditions typically impact decisions in unanticipated ways. Two of the unanticipated ways that are partially triggered by inadequate information and lack of control are risk propensity and problem framing.

Risk Propensity

Risk propensity is the tendency of an individual or team to make or avoid decisions in which the anticipated outcomes are unknown.[19] It captures individual's risk-taking behaviors. The probability of loss is overestimated relative to the probability of gain. Therefore, the decision maker requires a high probability of gain to tolerate exposure to failure. Conversely, a risk-seeking decision maker or team focuses on potentially positive outcomes. The probability of gain is overestimated relative to the probability of loss. Risk seekers may be willing to tolerate exposure to failure with a lower probability of gain.

Some decisions can be understood in terms of a desire to avoid the unpleasant consequences of a decision that turns out poorly. A choice can be personally threatening because a poor result can undermine the decision maker's sense of professional competence, create problems for the organization, and even get the decision maker demoted or fired. Many individuals have a low propensity for risk. They purchase many types of insurance to avoid the risk of large but improbable losses. They invest in savings accounts, CDs, and money market funds to avoid the risk of extreme fluctuations in stocks and bonds. Generally, they prefer decision alternatives that produce satisfactory results more than risky decisions that have the same or higher expected outcomes.[20]

Problem Framing

Problem framing is the tendency to interpret issues and options in either positive or negative terms. Individuals or teams in favorable circumstances tend to be more risk averse because they think that they have more to lose. In contrast, individuals or teams in unfavorable situations tend to think that they have little to lose and therefore may be more risk seeking. Focusing on potential losses increases the importance of risk. In contrast, focusing on potential gains reduces the importance of risk. Thus, a positively framed situation fosters risk taking by drawing managerial attention to opportunities rather than the possibility of failure. An example of positive versus negative framing is that of the certainty of winning $6,000 or the 80 percent probability of winning $10,000. Most people prefer the certain gain to the uncertain chance of larger gain. Which would you choose? Although risk aversion commonly is assumed to hold for most decisions, many exceptions have been documented. For example, people tend to prefer taking risks when making a choice between a certain loss and a risky loss.[21]

Insights for Leaders

Decision rules are a part of the bounded rationality model. They are often referred to as *heuristics*. They provide quick and easy ways for managers to reach a decision without a detailed analysis and search. They are written down, easily applied, and sometimes thought of as "rules of thumb." One type of heuristic is the **dictionary rule**, *which involves ranking items the same way a dictionary does: one criterion (analogous to one letter) at a time.* The dictionary rule gives great importance to the first criterion. It is valid in decision making only if this first criterion is known to be of overriding importance.[22]

Consider what can happen, however, when management too hastily uses the dictionary rule. The director and his staff at the Ohio Department of Claims experienced a growing backlog of social benefit appeals. They implemented a change in handling procedures. Their brief analysis led to a pooling idea that grouped similar claims for mass handling. However, the analysis failed to focus on the reason for the growing number of claims. After the backlog grew to the point that claims took a year to process, the director discovered a loophole in the legislation that had inadvertently eased eligibility requirements. The director made the legislature aware of the oversight and the loophole was closed. In the meantime, the agency was subjected to constant criticism and legal action for its slow, error-prone claims management. As the incident suggests, leaders often want to find out quickly what is wrong and fix it immediately. The all-too-common result is poor problem definition and a choice of criteria that proves to be misleading. Symptoms are analyzed while more important concerns may be ignored.[23]

Individuals and leaders may fall prey to various biases when they make decisions. These biases cause individuals to use inadequate information in decision making. They can even influence what problems are recognized and how they are interpreted. The potential for such biases most likely occur under conditions of high risk and uncertainty.

Competent and experienced leaders attempt to minimize these biases. Past experience may enable them to gain an accurate sense of what's going on in the situation. They recognize typical and effective ways of reacting to problems. Their past experience enables them to see patterns and anomalies that serve as warning signs. Successful leaders do not settle on the first thought—definition of the problem or solution—that comes to mind. They have typically encountered the adverse consequences of this approach in the past and have thus learned from experience.[24] At the same time, effective leaders guard against preconceived notions. This is suggested by Jeffrey McKeever, the CEO of MicroAge, a company that assists organizations with selecting, sourcing, and servicing their needs. McKeever comments on the importance of guarding against bounded rationality and biases in decision making:

> *When someone comes to you, you often have a bias about what they are talking about. If you have been in business for 20 to 30 years, chances are you've been there and done that. Their idea is generally not so new or innovative as they think. You have a strong prejudice about outcomes. That is a dangerous thing. One of the things you have to do very cognitively to be a good leader is not let your biases or your filters totally cloud the message someone's trying to deliver.*[25]

Recall one of the comments by Herbert Simon in an earlier quote: "The level of satisficing can be raised—by personal determination, setting higher individual or organizational standards, and by the use of an increasing range of sophisticated management science and computer-based decision-making and problem-solving techniques." As discussed next, knowledge management has emerged as one way for doing so.

Knowledge Management

Knowledge management (KM) *is the art of adding or creating value by systematically capitalizing on the know-how, experience, and judgment found both within and outside an organization.* Knowledge management is a means of raising the level of satisficing. Knowledge is different from data and information. *Data* represent observations or facts that have no context and are not immediately or directly useful. *Information* results from placing data within some meaningful context, often in the form of a message. *Knowledge* is that which a person comes to believe and value on the basis of the systematic organized accumulation of information through experience, communication, and inference. Knowledge can be viewed both as a *thing* to be stored and manipulated and as *process* of applying expertise.[26]

Knowledge management requires developing a system for collecting and maintaining data, information, experiences, and lessons, as well as improving communication. Decision making and planning have always benefited from having the right knowledge at the right place and at the right time. KM helps to achieve this. Knowledge management is generally viewed as consisting of three main components[27]:

- *Explicit knowledge:* published in internally generated reports and manuals, books, magazines, journals, government data and reports, online services newsfeeds, and the like. The KM software adopted by OMR Architects, headquartered in West Action, Massachusetts, provides for 24/7 access to and updating of documents, drawings, specifications, and contracts for each project.[28]

- *Tacit knowledge:* the information, competencies, and experience possessed by employees, including professional contacts and social networks. David Hoover, the CEO of Ball Corporation, has a reputation for having developed insightful tacit knowledge. This knowledge may be difficult to express because it is often developed from direct experiences and action. It is typically shared through conversations involving storytelling and shared experiences. OMR Architects recognizes the importance of tacit knowledge by organizing into five specialty groups so that its professionals in each group can develop deep insights, contacts, and relationships related to their specialty.

- *Enabling technologies:* intranets, the Internet, search engines, work-flow software. OMR Architects' adoption of KM software and related technologies enables the firm to foster knowledge management on a 24/7 basis for those involved in each project. Web-based (Internet) KM software substantially improves the work flow of each project.

Enabling Technology

Technology is one of the KM enablers. It provides the foundation for solutions that automate and centralize the sharing of knowledge, foster innovation, and improve decision making to reduce bounded rationality. Choosing a set of technologies on which to build KM should involve addressing at least two critical issues. First, the technologies should deliver only the relevant information to users, but quickly and from every feasible source. A by-product of the speed at which technologies change is the creation and storage of knowledge in many different places. The technology used should support exploration of new ideas and solutions to problems and make existing knowledge easily available to both developers and users. Second, because of the increasing mobility of knowledge workers, technologies used need to comprise a variety of devices—from cell phones to laptop computers to BlackBerry PDAs. The ability to obtain and deliver information is useless if it cannot be transmitted to the place where a decision needs to be made and on a timely basis. We have identified some of these enabling technologies in this and previous chapters—the Internet, websites, extranets, intranets, and so forth.

The increasing use of radio-frequency identification tags is an example of knowledge management technology. **Radio-frequency identification (RFID)** *is an* *automatic identification method that relies on storing and remotely retrieving data using devices called RFID tags or transponders.* An RFID tag is a small object that can be attached to or incorporated into a product, animal, or person. These tags contain silicon chips and antennas that enable them to receive and respond to radio-frequency signals from an RFID transceiver. Passive tags require no internal power source, whereas active tags require a power source. Most RFID tags are passive, such as those attached to clothing or books.[29]

The following Change Competency feature reports on the adoption of RFID and related technologies at St. Clair Hospital in Pittsburgh, Pennsylvania.[30] These technologies aid the hospital's knowledge management initiatives, which help reduce bounded rationality. St. Clair's is a 327-bed, independent, acute care facility with 525 physicians and more than 2,000 employees.[31]

Change competency

St. Clair Hospital Adopts RFID and Related Technologies

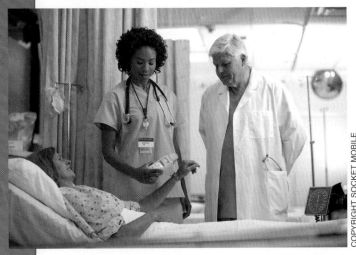

COPYRIGHT SOCKET MOBILE

The Socket SoMo® 650 handheld computer is at the heart of knowledge management technology.

When nurses give pills, intravenous fluids, or other medications to patients, there are many risks involved. These include providing the wrong type of medication or the incorrect dosage or administering it at the improper time. The Institute of Medicine estimates that more than 44,000 Americans die each year in hospitals from medical errors, with 7,000 resulting from medication-related errors alone.

St. Clair Hospital of Pittsburgh is reducing medication errors with its innovative Five Rights Medication Verification System. This system enables nurses to confirm in real time, right from a patient's bedside, that they are correctly administering medications to patients. The system has enabled the hospital to identify and prevent 5,000 potential medication errors in one year. Besides saving the lives of patients, it also saves time for nurses so that they can provide more attention to patients in their care.

At the heart of knowledge management technology is the Socket SoMo® 650 handheld computer, a durable Windows Mobile–powered device designed specifically for business situations. Inserted into the SoMo 650 is a Socket CompactFlash RFID Reader-Scan Card 6M. The first system of its kind, the card is a small plug-in card that provides both RFID and bar code scanning capabilities. Running on the SoMo 650 is VeriScan software from Hospira, a global specialty pharmaceutical and medication delivery company.

Before administering medication, nurses first read the RFID tag in their badge to log in. They then scan the bar code on the medication package and the RFID tag in a patient's wristband. The data are sent wirelessly from the SoMo 650 over the hospital's Wi-Fi network to the main clinical database, where the information is compared with the doctor's latest orders.

Voice commands on the SoMo 650 immediately announce "Patient identification confirmed" or, in the case of discrepancies, "Access denied." Information is also presented on-screen, including a photo of the correct patient, which was taken during the patient's admission to the hospital. Because the SoMo 650 is connected to the hospital's wireless network, nurses know immediately about any new medication orders, order changes, or cancellations.

By using RFID technology, nurses can quickly and easily scan their badges and patients' wristbands by simply waving the SoMo 650 within inches of the RFID tag, and the RFID card will instantly read the information. Unlike bar code scanning, no line of sight is needed. Nurses can read data without removing blankets or bothering sleeping patients to turn their wrists. "With the [previous system], you had to twist the wristband until the bar code was facing you, then you had to aim the scanner, and if the badge wasn't flat, maybe you wouldn't get a good scan," described Tom Ague, COO and executive VP of St. Clair Hospital. Eliminating physical contact also helps to prevent infections from spreading. Besides patient identity, the RFID wristband can also hold other critical information such as drug allergies.

To learn more about St. Clair Hospital Pittsburgh, go to **www.stclair.org**.

Evidence-Based Management

3. *Discuss and apply the elements of the evidence-based management.*

Evidence-based management *proceeds from the premise that using a better, deeper diagnosis and employing facts to the extent possible enable managers and leaders to do their jobs better.*[32] Its roots are in evidence-based medicine, a quality movement designed to apply the scientific method to medical practice.[33] Like knowledge management, it recognizes and attempts to reduce the problems identified through bounded rationality.

Jeffrey Pfeffer and Robert Sutton, two of the leading developers of evidence-based management, comment:

> *As with medicine, management is and will likely always be a craft that can be learned only through practice and experience. Yet, we believe that managers can practice their craft more effectively if they are routinely guided by the best logic and evidence—and if they relentlessly seek new knowledge and insight, from both inside and outside their companies, to keep updating their assumptions, knowledge, and skills.*[34]

Evidence-based management emphasizes the dangers of being "seduced" by the "quick fix" or "fad." It reminds us that managerial decision making is often complex and time consuming, and it requires a tough, disciplined mind-set. Beware of easy and simpleminded answers.[35]

Diagnostic Questions

According to evidence-based management, one way to help leaders and others avoid simpleminded quick fixes is to carefully consider five critical diagnostic questions[36]:

1. What assumptions does the idea or practice make about people and organizations? What would have to be true about people and organizations for the idea or practice to be effective?

2. Which of these assumptions seem reasonable and correct to you and your colleagues? Which seem wrong and suspect?

3. Could this idea or practice still succeed if the assumptions turned out to be wrong?

4. How might you and your colleagues quickly and inexpensively gather some data to test the reasonableness of the underlying assumptions?

5. What other ideas or management practices can you think of that would address the same problem or issue and be more consistent with what you believe to be true about people and organizations?

Evidence-based management helps to reduce the mental blinders and bounded rationality that prevent leaders and others from seeing, seeking, using, or sharing relevant and accessible information during the decision-making process.[37] The most problematic aspect of the failure to seek information occurs when a leader is motivated or biased to favor a particular course of action. As a result, there is often an absence of seeking out or listening to disconfirming evidence.

Role of Wisdom

Beyond diagnostic questions, Pfeffer and Sutton emphasize the need for wisdom by decision makers. They state:

> . . . wisdom means "knowing what you know and knowing what you don't know," especially striking a balance between arrogance (assuming you know more than you do) and insecurity (believing that you know too little to act). This attitude enables people to act on their present knowledge while doubting what they know. It means they do things now, as well as keep learning along the way.[38]

This involves learning principles, models, and concepts (knowing what) as well as processes and procedures (knowing how).[39] Our book has implemented this learning process through the presentation of models and concepts (knowing what) and their application (knowing how) through the Learning from Experience features, competency features, experiential exercises, and cases. In their day-to-day decision making, leaders would be well served by learning from books such as this one and the key sources we have cited as they address issues and problems related to perceptions, stress, conflict, communication, culture, leadership, organization design, change, decision making, and the like.

Self Insight

A good decision maker will always weigh the evidence. Although it's clear that we all rely on our personal experiences and values to guide our decision making, leaders who differentiate themselves from others time and again are the ones who trust their intuition but also use properly researched evidence to make decisions. That does not mean that their well-honed intuition is without value, but it should drive their demands for evidence, rather than replace it altogether.

Chris Hyman, CEO, Serco Group

Insights for Leaders

Let's consider a few of the insights and prescriptions advanced by Pfeffer and Sutton for using evidence-based management:

- Leaders should be cautious about blindly embracing and implementing practices and ideas that are sold as new and novel, but are really old ideas and practices under new labels. Employees subjected to such "new" ideas and practices soon discover that higher management is simply advancing "old wine in a new bottle," which creates cynicism, skepticism, and distrust toward management.

- Leaders should constructively question the *big* idea or technique that is claimed to create breakthroughs for the organization. In general, most claimed breakthroughs—or "silver bullets"—represent incremental improvements in the best case scenario or counterproductive changes if they do not fit the context and tasks performed by employees in specific units.

- Leaders should be cautious of celebrating and embracing lone "geniuses" or gurus. Knowledge that effectively guides decision making is rarely generated by a lone guru. Moreover, gurus too often oversimplify leadership challenges and the decision context in prescribing their ready-made solutions.

- Leaders should recognize and diagnose the potential drawbacks, not just virtues, of a particular *new* idea or practice both before and during its implementation. In medicine, few drugs are without potential negative side effects, and few surgical procedures are without potential risks and problems. These potential downsides are typically made explicit in the practice of medicine, but rarely so in the "selling" of a new idea, technique, or program that is claimed to solve one or more problems in organizations.

Limitations

Let's now turn to a few of the limitations in the use of evidence-based management. First, the notions of "substituting facts for conventional wisdom" and "being committed to fact-based decision making" can be a challenge to put in practice. For example, it can be challenging ". . . to define what a fact is—who decides which facts count, get included, get dismissed, and so forth?"[40] Leaders and others may disagree on which goals, data, evidence, and logic are relevant to or should be used in the decision-making process. Second, evidence-based management does not adequately address the value of intuition and judgment, especially when the decision-making situation involves high risk, uncertainty, or novelty due to the lack of "facts" that can "predict" the outcome of decision alternatives.[41] Strategic decisions (e.g., acquisitions, mergers) made by leaders often involve uncertainty because data and evidence look backward, even though the decisions made today with that data are about the future, which may or may not be influenced by the past when the competitive environment is highly complex and rapidly changing. Third, evidence for decision making, especially under conditions of uncertainty, may be contradictory, not always easy to understand, and subject to different interpretations among leaders as well as influential stakeholders. While recognizing these potential limitations, evidence-based management has much to offer for improving the day-to-day decision making that takes place in organizations.

The following Diversity Competency feature reports on the evidence-driven business case for diversity at the Chubb Group of Insurance Companies.[42] Chubb is the 11th largest property and casualty insurer in the United States and has a worldwide network of some 120 offices in 27 countries staffed by 10,400 employees. Chubb has $48 billion in assets and more than $13 billion in revenues. It is the 203rd largest U.S.-based corporation. *Forbes* listed Chubb as one of America's 400 Best Big Companies. It has direct relationships with customers and also markets through 8,500 independent agents and brokers. Chubb has received a variety of awards for its evidence-based diversity initiatives.[43] It is headquartered in Warren, New Jersey.

Diversity competency

Chubb's Business Case for Diversity

This feature presents Chubb's evidence-driven business case for diversity. Chubb's leaders contend that those who perceive diversity as exclusively a moral imperative or societal goal are missing the larger point. Workforce diversity needs to be viewed as a competitive advantage and a business opportunity. That's why Chubb makes diversity a business priority and strives to achieve a fully inclusive diverse workforce.

Defining Diversity. Diversity is about recognizing, respecting and valuing differences based on ethnicity, gender, color, age, race, religion, disability, national origin and sexual orientation. It also includes an infinite range of unique individual characteristics and experiences, such as communication style, career path, life experience, educational background, geographic location, income level, marital status, military experience, parental status and other variables that influence personal perspectives.

These life experiences and personal perspectives make us react and think differently, approach challenges and solve problems differently, make suggestions and decisions differently, and see different opportunities. Diversity, then, is also about diversity of thought. Superior business performance requires tapping into these unique perspectives.

Diverse Workforce. As our U.S. and global customer base becomes steadily more diverse, significant portions of Chubb's future growth must come from tapping into these diverse markets. If we are to form lasting business relationships with our customers and become a true global leader in the industry, we must understand our customers' diverse cultures and decisional processes, not merely their languages. To do so, we must begin with a diverse workplace.

Demographics. Once a largely homogeneous group, the faces of customers,

claimants, producers, employees and suppliers have been transformed into a dynamic mix of people comprised of various races, cultures and backgrounds. "Minorities" are roughly one-third of the U.S. population, by 2042 "minorities" will be the majority.

Buying Power. If we disregard the data on changing demographics, we also disregard the substantial growth in buying power of diverse markets. Not only are these diverse minority groups increasing as a percentage of the U.S. population, but so too is the buying power they wield.

Business Imperative. In order for Chubb to remain competitive for talent and for customers, it is imperative that we attract and value diverse talent and enable that talent to attract and value diverse customers.

To learn more about the Chubb Group of Insurance Companies, go to **www.chubb.com.**

Political Decision Making

Learning Goal

4. *Describe the attributes of political decision making.*

Political decision making *describes situations where the parties have separate and different interests, goals, and values and, therefore, employ self-serving tactics.* It stands in contrast to the evidence-based management because of its focus on self-interest goals. Those may not change as new information is learned. Problem definition, data search and collection, information exchange, and evaluation criteria are methods used to bias the outcome in favor of the individual, group, or unit.[44]

The distribution of power in an organization and the effectiveness of the tactics used by managers and employees influence the impact of the decisions.[45] Political decision making doesn't explicitly recognize ethical dilemmas. However, it often draws on two of the self-serving ethical principles discussed in Chapter 2: (1) the hedonistic principle—do whatever you find to be in your own self-interest; and (2) the might-equals-right principle—you are strong enough to take advantage without respect to ordinary social customs.

Political decision making is found in all organizations. For example, French culture values relatively high power distance. Relationships between superiors and subordinates are unequal, with different levels of status and privilege. Political decision making in French organizations, such as Altedia, Société Allen SA, and Groupe Ares, is based on various underlying assumptions and expected behaviors, three of which follow:

- Power, once attained, should not be shared except with a small group of senior leaders. Some people are born to lead and others to follow; it is difficult for people to change. Secretaries are there to follow orders. Middle managers need to consult with their bosses as well as many others in the organization before making a decision.

- If individuals have been recognized as having top-leadership competencies, it does not matter if they are put in a job where they have no experience. They should be able to learn how to do their jobs with experience because of their competencies.

- It is harmful to reveal information unnecessarily because then the decision-making process cannot be controlled. When, where, and how to communicate information is a delicate question that often only the upper echelons can decide.[46]

Political decision-making processes are most likely to be used when issues involve powerful stakeholders who have a divergence in problem definition, a divergence in goals, or a divergence in preferred solutions.[47]

Divergence in Problem Definition

In political decision making, stakeholders attempt to define problems to their own advantage. Conflicts occur when various stakeholders have different perceptions about the nature and sources of problems.

When things go wrong in a politically based organization, one or more individuals may be singled out as the cause of the problem. **Scapegoating** *is the casting of blame for problems or shortcoming on an innocent or only partially responsible individual, team, or department.* By implication, the other people who might be responsible for the problem are considered to be free from blame. Individuals or organizational units may use scapegoating to preserve a position of power or maintain a positive image. Whistle-blowers, who report what they see as wrongdoing to outside agencies, are sometimes subject to scapegoating. This has been of concern to the American Institute of Certified Public Accountants. The institute's position is that whistle-blowing may be necessary to meet the ethical standards of certified public accountants (CPAs) who are employed by the firm. That very act, however, too often results in the CPAs being scapegoated as the real problem by higher management and labeled as "snitches," "disgruntled employees," or "poor team players." Of course, this situation is more likely to occur when higher management is the source of the misleading or questionable practices and statements.[48]

When corporations lose money for several quarters or years, there may be efforts to lay blame for the problems on external sources. For example, the top management of General Motors often suggested that rising health-care and pension costs due to labor demands, global overcapacity, falling prices, unstable fuel prices, and increasing competition as the problems that triggered its financial problems.[49] Others suggest that GM's major bankruptcy problems were poor executive leadership; nonresponse to changing consumer preferences for more style and fuel efficiency in vehicles; too many car lines, which reduces production efficiencies; lagging quality relative to competitors; slow and excessively bureaucratic decision making with too many levels of management; weak management reactions to union demands over many years; and so forth. You will note that the first set of problems presented by the senior management of GM is seen as external and beyond their immediate control or influence. In contrast, the second set of problems is seen as due to the actions, reactions, and inactions by the senior management of GM over a period of years.

Divergence in Goals

Political decision making recognizes the likelihood of conflicting goals among stakeholders. Thus, an organization's choice of goals will be influenced by the relative power of these stakeholders. Often no clear "winner" emerges. If power is concentrated in one stakeholder, the organization's primary goals will likely reflect that stakeholder's goals.

A balance of power among several stakeholders may lead to negotiation and compromise in the decision-making process. Although a balance of power may lead to a compromise, as in most union–management negotiations, it also may lead to stalemate. A common political strategy is to form a coalition (alliance) in which no one person, group, or organization has sufficient power to select or implement its preferred goal. Many health-related organizations and associations—such as the American Cancer Society, American Heart Association, and American Medical Association—have formed an informal coalition with Congress to fight smoking and the tobacco interests. Recently, Congress passed new legislation regarding the advertising that tobacco companies can use.

Divergence in Solutions

Some goals or the means used to achieve them may be perceived as win–lose situations; that is, my gain is your loss, and your gain is my loss. In such a situation, stakeholders often distort and selectively withhold information to further their own interests. Such actions can severely limit a leader's ability to make adaptive and innovative decisions, which, by definition, require utilizing all relevant information, as well as exploring a full range of alternative solutions.

Stakeholders within the organization often view information as a major source of power and use it accordingly. Evidence-based decision making calls for all employees to present all relevant information openly. However, managers and employees operating under political decision making would view free disclosure as naïve, making achievement of their personal, team, or departmental goals more difficult.[50] To complicate the picture, information often is (1) piecemeal and based on informal communication (Did you know that. . .?); (2) subjective rather than based on hard facts (Those computer printouts don't really matter around here); and (3) defined by what powerful stakeholders consider to be important (What does the boss think? How will the board respond?).

Self Insight

Some ruthless office politickers make it to the top. In the long run, though, those who relentlessly refuse to play the game win the organization's trust and reputation for integrity. They're known to hold no grudges and harbor no hidden agendas.

Jack and Suzy Welch, Contributors to Business Week; *Jack Welch is the former CEO of General Electric*

Insights for Leaders

Despite the popular view, political decision making is not always bad. It can be useful and appropriate, especially for resolving conflicts among stakeholders with divergent goals and/or divergent preferences for actions to be taken. If the political decision making is implemented with an underpinning of basic ethical principles as discussed in Chapter 2, it can lead to constructive decisions and outcomes.

Political decision making reflects a variety of influence methods used to exert power or impact others' behaviors. The political influence methods presented at the top of Table 14.2—rational persuasion, inspirational appeal, and consultation—often are the most effective in many situations. The least effective methods seem to be coalition, legitimating, and pressure. To assume that certain methods will always work or that others will always fail is a mistake. Differences in effectiveness occur when attempts to influence are downward rather than upward in the organizational hierarchy. Differences in effectiveness appear when various methods are used in combination rather than independently. The political influence process is complex. To understand fully the effectiveness of various influence strategies, you need to know the power sources available, the direction of attempts to influence (i.e., upward, downward, or laterally), the goals being sought, and the cultural values of the organization.[51]

Having the *capacity* (power) to influence the behaviors of others and effectively using it are not the same thing. Leaders who believe that they can always effectively influence the behaviors of others by acquiring enough power simply to order other people around generally are ineffective. The ineffective use of power has many negative implications, both for the individual and the organization. For example, the

TABLE 14.2 Influence Strategies

INFLUENCE STRATEGY	DEFINITION
• Rational persuasion	Use logical arguments and factual evidence.
• Inspirational appeal	Appeal to values, ideals, or aspirations to arouse enthusiasm.
• Consultation	Seek participation in planning a strategy, activity, or change.
• Ingratiation	Attempt to create a favorable mood before making request.
• Exchange	Offer an exchange of favors, share of benefits, or promise to reciprocate at later time.
• Personal appeal	Appeal to feelings of loyalty or friendship.
• Coalition	Seek aid or support of others for some initiative or activity.
• Legitimating	Seek to establish legitimacy of a request by claiming authority or by verifying consistency with policies, practices, or traditions.
• Pressure	Use demands, threats, or persistent reminders.

Source: Adapted from Yukl, G., Guinan, P. J., and Sottolano, D. Influence tactics used for different objectives with subordinates, peers, and superiors. *Group & Organization Management*, 1995, 20, 275; Buchanan, D., and Badham, R. *Power, Politics and Organizational Change.* London: Sage, 1999, 64.

consequences of an overreliance on the pressure method are often negative. Leaders who are aggressive and persistent with others—characterized by a refusal to take *no* for an answer, reliance on repeated reminders, frequent use of face-to-face confrontations, and the like—usually suffer negative consequences. Compared to others, the leaders who rely heavily on the pressure method typically (1) receive the lowest performance evaluations, (2) earn less money, and (3) experience the highest levels of job tension and stress.[52] Also, recall our discussion of *impression management* strategies—ingratiation, self-promotion, and face-saving—and *political skill* in Chapter 9.

Creative Decision Making

Learning Goal

5. *Explain the blocks, stages, and several methods of creative decision making.*

Creativity *is the ability to visualize, generate, and implement new ideas or concepts or new associations between existing ideas or concepts that are novel and useful.*[53] Creative decision making helps to identify problems, increases the quality of solutions to problems, stimulates innovation, revitalizes motivation and commitment by challenging individuals, and serves as a catalyst for effective team performance. For organizations, creativity is no longer optional—it is imperative. In particular, for innovative initiatives to succeed, leaders and employees alike need creative decision-making skills.[54]

The simulation of creativity is in the hands of leaders as they think about and establish the work environment. For example, poorly designed motivational and reward systems are likely to result in turnover, absenteeism, low morale, and so forth. One creativity expert comments: "The thing about creativity is that you can't tell at the outset which ideas will succeed and which will fail. . . . Now, leaders pay a lot of lip service to the notion of rewarding failure. . . . Often, they have a forgive-and-forget policy. Forgiveness is crucial but it's not enough. In order to learn from mistakes, it's even more important to forgive and *remember*."[55] Three broad categories of blocks are perceptual, cultural, and emotional[56]:

1. *Perceptual blocks* include such factors as the failure to use all of the senses in observing, failure to investigate the obvious, difficulty in seeing remote relationships, and failure to distinguish between cause and effect.

2. *Cultural blocks* include a desire to conform to established norms, overemphasis on competition or conflict avoidance and smoothing, the drive to be practical and narrowly economical above all else, and a belief that indulging in fantasy or other forms of open-ended exploration is a waste of time.

3. *Emotional blocks* include the fear of making a mistake, fear and distrust of others, grabbing the first idea that comes along, and the like. For many organizations, fostering creativity and innovation is essential to their ability to offer high-quality products and services.

Creative Stages

One way of viewing the creative process, as suggested in Figure 14.3, is through five interconnected stages: preparation, concentration, incubation, illumination, and verification.[57] These are not easy or quick stages to master for a meaningful creative process.

The *preparation stage* involves thoroughly investigating an issue or problem to ensure that all of its aspects have been identified and understood. This stage involves searching for and collecting facts and ideas. Extensive formal education or many years of relevant experience are needed to develop the expertise required to identify substantive issues and problems. The preparation and concentration stages are consistent with Thomas Edison's statement that "Creativity is 90 percent perspiration and 10 percent inspiration." Edison was responsible for more than a thousand patents, the most famous of which is the 1879 patent for the electric light bulb.[58]

The *concentration stage* involves focusing energies and resources on identifying and solving an issue or problem. A commitment must be made at this stage to implement a solution.

The *incubation stage* is an internal and unconscious ordering of information. This stage may involve an unconscious personal or team conflict between what is currently accepted as reality and what may be possible. Relaxing, sometimes distancing oneself or the team from the issue, and allowing the mind to search for possible issues or problems and solutions is important. A successful incubation stage yields fresh ideas and new ways of thinking about the nature of an issue or a problem and alternative solutions.

The *illumination stage* is the moment of discovery, the instant of recognition, as when a light bulb seems to be turned on mentally. The mind instantly connects an issue or a problem to a solution through a remembered observation or occurrence.

The *verification stage* involves the testing of the created solution or idea. At this stage, confirmation and acceptance of the new approach are sought. The knowledge and insights obtained from each stage of the creative process are often useful in addressing new issues and problems at the next *preparation stage*.

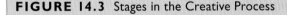

FIGURE 14.3 Stages in the Creative Process

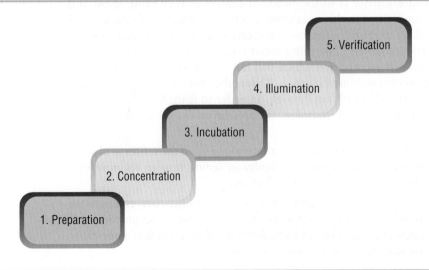

The *Personal Creativity Inventory* at the end of this chapter is a way for you to assess barriers to your own creative thought and innovative action. For now, we present several methods for helping to stimulate creative decision making by an individual or team. We are mindful that there are numerous creativity methods.[59]

De Bono's Lateral Thinking

The **lateral thinking method** *is a deliberate process and set of techniques for generating new ideas by changing an individual's or team's way of perceiving and interpreting information.* We can best explain this method by contrasting it with the **vertical thinking method,** *which is a logical step-by-step process of developing ideas by proceeding continuously from one bit of information to the next.* Table 14.3 presents the primary differences between lateral thinking and vertical thinking. Edward de Bono, the British physician and psychologist who developed the lateral thinking method, stated that the two processes are complementary and not at odds with each other.[60]

Lateral thinking fosters the generation of unique ideas and approaches. Vertical thinking is useful for assessing them. Lateral thinking enhances the effectiveness of vertical thinking by offering it more from which to select. Vertical thinking improves the impact of lateral thinking by making good use of the ideas generated. You probably use vertical thinking most of the time, but when you need to use lateral thinking, vertical thinking capabilities won't suffice.

The lateral thinking method includes a variety of techniques for (1) developing an awareness of current ideas and practices, (2) stimulating alternative ways of identifying or looking at a problem, and (3) aiding in the development of new ideas. Here, we consider only three of the techniques for fostering the development of new ideas: reversal, analogy, and cross-fertilization.

Reversal Technique

The **reversal technique** *involves examining a problem by turning it completely around, inside out, or upside down.* Engineers at Conoco asked, "What's good about toxic waste?" By so doing, they discovered a substance in refinery waste that they now are turning into both a synthetic lubricant and—they hope—a promising new market. Ronald Barbaro, president of Prudential Insurance, considered the idea "You die before you die" and came up with "living benefit" life insurance. It pays death benefits to people

---

TABLE 14.3 Characteristics of Lateral versus Vertical Thinking

LATERAL THINKING	VERTICAL THINKING
1. Tries to find new ways for looking at things; is concerned with change and movement.	1. Tries to find absolutes for judging relationships; is concerned with stability.
2. Avoids looking for what is "right" or "wrong." Tries to find what is different.	2. Seeks a "yes" or "no" justification for each step. Tries to find what is "right."
3. Analyzes ideas to determine how they might be used to generate new ideas.	3. Analyzes ideas to determine why they do not work and need to be rejected.
4. Attempts to introduce discontinuity by making "illogical" (free association) jumps from one step to another.	4. Seeks continuity by logically proceeding from one step to another.
5. Welcomes chance intrusions of information to use in generating new ideas; considers the irrelevant.	5. Selectively chooses what to consider for generating ideas; rejects information not considered to be relevant.
6. Progresses by avoiding the obvious.	6. Progresses using established patterns; considers the obvious.

Source: Based on de Bono, E. *Lateral Thinking: Creativity Step by Step.* New York: Harper & Row, 1970; de Bono, E. *Six Thinking Hats.* Boston: Little, Brown, 1985.

suffering from terminal illnesses before they die. Prudential has sold more than a million such policies.[61]

Analogy Technique

The **analogy technique** *involves developing a statement about similarities among objects, persons, and situations.* Some examples of analogies are "This organization operates like a beehive" or "This organization operates like a fine Swiss watch." The technique involves translating the problem into an analogy, refining and developing the analogy, and then retranslating the problem to judge the suitability of the analogy. If an analogy is too similar to the problem, little will be gained. Concrete and specific analogies should be selected over more abstract ones. Analogies should describe a specific, well-known issue or process in the organization. For an organization that is ignoring increased environmental change, an analogy might be "We are like a flock of ostriches with our heads buried in the sand."

Cross-Fertilization Technique

The **cross-fertilization technique** *involves asking experts from other fields to view the problem and suggest methods for solving it from their own areas of expertise.* For the technique to be effective, these outsiders should be from fields entirely removed from the problem. An attempt can then be made to apply new methods to the problem. Each year, Hallmark Cards brings to its Kansas City headquarters 50 or more speakers who might provide fresh ideas to the firm's more than 700 artists, designers, writers, editors, and photographers. Hallmark staffers often go from Hallmark's midtown headquarters to a downtown loft, where teams of writers and artists get away from phones to exchange ideas. They also may spend days in retreat at a farm in nearby Kearney, Missouri, taking part in fun exercises.[62]

Osborn's Creativity Process

Osborn's creativity process *is a three-phase decision-making process that involves fact finding, idea finding, and solution finding.* It is designed to help overcome blockages to creativity and innovation, which may occur for a variety of reasons. It is intended to stimulate the freewheeling thinking, novel ideas, curiosity, and cooperation that in turn lead to innovative decisions.[63] It can be used with all types of groups and teams. Sufficient time and freedom must be allowed for the model to work well, and some degree of external pressure and self-generated tension are helpful. However, too much pressure or threats from the wrong sources (e.g., an order from top management for the team to determine within 10 days why quality has deteriorated) can easily undermine the process.

Fact-Finding Phase

Fact finding involves defining the issue or problem and gathering and analyzing relevant data. Although the Osborn creativity process provides some fact-finding procedures, they aren't nearly as well developed as the idea-finding procedures that are discussed next.[64] One way to improve fact finding is to begin with a broad view of the issue or problem and then proceed to define subissues or subproblems. This phase requires making a distinction between a symptom of an issue or a problem and an actual issue or problem. For example, a leader might claim that low morale is a problem. A deeper investigation might reveal that low morale is only a symptom of a festering issue. The issue may be a lack of any positive feedback and rewards to employees when they are performing well.

Idea-Finding Phase

Idea finding starts by generating tentative ideas and possible leads. Then the most likely of these ideas are modified, combined, and added to, if necessary. Osborn maintained that individuals can generate more good ideas by following two principles. First, defer judgment. Individuals can think up almost twice as many good ideas in the same length of time if they defer judgment on any idea until after they create a list of possible leads to a solution. Second, quantity breeds quality: The more ideas that individuals think up, the more likely they are to arrive at the potentially best leads to a solution.

To encourage uninhibited thinking and generate lots of ideas, Osborn developed 75 general questions to use when brainstorming a problem. **Brainstorming** *is an unrestrained flow of ideas in a group or team with all critical judgments suspended.* The group or team leader must decide which of the 75 questions are most appropriate to the issue or problem being addressed. Moreover, the leader isn't expected to use all of the questions in a single session. The following are examples of questions that could be used in a brainstorming session:

- How can this issue, idea, or thing be put to other uses?
- How can it be modified?
- How can it be substituted for something else, or can something else be substituted for part of it?
- How could it be reversed?
- How could it be combined with other things?

A brainstorming session should follow four basic rules:

1. *Criticism is ruled out.* Participants must withhold critical judgment of ideas until later.
2. *Freewheeling is welcomed.* The wilder the idea, the better; taming down an idea is easier than thinking up new ones.
3. *Quantity is wanted.* The greater the number of ideas, the greater the likelihood that some will be useful.
4. *Combination and improvement are sought.* In addition to contributing ideas of their own, participants should suggest how ideas of others can be turned into better ideas or how two or more ideas can be merged into still another idea.

These rules are intended to separate creative imagination from judgment. The two are incompatible and relate to different aspects of the decision-making process. The leader of one brainstorming group put it this way: "If you try to get hot and cold water out of the same faucet at the same time, you will get only lukewarm water. And if you try to criticize and create at the same time, you will not do either very well. So let us stick solely to *ideas*—let us cut out *all* criticism during this session."

A brainstorming session should have from 5 to 12 or so participants in order to generate diverse ideas. This size range permits each member to maintain a sense of identification and involvement with the group or team. A session should normally run not less than 20 minutes or more than an hour. However, brainstorming could consist of several idea-generating sessions. For example, follow-up sessions could address individually each of the ideas previously generated. Table 14.4 presents the guidelines for leading a brainstorming session.

Solution-Finding Phase

Solution finding involves generating and evaluating possible courses of action and deciding how to implement the chosen course of action. This phase relies on judgment, analysis, and criticism. A variety of planning and decision aids—such as those presented in this chapter and elsewhere in the book—can be used. To initiate the solution-finding phase, the leader could ask the team to identify from one to five of the most important ideas generated. The participants might be asked to jot down these ideas individually on a piece of paper and evaluate them. A very important idea might get five points, a moderately important idea could get three points, and an unimportant idea could be assigned one point. The highest combined scores may indicate the actions or ideas to be investigated further.

TABLE 14.4 Guidelines for Conducting a Traditional Brainstorming Session

Basic Facilitator

- Make a brief statement of the four basic rules.
- State the time limit for the session.
- Read the problem and/or related question to be discussed and ask, "What are your ideas?"
- When an idea is given, summarize it by using the speaker's words insofar as possible. Have the idea recorded by a recorder or on an audiotape machine. Number each idea. Follow your summary with the single word "Next."
- Say little else. Whenever the facilitator participates as a brainstormer, group productivity usually falls.
- Consider asking participants to spend 10 minutes on doing individual brainstorming prior to the start of the session by having them record their initial ideas on cards that are provided.

Handling Issues

- When someone talks too long, wait until he or she takes a breath (everyone must stop to inhale sometime), break into the monologue, summarize what was said for the recorder, point to another participant, and say "Next."
- When someone becomes judgmental or starts to argue, stop him or her.
- When the discussion stops, relax and let the silence continue. Say nothing. The pause should be broken by the group and not the facilitator. This period of silence is called the mental pause because it is a change in thinking. All the obvious ideas are exhausted; the participants are now forced to rely on their creativity to produce new ideas.
- When someone states a problem rather than idea, repeat the problem, raise your hand with five fingers extended, and say, "Let's have five ideas on this problem." You may get only 1 or you may get 10, but you're back in the business of creative thinking.
- Strongly enforce the rule that only one person speaks at a time.
- Provide note cards for people who get ideas while someone else is speaking to minimize production blocking.

Source: Adapted from Wilson, C. E. Brainstorming pitfalls and best practices. *Interactions, September/October* 2006, 50–53; Dharmarajan, K. *Eightstorm: Eight Step Brain Storming for Innovative Managers.* Las Vegas, NV: BookSurge Publishing, 2007.

Osborn's creativity process has been modified often and applied in a variety of ways. The following Team Competency feature highlights how IDEO Product Development, headquartered in Palo Alto, California, uses brainstorming.[65] The company is a renowned professional services firm that helps clients design and develop new products and, in the process, become more innovative. The creative process at IDEO is enriched through the extensive use of empowered design teams. These teams are staffed to take advantage of diverse perspectives, technical and creative skills, and the ability to achieve goals jointly. Diverse views are encouraged and used to enhance the quality and creativity of decisions. At the same time, cooperation is fostered, and the teams are kept moving toward their goals.

Teams competency

IDEO Brainstorms

IDEO projects last from a few weeks to several years, with the average being 10 to 12 months. Depending on the client's needs, results can range from sketches of products to crude working models to complete new products. Clients vary from venture-funded start-ups to multinational corporations in North America, Europe, and Japan. IDEO has developed part or all of more than 3,000 products in dozens of industries. For example, IDEO recently worked with Ford Motor on a totally new dashboard design for the 2010 Ford Fusion and Mercury Milan hybrids. It is called "SmartGauge with EcoGuide." The gauges and configurations serve as tools that communicate with drivers to better enable them to maximize fuel economy.

IDEO is unique in that it encourages clients to participate in brainstorming sessions conducted by its design teams. By going to a "brainstormer," clients gain insight and learn because they join IDEO designers in the creative process. Brainstorming sessions usually are initiated by a design team. The team members then invite other IDEO designers to help generate ideas for the project. These sessions are held in rooms with five brainstorming rules written on the walls: (1) Defer judgment, (2) build on the ideas of others, (3) one conversation at a time, (4) stay focused on the topic, and (5) encourage wild ideas.

Designers are also skilled facilitators who lead the brainstorming sessions, enforce rules, write suggestions on the board, and encourage creativity and fun. Nearly all of the designers are experienced at brainstorming. Typically, project members (or clients) introduce the project and describe the design issue or problem they face (e.g., How do you make fishing more fun and easier for beginners?). Participants

COURTESY OF FORD MOTOR COMPANY

IDEO recently worked with Ford Motor to design a new dashboard for the 2010 Ford Fusion.

then generate ideas (e.g., use a "slingshot" to launch lures), often sketching them on paper or whiteboards. Many new projects start with a flurry of brainstorming sessions. Clients often attend them to describe their existing products and the new products that they want designed. Clients may also give detailed demonstrations before a brainstormer to explain the product or service, such as when clients from a chain of hair salons did haircuts at the Palo Alto office to demonstrate their work process. Twenty or so IDEO employees may be invited to brainstorming sessions in the early weeks of a project.

To learn more about IDEO, go to **www.ideo.com.**

Electronic Brainstorming

Electronic brainstorming *involves the use of collaborative software technology to anonymously enter and automatically disseminate ideas in real time to all team members, each of whom may be stimulated to generate other ideas.* For example, GroupSystems, headquartered in Broomfield, Colorado, is one of the leading providers of electronic brainstorming software. For this approach to work, each team member must have a computer terminal that is connected to all other members' terminals. The software allows individuals to enter their ideas as they think of them. Every time an individual enters an idea, a random set of the team's ideas is presented on each person's screen. The individual can continue to see new random sets of ideas by pressing the appropriate key.[66]

Research on electronic brainstorming is encouraging. It tends to produce more novel ideas than traditional face-to-face brainstorming. It also removes the main barrier of traditional brainstorming: Members seeing and hearing which ideas are whose. Electronic brainstorming permits anonymity and lets team members contribute more freely to idea generation. They need not fear they will "sound like a fool" to other employees and managers when spontaneously generating ideas. These advantages appear to be greater for teams of seven or more people or where there is distrust and rampant politics among team members.[67]

Insights for Leaders

Methods for enhancing creative decision making are based on the assumption that employees have the potential for greater creativity and innovation than they currently demonstrate. Some research suggests that the same number of individuals working alone may generate more ideas and more creative ideas than do groups.[68] Whether creativity methods in a work setting are more or less effective than individuals working alone to generate ideas remains an open question.

Creative decision making, with or without the aid of creativity methods, will not occur or will be minimal if perceptual, cultural, or emotional blocks are dominant in the organization.[69] From an organization perspective, Chapter 16 addresses a number of the dynamics of organizational culture that can serve to block or support creative decision making. Chapter 11, in particular, addressed several leadership approaches that support creative decision making at all levels of the organization, especially the authentic leadership and transformational leadership approaches.

Chapter Summary

1. *Explain certainty, risk, and uncertainty and how these influence decision making.*

Individuals make decisions that represent the probability of events occurring over which they have no control but that may affect the outcomes of those decisions. Such conditions may be viewed as a continuum from certainty to risk to uncertainty. Decision making becomes more challenging with increasing levels of risk and uncertainty. Important decisions by managers and leaders are often made under the conditions of risk (subjective probabilities) and uncertainty.

2. *Explain the core concepts of bounded rationality and how knowledge management helps leaders to reduce it.*

Bounded rationality describes a pattern that tends to be more descriptive of how leaders and others make what they consider to be thoughtful decisions. It represents tendencies to satisfice, engage in a limited search for alternative solutions, work with inadequate information, and use various biases to obtain and process information. It recognizes the practical limitations of individuals when they attempt to make decisions. Over time, the level of satisficing can be raised through various actions, such as the various elements and technologies associated with knowledge management.

3. *Discuss and apply elements of evidence-based management.*

Evidence-based management, like knowledge management, strives to reduce the natural tendency toward bounded rationality. It proceeds from the premise that using a deeper diagnosis enables leaders to do their jobs better. We presented five critical diagnostic questions and the key insights for leaders that are central to evidence-based management.

4. *Describe the attributes of political decision making.*

Political decision making emphasizes the impact of multiple stakeholders who have the power to influence decisions. It may be triggered when interdependent stakeholders hold divergent views about problem definitions, desired goals, and/or preferred solutions. Various political strategies, such as scapegoating and impression management tactics, may come into play under such circumstances. The most effective influence methods over the long run tend to be rational persuasion, inspirational appeal, and consultation.

Common blocks to creativity are found in three major categories: perceptual, cultural, and emotional. One way of viewing the creative process is through five interconnected stages: preparation, concentration, incubation, illumination, and verification. Two of the many approaches for stimulating creativity were highlighted: de Bono's lateral thinking method and related techniques, and Osborn's creativity process. Osborn's creativity process includes three phases: fact finding, idea finding, and solution finding. Brainstorming is one of the key methods of Osborn's creativity process that is used to help stimulate idea finding by teams. Electronic brainstorming may be an effective alternative to traditional face-to-face brainstorming in various situations.

5. *Explain the blocks, stages, and several methods of creative decision making.*

Key Terms and Concepts

Analogy technique, **434**
Bounded rationality, **419**
Brainstorming, **435**
Certainty, **415**
Creativity, **431**
Cross-fertilization technique, **434**
Decision making, **414**
Dictionary rule, **422**
Electronic brainstorming, **437**
Escalating commitment, **420**
Evidence-based management, **425**
Knowledge management (KM), **423**
Lateral thinking method, **433**
Objective probability, **416**

Osborn's creativity process, **434**
Political decision making, **428**
Probability, **416**
Problem framing, **421**
Radio-frequency identification (RFID), **423**
Reversal technique, **433**
Risk, **416**
Risk propensity, **421**
Satisficing, **419**
Scapegoating, **429**
Subjective probability, **416**
Uncertainty, **417**
Vertical thinking method, **433**

Discussion Questions

1. In the Learning from Experience feature, David Hoover comments: "We've got lots of challenges ahead of us. I spend about 75% of my time solving problems. . . ." Go to the Ball Corporation's website at www.ball.com. Click on "Sustainability" and review Ball's most recent annual "Sustainability Report" and read the "Chairman's Letter" from David Hoover. What ethical issues and potential problems are discussed by Hoover in this letter?

2. Review the Diversity Competency feature entitled "Chubb's Business Case for Diversity." In what three ways do you agree and/or disagree with this business case for diversity?

3. Give three examples of a "personal problem/decision" that you have experienced: one that involved the condition of certainty, one that involved risk (subjective probability), and one that involved uncertainty.

4. Review the "Shoes For Crews Reduces Risk and Uncertainty" Change Competency feature, then visit the company's website at www.shoesforcrews.com. Has this firm effectively communicated how its shoes help to reduce safety risks and uncertainty for employees and firms? Explain.

5. Review the Change Competency feature entitled "St. Clair Hospital Adopts RFID and Related Technologies." What specific components and applications of knowledge management are illustrated in this feature?

6. Think of an organization in which you are or have been an employee. Describe a decision situation that seemed to be based on the bounded rationality process in relation to the concepts of satisficing, limited search, and inadequate information and control.

7. What are three differences between evidence-based management and political decision making?

8. Think of an important decision that you have made during the past year. In what ways did your decision making match or vary from each factor in the political decision-making process? Explain.

9. Review the characteristics of lateral versus vertical thinking in Table 14.3. Try to think of a "personal" decision situation in which you would have benefited from lateral thinking but you instead used primarily vertical thinking. Why do you think lateral thinking would have been useful?

Experiential Exercise and Case

Experiential Exercise: Self Competency

Personal Creativity Inventory[70]

Introduction and Instructions

This inventory provides you the opportunity to assess, reflect on, and reduce possible personal barriers to creativity. For each of the statements in the inventory, use the following scale to express which number best corresponds to your agreement or disagreement with the statement. Write that number in the blank to the left of each statement. Please do not skip any statements.

Strongly Agree	Agree Somewhat	Agree	Disagree	Strongly Disagree
1	2	3	4	5

Statements

_____ 1. I evaluate criticism to determine how it can be useful to me.

_____ 2. When solving problems, I attempt to apply new concepts or methods.

_____ 3. I can shift gears or change emphasis in what I am doing.

_____ 4. I get enthusiastic about problems outside of my specialized area of concentration.

_____ 5. I always give a problem my best effort, even if it seems trivial or fails to arouse enthusiasm.

_____ 6. I set aside periods of time without interruptions.

_____ 7. It is not difficult for me to have my ideas criticized.

_____ 8. In the past, I have taken calculated risks and I would do so again.

_____ 9. I dream, daydream, and fantasize easily.

_____ 10. I know how to simplify and organize my observations.

_____ 11. Occasionally, I try a so-called unworkable answer in hopes that it will prove to be workable.

_____ 12. I can and do consistently guard my personal periods of privacy.

_____ 13. I feel at ease with peers even when my ideas or plans meet with public criticisms or rejection.

_____ 14. I frequently read opinions contrary to my own to learn what the opposition is thinking.

_____ 15. I translate symbols into concrete ideas or action steps.

_____ 16. I see many ideas because I enjoy having alternative possibilities.

_____ 17. In the idea-formulation stage of a project, I withhold critical judgment.

_____ 18. I determine whether an imposed limitation is reasonable or unreasonable.

_____ 19. I would modify an idea, plan, or design, even if doing so would meet with opposition.

_____ 20. I feel comfortable expressing my ideas even if they are in the minority.

_____ 21. I enjoy participating in nonverbal, symbolic, or visual activities.

_____ 22. I feel the excitement and challenge of finding solutions to problems.

_____ 23. I keep a file of discarded ideas.

_____ 24. I make reasonable demands for good physical facilities and surroundings.

_____ 25. I would feel no serious loss of status or prestige if management publicly rejected my plan.

_____ 26. I frequently question the policies, goals, values, or ideas of an organization.

_____ 27. I deliberately exercise my visual and symbolic skills in order to strengthen them.

_____ 28. I can accept my thinking when it seems illogical.

_____ 29. I seldom reject ambiguous ideas that are not directly related to the problem.

_____ 30. I distinguish between trivial and important physical distractions.

_____ 31. I feel uncomfortable making waves for a worthwhile idea even if it threatens team harmony.

_____ 32. I am willing to present a truly original approach even if there is a chance it could fail.

_____ 33. I can recognize the times when symbolism or visualization would work best for me.

_____ 34. I try to make an uninteresting problem stimulating.

_____ 35. I consciously attempt to use new approaches toward routine tasks.

_____ 36. In the past, I have determined when to leave an undesirable environment and when to stay and change the environment (including self-growth).

Scoring

Transfer your responses to the statements above and record them in the blanks provided below. Then add the numbers in each column, and record the column totals.

A	B	C	D	E	F
1. _____	2. _____	3. _____	4. _____	5. _____	6. _____
7. _____	8. _____	9. _____	10. _____	11. _____	12. _____
13. _____	14. _____	15. _____	16. _____	17. _____	18. _____
19. _____	20. _____	21. _____	22. _____	23. _____	24. _____
25. _____	26. _____	27. _____	28. _____	29. _____	30. _____
31. _____	32. _____	33. _____	34. _____	35. _____	36. _____

Totals: _____ _____ _____ _____ _____ _____

Interpretation

Take your scores from the scoring sheet and mark them with a dot in the score categories (cells) on the following graph. The vertical axis, which represents the possible column totals, ranges from 6 to 36. The horizontal axis represents the columns on your scoring sheet and ranges from A to F. The Key to Barriers legend at the end of this exercise identifies the category of barriers in each column. Connect the dots you have marked with a line. The high points represent your possible barriers to creativity as you see them. The higher the number in each column, the greater the barrier that factor represents in realizing your creative potential.

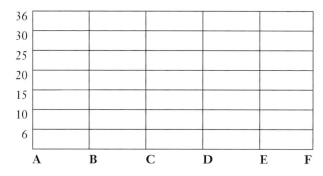

Key to Barriers

A = Barriers related to self-confidence and risk taking
B = Barriers related to need for conformity
C = Barriers related to use of the abstract
D = Barriers related to use of systematic analysis
E = Barriers related to task achievement
F = Barriers related to the physical environment

Questions

1. Based on these results, what competencies can you use to change or improve your creativity?
2. What barriers are linked to your potential creativity? Explain.

Case: Self Competency

A Manager's Dilemma: Who Gets the Project?[71]

"It seemed like a real ego booster when I got to take over my boss's job during his vacation," thought Dave Peterson. "Now I'm not so sure. Both Seamus and Jeremy really want to be in charge of this new project. I have to decide between them and I will still have to work with them as a peer after this is all over."

Background

CMT is a leading innovator in the telecommunications industry. Rapid growth and persistence in the face of early company setbacks have generated a culture based on problem solving and meeting customer expectations. The primary guidelines directing action are "If you see a problem that needs to be fixed, it becomes your problem" and "Do what you have to do to satisfy the customer." This environment has led to frequent conflicts and job stress but also provided opportunities for job enrichment and advancement. Additional company characteristics follow:

- *History:* 10 years old, telecommunications industry, rapid growth, $50M/annual revenue
- *Culture:* innovative, encourages individual initiative, respect for technical expertise, conflict accepted as part of company life.

Dave is the manager of Customer Software Support. His department provides support to customer and field staff when software problems occur. Dave had worked as a systems analyst in Customer Software Support prior to his promotion to manager. He and his staff have considerable experience with CMT's products and many contacts with CMT's software developers.

Seamus is in charge of the Technical Publications Department, which provides technical and user manuals and other materials for customers and CMT field staff. These manuals detail the technical operations of CMT Corporation's equipment and software. Seamus and his staff work closely with designers and have a good reputation for translating engineering terminology into more user-friendly materials that can be understood by those without engineering training.

Jeremy Olson manages the Software Training Department. This department offers courses that explain CMT Corporation's software products and trains customer and company employees on the proper use of the products. The Software Training Department utilizes documentation generated by the Technical Publications Department for its training courses. Jeremy and his staff members are especially good at designing courses that communicate technical information in a way that customers can readily understand. Course design and presentation are particularly important due to the high degree of modularity of CMT software.

The New Project

A new hardware product is under development with associated software. Due to the low target price for the product and the need for inexpensive training, CMT's Sales Department had requested that a CD-ROM self-study course be developed for customers of the new product. At this time, CMT Corporation has not yet begun using CD-ROM technology for training.

Both Seamus and Jeremy have been lobbying heavily to be allowed to develop the new course. Seamus argued that he and his staff had superior technical expertise due to their close working relationship with engineers during the development of technical manuals for the new product. In addition, some of his staff had previously developed CD-ROM presentations.

Jeremy noted that the primary purpose of the course was to train employees and customers in a situation where there were no company consultants or trainers available to answer questions. Thus, he argued, the presentation of the material and the pedagogy used were critical for the success of the CD-ROM. Both managers presented their respective cases to their supervisor, Henry Mathews, the Director of Software Support.

During the next two months, the lobbying intensified and the level of conflict escalated to the point where both Jeremy and Seamus openly declared that the other department simply "lacked the needed skills to get the job done" and "if the project was not assigned to their respective department, it would surely fail." Both managers had approached Dave asking for his support.

The culture at CMT accepts conflict that was based on doing the best job for the customer. In spite of this, Dave feels that the conflict between Seamus and Jeremy has gotten out of hand. If it goes on much longer, Dave feels the conflict might spill over into other areas where all three departments need to cooperate.

The Decision

Henry took a two-week vacation and when he left on Friday, he put Dave temporarily in charge of the entire unit. The following Monday, both Seamus and Jeremy informed Dave that a decision on the new project had to be made right away. The purchase order for the filming equipment needed to be placed immediately in order for it to arrive in time. They, of course, disagreed on the type of equipment that should be used so a decision needed to be made as to the long-term assignment of the project. Furthermore, the project was now behind schedule given the needed development time based on the projected product release date.

Dave realized that how he handled this decision would reflect on his management competencies and possibly influence his opportunity for advancement. "I know if I assign this project to either Seamus or Jeremy someone is going to be very upset," David pondered, "and I don't know if I can get these two to talk to each other, let alone to agree on a compromise. The only thing I do know is that I have to make a decision on this before Henry returns."

Questions
1. What examples of bounded rationality are evident in this case?
2. What examples of the political decision-making process can you identify?
3. How would evidence-based management help to address this situation?
4. What decision should be made by Dave? Explain.

chapter 15

Organization Design

Learning Goals

After studying this chapter, you should be able to:

1
Explain the environmental and strategic factors that affect the design of organizations.

2
State the two basic fundamentals of organizing.

3
Describe the major concepts of vertical organizational design.

4
Describe four types of horizontal organizational design.

Learning Content

Learning from Experience
  Lowe's Companies, Inc.

Key Factors in Organization Design

Change Competency
  KFC in China

Fundamentals of Organizing

Vertical Organizational Design

Ethics Competency
  Enron

Across Cultures Competency
  Eureka

Horizontal Organizational Design

Communication Competency
  DreamWorks Animation SKG

Experiential Exercise and Case

Experiential Exercise: Communication Competency
  Analyzing Your Organization's Design

Case: Change Competency
  FedEx Office and Print Services, Inc.

Lowe's Companies, Inc.

In 1946, Carl Buchan transformed his North Wilkesboro hardware store in North Carolina into Lowe's by eliminating some general merchandise and focusing on hardware and building materials. Today, Lowe's Companies vision is to provide customer-valued solutions with the best prices, products, and services to make Lowe's the first choice for home improvement. Lowe's has more than 228,000 employees working in its stores' 20 departments to implement its vision. It stocks more than 40,000 products and generates revenues of more than $48 billion. More than 14 million customers a week visit its 1,650 superstores. It has recently expanded in Canada and plans to have 100 stores open in Canada in the near term. It also plans to open stores in Monterrey, Mexico (rival Home Depot already has 55 stores in Mexico). Home Depot, the leader in the home improvement industry, has sales that exceed $91 billion from its more than 2,000 stores.

When Buchan started Lowe's, he focused on small and medium-sized markets. Today, Lowe's has expanded into major metropolitan markets with populations of 500,000 or more. But the company is not forgetting its roots and plans to open half of its 150 new stores in rural markets to serve farmers and small business owners. To improve its nationwide sales, Lowe's purchased a 38-store chain, Eagle Hardware and Garden. To supply these stores, Lowe's is expanding its distribution network. Recently, it has built new warehouses in Mississippi, Pennsylvania, Oregon, and North Carolina.

Lowe's organization design has been created to handle an increasing number of customers and their desires for product diversity. Lowe's is trying to take advantage of five major trends in the marketplace. First, Lowe's is putting an emphasis on installation services in more than 40 categories, such as flooring, cabinets, and appliances, and has created a department to handle customers' installations. Lowe's second goal is to appeal to female urban shoppers. Female shoppers make about 80 percent of the home improvement decisions. These shoppers want installation services in major categories, such as cabinets and flooring. Third, Lowe's opened its first urban store, with a focus on satisfying the home improvement needs of inner-city dwellers and building superintendents, in New York City. Fourth, to retain the professional builder as a customer, Lowe's entered into a joint venture with Kobalt-brand professional mechanics' tools manufactured by Snap-on. Finally, Lowe's wants to attract more baby boomers who want less hassle, one-stop shopping, and someone they can trust to help them with home improvement projects.[1]

MICHAEL FEIN/BLOOMBERG NEWS/LANDOV

To learn more about Lowe's, go to www.lowes.com.

The basis for any successful organization is for people to work together and understand how their behaviors support the organization's strategy. Yet, talented people in even the best managed organizations are sometimes left trying to understand how their own activities contribute to their organization's success. An organization's design is crucial in clarifying the roles of the leaders and employees who hold the organization together. **Organization design** *is the process of selecting a structure for the tasks, responsibilities, and authority relationships within an organization.*[2] An organization's design influences communication patterns among individuals and teams and determines which person or department has the political power to get things done. The structure of an organization influences the behavior of employees. Therefore, an organization's design plays a critical role in the success of an organization.

In this chapter, we first note how environmental factors and leaders' strategic choices influence the design of an organization.[3] Strategic choices made by leaders also influence how the organization differentiates and integrates its structure. An organization's design should also ease communication among employees and departments to accomplish the goals of the organization. Our discussion on the vertical design of an organization focuses on practices that assist leaders in achieving these goals. Finally, we describe the functional, product, geographical, and network types of horizontal organizational design. All of these designs are intended to help leaders reach their organization's goals in the face of complex and changing environments.

Key Factors in Organization Design

Learning Goal

1. *Explain the environmental and strategic factors that affect the design of organizations.*

Every organization's design decision solves one set of problems but creates others. Organization design decisions often involve the diagnosis of multiple factors, including an organization's culture, power and political behaviors, and job design. Organization design represents the outcomes of a decision-making process that includes environmental factors, strategic choices, and technological factors. Specifically, organization design should:

*   promote the flow of information and speed decision making in meeting the demands of customers, suppliers, and regulatory agencies;
*   clearly define the authority and responsibility for employees, teams, departments, and divisions; and
*   create the desired balance between integration (coordination) and differentiation to account for responses to changes in the environment.

We frequently refer to departments and divisions as we discuss organization design. The term *department* typically is used to identify a specialized function within an organization, such as human resources, production, accounting, and purchasing. In contrast, the term *division* typically is used to identify a broader, often autonomous part of an organization that performs many, if not all, of the functions of the parent organization with respect to a product or large geographic area.

The formal connections among various divisions or departments in an organization can be represented in the form of an organization chart. An **organization chart** *is a representation of an organization's internal structure, indicating how various tasks or functions are interrelated.* How is Lowe's organized to compete in the home improvement industry? Figure 15.1 shows an abridged organization chart for Lowe's. Each box represents a specific job, and the lines connecting them reflect the formal lines of communication between individuals performing those jobs. That is, the senior vice president for the North Central Division reports to the executive vice president for store operations, who reports to the CEO.

An organization chart provides several benefits. First, it gives some insight into how the entire organization fits together. Everyone presumably knows who reports to whom and where to go with a particular problem. Second, the chart may indicate

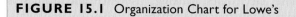

FIGURE 15.1 Organization Chart for Lowe's

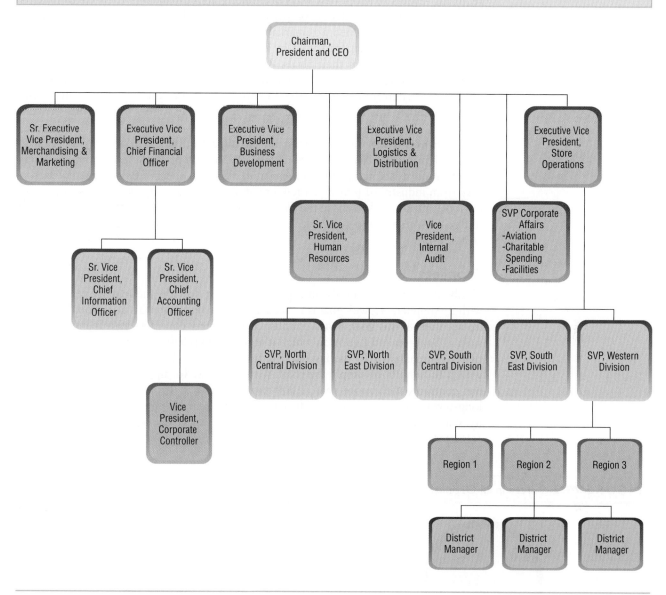

gaps or duplication of activities. Unfortunately, the chart doesn't show how things really get done in an organization or who really has the political clout to make things happen. By definition, the choice of organization design entails a set of trade-offs because every organization design has some drawbacks. The key is to select one that minimizes the drawbacks. Two primary factors—environmental and strategic—that impact organization design decisions will be reviewed in this section. Other factors (e.g., government, state of the economy, and politics) can also affect the design of an organization, but we have chosen these two as most important.

Environmental Factors

The environmental factors that leaders and employees need to be aware of are (1) the characteristics of the present and possible future environments and (2) how those characteristics affect the organization's ability to function effectively. Hypercompetition in some industries, including consumer electronics, banking, insurance, and airlines, is requiring leaders to adopt new ways of thinking about managing their environments. As markets become global and competition escalates, the quest for productivity, quality, and speed has spawned a remarkable number of new organization designs. Yet, many leaders have been frustrated by their inability to redesign themselves quickly enough to stay ahead of their rivals. After realizing disappointing sales, top leaders of Zales, a national jewelry store chain, redesigned Zales by giving regional leaders more decision-making authority to compete more effectively with local jewelry stores. Whether this redesign results in more sales and higher profitability remains to be seen.

Perhaps the best way to understand the impact of the environment on organization design is to look at the various factors that comprise the environment. Every organization exists in an environment and, although specific environmental factors vary from industry to industry, a few broad ones exert an impact on the strategies of most organizations. We chose the four that we believe are among the most important to discuss.[4] As shown in Figure 15.2, they are suppliers, distributors, competitors, and customers.

Suppliers

To obtain required materials, an organization must develop and manage relationships with its suppliers. Lowe's goal is to secure high-quality materials at reasonable prices. To accomplish this goal, it has established long-term contracts with many suppliers, such as Snap-on and Lenox, in which it agrees to purchase from them certain quantities of merchandise. In the fast-food industry, McDonald's has a long-term contract with J. R. Simplot to supply the chain with potatoes. To supply McDonald's, Simplot has contracts with more than 1,000 potato growers throughout the world. Such long-term contracts ensure product uniformity, cost stability, and delivery reliability. Customers are drawn to familiar brands and expect reasonable cost and product consistency.

FIGURE 15.2 Forces in an Organization's Environment

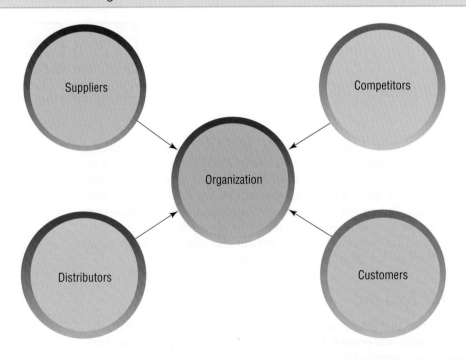

Distributors

An organization must establish channels of distribution that give it access to customers. Distributors are the various organizations that help other organizations deliver and sell its products. Manufacturers, such as Lenox and Whirlpool, do not typically distribute their products directly to the customer; instead, they deliver their products to one of Lowe's regional warehouses, which then fill store orders.

In other businesses, store managers can develop personalized relationships with customers and devise ways to offer them good quality in both sales and service. Sam Su, who heads up YUM! Brands (e.g., KFC, Pizza Hut) China, has found distribution in Shanghai to be vastly different than in the United States. Because traffic is so congested, pizza delivery is usually made by drivers on motor scooters who weave and dodge through snarled terrific or by delivery people who use peddle bikes with warming ovens strapped onto their bikes to deliver pizzas to customers. As an alternative, he recently has converted apartments into pizza parlors and simply has delivery people deliver pizza via elevator to residents in multistory apartment buildings.[5]

Competitors

Competitors can also influence the design of an organization because they drive the organization to become more productive. Lowe's major competitors are Home Depot, Sears, and Menards. To compete at low cost requires organization designs that are simple and easy to manage. Cost savings must be gained at every step of the process, including labor, raw materials, acquisition of land, logistics, and human resources. For example, Lowe's turns over its store inventory about 4.5 times a year, compared to Home Depot's 5.0, and holds goods in inventory about 10 days longer than Home Depot. Lowe's is trying to turn its inventory faster and reduce the number of days goods are in inventory to remain cost competitive with Home Depot and other competitors.

Customers

Relationships with customers are vital. Customers can easily evaluate the costs of various products and easily switch buying habits with minimal inconvenience by shopping on-line. Lowe's tries to manage customer relationships in several ways. On a global level, the company engages in massive country-wide advertising campaigns to create product awareness in customers. As shown earlier in Figure 15.1, Lowe's has a senior executive vice president of merchandising and marketing who manages Lowe's multi-million-dollar advertising campaign. Recently, it ranked second behind Costco in an American Consumer Satisfaction survey, in which Home Depot placed last. Three of the reasons for Lowe's customer satisfaction are the installation of self-checkouts in most stores, use of the Internet, and the offering of installation services. Offering self-checkouts cuts down customer waiting time for service, a major complaint for most customers. Permitting customers to shop on the Internet offers them the speed of Internet service, but also places an additional burden on Lowe's by offering customers the convenience of easily returning items they do not want. The challenge for Lowe's is to bridge two different retailing models (retail stores and websites). Finally, offering installation services has also helped Lowe's customer satisfaction rankings. The challenge for Lowe's is to hire competent outside contractors to actually perform the work that Lowe's has promised the customer.

Strategic Factors

Many strategic factors affect organization design decisions. We focus on one of the most popular frameworks of competitive strategy, which was developed by Michael Porter of Harvard University. According to Porter, organizations need to distinguish and position themselves differently from their competitors in order

Change Insight

Failure to factor the environmental issue into corporate strategy greatly increases the probability that the company strategy will turn into a nightmare for many firms. A company needs to think proactively about how to create a reputation for a clean company that helps develop the economy in environmentally sustainable ways.

Elizabeth Economy, Senior Fellow U.S. Council on Foreign Relations

to build and sustain a competitive advantage.[6] Organizations have attempted to build competitive advantages in various ways, but three underlying strategies appear to be essential to doing so: cost leadership (that is, a low-cost strategy), differentiation, and focused strategies, which are illustrated in Figure 15.3.

Cost Leadership Strategy

A **cost leadership strategy**, *also known as a low-cost strategy, is based on an organization's ability to provide a product or service at a lower cost than its rivals.* An organization that chooses the cost leadership strategy seeks to gain a significant cost advantage over other competitors and pass the savings on to consumers in order to gain market share. Such a strategy aims at selling a standardized product that appeals to an "average" customer in a broad market. Customers buy from these companies because they feel that these companies have been around for a long time and are less risky to buy from than others. The organization must attain significant economies of scale in key business activities (e.g., purchasing and logistics). Because the environment is stable, few product modifications are needed to satisfy customers. The organization's design is functional, with accountability and responsibility clearly assigned to various departments. Lowe's has adopted a cost leadership business strategy.

Other organizations that have successfully used a cost leadership strategy include Dollar General, BIC (maker of ballpoint pens), and Walmart discount stores. The risks involved in following this strategy are (1) getting "locked in" to a technology and organization design that is expensive to change, (2) the ability of competitors to copy the strategy (e.g., Target copying Walmart), or, most important, (3) management not paying attention to shifts in the environment (e.g., customer demand for different types of products and/or services and losing market share, as happened at Kmart).

FIGURE 15.3 Strategies Model

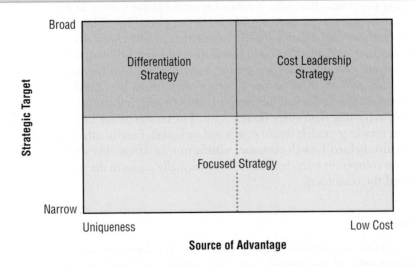

The cost leadership strategy is based on locating and taking advantage of opportunities for an organization to seek cost-based advantages in all of its activities, including human resources, marketing, manufacturing, and information systems. Tune Hotels operates hotels in Kuala Lumpur, Malaysia. It builds rooms for $22,000, a cost that includes land. Competitors' rooms cost three times as much to build. The Tune Hotels rooms, which cost as little as US $16 per night, come with a King Koil mattress, an electronic door lock, one power outlet, and a bathroom with a shower. Some rooms have a window and others do not. Clothes are hung on hooks on the walls instead of in closets, which saves space, allowing more rooms per floor. The floors are concrete. There are no towels, soap, phone, or radio, although towels and soap can be purchased in the hotel's 24-hour store. Air conditioning and televisions also cost extra. Only the toilet paper is free says Tony Fernandes, the CEO for Tune Hotels. To keep rates low, Tune leases space to a fast-food restaurant on the first floor and sells advertising space on room walls, room keys, in hallways, and in the lobby. The hotels run about 92 percent occupancy.[7]

Differentiation Strategy

A **differentiation strategy** *is based on providing customers with something unique that makes the organization's product or service distinctive from its competition.* This is the strategy chosen by St. Regis Resorts, Ritz-Carlton Hotels, and Maytag Corporation, among others. An organization that uses a differentiation strategy typically uses a product organization design whereby each product has its own manufacturing, marketing, and R&D departments. The key managerial assumption behind this strategy is that customers are willing to pay a higher price for a product that is distinctive in some way. Superior value is achieved through higher quality, technical superiority, or some special appeal. Organizations pursuing differentiation must still control expenses to balance somewhat higher costs with a distinctive edge in key activities, such as manufacturing. Therefore, an organization selecting a differentiation business strategy must aim at achieving cost parity by keeping costs low in areas not related to differentiation and by not spending too much to achieve differentiation.

In almost all differentiation strategies, attention to product quality and service represents the ways in which organizations build their competitive advantage. For example, Toyota's strategy with Lexus is based on exceptional manufacturing quality, the use of genuine wood paneling, advanced sound systems, high engine performance, and comparatively high fuel economy (for luxury cars). After-sales service is hard for other dealers to duplicate. Other organizations that have successfully used a differentiation strategy include American Express in credit cards, Nordstrom in department stores, and Krups in coffeemakers and espresso makers. The biggest disadvantage that these organizations face is maintaining a price premium as the product becomes more familiar to customers. Price is especially an issue when a product or service becomes mature. Organizations may also overdo product differentiation, which places a burden on their R&D departments, as well as a drain on their financial and human resources.

When Sam Su entered China in 1987 as president of YUM! Brands, the two brands he was responsible for developing—KFC and Pizza Hut—faced tremendous problems. (Remember the earlier discussion about Su converting apartments into pizza parlors because delivery on the crowded streets of Shanghai was so difficult?) Many of the roads in China were unpaved making delivery very difficult, time consuming, and expensive. Trucks were constantly delayed because of broken axles and flat tires. Also, there were few modern distribution facilities and no established network of domestic suppliers. Importing foodstuffs was too costly, so he needed to develop networks of suppliers in China who could supply these two brands. The following Change Competency feature highlights some of the problems Su faced as he tried to implement a differentiation strategy for KFC in China.[8]

Change competency

KFC in China

KFC restaurant in China.

When Sam Su entered China, his first problem was to educate the Chinese government on what franchising meant. Chinese governmental officials had never heard of the term. Because intellectual property laws were weak, government officials interpreted these as they saw fit. Second, there were no known foreign brands. For organizations that have adopted a differentiation strategy, a brand is what sets them apart from their competition and provides a customer recognition factor that they need to succeed. Third, Su learned very quickly that without government involvement, he couldn't do business in China. Informal relationships with government officials, also known as *guanxi*, were critical to foster. In China's Confucian society, the web of social networks maintained through informal communications is critical. Through these informal relationships, a leader can cut through the layers of bureaucracy that pervade the Chinese government.

Another problem facing Su was to develop a marketing program that attracted customers to KFC instead of McDonald's. Su knew that kids didn't come alone but had friends. To attract kids, he needed to tailor the menu (e.g., combo meals) and provide entertainment. Combo meals not only attract kids, but also simplify communication and choice. At many KFCs, kids have a corner reserved for them. The corner is staffed with a professional hostess whose job is to talk with the kids. The hostess sings and dances with the kids. Today, the average KFC hosts more than 400 birthday parties annually.

Su also knew that he had to clearly differentiate KFC's products not only from McDonald's products, but also from the millions of mom-and-pop restaurants along the streets. Therefore, he needed to pay close attention to Chinese values.

First, when a KFC restaurant opened, it celebrated with a traditional "Lion Dance" to bring good luck. Even though traditional Chinese fast-food restaurants have a lot of choices on their menus and are cheap, controlling their standard of cooking and cleanliness is difficult. KFC prides itself on its consistency and cleanliness. It forbids smoking, bathrooms are clean, and no parents are allowed in the kids' corner. Its lack of noise also differentiates KFC from other restaurants. Su learned that the menu at a KFC provides an important intangible: social freedom. In many Chinese restaurants, what you order has social and status implications (e.g., I can afford this). The wrong order can cause the person to lose "face" with friends. A standard and restricted menu with a limited price range frees the diner from this concern.

To learn more about YUM! Brands in China, go to **www.yum.com**.

Focused Strategy

A **focused strategy** *is designed to help an organization target a specific niche in an industry,* unlike both the low-cost and differentiation strategies, which are designed to target industry-wide markets. An organization that chooses a focused strategy may utilize any of a variety of organization designs, ranging from functional to product to network, to satisfy its customers' preferences. The choice of organization design reflects the niche of a particular buyer group, a regional market, or customers who have special tastes, preferences, or requirements. The basic idea is to specialize in ways that other organizations can't effectively match.

A major assumption for companies who adopt a focus strategy is that they can attract a growing number of new customers and continue to attract repeat buyers. Attracting repeat buyers is very important because they are knowledgeable about the firm's offerings and are less likely to be price sensitive. Repeat buyers often become emotionally attached to the firm's products/services and act as spokespeople for the firm. Harley-Davidson has captured this emotional appeal—can you think of any another firm whose customers have tattoos on their body advertising their product?

Organizations that have successfully used a focused strategy include Karsten Manufacturing, Midas Mufflers, and Jiffy Lube. Karsten Manufacturing has implemented its focused strategy by designing and producing a line of golf clubs under the Ping label. It was able to carve out a defensible niche in the hotly contested golf equipment business. Karsten uses ultrasophisticated manufacturing equipment and composite materials to make golf clubs almost on a customized basis. Midas Mufflers and Jiffy Lube use a focused strategy to compete in their industries because they specialize in parts of the car—exhaust and lubrication systems, respectively.

The greatest disadvantage that an organization faces in using a focused strategy is the risk that its underlying market niche may gradually shift toward a broader market. Distinctive customer tastes may "blur" over time, thus reducing the defensibility of the niche. For example, when Calloway Golf introduced its own line of golf equipment, it targeted the same customers that Karsten had targeted. In an attempt to differentiate Ping from Calloway, Karsten introduced a broader line of clubs that would appeal to the wider golfing public, thus facing losing its distinctive niche in the marketplace.

Another risk faced by firms pursuing a focused strategy is that of expanding their distribution channels too quickly. To be successful pursuing a focused strategy, customers must love the firm's products so that they become buyers. For more than 15 years, Krispy Kreme Doughnuts was able to create a cultlike group of customers who were willing to stand in line at 5:00 A.M. for high-priced, fresh-from-the-oven doughnuts. Krispy Kreme diluted its premium image by selling its doughnuts in gas stations, large supermarket chains, and even in Target stores. As a result, customers felt less desire to pay the high price of a Krispy Kreme doughnut after it had lost its special appeal.

Fundamentals of Organizing

Learning Goal

2. State the two basic fundamentals of organizing.

As you can imagine, leaders must contend with many different environments. For example, leaders in the rapidly changing video game industry face different challenges than leaders at Lowe's. In the video game industry, many external factors are changing simultaneously. Similarly, leaders at Google, Yahoo!, MySpace, and Facebook confront a different set of challenges in China than they do domestically because of the role of China's government in the Internet industry. The question confronting these leaders is: "How do we organize our firm to be successful in these differing environments?" When leaders answer this question, they often rely on two basic principles around which all organizations are organized: *differentiation* and *integration*.

Differentiation

Differentiation *means that the organization is composed of units that work on specialized tasks using different work methods and requiring employees with unique competencies.* Michael Brown is the executive vice president for store operations at Lowe's. In his job, he is concerned with the operations of all 1,650 Lowe's stores. Bill Edwards is the senior vice president for store operations for the Southeast Division. He is responsible for the operations of all stores in his region. Each person faces a unique set of problems, and each will organize his unit differently to handle these problems.

Differentiation is created through a division of labor and job specialization. **Division of labor** *means that the work of the organization is divided into smaller tasks.* Look back at the organization chart for Lowe's in Figure 15.1. There are five executive vice presidents. Each one is in charge of performing a different set of tasks: merchandising and marketing, chief financial officer, business development, logistics and distribution, and store operations. Each of Lowe's stores has 20 departments, including appliances, building supplies, flooring, hardware, and the like.

Specialization *is the process of identifying particular tasks and assigning them to departments, teams, or divisions.* Division of labor and specialization are closely related concepts. The numerous tasks that must be carried out in an organization make division of labor and specialization necessary. Otherwise, the complexity of running the entire organization would be too great for any one person. At a typical Lowe's home improvement center, a manager is in charge of one of the 20 departments, for example, windows and doors or tools or the garden center.

Integration

Integration *means that the various units coordinate their work to achieve common goals.* Rules and procedures are one means used by leaders to coordinate the ongoing activities of an organization's various units. If departments have common goals, are organized similarly, and work together to achieve the organization's goals, the organization is highly integrated.

As organizations differentiate their designs, leaders are also concerned with issues of integration. An organization is more than the sum of its parts; it is an integration of its parts. Because different units are part of the larger organization, some degree of coordination is needed among them for an organization to be effective. When Lowe's grew during the mid-1990s, for example, merchandising decisions were made by various regional presidents. With Home Depot, TrueValue, Ace Hardware, and other organizations entering the market, senior management recognized that Lowe's needed to become more efficient in its merchandising function. Therefore, they coordinated all merchandising decisions at Lowe's headquarters and put a senior executive vice president in charge of this function.

> ### Teams Insight
>
> Coordination is like professional sports: It looks easy, but when you're on the field, you see how difficult it is. The more people need to work with each other to reach the organization's goal, the more coordination is needed. However, there is a cost (meeting time, travel, uniform policies) to achieving integration.
>
> *Mike Lazaridis, President, Research in Motion, Waterloo, Ontario, Canada*

To achieve organizational goals, employees, projects, and tasks have to be coordinated regardless of the task. Without it, employees' efforts are likely to result in delay, frustration, and waste. Integration is one of the basic elements of organizing.

Many leaders believe that good people can make any organization design work. Although such leaders may be overstating the case, employees who work well together are extremely valuable assets. A good analogy is basketball, where teamwork is essential. During practice sessions, coaches try to transform the individual players into one smoothly functioning team. Players learn their functions—guards, forwards, center—as part of a cooperative effort, learn how each task relates to every other task, and relate these tasks to the whole. Coordination is required as the players execute their functions, particularly when they are called on to make adjustments in a game situation. Leaders can use mechanistic and/or organic practices to integrate the activities of their employees and achieve the goals of their organization.

Mechanistic and Organic Management Practices

We have identified two types of management practices—mechanistic and organic—that leaders have used for integrating employees and the tasks they perform.[9] **Mechanistic management practices** *break down activities into separate, highly specialized tasks, rely* *extensively on standardized rules, and centralize decision making at the top.* Another word for mechanistic is bureaucratic. This type of system may be most appropriate when an organization's environment is relatively stable and predictable, as found in companies such as Home Depot, Lowe's, McDonald's, and the IRS. Table 15.1 highlights these characteristics. Mechanistic management practices are most effective when (1) the organization needs to process large amount of standard information (as in credit card and insurance companies and traffic courts), (2) the needs of the customer are well known and are not likely to change, (3) the technology is routine and stable so employees can be easily and quickly taught how to operate it, and (4) the organization has to coordinate the activities of numerous employees in order to deliver a standardized product or service.

Organic management practices *encourage leaders and subordinates to work together in teams and to communicate openly with each other*. In fact, employees are encouraged to communicate with anyone who might help them solve a problem. Decision making tends to be decentralized. Authority, responsibility, and accountability flow to employees having the expertise required to solve problems as they arise. As a result, an organic organization is well suited to a changing environment. Table 15.1 summarizes the characteristics of an organic system.

Raymond Bingham, chairman of Flextronics International, has used many of the ideas of an organic system to create a very successful organization that manufactures and assembles printed circuit boards for Cisco Systems, Dell, and Eastman Kodak.[10] The company's services range from design engineering through manufacturing and assembly for makers of networking and telecommunications equipment. Located in Singapore, the organization employs more than 162,000 people in more than 20 countries located in the Americas, Asia, and Europe. In the past 10 years, its revenues have gone from $93 million to more than $27.5 billion by acquiring competitors. The operating manual has 80 pages—all of them blank. Sometimes Bingham lets subordinates do multimillion-dollar acquisitions without showing him the paperwork. He asks four questions: One, what is their line of business; two, what is their manufacturing capacity; three, how big and what is their customer base; and four, what are their cultural values? If his leaders answer all of these questions, then the acquisition is verbally agreed on and as far as Bingham is concerned, it's a done deal. He hates staff meetings and has refused to draw up an organization chart outlining his leaders' responsibilities.

As Bingham sees it, the business of global contract manufacturing is all about speed. The time it takes to get a prototype in mass production and onto retail

---

TABLE 15.1   Organic versus Mechanistic Systems

ORGANIC	MECHANISTIC
• Tasks tend to be interdependent.	• Tasks are highly specialized.
• Tasks are continually adjusted and redefined through interaction and as situations change.	• Tasks tend to remain rigidly defined unless changed by top management.
• Generalized roles (responsibility for task accomplishment beyond specific role definition) are accepted.	• Specific roles (rights, obligations, and technical methods) are prescribed for each employee.
• Network structure of control, authority, and communication.	• Hierarchical structure of control, authority, and communication.
• Communication and decision making are both vertical and horizontal, depending on where needed information and expertise reside.	• Communication and decision making are primarily vertical, top-down.
• Communication emphasizes the form of mutual influence and advice among all levels.	• Communication emphasizes directions and decisions issued by superiors.

shelves across the globe can determine whether or not the digital gadget succeeds or flops. Bingham thinks the biggest mistake is to miss important opportunities rather than make a mistake or two. So he doesn't want to tie down his top leaders with bureaucracy. This means that Flextronics' global leaders can utilize the company's worldwide information technology to solve a local customer's problem or send a project to other global leaders to solve without going through a lot of red tape.

The basketball hoops hanging in Bingham's modest, somewhat messy office seem to sum up his organization. He's convinced that he can retain the agile management style of a start-up, while making Flextronics a global organization.

Now that we have introduced you to the two basic principles of organizing—differentiation and integration—we will discuss the vertical structure of an organization. In one sense, an organization's vertical structure acts as a "harness" to integrate employees' activities.

There are few hard and fast rules for designing or redesigning an organization. An organization's vertical structure is often the result of many decisions and its past. It may reflect political biases, the preferences of powerful external stakeholders, and historical circumstances.[11]

Learning Goal

3. *Describe the major concepts of vertical organizational design.*

Vertical Organizational Design

An organization's design should ease the communication among employees and departments to accomplish the goals of the organization. That is, employees at lower levels should carry out activities consistent with senior leaders' goals, and senior leaders need to be informed about the activities and accomplishments of lower level employees. Organizations may use any one of five ways to achieve these results.[12]

Hierarchy

The **hierarchy** *is a pyramid showing relationships among levels.* The CEO occupies the top position and is the senior member of top management. The CEO and members of the top leadership team set the strategic direction of the organization. In Figure 15.1, this would include the CEO and the five senior executive vice presidents at Lowe's. Reporting to these people are senior vice presidents in charge of specific areas, such as chief information officer, accounting, human resources, and corporate affairs. At the next level are various vice presidents (internal audit and corporate controller). The Western Division's senior vice president is responsible for three regional leaders who manage six district leaders (only three are shown in the figure). Each district manager is responsible for eight stores.

During the past few years, many U.S. companies, including GE, Wells Fargo Bank, and Farmers Insurance, have reduced the number of hierarchical levels in their organizations. For example, GE used to have more than 20 hierarchical levels between the CEO and its first-line employees. Today, it has 5. Why? Most executives think that having fewer layers creates a more efficient organization that can react faster to competition and is more cost effective. Ten of thousands of employees laid off during the recent global recession have reduced the cost of doing business for many organizations, including Dell, GM, GE, and Hewlett Packard. According to Andy Kohlberg, president of Kisco Senior Living Communities, with fewer employees and levels, top leaders can hear "bad" news more frequently and quickly and, hence, take quicker corrective action to solve the problem before it spins out of control. Also, having fewer hierarchical levels permits more people to participate in the decision-making processes.

Span of Control

Span of control *refers to the number of employees directly reporting to a person*. In the case of Lowe's, the CEO has a span of control of five. The implications for different spans of control on the vertical design of an organization are clear. By holding size constant, narrow spans of control lead to more hierarchical levels. Wider spans create a flatter organization with fewer hierarchical levels. The span of control can either be too wide, too narrow, or appropriate. The optimal span of control is not so narrow that the manager "micromanages" subordinates or too broad so that the manager loses the ability to lead subordinates.

Insights for Leaders

What is the optimal number of subordinates? There is no "correct" number of subordinates that a manager can supervise effectively. The following four key factors can influence the span of control in any situation[13]:

1. *The competence of both the manager and the employee.* If leaders and/or employees are new to a task, they require more supervision than do knowledgeable veteran leaders and employees.

2. *The similarity or dissimilarity of tasks being supervised.* At Starbucks, the span of control in the retail store area is broad because all leaders can focus on one main product: coffee and its accessories. The more numerous and dissimilar the products, the narrower the span of control should be.

3. *The incidence of new problems in the manager's department.* A manager should know enough about the operations of the department to understand precisely the problems that subordinates are likely to face. The more the manager knows about these factors, the broader the span of control can be.

4. *The extent of clear operating standards and rules.* Clear rules and standard operating procedures (SOPs) leave less to chance and reduce the need for improvisation. At Lowe's, rules govern the tasks and behaviors of store employees in serving customers. For example, when a customer wants to exchange an item, the store clerk should know the procedure to follow. This makes it possible for leaders to have larger spans of control. The greater the reliance on rules and SOPs, the broader the span of control may be because the rules do part of the controlling for the manager.

Authority, Responsibility, and Accountability

Authority *is the right to make a decision*. Authority is the glue that holds the vertical and horizontal parts together.[14] Generally, but not always, people at higher levels have the authority to make decisions and tell lower level people what to do. For example, the manager of the paint department at Lowe's has the authority to schedule worker overtime. The manager of the store has the authority to review the overtime scheduled by the paint department manager. Robert Niblock, the CEO of Lowe's, has the authority to make decisions that require spending money opening stores in Canada.

Authority implies both responsibility and accountability. That is, by exercising authority, employees accept the responsibility for acting and are willing to be held accountable for success or failure. **Responsibility** *is an employee's duty to perform the assigned task*. Employees take on this obligation when they accept a job assignment. When giving an employee responsibility, the leader should give the subordinate enough authority to get the job done; oftentimes, however, that is not possible. Under these conditions, the subordinate must use her informal influence instead of relying on formal authority.

When a leader delegates authority and responsibility to an employee, that person is accountable for achieving the desired results. **Accountability** *is the manager's expectation that the employee will accept credit or blame for his work*. No leader can check everything an employee does. Therefore, leaders normally establish guidelines and performance standards within which responsibilities are carried out. As such, accountability flows from the bottom to the top. The manager of the garden department at Lowe's is accountable to the store leaders for their operation. Accountability is the point at which authority and responsibility meet and is essential for high performance. When either authority or responsibility is lacking, leaders cannot judge a subordinate's accomplishments fairly. When leaders are reluctant to hold their subordinates accountable, subordinates can easily pass the buck for nonperformance onto others.

While these three concepts seem simple to understand, a close look at business practices at Enron, one of America's biggest business failures, illustrates that these concepts are often difficult to implement. Many of you can recall the headlines that this Houston-based energy company made for months in the newspapers and business press. The top three leaders—Lay, Skilling, and Fastow—were all convicted of fraudulently using Enron funds to make poor deals look profitable. These unscrupulous actions were gambles to keep the deception of profitability going and inflate Enron's stock prices—because as long as Enron's stock prices increased, investors would keep buying its stock. Today, after several years and mountains of conflicting testimony by Jeff Skilling, Andy Fastow, Ken Lay, and other top leaders at Enron, a picture has emerged that indicates these people often didn't follow the basic principles of accountability, responsibility, and authority. Who are senior leaders accountable to? Who has the authority to make decisions? Who is responsible for making a decision? We have asked questions to highlight these three basic management principles in the following Ethics Competency feature.[15]

Ethics competency

Enron

After the fall of Enron in December 2001, employees sat outside the company's Houston headquarters.

DAVID J. PHILLIP/AP PHOTO

One of the more interesting testimonies in the Enron trial occurred right after Jeffrey Skilling, Enron's chief executive officer, resigned in August 2001. Greg Whalley, the company's soon-to-be president, after meeting with worried investors in New York, flew home to Houston so he didn't have to lie too much if he stayed in New York. Who is a president accountable to?

Both Andy Fastow, chief financial officer, and former Enron treasurer Ben Glisan testified at a meeting of Enron's top executives in September 2001 that the company was roughly $500 million short of its earnings target. Whalley said "Don't worry about it. I'll cover it with reserves." Whalley had asked an employee to hide hundreds of millions of dollars in losses in a separate account. Unfortunately for Whalley, this employee gave the government some of the most powerful testimony against Whalley, Skilling, Fastow, and Lay during the trial. Did Whalley have the authority to make the decision to cover the reserves?

The poor financial condition of Enron's international assets and its water business was another issue that arose during the trial. Whalley said that all of the heads of the international business division should be fired because they had done billions of dollars worth of bad deals. Skilling disagreed and no one was fired when Skilling overvalued the assets by billions of dollars to hide the losses. Skilling told Ken Lay, Enron's chairman, that everything was fine.

Merrill Lynch agreed to buy three Nigerian power barges from Enron. A verbal guarantee had been made that the three barges would be repurchased six months later at a guaranteed profit for Merrill Lynch. Jeff McMahon, who was working for Fastow at the time, was in charge of the deal. After six months, there was no profit, and losses were mounting. McMahon told Fastow of the problem. The money Fastow got to pay off Merrill Lynch came from "offshore" deals that he and other senior leaders at Enron had made

off the books. Fastow and Skilling told Lay that "you can always hit the earnings target. We just need to sell more business." Who is responsible for the power barge losses?

While admitting to two major business mistakes—Enron's failed broadband venture and its inability to unload its international assets—Skilling and Lay passionately maintain that they did nothing wrong with a company they called the "finest in the world" back in August 2001. Skilling claimed that most of the people who testified against him were really lying when they say that he committed crimes at Enron.

In May 2006 a jury convicted both Skilling and Lay, who died on July 5, 2006, on many counts of fraud and unethical behaviors.

To learn more about Enron, go to **www.enron.com**.

Delegation

Delegation *is the process of giving authority to a person (or group or team) to make decisions and act in certain situations.* In addition to holding an employee accountable for the performance of certain job responsibilities, the manager should give the employee the authority to carry out the responsibilities effectively. Delegation starts when the design of the organization is being established and work is divided. Delegation continues as new jobs and tasks are added during day-to-day operations.

Insights for Leaders

Delegation should occur in conjunction with the assignment of responsibilities. David Stoner, president of ViewCast, asked Laurie Latham, chief financial officer, to undertake a financial analysis of Ancept, a company that ViewCast was considering purchasing, and make a recommendation to the Board of Directors after her analysis. In this case, Stoner is delegating authority to Latham to make a decision whether to buy Ancept based on her financial analysis. In this case, Stoner delegated the authority to make a recommendation to Latham, his subordinate.

The following practices are useful for achieving effective delegation[16]:

1. *Establish goals and standards*. Individuals or teams should participate in developing the goals that they will be expected to meet. Ideally, they should also agree to the standards that will be used to measure their performance.

2. *Ensure clarity*. Individuals or teams should clearly understand the work delegated to them, recognize the scope of their authority, and accept their accountability for results.

3. *Involvement*. The challenge of the work itself won't always encourage individuals or groups to accept and perform delegated tasks well. Leaders can motivate them by involving them in decision making, by keeping them informed, and by helping them improve their skills and abilities.

4. *Expect completed work*. Individuals or teams should be expected to carry a task through to completion. The leader's job is to provide guidance, help, and information—not to finish the task.

5. *Provide training.* Delegation is only as effective as the ability of people to make the decisions necessary to perform the work and then actually to do the work. Leaders should continually appraise delegated responsibilities and provide training aimed at building on strengths and overcoming deficiencies.

6. *Timely feedback.* Timely, accurate feedback should be provided to individuals or teams so that they can compare their performance to stated expectations and correct any deficiencies.

Barriers to Delegation

Delegation is only as effective as the ability of leaders to delegate. The greatest psychological barrier to delegation is fear. A leader may be afraid that if subordinates don't do the job properly, the manager's own reputation will suffer. Such a manager may rationalize that "I can do it better myself" or "My subordinates aren't capable enough" or "It takes too much time to explain what I want done." In addition, some leaders also may be reluctant to delegate because they fear that subordinates will do the work their own way, or do it too well and outshine them!

Among the organizational barriers that may block delegation is a failure to define authority and responsibility clearly. If leaders themselves don't know what is expected or what to do, they can't properly delegate authority and responsibility to others.

The six practices for achieving effective delegation that we presented earlier provide a strong foundation for reducing barriers to delegation. In addition, leaders need to accept that there are several different ways to deal with problems and that their particular way of dealing with a problem is not necessarily the way their subordinates will choose to deal with it. Employees will make mistakes, but, whenever possible, they should be allowed to develop their own solutions to problems and learn from their mistakes.

Another barrier to delegation is culture.[17] Japanese leaders tend not to delegate decisions to others because of Japan's high power distance ranking (see Chapter 3, page 73). Most Japanese organizations operate like centralized hubs into which information flows and decisions are announced by leaders. Nearly all senior management positions in Japanese companies are held by Japanese leaders who rarely give foreign leaders access to decision-making processes. Many U.S. and other foreign employees complain about the "bamboo ceiling," a term used to refer to the exclusion of foreigners from key decision-making roles.

Centralization and Decentralization

Centralization and decentralization of authority are basic, overall management philosophies that indicate where decisions are to be made. **Centralization** *is the concentration of authority at the top of an organization or department.* **Decentralization** *is the delegation of authority to lower level employees or departments.* Decentralization is an approach that requires leaders to decide what and when to delegate, to select and train personnel carefully, and to formulate adequate controls.

Insights for Leaders

Neither centralization nor decentralization is absolute in an organization. No one manager makes all the decisions, even in a highly centralized setting such as the IRS. Total centralization would end the need for middle and first-line leaders. Thus, there are only degrees of centralization and decentralization. In many organizations, some tasks are relatively centralized (e.g., payroll systems, purchasing, and human resource policies), whereas others are relatively decentralized (e.g., marketing and production).

Potential benefits to decentralization include the following:

1. It frees top leaders to develop organizational plans and strategies. Lower level leaders and employees handle routine, day-to-day decisions.

2. It develops lower level leaders' self-management and planning and administration competencies.

3. Because subordinates often are closer to the action than higher level leaders, they may have a better grasp of the facts. This knowledge may enable them to make sound decisions quickly. Valuable time can be lost when a subordinate or team must check everything with a manager.

4. It fosters a healthy, achievement-oriented atmosphere among employees.

A variety of factors can affect management's decisions to centralize or decentralize authority in various areas of decision making. We briefly consider five of these factors:

1. *Cost of decisions*. Cost is perhaps the most important factor in determining the extent of centralization. As a general rule, the more costly the outcome, the more likely top management is to centralize the authority to make the final decision.

2. *Uniformity of policy*. Leaders who value consistency favor centralization of authority. These leaders may want to assure customers that everyone is treated equally in terms of quality, price, credit, delivery, and service. At Lowe's, for example, a nationwide home improvement sales promotion on paint requires that all stores charge the same price. Uniform policies have definite advantages for cost accounting, production, and financial departments. They also enable leaders to compare the relative efficiencies of various departments. In organizations with unions, such as Delta, United Airlines, and Northwest Airlines, uniform policies also aid in the administration of labor agreements regarding wages, promotions, fringe benefits, and other human resource matters.

3. *Competency levels*. Many organizations work hard to ensure an adequate supply of competent leaders and employees—an absolute necessity for decentralization. Royal Dutch Shell, Harley-Davidson, and Brinker, among others, recognize that extensive training and practical experiences are essential to developing the competencies needed by people in a decentralized organization. These organizations decentralize many decisions to employees because leaders are willing to permit employees to make mistakes involving small costs so as to learn from them.

4. *Control mechanisms*. Even the most avid proponents of decentralization, such as Philips, Cisco, and Marriott, insist on controls and procedures to prevent costly mistakes and to determine whether actual events are meeting expectations. For example, each Marriott Hotel centralizes the analysis of key data, including number of beds occupied, employee turnover, number of meals served, and the average amount that guests spend on food and beverages. Analysis of these data helps leaders control important aspects of the hotel's operation and compare it against the performance of others in the chain. If a hotel's operations don't fall within certain guidelines, top management may step in to diagnose the situation.

5. *Environmental influences*. External factors (e.g., unions, federal and state regulatory agencies, and tax policies) affect the degree of centralization in an organization. For example, laws and government regulations regarding hours, wages, working conditions, and safety make it difficult to decentralize authority in those areas.

The following Across Cultures Competency feature illustrates some of the leadership challenges Eureka faced in its global operations. Originally founded in 1912, this Swedish company became best known for its Electrolux vacuum cleaners. By the early 1960s, the company was in serious financial difficulty primarily because of the factors we have just reviewed as aspects of an organization's vertical design. The company was purchased by the Wallenbergs, a Swedish family that had interests in Ericsson (telecommunications), Saab (automobiles), and Astra (pharmaceuticals). In 2004, the company was purchased by AB Electrolux, a Swedish company. It changed its name back to Eureka shortly after the purchase. Today, the company makes and markets more than 130 vacuum models under the brand names of Electrolux, Sanitaire, Beam, and Eureka and sells these products at Lowe's, Sam's Club, Best Buy, Target, and Costco. After reading this feature, you should be able to point out some of the vertical organizational design challenges that faced Eureka's leaders.[18]

Across Cultures competency

Eureka

When AB Electrolux purchased Eureka in 2004, it had to redesign itself to become a viable global organization. This required several changes to Eureka's organizational design. First, the company needed to centralize its planning process so that products could be introduced in several European countries simultaneously. Local plants needed to be coordinated and share resources to achieve the organization's goal. Second, it needed to change how the plant leaders' managed their plant. For example, the Italian plant manager believed in a highly centralized (e.g., mechanistic) decision-making process, whereas the plant manager in Sweden practiced a more decentralized (e.g., organic) control system. Leaders in Sweden were known by their first names throughout the plant, whereas Italian leaders were only known by their job title. Third, inefficiencies were rampant. Because of tailor-made specifications for different markets (e.g., Spain, Italy, France), plants weren't being used efficiently. At one point, plants were producing hundreds of different motors for vacuum cleaners and refrigerators, even though market research had indicated that the firm needed fewer than 10 different models. Plant utilization was quite low, employment

levels were high, and output per employee was unacceptably low. Similarly, the Italian plant had too many staff people in relation to its production workers.

To gain manufacturing efficiencies needed to compete in a global market, leaders made the following changes. First, motor designs and horsepower were standardized. This permitted leaders to develop global product development strategies. When Eureka introduced its new "Jet-System" washing machine that allowed people to use less detergent and reduced water consumption by one-third, it was able to introduce this product throughout Europe because all machines used similar motors. Second, to achieve cost savings in raw materials, headquarters leaders began negotiating with a few suppliers for all product lines, thus achieving considerable materials savings. By centralizing these decisions, it removed these decisions from plant leaders. Senior leaders also required all suppliers to make a commitment to quality and to use just-in-time delivery systems. Third, plant leaders are now responsible for all functions, including manufacturing, human resource management, advertising, and sales. Each plant manager is now judged by the profits his or her plant earns.

To learn more about Eureka, go to **www.eureka.com.**

In this section, we examined the five basic vertical parts of an organization. Issues of hierarchy, span of control, authority, delegation, and centralization/decentralization are important because they give you an idea of how leaders and employees relate to each other at different levels. These five parts can be combined in many different ways to build a vertical design. Accordingly, leaders need the right combination of hierarchical levels, spans of control, and delegation to implement the organization's strategy. Leaders can use a number of practices, procedures, or rules to achieve consistent performance.

Horizontal Organizational Design

The basis for a successful organizational design rests on people working together in an organization. They must be able to understand its strengths and limitations. A company's choice of a particular structure will go a long way toward supporting its strategy.[19] In this section we illustrate four basic designs and provide guidelines for using them. The four most commonly used types of horizontal design are (1) functional, (2) product, (3) geographical, and (4) network. Each of these designs involves different choices with respect to the vertical integration factors that you have just read about.

Functional Design

Functional design *means grouping leaders and employees according to their areas of expertise and the resources they use to perform their jobs.* Functions vary widely according to the type of organization. For example, Presbyterian Hospital doesn't have a production unit, but it has functional units for admitting, emergency rooms, surgery, and maintenance. Similarly, Lowe's has functional departments shown in Figure 15.1, but doesn't have admitting and emergency rooms. Functional designs are usually found in organizations that have adopted a low-cost business strategy and distribute or produce a high volume of products. Functional designs are also particularly suited for these organizations because authority, responsibility, and accountability can be pinpointed and will not radically change over time.

As shown in Figure 15.4, Harley-Davidson has chosen a functional form of departmentalization.[20] Harley has more than 1,300 worldwide dealers, produces 33 different models of motorcycles, and has eight functional vice presidents as shown in Figure 15.4. Grouping activities by way of a functional structure is efficient and cost effective. That is, a set of functional leaders oversees activities for each major area of the organization.

Potential Benefits

Designing by function is economical because it results in a simple design. Leaders create one department for each primary function to be performed (e.g., production, marketing, and human resources). This design keeps administrative expenses low because everyone in a department shares training, experience, and resources. Senior

---

FIGURE 15.4 Harley-Davidson Organization Chart

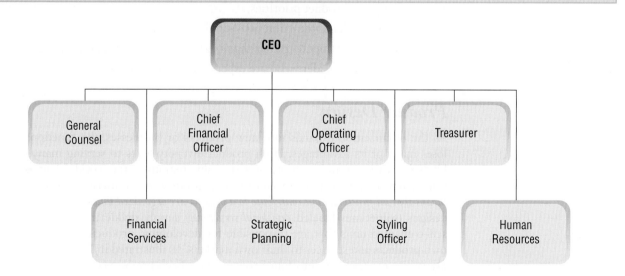

leaders can easily identify and promote those people who have the necessary competencies to manage their particular functional unit. Also, employees can see clearly defined career paths within their own departments. As a result, the organization can more easily hire and promote employees who have or develop good problem-solving skills in each area of specialization.

In brief, the potential benefits of functional design include:

- supporting skill specialization,
- reducing duplication of resources and increasing coordination within the functional area,
- enhancing career development and training within the functional area,
- allowing superiors and subordinates to share common expertise, and
- promoting high-quality technical decision making.

Potential Pitfalls

The pitfalls of functional design become apparent when an organization provides highly diverse products (goods and/or services) or serves highly diverse customers. Making decisions quickly becomes difficult when employees have to coordinate with other units. For example, a sales rep at Harley-Davidson in Chicago, Illinois, may lose a sale because he or she has to wait for the sales manager to get the production manager in Kansas City to make a scheduling decision. In addition, when friction exists between units, leaders have to spend time resolving the issues involved. Pinpointing the accountability and performance levels of employees who are performing separate functions may also be difficult. In other words, a top manager may not be able to determine easily which department—production, sales, or credit—is responsible for delays and declining profits.

Another pitfall is that top management may have a hard time coordinating the activities of employees in different departments. At ViewCast, manufacturing and marketing are in different physical locations in Plano, Texas, and employees in those departments report to different leaders, each of whom has different goals for his or her departments. The plant manager wants long and steady production runs to minimize changes and save costs, whereas the sales manager wants to make last-minute changes to satisfy a customer's demands. Moreover, functional designs tend to de-emphasize the overall goals of the organization, with employees often focusing on departmental goals (e.g., meeting their own budgets and schedules).

In brief, the potential pitfalls of functional design include:

- inadequate communication between units,
- conflicts over product priorities,
- difficulties with coordination between departments,
- a focus on departmental rather than organizational issues and goals, and
- development of leaders who are experts only in narrow fields.

Product Design

As the organization expands into new products or businesses, the functional design loses many of its advantages. High product diversity leads to serving many different kinds of customers and a variety of geographic regions of the world. Many organizations group all of their functions into a single product line or division. **Product design** *means that all functions that contribute to a product are organized under one leader.* Product designs (sometimes labeled *divisional structures*) simply divide the organization into self-contained units that are responsible for developing, producing, and selling their own products and services to their own markets. As illustrated in Figure 15.5, General Dynamics is organized into four product lines. Each product competes against competitors in its own market.[21]

FIGURE 15.5 General Dynamics Organization Chart

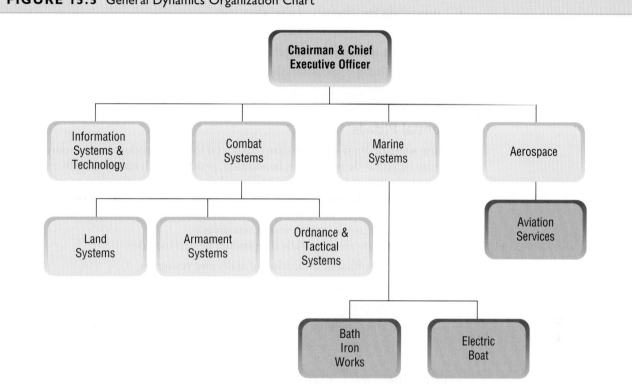

Product design is the most commonly used design for companies in the Fortune 500 pursing a differentiation business strategy. In large companies, such as Komatsu, General Dynamics, or Procter & Gamble, the product divisions remain fairly autonomous, with each division competing against a different set of competitors. Thus, leaders and employees assigned to a particular product often become experts about that division's products and markets. Each product also has its own functional specialists and resources needed to support the product. Therefore, a product design encourages decentralization of authority to the product manager by tailoring functional activities to the needs of the particular product. In the case of General Dynamics, the leader in charge of the Bath Iron Works has various functional leaders, such as manufacturing, finance, and human resources, reporting to him.

Product designs are evaluated on the basis of their profit contributions to the entire organization. Because each division represents a product or group of products, senior management can measure the financial performance of each division. For example, at General Dynamics, the profitability of Bath Iron Works can be compared against the profitability of the Electric Boat division to see which division is more profitable. In many respects, separate divisions act almost as separate businesses and work independently to accomplish their goals and those of the organization.

Potential Benefits

This form of organization enables leaders and employees to become specialized and expert in a particular product (good or service) line. This benefit lessens only as the number and diversity of products provided by an organization increase. Management also can pinpoint costs, profits, problems, and successes accurately for each product line.

In brief, the potential benefits of product design include:

- permitting fast changes in a product line,
- allowing greater product line visibility,
- fostering a concern for customer demands,
- clearly defining responsibilities for each product line, and
- developing leaders who can think across functional lines.

Potential Pitfalls

Because some or many functions are duplicated for each product line, resource utilization may be relatively inefficient. In addition, products with seasonal highs and lows in sales volumes may result in higher personnel costs. Coordination across product lines usually is difficult. Employees tend to focus on the goals for their particular products, rather than on broader company goals. This situation may create unhealthy competition within an organization for scarce resources.

In brief, the potential pitfalls for product design include:

- not allowing efficient utilization of skills and resources,
- not fostering coordination of activities across product lines,
- encouraging politics and conflicts in resource allocation across product lines, and
- limiting career mobility for personnel outside their own product lines.[22]

Geographical Design

Some organizations, such as Nestlé, Sheraton Hotels, and Celanese Chemical, operate in a number of geographic regions. Such organizations often find that functional and product designs are inefficient because they do not provide a way for leaders to coordinate activities within a geographic region. **Geographical design** *organizes activities around location*. Geographical designs allow organizations to develop competitive advantage in a particular region according to that area's customers, competitors, and other factors. This form of horizontal design permits leaders to specialize in particular markets.

Geographical designs are extremely versatile. If each manager is in close contact with customers in his or her market, the manager can quickly adapt to changing market conditions. The practices, procedures, and standards used in a geographical design can vary according to regional conditions, as well as the priorities senior management assigns to each region. Leaders at local sites become familiar with local labor force practices, governmental requirements, and cultural norms that could impact their operations. When Celanese Chemical opened its plant in Singapore to serve the Asian market for its chemicals, quality control, human resources, engineering, and manufacturing departments were established. All of the necessary functional activities to reach the organization's goals were established in Singapore.

Potential Benefits

Geographical designs allow an organization to focus on customer needs within a relatively small geographic area and to minimize the costs associated with transportation of goods or services. In brief, the potential benefits of geographical design include:

- having facilities and the equipment used for production and/or distribution all in one place, saving time and costs;
- being able to develop expertise in solving problems unique to one location;
- gaining an understanding of customers' problems and desires; and
- getting production closer to raw materials and suppliers.

Potential Pitfalls

Organizing by location typically increases problems of control and coordination for top management. To ensure uniformity and coordination, organizations that use geographical designs, such as Starbucks and the IRS, make extensive use of rules that apply to all locations. One reason for doing so is to guarantee a standard level of quality regardless of location, which would be difficult if units in various locations went their own separate ways.

In brief, the potential pitfalls of geographical design include:

- duplication of functions, to varying degrees, at each regional or individual unit location;
- conflict between each location's goals and the organization's goals; and
- added levels of management and extensive use of rules and regulations to coordinate and ensure uniformity of quality among locations.[23]

Network Design

Recently, a number of organizations have started to rely on a network design. A **network design** *subcontracts some or many of its operations to other firms and coordinates them to accomplish specific goals.*[24] Sometimes also called a *virtual organization*, leaders need to coordinate and link people (from many organizations) to perform activities in many locations. Contacts and working relationships in the network are facilitated by electronic means, as well as through face-to-face meetings. The use of computer-based technologies permits leaders to coordinate suppliers, designers, manufacturers, distributors, and others on an instantaneous, real-time basis. Often, leaders in a network design work as closely with their suppliers and customers as they do with their own employees.

By connecting people regardless of their location, the network design enhances fast communications so that people can act together. Numerous organizations in the fashion, toy, publishing, software design, and motion picture industries use this design. Organizing as a network design allows the organization to compete on the basis of speed and ability to quickly transfer knowledge. For example, Cisco Systems outsources most of its manufacturing to other organizations that are better able to manage this function than Cisco. In turn, Cisco focuses on product development and customer relationships.

Potential Benefits

All organizations seek to combine the stability and efficiency of their existing designs with a capability for fast response to competitors. However, relying on functional, product, or geographical designs to attain such a balance is very difficult. To meet the dual needs of high efficiency and fast response, many organizations are becoming much more focused and specialized in what they will do in-house. As a result, some activities that used to be performed within the organization are now given to other firms.

The network design offers many potential benefits for an organization pursuing a focused business strategy. First, the organization brings together the special knowledge and skills of others to create value rather than hiring employees to perform this task. The network design enables leaders to focus on one set of activities and rely on others to contribute. Second, the network design has the advantage of bringing together people with different insights into teams that work exclusively on a given project. Thus, network designs enhance the search for new ideas and creative solutions. Yet, it is important for employees working on such a project to have strong self-management, teamwork, communication, and planning and administration competencies. When a given project is completed, these teams will be disassembled.

Third, organizations choosing a network design can work with a wide variety of different suppliers, customers, and other organizations. This gives leaders a high degree of flexibility to respond to different customer demands.

In brief, the potential benefits of a network design include:

- utilization of part-time specialists to solve complex problems,
- bringing outside experts together to work on one project,
- gaining an understanding of customers and their problems quickly, and
- minimizing bureaucracy.

Potential Pitfalls

With many people working from different locations and often linked by electronic means, potential pitfalls exist. First, other organizations can sometimes fail to live up to the deadlines that were established. Because network designs work in real time, a delay in one part of the process has ripple effects throughout the system. How many times have you waited for a doctor in an office? In instances where time is critical, delays can be very costly because the entire system must wait until a decision is made. Thus, dependence on other organizations can create an operational risk. Often, additional resources or coordination is needed, thus increasing the cost to the consumer. Second, because the network design does not provide leaders with knowledge to complete the process on their own, they must constantly monitor the quality of work provided by those in other organizations. Knowledge resides in people's minds. Thus, the network organization is only as competitive as the quality and resources assigned to the project by another organization. Assigning employees with weak communication and team competencies, for example, can lead to reduced effectiveness. Third, employees in the outsourced organization may not commit to the same values and sense of time urgency to which employees in the networked organization are committed. Therefore, it is crucial that all people working in a network organization understand the critical nature of projects. Last, the network design involves leaders working with many organizations. Lines of authority, responsibility, and accountability are not always clear. Projects may be delayed and cost overruns can occur.

The production of movies has for a long time illustrated many characteristics of the network design. Filmmakers, directors, producers, actors, agents, makeup artists, costume designers, special-effects artists, technicians, and lawyers come together from many different organizations and agencies to produce a film. Although they are all independent, the producer and director need to closely orchestrate and communicate with each of these specialists to produce a film according to very exact specifications. After the production is complete and the film is released, these various people disband and then regroup (often with different people) to produce another film with a different set of actors, producers, directors, and so forth. Thus, the movie industry is actually composed of many different specialized organizations, each of which is critically dependent on the people, knowledge, and skills of other organizations to create a product that is often beyond the scope, capabilities, and means of any one firm.

Some of the pitfalls of a network design include:

- a potential conflict of interest between the long-term interests of the company and the short-term interests of employees,
- managers who lack complete knowledge of the product,
- staffing requirements that vary project by project,
- concerns about whether the best people are available to work on your company's project,
- the difficulty company leaders have establishing clear lines of authority with outside employees, and
- difficulties surrounding the supervision of people in different physical locations.

The following Communication Competency feature illustrates how DreamWorks Animation SKG uses a network design to make movies.[25] Created in 1994 by Steven Spielberg, Jeffrey Katzenberg, and David Geffen, this multibillion-dollar company produced such mega box office hits as *Kung Fu Panda*, *Madagascar*, and *Shark Tale*. The company also produced other movies, such as *Amistad* and *Mouse Hunt*, which had mediocre box office sales.

DreamWorks Animation has also produced television shows, as well as music albums for a number of pop artists, and it produced a string of TV flops before producing Michael Fox's successful comedy *Spin City*. In 2003, the company had to exit the music business because of lagging sales and high costs. After facing a multitude of environmental protests, cost overruns, and construction delays, the three founders sold DreamWorks to Paramount Pictures in 2006 for $1.6 billion, giving Paramount the distribution rights for DreamWorks Animation films until 2013. Roger Enrico, former chairman of PepsiCo, was appointed chairman and Lew Coleman was appointed president of DreamWorks Animation.

Communication Competency

DreamWorks Animation SKG

At DreamWorks Animation, senior leaders divide their responsibilities by function. Bill Damaschke is co-president for production and feature animation, Derek Chan is the head of digital operations, Jane Hartwell is the head of global production, Anne Globe is the head of worldwide marketing, and Alex Schwartz is the head of development. These people and a few more comprise the senior management circle shown in Figure 15.6.

DreamWorks relies heavily on many other organizations to provide the critical resources, people, and skills needed to produce a film. As shown in Figure 15.6, makeup artists, costume designers, actors, and agents are not a part of DreamWorks Animation. These people are hired as contract employees at the time they are needed. Likewise, DreamWorks Animation works with other specialized organizations to develop many of the newest technologies used to create computer-generated, animated films. A central task for the senior leaders of the company is communicating with people from different backgrounds, expertise, and competencies to produce blockbuster entertainment. It is the job of leaders to rapidly find the competencies needed to complete a project on time and within budget, assemble the team(s), and then disband the team when the project is finished.

MONICA ALMEIDA/THE NEW YORK TIMES/REDUX PICTURES

DreamWorks uses a networked organization to create characters.

DreamWorks Animation signed with computer giant Hewlett-Packard (HP) to develop cutting-edge technologies for new forms of animation. HP provided all of the computing resources for DreamWorks Animation's next-generation digital studio at its Glendale, California, location. Working with HP permitted DreamWorks Animation to create the latest computer-designed animation more quickly and more cost effectively than previous technology. HP supplied all of the workstations, servers, printers, and networking devices needed. HP also helped

FIGURE 15.6 DreamWorks Network Design

DreamWorks Animation develop technologies that fostered closer collaboration among producers, directors, animators, and other technicians working from many distant locations. Hewlett-Packard had effectively become a key provider of computer hardware and other technologies that allowed DreamWorks Animation, which could not develop the technology as effectively or in as timely a manner on its own, to produce even more realistic animation.

Many of DreamWorks Animation's popular movies have become the basis for the newest video game ideas. Yet, DreamWorks Animation does not currently seek to invest in this industry by itself, especially after having encountered some product failures in the late 1990s. DreamWorks realizes that it does not have the skills or the resources to successfully invest in or compete in the video game industry. Yet, leaders at DreamWorks Animation recognize that the video game market is a new channel that could help spark interest in both current and future films. So DreamWorks Animation signed a deal with Activision to publish games based on three DreamWorks films: *Sharkslayer*, *Madagascar*, and *Over the Hedge*. In this relationship, Activision has helped DreamWorks Animation develop a video game franchise for interactive entertainment, but DreamWorks Animation does not actually develop the games.

To learn more about DreamWorks, go to **www.dreamworksanimation.com.**

Chapter Summary

We reviewed how the four major environmental factors—suppliers, distributors, competitors, and customers—can affect the design of an organization. Although these four factors vary by industry, leaders need to assess them before choosing a business strategy. A business strategy indicates how the organization intends to compete in its industry. A cost leadership (low-cost) strategy focuses on achieving cost efficiencies that let the organization compete favorably against its rivals. An organization pursuing a differentiation strategy attempts to provide customers with a unique product and/or service. Organizations pursing a focused strategy target a narrow market or niche for their product or service.

1. *Explain the environmental and strategic factors that affect the design of organizations.*

There are two fundamentals of organizing: differentiation and integration. Differentiation is created through a division of labor and job specialization. As organizations grow, they create departments to handle certain activities, such as payroll, manufacturing, and human resources. Because different units are part of the larger organization, some degree of integration (coordination) is needed among them for an organization to be effective. Integration is achieved through the use of mechanistic and organic management practices.

2. *State the two basic fundamentals of organizing.*

The vertical design of an organization has five major parts. The hierarchy shows relationships among the various management levels in an organization. These relationships are shown in the organization chart. The span of control refers to the number of subordinates reporting to each manager. Authority, responsibility, and accountability are the glue that holds an organization together because these indicate who has the right to make a decision, who will be held responsible for the decision, and who is accountable for the results. Delegation is the process of giving authority to a person (or group) to make decisions. Delegation should go hand in hand with responsibility and accountability. Centralization/decentralization refers to the overall philosophy of management as to where decisions are to be made.

3. *Describe the major concepts of vertical organizational design.*

The four primary types of design are (1) functional design—groups employees according to common tasks to be performed; (2) product design—groups employees by product or service in self-contained units, each responsible for its own goods or services; (3) geographical design—groups functions and employees by location; and (4) network design—subcontracts some or many of its operations to other organizations and coordinates them to accomplish specific goals.

4. *Describe four types of horizontal organizational design.*

Key Terms and Concepts

Discussion Questions

1. We discussed many features of Lowe's organizational design. If Lowe's continues to grow, what are some of the possible changes that might be considered in its organization design? You might want to go to Lowe's website (www.lowes.com), search for "About Lowe's" and then go to "Investors Report" and download Lowe's annual report.
2. What are some organizational design mistakes you learned from reading the Ethics Competency feature about Enron?
3. What impact does the choice of business strategy have on how your organization or university is organized?
4. Give examples of authority, responsibility, and accountability for a course in which you have been enrolled.
5. The following are some reasons why organizations fail:
   - *Lack of goal clarity*—strategic goals are not clear or linked to the organization's design.
   - *Lack of internal alignment*—the design of the organization doesn't pinpoint authority, responsibility, and accountability.
   - *Ineffective attention to customers' needs*—the strategy and design are out of touch with the needs of customers.
   - *Lack of external fit*—the design does not match the demands of suppliers, distributors, and customers.

   Identify and briefly describe one organization (e.g., General Motors, Chrysler, Citigroup) whose ineffectiveness you believe reflects these reasons.
6. Think of a leader for whom you have worked. Based on the guidelines presented for effective delegation, did this manager do a good job of delegating? Explain your answer.
7. What are some advantages and disadvantages of organizing by product?
8. What are some warning signs that an organization's design is not working?
9. What implications for managerial spans of control can be expected as organizations downsize? What additional managerial competencies might be required of leaders who remain in a downsized organization?
10. What are some of the challenges facing leaders of a network organization?

Experiential Exercise and Case

Experiential Exercise: Communication Competency

Analyzing Your Organization's Design[26]

Instructions

Listed are statements describing an organization's design. Indicate the extent to which you agree or disagree with each statement as a description of an organization you currently work for or have worked for in the past. Circle the appropriate number next to the statement.

PART I: PERFORMANCE MANAGEMENT CONTEXT

Leaders in my organization . . .	Not at all			Neutral			To a very great extent
1. Set challenging/aggressive goals.	1	2	3	4	5	6	7
2. Issue creative challenges to their people instead of narrowly defining tasks.	1	2	3	4	5	6	7
3. Make a point of stretching their people.	1	2	3	4	5	6	7
4. Use business goals and performance measures to run their businesses.	1	2	3	4	5	6	7
5. Hold people accountable for their performance.	1	2	3	4	5	6	7
6. Encourage and reward hard work through incentive compensation.	1	2	3	4	5	6	7

Add the points for statements 1 through 6. This is your score for the performance management context _____

PART II: SOCIAL SUPPORT CONTEXT

Leaders in my organization . . .	Not at all			Neutral			To a very great extent
7. Devote considerable effort to developing subordinates.	1	2	3	4	5	6	7
8. Push decisions down to the lowest appropriate level.	1	2	3	4	5	6	7
9. Have access to the information they need to make good decisions.	1	2	3	4	5	6	7
10. Quickly replicate best practices across organizational boundaries.	1	2	3	4	5	6	7
11. Treat failure in a good effort as a learning opportunity, not as something to be ashamed of.	1	2	3	4	5	6	7
12. Are willing and able to take prudent risks.	1	2	3	4	5	6	7

Add the points for statements 7 through 12. This is your score for the social support context _____

Now plot your scores on the graph provided by dividing by 6 your score for questions 1–6 (performance management context) and dividing by 6 your score for questions 7–12 (social support context).

PLOT SCORES ON THE GRAPH

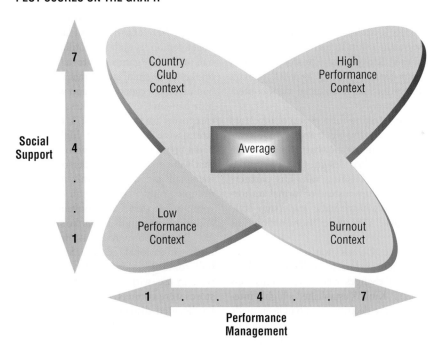

Questions
1. Using the data you plotted, what is the context orientation of your organization design?
2. What are some consequences for employees working in a Country Club context? A Burnout context?
3. What organization design decisions are needed to make your organization's context more effective?

Case: Change Competency

FedEx Office and Print Services, Inc.[27]

Kinko's (now FedEx Office and Print Services) has come a long way since its humble beginnings as a college town copy shop. Kinko's was the creation of Paul Orfalea, who started selling pencils and spiral notebooks on the campus of the University of California, Santa Barbara, in 1972. However, when he realized that it cost 10 cents per page to use the photocopy machine in the library, he realized that selling copies would be more profitable than pencils and notebooks. He borrowed $5,000 and opened his first Kinko's shop in a tiny office measuring 100 square feet. He sold school supplies and made copies on a copy machine that he moved outside when it was in use because the shop was so small.

When Orfalea decided to expand his business into college towns nationwide, he didn't seek out local entrepreneurs to buy franchise rights. Rather, he invited his friends and relatives to become his partners. These partners enjoyed a large share of the store's profits, usually around 50 percent. Many of the partners shared profits with their employees. By 1979 Kinko's had expanded to more than 80 stores in 28 states. Then in the early 1990s, Kinko's was no longer just serving colleges and small businesses. It established a partnership with Federal Express, and FedEx drop boxes were handily placed in all Kinko's outlets following a shift in focus to the growing home office market. By then Kinko's had 420 stores and was positioning itself as "Your Branch Office." In 1992, Kinko's formed an alliance with Sprint and introduced videoconferencing services in many of its stores.

In 1996, Orfalea started looking for a group of investors who were interested in reorganizing his company. He realized his organization had become somewhat unmanageable because it had outgrown its original design. Orfalea himself was the hub around which the business ran. His partners relied on interpersonal relationships instead of formal authority and responsibility. Orfalea's charismatic leadership style had worked early on because very little coordination was needed among the partners.

Clayton Dubilier & Rice (CD&R) was a private investment firm that could see bright prospects for Kinko's, as long as some organization design changes were made. This new structure was created in 1997. Kinko's established a highly integrated organization. Many of the decisions that had been made in the stores were now being made by top management. The company was reorganized by geographical region—East, West, Central, and International. (Kinko's shops had been located in Japan and the Netherlands since 1992.) Partners who owned the largest group of stores headed up their regional divisions.

After the reorganization, a search was begun for a new CEO because Orfalea resigned as chairman in 2000. Gary Kusin joined the company in 2001 in that position. Kusin decided to relocate the company headquarters from Ventura, California, to Dallas, Texas, a move that Orfalea criticized as unnecessary. The move was completed in 2002. Dallas was chosen because it was more centrally located in the United States and a less expensive city in which to do business than was Southern California.

All but three of Kinko's top executives had been replaced by the end of 2002. The common thread in the new top team was that each person was a strong team player, had previously been with a successful organization, and had each held jobs with high accountability. The team members had diverse managerial competencies. Their primary job was to implement the programs that Kusin and his team had put together to improve the overall performance of Kinko's.

The team zeroed in on improving efficiency and reducing corporate overhead in each store in order to reduce costs. Management layers in the company's hierarchy were reduced from 12 to 6. An executive vice president of operations was named for the retail side of the business. The vice president of marketing and two general leaders for retail operations, operations support, and real estate reported directly to him. These general leaders were put in charge of 18 operations directors, each of whom was responsible for the profit and loss in a distinct geographical market. Seventy-four district leaders and the human resource and technology staff report directly to these operations directors. All 1,100 branches of Kinko's report up through the individual districts.

Further expansion of Kinko's commercial business depended on its ability to utilize its store network. The stores had been reorganized into a hub-and-spoke configuration. Spokes were small stores that reported to larger facilities that had extensive capabilities and were open 24 hours a day. Each hub had one or two spokes. Kinko's also added two other categories to their stores: a flagship and a node. Flagship stores were large hubs in high-demand areas and each one had a broad range of technologies. Nodes were smaller stores that were staffed by one person. These nodes were designed for small and sporadic walk-in customers. They sometimes occupied only a corner in an office building. Nodes had low volume, but they were convenient to use and exposed more and more customers to Kinko's.

Large, commercial customers were not forgotten during the organizational redesign. Stand-alone locked facilities were built for large batch jobs. By 2003, four of these large facilities were in use, with four per district planned for the future. All stores were connected through the Internet so that jobs could be allocated, distributed, or shared, as the need arose. This was possible because Kinko's had calibrated all machines in these facilities so that all color copies were identical, regardless of where they were produced.

The senior vice president of sales had 18 sales directors reporting directly to him. Each sales director was responsible for profit and loss in his geographical district. Twenty-four digital sales consultants were added to call on clients and suggest money-saving processes to customers. These consultants reported to the sales directors. Ten engagement leaders had been located on-site at the largest Kinko's facility, and there were 74 sales leaders, all organized by district, who reported to the sales directors.

FedEx purchased Kinko's in 2004 and changed the company's name to FedEx Kinko's Office and Print Services, Inc.

Kusin stepped down in 2006 and today the company is run by Brian Philips. Also in 2006, the company dropped the Kinko's references from its name and became FedEx Office and Print Services.

Today, FedEx Office and Print Services operates more than 1,950 locations in more than 11 countries. It serves more than 100 million customers each year. It is the only brand that offers customers 24-hour-a-day, seven-days-a-week, walk-in access to a full range of office and shipping services in many of their locations.

Questions

1. What aspects of differentiation and integration are illustrated in this case?
2. What concepts of vertical design are highlighted?
3. What is FedEx Office and Print Services' business strategy? That is, how does it compete in the printing services industry?

chapter 16

Cultivating Organizational Culture

Learning Goals

After studying this chapter, you should be able to:

1
Explain how an organization's culture is formed, sustained, and changed.

2
Describe four types of organizational culture.

3
Discuss how organizational culture can influence ethical behaviors of leaders and employees.

4
Explain why fostering cultural diversity is important.

5
Describe the process of organizational socialization and its effect on culture.

Learning Content

Zappos

Zappos, the Las Vegas based e-commerce call center site with more than 1,500 employees and revenue exceeding $1 billion annually, sells shoes, apparel, and electronics. The CEO, Tony Hsieh, calls himself the leader of the Zapponians. Hsieh pays himself $36,000, leads parades, and has devised Zappos' "Ten Commandments." These ten commandments are a list of Zappos' core values and include commandments such as "Deliver WOW through service," "Be humble," "Create fun and a little weirdness," and "Build open and honest relationships with communication." These core values drive all key decisions from deciding where to locate its distribution facilities, to hiring, to customer relations and, most recently, to downsizing. To instill WOW customer service, repeat customers are routinely given free overnight service or sent a personal thank-you note or flowers. All suppliers have access to an extranet revealing the same inventory and sales data that top leaders get.

When Zappos had to lay off people because of the economic downturn, Hsieh wanted to take care of employees who had helped turn Zappos into a successful company. Employees with less than two years of service were paid until the end of the year. Those with longer service were given four weeks of pay for every year of service. All laid-off employees received six months of health insurance.

The company annually publishes its *Culture Book*, which it distributes to all employees. In that book, Hsieh describes the culture as fun, family,

smile, proud, weird, and with a lot of thank-yous. To make his words come alive, Hsieh attends regular happy hours (ice cream socials), has pajama parties at his house, provides free lunches (cold cuts), offers profit sharing to all employees, and pays all employees health care insurance. He also employs a full-time life coach, who listens to employees' gripes, gives them confidential advice, or is just there for them. When meeting with the coach, employees usually sit on a red velvet throne. Zappos' leaders are encouraged to spend between 10 and 20 percent of their time with team members outside of the office

BRAD SWONETZ/REDUX PICTURES

To learn more about Zappos, go to www.zappos.com

where they hike together or share a dinner. Any employee can give another employee a $50 bonus for a job well done.

Hsieh knows that Zappos isn't for everyone. Most employees are hourly and cannot get rich on a call center salary. Also, people might not like employees ringing cowbells and singing while working. If a person prefers to separate his or her work and home lives, that person would probably not get hired at Zappos. The Zappos human resource team uses off-beat cartoony applications and wacky interview questions, such as "How weird are you?" or "What's your theme song?" These and other questions are used to screen applicants for creativity and individuality while attempting to screen out egomaniacs and wallflowers. The application form looks like a crossword puzzle. All new hires must complete four weeks of training, including two weeks on the phones, beginning every day at 7:00 A.M. They cannot be late or call in sick. Hsieh believes that anyone who thinks they're too good to work the phones isn't Zappos material. During the last week of training, recruits are offered a $2,000 bribe to leave the company. (Only three people took it during 2008.) The human resources team puts on *Saturday Night Live*–style skits to demonstrate to new recruits offenses that can get them fired. Hsieh regularly twitters all employees informing them about the financial side of the business. The net effect is that Hsieh and his team have created a culture of extroversion and nose rings.[1]

The competencies and values of employees and leaders play a large role in determining the effectiveness and success of an organization. As illustrated by the Learning from Experience feature, the style, character, and ways of doing things at Zappos are driven by the core values of the firm and the leader. Fully understanding the soul of an organization requires plunging below the charts, financial numbers, machines, and buildings into the world of organizational culture.[2]

In this chapter, we examine the concept of organizational culture and how cultures are formed, sustained, and changed. We also explore some possible relationships between organizational culture and performance, the relationship between organizational culture and ethical behavior, the challenge of managing a culturally diverse workforce, and, finally, how organizations socialize individuals into their particular cultures. We begin with a brief overview of what organizational culture is and how organizational cultures are formed, sustained, and changed.

Dynamics of Organizational Culture

Learning Goal

1. *Explain how an organization's culture is formed, sustained, and changed.*

In Chapter 2, we defined *organizational culture* as the shared and learned values, beliefs, and attitudes of its members.[3] Unlike Zappos, most organizational cultures evolve slowly over time. Contrary to mission and vision statements, cultures are not usually written down, but are the soul of an organization. A culture is a collection of unspoken rules and traditions that operate 24 hours a day. Culture plays a large part in determining the quality of organizational life. Some leaders have sought to replicate the strong cultures of successful companies like Southwest Airlines, the Mayo Clinic, and Zappos, whereas others have tried to engineer their own culture in the hope of increasing loyalty, productivity, and/or profitability.

Culture is rooted in the countless details of an organization's life and influences much of what happens to employees within an organization. The culture of an organization influences who gets promoted, how careers are either made or derailed, and how resources are allocated. Each of these decisions conveys some unique aspect of an organization's culture. Although leaders are aware of their organization's culture(s), they are often unsure about how to influence it. If cultures are powerful influencers of behavior, they must be created and managed. More specifically, organizational culture includes:

- routine ways of communicating, such as organizational rituals and ceremonies and the language commonly used;

- the norms shared by individuals and teams throughout the organization, such as no reserved parking spaces;

- the dominant values held by the organization, such as product quality or customer service;

- the philosophy that guides management's policies and decision making, including determining which groups are included or consulted on decisions;

- the rules of the game for getting along in the organization, or the "ropes" that a newcomer must learn in order to become an accepted member; and

- the feeling or climate conveyed in an organization by the physical layout and the way in which leaders and employees interact with customers, suppliers, and other outsiders.[4]

None of these components individually represents the culture of the organization. Taken together, however, they reflect and give meaning to the concept of organizational culture. Using these six components, how would you describe the culture of Zappos?

As indicated in Figure 16.1, trying to diagnose an organization's culture is analogous to trying to guess the size of an iceberg based on what is visible. We know that 66 percent of an iceberg is below water and, hence, can only guess its shape and size. The norms, values, and assumptions are of an organization's culture are often hidden and resistant to change. They can only be inferred from a culture's more visible

FIGURE 16.1 The Culture Iceberg

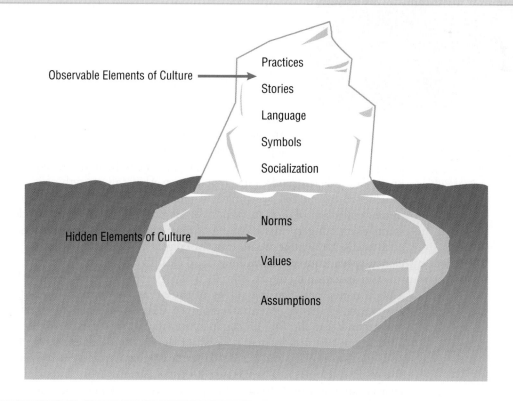

elements—its socialization activities, symbols, language, stories, and practices. At Zappos, the core value of "creating a little weirdness" is expressed through its hiring procedure, Hsieh's pajama parties, and the like.

Organizational cultural values *represent collective beliefs, assumptions, and feelings about what things are good, normal, rational, and valuable.*[5] Cultural values can be quite different from organization to organization. In some cultures, employees may care deeply about money, but in others they may care more about technological innovation or employee well-being. These values tend to persist over time, even when organizational membership changes.

Shared behaviors, *including norms, are more visible and somewhat easier to change than values.* Zappos' *Culture Book* details those behaviors that employees need to demonstrate on a daily basis to find their work fulfilling.

The most superficial level of organizational culture consists of symbols. **Cultural symbols** *are words (jargon or slang), gestures, and pictures or other physical objects that carry a particular meaning within a culture.*[6] Someone entering a New York City Police Department precinct station encounters symbols of authority and Spartan surroundings, including physical barriers between officers and civilians; the attire of the duty officer; emblems of authority, such as the American flag, seals, certificates, photos of various city leaders, and signs prohibiting certain behaviors; and hard straight chairs, vending machines, and instructions. In contrast, someone entering the lobby of a Ritz-Carlton hotel encounters warmth, including comfortable chairs and soft couches, decorative pictures, plants and flowers, and reading materials. When A. G. Lafley took over the CEO's job at Procter & Gamble, he wanted to show the value he placed on teamwork. To encourage people to work together, he rebuilt the executive floor to open it up and encourage conversations. He added a "living room" area for casual meetings. Mini espresso cafes, where employees relax and watch the news on large flat-screen TVs, were added to other floors.

The cultural symbols of McDonald's also convey a standard meaning. McDonald's restaurants are typically located in rectangular buildings with large windows to let the sun in and with neatly kept surroundings. Parking lots are large and paved; there is rarely any visible litter. A drive-thru window indicates that speedy service is available. The most prominent symbol is the golden arch sign that towers over the building (where zoning laws permit). Inside, bright colors and plants create a homey atmosphere. Glistening stainless steel appliances behind the counter provide an up-to-date, efficient, and sanitary appearance. Above all, everything is *clean.* Cleanliness is achieved by endless sweeping and mopping of floors, rapid removal of garbage, instant collecting of dirty trays and cleaning of spills, washing of windows to remove smudges and fingerprints, cleaning of unoccupied tables, and constant wiping of the counter. Both the interior and exterior convey cultural symbols of predictability, efficiency, speed, courtesy, friendliness, and cleanliness.

Organizational culture is important for employees and leaders alike. Achieving a good match between the values of the organization and those of the employee first requires that a potential employee figure out what an organization values and second that she find an organization that shares her personal values. You can address the first task by making a list of the 8 values that are most characteristic of your ideal workplace and the 8 that are least characteristic of it from the 54 values shown in Table 16.1. Then return to the Learning from Experience feature and answer the question "What are Zappos' values?" Would you like to work for this organization?

MARK HUMPHREY/AP PHOTO

Someone entering a hotel lobby is likely to see cultural symbols of warmth, including comfortable chairs and plants and flowers.

TABLE 16.1 What Do You Value at Work?

We have listed 54 values below. These are divided into two groups of 27 each. Select four values in the **YOU ARE** group and four values from the **YOUR COMPANY** group that you desire. Place these in your top eight choices. Next, take four values that are least descriptive of you and four values that are least descriptive of your company and place these in your bottom eight choices. Is there a match?

Top Eight Choices

Bottom Eight Choices

The Choice Menu

You Are: 1. Flexible 2. Adaptable 3. Innovative 4. Able to seize opportunities 5. Willing to experiment 6. Risk-taking 7. Careful 8. Autonomy-seeking 9. Comfortable with rules 10. Analytical 11. Attentive to detail 12. Precise 13. Team-oriented 14. Ready to share information 15. People-oriented 16. Easygoing 17. Calm 18. Supportive 19. Aggressive 20. Decisive 21. Action-oriented 22. Eager to take initiative 23. Reflective 24. Achievement-oriented 25. Demanding 26. Comfortable with individual responsibility 27. Comfortable with conflict

Your Company Offers: 28. Competitive 29. Highly organized 30. Results-oriented 31. Having friends at work 32. Collaborative 33. Fitting in 34. People enthusiastic about their jobs 35. Stability 36. Predictability 37. High expectations of performance 38. Opportunities for professional growth 39. High pay for good performance 40. Job security 41. Praise for good performance 42. A clear guiding philosophy 43. A low level of conflict 44. An emphasis on quality 45. A good reputation 46. Respect for the individual's rights 47. Tolerance 48. Informality 49. Fairness 50. A unitary culture throughout the organization 51. A sense of social responsibility 52. Long hours 53. Relative freedom from rules 54. The opportunity to be distinctive, or different from others

Source: Adapted from Siegel, M. The perils of culture conflict. *Fortune*, November 9, 1998, 259; Chatman, J. A. and Jehn, K. A. Assessing the relationship between industry characteristics and organizational culture: How different can they be? *Academy of Management Journal*, 1994, 37, 522–553.

Forming a Culture

An organizational culture forms in response to two major challenges that confront every organization: (1) external adaptation and survival and (2) internal integration.[7]

External adaptation and survival *refer to how the organization will find a niche in and cope with its constantly changing external environment*. How leaders respond to their external environment is partly based on the cultural values of society. In Chapter 3, we indicated how a country's cultural values (e.g., individualism–collectivism, power distance, uncertainty avoidance, gender role orientation, long-term orientation) can influence employees' behavior. The pressures for employees to conform to their country's culture cannot be ignored by leaders.[8] Leaders in Indonesia, Italy, and Japan, for example, believe that the purpose of an organization's design is to let everyone know who his or her boss is. Leaders in the United States and Great Britain, on the other hand, believe that an organization's design is intended to coordinate group behavior.

Siemens is an organization based in Germany, a country with a high uncertainty avoidance–based culture. Leaders at Siemens strive to survive and adapt to changes in the company's external environment by closely following the rules and regulations of Germany. In Germany long-term employment is common because job security is highly valued. When Peter Löscher took over as CEO several years ago, he created quite a revolution at Siemens because he cut more than 17,000 jobs worldwide and slashed expenses by $1.6 billion. He also started to dismantle the bureaucracy that had kept Siemens from being competitive. This included reducing the number of management boards, and reorganizing 70 regional fiefdoms into 20. He installed control mechanisms so that risks are properly recorded and understood. The purpose of these changes was to make Siemens a great marketing company.

Insights for Leaders

External adaptation and survival requires leaders to consider and address the following issues:

- *Mission and strategy:* Identify the primary purpose of the organization and select strategies to pursue this mission.
- *Goals:* Set specific targets to achieve.
- *Means:* Determine how to pursue the goals, including selecting an organizational structure and reward system.
- *Measurement:* Establish criteria to determine how well individuals, teams, and departments are accomplishing their goals.

Internal integration *refers to the establishment and maintenance of effective working relationships among the members of an organization.* Internal integration involves addressing the following issues:

- *Language and concepts:* Identify methods of communication and develop a shared meaning of key values.
- *Group and team boundaries:* Establish criteria for membership in groups and teams.
- *Power and status:* Determine rules for acquiring, maintaining, and losing power and status.
- *Rewards and punishments:* Develop systems for encouraging desirable behaviors and discouraging undesirable behaviors.[9]

An organizational culture emerges when members share knowledge and assumptions as they discover or develop ways of coping with issues of external adaptation and internal integration. Figure 16.2 shows a common pattern in the emergence of organizational cultures. In relatively young organizations, such as Akami Technologies, Zappos, or CyberSource, the founder or a few key individuals may largely influence the organization's culture. Later in the life of the organization, its culture will reflect a complex mixture of the assumptions, values, and ideas of the founder or other early top leaders and the subsequent experiences of leaders and employees.

Societal and Organizational Cultures

Throughout this book, we have indicated that a country's cultural values, customs, and societal norms are critically important for leaders to understand in order to motivate, lead, build high-performance teams, and handle conflict in their

---

FIGURE 16.2 How Cultures Emerge

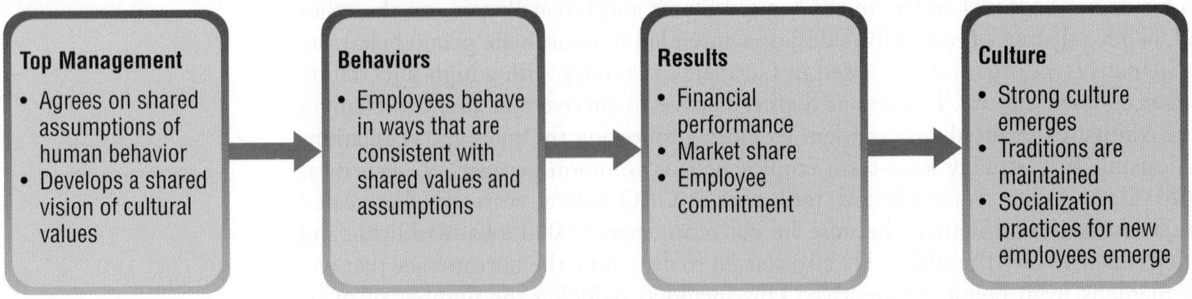

Top Management
- Agrees on shared assumptions of human behavior
- Develops a shared vision of cultural values

Behaviors
- Employees behave in ways that are consistent with shared values and assumptions

Results
- Financial performance
- Market share
- Employee commitment

Culture
- Strong culture emerges
- Traditions are maintained
- Socialization practices for new employees emerge

organizations more effectively. The dominant value of a country's culture also affects an organization's culture.

Throughout our book, we have discussed how the cultural values of various countries impact on behaviors of leaders and employees. In Chapter 3, we discussed the five factors that can be used to understand a culture's value system: individualism–collectivism, power distance, uncertainty avoidance, gender role orientation, and long-term orientation. When Ricardo Semler took over as CEO of Semco Manufacturing, a Brazilian organization, it was almost bankrupt. Born in Sao Paulo, Brazil, he understood that to make this company successful, he would have to make changes that would go against many of Brazil's cultural values. Brazil is a country in which the ideal boss is a well-meaning autocrat, decisions are made by senior leaders, there is strong loyalty to the organization, few women have joined the managerial ranks, leaders are expected to be decisive and assertive, and there are large pay gaps between leaders and employees.

To turn Semco into a successful organization, Semler knew that he had to radically change the behaviors of employees. The following Across Cultures Competency feature illustrates how his leadership allowed him to overcome some of these cultural values.[10]

Self Insight

I wanted to create a unique corporate culture. I knew that I had only one chance to establish a culture that would set the norms, expectations, and performance standards for the entire organization when we made the acquisition. Without a strong culture, we would lose our competitive advantage.

Andy Kohlberg, CEO, Kisco Senior Living

Across Cultures competency

Ricardo Semler, CEO of Brazil's Semco Manufacturing

When Ricardo Semler took over the organization in 1979, Semco operated like many other Brazilian companies. Leaders used fear of unemployment as a governing principle. Armed guards patrolled the factory floor, timed employees' trips to the rest rooms, and frisked employees for contraband when they left the building. Employees who broke equipment had their paychecks docked to replace it. Revenues from the manufacturing of industrial pumps, mixers, and other products were $35 million. Today, revenues have increased to more than $160 million.

Semler decided to replace fear with freedom. He reduced the organization's hierarchy from eight levels to three. The new levels were designed as concentric circles. One circle contains eight employees who develop business strategies and coordinate the manufacturing activities of the entire company. These employees are elected by their fellow employees. The second circle contains the heads of the various functional areas. The third circle contains all other employees.

Employees are called associates. Associates make most of the day-to-day decisions, dress as they want, choose their own supervisors, and have no time clocks. All associates attend classes to learn how to read and understand financial statements. A union leader teaches the course—not someone from the human resources department. Every month, each associate gets a balance sheet, a profit-and-loss analysis, and a cash flow statement for his or her product line. Almost one-third of the associates set their own salaries. All meetings are voluntary.

Associates also evaluate their supervisors. These evaluations are posted for everyone to see. If a supervisor's evaluation is consistently low, that person is asked to step down. Senior leaders are also evaluated by their subordinates.

To learn more about Semco and Ricardo Semler, go to **www.semco.com**.

Sustaining a Culture: Insights for Leaders

The ways in which an organization functions and is led may have both intended and unintended consequences for maintaining and changing organizational culture. Figure 16.3 illustrates a basic approach for sustaining an organization's culture: (1) The organization hires individuals who seem to fit its culture and (2) the organization sustains its culture by removing employees who consistently or markedly stray from accepted behaviors and activities.

Specific methods of sustaining organizational culture, however, are a great deal more complicated than just hiring the right people and firing those who don't work out. The most powerful indicators of the organization's culture are (1) what leaders and teams pay attention to, measure, and control; (2) the ways in which leaders (particularly top leaders) react to critical incidents and organizational crises; (3) managerial and team role modeling, teaching, and coaching; (4) criteria for allocating rewards and status; (5) criteria for recruitment, selection, promotion, and removal from the organization; and (6) organizational rites, ceremonies, and stories.[11]

What Leaders and Teams Pay Attention To

One of the more powerful methods of sustaining organizational culture involves the processes and behaviors that leaders, individual employees, and teams pay attention to—that is, the events that get noticed and commented on. Dealing with events systematically sends strong signals to employees about what is important and expected of them. For example, Gary Klembara, vice president of sales for ViewCast, a media encoding company, holds a 30-minute meeting every Friday at 7:25 A.M. sharp with his salespeople, who use cell phones to call in from the road. They share their challenges and results from the previous week.

Reactions to Incidents and Crises

When an organization faces a crisis such as terrorism attacks or loss of a major customer, the handling of that crisis by leaders and employees reveals a great deal about its culture. The manner in which the crisis is dealt with can either reinforce the existing culture or bring out new values and norms that change the culture in some way. Gary Kelly, CEO of Southwest Airlines, tells a story about a customer who had gotten

FIGURE 16.3 Methods of Sustaining Organizational Culture

gasoline on her clothes while refueling her rental car. The customer was (understandably) stopped by TSA officials, who won't allow anyone on a plane with gas-soaked clothing. Stephanie Gamble, a Southwest supervisor, took down the customer's clothing and shoe size, and left for a nearby department store to buy her something to wear. On the flight home with her new clothes the customer, who had left money in an envelope for the supervisor to mail her items back, was handed the same envelope with this note: "Stephanie won't take your money for clothes or postage. Have a good flight." This incident says a lot about the caring and nurturing culture that Southwest Airlines has created for its customers.[12]

Role Modeling, Teaching, and Coaching

Aspects of an organization's culture are communicated to employees by the way leaders treat them. At the Ritz-Carlton Hotels and Resorts, all new trainees are shown films that emphasize customer service. Leaders also demonstrate good customer or client service practices in their interactions with customers. For example, the story is told of the beach attendant who was busy stacking chairs for an evening event when he was approached by a guest who asked him to leave two chairs out because he wanted to return to the beach that evening with his girlfriend and propose. Although the beach attendant was going off duty, he didn't just have two chairs on the beach; he put on a tuxedo and brought flowers, champagne, and candles. He met the couple when they arrived at the beach later that evening. He escorted them to the chairs, presented the flowers, lit the candles, and served the champagne to them. The repeated emphasis on good customer relations in both training and day-to-day behavior helps create and maintain a customer-oriented culture throughout the Ritz-Carlton Hotel and Resorts chain.[13]

Allocation of Rewards and Status

Employees also learn about an organization's culture through its reward system. The rewards and punishments attached to various behaviors convey to employees the priorities and values of both individual leaders and the organization. At Zappos, rewards are based on overall company performance, whereas at Sara Lee, the baked goods company, programs encourage leaders at different levels to own stock in the company. The rationale is that leaders should have a stake in the financial health of the firm, based on its overall performance.

In many organizations the status system maintains certain aspects of its culture. The distribution of perks (a corner office on an upper floor, executive dining room, carpeting, a private secretary, or a private parking space) demonstrates which roles and behaviors are most valued by an organization. At Chase Manhattan Bank in New York City, Jim Donaldson was promoted to vice president for global trusts. His new office was well furnished with most of the symbols of relatively high status. Before he was allowed to move in to his new office, however, his boss ordered the maintenance department to cut a 12-inch strip from the entire perimeter of the carpet. At Chase Manhattan, wall-to-wall carpeting is a status symbol given only to senior vice presidents and above.

An organization may use rewards and status symbols ineffectively and inconsistently. If so, it misses a great opportunity to influence its culture. An organization's reward practices and its culture are strongly linked in the minds of its members. In fact, some authorities believe that the most effective method of influencing organizational culture may be through the reward system. Within NASA, the crash of the space shuttle *Columbia* and the explosion in space over Texas of the *Challenger* have been attributed to a change in the reward system from one that rewarded space safety and technical brilliance to a reward system that focused on efficiency and reuse of the space shuttle. NASA's motto of "faster, better, and cheaper" put an emphasis on meeting schedules and avoiding cost overruns. This motto became a symbol of how rewards were allocated.[14]

Recruitment, Selection, Promotion, and Removal

As Figure 16.3 suggests, one of the fundamental ways in which organizations maintain a culture is through the recruitment process. As discussed in the opening feature, recall the Zappos hiring program. How would you answer these questions from Zappos' leaders?: "How weird are you?" or "What's your theme song?" In addition, a few of the criteria used by other organizations to determine who is assigned to specific jobs or positions, who gets raises and promotions and why, who is removed from the organization by firing or early retirement, and so on, reinforce and demonstrate basic aspects of an organization's culture. These criteria become known informally throughout the organization. They serve to help maintain or change an existing culture.

Organizational Rites and Ceremonies

Organizational rites and ceremonies **are planned activities or rituals that have personal and emotional meaning to employees.** Certain managerial or employee activities can become rituals that are interpreted as part of the organizational culture. Rites and ceremonies that sustain organizational culture include rites of passage, degradation, enhancement, and integration. Table 16.2 contains examples of each of these four types of rites and ceremonies, including some of their desirable consequences.[15]

A ceremony used at Mary Kay Cosmetics Company provides a good example of rites of enhancement. During elaborate awards ceremonies, gold and diamond pins, fur stoles, and pink Cadillacs are presented to salespeople who achieve their sales quotas. Music tends to arouse and express emotions, and all the participants know the Mary Kay song, "I've Got that Mary Kay Enthusiasm." It was written by a member of the organization to the tune of the hymn "I've Got that Old Time Religion." This song is a direct expression of the Mary Kay culture and is fervently sung during the awards ceremonies. The ceremonies are reminiscent of a Miss America pageant, with all of the participants dressed in glamorous evening clothes. The setting is typically an auditorium with a stage in front of a large, cheering audience. The ceremonies clearly are intended to increase the identity and status of high-performing employees and emphasize the company's rewards for excellence.[16]

Organization Stories

Many of the underlying beliefs and values of an organization's culture are expressed as stories that become part of its folklore. These stories transmit the existing culture from old to new employees and emphasize important aspects of that culture—and some may persist for a long time. The Mayo Clinic in Rochester, Minnesota, is famous for its patient care. A story is told about the critically ill mother of a bride. The bride told the physicians how much she wanted her mother to be part of her wedding ceremony.

TABLE 16.2 Organizational Rites and Ceremonies

TYPE	EXAMPLE	POSSIBLE CONSEQUENCES
Rites of passage	Basic training, U.S. Army	Facilitate transition into new roles; minimize differences in way roles are carried out
Rites of degradation	Firing a manager	Reduce power and identity; reaffirm proper behavior
Rites of enhancement	Mary Kay Cosmetics Company ceremonies	Enhance power and identity; emphasize value of proper behavior
Rites of integration	Office party	Encourage common feelings that bind members together

Source: Adapted from Trice, H. M., and Beyer, J. M. *The Cultures of Work Organizations.* Englewood Cliffs, NJ: Prentice-Hall, 1993, 111.

The physicians conveyed this message to the critical care leader. A team of physicians worked hard to stabilize her mother's condition. Within hours, the hospital atrium was transformed for the wedding service, complete with flowers, balloons, and confetti. Staff members provided a cake, and nurses arranged for the mother's hair and makeup, dressed her, and wheeled her bed to the atrium. A volunteer played the piano and the chaplain performed the ceremony. On every floor, hospital staff and visiting family members ringed the atrium balconies "like angels from above" to quote the bride. This scene not only provided evidence of caring to the patient and her family, but a strong reminder to the staff that patients' needs come first.[17]

> ### Change Insight
>
> Culture change does not occur in a vacuum. All employees must embrace the change. Senior leaders need to celebrate behaviors that reinforce and reward the new culture's values.
>
> *David Novak, CEO, YUM! Brands*

Changing a Culture

The same practices used to maintain an organization's culture may be used to modify it. That is, culture might be modified by changing (1) what leaders and teams pay attention to, (2) how crises are handled, (3) criteria for recruiting new members, (4) criteria for allocating rewards, (5) criteria for promotion within the organization, and (6) organizational rites, ceremonies, and stories.

Changing an organization's culture can be tricky because an accurate assessment of an organization's culture is difficult. Most large, complex organizations actually have more than one culture. Organizations, such as Procter & Gamble, HP, and Siemens, with different divisions that serve different customers usually have different cultures in each division. *When multiple cultures are present within an organization, they are referred to as* subcultures. Often, if an organization has subcultures they will reflect the following three types: an operating culture (line employees), an engineering culture (technical and professional people), and an executive culture (top management). Each culture stems from very different views typically held by these groups of individuals.[18] Faced with a variety of subcultures, top-level leaders may have difficulty (1) accurately assessing them and (2) implementing needed changes, especially when these subcultures are based in units in different locations.

Why is changing a culture so hard? There are at least three reasons.[19] First, cultures give employees an organizational identity. It tells customers and others what the organization stands for. Zappos, for example, is known as a fun place to work that values customer satisfaction and customer loyalty before corporate profits. By going to the Zappos website, anyone can watch videos and read white papers on how the company hires, deals with vendors, and evaluates employees. Second, culture provides stability. Zappos is known for having parties and celebrating. These parties and celebrations reflect its positive and reinforcing work environment. Third, culture helps focus its employees' behaviors. One of the functions of a culture is to help employees understand why the organization does what it does and how it intends to accomplish its long-term goals. Zappos does this through some of its ten commandments, such as "deliver WOW service."

Despite obstacles to changing an organization's culture, change is feasible. In the case of failing organizations or significant shifts in an organization's external environment, changing the culture is essential. Successfully changing organizational culture requires:

- understanding the old culture first because a new culture can't be developed unless leaders and employees understand where they're starting from;
- providing support for employees and teams who have ideas for a better culture and are willing to act on those ideas;
- finding the most effective subculture in the organization and using it as an example from which employees can learn;

- not attacking culture head-on unless the organization is rapidly failing (e.g., Siemens, Chrysler, GM), but finding ways to help employees and teams do their jobs more effectively;

- treating the vision of a new culture as a guiding principle for change, not as a miracle cure;

- recognizing that top leadership commitment to significant organization-wide cultural change may take several years; and

- living the new culture by leaders early on because actions speak louder than words.

As discussed in the following Change Competency feature, Harley-Davidson is one example of how a company changed its culture in a relatively short period of time through transformational leadership. This culture persists today because of the fundamental changes made by its CEO, Richard Teerlink, and his successors. To change a company's culture, its reward systems, leader behaviors, and organizational structures must be changed.[20]

Change **competency**

Harley-Davidson's Culture

Richard Teerlink set out to change the culture of Harley-Davidson.

When Richard Teerlink took over as president of Harley-Davidson in 1987, the differences in quality between Harley-Davidson and its competitors were striking. For example, only 5 percent of Honda's motorcycles failed to pass inspection; more than 50 percent of Harleys failed the same test. Honda's value added per employee was three times that of Harley's. Harley's relations with its dealers were poor because they were forced to provide customers with free service because of factory defects. So what did Teerlink do? He set out to change the culture of Harley-Davidson, which he accomplished before retiring in 1999.

First, he emphasized that although Harley was a manufacturer of motorcycles, it was also in the "experience business." He said that the real product is not a machine, but a lifestyle, an attitude, a way of being, a perspective on life that had its beginnings before Bill Harley and Arthur Davidson built the first motorized bicycle in 1901. It is the strength and courage that come from feelings of individuality. Therefore, riding a Harley is the stuff adventure and legends are made of.

Second, he began emphasizing organizational and individual learning at all levels through a Leadership Institute. The institute was designed to introduce new workers to Harley's goals and culture while providing current workers with a better understanding of the organization's design and effects of competition on Harley's performance. Leaders prepared a series of nontechnical explanations of how cash flow and flexible production affect financial success. Line workers were taught how products, sales, and productivity affect profitability. Substantial changes in employee job descriptions, responsibilities, and production processes were undertaken in an effort to increase job enrichment and worker empowerment. These efforts were implemented through cross-training and expansion of job responsibilities.

Third, Teerlink eliminated the positions of vice presidents of marketing and operations because these jobs didn't add value to the product. Teams of employees, such as a "create-demand team," which is in charge of producing products, and a "product-support team," now make marketing and operations decisions. First-line employees participated in problem-solving teams and came up with ideas for improving quality. Employees created a peer review system to evaluate each other's performance instead of relying solely on first-line supervisors' evaluations. These evaluations help determine employees' pay.

Fourth, to recapture the Harley mystique, Teerlink revitalized the Harley Hogs, a customer group formed to get people more actively involved in motorcycling. To attract female riders, the Ladies of Harley group was formed to increase ridership and interest among young female motorcyclists. Teerlink and his staff regularly attended road rallies and helped clubs sponsor various charitable events. Harley also issued a credit card to thousands of riders and encouraged them to use the card for the purchase of a motorcycle, service, and accessories. The sale of merchandise, including T-shirts, clothing, jewelry, small-leather goods, and numerous other products, permits customers to identify with the company. As Teerlink noted, "There are very few products that are so exciting that people will tattoo your logo on their body."

Since Teerlink's retirement, incoming CEO James Zimmer worked hard to sustain Harley's culture. When Keith Wendell succeeded Zimmer in 2009, it appeared that Wendell would be able to sustain the culture Teerlink and Zimmer had created.

To learn more about Harley-Davidson, go to **www.harley-davidson.com.**

We cover planned organizational change extensively in Chapter 17. Specific approaches and methods for changing organizational behaviors are presented in that chapter. These may be used to change an organization's culture. Indeed, any comprehensive program of organizational change is likely to involve transforming an organization's culture.

We cannot overemphasize how difficult deliberately changing organizational cultures may be. In fact, the incompatibility of organizational cultures and their resistance to change has been one of the most significant barriers to successful corporate mergers. It is estimated that 60 percent of all mergers fail to achieve their financial goals because of cultural differences. For a merger to be effective, at least one (and sometimes both) of the merging organizations may need to change its culture.

Types of Organizational Culture

Learning Goal

2. Describe four types of organizational culture.

Cultural elements and their relationships create a pattern that is distinct to an organization (e.g., the fun-loving culture of Zappos versus the bureaucratic culture of GM). These differences or similarities may be assessed in relation to various factors.[21] One proposed framework is presented in Figure 16.4. The vertical axis reflects the relative control orientation of an organization, ranging from stable to flexible. The horizontal axis reflects the relative focus of attention of an organization, ranging from internal functioning to external functioning. The extreme corners of the four quadrants represent four pure types of organizational culture: bureaucratic, clan, entrepreneurial, and market. In a culturally homogeneous organization such as Mary Kay, one of these basic types of culture will dominate. IBM, General Electric, Cisco, and other large organizations all have subcultures within their divisions that often function within an umbrella-like overall culture.

FIGURE 16.4 Framework of Types of Culture

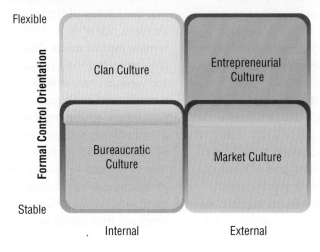

Source: Adapted from Hooijberg, R., and Petrock, F. On cultural change: Using the competing values framework to help leaders execute a transformational strategy. *Human Resources Management*, 1993, 32, 29–50; Quinn, R. E., *Beyond Rational Management: Mastering the Paradoxes and Competing Demands of High Performances.* San Francisco: Jossey-Bass, 1988.

For example, at General Electric, its NBC and its GE Capital division will have different practices that represent innovation, a core of GE's corporate culture.

As is true of organization designs, different organizational cultures may be appropriate under different conditions. There is no one type of cultural ideal for every situation. Of course, some employees may prefer one culture to others. As you read about each type of culture, consider which one best fits your preferences. Employees who work in an organization with a culture that fits their own view of an ideal culture tend to be committed to the organization and optimistic about its future. We recognize that many new employees do not have predetermined ideas of their ideal organizational culture. Through seeing who gets promoted, large raises, or important assignments, they will come to understand their organization's culture. Also, a culture should reflect the organization's goals.

Bureaucratic Culture

An organization that practices formality, rules, standard operating procedures, and hierarchical coordination has a **bureaucratic culture**. Recall from Chapter 15 that the goals of a bureaucracy are predictability, efficiency, and stability. Its members highly value standardized goods and customer service. Behavioral norms support formality over informality. Leaders view their roles as being good coordinators, organizers, and enforcers of written rules and standards. Tasks, responsibilities, and authority for all employees are clearly defined. The organization's many rules and processes are spelled out in thick manuals, and employees believe that their duty is to "go by the book" and follow legalistic procedures.

Richard Dugas, CEO of Pulte Homes, has built the company into a $6.3 billion home builder by designing a bureaucratic culture. Pulte is one of America's largest homebuilders, building homes under its own name and also homes in its Del Webb retirement communities. Pulte recently acquired Centex, another major home builder. Dugas and his team have segmented the home market into 11 categories, from first-time buyers to retirees. Employees study potential land acquisitions to target customers in one of these categories. Once a location is chosen, Pulte uses it extensive database to reduce costs. For example, it discovered that 80 percent of its home buyers end up selecting the same countertops, floors, carpets, toilets, and other options. At one time, the company was offering customers a choice of 35 toilet models from six different manufacturers, windows from 17 different suppliers, and more than 2,000 floor plans. After hiring a supply chain manager from Walmart, Pulte reduced the floor plan options to fewer than 1,000 and has begun to standardize how each home is built. All homes use nails, concrete, lumber, wiring, and roofing materials from an approved list of suppliers. The list of suppliers is based on cost and performance measures.[22]

Clan Culture

Tradition, loyalty, personal commitment, extensive socialization, teamwork, self-management, and social influence are attributes of a **clan culture**. Its members recognize an obligation beyond the simple exchange of labor for a salary. They understand that contributions to the organization (e.g., hours worked per week) may exceed any contractual agreements. The individual's long-term commitment to the organization (loyalty) is exchanged for the organization's long-term commitment to the individual (security). Because individuals believe that the organization will treat them fairly in terms of salary increases, promotions, and other forms of recognition, they hold themselves accountable to the organization for their actions. Organizations such as Zappos, Mayo Clinic, and Southwest Airlines have developed strong clan cultures. Herb Kelleher, the former chairman of Southwest Airlines, stated: "Culture is one of the most precious things a company has so you must work harder at it than anything else." For organizations with clan cultures, this is especially true.

A clan culture achieves unity by means of a long and thorough socialization process. Long-time clan members serve as mentors and role models for newer members. The clan is aware of its unique history and often documents its origins and celebrates its traditions in various rites. Members have a shared image of the organization's style and manner of conduct. Public statements and events reinforce its values. The restaurant support center (i.e., the headquarters) of YUM! Brands, which owns the KFC, Pizza Hut, Long John Silver's, A&W Root Beer, and Taco Bell chains among others, operates as a clan culture. David Novak, CEO, and Gregg Dedrick, who was the company's chief people officer, developed a common framework for YUM's culture called "How We Work Together." A plaque hangs at headquarters with the "Founding Truth" and "How We Work Together Principles" proudly displayed for all to see. Statements on these plaques communicate the culture of YUM!, such as "Great operations and marketing drive sales," "No finger pointing," and "The restaurant manager is #1, not senior management." Within each restaurant, these principles are proudly displayed.[23]

In a clan culture, members share feelings of pride in membership. They have a strong sense of identification and recognize their common fate in the organization. At YUM!, general managers and area coaches can earn YUMBUCKS for increasing their restaurant's profits and also bonuses based on the performance of their restaurant. YUMBUCKS can be used to pay for college tuition or buy YUM! stock. The up-through-the-ranks career pattern results in an extensive network of colleagues whose paths have crossed and who have shared similar experiences. Shared goals, perceptions, and behavioral tendencies foster communication, coordination, and integration.

A clan culture generates feelings of personal ownership of a business, a product, or an idea. In addition, peer pressure to adhere to important norms is strong. The richness of the culture creates an environment in which few areas are left totally free from normative pressures. Depending on the types of its norms, the culture may or may not generate risk-taking behavior or innovation. Success is assumed to depend substantially on sensitivity to customers and concern for people. Teamwork, participation, and consensus decision making are believed to lead to this success.

Entrepreneurial Culture

High levels of risk taking and creativity characterize an **entrepreneurial culture.** There is a commitment to experimentation, innovation, and being on the leading edge. This culture doesn't just quickly react to changes in the environment—it creates change. Many of today's hi-tech companies, such as Apple, Google, and Nintendo, have developed entrepreneurial cultures. Effectiveness means providing new and unique products and rapid growth. Individual initiative, flexibility, and freedom foster growth and are encouraged and well rewarded.

Entrepreneurial cultures are often found in small to midsized companies that are still run by a founder. Innovation and entrepreneurship are values held by the founder. Texas Nameplate, a privately held firm headquartered in Dallas, Texas, has 43 employees and makes nameplates, identification tags, and labels for a variety of products. Founded by Dale Crownover, the company has won the Malcolm Baldrige National Quality Award twice—in 1998 and 2004—for their entrepreneurial success.[24]

Communications competency

Texas Nameplate Company

Dale Crownover says that quality is everyone's responsibility at Texas Nameplate Company (TNC). The company has a flat organization structure that places the authority to make a decision in the hands of the employee who knows most about the decision. Leaders respect everyone's contributions as equally desirable and work with employees together to satisfy the customer.

John Darrouzet, the vice president and general counsel, comments: "We all have a role to play. We call it mutual respect. We guide the business on the quote: 'Fear is useless, what is needed is trust.' In the end, fear doesn't motivate anyone. Leaders need to trust their people and ensure their people trust them."

New Hotrod is the name of TNC's employee intranet. Besides hosting each employee's personal web page, this site also helps make the company's meetings open to all. This intranet site is projected onto the wall of meeting rooms. The teams use Microsoft Front Page to take notes, which immediately become available to all employees. There is no paperwork involved, which has helped TNC become a paperless company and speed up communications and decisions.

On TNC's intranet, Crownover shares his thoughts about effective communications. "First, meetings can waste time. Employees are asked to use e-mails to exchange standard information. Second, as a small entrepreneurial company, we cannot waste time chasing projects and communicating with potential customers that are outside of our core business. We need to focus on making high quality nameplates. Third, I tell my direct reports to let employees decide when and where to make a product for a customer so they can be happy and productive. As long as the customer is satisfied and TNC makes a profit, let teams of employees decide what to do."

Simplicity is one of TNC's guiding principles. At meetings, leaders and employees review the financial progress of the company, including charts with targeted goals. The leaders share comments about the results of a variety of meetings from customers, bankers, etc. There is a continuing effort to encourage all team members to share what they have learned from each other. There is an individual and team-based reward system that focuses on guaranteeing the customer that TNC products are free from defects.

To learn more about Texas Nameplate, go to **www.nameplate.com.**

Market Culture

The achievement of measurable and demanding goals, especially those that are financial and market based (e.g., sales growth, profitability, and market share), characterize a **market culture**. PepsiCo, Bank of America, and Goldman Sachs, among others, have many of the characteristics found in market cultures. Hard-driving competitiveness and a profit orientation prevail throughout a market culture organization. CEO Christos Cotsakos describes the market culture of E*Trade this way: "At E*Trade we're an attacker. We're predatory. We believe in the right to take market share from any competitor."

In a market culture, the relationship between individual and organization is contractual. That is, the obligations of each party are agreed on in advance. In this sense, the control orientation is formal and quite stable. The individual is responsible for some level of performance, and the organization promises a specified level of rewards in return. Increased levels of performance are exchanged for increased rewards, as outlined in an agreed-on schedule. Neither party recognizes the right of the other to demand more than was originally specified. The organization doesn't promise (or imply) security, and the individual doesn't promise (or imply) loyalty. The contract, renewed annually if each party adequately performs its obligations, is utilitarian because each party uses the other to further its own goals. Rather than promoting a feeling of membership in a social system, the market culture values independence and individuality and encourages members to pursue their own financial goals.

In market cultures, superiors' interactions with subordinates largely consist of negotiating performance–reward agreements and/or evaluating requests for resource allocations. Leaders aren't formally judged on their effectiveness as role models or mentors. The absence of a long-term commitment by both parties results in a weak socialization process. Social relations among coworkers aren't emphasized, and few economic incentives are tied directly to cooperating with peers. Leaders are expected to cooperate with managers in other departments only to the extent necessary to achieve their performance goals. As a result, they may not develop an extensive network of colleagues within the organization. The market culture often is tied to monthly, quarterly, and annual performance goals based on profits. At Goldman Sachs and many other Wall Street financial firms, key employees are driven by profit and bonus incentives to make their numbers.[25]

Culture–Performance Relationships

Organizational culture has the potential to enhance organizational performance, individual satisfaction, the sense of certainty about how problems are to be handled, and so on. If an organizational culture gets out of step with the changing expectations of internal and/or external stakeholders, the organization's effectiveness can decline as has occurred with General Motors, Chrysler, and other organizations. Organizational culture and performance clearly are related, although the evidence regarding the exact nature of this relationship is mixed. Studies show that the relationship between many cultural attributes (featured in the popular press as being important for performance) and high performance hasn't been consistent over time.[26] Based on what we know about culture–performance relationships, a contingency approach seems to be a good one for leaders and organizations to take. Further investigations of this issue are unlikely to discover one "best" organizational culture (either in terms of strength or type).

We do know the following about the relationships between culture and performance:

- Organizational culture can have a significant impact on a firm's long-term economic performance.

- Organizational culture will probably be an even more important factor in determining the success or failure of firms during the next decade.

- Organizational cultures that inhibit strong long-term financial performance are not rare; they develop easily, even in firms that are filled with reasonable and intelligent people.
- Although difficult to change, organizational cultures can be made more performance enhancing if leaders understand what sustains a culture.

Insights for Leaders

We can summarize the effects of organizational culture on employee behavior and performance with four key ideas. First, knowing the culture of an organization allows employees to understand both the firm's history and current methods of operation. This insight provides guidance about expected future behaviors. Second, organizational culture can foster commitment to corporate philosophy and values. This commitment generates shared feelings of working toward common goals. Third, organizational culture, through its norms, serves as a control mechanism to channel behaviors toward desired behaviors and away from undesired behaviors. Finally, certain types of organizational cultures may be related directly to greater effectiveness and productivity than others.

There is an ongoing need to determine which attributes of an organization's culture should be preserved and which should be modified. In the United States during the 1980s, many organizations began changing their cultures to be more responsive to customers' expectations of product quality and service. During the late 1990s, many organizations began to reassess how well their cultures fit the expectations of the workforce. The U.S. workforce has changed to become much more diverse. More and more employees have begun to feel that organizational cultures established decades ago are out of step with contemporary expectations. In the remainder of this chapter, we address the challenge of adjusting established organizational cultures to meet the growing expectations for ethical behaviors in a diverse workforce.

Learning Goal

3. *Discuss how organizational culture can influence ethical behaviors of leaders and employees.*

Ethical Behavior and Organizational Culture

From the insider trading scandals of the 1980s and loan scandals of the 1990s to the more widespread recent fraud and manipulation of financial information by some organizations, there have been widespread charges of unnecessary chronic breakdowns in ethical conduct.[27] These problems seem to be enduring over a number of years despite repeated considerable public outcry, governmental action, and business attempts to create new ethical programs. In Chapter 2, we pointed out that ethical problems in organizations continue to concern leaders and employees greatly. One organization, Deloitte Touche Tohmatsu, a professional-service firm, has created a web-based ethics course for all employees in the 150 countries in which it operates. It has the kind of 1-800 hotline mandated by the Sarbanes-Oxley Act of 2002 for the anonymous reporting of wrongdoings. It has also customized its ethics program on a country-by-country basis. For instance, in some cultures, having a 1-800 hotline would not be culturally acceptable.[28]

Impact of Culture

Organizational culture involves a complex interplay of formal and informal systems that may support either ethical or unethical behavior. As discussed previously, formal systems include leadership, structure, policies, reward systems, orientation and training programs, and decision-making processes. Informal systems include norms, heroes, rituals, language, myths, sagas, and stories. Organizational culture appears to affect ethical behavior in several ways.[29] For example, a culture that emphasizes ethical norms provides support for ethical behavior. In addition, top management plays a key role in fostering ethical behavior by exhibiting the correct behavior.

Organizations identified as having strong ethical cultures include Ben & Jerry's, Medtronic, Patagonia, and Tom's of Maine. Top leaders in these organizations have a culture that rewards ethical priorities and influences how employees behave. If lower level employees observe top-level managers sexually harassing others, falsifying expense reports, diverting shipments to preferred customers, misrepresenting the organization's financial position, and other forms of unethical behavior, they may assume that these behaviors are acceptable and will be rewarded in the future. Thus, the presence or absence of ethical behavior in managerial actions both influences and reflects the culture. The organizational culture may promote taking responsibility for the consequences of actions, thereby increasing the probability that individuals will behave ethically. Alternatively, the culture may diffuse responsibility for the consequences of unethical behavior, thereby making such behavior more likely. In short, ethical behaviors and practices stem from ethical organizational cultures.

Employees might take various steps to reduce unethical behavior, including these:

- Secretly or publicly report unethical actions to a higher level within the organization.
- Secretly or publicly report unethical actions to someone outside the organization.
- Secretly or publicly threaten an offender or a responsible leader with reporting unethical actions.
- Quietly or publicly refuse to implement an unethical order or policy.

Whistle-Blowing

Whistle-blowing *is the disclosure by current or former employees of illegal, immoral, or illegitimate organizational practices to people or organizations that may be able to change the practice*. The whistle-blower lacks the power to change the undesirable practice directly and so appeals to others either inside or outside the organization.[30]

The collapse of Enron started when Sherron Watkins sat down at her computer on August 14, 2001, and began typing a questioning and now famous memo to her boss, Kenneth Lay. "I am incredibly nervous that we will implode in a wave of accounting scandals," she wrote. Watkins' seven-page memo became the smoking gun in an investigation of alleged financial misdealing at Enron and Arthur Andersen, an accounting firm, which ultimately led to the collapse of both firms. Watkins found herself confronting fraudulent behavior that was illegal and could be related to individuals. Her concerns also had to do with the mismanagement of information and ineffective leadership. She acted when the evidence became overwhelming that a significant wrongdoing had occurred, even though she feared retaliation.

What do you consider a whistle-blowing offense? The following Ethics Competency feature asks you to decide what a wrongdoing is, and asks you if you would blow the whistle on a person who you observed engaging in a certain practice. We also ask you to indicate whether the types of retaliation listed would happen to you if you reported such a wrongdoing to your manager and/or the organization's ethics officer. For the purpose of this illustration, you may assume that the average cost of the wrongdoing is $35,000 and that you had observed this wrongdoing frequently. We realize that oftentimes a dollar amount is difficult to place on a wrongdoing (e.g., a safety violation, sexual harassment, mismanagement). On page 507, you can compare your answers to those of people who have actually blown the whistle at work.[31]

Ethics competency

What Would You Do?

We realize that the eight types of wrongdoing presented will be significantly affected by the cost of the wrongdoing. The cost, quality of evidence, and frequency of activity of the wrongdoing are all related to whether you would actually blow the whistle or just threaten to do so. The type of retaliation also varies by the type of wrongdoing and the cost. We want you to indicate the type of retaliation most likely suffered by the whistle-blower.

TYPE OF WRONGDOING	WOULD YOU REPORT TO TOP MANAGEMENT?	
Stealing	YES	NO
Waste	YES	NO
Mismanagement	YES	NO
Safety problems	YES	NO
Sexual harassment	YES	NO
Unfair discrimination	YES	NO
Legal violation	YES	NO
Financial reporting	YES	NO

TYPE OF RETALIATION	WOULD THIS HAPPEN TO YOU?	
Coworkers not associating with person	YES	NO
Pressure from coworkers to stop complaint	YES	NO
Withholding of information needed to perform job	YES	NO
Poor performance appraisal	YES	NO
Verbal harassment or intimidation	YES	NO
Tighter scrutiny of daily work by management	YES	NO
Reassignment to a different job	YES	NO
Reassignment to a different job with less desirable duties	YES	NO
Denial of a promotion	YES	NO

Insights for Leaders

As suggested in Chapter 2, the constructive actions by leaders to help create an organizational culture that encourages ethical behavior include the following:

- Be realistic in setting values and goals regarding employment relationships. Do not promise what the organization cannot deliver.

- Encourage input from throughout the organization regarding appropriate values and ethical practices for implementing the culture. Choose values that represent the views of both employees and leaders.

- Opt for a *strong* culture that encourages and rewards diversity and principled dissent, such as grievance or complaint mechanisms or other internal review procedures.

- Provide training programs for leaders and teams on adopting and implementing the organization's ethical values. These programs should stress the underlying ethical and legal principles and cover the practical aspects of carrying out ethical procedural guidelines.

An effective organizational culture should encourage ethical behavior and discourage unethical behavior. Admittedly, ethical behavior may "cost" the organization and individuals in the short run. A global firm that refuses to pay a bribe to secure business in a particular country may lose sales. An individual may lose financially by not accepting a kickback. Similarly, an organization or individual might seem to gain from unethical actions. An organization may flout U.S. law by quietly paying bribes to officials in order to gain entry to a new market. A purchasing agent for a large corporation might take kickbacks for purchasing all needed office supplies from a particular supplier. However, such gains are typically short term.

In the long run, an organization can't successfully operate if its prevailing culture and values don't reflect strong ethics. In the long run, an organization cannot survive unless it provides high-quality goods and services that society wants and needs. An organizational culture that promotes ethical behavior is not only compatible with prevailing cultural values in the United States and other developed nations, but it also makes good business sense.

Fostering Cultural Diversity

Learning Goal

4. *Explain why fostering cultural diversity is important.*

In Chapter 2, we noted that diversity represents individual differences and similarities that exist among people. We indicated that there are three important issues surrounding diversity.[32] First, there are many different dimensions of diversity. We indicated that diversity is not about age, gender, or race. It is also not about being gay, heterosexual, or lesbian, or having certain religious beliefs. Diversity pertains to all those individual differences that make each one of us unique. Second, diversity is not synonymous with differences. Diversity encompasses both similarities and differences. For the leader, this means managing both similarities and differences among employees. In Chapter 2, we discussed how generational differences pose some real challenges for all leaders. Gen Y employees have different needs and face different personal challenges than the baby boomers. Finally, diversity includes all differences and similarities and not just pieces. In Chapter 3, we discussed how various personality dimensions, such as openness, conscientiousness, self-esteem, and locus of control, contribute to each person's unique personality. Leaders need to deal not only with these dimensions, but also with a person's attitudes, cultural values, and the like.

Organizations are becoming increasingly diverse in terms of gender, race, ethnicity, and nationality. More than half of the U.S. workforce consists of women, minorities, and recent immigrants. The growing diversity of employees in many organizations can bring substantial benefits, such as more successful marketing strategies for different types of customers, improved decision making, and greater creativity and innovation. The U.S. Department of Labor forecasts that by 2015, 60 percent of all new employees entering the U.S. workforce will be women or people of color. Whether motivated by economic necessity or choice, organizations will be competing in this marketplace for talent.

At DuPont, a group of African-American workers recently opened promising new markets for the firm by focusing on black farmers. A multicultural team gained the company about $45 million in new business by changing the way DuPont designs and markets decorating materials (e.g., countertops, roofing materials) in order to appeal more to overseas customers. At Target, CEO Bob Ulrich says that "Our ability to offer an exceptional shopping experience depends on team members who understand the diverse communities we serve." Forty-one percent of Target employees are classified as diverse. Target offers all employees a series of classes on appreciating differences, communication styles, managing inclusion, and the multicultural workforce.[33]

Challenges

In Chapter 2, we indicated that along with its benefits, cultural diversity brings costs and concerns, including communication difficulties, intraorganizational conflict, and turnover. Effectively fostering cultural diversity promises to continue to be a significant challenge for organizations for a long time. For example, programs such as day care and elder care, flexible work schedules, paternal leaves, and management of contingent workers are major issues facing organizations. United Technologies uses a variety of diversity management approaches. During succession planning, a diversity manager participates to ensure that a diverse pool of employees is considered for career advancement. The company also provides performance appraisal training to help leaders make judgments that accurately reflect each person's efforts and contributions. It sponsors forums for women and minorities and encourages membership in employee mentoring networks, such as the Society for Women Engineers, National Society of Black Engineers, and the National Society for Hispanic MBAs. The challenge for United Technologies is to ensure that all employees working for the company feel comfortable and committed to its goals.[34]

Insights for Leaders

There are no easy answers to the challenges of fostering a culturally diverse workforce. However, there are some common characteristics in organizations with effective diversity management programs. These characteristics have been distilled into the following insights and guidelines for leaders:

- Leaders and employees must understand that a diverse workforce will embody different perspectives and approaches to work and must truly value variety of opinion and insight.

- Leaders must recognize both the learning opportunities and the challenges that the expression of different perspectives presents for the organization.

- The organizational culture must create an expectation of high standards of performance and ethics from everyone.

- The organizational culture must stimulate personal development.

- The organizational culture must encourage openness and respect for diversity.

- The organizational culture must make diverse employees feel valued.[35]

Table 16.3 contains a questionnaire that you can use to examine your awareness of diversity issues. Take a moment to complete it now. What did you learn about yourself?

TABLE 16.3 Diversity Questionnaire

Directions

Indicate your views by placing a T (true) or F (false) next to each of these nine statements.

1. I know about the rules and customs of several different cultures. _____
2. I know that I hold stereotypes about other groups. _____
3. I feel comfortable with people of different backgrounds from my own. _____
4. I associate with people who are different from me. _____
5. I find working on a multicultural team satisfying. _____
6. I find change stimulating and exciting. _____
7. I enjoy learning about other cultures. _____
8. When dealing with someone whose English is limited, I show patience and understanding. _____
9. I find that spending time building relationships with others is useful because more gets done. _____

Interpretation

The more true responses you have, the more adaptable and open you are to diversity. If you have five or more true responses, you probably are someone who finds value in cross-cultural experiences.

If you have less than five true responses, you may be resistant to interacting with people who are different from you. If that is the case, you may find that your interactions with others are sometimes blocked.

Source: Adapted from Gardenswartz, L., and Rowe, A. What's your diversity quotient? *Managing Diversity Newsletter,* New York: Jamestown (undated).

Socialization of New Employees

Socialization is the process by which older members of a society transmit to younger members the social skills and knowledge needed to function effectively in that society. Similarly, **organizational socialization** *is the systematic process by which an organization brings new employees into its culture.*[36] In other words, organizational socialization involves the transmission of an organization's cultural values from leaders and senior employees to new employees, providing them with the social knowledge and skills needed to perform organizational roles and tasks successfully. Socialization takes an outsider and attempts to change that person into an insider by promoting and reinforcing the organization's core values and beliefs.

It is during the organizational socialization process that the newcomer reaches a psychological contract with the organization. A **psychological contract** *refers to a person's overall set of expectations regarding what they will contribute to the organization and what the organization will provide in return.* Unlike a business contract, a psychological contract is not written on paper, nor are its terms clearly defined. It is an understanding reached between the person and the organization. In the Learning from Experience feature, we noted how Zappos' hiring program is one cornerstone to its socialization program. Thus, if you choose to work at Zappos, you need to accept its cultural values as a part of your psychological contract with Zappos.

Organizational socialization provides the means by which new employees learn which "ropes" to pay attention to and which to ignore. It includes learning work group, departmental, and organizational values, rules, procedures, and norms; developing social and working relationships; and developing the skills needed to perform a job.

Organizational Socialization Process

Figure 16.5 presents an example of an organizational socialization process. It doesn't represent the socialization process of every organization. However, many firms with strong cultures—such as Disney, Zappos, and Texas Nameplate—frequently follow at least some of these steps in socializing new employees:

Step 1. Entry-level candidates are selected carefully. Trained recruiters use standardized procedures and seek specific capabilities that are related to the success of the business.

Step 2. Challenging early work assignments in the first year on the job are critical. For years, KeySpan Energy, a gas utility company in Brooklyn, New York, held a two-day executive retreat at a resort in Seaview, New Jersey. Newly hired employees had to be nominated by their leader to attend this retreat. After a day of playing golf, fishing, and so forth, and a night of dinner and cards, the next morning at breakfast the CEO would pick a new employee to lead the group in a discussion of a current issue confronting the company. The employee would have 90 minutes or so to prepare and make the presentation shortly thereafter. Careers were made or broken on these presentations. Those who successfully survived this "baptism by fire" were given plum job assignments in powerful departments.

Step 3. Tough on-the-job training leads to mastery of one of the core disciplines of the business. Promotion is then tied to a proven track record. At KFC, for example, many restaurant managers have been chefs, waiters, greeters, and even members of the bus staff.

Step 4. Careful attention is given to measuring results and rewarding performance. Reward systems are true indicators of the values that underlie an organization's culture. At KFC, David Novak, its CEO, passes out floppy rubber chickens (all of which are numbered and have a personal note on them) as a reward and to recognize employees for their outstanding contributions to KFC.

FIGURE 16.5 Steps in Socialization Process

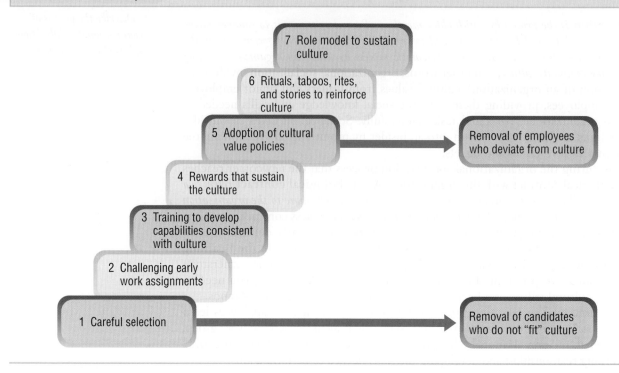

7 Role model to sustain culture

6 Rituals, taboos, rites, and stories to reinforce culture

5 Adoption of cultural value policies → Removal of employees who deviate from culture

4 Rewards that sustain the culture

3 Training to develop capabilities consistent with culture

2 Challenging early work assignments

1 Careful selection → Removal of candidates who do not "fit" culture

Disney World has an effective socialization process that often ends with new cast members wearing costumes.

GENE DUNCAN/DISNEY/AP PHOTO

Step 5. Adherence to the organization's values is emphasized. Identification with common values allows employees to justify the personal sacrifices caused by their membership in the organization.

Step 6. Reinforcing folklore provides legends and interpretations of important events in the organization's history that validate its culture and goals. Folklore reinforces a code of conduct for "how we do things around here."

Step 7. Consistent role models and consistent traits are associated with those recognized as being on the fast track to promotion and success.[37]

How effectively have you been socialized by either your current or past employer? Take a few minutes and answer the statements found in Table 16.4. Do you think the degree of socialization by your employer affected your job satisfaction? Job performance?[38]

Disney World has an effective socialization process that uses some of these seven steps to help ensure that tens of thousands of visitors a day will have fun.[39] Disney annually hires more than 2,000 people and employs more than 27,500 at Disney World. Those who cannot afford housing around the Disney World site are housed in a separate Disney gated complex. Disney carefully screens all potential members (Step 1). After recruits complete their applications, they are screened for criminal records. Those who have a record are dropped from consideration.

All workers at Disney World must strictly follow Disney rules (e.g., no mustaches, visible tattoos, or dangling body piercing items, and no hair color outside of the "normal" colors) and norms (such as always taking the extra step to make sure guests have a good experience) and behave in a certain way. To learn these rules, norms, and behaviors, new cast members (recruits) receive formal training at Disney University in

TABLE 16.4 How Effectively Have You Been Socialized?

Instructions: Complete the following survey items by considering either your current job or one you held in the past. If you have never worked, identify a friend who is working and ask that individual to complete the questionnaire for his or her organization. Read each item and circle your response by using the rating scale shown below. Remember, there are no right or wrong answers. On completion, compute your total score by adding up your responses and compare it to the scoring norms.

		Strongly Disagree	Disagree	Neutral	Agree	Strongly Agree
1.	I have been through a set of training experiences that are specifically designed to give newcomers a thorough knowledge of job-related skills.	1	2	3	4	5
2.	This organization puts all newcomers through the same set of learning experiences.	1	2	3	4	5
3.	I did not perform any of my normal job responsibilities until I was thoroughly familiar with departmental procedures and work methods.	1	2	3	4	5
4.	There is a clear pattern in the way one role leads to another, or one job assignment leads to another, in this organization.	1	2	3	4	5
5.	I can predict my future career path in this organization by observing other people's experiences.	1	2	3	4	5
6.	Almost all of my colleagues have been supportive of me personally.	1	2	3	4	5
7.	My colleagues have gone out of their way to help me adjust to this organization.	1	2	3	4	5
8.	I received much guidance from experienced organizational members as to how I should perform my job.	1	2	3	4	5
9.	In the last several months, I have been extensively involved with other new recruits in common, job-related activities.	1	2	3	4	5
10.	I am gaining a clear understanding of my role in this organization from observing my senior colleagues.	1	2	3	4	5

Total score = _____

Scoring Norms

10–20 = Low socialization
21–39 = Moderate socialization
40–50 = High socialization

groups of 45. The training follows a rigid program. During the Tradition I program, which lasts a day and a half, new cast members learn the Disney language and the four Disney values: safety, courtesy, show or entertainment, and efficiency. They also receive training in how to answer guests' questions no matter how simple or difficult the question (Step 5). About 40 percent of new cast members complete Tradition I training. Many simply quit when they understand what their jobs and the rules entail.

Once the cast members have completed the Tradition I phase, they move on to further socialization in the attraction areas (Adventureland, Fantasyland, and so on) that they will join. This session, which can last as long as a day and a half, covers rules for each area. Last but not least is on-the-job training by experienced cast members who actually work in an attraction (Step 3). This part of the socialization process can take up to two and a half weeks to complete, during which the new cast members wear a costume, learn to sing a song (where appropriate), and begin to relate effectively with other cast members and guests.

Insights for Leaders

All organizations and groups socialize new members in some way, but the steps can vary greatly in terms of how explicit, comprehensive, and lengthy the process is. Generally, rapid socialization is advantageous. For the individual, it quickly reduces the uncertainty and anxiety surrounding a new job. For the organization, it helps the new employee become productive quickly. Organizations with strong cultures may be particularly skillful at socializing individuals. If the culture is effective, socialization will contribute to organizational success. However, if the culture needs changing, strong socialization reduces the prospects for making needed changes.

Socialization creates additional dilemmas.[40] For example, GE, Xerox, Disney, and other organizations use management development programs to socialize employees. How strong should the socialization be? Does the organization want its new hires to think alike, at least in terms of a certain level of logic and intelligent analysis? To have the same business values and sense of professionalism? In some sense, the answer to these questions has to be *yes*. Yet, oversocialization runs the risk of creating rigid, narrow-minded corporate men and women. The goal of most organizations' socialization processes is to develop independent thinkers committed to what they believe to be right, while at the same time helping them become collaborative team players who have good interpersonal skills. This goal poses a challenge for socialization, which, to be effective, must balance these two demands.

The socialization process may affect employee and organizational success in a variety of ways. Table 16.5 lists some possible socialization outcomes. These outcomes aren't determined solely by an organization's socialization process. For example, job satisfaction is a function of many things, including the nature of the task, the individual's personality and needs, the nature of supervision, opportunities to succeed and be rewarded, and the like (see Chapter 3). Note that successful socialization may contribute to job satisfaction, whereas unsuccessful socialization may contribute to job dissatisfaction.

TABLE 16.5 Possible Outcomes of the Socialization Process

SUCCESSFUL SOCIALIZATION IS REFLECTED IN	UNSUCCESSFUL SOCIALIZATION IS REFLECTED IN
• Job satisfaction	• Job dissatisfaction
• Role clarity	• Role ambiguity and conflict
• High work motivation	• Low work motivation
• Understanding of culture, perceived control	• Misunderstanding, tension, perceived lack of control
• High job involvement	• Low job involvement
• Commitment to organization	• Lack of commitment to organization
• Tenure	• Absenteeism, turnover
• High performance	• Low performance
• Internalized values	• Rejection of values

Chapter Summary

Organizational culture is the pattern of beliefs and expectations shared by members of an organization. It includes a common philosophy, norms, and values. In other words, it expresses the "rules of the game" for getting along and getting things done and ways of interacting with outsiders, such as suppliers and customers. Some aspects of organizational culture are cultural symbols, heroes, rites, and ceremonies. Organizational culture develops as a response to the challenges of external adaptation and survival and of internal integration. The formation of an organization's culture also is influenced by the culture of the larger society within which the organization must function.

1. Explain how an organization's culture is formed, sustained, and changed.

The primary methods for both sustaining and changing organizational culture include (1) identifying what leaders and teams pay attention to, measure, and control; (2) recognizing the ways in which leaders and employees react to crises; (3) using managerial and team role modeling, teaching, and coaching; (4) developing and applying fair criteria for allocating rewards and status; (5) utilizing consistent criteria for recruitment, selection, and promotion within the organization and removal from it; and (6) emphasizing organizational rites, ceremonies, and stories.

Although all organizational cultures are unique, four general types are identified and discussed: bureaucratic, clan, entrepreneurial, and market. They are characterized by differences in the extent of formal controls and focus of attention.

2. Describe four types of organizational culture.

Organizational culture also can have a strong effect on the ethical behavior of leaders and employees alike. One concept linking culture to ethical behavior is principled organizational dissent. Cultures that encourage dissent and permit whistle-blowing provide guidelines for ethical behaviors.

3. Discuss how organizational culture can influence ethical behaviors of leaders and employees.

Fostering cultural diversity is expected to be one of the principal challenges facing the leaders of organizations for years to come. How leaders respond to this challenge will determine the effectiveness of culturally diverse teams, an organization's communication process, and employees' personal development.

4. Explain why fostering cultural diversity is important.

Socialization is the process by which new members are brought into an organization's culture. At firms having a strong culture, socialization steps are well developed and the focus of careful attention. All organizations socialize new members, but depending on how it is done, the outcomes could be either positive or negative in terms of job performance, satisfaction, and commitment to the organization. We presented a seven-step process for socializing new employees.

5. Describe the process of organizational socialization and its effect on culture.

Key Terms and Concepts

Bureaucratic culture, **490**
Clan culture, **491**
Cultural symbols, **480**
Entrepreneurial culture, **492**
External adaptation and survival, **481**
Internal integration, **482**
Market culture, **493**
Organizational cultural values, **480**

Organizational rites and ceremonies, **486**
Organizational socialization, **499**
Psychological contract, **499**
Shared behaviors, **480**
Socialization, **499**
Subcultures, **487**
Whistle-blowing, **495**

Discussion Questions

1. Tony Hsieh, leader of Zappos, has some very strong norms about what behaviors are rewarded and what are punished. To more fully understand Zappos' cultural values go to www.zappos.com and click on "What are Zappos employees doing right now?" at the bottom of the homepage. Are there any ethical issues here?
2. Go to www.zappos.com. How does this website illustrate cultural diversity?
3. Provide two examples of how organizational culture is expressed at your college or university.
4. Describe how the organizational culture at your college or university affects your behavior using the values listed in Table 16.1.
5. What are the primary methods that Richard Teerlink used to change the culture of Harley-Davidson?

6. Describe how organizations use symbols and stories to communicate values and beliefs. Give some examples of organizations' symbols or stories with which you are familiar.
7. Use the values listed in Table 16.1 to describe what it would be like to work at Semco and for Ricardo Semler.
8. What role does communications play is sustaining Texas Nameplate's entrepreneurial culture?
9. How might an organization use its culture to increase the probability of ethical behavior and decrease the probability of unethical behavior by its leaders and employees?
10. Dave Stoner, CEO of ViewCast, a video encoding company, says that changing a culture is among the hardest things he has ever done. Why is changing a culture so difficult?

Experiential Exercise and Case

Experiential Exercise: Self Competency

Assessing the Culture of Your Organization[41]

Instructions

Think of an organization that you currently work for or used to work for. This questionnaire will help you look at some aspects of that organization's culture. The following 40 statements indicate some organizational values. If these values are held by top management, they generally will be shared by other members of the organization. Read each statement and indicate in the blank to the left of the statement how much the behavior contained in the statement is valued in that organization. Use the following key for your responses:

4 = Very highly valued in the organization.
3 = Valued in the organization.
2 = Given rather low value in the organization.
1 = Not valued in the organization.

_____1. Free communication among employees, each respecting the feelings, competence, and judgment of others.
_____2. Facing problems, not shying away from them.
_____3. Offering moral support and help to employees and colleagues in crisis.
_____4. Match between feelings and expressed behavior.
_____5. Preventive action on most matters.
_____6. Employees taking independent action relating to their jobs.
_____7. Teamwork and team spirit.
_____8. Employees trying out innovative ways of solving problems.
_____9. Genuine sharing of information, feelings, and thoughts in meetings.
_____10. Going deeper rather than doing surface-level analysis of interpersonal problems.

_____11. Interpersonal contact and support among employees.
_____12. Tactfulness, cleverness, and even a little manipulation to get things done.
_____13. Superiors encouraging their subordinates to think about their development and take action in that direction.
_____14. Close supervision and direction of employees regarding their behaviors.
_____15. Accepting and appreciating help offered by others.
_____16. Encouraging employees to take a fresh look at how things are done.
_____17. Free discussion and communication among superiors and subordinates.
_____18. Facing challenges inherent in the work situation.
_____19. Confiding in superiors without fear that they will misuse the trust.
_____20. "Owning" mistakes made.
_____21. Considering both positive and negative aspects before taking action.
_____22. Obeying and checking with superiors rather than being concerned about larger organizational goals.
_____23. Performing immediate tasks rather than being concerned about larger organizational goals.
_____24. Making genuine attempts to change behavior on the basis of feedback received.

Use the following key for the remainder of your responses:

4 = This belief is very widely shared in the organization.
3 = This belief is fairly well shared in the organization.
2 = Only some people in the organization share this belief.
1 = Few or no people in the organization share this belief.

_____25. Effective leaders suppress their feelings.
_____26. Pass the buck to others tactfully when there is a problem.
_____27. Trust begets trust.
_____28. Telling a polite lie is preferable to telling the unpleasant truth.
_____29. Prevention is better than cure.
_____30. Freedom for employees breeds lack of discipline.
_____31. Emphasis on teamwork dilutes individual accountability.
_____32. Thinking and doing new things are important for organizational vitality.
_____33. Free and candid communication among various levels helps in solving problems.
_____34. Surfacing problems is not enough; we should find the solution.
_____35. When the situation is urgent and has to be dealt with, you have to fend for yourself.
_____36. People are what they seem to be.
_____37. A stitch in time saves nine.
_____38. A good way to motivate employees is to give them autonomy to plan their work.
_____39. Employee involvement in developing the organization's mission and goals contributes to productivity.
_____40. In today's competitive situation, consolidation and stability are more important than experimentation.

Organizational Cultural Values Profile

The Organizational Cultural Values Profile assesses eight dimensions of an organization's culture. Each dimension is listed, along with the items related to it. For each aspect, add the ratings you assigned to the item numbers indicated. **Important:** For each bold item with an asterisk, you must convert your rating as follows: 1 becomes 4; 2 becomes 3; 3 becomes 2; and 4 becomes 1.

Openness

Items 1	_____
9	_____
17	_____
25*	_____
33	_____
Total	_____

Confrontation

Items 2	_____
10	_____
18	_____
26*	_____
34	_____
Total	_____

Trust

Items 3	_____
11	_____
19	_____

Proaction

Items 5	_____
13	_____
21	_____
29	_____
37	_____
Total	_____

Autonomy

Items 6	_____
14*	_____
22*	_____
30*	_____
38	_____
Total	_____

Collaboration

Items 7	_____
15	_____
23*	_____

27	_____	**31***	_____
35*	_____	39	_____
Total	_____	Total	_____

Authenticity

Items 4	_____
12*	_____
20	_____
28*	_____
36	_____
Total	_____

Experimentation

Items 8	_____
16	_____
24	_____
32	_____
40*	_____
Total	_____

Organizational Cultural Values Interpretation Sheet

The eight organizational cultural values are **O**penness, **C**onfrontation, **T**rust, **A**uthenticity, **P**roaction, **A**utonomy, **C**ollaboration, and **E**xperimentation. The following definitions may help to clarify the values:

1. **O**penness: Spontaneous expression of feelings and thoughts and sharing of these without defensiveness.
2. **C**onfrontation: Facing—not shying away from—problems; deeper analysis of interpersonal problems; taking on challenges.
3. **T**rust: Maintaining confidentiality of information shared by others and not misusing it; a sense of assurance that others will help when needed and will honor mutual obligations and commitments.
4. **A**uthenticity: Match between what one feels, says, and does; owning one's actions and mistakes; unreserved sharing of feelings.
5. **P**roaction: Initiative; preplanning and preventive action; calculating payoffs before taking action.
6. **A**utonomy: Using and giving freedom to plan and act in one's own sphere; respecting and encouraging individual and role autonomy.
7. **C**ollaboration: Giving help to, and asking for help from, others; team spirit; working together (individuals and groups) to solve problems.
8. **E**xperimentation: Using and encouraging innovative approaches to solve problems; using feedback for improving; taking a fresh look at things; encouraging creativity.

Norms for the Organizational Culture Value Profile

	Low	High
1. Openness	13	17
2. Confrontation	10	16
3. Trust	10	16
4. Authenticity	10	14
5. Proaction	12	18
6. Autonomy	11	16
7. Collaboration	13	17
8. Experimentation	11	16

Based on the studies of the value profile so far, these are the high- and low-scoring norms.

High scores indicate a strong belief in the values and, thus, a strong organizational culture. Low scores illustrate a weak set of cultural values. If the average or mean score for your organization is low, the questions on the profile can be used as the basis for action planning to improve the organization's culture and to increase openness, creativity, and collaboration. Remember that items 12, 14, 22, 23, 25, 26, 28, 30, 31, 35, and 40 are reverse scored.

Questions

1. What approaches might you use to change these cultural values?
2. Using these eight cultural values, analyze the culture at Zappos. What is its profile and how does it influence employees' behaviors?

Case: Self Competency[42]

Wegmans

Wegmans, which has been named one of *Fortune*'s 100 Best Companies to work for in 2009, is highly respected as a tough competitor in the supermarket industry in New Jersey, New York, Pennsylvania, Virginia, and Maryland. Known for its gourmet cooking classes and extensive employee-training programs, Wegmans operates 70 stores in these states and has sales exceeding $4.5 billion annually. Founded in 1916, Wegmans is still owned and operated by the family of the founder, John Wegman.

One of the reasons why Wegmans is so successful is its values. When John and Walter Wegman opened their first store in Rochester, New York, it featured a café that served gourmet foods and sat nearly 300 customers. The store's immediate focus on fine foods quickly separated it from other grocers. Many of the employees were hired by Wegmans because of their interest in fine foods, a tradition that still holds today. People who do not express an interest in food may not fit in and are sometimes not hired.

In 1950, Walter's son, Robert, became president and immediately added a generous number of benefits for all employees, including profit sharing and medical insurance, both of which were paid for by the company. The reason that he offered these benefits was "I was no different from them," referring to the company's employees. Though the benefits are still generous at Wegmans, today employees pay a small amount into these plans.

Today, Daniel (Danny), Robert's son, is the president and he has continued the tradition of taking care of Wegmans' employees. Wegmans has paid millions of dollars into college scholarships for both full-time and part-time employees. In addition to benefits, employees receive pay well above the average for the market. As a result, employee turnover is around 6 percent, well below the national average of 25 percent according to the Food Marketing Institute.

The culture that has developed at Wegmans is an important part of the company's success. Employees are proud to work there because of the way they are treated. Sara Goggins, a college student who worked part time for Wegmans during her college days, recalls the day that Danny Wegman personally complemented her on her in-store display that she helped set up. "I love this place," she said. "If teaching doesn't work out, I would love to work at Wegmans." Kelly Schoeneck, a store manager, recalls that her manager asked her to analyze a frequent-shopper program that a competitor had recently adopted. She naturally assumed that he would take credit for this analysis, but was totally surprised when her supervisor asked her to make the presentation to Robert Wegman.

Maintaining a culture of driven, satisfied, and loyal employees who are eager to help one another is not easy. For example, when the company opened a new $100 million distribution center in Pennsylvania to serve its newer Mid-Atlantic stores, it needed truck drivers. Rather than hire experienced drivers, Wegmans allowed current store employees to apply for the job. Twenty-one weeks later Wegmans had 24 drivers with commercial licenses. Since day one, Wegmans has carefully selected each employee.

The emphasis on developing people attracts people who never thought that they would work in retail. Heather Pawlowski, an electrical engineering major at Cornell who began her career at National Semiconductor, thought of herself at a "techie." But she had always enjoyed walking through the aisles of retailers wondering why people bought different brands. After getting her MBA, she entered a Wegmans store in Rochester, New York, and introduced herself to the store manager. Shortly thereafter, she found herself in Wegmans' store manager training program. While many of her classmates were off to Wall Street, she wore long underwear and got up to her elbows in fish guts, just like all other store trainees. As she moved from packing fish to cutting meat to baking bread, she learned all aspects of store operations.

When a new store is opened, employees from existing stores are brought in to the new store to establish Wegmans' culture. The job of these employees is to help the new employees "learn the ropes to skip and those to know." When Wegmans opened its Dulles store, for example, all its managers came from different Wegmans locations and dozens of other employees drove to the store to temporarily get the place up and running. Wegmans spent $5 million on training to open its Dulles store. New employees learn what behaviors are rewarded and those that are not rewarded. Wegmans never opens a store until its employees are fully prepared.

More than half of all Wegmans' managers started working at a Wegmans during high school as part-time help. Edward McLaughlin, director of Cornell's Food Industry Management program, says, "When you're a 16-year-old kid, the last thing you want to do is wear a geeky shirt and work for a supermarket. But at Wegmans, it's a badge of honor. You are not simply a cashier. You are a part of the social fabric."

Jack DePeters, chief of operations at Wegmans, says "We're a billion dollar company run by 16-year-old cashiers. The key is to motivate them."

Questions
1. Using the values listed in Table 16.1, describe the culture of Wegmans.

2. What is the primary source of Wegmans' culture? How has Wegmans been able to sustain the culture? Go to www.wegmans.com and search under "About Us."
3. What are some threats to sustaining Wegmans' culture? How can these be overcome?

Answers to Ethics Competency
What Would You Do?

Types of Wrongdoings	Percentage of People Who Would Report the Wrongdoing to Management
Stealing	25%
Waste	17
Mismanagement	42
Safety problems	23
Sexual harassment	40
Unfair discrimination	27
Legal violations	53
Financial reporting	52

Type of Retaliation	Percentage Who Experienced It
Coworkers not associating with person	12%
Pressure from coworkers to stop complaint	5
Withholding of information needed to perform job	10
Poor performance appraisal	15
Verbal harassment or intimidation	12
Tighter scrutiny of daily work by management	14
Reassignment to a different job	8
Reassignment to a different job with less desirable duties	7
Denial of a promotion	7

chapter 17

Managing Organizational Change

Learning Goals

After studying this chapter, you should be able to:

1
Identify key pressures for change.

2
Discuss the nature of planned organizational change.

3
Identify common reasons for individual and organizational resistance to change.

4
Identify two key elements in organizational diagnosis.

5
Discuss three methods for promoting change.

Learning Content

Learning from Experience
José Sergio Gabrielli de Azevedo of Petrobras

Pressures for Change
Diversity Competency
Managing across Generations

Planned Organizational Change

Resistance to Change
Self Competency
Are You Ready to Change?
Change Competency
Target

Organizational Diagnosis

Change Methods
Communication Competency
United Technologies' Diversity Programs

Experiential Exercise and Case
Experiential Exercise: Self Competency
Assessing an Organization's Readiness for Change

Case: Communication Competency
Carolyn Bivens: Change Agent at the Ladies Professional Golf Association

José Sergio Gabrielli de Azevedo of Petrobras

In January 2000, a leak in a pipeline spilled thousands of gallons of crude oil into Guanabara Bay, a tourist attraction near Rio de Janeiro, Brazil. Because the company that owned the pipeline, Petrobras, had not installed sensors to detect the spill, it was fined more than $25 million by the Brazilian government. Environmental groups and local fisherman protested outside of Petrobras's headquarters and some protesters chained themselves to the entrance of the building. Six months later, an oil leak from a refinery spilled more than one million gallons of oil into two rivers. The government fined Petrobras another $115 million for having inadequate staffing and emergency plans in place. A local TV station said that Petrobras's management exhibited an "embarrassing level of incompetence." In March 2001, a $350 million oil rig owned by Petrobras sank in the ocean, killing two employees and untold numbers of fish.

In response to these disasters, the company created a new director position for health and safety and launched a $4 billion dollar initiative designed to prevent accidents. When José Sergio Gabrielli de Azevedo later took over the reins as CEO in 2005, his goal was to have the company become a benchmark company for outstanding environmental performance. To reach that goal, he led the following changes.

First, leaders in the company set out guidelines for required performance in 15 areas, such as regulatory compliance, risk evaluation and management, and accident analysis.

The goal was to meet and/or exceed all international health, safety, and environmental standards. Azevedo and other top leaders participated in more than 1,000 on-site audits at oil refineries, off-shore platforms, and pipelines to send a message to all employees that he was serious about achieving these standards.

Second, Petrobras decided to give preference to ordering supplies from local Brazilian companies if these companies could meet the environmental standards set by Petrobras. Recently, Petrobras spent more than $40 billion on goods and services purchased from more than 4,000 domestic suppliers. To motivate the suppliers, Petrobras developed a scoring system to monitor their suppliers' adherence to its health, safety, and environmental standards. Every supplier was ranked according to how well they met these criteria. Suppliers with low rankings were encouraged to change their behavior

FRANCK ROBICHON/EPA/CORBIS

To learn more about Petrobras, go to www.petrobras.com.

or be dropped. Petrobras is also pushing its suppliers to develop their own R&D capabilities to improve their social and environmental performance.

Third, Petrobras developed a long-term plan to become one of the five largest integrated energy companies in the world. With recent oil discoveries, its oil production should rival that of Exxon/Mobil by 2012. As an integral part of its strategy, it needs to develop its biofuels program. To reach its biofuel goal, $1.5 billion has been dedicated to achieving this result by 2012.[1]

Understanding and managing organizational change are tasks that present complex challenges. Planned change may not work, or it may have consequences far different from those intended. Today, organizations must have the capacity to adapt quickly and effectively in order to survive. Often the speed and complexity of change severely test the capabilities of leaders and employees to adapt rapidly enough, but if organizations fail to change, the cost of that failure may be quite high. Hence, leaders and employees must understand the nature of the changes needed and the likely effects of alternative approaches to bring about that change.

Because organizations exist in changing environments, bureaucratic organizations are increasingly ineffective. Organizations with rigid hierarchies, high degrees of functional specialization, narrow and limited job descriptions, inflexible rules and procedures, and impersonal, autocratic management cannot respond adequately to demands for change. As we emphasized in Chapter 15, organizations need designs that are flexible and adaptive. Organizations also need reward systems and cultures that allow greater participation in decisions by employees and leaders alike.

In this chapter, we examine the pressures on organizations to change, types of change programs, and why accurate diagnosis of organizational problems is crucial. We explore the difficult issue of resistance to change at both the individual and organizational levels and examine ways to cope with that inevitable resistance. In addition, we identify three methods for promoting organizational and behavioral changes.

Pressures for Change

Learning Goal

1. *Identify key pressures for change.*

Why Change?

As José Sergio Gabrielli de Azevedo of Petrobras found out, change can be difficult and takes time. Despite the challenges, many organizations successfully make needed changes, but failure also is common. There is considerable evidence that adaptive, flexible organizations have a competitive advantage over rigid, static organizations.[2] As a result, managing change has become a central focus of leaders in most organizations.

Most organizations around the world have tried to change themselves—some more than once—during the past decade. Yet for every successful change, there is an equally prominent failure. Walmart's dramatic performance improvement stands in stark contrast to a string of disappointments that have plagued Kmart. The rise of Target and Kohl's as leaders in the retailing industry merely emphasizes Kmart's inability to reverse its declining market share in retailing.

Organizations that are well positioned to change will prosper, but those that ignore change will flounder. When Bill McComb, CEO of Liz Claiborne, took over in 2006, he attempted an incredible balancing act of upgrading the company's image by selling off profitable brands that appealed to older women, like Ellen Tracy and Laundry by Design, and promoting younger ones like Juicy Couture, Lucky Brand Jeans, Kate Spade, and Mexx. While making these changes, Claiborne's stock dropped 87 percent. As Claiborne struggles to reinvent itself, it has chosen to open its own retail boutiques, as opposed to relying on department stores, such as Macy's, JCPenney, and Dillard's, to sell its merchandise. This is a more costly alternative, but McComb believes that it will give Claiborne more control over the way merchandise is displayed and when it is marked down. McComb has also eliminated more than 1,300 jobs and stopped selling 13 brands. Only time will tell whether these drastic moves will save the company that was founded by Liz Claiborne in 1976 to dress working women.[3]

An almost infinite variety of *pressures for change* exists in today's word. In this section, we examine four of the most significant ones: (1) globalization of markets, (2) technology, (3) social networks, and (4) generational differences.

Globalization

Organizations today face global competition on an unprecedented scale. **Globalization** *means that many markets are worldwide and are served by international or multinational corporations.* These firms create pressures on domestic corporations to international-ize and redesign their operations. Global markets now exist for most products, but to compete effectively in these markets, firms often must transform their cultures, structures, and operations. Lenovo, a computer company that started in China, has now become a dominant user of software in the PC market after it purchased IBM's laptop manufacturing facilities. Until this purchase, few people outside of China had ever heard of Lenovo.

In his book, *The World Is Flat*, Thomas Friedman outlined the most important global forces that leaders faced in the late 20th and early 21st centuries[4]:

- the fall of the Berlin Wall and the opening of Eastern European markets,
- the start of the Internet,
- development of software to manage Internet communications,
- development of self-organizing communities via the Internet,
- outsourcing, and
- the founding of Google, Yahoo, and MSN web search engines.

These and other powerful globalization forces required domestic firms to abandon "business as usual" in order to remain competitive. In some industries, such as steel, apparel, and shoes, global strategies are replacing country-by-country approaches. Although globalization strategies aren't easy to implement, many organizations have effectively moved outside their domestic markets. Procter & Gamble, YUM! Brands (KFC, Pizza Hut, Taco Bell, Long John Silver's, and A&W Root Beer), and Mary Kay Cosmetics have highly successful Asian operations. Mary Kay sells more products in China than in the United States. KFC and Pizza Hut serve more customers in China and earn more profits from these operations than anywhere else in the world. Procter & Gamble and Gillette merged to form an $83 billion consumer products company that serves customers in more than 80 countries and employs more than 138,000 people. Together, they hope to do what each has struggled to do on its own—ramp up sales in the developing markets of China and Eastern Europe, bring global products to market more quickly, increase their lever-age over Walmart and Costco, and gain savings with media companies from which they buy advertising.[5]

Going global does not mean that the firm provides exactly the same goods or services in all countries. For example, Campbell Soup Company has long wanted to sell its soups in Russia. In the early 1990s, however, it gave up trying to sell canned soups in Russia because women weren't buying them. To understand why women weren't buying their soup, Campbell hired cultural anthropologists to visit homes in Russia to watch how consumers prepare and eat soup. What did they learn? Russians

COURTESY OF CAMPBELL SOUP

Highly decentralized organizations, such as Campbell Soup, have operating units and sell products throughout the world.

eat soup more than five times a week, compared with America's once-a-week habit. Russians consume more than 32 billion bowls annually, compared to just 14 billion in the United States. The anthropologists also found that Russians consider themselves to be the world's foremost experts on soup. Russians have words that they use only for soup. Armed with this information, Campbell now plans to sell a beef broth soup with pieces of meat, onions, and potatoes; a chicken broth with chicken, onions, and potatoes; and a mushroom soup with large pieces of mushrooms, onions, and seasonings. Campbell's strategy is to encourage Russians to use these soups as a base for their homemade soups. Campbell also knows that for century's mothers have done the bulk of the soup preparation, with daughters helping out by cutting vegetables. Therefore, instead of trying to change this tradition, it is targeting newlywed women as they take on the role of soup-maker. Campbell gives out discount coupons and recipes at buildings where couples register their marriages.[6]

Technology

Coping with global competition requires a flexibility that many organizations often do not possess. Fortunately, the revolution in information technology (IT) permits organizations to develop the needed flexibility. IT is having a profound impact on individual employees, teams, and organizations. For example, experts who have studied its impact on organizations have observed that IT:

- changes almost everything about an organization—its structure, its products, its markets, and its manufacturing processes;

- increases the value of invisible assets, such as knowledge, competencies, and training;

- democratizes a company because employees have more information and can communicate with anyone else in the organization;

- increases the flexibility of work by allowing more employees to work at home, on the road, or at hours that suit them; and

- allows organizations to unify their global operations and to work a 24-hour day spanning the world.[7]

Imagine employees who work 16 hours a day, seven days a week, are never sick or late, and demand no benefits or health insurance. They spend every minute maximizing their productivity. Who are these employees? Robots. Staples, an office supply chain, uses robots to fill orders in its 500,000-square-foot warehouse in Chambersburg, Pennsylvania. Staples realized that the order fulfillment process was the weakest link in its supply-chain management system. The company had traditionally used a conveyor belt where employees gathered goods just like you do when shopping at a grocery store. Instead of a shopping cart, employees put their goods on the conveyor belt and then additional employees packaged them for shipment. Today, when an order is received, the computer tells the robots where to find the rack with the goods. Through the use of bar-code stickers on the floor, the robot goes to the rack and waits for an employee to pull the correct items and place them in a box. When the order is completed, the robot packs the box and puts on a shipping label. A central computer instructs the robot where to leave the package for delivery. Before robots arrived, the warehouse processed 13,000 orders daily. With the use of robots, it now handles 18,000 orders daily.[8]

However, the potential effects of IT aren't uniformly positive. Organizations that rely on sophisticated information technologies are more vulnerable to sabotage, espionage, and vandalism. The violation of intellectual property rights in China has forced Microsoft to work more closely with the Chinese government. Instead of pursuing courts and other legal means to curb violation of its Windows and other propriety products, Microsoft has decided to take a more collaborative approach and work with the Chinese government. This required Microsoft to finance computer classrooms in rural China and establish training for teachers and software entrepreneurs for free. As a result of these and other efforts, employees in Beijing city government have stopped using pirated software and are downloading legal software on their computers.[9]

The globalization phenomenon and information technologies are linked in interesting ways. Highly decentralized organizations, such as Procter & Gamble and Campbell Soup, with operating units scattered throughout the world, face some significant challenges in terms of coordination and cooperation. However, advanced computer and telecommunication technologies provide mechanisms to link employees in ways only imagined in the past. For example, many multinational corporations rely on the use of virtual teams to accomplish their work. As discussed in Chapter 12, *virtual teams* are groups of geographically and/or organizationally dispersed coworkers who are assembled via a combination of telecommunications and information technologies to accomplish organizational tasks. Such teams rarely meet or work together face to face. Virtual teams may be set up on a temporary basis and used to accomplish a specific task, or they may be relatively permanent and used to address ongoing strategic planning issues. The membership of virtual teams may be quite fluid, with members changing according to task demands even for those teams with an ongoing assignment.[10]

Social Networks

In the chapter on teams, Chapter 12, we discussed the impact of social networking on friendship groups. We pointed out that the Internet has changed the ability of people to form social networks. Facebook, a popular social networking website founded in 2004, claims to sign up more than 150,000 new members each day. MySpace, another social networking site, claims that it adds 250,000 a day, and LinkedIn, a business networking site, adds thousands of new members each day. All of these forms of social networking are changing the way people communicate, search for jobs, and form groups. Leaders must understand these forms of social networking in order to be effective. Why? Social networking allows employees to ignore the rules and find solutions to problems without going through the organization's chain of command. For example, Bell Canada uses social networks in which leaders freely share ideas about best practices. These networks also work on problems identified as hindering business, such as managing people from different generations and the bureaucracy associated with hiring new employees. Bell Canada found that employees' job satisfaction rose when they participated in such groups and even helped bring out needed changes.

Generational Differences

Along with 85 million baby boomers in the United States (those born between 1946 and 1964) and 50 million Gen X'ers (those born between 1965 and 1977), there has been an influx of 76 million younger Gen Y'ers (those born between 1978 and 1999) into the workforce.[11] Most Gen Y'ers have never experienced life without a microwave, computer, ATM card, or a television remote. They will be the first generation to have used e-mail, instant messaging, and cell phones since childhood. Due to a variety of factors, instant gratification is causing some Gen Y'ers to have unrealistic expectations about their careers. Many are unwilling to work hard and make personal sacrifices to get ahead. Gen Y'ers are impatient. They want things yesterday and this may cause them to become inefficient, says Barbara Dwyer, CEO of the Job Journey. Another disadvantage is that they lack the patience to work through a complex problem. E-mail and instant messaging also reduce the opportunity for employees to develop strong interpersonal competencies, which could derail their careers in the future.

Motivating these three diverse generations of employees requires leaders to adapt their management styles. At IBM, Kari Barbar, vice president of human resources, offers different learning venues to different generations. Boomers are accustomed to learning in a classroom with a teacher and want to work through the problem. Gen X'ers prefer web courses so they can learn by themselves and at their own pace. Networking-prone Gen Y'ers enjoy working on blogs with others to solve a problem. Some organizations are also tailoring programs to retain and attract all generations. For example, Gen Y'ers are opting out of putting in the long hours common for boomers, and have high expectations for personal growth on the job. More than half of the Gen Y'ers have college degrees, but many take time off to travel before they start to look for a job, which used to be a "red flag" for baby boomers back when leaders were considering hiring them.[12]

With more career options, Gen Y employees are nudging some organizations to think more creatively about the work/life balance. Deloitte Consulting has created programs that help Gen Y employees think about their careers. It learned that Gen Y employees are motivated by friendship and will choose a job just to be with friends and Gen X'ers. Boston-based Gentle Moving once hired an entire athletic team. "It looked like a great work environment because of the people," said Niles Kuronen, a rower. "It was huge to be able to work with friends." Gen Y employees use their BlackBerrys or iPods to check in with their friends, and they want flexibility during the week. Today's technologies allow employees to be perpetually connected with their peers.

The line between work and friends is blurred for the Gen Y'ers, who look to their friends for advice and career direction. For baby boomers going to college, a student called home once a week—maybe. Boomers couldn't wait to claim their independence from their parents. Today, students call their parents three or four times a day to keep in contact with them. Sun Microsystems's telecommuting program was started to appeal to Gen Y employees and more than half of all employees are now on this program.

Gen Y employees are also searching for meaning in their work. More than half of the workers in their twenties prefer employment in companies that provide volunteer opportunities. Employees at www.salesforce.com, for example, did 50,000 hours of community service recently. According to Marc Benioff, its CEO, this has helped attract and retain employees.

The following Diversity Competency feature illustrates some of the leadership challenges associated with managing across generations. Understanding these differences is important to increase leaders' ability to attract and retain high-quality employees.[13]

Diversity **competency**

Managing across Generations

What attracts an organization to Gen Y'ers? According to Jared Larrabee of Deloitte Consulting: Gen Y'ers bring to the job several desirable traits:

- *Tech-savvy.* They can locate details about anything in seconds because they have grown up with the Internet.
- *Adept at global and diversity issues.* Through online social networks, they have found ways to reach beyond their own location and have established relationships with others through Facebook, MySpace, and other social networking portals.
- *Team oriented.* Gen Y'ers measure their accomplishments by their peers.
- *Multitaskers.* Most Gen Y'ers feel that listening to an iPod while working improves their job satisfaction and productivity.
- *Focus on work/life balance.* Having flexibility about when and where to work is very important for keeping them loyal to their organization.

Gen Y'ers also bring some behaviors that organizations need to be aware of:

- *Lack of independence.* Because they are so connected to others, including their parents, they often need more direction than Gen X'ers or boomers.
- *Lack of discretion.* Because many of the Gen Y'ers have discussed everything from musical tastes to dating habits with their friends, this lack of confidentiality can have a major impact on the organization. There will be no secrets between manager and subordinate. Gen Y'ers will need to adopt acceptable standards of behavior. They will have to figure out what they can share with their friends and what they should not share.
- *Unrealistic expectations.* Gen Y'ers believe that they can change the world quickly. The problem is that they lack the experience and political savvy to make it happen.
- *Impatience.* Gen Y'ers have played video games that show players how they are doing instantly. In organizations, they will need to learn to wait for semiannual or annual performance reviews that rely on a manager's subjective evaluations in the areas of leadership, teamwork, and communications.
- *Relaxed work ethic.* Many are unwilling to work hard and make personal sacrifices to get ahead.
- *Weak interpersonal competencies.* E-mail and instant text messaging reduce opportunities for face-to-face communications, but strong interpersonal competencies are required to be successful in most organizations.

Compared to baby boomers or Gen X'ers, Gen Y'ers spend 50 percent more time than others on their computers either socializing or blogging. The use of electronic social interactions with friends has replaced face-to-face interactions. Technology has made it easier to maintain a network of valued friendships. Therefore, Gen Y'ers often do not recognize a manager's authority in the same way as boomers and Gen X'ers do. They are more inclined to discuss an instruction with friends before obeying it. They want to be treated as equals, partnering with their manager and coworkers in making decisions that affect them.[14]

Planned Organizational Change

Learning Goal

2. *Discuss the nature of planned organizational change.*

Distinguishing between change that inevitably happens to all organizations and change that is deliberately planned by members of an organization is important. Our focus is primarily on intentional, goal-oriented organizational change. **Planned organizational change** *represents a deliberate attempt by leaders and* *employees to improve the functioning of teams, departments, divisions, or an entire orga-nization in some important way.*

Two radically different approaches are used to achieve organizational change: economic and organizational development.[15] Each approach is guided by a different set of assumptions about the purpose and means for change. We have highlighted these differences in Table 17.1.

Economic Approach

The economic approach *refers to initiating change for the purpose of creating shareholder value.* Change is driven by top management, whose members use financial incentives to motivate employees to change their behaviors. Change is planned and focused. Leaders who create change using this approach set goals based on expectations of the financial markets. They do not involve their management team or employees in discussing ways to reach financial goals. These change agents focus on decisions that affect the strategy, structure, and systems of their organization. The economic approach is mainly used by turnaround artists, and not by people who want to build the organization.

On August 5, 2007, Robert Nardelli was announced as the CEO of Chrysler after leaving Home Depot. Chrysler's German partner, Mercedes-Benz, sold Chrysler to Cerberus Capital Management because Mercedes-Benz decided that it didn't want to be part of a merger among equals. Cerberus hired Nardelli to turn the bankrupt company around, as he had done at Home Depot. Cerberus chose Nardelli for his reputation as an "in-your-face" cost-cutting leader. Cerberus knew that he alienated both employees and senior leaders at Home Depot because he lacked corporate diplomacy but got the job done at Home Depot. His laser-like focus on executing cost-effective strategies at Home Depot (and at GE before that) made him an ideal CEO for Chrysler.

Using the same change strategy at Chrysler that he used at GE and Home Depot, Nardelli cut 23,000 employees and stopped production of three models, the Pacifia, PT Cruiser convertible, and Dodge Magnum. He also made numerous changes to his top management team. Under Cerberus, Nardelli tried to improve Chrysler's image and boost quality, but the bottom fell out of the U.S. auto market in 2008, and losses began piling up. In 2008, Nardelli rattled employees by declaring the company to be "opera-tionally bankrupt." He claimed that he used these words to create a sense of urgency at Chrysler, but the resulting uproar by the union and dealers made Nardelli retract his statement. In 2009, Nardelli left Chrysler with no "golden parachute." Chrysler became owned by Fiat and the U.S. government. Nardelli acknowledged that he failed to remake Chrysler into a competitive automobile company. He said, "It's like we came to the last pit stop, the car was tuned up, and we had one of the fastest cars on the track and we ran out of gas." In June 2009, Chrysler closed 789 of their dealerships.[16]

Organizational Development Approach

The organizational development approach *refers to developing employees' competencies to solve problems by enabling them to identify and become emotionally committed to improving*

TABLE 17.1 Approaches to Change		
MEANS	**ECONOMIC**	**ORGANIZATIONAL DEVELOPMENT**
Purpose	Profit	Develop employees' competencies
Leadership	Top-down	Participative
Focus	Structure and strategy	Culture
Motivation	Incentives lead performance	Incentives lag performance

the performance of the firm. This approach emphasizes the building of partnerships, trust, and employee commitment. If commitment is developed, it is assumed that the extensive use of rules and regulations will be unnecessary. The organizational development approach requires leaders to engage people emotionally in examining why the existing structure and systems are not meeting the new challenges facing the organization.

In Chapter 16, we introduced you to Wegmans, a grocery store chain headquartered in Rochester, New York, that operates grocery stores in the Northeast. It uses the organizational development approach to empower employees to make changes. It has created a work environment where employees' contributions count and there are few rules. Wegmans knows that shoppers who are emotionally connected to a store spend 46 percent more at the checkout stand than those who aren't. It is each employee's job to create this emotional bond for the shopper by changing the way Wegmans does business. Wegmans selects people who are passionate about customer service, have a genuine interest in food, and are capable of making decisions on their own. To instill the Wegmans approach to change, all management employees go through a store manager training program, where they learn how to greet customers, sweep floors, gut fish, bake bread, walk a customer to the car, and the like. All members of the Wegmans family have also been through the same training program.[17]

> ### Self Insight
>
> While the command-and-control approach is expedient, I work as a collegial leader. I work with my senior leaders to create change. I want to hear people's solutions to problems.
>
> *José Sergio Gabrielli de Azevedo, CEO, Petrobras*

Effective Change Programs

Leaders who face major changes need to think through the long-term consequences of using either the economic approach or the organizational development approach. Moreover, finding leaders with the managerial competencies needed to achieve large-scale organization change properly is difficult.

In 2004, Fiat had reported huge losses and endured a long strike when Sergio Marchionne showed up as CEO. Many insiders thought that they would have to spend years teaching this outsider about the car business. Since Marchionne showed up, Fiat has introduced the Cinquecento, one of the world's smallest cars, and taken a major stake in Chrysler. According to Marchionne, he had to make major changes in the way Fiat was run. Traditionally, all important decisions in Italian companies were made by the CEO. Therefore, senior leaders were not used to taking responsibility and were working in a status-quo environment. To create a sense of urgency, Marchionne laid top leaders off because they had too many "bad habits ingrained in them." Fiat's culture had been dominated by engineers and while Fiat has developed some global diesel engines, Marchionne believed that it took its eyes off its brands. For example, he not only started promoting marketing people, but started to benchmark Fiat's marketing efforts against companies like Apple and P&G. He replaced them with younger leaders and gave them authority and responsibility to turn around Alfa and Fiat. Next, he spent five months conducting performance appraisals of the top 700 people. He not only looked at their numbers (cars sold, factory utilization, etc.), but how they lead people and lead change.

He also started to share new ideas across the organization as well. More than a third of his top leadership team has been recruited from the agricultural and construction businesses run by Fiat. This diverse team focuses on operational efficiency and flexibility. One of the recommendations from this team was to improve the company's relationship with its employees. Marchionne agreed and opened kindergartens and grocery stores next to plants to make it easier for employees to balance work and family obligations. He also redid all dressing rooms and bathrooms because he believes that these changes were needed to show employees that senior leaders were committed to make the workforce happy and productive.[18]

Insights for Leaders

Most successful change approaches share some common characteristics. For example, effective change programs typically involve:

- motivating change by creating a readiness for the change among leaders and employees and attempting to overcome resistance to change (which we discuss in detail shortly);
- creating a shared vision of the desired future state of the organization;
- developing political support for the needed changes;
- managing the transition from the current state to the desired future state; and
- sustaining momentum for change so that it will be carried to completion.

The initiatives that contribute to effective change programs are summarized in Figure 17.1.

FIGURE 17.1 Initiatives Contributing to Effective Change Management

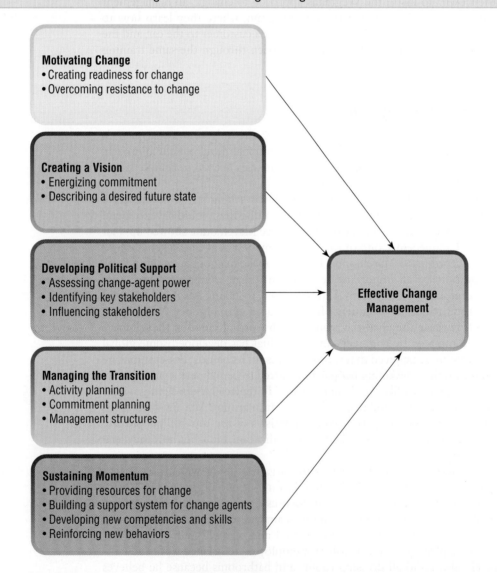

Source: From Cummings, J. G., and Worley, C. G. *Organization Development and Change,* 6th ed. Cincinnati, OH. © 1997. South-Western, a part of Cengage Learning, Inc. Reproduced by permission. www.cengage.com/permissions.

Similarly, the conditions necessary for successfully carrying out effective change programs include the following:

- The organization's members must be the key source of energy for change, not some party external to the team or organization.
- Key members of the organization must recognize the need for change and be attracted by the potentially positive outcomes of the change program.
- A willingness to change norms and procedures must exist.

Economic and organizational development programs and the conditions necessary for their use are similar in certain respects. Change must come from within the organization. People must be aware of the need for change, believe in the potential value of the proposed changes, and be willing to change their behaviors in order to make the team, department, or organization more effective. Absent these beliefs and behaviors, effective organizational change is problematic. Leaders must be open to trying different approaches at different times.

Resistance to Change

Learning Goal

3. *Identify common reasons for individual and organizational resistance to change.*

Change involves moving from the known to the unknown. Because the future is uncertain and may negatively affect people's careers, salary, and competencies, organization members generally do not support change unless compelling reasons convince them to do so. Resistance to change often is baffling because it can take so many forms. Overt resistance may be expressed through strikes, reduced productivity, shoddy work, and even sabotage. Covert resistance may be expressed by increased tardiness and absenteeism, requests for transfers, resignations, loss of motivation, lower morale, and higher accident or error rates. One of the most damaging forms of resistance is passive resistance by employees—a lack of participation in formulating change proposals and ultimately a lack of commitment to the proposals, even when they have had an opportunity to participate in making such decisions.

Figure 17.2 shows three ways to decode resistance to change.[19] Leaders often describe resistance to change by employees as not buying into the program, foot-dragging, and, sometimes, overt sabotage. Moreover, whether or not something constitutes a resistance to change is subjective. When leaders believe resistance is a threat, they may become competitive, defensive, and uncommunicative. They are sometimes more concerned about being right—and not looking bad—such that they lose sight of their original goals. In trying to push things through without decoding the sources of resistance, they sacrifice goodwill, put valuable relationships in jeopardy, and kill the opportunity to communicate effectively with the dissenters. They often don't hear about vital information that others might have about how to successfully achieve change. Although it is true that resistance can be self-serving, leaders need to learn from this form of feedback. If leaders dismiss this form of feedback, it will rob them of the opportunity to learn.

Individual Resistance

There are six reasons why individuals might not be aware of the need for change. We suggest some ways in which this resistance can be reduced.

Perceptions

In Chapter 4, we discussed the notion of perceptual defense—a perceptual error whereby people tend to perceive selectively those things that fit most comfortably with their current view of the world. Once individuals have established an understanding of reality, they may resist changing it. Among other things, people may resist the possible impact of change in their lives by (1) reading or listening only to what they agree with,

FIGURE 17.2 Three Practices That Can Help Reduce Resistance to Change

(2) conveniently forgetting any knowledge that could lead to other viewpoints, and (3) misunderstanding communication that, if correctly understood, wouldn't fit their existing attitudes and values. For example, leaders enrolled in management training programs at Baylor Health Care are exposed to different managerial philosophies and change techniques. In the classroom, they may competently discuss and answer questions about these new ideas, yet carefully separate in their minds the approaches that they believe wouldn't work from those that they believe would work or that they already practice.

What happens if a person changes his or her perception and tackles the problem from a different perspective? That's what Hinda Miller and Lisa Lindahl did. In 1977, Miller was working as a costume designer at a Shakespeare festival in Vermont. She and Lindahl were avid runners and were unhappy with the lack of jogging gear available for women. One day while discussing the problem, Lindahl's husband held a jockstrap up to his chest, laughing, and said, "Look, a jock bra." Miller and Lindahl had never viewed a jockstrap like that. That afternoon, Miller and Lindahl went to the campus bookstore, bought two jockstraps, and sewed them together, thus creating the first sports bra. Their invention, the jogging bra, made them a fortune. Sara Lee eventually acquired the business.[20]

Personality

Some aspects of an individual's personality may predispose that person to resist change. In Chapter 3, we indicated that self-esteem is an important personality characteristic that determines how a person behaves in an organization. People with low self-esteem are more likely to resist change than those with high self-esteem because low self-esteem people are more likely to perceive the negative aspects of change than the positive aspects. Low self-esteem people are not as likely as high self-esteem people to work hard to make change succeed. Another personality characteristic is adjustment (see the Big Five personality profile in Chapter 3). People who are nervous, self-doubting, and moody typically have a difficult time changing their behaviors. They may resist change until those people they depend on endorse it. These employees are highly dependent on their supervisors for performance feedback. They probably won't accept any new techniques or methods for doing their jobs unless their supervisors personally support the changes and indicate how these changes will improve performance and/or otherwise benefit the employees.[21]

Leaders must be careful to avoid overemphasizing the role played by personality in resistance to change because they can easily make the fundamental attribution error (see Chapter 4). There is a tendency to "blame" resistance to change in the workplace on individual personalities. Although personality may play a role (as we have just discussed), it seldom is the only important factor in a situation involving change.

Habit

Unless a situation changes dramatically, individuals may continue in their usual ways. A habit can be a source of comfort, security, and satisfaction for individuals because it allows them to adjust to the world and cope with it. Whether a habit becomes a primary source of resistance to change depends, to a certain extent, on whether individuals perceive advantages from changing their behaviors. For example, read the following sentences:

> Cna yuo raed tihs? I cdn'uolt blveiee taht I cluod aulclty uesdnatnrd wahtI wsa rdanieg. It dseno't myaetr in what oerdr the ltteres in a wrod are in. Slpeling ins't ipmorant.[22]

Why could you read this? The mind does not let you read every letter, but lets you read the whole word. Having the first and last letter in the proper place is the key. The reason why you can easily understand the sentences is because of a habit. People are used to straightening our miscues, discovering hidden meanings, and the like because they have developed habitual ways of behaving.

Threats to Power and Influence

Some employees may view change as a threat to their power or influence. The control of something needed by others, such as information or resources, is a source of power in organizations. Once a power position has been established, individuals or teams often resist changes that they perceive as reducing their ability to influence others. When José Sergio Gabrielli de Azevedo took over as CEO of Petrobras, he was keenly aware of the environmental issues facing the company. Being an informal person, he preferred to go to inexpensive restaurants, wear jeans on casual Fridays to work, and wear his ID badge like other employees. Although his leadership style was genuine, it led to the perception that he lacked power and couldn't make difficult decisions. His informal style also raised questions when he was dealing with the powerful Brazilian government because Brazil has less of an individualistic culture and more of a collective culture with strong norms about the government's role in business. To undertake the change initiatives, he took the company private and thus prevented Petrobras from becoming a quasi-governmental company. Now the company didn't need to answer to stockholders, and governmental officials had less influence on the decisions made by top leaders.

Fear of the Unknown

Confronting the unknown makes most people anxious. Each major change in a work situation carries with it an element of uncertainty. When Merrill Fernando, Sri Lanka tea producer Dilmah's founder, decided to invest in tea shops to compete in the $70 billion global hot-beverage market, people thought he was crazy. Dilmah's major competitors, like Unilever whose Lipton brand has a 15 percent share of the world's tea market, and Associated British Foods, second with its Twinings tea at 6 percent market share, had tried and failed to compete

Dilmah's founder has had to face many unknown factors to make his "T-Bars" successful in the world market.

SENA VIDANAGAMA/AFP/GETTY IMAGES

successfully against Starbucks and other coffee shops. Dilmah's "T-Bars," as Fernando named them, are stand-alone, chic and trendy outlets targeting the Buddha bar set. He opened 65 T-Bars in Poland, Belarus, Kazakhstan, and other places where Starbucks had a lesser presence. He had to face many unknown factors, such as how to get the tea from the plantations to the shops in countries where roads are in poor conditions. He also found that in Colombo, roads were shut down for military security checks at random times, increasing the time it took tea to travel from the plantation to the shop. Oftentimes, a 100-mile trip took seven or more hours, making the tea less fresh because of the excessive heat. Similarly, worried shippers have abandoned Sri Lanka out of fear that their trucks will be attacked by warring tribes engaged in the country's civil war. Although Fernando has successfully overcome these unknowns, he is sure that he will face others.[23]

Economic Reasons

Money weighs heavily in people's considerations, and they certainly can be expected to resist changes that might lower their incomes. In a very real sense, employees have invested in the status quo in their jobs. That is, they have learned how to perform their work well, how to get good performance evaluations, and how to interact effectively with others. Changes in established work routines or job duties may threaten their economic security. Employees may fear that, after changes are made, they won't be able to perform as well and thus may not be as valuable to the organization, their supervisors, or their coworkers.

Sometimes the problems and dissatisfaction in a company are so serious that a general readiness for change exists. For instance, during the economic meltdown that began in late 2008, employees at the major global automobile manufacturers knew that major changes in wages and medical and retirement benefits were necessary if their organizations were to survive. However, the real challenge is for leaders to create a sense of readiness for change while things seem to be going well instead of after a company begins to experience problems. The following Self Competency feature can help you assess your readiness for change.[24] If your readiness score is low, what competencies do you need to develop to increase your readiness for change?

Self competency

Are You Ready to Change?

Instructions

Read each of the following statements and then use the scale shown to reflect your opinion. Record your answer in the blank at the left of the question's number.

1	2	3	4	5	6	7
Completely disagree			Neither agree nor disagree			Completely agree

_____1. I believe that an expert who doesn't come up with a definitive answer probably doesn't know too much.

_____2. I think it would be fun to live in a foreign country for a period of time.

_____3. The sooner we all agree on some common values and ideals, the better.

_____4. A good teacher is one who makes you wonder about your way of looking at things.

_____5. I enjoy parties where I know most of the people more than ones where all or most of the people are strangers.

_____6. A manager who hands out a vague assignment gives me a chance to show initiative and originality.

_____ 7. People who lead even, regular lives—in which few surprises or unexpected events arise—really have a lot to be grateful for.

_____ 8. Many of our most important decisions are actually based on insufficient information.

_____ 9. There is really no such thing as a problem that can't be solved.

_____ 10. People who fit their lives to a schedule probably miss most of the joy of living.

_____ 11. A good job is one in which what is to be done and how it is to be done are always clear.

_____ 12. It is more fun to tackle a complicated problem than to solve a simple one.

_____ 13. In the long run, it is possible to get more done by tackling small, simple problems than large, complicated ones.

_____ 14. Often the most interesting and stimulating people are those who don't mind being different or original.

_____ 15. What we are used to is always preferable to what is unfamiliar.

_____ 16. People who insist on a "yes" or "no" answer just don't know how complicated things really are.

Interpretation

To get your total score, you need to do several things. First, sum your responses to the *odd*-numbered items and write your score here: _____. Second, add 64 points to that score to create the first subtotal and record it here: _____. Third, sum your responses to the *even*-numbered items and write your score here: _____. Then subtract that number from the subtotal for the odd-numbered items to determine your overall score.

Your overall score is _____. Total scores may range from 16 to 112. The lower your overall score, the more willing you may be to deal with the uncertainty and ambiguity that typically go with change. Higher scores suggest a preference for more predictable and structured situations and indicate that you may not respond as well to change. Research data show scores typically range from 20 to 80, with a mean of 45. How does your score compare to these norms?

Reducing Resistance through Engagement

Buy-in can be a simple matter of being heard. When Randall Stephenson took over as CEO of AT&T in 2007, the firm faced a series of challenges. More than 31 million homes rely on AT&T for phone service, and every company on the *Fortune 500* list uses AT&T for data and phone connections. Stephenson recognized that this $124 billion dollar company, with more than 300,000 employees, needed to change. What was its main business? Local phone service was shrinking as cable operators continued to take customers. Competitors such as Verizon, Sprint, and Vonage were keeping prices low to attract customers.

To engage employees, Stephenson frequently sends text messages to thousands of employees and uses YouTube-style video e-mails to engage his employees. The former CEO, Ed Whitacre, didn't even have a computer in his office. To engage customers and listen to their concerns, Stephenson created a new global marketing position that was filled by a long-time employee, Cathy Coughlin. After listening to the concerns of millions of customers, she recommended that AT&T join with Apple to introduce a new mobile phone. Working with Apple, her team introduced the iPhone, a deal that allowed AT&T to lure 3 million customers away from competitors. Appealing specifically to the Gen Y users, Coughlin believes that customers want mobility. They use the web more because it's getting easier to access it from anywhere and the iPhone can access the web.[25]

Reducing Organizational Resistance

To a certain extent, the nature of organizations is to resist change. Organizations often are most efficient at doing routine tasks and tend to perform more inefficiently, at least initially, when doing something for the first time. Thus, to ensure operational efficiency and effectiveness, some organizations may create strong defenses against change. Moreover, change often opposes vested interests and violates certain territorial rights or decision-making prerogatives that departments, teams, and informal groups have established and accepted over time.

Organization Design

In Chapter 15, we discussed a variety of organization designs. We emphasized that organic organizations are more attuned to anticipating and responding to the need for change than mechanistic ones (see Table 15.1). Many leaders believe that organizations need stability and continuity in order to function effectively. Indeed, the term *organization* implies that the individual, team, and department have a certain structure. Individuals have assigned roles, established procedures for getting the job done, consistent ways of getting needed information, and the like. However, this legitimate need for structure also may lead to resistance to change. For example, in AOL's organization structure, employees were assigned to centralized departments according to function. When a new project began, leaders would assemble a team from those areas. Given "turf" battles between functions, decision making took a long time. In some instances, eight months elapsed before warring departments were able to make a decision. Because everything was decided by committee, there was little accountability when something went wrong. Many people couldn't identify their bosses. This design gave rise to a situation where self-preservation was more important than making a decision.[26]

Bureaucratic organizations have narrowly defined jobs, clearly identified lines of authority and responsibility, and a limited flow of information from top to bottom. These were the types of problems facing Sergio Marchionne when he took over Fiat. The use of a rigid design and an emphasis on the authority hierarchy caused employees to use only certain specific channels of communication and to focus narrowly on their own duties and responsibilities. Typically, the more mechanistic the organization, the more numerous are the levels through which an idea must travel (see Chapter 15). The mechanistic type of design, then, increases the probability that any new idea will be screened out because it threatens the status quo. More adaptive and flexible organizations are designed to reduce the resistance to change created by rigid organizational structures.

Organizational Culture

Organizational culture plays a key role in change. Cultures are not easy to modify and may become a major source of resistance to needed changes (see Chapter 16). One aspect of an effective organizational culture is whether it has the flexibility to take advantage of opportunities to change. An ineffective organizational culture (in terms of organizational change) is one that rigidly socializes employees into the old cultural values even in the face of evidence that they no longer work. As we noted in Chapter 16, a culture takes a long time to form and once it is established, it tends to become stable. Strong cultures, like those at Southwest Airlines, JCPenney, and IBM, are particularly resistant to change because employees have become committed to them and their behaviors are rewarded for following cultural norms.[27]

Resource Limitations

Some organizations want to maintain the status quo, but others would change if they had the resources to do so. Change requires capital, time, and individuals with a lot of competencies. At any particular time, an organization's leaders and employees may have identified changes that could or should be made, but they may have had to defer or abandon some of the desired changes because of resource limitations. The recent financial woes in the global automobile industry have forced companies to merge and/or seek government funding to sustain their operations. Similar resource limitations have hit companies in the senior housing (nursing homes) market, electronics, apparel, and other industries.

According to Jay Parkinson, cofounder of Hello Health, the U.S. health-care system is a $2.4 trillion industry run on handwritten notes. He has devised a Facebook-like platform that uses technology to restore doctor–patient relationships. A Canadian software company, Myca Health, has persuaded Parkinson to join them in an effort to market his system. Myca has developed a portal that requires no receptionist so that doctors greet patients as they arrive. Doctors using this platform set their own fees, and Myca takes a cut of each transaction. Patients pay a $35 monthly subscription fee and $100 to $200 an hour for online or office visits. Brief e-mail queries are free. Myca maintains that there is no shortage of companies looking for health-care options for employees that could eliminate lost productivity through absenteeism or waiting in doctor's offices. Companies are hoping that through President Obama's promise to invest $634 billion in health-care reform, companies will have the resources to invest in this system.[28]

Interorganizational Agreements

Agreements between organizations usually impose obligations on them that can restrain their actions. Labor negotiations and contracts provide some examples. Nike's relationship with colleges and various NFL teams precludes Adidas and other sporting apparel manufacturers from negotiating with them until the current Nike contract expires. Some universities, however, have recently dropped Nike because of their ability to negotiate better terms with Adidas. Ways of doing things that once were considered the rights of management (the right to hire and fire, assign tasks, promote and demote, and the like) may become subject to negotiation and fixed in a union–management contract.

Other types of contracts also may constrain organizations. For example, proponents of change may face delay because of arrangements with competitors, commitments to suppliers and other contractors, and pledges to public officials in return for licenses, permits, financing, or tax abatement. Several years ago when the Dallas Cowboys football team announced that it had plans to move to a new location in 2009 from its home in Irving, Texas, the city of Arlington, Texas, gave the team $325 million dollars as an inducement to choose Arlington to build their new $1.2 billion, 80,000-seat stadium. The city issued a bond for that amount. This arrangement requires that the Cowboys stay in the city for at least the next 30 years, play all their home games at that stadium, and pay $2 million dollars in rent (with increases depending on inflation) per year for the duration of the contract.[29]

Force Field Analysis

Realistically, resistance to change will never cease completely. Leaders and employees, however, can learn to identify and minimize resistance and thus become more effective change agents. People often have difficulty with clearly understanding situations that involve change. Part of the reason is because even the initial task of analyzing a change problem can be quite complex when a large number of variables must be considered.

Kurt Lewin, a pioneering social psychologist, developed a way of looking at change that has been highly useful for leaders and employees when faced with the challenge of change. Lewin viewed change not as an event but rather as a dynamic balance of forces working in opposite directions. His approach, called **force field analysis,** *suggests that any situation can be considered to be in a state of equilibrium resulting from a balance of forces constantly pushing against each other*. Certain forces in the situation—various types of resistance to change—tend to maintain the status quo. At the same time, various pressures for change are acting opposite to these forces. The combined effect of these two sets of forces is illustrated in Figure 17.3.[30]

To initiate change, an organization must take one or more of three actions to modify the current equilibrium of forces:

- Increase the strength of pressure for change.

FIGURE 17.3 Force Field Analysis

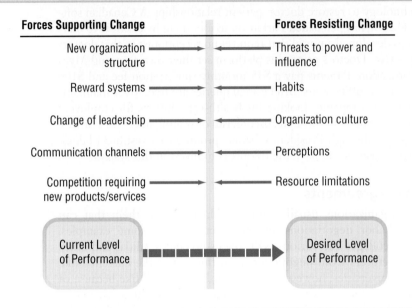

- Reduce the strength of the resisting forces or remove them completely from the situation.
- Change the direction of a force—for example, by changing a resistance into a pressure for change.

Change Insight

Changing the attitude and behavior of hundreds of thousands of people is very, very hard to accomplish. You cannot mandate it, or engineer it. What you can do is create the conditions for transformation by providing incentives, defining marketplace realities and goals. But at some point you must trust.

Lou Gerstner, Chairman, Carlyle Team

Using force field analysis to understand the process of change has two primary benefits. First, leaders and employees are required to analyze the current situation. By becoming competent at diagnosing the forces pressing for change and those resisting change, individuals should be able to understand better the relevant aspects of a change situation. Second, force field analysis highlights the factors that can be changed and those that cannot be changed. People typically waste time considering actions related to forces over which they have little, if any, control. When individuals and teams focus on the forces over which they do have some control, they increase the likelihood of being able to change the situation.

Of course, careful analysis of a situation doesn't guarantee successful change. For example, people in control have a natural tendency to increase the pressure for change to produce the change they desire. Increasing such pressure may result in short-run changes, but it also may have a high cost: Strong pressure on individuals and teams may create conflicts that disrupt the organization. Often the most effective way to make needed changes is to identify existing resistance to change and focus efforts on removing resistance or reducing it as much as possible.

An important part of Lewin's approach to changing behaviors consists of carefully managing and guiding change through a three-step process:

1. *Unfreezing.* This step usually involves reducing those forces that are maintaining the organization's behavior at its present level. Unfreezing is sometimes accomplished by introducing information to show discrepancies between behaviors desired by employees and behaviors they currently exhibit.

2. *Moving*. This step shifts the organization's behavior to a new level. It involves developing new behaviors, values, and attitudes through changes in organizational structures and processes.

3. *Refreezing*. This step stabilizes the organization's behavior at a new state of equilibrium. It is frequently accomplished through the use of supporting mechanisms that reinforce the new organizational state, such as organizational culture, norms, policies, and structures.

The following Change Competency feature illustrates how Target has been able to avoid the bankruptcy fate that Kmart, Caldor, Bradlees, and other department stores have suffered. Target was originally Dayton Hudson, a store started in 1909 by George Dayton. In 1962, the same year that Walmart and Kmart both began, Dayton Hudson changed its name to Target because the name suggested value and had a visual impact. Target has annual sales in excess of $65 billion that are generated from its 1,680 Target and SuperTarget stores. Target employs approximately 360,000 employees. Ninety-seven percent of Americans recognize Target's red bull's-eyed white dog.[31]

Change **competency**

Target

Gregg Steinhafel is the chairman, president, and chief executive officer of Target. He and his leadership team know that the United States' retail scene is dominated by Walmart, but Target has also been performing financially very well despite the recent recession. Why? First, Target's marketing department provides detailed information about which products are moving and where. To understand the consumer, Target created a "creative cabinet," a secret team of 12 diverse customers. Each of these members is asked to voice his or her opinion on products from Go International, a series of high-end designer clothes, to a new slimmed-down cereal box with a self-locking top. These members are a virtual team. The job of integrating their findings belongs to the marketing department. Along with this creative cabinet, Target uses its suppliers to figure out what should be on the shelves. In that way, Target hopes to gain highly creative ideas from non-Target sources. It was from these sources that Target decided to enter the grocery store business and introduce its own house brands (Archer Farms and Market Pantry).

To encourage a steady stream of bold new ideas, leaders vie against each other for portions of their budgets every year. The head of the

SCOTT OLSON/GETTY IMAGES

Target strives to deliver to customers a great experience and unique, exciting products.

marketing department holds back a huge percent of marketing dollars each year to be spent on new, bold, and creative advertising ideas, such as a temporary virtual store floating down the Hudson river and a fashion show where acrobats "walked" down the side of a building (*unfreezing*).

Steinhafel says that if Walmart wants to be known as the king of logistics with enough muscle to force vendors to deliver on price, Target wants to be known as the king that delivers a great experience and offers exciting products

that are unique to customers. To achieve this goal, old products lines have been discontinued and new ones added. Target's designers include Amy Coe (children's bedding and accessories), Liz Lange (maternity), and architect Michael Graves (housewares). It has created an online division (Target.com) for customers who want to shop online. Target is also trying to attract business-to-business customers and operates six showrooms that provide products and services for office environments (*moving*).

To learn more about Target, go to **www.target.com.**

Learning Goal

4. *Identify two key elements in organizational diagnosis.*

Organizational Diagnosis

Organizational diagnosis *is the process of assessing the functioning of the organization, department, team, or job to discover the sources of problems and areas for improvement.* It involves collecting data about current operations, analyzing those data, and drawing conclusions for potential change and improvement. An accurate diagnosis of organizational problems and functioning is absolutely essential as a starting point for planning organizational change.[32]

Information Needed

Information needed to diagnose organizational problems may be gathered by questionnaires, interviews, or observation—and from the organization's records. Typically, some combination of these data gathering methods is used. An advantage of the information collecting process is that it increases awareness of the need for change. Even with widespread agreement on the need for change, people may have different ideas about the approach to be used and when, where, and how it should be implemented.

To diagnose an organization, leaders need to have an idea about what information to collect and analyze. Choices on what to look for invariably depend on leaders' perceptions, the leadership practices used, how the organization is structured, its culture, and the like. Potential diagnostic models provide information about how and why certain organizational characteristics are interrelated. We illustrate one such model in Figure 17.4. Based on concepts presented throughout this book, this model illustrates how a change in one element usually affects others. For example, a change in an organization's reward system from one based on individual performance to a team-based system will affect the type of individuals joining the organization. ViewCast Corporation, a company that digitizes programming for transmission over the Internet, undertook such a reward system change because it reflected the needs that employees wanted to satisfy on the job, how leaders made decisions, the type of decisions that teams could make, the structure of the department or division, and the culture of the organization. The new reward system required that leaders from various product lines frequently communicate with each other and share best practices. It also helped change the culture from a market one to a clan culture.

Capacity for Change

Any planned change program also requires a careful assessment of individual and organizational capacity for change. Two important aspects of individual readiness for

FIGURE 17.4 Diagnostic Model of Change

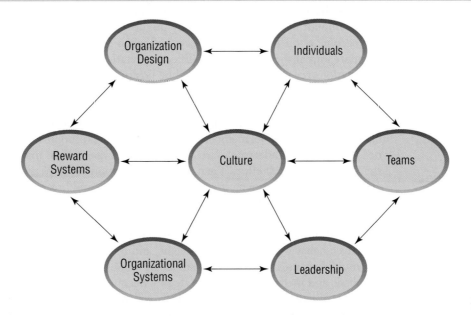

change are the degree of employee satisfaction with the status quo and the perceived personal risk involved in changing it. Figure 17.5 shows the possible combinations of these concerns. When employees are dissatisfied with the current situation and perceive little personal risk from change, their readiness for change probably would be high. In contrast, when employees are satisfied with the status quo and perceive high personal risk in change, their readiness for change probably would be low. This was the situation facing José Sergio Gabrielli de Azevedo when he took over as CEO of Petrobras. He created a sense of urgency by changing performance standards not only for Petrobras's employees, but its suppliers.

FIGURE 17.5 Employee Readiness for Change

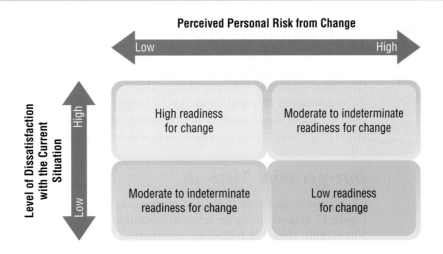

Source: Adapted from Zeira, Y., and Avedisian, J. Organizational planned change: Assessing the chances for success. *Organizational Dynamics*, Spring 1989, 37.

With regard to individual readiness for change, another important aspect is employee expectations regarding the change effort because expectations play a crucial role in behavior. If people expect that nothing of significance will change, regardless of the amount of time and effort they might devote to making it happen, this belief can become a self-fulfilling prophecy. And when employee expectations for improvement are unrealistically high, unfulfilled expectations can make matters worse. Ideally, expectations regarding change should be positive yet realistic.

In addition, the organization's capacity for change must be accurately assessed. Approaches that require a massive commitment of personal energy and resources from organizations (such as at Fiat and Hewlett-Packard) probably will fail if the organization has few resources and its members don't have the time or opportunity to implement the needed changes. Under such circumstances, the organization may benefit most from starting with a modest effort. Then, as the organization develops the necessary resources and employee commitment, it can increase the depth and breadth of the change.

When leaders and employees conduct an organizational diagnosis, they need to recognize two additional important factors. First, organizational behavior is the product of many things, as shown in Figure 17.4. Therefore, what is observed or diagnosed—employee behaviors, issues and problems, and the current state of the organization—has multiple causes. Trying to isolate single causes for complex problems can lead to simplistic and ineffective change strategies. Second, much of the information gathered about an organization during a diagnosis will represent symptoms rather than causes of problems. Obviously, change strategies that focus on symptoms won't solve underlying problems. For example, at one Marriott Hotel, an awards program that recognized perfect attendance failed to reduce absenteeism because it didn't deal with the causes of the problem. Careful diagnosis revealed that employees were absent from work because of poor bus service, lack of child care, and family pressures. The awards offered weren't sufficient to change employee behaviors and, more important, didn't address the employees' problems.[33]

Potential resistance to change represents another important aspect of readiness and motivation for change. Both individual and organizational resistance to change must be diagnosed. The main objective of planned organizational change is to alter the behavior of individuals within the organization. In the final analysis, organizations survive, grow, prosper, decline, or fail because of the things that employees do or fail to do. Behavior, therefore, should be a primary target of planned organizational change. In other words, to be successful, change programs must have an impact on employee roles, responsibilities, and working relationships.

Change Methods

Learning Goal

5. *Discuss three methods for promoting change.*

At some fundamental level, all organizational change depends on changes in behavior. Of course, managing effective change also depends on identifying specific aspects of the organization that will be the initial target of change efforts. We use Figure 17.4 from earlier in the chapter as an organizing framework to explore three methods for promoting change: interpersonal, team, and organizational.

Interpersonal Methods

Change programs that focus on interpersonal behavior (the *individual's* variable in Figure 17.4) tend to rely on active involvement and participation by many employees. Successfully changing behaviors can improve individual and team processes in decision making, problem identification, problem solving, communication, working relationships, and the like. Studies have shown that interpersonal methods for achieving change usually include the following components[34]:

1. *Empathy and support.* Understanding how employees are experiencing change is useful. It helps identify those who are troubled by the changes and helps management to understand the nature of their concerns. When employees feel that those managing change are open to their concerns, they are more willing to provide information. This openness, in turn, helps establish collaborative problem solving, which may overcome barriers to change.

2. *Communication.* People are more likely to resist change when they are uncertain about its consequences. Effective communication can reduce gossip, rumors, and unfounded fears. Adequate information helps employees prepare for change.

3. *Participation and involvement.* Perhaps the single most effective strategy for overcoming resistance to change is to involve employees directly in planning and implementing change. Involved employees are more committed to implementing the planned changes and more likely to ensure that they work than are employees who have not been involved.

One popular approach to focus on people who are having problems fitting in with others or dealing with change is to use survey feedback. We examine that approach next.

Survey Feedback

In **survey feedback** *information is (1) collected (usually by questionnaire) from members of an organization, department, or team; (2) organized into an understandable and useful form; and (3) fed back to the employees who provided it.*[35] In Chapter 9, we discussed how 360-degree feedback is used by leaders to improve the performance of employees; 360-degree feedback is just one form of survey feedback. It leads to a comprehensive assessment of an employee's performance and usually leads to change methods that increase the likelihood that the person's competencies will be taken into account. This information provides the basis for planning actions to deal with specific issues and problems.

The primary objective of all interpersonal methods is to improve the relationships among team members through the discussion of common problems, rather than to introduce a specific change, such as a new computer system. Leaders who want to use survey feedback design a questionnaire that is sent to all members of a company and/or department. The questionnaire typically asks members for their perceptions and attitudes on a broad range of issues, including communications, job satisfaction, satisfaction with one's supervisor, and the like. The diversity questionnaire in Table 17.2 is one such questionnaire.[36] This survey instrument is used by many organizations to understand the diversity of an organization and your level of comfort with diversity issues.

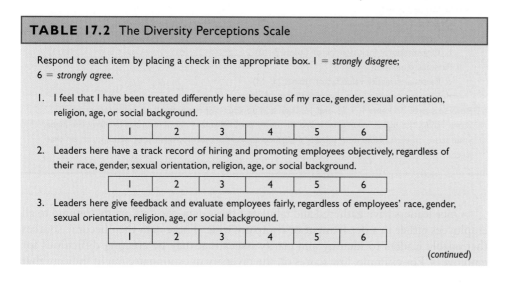

TABLE 17.2 The Diversity Perceptions Scale

Respond to each item by placing a check in the appropriate box. 1 = *strongly disagree;* 6 = *strongly agree.*

1. I feel that I have been treated differently here because of my race, gender, sexual orientation, religion, age, or social background.

1	2	3	4	5	6

2. Leaders here have a track record of hiring and promoting employees objectively, regardless of their race, gender, sexual orientation, religion, age, or social background.

1	2	3	4	5	6

3. Leaders here give feedback and evaluate employees fairly, regardless of employees' race, gender, sexual orientation, religion, age, or social background.

1	2	3	4	5	6

(continued)

TABLE 17.2 The Diversity Perceptions Scale (Continued)

4. Leaders here make layoff decisions fairly, regardless of factors such as employees' race, gender, sexual orientation, religion, age, or social background.

| 1 | 2 | 3 | 4 | 5 | 6 |

5. Leaders interpret human resource policies (such as sick leave) fairly for all employees.

| 1 | 2 | 3 | 4 | 5 | 6 |

6. Leaders give assignments based on the skills and abilities of employees.

| 1 | 2 | 3 | 4 | 5 | 6 |

7. Management here encourages the formation of employee network support groups.

| 1 | 2 | 3 | 4 | 5 | 6 |

8. There is a mentoring program in use here that identifies and prepares all minority and female employees for promotion.

| 1 | 2 | 3 | 4 | 5 | 6 |

9. The "old boys' network" is alive and well here.

| 1 | 2 | 3 | 4 | 5 | 6 |

10. The company spends enough money and time on diversity awareness and related training.

| 1 | 2 | 3 | 4 | 5 | 6 |

11. Knowing more about the cultural norms of diverse groups would help me be more effective in my job.

| 1 | 2 | 3 | 4 | 5 | 6 |

12. I think that diverse viewpoints add value.

| 1 | 2 | 3 | 4 | 5 | 6 |

13. I believe diversity is a strategic business issue.

| 1 | 2 | 3 | 4 | 5 | 6 |

14. I feel at ease with people from backgrounds different from my own.

| 1 | 2 | 3 | 4 | 5 | 6 |

15. I am afraid to disagree with members of other groups for fear of being called prejudiced.

| 1 | 2 | 3 | 4 | 5 | 6 |

16. Diversity issues keep some work teams here from performing to their maximum effectiveness.

| 1 | 2 | 3 | 4 | 5 | 6 |

Scoring

This scale measures two dimensions—the organizational and the personal—each of which contains two factors as follows:

   I. Organizational dimension
      a. Organizational fairness factor (items 1–6)
      b. Organizational inclusion factor (items 7–10)
   II. Personal dimension
      c. Personal diversity value factor (items 11–13)
      d. Personal comfort with diversity (items 14–16)

Reverse scores on items 1, 9, 15, and 16. Then add up your responses to all 16 items (maximum score = 96). The higher your total score, the more positive your view of diversity. Similarly, the higher your score on each of the item subsets described above, the more positive your perceptions on that factor.

Once leaders have gathered and tabulated these data, the data are distributed to all employees either in a department or company wide. These data then become sources that enable leaders to identify and clarify issues that may be creating difficulties for employees. For example, low scores on the diversity questionnaire might indicate that employees of different ages, races, and ethnic backgrounds do not feel welcome in the organization and believe that leaders of the organization treat people differently based on their diversity. Leaders then may pay special attention to supporting activities that surround these diversity issues. For example, if your organization scores low, some possible solutions are to change the colleges that the organization interviews with to be more inclusive in interviewing job candidates (e.g., interviewing at historically African American and women's colleges), making promotion and salary raise decisions based on objective facts and not stereotypes, and making sure management supports diverse employees' groups. For example, to promote employees' diversity awareness, JCPenney has members of various diversity groups celebrate holidays in its cafeteria. All employees are encouraged to attend these events. If you scored low on the diversity perceptions scale, you might attend meetings with a diverse set of employees, eat with people of different races and gender while at work, or join social groups that cater to people who hold widely differing beliefs. Because of its value in organizational diagnosis, survey feedback often is utilized as part of large-scale, long-term change programs in combination with other approaches and techniques.

Team Methods

The purpose of team methods is to get a handle on team performance problems.[37] Team performance is influenced by the competencies of its members, organizational structure, the organization's reward system, organizational culture, and other factors. When these factors have been successfully implemented, teams can go from merely being working groups to high-performing teams, as illustrated in Figure 17.6.

Team methods are designed to improve interpersonal relationships among team members, clarify each member's role and responsibilities, and reveal dysfunctional team behaviors that are hindering the team's overall performance. You might wish to review the materials in the chapter on teams (Chapter 12) for more information on the characteristics of successful teams and how leaders can change the behaviors of team members to become more effective.

Team Building

In **team building**, *team members diagnose how they work together and plan changes to improve their effectiveness.* Team building begins when members recognize a problem.[38] An effective team can recognize barriers to its own effectiveness and design and take actions to remove them. During team building, members of the team contribute information concerning their perceptions of issues, problems, and working relationships. Usually information is gathered during team meetings or prior to meetings, using interviews or questionnaires. Leaders then analyze the information and diagnose work-related problems. Using problem diagnosis as the starting point, team members plan specific actions and assign individuals to implement them.

At some later stage, team members evaluate their plans and progress to determine whether their actions solved the problems identified. As team effectiveness grows, the potential impact on organizational performance increases. Another good way to define team building is that it consists of the activities designed to move the team up the performance curve shown in Figure 17.6.

Insights for Leaders

The goal of many team-building methods is to change the culture of the organization. In Chapter 16, we explored changing organizational culture and pointed out just how difficult such changes can be. Among other issues and problems, just assessing accurately the organization's culture before any plans for changes can be developed may be a daunting task. In addition, some aspects of culture (e.g., the deepest core values shared by employees) may be almost impossible to change.

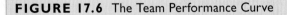

FIGURE 17.6 The Team Performance Curve

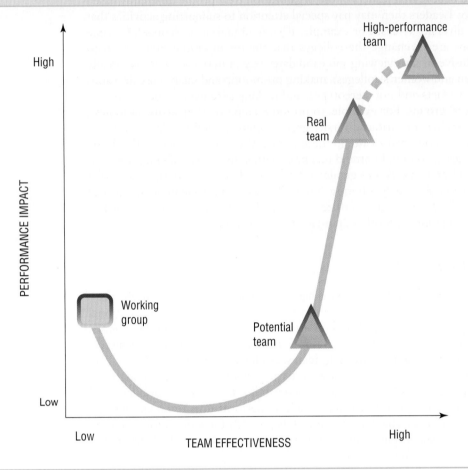

Source: Adapted from Katzenbach, J. R., and Smith, D. K. *The Wisdom of Teams*. Boston: Harvard Business School Press, 1993, 84.

Despite these challenges, some organizations have successfully changed their cultures. How did they do it? A detailed examination of successful cultural change suggests that the odds for success can be increased by giving attention to seven main issues:

1. *Capitalize on dramatic opportunities.* The organization needs to take advantage of the moment when obvious problems or challenges that are not being met "open the door" to needed change. When Sergio Marchionne took over the leadership of Chrysler, everyone knew that a change was needed in order for Chrysler to survive.

2. *Combine caution with optimism.* Leaders and employees need to be optimistic with regard to the advantages of cultural change; otherwise they will be unwilling to make the attempt. Yet, because cultural change can have negative impacts, the organization needs to proceed with caution. Expectations for improvement must be positive, yet realistic.

3. *Understand resistance to cultural change.* Resistance to change needs to be diagnosed. Identifying and reducing sources of resistance is valuable in cultural change as well as in other change programs.

4. *Change many elements but maintain some continuity.* "Don't throw the baby out with the bathwater" is a common saying that sums up the importance of recognizing what is of value and retaining it. Southwest Airlines has grown and prospered

since its founding in the early 1970s, yet it managed to retain the core of cultural ideas and beliefs that Herb Kelleher instilled when he founded the organization. Although Kelleher is no longer involved in the day-to-day operations, CEO Gary Kelly and other long-time employees have been able to sustain the culture that Kelleher created.

5. *Recognize the importance of implementation.* A survey indicated that more than 90 percent of planned changes in strategy and culture are never fully implemented. A large percentage of failed change programs are failures of implementation rather than failures of ideas. Management needs to recognize that having a vision and a plan, although important, are only part of the battle. Planned changes must be carried through.

6. *Modify socialization tactics.* Socialization is the primary way in which people learn about a culture (see Chapter 16). Thus, changing socialization processes can be an effective approach to implementing cultural change.

7. *Find and cultivate innovative leadership.* Cultural change must begin at the top of the organization, and good leadership is crucial. When Robert Fornaro took over as CEO of AirTran in 2007, the airline was in financial trouble. Today, it is one of the low-cost airlines that is making money. He focused on cutting costs, flying lucrative short-haul flights, adding routes to smaller markets, and buying fuel-efficient Boeing 737s and 717s. AirTran differentiates itself from its competitors, such as Southwest and JetBlue, which fly point-to-point routes, by having Atlanta as its hub and by providing reserved seats and business-class service. It also doesn't fly long-haul flights from major markets like New York and Los Angeles, but instead focuses on flying to Orlando and other Florida cities. Another way in which AirTran differentiates itself from its competitors and maintains its low costs is through cross-training of its employees to perform multiple jobs. When Zakiya Cheris, for example, an employee based in Philadelphia, moves from the counter to the conveyor belt to the runway at the airport, she is helping the airline reduce its labor costs.[39]

Organizational Methods

In the past decade, a large number of organizations have radically changed how they operate to satisfy customers' demands. Increased competition has forced many organizations to downsize, become leaner and more efficient, and be flexible. Organizations are unlikely to undertake major organizational changes unless there are compelling reasons to do so. Power, habit, culture, and vested interests are organization-wide norms that are difficult to change. Many organizations, such as General Motors, Citigroup, and Bank of America, had to experience a severe threat to their survival before they were motivated to undertake such change.[40]

Organization-wide change programs frequently are aimed at changing an organization's design, reward systems, culture, and organizational systems. Approaches to change that focus on organizational methods involve redefining positions or roles and relationships among positions and redesigning departmental, divisional, and/or organizational structure. Unfortunately, implementing design or structural change has sometimes been used as an excuse for organizations simply to downsize their workforces without identifying and exploring the reasons for inefficiency and poor performance.

A key feature of organizational change methods is the active role of top leaders in all phases of the change process. Because leaders are responsible for the strategic direction and operation of the organization, they decide when to initiate such changes, what the changes should be, how they should be implemented, and who should be responsible for implementing them. In organizations undergoing organization-wide changes, senior leaders need to play three roles:

- *Envisioning.* Top management must articulate a clear and credible vision for the change. They must also set new standards of performance.

- *Energizing.* Top management must demonstrate personal excitement for the changes and model behaviors that are expected of others. They must constantly communicate with all employees.
- *Enabling.* Top management must provide the resources necessary for undertaking significant change and use rewards to reinforce new behaviors.[41]

Organization-wide change needs to start with senior leaders taking charge and supporting these change programs. One of the problems facing senior leaders of global corporations is being able to attract and retain a highly diverse group of people to work for them. As baby boomers retire and Gen Y individuals enter the workforce, new diversity practices will be needed for organizations to remain competitive. Organizations that succeed in managing diversity do so because senior leaders are committed to achieving compliance, instituting a positive organizational culture, and using diversity to create a more successful organization. As organizations compete for the best talent from all cultures and genders, companies strive to be rated by business magazines as one of the best places to work, says Ossie Reid, director for diversity at United Technologies. To achieve that, United Technologies has to offer a culturally diverse environment for its more than 223,000 employees. In response to changing employee demographics, the company introduced diversity programs in the early 1990s and received the Department of Labor's Opportunity 2000 award for advancement of women and minorities in the workforce. The following Communication Competency feature describes an organization-wide change program at United Technologies that was led by Thomas Bowler, senior vice president of human resources and organization. United Technologies provides high-tech products and support to aerospace industries and the building-system industry. Its headquarters are located in Hartford, Connecticut.[42]

Communication competency

United Technologies' Diversity Programs

At United Technologies, leaders aim to create an environment that accommodates cultural, religious, and intellectual diversity. They want to make sure everyone has an opportunity to participate in the organization, regardless of gender, background, or race. The goals for its diversity program are to:

- make all associates feel valued,
- provide an inclusive environment,
- remove attitudinal barriers, and
- build community.

To achieve these goals, United Technologies uses a variety of diversity and communication practices. During succession planning, a diversity manager participates in the discussions to ensure that a diverse pool of associates is considered for career advancement. The company also provides all leaders with performance appraisal training to help them make judgments that accurately reflect each associate's performance and contributions. The firm sponsors mentoring networks and also forums and symposia for women and minorities. At these forums, senior leaders, such as Thomas Bowler, CEO Louis Chênevert, and Ari Bousbib, executive vice president for commercial companies, are usually in attendance to address the associates and answer questions. To attract associates, United Technologies partners with organizations such as the National Society of Black Engineers, the National Society of Hispanic MBAs, and the Society of Women Engineers. Since the start of its diversity programs in the 1990s, the percentage of women in executive positions has increased more than 60 percent and the percentage of people of color in managerial positions has increased 35 percent.

As United Technologies' workforce changes, the company's efforts to build a diverse inclusive culture will evolve. George David, chairman, states: "We must treasure openness in every single thing we do, from ideas to beliefs to people. This is the business benefit of strong and committed diversity in our ranks. It's also a personal benefit, because this is how we learn. We remain totally committed to diversity within our workforce and to opportunities for advancement for all. I expect our entire senior leadership team to value and practice these beliefs. When our associates know that senior leaders 'walk the talk,' change will happen."

To learn more about United Technologies, go to **www.utc.com**.

Chapter Summary

A rapidly changing environment places many demands on leaders and employees, including the need to plan for and manage organizational change effectively. Pressures for change stem from globalization, the increasing use of information technology as a communication channel, the rise in the number of powerful social networking groups, and the mixing of different generations of employees in many organizations. Each of these pressures for change requires leaders to adapt their behaviors in order to achieve their organization's goals.

1. Identify key pressures for change.

The two major approaches to achieving planned organizational change are economic and interpersonal. The economic approach focuses on changing the organization's design, reward system, and technology to achieve change and improve stockholder value. The organizational development approach focuses on the development of employees' interpersonal competencies. This approach requires employees and leaders to become emotionally involved with the organization and be committed to its values and goals. Many successful planned change programs sequence these two basic approaches, starting first with the economic and then shifting to the organizational development approach.

2. Discuss the nature of planned organizational change.

Individuals may resist change because of their perceptions or personalities. In addition, habits, threats to established power and influential relationships, fear of the unknown, and economic insecurities may generate further resistance to change. Organizational resistance to change may be caused by organizational design and culture, resource limitations, and interorganizational agreements. By performing a force field analysis, various resistances to change can be explored in more detail.

3. Identify common reasons for individual and organizational resistance to change.

Organizational diagnosis involves collecting information about the change and then developing the organization's capacity to change. Oftentimes employees have information about needed changes but are reluctant to share this information for fear of looking foolish or not being rewarded for making suggestions. An organization's capacity for change focuses on leaders creating a sense of urgency to break the status quo and managing employees' expectations about the change.

4. Identify two key elements in organizational diagnosis.

Three methods are available for promoting organizational change: interpersonal, team, and organizational. The interpersonal method focuses on changing employees' behaviors so that they can become more effective performers. This method usually involves some use of survey feedback. The team method focuses on ways to improve the performance of entire teams, and team-building activities are its foundation. The organizational method is aimed at changing the organization's structure, reward system, level at which decisions are made, and the like.

5. Discuss three methods for promoting change.

Key Terms and Concepts

Economic approach, **516**
Force field analysis, **525**
Globalization, **511**
Organizational development approach, **516**

Organizational diagnosis, **528**
Planned organizational change, **515**
Survey feedback, **531**
Team building, **533**

Discussion Questions

1. Go to www.petrobras.com, click on "About us," and read about the oil company. What are the key pressures for change reported in these statements?
2. From your answers on the diversity questionnaire in Table 17.2, what competencies might you need to develop to increase your diversity competency? What action steps do you plan to take? How will others know that you have taken these?
3. Why is organizational diagnosis essential to the success of any change effort?
4. Think of a situation in which someone asked you to change your behavior. Did you change? Why or why not?
5. Rosabeth Kanter, a leading authority on change, stated that trying to change an organization is like trying to teach elephants to dance. Why is changing an organization's direction so difficult?
6. Based on the discussion about force field analysis, why is it hard for people to lose weight and keep it off?
7. From your own experience, describe a team, department, or organization that needed to change. Which of the change approaches presented in this chapter was used? Was it successful?
8. Identify and describe an ethical dilemma or issue created by some organizational change effort with which you are familiar. How was the ethical problem handled? What, if anything, would you do differently?
9. After reading the Communication Competency about United Technologies, identify the key behaviors demonstrated by senior leaders to reinforce the company's diversity programs.
10. Rahm Emanuel, White House chief of staff for President Obama, said: "You never want a serious crisis to go to waste because it gives leaders a tremendous opportunity to make difficult, yet necessary, organizational changes." Do you agree or disagree with this statement?

Experiential Exercise and Case

Experiential Exercise: Self Competency[43]

Assessing an Organization's Readiness for Change

Instructions

This questionnaire is designed to help you understand the level of support or opposition to change within an organization. Please respond to each of the following 16 items according to how true it is in terms of an organization with which you are familiar. Circle the appropriate number on the scale that follows the question.

3 = Yes
2 = Somewhat
1 = No

1. Is the change effort being sponsored by top management?
   3 2 1
2. Are all levels of management committed to the change?
   3 2 1
3. Does the organization's culture encourage change?
   3 2 1

4. Does the organization reward continuous improvement?
   3 2 1
5. Has top management clearly stated the reason for change?
   3 2 1
6. Has top management presented a clear vision of the future?
   3 2 1
7. Does the organization use objective indicators to measure its performance?
   3 2 1
8. Does the change effort support other major ongoing activities in the organization?
   3 2 1
9. Has the organization benchmarked itself against world-class organizations?
   3 2 1
10. Do all employees understand the customers' needs?
    3 2 1
11. Does the organization reward employees for being innovative and looking for causes of problems?
    3 2 1
12. Is the organization's design adaptable?
    3 2 1

13. Do senior leaders communicate effectively to all
    employees?   3 2 1
14. Has the organization recently implemented a successful
    change?   3 2 1
15. Do employees assume responsibility for their own
    behavior?   3 2 1
16. Do senior leaders make decisions quickly?   3 2 1

Norms:
40–48 = High readiness for change
24–39 = Moderate readiness for change
16–23 = Low readiness for change

Questions
1. What type of change program (economic or organizational development) might work best in your
   organization?
2. Depending on your score, what are some individual
   and organizational resistances to change that you might
   encounter when making changes in your organization?
   How do you plan to overcome these?
3. What ethical problems might you face when implementing changes in your organization?

Case: Communication Competency

Carolyn Bivens: Change Agent at the Ladies Professional Golf Association[44]

In 2005 when Carolyn Bivens became commissioner of the Ladies Professional Golf Association (LPGA), she was surprised to learn that 70 percent of tournaments were losing money. Many of these events hardly compensated the tour for its support. She also inherited unsigned contracts and different financial practices for different tournaments. She was also shocked to see the differences between the PGA and LPGA. At many events, women forego the smaller women's locker rooms to use the more spacious men's locker rooms, where pots of geraniums sometimes disguise urinals. The difference between winning a PGA event and an LPGA event often approaches 1 million dollars.

Having a deficit was not an option that Bivens could live with. She moved quickly and unilaterally, bluntly telling tournament owners that they needed to pay for services rendered. In some cases, fees were raised from $15,000 to $100,000. Tournament sponsors balked at the increase and some left, including Corning Glass, who had been a sponsor of the Corning Glass tournament for more than 31 years, and McDonald's. Corning Classic's sponsorship dollars had declined more than 20 percent and Corning's board chairman, Jack Benjamin, said, "We want to be part of the LPGA, but I want to make sure that everybody understands this—if the revenue side of the ledger does not match with the expense side—we cannot support the LPGA." Even long-time partner Anheuser-Busch, sponsor of the Michelob Ultra Classic, is rethinking its sponsorship.

Bivens has been described as the proverbial bull in a china shop, causing controversy since she replaced Charlie Mechem, whom players called affectively "Uncle Charlie." To keep the LPGA on solid financial footing, after looking at each event's profits and losses and severing ties with long-time sponsors, she found new sponsors who were willing to pay bigger purses. For example, she secured Ginn as a sponsor for two new LPGA events and touted the real estate developer as a new partner who could offer the bigger purses that her players deserved. She moved some long-standing tournament dates around to satisfy Ginn, causing some long-time sponsors to question her judgment. Unfortunately, when the real estate market crashed in 2008 and 2009, Ginn foreclosed on its

tournament commitments. Bivens has battled the media over control of image rights, and imposed an English-proficiency policy for the tour's international players. She took the latter action to make the tour and its players more marketable. This action caused such an uproar that she had to rescind the policy.

Bivens maintains a vision that she can make the LPGA a model for 21st-century sports organizations. She landed a 10-year deal with the Golf Channel that is worth between $3 and $4 million a year depending on the tour's ability to get TV sponsors. Historically, the LPGA has jumped among channels, on network and cable, making it difficult to develop a fan following. She is also working on improving the meager LPGA pension plan. Currently, the LPGA has no medical benefits for its members. She is planning to leverage the LPGA brand by going international. She signed a five-year broadcasting-rights tour exclusive contract with J. Golf, a South Korean TV company, for more than $4 million dollars a year. This was a major feat during the recession of 2009 when most companies dramatically cut sports marketing programs. In 2009, she traveled to India, Abu Dhabi, and Dubai to determine interest in those countries. She says that players will have to adjust to a globetrotting schedule if that's what it takes to make the tour financially viable.

For the most part, the LPGA doesn't own its events; it extends contracts to third parties to host them. But in 2010, the LPGA will own its major championship, the LPGA Championship. Unfortunately, McDonald's has ended its sponsorship of that event and many now question Bivens' ability to raise more than $3 million to stage it. The loss of sponsors and rising operating costs is taking its toll on other LPGA tour events as well. The title sponsorship of a regular PGA tour event, such as the HP Byron Nelson or Shell Houston Open, costs $6 to $8 million annually (including a TV commitment of $3 million). Sixty-eight percent of the LPGA tour's future events do not have sponsors. That means that the tour's schedule is cloaked with uncertainty. In fact, Bivens says that "it's high risk and high reward" time for the LPGA.

Adding to the LPGA's challenge is the recent backlash against golf sponsorships in general. Bivens knows that companies still want the business opportunities that tournaments create, but with less fanfare and spectacle to avoid public backlash. At the 2009 Michelob Ultra Open at Kingsmill, Virginia, for example, Anheuser-Busch cancelled its annual champions' dinner, which mingles past champions with Anheuser-Busch executives, because InBev, the Belgian brewer than now owns Anheuser-Busch, thought that such expense was not needed. Even so, Bivens believes that the LPGA's hospitality benefits will save the LPGA. It is the networking that occurs in the Wednesday pro-amateur rounds that cannot be duplicated anywhere else. "The fact that a sponsor can spend five hours with its biggest three or four customers away from the office is something that money can't buy," she says. The LPGA pro-ams are played in a scramble format, ensuring participants the opportunity to share their experience with their LPGA hosts. Because of all these issues, in July 2009 Bivens resigned her position as commissioner of the LPGA.

Questions

1. Which forces facing Bivens supported change and which resisted change?
2. Did she use an economic or an organizational development approach to create change? Was it effective?
3. Using the diagnostic model for change in Figure 17.4, analyze the factors affecting the LPGA.

part 5

Integrating Cases

A Day in the Life of Yolanda Valdez

Yolanda Valdez, senior vice president for marketing of ClearVision Optical Group, arrived at her office at 7:25 A.M. Settling in at her desk, she began to think about the problems she needed to handle in the course of the day.

ClearVision Optical Group is a specialty retailer operating under the name of ClearVue with annual sales of over $20 million. The optical group owns 750 stores in 40 states, Canada, Mexico, Puerto Rico, The Netherlands, and England. It is the United States' largest provider of eye care products and services, and it seeks to expand its market share in other free world countries. ClearVision is one group of S. G. Davis, an Illinois-based company that also has pharmaceutical and medical product groups. The optical group is planning to expand into other broadly based health-care markets, and in 2010 it began experimenting with small shops that sell only sunglasses. ClearVision is a marketing-oriented company that bases its strategy on understanding customer needs and developing and delivering distinctive characteristics that appeal to customers. An example of this is ClearVue's in-store labs that cut lenses for eyeglass frames on a "while-you-wait" basis, often getting the customer's prescription filled within an hour. This service differentiates ClearVue from its competitors, who typically do not offer such speedy service.

Valdez' duties as senior vice president for marketing broadly include determination and evaluation of the strategic and operational directions for the company. Her specific responsibilities include marketing research, advertising programs, the eyeglass frame line, contact lenses, and in-store merchandising-display programs.

A high-priority item on Valdez' list of things to accomplish today was to construct a questionnaire to survey customer attitudes about the firm's line of frames. This was to be circulated to each of ClearVue's retail store managers to determine whether the current frame styles were preferred by customers and if the selection of frames was adequate at each price level. Valdez realized that she would have a greater likelihood of uninterrupted work before most of the other employees came at 8:30, so she began working on the questionnaire at 7:45. She had scarcely begun clarifying her definition of the problem and stating her objectives when her secretary, Linda Brown, came in with a list of activities planned for the day.

A meeting with the research analysis group working on contact lenses was scheduled for 9:15. There was another meeting set for 10:15 with the group working on fall displays for use in the stores. Valdez was scheduled to lunch with a representative of a prospective advertising agency at 12:00, and she had an appointment with the president at 3:00 P.M. to discuss progress on an evaluation of the firm's frame suppliers. She told her secretary she needed some letters typed and put in the mail before the afternoon and a summary of the supplier evaluation typed before her meeting with the president. Her secretary reminded Valdez that the vice president for finance wanted to see her that day to discuss the details of financing for the new sunglass stores.

When Linda left, Valdez settled back to work on the questionnaire. She outlined what she hoped to accomplish and wrote down a list of specific pieces of information she wanted to get from the store managers. At 8:20 the senior vice president for operations in the Western Division called and asked Valdez if she could get a cup of coffee with him and discuss some new ideas he had for marketing children's eyewear. Yolanda agreed to meet him in five minutes. They discussed the plans she was currently considering and how the new suggestions would modify those plans. As she was walking back to her office at 8:45, a woman who worked in the optical lab on the premises asked her if she could give her some advice. Yolanda said she could spare a moment. The woman questioned her on career opportunities in marketing, both in the company and in the entire field. She confessed that she had wanted to get more training and go into marketing, but had never taken the opportunity. Yolanda told her about her experiences in the field and advised her about the best route to take to get into the company's marketing department. After she left, Valdez called the president and asked for his opinion of a major new advertising and display campaign for children's eyewear based on the suggestions she had received. They discussed various ways in which the advertising budget could be reallocated to finance such a campaign. They decided that some funds could be taken from fashion eyewear programs, and some additional money could be trimmed from other elements of the budget and allocated to this campaign. The president mentioned that he would like to see the ideas Valdez had for this campaign before they were sent to an advertising agency.

As Valdez hung up, she realized it was time for the meeting with the contact lens group. She walked into the conference room and sat down at the head of the table. She chatted informally with a few of the people in the group before they got down to business. Valdez listened to their presentation, and after they were finished, she stated some new ideas on the situation and thanked them for the results. She set some goals for the contact lens group that she wanted accomplished before the next meeting. This meeting was over at 10:15, and the group working on fall store displays came in for their meeting. Valdez told them about the children's eyewear. The meeting ended at 11:20.

As Valdez walked out of the conference room, she was stopped by a man from the display group. He talked to Valdez for a few moments about some ideas he had for different types of displays for the sunglass stores. Then he hesitated for a moment and asked Valdez if he could speak to her about a situation that had been troubling him. Valdez said she would like to help with the problem if possible. The man told her that he had been experiencing conflict with his team leader in the display group: He felt she had not been allowing free expression of ideas and "had it in" for him. The man admitted that he did not know how to cope with the situation and had been considering looking for another job. Valdez promised to look into the matter further.

When she returned to her office and found a stack of phone messages waiting for her, she first returned the call of the vice president for finance and arranged to meet with him at 1:30. She also returned the call of the vice president for manufacturing. He needed to talk to her about manufacturing problems with one of the new specialty lenses, so they set up a time to discuss the problem at 2:00. Leaving the rest of the messages on her desk, Valdez left for her lunch appointment with the ad agency representative. At lunch, she discussed plans for network TV advertising and asked for ideas and strategies for effective new messages and the most effective timing for ads. All the time, she was attempting to evaluate whether or not ClearVision should hire this new agency for its next campaign. Since this would be ClearVision's first use of network TV advertising, it was a particularly important decision.

Valdez was back in her office at 1:15. She made some routine calls to subordinates to check on their progress on certain projects until 1:30. Then the vice president for finance came in to discuss the acquisition of an existing chain of sunglass stores. They talked about integrating these stores into ClearVision Optical Group's strategic plan until Keisha Jackson, the vice president for personnel, knocked on the door. The vice president for finance stayed to hear what Jackson had to say, and the three discussed possible solutions to the new company employee benefits program.

Both vice presidents left at 2:30. Valdez collected her phone messages and began returning calls. She had just finished talking with a frame supplier representative in New York and an ad agency reporting the completion of a print ad campaign for the next quarter when she had to leave for her meeting with the president. Valdez talked with him for half an hour about expansion strategy and another half-hour about her evaluation of the frame suppliers the firm was currently using.

At 4:00 Valdez went back to her office and found a report on her desk about an inventory control model that gave appropriate purchase quantities and intervals for the current frame line. One of her subordinates in the frame management group had researched the matter and felt that frame purchasing could be more efficient. Valdez recalled that she had told the man to come up with a better method if he could, and this report gave his findings on the matter. Valdez read the report carefully and thought about its implications. She called the man in and asked him to explain some aspects of the model more clearly. They discussed how the model would work in practice and the dollar savings that would result from it. The man left Valdez' office at 4:45, and Valdez began working on the frame line questionnaire again. Five minutes later, Linda Brown came in with some letters for her to sign and some personnel evaluations the head of personnel had sent over to be filled out. She decided to forget about the questionnaire and work on it at home, where she was less likely to be interrupted. She worked on the performance evaluations until 5:45, when she packed her papers in her briefcase and headed for home.

Questions

1. What competencies are illustrated in the case?
2. Using the Communication Inventory presented as an Experiential Exercise with Chapter 9, evaluate Valdez' communication effectiveness. In what area(s) does she excel?
3. Is Valdez an effective team leader?

Alan Mulally, CEO, Ford Motor Company

Alan Mulally, who was hired as CEO of Ford in September 2006, had not engineered, designed, or built any cars. He came from Boeing. After joining Ford, he devised a plan that identified specific goals for the company, created a process that moved it toward those goals, and installed a management system to make sure the company reaches those goals. Mulally demands weekly, sometimes daily, updates. "Alan's style is pretty relentless," says chief financial officer Lewis Booth, a 31-year Ford veteran. "He says, 'If this is the reality, what are we going to do about it?' not 'We're going to work our way through it.'"

Mulally's leadership has resulted in Ford making some strategic moves. When Mulally arrived in September 2006, Ford was known mainly for its pickup trucks and the Mustang. The company was on the verge of financial collapse. It lost $12.6 billion in 2006 and another $2.7 billion in 2007. Sensing a recession in 2006, Mulally decided to borrow $23 billion against Ford's assets. Taking on more debt wasn't easy, but the extra cash meant that Ford could say no to government loans when sales declined in 2008 and 2009. He wants Ford to maintain its independence.

Mulally is moving to integrate the company globally, despite several failed attempts in the past. In 2010, Ford will be selling small cars (e.g., Fiesta and Focus) in the United States that were developed in Europe. Mulally persuaded Bill Ford to sell off Jaguar and Land Rover and focus its resources on the Ford brand. He sold Jaguar, Aston Martin, and Land Rover to India's Tata in 2007 when there was still a market for makers of luxury vehicles, and he has been trying to sell Volvo. Mulally felt that these cars were a "dangerous" distraction from Ford's core business. Mulally believes that fewer models mean better economies of scale and significantly improved profitability.

Mulally's decisions have helped Ford separate itself from its major competitors, GM and Chrysler/Fiat. "As we come through this recession of 2008–2009, we're going to be a turbo machine when the economy turns around," he says. He has promised that Ford's core North American operations, as well as the entire company, will be profitable by 2011. It had better, because it can't keep losing money indefinitely while GM and Chrysler/Fiat recover with the help of loans from the federal government. Ford recorded a loss of $14.7 billion in 2008 and another $1.4 billion in 2009's first quarter. If the U.S. and other global economies continue to slump, Ford's survival could be in question. "The test of Ford's profitability will be how low vehicle sales go this year, when they recover, and what levels they recover to in 2010 and 2011," notes analyst Shelly Lombard of Gimme Credit.

If the economy recovers in 2010, Ford will be in a good competitive position. To meet stricter government fuel-economy standards, it is introducing a line of more efficient cars such as the Ford Fusion, Focus, and Fiesta. It will start manufacturing electric cars in 2010. Mulally hopes that Ford will be able to take business from GM and Chrysler/Fiat. Goldman Sachs' Patrick Archambault sees Ford picking up 25 percent of the sales the two competitors have lost, the equivalent of 1.4 points of market share.

So how does an industry outsider like Mulally come into a company as large as Ford—with its 205,000 employees, multiple product lines, and international operations—and straighten it out? "I arrived here, and the first day I said, 'Let's go look at the product lineup.' And they laid it out. I said, 'Where's the Taurus?' Senior leaders said, 'Well, we killed it.' I said, 'What do you mean, you killed it?' 'Well, we made a couple that looked like a football. They didn't sell very well, so we stopped it.' 'You stopped the Taurus?' I said. 'How many billions of dollars does it cost to build brand loyalty around a name?' 'Well, we thought it was so damaged that we named it the Five Hundred.' I said, 'Well, you've got until tomorrow to find a vehicle to put the Taurus name on because that's why I'm here. Then you have two years to make the coolest vehicle that you can possibly make.'" The 2010 Taurus is now in dealer showrooms.

Ford's long-tenured executives were shocked by Mulally's arrival. Fierce loyalties and frequent turf battles became features of Ford's corporate culture—and the tough guys won. Despite nearly 40 years in the commercial airplane business—one of the most international of all industries—Mulally looks youthful. He dresses casually in a blue blazer, button-down shirt, and kiltie loafers, and his smile makes him appear bemused or even a bit puzzled by what goes on around him. His appearance, however, masks confidence, discipline, and a fierce desire to win.

"Communicate, communicate, communicate," Mulally states. "Everyone has to know the plan, its status, and areas that need special attention." Mulally is determined to reduce Ford's dependence on light trucks as gas becomes more expensive. He has let the entire organization know that in the bluntest possible language. "Everybody says you can't make money off small cars," he says. "Well, you'd better damn well figure out how to make money, because that's where the world is going."

Mulally's openness has won him support throughout the organization. Manufacturing VP Joe Hinrichs says, "Alan brings infectious energy. This is a person people want to follow." Mulally wrote a one-page summary of his managerial abilities. Titled "Alan's Leadership," it includes "proven successful leader . . . business acumen and judgment . . . steady . . . true North." It also lists some less quantifiable traits: "expects the very best of himself and others, seeks to understand rather than to be understood." Few other CEOs have made such a list public. Bill Ford sums Mulally up this way: "Alan is not a very complicated person. He is very driven."

Prior to arriving at Ford, Mulally studied up on Ford like a student cramming for an exam, interviewing dozens of employees, analysts, and consultants. He filled five binders with typed notes. The research allowed him to develop a strategy about the auto business that now influences all of his decisions. His strategy draws heavily from his experience at Boeing: Focus on the Ford brand ("nobody buys a house of brands"); compete in every market segment with carefully defined products (small, medium, and large; cars, utilities, and trucks); market fewer products (40 worldwide by 2013, down from 97 worldwide in 2006); and become best in class in quality, fuel efficiency, safety, and value. To let everyone know what he had in mind, Mulally created plastic cards with four goals on one side ("Expected Behaviors") and a revised definition of the company ("One Ford") on the other. The expected behaviors are:

- **Foster Functional and Technical Excellence**
  - Know and have a passion for our business and our customers

- Demonstrate and build functional and technical excellence
- Ensure process discipline
- Have a continuous improvement philosophy and practice

- **Own Working Together**
  - Believe in skilled and motivated people working together
  - Include everyone; respect, listen to, help, and appreciate others
  - Build strong relationships; be a team player; develop ourselves and others
  - Communicate clearly, concisely, and candidly

- **Role Model Ford Values**
  - Show initiative, courage, integrity, and good corporate citizenship
  - Improve quality, safety, and sustainability
  - Have a can do, find-a-way attitude and emotional resilience
  - Enjoy the journey and each other; have fun—never at others' expense

- **Deliver Results**
  - Deal positively with our business realities; develop compelling and comprehensive plans, while keeping an enterprise view
  - Set high expectations and inspire others
  - Make sound decisions using facts and data
  - Hold ourselves and others responsible and accountable for delivering results and satisfying our customers

On the other side of the card is Mulally's revised definition of the company:

One Ford

One Team   People working together as a lean, global enterprise for automotive leadership, as measured by:

Customer, Employee, Dealer, Investor, Supplier, Union/Council, and Community Satisfaction

One Plan

- Aggressively restructure to operate profitably at the current demand and changing model mix.
- Accelerate development of new products our customers want and value.
- Finance our plan and improve our balance sheet.
- Work together effectively as one team.

One Goal   An exciting viable Ford delivering profitable growth for all.

"I am here to save an American and global icon," Mulally said upon his arrival in 2006. He drives performance the way he did at Boeing, with the Business Plan Review. He holds an early meeting with his direct reports every Thursday. "I live for Thursday morning at 8 A.M.," he says. First discussed are Ford's four profit centers: the Americas, Europe, Asia Pacific, and Ford Credit. Then come presentations from 12 functional areas (from product development and manufacturing to human resources and government relations). "When I arrived there were six or seven people reporting to Bill Ford, and the IT person wasn't there, the human resources person wasn't there," says Mulally. "Today every functional discipline on my team is included because everybody in this place had to be involved and had to know everything."

The Thursday meetings are held in the Thunderbird Room, around a circular dark wood table fitted with three pairs of video screens in the center. Eight clocks, one for each Ford time zone, are mounted on the wall. There are seats for 18 executives around the table, with additional ones on the perimeter. ("Here's where I sit," says Mulally, indicating a chair: "Pilot's seat.") There are no pre-meetings or briefing books. "They don't bring their big books anymore because I'm not going to grind them with as many questions as I can to humiliate them," Mulally says. "We'll see them next week. If we don't take action on a plan—I'm going to see the person next week." No BlackBerrys are allowed, and no side conversations either. Mulally is insistent about that. "If somebody starts to talk or they don't respect each other, the meeting just stops. They know I've removed vice presidents at Boeing because they couldn't stop talking. They thought they were so damn important."

Mulally instituted color coding for reports: green for good, yellow for caution, red for problems. Managers coded all of their operations green at the first couple of meetings to show how well they were doing, but Mulally questioned them. "You guys, you know we lost a few billion dollars last year," he told the group. "Is there anything that's not going well?" After that statement the communications loosened up. Americas boss Mark Fields spoke up first. He admitted that the Ford Edge had some technical problems with the rear lift gate and wasn't ready for the start of production. "The whole place was deathly silent," says Mulally. "Then I clapped, and I said, 'Mark, I really appreciate that clear visibility.' And the next week the entire set of charts were all rainbows." "If something is off-track, we are much better at identifying it and resolving it," says CFO Booth. "Not everything turns to green. If it doesn't, we have to modify the plan."

To monitor operations during the week, Mulally visits two rooms whose walls are lined with 280 performance charts, arranged by area of responsibility (e.g., manufacturing, design, dealer relationships) with a photo of the executive in charge in case there are any doubts. Every leader at the Thursday meeting also gets wall space. The message, though, comes through clearly: Mulally has his finger on every piece of this large and complex company. Ford's board of directors sees a subset of the same data. There are no secrets at Ford anymore. "This is a huge enterprise, and the magic is, everybody knows the plan," says Mulally.

Former chief financial officer Don Leclair had became a company hero for arranging the $23 billion loan in 2006. But other executives found him hard to work with, and Leclair was urged to retire. Mulally doesn't want to have to settle arguments between executives, either. "They can either work together or they can come see me," he says. He notes that few people are waiting to see him.

So far Mulally has been managing the Ford product line since he arrived. The first new model to bear his vision is the restyled 2010 Taurus that went on sale in June 2009. His plan for "One Ford" won't get a real test until 2010 when two small, fuel-efficient cars, the Fiesta and the Focus,

are imported from Europe to the United States. It remains an open question whether Americans will be willing to pay more for the smaller, higher content vehicles—they will have to if Mulally is to succeed in reducing Ford's dependence on pickup truck profits.

The biggest unanswered questions about Mulally are how long he will stay at Ford and who will succeed him. Bill Ford has been saying that he hopes Mulally never leaves, but having spent nearly 40 years in Seattle, he isn't likely to settle in Dearborn, Michigan. The company spent more than $344,000 in 2008 flying Mulally and his family between the two cities and elsewhere. If Mulally leaves when he turns 65 in 2010, there are two insiders that he has developed that can take over.

At one of his early meetings with employees upon joining Ford in 2006, Mulally was asked whether Ford would be able to remain in business: "Is Ford going to make it?" "I don't know," Mulally replied. "But we have a plan, and the plan says we are going to make it."

Questions

1. Using the Big Five personality dimensions (see Chapter 3), diagnose Mulally's personality. How have these dimensions influenced his leadership at Ford?
2. What is Mulally's leadership style? What evidence supports your choice?
3. Evaluate Mulally's change methods. Are these effective?
4. Are there indicators of the use of evidence-based management? Explain.
5. How would you assess Mulally on each of the elements of communication openness? (See Figure 9.4.)

Source: Adapted from Taylor III, A. Ford's comeback kid. *Fortune*, May 25, 2009, 44–51. Ritson, M. Ford's clarity of focus. *Marketing*, May 27, 2009, 22; Wilson, A. Detroit. *Automotive News*, March 30, 2009, 6; Kiley, D. Ford heads out on a road of its own. *Business Week*, January 19, 2009, 47; Ford's Mulally hits the road. *Business Week Online*, December 3, 2008; Vlasic, B. Family loyalty anchors Ford in risky times. *New York Times*, June 23, 2009, A1.

Conflict Resolution at General Hospital

General Hospital was founded in 1968 as a nonprofit community hospital in the Northeast. In 1981, the facility was expanded from 175 beds to 275 beds, and the emergency room was upgraded. Also, General Hospital signed an agreement with a nearby medical center to provide patient services that it wasn't able to provide itself.

During the 1980s, approximately 90 percent of General Hospital's beds were occupied. However, a few years ago, the nearby medical center underwent renovations and obtained state-of-the-art equipment. As a result, General Hospital's patient occupancy rate had dropped to 65 percent recently. It had to eliminate services in areas in which it couldn't compete. General Hospital also experienced a 35 percent increase in Medicare and Medicaid patients during this time. These government health insurance plans generate significantly less revenue than many private health insurance plans.

General Hospital's CEO Mike Hammer realized that his hospital was in a nosedive and that a long-term, high-speed fix was in order. Without it, the hospital would soon begin to face survivability issues and possibly lose its accreditation. An experienced health-care executive, Hammer knew that he had to cut costs and increase revenues so that promising current services could be expanded and new services added in areas in which General Hospital could successfully compete against the medical center. Hammer felt that under his leadership the current management team could get the job done with one exception: cost control.

In Mike Hammer's experience, physicians were a major factor in the inability of hospitals to regulate costs. He believed that physicians in the main didn't understand, nor were they interested in, the role of costs in determining the viability of hospitals. He felt that this lack of concern stemmed from the physicians' strong allegiance to their profession as opposed to the hospitals in which they had patient privileges.

In the past, Hammer had tried two approaches to controlling physician-driven costs, each of which had failed. Early in his tenure as General Hospital's CEO, he had tried to convince Director of Medicine Dr. Mark Williams to get the staff physicians to become cost sensitive in their decision making. Even when Hammer spotted a wasteful practice, physicians defended their actions as "the practice of good medicine." He rarely won any of these battles. Also, in 1993, he hired a consultant who studied the situation and recommended a formal comprehensive cost containment program. However, the hospital's board of trustees failed to support the program because the director of medicine vehemently opposed it. Even private meetings with Dr. Williams could not get him to change his mind or even to use the proposed program as a focus for constructive change. Dr. Williams felt that Hammer was asking for a cultural change that was impossible. Forcing them to adhere to the plan would make it significantly more difficult to attract and keep talented physicians. Therefore the plan was not implemented.

The failure to achieve comprehensive cost control led Hammer to believe that physician-controlled costs had to be addressed on a step-by-step basis, one physician at a time. He theorized that, once a series of cost containment steps had been taken and reductions accrued, the culture would begin to change and more ambitious attempts at cost control would stand a better chance of success. Hammer had just hired a new hospital administrator, Marge Harding, who was effectively the hospital's chief operating officer (COO). He thought that perhaps the time had arrived to test his theory and see if cost control could begin to become a reality.

The Meeting

Hammer met with Harding and suggested a course of action:

Hammer: As I mentioned last week, we have to get aggressive in the cost area. Here's what I want you to do. Select something that the physicians are doing that can be done at less cost and implement the change. And remember, as COO you have the unilateral authority to place contracts and fire employees who are in an at-will employment status. In fact, don't tell me what you're doing. That will allow us more time and help us play good cop–bad cop with the doctors.

Harding: I'll get right on it. I'm sure that I can get some good results.

Hammer: Good, Marge! That's all I have for now.

Harding was delighted that Hammer had given her a cost-reduction assignment. In her 10 years in the health-care field, she had seen many financial abuses but until now never had the authority to do anything about them. She judged that her registered nurse experience, a 3-year stint as assistant hospital administrator at another hospital, her baccalaureate degree in finance, and her master's degree in health-care administration would serve her well in a cost-cutting role. Also, her dad and one of her brothers were physicians, so she wasn't awed by medical doctors. In fact, she rather enjoyed challenging them, as she considered many of them to be one dimensional. She felt that physicians knew the scientific elements of medicine well, but lacked the sensitivity, knowledge, and skill needed to deliver patient care in a cost-effective manner. Harding also knew that health-care reform was a hot item and that if she could improve the cost of operating General Hospital significantly, she would have a good chance of getting a CEO position, perhaps within the next 5 years, before she reached 40.

The Change

That night in the solitude of her condo while listening to a CD, Marge reviewed in her mind the orientation tour that she had gone through two weeks earlier at General Hospital. As she identified candidates for cost cutting, she listed the pros and cons of each. Next, she telephoned her friend, Joel Cohen, a 4.0 GPA MBA graduate of a prestigious business school. She got him to help her identify more clearly some cost-cutting alternatives, to formulate additional advantages and disadvantages, and to finalize her first choice: to computerize the interpretation of EKG readings.

All EKG readings at General Hospital were interpreted by Dr. James Boyer, an attending cardiologist. Dr. Boyer had been approved by both the board of trustees and the hospital medical staff to interpret EKGs. Furthermore, he was held in high esteem by his colleagues for accurate and timely reports. He had hardly ever missed a day of work in 15 years and had always arranged for a suitable replacement when he went on vacation. Dr. Boyer was particularly valuable at dovetailing his services with the many other hospital activities involved in elective admissions.

Marge Harding knew that computerized EKG interpretations were the norm today. Furthermore, she determined that replacing Dr. Boyer with a computerized EKG interpretation service would save General Hospital at least $100,000 per year for the next three years and provide nearly instantaneous results.

She signed a one-year contract on behalf of General Hospital with Health Diagnostics. The equipment was installed and the hospital's EKG technicians were trained. Finally, the computerized EKG interpretation system was put online and Harding issued two directives, one to the EKG department to use the system and another to her assistant, John Will. She was taking a week's vacation and was instructing Will to provide liaison between the contractor and the hospital and to introduce the system and its benefits to the medical and nursing staffs. Finally, just prior to catching a plane to her vacation paradise, Harding sent a letter to Dr. Boyer notifying him that his services were no longer needed and that he was involuntarily separated from General Hospital unless he successfully competed for a vacant position within the next 30 days.

Early Problems

During the first week of computerized operations, many EKG problems emerged. Some EKG interpretations came back on time, others were a few hours late, and still others never arrived at General Hospital. At times, reports were returned inadvertently with a different patient's EKG analyses on them. Such mix-ups resulted in misfiling and at times confused physicians and even caused a few misdiagnoses. At other times, the patients were actually at other hospitals! The overwhelming problem was incorrect EKG interpretations in 25 percent of the reports.

The physicians were furious. They did not recognize the physicians who had certified the EKG reports. "What happened to Dr. Boyer?" became an echo. When they discovered that Dr. Boyer had been fired, they vehemently complained to Dr. Williams. Dr. Boyer's colleagues felt strongly that, because Dr. Boyer was part of the medical staff, a review of his termination was in order. Dr. Williams worried about the potential for legal liabilities resulting from inaccurate readings, as well as EKG reports signed by physicians not certified by General Hospital's certification committee. The nursing director, Nancy Ames, was unaware of the extent of the change and the ensuing problems.

The overall result was that the hospital's operation was quickly becoming seriously jeopardized. John Will was powerless to discontinue the computerized EKG service because he had no legitimate authority to do so.

The Following Monday

At 10:00 A.M. the following Monday, the medical staff convened to discuss the problem. Dr. Williams strongly urged Harding to come to the meeting, but she didn't attend. Instead she sent John Will with a message: "General Hospital needs to stay abreast of ongoing technological developments in science and medicine, especially when costs are reduced. The computerized EKG system stays." This incensed the medical staff. Dr. Williams sent Will back to Harding with a rebuttal message: "Either speak to us today and resolve this problem, or we will admit all new patients to other hospitals." Dr. Williams was totally frustrated. He had brought the matter up with Mike Hammer that morning but felt that he had been brushed off. Hammer said that he was very busy and that, hopefully, the problem would get resolved by those directly involved.

Questions
1. What conflict management styles are evidenced in this case?
2. How would you characterize Hammer's leadership style?
3. What type of change approach was used by Hammer? Was it successful?

Source: This case was prepared by James W. Lawson and Charles Connant of St. Peter's College, Jersey City, New

Jersey. It was presented to and accepted by the referred Society for Case Research. All rights reserved to the authors. Copyright © 1994. It was edited for *Organizational Behavior*, 13th edition, and used with permission.

Bob Knowlton

Bob Knowlton was sitting alone in the conference room of the laboratory. The rest of the group had gone. One of the secretaries had stopped and talked for a while about her husband's coming induction in the Army, and had finally left. Knowlton, alone in the laboratory, slid a little farther down in his chair, looking with satisfaction at the results of the first test run of the new photon unit.

He liked to stay after the others had gone. His appointment as project head was still new enough to give him a deep sense of pleasure. His eyes were on the graphs before him, but in his mind he could hear Dr. Jerrold, the head of the laboratory, saying again. "There's one thing about this place that you can bank on. The sky is the limit for a person who can produce." Knowlton felt again the tingle of happiness and embarrassment. Well, dammit, he said to himself, he had produced. He had come to Simmons Laboratories two years ago. During a routine testing of some rejected Clanson components he had stumbled on the idea of the photon correlator, and the rest just happened. Jerrold had been enthusiastic; a separate project had been set up for further research and development of the device, and he had gotten the job of running it. The whole sequence of events still seemed a little miraculous to Knowlton.

He had shrugged off his reverie and bent determinedly over the sheets when he heard someone come into the room behind him. He looked up expectantly. Jerrold often stayed late himself, and now and then dropped in for a chat. This always made his day's end especially pleasant. But it wasn't Jerrold. The man who had come in was a stranger. He was tall, thin, and rather dark. He wore steel-rimmed glasses and had on a very wide leather belt with a large brass buckle. The stranger smiled and introduced himself. "I'm Simon Fester. Are you Bob Knowlton?" Bob said "yes," and they shook hands. "Doctor Jerrold said I might find you in. We were talking about your work, and I'm very much interested in what you're doing." Knowlton waved him to a chair. Fester didn't seem to belong in any of the standard categories of visitors: customers, visiting fireman, shareholder. Bob pointed to the sheets on the table. "These are the preliminary results of a test we're running. We've got a new gadget by the tail and we're trying to understand it. It's not finished, but I can show you the section that we're testing." He stood up, but Fester was deeply engrossed in the graphs. After a moment he looked up with an odd grin. "These look like plots of a Jennings surface. I've been playing around with some autocorrelation functions of surfaces—you know that stuff." Knowlton, who had no idea what Fester was referring to, grinned back and nodded, and immediately felt uncomfortable. "Let me show you the monster," he said, and led the way to the workroom.

After Fester left, Knowlton slowly put the graphs away, feeling vaguely annoyed. Then, as if he had made a decision, he quickly locked up and took the long way out so that he would pass Jerrold's office. But the office was locked. Knowlton wondered whether Jerrold and Fester had left together.

The next morning Knowlton dropped into Jerrold's office, mentioned that he had talked with Fester, and asked who he was.

"Sit down for a minute," Jerrold said. "I want to talk to you about him. What do you think of him?" Knowlton replied truthfully that he thought Fester was very bright and probably very competent. Jerrold looked pleased.

"We're taking him on," he said. "He has a very good background at a number of laboratories, and he seems to have ideas about the problems we're tackling here." Knowlton nodded in agreement, instantly wishing that Fester not be placed with him.

"I don't know yet where he will finally land," Jerrold continued, "but he seems interested in what you're doing. I thought he might spend a little time with you by way of getting started." Knowlton nodded thoughtfully. "If his interest in your work continues, you can add him to your group.

"Well, he seemed to have some good ideas even without knowing exactly what we are doing," Knowlton answered. "I hope he stays; I'd be glad to have him."

Knowlton walked back to the lab with mixed feelings. He told himself that Fester would be good for the group. He was no dunce; he'd produce. Knowlton thought again of Jerrold's promise when he had promoted him: "The person who produces gets ahead in this outfit." The words now seemed to him to carry the overtones of a threat.

The next day, Fester didn't appear until midafternoon. He explained that he had had a long lunch with Jerrold, discussing his place in the lab. "Yes," said Knowlton, "I talked with him this morning about it, and we both thought you might work with my group for a while."

Fester smiled in the same knowing way that he had smiled when he mentioned the Jennings surfaces. "I'd like to," he said.

Knowlton introduced Fester to the other members of the lab. Fester and John Link, the mathematician of the group, hit it off well together. They spent the rest of the afternoon discussing a method of analysis of patterns that Link had been worrying over for the last month.

It was 6:30 when Knowlton finally left the lab that night. He had waited almost eagerly for the end of the day to come—when all the lab personnel would all be gone and he could sit in the quiet room, relax, and think it over. Think what over? He asked himself. He didn't know. Shortly after 5:00 they had all gone except Fester, and what followed was almost a duel. Knowlton was annoyed that he was being cheated out of his quiet period, and finally resentful, determined that Fester should leave first.

Fester was sitting at the conference table reading, and Knowlton was sitting at his desk in the little glass-enclosed office that he used during the day when he needed to be undisturbed. Fester had gotten last year's progress reports out and was studying them carefully. Time dragged. Knowlton doodled on a pad, the tension growing inside him. What the hell did Fester think he was going to find in the reports?

Knowlton finally gave up, and they left the lab together. Fester took several of the reports with him to study that evening. Knowlton asked him if he thought the reports gave a clear picture of the lab's activities.

"They're excellent," Fester answered with obvious sincerity. "They're not only good reports; what they report is damn good too!" Knowlton was surprised at the relief he felt, and grew almost jovial as he said goodnight.

Driving home, Knowlton felt more optimistic about Fester's presence in the lab. He had never fully understood the analysis that Link was attempting. If there was anything wrong with Link's approach, Fester would probably spot it.

And if I'm any judge, he thought, he won't be especially diplomatic about it.

He described Fester to his wife, Lucy, who was amused by the broad leather belt and the brass buckle.

"It's the kind of belt the Pilgrims must have worn," she laughed.

"I'm not worried about how he holds his pants up," Knowlton laughed with her. "I'm afraid that he's the kind that just has to make like a genius twice each day. And that can be pretty rough on the group."

Knowlton had been asleep for several hours when he was jarred awake by the telephone. He realized it had rung several times. He swung off the bed, muttering about damn fools and telephones. It was Fester. Without any excuses, apparently oblivious of the time, he plunged into an excited recital of how Link's patterning problem could be solved.

Knowlton covered the mouthpiece to answer his wife's stage whisper, "Who is it?" "It's the genius."

Fester, completely ignoring the fact that it was 2:00 in the morning, proceeded excitedly to explain a completely new approach to certain of the photon lab problems that he had stumbled onto while analyzing some past experiments. Knowlton managed to put some enthusiasm in his own voice and stood there, still half-dazed and very uncomfortable, listening to Fester talk endlessly, it seemed, about what he had discovered. He said that he not only had a new approach but also an analysis that showed how inherently weak the previous experiment was. He finally concluded by saying that further experimentation along that earlier line certainly would have been inconclusive.

The following morning, Knowlton spent the entire morning with Fester and Link, the usual morning group meeting having been called off so that Fester's work of the previous night could be gone over intensively. Fester was very anxious that this be done, and Knowlton wasn't too unhappy to call the meeting off for reasons of his own.

For the next several days, Fester sat in the back office that had been turned over to him and did nothing but read the progress reports of the work that had been done in the last six months. Knowlton caught himself feeling apprehensive about the reaction that Fester might have to some of his work. He was a little surprised at his own feelings. He had always been proud—although he had put on a convincingly modest face—of the way his team had broken new ground in the study of photon measuring devices. Now he wasn't sure. It seemed to him that Fester might easily show that the line of research they had been following was unsound or even unimaginative.

The next morning, as was customary, the members of Knowlton's group, including the secretaries, sat around the table in the conference room for a group meeting. He had always prided himself on the fact that the team as a whole guided and evaluated its work. He would point out that often what started out as a boring recital of fundamental assumptions to a naïve listener uncovered new ways of regarding these assumptions that wouldn't have occurred to the lab member who had long ago accepted them as a necessary basis for the research he was doing. These group meetings also served another purpose. He admitted to himself that he would have felt far less secure if he had had to direct the work completely on his own. Team meetings, as a principle of leadership, justified the exploration of blind alleys because of the general educative effect of the team. Fester and Link were there, as were Lucy Martin and Martha Ybarra. Link sat next to Fester, the two of them continuing their conversation concerning Link's mathematical study from yesterday. The other group members, Bob Davenport, George Thurlow, and Arthur Oliver, sat there waiting quietly.

Knowlton, for reasons that he didn't quite understand, brought up a problem that all of them had previously spent a great deal of time discussing. The team had come to an implicit conclusion that a solution was impossible and that there was no feasible way of treating it experimentally. Davenport remarked that there was hardly any use going over it again. He was satisfied that there was no way of approaching the problem with the equipment and the physical capacities of the lab.

This statement had the effect of a shot of adrenaline on Fester. He said he would like to know in detail what the problem was, and walking to the blackboard, began both discussing the problem and simultaneously listing the reasons why it had been abandoned. Very early in the description of the problem it became evident that Fester was going to disagree about the impossibility of solving it. The group realized this and finally the descriptive materials and their recounting of the reasoning that had led to its abandonment dwindled away. Fester began his analysis, which as it proceeded might have well been prepared the previous night although Knowlton knew that to be impossible. He couldn't help being impressed with the organized and logical way that Fester was presenting ideas that must have occurred to him only a few minutes before.

However, Fester said some things that left Knowlton with a mixture of annoyance, irritation, and, at the same time, a rather smug feeling of superiority in at least one area. Fester was of the opinion that the way that the problem had been analyzed was typical of what happened when such thinking was attempted by a team, and with an air of sophistication that made it difficult for a listener to dissent, he proceeded to make general comments on the American emphasis on team ideas, satirically describing the ways in which they led to a "high level of mediocrity."

Knowlton observed that Link stared studiously at the floor and was conscious of George Thurlow's and Bob Davenport's glances at him at several points during Fester's little speech. Inwardly, Knowlton couldn't help feeling that this was one point at least in which Fester was off on the wrong foot. The whole lab, following Dr. Jerrold's lead, talked, if not actually practiced, the theory of small research teams as the basic organization for effective research. Fester insisted that the problem could be solved and that he would like to study it for a while himself.

Knowlton ended the session by remarking that the meetings would continue and that the very fact that a supposedly insoluble experimental problem was now going to get another look was yet another indication of the value of such meetings. Fester immediately remarked that he was not at all averse to meetings for the purpose of informing the group of the progress of its members. He went on to say that the point he wanted to make was that creative advances were seldom accomplished in such meetings, that they were made by the individual "living with" the problem closely and continuously, forming a sort of personal relationship with it. Knowlton responded by saying that he was glad Fester had raised these points and that he was sure the team would profit by reexamining the basis on which they had been operating. Knowlton agreed that individual effort was probably the basis for making major advances but that he considered the group meetings useful primarily because of the effect they had on keeping the team together and on helping the weaker members of the team keep up with the advances of the ones who were able to move more easily and quickly when analyzing problems.

As days went by and the meetings continued, Fester came to enjoy them because of the direction the meetings soon took. Typically, Fester would hold forth on some subject, and it became clear that he was, without question, more brilliant and better prepared on the topics germane to the problems being studied. He probably was more capable of going ahead on his own than anyone there, and Knowlton grew increasingly disturbed as he realized that his leadership of the team had been, in fact, taken over. In Knowlton's occasional meetings with Dr. Jerrold, whenever Fester was mentioned, he would comment only on Fester's ability and obvious capacity for work, somehow never quite feeling that he could mention his own discomforts. He felt that they revealed a weakness on his own part. Moreover, Dr. Jerrold was greatly impressed with Fester's work and with the contacts he had with Fester outside the photon laboratory.

Knowlton began to feel that the intellectual advantages that Fester had brought to the team might not quite compensate for evidences of a breakdown in the cooperative spirit that had been evident in the group before Fester's coming. More and more of the morning meetings were skipped. Fester's opinion concerning the abilities of others of the team, with the exception of Link's, was obviously low. At times during morning meetings or in smaller discussions, he had been rude, refusing at certain times to pursue an argument when he claimed that it was based on the other person's ignorance of the facts involved. His impatience with the others also led him to make remarks of this kind to Dr. Jerrold. This Knowlton inferred from a conversation he had had with Jerrold. The head of the lab had asked whether Davenport and Oliver were going to be retained, but he hadn't mentioned Link. This conversation led Knowlton to believe that Fester had had private conversations with Jerrold.

Knowlton had little difficulty making a convincing case regarding whether Fester's brilliance actually was sufficient recompense for the beginning of his team's breaking up. He spoke privately with Davenport and Oliver. Both clearly were uncomfortable with Fester's presence. Knowlton didn't press the discussion beyond hearing them in one way or another say that they sometimes felt awkward around Fester. They said that sometimes they had difficulty understanding the arguments he advanced. In fact, they often felt too embarrassed to ask Fester to state the grounds on which he based such arguments. Knowlton didn't talk to Link in this manner.

About six months after Fester's coming to the photon lab, meetings were scheduled at which the sponsors of much of the ongoing research were coming to get some idea of its progress. At special meetings, project heads customarily presented the research being conducted by their groups. The other members of the laboratory groups were invited to other, more general meetings later in the day and open to all. The special meetings usually were restricted to project heads, the head of the laboratory, and the sponsors. As the time for his special meeting approached, Knowlton felt that he must avoid the presentation at all costs. He felt that he couldn't present the ideas that Fester had advanced—and on which some work had been done—in sufficient detail and answer questions about them. However, he didn't feel that he could ignore these newer lines of work and present only the work that had been started or completed before Fester's arrival (which he felt perfectly competent to do). It seemed clear that keeping Fester from attending the meeting wouldn't be easy in spite of the fact that he wasn't on the administrative level that had been invited. Knowlton also felt that it wouldn't be beyond Fester, in his blunt and undiplomatic way, if he was present at the meeting, to comment on Knowlton's presentation and reveal the inadequacy that he felt.

Knowlton found an opportunity to speak to Jerrold and raised the question. He remarked to Jerold that, of course, with the interest in the work and Fester's contributions he probably would like to come to these meetings. Knowlton said that he was concerned about the feelings of the others in the group if Fester were invited. Jerrold brushed this concern aside by saying that he felt the group would understand Fester's rather different position. He thought that, by all means, Fester should be invited. Knowlton then immediately said that he had thought so too and further that Fester should make the presentation because much of it was work that he had done. As Knowlton put it, this would be a nice way to recognize Fester's contributions and to reward him because he was eager to be recognized as a productive member of the lab. Jerrold agreed, and so the matter was decided.

Fester's presentation was very successful and, in some ways, dominated the meeting. He held the interest and attention of those attending, and following his presentation the questions persisted for a long period. Later that evening at the banquet, to which the entire laboratory was invited, a circle of people formed about Fester during the cocktail period before the dinner. Jerrold was part of the circle and discussion concerning the application of the theory Fester was proposing. Although this attention disturbed Knowlton, he reacted and behaved characteristically. He joined the circle, praised Fester to Jerrold and the others, and remarked how able and brilliant some of his work was.

Knowlton, without consulting anyone, began to consider the possibility of a job elsewhere. After a few weeks, he found that a new laboratory of considerable size was being organized in a nearby city. His training and experience would enable him to get a project-head job equivalent to the one he had at the lab, with slightly more money.

When it was offered, he immediately accepted the job and notified Jerrold by letter, which he mailed on a Friday night to Jerrold's home. The letter was brief, and Jerrold was stunned. The letter merely said that Knowlton had found a better position; that there were personal reasons why he didn't want to work at the lab anymore; that he would be glad to come back later (he would be only 40 miles away) to assist if there was any problems with the past work; that he felt sure that Fester could, however, supply any leadership that was required for the group; and that his decision to leave so suddenly was based on some personal problems (he hinted at family health problems involving his mother and father, which were fictitious). Dr. Jerrold took it at face value but still felt that Knowlton's behavior was very strange and quite unaccountable. Jerrold had always felt that his relationship with Knowlton had been warm; that Knowlton was satisfied and, as a matter of fact, quite happy and productive.

Jerrold was considerably disturbed because he had already decided to place Fester in charge of another project that was going to be set up soon. He had been wondering how to explain this decision to Knowlton in view of the obvious help, assistance, and value Knowlton had been getting from Fester and the high regard in which Knowlton held him. In fact, Jerrold had considered letting Knowlton add to his staff another person with Fester's background and training, which apparently had proved so valuable.

Jerrold did not make any attempt to contact Knowlton. In a way, he felt aggrieved about the whole thing. Fester, too, was surprised at the suddenness of Knowlton's departure and when Jerrold, in talking to him, asked him whether he preferred to stay with the photon group rather than to head the Air Force project that was being organized, he chose the Air Force project and moved into that job the following week. The photon lab was hard hit. The leadership of the photon group was given to Link, with the understanding that it would be temporary until someone else could be brought in to take over.

Questions
1. One might say that there was a "personality" clash between Knowlton and Fester. What personality model could you use to describe the clash?
2. What leadership style did Knowlton need from Dr. Jerrold after Fester arrived? Did he receive this? Explain.
3. Was Knowlton's team effective before Fester arrived? After Fester arrived? Why? Why not?
4. What changes in conflict management should Dr. Jerrold make to prevent another Knowlton problem?

Source: This case was developed by Dr. Alex Bavelas. It was edited for *Organizational Behavior*, 13th edition, and used with permission.

BMW's Dream Factory and Culture

BMW, with more than $73 billion in sales, is much smaller than its American rivals. However, the U.S. auto giants could still learn some things from BMW. Detroit's rigid bureaucracies have been slow to respond to competitive threats and market trends. In contrast, BMW's management system is flat, flexible, entrepreneurial—and fast.

Few companies have been as consistent at producing an ever-changing product line, with near-flawless quality, that consumers like. BMW has redefined luxury design with its 7 Series, created enthusiasm for its Mini, and maintained some of the highest profit margins in the auto industry.

A sporty four-wheel-drive coupe and a stylish minivan called the Luxury Sport Cruiser rolled off the production line in 2008. These models promise to continue BMW's run of cool cars under its new chief executive, Norbert Reithofer. (His predecessor, Helmut Panke, stepped down upon reaching the mandatory retirement age of 60.) Says Reithofer: "We push change through the organization to ensure its strength. There are always better solutions." Panke once insisted that all six members of the management board take an advanced driving course so they would have a better feel for BMW cars.

Virtually everyone at BMW is expected to help find those solutions. When demand for the 1 Series compact soared, plant manager Peter Claussen volunteered to temporarily use the brand new factory in Leipzig, Germany—which had been designed for the 3 Series—to produce 5,000 of the compacts. Claussen and his associates quickly figured out how to do it while maintaining high quality. Recently, line workers in Munich, Germany, suggested adding a smaller diesel engine in the 5 Series. They contended that it would have enough power to handle like a Bimmer and be a big seller among those on a tighter budget. They were right.

Culture

Much of BMW's success stems from an entrepreneurial culture that's rare in corporate Germany. Management in Germany is usually top-down. The cultural gulf between workers and managers is significant. BMW's 100,000 employees have become a network of committed associates with few hierarchical barriers to hinder innovation. From the moment they set foot inside the company, associates are overcome with a sense of place, history, and mission. Individuals from all levels of BMW work side by side. They create informal networks where even the most unorthodox ideas can be thought of for making better Bimmers or boosting profits. BMW buyers may not know it, but when they slide behind the wheel, they are driving a vehicle born of thousands of impromptu brainstorming sessions. BMW, in fact, might just be the chattiest auto company ever. Claussen comments: "The difference at BMW is that [managers] don't think we have all the right answers. Our job is to ask the right questions."

That's not to say this freewheeling idea factory hasn't made its share of blunders over the years. In 2001, BMW alienated customers with its iDrive control system. The device was designed to help drivers quickly move through hundreds of information and entertainment functions with a single knob. It proved incomprehensible to many buyers. Rival Audi is narrowing the gap with BMW in Europe by producing a new generation of stylish, high-performance cars that have topped consumer polls. Toyota's Lexus also has BMW in its sights as it makes a move to gain in Europe with sportier, better handling cars. Reithofer comments: "We will be challenged—no question. We have to take Lexus seriously."

In BMW's favor is an enduring sense that things can go wrong. New hires quickly learn that the BMW world as they know it began in 1959. That's when the company nearly went bankrupt and was just a step away from being acquired by Mercedes. This long-ago trauma remains the pivotal moment in BMW folklore. Reithofer continues: "We never forget 1959. It's in our genes, and it drives our performance." BMW wouldn't exist today if it weren't for a bailout by Germany's wealthy Quandt family—still the controlling shareholder, with a 47 percent stake—and a pact with labor to keep the company afloat. "Near-death experiences are very healthy for companies," says David Cole, a partner at the Center for Automotive Research in Ann Arbor, Michigan. "BMW has been running scared for years."

The story of 1959 is told and retold at each orientation of new plant associates. Works Council Chief Manfred Schloch, a 26-year veteran, holds up old, grainy black-and-white photos of two models from the 1950s. The big one was too pricey for a struggling postwar Germany. The other, a tiny two-seater, looked like a toy and was too small to be practical, even by the standards of that era. The company badly misjudged the market, he says. Schloch pulls out a yellowed, typewritten 1959 plan for turning the company around with a new class of sporty sedans. Schloch then hands out photos of Herbert Quandt and the labor leader of the period, Kurt Golda. Schloch states: "I explain how we rebuilt the company with Quandt's money and the power of the workforce. And I tell them that's the way it works today, too."

Motivated Workers, Better Cars

BMW derives much of its strength from an almost unparalleled labor harmony rooted in that long-ago pact. In 1972 and years before the rest of European companies began to think about pay for performance, the company included all employees in profit sharing. It set up a plan that distributes as much as one and a half months' extra pay at the end of the year, provided BMW meets financial targets. In return, employees are flexible. When a plant is introducing new technology or needs a volume boost, it's not uncommon for associates from other BMW factories to move into temporary housing far from home for months and put in long hours on the line. Union leaders have made it easy for BMW to quickly adjust output to meet demand. Without paying overtime, the company can increase the production schedule to as much as 140 hours a week (20 hours per day, 7 days a week) or scale it back to as little as 60 hours. The system enables BMW to provide a high level of job security. Since 2000, BMW has hired new associates even as General Motors Corporation, Chrysler, and Ford Motor Company have slashed tens of thousands of jobs.

BMW's human resources department receives more than 200,000 applications annually. Those who make it to an interview undergo elaborate day-long drills in teams that screen out big egos. For the lucky few who are hired, a Darwinian test of survival ensues. BMW promotes talented managers rapidly and provides little training along the way. It requires them to reach out to others to learn the ropes. With no one to formally coach them in a new job, managers need to stay humble and work closely with subordinates and their peers. This minimizes traditional corporate turf battles. Anyone who wants to push an innovative new idea learns the key to success fast. "You can go into fighting mode or you can ask permission and get everyone to support you," says Stefan Krause, BMW's 44-year-old chief financial officer. "If you do it without building ties, you will be blocked."

Work Environment

The construction of the Leipzig factory is a testament to the power of such ties. When plant manager Claussen first proposed a competition to lure top architects, executives at headquarters were taken back. Krause comments: "People said to me, 'What's wrong with these guys in Leipzig? We don't need beautiful buildings, we need productive buildings.'" Claussen convinced Krause and others that the unconventional approach wouldn't just produce a pretty factory but one whose open, airy spaces would improve communications between line workers and managers and create an environment that helps the company build cars better.

Even before Claussen began pushing his architectural vision, others were busy designing the inner workings of the plant. Jan Knau, an engineer, was only 27 when he was asked to come up with a flexible assembly line for the factory. Knau, then just a junior associate, contacted BMW's top 15 assembly engineers. He invited them to a two-day workshop at a BMW retreat near the Austrian Alps. After a series of marathon sessions that included discussions of every facet of the ideal assembly line, Knau sketched a design with four "fingers," or branches, off the main spine. The branches could extend to add equipment needed to build new models. This made it possible to keep giant robots along the main line in place rather than moving them for each production change, an expensive and time-consuming process.

The Leipzig plant opened in 2005. It represents Claussen's vision of teamwork enhanced through design by Knau's creative engineering concepts. With pillars of sunlight streaming through soaring glass walls, architect Zaha Hadid's design looks more like an art museum than a car factory. Open workspaces cascade over two floors. Unfinished car bodies move along a track with enhanced lighting that runs above offices and an open cafeteria. If the pace of the half-finished cars slows, engineers know it immediately and can quickly investigate the problem. The weekly quality audits—in a plaza workers pass on their way to lunch—ensure that everyone is quickly aware of any production snafus. The combination of togetherness and openness sparks impromptu dialogue among line workers, logistics engineers, and quality experts. Knau states: "They meet simply because their paths cross naturally. And they say, 'Ah, glad I ran into you, I have an idea.'"

Flexibility and Innovation

The flexibility of BMW's factories allows for a wide range of variations on basic models. At Leipzig, for instance, parts ranging from dashboards and seats to axles and front ends snake onto overhead conveyer belts to be lowered into the assembly line in precise sequence according to customers' orders. BMW buyers can select everything from engine type to the color of the gear-shift box to a seemingly limitless number of interior trims—and then change their mind and order a completely different configuration as little as five days before production begins. Customers request some 170,000 changes a month in their orders, mostly higher priced options such as a bigger engine or a more luxurious interior. There are so many choices that line workers assemble exactly the same car only about once every nine months.

This kind of customization would swamp most automakers with budget-busting complexity. But BMW has emerged as a sort of anti-Toyota. Toyota excels in simplifying automaking. BMW excels in mastering complexity and tailoring cars to customers' tastes. That's what differentiates BMW from Lexus and the rest of the premium pack. "BMW drivers never change to other brands," says Yoichi Tomihara, president of Toyota Deutschland. He concedes that Toyota lags behind BMW in the sort of customization that creates emotional appeal.

Bottom-up ideas help keep BMW's new models fresh and edgy year after year. Young designers in various company studios from Munich headquarters to DesignWorks in Los Angeles are constantly pitted against one another in constructive competitions. Unlike many car companies, where a design chief dictates a car's outlines to the staff, BMW designers are given only a rough goal. Otherwise, they are free to come up with their best concepts.

To get the most out of its associates, BMW likes to bring together designers, engineers, and marketing experts to work intensively on a single project. The redesign of the Rolls-Royce Phantom, for instance, was dubbed "The Bank." The 10 team members worked out of an old bank building at London's Marble Arch, where dozens of Rollses roll by daily. "We took designers from California and Munich and put them in a new environment" to immerse them in the Rolls Royce culture, says Ian Cameron, Rolls's chief designer. The result was the new Phantom, a 19-foot vehicle that remains true to Rolls's DNA, but with 21st-century lines and BMW's technological sophistication under the hood. With sales of the $385,000 car running at about 700 a year, the Phantom is the best-seller in the superluxury segment, outstripping both the Bentley Arnage and the Mercedes Maybach.

Much of BMW's innovation doesn't come via formal programs such as The Bank. In 2001, management decided to pull the plug on the disappointing Z3 sports coupe. That didn't stop a 33-year-old designer named Sebastian Trübsbach from doodling a sketch of what a Z3 successor might look like. Ulrich Bruhnke, head of BMW's high-performance division, loved it. In Trübsbach's drawing, Bruhnke saw a car that could rival Porsche's Cayman S in performance but at a lower price. He persuaded a few designers and engineers to carve out some time for the renegade project. Next, Bruhnke gathered a team to map out the business case. The small group worked for 10 months to build a prototype.

The moment of truth came in 2004 at a top-secret test track near Munich. Cars were lined up so the board could examine their styling and proportions in natural light. Only one was covered by a tarp. Former board chairman Panke approached the mystery model. "What is this interesting silhouette?" he asked Bruhnke, who invited his boss to take a look. Panke yanked back the cloth, exposing a glittering, bronze metallic prototype for what would become the Z4 coupe. Bruhnke breathed a sigh of relief when he saw Panke's eyes light up as they viewed the car's design. Panke and the board quickly gave the go ahead. The Z4 coupe sped to production in just 17 months, hitting showrooms in 2007.

Questions

1. How would you describe the culture at BMW?
2. What model of leadership is illustrated at BMW? How does this impact BMW's culture?

3. Using the concepts illustrated in the Job Characteristics Model, analyze why employees derive high job satisfaction at BMW.

4. What attributes of organizational creativity are fostered at BMW?

Source: Adapted from G. Edmondson. BMW's dream factory. *Business Week*, October 16, 2006, 70–80; Kurylko, D. T. Job swap works for BMW. *Automotive News*, July 9, 2007, 48; Cokayne, R. BMW plan offers workers stable income. *BusinessReport*, September 3, 2007. www.busrep.co.za/index.php?fSectionId=563&fArticleId=4015366 (September 2007); Pries, L. Emerging production systems in the transnationalization of German carmakers: Adaptation, application or innovation? *New Technology: Work and Employment*, 2003, 18, 82–100; BMW Group. www.bmwgroup.com (September 2009).

ROWE Program at Best Buy

Jennifer Janssen works in the finance department at the headquarters of Best Buy, located in Minneapolis, Minnesota. One of Best Buy's electronics suppliers is furious because he claims he has not been paid. Janssen states: "He told me, 'I'm not going to ship any more products to your company unless I get this issue resolved.'" She has to resolve the problem by the end of the day. The mother of twins also has to pick up her children from day care. What choices does she have? Perhaps Janssen makes a call to her husband, asking if he could skip out early while she puts out the fire at work. (Again?) Maybe Janssen scrambles to find someone who can handle the issue in time for her to leave at 4:00 P.M. (Did anyone see me?) Or perhaps, after another late night, Janssen spends the car ride home wondering whether she should just quit. (This time, I swear!)

Janssen is calm as she looks around the finance department, trying to find someone who can cover for her. As she figures out what happened to her vendor's payment, Janssen knows that she can leave the office at 4:00—without guilt, without looking over her shoulder. Even if a solution isn't found by then, she can keep working on it from her laptop at home. No one remarks that she's leaving and no one notices. Janssen is part of the program to solve the problem of overwork at Best Buy. Like many other U.S. companies, Best Buy strives to meet the demands of its business—how to do things better, faster, and cheaper than its competitors—with an increasingly stressed-out workforce.

The company's culture used to embrace long hours and sacrifice. One manager even gave a plaque to the employee "who turns on the lights in the morning and turns them off at night." Darrell Owens, a Best Buy veteran, once stayed up for three days in a row to write a report that was suddenly due. He received a bonus and a vacation. But, Owens stated, "I ended up in the hospital." Cali Ressler, a human resources executive, had noticed an alarming trend: Women were accepting the reduced pay and status of a part-time position but doing the same work because it was the only way to get the family flexibility they needed. Ressler states: "If we keep moving the way we're moving, women are going to be in the same place we were 40 years ago."

ROWE Program

The number of people in the United States who say they are overworked has been rising, from 28 percent of Americans in 2001 to 44 percent in 2009, according to the Families and Work Institute. Instead of launching a "work–life balance" program, Best Buy rethought the very concept of work. Under the *Results-Only Work Environment* program, or ROWE, employees can work when and where they like, as long as they get the job done.

As of 2009, the program was six years old and was started at Best Buy's Minneapolis headquarters, which has 4,000 employees. Recently, Best Buy started introducing the ROWE program to its 150,000 employees in retail stores. The firm is still figuring out how the program can be applied in stores, since retail requires "time clocks" and working to schedules, which are against the program's operating philosophy.

The ROWE program is based on 13 principles and rules. The key ones include:

*   There are no work schedules in the traditional sense.

*   Every meeting is optional, with a few key exceptions.

*   Employees are not to judge how colleagues spend their time. Thus, there is to be no focus on "how many hours did you work."

*   Work is not a place you go, it's something you do.

*   As long as the work gets done, employees do whatever they want whenever they want.

*   In brief, ROWE is all about results. No results, no job. It's that simple.

Entire departments join at once, so that no single employee is left out and made to feel less dedicated. Thus far, 75 percent of the 4,000 employees at Best Buy's headquarters are in the ROWE program. Each group finds a different way to keep flexibility from turning into chaos. The public relations team has pagers to make sure someone is always available in an emergency. Janssen has software that turns voice mail into e-mail files accessible from anywhere, making it easier for her to work at home. Many teams realized that they need only one regular weekly or monthly staff meeting, so they eliminated the unproductive ones.

Early Results

Results from and reactions to ROWE have been encouraging. Productivity increased an average of 35 percent within six to nine months in Best Buy units that implemented ROWE. Voluntary turnover has dropped between 52 percent and 90 percent in three Best Buy divisions that have implemented ROWE. The three divisions were chosen because they were otherwise unaffected by company reorganizations or other initiatives. This voluntary turnover figure is viewed as an indication that employees who once would have left Best Buy decided to stay put after ROWE was implemented. One procurement division saw voluntary turnover drop from 37 percent a year to less than 6 percent annually.

Jody Thompson helped introduce ROWE and is now a principal of Culture Rx, a division of Best Buy. Culture Rx offers customized consulting services tailored to the needs of clients with ROWE at the core of its philosophy. A Culture Rx study of attitudes of ROWE participants found that feelings of pressure and a sense of working too hard have changed. Thompson states: "They feel happier about work. They feel more ownership of their work. They feel clearer about what they're doing for the company, and they see ROWE as a benefit that's almost more important than any other. They talk about it as if to say, 'Someone else could offer me more money, but I wouldn't go because I now have control over my time.'"

Change Process

The ROWE experiment started quietly. Cali Ressler used to manage Best Buy's work–life balance programs and is now a principal with Thompson at Culture Rx. She helped a troubled division of the retail group in Minneapolis deal with poor employee morale. Ressler encouraged the manager to try flexible scheduling, trusting his team to work as it suited them. As she recalls: "He said, 'Well, trust doesn't cost me anything.'" The innovation was that the whole team did it together. While the sample size was fewer than 300 employees, the early results were promising. Turnover in the first three months of employment fell from 14 percent to zero, job satisfaction rose 10 percent, and team-performance scores rose 13 percent.

When Jody Thompson, who then led Best Buy's "organizational change" initiatives, heard about Ressler's work, she pushed the company's top management to make total flexibility available to everyone. No one is forced into it; teams sign up when they're ready. Best Buy expects that ROWE one day will apply to the whole company in one form or another.

The transition to a flexible workplace in Minneapolis was slow. "There was a lot of trepidation," says Traci Tobias, who manages travel reimbursements for Best Buy. "A lot of 'Can I really do this? Do I need to stop and tell someone? What will people think of me?'" Each ROWE team had to deal with those fears. "We took baby steps," Tobias says. The first step was an online calendar in which everyone entered exactly where they were at any given time. After a few weeks, the employees abandoned the calendar and now just use an ad hoc combination of out-of-office messages and trust. "There is no typical day," Tobias says. On a recent Wednesday, she slept in, went to a doctor's appointment, and arrived in the office around 10 A.M.

When Tobias needs to find people, she checks the whiteboards hanging outside their cubes, where she and her coworkers write down where they are on any given day: "In the office today." "Out of the office this afternoon, available by e-mail." The impromptu meetings are gone, but business done by cell phone is way up. Because she no longer assumes that everyone is around, Tobias makes more of an effort to catch up with her colleagues by phone or e-mail instead of just dropping by someone's office. "You can still have those conversations," she says, just not always in person. She noticed that e-mails have gotten more concise and meaningful, with much less "FYI." And as everyone started to rethink their priorities, Tobias states: "We spend a lot less time in meetings." They used to have a two-hour weekly staff meeting that often devolved into chit-chat. Now, if they don't need to meet, they don't.

The transition required a lot of changing of old attitudes, and it produced a lot of stress. Some employees broke down and cried in ROWE training sessions. Ressler states: "People in the baby-boom generation realize what they gave up to get ahead in the workplace, and a lot of times it's their families. They realize that it doesn't have to be that way." In particular, men thank her and Thompson, who run the sessions, for giving them permission to spend more time with their families. "They know now they can do it and not be judged," says Thompson.

The change also has exposed some ugly attitudes among managers. When Thompson proposed extending flexibility to hourly workers, the managers resisted, arguing that "there are certain people that need to be managed differently than other people. 'Because we believe that administrative assistants need to be at their desks to *serve* their bosses,'" she says. That issue is not yet resolved, but Thompson says ROWE is requiring the company to confront it.

Denise LaMere, a Best Buy corporate strategist, has struggled to figure out how to prove herself in the new environment. "It made me very nervous," LaMere says. Without children, she once had an advantage—she could always be the first one in and the last one out. She states: "I had all this panic. Everything we knew about success was suddenly changing."

The change begins with what Best Buy calls "sludge sessions." These sessions are where employees dig out the cultural barriers to change—the jokes and comments that reinforce overwork. Tobias comments: "It's like, coming in at 10 o'clock and someone says, 'Wow, I wish I could come in at 10 A.M.' It's really hard to let that bounce off and not be defensive." LaMere admits that she used to gossip about who was taking an extra-long lunch break. "We were all watching each other. You don't want to be seen eating in the cafeteria." LaMere always ate at her desk.

During the first few weeks in ROWE, employees call "sludge" out loud when they hear an offending comment. They try to keep a sense of humor about it—some teams put a dollar into a kitty for every sludge infraction. Yes, it sounds weird, but it can help people break their bad habits, says Phyllis Moen, a sociologist at the University of Minnesota who has studied Best Buy's ROWE employees. "These are all examples of the way we use time to say how valuable we are," she says.

Sources of Resistance

Managers have put up the most resistance. The hardest part of the transition to ROWE, says Tom Blesener, one of the first to go through it, was accepting responsibility for the stress his employees felt. "It was me," he says. "That was hard." Blesener also had to learn how to stop treating his employees as if they were "unruly children," he says. Blesener manages 27 people who handle the company's extended-warranty services. His 20 hourly employees told him they were sick of punching time clocks. "They felt it was almost inhumane," he says. Now these data-entry clerks and claims processors focus on how many quality forms they get through in a week, rather than when they do it. They still count their hours (Best Buy has to follow governmental overtime rules for hourly workers), but they have more freedom to schedule their work around their families' needs.

In the end, Blesener had to give up some of his control. When a client needed someone to be available on Saturdays,

Blesener left it up to his team to decide how to handle the coverage. Under ROWE, he can't stop by his employees' desks and spring deadlines on them—they might not be there. He now plans his whole team's work more carefully and meets with each of his direct reports weekly. "It requires you to get to know your people on a much deeper level," he says.

Total flexibility may not be for everyone. For instance, Best Buy's legal department so far has resisted the new way of working, partly because the in-house attorneys are worried that it will reduce their pay, says one of them, Jane Kirshbaum. Best Buy's lawyers are compensated in part based on how well they serve their clients—other departments that have legal issues—and they are not connected to any revenue-generating part of the business. Kirshbaum wonders if they will be criticized as unresponsive if they take off one afternoon. She admires the freedom the employees in the ROWE program seem to enjoy. She changed to a four-day schedule after the birth of her second child and struggles every day with the push of work and the pull of family. Still, she is not convinced that ROWE will work for her. She already checks e-mail and voice mail on her "day off." Will ROWE push even more work into her downtime? Without everyone in the office, she asks, "How do you make sure that the person who's left is not the person who's dumped on?"

In exchange for more autonomy, Best Buy employees give up the guidelines that signal where work ends and leisure begins. Janssen says the hardest adjustment was "not working 24 hours a day. Because you have that ability now. I had to learn when enough is enough." Moen says the old rigid system is comforting for routine-loving workers. ROWE, she says, "could be harder for people who want order in their lives."

Despite all the challenges, employees who have already made the switch say the benefits of "ROWE-ing," as they call it, are profound. Tobias says she has stopped avoiding her children. "I was getting up in the morning, rushing to get out of the door before my kids were awake," she says. If her children saw her, they would beg her to stay for breakfast. Now, because her quarterly goals are very clearly spelled out, she knows exactly what she has to finish in a given week—negotiate a rental-car contract or audit expense reports, for example. She can decide how and when to do it. If she wants to have a leisurely breakfast, she will. "My kids have stopped saying every morning, 'Mommy, I don't want you to go to work,'" she says. It isn't perfect. "The family doesn't always win," she says. But the family doesn't always lose either. "I don't feel guilty anymore."

Janssen, for her part, had considered leaving when she was pregnant. "Now, it's not even an issue," she says. As for Blesener, the retail supervisor, he went to his first parent–teacher conference, a task that had always fallen to his wife, a stay-at-home mother to their two sons. Joe Pagano, a vice president who works in merchandising, looks back in sadness at all the sacrifices he made. His wife stayed at home with their son and daughter. He states: "I basically worked every Saturday, and some Sundays. It's one of the biggest regrets of my life." After his department switched to the new system, he started taking an afternoon here and there to play golf. He went to Special Persons Day at his grandson's school. Pagano continues: "If things had been different, I probably would have been a better father and husband, and a better manager. I'm doing this so other people do not do what I did wrong."

Key Rationale

The corporate management team, led by CEO Brad Anderson, was initially skeptical about the ROWE program and whether it should be expanded. The initial experiments with ROWE showed that it helped to reduce voluntary turnover, improve productivity, and increase employee morale. As a result of these outcomes, top management allowed managers throughout corporate headquarters to adopt the ROWE program at their discretion. As noted, experiments with the introduction of ROWE in retail stores are in the early phase.

Ultimately, for Best Buy, the new approach to work is about staying competitive, not just helping its employees. Like many other companies facing global competition, Best Buy expects more training, more initiative, and more creativity from all of its employees. The company doesn't guarantee job security: Management has realized that it can't expect so much from its employees without giving something in return. "We can embrace that reality and ride it, or we can try to fight it," says Shari Ballard, an executive vice president.

Questions
1. What approach to organizational change does the ROWE program illustrate?
2. Identify some resistances, both organizational and individual, that the ROWE program had to overcome.
3. What sources of stress are apparent in this case?
4. How would you describe the culture of Best Buy? How has the culture helped the change?

Source: Adapted from Thottam, J. Reworking work. *Time*, July 25, 2005. www.time.com/time/magazine/article/0,9171,1083900,00.html (September 2007); Conlin, M. Smashing the clock: No fixed schedules. No mandatory meetings. Inside Best Buy's radical reshaping of the workplace. *Business Week*, December 11, 2006, 60ff; Halkias, M. It comes from the job. *Dallas Morning News*, February 21, 2007, D1, D6; Brandon, J. Rethinking the time clock. *Business 2.0*, March 2007, 24; Jossi, F. Clocking out. *HRMagazine*, 2007, 52(6), 46–50; About CultureRx. www.culturerx.com/about (April 2009); Finding freedom at work. *Time*, May 30, 2008, www.time.com/business/article/0,8599,1810690,00.html.

Whole Foods Market

Whole Foods Market was founded in 1980 as one small store in Austin, Texas. It is now a leading retailer of natural and organic foods. Its more than 330 locations in the United States, United Kingdom, and Canada include retail, distribution centers, bake houses, commissary kitchens, seafood processing facilities, a coffee roasting operation, and global and regional support offices. Whole Foods Market has a focused mission. It is highly selective about what it sells and is dedicated to stringent quality standards. The firm is committed to sustainable agriculture. In 2007, Whole Foods acquired Wild Oats Markets, a natural and organic foods retailer with 109 stores.

John Mackey

John Mackey founded Whole Foods Market and currently serves as the company's CEO and president. He is known for being casual, opinionated, and very direct. On a scale of CEO directness, Mackey might rate an 8 or 9. On a scale of CEO competitiveness, he is off the charts as judged by most observers.

Current and former colleagues describe Mackey as spiritual and calculating, forthright and aloof, humble and arrogant, good-natured and prickly, rebellious and open-minded, and impatient and impetuous. Mackey himself does little to dispel the contradictions. He says he is pro-employee but is avowedly anti-union. Mackey calls himself pro-customer but acknowledges that he runs a store with higher profit margins (and prices, often) than almost any other grocer. He is avowedly pro-capitalism but also pro-love. Asked once to list the principles he lives by, Mackey commented: "Love is the only reality. Everything else is merely a dream or illusion."

Mackey remarks: "Americans love to shop, right? We love to shop. And Americans love to eat. We're the fattest nation on earth. But, paradoxically, we don't love to shop for food. Grocery shopping in America, for the most part, is a chore." Mackey tried to address this problem before almost anybody else. Yet, he began as a food entrepreneur not so much to introduce style into the supermarket aisles as to influence the health and eating habits of the next generation of Americans. His original stores were big on nuts and grains and loaves dense as doorstops. It was food that took some serious chewing. Mackey comments: "The produce often came from farmers who showed up unannounced at the backdoor with muddy boots and battered pickup trucks. Tomatoes, turnips, carrots, basil—it might be local, it might be organic, it might be both: it just depended on the day."

Mackey's next project, after more than two decades spent trying to reinvent the supermarket, is to change the value and reputation of business in America. He remarks: "Business is always painted as the bad guys. They're the ones who are greedy, selfish, the ones who despoil the environment. They're never the heroes. Business has done a terrible job of portraying itself as invaluable. And it never will be accepted by society as long as business says it has no responsibility except for maximizing profits." Mackey's efforts at rehabilitating the good name of business have involved speaking to college students and talking up the Whole Foods "stakeholder" philosophy, which emphasizes the importance of satisfying customers and employees before shareholders. His argument is that a responsible business benefits all of its stakeholders, including the local community and the environment; he also asserts that such a business will naturally enjoy a higher stock price.

In the meantime, he intends to make some waves. Tired of the way Wall Street's analysts enlist corporate executives in the setting of important quarterly earnings targets—often with the effect of punishing the stock of companies that fail to meet them—Mackey has decided Whole Foods will not play the short-term expectations game. "It's stupid," he says.

In November 2006, Mackey sent a letter to all team members at Whole Foods Market. It stated, in part:

> The tremendous success of Whole Foods Market has provided me with far more money than I ever dreamed I'd have and far more than is necessary for either my financial security or personal happiness.... I am now 53 years old and I have reached a place in my life where I no longer want to work for money, but simply for the joy of the work itself and to better answer the call to service that I feel so clearly in my own heart. Beginning on January 1, 2007, my salary will be reduced to $1, and I will no longer take any other cash compensation.... My intention is for the board of directors to donate all of the future stock options I would be eligible to receive to our two company foundations.

Working at Whole Foods Market

Whole Foods Market slowly opens larger stores in labor markets where untraditional management practices may seem, simply, weird. Whole Foods opened a store in Manhattan, within the Time Warner building at Columbus Circle. It is the largest supermarket in Manhattan, with 68,000 square feet. The ceilings are airy, the café is sky lit, the aisles are so wide that two shopping carts and a baby stroller—three abreast—can easily slide past one another. The Columbus Circle Whole Foods provides an array of choices. The prepared-foods area includes a sushi bar, staffed at lunch with 11 people; a pizza bar with 14 kinds of pizza; a coffee and tea bar; a salad bar with 40 items; and a daily hot-lunch bar that includes separate arrays of Asian, Indian, and Latin food. The produce section recently offered 15 different varieties of organic greens, including dinosaur kale; the meat case held four dozen kinds of meat. The store has 30 checkout stations, a single bank-style line, and a line monitor to speed customers to the next open cashier.

Columbus Circle opened with 292 people on staff, which means some of the 14 teams had 50 or more members, a hard group to stay focused on their goal. Of those 292 staff members, 70 came from other stores. With their understanding of the company, they were the starter culture, in Mackey's metaphor, a yogurt culture. The store has a team leader, marketing team leader, and three associate store team leaders, all of whom were previously running their own stores in Georgetown, Maryland, and Albuquerque, New Mexico, before coming to New York. Five years after opening, Columbus Circle now has 615 team members, including 140 people on the cashier/front-end team alone, more people than used to work in a whole store.

Aaron Foster came to Columbus Circle from a Philadelphia Whole Foods. He's a cheese buyer, and standing at the cheese display, he's pondering the tension in Whole Foods' values—as he puts it, to "further the goals of sustainable agriculture and natural food production while being as big as we are and growing as fast as we are." A customer comes up to Foster. She states: "Excuse me. I'm looking for a certain cheese. It begins with a C. It's one syllable." Foster focuses on the roster of C cheeses in his brain. "I bought it yesterday at Dean & DeLuca!" the customer comments. Foster replies: "Comte." "That's it!" the customer says, and they head off to get her some.

Barry Keenan is working the fresh seafood case. He calls out the weights of the salmon and the shrimp he is selling before the scale can display them. He states: "I shopped at the Whole Foods in Chelsea all the time. I figured I'd put in my application, and they hired me in September."

Chris Hitt, who was at Whole Foods for 16 years and left as president in 2001, says, "Customers experience the food and the space, but what they really experience is the work culture. The true hidden secret of the company is the work culture. That's what delivers the stores to the customers."

Wendy Steinberg has worked at Whole Foods since 1992 (her husband works at Whole Foods, too), and she is now one of the associate team leaders at Columbus Circle. She has a story from her first year at the company, when she was working in a store in Providence, Rhode Island:

> *I was on break, in the break room. I hadn't been a team member more than six months, and there was this guy in the break room. He was sitting there, with his hands crossed, with this big 1970s style Afro, just checking things out. We talked. He asked me a lot of questions. I had no idea who he was. I figured he was just another team member."* Finally, she says *"I was like, who are you, anyway?"* He answers *"John Mackey."*

Market/Cultural Shifts

Mackey says he thinks Whole Foods benefits from the fact that the American culture, and especially the food culture, is shifting profoundly. The old idea was A&P and Shop Rite. The milk always in one place and the meat in another; the Muzak and fluorescent lights and wheels rolling over linoleum producing a supermarket trance that was exactly the same in Connecticut as in California. The old idea was Mom going to the store once a week and rarely reading labels. The old idea was male grocery executives and store managers and a clientele that was almost exclusively women.

In Mackey's view, consumer evolution requires a change in the look and feel of grocery stores. It obliges retailers to understand that a sizable portion of consumers (up to 65 percent) are willing to pay more for organic food. It demands a new kind of empathy for an American family that has changed its eating habits (cooking less, shopping more often, and buying more prepared foods) and its makeup (more single parents, fewer children). A large number of women hold executive positions within Whole Foods, Mackey points out, and store designs depend greatly on women's preferences. "We have a lot more feminine energy here," he says.

Whole Foods has also been helped by the entrepreneurs who have been driving the organic and natural-foods movement for the past three decades. The company has incorporated ideas and employees from the chains it has bought—Bread & Circus and Fresh Fields in the Northeast, Mrs. Gooch's in the West, Wellspring in North Carolina—even as many of its vendors have followed the same path from fringe to hip to the edge of mainstream. There seems to be some agreement among Mackey and businessmen like Joe Scalzo, the CEO and president of White Wave, which makes Silk soy milk. They contend that the battles for consumer attention (good tastes, recognizable brands), as well as the fight for agricultural validation (sustainable farming, no antibiotics), have largely been won. It's the push to get their ideas about socially responsible business into the mainstream that is just beginning. Scalzo says: "Wall Street—that's where the fun begins. They only measure one thing, the bottom line. My goal is to demonstrate that the principle-based business model is more profitable than its counterpart, and when we do, Wall Street will chase us instead of the other way around."

Mackey, of course, is just as fervent a capitalist—or neocapitalist, as he calls himself, since he characterizes his early political views as socialist and says his commitment to free markets came late in life. He simply maintains that there is no conflict between an aggressively capitalistic enterprise and a socially responsible enterprise like Whole Foods Market. He is steadfast that his company will never compromise with Wall Street on its values—the minimum of 5 percent of profits given every year to a wide variety of community and nonprofit organizations, the installation of solar panels on the tops of some stores, the payment to employees for their community service. At the same time, Mackey says the company won't compromise its intentions to make as much money as possible along the way. Mackey comments: "One of the things that's held back natural foods for a long time is that most of the other people in this business never really embraced capitalism the way I did."

Our Quality Standards

- We carefully evaluate each and every product we sell.
- We feature foods that are free from artificial preservatives, colors, flavors, sweeteners, and hydrogenated fats.
- We are passionate about great-tasting food and the pleasure of sharing it with each other.
- We are committed to foods that are fresh, wholesome, and safe to eat.
- We seek out and promote organically grown foods.
- We provide food and nutritional products that support health and well-being.

It irks Mackey that some of his oldest customers don't accept that the road to profitability runs directly into the mainstream. He comments: "I don't know how many letters we get from people who resent that. 'You've sold out,' they say, or 'Don't forget about the little people who supported you when you were nothing.'" He adds: "It's interesting that when an idea that began on the fringe hits the mainstream, it's no longer hip and cool, even if it preserves its integrity and values. America has a love affair with small businesses. But when they get to be big, they're no longer good, they must be evil." Mackey's commitment, along with the team members at Whole Foods Market, to multiple stakeholders is suggested in the firm's formal statement of its "Declaration of Interdependence."

Declaration of Interdependence

With the support and leadership of Mackey, the Declaration of Interdependence was created originally in 1985 by 60 team members who volunteered their time. This was five years after Mackey founded the firm. It has been updated in 1988, 1992, and 1997, which remains in effect. We present excerpts of that declaration here:

> *Our motto—Whole Foods, Whole People, Whole Planet— emphasizes that our vision reaches far beyond just being a food retailer. Our success in fulfilling our vision is measured by customer satisfaction, Team Member excellence and happiness, return on capital investment, improvement in the state of the environment, and local and larger community support.*

Our ability to instill a clear sense of interdependence among our various stakeholders (the people who are interested and benefit from the success of our company) is contingent upon our efforts to communicate more often, more openly, and more compassionately. Better communication equals better understanding and more trust.

- Selling the highest quality natural and organic products available
- Satisfying and delighting our customers
- Supporting team member happiness and excellence
- Creating wealth through profits & growth
- Caring about our communities & our environment
- Creating ongoing win-win partnerships with our suppliers.

Natural and Organic Products We appreciate and celebrate that great food and cooking improves the lives of all of our stakeholders. Breaking bread with others, eating healthfully and eating well—these are some of the great joys of our lives.

Our goal is to sell the highest quality products that also offer high value for our customers. High value is a product of high quality at a competitive price. Our product quality goals focus on ingredients, freshness, taste, nutritive value, safety and/or appearance. While we have very high standards for product quality, we believe that it is important to be inclusive and open minded, and not overly restrictive or dogmatic.

Customers Our customers are the most important stakeholder in our business. Therefore, we go to extraordinary lengths to satisfy and delight our customers. We want to meet or exceed their expectations on every shopping trip. We know that by doing so we turn customers into advocates for whole foods. We guarantee our customers 100% product satisfaction or their money will be refunded.

Outstanding customer service is a result of both our Team Members' competencies and enthusiasm in serving our customers and their in-depth knowledge and excitement about the products we sell. We nurture a quality business relationship with our customers by daily demonstrating our customer service beliefs:

- Customers are the lifeblood of our business and we are interdependent on each other.
- Customers are the primary motivation for our work—they are not an interruption of our work.
- Customers are people who bring us their wants and desires and our primary objective is to satisfy them as best we can—they are *not* people to argue or match wits with.
- Customers are fellow human beings with feelings and emotions like our own; they are equals to be treated with courtesy and respect at all times.

We continually experiment and innovate in order to raise our retail standards. We create store environments that are inviting, fun, unique, informal, comfortable, attractive, nurturing, and educational. We want our stores to become community meeting places where our customers come to join their friends and to make new ones. Our stores are "inclusive." Everyone is welcome, regardless of race, gender, sexual orientation, age, beliefs, or personal appearance. We value diversity—whole foods are for everyone.

Team Members Our success is also dependent upon the collective energy and intelligence of all our Team Members. In addition to receiving fair wages and benefits, belief in the value of our work and finding fulfillment from our jobs is a key reason we are part of Whole Foods Market. Therefore, we design and promote safe work environments where motivated Team Members can flourish and reach their highest potential. And no matter how long a person has worked or plans to work with us, each and every Team Member is a valued contributor.

There are many Team Members in our company who "work behind the scenes" to produce product, distribute product and generally support our retail Team Members and customers. Although they are not as visible as our retail Team Members, they are integral to the success of our business.

Achieving unity of vision about the future of our company, and building trust between Team Members is a goal of Whole Foods Market. At the same time, diversity and individual differences are recognized and honored. We aim to cultivate a strong sense of community and dedication to the company. We also realize how important leisure time, family, and community involvement outside of work are for a rich, meaningful and balanced life. We must remember that we are not "Whole Life Market."

We strive to build positive and healthy relationships among Team Members. "Us versus them" thinking has no place in our company. We believe that the best way to do this is to encourage participation and involvement at all levels of our business. Some of the ways we do this are:

- Self-Directed Teams that meet regularly to discuss issues, solve problems and appreciate each other's contributions.
- Increased communication through Team Member forums and Advisory Groups, and open book, open door, and open people practices.
- Labor gainsharing and other Team Member incentive programs.
- Team Member Stock Options and Stock Purchase Plan.
- Commitment to make our jobs more fun by combining work and play and through friendly competition to improve our stores.
- Continuous learning opportunities about company values, food, nutrition and job skills.
- Equal opportunity for employment, with promotion mostly from within the company.

Profits and Growth We earn profits every day through voluntary exchange with our customers. We know that profits are essential to create capital for growth, job security and overall financial success. Profits are the "savings" every business needs in order to change and evolve to meet the future. They are the "seed corn" for next year's crop. We are the stewards of our shareholder's investments and we are committed to increasing long-term shareholder value.

As a publicly traded company, Whole Foods Market intends to grow. We will grow at such a pace that our quality of work environment, Team Member productivity and excellence, customer satisfaction, and financial health continue to prosper.

There is a community of self interest among all of our stakeholders. We share together in our collective vision for the company. To that end, we have a salary cap that limits the maximum cash compensation (wages plus profit incentive bonuses) paid to any Team Member in the calendar year to 14 times the company-wide annual average salary of all full-time Team Members.

Our Communities Our business is intimately tied to the neighborhood and larger community that we serve and in which we live. The unique character of our stores is a direct reflection of the customers who shop with us. Without their support, both financial and philosophical, Whole Foods Market would not be in business. Our interdependence at times goes beyond our mutual interest in quality food, and where appropriate, we will respond.

Environmental Stewardship We see the necessity of active environmental stewardship so that the earth continues to flourish for generations to come. We seek to balance our needs with the needs of the rest of the planet through the following actions:

- Supporting sustainable agriculture. We are committed to greater production of organically and biodynamically grown foods in order to reduce pesticide use and promote soil conservation.

- Reducing waste and consumption of non-renewable resources. We promote and participate in recycling programs in our communities. We are committed to re-usable packaging, reduced packaging, and water and energy conservation.

- Encouraging environmentally sound cleaning and store maintenance programs.

Balance and Integration Satisfying all of our stakeholders and achieving our standards is our goal. One of the most important responsibilities of Whole Foods Market's leadership is to make sure the interests, desires and needs of our various stakeholders are kept in balance. We recognize that this is a dynamic process. It requires participation and communication by all of our stakeholders. It requires listening compassionately, thinking carefully and acting with integrity. Any conflicts must be mediated and win–win solutions found. Creating and nurturing this community of stakeholders is critical to the long-term success of our company.

Is Whole Foods Market's Declaration of Interdependence too good to be true? One indicator that it is more than a public relations statement is the recognition in 2009—the 12th year in a row—that its 54,000 team members have ranked their company as one of *Fortune* magazine's "100 Best Companies to Work For." Other indicators are the continuing and strong increases within store sales and the opening of new stores—a reflection of customer satisfaction. Sales increased to more than $8 billion in 2009, including sales of approximately $1.2 billion due to the acquisition of Wild Oats Markets.

Mackey's View of Stakeholders

Consistent with Whole Foods declaration of interdependence, Mackey has expressed his sense of obligation to multiple stakeholders and the special leadership challenges that go with this value in these words.

> *I think the hardest thing about my job is the way Whole Foods Market views itself philosophically is that we are a business dedicated to meeting all the various stakeholders of the company's best interests. And by stakeholders we mean customers, team members, stockholders, community, and the environment. Sometimes what is in the best interest of one stakeholder may not be in the best interest of another stakeholder and, as the CEO, I have to balance the various interests of the different constituencies and stakeholders to create win, win, win scenarios. That can sometimes be very difficult to do. Everybody wants something from the CEO.*

Questions
1. Using the Big Five personality dimensions (see Chapter 3), describe John Mackey's personality. How does his personality impact his running of Whole Foods?
2. What is motivating John Mackey?
3. Using the dimensions of authentic leadership, describe Mackey's leadership style.
4. What aspects of self-managed teams are illustrated in this case?
5. What are the cultural characteristics of Whole Foods?

Source: Adapted from Gertner, J. The virtue in 6 heirloom tomatoes. *New York Times*, June 6, 2004, 44–50; Lubove, S. Food porn. *Forbes*, February 14, 2005, 102–112; Fishman, C. The anarchist's cookbook. *Fast Company*, July 2004, 70–78; Mackey, J. I no longer want to work for money. *Fast Company*, February 2007, 112–113; Gray, S. Boss talk: John Mackey. *Wall Street Journal*, December 4, 2006, B1; John Mackey quotes. www.woopidoo.com/business_quotes/authors/john-mackey/index.htm; About Whole Foods Market. www.wholefoodsmarket.com/company/index.php (April 2009).

The Road to Hell

John Baker, chief engineer of the Caribbean Bauxite Company Limited of Barracania in the West Indies, was making his final preparations to leave the island. His promotion to production manager of Keso Mining Corporation near Winnipeg—one of Continental Ore's fast-expanding Canadian enterprises—had been announced a month before, and now everything had been attended to except the last vital interview with his successor, the able young Barracanian Matthew Rennalls. It was vital that his interview be a success and that Rennalls leave Baker's office uplifted and encouraged to face the challenge of his new job. A touch on the bell would have brought Rennalls walking into the room, but Baker delayed the moment and gazed thoughtfully through the window, considering just exactly what he was going to say and, more particularly, how he was going to say it.

Baker, an English expatriate, was 45 years old and had served his 23 years with Continental Ore in many different places: the Far East, several countries of Africa; Europe; and for the last two years, the West Indies. He had not cared much for his previous assignment in Hamburg and was delighted when the West Indian appointment came through. Climate was not the only attraction. Baker had always preferred working overseas in what were called the "developing countries" because he felt he had an innate knack—more than most other expatriates working for Continental Ore—for knowing just how to get on with regional staff. After only 24 hours in Barracania, however, he realized that he would need all of his innate knack if he were to deal effectively with the problems in this field that now awaited him.

Matthew Rennalls

At his first interview with Glenda Hutchins, the production manager, the whole problem of Rennalls and his future was discussed. Then and there, it was made quite clear to Baker that one of his important tasks would be the grooming of Rennalls as his successor. Hutchins had pointed out that not only was Rennalls one of the brightest Barracanian prospects on the staff of Caribbean Bauxite—at London University, he had taken first-class honors in the B.Sc. engineering degree— but, being the son of the minister of finance and economic planning, he also had political pull.

Caribbean Bauxite had been particularly pleased when Rennalls decided to work for it, rather than for the government in which his father had such a prominent post. The company ascribed his action to the effect of its vigorous and liberal regionalization program that, since World War II, had produced 18 Barracanians at the middle management level and had given Caribbean Bauxite a good lead in this respect over all other international concerns operating in Barracania. The success of this timely regionalization policy had led to excellent relations with the government—a relationship that gained added importance when Barracania, three years later, became independent, an occasion that encouraged a critical and challenging attitude toward the role foreign interests would play in the new Barracania. Hutchins, therefore, had little difficulty convincing Baker that the successful career development of Rennalls was of prime importance.

The interview with Hutchins was now two years in the past, and Baker, leaning back in his office chair, reviewed just how successful he had been in the grooming of Rennalls. What aspects of the latter's character had helped, and what had hindered? What about his own personality? How had that helped or hindered? The first item to go on the credit side, without question, would be the ability of Rennalls to master the technical aspects of his job. From the start, he had shown keenness and enthusiasm, and he had often impressed Baker with his ability in tackling new assignments and the constructive comments he invariably made in departmental discussions. He was popular with all ranks of Barracanian staff and had an ease of manner that stood him in good stead when dealing with his expatriate seniors.

Those were all assets, but what about the debit side? First and foremost was his racial consciousness. His four years at London University had accentuated this feeling and made him sensitive to any sign of condescension on the part of expatriates. Perhaps to give expression to this sentiment, as soon as he returned home from London, he threw himself into politics on behalf of the United Action Party, which was

later to win the preindependence elections and provide the country with its first prime minister.

The ambitions of Rennalls—and he certainly was ambitious—did not, however, lie in politics. Staunch nationalist that he was, he saw that he could serve himself and his country best—was not bauxite responsible for nearly half the value of Barracania's export trade?—by putting his engineering talent to the best use possible. On this account, Hutchins found that she had an unexpectedly easy task in persuading Rennalls to give up his political work before entering the production department as an assistant engineer.

It was, Baker knew, Rennalls' well-represented sense of racial consciousness that had prevented their relationship from being as close as it should have been. On the surface, they could not have seemed more agreeable. Formality between the two was minimal. Baker was delighted to find that his assistant shared his own peculiar "shaggy dog" sense of humor, so jokes were continually being exchanged. They entertained one another at their houses and often played tennis together—and yet the barrier remained invisible, indefinable, but ever present. The existence of this screen between them was a constant source of frustration to Baker, since it indicated a weakness that he was loath to accept. If successful with people of all other nationalities, why not with Rennalls?

At least he had managed to break through to Rennalls more successfully than had any other expatriate. In fact, it was the young Barracanian's attitude—sometimes overbearing, sometimes cynical—toward other company expatriates that had been one of the subjects Baker raised last year when he discussed Rennalls' staff report with him. Baker knew, too, that he would have to raise the same subject again in the forthcoming interview, because Martha Jackson, the senior person in charge of drafting, had complained only yesterday about the rudeness of Rennalls. With this thought in mind, Baker leaned forward and spoke into the intercom: "Would you come in, Matt, please? I'd like a word with you." Rennalls came in, and Baker held out a box and said "Do sit down. Have a cigarette."

Baker and Rennalls' Meeting

He paused while he held out his lighter and then went on. "As you know, Matt, I'll be off to Canada in a few days' time, and before I go, I thought it would be useful if we could have a final chat together. It is indeed with some deference that I suggest I can be of help. You will shortly be sitting in this chair doing the job I am now doing, but I, on the other hand, am ten years older, so perhaps you can accept the idea that I may be able to give you the benefit of my longer experience."

Baker saw Rennalls stiffen slightly in his chair as he made this point, so he added in explanation, "You and I have attended enough company courses to remember those repeated requests by the human resources manager to tell people how they are getting on as often as the convenient moment arises, and not just the automatic once a year when, by regulation, staff reports have to be discussed."

Rennalls nodded his agreement, so Baker went on, "I'll always remember the last job performance discussion I had with my previous boss back in Germany. She used what she called the 'plus and minus technique.' She firmly believed that when managers seek to improve the work performance of their staff by discussion, their prime objective should be to make sure the latter leave the interview encouraged and inspired to improve. Any criticism, therefore, must be constructive and helpful. She said that one very good way to encourage a person—and I fully agree with her—is to discuss good points, the plus factors, as well as weak ones, the minus factors. So I thought, Matt, it would be a good idea to run our discussion along these lines."

Rennalls offered no comment, so Baker continued, "Let me say, therefore, right away, that as far as your own work performance is concerned, the pluses far outweigh the minuses. I have, for instance, been most impressed with the way you have adapted your considerable theoretical knowledge to master the practical techniques of your job—that ingenious method you used to get air down to the fifth shaft level is a sufficient case in point. At departmental meetings, I have invariably found your comments well taken and helpful. In fact, you will be interested to know that only last week I reported to Ms. Hutchins that, from the technical point of view, she could not wish for a more able person to succeed to the position of chief engineer."

"That's very good indeed of you, John," cut in Rennalls with a smile of thanks. "My only worry now is how to live up to such a high recommendation."

"Of that I am quite sure," returned Baker, "especially if you can overcome the minus factor which I would like now to discuss with you. It is one that I have talked about before, so I'll come straight to the point. I have noticed that you are more friendly and get on better with your fellow Barracanians than you do with the Europeans. In point of fact, I had a complaint only yesterday from Ms. Jackson, who said you had been rude to her—and not for the first time, either.

"There is, Matt, I am sure, no need for me to tell you how necessary it will be for you to get on well with expatriates, because until the company has trained sufficient personnel of your caliber, Europeans are bound to occupy senior positions here in Barracania. All this is vital to your future interests, so can I help you in any way?"

While Baker was speaking of this theme, Rennalls sat tensed in his chair, and it was some seconds before he replied. "It is quite extraordinary, isn't it; how one can convey an impression to others so at variance with what one intends? I can only assure you once again that my disputes with Jackson—and you may remember also Godson—have had nothing at all to do with the color of their skins. I promise you that if a Barracanian had behaved in an equally peremptory manner, I would have reacted in precisely the same way. And again, if I may say it within these four walls, I am sure I am not the only one who has found Jackson and Godson difficult. I could mention the names of several expatriates who have felt the same. However, I am really sorry to have created this impression of not being able to get on with Europeans—it is an entirely false one—and I quite realize that I must do all I can to correct it as quickly as possible. On your last point, regarding Europeans holding senior positions in the company for some time to come, I quite accept the situation. I know that Caribbean Bauxite—as it has been doing for many years now—will promote Barracanians as

soon as their experience warrants it. And, finally, I would like to assure you, John—and my father thinks the same, too—that I am very happy in my work here and hope to stay with the company for many years to come."

Rennalls had spoken earnestly, and Baker, although not convinced by what he had heard, did not think he could pursue the matter further except to say, "All right, Matt, my impression may be wrong, but I would like to remind you about the truth of that old saying 'What is important is not what is true, but what is believed.' Let it rest at that."

But suddenly Baker knew that he did not want to "let it rest at that." He was disappointed once again at not being able to break through to Rennalls and at having again had to listen to his bland denial that there was any racial prejudice in his makeup.

Baker, who had intended to end the interview at this point, decided to try another tack. "To return for a moment to the plus and minus technique I was telling you about just now, there is another plus factor I forgot to mention. I would like to congratulate you not only on the caliber of your work but also on the ability you have shown in overcoming a challenge that I, as a European, have never had to meet.

"Continental Ore is, as you know, a typical commercial enterprise—admittedly a big one—that is a product of the economic and social environment of the United States and Western Europe. My ancestors have all been brought up in this environment for the past two or three hundred years, and I have, therefore, been able to live in a world in which commerce (as we know it today) has been part and parcel of my being. It has not been something revolutionary and new that has suddenly entered my life. In your case," went on Baker, "the situation is different, because you and your forebears have only had some fifty and not two or three hundred years. Again, Matt, let me congratulate you—and people like you—on having so successfully overcome this particular hurdle. It is for this very reason that I think the outlook for Barracania—and particularly Caribbean Bauxite—is so bright."

Rennalls had listened intently, and when Baker finished, he replied, "Well, once again, John, I have to thank you for what you have said, and, for my part, I can only say that it is gratifying to know that my own personal effort has been so much appreciated. I hope that more people will soon come to think as you do."

There was a pause, and, for a moment, Baker thought hopefully that he was about to achieve his long-awaited breakthrough. But Rennalls merely smiled back. The barrier remained unbreached. There were some five minutes' cheerful conversation about the contrast between the Caribbean and Canadian climates and whether the West Indies had any hope of beating England in a soccer game before Baker drew the interview to a close. Although he was as far as ever from knowing the real Rennalls, he was nevertheless glad that the interview had run along in this friendly manner and, particularly, that it had ended on such a cheerful note.

Rennalls' Memo

This feeling, however, lasted only until the following morning. Baker had some farewells to make, so he arrived at the office considerably later than usual. He had no sooner sat down at his desk than his secretary walked into the room with a worried frown on her face. Her words came fast. "When I arrived this morning, I found Mr. Rennalls already waiting at my door. He seemed very angry and told me that he had a vital letter to dictate that must be sent off without any delay. He was so worked up that he couldn't keep still and kept pacing about the room, which is most unlike him. He wouldn't even wait to read what he had dictated. Just signed the page where he thought the memo would end. It has been distributed, and your copy is in your tray."

Puzzled and feeling vaguely uneasy, Baker opened the envelope marked "confidential" and read the following memo:

FROM: Assistant Engineer
TO: Chief Engineer Caribbean Bauxite Limited
SUBJECT: Assessment of Interview between Messrs. Baker and Rennalls

It has always been my practice to respect the advice given to me by seniors, so after our interview, I decided to give careful thought once again to its main points and to make sure that I had understood all that had been said. As I promised you at the time, I had every intention of putting your advice to the best effect.

It was not, therefore, until I had sat down quietly in my home yesterday evening to consider the interview objectively that its main purpose became clear. Only then did the full enormity of what you said dawn on me. The more I thought about it, the more convinced I was that I had hit upon the real truth—and the more furious I became. With a facility in the English language which I—a poor Barracanian—cannot hope to match, you had the audacity to insult me (and through me every Barracanian worth his salt) by claiming that our knowledge of modern living is only a paltry fifty years old, while yours goes back two hundred to three hundred years. As if your materialistic commercial environment could possibly be compared with the spiritual values of our culture! I'll have you know that if much of what I saw in London is representative of your most boasted culture, I hope fervently that it will never come to Barracania. By what right do you have the effrontery to condescend to us? After all, you Europeans think us barbarians, or, as you say amongst yourselves, we are "just down from the trees."

Far into the night I discussed this matter with my father, and he is as disgusted as I. He agrees with me that any company whose senior staff think as you do is no place for any Barracanian proud of his culture and race. So much for all the company claptrap and specious propaganda about regionalization and Barracania for the Barracanians.

I feel ashamed and betrayed. Please accept this letter as my resignation, which I wish to become effective immediately.

cc: Production Manager
      Managing Director

Questions

1. What were Baker's intentions in the conversation with Rennalls? Were they fulfilled or not, and why?

2. Was Baker alert to nonverbal signals? What did both Baker and Rennalls communicate to one another by nonverbal means?

3. How did Baker's view of himself affect the impression he formed of Rennalls?

4. What kind of interpersonal relationship had existed between Baker and Rennalls prior to the conversation described in the case? Was the conversation consistent or inconsistent with that relationship?

5. What, if anything, could Baker or Rennalls have done before, during, or after the conversation to improve the situation?

6. How would you characterize the personality attributes of Baker and Rennalls?

7. What perceptual errors and attributions are evident?

Source: Prepared and adapted with permission from G. Evans, late of Shell International Petroleum Co. Ltd., London, for Shell-BP Petroleum Development Company of Nigeria, Limited.

How Personal Can Ethics Get?

Valerie Young was a marketing manager at an international cosmetics and fragrance company, Wisson, in Chicago. Wisson underwent a major reorganization due to cost cutting, and Valerie's department was downsized from 25 to 10 people the year before. They did survive as a small team though, and their role within the organization was unique—acting as an agency, delivering designs for bottles and packaging and developing the fragrances for their brands.

Valerie's boss, Lionel Waters, had been with the department for 14 years. He was hired by Wisson's CEO at the time, after he had worked for big names in the fragrance industry, and launched one of the most successful female fragrances in the industry several years before. Waters joined the company in order to start new product lines for the company in the mass fragrance market. He then hired two close friends as executives with salaries well above industry standards and gave them each six weeks of vacation. Teams were formed around them quickly and after three years, each team had its own line of fragrances that were launched worldwide.

Valerie was hired to contribute organizational, financial, and marketing skills. The rest of the team was mainly comprised of creative individuals who had basically no interest whatsoever in the dry theoretical world of calculating numbers and strategies. Valerie had not worked in the beauty industry before, but was eager to learn everything about the world of scents and how they were developed. At that time, the department worked with many different perfumers from several fragrance companies. The perfumers themselves, or their representatives, came to present their creations for new projects, or the Wisson teams went to their suppliers' offices in France to conduct so called "fragrance sessions."

It takes time to develop a fragrance product that will end up being a perfect creation on the counters of the world's department stores. The name, concept, design of bottle and packaging, advertising, and, last but not least, the fragrance has to be put together to create an innovative and uniquely new product. Fragrance development itself takes a tremendous amount of time.

First, the perfumers are briefed about the new project so that they can base their creations on already firm ideas about the end product. Then, for every new project in the department, at least 300 to 400 samples are submitted by the perfumers. The majority of those samples are usually discarded right away after "smelling" for the first time because the scent did not match the concept or simply did not smell good enough. Some are set aside, smelled again and again, and during that process, the perfumers get feedback about what to change. Sometimes Valerie's team got 20 reworked submissions for one scent and it often happened that after all that work, the original was picked as the best choice. In the final phase, three to four fragrances remain and only those few go on to the market research testing phase.

During Valerie's first year at the company, the team worked with as many as eight different fragrance companies to have a good diversity of new scent ideas. After a while, they began using only perfumers from two fragrance companies for their projects. She was wondering why they stopped working with the other perfumers, because their submissions were not bad at all and they also successfully supply Wisson's competitors. Why were these perfumers not good enough for Wisson? It did not take long for the team members to realize that Waters was not to be questioned. The team then went forward and developed great relationships with the perfumers of the two remaining fragrance houses.

And then one day, it all became clear to Valerie. She had some copies to make and walked to the copy room in the office area. As she was putting her originals in the copy machine, she saw that there was a paper jam, and the person who caused it left without taking care of it. She started to open the drawers of the paper supply and checked the output tray. There were some sheets that someone must have forgotten and she was going to throw them in the recycling container next to the copy machine. As soon as she grabbed the sheets, she saw that they looked like her boss's private company's stationary (he had a consulting company on the side). So Valerie looked closer and realized that what was in her hand were invoices from Waters to the two fragrance companies Wisson worked with for "commissions and fees" totaling almost $35,000 per month! So that was the reason Wisson stopped working with other companies–they probably refused to pay Waters' kickbacks!

Valerie was stunned. She was left shocked and speechless. Almost as if it were like a reflex action, she took all her papers and the invoices and walked back to her office. Sitting there for a while, she tried to calm down. So many questions were running through her head: Does anyone else know about this? Are even other people of our team involved? Is this normal in the industry? Should I talk to anyone about it?

All kinds of thoughts were spinning inside her, and she spent the rest of that workday walking around as if she were in a cloud. Fortunately her boss was not in that day. He was probably on vacation, just like the 20 other weeks per year of time off he grants himself.

When Valerie came home the night of her discovery, she told her boyfriend about it. This is one of those situations when you have to tell somebody; otherwise you think you are going to explode. Her boyfriend was not directly affected by this, so she could confide in him and be sure of his honest opinion. First, he did not quite understand what she was saying because it sounded so outrageous, but then he realized what had happened. He asked her if she had told anyone else about it, and when she assured him that she had not, he recommended that she keep this information to herself for the time being, not because he is not an ethical person himself, but because he knew that her career in Chicago could be in danger if something happened to her boss. After all, he was the person in charge of the department and if he was gone, the already small team might not survive either.

Valerie did not have a green card in the United States, only a special working visa, which allows non-U.S. citizens with unique skills to work in this country for a certain amount of time. This kind of visa is completely dependent on the "fairness" of the company someone is working for, and means that Valerie could lose the right to work, or even the right to stay in the United States if she did not have this job any longer.

And that was not all. She had just been accepted in a master's of science program at the University of Chicago and was looking forward to that. Tuition would be reimbursed by the company if she got A's and B's in her classes. This was a huge opportunity to gear her career toward greater challenges and successes.

But what about ethics? What about her own values? In this situation, there was so much more at stake than just right or wrong. The decision she had to make would influence other people's lives as well as her own. Her colleagues had become her friends, and even though her boss disregarded good management and leadership principles, these individuals formed friendships among themselves, particularly since they had been reduced to only a handful of people. Instead of joining his team in building up not only professional but also friendly relationship with his employees, Waters preferred to look for only one goal—to enrich himself. He did not care about relationships with other fragrance companies either. Perfumers are somewhat like artists; they sometimes work well under pressure and they are often inspired by their customers as well. To have the greatest diversity of fragrance submissions, Waters should have worked with perfumers from more than only two companies. This would have given Wisson's products a big competitive advantage.

Waters was a constant example of how not to be ethical in handling business and employees. Instead of being a leader who would help activate ethics mindfulness in others, he was the polar opposite. He seemed to have made it one of his goals to spend as much of the company's money as possible. Launch events went overboard with extravagances and expenses; on one occasion, just to show off his horseback riding talent, he rented an entire stable outside of Chicago for one hour—the cost: $25,000—and he expensed it to the company.

Usually he showed up late for meetings or canceled them entirely even when the attendees were already in the office. Or, he would tell someone "something really important" came up, and then relate a completely different version to somebody else. Waters' team did all the work and had to make most decisions without him because he was rarely around. Mondays and Fridays he usually stayed home or at his other office, and with some traveling and all that vacation time, there was never much opportunity to actually work with him. So they learned to be efficient and productive by themselves without the person who was supposed to be their team leader, teacher, and supervisor. It finally deteriorated to the point that even the most positive colleagues realized that Waters contributed nothing to either the work level or to morale, both of which were already low. And that was without even being burdened with the things Valerie now knew!

Could she let her boss get away with this? Was she not obligated to report this? After all, in the company's policies it was clearly stated:

> Personal payments, bribes or kickbacks to customers or suppliers or the receipt of kickbacks, bribes or personal payments by employees are absolutely prohibited.

How could she even work with Waters any longer under these circumstances?

She felt her anger toward him growing stronger. What kind of person was this man? Was he just a greedy human being? Didn't he make enough money already? He always acted as if he was the most naïve person in the office, and then she discovered this! She wished she had never seen those papers. It would have been much easier for her to continue her work and conduct "business as usual."

What Valerie had to do, or not do, somehow became an easy decision. It was clear that she was unable to report this before she had another job or even before she graduated from the M.S. program, which was her ultimate short-term goal. Getting another job is not easy without a green card. The Immigration and Naturalization Service had recently made it more difficult for non-U.S. citizens to work in the United States, so companies hesitate to hire people like Valerie because it means a lot of paperwork and expenses for them. Also, workers with Valerie's type of visa have only 30 days to find a new job in the event they lose theirs; otherwise, they are required to leave the country.

Basically, Valerie did not really have a choice if she did not want to become a martyr for the ethics cause. She decided to wait for a while before bringing these findings to light, at least until she was close to graduating from the M.S. program so that she could receive her degree. It seemed that the highly ethical stance would be to report this right away, but it also seemed silly to sacrifice herself and her own future for the sake of "outing" someone who had been so unethical. Did she act morally and ethically correctly? She felt that she put her own interests before ethics for now, and that bothered her deeply, but she knew she was going to do what had to be done as soon as her circumstances allowed for it.

Valerie's discovery changed everything, and nothing. She still had to set up meetings with their long-time perfumers, and participate and act as if she knew nothing about what happened. She did try talking to Waters about involving other fragrance companies again. Her stated reason to him was that Wisson only receives approximately 100 submissions per project now, instead of the 300 to 400 in prior years. He was not willing to discuss that topic at all though, which obviously did not surprise her. She wondered whether the perfumers knew about these sweet deals too, or if they believed that their hard work won them their projects. Every time Waters said something regarding the importance of keeping the fragrance development as this team's responsibility, she said to herself, "Yes, and I know why!"

When the timing is right, and Valerie makes this crucial information "public," of course Waters and his future will be affected. He will certainly lose his job, could possibly face criminal charges, and his reputation in the industry will be destroyed. For the team, the question will be whether it can survive without him. The teams do have a very strong brand manager among them, who has an excellent reputation within the Wisson organization. Perhaps he will be able to take over the team and restart this department the right way.

Questions
1. What ethical dilemmas are facing Valerie?
2. If you were Valerie, what would you do?

Source: Dench, S. How personal can ethics get? *Journal of Management Development*, 2006, 10, 1013–1017. Used with permission.

Chapter 1: *In Good Company*

A corporate takeover brings star advertising executive Dan Foreman (Dennis Quaid) a new boss who is half his age. Carter Duryea (Topher Grace), Dan's new boss, wants to prove his worth as the new marketing chief at *Sports America*, Waterman Publishing's flagship magazine. Carter applies his unique approaches while dating Dan's daughter, Alex (Scarlett Johansson).

Organizational Behavior and Management: *Sports America* Magazine

This sequence starts with Carter Duryea entering Dan Foreman's office. It follows Foreman's reaction toward the end of a speech given by Globecom CEO Teddy K. (Malcolm McDowell). Carter enters while saying, "Oh, my God, Dan. Oh, my God." Marketing Manager Mark Steckle (Clark Gregg) soon follows. The sequence ends with Carter asking, "Any ideas?" Dan Foreman says, "One."

What to Watch For and Ask Yourself
1. The film sequence shows three people interacting in a work environment. Which aspects of organizational behavior discussed in this chapter appear in this sequence?
2. The three people in this sequence represent different hierarchical levels in the company. Which hierarchical levels do you attribute to Carter Duryea, Dan Foreman, and Mark Steckle? Do they behave as leaders or managers as described in this chapter?
3. This chapter emphasized key competencies as central to behavioral effectiveness of individuals, teams, and entire organizations. Which of those competencies do you see in this film sequence? Give behavioral examples from the sequence for each competency you choose.

Chapter 2: *The Emperor's Club*

William Hundert (Kevin Kline), a professor at the exclusive Saint Benedict's Academy for Boys, believes in teaching his students about living a principled life. He also wants them to learn his beloved classical literature. A new student, Sedgewick Bell (Emile Hirsch), challenges Hundert's principled ways. Bell's behavior during the 73rd annual Mr. Julius Caesar Contest causes Hundert to suspect that Bell leads a less-than-principled life, a suspicion confirmed years later during the competition's reenactment.

Ethics and Ethical Behavior: An Assessment of Sedgewick Bell

Mr. Hundert is the honored guest of his former student Sedgewick Bell (Joel Gretsch) at Bell's estate. Deepak Mehta (Rahul Khanna), Bell, and Louis Masoudi (Patrick Dempsey) compete in a reenactment of the Julius Caesar competition.

Bell wins the competition, but Hundert notices that Bell is wearing an earpiece. Earlier in the film, Hundert had suspected that young Bell wore an earpiece during the competition, but Headmaster Woodbridge (Edward Herrmann) urged him to ignore his suspicion.

This scene appears near the end of the film after the competition reenactment. Bell announced his candidacy for the U.S. Senate just before he talks to Hundert in the bathroom. In his announcement, he carefully described his commitment to specific values he would pursue if elected.

What to Watch For and Ask Yourself
1. What are William Hundert's ethical values?
2. What are Sedgewick Bell's ethical values?
3. What consequences do you predict for Sedgewick Bell because of his ethical values?

Chapter 3: *Because I Said So*

Meet Daphne Wilder (Diane Keaton)—your typical meddling, overprotective, and divorced mother of three daughters. Two of her three beautiful daughters have married. That leaves Millie (Mandy Moore) as the focus of Daphne's undivided attention and compulsive need to find Millie a mate. Daphne places some online advertising, screens the applicants, and submits those she approves to Millie. Along the way, Daphne meets Joe (Stephen Collins), the father of one applicant. Romance emerges and the film comes to a delightful, though expected, conclusion.

Personality Assessment: Daphne and Millie

This scene starts after Daphne answers her cellular telephone and says the person has the wrong number. It follows the frantic rearrangement of the sofa, which ends up in the same place it started. The film cuts to Millie and Jason (Tom Everett Scott) dining at his place.

What to Watch For and Ask Yourself
1. Which Big Five personality traits best describe Daphne? Give examples of behavior from the film scene to support your observations.
2. Which Big Five personality traits best describe Millie? Give examples of behavior from the film scene to support your observations.
3. Review the discussion of *locus of control* in this chapter. Assess both Daphne and Millie from the perspectives of internal locus of control and external locus of control.

Chapter 4: *The Breakfast Club*

John Hughes's careful look at teenage culture in a suburban Chicago high school focuses on a group of teenagers from the school's different subcultures. They start their Saturday detention with nothing in common, but over the course of a day, they learn each other's innermost secrets. The highly memorable characters—the Jock, the Princess, the Criminal, the Kook, and the Brain—leave lasting impressions.

Person Perception: Lunchtime

This sequence shows the detainees at lunchtime. It is an edited version of the "Lunchtime" sequence that appears in the first third of the film. Carefully study each character's behavior to answer the following questions. The rest of the film shows the growing relationships among the five detainees as they try to understand each other.

What to Watch For and Ask Yourself
1. Review the text section titled "Perceptual Process," especially Figure 4.1. Apply each step to this scene to develop your perception of each person.
2. This chapter's section titled "Perceptual Selection" described some external and internal factors that people use in forming their perceptions. Which factors did you use to form your perception of each person?
3. Person perception is the process of attributing traits or characteristics to other people. What aspects of the perceived person, and yourself as the perceiver, do you believe affected your emerging person perception?

Chapter 5: *Take the Lead*

Dance academy owner and instructor Pierre Dulaine (Antonio Banderas) offers to help troubled detention students in a South Bronx high school. His formal ballroom style sharply differs from their hip-hop moves. After watching a hot tango sequence between Pierre and dance instructor Morgan (Katya Virshilas), the students begin to warm up to Pierre's approach. His work with the students proves successful and they compete in the 25th Annual Grand Ballroom Competition.

Operant Conditioning: Learning Ballroom Dancing

This film sequence has two parts with a title screen between them. The first part starts with Pierre saying, "So, as your principal has made me your executioner, you will report to me every morning here at 7:30 A.M." This part ends after Pierre sings, "You're dancing, you're dancing. . . ."

The second part begins with Pierre saying "The waltz. It cannot be done without trust between partners." This sequence ends with Rock (Rob Brown) and LaRhette (Yaya DaCosta) continuing with their practice.

What to Watch For and Ask Yourself
1. Review the "Contingencies of Reinforcement" section in this chapter. Identify examples of antecedent, behavior, and consequence in Part I of the film sequence.
2. This chapter defined reinforcement as "a behavioral contingency that increases the frequency of a particular

behavior that it follows." Which type of reinforcement appears in the film sequence? Give examples from Part I of the film sequence to support your answer.
3. Part II of the film sequence primarily shows Rock and LaRhette. Which concepts in the chapter section "Contingencies of Reinforcement" apply to this part of the film sequence? Give examples to support your answer.

Chapter 6: *Friday Night Lights* (I)

The Odessa, Texas, passion for Friday night high school football (Permian High Panthers) comes through clearly in this cinematic treatment of H. G. (Buzz) Bissinger's well-regarded book of the same title.[1] Coach Gary Gaines (Billy Bob Thornton) leads them to the 1988 semifinals where they must compete against a team of much larger players. Fast-moving pace in the football sequences, and a slower pace in the serious, introspective sequences, give this film many fine moments.

Motivation: "Can You Get the Job Done, Mike?"

This scene starts with a panning shot of the Winchell's house. Coach Gaines says to Mike Winchell (Lucas Black), "Can you get the job done, Mike?" The scene follows a harsh practice and Mike talking to someone from a telephone booth. The film continues with the Odessa-Permian vs. Cooper football game.

What to Watch For and Ask Yourself
1. This chapter defined motivation as a set of internal or external forces that focus a person on specific, goal-directed behavior. Does Mike Winchell show the characteristics of this definition early in the scene? Do you expect him to show any of the characteristics after the scene ends and he returns to the team?
2. Which needs discussed in this chapter does Mike appear to be satisfying? Which needs become his focus later in the scene?
3. Apply McClelland's learned needs model to this scene. Which parts of that motivation model appear in this scene? Give specific examples.

Chapter 7: *Gracie*

The setting is 1978 South Orange, New Jersey. Grace Bowen's (Carly Schroeder) soccer-crazed family suffers a tragedy with the death of her soccer star brother Johnny (Jesse Lee Soffer). She wants to replace him on the boy's team but meets resistance from many sources. Gracie persists with her solid determination and wins a place on the team. Time and successful playing help her win the confidence of teammates and coaches.

---

[1] J. Craddock, Ed., *VideoHound's Golden Movie Retriever* (Detroit, MI: Gale Cengage Learning, 2008), p. 368.

Goal Setting and Rewards: Gracie Knows What to Do

This sequence is a composite built from scenes in two different parts of the film. A title screen appears between the two parts. Apply the first two questions to Part I. Answer them before viewing Part II.

The Part I sequence begins as Gracie enters the kitchen. Her dad, Brian Bowen (Dermot Mulroney), tells her he is going back to work. This part of the sequence follows Gracie's discussion with Coach Colasanti (John Doman). He has told her she will play Junior Varsity, not on the regular boy's team. This scene ends after her dad tells her, "You know what to do."

The Part II sequence follows the final game against Kingston. Grace and her dad call to each other. Make the prediction asked in the third question below before viewing Part II.

What to Watch For and Ask Yourself
1. What goal is Gracie's dad trying to set for her? Does she appear to accept the goal?
2. This chapter described ability and goal commitment as moderators of the relationship between goals and performance. What is Gracie's level on each of those moderators?
3. What do you predict as Gracie's performance in the final game against Kingston? Note your prediction before viewing Part II of the film sequence.

Chapter 8: *The Upside of Anger*

Terry Ann Wolfmeyer (Joan Allen) turns to ferocious anger and alcohol after her husband leaves her for his secretary. Neighbor Denny Davies (Kevin Costner), a retired Detroit Tigers pitcher and a radio talk show host, tries to befriend Terry and help her cope as a drinking buddy. Add four beautiful daughters and the interpersonal interactions become complex and sometimes comedic.

Stressors and the Stress Response: Terry and Denny

This sequence has two parts with a title screen separating them. Part I follows the family dinner with Denny as a guest. Terry is standing on the porch holding her drink against her forehead. Denny enters the porch. Part I ends with Terry saying, "Then leave. Any other reason than that for you to be here, frankly, is just pitiful." She returns to the house while Denny stays on the porch.

Part II follows the bungee jumping scene and Denny driving Lavender "Popeye" Wolfmeyer (Evan Rachel Wood) home. It begins with Terry and Denny eating ice cream from the same container. Denny tells her that "Popeye" suggested he marry her mother. The sequence ends after Denny kicks down the bathroom door. Terry screams, jumps into the bathtub, and Denny approaches silently.

What to Watch For and Ask Yourself
1. Assess the stressors affecting Terry and Denny. View Part I for Terry and Part II for Denny. These film sequences show life stressors, not work stressors.
2. Are Terry and Denny having the distress response described at the beginning of Chapter 8's "Concept of Stress" section? Give examples of behavior in the film sequences to support your observations.
3. Review the text section titled "Severe Stress." What effects do you observe or predict for Terry and Denny?

Chapter 9: *Friday Night Lights* (II)

The Odessa, Texas, passion for Friday night high school football (Permian High Panthers) comes through clearly in this cinematic treatment of H. G. (Buzz) Bissinger's well-regarded book of the same title.[2] Coach Gary Gaines (Billy Bob Thornton) leads them to the 1988 semifinals where they must compete against a team of much larger players. Fast-moving pace in the football sequences, and a slower pace in the serious, introspective sequences, give this film many fine moments.

Communication: Half-Time

This sequence[3] begins with a shot of Coach Gaines and the team gathered around him during the half-time break. He starts his speech to the team by saying, "Well, it's real simple. You got two more quarters and that's it." It ends after Gaines says, "Boys, my heart is full. My heart's full." He calls to Ivory Christian (Lee Jackson) to begin the team prayer.

What to Watch For and Ask Yourself
1. This chapter described an interpersonal communication model (see Figure 9.1). What examples from this film sequence represent each part of the model?
2. Assess the effectiveness of this communication event. How do you expect team members and the assistant coaches to react in the second half of the game?
3. Do any interpersonal barriers exist within this communication event? See the "Interpersonal Barriers" section in Chapter 9 for a discussion of personal and direct barriers to communication.

Chapter 10: *Doomsday*

The Reaper virus strikes Glasgow, Scotland, on April 3, 2008. It spreads and devastates the population throughout Scotland. Authorities seal off the borders, preventing anyone from

---

[2] J. Craddock, Ed., *VideoHound's Golden Movie Retriever* (Detroit, MI: Gale Cengage Learning, 2008), p. 368.
[3] This sequence draws from the DVD, Chapter 27, "Half-Time." However, we edited in scenes from other parts of the film to reduce the number of identifiable talent to whom we must pay a fee. If you have seen this film, you will know that this exact sequence does not exist at any point in the film.

entering or leaving the country. They also prohibit aircraft flyovers. Social decay spreads, and cannibalistic behavior develops among the few remaining survivors. Eventually, no one is left alive in the quarantined area. The Reaper virus reemerges in 2032 in London, England. Classified satellite images show life in Glasgow and Edinburgh. Prime Minister John Hatcher (Alexander Siddig) and his assistant Michael Canaris (David O'Hara) assign the task of finding a cure to Security Chief Bill Nelson (Bob Hoskins).

Leadership: No Rules, No Backup

This sequence starts with a shot of the Department of Domestic Security emblem. The film cuts to Major Eden Sinclair (Rhona Mitra) standing in the rain smoking a cigarette while waiting for Chief Nelson. The sequence ends after Michael Canaris leaves the helicopter while saying to Sinclair, "Then you needn't bother coming back." He closes the helicopter's door. Major Sinclair blows her hair from her face while pondering his last statement. The film cuts to the helicopter lifting off the tarmac.

What to Watch For and Ask Yourself
1. Assess the leadership behaviors of both Major Sinclair and Michael Canaris. Which leadership traits described in this chapter appear in their behavior?
2. Apply the behavioral model of leadership to Sinclair and Canaris's behavior. Draw specific examples from the film sequence.
3. Analyze this film sequence using the Situational Leadership® Model described in this chapter. Use Figure 10.2 as a guide for your analysis.

Chapter 11: *Hot Fuzz*

Nicholas Angel (Simon Pegg) is simply too good of a London police officer for the department. His 400 percent arrest record makes the other officers look bad. The department reassigns him to the allegedly sleepy town of Sandford. Angel's new partner Danny Butterman (Nick Frost) has more interest in films than police work [his father is Inspector Frank Butterman (Frank Broadbent)]. Their team relationship develops over time leading to a genuine partnership and the discovery that Sandford is not as sleepy as it appears.

Leadership: Transactional and Transformational

This two-part sequence comes from different parts of the film. A title screen separates each part. Part I opens with Danny Butterman sliding his chair to get closer to Nicholas Angel. He asks, "What's it like being stabbed?" This part ends in the locker room after Butterman says, "Same again tomorrow?" Angel responds "Yeah" as he removes his civilian clothes from the locker.

Part II begins as Angel enters the corridor that leads to his apartment. It ends at the station with Angel and Butterman talking at the table. Butterman says, "People have accidents every day." Angel laughs with his head on the table.

What to Watch For and Ask Yourself
1. This chapter opens with the observation, "Leadership is future oriented. It involves influencing people to move from where they are (here) to some new place (there)." Does this film sequence provide examples of these aspects of leadership?
2. The chapter discussed the authentic leadership model. Which aspects of the film sequence showed such leadership behavior?
3. This chapter also discussed transformational leadership. Which film sequence aspects showed transformational leadership behavior?

Chapter 12: *Friends with Money*

This film focuses on four female friends at various stages of life development. Three are married; some with children. Some couples are extremely wealthy; others are not. Olivia (Jennifer Anniston), a former schoolteacher and now a maid, is single. The film focuses on interactions among them and the dynamics of their lives.

A Small Team: The Aaron Team in Action

This sequence comes from two sequences that appear at different places in the film. A title screen separates the sequences.

The first sequence begins with The Other Aaron (Ty Burrell) saying to Aaron (Simon McBurney), "I've—Excuse me, I've . . . . I've seen you in here a lot." This sequence ends after they discuss Aaron's socks.

Sequence 2 is DVD, Chapter 15, "Friendship Grows." The two Aarons come out of a movie theater. Aaron says, "On top of it, I don't get the part where the guy tells the other guy not to come to the house." The sequence ends as The Other Aaron says, "I love your shirt, by the way."

What to Watch For and Ask Yourself
1. This chapter defined a group as any number of people with shared goals who communicate with each other and few enough to communicate person to person. Does this film sequence have examples of each part of that definition? Identify specific moments that fit the definition.
2. Review the "Stages of Team Development" section. Apply the model of development stages to this entire film sequence. You should see examples of each stage.
3. Chapter 12 defines cohesiveness as "the strength of the members' desire to remain in a team and their commitment to it." Is this a cohesive group? Cite some specific moments from the film sequence to support your conclusion.

Chapter 13: *Welcome Home Roscoe Jenkins*

Hollywood talk show host Roscoe Jenkins (Martin Lawrence) returns to his Georgia home for his parents' 50th wedding anniversary. Cultures clash between the big-city Roscoe and other family members. The culture clash becomes even more severe because of the presence of his upper-class fiancée, Bianca Kittles (Joy Bryant), who does not understand this family and feels superior to them.

Conflict: It Can Sneak Up on You

This sequence starts with Roscoe and his brother, Sheriff Otis Jenkins (Michael Clarke Duncan), carrying a tub of fish and ice from Monty's butcher shop to Sheriff Jenkins's pickup truck. It follows the baseball game during which Roscoe hit a ball that struck Mama Jenkins (Margaret Avery) in the head. This sequence ends after Sheriff Jenkins knocks out his brother.

What to Watch For and Ask Yourself
1. Chapter 13 opened with definitions of conflict and conflict management and a discussion of desirable and destructive conflict. Apply those definitions and discussions to this film sequence. Draw examples from the sequence.
2. Which conflict levels shown in Figure 13.1 appear in this sequence? Give examples for the levels you choose.
3. Which interpersonal conflict-handling style best fits the behavior shown in the film sequence? Give some examples from the sequence.

Chapter 14: *Failure to Launch*

Meet Tripp (Matthew McConaughey), 35 years old, nice car, loves sailing, and lives in a nice house—his parents'. Tripp's attachment to his family usually annoys any woman with whom he becomes serious. Mother Sue (Kathy Bates) and father Al (Terry Bradshaw) hire Paula (Sarah Jessica Parker). She specializes in detaching people like Tripp from their families. The term "failure to launch" refers to the failure to move out of the family home at an earlier age.

The Bird Problem: Fast Decision Making!

This fast-moving sequence begins with the sound of a bird chirping as it perches on a tree limb. Kit (Zooey Deschanel) and Ace (Justin Bartha) have waited patiently for the bird's arrival. This bird has annoyed Kit for many days. Ace believes that Kit only pumped the shotgun twice. The sequence ends after the bird leaves the house.

What to Watch For and Ask Yourself
1. Assess the degree of certainty or uncertainty that Kit and Ace face in this decision. What factors set the degree of certainty or uncertainty?
2. "The Bird Problem" presents examples of bounded rationality discussed early in Chapter 14. What features of their problem fit different aspects of bounded rationality?
3. Review the chapter section describing Osborn's creativity process. Which steps in that process appear in "The Bird Problem?" Note the examples of each step that you see.

Chapter 15: *Rendition*

U.S. government operatives suddenly take Anwar El-Ibrahimi (Omar Metwally) from his flight from Cape Town, South Africa, after it arrives in Washington, D.C. He is a suspected terrorist whom the government sends to North Africa for torture and interrogation (extraordinary rendition). Douglas Freeman (Jake Gyllenhaal), a CIA analyst, becomes involved. He reacts negatively to the torture techniques and urges El-Ibrahimi's release. The story has other complications in the form of El-Ibrahimi's pregnant wife at home who desperately works for her husband's safe return.

Designing Organizations: A Simple Look

This scene opens with a night shot of the Washington Monument. It follows Kahlid's (Moa Khouas) discussion with Hamadi (Hassam Ghancy), the leader of the terrorist bomb group. Congressional aide Alan Smith's (Peter Sarsgaard) voice-over says, "She called you?" The scene ends after Senator Hawkins (Alan Arkin) tells Alan to back off. The film cuts to a panning shot of a market area and Douglas Freeman drinking.

Alan Smith's question, "She called you?" refers to Corrine Whitman (Meryl Streep), head of U.S. intelligence. She authorized the extraordinary rendition of El-Ibrahimi. Alan Smith, earlier in the film, pressed her for El-Ibrahimi's release and his return to the United States. Whitman lied about El-Ibrahimi's existence. This scene does not explicitly discuss organizational design, but you can infer several aspects of design from the scene.

What to Watch For and Ask Yourself
1. Which type of management practice best fits Senator Smith's office—mechanistic or organic?
2. What reporting relationships does this scene show or imply? Does it show or imply a hierarchy? Draw examples from the scene.
3. Can you sense the division of labor represented by Senator Hawkins and Alan Smith? Corrine Whitman does not appear in this scene but is also part of a division of labor.

Chapter 16: *Charlie Wilson's War*

Democratic Congressman Charlie Wilson (Tom Hanks) from East Texas lives a reckless life that includes heavy drinking and chasing attractive women. The film focuses on the Afghanistan rebellion against the Soviet troop invasion in the 1980s. Wilson becomes the unlikely champion of the Afghan cause through his role in two major congressional committees that deal with foreign policy and covert operations. Houston socialite Joanne Herring (Julia Roberts) strongly urges the intervention. CIA agent Gust Avrakotos (Philip Seymour Hoffman) helps with some details.

Organizational Culture: Some Observations on the U.S. Congress

This sequence appears early in the film after the scene showing Charlie Wilson, Paul Brown (Brian Markinson), Crystal Lee (Jud Tyler), and two strippers drinking and partying in a hot tub. It opens with a shot of the Capitol building. Congressman Charlie Wilson talks to his assistant Bonnie Bach (Amy Adams) while walking to chambers for a vote. The sequence ends after Wilson enters the chambers. The film cuts to Wilson's office where Larry Liddle (Peter Gerety) and his daughter Jane (Emily Blunt) wait for Wilson to arrive.

What to Watch For and Ask Yourself
1. Organization members will unconsciously behave according to organizational cultural values. Which cultural values appear in this sequence?
2. Shared behaviors are another level of organizational culture. You also can infer these shared behaviors from the behavior of organizational members. Which shared behaviors appear in this sequence?
3. Cultural symbols are the last level and the easiest to see. Which cultural symbols did you observe? How do these symbols reinforce the cultural values?

Chapter 17: *Field of Dreams*

Ray Kinsella (Kevin Costner) hears a voice while working in his Iowa cornfield that says, "If you build it, he will come." Ray concludes that "he" is legendary "Shoeless Joe" Jackson (Ray Liotta), a Chicago White Sox player suspended for rigging the 1919 World Series. With the support of his wife Annie (Amy Madigan), Ray jeopardizes his farm by replacing some cornfields with a modern baseball diamond. "Shoeless Joe" soon arrives, followed by the rest of the suspended players. This charming fantasy film, based on W. P. Kinsella's novel *Shoeless Joe*, shows the rewards of pursuing a dream.

Forces for Change: Some Internal and External Forces

This scene is part of the "People Will Come" sequence toward the end of the film. By this time in the story, Ray has met Terrence Mann (James Earl Jones). They have traveled together from Boston to Minnesota to find A. W. "Moonlight" Graham (Burt Lancaster). At this point, the three are at Ray's Iowa farm.

This scene follows Mark's (Timothy Busfield) arrival to discuss the foreclosure of Ray and Annie's mortgage. Mark, who is Annie's brother, cannot see the players on the field. Karin (Gaby Hoffman), Ray and Annie's daughter, has proposed that people will come to Iowa City and buy tickets to watch a baseball game. Mark does not understand her proposal. The film continues to its end.

What to Watch For and Ask Yourself
1. Who is the target of change in this scene?
2. Apply a force field analysis to this scene. What are the forces for change? What are the forces for the status quo?
3. Chapter 17 discussed the role and importance of a vision of a future state in the organizational change process. Does a vision emerge in this scene? If yes, what is that vision and who expresses it?

References

Chapter 1

1. *Adapted from* Nooyi, I. The best advice I ever got. http://cnnmoney.com (November 2008); Bingham, T., and Galagan, P. Doing good while doing well. *T&D*, 2008, 62(6), 32–34; Morris, B. The Pepsi challenge. *Fortune*, March 3, 2008, 55–66; PepsiCo, Inc. *Yahoo! Finance*. http://finance.yahoo.com (January 2009).

2. *Adapted from* Organizational Behavior Division domain statement of the Academy of Management. www.aomonline.org (January 2009).

3. Tichy, N. M. The teachable point of view. *Journal of Business Strategy*, January/February 1998, 29–33; Tichy, N. M. *The Cycle of Leadership: How Great Leaders Teach Their Companies to Win*. New York: HarperBusiness, 2004; Tichy, N. M., and DeRose, C. Leadership judgment at the front line. *Leader to Leader*, Summer 2006, 31–37.

4. McCartney, W. W., and Campbell, C. R. Leadership, management, and derailment: A model of individual success and failure. *Leadership & Organization Development Journal*, 2006, 27, 190–202.

5. White Stag Leadership Development. Principles of leadership. www.whitestag.org (January 2009).

6. Kouzes, J. M., and Posner, B. Z. *The Leadership Challenge*, 4th ed. San Francisco: Jossey-Bass, 2008.

7. *Adapted from* Bingham and Galagan. Doing good while doing well, 32–34.

8. Competency Model Clearinghouse. Building blocks for competency models. www.careeronestop.org /competencymodel (January 2009); Kahane, E. Competency management: Cracking the code for organizational impact. *T&D*, 2008, 62(5), 71–76; Naquin, S. S., and Holton, E. Leadership and managerial competency models: A simplified process and resulting model. *Advances in Developing Human Resources*, 2006, 8, 144–165; for a discussion of the uses and limitations of competency frameworks, see Levenson, A. R., van der Stede, W. A., and Cohen, S. G. Measuring the relationship between managerial competence and performance. *Journal of Management*, 2006, 32, 360–380.

9. Competency models. http://www.salary.com/Competencies/ competency_models.asp (January 2009); see also Sanghi, S. *The Handbook of Competency Mapping: Understanding, Designing and Implementing Competency Models in Organizations*, 2nd ed. Thousand Oaks, CA: Sage, 2007.

10. This section draws from Thiroux, J. P., and Krasemann, K. W. *Ethics: Theory and Practice*, 10th ed. Upper Saddle River, NJ: Prentice-Hall, 2009; MacKinnon, B. *Ethics: Theory and Contemporary Issues*, Boston: Wadsworth/ Cengage Learning, 2009.

11. McNamara, C. *Complete Guide to Ethics Management: An Ethics Toolkit for Managers*. 2006. http://managementhelp .org/ethics/ethxgde.htm (January 2009); Geva, A. A typology of moral problems in business: A framework for ethical management. *Journal of Business Ethics*, 2006, 69, 133–147.

12. Treviño, L. K., and Nelson, K. *Managing Business Ethics: Straight Talk about How to Do It Right*. New York: Wiley, 2006.

13. Cohen, M. *101 Ethical Dilemmas*, 2nd ed. New York: Routledge, 2007.

14. Mattel: About us. www.mattel.com (January 2009).

15. Levick, R. Lessons from the Mattel crisis. *CRO Today*, March 5, 2008. www.thecro.com (December 2008).

16. *Adapted from* Eckert, R. A. Commitment to ethical path. *Ethisphere Magazine*, June 3, 2008. www.ethisphere .com/committed (December 2008); Dee, J. Toy maker's conscience. *New York Times Magazine*, December 23, 2007, 34–39.

17. *Adapted from* Brady, O. Indra Nooyi: Keeping cool in hot water. *Business Week*, June 17, 2007, 49; McKay, B. Boss talk: PepsiCo CEO adapts to tough climate. *Wall Street Journal*, September 11, 2008, B1; Krischer Goodman, C. PepsiCo CEO defines good work. *Knight Ridder Tribune Business News*, September 11, 2007, 1; Morris. The Pepsi challenge, 55–66; Indra Nooyi. http://en.wikipedia.org/ wiki/Indra_Nooyi (November 2008).

18. Harrington, B., and Hall, D. T. *Career Management & Work/Life Integration: Using Self-Assessment to Navigate Contemporary Careers*. Thousand Oaks, CA: Sage, 2007; Kets de Vries, M. *Reflections on Leadership and Career Development*. New York: Wiley, 2009.

19. Inkson, K. *Understanding Careers: The Metaphors of Working Lives*. Thousand Oaks, CA: Sage, 2006; Heslin, P. A. Experiencing career success. *Organizational Dynamics*, 2005, 34, 376–390.

20. Hunt, J. M., and Weintraub, J. R. *The Coaching Organization: A Strategy for Developing Leaders*. Thousand Oaks, CA: Sage, 2006; Dries, N. Pepermans, R. and Carlier, O. Career success: Constructing a multidimensional model. *Journal of Vocational Behavior*, 2008, 73, 254–267.

21. This section draws from Greene, A., and Greene, M. *Diversity Management*. New York: Routledge, 2009; G. Moss (Ed.). *Profiting from Diversity*. New York: Palgrave Macmillan, 2009; Maltbia, T., and Power, A. *A Leader's Guide to Leveraging Diversity*. Boston: Butterworth-Heinemann, 2008.

22. Bingham and Galagan. Doing good while doing well, 34.

23. *Adapted from Demonstrating Social Responsibility and Integrity: 2008*. Hartford, CT: Aetna, 2008; *Aetna's Diverse Discoveries Program*. www.aetna.com (December 2008); Best practices & outstanding initiatives. *Training*, 2008, 45(2), 114–120; The editors. The 40 best companies for diversity. *Black Enterprise*, 2008, 38(12), 94–112.

24. Aetna, Inc. *Hoover's*. http://hoovers.com (December 2008); About Aetna. www.aetna.com/about (December 2008).

25. Moran, R. T., Harris, P. R., and Moran, S. V. *Managing Cultural Differences: Global Leadership Strategies for the 21st Century*, 7th ed. New York: Elsevier, 2008; Moodian, M. A. *Contemporary Leadership and Intercultural*

Competence: Exploring the Cross-Cultural Dynamics within Organizations. Thousand Oaks, CA: Sage, 2008.

26. Adler, N. J., and Gunderson, A. *International Dimensions of Organizational Behavior*, 5th ed. Mason, OH: South-Western/Cengage Learning, 2008.

27. Gannon, M. J., and Pillai, R. *Understanding Global Cultures: Metaphorical Journeys Through 29 Nations, Clusters of Nations, Continents, and Diversity*, 4th ed. Thousand Oaks, CA: Sage, 2009.

28. Carlos Ghosn. www.nissanusa.com (December 2008); www.renault.com (December 2008).

29. *Adapted from* The transcultural leader: Carlos Ghosn. http://knowledge.insead.edu (December 2008); Rivas-Micoud, M. *The Ghosn Factor: 24 Inspiring Lessons from Carlos Ghosn, the Most Successful Transnational Leader.* New York: McGraw-Hill Education, 2005.

30. This section draws from Smith, S. W., and Wilson, S. R. (Eds.). *New Directions in Interpersonal Communication Research.* Thousand Oaks, CA: Sage, 2009; Wood, J. T. *Interpersonal Communication.* Mason, OH: South-Western/Cengage Learning, 2009; Lane, S. D. *Interpersonal Communication: Competence and Contexts*, 2nd ed. Boston: Allyn & Bacon, 2009.

31. *Adapted from* Bingham and Galagan. Doing good while doing well, 32–34.

32. *Adapted from* Wademan Dowling, D. Maureen Chiquet on the best advice I ever got. *Harvard Business Review*, 2008, 86(11), 30; Berner, R. Chanel's American in Paris, *Business Week*, January 29, 2007, 70.

33. Chanel S.A. *Hoover's*. http://hoovers.com (December 2008); Chanel. www.chanel.com (December 2008); Chanel. http://en.wikipedia.org/wiki/Chanel (December 2008).

34. Levi, D. *Group Dynamics for Teams*, 2nd ed. Thousand Oaks, CA: Sage, 2007; LaFasto, F. M. J., and Larson, C. E. *When Teams Work Best: 6000 Team Members and Leaders Tell What It Takes to Succeed.* Thousand Oaks, CA: Sage, 2002.

35. Guttman, H. *Great Business Teams: Cracking the Code for Outstanding Performance.* New York: Wiley, 2008.

36. Allgaier, L., and Reid, G. Think horizontal: The case for organizing your company teams. *Conference Board Review*, November/December 2008, 53.

37. Scearce, C. *100 Ways to Build Teams.* Thousand Oaks, CA: Sage, 2007.

38. *Adapted from* Allgaier and Reid. Think horizontal, 52–57.

39. This section draws from Spector, B. *Implementing Organizational Change: Theory and Practice*, 2nd ed. New York: Prentice-Hall, 2009; W. W. Burke, D. G. Lake, and J. Waymire Paine (Eds.). *Organizational Change: A Comprehensive Reader.* San Francisco: Jossey-Bass, 2009; Kotter, J. P. *A Sense of Urgency.* Boston: Harvard Business Press, 2008.

40. Allgaier and Reid. Think horizontal, 58.

41. Neal, J. *Edgewalkers: People and Organizations That Take Risks, Build Bridges, and Break New Ground.* Westport, CT: Greenwood Publishing, 2007.

42. *Adapted from* McKay, B. Interview of Indra Nooyi. *Wall Street Journal*, November 10, 2008, R3; PepsiCo working on nutritious products, *Businessline*, September 22, 2008, 1; McKay, B. Boss talk: PepsiCo CEO adapts to

tough climate. *Wall Street Journal*, September 11, 2008, B1; Morris. The Pepsi challenge, 55–66; *Performance with Purpose* www.pepsico.com/Articles/Performance-with-Purpose.html (December 2008).

43. This section draws from Chesbrough, H. *Open Business Models: How to Thrive in the New Innovation Landscape.* Boston: Harvard Business School Press, 2007; Allen, T. J., and Henn, G. *Organization and Architecture: Managing the Flow of Technology.* Burlington, MA: Elsevier Science & Technology Books, 2007.

44. Barsh, J. Innovative management: A conversation with Gary Hamel and Lowell Bryan. *McKinsey Quarterly*, 2008, 1, 1–10.

45. Davis, S., and Meyer, C. *Blur: The Speed of Change in the Connected Economy.* New York: Warner Books, 1999, 5; Davis, S. *Lessons from the Future: Making Sense of the Blurred World.* Mankato, MN: Capstone Press, 2001.

46. *Adapted from* Klun, S. Work–life balance is a cross-generational concern—and a key to retaining high performers at Accenture. *Global Business and Organizational Excellence*, 2008, 27(6), 14–20; Accenture: Inclusion and diversity. www.accenture.com (December 2008); New Horizon for Women *One Step Ahead of 2011*. Accenture. https://microsite.accenture.com/mpw/experience/Pages/StepAhead2011.aspx (December 2008).

Chapter 2

1. *Adapted from* Donlon, J. P. The X-factor. *Chief Executive*, June 2008, 26–31; Deckert, A. Mulcahy describes the keys to Xerox turnaround. *Rochester Business Journal*, 2007, 23(31), 3–4; Tennant, D. The grill: Anne Mulcahy. *Computerworld*, September 1, 2008, 22–24; Xerox Corporation. *Hoovers*, http://hoovers/wiki/Chanel.com (January 9, 2009).

2. Leviscky, G. E., Treviño, L. K., and Jacobs, R. R. Assessing managers' ethical decision-making: An objective measure of managerial moral judgment. *Journal of Business Ethics*, 2007, 73, 263–285; Tenbrunsel, A. E., and Smith-Crowe, K. Ethical decision making: Where we've been and where we're going. *Academy of Management Annals*, 2008, 2, 545–607.

3. Ethical dilemma. http://en.wikipedia.org/wiki/Ethical_dilemma (January 2009); Boyle, B. A., Dahlstrom, R. F., and Kellaris, J. J. Points of reference and individual differences as sources of bias in ethical judgments. *Journal of Business Ethics*, 2008, 17, 517–525; Adler, G. S., Schminke, M., Noel, T. W., and Kuenzi, M. Employee reactions to Internet monitoring: The moderating role of ethical orientation. *Journal of Business Ethics*, 2008, 80, 481–498.

4. Kohlberg, L. *The Psychology of Moral Development: The Nature and Validity of Moral Stages and the Idea of Justice.* New York: Harper & Row, 1984; Boxter, G. D., and Rarick, C. A. Education and moral development of managers: Kohlberg's stages of moral development and integrative education. *Journal of Business Ethics*, 6, 1987, 243–248; Schminke, M., Ambrose, M. L., and Neubaum, D. O. The effect of leader moral development on ethical climate and employee attitudes.

Organizational Behavior and Human Decision Processes, 2005, 97, 131–151; Reynolds, J. S. Moral awareness and ethical predispositions: Investigating the role of individual differences in the recognition of moral issues. *Journal of Applied Psychology*, 2006, 91, 233–243.

5. Kohlberg's stages of moral development. http://en.wikipedia.org/wiki/Kohlberg_stages_of_moral_development (January 2009). Also see Bandura, A. Moral disengagement in the perpetration of inhumanities. *Personality and Social Psychology Review*, 1999, 3, 193–209.

6. Lennick, D., and Kiel, F. Moral intelligence for successful leadership. *Leader to Leader*, Spring 2006, 13–16; White, D. W., and Lean, E. The impact of perceived leader integrity on subordinates in a work team environment. *Journal of Business Ethics*, 2008, 81, 765–778.

7. Lennick, D., and Kiel, F. *Moral Intelligence: Enhancing Business Performance and Leadership Success*. Philadelphia: Wharton School Publishing, 2005; Sama, L. M., and Shoof, V. Ethical leadership for the professions: Fostering a moral community. *Journal of Business Ethics*, 2008, 78, 39–46.

8. *Adapted from* Mulcahy, A. Annual letter to employees on business ethics. www.xerox.com. Click on "citizenship." (December 2008).

9. *Adapted from* Ethics Resource Center. Why ethics & compliance programs should be spared from cost cutting programs. December 2, 2008. www.ethics.org (December 2008); Ethics Resource Center. National business ethics survey. www.ethics.org (December 2008); Also see Brown, M. T. *Corporate Integrity: Rethinking Organizational Ethics and Leadership*. New York: Cambridge University Press, 2005; Gibson, K. *Ethics and Business: An Introduction*. New York: Cambridge University Press, 2007.

10. This discussion is based primarily on James, T. M. Ethical decision making by individuals in organizations: An issue-contingent model. *Academy of Management Review*, 1991, 16, 366–395; Tsalikis, J. Seaton, B., and Shepherd, P. Relative importance measurement of the moral intensity dimensions. *Journal of Business Ethics*, 2008, 80, 613–626; McMahon, J., and Harvey, R. J. The effect of moral intensity on ethical judgment. *Journal of Business Ethics*, 2007, 72, 335–357.

11. Ellis, D. Citigroup to cut more than 50,000 jobs. http://money.cnn.com/2008 (December 2008).

12. Kolbe, R. W. (Ed.). *Encyclopedia of Business Ethics and Society*. Thousand Oaks, CA: Sage, 2008; Quatro, S. A., and Sims, R. R. (Eds.). *Executive Ethics: Ethical Dilemmas and Challenges for the C-Suite*. Charlotte, NC: Information Age Publishing, 2008.

13. Craig, S. Thain spars with board over bonus at Merrill. *Wall Street Journal*, December 8, 2008, A1, A16; Fitzpatrick, D., and Or, A. Bank of America's chief decides to forgo bonuses. *Wall Street Journal*, January 7, 2009, C1; Fitzpatrick, D., Craig, S., and Mollenkamp, C. Thain ousted in clash at Bank of America. *Wall Street Journal*, January 29, 2009, A1, A2.

14. Weiss, J. W. *Business Ethics: A Stakeholder and Issues Management Approach*, 5th ed. Mason, OH: South-Western/Cengage Learning, 2009; Puncheva, P. The role of corporate reputation in the stakeholder decision-making process. *Business & Society*, 2008, 47, 272–290.

15. Staples, W. G. (Ed.). *Encyclopedia of Privacy: Are U.S. Civil Rights Under Siege?* Westport, CT: Greenwood Press, 2007; Rule, J., and Greenleaf, G. *Global Privacy Protection: The First Generation*. Northampton, MA: Edward Elger, 2009.

16. Kerr, I. (Ed.). *Lessons from the Identity Trail: Anonymity, Privacy and Identity in a Networked Society*. New York: Oxford University Press, 2009.

17. Workplace privacy. Privacy Rights Clearinghouse. www.privacyrights.org (January 2009); Aspen's Publishers Editorial Staff. *Employers Guide to Workplace Privacy 2009*. New York: Aspen Publishers, 2009.

18. Etzioni, A. *The Limits of Privacy*. New York: Basic Books, 2000; Cohen, M. *101 Ethical Dilemmas*, 2nd ed. New York: Routledge, 2007.

19. U.S. Equal Employment Opportunity Commission. Discrimination by type: Facts and guidance. www.eeoc.gov (January 2009).

20. Feldman, S. P. Moral business cultures: The keys to creating and maintaining them. *Organizational Dynamics*, 2007, 36, 156–170; Kitson, A., and Campbell, R. *The Ethical Organization*. New York: Palgrave Macmillan, 2008.

21. Harned, P. J. Rule #1: It takes more than rules. *Ethics Today*, October 28, 2008. www.ethics.org/ethics-today (January 2009).

22. *Code of Conduct: A Handbook for Xerox People*. www.xerox.com (January 2009).

23. Lawrence, A. T., and Weber, J. *Business and Society: Stakeholders, Ethics, Public Policy*, 12th ed. Burr Ridge, IL: McGraw-Hill/Irwin, 2008.

24. *Adapted from* United National Global Compact. www.unglobalcompact.org (January 2009).

25. Cushway, B. *The Employer's Handbook*, 6th ed. London: Kogan Page Ltd., 2008.

26. Stone, K. V. Revisiting the at-will employment doctrine: Imposed terms, implied terms, and the normative world of the workplace. *Industrial Law Journal*, 2007, 36, 84–101.

27. Greenpeace calls on Detroit to make real changes in the way it does business to save the climate. www.greenpeace.org/usa/press-center/releases2/washington-in-response-to-the (December 2008).

28. Uhl-Bien, M., and Carsten, M. K. Being ethical when the boss is not. *Organizational Dynamics*, 2007, 36, 187–201.

29. Brown, M. E. Misconceptions of ethical leadership: How to avoid potential pitfalls. *Organizational Dynamics*, 2007, 36, 140–155; Zahra, S. A., Priem, R. L., and Rasheed, A. A. Understanding the causes and effects of top management fraud. *Organizational Dynamics*, 2007, 36, 122–139; Schminke, M., Arnaud, A., and Kuenzi, M. The power of ethical work climates. *Organizational Dynamics*, 2007, 36, 171–186.

30. Witzium, A. Corporate rules, distributive justice and efficiency. *Business Ethics Quarterly*, 2008, 18, 85–116.

31. Fortin, M. Perspectives on organizational justice: Concept clarification, social context integration, time and links with morality. *International Journal of Management Reviews*, 2008, 10, 93–126.

32. Greenberg and Colquitt. *Handbook of Organizational Justice*.

33. Beugre, C. D. *A Cultural Perspective on Organizational Justice*. Charlotte, NC: Information Age Publishing, 2007.

34. Forret, M., and Love, M. S. Employee justice perceptions and coworker relationships. *Leadership & Organization Development Journal*, 2008, 29, 248–260.

35. Bies, R. J. Are procedural and interactional justice conceptually distinct? In Greenberg and Colquitt. *Handbook of Organizational Justice*, 85–112; Dayan, M., and Di Benedetto, A. Procedural and interactional justice perceptions and teamwork quality. *Journal of Business and Industrial Marketing*, 2008, 23, 566–576; Chiaburu, D. S. From interactional justice to citizenship behaviors: Role enlargement or role discretion? *Social Justice Research*, 2007, 20, 207–227.

36. *Adapted from* Posthuma, R. A., and Campion, M. A. Twenty best practices for just employer performance reviews. *Compensation & Benefits Review*, 2008, 40(1), 47–55; Cloutier, J., and Vilhuber, L. Procedural justice criteria in salary determination. *Journal of Managerial Psychology*, 2008, 23, 713–740; Zapata, C. P., Colquitt, J. A., Scott, B. A., and Livingston, B. Procedural justice, interactional justice, and task performance: The mediating role of intrinsic motivation. *Organizational Behavior and Human Decision Processes*, 2009, 108, 93–105.

37. *Adapted from* W. James McNerney. Testimony to U.S. Armed Services Committee, August 1, 2006. www.boeing.com/news/speeches (January 2009); Kidder, R. M. Boeing's $40 billion ethics bill. *Institute for Global Ethics*, March 3, 2008. www.globalethics.org/newsline. (January 2009); Bigelow, B. V. Boeing CEO oversees a culture shift. *Knight Ridder Tribune Business News*, April 28, 2006, 1; Wayne, L. Senate critic now praises Boeing chief. *New York Times*, August 2, 2006, C2; Brown, M. E. Misconceptions of ethical leadership: How to avoid potential pitfalls. *Organizational Dynamics*, 2007, 36, 140–155; Boeing ethics. www.boeing.com. Click on "Ethics." There is an extensive portfolio of initiatives and guidelines to nurture an ethical culture at Boeing. (January 2009).

38. Boeing: About us. www.boeing.com/companyoffices/aboutus (January 2009); The Boeing Company. *Hoovers*. http://premium.hoovers.com (January 2009).

39. Kujala, J., and Pietiläinen, T. Developing moral principles and scenarios in the light of diversity: An extension to the multidimensional ethics scale. *Journal of Business Ethics*, 2007, 20, 141–150.

40. Brief, A. P. (Ed.). *Diversity at Work*. New York: Cambridge University Press, 2008.

41. Stevens, F. G., Plaut, V. C., and Sanchez-Burks, J. Unlinking the benefits of diversity: All-inclusive multiculturalism and positive organizational change. *Journal of Applied Behavioral Sciences*, 2008, 44, 116–133; Ashburn-Nardo, L. Morris, K. A., and Goodwin, S. A. The confronting prejudice responses (CPR) model: Applying CPR in organizations. *Academy of Management Learning & Education*, 2008, 332–342; Greene, A.-M., and Kirton, G. *Diversity in Management*. New York: Cambridge University Press, 2009; Johnson, C. D. It's more than the five to do's: Insights on diversity education and training from Roosevelt Thomas. *Academy of Management Learning & Education*, 2008, 7, 406–417.

42. Hubbard, A. S. The boundary of diversity. *Mortgage Banking*, June 2008, 101; see also Harrison, D. A., and Klein, K. J. What's the difference? Diversity constructs as separation, variety or disparity in organizations. *Academy of Management Review*, 2007, 1119–1228.

43. Jarnagin, C., and Slocum, J. Creating corporate cultures through mythopoetic leadership. *Organizational Dynamics*, 2007, 36, 788–302.

44. Feldman, S. P. Moral business cultures; The keys to creating and maintaining them. *Organizational Dynamics*, 2007, 36, 156–170.

45. *How Xerox Diversity Breeds Business Success*. www.xerox.com (January 2009).

46. Roberson, L., and Kulik, C. T. Stereotype threat at work. *Academy of Management Perspective*, 2007, 21(2), 24–40.

47. Pendry, L. F., Driscoll, D. M., and Susannah, C. T. Diversity training: Putting theory into practice. *Journal of Occupational and Organizational Psychology*, 2007, 80, 27–51.

48. *Adapted from* Dial, J. J. Retiring the generation gap—10 principles for working across generations. *Leading Effectively Newsletter*, January 2007. www.ccl.org (January 2009); Dial, J. J. *Retiring the Generation Gap: How Employees Young and Old Can Find Common Ground*. San Francisco: Jossey-Bass, 2007.

49. *2008 USA World of Work*. Atlanta, GA: Randstad USA, 2008. www.us.randstad.com (January 2009).

50. Josephson Institute. *The Ethics of American Youth 2008*. Los Angeles, CA: Josephson Institute, 2008. http://josephsoninstitute.org (January 2009).

51. Bowling, N. A., and Beehr, T. A. Workplace harassment from the victim's perspective: A theoretical model and meta-analysis. *Journal of Applied Psychology*, 2006, 91, 998–1012; Harassment. http://en.wikipedia.org/wiki/Harassment (January 2009).

52. This discussion is based on Sexual harassment. http://en.wikipedia.org/wiki/Sexual_harassment (January 2009); Division for Public Education, American Bar Association. Sexual harassment. www.abanet.org (January 2009); Conte, A. *Sexual Harassment in the Workplace—Law and Practice*. New York: Aspen, 2009.

53. Equal Opportunity Commission. Sexual harassment. www.eeoc.gov/types/sexual_harassment.html (January 2009); Gordon-Howard, L. *The Sexual Harassment Handbook*. Franklin Lakes, NJ: Career Press, 2007.

54. State of California. *Fair Employment and Housing Act*. www.dfeh.ca.gov (January 2009); OfficeWorksRX sexual harassment policy. www.officeworksrx.com (January 2009).

55. Walsh, D. J. *Employment Law for Human Resource Practice*, 3rd ed. Mason, OH: South-Western/Cengage Learning, 2010.

56. Ilies, R., Hauserman, N., Schwochau, S., and Stibal, J. Reported incidence rates of work-related sexual harassment in the United States. *Personnel Psychology*, 2003, 56, 607–632; Chamberlain, L. J., Crowley, M., Tope, M.,

and Hodson, R. Sexual harassment in organizational context. *Work and Occupations*, 2008, 35, 262–295.

57. Catrell, C., and Swan, E. *Gender and Diversity in Management*. Thousand Oaks: CA: Sage, 2008.

58. Stevens, F. G., Plaut, V. C., and Sanchez-Burks, J. Unlocking the benefits of diversity: All inclusive multiculturalism and positive organizational change. *Journal of Applied Behavioral Science*, 2008, 44, 116–133; Stone, D., and Stone-Romero, E. E. (Eds.). *The Impact of Culture on Human Resource Management Processes and Practices*. New York: Routledge, 2007.

59. Chavex, C. I., and Weisinger, J. Y. Beyond diversity training: A social infusion for cultural inclusion. *Human Resource Management*, 2008, 47, 331–350; Ozbiligin, M. F. *Equality, Diversity and Inclusion at Work*. Northampton, MA: Edward Elgar, 2009.

60. Verizon Communication Inc. *Hoovers.* http://premium.hoovers.com (January 2009).

61. Verizon: Making progress through diversity. http://multimedia.verizon.com/diversity (January 2009); *Verizon: Your Code of Conduct*. New York: Verizon, 2009. Available at http://verizon.com. Enter "code of conduct" in search field.

62. Goodstein, J. D., and Wicks, D. C. Corporate and stakeholder responsibility: Making business ethics a two-way conversation. *Business Ethics Quarterly*, 2007, 17, 375–398.

63. O'Riordan, L., and Fairbrass, J. Corporate social responsibility (CSR): Models and theories in stakeholder dialogue. *Journal of Business Ethics*, 2009, 83, 745–758.

64. Jenkins, Jr., H. W. The bailout so far. *Wall Street Journal*, December 3, 2008, A15.

65. Radoilska, L. Truthfulness and business. *Journal of Business Ethics*, 2008, 79, 21–28.

66. Hunt, S. D., and Hansen, J. M. Understanding ethical diversity in organizations. *Organizational Dynamics*, 2007, 36, 202–216.

67. Ibid., 202–216.

68. Johnson & Johnson. Our Credo. www.jnj.com/connect/about-jnj/jnj-credo/?flash=true. (Click on the "Our Credo" link for a PDF.) (January 2009).

69. Johnson & Johnson. *Hoovers.* http://premium.hoovers.com (January 2009).

70. Johnson & Johnson: Awards & Recognition. www.jnj.com/connect/about-jnj/diversity/awards (January 2009).

71. Xerox recognized for global sustainable business practices. www.xerox.com/citizenship (January 2009); see also Blake, D. H. Interview of Anne M. Mulcahy on role of ethical business leadership. *BGS International Exchange*, Winter 2008, 14–15.

72. *Adapted from* Sustainable development. http://en.wikipedia.org/wiki/Sustainable_development (January 2009).

73. UN Division for Sustainable Development. *Indicators of Sustainable Development: Guidelines and Methodologies*, 3rd ed. New York: United Nations, 2008.

74. Atkinson, G., Dietz, S., and Neumayer, E. *Handbook of Sustainable Development*. Northampton, MA: Edward Elgar, 2009; Kristensen, K. (Ed.). *Encyclopedia of Sustainability*. Great Barrington, MA: Berkshire Publishing, 2009.

75. The golden arches' golden rules for energy efficiency and sustainability. December 10, 2008. www.greenbiz.com/news/2008/12/11/golden-arches-golden-rules-energy-efficiency-and-sustainability (January 2009).

76. *McDonald's Corporate Responsibility Values in Practice Report.* 2008. www.crmcdonalds.com (January 2009).

77. Ambec, S., and Lanoie, P. Does it pay to be green? A systematic overview. *Academy of Management Perspectives*, 2008, 22(4), 45–62; McPeak, C., and Tooley, N. Do corporate responsibility leaders perform better financially? *Journal of Global Business Issues*, 2008, 2(2), 1–6; McManus, J., and White, D. A governance perspective. *Management Services*, 2008, 52(2), 14–20.

78. *Adapted from* Heslin, R. A., and Ochoa, J. D. Understanding and developing strategic corporate social responsibility. *Organizational Dynamics*, 2008, 37, 125–144.

79. *Adapted from* Best practices. *Calvert Online.* http://calvert.com (January 2009); Crane, A., McWilliams, A., Matten, D., Moon, J., and Siegel, D. S. (Eds.). *The Oxford Handbook of Corporate Social Responsibility*. New York: Oxford University Press, 2008.

80. About Global Reporting Initiative. www.globalreporting.org (January 2009).

81. Xerox Corporation. *Our Commitment to Global Citizenship: The 2008 Report.* www.xerox.com (January 2009).

82. *Adapted from* Liberman, V. Scoring on the job. *Across the Board*, November/December 2003, 47–51; Vogt, P. Test your business ethics. http://resources.monster.com/tools (January 2009); Right versus right: Ethical dilemmas in business. http://www.globalethics.org/dilemmas (January 2009).

83. *Adapted from* Tyler, K. Sign in the name of love. *HRMagazine*, 2008, 53(2), 41–43; Carrello, J. A., and Shinaman, T. R. Love contracts in the workplace: "What's love got to do with it?" *Employment Law Alert* (newsletter of Nixon Peabody LLP, Attorneys at Law), February 13, 2008, 1–3; Martinez, M. N. Working relationships: Finding love at work could force you to kiss and tell. www.graduatingengineer.com (January 2009); Richards, S. E. Before we hook up, please sign this. http://dir.salon.com (January 2009); Hernandez, A. V. Finding love at the water cooler. *McClatchy—Tribune Business News*, December 11, 2007, B1.

Chapter 3

1. *Adapted from* www.apple.com (February 2009); Elkind, P. The trouble with Steve. *Fortune*, March 17, 2008, 88ff; Lashinsky, A. Steve's leave. *Fortune*, February 2, 2009, 97–102.

2. Judge, T. A., Jackson, C. L., and Shaw, J. C. Self-efficacy and work-related performance: The role of individual differences. *Journal of Applied Psychology*, 2007, 92, 101–127; Payne, S. C., Youngcourt, S. S., and Beaubien, J. M. A meta-analytic examination of the goal orientation nomological net. *Journal of Applied Psychology*, 2007, 92, 128–150.

3. Anderson, C., Spataro, S. E., and Flynn, F. J. Personality and organizational culture as determinants of influence.

Journal of Applied Psychology, 2008, 93, 702–711; Schmidt, F. L., Shaffer, J. A., and Oh, I. Increased accuracy for range restriction corrections: Implications for the role of personality and general mental ability in job and training performance. *Personnel Psychology*, 2008, 61, 827–869.

4. Nettle, D. The evolution of personality variation in humans. *American Psychologist*, 2006, 61, 6522–6531.

5. Pinker, S. *The Blank Slate*. New York: Penguin Books, 2003.

6. Church, A. T. Culture, cross-role consistency, and adjustment: Testing trait and cultural psychology perspectives. *Journal of Personality and Social Psychology*, 2008, 95, 739–756; Shaffer, M. A., Harrison, D. A., Gregersen, H., Black, J. S., and Ferzandi, L. A. You can take it with you: Individual differences and expatriate effectiveness. *Journal of Applied Psychology*, 2006, 91, 109–126.

7. Kitayama, B. M., and Karasawa, M. Cultural affordance and emotional experience. *Journal of Personality and Social Psychology*, 2006, 91, 890–904.

8. Hofstede, G. *Cultures Consequences*, 2nd ed. Thousand Oaks, CA: Sage, 2001.

9. Alion, G. Mirror, mirror on the wall: Culture's consequences in a value test of its own design. *Academy of Management Review*, 2008, 33, 885–905.

10. Cannon, E. A., Schoppe-Sullivan, S. J., Mangelsdorf, S. C., Brown, G. L., and Sokolowski, M. S. Parent characteristics as antecedents of maternal gatekeeping and fathering behavior. *Family Process*, 2008, 47, 501–520.

11. *Adapted from* Arnoult, S. New horizons for JetBlue. *Air Transport World*, 2005, 42(11), 73–75; Neeleman, D. Lessons from the slums of Brazil. *Harvard Business Review*, 2005, 83(1), 24; Newman, R. Preaching JetBlue. *Chief Executive*, October 2004, 26–30; Brodsky, N. Street Smarts: Learning from JetBlue. *Inc.*, March 2004, 59ff.

12. Felps, W., Mitchell, T. R., and Byington, E. How, when and why bad apples spoil the barrel: Negative group members and dysfunctional groups. *Research in Organizational Behavior*, 2006, 27, 175–222.

13. Daniels, C. Does this man need a shrink? *Fortune*, February 5, 2001, 205.

14. *Adapted from* Donnellan, M. B., Oswald, F. L., Baird, B. M. and Lucas, R. E. The mini-IPIP scale: Tiny-yet-effective measures of the Big Five factors of personality. *Psychological Assessment*, 2006, 18, 192–203; Big five personality traits. http://en.wikipedia.org/wiki/Big_Five_personality_traits (February 2009).

15. The discussion of the personality characteristics has been drawn from Big Five personality traits. http://en.wikipedia.org/wiki/Big_Five_personality_traits (February 2009); Barrick, M. R., and Mount, M. K. The big five personality dimensions and job performance: A meta-analysis. *Personnel Psychology*, 1991, 44, 1–26; Mayer, D., Nishii, L., Schneider, B., and Goldstein, H. The precursors and products of justice climates: Group leader antecedents and employee attitudinal consequences. *Personnel Psychology*, 2008, 60, 929–963; Hirschfeld, R. R., Jordan, M. H., Thomas, C. H., and Field, H. S. Observed leadership potential in a team setting: Big five traits and proximal factors as predictors.

International Journal of Selection and Assessment, 2008, 16, 385–403.

16. Gale, S. F. Three companies cut turnover with tests. *Workforce*, 2002, 81(4), 66–69; Gales, S. F. Putting job candidates to the test. *Workforce*, 2003, 82(4), 64–68; Hogan, R. *Personality and the fate of organizations*. Mahwah, NJ: Lawrence Erlbaum, 2006.

17. Goffin, R. D., and Anderson, D. W. The self-rater's personality and self-other disagreement in multi-source performance ratings: Is disagreement healthy? *Journal of Managerial Psychology*, 2007, 22, 271–289; Judge, T. A., and Bono, J. E. Relationship of core self-esteem traits—self-esteem, general self-efficacy, locus of control, and emotional stability—with job satisfaction and job performance: A meta-analysis. *Journal of Applied Psychology*, 2001, 86, 80–92.

18. Furnham, A., Jensen, T., and Crump, J. Personality, intelligence and assessment centre expert ratings. *International Journal of Selection and Assessment*, 2008, 16, 356–366.

19. Ibid.

20. Goleman, D. *Working with Emotional Intelligence*. New York: Bantum Press, 1998.

21. Austin, E. J., Farrelly, D., Black, C., and Moore, H. Emotional intelligence, Machiavellianism and emotional manipulation: Does EI have a dark side? *Personality and Individual Differences*, 2007, 43, 179–190; Cote, S., and Miners, C. T. H. Emotional intelligence, cognitive intelligence, and job performance. *Administrative Science Quarterly*, 2005, 51, 1–29.

22. Personal interview with Jarnagin, C., Consultant, Lattice Consulting, LLP, Addison, TX, February, 2009.

23. Ford, M. T., Heinen, B. A., and Langkamer, K. L. Work and family satisfaction and conflict: A meta-analysis of cross-domain relations. *Journal of Applied Psychology*, 2007, 91, 57–80; Judge, T. A., and Hurst, C. How the rich (and happy) get richer (and happier): Relationship of core self-evaluation to trajectories in attaining work success. *Journal of Applied Psychology*, 2008, 93, 849–864.

24. Snyder, C. R., Berg, C., and Woodward, J. T. Hope against the cold. *Journal of Personality*, 2005, 73, 287–312; Youssef, C. M., and Luthans, F. Positive organizational behavior in the workplace: The impact of hope, optimism, and resilience. *Journal of Management*, 2007, 33, 321–349; Stajkovic, A. D. Development of a core confidence-higher order construct. *Journal of Applied Psychology*, 2006, 91, 1208–1224.

25. Luthans, F., Youssef, C. M., and Avolio, B. J. *Psychological Capital: Developing the Human Competitive Edge*. New York: Oxford University Press, 2007, 68–70; Peterson, S. J., and Byron, K. Exploring the role of hope in job performance: Results from four studies. *Journal of Organizational Behavior*, 2008, 29, 785–804.

26. Edwards, B. D., Bell, S. T., Arthur, W., and Decuir, A. D. Relationships between facets of job satisfaction and task and contextual performance. *Journal of Applied Psychology*, 2008, 57, 441–466; Riketta, M. The causal relation between job attitudes and performance: A meta-analysis of panel studies. *Journal of Applied Psychology*, 2008, 93, 472–482; Lester, S. W., Meglino, B. M., and Korsgaard, M. A. The role of other orientation in organizational citizenship behavior. *Journal of Organizational Behavior*, 2008, 29, 829–882.

27. LePine, J. A., Piccolo, R. F., Jackson, C. L., Mathieu, J. E., and Saul, J. R. A meta-analysis of teamwork processes: Tests of a multidimensional model and relationships with team effectiveness criteria. *Personnel Psychology*, 2008, 61, 273–308.

28. www.nokia.com (January 2009); Apfelathaler, G., Muller, H. J., and Rehder, R. R. Corporate culture as a competitive advantage: Learning from Germany and Japan in Alabama and Austria. *Journal of World Business*, 2002, 37, 108–118.

29. Nishi, L. H., Lepak, D. P., and Schneider, B. Employee attributions of the "why" of HR practices: Their effects on employee attitudes and behaviors and customer satisfaction. *Personnel Psychology*, 2008, 61, 503–548; Solinger, O. N., Van Olffen, W., and Roe, R. A. Beyond the three-component model of organizational commitment. *Journal of Applied Psychology*, 2008, 93, 70–84; Mowday, R. T., Porter, L. W., and Steers, R. M. *Employee–Organization Linkages: The Psychology of Commitment, Absenteeism, and Turnover.* New York: Academic Press, 1982.

30. Graves, L. M., Ohlott, P. J., and Ruderman, M. N. Commitment to family roles: Effects of managers' attitudes and performance. *Journal of Applied Psychology*, 2007, 92, 44–57.

31. Hellriegel, D., Jackson, S. E., and Slocum, J. W., Jr. *Managing: A Competency-Based Approach.* Mason, OH: South-Western/Cengage Learning, 2008, 614–615.

32. The seminal work in the field was done by Lazarus, R. *Emotion and Adaption.* New York: Oxford University Press, 1991; Byron, K. Male and female managers' ability to "read" emotions: Relationships with supervisor's performance ratings and subordinates' satisfaction ratings. *Journal of Occupational and Organizational Psychology*, 2007, 80, 713–725; Bono, J. E., Foldes, H. J., Vinson, G., and Muros, J. P. Workplace emotions: The role of supervision and leadership. *Journal of Applied Psychology*, 2007, 92, 1357–1368.

33. Bagozzi, R. P., Wong, N., and Yi, Y. The role of culture and gender in the relationship between positive and negative emotions. *Cognition and Emotion*, 1999, 16, 641–672.

34. Kakuchi, S. Put on a happy face. *Asian Business*, 2000, 36, 56; Barger, P. B., and Grandey, A.A. Service with a smile and encounter satisfaction: Emotional contagion and appraisal. *Academy of Management Journal*, 2006, 49, 1229–1238; Laabs, J. J. Hotels train to help Japanese quests. *Personnel Journal*, 1994, 73(9), 28–32.

35. *Used by permission from* P. Dorfman and J. Howell. *Cultural Values Questionnaire.* Las Cruces, NM: New Mexico State University, 2007.

36. *Adapted from* Schutte, N. S., Malouff, J. M., Hall, L. E., Haggerty, D. J., Cooper, J. T., Golden, C. J., and Dornheim, L. Development and validation of a measure of emotional intelligence. *Personality and Individual Differences*, 1998, 25, 167–177; see also Pratti, L. M., Liu, Y., Perrewé, P. L., and Ferris, G. R. Emotional intelligence as moderator of the surface acting-strain relationship. *Journal of Leadership and Organizational Studies*, 2009, 15, 368–380.

37. www.oracle.com (February 2009); Simmers, T. Larry Ellison: Visionary or modern day Genghis Khan? *Oakland Tribune*, July 27, 2003.

Chapter 4

1. *Adapted from* Chu, J., and Rockwood, K. Thinking outside the big box. *Fast Company*, November 2008, 128ff; www.costco.com (December, 2008); www.google.com (February 2009); Davis, M. K. Integrity and values. *New England Journal of Entrepreneurship*, 2008, 11(2), 9–12.

2. McAllister, D. J., Morrison, E. W., Kamdar, D., and Turban, D. B. Disentangling role perceptions: How perceived role breadth, discretion, instrumentality and efficacy relate to helping and talking charge. *Journal of Applied Psychology*, 2007, 92, 1299–1321.

3. Feng shui. http://en.wikipedia.org/wiki/Feng_shui (December 2008); Steinhauer, J. I'll have a Big Mac, serenity on the side. *New York Times*, March 2, 2008, A21; Do you want fries with that Zen?: California McDonald's aims to boost sales with feng shui. www.msnbc.msn.com/id/23300489, February 25, 2008 (December 2008).

4. *Adapted from* www.china.org.cn/culture/2008-02/08/content_124342.htm (February 8, 2008); Kerwin, T. Building tall (and designing deep) in China. *Architectural Review*, 2008, 224, 78ff.

5. Personal communication with Alberto de La Guardia, Manager, Frito-Lay Company, Plano, TX, February 2009.

6. Rosen, C. C., Levy, P. E., and Hall, R. J. Placing perceptions of politics in the context of the feedback environment, employee attitudes and job performance. *Journal of Applied Psychology*, 2006, 91, 221–232.

7. Chan, D. Interactive effects of situational judgment effectiveness and proactive personality on work perceptions and work outcomes. *Journal of Applied Psychology*, 2006, 91, 475–482.

8. Diener, E. What is positive about positive psychology: The curmudgeon and Pollyanna. *Psychology Inquiry*, 2003, 14(2), 115–120.

9. Frost, B. C., Ko, C. E., and James, L. R. Implicit and explicit personality: A test of a channeling hypothesis for aggressive behavior. *Journal of Applied Psychology*, 2007, 92, 1299–1320.

10. McCrae, R. R., and Terracciano, A. Universal features of personality traits from the observer's perspective: Data from 50 cultures. *Journal of Personality and Social Psychology*, 2005, 88, 547–561.

11. Kim, J., and Slocum, J. W., Jr. Individual differences and expatriate assignment effectiveness: The case of U.S. based Korean expatriates. *Journal of World Business*, 2008, 43, 109–126; Young, J. *Global Relocation Trends Survey.* Woodridge, IL: GMAC Relocation Services, 2008.

12. Collings, D. G., Scullion, H., and Morley, M. J. Changing patterns of global staffing in the multinational enterprise: Challenges to the conventional expatriate assignment and emerging alternatives. *Journal of World Business*, 2007, 42, 198–213; Shaffer, M. A., Harrison, D. A., Gregersen, H., Black, J. S., and

Ferzandi, L. A. You can take it with you: Individual differences and expatriate effectiveness. *Journal of Applied Psychology*, 2006, 91, 109–126.

13. Wang, M., and Takeuchi, R. The role of goal orientation during expatriation: A cross-sectional and longitudinal investigation. *Journal of Applied Psychology*, 2007, 92, 1437–1446.

14. Janssens, M., Cappellen, T., and Zanoni, P. Successful female expatriates as agents: Positioning oneself through gender, hierarchy, and culture. *Journal of World Business*, 2006, 41, 133–148; Verma, A., Toh, S. M., and Budhwar, P. A new perspective on the female expatriate experience: The role of host country national categorization. *Journal of World Business*, 2006, 41, 112–120.

15. *Adapted from* Arabian business and cultural guide. www.traderscity.com/abcg/culture8.htm (May 2005).

16. Chen, Y., Tsai, W., and Hu, C. The influences of interviewer-related and situational factors on interviewer reactions to high structured job interviews. *International Journal of Human Resource Management*, 2008, 19, 1056–1072; Levashina, J., and Campion, M. A. Measuring faking in the employment interview: Development and validation of an interview faking behavior scale. *Journal of Applied Psychology*, 2007, 92, 1638–1657.

17. Cable, D. M., and Judge, T. A. The effect of physical height on workplace success and income: Preliminary test of a theoretical model. *Journal of Applied Psychology*, 2004, 89, 428–441; Cialdini, R. B. *Influence: Science and Practice*, 5th ed. Boston: Allyn & Bacon, 2009.

18. Lorenz, K. Do pretty people earn more? www.careerbuilder.com (September 2007); Anderson, S. L., Adams, G., and Plaut, V. C. The cultural grounding of personal relationship: The importance of attractiveness in everyday life. *Journal of Personality and Social Psychology*, 2008, 95, 352–369; Peluchette, J. V., Karl, K., and Rust, K. Dressing to impress: Beliefs and attitudes regarding workplace attire. *Journal of Business and Psychology*, 2006, 21(1), 45–63.

19. Heuze, J., Nicolas, R., and Manual, M. Relations between cohesion and collective effectiveness within male and female professional basketball teams. *Canadian Journal of Behavioural Science*, 2006, 38(1), 81–91; www.costco.com (February 2009).

20. Dennis, I. Halo effects in grading student projects. *Journal of Applied Psychology*, 2007, 92, 1169–1177; Roesenzweig, P. Misunderstanding the nature of company performance: The halo effects and other business delusions. *California Management Review*, 2007, 49, 6–20; Rosenzweig, P. *The Halo Effect*. New York: The Free Press, 2007.

21. Natanovich, G., and Eden, D. Pygmalion effects among outreach supervisors and tutors: Extending sex generalizability. *Journal of Applied Psychology*, 2008, 93, 1382–1400.

22. McElroy, J. C., and Crant, J. M. Handicapping: The effects of its source and frequency. *Journal of Applied Psychology*, 2008, 93, 893–901.

23. Harris, K. J., Kacmar, K. M., and Zivuska, S. The impact of political skills on impression management effectiveness. *Journal of Applied Psychology*, 2007, 92, 278–285; Bolino, M. C., Varela, J. A., Bande, B., and Turnley, W. H. The impact of impression-management tactics on supervisory rating of organizational citizenship behavior. *Journal of Organizational Behavior Management*, 2006, 27, 281–298; Bolino, M. C., and Turnley, W. H. Measurement of impression management: A scale development based on Jones and Pittman taxonomy. *Organizational Research Methods*, 1999, 2, 187–206.

24. Ibid.

25. Buillett, M. T., and Qian, Y. Are overconfident CEOs born or made? Evidence of self-attribution bias from frequent acquires. *Management Science*, 2008, 54, 1037–1052.

26. Ibid.

27. Ployhart, R. E., Ehrhart, K., Holcombe, and Hayes, S. C. Using attributions to understand the effects of applicant reactions. *Journal of Applied Social Psychology*, 2005, 35, 259–296.

28. Moore, D. A., and Healy, P. J. The trouble with overconfidence. *Psychological Review*, 2008, 115, 502–518; Forgas, J. P. On being happy and mistaken: Mood effects on the fundamental attribution error. *Journal of Personality and Social Psychology*, 1998, 25, 318–331.

29. Nurcan, E., and Murphy, S. E. Cross-cultural variations in leadership perceptions and attribution of charisma to the leader. *Organizational Behavior and Human Decision Processes*, 2003, 92(1–2), 52–66.

30. *Adapted from* www.gap.com. (February 2009).

31. Dixon, A. L., and Schertzer, S. M. B. Bouncing back: How salesperson optimism and self-efficacy influence attributions and behaviors following failure. *Journal of Personal Selling & Sales Management*, 2005, 25, 361–370.

32. Hochwarter, W. A., Witt, L. A., and Treadway, D. C. The interaction of social skill and organizational support on job performance. *Journal of Applied Psychology*, 2006, 91, 482–489; Treadway, D. C., Ferris, G. R., and Hochwarter, W. The role of age in the perceptions of politics–job performance relationship: A three study constructive replication. *Journal of Applied Psychology*, 2005, 90, 872–881.

33. Mendenhall, R., Kalil, A., Spindel, L. J., and Hart, C. Job loss at mid-life: Managers and executives face "the new risk economy." *Social Forces*, 2008, 87, 185–210.

34. *Adapted from* Fandt, P. M. *Management Skills: Practice and Experience*. Minneapolis, MN: West Publishing, 1994. Reprinted with permission.

35. *Adapted from* Gardenwartz, L., and Rowe, A. *Diverse Teams at Work*. New York: McGraw-Hill, 1994, 169.

Chapter 5

1. Personal communication with Cal Peveto, Business Leader, Southwest Region of UPS, Dallas, TX, January, 2009; www.ups.com (search "careers" in the search bar) (January 2009).

2. www.ascentgroup.com (January 2009).

3. Weiss, H. M. Learning theory and industrial and organizational psychology. In Dunnette, M. D., and Hough, L. M. (Eds.), *Handbook of Industrial & Organizational Psychology*, 2nd ed. Palo Alto, CA: Consulting Psychologist Press, 1990, 170–221; Bouton, M. E. *Learning and Behavior: A Contemporary Synthesis*. Sunderland, MA: Sinauer Associates, 2006.

4. Oaks, S. Absenteeism: Positive reinforcement works. *ASHCSP Angle*, March 2007. For other examples, see Investing in employees' interests leads to business success: Investment also results in lower administrative costs and high productivity. *Medicine & Health*, 2008, 62(13), 7ff.

5. Kanfer, R. Motivation theory and industrial and organizational psychology. In Dunnette and Hough, *Handbook of Industrial & Organizational Psychology*, 75–169; Daniels, A. C. *Bringing Out the Best in People*, 2nd ed. New York: McGraw-Hill, 2000, 25–78.

6. Skinner, B. F. *About Behaviorism*. New York: Knopf, 1974. For examples, see Tucker, P. Video games and behavioral modification: New technological methods foster self-esteem. *The Futurist*, 2009, 43, 8–10.

7. www.virginhealthmiles.com (January 2009); Rawe, J. Fat chance. *Time*, June 11, 2007, 62; Cullen, L. T. The company doctor. *Time*, June 25, 2007, Global 4.

8. Thang, L. C., Rowley, C., Quang, T., and Warner, M. To what extent can management practices be transferred between countries? The case of human resource management in Vietnam. *Journal of World Business*, 2007, 42, 113–127.

9. Bland, C., Brown, J., Ewing, J., Kavi, S., Morehead, G., and Sims, C. *Wal-Mart China* (unpublished Executive MBA paper). Dallas, TX: Cox School of Business, Southern Methodist University, March 2007.

10. www.costco.com (January 2009).

11. Roberson, J. Coming in today? *Dallas Morning News*, December 4, 2008, D1–D3; Hausknecht, J. P., Hiller, N. J., and Vance, R. J. Work-unit absenteeism: Effects of satisfaction, commitment, labor market conditions and time. *Academy of Management Journal*, 2008, 51, 1223–1245.

12. Daniels, *Bringing Out the Best*, 59–60; Deeprose, D. *How to Recognize and Reward Employees: 150 Ways to Inspire Peak Performance*. New York: AMACOM, 2006.

13. Roberson, J. Coming in today? *Dallas Morning News*, December 4, 2008, D3.

14. Besser, T. L. Rewards and organizational goal achievement: A case study of Toyota Motor manufacturing in Kentucky. *Journal of Management Studies*, 1995, 32, 383–401; Lustgarten, A. Elite factories. *Fortune*, September 6, 2004, 240ff; Takeda, H. *Synchronized Production System: Going Beyond Just in Time through Kaizen*. London: Kogan Page, 2006.

15. Hinkin, T. R., and Schriesheim, C. A. An examination of "nonleadership": From laissez-faire leadership to leader reward omission and punishment omission. *Journal of Applied Psychology*, 2008, 93, 1234–1249.

16. *Adapted from* Falkenberg, K. Time off for bad behavior. *Forbes*, January 12, 2009, 64–65. Also see Fragale, A. R., Rosen, B., Xu, C., and Merideth, I. The higher they are, the harder they fall: The effects of wrongdoer status on observer punishment recommendations and intentionality attributions. *Organizational Behavior and Human Decision Processes*, 2009, 108, 53–65; Parloff, R. Wall Street: It's payback time. *Fortune*, January 19, 2009, 57ff.

17. Luthans, F., Youssef, C. M., and Avolio, B. J. *Psychological Capital*. New York: Oxford University Press, 2007; Luthans, F., and Avolio, B. J. The "point" of positive organizational behavior. *Journal of Organizational Behavior*, 2009, 30, 291–307.

18. *Adapted from* Mackintosh, J. How BMW put the Mini back on track. *Financial Times*, March 19, 2003, 14.

19. Onkvisit, S., and Shaw, J. J. *International Marketing: Strategy and Theory*, 5th ed. New York: Rutledge, 2009, 85, 206; Kincaid, J. Flowers of evil in the garden. *The New Yorker*, 1992, 68(33), 154–159.

20. Smyth, R., Wang, J., and Deng, X. Equity-for-debt swaps in Chinese big business: A case study of restructuring in one large state-owner enterprise. *Asia Business Review*, 2004, 10(3/4), 382–401; Selmer, J. Cultural novelty and adjustment: Western business expatriates in China. *International Journal of Human Resource Management*, 2006, 17, 1209–1222.

21. *Adapted from* Sims, S. Truly a pioneer. *US Business Review*, November 2006, 116–117; French, L. Staying connected. *American Executive*, 2005, 3(6), 37–41.

22. Bandura, A. *Social Learning Theory*. Upper Saddle River, NJ: Prentice Hall, 1977; Bandura, A. *Self-Efficacy: The Exercise of Self-Control*. New York: W. H. Freeman, 1997.

23. Terlaak, A., and Gong, Y. Vicarious learning and inferential accuracy in adoption processes. *Academy of Management Review*, 2008, 33, 846–869; Kim, J., and Miner, A. S. Vicarious learning from the failures and near-failures of others: Evidence from the U. S. commercial banking industry. *Academy of Management Journal*, 2007, 50, 687–715.

24. Gibson, C. B., Benson, G. S., Porath, C. L., and Lawler, E. E. What results when firms implement practices: The differential relationship between specific practices, firm financial performance, customer service and quality. *Journal of Applied Psychology*, 2007, 92, 1467–1481; Chen, G., Kanfer, R., Kirkman, B. L., Allen, D., and Rosen, B. A multilevel study of leadership. Empowerment, and performance in teams. *Journal of Applied Psychology*, 2007, 92, 331–347.

25. *Adapted from* www.steelcase.com (January 2009); Hackett, J. P. Preparing for the perfect product lunch. *Harvard Business Review*, April 2007, 45–50; Hawthorne, C. Steelcase house. *Architecture*, November 2000, 67.

26. Walumbwa, F. O., Avolio, B. J., and Zhu, W. How transformational leadership weaves its influence on individual performance: The role of identification and efficacy beliefs. *Personnel Psychology*, 2008, 61, 793–825; Zellars, K. L., Perrewe, P. L., Rossi, A. M., Tepper, B. J., and Ferris, G. R. Moderating effects of political skill, perceived control, and job-related self-efficacy on the relationship between negative affectivity and physiological strain. *Journal of Organizational Behavior*, 2008, 29, 549–572.

27. Stajkovic, A. D. Development of a core confidence-higher order construct. *Journal of Applied Psychology*, 2006, 91, 208–1224.

28. Luthans, Youssef, and Avolio. *Psychological Capital*, 33–62.

29. *Adapted from* Lee, C., and Bobko, P. Self-efficacy beliefs: Comparison of five measures. *Journal of Applied Psychology*, 1994, 79, 364–370; Maurer, T. J., and Pierce, H. R. A comparison of Likert scale and traditional measures

of self-efficacy. *Journal of Applied Psychology*, 1998, 83, 324–330.

30. Personal communication with Joe Salatino, President, Great Northern American, Dallas, TX, January 2009.

Chapter 6

1. *Adapted from* www.starbucks.com (February 2009). LaFave, C. The ten-minute manager's guide to hiring and keeping GenY workers. *Restaurants and Institutions*, 2008, 118(2), 22–23; Goetz, S. J., and Shrestha, S. S. Explaining self-employment success and failure: Wal-mart versus Starbucks or Schumpeter versus Putnam. *Social Science Quarterly*, 2009, 90, 22–39; Ruzich, C. M. For the love of Joe: The language of Starbucks. *Journal of Popular Culture*, 2008, 41, 428–443.

2. Erickson, T. J. *Plugged In: Generation Y Guide to Thinking at Work*. Cambridge, MA: Harvard Business School Press, 2008; Allison, M. More layoffs expected at Starbucks. *Seattle Times*, January 24, 2009. http://seattletimes.nwsource.com/html/businesstechnology/2008665670_starbucks24.html (May 2009).

3. LePine, J. A., LePine, M. A., and Jackson, C. L. Challenge and hindrance stress: Relationships with exhaustion, motivation to learn and learning performance. *Journal of Applied Psychology*, 2004, 98, 883–891.

4. Cascio, W. F., and Cappelli, P. Lessons from the financial services crisis. *HR Magazine*, January 2009, 47–50; Kerr, S. *Reward Systems*. Boston, MA: Harvard Business School Press, 2009.

5. Zyphur, M. J., Cjhaturvedi, S., and Arvey, R. D. Job performance over time is a function of latent trajectories and previous performance. *Journal of Applied Psychology*, 2008, 93, 217–225.

6. Tolli, A. P., and Schmidt, A. M. The role of feedback, causal attributions and self-efficacy in goal revision. *Journal of Applied Psychology*, 2008, 93, 692–702.

7. Maslow, A. H. *Motivation and Personality*. New York: Harper & Row, 1970. For an excellent overview of motivation models, see Pinder, C. C. *Work Motivation in Organizational Behavior*, 2nd ed. Clifton, NJ: Psychology Press, 2008.

8. Kim, K., and Slocum, J. W. Individual differences and expatriate assignment effectiveness: The case of U.S.-based Korean expatriates. *Journal of World Business*, 2008, 43, 109–126.

9. Kim, T., and Leung, K. Forming and reacting to overall fairness: A cross-cultural comparison. *Organizational Behavior and Human Decision Processes*, 2007, 104, 83–96; Gelfand, M. J., Nishii, L. H., and Raver, J. L. On the nature of the importance of cultural tightness-looseness. *Journal of Applied Psychology*, 91, 2006, 1225–1244.

10. Metlen, S. Relationships among facets of employee satisfaction: Why managers should care. *International Journal of Business Strategy*, 2007, 7(1), 147–158; Koltko-Rivera, M. E. Rediscovering the later version of Maslow's hierarchy of needs. *Review of General Psychology*, 2006, 10, 302–317.

11. McClelland, D. C., and Burnham, D. H. Power is the great motivator. *Harvard Business Review*, March/April 1976, 100–111; Payne, D. K. *Training Resources Group*. Boston: McBer & Company, 1998.

12. Rath, T. *Vital Friends*. New York: Gallup Press, 2006.

13. Personal communication with Susan Reed, General Manager, Innovative Hospice Care, Fort Worth, TX, March 2007.

14. *Adapted from* www.papajohns.com (February 2009); Decarbo, B., Adamy, J., Casselman, B., and Martin, L. Scoring a pizza delivery. *Wall Street Journal*, December 18, 2008, D4ff.

15. Magee, J. C., and Langner, C. How personalized and socialized power motivation facilitate antisocial and prosocial decision-making. *Journal of Research in Personality*, 2008, 42, 1547–1559; Spreier, S. W., Fontaine, M. H., and Malloy, R. L. Leadership run amok: The destructive potential overachievers. *Harvard Business Review*, 2006, 84(6), 72–83.

16. Collins, C. J., Hanges, P. J., and Locke, E. A. The relationship of achievement motivation to entrepreneurial behavior: A meta-analysis. *Human Performance*, 2004, 17, 95–117.

17. Manager Joanne Reichardt. www.randstad.com (March 2007).

18. Herzberg, F. I., Mausner, B., and Snyderman, B. B. *The Motivation to Work*. New York: John Wiley & Sons, 1959; Story, P., Hart, J. W., Stasson, M. F., and Mahoney, J. M. Using a two-factor theory of achievement motivation to examine performance-based outcomes and self-regulatory processes. *Personality & Individual Differences*, 2009, 46, 391–395.

19. Hackman, J. R., and Oldham, G. R. *Work Redesign*. Reading, MA: Addison-Wesley 1980; Strubler, D. C., and York, K. M. An exploratory study of team characteristics model using organizational teams. *Small Group Research*, 2007, 38, 670–695.

20. www.athleta.com (February 2009).

21. *Adapted from* www.seic.com (February 2009); Sung, J. Designed for interaction. *Fortune*, January 8, 2001, 150–151.

22. Gómez, C. The influence of environmental, organizational, and HRM factors on employee behaviors in subsidiaries: A Mexican case study of organizational learning. *Journal of World Business*, 2004, 39, 1–11; Gelfand et al. On the nature of the importance of cultural tightness-looseness.

23. Vroom, V. H. *Work and Motivation*. New York: John Wiley & Sons, 1964.

24. Dickhauser, O., and Reinhard, M. The effects of affective states on formation of performance expectancies. *Cognition & Emotion*, 2008, 22, 1542–1554.

25. Adler, N. *International Dimensions of Organizational Behavior*, 4th ed. Mason, OH: South-Western, 2002, 179–182.

26. Brown, D. J., Ferris, D. L., Heller, D., and Keeping, L. M. Antecedents and consequences of the frequency of upward and downward social comparisons at work. *Organizational Behavior & Human Decision Processes*, 2007, 102, 59–78.

27. Personal interview with T. Johnson, Clinical Therapy Representative, Smith and Nephew, Corpus Christi, TX, March 2007.

28. www.intuit.com (February 2009).

29. Adams, J. S. Toward an understanding of inequity. *Journal of Abnormal and Social Psychology*, 1963, 67, 422–436.

30. Kim and Leung, Forming and reacting to overall fairness; Bolino, M. C., and Turnley, W. H. Old faces, new places: Equity theory in cross-cultural contexts. *Journal of Organizational Behavior*, 2008, 29, 29–51.

31. Hellriegel, D., Jackson, S. E., and Slocum, J. W. *Managing: A Competency Based Approach*. Mason, OH: South-Western/Thomson, 2008, 473–474.

32. Nath, L., and Lovaglia, M. Cheating on multiple-choice exams. *College Teaching*, 2009, 57(1), 3–6; Reynolds, S. J., and Ceranic, T. L. The effects of moral judgment and moral identity on moral behavior. *Journal of Applied Psychology*, 2007, 92, 1610–1625.

33. Magoshi, E., and Chang, E. Diversity management and the effects on employees' organizational commitment: Evidence from Japan and Korea. *Journal of World Business*, 2009, 44, 31–40; Zapata-Phelan, C. P., Colquitt, J. A., Scott, B. A., and Livingston, B. Procedural justice, interactional justice, and task performance: The mediating role of intrinsic motivation. *Organizational Behavior and Human Decision Processes*, 2009, 108, 93–105; Barsky, A., and Japlan, S. A. If you feel bad, it's unfair: A quantitative synthesis of affect and organizational justice perceptions. *Journal of Applied Psychology*, 2007, 92, 286–296; Li, H., Bingham, J. B., and Umphress, E. E. Fairness from the top perspective: Perceived procedural justice and collaborative problem solving in new product development. *Organization Science*, 2007, 18, 200–216.

34. Liao, H., Chuang, A., and Joshi, A. Perceived deep-level dissimilarity: Personality antecedents and impact on overall job attitude, helping, work withdrawal and turnover. *Organizational Behavior & Human Decision Processes*, 2008, 106, 106–125; Craig, W. J., Edwards, B. D., Shull, A., and Finch, D. M. Examining the consequences in tendency to suppress and reappraise emotions on task related job performance. *Human Performance*, 2009, 22, 23–43.

35. Kamdar, D., McAllister, D. J., and Turban, D. B. All in a day's work: How follower individual differences and justice perceptions predict OCB role definitions and behavior. *Journal of Applied Psychology*, 2006, 91, 841–855.

36. Whiting, S. W., Podsakoff, P. M., and Pierce, J. R. Effects of task performance, helping, voice and organizational loyalty on performance appraisal ratings. *Journal of Applied Psychology*, 2007, 92, 1131–1140.

37. Class discussion with EMBAs, Cox School of Business, SMU, Dallas, TX (February 2009); Hellriegel, D., and Slocum, J. *Organizational Behavior*, 10th ed. Cincinnati, OH: South-Western, 2004, 141.

38. *Adapted from* www.sas.com. (February 2009); Business: Doing well by being rather nice. *The Economist*, December 1, 2007, 82; SAS Institute. http://en.wikipedia.org/wiki/SAS_Institute (February 2009). 100 Best places to work in IT 2008. *Computerworld*, June–July 7, 2008, 18–50.

Chapter 7

1. *Adapted from* www.enterprise.com (February 2009); 50 Most Powerful Women, *Fortune*, October 13, 2008, 1ff (Nicholson was ranked 44th); Landes, L. Cracking the culture code. *Communication World*, 2008, 25(6), 24–28.

2. Rewards & recognition best practices. www.ascentgroup.com (March 2009).

3. Schantz, A., and Latham, G. An exploratory field experiment of the effect of subconscious and conscious goals on employee performance. *Organizational Behavior and Human Decision Processes*, 2009, 109, 9–18; Tolli, A. P., and Schmidt, A. M. The role of feedback, causal attributions, and self-efficacy in goal revision. *Journal of Applied Psychology*, 2008, 93, 692–702; Latham, G. P. The motivational benefits of goal-setting. *Academy of Management Executive*, 2004, 18, 126–129.

4. Locke, E. A., and Latham, G. P. *A Theory of Goal Setting and Task Performance*. Englewood Cliffs, NJ: Prentice-Hall, 1990; Locke, E. A., and Latham, G. P. Building a practically useful theory of goal setting and task motivation: A 35-year odyssey. *American Psychologist*, 2002, 57, 705–717.

5. Latham, G. P. A five step approach to behavior change. *Organizational Dynamics*, 2003, 32, 309–318.

6. Blue, L. Making good health easy. *Time*, February 23, 2009, Wellness 1–2; Garrow, V., and Hirsh, W. Talent management: Issues of focus and fit. *Public Personnel Management*, 2008, 37(4), 389–403; Moss, B. These workers heed their health, then reap rewards. *Dallas Morning News*, December 19, 2004, D7ff.

7. Tolli and Schmidt, The role of feedback; Bandura, A., and Locke, E. A. Negative self-efficacy and goal effects revisited. *Journal of Applied Psychology*, 2003, 88, 87–99.

8. *Adapted from* www.jeffgordon.com (March 2009); Anderson, L. NASCAR. *Sports Illustrated*, April 9, 2007, 84; Beech, M. Projected chase field. *Sports Illustrated*, February 16, 2009, 59–60; Anderson, L. A bang-up revival. *Sports Illustrated*, February 23, 2009, 40–43.

9. Chen, G., and Mathieu, J. E. Goal orientation dispositions and performance trajectories: The roles of supplementary and complementary situational inducements. *Organizational Behavior & Human Decision Processes*, 2008, 106, 21–39; Bell, B. S., and Kozlowski, S. W. J. Active learning: Effects of core training design elements on self-regulatory processes, learning, and adaptability. *Journal of Applied Psychology*, 2008, 92, 296–317.

10. *Adapted from* Wright, P. M., O'Leary-Kelly, A. M., Cortina, J. M., Klein, H. J., and Hollenbeck, J. R. On the meaning and measurement of goal commitment. *Journal of Applied Psychology*, 1994, 79, 795–808; Klaus-Helmut, S. Organizational commitment: A further moderator in the relationship between work stress and strain. *Journal of Stress Management*, 2007, 14, 26–40.

11. Litchfield, R. C. Brainstorming reconsidered: A goal-based review. *Academy of Management Review*, 2008, 33, 649–669.

12. Interview with Carl Couch, Senior Consultant for Clinical Excellence & Medical Director–HTPN, HealthTexas, Dallas, TX, March 2009.

13. Tolli and Schmidt, The role of feedback; Leonard, N. H., and Harvey, M. Negative perfectionism: Examining negative excessive behavior in the workplace. *Journal of Applied Social Psychology*, 2008, 38, 585–611; Remus, I., and Judge, T. A. Goal regulation across time: The effects of feedback and affect. *Journal of Applied Psychology*, 2005, 90, 453–467; Mellalieu, S. D., Sheldon, H., and O'Brien, M. The effects of goal setting on rugby performance. *Journal of Applied Behavior Analysis*, 2006, 39(2), 257–262.

14. Garrison, A. M. Walking for wellness. *Parks & Recreation*, 2009, 44(1), 14–15; Heath, D., and Heath, C. Time to aim lower. *Fast Company*, March 2009, 45–46.

15. Heath, D., and Heath, C. The curse of incentives. *Fast Company*, February, 2009, 48–49; Spolsky, J. Employee will always game incentive plans because the geniuses who design them don't anticipate how employees will respond. *Inc.*, October 2008, 85–86.

16. *Adapted from* Hellriegel, D., Jackson, S. E., and Slocum, J. W. *Management: A Competency-Based Approach*. Mason, OH: Thomson/South-Western, 2008, 391; www.hp.com (March 2009).

17. Borton, L. Working in a Vietnamese voice. *Academy of Management Executive*, 2000, 14(4), 20–31; Smith, E. D., Jr., and Pham, C. Doing business in Vietnam: A cultural guide. *Business Horizons*, May/June 1996, 47–51.

18. Latham, G. P. The motivational benefits of goal-setting. *Academy of Management Executive*, 2004, 18(4), 125–126; Goldman, B. M., Masterson, S. S., and Locke, E. A. Goal-directedness and personal identity as correlates of life outcomes. *Psychological Reports*, 2002, 91, 152–166.

19. *Adapted from* Baier, K. Diversity dialogue. *Communication World*, 2008, 25(5), 40–41; see also www.lockheedmartin.com.

20. Latham, G. P., and Locke, E. A. Enhancing the benefits and overcoming the pitfalls of goal setting. *Organizational Dynamics*, 2006, 35, 332–341.

21. *Adapted from* Dess, G. P., and Picken, J. C. *Beyond Productivity*. New York: American Management Association, 1999, 164–167.

22. Locke, E. A. Setting goals for life and happiness. In Snyder, C. R., and Lopez, S. J. (Eds.), *Handbook of Positive Psychology*. London: Oxford University Press, 2002, 299–312; Kerr, S., and Landauer, S. Using stretch goals to promote organizational effectiveness and personal growth: General Electric and Goldman Sachs. *Academy of Management Executive*, 2004, 18, 134–138.

23. www.ascentgroup.com (March 2009); Kalleberg, A. L., Marsden, P. V., Reynolds, J., and Knoke, D. Beyond profit? Sectoral differences in high-performance work practices. *Work and Occupations*, 2006, 33(3), 271–303.

24. Heath and Heath, The curse of incentives.

25. Nelson, B. Informal rewards as a performance-management tool. *The 1998 Annual: Consulting*, Vol. 2, 1998, 303–314.

26. Ibid.

27. Personal conversation with Steve Watson, Partner, Stanton Chase International, Dallas, TX, March 2009; see also Williams, M. L., McDaniel, M. A., and Nguyen, N. T. A meta-analysis of the antecedents and consequences of pay level satisfaction. *Journal of Applied Psychology*, 2006, 91, 392–413.

28. Personal conversation with John Semyan, Partner, TNS Associates, Dallas, TX, March 2009.

29. *Adapted from* www.nucor.com (March 2009); Byrnes, N., and Arndt, M. The art of motivation. *Business Week*, May 1, 2006, 56–62; Forging a winning workforce. *Business Week*, May 1, 2006, 56–59; Helman, B. Test of mettle. *Forbes*, May 11, 2009, 81–82.

30. Lee, C., Law, K. S., and Bobko, P. The importance of justice perceptions on pay effectiveness: A two-year study of a skilled-based pay plan. *Journal of Management*, 1999, 25, 851–873.

31. Dierdorff, E. C., and Surface, E. A. If you pay for skills, will they learn? Skill change and maintenance under skill-based pay system. *Journal of Management*, 2008, 34, 721–743.

32. Guthrie, J. P. Alternative pay practices and employee turnover: An organization economics perspective. *Group & Organization Management*, 2000, 25, 419–439.

33. Personal conversation with Leslie Ritter, Principal, Sagen Consulting, Addison, TX, March 2009.

34. Heath and Heath, The curse of incentives; Lambert, E. The right way to pay. *Forbes*, May 11, 2009, 78–80; Jones, D., and Hansen, B. Companies get creative to boost CEO pay. *USA Today*, May 4, 2009, 1ff;

35. Hofstede, G. *Cultures Consequences*, 2nd ed. Thousand Oaks, CA: Sage, 2001.

36. Tosi, H. L., and Greckhamer, T. Culture and CEO compensation. *Organization Science*, 2004, 15, 657–670. Carlo, G., Roesch, S. C., and Knight, G. P. Between or within cultural variation: Cultural group as a moderator of the relations between individual differences and resource allocation preferences. *Journal of Applied Development Psychology*, 2001, 22, 559–579.

37. *Adapted from* Locke and Latham, *A Theory of Goal Setting and Task Performance*, 355–358.

38. *Adapted from* www.allstate.com (March 2009); Allstate: 3rd time on the top 50 diversity list. *American Banker*, April 20, 2004, 9.

Chapter 8

1. *Adapted from* Powell, C. Doctors say stress-related ailments are rising in recession. *McClatchy-Tribune Business News*, December 13, 2008, 1; Calos, K. Surviving a layoff. *McClatchy-Tribune Business News*, January 4, 2009, 1; Conwell, V. Better health: Season's burdens. *Atlanta Journal-Constitution*, December 17, 2008, E1; Gardner, M. Marriages follow the ups and downs of the economy. *Christian Science Monitor*, November 17, 2008, 17.

2. Economic worries drive stress and drain productivity. *HR Focus*, 2008, 85(11), 8.

3. American Institute of Stress. Job stress. www.stress.org (February 2009).

4. Seward, B. L. *Managing Stress: Principles and Strategies for Health and Well Being*, 6th ed. Sudbury, MA: Jones & Bartlett, 2009.

5. Fink, G. (Ed.). *Encyclopedia of Stress*, 2nd ed. New York: Elsevier, 2007.

6. Selye, H. History of the stress concept. In Goldberger, L., and Breznitz, S. (Eds.). *Handbook of Stress*, 2nd ed. New York: Free Press, 1993, 7–20; Friedman, H. S., and

Silver, R. C. (Eds.). *Foundations of Health Psychology*. New York: Oxford University Press, 2007.

7. Richardson, H. A., Jang, J., Vandenberg, R. J., DeJoy, D. M., and Wilson, M. G. Perceived organizational support's role in stressor–strain relationships. *Journal of Managerial Psychology*, 2008, 23, 789–810.

8. Grant, S., and Langan-Fox, J. Personality and the occupational stressor–strain relationship: The role of the big five. *Journal of Occupational Health Psychology*, 2007, 12, 20–33.

9. Gilboa, S., Shirom, A., Fried, Y., and Cooper, C. A. Meta-analysis of work demand stressors and job performance: Examining main and moderating effects. *Personnel Psychology*, 2008, 61, 227–271.

10. Moen, P., Kelly, E., Huang, Q. Work, family and life-course fit: Does control over work time matter? *Journal of Vocational Behavior*, 2008, 73, 414–425.

11. Donaldson-Feilder, E. Yorker, R., and Lewis, R. Line management competence: The key to preventing and reducing stress. *Strategic HR Review*, 2008, 18, 11–20.

12. Weisman, R. Globe plans to cut staff in newsroom. *Boston Globe*, January 16, 2009, B5.

13. *Adapted from* Hall, C. Post-traumatic layoff syndrome hurts survival productivity. *Dallas Morning News*, January 21, 2009, D1, D5.

14. Anderson, L. M., and Pearson, C. M. Tit for tat? The spiraling effect of incivility in the workplace. *Academy of Management Review*, 1999, 24, 452–472.

15. Crampton, S. M., and Hodge, J. W. Rudeness and incivility in the workplace. *Journal of Leadership, Accountability and Ethics*, Fall 2008, 41–49; Estes, B., and Wang, J. Workplace incivility: Impacts on individual and organizational performance. *Human Resource Development Review*, 2008, 7, 218–240; Porath, C. L., and Erez, A. Does rudeness really matter? The effects of rudeness on task performance and helpfulness. *Academy of Management Journal*, 2007, 50, 1181–1197.

16. *Adapted from* Maitland, A. Bosses with no time to be nice. *Financial Times*, May 12, 2006, 10; Chao, L. Not so nice costs. *Wall Street Journal*, January 17, 2006, B4; Pearson, C. M., Andersson, L. M., and Porath, C. L. Assessing and attacking workplace incivility. *Organizational Dynamics*, 2000, 29(2), 123–137; Lim, S. Cortina, L. M., and Vicki, J. Personal and workgroup incivility: Impact on work and health outcomes. *Journal of Applied Psychology*, 2008, 93, 95–107.

17. Jones, F., Burke, R. J., and Westman, M. (Eds.). *Work–Life Balance: A Psychological Perspective*. New York: Psychology Press, 2006.

18. Hobson, C. J., Kamen, J., Szostek, J., Nethercut, C. M., Tiedman, J. W., and Wojnarowicz, S. Stressful life events: A revision and update of the social readjustment rating scale. *International Journal of Stress Management*, 1998, 5, 1–23.

19. Kreiner, G. E., Clark, M. A., and Fugate, M. Normalizing dirty work: Managerial tactics for countering occupational taint. *Academy of Management Journal*, 2007, 50, 149–174.

20. Baum, A., and Contrada, R. *The Handbook of Stress Science: Psychology, Medicine, and Health*. New York: Springer, 2009.

21. Workplace stress: The business case. *Employee Benefits*, June 9, 2008, S10, S11.

22. Haines, J., Williams, C. L., and Carson, J. Workers' compensation for psychological injury: Demographic and work-related correlates. *Work*, 2006, 26, 57–66.

23. National Institute of Mental Health. Post-traumatic stress disorder. www.nimh.nih.gov (February 2009).

24. Casserley, T., and Megginson, D. *Learning from Burnout: Developing Sustainable Leaders and Avoiding Career Derailment*. Burlington, MA: Butterworth-Heinemann, 2009; LeFevre, M., Kolt, G. S., and Matheny, J. Eustress, distress, and their interpretation in primary and secondary occupational stress interventions: Which way first? *Journal of Managerial Psychology*, 2006, 21, 547–565.

25. Reinardy, S. It's gametime: The Maslach burnout inventory measures burnout of sports journalists. *Journalism and Mass Communication Quarterly*, 2006, 83, 397–412.

26. Halbesleben, J. R., and Bowler, M. Emotional exhaustion and job performance: The mediating role of motivation. *Journal of Applied Psychology*, 2007, 92, 93–106.

27. Maslach, C., and Leiter, M. P. Early predictors of job burnout and engagement. *Journal of Applied Psychology*, 2008, 93, 498–512.

28. Reyes, G., Elhai, J. D., and Ford, J. D. *The Encyclopedia of Psychological Trauma*. New York, Wiley, 2009.

29. Type A and Type B personality theory. http://en.wikipedia.org/wiki/Type_A_personality (February 2009).

30. Friedman, M., and Rosenman, R. *Type A Behavior and Your Heart*. New York: Knopf, 1974.

31. Cooper, C. L. (Ed.). *Handbook of Stress Medicine and Health*, 2nd ed. Boca Raton, FL: CRC Press, 2005.

32. Maddi, S. R., Harvey, R. H., Khoshaba, D. M., Lu, J. L., Persico, M., and Brow, M. The personality construct of hardiness, III: Relationships with repression, innovativeness, authoritarianism, and performance. *Journal of Personality*, 2006, 74, 575–597.

33. Turnipseed, D. L. Hardy personality: A potential link with organizational citizenship behavior. *Psychological Reports*, 93, 2003, 529–543; Hardiness Institute for Performance Enhancement and Leadership Training. The hardiness concepts. www.hardinessinstitute.com (February 2009).

34. *Adapted from* McClam, E. Pilot's maneuvers built over lifetime. *Eagle*, January 17, 2009, A1, A4; Baker, D. US Airways pilot a mix of modesty and professionalism, *Union-Tribune*, January 16, 2009, A1; Burke, K., Donahue, P., and Siemaszko, C. US Airways airplane crashes in Hudson River. *NY Daily News*, January 16, 2009, A1; Kolker, R. My aircraft: Why Sully may be the last of his kind. *New York Magazine*, February 1, 2009. Available at www.nymag.com/news/features/53788 (February 2009).

35. Seward, *Managing Stress*.

36. Childre, D. *De-Stress Kit for the Changing Times*. Boulder Creek, CA: Institute of HeartMath, 2008. Available free at www.heartmath.org/for-you/destress-kit-for-the-changing-times.html (February 2009); Luskin, F., and Pelletier, K. *Stress Free for Good: 10 Scientifically Proven Life Skills for Health and Happiness*. San Francisco: HarperSanFrancisco, 2005.

37. Richardson, K. M., and Rothstein, H. R. Effects of occupational stress management intervention programs:

A meta-analysis. *Journal of Occupational Health Psychology*, 2008, 13(1), 69–93.

38. *Adapted from* Jacobs, M. IT is most stressful job, survey says. *Dallas Morning News*, January 21, 2007, 1J, 6J; Chordial Solutions. www.chordial.com (February 2009).

39. Grazier, K. L. Interview with Larry Sanders. *Journal of Healthcare Management*, 2006, 51(4), 212–214; to learn more about Larry Sandlers and Columbus Regional Healthcare System, go to www.columbusregional.com (February 2009).

40. Peyton, J. Wellness programs in the workplace. www.wellnessproposals.com (February 2009).

41. For extensive information on wellness programs, go to the website for the Wellness Council of America at www.welcoa.org (February 2009); see also Murta, S. G., Sanderson, K., and Oldenburg, B. Process evaluation in occupational stress management programs: A systematic review. *American Journal of Health Promotion*, 2007, 21, 248–254.

42. Cunningham, J. L., Weathington, D. L., and Burke, L. A. Riding the wave of wellness: Implications for organizations. *Employee Benefit Plan Review*, November 2008, 7–9; Wells, S. J. Finding wellness' return on investment, *HR Magazine*, 2008, 53(6), 75–84.

43. *Adapted from* Waltzer, D. Firm means business when it comes to health: Ortho-Clinical Diagnostics, Inc. *Rochester Business Journal*, 2008, 24(9), 25–26.

44. Ortho-Clinical Diagnostics: Who we are. www.orthoclinical.com/en-us/localehome/whoweare/Pages/OverviewHistory.aspx (February 2009); Johnson & Johnson. www.jnj.com. Enter "protecting our people" in the search box. (February 2009).

45. *Adapted from* Douglas, S. C., Kiewitz, C., Martinko, M. J., Harvey, P., Kim, Y., and Uk Chun, J. Cognitions, emotions, and evaluations: An elaboration likelihood model of workplace aggression. *Academy of Management Review*, 2008, 33, 425–451; Geddes, D., and Roberts Callister, R. Crossing the line(s): A dual threshold model of anger in organizations. *Academy of Management Review*, 2007, 32, 721–746.

46. Stewart, S. M. An integrative framework of workplace stress and aggression. *Business Review, Cambridge*. 2007, 8(1), 223–233.

47. Schat, A. C. H., Frone, M. R., and Kelloway, E. K. Prevalence of workplace aggression in the U.S. workforce. In Kelloway, E. K., Barling, J., Hurrell, Jr., J. J. (Eds.). *Handbook of Workplace Violence*. Thousand Oaks, CA: Sage, 2006, 47–91; Workplace violence update: What you should know now. *HRFocus*, 2008, 85(6), 7, 10–11.

48. James, L. R., and Associates. A conditional reasoning measure for aggression. *Organizational Research Methods*, 2005, 8, 69–99; Cavell, T. A., and Malcolm, K. T. (Eds.). *Anger, Aggression, and Interventions for Interpersonal Violence*. Mahwah, NJ: Lawrence Erlbaum Associates, 2007.

49. *Adapted from* LaVan, H., and Martin, W. M. Bullying in the U.S. workplace: Normative and process-oriented ethical approaches. *Journal of Business Ethics*, 2008, 83, 147–165; Heames, J., and Harvey, M. Workplace bullying: A cross-level assessment. *Management Decision*, 2006, 44, 1214–1230.

50. Lutgen-Sandvik, P., Tracy, S. J., and Alberts, J. K. Burned by bullying in the American workplace. *Journal of Management Studies*, 2007, 44, 837–862.

51. Workplace Bullying Institute. Bullying in depth. www.bullyinginstitute.org (February 2009); Kilmartin, C., and Allison, J. *Men's Violence against Women: Theory, Research, and Activism*. Mahwah, NJ: Lawrence Erlbaum Associates, 2007.

52. Lutgen-Sandvik, P. Intensive remedial identity work: Responses to workplace bullying trauma and stigmatization. *Organization*, 2008, 15, 97–119; Hodson, R., Roscigno, V. J., and Lopez, S. J. Chaos and the abuse of power: Workplace bullying in organizational and interactional context. *Work and Occupations*, 2006, 33, 382–416.

53. Canada Safety Council. Bullying in the workplace. www.safety-council.org/info/OSH/bullies.html (February 2009).

54. Tuna, C. Theory & practice: Lawyers and employers take the fight to "workplace bullies." *Wall Street Journal*, August 4, 2008, B6; Von Bergen, C. W., Zavaletta, J. A., and Soper, B. Legal remedies for workplace bullying: Grabbing the bully by the horns. *Employee Relations Law Journal*, 2006, 32(3), 14–40.

55. Olson-Buchanan, J. B., and Boswell, W. R. An integrative model of experiencing and responding to mistreatment at work. *Academy of Management Review*, 2008, 33, 76–96; Estes, B., and Wang, J. Workplace incivility: Impacts on individual and organizational performance. *Human Resource Development Review*, 2008, 7, 218–240.

56. Westhues, K. Summary of workplace mobbing conference. Brisbane, Australia: Workplace Mobbing Conference, October 14–15, 2004.

57. Davenport, N., Schwartz, R. D., and Elliott, G. P. *Mobbing: Emotional Abuse in the American Workplace*, 3rd ed. Ames, IA: Civil Society Publishing, 2005; Ferris, D. L., Brown, D. J., Berry, J. W., and Lian, H. The development and validation of the workplace ostracism scale. *Journal of Applied Psychology*, 2008, 93, 1348–1366.

58. Gates, G. Bullying and mobbing. *Pulp & Paper*, 2004, 78(10), 31–33.

59. Emotional abuse in the American workplace: Mobbing–U.S.A. www.mobbing-usa.com (February 2009).

60. Mitchell, M. S., Koen, C. M., and Crow, S. M. Harassment: It's not (all) about sex! Part I: The evolving legal environment. *Health Care Manager*, 2008, 27, 13–21; Mitchell, M. S., Koen, C. M., Crow, S. M. Harassment: It's not (all) about sex! Part II: Plaintiffs, supervisors, and preventive protocol. *Health Care Manager*, 2008, 27, 137–146.

61. This discussion is based on Sexual harassment. http://en.wikipedia.org/wiki/Sexual_harrassment (February 2009); Division for Public Education, American Bar Association. Sexual harassment. www.abanet.org/publiced/practical/sexualharassment.html (February 2009); Conte, A. *Sexual Harassment in the Workplace: Laws & Practice*. 3rd ed. New York: Wolters Kluwer Law & Business, 2009.

62. Equal Opportunity Commission. Sexual harassment. www.eeoc.gov/types/sexual_harassment.html (February 2009); Olson-Buchanan, J. B., and Boswell, W. *Mistreatment in*

the Workplace: Prevention and Resolution for Managers and Organizations. New York: Wiley-Blackwell, 2009.

63. *Adapted from* Know your rights: Sexual harassment at work. www.equalrights.org/publications/kyr/shwork.asp (February 2009); Lazar, M. How to stop sexual harassment at work. www.ehow.com/how_2178593_stop-sexual-harassment-work.html (February 2009).

64. Workplace violence. http://en.wikipedia.org/wiki/Workplace_violence (February 2009).

65. Canadian Centre for Occupational Health and Safety. Violence in the workplace. www.ccohs.ca (February 2009); Cappell, D., and DiMartino, V. *Violence at Work*, 3rd ed. Geneva, Switzerland: International Labour Organization, 2006.

66. Mannila, C. How to avoid becoming a workplace violence statistic. *T+D*, 2008, 62(7), 60–65; Survey of workplace violence prevention. Washington, DC: U.S. Department of Labor, October 27, 2006.

67. Geffner, R., Baverman, M., Galasso, J., and Marsh, J. (Eds.). *Aggression in Organizations: Violence, Abuse, and Harassment at Works and Schools.* Binghamton, NY: Haworth Press, 2004.

68. Hershcovis, M. S., Turner, N., Barling, J., Arnold, K. A., Dupré, K. E., Inness, M., LeBlanc, M. M., and Sivanathan, N. Predicting workplace aggression: A meta-analysis. *Journal of Applied Psychology*, 2007, 92, 228–238.

69. Perline, I. H., and Goldschmidt, J. *The Psychology and Law of Workplace Violence.* Springfield, IL: Charles C. Thomas, 2004; Galperin, B. L., and Leck, J. D. Understanding the violent offender in the workplace. *Journal of American Academy of Business*, 2007, 10, 114–120.

70. Van Fleet, D. D., and Van Fleet, E. W. Preventing workplace violence: The violence volcano metaphor. *Journal of Applied Management and Entrepreneurship*, 2007, 12(3), 17–36; Lucero, M. A., and Allen, R. E. Implementing zero tolerance policies: Balancing strict enforcement with fair treatment. *S.A.M. Advanced Management Journal*, 2006, 71(1), 35–42.

71. O'Leary-Kelly, A., Lean, E. Reeves, C., and Randel, J. Coming into the light: Intimate partner violence and its effects at work. *Academy of Management Perspectives*, 2008, 22(2), 57–72.

72. *Corporate Leaders and America's Workforce on Domestic Violence.* Bloomington, IL: Corporate Alliance to End Partner Violence with Others, 2008. Available at www.caepv.org (February 2009).

73. *Adapted from* Morris, B. You have victims working for you. You have batterers working for you too. *Fortune*, November 24, 2008, 122–132.

74. Darwin Realty & Development Corporation. Company profile. www.darwinrealty.com (February 2009).

75. Olson, B. J., Nelson, D. L., and Parayitam, S. Managing aggression in organizations: What leaders must know. *Leadership & Organization Development Journal*, 2006, 27, 384–398; Viollis, P., Roper, M. J., and Dicker, K. Avoiding the legal aftermath of workplace violence. *Employee Relations Law Journal*, 2005, 31(3), 65–70.

76. *Adapted and modified from* Lawrence, S. A., Garner, J., and Callan, V. J. The support appraisal work stressors

inventory: Construction and initial validation. *Journal of Vocational Behavior*, 2007, 70, 172–204.

77. *Adapted from* Der Hovanesian, M. Sex, lies, and mortgage deals. *Business Week*, November 24, 2008, 71–74; Gwilliam, I., and Chiasso, C. Women forced out of their jobs for reporting fraudulent sub-prime home loans win appellate decision. *MortgageMag News*, October 3, 2007, 1–2.

Chapter 9

1. *Adapted from* Investor overview: DineEquity. www.dineequity.com (March 2009); Farkas, D. IHOP CEO Julia Stewart. *Chain Leader*, November 2007, 1–31; Chapman, M. Julia Stewart works to keep IHOP's turnaround spirit live. *Chain Leader*, September 2007, 1–8; Ryssdal, K. Interview transcript: Julia Stewart. *Marketplace*, September 25, 2008, 1–6; Mero, J. The pancake pusher. *Fortune*, October 15, 2007, 48; Horovitz, B. Executive suite: Comeback is on the menu at Applebee's. *USA Today*, April 28, 2008, 1–2.

2. Wood, J. T. *Interpersonal Communication: Everyday Encounters*, 6th ed. Belmont, CA: Wadsworth/Cengage Learning, 2010.

3. Showkeir, J., and Showkeir, M. *Authentic Conversations: Moving from Manipulation to Truth and Commitment.* San Francisco: Berrett-Koehler, 2009.

4. Russ, G. S., Daft, R. L., and Lengel, R. H. Media selection and managerial characteristics in organizational communications. *Management Communication Quarterly*, 1990, 4, 151–175; Rockmann, K. W., and Northcraft, G. B. To be or not to be trusted: The influence of media richness on defection and deception. *Organizational Behavior and Human Decision Sciences*, 2008, 107, 106–122.

5. Duck, S., and McMahan, D. T. *The Basics of Communication: A Relational Perspective.* Thousand Oaks, CA: Sage, 2009.

6. *Adapted from* Molinsky, A., and Margolis, J. The emotional tightrope of downsizing: Hidden challenges for leaders and their organizations. *Organizational Dynamics*, 2006, 35, 145–159.

7. Smith, S. W., and Wilson, S. R. (Eds.). *New Directions in Interpersonal Communication Research.* Thousand Oaks, CA: Sage, 2009.

8. Adler, R. B., and Rodman, G. *Understanding Human Communication*, 10th ed. New York: Oxford University Press, 2009; French, S. Critiquing the language of strategic management. *Journal of Management Development*, 2009, 28, 6–17.

9. Scott, J. C. Differences in American and British vocabulary: Implications for international business. *Business Communication Quarterly*, 2000, 63(4), 27–39.

10. About Intel. www.intel.com/intel/index.htm?iid=gg_about+intel_aboutintel (March 2009).

11. Brinson, S. L., and Benoit, W. L. The tarnishing star. *Management Communication Quarterly*, 1999, 12, 483–510; Labich, K. No more crude at Texaco. *Fortune*, September 6, 1999, 205–212.

12. Spitzberg, B. H., and Cupach, W. R. (Eds.). *The Dark Side of Interpersonal Communication*, 2nd ed. Mahwah, NJ: Lawrence Erlbaum Associates, 2007.

13. Burns, S. Madoff caused massive damage. *Eagle*, December 28, 2008, B2; see also this website for more information on financial transparency: http://assetbuilder.com (March 2009).

14. Arnett, R. C., Harden Fritz, J. M., and Bell, L. M. (Eds.). *Communication Ethics Literacy: Dialogue and Difference*. Thousand Oaks, CA: Sage, 2009.

15. Lopez, S. J. (Ed.). *The Encyclopedia of Positive Psychology*. New York: Wiley-Blackwell, 2009.

16. Bolino, M. C., Kacmar, K. M., Turnley, W. H., and Gilstrap, J. B. A multi-level review of impression management motives and behaviors. *Journal of Management*, 2008, 34, 1080–1109.

17. Bokeno, R. M. Dialogue at work: What it is and isn't. *Development and Learning in Organizations*, 2007, 21, 9–11; Conklin, J. *Dialogue Mapping: Building Shared Understanding of Wicked Problems*. New York: Wiley, 2006.

18. *Adapted from* Farkas, D. IHOP CEO Julia Stewart. *Chain Leader*, November 2007, 1–2; Julia Stewart of IHOP: Making the partnership work. Franchising.com. February 15, 2004. www.franchising.com/articles/66 (February 2009).

19. Ayoko, O. B., and Pekerti, A. A. The mediating and moderating effects of conflict and communication openness on workplace trust. *International Journal of Conflict Management*, 2008, 19, 297–318; Jablin, F. M. Courage and courageous communication among leaders and followers in groups, organizations, and communities. *Management Communication Quarterly*, 2006, 20, 94–1101.

20. Tomlinson, E. C., and Mayer, R. C. The role of causal attribution dimensions in trust repair. *Academy of Management Review*, 2009, 34, 85–104; Gillespie, N., Dietz, G. Trust repair after an organization-level failure. *Academy of Management Review*, 2009, 34, 127–145.

21. London, M. *Job Feedback: Giving, Seeking, and Using Feedback for Performance Improvement*, 2nd ed. Mahwah, NJ: Lawrence Erlbaum Associates, 2003.

22. Hezlett, S. A. Using multisource feedback to develop leaders: Apply theory and research to improve practice. *Advances in Developing Human Resources*, 2008, 10, 703–720; Lepsinger, R. *The Art and Science of 360 Degree Feedback*, 2nd ed. San Francisco: Pfeiffer, 2009; Smither, J. W., Brett, J. F., and Atwater, L. E. What do leaders recall about their multisource feedback? *Journal of Leadership & Organizational Studies*, 2008, 14, 202–218.

23. Sias, P. M. *Organizing Relationships: Traditional and Emerging Perspectives on Workplace Relationships*. Thousand Oaks, CA: Sage, 2009; Kirkpatrick, D. C., Duck, S., and Foley, M. K. *Relating Difficulty: The Process of Constructing and Managing Difficult Interactions*. Mahwah, NJ: Lawrence Erlbaum Associates, 2006.

24. Brownell, J. *Listening: Attitudes, Principles, and Skills*, 3rd ed. Boston: Allyn & Bacon, 2006.

25. *Adapted from* Hoppe, M. *Active Listening: Improve Your Ability to Listen and Lead*. Greensboro, NC: Center for Creative Leadership, 2006.

26. *Adapted from* Holmes, A. The art of influence: Without it you'll never get anything done. *CIO*, 2006, 20(3), 1–5; Waigum, T. Coping with project backlog. *CIO*,

January 7, 2008, 1–2. www.cio.com (February 2009); CIO values: Sue Powers, CIO, Travelport GDS. July 12, 2008. www.informationweek.com (February 2009).

27. About Travelport. www.travelport.com/about.aspx (February 2009).

28. *This section draws material from* Burgoon, J. K., Guerrero, L. K., and Floyd, K. *Nonverbal Communication*. Upper Saddle River, NJ: Allyn & Bacon, 2010; Knapp, M. L., and Hall, J. A. *Nonverbal Communication*. Belmont, CA: Wadsworth/Cengage Learning, 2010; Reiman, T. *The Power of Body Language*. New York: Pocket, 2008.

29. Hickson, M., Stacks, D. W., and Moore, N. *Nonverbal Communication: Studies and Applications*. New York: Oxford University Press, 2007; Manusov, V., and Patterson, J. L. (Eds.). *The SAGE Handbook of Nonverbal Communication*. Thousand Oaks, CA: Sage, 2006.

30. *Adapted from* Beall, A. E. Body language speaks. *Communication World*, March/April 2004, 18–20; Knapp, M. L., and Hall, J. A. *Nonverbal Communication in Human Interaction*, 7th ed. Belmont, CA: Wadsworth/Cengage Learning, 2009. Beall, A. E. Reading hidden communications of respondents. www.beallresearchandtraining.com (March 2009).

31. Zeer, D. *Office Feng Shui: Creating Harmony in Your Work Space*. San Francisco: Chronicle Books, 2004; Feng shui. www.fastfengshui.com (March 2009).

32. Tsang, E. W. Toward a scientific inquiry into superstitious business decision-making. *Organization Studies*, 2004, 25, 923–946.

33. American Feng Shui Institute. www.amfengshui.com (March 2009).

34. *Adapted from* Mattioli, D. Layoff sign: Boss's cold shoulder. *Wall Street Journal*, October 23, 2008, D6; Patton, C. Handle with care. *Incentive*, 2009, 182(9), 54–56; Holtz, S. Nine tips for communicating layoffs. http://blog.holtz.com (March 2009).

35. Lee, T. J. Actions speak loudly. *Communication World*, 2008, 25(4), 24–28; Fellon, A. Using informal and formal status symbols in your organization to advance your career. http://ezinearticles.com/?Using-Informal-and-Formal-Status-Symbols-in-Your-Organization-to-Advance-Your-Career?id=207807 (March 2009); Pentland, A. *Honest Signals: How They Shape Our World*. Cambridge, MA: The MIT Press, 2008.

36. Pease, B., and Pease, A. *The Definitive Book of Body Language*. New York: Bantam, 2006; Raghaven, R. Watch your body language. *Forbes*, March 16, 2009, 92–93.

37. Beamer, L., and Varner, I. *Intercultural Communication in the Global Workplace*, 4th ed. New York: McGraw-Hill, 2008.

38. Mozveni, A. Solving the riddles of Iran. www.martinfrost.ws/htmlfiles/aug2006/iran_riddles.html (March 2009).

39. Slackman, M. The fine art of hiding what you mean to say. *New York Times*, August 6, 2006, 4–5.

40. O'Rourke, J. S., and Tuleja, E. A. *Intercultural Communication for Business*, 2nd ed. Mason, OH: South-Western/Cengage Learning, 2009.

41. Ethnocentrism. http://en.wikipedia.com/wiki/Ethnocentrism (March 2009); Gudykunst, W. B. (Ed.). *Theorizing about Intercultural Communication*. Thousand Oaks, CA: Sage, 2005.

42. *Adapted from* Neuliep, J. W. *Intercultural Communication: A Contextual Approach*, 4th ed. Thousand Oaks, CA: Sage, 2009.

43. *Adapted from* Ulysses program. www.pwc.com (March 2009); Tahir Ayub, CA, partner. https://secure.ca.pwc.com (March 2009); Marquez, J. Companies send employees on volunteer projects abroad to cultivate leadership skills. *Workforce Management*, November 2005, 50–52.

44. About us: PwC. www.pwc.com/us/en/about-us/index.jhtml (March 2009).

45. Bowe, H., and Martin, K. *Communication across Cultures: Mutual Understanding in a Global World*. New York: Cambridge University Press, 2007; Newsom, D. *Bridging the Gaps in Global Communication*. Boston: Blackwell Publishing, 2007.

46. Bluedorn, A. C., Kaufman, C. F., and Lane, P. M. How many things do you like to do at once? An introduction to monochronic and polychronic time. *Academy of Management Executive*, 1992, 6(4), 17–26; Kaufman-Scarborough, C., and Lindquist, J. D. Time management and polychronicity comparisons, contrasts, and insights for the workplace. *Journal of Managerial Psychology*, 1999, 14, 288–312; Crossan, M., Cunha, M. P., Vera, D., and Cunha, J. Time and organizational improvisation. *Academy of Management Review*, 2005, 30, 129–145; Bluedorn, A. C., and Jaussi, K. S. Leaders, followers, and time. *Leadership Quarterly*, 2008, 19, 654–658.

47. Chronemics. http://en.wikipedia.org/wiki/chronemics (March 2009).

48. Jandt, F. E. *An Introduction to Intercultural Communication*. Thousand Oaks, CA: Sage, 2009; Samovar, L. A., Porter, R. E., and McDaniel, E. R. *Communication between Cultures*, 7th ed. Belmont, CA: Wadsworth/Cengage Learning, 2010.

49. Latane, B., Liu, J. H., Nowak, A., Bonevento, M., and Zheng, L. Distance matters: Physical space and social impact. *Personality and Social Psychology Bulletin*, 1995, 21, 795–805.

50. *Adapted from* Baber, D., and Wayman, L. Internal networking: The key to influence. *Canadian HR Reporter*, June 17, 2002, 12–13.

51. Amand, N., and Conger, J. A. Capabilities of the consummate networker. *Organizational Dynamics*. 2007, 36, 13–27; Ng, I., and Chow, I. H. Does networking with colleagues matter in enhancing job performance? *Asia Pacific Journal of Management*, 2005, 22, 405–421.

52. Ahearn, K. K., Ferris, G. R., Hochwarter, W. A., Douglas, C., and Ammeter, A. P. Leader political skill and team performance. *Journal of Management*, 2004, 30, 309–327.

53. Ferris, G. R., Treadway, D.C., Kolodinsky, R. W., Hochwarter, W. A., Kacmar, C. J., Douglas, C., and Frank, D. D. Development and validation of the political skill inventory. *Journal of Management*, 2005, 31, 128; Ferris, G. R., Blicke, G., Schneider, P. B., Kamer, J., et al. Political skill construct and criterion-related validation: A two study investigation. *Journal of Managerial Psychology*, 2008, 23, 744–771.

54. Longenecker, C. O., Neubert, M. J., and Fink, L. S. Causes and consequences of managerial failure in rapidly changing organizations. *Business Horizons*, 2007, 50, 145–155; see also Finkelstein, S., Whitehead, J. and Campbell, A. *Think Again: Why Great Leaders Make Bad Decisions and How to Keep It from Happening to You*. Boston: Harvard Business School Press, 2009.

55. Trenholm, S. *Thinking through Communication: An Introduction to the Study of Human Communication*, 5th ed. Boston: Allyn & Bacon, 2007.

56. Bordia, P., Jones, E., Gallois, C., and Difonzia, N. Management are aliens! Rumors and stress in organizational change. *Groups and Organization Management*, 2006, 31, 601–621; van Iterson, A., and Clegg, S. R. The politics of gossip and denial in interorganizational relations. *Human Relations*, 2008, 61, 1117–1137.

57. *Adapted from* Burke, L. A., and Morris Wise, J. The effective care, handling and pruning of the office grapevine. *Business Horizon*, 2003, 46(3), 71–76.

58. Kemmel, A. J. *Rumors and Rumor Control: A Manager's Guide to Understanding and Combatting Rumors*. Mahwah, NJ: Lawrence Erlbaum Associates, 2004.

59. Michelson, G., and Mouly, V. S. Do loose lips sink ships? The meaning, antecedents and consequences of rumor and gossip in organizations. *Corporate Communications: An International Journal*, 2004, 9, 189–201.

60. Cross, R., Thomas, B., Dutra, A., and Newberry, C. Using network analysis to build a business. *Organizational Dynamics*, 2007, 36, 346–362; Belasen, A. T. *The Theory and Practice of Corporate Communication: A Competing Values Perspective*. Thousand Oaks, CA: Sage, 2007.

61. *Adapted from* Vantuono, W. C. Railroader of the Year: Michael J. Ward. *Railway Age*, 2009, 210(1), 22–51.

62. About CSX. www.csx.com/?fuseaction=about.main (March 2009).

63. Kruger, J., Epley, N., Parker, J., and Ng, Z. Egocentrism over e-mail: Can people communicate as well as they think? *Journal of Personality and Social Psychology*, 2005, 89, 925–936; Taylor, H., Fieldman, G., Altman, Y. E-mail at work: A cause for concern? The implications of the new communication technologies for health, wellbeing and productivity at work. *Journal of Organisational Transformation and Change*, 2008, 5, 159–173.

64. Enemark, D. It's all about me: Why e-mails are so easily misunderstood. *Christian Science Monitor*, May 15, 2006, 13–14.

65. Whipple, R. T. *Understanding E-Body Language: Building Trust Online*. Rochester, NY: Productivity Publications, 2006; Byron, K. Carrying too heavy a load? The communication and miscommunication of emotion by email. *Academy of Management Review*, 2008, 33, 309–327.

66. Chatzky, J. Confessions of an e-mail addict. *Money*, March 2007, 28–29.

67. Whipple, R. E-body language: Decoded. *T&D*, February 2006, 20–22.

68. Text messaging. www.pcmag.com (February 2009).

69. Chen, K., Yen, D. C., Hung, S., and Huang, A. H. An exploratory study of the selection of communication media: The relationship between flow and communication outcomes. *Decision Support Systems*, 2008, 45, 822–832.

70. Walden, J. As text messaging grows, generations begin bridging gap. *Arkansas Business*, January 12, 2009, 1–2.

71. Tyson, J., and Cooper, A. How instant messaging works. http://communication.howstuffworks.com/instant-messaging.htm (March 2009).

72. Instant messaging. http://en.wikipedia.org/wiki/Instant_messaging (March 2009).

73. Instant messaging emerging as mission critical business tool. www.continuitycentral.com/news03330.htm (February 2009); About Gartner. www.gartner.com (March 2009).

74. Falls, J. Instant messaging as a business tool. www.socialmediaexplorer.com/2008/01/17/intant-messaging-as-a-business-tool (February 2009).

75. *Adapted from* Castican, J. I., and Schmeidler, A. Communication climate inventory. In Pfeiffer, J. W., and Goodstein, L. D. (Eds.). *The 1984 Annual: Developing Human Resources*. San Diego, CA: Pfeiffer and Company, 1984, 115–118.

76. *Adapted from* Douglas Roberts, formerly manager of training, LTV Missiles and Fire Control Group, Grand Prairie, TX. Used with permission.

Chapter 10

1. *Adapted from* Horowitz, B. CEO profile: Campbell exec nears extraordinary goal. *USA Today*, January 25, 2009, 1, 3; Donnelly, R. Two CEOs, One strategy. *CEO Magazine*, November/December 2008, 47–51; Carter, A. Lighting a fire under Campbell: How Doug Conant's quiet, cerebral style got things bubbling again. *BusinessWeek*, December 4, 2006, 96–101; Brubaker, H. Souper saver. *Knight Ridder Tribune Business News*, July 26, 2006, 1, 2. Our company: Campbell Soup Company. www.campbellsoupcompany.com (March 2009).

2. Vecchio, R. P. (Ed.). *Leadership: Understanding the Dynamics of Power and Influence in Organizations*, 2nd ed. Notre Dame, IN: University of Notre Dame Press, 2008; Ferris, G. R., Davidson, S. L., and Perrewe, P. L. *Political Skill at Work: Impact on Work Effectiveness*. Mountain View, CA: Davies-Black Publishing, 2005.

3. French, J. R. P., and Raven, B. The bases of social power. In Cartwright, D. (Ed.). *Studies in Social Power*. Ann Arbor: University of Michigan Institute of Social Research, 1959, 150–167; Fleming, P., and Spicer, A. Beyond power and resistance: New approaches to organizational politics. *Management Communication Quarterly*, 2008, 21, 301–309.

4. See, for example, the classic work by Barnard, C. I. *The Functions of the Executive*. Cambridge, MA: Harvard University Press, 1938, 110.

5. Executive team—Douglas R. Conant. www.campbellsoupcompany.com (March 2009).

6. Blass, F. R., and Ferris, G. R. Leader reputation. The role of mentoring, political skill, contextual learning, and adaptation. *Human Resource Management*, 2007, 46, 5–19; Dubrin, A. J. *Political Behavior in Organizations*. Thousand Oaks, CA: Sage, 2008.

7. Cross, R., Parker, A., and Cross, R. L. *The Hidden Power of Social Networks: Understanding How Work Really Gets Done in Organizations*. Boston: Harvard Business School Press, 2004; Nye, J. S. *The Power to Lead*. New York: Oxford University Press, 2008.

8. Ferris, G. R., Blicke, G., Schneider, P. B., Kramer, J., Zettler, I., Solga, J., Noethen, D., and Meurs, J. A. Political skill construct and criterion-related validation: A two-study investigation. *Journal of Managerial Psychology*, 2008, 23, 744–771.

9. Madison, D. L., Allen, R. W., Porter, L. W., Renwick, P. A., and Mayes, B. T. Organizational politics: An exploration of managers' perceptions. *Human Relations*, 1980, 33, 79–100; Benschop, Y. The micro-politics of gendering in networking. *Gender, Work and Organizations*, 2009, 16, 217–237.

10. Strategies and values. http://careers.campbellsoupcompany.com (March 2009).

11. Valle, M. The power of politics: Why leaders need to learn the art of influence. *Leadership in Action*, 2006, 26(2), 8–12; Harris, R. B., Harris, K. J., and Harvey, P. A test of competing models of the relationships among perceptions of organizational politics, perceived organizational support and individual outcomes. *Journal of Social Psychology*, 2007, 147, 631–655.

12. Higgins, C., Judge, T. A., and Ferris, G. R. Influence tactics and work outcomes. A meta-analysis. *Journal of Organizational Behavior*, 2003, 24, 89–106.

13. Hochwarter, W. A., Ferris, G. R., Gavin, M. B., and Perrewé, P. L. Political skill as neutralizer of felt accountability—job tension effects on job performance ratings: A longitudinal investigation. *Organizational Behavior and Human Decision Processes*, 2007, 102, 226–254.

14. Catano, V. M., Darr, W., and Campbell, C. A. Performance appraisal of behavior-based competencies: A reliable and valid procedure. *Personnel Psychology*, 2007, 60, 60–89; Gordon, M. E., and Stewart, L. P. Conversing about performance: Discursive resources for the appraisal interview. *Management Communication Quarterly*, 2009, 22, 473–501.

15. *Adapted from* Shankland, S. Carol Bartz's Yahoo reorganization announcement. February 26, 2009. http://news.cnet.com/8301-1023_3-10172685-93.html?tag=mncol (March 2009); Helft, M. Yahoo chief rearranges managers once again. *New York Times*, February 27, 2009, B5; Hof, R. D. Yahoo's Bartz shows who's boss. *BusinessWeek (Online)*, February 27, 2009; Hof, R. D. The difficulties Bartz faces at Yahoo. *BusinessWeek (Online)*, January 24, 2009.

16. Yahoo! Inc. *Hoover's*. http://premium.hoovers.com (March 2009).

17. Yukl, G. A. *Leadership in Organizations*, 7th ed. Upper Saddle River, NJ: Pearson Prentice-Hall, 2010; Belasen, A., and Frank, N. Competing values leadership: Quadrant roles and personality traits. *Leadership & Organization Development Journal*, 2008, 29, 127–143.

18. Bass, B. M. *Bass Handbook of Leadership: Theory, Research, and Managerial Applications*, 4th ed. New York: Free Press, 2009.

19. McGregor, D. The human side of enterprise. *Management Review*, 46(11), 1957, 22–28, reprinted in *Reflections: The SOL Journal*, Fall 2000, 6–14; Heil, G., Stephens, D. C., McGregor, D., and Bennis, W. G. *Douglas McGregor, Revisited: Managing the Human Side of the Enterprise*. New York: John Wiley & Sons, 2000.

20. McGregor, D., *The Human Side of the Enterprise*. New York: McGraw-Hill, 1960; see also Kopelman, R. E.,

Prottas, D. J., and Davis, A. L. Douglas McGregor's Theory X and Theory Y: Toward a construct-valid measure. *Journal of Managerial Issues*, 2008, 20, 255–271.

21. Survey: The X and Y factors. *Economist*, January 21, 2006, 19–20; Kellaway, L. The infinite potential to get out of bed in the morning. *Financial Times*, September 5, 2005, 10.

22. Judge, T. A., Piccolo, R. F., and Ilies, R. The forgotten ones? The validity of consideration and initiating structure in leadership research. *Journal of Applied Psychology*, 2004, 89, 36–51; Fleishman, E. A. Consideration and structure: Another look at their role in leadership research. In Damserau, F., and Yammarino, F. J. (Eds.). *Leadership: The Multi-Level Approaches*. Greenwich, CT: JAI Press, 1998, 285–302.

23. *Adapted from* Greengard, S. Lessons in leadership: Colin Powell. *PM Network*, August 2008, 60–63; Harari, O. *The Powell Principles (Mighty Manager)*. New York: McGraw-Hill, 2004; Harari, O. *Leadership Secrets of Colin Powell*. New York: McGraw-Hill, 2003.

24. Colin Powell. http://en.wikipedia.org/wiki/Colin_Powell (March 2009).

25. Hersey, P., et al. *The Management of Organizational Behavior: Leading Human Resources*, 8th ed. Escondido, CA: Center for Leadership Studies, 2001; Center for Leadership Studies. Situational leadership. www.situational.com (March 2009).

26. Hersey, P., Blanchard, K. H., and Johnson, D. E. *The Management of Organizational Behavior: Leading Human Resources*. © 2001 Center for Leadership Studies. Used with permission.

27. *Adapted from* Greisman, D. Being their own bosses. *Keene Sentinel*, January 17, 2009. www.keenesentinel.com (March 2009); Clark Steiman, H. A socialist grows up: His company tries, too. *INC*, July 2008, 45–46; Fleisher, C. Corporate culture allows for worker autonomy at Rockingham, Vermont, tech firm. *Knight Ridder Tribune Business News*, December 19, 2004, 1, 3.

28. Chroma Technology: Company profile. www.chroma.com (March 2009).

29. Sims, Jr., H. P., Faraj, S., and Yun, S. When should a leader be directive or empowering? How do you develop your own situational theory of leadership? *Business Horizons*, 2008, 52(2), 149–158; Oshagbemi, T. The impact of personal and organizational variables on the leadership styles of managers. *International Journal of Human Resource Management*, 2008, 19, 1886–1910.

30. Vroom, V. H., and Jago, A. G. *The New Leadership*. Englewood Cliffs, NJ: Prentice-Hall, 1988; see also Sternberg, R. J., and Vroom, V. The person versus the situation in leadership. *Leadership Quarterly*, 2002, 13, 321–323.

31. The discussion of the revised model is based on Vroom, V. H. New developments in leadership and decision making. *OB News*. Briarcliff Manor, NY: Organizational Behavior Division of the Academy of Management, headquartered at Pace University, Spring 1999, 4–5; Vroom, V. H. Leadership and the decision-making process. *Organizational Dynamics*, Spring 2000, 82–93; Vroom, V. H. Educating managers for decision making and leadership. *Management Decision*, 2003, 41, 968–978.

32. *Adapted from* Vroom, Leadership and the decision-making process, 90–91; see also Duncan, W. J., LaFrance, K. G., and Ginter, P. M. Leadership and decision making: A retrospective application and assessment. *Journal of Leadership & Organizational Studies*, 2003, 9, 1–20.

33. *Adapted from* Reddy, W. B., and Williams, G. The visibility/credibility inventory: Measuring power and influence. In Pfeiffer, J. W. (Ed.). *The 1988 Annual: Developing Human Resources*. San Diego: University Associates, 1988, 115–124; see also Ferris, G. R., Treadway, D. C., Kolodinsky, R. W., Hochwarter, W. A., Kacmar, C. J., Douglas, C., and Frink, D. D. Development and validation of the political skill inventory. *Journal of Management*, 2005, 31, 126–152.

34. *Adapted from* Konrad, D. M., Kramer, V., and Erkuit, S. The impact of three or more women on corporate boards. *Organizational Dynamics*, 2008, 37, 145–168; Meany, M. C. Seeing beyond the woman: An interview with a pioneering academic and board member. *McKinsey Quarterly*, September 2008, 1–8; Reals Ellig, J., and Lang, I. H. Getting from a good to a great board. *Boards & Directors*, Fourth quarter 2008, 22–25; St. Anthony, N. A good reason to aspire for more women on boards. *McClatchy-Tribune Business News*, March 3, 2009, 1, 3; Patel, P. Moneymakers: Five questions with Laureen Wishom. *McClatchy-Tribune News*, June 7, 2008, 1, 3.

Chapter 11

1. *Adapted from* About Symantec. www.symantec.com/about (April 2009); Thompson, J. W. Managing more: Making sense of the information explosion. Remarks at Symantec VISION 2008 conference. June 10, 2008. Available at www.symantec.com (April 2009); Worthen, B. Symantec chief to retire in April, remain chairman, *Wall Street Journal*, November 18, 2008, B6; John W. Thompson. http://en.wikipedia.org/wiki/John_W._Thompson (April 2009); Hooper, L. John W. Thompson, Symantec. *CRN*, November 11, 2005. www.crn.com (April 2009); With the retirement of John W. Thompson, Symantec may be losing its best asset. Blog posted November 18, 2008. http://blogs.itworldcanada.com/cdn/2008/11/18 (April 2009).

2. Puccio, G. J., Murdock, M. C., and Mance, M. *Creative Leadership: Skills That Drive Change*. Thousand Oaks, CA: Sage, 2006; Kameron, K. *Positive Leadership: Strategies for Extraordinary Performance*. San Francisco: Berrett-Koehler, 2008.

3. Bass, B. M. Does the transactional-transformational leadership paradigm transcend organizational and national boundaries? *American Psychologist*, 1997, 52, 130–139; Leadership. www.changingminds.org (April 2009).

4. Avolio, B. J. *Leadership Development in Balance: Made/Born*. Mahwah, NJ: Lawrence Erlbaum Associates, 2005, 15.

5. Drucker, P. F. What makes an effective executive. *Harvard Business Review*, 2004, 82(6), 58–63; Hackman, J. R., and Wageman, R. Ask the right questions about leadership: Discussion and conclusions. *American Psychologist*, 2007, 62, 43–47.

6. Oke, A. Munski, N., and Walumbwa, F. O. The influence of leadership on innovation processes and activities. *Organizational Dynamics*, 2009, 38, 64–72; Bryant, S. E. The role of transformational and transactional leadership

in creating, sharing and exploiting organizational knowledge. *Journal of Leadership & Organizational Studies*, 2003, 9(4), 32–44; Judge, T. A., and Piccolo, R. F. Transformational and transactional leadership: A meta-analytic test of their relative validity. *Journal of Applied Psychology*, 2004, 89, 755–768.

7. *Adapted from* Lashinsky, A. Mark Hurd's moment. *Fortune*, March 16, 2009, 91–100; HP to slash 24,600 jobs over 3 years; Most cuts will come from EDS workforce. *Chicago Tribune*, September 16, 2008, 3; Fortt, J. Mark Hurd, Superstar. *Fortune*, June 9, 2008, 35–36; Mark Hurd. http://en.wikipedia.org/wiki/Mark_Hurd (April 2009); Paczkowski, J. HP CEO Mark Hurd's memo to the troops on pay cuts. February 19, 2009. http://digitaldaily.allthingsd.com/20090219/hp-ceo-mark-hurds-memo-to-the-troops (April 2009); Kim, R. Chron 200: CEO of the year. Mark Hurd has earned a name at Hewlett-Packard. April 20, 2008. www.sfgate.com/cgi-bin/article.cgi?f=/c/a/2008/04/20/BUG510520P.DTL (April 2009).

8. HP: About us. www.hp.com/hpinfo/abouthp (April 2009); Hoover's. Hewlett-Packard Company. http://premium.hoovers.com (April 2009).

9. This discussion, related studies, and other versions of this model are available in Graen, G. B., and Uhl-Bien, M. Relationship-based approach to leadership. Development of leader-member exchange (LMX) theory of leadership over 25 years: Applying a multi-level multidomain perspective. *Leadership Quarterly*, 1995, 6, 219–247; Graen, G. B. (Ed.). *LMX Leadership: The Series*. Charlotte, NC: Information Age Publishing, multiple editions published in 2008, 2007, 2006, 2005, 2004, and 2003; Scandura, T. A., and Pellegrini, E. K. Trust and leader member exchange: A closer look at relational vulnerability. *Journal of Leadership & Organizational Studies*, 2008, 15, 101–110; Mardanov, I. T., Heischmidt, K., and Henson, A. Leader-member exchange and job satisfaction bond and employee turnover. *Journal of Leadership & Organizational Studies*, 2008, 15, 159–175; Nahrgang, J. D., Morgeson, F. R., and Ilies, R. The development of leader-member exchanges: Exploring how personality and performance influence leader and member relationships over time. *Organizational Behavior and Human Decision Sciences*, 2009, 108, 256–266; Landry, G., and Vandenberghe, C. Role of commitment of the supervisor, leader-member exchange, and supervisor-based self-esteem in employer–supervisor conflicts. *Journal of Social Psychology*, 2009, 149, 5–27; Brouer, R. L., Duke, A. Treadway, D. C., and Ferris, G. R. The moderating role of political skill on the demographic dissimilarity—Leader-member exchange quality relationship. *Leadership Quarterly*, 2009, 20, 61–69; Sekiguchi, T., Burton, J. P., and Sablynski, C. J. The role of job embeddedness on employee performance: The interactive effects of leader-member exchange and organizational-based self-esteem. *Personnel Psychology*, 2008, 61, 761–792; Hsiung, H. H., and Tsai, W-C. Job definition discrepancy between supervisors and subordinates: The antecedent role of LMX and outcomes. *Journal of Occupational and Organizational Psychology*, 2009, 82, 89–112.

10. Mardanov, Heischmidt, and Henson, Leader-member exchange and job satisfaction bond and predicted employee turnover, 159–170.

11. Baker, H-A., Mustaffa, C-S., and Mohanad, B. LMX quality, supervisory communication and team-oriented commitment: A multilevel analysis approach. *Corporate Communications: An International Approach*, 2009, 14, 11–33.

12. Nahrgang, Morgeson, and Ilies, The development of leader-member exchanges.

13. Douglas, C., Ferris, G. R., Buckley, M. R., and Gundlach, M. J. Organizational and social influences on leader-member exchange processes: Implications for the management of diversity. In Graen, G. B. (Ed.). *Dealing with Diversity*. Greenwich, CT: Information Age Publishing, 2003, 59–90.

14. Brouer, Duke, Treadway, and Ferris, The moderating effect of political skill on the demographic dissimilarity; see also Piccolo, R. F., Bardes, M., Mayer, D. M., and Judge, T. A. Does high quality leader-member exchange accentuate the effects of organizational justice. *European Journal of Work and Organizational Psychology*, 2008, 17, 273–298.

15. For an extended definition and conceptualization of authentic leadership, see Walumbwa, F. O., Avolio, B. J., Gardner, W. L., Wernsing, T. S., and Peterson, S. J. Authentic leadership: Development and validation of a theory-based measure. *Journal of Management*, 2008, 34, 89–126.

16. This discussion draws from Avolio, B. J. Promoting more integrative strategies for leadership theory-building. *American Psychologist*, 2007, 62, 25–33; Novicevic, M. M., Harvey, M. G., Buckley, M. R., Brown-Radford, J. A., and Evans, R. Authentic leadership: A historical perspective. *Journal of Leadership and Organizational Studies*, 2006, 13, 64–75; George, B., with Sims, P. *True North: Discover Your Authentic Leadership*. San Francisco: Jossey-Bass, 2007; Snyder, C. R., and Lopez, S. J. *Handbook of Positive Psychology*. New York: Oxford University Press, 2009.

17. Mayer, D. M., Bardes, M., and Piccolo, R. F. Do servant leaders help satisfy follower needs? An organizational justice perspective. *European Journal of Work and Organizational Psychology*, 2008, 17, 180–197; see also Fry, L. W., and Slocum Jr., J. W. Maximizing the triple bottom line through spiritual leadership. *Organizational Dynamics*, 2008, 37, 86–96.

18. *Adapted from* George, G. Seven lessons for leading in a crisis. *Wall Street Journal*, February 24, 2009, A11; Craig, N. How to be your best when things are at their worst. Authentic Leadership Institute. http://authleadership.com (April 2009); Bernstein, A. Bill George: The thought leader interview. *Strategy & Business*, Winter, 2007, 1–7.

19. George and Sims, *True North: Discover Your Authentic Leadership*.

20. Based on and for more information, go to Authentic Leadership Institute. http://authleadership.com (April 2009).

21. Colbert, A. E., Kristof-Brown, A. L., Bradley, B. H., and Barrick, M. R. CEO transformational leadership: The role of goal importance congruence in top management teams. *Academy of Management Journal*, 2008, 51, 81–96.

22. This section draws from Bass, B. M., and Bass, R. *The Bass Handbook of Leadership: Theory, Research, and Managerial Applications*, 4th ed. New York: Free Press, 2009; Bass, B. M., and Riggio, R. E. *Transformational Leadership*, 2nd ed. Florence, KY: Lawrence Erlbaum Associates, 2005; Bedeian, A. G., and Field, H. S. The measurement equivalence of web-based and paper-and-pencil measures of transformational leadership. *Organizational Research Methods*, 2006, 9, 339–368; Herold, D. M., Fedor, D. B., Caldwell, S., and Liu, Y. The effects of transformational and change leadership on employees' commitment to a change: A multilevel study. *Journal of Applied Psychology*, 2008, 93, 346–357; Sarros, J. C., Cooper, B. K., and Santora, J. C. Building a climate for innovation through transformational leadership and organizational culture. *Journal of Leadership & Organizational Studies*, 2008, 15, 145–158; Ling, Y., Simsek, Z., Lubatkin, M. H., and Veiga, J. F. Transformational leadership's role in promoting corporate entrepreneurship. Examining the CEO-TMT interface. *Academy of Management Journal*, 2008, 51, 557–576.

23. *Adapted and modified from* GE leadership effectiveness survey. www.1000ventures.com/business_guide/crosscuttings/tests_leadership_ef_byge.html (May 2009).

24. Kearney, E., and Gebert, D. Managing diversity and enhancing team outcomes: The promise of transformational leadership. *Journal of Applied Psychology*, 2009, 94, 77–89.

25. The Center for Creative Leadership is a good source, among others, to learn about leadership development programs. Go to www.ccl.org (April 2009).

26. Wolfam, H-J., and Mohr, G. Transformational leadership, team goal fulfillment, and follower work satisfaction. *Journal of Leadership & Organizational Studies*, 2009, 15, 260–274; Osborn, R. N., and Marlon, R. Contextual leadership, transformational leadership and the performance of international innovation seeking alliances. *Leadership Quarterly*, 2009, 20, 191–206; Walumbwa, F. O., Avolio, B. J., and Zhu, W. How transformational leadership weaves its influence on individual job performance: The role of identification and efficacy beliefs. *Personnel Psychology*, 2008, 61, 793–825.

27. *Adapted from* Puffer, S. M., and McCarthy, D. J. Ethical turnarounds and transformational leadership: A global imperative for corporate social responsibility. *Thunderbird International Business Review*, 2008, 50, 303–314; Shekshnia, S., and Kets de Vries, M. Interview with a Russian entrepreneur: Ruben Vardanian. *Organizational Dynamics*, 2008, 37, 288–299; Shekshnia, S. V. Interview: Troika Dialog's founder Ruben Vardanian on building Russia's first investment bank. *Academy of Management Executive*, 2001, 15(4), 16–23; see also McCarthy, D. J., and Puffer, S. M. Interpreting the ethicality of corporate governance decisions in Russia: Utilizing integrative social contracts theory to evaluate the relevancy of agency theory norms. *Academy of Management Review*, 2008, 33, 11–31.

28. Troika Dialog. Ruben Vardanian. www.troikadialog.ru/eng/About/Management/Ruben_Vardanian.wbp (April 2009).

29. Troika Dialog: About us. www.troikadialog.ru/eng/About/About_Troika/About_Us.wbp (April 2009); see also Belton, C., and Burgis, T. Standard strikes Russian deal. *Financial Times*, March 6, 2009, 13.

30. Global Leadership and Organizational Behavior Effectiveness (GLOBE) project. www.thunderbird.edu (April 2009). We express appreciation to Mansour Javidan (Thunderbird School of Global Management) and Peter Dorfman (New Mexico State University) for their review and constructive inputs on a draft of our discussion of the GLOBE model. Their inputs have been incorporated in this presentation.

31. This section is based on Chhokar, J. S., Brodbeck, F. C., and House, R. J. (Eds.). *Culture and Leadership across the World: The GLOBE Book of In-Depth Studies of 25 Societies*. Florence, KY: Lawrence Erlbaum Associates, 2007; House, R. J., Hanges, P. J., Javidan, M., Dorman, P. W., and Gupta, V. (Eds.). *Culture, Leadership, and Organizations: The GLOBE Study of 62 Societies*. Thousand Oaks, CA: Sage, 2004; House, R. J., Javidan, M., Dorfman, P. W., and de Luque, M. S. A failure of scholarship: Response to George Graen's critique of GLOBE. *Academy of Management Perspectives*, 2006, 20(4), 102–114; Javidan, M. House, R. J., Dorfman, P. W., Hanges, P. J., and de Luque, M. S. Conceptualizing and measuring cultures and their consequences: A comparative review of GLOBE's and Hofstede's approaches. *Journal of International Business Studies*, 2006, 37, 897–914; Javidan, M., and Dastmalchian, A. Managerial implications of the GLOBE project: A study of 62 societies. *Asia Pacific Journal of Human Resources*, 2009, 47, 41–58.

32. *Based on* Grove, C. N. Worldwide differences in business value and practices: Overview of GLOBE research findings. Glovewell LLC. www.glovewell.com (April 2009); Muczyk, J. P., and Holt, D. T. Toward a cultural contingency model of leadership. *Journal of Leadership and Organizational Studies*, 2008, 14, 277–286.

33. House et al., *Culture, Leadership, and Organization*, 275–276.

34. Grove, Worldwide differences in business values and practices; see also Caligiuri, P., and Tarique, I. Predicting effectiveness in global leadership activities. *Journal of World Business*, 2008, 43, 1–11; Smith, P. B., and Best, D. L. (Eds.). *Cross-Cultural Psychology*, four-volume set. Thousand Oaks, CA: Sage, 2009.

35. *Adapted from* Howell, J. P., DelaCerda, J., Martinez, S. M., Prieto, L., Bautista, J. A., Ortiz, J., Dorfman, P., and Mendez, M. J. Leadership and culture in Mexico. *Journal of World Business*, 2007, 42, 449–462; Matviuk, S. Cross-cultural leadership behavior expectations: A comparison between United States managers and Mexican managers. *Journal of American Academy of Business*, 2007, 11, 253–260; Miramontes, G. *A Qualitative Study of Examining Leadership Characteristics of Mexican Leaders*. Malibu, CA: Pepperdine University, 2008 (doctoral dissertation).

36. *Adapted from* Leader Behaviors (Sections 2 and 4). GLOBE Research Survey: Form Alpha. The research-based versions of these leadership and culture scales within the GLOBE project are available on the GLOBE website at the Thunderbird School of Global Management. www.thunderbird.edu/sites/globe (April 2009). This adapted instrument is from House et al., *Culture Leadership and Organizations*, Chapter 8. Used, adapted, and shortened with permission of Mansour Javidan, President and CEO of GLOBE and Director of the Garvin Center for Cultures

and Languages of International Management, Thunderbird School of Global Management (April 2009).

37. *Adapted from* Branson, R. *Business Stripped Bare: Adventures of a Global Entrepreneur.* New York: Virgin Books, 2008; Hoovers. Virgin Group Ltd. http://premium.hoovers.com (April 2009); Questions for . . . Sir Richard Branson. *Fortune*, November 10, 2008, 38–39; About Virgin: Ask Richard. www.virgin.com/virgin, click on "About Richard Branson" and see the "Ask Richard" section (April 2009); Crooks, E. Five fighters of climate change. *Financial Times*, March 19, 2009, 14–15; Thomson, M., Emery, S., and Porras, J. Integrity to what matters. *Association Now*, December 2006, 39–43; Coleman, A. Make me good, but not yet. . . . *Director*, 2007, 60(9), 46–50; Kets de Vries, M. F. R. *The New Global Leaders: Richard Branson, Percy Barnevik, and David Simon.* San Francisco: Jossey-Bass, 1999; Gimbel, B. Sir Richard Branson. *Fortune*, November 10, 2008, 38–39.

Chapter 12

1. *Adapted from* Boeing: About us. www.boeing.com/companyoffices/aboutus (May 2009); Matson, E. How Boeing's leaders fly. www.fastcompany.com/magazine/09/boeing.html (May 2009); Jacobsen, J. Teamwork makes the difference. *Journal for Quality and Participation*, 2008, 31(3), 30–38.

2. Homans, G. C. *The Human Group.* New York: Harcourt, Brace and World, 1959, 2.

3. Levi, D. *Group Dynamics for Teams*, 2nd ed. Thousand Oaks, CA: Sage, 2007; Edmondson, A. C. *Teams That Learn: What Leaders Must Do to Foster Organizational Learning.* New York: Wiley, 2006.

4. Wheelan, S. A. *Creating Effective Teams: A Guide for Members and Leaders*, 2nd ed. Thousand Oaks, CA: Sage, 2005.

5. Oh, H., Labianca, G., and Chung, M. A multilevel model of group social capital. *Academy of Management Review*, 2006, 31, 569–582.

6. Morton, S. C., Brookes, N. J., Smart, P. K., Backhouse, C. J., and Burns, N. D . Managing the informal organization: Conceptual model. *International Journal of Productivity and Performance Management*, 2004, 53, 214–227.

7. LaFasto, F., and Larson, C. *When Teams Work Best.* Thousand Oaks, CA: Sage, 2001.

8. Adrian, N. Boeing team uses quality to create a safer work environment. *Quality Progress*, 2008, 41(3), 44–50.

9. Herrenkohl, R. C. *Becoming a Team: Achieving a Goal*, 2nd ed. Mason, OH: South-Western/Cengage, 2008; LePine, J. A., Piccolo, R. F., Jackson, C. L., Mathieu, J. E., and Saul, J. R. A meta-analysis of teamwork processes: Tests of a multidimensional model and relationships with team effectiveness criteria. *Personnel Psychology*, 2008, 61, 273–307; Mathieu, J., Maynard, M. T., Rapp, T., and Gilson, L. Team effectiveness 1997–2007: A review of recent advances and a glimpse into the future. *Journal of Management*, 2008, 34, 410–476.

10. Kirkman, B. I., and Rosen, B. Beyond self-management: Antecedents and consequences of team empowerment. *Academy of Management Journal*, 1999, 42, 58–74; Chen, G., Kirkman, B. L., Kanfer, R., Allen, D., and Rosen, B. A multilevel study of leadership, empowerment, and performance in teams. *Journal of Applied Psychology*, 2007, 92, 331–346; Mathieu, J. E., Gilson, L. L., and Rudy, T. M. Empowerment and team effectiveness: An empirical test of an integrated model. *Journal of Applied Psychology*, 2006, 91, 97–108.

11. *Adapted from* Our culture: A team-based flat lattice organization. www.gore.com/en_xx/aboutus/culture (May 2009); Champagne, R. Gore at 50. *Delaware Today*, July 2008, 1–4; Faragher, J. The world is flat. *Personnel Today*, July 22, 2008, 18–20; Small groups, big ideas. *Workforce Management*, February 26, 2006, 22–27; Deutschman, A. The fabric of creativity. *Fast Company*, December 2004, 54–62.

12. About Gore and Fast facts about Gore. www.gore.com/en_xx/aboutus (May 2009); Hoovers, W. L. Gore & Associates, Inc. www.hoovers.com (May 2009); 50 of the world's most innovative companies. *Fast Company*, March 2009, 52–97.

13. Rico, R., Sanchez-Manznares, M., Gil, F., and Gibson, C. B. Team implicit coordination processes: A team knowledge-based approach. *Academy of Management Journal*, 2008, 33, 163–184; Molleman, E. Attitudes toward flexibility: The role of task characteristics. *Group & Organization Management*, 2009, 34, 241–268.

14. Tuckman, B. W. Development sequence in small groups. *Psychological Bulletin*, 1965, 62, 384–399; Tuckman, B. W., and Jensen, M. A. Stages of small group development revisited. *Group & Organization Studies*, 1977, 2, 419–427; see also Gersick, C. J. G. Marking time: Predictable transitions in task groups. *Academy of Management Journal*, 32, 1989, 274–309; Chang, A., Bordia, P. and Duck, J. Punctuated equilibrium and linear progression: Toward a new understanding of group development. *Academy of Management Journal*, 46, 2003, 106–117; Ito, J. K., and Brotheridge, C. M. Do teams grow up one stage at a time? Exploring the complexity of group development models. *Team Performance Management*, 2008, 14, 214–232.

15. Ancona, D., and Bresman, H. *X-teams: How to Build Teams that Lead, Innovate, and Succeed.* Boston: Harvard Business School Press, 2007; Guttman, H. M. *Great Business Teams: Cracking the Code for Standout Performance.* New York: Wiley, 2008; Mesmer-Magnus, J. R., and De Church, L. A. Information sharing and team performance: A meta-analysis. *Journal of Applied Psychology*, 2009, 94, 535–546.

16. *Adapted from* Johnson, K. Stoner: Built on a strong foundation. *Quality Progress*, August 2004, 40–47; Stoner: 60 years of innovation. www.stonersolutions.com/AboutStoner.htm (May 2009).

17. Dubinsky, R., Druskat, V. U., Mangino, M., and Flynn, E. What makes good teams work better: Research-based strategies that distinguish top-performing cross-functional drug development teams. *Organization Development Journal*, 2007, 25, 179–186; Applebaum, S. A., and Gonzalo, F. Effectiveness and dynamics of cross-functional teams: A case study of Northerntranspo Ltd. *Journal of American Academy of Business*, 2007, 10(2), 36–44.

18. Pessin, A. US seeking new approaches to Somali piracy. April 14, 2009. www.voanews.com/english/archive/

2009-04/2009-04-14-voa58.cfm (May 2009); Blenky, N. Rampant piracy takes shipping hostage. *Marine Log*, 2008, 113(11), 62–69; Phillips, Z. Some ships arm as pirate attacks rise. *Business Insurance*, December 22, 2008, 1–2.

19. Hiscox Insurance Company (Bermuda) Ltd. www.hiscox.com (May 2009).

20. Douglas, C. Martin, J. S., and Krapels, R. H. Communication in the transition to self-directed work teams. *Journal of Business Communication*, 2006, 43, 295–321.

21. Proenca, T. Self-managed work teams: A lean or an autonomous teamwork model. *International Journal of Human Resources Development and Management*, 2009, 9, 59–80.

22. DeVaro, J. The effects of self-managed and closely managed teams on labor productivity and product quality: An empirical analysis of a cross-section of establishments. *Industrial Relations*, 2008, 47, 659–697.

23. Solansky, S. T. Leadership style and team processes in self-managed teams. *Journal of Leadership & Organizational Studies*, 2008, 14, 332–341.

24. Escriba-Moreno, M. A., Canet-Giner, M. T., and Moreno-Luzon, M. TQM and teamwork effectiveness: The intermediate role of organizational design. *Quality Management Journal*, 2008, 15(3), 41–59.

25. Kirkman, B. L., and Rosen, B. Powering up teams. *Organizational Dynamics*, 2000, 28(3), 48–66; Manning, T., Pogson, G., and Morrison, Z. Interpersonal influence in the workplace—part three: Some research findings: Influencing behaviour and team role behavior. *Industrial and Commercial Training*, 2008, 40, 328–334.

26. Nemiro, J., Beyerlein, M. M., Bradley, L., and Beyerlein, S. (Eds.). *The Handbook of High Performance Virtual Teams: A Toolkit for Collaborating across Cultures*. San Francisco: Jossey-Bass, 2008.

27. Edwards, A., and Wilson, J. R. *Implementing Virtual Teams*. Abingdon, Oxon, UK: Gower Publishing, 2004; Jones, R., Oyung, R., and Pace, L. *Working Virtually: Challenges of Virtual Teams*. Hershey, PA: IRM Press, 2005.

28. Malhotra, A., and Majchrzak, A. Virtual workspace technologies. *Sloan Management Review*, 2005, 46(2), 11–14; Curseu, P. L., Schalk, R., and Wessel, I. How do virtual teams process information? A literature review and implications for management. *Journal of Managerial Psychology*, 2008, 23, 628–652.

29. Greene, T. Cisco rolls out low-end telepresence system. *Network World*, March 31, 2009; Telepresence. http://en.wikipedia.org/wiki/Telepresence (May 2009).

30. Cisco's TelePresence technology selected for NBA all-star game. *Telecomworldwire*, February 16, 2009, 1.

31. Collaborative software. http://en.wikipiedia.org/wiki/Collaborative_software (May 2009).

32. IBM. IBM Lotus software. www-01.ibm.com/software/lotus (May 2009).

33. Kock, N. *Virtual Team Leadership and Collaborative Engineering Advancements: Contemporary Issues and Implications*. Hershey, PA: Information Science Reference, 2009.

34. Brake, T. *Where in the World Is My Team: Making a Success of Your Virtual Global Workplace*. New York: Wiley,

2009; Bergiel, B. J., Bergiel, E. G., and Balsmeier, P. W. Nature of virtual teams: A summary of their advantages and disadvantages. *Management Research News*, 2008, 31(2), 99–110; Stevens, E., Karkkainen, H., and Lampela, H. Contribution of virtual teams to learning and knowledge generation in innovation-related products. *International Journal of Product Development*, 2009, 8, 1–21.

35. Oshri, I., and Kotlarsky, J. *Managing Component-Based Development in Global Teams*. Hampshire, England: Macmillan Publishers, Ltd., 2009.

36. Ahlstrom, D., and Bruton, G. D. *International Management: Strategy and Culture in the Emerging World*. Florence, KY: South-Western/Cengage, 2010; Hitt, M. A., Ireland, R. D., and Hoskisson, R. E. *Strategic Management: Competitiveness and Globalization, Concepts and Cases*. Florence, KY: South-Western/Cengage, 2009.

37. Cohen, E. *Leadership without Borders: Successful Strategies from World-Class Leaders*. New York: Wiley, 2007; Monalisa, M., Daim, T., Mirani, F., Dash, P., Khamis, R., and Bhusari, V. Managing global design teams. *Research Technology Management*, 2008, 51(4), 48–59.

38. Barczak, G., McDonough, E. F., and Athanassiou, N. So you want to be a global project leader? *Research Technology Management*, 2006, 49(3), 28–35.

39. *Adapted from* Jordery, J., Soo, C., Kirkman, B., Rosen, B., and Mathieu, J. Leading parallel global virtual teams: Lessons from Alcoa. *Organizational Dynamics*, 2009, 38, in press.

40. Ibid.

41. About Alcoa. www.alcoa.com/global/en/about_alcoa/overview.asp (May 2009).

42. Doolen, T. L., Hacker, M. E., and Van Aken, E. Managing organizational context for engineering team effectiveness. *Team Performance Management*, 2006, 12, 138–154; Rico, R., Sanchez-Manzanares, M., Gil, F., and Gibson, C. B. Team implicit coordination processes: A team knowledge-based approach. *Academy of Management Review*, 2008, 33, 163–184.

43. Berry, L. L. Leadership lessons from Mayo Clinic. *Organizational Dynamics*, 2004, 33, 228–242; see also Berry, L. L., and Seltman, K. D. *Management Lessons from Mayo Clinic*. New York: McGraw-Hill, 2008.

44. Gibson, C. B., and Cooper, C. D. Do you see what we see? The complex effects of perceptual distance between leaders and teams. *Journal of Applied Psychology*, 2009, 94, 62–76; Saren, S., and Colarelli O'Connor, G. First among equals: The effect of team leader characteristics on the internal dynamics of product development teams. *Journal of Product Innovation Management*, 2009, 26, 188–205.

45. *Adapted from* Armour, S. CEO helps people keep their homes. *USA Today*, April 27, 2009, 4B; Cavuto, N. CitiMortgage—CEO interview. *CEO Wire*, March 4, 2009, 1.

46. About CitiMortgage. www.citimortgage.com (May 2009).

47. Ordónez, L. D., Schweitzer, M. D., Galinsky, A. D., and Bazerman, M. H. Goals gone wild: The systematic side effects of overprescribing goal setting. *Academy of Management Executive*, 2009, 23, 6–16.

48. About Mayo Clinic: Mission, values, and core principles. www.mayoclinic.org/about (May 2009).

49. Tasa, K., Taggar, S., and Seijts, G. H. The development of collective efficacy in teams: A multilevel and longitudinal perspective. *Journal of Applied Psychology*, 2007, 92, 17–27.

50. De Rue, D. S., Hollenbeck, J. R., Johnson, M. D., Ilgen, D. R., and Jundt, D. K. How different team downsizing approaches influence team-level adaptation and performance. *Academy of Management Journal*, 2008, 51, 182–196.

51. Aritzeta, A., Swailes, S., and Senior, B. Belbin's team role model: Development, validity and applications for team building. *Journal of Managerial Studies*, 2007, 44, 96–118; Manning, T., Parker, R., and Pogson, G. A revised model of team roles and research findings. *Industrial and Commercial Training*, 2006, 38, 287–296.

52. Bales, R. F. *Interaction Process Analysis*. Cambridge, MA: Addison Wesley, 1950; Klein, K. J., Lim, B., Saltz, J. L., and Mayer, D. M. How do they get there? An examination of the antecedents of centrality in team networks. *Academy of Management Journal*, 2004, 47, 952–963.

53. Humphrey, S. E., Manor, M. J., and Morgeson, F. P. Developing a theory of the strategic core of teams. A role composition model of team performance. *Journal of Applied Psychology*, 2009, 94, 48–61; Postrel, S. Multitasking teams with variable complimentarity: Challenges for capability management. *Academy of Management Review*, 2009, 34, 273–296.

54. Ozbilgin, M. F. (Ed.). *Equality, Diversity, and Inclusion at Work: Theory and Scholarship*. Northampton, MA: Elgar, 2009; Harrison, D. A., and Klein, K. J. What's the difference? Diversity constructs as separation, variety, or disparity in organizations. *Academy of Management Review*, 2007, 32, 1199–1228.

55. Rico, R., Molleman, E., Sánchez-Manzannes, M., and Van der Vegt, G. S. The effects of diversity faultlines and team task autonomy on decision quality and social integration. *Journal of Management*, 2007, 33, 111–132; Pearsall, M. J., Ellis, A. P., and Evans, J. M. Unlocking the effects of gender faultlines on team creativity: Is activation the key? *Journal of Applied Psychology*, 2008, 93, 225–234.

56. Kearney, E. When and how diversity benefits teams: The importance of team members' need for cognition. *Academy of Management Journal*, June 2009, 52, in press; Kearney, E., and Gebert, D. Managing diversity and enhancing team outcomes: The promise of transformational leadership. *Journal of Applied Psychology*, 2009, 94, 77–89.

57. Stevens, F. G., Plaut, V. C., and Sanchez-Burks, J. Unlocking the benefits of diversity: All inclusive multiculturalism and organizational change. *Journal of Applied Behavioral Science*, 2008, 44, 116–133; Joshi, A. The role of context in work team diversity research: A meta-analytic review. *Academy of Management Journal*, June 2009, 52, in press.

58. *Adapted from* Special feature on WellPoint, Inc. Diversity: Innovation, creativity, success. *Profiles in Diversity Journal*, 2008, 10(3), 1–59; WellPoint. 2007–2008 diversity annual report. www.wellpointdiversity.com (click on "Diversity Annual Report" for the full pdf) (May 2009); O'Hara, K. J. Guided by principles: How Angela Braly leads WellPoint based on clear goals and a strong sense of purpose. *Smartbusiness Online*. www.sbnonline.com/Local/Article/12852/65/0/Guided_by_principles.aspx (May 2009).

59. WellPoint: Our business. www.wellpoint.com/business/default/asp; Wellpoint: Diversity. www.wellpointdiversity.com (May 2009).

60. Taggar, S., and Ellis, R. The role of leaders in shaping formal team norms. *Leadership Quarterly*, 2007, 18, 105–120.

61. Bamberger, P., and Biron, M. Group norms and absenteeism: The role of peer referent others. *Organizational Behavior and Human Decision Processes*, 2007, 103, 179–196.

62. Feldman, D. C. The development and enforcement of group norms. *Academy of Management Review*, 1984, 9, 47–53; Ellemers, N., Pagliaro, S., Barreto, M., and Leach, C. W. Is it better to be moral than smart? The effects of morality and competence norms on the decision to work at group status improvement. *Journal of Personality and Social Psychology*, 2008, 95, 1397–1410.

63. Ehrhart, M. G., and Naumann, S. E. Organizational citizenship behavior in work groups: A group norms approach. *Journal of Applied Psychology*, 2004, 89, 960–974.

64. West, B. J., Patera, J. L., and Carsten, M. K. Team level positivity: Investigating positive psychological capacities and team level outcomes. *Journal of Organizational Behavior*, 2009, 30, 249–267.

65. Lencioni, P. M. *The Five Dysfunctions of a Team: A Leadership Fable*. San Francisco: Jossey-Bass, 2002; Lencioni, P. M. *Overcoming the Five Dysfunctions of a Team: A Field Guide for Leaders, Managers, and Facilitators*. San Francisco: Jossey-Bass, 2005.

66. Janis, I. L. *Groupthink*, 2nd ed. Boston: Houghton Mifflin, 1982; Whyte, G. Groupthink reconsidered. *Academy of Management Review*, 1989, 14, 40–56; Brownstein, A. L. Biased decision processing. *Psychological Bulletin*, 2003, 129, 545–591.

67. Hackman, J. R. Why teams don't work. *Harvard Business Review*, 2009, 87(5), 98–105; see also Chapman, J. Anxiety and defective decision making: An elaboration of the groupthink model. *Management Decision*, 2006, 44, 1391–1404; Schültz, P., and Bloch, B. The "silo-virus": Diagnosing and curing departmental groupthink. *Team Performance Management*, 2006, 12, 31–43.

68. Taggar, S., and Neubert, M. J. A cognitive (attributions)-emotion model of observer reactions to free-riding poor performers. *Journal of Business Psychology*, 2008, 22, 167–177; Anesi, V. Moral hazard and free riding in collective action. *Social Choice and Welfare*, 2009, 32, 197–219.

69. Schnake, M. E. Equity in effort: The "sucker effect" in co-acting groups. *Journal of Management*, 1991, 17, 41–55; Murphy, S. M., Wayne, S. J., Liden, R. C., and Erdogan, B. Understanding social loafing: The role of justice perceptions and exchange relationships. *Human Relations*, 2003, 56, 61–84.

70. Felps, W., Mitchell, T. R., and Byington, E. How, when, and why bad apples spoil the barrel: Negative group members and dysfunctional groups. *Research in Organizational Behavior*, 2006, 27, 175–222.

71. Tang, L-P., Chen, Y-J., and Sutarso, T. Bad apples in bad (business) barrels. *Management Decision*, 2008, 46, 243–263.

72. Mooradian, T., Renzl, B., and Matzler, K. Who trusts? Personality, trust and knowledge sharing. *Management Learning*, 2006, 37, 523–540; Kenworthy, J. B., and Jones, J. The role of group importance and anxiety in predicting depersonalized ingroup trust. *Group Processes & Intergroup Relations*, 2009, 12, 227–239.

73. Cottrell, C. A., Li, N. P., and Neuberg, S. L. What do people desire in others? A sociofunctional perspective on the importance of different valued characteristics. *Journal of Personality and Social Psychology*, 2007, 92, 208–231.

74. Boomer, L. G. Build a winning team and fight firm dysfunction. *Accounting Today*, February 24–March 16, 2003, 1, 21.

75. *Adapted from* The Student Audit Instrument. Developed by Jon M. Werner, faculty member, Department of Management at the University of Wisconsin–Whitewater; see also Senior, B., and Swailes, S. Inside management teams: Developing a teamwork survey instrument. *British Journal of Management*, 2007, 18, 138–153; Wageman, R., Hackman, J. R., and Lehman, E. Team diagnostic survey: Development of an instrument. *Journal of Applied Behavioral Science*, 2005, 373–398.

76. *Source:* This case was prepared by Kenneth S. Rhee. Case appeared in Fransson, M. C. (Ed.), *Society for Case Research 2005 Proceedings*, 68–69. It is intended to be used as a basis for class discussion rather than to illustrate either effective or ineffective handling of the situation. Copyright © 2005 by Kenneth S. Rhee. The views presented here are those of the case authors and do not necessarily reflect the views of the Society for Case Research. The names of the organization, individuals, location, and financial information have been disguised to preserve anonymity. Edited for *Organizational Behavior*, 13th edition, and used with permission.

Chapter 13

1. *Adapted from* Olsen, L. Powerful judge's downfall began with a "small voice." *Houston Chronicle*, May 12, 2009, A1, A7; Flood, M., Kent receives 33 months, impeachment may be next. *Houston Chronicle*, May 12, 2009, A1, A7; Casey, R. Judge Kent film would write itself. *Houston Chronicle*, May 13, 2009, B1, B3; Samuel B. Kent. http://en.wikipedia.org/wiki/Samuel_B._Kent (June 2009); Powell, S., and Olsen, L. Kent shows he won't go away easily: Judge's plan to collect year of pay galvanizes Congress on impeachment. *Houston Chronicle*, June 3, 2009, A1, A9.

2. Rahim, M. A. *Managing Conflict in Organizations*, 3rd ed. Westport, CT: Quorum Books, 2001.

3. Tjosvold, D. The conflict-positive organization: It depends on us. *Journal of Organizational Behavior*, 2008, 29, 19–28; De Dreu, C. K. The virtue and vice of workplace conflict: Food for (pessimistic) thought. *Journal of Organizational Behavior*, 2008, 29, 5–18.

4. De Dreu, C. K., and Gelfand, M. J. (Eds.). *The Psychology of Conflict and Conflict Management in Organizations*. Clifton, NJ: Psychology Press, 2008.

5. Mohr, A. T., and Puck, J. F. Role conflict, general manager job satisfaction and stress, and the performance of IJVs. *European Management Journal*, 2007, 25, 25–35; Kinman, G., and Jones, F. Effort–reward imbalance: Overcommitment and work–life conflict: Testing an expanded model. *Journal of Managerial Psychology*, 2008, 23, 236–251.

6. Li, A., and Bagger, J. Role ambiguity and self-efficacy: The moderating effects of goal orientation and procedural justice. *Journal of Organizational Behavior*, 2008, 13, 368–375.

7. Gordon, G., and Nicholson, N. *Family Wars: Classic Conflicts in Family Business and How to Deal with Them*. London: Kogan Page, 2008; Kets de Vries, M. F., Carlock, R. S., and Florent-Treacy, E. *Family Business on the Couch: A Psychological Perspective*. New York: Wiley, 2008.

8. Pervin, A. Managing the relationships that bind or bond. www.pervinfamilybusiness.com/library/booklets/managing-the-relationships/pdf/managing-the-relationships.pdf (June 2009).

9. Daft, R. L. *Organization Theory and Design*, 10th ed. Mason, OH: South-Western/Cengage, 2010; Fiol, C. M., Pratt, M. G., and O'Connor, E. J. Managing intractable identity conflicts. *Academy of Management Review*, 2009, 34, 32–55.

10. *Adapted from* Weiss, J., and Hughes, J. Want collaboration? Accept—and actively manage—conflict. *Harvard Business Review*, 2005, 83(3), 93–101; Frausnheim, E. A leader in leadership, *Workforce Management*, May 21, 2007, 19–23; IBM Jam program office. www.collaborationjam.com (June 2009).

11. IBM. www.hoovers.com/ibm/--ID__10796--/free-co-factsheet.xhtml (June 2009).

12. Thomas, K. W. Conflict and negotiation processes in organizations. In Dunnette, M. D., and Hough, L. M. (Eds.). *Handbook of Industrial and Organizational Psychology*, Vol. 3, 2nd ed. Palo Alto, CA: Consulting Psychologists Press, 1992, 651–717; Hede, A. Toward an explanation of interpersonal conflict in work groups. *Journal of Managerial Psychology*, 2007, 22, 25–39.

13. Runde, C. E., and Flanagan, T. A. Conflict competent leadership. *Leader to Leader*. Winter 2008, 46–51; Runde, C. E., and Flanagan, T. A. *Building Conflict Competent Teams*. San Francisco: Jossey-Bass, 2008.

14. Zarankin, T. G. A new look at conflict styles: Goal orientation and outcome preferences. *International Journal of Conflict Management*, 2008, 19, 167–184; Aritzeta, A., Ayestaran, S., and Swailes, S. Team role preference and conflict management styles. *International Journal of Conflict Resolution*, 2005, 16, 157–182.

15. *Adapted from* Sandberg, J. Avoiding conflicts, the too-nice boss makes matters worse. *Wall Street Journal*, February 26, 2008, B1; Dalton, F. Poisonous passivity. *SuperVision*, 2008, 69(8), 18–19; Hite, B. Employers rethink how they give feedback. *Wall Street Journal*, October 13, 2008, B5.

16. Lewicki, R. J., Saunders, D. M., and Barry, B. *Negotiation*, 6th ed. New York: McGraw-Hill, 2010; Lewicki, R. J., and Hiam, A. *Mastering Business Negotiation: A Working Guide to Making Deals and Resolving Conflict*. San Francisco: Jossey-Bass, 2006.

17. Masters, M. F. *Business of Negotiating*. Upper Saddle River, NJ: Prentice Hall, 2008; Raiffa, H., with Richardson, H., and Metcalfe, D. *Negotiation Analysis: The Science and Art of Collaborative Decision Making*, 2nd ed. Cambridge, MA: Belknap Press, 2007.

18. Walton, R. E., and McKersie, R. B. *A Behavioral Theory of Labor Negotiations: An Analysis of a Social Interaction System*, 2nd ed. Ithaca, NY: ILR Press, 1991; Walton, R. E., Cutcher-Gershenfeld, J. E., and McKersie, R. B. *Strategic Negotiations: A Theory of Change in Labor–Management Relations*. Ithaca, NY: ILR Press, 2000.

19. Fisher, R., and Ury, W. *Getting to Yes: Negotiating Agreement without Giving In*, 2nd ed. New York: Penguin Books, 1991; Spector, B. Introduction: An interview with Roger Fisher and William Ury. *Academy of Management Executive*, 2004, 18(3), 101–108; Fisher, R., and Shapiro, D. *Beyond Reason: Using Emotions as You Negotiate*. New York: Penguin, 2006.

20. Ertl, D., and Gordon, M. *The Point of the Deal: How to Negotiate When Yes Is Not Enough*. Boston: Harvard Business School Press, 2007; Bercovitch, J., Kremenyuk, V., and Zartman, I. W. (Eds.). *Sage Handbook of Conflict Resolution*. Thousand Oaks, CA: Sage, 2009.

21. Program on negotiation: Harvard Negotiation Project. www.pon.harvard.edu/hnp. (June 2009).

22. Fisher and Ury, *Getting to Yes*; Malhotra, D., and Bazerman, M. *Negotiation Genius: How to Overcome Obstacles and Achieve Brilliant Results at the Bargaining Table and Beyond*. New York: Bantam, 2007.

23. *Adapted from* Powers of persuasion. *Fortune*, October 12, 1998, 160–164; Shapiro, R., and Jankowski, M. *The Power of Nice: How to Negotiate So Everyone Wins—Especially You*, rev. ed. New York: John Wiley & Sons, 2002; Shapiro Negotiation Institute. www.shapironegotiations.com (June 2009).

24. *Excerpts from* Tyler, K. The art of give-and-take. *HR Magazine*, November 2004, 107–116; Ury, W. *The Power of a Positive No: How to Say No and Still Get to Yes*. New York: Bantam, 2008.

25. Beacon, N., and Blyton, P. Conflict for mutual gains. *Journal of Management Studies*, 2007, 44, 814–834.

26. Ogilvie, J. R., and Kidder, D. L. What about negotiator styles? *International Journal of Conflict Management*, 2008, 19, 132–147; Katz, H., Kochan, T. A., and Colvin, A. J. *An Introduction to Collective Bargaining & Industrial Relations*, 4th ed. New York: McGraw-Hill/Irwin, 2008; Rousseau, D. M., and Batt, R. Global competition's perfect storm: Why business and labor cannot solve their problems alone. *Academy of Management Perspectives*, 2007, 21(2), 16–23.

27. *Adapted from* Stoll, J. D., and Terlop, S. GM clears UAW hurdle as deadline looms. *Wall Street Journal*, May 30, 2009, B5; Stoll, J. D. GM nears crucial deal with UAW. *Wall Street Journal*, May 15, 2009, B1, B2; Simon, B. UAW gears up to join boards of carmakers. www.ft.com/cms/s/0/4acca122-351f-11de-940a-00144feabdc0.html?nclick_check=1 (April 30, 2009); Green, J., and Miles, G. GM may trim imports 'substantially' in UAW talks (Update1). www.bloomberg.com/apps/news?pid=newsarchive&sid=ajybcNSH36tI (May 14, 2009).

28. Chatterjee, C. *Alternative Dispute Resolution*. New York: Routledge, 2008; Coltri, L. G. *Alternative Dispute Resolution: A Conflict Diagnosis Approach*, 2nd ed. Upper Saddle River, NJ: Prentice-Hall, 2009.

29. Friedman, G. *Challenging Conflict: Mediation through Understanding*. Washington, DC: American Bar Association, 2009; Olson-Buchanan, J. B., and Boswell, W. R.

Mistreatment in the Workplace: Prevention and Resolution for Managers and Organizations. Malden, MA: Wiley-Blackwell, 2009.

30. Graham, J. L., and Requejo, W. H. Managing face-to-face international negotiations. *Organizational* Dynamics, 2009, 38, 167–177; Salacuse, J. W. Ten ways that culture affects negotiating style: Some survey results. *Negotiation Journal*, 1998, 14, 221–240; Salacuse, J. W. Negotiating: The top ten ways that culture can affect your negotiation. *Ivey Business Journal*, March/April 2005, 1–6; Katz, L. *Negotiating International Business: The Negotiator's Reference to 50 Countries Around the World*. Charleston, SC: BookSurge Publishing, 2007.

31. Culture and negotiation. www.negotiations.org (June 2009); Brett, J. M. *Negotiating Globally: How to Negotiate Deals, Resolve Disputes, and Make Decisions across Cultural Boundaries*, 2nd ed. San Francisco: Jossey-Bass, 2007.

32. Metcalf, L. E., Bird, A., Shankarmahesh, M., Aycan, Z., Larimo, J., and Valdelamar, D. D. Cultural tendencies in negotiation: A comparison of Finland, Mexico, Turkey, and the United States. *Journal of World Business*, 2006, 41, 382–394.

33. Salacuse, J. W., Johnson, J. P., Lenartowicz, T., and Apud, S. Cross-cultural competence in international business: Toward a definition and a model. *Journal of International Business Studies*, 2006, 37, 525–543.

34. Moriomoto, I., Saijo, M., Nohara, K., Takagi, K., Otsuka, H., Suzuki, K., and Okumura, M. How do ordinary Japanese reach consensus in group decision making?: Identifying and analyzing "naïve negotiation." *Group Decision and Negotiation*, 2006, 15, 157–169.

35. *Adapted from* Jassawalla, A., Truglia, C., and Garvey, J. Cross-cultural conflict and expatriate manager adjustment: An exploratory study. *Management Decision*, 2004, 42, 837–849; Ang, S., and Van Dyne, L. (Eds.). *Handbook of Cultural Intelligence: Theory, Measurement, and Application*. Armonk, NY: M. E. Sharpe, 2008; Crowne, K. A. What leads to cultural intelligence. *Business Horizons*, 2008, 51, 391–399; Cultural Intelligence Center. http://culturalq.com (June 2009).

36. Griffin, T. J., and Daggatt, W. R. *The Global Negotiator: Building Strong Business Relationships Anywhere in the World*. New York: HarperBusiness, 1992, 29–30.

37. *Adapted from* Ghauri, P., and Usunier, J. (Eds.). *International Business Negotiations*. New York: Pergamon, 2006; Starkey, B., Boyer, M. A., and Wikenfeld, J. *Negotiating in a Complex World: An Introduction to International Negotiation*, 2nd ed. London: Littlefield Brown Publishers, 2005; Brett, J., Behfar, K., and Kern, M. C. Managing multicultural teams. *Harvard Business Review*, 2006, 84(1), 84–91.

38. *Adapted from* Rodrigues, C. *International Management: A Cultural Approach*. Thousand Oaks, CA: Sage, 2009, 366–367, 388–390; Hill, J. S. *World Business: Globalization Strategy and Analysis*. Mason, OH: South-Western/Cengage, 2005, 471–472; Lewis, R. D. *When Cultures Collide: Managing Successfully Across Cultures*, 3rd ed. Boston: Nicholas Brealey Publishing, 2006, 223–232, 262–268.

39. *Adapted from* Baskerville, D. M. How do you manage conflict? *Black Enterprise*, May 1993, 63–66; Thomas, K. W., and Kilmann, R. H. *The Thomas-Kilmann Conflict Mode*

Instrument. Tuxedo, NY: Xicom, 1974; Rahim, M. A. A measure of styles of handling interpersonal conflict. *Academy of Management Journal*, 1983, 26, 368–376.

40. *Adapted from* Zoll, III, A. A. *Explorations in Managing.* Reading, MA: Addison-Wesley, 1974.

Chapter 14

1. *Adapted from* Dalton, C. M. From canning jars to aerospace: An interview with R. D. Hoover, chairperson, chief executive officer, and president of Ball Corporation. *Business Horizons*, 2006, 49, 97–104; About Ball. www.ball.com (July 2009); *Ball Corporation 2008 Annual Report.* www.ball.com (July 2009); R. David Hoover elected to Lily Board of Directors. *PR Newswire*, June 2, 2009, 1.

2. Decision making. http://en.wikipedia.org/wiki/Decision_making (July 2009).

3. *Ball Corporation 2008 Annual Report.*

4. Dalton, From canning jars to aerospace, 103.

5. Stanovich, K. E. *Decision Making and Rationality in the Modern World.* New York: Oxford University Press, 2009.

6. About Avis Budget Group, Inc. www.avisbudgetgroup .com/about (July 2009); Avis FAQs. www.avis.com (July 2009); Deaver, S., and Beasty, C. Secret of my success. *Customer Relationship Management*, 2005, 9(12), 44–45.

7. Risk World: Covering risk news and views. www.riskworld .com (July 2009).

8. Introduction to probability. http://mathforum.org/ dr.math/faq/faq.prob.intro.html (July 2009).

9. *Adapted from* Form 10-K for the Ball Corporation. Filed with the U.S. Securities and Exchange Commission. Filed February 25, 2009. Available thru http://phx.corporate-ir .net/phoenix.zhtml?c=115234&p=irol-IRHome (July 2009).

10. Halpern, J. Y. *Reasoning about Uncertainty.* Cambridge, MA: MIT Press, 2006.

11. Mitroff, I. I., and Silvers, A. *Dirty Rotten Strategies: How We Trick Ourselves and Others Into Solving the Wrong Problems Precisely.* Stanford, CA: Stanford Business Books, 2010; Alpaslan, C. M., Green, S. E., and Mitroff, I. I. Corporate governance in the context of crises: Towards a stakeholder theory of crisis management. *Journal of Contingencies and Crisis Management*, 2009, 17, 38–49.

12. *Adapted from* Shoes For Crews. www.shoesforcrews .com (July 2009). Click on "About us," then search under "customer service" and "corporate shoe programs"; Tierney, J. Shoes For Crews: Surefooted recession. *Multichannel Merchant*, 2009, 26(6), 8; Gill, D. Or your money back. *INC.*, September 2005, 46–47.

13. Moore, D. A., and Flynn, F. J. The case for behavioral decision research in organizational behavior. *Academy of Management Annals*, 2008, 2, 399–431.

14. Simon, H. A. *Administrative Behavior: A Study of Decision-Making Processes in Administrative Organizations*, 4th ed. New York: Free Press, 1997; also see Clegg, S. The bounds of rationality: Power/history/imagination. *Critical Perspectives on Accounting*, 2006, 17, 847–863.

15. Roach, J. M. Simon says: Decision making is "satisficing" experience. *Management Review*, January 1979, 8–9; also see deBoer, L., Gaytan, J., and Arroyo, P. A satisficing

model of outsourcing. *Supply Chain Management*, 2006, 11, 444–455.

16. Knudsen, T., and Levinthal, D. A. Two faces of search: Alternative generation and alternative evaluation. *Organization Science*, 2007, 18, 39–54; Tiawana, A., Wang, J., Keil, M., and Ahulwalia, P. The bounded rationality bias in managerial evaluation of real options: Theory and evidence from IT projects. *Decision Sciences*, 2007, 38, 157–181.

17. Staw, B. M. The escalation of commitment to a course of action. *Academy of Management Review*, 1981, 6, 577–587; Schulz-Hardt, S., Thurow-Kröning, B., and Frey, D. Preference-based escalation: A new interpretation for the responsibility effect in escalating commitment and entrapment. *Organizational Behavior and Human Decision Science*, 2009, 108, 175–186.

18. Montealegre, R., and Keil, M. Deescalating information technology projects: Lessons from the Denver International Airport. *MIS Quarterly*, 2000, 24, 417–447; Denver International Airport. http://en.wikipedia.org/ wiki/Denver_International_Airport (July 2009).

19. Stulz, R. M. Six ways companies mismanage risk. *Harvard Business Review*, 2009, 87(3), 86–93; Hillson, D., and Murray-Webster, R. *Understanding and Managing Risk Attitude.* Aldershot, Hampshire, UK: Gower Publishing, 2007.

20. Lehrer, J. *How We Decide.* Boston: Houghton Mifflin, 2009. For a discussion of the relationship between escalating commitment and risk propensity, see Wong, K. F. The role of risk in making decisions under escalation situations. *Applied Psychology*, 2005, 54, 584–607.

21. Kahneman, D. A perspective on judgment and choice: Mapping bounded rationality. *American Psychologist*, 2003, 58, 697–720; Maitlis, S., and Lawrence, T. B. Triggers and enablers of sensemaking in organizations. *Academy of Management Journal*, 2007, 50, 58–84.

22. Schoemaker, P. J. H., and Russo, J. E. A pyramid of decision approaches. *California Management Review*, Fall 1993, 9–31; Walker, E. D., and Cox III, J. F. Addressing ill-structured problems using Goldratt's thinking processes. *Management Decision*, 2006, 44, 137–154; Browne, G. J., Pitts, M. G., and Wetherbe, J. C. Cognitive stopping rules for terminating information search in online tasks. *MIS Quarterly*, 2007, 31, 89–104.

23. Nutt, P. C. Expanding the search for alternatives during strategic decision-making. *Academy of Management Executive*, 2004, 18(4), 13–28; Nutt, P. C. Intelligence gathering for decision making. *Omega*, 2007, 35, 604–622; Gilovich, T., Griffin, D., and Kahneman, D. *Heuristics and Biases: The Psychology of Intuitive Judgment.* New York: Cambridge University Press, 2002.

24. Lei, D., and Slocum, J. W. The tipping points of business strategy: The decline and rise of competitiveness. *Organizational Dynamics*, 2009, 38, 131–147.

25. Doran, G. T., and Gunn, J. Decision making in high-tech firms: Perspectives of three executives. *Business Horizons*, 2006, 45(6), 7–16; About MicroAge. www.microage.com/ about-microage.aspx (July 2009).

26. Geisler, E., and Wickramasinghe, N. *Principles of Knowledge Management: Theory, Practice, and Cases.* Armonk, NY: M. E. Sharpe, 2009.

27. Jasimuddin, S. M. *Knowledge Management: An Interdisciplinary Perspective.* Armonk, NY: M. E. Sharpe, 2010.

28. Our firm: Office of Michael Rosenfield, Inc. Architects. www.omr-architects.com/index2.html (July 2009).

29. Radio-frequency identification (RFID). http://en.wikipedia.org/wiki/Radio-frequency_identification (July 2009).

30. *Adapted from* Case study: St. Clair hospital saves lives with Socket Mobile and Hospira. *RFID Journal*, 2008, 1–4. www.aimglobal.org/members/news/articlefiles/3406-st-clair-hospital_case-study.pdf (June 2009).

31. About St. Clair. http://www.stclair.org/2/about (July 2009).

32. *This section is based on* Pfeffer, J., and Sutton, R. I. Management half-truths and nonsense: How to practice evidence-based management. *California Management Review*, 2006, 46(3), 77–100; Pfeffer, J., and Sutton, R. I. *Hard Facts, Dangerous Half-Truths & Total Nonsense: Profiting from Evidence-Based Management*. Boston: Harvard Business School Press, 2006. Evidence-based management. www.evidence-basedmanagement.com (July 2009).

33. Fine, D. J., D'Aquila, R., and Kovner, A. R. *Evidence-Based Management in Healthcare*. Chicago: Health Administration Press, 2009.

34. Pfeffer, J., and Sutton, R. I. Evidence-based management. *Harvard Business Review*, 2006, 84(1), 2.

35. Baack, S. Book review of *Hard Facts, Dangerous Half-Truths & Total Nonsense: Profiting from Evidence-Based Management*. *Academy of Management Learning & Education*, 2007, 6, 139–141.

36. Pfeffer and Sutton, *Hard Facts, Dangerous Half-Truths & Total Nonsense*, 22.

37. Bazerman, M. H., and Chugh, D. Decisions without blinders. *Harvard Business Review*, 2006, 84(1), 88–97; Thaler, R. H., and Sunstein, C. R. *Nudge: Improving Decisions about Health, Wealth, and Happiness*. New Haven, CT: Yale University Press, 2008.

38. Pfeffer and Sutton, Management half-truths and nonsense, 96–97.

39. Rousseau, D. M., Manning, J., Denyer, D. Evidence in management and organizational science. *Academy of Management Annals*, 2008, 2, 475–515.

40. Baack, Book review, 139–141; also see other reviews of this book in the same issue by Miller, S., Williams, J., Dierdorff, E. C., and Bielmeier, P., 141–149. These reviews address the strengths and potential limitations of the evidence-based management model. Learmonth, M. Evidence-based management: A backlash against pluralism in organizational studies. *Organization*, 2008, 15, 283–291.

41. Gigerenzer, G. *Gut Feelings: The Intelligence of the Unconscious*. New York: Viking Press, 2007; Dane, E., and Pratt, M. G. Exploring intuition and its role in managerial decision making. *Academy of Management Review*, 2007, 32, 33–54.

42. *Adapted from* Chubb's business case for diversity and Chubb's diversity objectives. www.chubb.com/diversity/chubb4510.html (July 2009); Souter, G. Diversity winning the fight for talent. *Business Insurance*, 2008, 42(8), 9–12.

43. Chubb at a glance. www.chubb.com/corporate/chubb3323.pdf (July 2009).

44. Clegg, S. R., and Maugaard, M. (Eds.). *The SAGE Handbook of Power*. Thousand Oaks, CA: Sage, 2009; Vigoda-Gadot, E., and Drory, A. (Eds.). *Handbook of Organizational Politics*. Northampton, MA: Edward Elgar Publishing, 2006.

45. Buchanan, D., and Badham, R. *Power, Politics, and Organizational Change: Winning the Turf War*. Thousand Oaks, CA: Sage, 2008.

46. Funk, S. Risky business. *Across the Board*, July/August 1999, 10–12.

47. Boutilier, R. *Stakeholder Politics: Social Capital, Sustainable Development, and the Corporation*. Sheffield, UK: Greenleaf Publishing, 2009; Pfeffer, J. *Managing with Power: Politics and Influence in Organizations*. Boston: Harvard Business School Press, 1992.

48. Gabbin, A. L., and Richardson, R. C. Professional responsibility and the fate of whistleblowers. *CPA Journal*, 76(4), 2006, 14–15; also see Paetzold, R. J., Dipboye, R. L., Elsbach, K. D. A new look at stigmatization in and of organizations. *Academy of Management Review*, 2008, 33, 186–193.

49. Stall, J. D., Helliker, K., and Boudette, N. E. A saga of decline and denial. *Wall Street Journal*, June 2, 2009, A1, A15; Ingrassia, P. How GM lost its way. *Wall Street Journal*, June 2, 2009, A21.

50. Buchanan, D. A. You stab my back, I'll stab yours: Management experience and perceptions of organization political behavior. *British Journal of Management*, 2008, 19, 49–64.

51. Breaux, D. M., Munyon, T. P., Hochwarter, W. A., and Ferris, G. R. Politics as a moderator of the accountability-job satisfaction relationship: Evidence across three studies. *Journal of Management*, 2009, 35, 307–326; Rosen, C. C., Harris, K. J., and Kacmar, K. M. The emotional implications of organizational politics: A process model. *Human Relations*, 2009, 62, 27–57.

52. Gilley, J. W. *The Manager as Politician*. Westport, CT: Praeger, 2006; Fox, A. Politics in the office. *HRMagazine*, 2008, 53(1), 38–42; Griskevicius, V., Cialdini, R. B., and Goldstein, N. J. Applying (and resisting) peer influence. *MIT Sloan Management Review*, 2008, 49(2), 84–88.

53. *Adapted from* Creativity. http://en.wikipedia.org/wiki/Creativity (July 2009).

54. Townley, B., and Buch, N. (Eds.). *Managing Creativity: Exploring the Paradox*. New York: Cambridge University Press, 2010; Bilton, C., and Cummings, S. *Creative Strategy: How Aligning Creativity and Strategy Can Invigorate Business*. New York: Wiley-Blackwell, 2009.

55. La Barre, P. Weird ideas that work. *Fast Company*, January 2002, 68–73.

56. Feinstein, J. S. *The Nature of Creative Development*. Stanford, CA: Stanford University Press, 2009; Napier, N. K., and Nilsson, M. *The Creative Discipline: Mastering the Art and Science of Innovation*. Santa Barbara, CA: Praeger, 2008.

57. *This section draws on* Ulrich, D. *Widening Stream: The Seven Stages of Creativity*. New York: Altria Books/Beyond Words, 2002; Bolton, C. *Management and Creativity: From Creative Industries to Creative Management*. New York: Wiley-Blackwell, 2006.

58. Israel, P. *Edison: A Life of Imagination*. New York: Wiley, 1999.

59. Creativity tools. www.mindtools.com/pages/main/newMN_CT.htm (July 2009).

60. *This section is based on* de Bono, E. *Creativity Workout: 62 Exercises to Unlock Your Most Creative Ideas.* Berkeley, CA: Ulysses Press, 2008; de Bono Group, LLC. www.debonogroup.com (July 2009); de Bono, E. *Lateral Thinking: Creativity Step by Step.* New York: Harper Colophon, 1973; Great thinkers: Edward de Bono. *Training Journal,* May 2007; 64–65; Waller, D. The gospel according to Edward de Bono. *Management Today,* August 2007, 48–51.

61. Amabile, T. M. How to kill creativity. *Harvard Business Review,* September/October 1998, 77–87.

62. Gryskiewicz, S. S., and Epstein, R. Cashing in on creativity at work. *Psychology Today,* September/October 2000, 62–67; Maurzy, J., and Harriman, R. A. Three climates for creativity. *Research Technology Management,* 2003, 46, 27–31; The Hallmark difference: Committed to creativity. http://corporate.hallmark.com/Company/The-Hallmark-Difference (July 2009).

63. Osborn, A. F. *Applied Imagination,* rev. ed. New York: Scribner, 1957.

64. Paulus, P. B., and Njstad, B. A. (Eds.). *Group Creativity: Innovation through Collaboration.* New York: Oxford University Press, 2003.

65. *Adapted from* Kelley, T. (with Littman, J.). *The Ten Faces of Innovation: IDEO's Strategies for Beating the Devil's Advocate & Driving Creativity Throughout Your Organization.* New York: Doubleday, 2005; Brown, T. Thinking design. *Harvard Business Review,* 2008, 86(6), 85–91; Tischler, L. A designer takes on his biggest challenge ever. *Fast Company,* February 2009, 78–101; IDEO to go. www.ideo.com/to-go (July 2009).

66. For a description of the wide array of collaborative software products and services offered by GroupSystems, visit this organization's home page at www.groupsystems.com (July 2009).

67. Dennis, A. R., and Reinicke, B. A. Beta versus VHS and the acceptance of electronic brainstorming technology. *MISQuarterly,* 2004, 28, 1–20; Reing, B. A., Briggs, R. O., and Nunamaker, Jr., J. F. On the measurement of ideation quality. *Journal of Management Information Systems,* 2007, 23, 143–161.

68. Goncalo, J. A., and Staw, B. M. Individualism-collectivism and group creativity. *Organizational Behavior and Human Decision Sciences,* 2006, 100, 96–109.

69. For discussions of additional influences on creativity in the workplace, see Litchfield, R. C. Brainstorming reconsidered: A goal-based view. *Academy of Management Review,* 2008, 33, 649–668; Hirst, G., van Knippenberg, D., and Zhou, J. Across level perspective on employee creativity: Goal orientation, team learning, and individual creativity. *Academy of Management Journal,* 52, 280–293.

70. Martin, L. P. Inventory of barriers to creative thought and innovation action. Reprinted from J. William Pfeiffer (Ed.). *The 1990 Annual: Developing Human Resources.* San Diego: University Associates, 1990, 138–141. Used with permission.

71. Polly, D., and Weber, P. A manager's dilemma: Who gets the project? In Benson, J. K. (Ed.). *Journal of Critical Incidents,* 2008, 1, 15–17. Presented to and accepted by the Society for Case Research. All rights reserved to SCR. *This case was prepared by the authors and is intended to be used as a basis for class discussion. The views represented here are those of the case authors and do not necessarily reflect the views of the Society for Case Research. The authors' views are based on their professional judgment. The names of the organization, individuals, and location have been disguised to preserve the organization's anonymity.* Edited for *Organizational Behavior,* 13th edition, and used with permission. Copyright Clearinghouse.

Chapter 15

1. *Adapted from* www.lowes.com (March 2009); personal conversation with H. Johnson, retired Vice President, Internal Auditing, Lowe's, March, 2009; Spindel, D. T. Lowe's Companies, Inc. *Better Investing,* March 2009, 46–48.

2. Daft, R. *Organization Theory and Design,* 9th ed. Mason, OH: Thomson/South-Western, 2007.

3. Lei, D., and Slocum, J. W. The tipping points of business strategy: The rise and decline of competitiveness. *Organizational Dynamics,* 2009, 38, 131–147; Mathieu, J. E., and Rapp, T. L. Laying the foundation for successful team performance trajectories: The role of team characters and performance strategies. *Journal of Applied Psychology,* 2009, 94, 90–104.

4. Anand, N., and Daft, R. What is the right organization design? *Organizational Dynamics,* 2007, 36, 329–344.

5. Personal conversation with Sam Su, President, YUM! Brands China, March 2009.

6. Porter, M. *Competitive Strategy.* New York: Free Press, 1980; see also Hambrick, D. C., and Fredrickson, J. W. Are you sure you have a strategy? *Academy of Management Executive,* 2001, 15, 48–59.

7. Doebele, J. Proletariat capitalist. *Forbes,* 2007, June 18, 128–130; www.tunehotels.com (March 2009).

8. Su, personal conversation.

9. Kang, S., and Snell, S. A. Intellectual capital architectures and learning: A framework for human resource management. *Journal of Management Studies,* 2009, 46, 65–93; Toh, S. M., Morheson, F. P., and Campion, M. A. Human resource configurations: Investigating fit with organizational context. *Journal of Applied Psychology,* 2008, 93, 864–883.

10. *Adapted from* www.flextronics.com (March 2009).

11. Thompson, K. R., and Mathys, N. J. An improved tool for building high performance organizations. *Organizational Dynamics,* 2008, 37, 378–393.

12. Lange, D., Boivie, S., and Henderson, A. D. The parenting paradox: How multibusiness diversifiers endorse disruptive technologies while their corporate children struggle. *Academy of Management Journal,* 2009, 52, 179–198; Sirmon, D. G., Gove, S., and Hitt, M. A. Resource management in dyadic competitive rivalry: The effects of resource bundling and deployment. *Academy of Management Journal,* 2008, 51, 919–936; Wolter, C., and Veloso, F. M. The effects of innovation on vertical structure: Perspectives and transaction costs and competencies. *Academy of Management Review,* 2008, 33, 496–520.

13. Anand and Daft, What is the right organization design?

14. *Adapted from* Weber, M. *The Theory of Social and Economic Organization* (trans. Parsons, T.). New York: Oxford University Press, 1947, 329–334.

15. *Adapted from* Elkind, P., and McLean, B. The luckiest people in Houston. *Fortune*, May 1, 2006, 36ff; McLean, B., and Elkind, P. The guiltiest guys in the room. *Fortune*, June 12, 2006, 26–28; Reddy, S., and Case, B. M. Decision expected to reinforce strict accountability. *Dallas Morning News*, May 26, 2006, Aff.

16. *Adapted from* Hellriegel, D., Jackson, S. J., and Slocum, J. W., Jr. *Managing: A Competency-Based Approach*, 11th ed. Cincinnati, OH: South-Western/ Cengage Learning, 2008, 361–362.

17. Itoh, H., Kikutani, T., and Hayashida, O. Complementarities among authority, accountability and monitoring: Evidence from Japanese business groups. *Journal of Japanese and International Economies*, 2008, 22(2), 207–229; Bakalis, S., Joiner, T. A., and Zie, Z. Decision-making delegation: Implications for Chinese leaders' performance and satisfaction. *International Journal of Human Resources Development and Management*, 2008, 7, 286–302.

18. *Adapted from* www.eureka.com (March 2009); www .hoovers.com (search under Eureka, March 2009).

19. Anand and Daft, What is the right organization design?

20. www.harley-davidson.com (March 2009); Kuglin, H., Kuglin, F. and Slocum, J. Building a route to competitive advantage: Harley Davidson. *Nanyang Business Review*, 2005, 4(1) 25–43.

21. www.generaldynamics.com (March 2009).

22. Anand and Daft, What is the right organization design?

23. DiGregorio, D. D., Musteen, M., and Thomas, D. E. International new ventures: The cross-border nexus of individuals and opportunities. *Journal of World Business*, 2008, 43, 186–196; Raisch, S. Balanced structures: Designing organizations for profitable growth. *Long Range Planning*, 2008, 41, 483–509.

24. Timmerman, C. E., and Scott, C. R. Virtually working: Communicative and structural predictors of media use and key outcomes in virtual work teams. *Communication Monographs*, 2006, 73, 108–137.

25. *Adapted from* www.dreamworksanimation.com (March 2009); Cripps, T. The dream team: The rise and fall of DreamWorks: Lessons from the New Hollywood. *CHOICE: Current Reviews for Academic Libraries*, 2007, 44(1), 1762–1763; see also Bengtsson, L., and Berggren, C. The integrator's new advantage—The reassessment of outsourcing and production competence in a global telecom firm. *European Management Journal*, 2008, 26, 314–325.

26. *Adapted from* Birkinshaw, J., and Gibson, C. B. Building ambidexterity into an organization. *MIT Sloan Management Review*, 2004, 45(4), 47–55.

27. *Adapted from* www.fedex.com (March 2009).

Chapter 16

1. *Adapted from* O'Brien, J. M. Zappos knows how to kick it. *Fortune*, February 2, 2009, 55–60; www.zappos.com (May 2009).

2. Jarnagin, C., and Slocum, J. W., Jr. Creating corporate cultures through mythopoetic leadership. *Organizational Dynamics*, 2007, 36, 288–302.

3. Organizational culture. http://en.wikipedia.org/wiki/ Organizational_culture (May 2009); Randel, A. E., and Early, C. P. Organizational culture and similarity among team members' salience of multiple diversity characteristics. *Journal of Applied Social Psychology*, 2009, 38, 804–833.

4. Islam, G., and Zyphur, M. J. Rituals in organizations: A review and expansion of current theory. *Group & Organization Management*, 2009, 34, 114–139.

5. Berson, Y., Oreg, S., and Dvir, T. CEO values, organizational culture and firm outcomes. *Journal of Organizational Behavior*, 2008, 29, 615–634.

6. Schein, E. H. *Organizational Culture and Leadership*. San Francisco: Jossey-Bass, 1985.

7. Ravasi, D., and Schultz, M. Responding to organizational identity threats: Exploring the role of organizational culture. *Academy of Management Journal*, 2006, 49, 433–459.

8. Gelfand, M. J., Nishii, L. H., and Raver, J. L. On the nature and importance of cultural tightness–looseness. *Journal of Applied Psychology*, 2006, 91, 1225–1244; Molinsky, A. Cross-cultural code-switching: The psychological challenges of adapting behavior in foreign cultural interactions. *Academy of Management Review*, 2007, 32, 595–621; Raghavan, A. No more excuses. *Forbes*, April 27, 2009, 120–123.

9. Chatman, J. A., and Spataro, S. E. Using self-categorization theory to understand relational demography-based variations in people's responsiveness to organizational culture. *Academy of Management Journal*, 2005, 48, 321–332.

10. *Adapted from* Brazilian CEO challenges hierarchal business structure, *Quality Progress*, 2004, 37(8), 16; Awe, S. The seven-day weekend: Changing the way work works. *Library Journal*, 2004, 129(6), 104–105; www.semco.com (May 2009).

11. McGuire, J. B., and Rhodes, G. B. *Transforming Your Leadership Culture*. San Francisco, CA: Jossey-Bass, 2009; Schein, E. H. Organizational culture. *American Psychologist*, 1990, 45, 109–119; Schein, *Organizational Culture and Leadership*.

12. Maxon, T. Supervisor goes above and beyond. *Dallas Morning News*, May 20, 2007, D5.

13. Morris, B. The new rules. *Fortune*, 2006, July 24, 70–84.

14. Mason, R. Lessons in organizational ethics from the *Columbia* disaster: Can culture be lethal? *Organizational Dynamics*, 2004, 33, 128–142.

15. Trice, H. M., and Beyer, J. M. *The Cultures of Work Organizations*. Englewood Cliffs, NJ: Prentice-Hall, 1993, 111.

16. Personal conversation with Fred Flores, Director, Mary Kay Cosmetics, Dallas, TX, April 2009.

17. Berry, L. L. Leadership lessons from the Mayo Clinic. *Organizational Dynamics*, 2004, 33, 228–242.

18. Naor, M., Goldstein, S. M., Linderman, K. W., and Schroeder, R. G. The role of culture as driver of quality management and performance: Infrastructure versus core quality practices. *Decision Sciences*, 2008, 39, 671–703.

19. Jarnagin and Slocum, Creating corporate cultures through mythopoetic leadership; Whitely, A., and Whitely, J. *Core Values and Organizational Change*. Singapore: World Scientific Publishing, 2007.

20. *Adapted from* www.harley-davidson.com (May 2009); Rollin, B. E. *Harley-Davidson and Philosophy: Full-*

Throttle Aristotle. Portland, OR: Open Court Publishing, 2006.

21. Kerr, J., and Slocum, J. W., Jr. Managing corporate cultures through reward systems. *Academy of Management Executive*, 1987, 1(2), 99–108.

22. www.pulte.com (May 2009)

23. Yum's formula for success starts with its people, *Nation's Restaurant News*, October 15, 2007, 44–48; Yang, L. A recipe for consistency. *Fortune*, October 29, 2007, 58ff; Barry, M., and Slocum, J. W., Jr. Changing culture at Pizza Hut and YUM! Brands, Inc. *Organizational Dynamics*, 2003, 32, 319–330.

24. *Adapted from* www.nameplate.com (May 2009).

25. Barry and Slocum, Changing culture at Pizza Hut and YUM! Brands, Inc.

26. Sorensen, J. B. The strength of corporate culture and the reliability of firm performance. *Administrative Science Quarterly*, 2002, 47, 70–91.

27. Balthazard, P. A., Cooke, R. A., and Potter, R. E. Dysfunctional culture, dysfunctional organization: Capturing the behavioral norms that form organizational culture and drive performance. *Journal of Managerial Psychology*, 2006, 21, 709–732.

28. Personal communication with Ralph Sorrentino, Partner, Deloitte Consulting, Dallas, TX, May 2009.

29. Feldman, S. P. Moral business cultures: The keys to creating and maintaining them. *Organizational Dynamics*, 2007, 36, 156–170; Elci, M., Kitapci, H., and Erturk, A. Effects of quality culture and corporate ethical values on employee work attitudes and job performance. *Total Quality Management & Business Excellence*, 2007, 18(3–4), 285–303; Organ, D. W., Podsakoff, P. M., and MacKenzie, S. B. *Organizational Citizenship Behavior: Its Nature, Antecedents and Consequences*. Thousand Oaks, CA: Sage, 2006.

30. Near, J. P., Rehg, M. T., VanScotter, J. R., and Miceli, M. P. Does type of wrongdoing affect the whistle-blowing process? *Business Ethics Quarterly*, 2004, 14, 219–242; Nam, D., and Lemak, D. J. The whistle-blowing zone: Applying Barnard's insights to a modern ethical dilemma. *Journal of Management History*, 2007, 13, 33–42; Moorhead, D. T. SOX and whistleblowing. *Michigan Law Review*, 2007, 15, 1757–1780.

31. *Adapted from* Near et al., Does type of wrongdoing affect the whistle-blowing process?

32. Umphress, E. E., Smith-Crowe, K., and Brief, A. P. When birds of a feather flock together and when they do not: Status composition, social dominance orientation and organizational attractiveness. *Journal of Applied Psychology*, 2007, 92, 396–409.

33. www.census.gov (May 2009); Roberson, Q. M., and Stevens, C. K. Making sense of diversity in the workplace. *Journal of Applied Psychology*, 2006, 91, 379–391; Roberson, L., and Kulik, C. Stereotype threat at work. *Academy of Management Perspectives*, 2007, 21(2), 24–40; Caminiti, S. Moving up the ranks. *Fortune*, June 25, 2007, S2–S6.

34. www.utc.com (May 2009).

35. Payne, S. C., Culbertson, S. C., Boswell, W. R., and Barger, E. J. Newcomer psychological contracts and employee socialization activities: Does perceived balance matter? *Journal of Vocational Behavior*, 2008, 73, 465–473;

Pendry, L. F., Driscoll, D. M., and Susannah, C. T. Diversity training: Putting theory into practice. *Journal of Occupational and Organizational Psychology*, 2007, 80, 27–51.

36. Cooman, R. D., Gister, S. D., Pepermans, R., Hermans, S., Du Bois, C., Caers, R., and Jegers, M. Person–organization fit: Testing socialization and attraction-selection attrition hypotheses. *Journal of Vocational Behavior*, 2009, 74, 102–108.

37. Payne et al., Newcomer psychological contracts and employee socialization activities.

38. Cooman et al., Person–organization fit.

39. www.disney.com (May 2009); Brannen, M. Y. When Mickey loses face: Recontextualization, semantic fit and semiotics of foreignness. *Academy of Management Review*, 2004, 29, 593–616.

40. Bowen, D. E., and Ostroff, C. Understanding HRM-firm performance linkages: The role of the "strength" of the HRM system. *Academy of Management Review*, 2004, 29, 203–221.

41. *Adapted from* Pareek, U. Studying organizational ethos: The Octapace profile. *The 1994 Annual: Developing Human Resources*. San Francisco: Jossey-Bass/Pfeiffer, 160–165. *Used with permission.*

42. *Adapted from* Wegmans Food Markets. http://en.wikipedia.com/wiki/Wegmans_Food_Markets (May 2009); www.wegmans.com (May 2009); Boyle, M. The Wegmans way. *Fortune*, January 24, 2005, 62–66.

Chapter 17

1. *Adapted from* Gabrielli de Azevedo, J. S. The greening of Petrobras. *Harvard Business Review*, March 2009, 43–47; www.petrobras.com (June 2009).

2. Marler, J. H., Fisher, S. L., and Ke, W. Employee self-service technology acceptance: A comparison of pre-implementation and post-implementation relationships. *Personnel Psychology*, 2009, 62, 327–349; Marshak, R. J. *Covert Process at Work: Managing the Five Hidden Dimensions of Organizational Change*. San Francisco, CA: Berrett-Koehler Publishers, 2007.

3. Kapner, S. Liz Claiborne's extreme makeover. *Fortune*, December 8, 2009, 141–146; www.lizclaiborne.com (June 2009).

4. Friedman, T. L. *The World Is Flat*. New York: Farrar, Straus and Giroux, 2005; Harvey, M. G., and Novicevic, M. M. The world is flat: A perfect storm for global business? *Organizational Dynamics*, 2006, 35, 207–220; Beck, N., Bruderi, J., and Woywode, M. Momentum of deceleration? Theoretical and methodological reflections of the analysis of change. *Academy of Management Journal*, 2008, 51, 413–436.

5. Personal communication with Su, S., President, YUM! Brands, Shanghai, China, June 2009.

6. Jargon, J. Can M'm, M'm good translate? *Wall Street Journal*, July 9, 2007, A16.

7. Haines, V. Y., III, and Lafleur, G. Information technology usage and human resource roles and effectiveness. *Human Resource Management*, 2008, 47, 525–540.

8. West, E. These robots play fetch. *Fast Company*, July/August 2007, 49–50.

9. Kirkpatrick, D. How Microsoft conquered China. *Fortune*, July 23, 2007, 78–84.

10. Purvanova, R. K., and Bono, J. E. Transformational leadership in context: Face-to-face and virtual teams. *The Leadership Quarterly*, 2009, 20, 343–358; Dube, L., and Robey, D. Surviving the paradoxes of virtual teamwork. *Information Systems Journal*, 2009, 19, 3–31.

11. Erickson, T. J. *Plugged In: The Generation Y Guide to Surviving at Work*. Boston: Harvard Business Press, 2008.

12. Fisher, A. When Gen X runs the show. *Time*, May 25, 2009, 48–49; Tyler, K. The tethered generation. *HRMagazine*, May 2007, 41–46.

13. *Adapted from* Litzpatrick, L. We're getting off the ladder. *Time*, May 25, 2009, 45; Godin, S. The last days of cubicle life. *Time*, May 25, 2009, 50; Larrabee, J. The virtuous cycle of community involvement. *Strategic HR Review*, May/June 2007, 24–27; Rowh, M. Managing younger workers. *Office Solutions*, 2007, 24(1), 29–31; Hewlett, S. A., Sherbin, L., and Sumberg, K. How Gen Y boomers will reshape your agenda. *Harvard Business Review*, July/August 2009, 71–77.

14. Stewart, K. Lessons for teaching Gen Y'ers. *College Teaching*, 2009, 57, 111–118.

15. Beer, M., and Nohria, N. Resolving the tension between theories E and O of change. In Beer, M., and Nohria, N. (Eds.). *Breaking the Code of Change*. Boston: Harvard Business School Press, 2000, 1–34; Cummings, T. G., and Worley, C. G. *Organizational Development and Change*, 8th ed. Mason, OH: Thomson/South-Western, 2008.

16. Welch, D. Bob Nardelli's wrong turns. *Business Week*, May 4, 2009, 26; Welch, D., Kiley, D. Chrysler files for bankruptcy. *Business Week Online*, May 1, 2009, 6; Maynard, M. Will Nardelli be Chrysler's Mr. Fix-It? *New York Times*, January 2008; B1ff; www.chrysler.com (June 2009).

17. Boyle, M. The Wegman's way. *Fortune*, January 24, 2005, 61–68.

18. Marchionne, S. Fiat's extreme makeover. *Harvard Business Review*, December 2008, 45–48.

19. Ford, J. D., and Ford, L. W. Decoding resistance to change. *Harvard Business Review*, April 2009, 99–102; Ford, J. D., Ford, L. W., and D'Amelio, A. Resistance to change: The rest of the story. *Academy of Management Review*, 2008, 33, 362–378; Furst, S. A., and Cable, D. M. Employee resistance to organizational change: Managerial influence tactics and leader-member exchange. *Journal of Applied Psychology*, 2008, 93, 453–563; Kotter, J. *Our Iceberg Is Melting: Changing and Succeeding Under Any Conditions*. New York: St. Martins Press, 2005; Ford, J. D., and Ford, L. W. Stop blaming resistance to change and start using it. *Organizational Dynamics*, 2010, in press.

20. Colan, L. J., and Cottrell, D. *Winners Always Quit*. Dallas, TX: CornerStone Leadership Institute, 2009, 40; Baruth, P. In search of Hinda Miller: The VDB interview. www.vermontdailybriefing.com/?p=187 (June 2009).

21. Luthans, F., Youssef, C. M., and Avolio, B. J. *Psychological Capital*. New York: Oxford University Press, 2007.

22. Colan and Cottrell, *Winners Always Quit*, 37.

23. Ellis, E. Vintage Ceylon. *Fortune*, July 23, 2007, 61–62.

24. *Adapted from* Nutt, P. C. *The Tolerance for Ambiguity and Decision Making*. Columbus, OH: Fisher School of Business, 2007.

25. Sloan, P. AT&T's new operator. *Fortune*, May 5, 2008, 139–144.

26. Lowry, T., Holahan, C. Breaking AOL in two. *Business Week Online*, February 7, 2008, 6; Case, D. Dead man walking. *Fast Company*, April, 2008, 112–119.

27. In focus: Lou Gerstner. CNN World Business. July 2, 2004. www.cnn.com/2004/BUSINESS/07/02/gerstner.interview/index.html.

28. Salter, C. The doctor of the future. *Fast Company*, May 2009, 64–70.

29. www.dallascowboys.com (June 2009).

30. Lewin, K. *Field Theory in Social Science*. New York: Harper & Row, 1951.

31. *Adapted from* Reingold, J. Target's inner circle. *Fortune*, March 31, 2008, 74–85.

32. Cummings and Worley, *Organizational Development and Change*; Fugate, M., Kinicki, A. J., and Prussia, G. E. Employee coping with organizational change: An examination of alternative theoretical perspectives and models. *Personnel Psychology*, 2008, 61, 1–37.

33. Whetten, D. A., and Cameron, K. S. *Developing Management Skills*, 7th ed. Upper Saddle River, NJ: Pearson/Prentice Hall, 2007, 537–594.

34. Ibid.

35. Cummings and Worley, *Organizational Development and Change*.

36. *Adapted from* Barak, M. *Managing Diversity: Toward a Globally Inclusive Workplace*. Thousand Oaks, CA: Sage, 2005, 293–294.

37. Gibson, C. B., Cooper, C. D., and Conger, J. A. Do you see what we see? The complex effects of perceptual distance between leaders and teams. *Journal of Applied Psychology*, 2009, 94, 62–77; Humphrey, S. E., Morgeson, F. P., and Mannor, M. J. Developing a theory of the strategic core teams: A role composition model of team performance. *Journal of Applied Psychology*, 2009, 94, 48–64.

38. Miles, S. A., and Bennett, N. 6 steps to rebuilding a top management team. *MIT Sloan Management Review*, 2008, 50, 60–65; Rushmer, R. What happens to team building during team building? Examining the change process that helps to build a team. *Journal of Management Development*, 1997, 16 316–328.

39. Goetzl, D. Fornaro aims to steer AirTran into bluer skies. *Advertising Age*, May 3, 1999, 44–46; www.airtran.com (June 2009); www.hoovers.com (June 2009).

40. Lei, D., and Slocum, J. W., Jr. The tipping points of business strategy: The rise and decline of competitiveness. *Organizational Dynamics*, 2009, 38, 131–147.

41. Cummings and Worley, *Organizational Development and Change*, 501.

42. www.utc.com (June 2009); www.dullesshrm.org/diversity/newsletter/current.html (May 13, 2009).

43. *Adapted from* Stewart, T. A. Rate your readiness to change. *Fortune*, February 7, 1994, 106–110.

44. *Adapted from* Schupak, A. Full speed ahead. *GolfWeek*, May 9, 2009, 15–22; Trimming down. *Time*, May 18, 2009, G10.

Subject and Organizational Index

U

Author Index

In the entry "Adams, G., R-8n.18(116)": R-8 refers to page R-8 in the References section; n.18 refers to note 18 on that page; and (116) refers to the *text* page where the note is called out. Page numbers followed by "f" indicate figures; "t" tables.